July 16-18, 2018
Vienna, Austria



Association for
Computing Machinery

*Advancing Computing as a Science & Profession*

# SPAA '18

**Proceedings of the 30th ACM**

## Symposium on Parallelism in Algorithms and Architectures

*Sponsored by:*

***ACM SIGACT & ACM SIGARCH***

*Supported by:*

***Akamai, Oracle Labs, Vienna Region, and Vienna Convention Bureau***

Association for
Computing Machinery

*Advancing Computing as a Science & Profession*

**The Association for Computing Machinery**
**2 Penn Plaza, Suite 701**
**New York, New York 10121-0701**



**ISBN:** 978-1-4503-5799-9 (Digital)

**ISBN:** 978-1-4503-6164-4 (Print)

Additional copies may be ordered prepaid from:

**ACM Order Department**
PO Box 30777
New York, NY 10087-0777, USA

Phone: 1-800-342-6626 (USA and Canada)
+1-212-626-0500 (Global)
Fax: +1-212-944-1318
E-mail: acmhelp@acm.org
Hours of Operation: 8:30 am – 4:30 pm ET

# Foreword

It is our great pleasure to welcome you to the *30th ACM Symposium on Parallelism in Algorithms and Architectures (SPAA 2018).* SPAA has a long history of bringing together the theory and practice of parallelism, defined broadly to include any computational settings where multiple operations can be performed simultaneously or concurrently. The program reflects the diversity of parallel settings and models.

This year's program includes 36 regular papers and 11 brief announcements, many of which combine both theory and practice, as well as two invited keynote lectures: "The Resurgence of Software Performance Engineering" by Charles E. Leiserson and "Massive-Scale Streaming Analytics: Models, Parallelism, and Real-World Applications" by David A. Bader. Several traditional topics are well-represented this year, including scheduling, graph algorithms, and parallel and concurrent data structures. The program also includes a significant number of papers that explore emerging memory technologies and parallelism in memory accesses.

The call for papers attracted 120 submissions as regular papers plus 6 as brief announcements. From the regular submissions, 36 papers were accepted (30%). The 11 brief announcements were selected from all submissions based on the committee's perception of interest from the SPAA community, with the goal that they serve as bases for further advances in parallelism. Extended versions of brief announcements may be published in other conferences or journals.

The best paper award for SPAA 2018 is awarded to two papers on parallel graph algorithms:

- Barbara Geissmann and Lukas Gianinazzi. Parallel Minimum Cuts in Near-Linear Work and Low Depth.
- Laxman Dhulipala, Guy E. Blelloch, and Julian Shun. Theoretically Efficient Graph Algorithms Can Be Fast and Scalable.

Geissmann and Gianinazzi give a parallel algorithm for minimum cut that is both highly parallel and nearly work efficient. Dhulipala, Blelloch, and Shun explore practical implementations of graph algorithms, showing that theoretically efficient graph algorithms can also be efficient in practice.

We would like to thank the program committee and external reviewers during the paper selection. The names of committee members and external reviewers appear later in these proceedings. The authors, external reviewers, and committee members made it possible to assemble the great collection of papers for this conference. We would also like to thank our sponsors and other financial supporters, including the ACM Special Interest Groups on Algorithms and Computation Theory (SIGACT) and Computer Architecture (SIGARCH), Akamai, Oracle Labs, and the Vienna Region and Vienna Convention Bureau. Finally, we would like to thank Guy Blelloch, who donated his honorarium as keynote speaker for SPAA 2017 toward the student travel fund.

**Jeremy Fineman**
*SPAA 2018 Program Chair*
*Georgetown University, USA*

**Christian Scheideler**
*SPAA 2018 General Chair*
*University of Paderborn, Germany*

# Table of Contents

## Session 4



## Keynote Address



## Session 5



## Session 6

## Session 10

Session Chair: Michael A. Bender *(Stony Brook University, USA)*

# SPAA 2018 Symposium Organization

**General Chair:** Christian Scheideler *(University of Paderborn, Germany)*

**Program Chair:** Jeremy Fineman *(Georgetown University, USA)*

**Local Arrangements Chair:** Jesper Larsson Träff *(TU Wien, Austria)*

**Publicity Chair:** Nodari Sitchinava *(University of Hawaii at Manoa, USA)*

**Treasurer:** David Bunde *(Knox College, USA)*

**Secretary:** Jeremy Fineman *(Georgetown University, USA)*

**Steering Committee:**
Guy Blelloch *(Carnegie Mellon University, USA)*
David Culler *(University of California, Berkeley, USA)*
Frank Dehne *(Carleton University, Canada)*
Pierre Friagniaud *(CNRS & University Paris Diderot, France)*
Phillip Gibbons *(Carnegie Mellon University, USA)*
Maurice Herlihy *(Brown University, USA)*
Tom Leighton *(Massachusetts Institute of Technology and Akamai Technologies, USA)*
Charles Leiserson *(Massachusetts Institute of Technology, USA)*
Fabrizio Luccio *(University of Pisa, Italy)*
Friedhelm Meyer auf der Heide *(University of Paderborn, Germany)*
Gary Miller *(Carnegie Mellon University, USA)*
Burkhard Monien *(University of Paderborn, Germany)*
Franco Preparata *(Brown University, USA)*
Vijaya Ramachandran *(University of Texas, Austin, USA)*
Arnold Rosenberg *(University of Massachusetts Amherst and Colorado State University, USA)*
Paul Spirakis *(Computer Technology Institute, Greece and University of Liverpool, England)*
Uzi Vishkin *(University of Maryland, USA)*

**Program Committee:**

Ittai Abraham *(VMware Research, USA)*
Kunal Agrawal *(Washington University in St Louis, USA)*
Grey Ballard *(Wake Forest University, USA)*
Michael Bender *(Stony Brook University, USA)*
Guy Blelloch *(Carnegie Mellon University, USA)*
Aydın Buluç *(Lawrence Berkeley National Lab, USA)*
Rezaul Chowdhury *(Stony Brook University, USA)*
Pierre Fraigniaud *(CNRS & University Paris Diderot, France)*
Seth Gilbert *(National University of Singapore, Singapore)*
Sungjin Im *(University of California, Berkeley, USA)*
Peter Kling *(University of Hamburg, Germany)*
I-Ting Angelina Lee *(Washington University in St Lous, USA)*
Victor Luchangco *(Oracle Labs, USA)*
Ryan Newton *(Indiana University, USA)*
Gopal Pandurangan *(University of Houston, USA)*
Erez Petrank *(Technion – Israel Institute of Technology, Israel)*
Vijaya Ramachandran *(University of Texas, Austin, USA)*
Peter Sanders *(Karlsruhe Institute of Technology, Germany)*
Thomas Sauerwald *(University of Cambridge, England)*
Oded Schwartz *(Hebrew University, Israel)*
Julian Shun *(Massachusetts Institute of Technology, USA)*
Nodari Sitchinava *(University of Hawaii at Manoa, USA)*
Edgar Solomonik *(University of Illinois, Urbana-Champaigne, USA)*
Michael Spear *(Lehigh University, USA)*
Denis Trystram *(University of Grenoble-Alpes, France)*

**Additional reviewers:**

Yaroslav Akhremtsev
John Augustine
Micheal Axtmann
Riyadh Baghdadi
Evripidis Bampis
Oren Becker
Naama Ben-David
Kyle Berney
Aaron Bernstein
Maciej Besta
Noam Birnbaum
Raphaël Bleuse
Uday Bondhugula
Costas Busch
Keren Censor-Hillel
Arthur Charguéraud
Soumyottam Chatterjee
Vincent Chau
Mehmet Deveci
Laxman Dhulipala
David Dice
Maya Dotan
Fanny Dufossé
Christoph Dürr
Reza Fathi
Mike Ferdman
Nitzan Gado
Ran Gelles
Robert Gmyr
Yan Gu
Demian Hespe
Rob Johnson
Elaye Karstadt
Nicholas Knight
Alexander Kononov
Grigorios Koumoutsos
Sriram Krishnamoorthy
Julian Labeit

**Additional reviewers: (cont'd)**

Dimitrios Letsios
Sarah Lutteropp
Pasin Manurangsi
Virendra Marathe
Alexander Matveev
Tyler Mayer
Samuel McCauley
Charith Mendis
Anisur Rahaman Molla
Clement Mommessin
Benjamin Moseley
Stefan Muller
Ofer Neiman
Calvin Newport
Kim Thang Nguyen
Roy Nissim
Stephen Olivier
Yishai Oltchik
Manuel Penchuk
Nguyen Pham
Mike Rainey
Veronika Rehn-Sonigo
Harald Räcke
Roy Schwartz
Michele Scquizzato
Ziv Scully
Gal Shahaf
Francesco Silvestri
Shikha Singh
Oliver Sinnen
Abhinav Srivastav
Yihan Sun
John Sylvester
Amitabh Trehan
Jesper Larsson Träff
Rob van Stee
Yuanhao Wei
Xiangyao Yu
Yunming Zhang

**Sponsors:** SIGACT, SIGARCH

**Supporters:** Akamai, Oracle Labs, VIENNA REGION (The Symphony of Opportunities.), VIENNA CONVENTION BUREAU

# Parallel Minimum Cuts in Near-linear Work and Low Depth

Barbara Geissmann
Department of Computer Science, ETH Zurich
Zurich, Switzerland
barbara.geissmann@inf.ethz.ch

Lukas Gianinazzi
Department of Computer Science, ETH Zurich
Zurich, Switzerland
lgianinazzi@acm.org

## ABSTRACT

We present the first *near-linear work* and *poly-logritharithmic depth* algorithm for computing a *minimum cut* in a graph, while previous parallel algorithms with poly-logarithmic depth required at least quadratic work in the number of vertices.

In a graph with $n$ vertices and $m$ edges, our algorithm computes the correct result with high probability in $O(m \log^4 n)$ work and $O(\log^3 n)$ depth. This result is obtained by parallelizing a data structure that aggregates weights along paths in a tree and by exploiting the connection between minimum cuts and approximate maximum packings of spanning trees.

In addition, our algorithm improves upon bounds on the number of cache misses incurred to compute a minimum cut.

## CCS CONCEPTS

• **Theory of computation → Parallel algorithms**;

## KEYWORDS

Minimum Cut; Graph Algorithms; Minimum Path Data Structure; Parallel Algorithms; Cache-oblivious Algorithms

**ACM Reference Format:**

Barbara Geissmann and Lukas Gianinazzi. 2018. Parallel Minimum Cuts in Near-linear Work and Low Depth. In *SPAA '18: 30th ACM Symposium on Parallelism in Algorithms and Architectures, July 16–18, 2018, Vienna, Austria.* ACM, New York, NY, USA, 11 pages. https://doi.org/10.1145/3210377.3210393

## 1 INTRODUCTION

Two trends have emerged in microprocessor design in the last two decades: (1) larger caches allow fast access to recently used memory locations and (2) many processing elements can be placed on the same chip, allowing for massively parallel processing. This has led to interest in both algorithms that take caches into account and parallel algorithm in a variety of different settings.

We consider *shared-memory parallel* algorithms for computing a *minimum cut* – a fundamental subject in graph theory, that has many applications in practice, such as in network reliability [15] and cluster analysis [4, 13, 28]. Our algorithm is based on one of the fastest known minimum cut algorithms, Karger's algorithm [15]. It exploits a random edge-sampling technique and returns the correct result with high probability. Recently, we presented a cache-efficient variant of that algorithm [10]. Now, we build on that result by parallelizing a key data structure in the algorithm and obtain a parallel minimum cut algorithm that has low overhead compared to the sequential one (only logarithmic in the number of vertices).

We identify two main challenges in parallelizing graph algorithms. The first challenge is how to parallelize graph searches, since traversing a graph in parallel is problematic, especially when the graph has large diameter. The second challenge is that many graph algorithms (including those for minimum cuts [16, 31]) employ intricate data structures for good performance. This is also problematic, because repeatedly accessing a data structure creates a sequential bottle-neck or can lead to concurrent accesses.

Our parallel minimum cut algorithm solves the first challenge by computing spanning trees that determine the order in which the edges of the input graph are accessed. In contrast to graphs, spanning trees can be traversed efficiently. Additionally, using parallel sorting, we rearrange the edges of the input graph to the order dictated by the traversal of the spanning tree, which avoids having to naively search the graph.

To solve the second challenge, we perform many data structure operations at once and in parallel. This works because the control flow of our algorithm does not depend on the result of the data structure operations until the very end, when the results from all data structure operations is aggregated efficiently in parallel.

### 1.1 Preliminaries

*1.1.1 Graphs.* We consider an undirected weighted graph $G$ with vertices $V$, edges $E$, and positive edge weights $w: E \mapsto \mathbb{N}^+$. The number of vertices $|V|$ is $n$ and the number of edges $|E|$ is $m$.

A nonempty proper subset of the vertices $V$ is a *cut* $C$ of the graph $G$. A cut $C$ induces a partition of the vertices into two nonempty sets $C$ and $\bar{C} = V - C$. An edge $\{u, v\}$ that has endpoints in different parts of the partition ($u \in C$ and $v \in \bar{C}$) *crosses* the cut $C$: it is a *crossing edge*. The total weight of the crossing edges of a cut $C$ is the *value* of $C$. A cut of smallest value is a *minimum cut*. In particular, a disconnected graph has a minimum cut of value 0.

In this work, we will also consider directed trees. For two vertices $u$ and $v$ in a directed tree, we say that $v$ is a *descendant* of $u$ (and $u$ is an *ancestor* of $v$) if there is a directed path from $u$ to $v$. In particular, every vertex is its own descendant and its own ancestor. We shall denote the set of all descendants of $v$ as $v^{\downarrow}$ and the set of all ancestors of $v$ as $v^{\uparrow}$.

*1.1.2 Model of Computation.* The well-known parallel random access machine (PRAM) model [27] consists of a set of $p$ processors each connected to an unbounded *shared memory*. This shared memory is organized into word-sized addressable locations. In each time step, every processor can read $O(1)$ memory locations and perform


*SPAA '18, July 16–18, 2018, Vienna, Austria*

ACM ISBN 978-1-4503-5799-9/18/07...$15.00
https://doi.org/10.1145/3210377.3210393

an $O(1)$ computable function on those words (this includes basic arithmetic, logic, control-flow, and addressing computations). Then, each processor can write back into $O(1)$ locations in the shared memory. The processors are *synchronous*, which means that they proceed at the same speed and complete a time step together.

The *runtime* of a PRAM algorithm is the number of time steps until the result is available in the shared memory. The runtime is determined by the processor that needs the most time steps.

We allow for multiple processors to read from the same memory location in the same time step, but forbid writing to the same location in the same time step. This is called the *concurrent-read exclusive-write* (CREW) PRAM setting.

The Work-Depth model [3] abstracts further from a concrete machine. In particular, a computation is viewed as a *directed acyclic graph* (DAG), where each node in the graph corresponds to a constant time operation. The out-edges of a node correspond to the outputs of the operation executed in this node, and its $O(1)$ in-edges correspond to the inputs to the operation. Consequently, the input of an algorithm is given at a designated set of nodes, and the output has to be available at another set of designated nodes.

The *work* of an algorithm is its number of nodes in the computation DAG (not counting the input nodes). The *depth* of an algorithm is the longest path from an input node to an output node.

Observe that the Work-Depth model and the PRAM model are closely related, as every PRAM algorithm can be viewed as generating a computation DAG. Conversely, the work and depth bounds translate to PRAM bounds. An algorithm with work $W$ and depth $D$ takes $O(W/p+D)$ time using $p$ processors in CREW PRAM [3, 5].

*1.1.3 Randomization.* We assume that in each time step, each processor has access to a uniformly random and independent bit. We distinguish between two types of randomized algorithms: A *Monte Carlo* randomized algorithm returns the correct result *with high probability*. This means that the probability to return the wrong result can be made smaller than $1/n^c$ for any constant $c$. In particular, increasing $c$ by a constant factor only changes the runtime by a constant factor. A *Las Vegas* randomized algorithm always returns the correct result, but the runtime bounds are probabilistic and hold with high probability.

## 1.2 Related Work

*1.2.1 Relation to Maximum Flow.* The minimum cut problem is a variant of the minimum $s$-$t$-cut problem, where the two designated vertices $s$ and $t$ must be in different parts of the partition.

The well-known Minimum-Cut-Maximum-Flow theorem [23] says that the value of a minimum $s$-$t$ cut equals the value of a maximum $s$-$t$ flow in the same network. Many maximum $s$-$t$ flow algorithms exist [8, 11, 19], the best of which obtain $O(mn+n^2 \log n)$ runtime in general [11].

A maximum $s$-$t$ flow can be computed with $O(n^2 \log n)$ depth [29], which provides some speedup for denser graphs. When the value of the maximum flow is small, better bounds are obtained [19].

*1.2.2 Deterministic Minimum Cut.* A minimum cut can be computed by fixing an arbitrary vertex $s$ and computing a maximum $s$-$t$ flow for all different vertices $t \neq s$. In general, such an approach leads to work $\Omega(mn^2)$ using the known algorithms. However, the ideas from computing maximum flows can be adapted [12] to a sequential algorithm with work $O(mn \log(n^2/m))$.

Slightly better bounds of $O(mn + n^2 \log n)$ are obtained by a relatively simple approach based on a graph search [31]. This approach is a simplification of an approach by Nagomochi and Ibaraki [22].

For *unweighted* graphs, a recent result [20] obtains near-linear work for a deterministic (sequential) minimum cut algorithm.

*1.2.3 Randomized Minimum Cut.* Randomized algorithms obtain both better work and depth than deterministic algorithms. Karger and Stein [18] give a Monte Carlo algorithm with $O(n^2 \log^3 n)$ work and $O(\log^3 n)$ depth, which is faster than any known maximum flow algorithm when $m = \Omega(n \log^3 n)$. Karger's algorithm [16] has the best known sequential bounds: it takes $O(m \log^3 n)$ work. However, the parallel variant of that algorithm uses $O(n^2 \log n)$ work to obtain $O(\log^3 n)$ depth.

## 1.3 Our Contributions

Our main contribution is a randomized parallel minimum cut algorithm that has near-linear work $O(m \log^4 n)$ and low depth $O(\log^3 n)$. It returns the correct result with high probability. Previous parallel algorithms [16, 18] with poly-logarithmic depth have quadratic work $\Omega(n^2 \log n)$ in the number of vertices. Our new algorithm, presented in Section 4, is thus much more work-efficient when the graphs are not too dense, that is, $m \leq o(n^2/\log^3 n)$. Consider Table 1 for an overview of our results compared to previous work.

As part of our solution, we present a parallel algorithm to solve a type of constrained minimum cut problem. Given a spanning tree $T$ of the graph, we find the cut of smallest value under the additional constraint that at most 2 crossing edges are part of the spanning tree $T$. See Figure 1 for an illustration of the problem. Our algorithm has work $O(m \log^2 n)$ and depth $O(\log^2 n)$, with high probability. The best previous algorithm [16] with poly-logarithmic depth has $\Theta(n^2)$ work and $\Omega(\log n)$ depth.

We solve the constrained minimum cut problem by parallelizing a data structure that maintains aggregates of weights along paths in a tree. In this data structure, we consider a fixed tree where every vertex has a variable weight. The queries find the smallest weight in a path of the tree. The updates add a fixed weight to every vertex in a path of the tree (potentially changing many weights). In Section 3, we show how to answer a batch of $k$ mixed queries and updates on a tree of $n$ vertices with $O(k \log n(\log n + \log k) + n \log n)$ work and $O(\log^2 n + \log n \log k)$ depth. Hence, the average work per query and update is $O(\log^2 k)$, when $k \geq \Omega(n)$.

Our new approach also improves the number of cache misses to compute a minimum cut in the cache-oblivious model [6, 9], where width of a cache line is $B$ and the size of the cache is $M$. As

**Table 1: Bounds for Computing a Minimum Cut. All algorithms are randomized and return correct results with high probability.**

| | Work | Depth |
|---|---|---|
| Lowest Work [16] | $\Theta(m \log^3 n)$ | $\Theta(m \log n)$ |
| Best Previous Polylog-Depth [16] | $\Theta(n^2 \log n)$ | $\Theta(\log^3 n)$ |
| *This Paper* | $O(m \log^4 n)$ | $O(\log^3 n)$ |

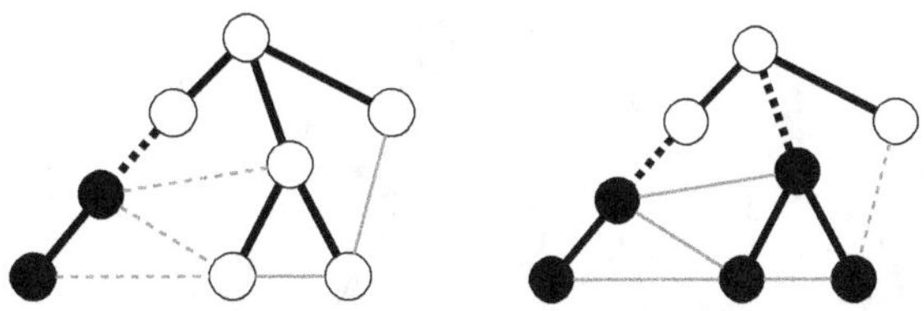

One edge of the bold tree is cut. Two edges of the bold tree are cut.

**Figure 1: Example illustrating the constrained optimization problem. The cuts are illustrated by the vertex shading. The left cut cuts one edge of the spanning tree and the right one cuts two edges of the spanning tree. Cuts that cut more edges of the spanning tree do not have to be considered in the constrained optimization problem.**

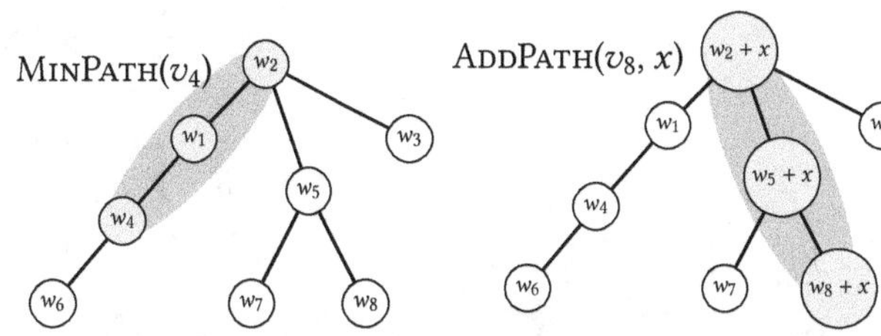


**Figure 2: Illustation of Minimum Path operations. Node $v_i$ stores value $w_i$. *Left:* MinPath($v_4$) computes the minimum of the weights of the highlighted nodes. *Right:* AddPath($v_8$, $x$) adds $x$ to the weight of the highlighted nodes.**

discussed in Section 5, it incurs $O(\lceil (m \log^4 n)/B \rceil)$ cache misses and takes $O(m \log^4 n)$ computation time. The best previous result [10] incurs $\Theta(\lceil (m(\log^4 n) \log_M n)/B \rceil)$ cache misses and takes $\Theta(m \log^5 n)$ computation time. Hence, the new algorithm improves the number of cache misses by a factor $\Theta(\log n / \log M)$, and the computation time by a factor $\Theta(\log n)$.

# 2 BACKGROUND

## 2.1 Karger's Minimum Cut Algorithm

On a high level, Karger's randomized algorithm [16] consists of two main steps:

(1) Find a set of spanning trees $S$ (with a special property as described below) in a graph $G$. Each of those trees gives rise to a more constrained optimization problem:
(2) For each spanning tree $T \in S$, compute the smallest cut $C$ of $G$ that has at most two crossing edges in $T$ (at most two edges of $T$ cross $C$). See Figure 1 for an illustration.

A key insight of Karger is a randomized procedure to find a set $S$ of only $O(\log n)$ spanning trees such that the smallest cut found in the second step is a minimum cut with high probability.

The set $S$ is constructed using an approximate maximum packing procedure [25]. This tree-packing procedure consists of sampling a sparse subgraph and performing a series of $O(\log^2 n)$ minimum spanning tree computations. It can therefore be parallelized using known algorithms.

Lemma 1 (Karger [16]). *In $O(\log^3 n)$ time using $O(m + n \log n)$ processors, a set of spanning trees $S$ of a graph $G$ can be computed with the following properties:*

*a) The set $S$ has size $O(\log n)$.*
*b) With high probability, there is a tree $T \in S$ such that a minimum cut of $G$ cuts at most 2 edges of $T$.*

The sequential bottleneck of Karger's algorithm lies in its second step. Although finding the smallest cut that cuts exactly *one edge* of a given spanning tree turns out to be relatively easy, finding the smallest cut that cuts exactly *two edges* of a given spanning tree is challenging. Karger gives a $O(\log^3 n)$ depth algorithm to do so, but it performs $\Theta(n^2 \log n)$ work. And for their faster $O(m \log^3 n)$ work algorithm no efficient parallelization is known.

## 2.2 Minimum Path

The problem left open by Karger is how to compute the smallest cut that cuts exactly *two edges* of a given spanning tree in parallel. The *sequential* $O(m \log^3 n)$ work minimum cut algorithm builds a data structure called *Minimum Path* on each of the spanning trees obtained in the first step and maintains weights on the vertices of the spanning tree, which correspond to certain estimates of the minimum cut.

Given a rooted tree $T$ with $n$ vertices where each vertex $v$ has a weight $w(v)$, a *Minimum Path* structure supports:

- MinPath($v$): Returns the smallest weight of a vertex on the path from $v$ to the root of $T$.
- AddPath($v$, $x$): Adds $x$ to the weight of all vertices on the path from $v$ to the root of $T$.

See Figure 2 for a illustration of the two operations.

This problem is a special case of dynamic trees [30], where $\Theta(\log n)$ time per query and update suffice. That this is optimal in the pointer machine setting follows from a recent lower bound on dynamic prefix sums [24]. The dynamic tree data structure [30] is difficult to parallelize because it is based on tree rotations. Therefore, for our *parallel* Minimum Path structure in Section 3, we will take a different approach.

## 2.3 Monotone Minimum Paths

We proceed with an overview of the data structure underlying the cache-oblivious algorithm minimum cut algorithm [10]. It is designed such that each operation accesses the memory in a monotone order (i.e., if an operation accesses location $x$ before location $y$ no operation accesses location $y$ before location $x$). This enables executing a batch of operations by sweeping through the memory only once, thus incurring a small number of cache misses. Similarly, this *monotonicity* is also crucial for our parallel variant in Section 3.

*2.3.1 Tree Decomposition.* The first step is to decompose the given tree $T$ into vertex-disjoint paths. To query or update a path $P$ in the tree $T$, simply perform an operation for each path in the decomposition that intersects the path $P$.

It is possible to decompose the tree such that each root-to-leaf path is decomposed into $O(\log n)$ parts [10, 30]. Figure 3 illustrates such a decomposition and how a query on the tree corresponds to a set of queries on the paths in the decomposition. We present a parallel procedure to compute a tree decomposition in Section 3.3.

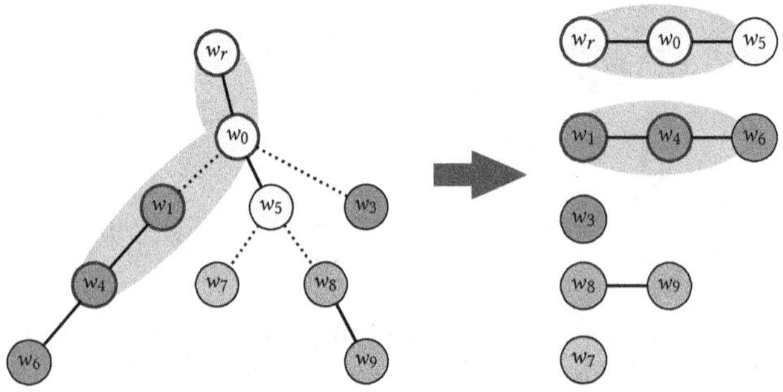

**Figure 3: An operation in the tree (left) is decomposed into operations on the paths in the decomposition (right).**

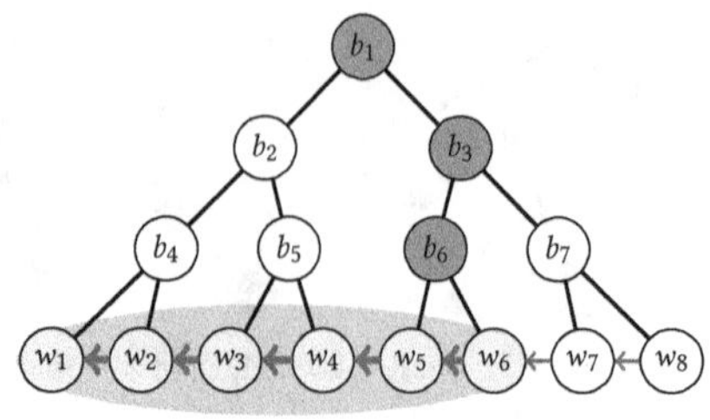

**Figure 4: At each inner node $b_i$, store the difference between the smallest weight in $b_i$'s right and left subtree. An update changes the differences on a single root-to-leaf path. The example above illustrates an update to the first six elements in the list.**

2.3.2 *List view.* We view each path of the decomposition as a list, where the vertex closest to the root is at the beginning (front) of the list. We call the deductive problem about querying and updating prefixes of lists *Minimum Prefix*. Specifically, we define *MinPrefix* analogously to MinPath and *AddPrefix* analogously to AddPath on a list $L$ of vertices $(v_1, \dots, v_n)$ with weights $(w_1, \dots, w_n)$:

MINPREFIX($v_i$) returns the smallest weight in the prefix $w_1, \dots, w_i$. The example below illustrates MinPrefix($v_6$) on a list with 8 nodes.

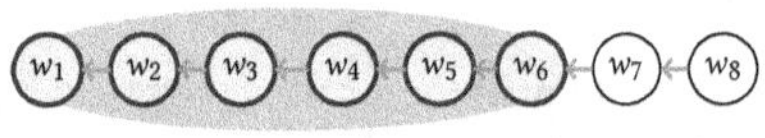

ADDPREFIX($v_i$, $x$) adds $x$ to the weights of the vertices in the prefix $v_1, \dots, v_i$. The example below illustrates AddPrefix($v_4$, $x$) on a list with 8 nodes.

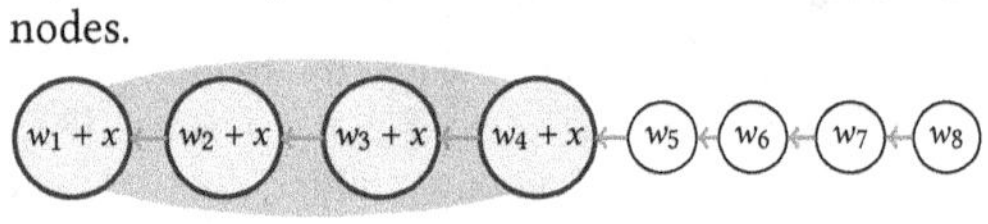

To perform Minimum Prefix operations on a list $l$ we build a complete binary tree $B$ on top the vertices $v_1, \dots, v_n$, such that the vertices form the leaves of the tree $B$. This tree holds auxiliary information that allows us to perform the prefix operations quickly. A naive attempt would be to store in each inner node of the tree $B$ the minimum value in its subtree. This approach answers queries in $O(\log n)$ time, but an update takes $\Omega(n)$ time (for example when the prefix covers the whole list).

A better approach is to store only differences of minima: Each inner node stores the difference between the smallest leaf in its right subtree and the smallest leaf in its left subtree. With this approach, only $O(\log n)$ values change when the list is updated, namely those on the path from the root of the binary tree to the leaf corresponding to the last vertex that is updated. See Figure 4 for an illustration.

Moreover, these differences (more specifically their signs) suffice to determine which subtree, and consequently, which vertex of the list contains the smallest value.

In the following, we we describe how to efficiently maintain these difference values and how to use them to compute the smallest weight in a given prefix of the list.

2.3.3 *AddPrefix.* For any node $b$ with right child $r$ and left child $l$, let $\min_i(b)$ be the smallest weight of any descendant of $b$ after the $i$-th update and let $\min_0(b)$ be the smallest weight of any descendant of $b$ in the initial state. Recall that this value is not stored directly for efficiency reasons, but instead, the data structure stores in each node $b$ at time $i$ the value

$$\Delta_i(b) := \min_i(r) - \min_i(l) \ .$$

Let ADDPREFIX($v$, $x$) be the $i$-th update and assume that we know by how much the update changes the minimum in the right subtree (i.e. $\min_i(r) - \min_{i-1}(r)$) and the minimum in the left subtree (i.e. $\min_i(l) - \min_{i-1}(l)$). Then, we can derive by how much the difference between the two subtree minima changes in this update. Therefore, we define $\phi_i(b) = \min_i(b) - \min_{i-1}(b)$. We have

$$\Delta_i(b) = \Delta_{i-1}(b) + \phi_i(r) - \phi_i(l) \ .$$

Of course, it would be too expensive to compute $\Delta_i(b)$ by recursively computing the values $\phi_i$ of both children, since all descendants would be traversed. However, we observe that at least one child of every node has a trivial value: If all descendant leaves of a node $b'$ are in the prefix of the list that is updated, then $\phi_i(b') = x$. If no descendant leaves of a node $u$ are in the prefix of the list that is updated, then $\phi_i(u) = 0$. This means that the value of $\phi_i$ is only non-trivial for the nodes on the path from $v$ to the root (which are also the only nodes where $\Delta$ changes). Hence, to perform the $i$-th update ADDPREFIX($v$, $x$), we walk up along this path in the tree starting in the leaf $v$ and compute $\phi_i(b)$ for each node $b$ along this path. For the leaf, this is $\phi_i(v) = x$. For an interior node $b$, Figure 5 and Figure 6 illustrate how the value of $\phi_i(b)$ is computed. There are two additional symmetric cases.

2.3.4 *MinPrefix.* The queries also proceed walking up the path from the last vertex in the prefix to the root. We consider the weights and state of the data structure at a fixed time and for simplicity, we omit the time subscripts.

When computing MINPREFIX($v_k$), it is tempting to directly compute for each node along this path the result of MINPREFIX($v_k$) restricted to the current subtree (namely $\min_{v_i \in b^{\downarrow}, i \le k} w_i$). Unfortunately, this is not possible using only the value of $\Delta(b)$. Instead, we compute the difference $d(b)$ between this quantity and the minimum of the current subtree $\min(b)$:

$$d(b) := \left( \min_{v_i \in b^{\downarrow}, i \le k} w_i \right) - \min(b) \ .$$

Once this difference is known for the root, we get the result of MINPATH($v_k$) by adding the overall minimum to this difference. See

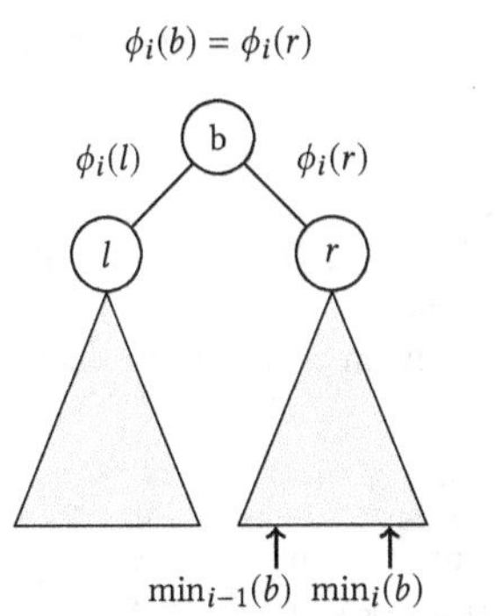


**Figure 5: AddPrefix (A): In case the minimum stays in the right subtree after the $i$-th update, the change in minimum at node $b$ is given directly by the change of minimum in the right subtree.**

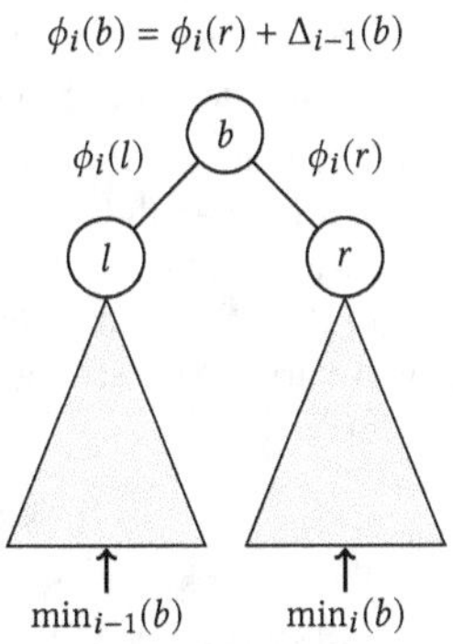


**Figure 6: AddPrefix (B): In case the minimum was in the left subtree before the $i$-th subtree, and is in the right subtree after the $i$-th update, the difference between the minimum of the two subtrees before the $i$-th update needs to be taken into account.**

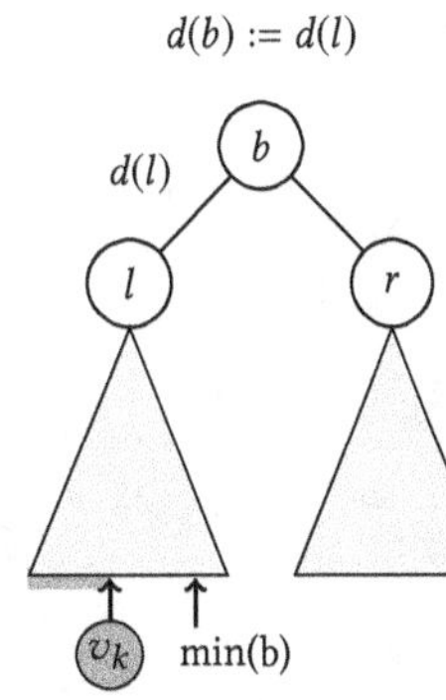


**Figure 7: MinPrefix (A). The easy case for MinPrefix($v_k$) is when both the query vertex $v_k$ and the smallest weight in $b$'s subtree min($b$) are in the left subtree $l$. Then, $d(b)$ is copied from the left child $l$.**

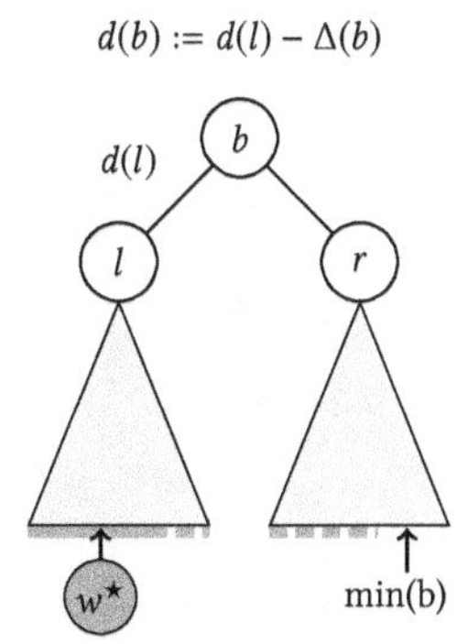


**Figure 8: MinPrefix (B): The smallest weight in the query prefix $w^\star = \min_{v_i \in b\downarrow, i \leq k} w_i$ is in the left subtree $l$, but the smallest weight in $b$'s subtree min($b$) is in the right subtree $r$. The difference $\Delta(b)$ between the minimum in the right subtree and the minimum in the left subtree needs to be taken into account.**

Figure 7 and Figure 8 for an illustration for how $d(b)$ is computed bottom-up. There is an additional case symmetric to Figure 7.

*2.3.5 Running time.* The runtime depends on the way we decompose the tree $T$ into paths. Each path in $T$ is decomposed into at most $O(\log n)$ lists. As we can perform MinPrefix and AddPrefix on each list in the decomposition in $O(\log n)$ time, the overall time to perform AddPath and MinPath is $O(\log^2 n)$.

# 3 PARALLEL MINIMUM PATH

The monotone Minimum Path structure from Section 2.3 can execute Queries and Updates one-by-one. Directly trying to parallelize such an approach leads to problems of *concurrency*: When many updates try to change the same memory location concurrently, these conflicts need to be resolved. Some general techniques to do so are known in practice, such as locks or lock-free methods [14]. However, these approaches essentially serialize accesses to the same memory location. Thus, locations that are accessed by many updates, such as the root in the minimum path structure, become sequential bottlenecks.

Therefore, we take a different approach. We start with two observations implied by cache-oblivious algorithm [10]:

(1) The complete sequence of updates and queries is known upfront: it is enough to find a parallel algorithm to perform a *batch* of minimum path operations.
(2) The data structure operations traverse the memory in a fixed order (namely walking bottom-up in some trees). This allows us to perform all of the updates at once, simulating the execution of all updates at the same time by logically sweeping the trees bottom-up and producing for each memory location all its intermediate states at once.

In the cache-oblivious algorithm, the batch of updates is simulated using a priority queue. This is inherently sequential. Moreover, it leads to a runtime of $\Theta(\log^3 n)$ per minimum path operation.

In Sections 3.1 and 3.2 we instead provide an explicit schedule for performing a batch of updates and queries *in parallel*, such that the overall work per minimum path operation is $\Theta(\log^2 n)$.

*3.0.1 Problem Statement.* We consider a *batch* of $k$ MinPath and AddPath operations $o_1, \ldots, o_k$. Each AddPath operation is of the form $o_i = (i, v(i), x(i))$ for a time $i$, a vertex $v(i)$, and a weight $x(i)$. Similarly, each MinPath operation $o_i$ is of the form $o_i = (i, v(i))$ for a time $i$ and a vertex $v(i)$. The goal is to compute the result of all MinPath operations at once in parallel, as if the operation sequence where executed sequentially.

As in the sequential case, we decompose the tree into a set of directed paths (See Section 3.3) and build a minimum prefix structure for each of those paths . We start with the presentation of *parallel* AddPrefix and *parallel* MinPrefix.

## 3.1 Parallel AddPrefix

We consider a batch of AddPrefix operations for a list of length $n$, where each operation $o_i$ is of the form $o_i = (i, v(i), x(i))$ for a time $i$, a vertex $v(i)$, and a weight $x(i)$. Conceptually, we build the same binary tree $B$ on top of the list as in the sequential case (see Section 2.3).

In order to allow for future queries, we need to produce all intermediate states of a particular node that arose when the updates were executed sequentially. From inspecting the update equation for a particular node $b$ with left child $l$ and right child $r$,

$$\Delta_i(b) = \Delta_{i-1}(b) + \phi_i(r) - \phi_i(l)\,,$$

we make the following key observation that it telescopes to

$$\Delta_i(b) = \Delta_0(b) + \left(\sum_{j=1}^{i} \phi_j(r)\right) - \left(\sum_{j=1}^{i} \phi_j(l)\right)\,.$$

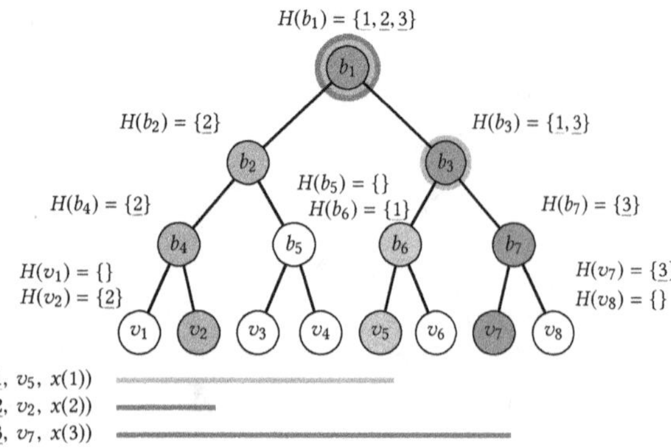


**Figure 9: Example illustrating the definition of $H$. The set $H(b_i)$ keeps track of the indexes of the updates that are relevant at node $b_i$. These are exactly those that update a prefix that ends in a descendant of $b_i$. The Figure indicates the value of $H$ for all inner nodes and the leafs $v_1$, $v_2$, $v_7$ and $v_8$.**

Therefore, given the all-prefix-sums for $\phi_1(r), \dots, \phi_k(r)$ and for $\phi_1(l), \dots, \phi_k(l)$, we can compute the values of $\Delta_1(b), \dots, \Delta_k(b)$ in $O(1)$ depth and $O(k)$ work. Moreover, given those values, the values $\phi_1(b), \dots, \phi_k(b)$ each only depend on a constant number of already computed terms. Therefore, they can also be computed in $O(1)$ depth and $O(k)$ work. Unfortunately, this naive interpretation still needs far too many processors: $\Omega(k)$ work at every node $b$, and hence $\Omega(nk)$ work overall.

Fortunately, not every update is relevant to every node: $\Delta_i(b)$ only changes for an update $o_i = (i, v(i), x(i))$ if $v(i)$ is a descendant of $b$. We can therefore restrict our attention to the times $i$ of those operations: Let $H(b)$ be the union over all times $i$ where the update is such that $v(i)$ is a descendant of $b$.

We continue with three important observations.

Observation 2. *$H(l)$ and $H(r)$ are disjoint, and $H(b) = H(l) \cup H(r)$. This implies that we can merge the updates relevant to the children to obtain the updates relevant to b. Note that an update is relevant to $\log n + 1$ nodes of the tree, namely those along the path from the root of B towards the last node in the list prefix that changes. See Figure 9 for an example.*

Observation 3. *The Observation 2 allows us leave out all the indices that do not occur in $H(b)$, as they are not relevant to b:*

$$\Delta_i(b) = \Delta_0(b) + \left( \sum_{j \in H(b)} \phi_j(r) \right) - \left( \sum_{j \in H(b)} \phi_j(l) \right), \text{ for any } i \in H(b).$$

Observation 4. *In a bottom up traversal of the tree, we get $\phi_i(l)$ for all $i \in H(l)$ and $\phi_i(r)$ for all $i \in H(r)$. This means that we have some "missing" values for the sums in Observation 3, namely the values of $\phi_i(r)$ for all $i \in H(l)$ and the values of $\phi_i(l)$ for all $i \in H(r)$. As explained for the sequential operation (see Section 2.3.3), these values are trivial to get:*

- *Updates $(i, v(i), x(i))$ with $i \in H(l)$ do not affect the descendants of $r$. Hence, for such an $i \in H(l)$ we have $\phi_i(r) = 0$.*
- *Updates $(i, v(i), x(i))$ with $i \in H(r)$ change all descendants of $l$ by the same amount: for such an $i \in H(r)$ we have $\phi_i(l) = x(i)$.*

The above Observations 2-4 suggest a parallel bottom-up procedure that produces for each node $b$:

- The values of $H(b)$ as an array in sorted order. In the following the $i$-th largest value in $H(b)$ is denoted $H(b)[i]$. This means that $H(b)[i]$ is the index (w.r.t. the batch of updates) of the $i$-th update relevant at node $b$.
- An array $X(b)$ storing the increment of the updates relevant at $b$:
$$X(b)[i] = x(j) \text{ , where } j = H(b)[i] \ .$$
This means that the $i$-th update relevant at $b$ is of the form AddPath($v(j)$, $X(b)[i]$) for some descendant $v(j)$ of $b$.
- An array $\Phi(b)$ storing $\phi_j(b)$ for the updates relevant at $b$. Specifically, we have
$$\Phi(b)[i] = \phi_j(b) \text{ , where } j = H(b)[i] \ .$$

Moreover, the procedure produces for each interior node $b$ the array $\Delta(b)$ containing the intermediate states of the data structure at all relevant times:

$$\Delta(b)[i] = \Delta_j(b) \text{ , where } j = H(b)[i] \ .$$

In the following, we explain how to obtain these values for leafs, inner nodes, and the root of the binary tree $B$.

*3.1.1 Leafs.* At the leafs, we just need to group the updates by vertex and keep track of the relevant quantities. First, apply a stable sort by vertex to the operation sequence. Now, the operation sequence is sorted by vertex and tuples with the same vertex are sorted by time. From this, we can easily find which operations belong to a given vertex $v$ (by a binary search for $v$ and its successor). Then, for each vertex $v$ initialize $H(v)$ as the times of the tuples that have $v$ as a vertex and initialize $X(v)$ with the corresponding increments. Set $\Phi(v)$ to $X(v)$ - recall that $\Phi(v)$ records how much the minimum in the subtree changed for every operation relevant at $v$ and at the leafs the minimum changes by the increment.

*3.1.2 Inner Nodes.* At an inner node $b$ with left child $l$ and right child $r$, we merge the results from its children, use prefix sums to generate $\Delta(b)$ in parallel, and construct $\Phi(b)$ based on $\Delta(b)$.

Using Observation 2, we merge the two sorted arrays $H(l)$ and $H(r)$ in parallel to receive $H(b)$ in sorted order. Similarly, we merge the update increments $X(l)$ and $X(r)$ to obtain $X(b)$ in sorted order.

Using Observation 4, we reconstruct the missing values for the right child $r$ and merge them with $\Phi(r)$ that we got from the right child. Proceed similarly for the left child $l$. Now, for all times $i$ relevant to $b$ (i.e. for all $i \in H(b)$), we have $\phi_i(l)$ and $\phi_i(r)$ each in an array sorted by increasing time $i$.

Using Observation 3, we construct $\Delta(b)$ as follows. We compute (in parallel) the all-prefix-sums over the array that contains the $\phi_i(l)$ for all $i$ in $H(b)$, and the array that contains the $\phi_i(r)$ for all $i$ in $H(b)$. Then, the observation immediately implies $\Delta_i(b)$ for all $i$ in $H(b)$ in parallel.

Finally, we compute each entry of $\Phi(b)$ in parallel:

$$\Phi(b)[i] = \begin{cases} \Phi(l)[i] & \text{if } \Delta(b)[i-1] > 0 \text{ and } \Delta(b)[i] > 0 \ , \\ \Phi(l)[i] - \Delta(b)[i] & \text{if } \Delta(b)[i-1] \le 0 \text{ and } \Delta(b)[i] > 0 \ , \\ \Phi(r) & \text{if } \Delta(b)[i-1] \le 0 \text{ and } \Delta(b)[i] \le 0 \ , \\ \Phi(r) + \Delta(b)[i] & \text{if } \Delta(b)[i-1] > 0 \text{ and } \Delta(b)[i] \le 0 \ . \end{cases}$$

*3.1.3 Root.* For the root $\rho$ of the binary tree, we proceed as for an internal node. Additionally, we generate the overall minimum weight after every update, which will be needed for the parallel MinPath queries. Observe that

$$\min_i(\rho) = \min_0(\rho) + \sum_{j=1}^{i} \phi_j(\rho) \ .$$

Hence, we compute all the values $\min_1(\rho), \ldots, \min_k(\rho)$ by a parallel all-prefix-sums computation on $\phi_1(\rho), \ldots, \phi_k(\rho)$.

*3.1.4 Running Time.* By the proceeding described above, we obtain the following bounds for parallel AddPrefix operations.

Lemma 5. *Performing a batch of k parallel AddPrefix operations on a list of length n takes $O(k(\log n + \log k) + n)$ work and $O(\log n \log k)$ depth.*

Proof. At the leafs, we sort the operation sequence and perform $O(k)$ parallel binary searches. This takes $O(k \log k)$ work and $O(\log k)$ depth.

At every inner node $b$, we perform a constant number of parallel all-prefix-sums operations and parallel merge operations on arrays of size $O(H(b))$. By the bounds of merging sorted arrays [7] and parallel prefix sums [27], the work at an inner node $b$ is $O(H(b)+1)$ and the depth is $O(\log(H(b)) + 1)$.

All nodes with the same distance to the root can be processed in parallel. Thus, the total work arising from nodes at distance $i$ to the root is $O(k + 2^i)$ and the depth is $O(\log k)$. Here, we used that summing $H(b)$ over all nodes at a fixed distance $i$ gives exactly $k$, because each leaf is the descendant of exactly one node at distance $i$. Nodes with different distance from the root need to be processed by decreasing distance (bottom up). Hence, the overall work arising at inner nodes is $O(k \log n + n)$ and the overall depth is $O(\log n \log k)$.

At the root, we perform an additional parallel all-prefix-sums operation on an array of size $k$. □

## 3.2 Parallel MinPrefix

The parallel update algorithm (batch of AddPath operations) produces all intermediate states for the data structure. If we store for each node in the data structure all the state it ever has (sorted by time), the value of a cell after the $i$-th update can be determined by doing a binary search on those states, taking $\Theta(\log k)$ time. Each query is then performed independently. Overall, this takes $\Theta(k \log n \log k)$ work and $\Theta(\log k \log n)$ depth. This however results in $\Omega(\log k)$ more work compared to the original data structure.

To get rid of this logarithmic factor in work, we also perform the queries in a batch and we use parallel merging to avoid the binary searches. We obtain the following bounds:

Lemma 6. *Performing a batch of k MinPrefix and AddPrefix operations on a list of length n takes $O(k(\log n + \log k) + n)$ work and depth $O(\log n \log k)$.*

The procedure is similar as for the updates. The queries are placed at the leafs and the nodes at the same distance from the root are processed in parallel.

For a single query $(i, v(i))$, the following happens: the query gets processed bottom-up in all nodes on the path $P_i$ from the leaf $v(i)$ to the root, such that every internal node $b$ obtains an intermediate result $d_i(c)$ from its child $c$, updates this result based on $\Delta_i(b)$ to $d_i(b)$, and passes this result to its parent node. Initially, leaf $v(i)$ sets $d_i(v(i)) = 0$. Then, every internal node $b$ with left child $l$ and right child $r$ updates this result to

$$d_i(b) = \begin{cases} d_i(l) & \text{if } \Delta_i(b) > 0, \\ d_i(r) & \text{if } v(i) \in r^{\downarrow}, \text{ and } d_i(r) + \Delta_i(b) < 0, \\ d_i(l) - \Delta_i(b) & \text{otherwise,} \end{cases}$$

where $d_i(b)$ and $d_i(r)$ have either been already computed, since the child lies on the path $P_i$, or are equal to zero.

To process all queries in parallel, every leaf now initiates an array that contains all its queries with the corresponding intermediate results sorted by time. Hence, an internal node $b$ obtains such an array $L$ from its left child and $R$ from its right child, which it merges (in parallel, by time) to an array $Q$ that now contains all queries and intermediate results relevant to $b$.

The last issue is to have the $\Delta$ values ready for each relevant query. In particular, we need the value that belongs to the last update before the query. Thus, we record the time when this value was set by translating the indices of $b$'s relevant updates to the times that correspond to it: $\Delta(b)[i]$ is mapped to the tuple $(H(b)[i], \Delta(b)[i])$. Then, we merge $Q$ and the relevant $\Delta$-values in parallel and sorted by time. The new array contains a mix of queries and $\Delta$-values, sorted by time, such that now each query just needs to read the last $\Delta$-value on its left. This is achieved by a segmented broadcast, where each $\Delta$-value broadcasts its value to all following queries. A segmented broadcast can be implemented using a variant of the parallel all-prefix-sums algorithm [27].

At the root, each query needs to read the overall minimum at the closest preceding time to the query. This can be achieved similarly using parallel merging and a segmented broadcast.

The overall runtime analysis is very similar to the one for the AddPrefix, since processing node $b$ has the same cost: it has work $O(H(b) + 1)$ and depth $O(\log(H(b)) + 1)$.

## 3.3 Tree Decomposition

To solve MinPath and AddPath for general trees, we find a suitable decomposition of the tree $T$ into paths. This section presents a parallel algorithm to compute the decomposition we also used in the cache-oblivious minimum cut algorithm [10]. The idea is to repeatedly remove certain subpaths that start at a leaf, as follows:

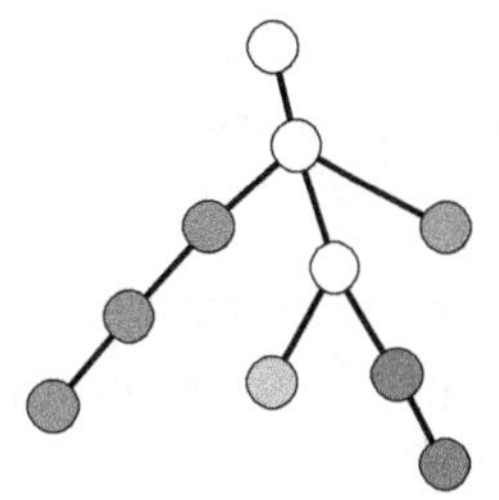

**Figure 10: The tree above has 4 boughs, indicated by the vertex colors. Each bough starts at a leaf and continues upwards until reaching the first node that has a sibling.**

We call a path that starts at a leaf and ends at the first vertex that has a sibling on the way up to the root, a *bough* of $T$. A bough ends at a vertex whose parent has multiple children or, if the tree $T$ is a path, at the root. See Figure 10 for an example.

The algorithm repeats the following until no edges remain:

(1) Identify the boughs of $T$. Each bough is in the decomposition.

(2) Remove all vertices that are part of a bough.

Note that shrinking boughs is also used for other parallel graph problems [26]. The algorithm is also related to a parallel tree contraction algorithm [21].

We obtain the following bounds for the decomposition:

Lemma 7. *A tree $T$ with $n$ vertices can be decomposed into a set of pairwise vertex-disjoint paths $P$ such that:*

- *Each root-to-leaf path in $T$ intersects at most $\log_2 n$ paths in $P$*
- *This takes work $O(n \log n)$ and depth $O(\log^2 n)$ (Las Vegas).*

Observe that, in each repetition, the number of leaves is at least halved. This is because each leaf in the new tree had at least two children before the contraction. Hence, there are at most $\log_2 n$ repetitions. This implies that every root-to-leaf path in $T$ is decomposed into at most $\log_2 n$ paths.

We give a randomized algorithm to find the boughs in parallel in Section 3.3.1. With high probability, it has work $O(n)$ and depth $O(\log n)$. Removing the vertices takes work $O(n)$ and depth $O(1)$. As the tree decomposition has $O(\log n)$ iterations, Lemma 7 follows.

*3.3.1 Finding the Boughs.* Next, we show how to find the boughs in parallel, implying the work and depth bounds from Lemma 8. Observe that the boughs are induced subpaths and thus we can use ideas from parallel list ranking [1].

We call a vertex in a tree a *branching vertex* if it has at least two children, and similarly we say that a vertex is *non-branching* if it has at most one child.

(1) As long as there are non-branching nodes in $T$, find an independent set of edges (i.e. edges that do not share endpoints) whose endpoints are both non-branching and contract this set of edges. When merging two vertices, keep track of the original labels of the vertices that were merged into that vertex. Specifically, keep the labels as linked lists with head and tail pointers.
(2) After the procedure converges, the leaf vertices contain the labels of the boughs (as a linked list).

Lemma 8. *The boughs of a tree with $n$ vertices can be identified with $O(n)$ work and $O(\log n)$ depth (Las Vegas randomized).*

Proof. We can find large independent sets with $O(N)$ work and $O(1)$ depth (where $N$ is the number of non-branching nodes), for example using the random-mate technique introduced for list ranking [1, 2]. This ensures that, with high probability, the number of non-branching internal vertices decreases by a constant factor at each repetition and $O(\log n)$ repetitions suffice until all internal vertices are branching. Merging two non-branching vertices takes $O(1)$ work because they have constant degree. As there can be at most $n - 1$ merge operations, the overall work from merging is $O(n)$. The depth to contract an independent set of edges connecting non-branching nodes is $O(1)$, as each such edge can be contracted completely parallel to the other edges and needs only $O(1)$ pointers to change. □

It is possible to make the algorithm deterministic by replacing the randomized independent set construction by a deterministic one: Construct a 3-coloring of the tree and choose the color $c$ with the largest number of non-branching internal vertices. For each internal non-branching vertex of that color, add the edge connecting it to its child to the independent set.

A 3-coloring of a tree is constructed deterministically in depth $O(\log^* n)$ and work $O(n \log^* n)$ [11]. Using this deterministic approach, the work to decompose the tree as in Lemma 7 increases to $O(n \log^2 n \log^* n)$ and the depth increases to $O(\log^2 n \log^* n)$.

## 3.4 Parallel MinPath and AddPath

Each MinPath and AddPath operation corresponds to $O(\log n)$ MinPrefix and AddPrefix operations, respectively, which can be processed in parallel. For the MinPath operations, the smallest result of the $O(\log n)$ MinPrefix queries can be found sequentially after they have completed. We conclude:

Lemma 9. *Performing a batch of $k$ MinPath and AddPath operations on a tree with $n$ nodes takes $O(k \log n(\log n + \log k) + n \log n)$ work and depth $O(\log n(\log k + \log n))$ (Las Vegas randomized).*

# 4 PARALLEL MINIMUM CUTS

The parallel *Minimum Path* structure is the missing puzzle-piece in a parallelization of Karger's algorithm. This solved, it remains to show how to create the batch of Minimum Path operations and how to combine the results of the Minimum Path structure into a minimum cut, achieving the following overall bounds.

Theorem 10. *The minimum cut of a graph can be computed with depth $O(\log^3 n)$ and work $O(m \log^4 n)$ (Monte Carlo randomized).*

In the following, we consider a (rooted) spanning tree $T$ of the input graph $G$ and we want to compute the smallest cut that cuts at most two edges of $T$. We will do so with work $O(m \log^3 n)$ and depth $O(\log^2 n)$. Together with Lemma 1 this implies the main result.

Karger already showed a parallel algorithm that computes the smallest cut that cuts *exactly one* edge of a given spanning tree. In fact, the algorithm computes for each vertex $v$, the value of the cut $v^{\downarrow}$ that has the descendants of $v$ on one side of the cut (and therefore cuts only the edge from $v$ to its parent in $T$).

Lemma 11 (Karger [16]). *A smallest cut that cuts exactly one edge of a given spanning tree can be computed with work $O(m)$ and depth $O(\log m)$.*

We therefore focus on giving a parallel algorithm for the case where *exactly two* edges of the spanning tree are cut.

## 4.1 Cutting two edges of a spanning tree

Our parallel algorithm uses ideas from Karger's sequential algorithm [17] to reduce the problem to a set of Minimum Path operations, which we already showed how to perform in parallel in Section 3.

We are given a spanning tree $T$ of $G$. Assume that the smallest cut $C$ that cuts at most two edges of $G$ cuts the edges $(u, v)$ and $(s, t)$ of $T$ (where $u$ is the parent of $v$ and $s$ the parent of $t$). Let us focus on the case where $u$ is not an ancestor of $s$ and vice versa. See Figure 11 for an example. The case where $u$ is an ancestor of $s$ is similar (we refer to Karger [17] for the details).

If we take the value of the cut $t^{\downarrow}$ and add the value of the cut $v^{\downarrow}$ we incorrectly count (twice) the edges that go between the descendants of $v$ and the descendants of $t$. We will use the Minimum

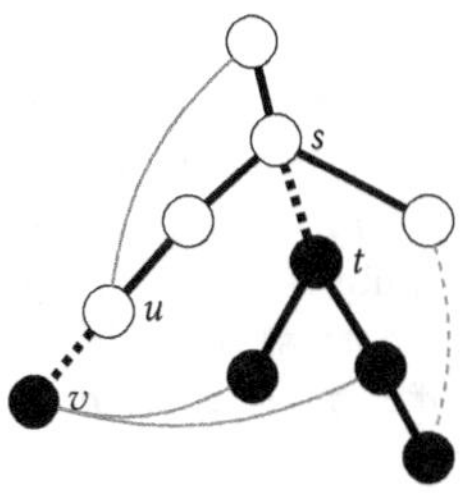


**Figure 11: The weight of the (black, white) cut that cuts $(u, v)$ and $(s, t)$ is given by the dashed edges. This equals the edges with at least one black endpoint minus the edges with two black endpoints.**

Path structure to keep track of these "extra" edges that go between the two parts of the tree.

In the following, we will explain how the algorithm handles possibilities for these four vertices, including for instance if one of $v$ or $t$ was a leaf. Since the algorithm does not know which two edges to cut is best, all possibilities need to be considered.

*4.1.1 Handling a leaf.* Without loss of generality, assume that $v$ is a leaf of $T$ (see Figure 11 for an illustration of this situation). The algorithm proceeds as follows:

(1) Initialize a Minimum Path Structure where the initial weight of each vertex $x$ is given by the value of the cut $x^{\downarrow}$. Recall that these values are computed by the algorithm from Lemma 11.
(2) Then, for each edge $e = (v, y)$ incident to $v$, perform AddPath($v$, $-2w(e)$).

Observe that after these steps, the weight in the minimum path structure of a vertex $x$ that is not an ancestor $v$ is exactly the value of the cut $x^{\downarrow}$ minus twice the weight of the edges between $v$ and the descendants of $x$. Moreover, since we assume that $C$ is a smallest cut of $G$ among those that cut at most two edges of $T$, at least one of $v$'s neighbors has to be a descendant of $t$. Otherwise, the cut $t^{\downarrow}$ would be smaller than the cut $C$, which leads to a contradiction. This implies that the value of $C$ is given by the value of the cut $v^{\downarrow}$ plus the minimum weight of a node $x$, such that $x$ is a neighbor but not an ancestor of $v$. Thus, we find the value of the cut $C$ as follows:

(1) Add $\infty$ to the weight of all ancestors of $v$ by AddPath($v$, $\infty$).
(2) For each neighbor $x$ of $v$, call MinPath($x$) and keep the smallest result.
(3) Add the value of the cut $v^{\downarrow}$. This is the value of the cut $C$.

*4.1.2 Handling a bough.* The observations from before can be generalized to also handle boughs. Recall from Section 3.3.1 that a bough is a maximal induced subpath that contains a leaf. Similar to the case where $v$ is a leaf, we use the Minimum Path Structure to keep track of the "extra" edges that go between $v^{\downarrow}$ and $t^{\downarrow}$. The following procedure handles the case where $v$ is in a bough.

(1) Initialize the minimum path structure just as in the leaf case.
(2) Start at the leaf of the bough and walk up the bough. At every node $y$ in the bough:
   (a) If $y$ is a leaf, perform AddPath($y$, $\infty$) .
   (b) Moreover, for every edge $e = (y, x)$ incident to $y$, perform AddPath($x$, $-2w(e)$).
   (c) Afterwards, for every neighbor $x$ of $y$, perform the query MinPath($x$). Record the smallest result.

Consider the state of the minimum path structure when the above procedure has processed some node $y$ in the bough. Consider another node $x$ that is not an ancestor of any node in the bough. Then, the weight of $x$ is equal to the value of the cut $x^{\downarrow}$ minus twice the weight of the "extra" edges that exist between $y^{\downarrow}$ and $x^{\downarrow}$.

Moreover, by the minimum assumption of $C$, it must hold that $v$ has a descendant that is a neighbor of a descendant of $t$.

Putting these two observations together, we conclude that it is indeed enough to perform a MinPath($y$) query for every neighbor $y$ of a node in the bough and record the smallest result. When we have processed $v$, the smallest result seen so far plus the value of the cut $v^{\downarrow}$ gives the value of the cut $C$.

*4.1.3 Handling a general tree.* To handle a general subtree we repeat the procedure for every bough. Then, we contract all edges (of the spanning tree and the overall graph) with at least one endpoint in a bough. Afterwards, we recurse in the new tree. We call such a phase a *bough-phase*. Note that this gives the same decomposition of the tree as in Section 3.3.

In each bough-phase, the boughs can be handled in any order. However, after handling a bough, we need to restore the weights to their initial state. This is done by reversing the order and the sign of all AddPath operations: We visit the nodes in the bough top-down and replace each AddPath($x$, $w$) by AddPath($x$, $-w$). In the end, we return the smallest cut value found.

## 4.2 Generating the batch of Minimum Path operations

We show how to generate the batch of minimum path operations for one bough-phase. We already saw how to identify the boughs in Lemma 8. The remaining difficulty is to compute (in parallel) the order in which the edges are accessed.

Observe that each edge is accessed at most four times: for each of its endpoints once on the way going upwards in the bough containing this endpoint, and once on the way down. We get the order and the operations as follows.

(1) Order each bough by list-ranking and give each leaf a unique identifier. Then, the order in which a vertex is visited is derived from the number of the leaf of its bough and its position in the list-ranking. See Figure 12 for an example.
(2) Each leaf creates an AddPath($v$, $\infty$) at the time of its first visit and an AddPath($v$, $-\infty$) at the time of its second visit.
(3) When a node $y$ in a bough is visited at times $t_1$ and $t_2$, then every neighbor $x$ of $y$ creates an update that corresponds to AddPath($y$, $-2w(e)$) at time $t_1$ and a query that corresponds to MinPath($y$) at time $t_1$. Moreover, it creates an update that corresponds to AddPath($y$, $2w(e)$) at time $t_2$ (this undoes the operation of the former update). Each edge in a graph is thus accessed at most four times, namely every time one of its endpoints is visited. See Figure 13 for an illustration.
(4) The queries and updates are sorted according to the visit times, where additionally operations with the same visit time are ordered such that updates come before queries. This gives the operation sequence that handles all the boughs in the tree.

Lemma 12. *Generating the batch of Minimum Path operations from Section 4.1 that handles all the boughs of a tree takes work $O(m \log n)$ and depth $O(\log n)$.*

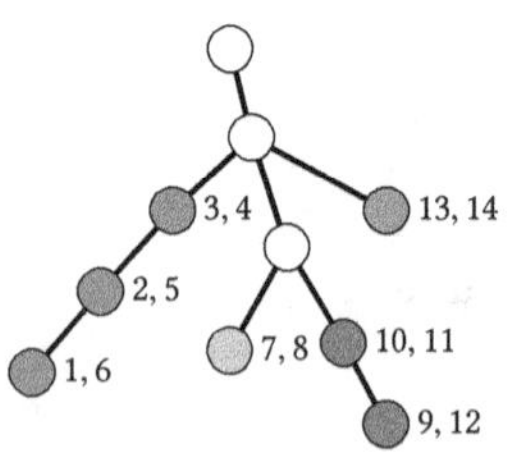


**Figure 12: The boughs of the tree are indicated by colors. The node labels indicate a possible order in which they are visited by the algorithm. Each node in a bough is visited twice. Once on a bottom-up traversal of its bough and then on a top-down traversal of its bough. The order between boughs is arbitrary.**

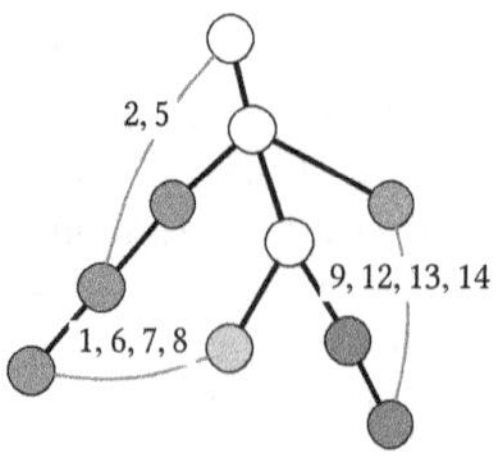


**Figure 13: The order in which the edges are visited is given by the order of the vertices. An edge is visited whenever one of its endpoints is visited. Thus, each edge is visited two or four times. The figure indicates the times when the non-tree edges (grey) are visited, based on the example on the left.**

Proof. List ranking of the boughs takes $O(\log n)$ depth and $O(m)$ work [1]. The vertices derive their visit time with $O(\log n)$ depth and $O(n)$ work, the edges can then be processed completely in parallel with $O(1)$ depth and $O(m)$ work. Finally, sorting the batch of $O(m)$ operations takes $O(\log n)$ depth and $O(m \log n)$ work [7]. □

### 4.3 Extracting the Minimum Cut.

To finally find the smallest cut of $G$ that cuts at most two edges of a given spanning tree $T$, we need to repeatedly apply such batches of operations in every bough-phase:

(1) For all vertices $x$, compute the value of the cut $x^{\downarrow}$ of $G$ that has the descendants of $x$ in $T$ on one side of the cut (using the algorithm from Lemma 11). In particular, this yields the smallest cut that cuts exactly one edge of $T$.
(2) Find the boughs of $T$. Contract all edges incident to a node in a bough (contract the edges in $T$ and $G$ at the same time) and recurse until the graph has a single vertex. This generates a sequence of graphs $G_1, G_2, \ldots, G_k$ and corresponding spanning trees $T_1, T_2, \ldots, T_k$. Note that $G_1 = G$ and $T_1 = T$.
(3) In parallel, for each of the pairs $T_i$ and $G_i$ in the sequence, run the algorithm from Section 4.2 to generate the necessary Minimum Path operations.
(4) For each of the trees $T_i$, execute the batch of Minimum Path operations in parallel (Section 3.4). Find the smallest value MinPath$(v) + C(v^{\downarrow})$ over all vertices $v$ (and all queries to $v$), where $C(v^{\downarrow})$ is the value of the cut of $G$ that has the descendants of $v$ in $T_i$ on one side of the value. These values have already been computed when finding the smallest cut that cuts one edge of $T$.
(5) The smallest value MinPath$(v) + C(v^{\downarrow})$ found overall is the value of the smallest cut that cuts exactly two edges of $T$.

The algorithm obtains the following bounds:

Lemma 13. *Finding the smallest cut of a graph $G$ that cuts at most two edges of a given spanning tree $T$ of $G$ takes work $O(m \log^3 n)$ and depth $O(\log^2 n)$ (Las Vegas randomized).*

Proof. Using Lemma 8, generating the graphs $G_1, G_2, \ldots, G_k$ and corresponding spanning trees $T_1, T_2, \ldots, T_k$ takes $O(m \log n)$ work and $O(\log^2 n)$ depth. Since the number of leaves is at least halved in each bough-phase, $k = O(\log n)$. Contracting the edges in the bough is just a matter of mapping each vertex in a bough to the vertex that is the parent of the topmost vertex in the bough, look up the value of the endpoints of each vertex in the mapping and remove loops. It is not necessary to combine parallel edges.

For each graph in $G_1, G_2, \ldots, G_k$, generating the queries takes $O(m \log n)$ work and $O(\log n)$ depth (by Lemma 12). Executing the batch of $O(m)$ minimum path operations and finding the minimum result takes $O(m \log^2 n)$ work and $O(\log^2 n)$ depth (by Lemma 6). As this can be done in parallel for each of the $O(\log n)$ graphs, the algorithm takes $O(m \log^3 n)$ work and $O(\log^2 n)$ depth overall.

The algorithm can be easily adapted to also output the edges of $T$ that define the cut, essentially by recording the edges that generated a Minimum Path query. □

Together with Lemma 1, Lemma 13 implies our main result as stated in Theorem 10.

## 5 CACHE-OBLIVIOUS ALGORITHM

The parallel minimum cut algorithm gives improved cache miss bounds to compute a minimum cut. The key difference to our previous cache-oblivious algorithm [10] is the implementation of the minimum path structure. The parallel minimum path algorithm from Section 3 uses operations (such as merging sorted lists and computing prefix sums) that are easily made cache-efficient.

The cache-oblivious model [6, 9] considers a fully-associative cache with optimal replacement strategy of size $M$ with cache lines of width $B$. The parameters $B$ and $M$ of the machine cannot be used in the algorithm description, hence the name cache-*oblivious*.

We obtain the following bounds to compute a minimum cut if we replace the minimum path structure in our previous cache-oblivious algorithm [10] with the the data structure from Section 3.

Theorem 14. *Finding a minimum cut incurs $O\left(\frac{m \log^4 n}{B} + 1\right)$ cache misses and takes $O(m \log^4 n)$ time (Monte Carlo randomized).*

## 6 CONCLUSION

Compared to the best sequential algorithm, our algorithm performs only $O(\log n)$ more work, namely $O(m \log^4 n)$ work and $O(\log^3 n)$ depth. It remains an open problem to find a work-optimal minimum cut algorithm that has poly-logarithmic depth.

The $\Omega(\log^3 n)$ depth of our algorithm comes from the algorithm to find the suitable spanning trees (where the minimum cut crosses at most two edges of one of the spanning trees). The rest of our algorithm has depth $O(\log^2 n)$. Consequently, a lower depth algorithm to find a suitable spanning tree would yield a lower depth minimum cut algorithm.

## REFERENCES

[1] Richard J. Anderson and Gary L. Miller. 1991. Deterministic Parallel List Ranking. *Algorithmica* 6, 6 (1991), 859–868. https://doi.org/10.1007/BF01759076
[2] Lars Arge, Michael T. Goodrich, and Nodari Sitchinava. 2010. Parallel external memory graph algorithms. In *24th IEEE International Symposium on Parallel and Distributed Processing, IPDPS 2010, 19-23 April 2010, Atlanta, Georgia, USA*. 1–11. https://doi.org/10.1109/IPDPS.2010.5470440

[3] Guy E. Blelloch. 1996. Programming Parallel Algorithms. *Commun. ACM* 39, 3 (March 1996), 85–97. https://doi.org/10.1145/227234.227246

[4] Rodrigo A. Botafogo. 1993. Cluster Analysis for Hypertext Systems. In *16th Annual International Conference on Research and Development in Information Retrieval, SIGIR 1993, Pittsburgh, PA, USA, June 27 - July 1, 1993.* 116–125. https://doi.org/10.1145/160688.160704

[5] Richard P. Brent. 1974. The Parallel Evaluation of General Arithmetic Expressions. *J. ACM* 21, 2 (1974), 201–206. https://doi.org/10.1145/321812.321815

[6] Gerth St. Brodal. 2004. Cache-Oblivious Algorithms and Data Structures. In *9th Scandinavian Workshop on Algorithm, SWAT 2004, Theory, Humlebaek, Denmark, July 8-10, 2004, Proceedings.* 3–13. https://doi.org/10.1007/978-3-540-27810-8_2

[7] Richard Cole. 1988. Parallel Merge Sort. *SIAM J. Comput.* 17, 4 (1988), 770–785. https://doi.org/10.1137/0217049

[8] E. A. Dinic. 1970. Algorithm for Solution of a Problem of Maximum Flow in a Network with Power Estimation. *Soviet Math Doklady* 11 (1970), 1277–1280. http://www.cs.bgu.ac.il/~

[9] Matteo Frigo, Charles E. Leiserson, Harald Prokop, and Sridhar Ramachandran. 1999. Cache-Oblivious Algorithms. In *40th Annual Symposium on Foundations of Computer Science, FOCS 1999, 17-18 October, 1999, New York, NY, USA.* 285–298. https://doi.org/10.1109/SFFCS.1999.814600

[10] Barbara Geissmann and Lukas Gianinazzi. 2017. Cache Oblivious Minimum Cut. In *10th International Conference on Algorithms and Complexity, CIAC 2017, Athens, Greece, May 24-26, 2017, Proceedings.* 285–296. https://doi.org/10.1007/978-3-319-57586-5_24

[11] Andrew V. Goldberg and Robert E. Tarjan. 1988. A new approach to the maximum-flow problem. *J. ACM* 35, 4 (1988), 921–940. https://doi.org/10.1145/48014.61051

[12] Jianxiu Hao and James B. Orlin. 1994. A Faster Algorithm for Finding the Minimum Cut in a Directed Graph. *J. Algorithms* 17, 3 (1994), 424–446. https://doi.org/10.1006/jagm.1994.1043

[13] Erez Hartuv and Ron Shamir. 2000. A clustering algorithm based on graph connectivity. *Inf. Process. Lett.* 76, 4-6 (2000), 175–181. https://doi.org/10.1016/S0020-0190(00)00142-3

[14] Maurice Herlihy and Nir Shavit. 2008. *The art of multiprocessor programming.* Morgan Kaufmann.

[15] David R. Karger. 1999. A Randomized Fully Polynomial Time Approximation Scheme for the All-Terminal Network Reliability Problem. *SIAM J. Comput.* 29, 2 (1999), 492–514. https://doi.org/10.1137/S0097539796298340

[16] David R. Karger. 2000. Minimum cuts in near-linear time. *J. ACM* 47, 1 (2000), 46–76. https://doi.org/10.1145/331605.331608

[17] David R. Karger. 2001. A Randomized Fully Polynomial Time Approximation Scheme for the All-Terminal Network Reliability Problem. *SIAM Rev.* 43, 3 (2001), 499–522. https://doi.org/10.1137/S0036144501387141

[18] David R. Karger and Clifford Stein. 1996. A New Approach to the Minimum Cut Problem. *J. ACM* 43, 4 (1996), 601–640. https://doi.org/10.1145/234533.234534

[19] Richard M. Karp and Vijaya Ramachandran. 1990. Parallel Algorithms for Shared-Memory Machines. In *Handbook of Theoretical Computer Science, Volume A: Algorithms and Complexity (A).* 869–942.

[20] Ken-ichi Kawarabayashi and Mikkel Thorup. 2015. Deterministic Global Minimum Cut of a Simple Graph in Near-Linear Time. In *47th Symposium on Theory of Computing, STOC 2015, Portland, OR, USA, June 14-17, 2015.* 665–674. https://doi.org/10.1145/2746539.2746588

[21] Gary L. Miller and John H. Reif. 1985. Parallel Tree Contraction and Its Application. In *26th Annual Symposium on Foundations of Computer Science, FOCS 1985, Portland, Oregon, USA, 21-23 October 1985.* 478–489. https://doi.org/10.1109/SFCS.1985.43

[22] Hiroshi Nagamochi and Toshihide Ibaraki. 1990. Computing Edge-Connectivity in Multiple and Capacitated Graphs. In *International Symposium on Algorithms, SIGAL 1990, Tokyo, Japan, August 16-18, 1990, Proceedings.* 12–20. https://doi.org/10.1007/3-540-52921-7_51

[23] Christos H. Papadimitriou and Kenneth Steiglitz. 1998. *Combinatorial optimization: algorithms and complexity, pages 117–120.* Courier Corporation. 117–120 pages.

[24] Mihai Patrascu and Erik D. Demaine. 2006. Logarithmic Lower Bounds in the Cell-Probe Model. *SIAM J. Comput.* 35, 4 (2006), 932–963. https://doi.org/10.1137/S0097539705447256

[25] Serge A. Plotkin, David B. Shmoys, and Éva Tardos. 1995. Fast Approximation Algorithms for Fractional Packing and Covering Problems. *Math. Oper. Res.* 20, 2 (1995), 257–301. https://doi.org/10.1287/moor.20.2.257

[26] Vijaya Ramachandran. 1997. Parallel Algorithms for Reducible Flow Graphs. *J. Algorithms* 23, 1 (1997), 1–31. https://doi.org/10.1006/jagm.1996.0820

[27] John H. Reif. 1993. *Synthesis of Parallel Algorithms* (1st ed.). Morgan Kaufmann Publishers Inc., San Francisco, CA, USA.

[28] Roded Sharan and Ron Shamir. 2000. Center CLICK: A Clustering Algorithm with Applications to Gene Expression Analysis. In *8th International Conference on Intelligent Systems for Molecular Biology, ISMB 2000, August 19-23, 2000, La Jolla / San Diego, CA, USA.* 307–316. http://www.aaai.org/Library/ISMB/2000/ismb00-032.php

[29] Yossi Shiloach and Uzi Vishkin. 1982. An $O(n^2 \log n)$ Parallel MAX-FLOW Algorithm. *J. Algorithms* 3, 2 (1982), 128–146. https://doi.org/10.1016/0196-6774(82)90013-X

[30] Daniel D. Sleator and Robert E. Tarjan. 1983. A Data Structure for Dynamic Trees. *J. Comput. Syst. Sci.* 26, 3 (1983), 362–391. https://doi.org/10.1016/0022-0000(83)90006-5

[31] Mechthild Stoer and Frank Wagner. 1997. A simple min-cut algorithm. *J. ACM* 44, 4 (1997), 585–591. https://doi.org/10.1145/263867.263872

# Wireless Expanders

Extended Abstract

Shirel Attali
The Weizmann Institute of Science
Rehovot, Israel
shirel.attali@weizmann.ac.il

Merav Parter
The Weizmann Institute of Science
Rehovot, Israel
merav.parter@weizmann.ac.il

David Peleg*
The Weizmann Institute of Science
Rehovot, Israel
david.peleg@weizmann.ac.il

Shay Solomon†
IBM Research, T. J. Watson Research Center
Yorktown Heights, New York
solo.shay@gmail.com

## ABSTRACT

This paper introduces an extended notion of expansion suitable for radio networks. A graph $G = (V, E)$ is said to be an $(\alpha_w, \beta_w)$-*wireless expander* if for every subset $S \subseteq V$ s.t. $|S| \leq \alpha_w \cdot |V|$, there exists a subset $S' \subseteq S$ s.t. there are at least $\beta_w \cdot |S|$ vertices in $V \backslash S$ that are adjacent in $G$ to exactly one vertex in $S'$. The main question we ask is the following: to what extent are ordinary expanders also good *wireless* expanders? We answer this question in a nearly tight manner. On the positive side, we show that any $(\alpha, \beta)$-expander with maximum degree $\Delta$ and $\beta \geq 1/\Delta$ is also a $(\alpha_w, \beta_w)$ wireless expander with $\alpha_w \geq \alpha$ and $\beta_w = \Omega(\beta/\log(2 \cdot \min\{\Delta/\beta, \Delta \cdot \beta\}))$. Thus the wireless expansion can be smaller than the ordinary expansion by at most a factor that is logarithmic in $\min\{\Delta/\beta, \Delta \cdot \beta\}$, which, in turn, depends on the *average degree* rather than the maximum degree of the graph. In particular, for low arboricity graphs (such as planar graphs), the wireless expansion matches the ordinary expansion up to a constant factor. We complement this positive result by presenting an explicit construction of a "bad" $(\alpha, \beta)$-expander for which the wireless expansion is $\beta_w = O(\beta/\log(2 \cdot \min\{\Delta/\beta, \Delta \cdot \beta\})$.

We also analyze the theoretical properties of wireless expanders and their connection to unique neighbor expanders, and then demonstrate their applicability: Our results (both the positive and the negative) yield improved bounds for the *spokesmen election problem* that was introduced in the seminal paper of Chlamtac and Weinstein from 1991 to devise efficient broadcasting for multihop radio networks. Our negative result yields a significantly simpler proof than that from the seminal paper of Kushilevitz and Mansour from 1998 for a lower bound on the broadcast time in radio networks.

## CCS CONCEPTS

• **Mathematics of computing** → *Network optimization*; • **Theory of computation** → *Expander graphs and randomness extractors*; • **Computing methodologies** → *Distributed algorithms*;

## KEYWORDS

expander; radio network; radio broadcast; unique neighbor expander; wireless network

**ACM Reference Format:**
Shirel Attali, Merav Parter, David Peleg, and Shay Solomon. 2018. Wireless Expanders: Extended Abstract. In *SPAA '18: 30th ACM Symposium on Parallelism in Algorithms and Architectures, July 16–18, 2018, Vienna, Austria.* ACM, New York, NY, USA, 10 pages. https://doi.org/10.1145/3210377.3210396

## 1 INTRODUCTION

### 1.1 Background and motivation

An expander is a sparse graph that has strong connectivity properties [11]. There are several definitions for expanders, with natural connections between them. We focus on the following combinatorial definition.

**Expanders:** Let $G = (V, E)$ be an undirected graph. For a set $S \subset V$, let $\Gamma(S)$ denote the set of neighbors of the vertices of $S$, and define $\Gamma^-(S) = \Gamma(S) \setminus S$. We say that $G$ is an $(\alpha, \beta)$ *expander*, for positive parameters $\alpha$ and $\beta$, if $|\Gamma^-(S)| \geq \beta \cdot |S|$ for every $S \subseteq V$ s.t. $|S| \leq \alpha \cdot |V|$.

One of the main advantages of expanders is that they enable fast and effective dissemination of information from a small group of vertices to the outside world. This property becomes less immediate when we consider using the expansion property in the context of wireless communication networks. Such networks can be represented by a specific kind of graphs, called *radio networks* [9]. A radio network is an undirected (multihop) network of processors that communicate in synchronous rounds in the following manner. In each step, a processor can either transmit or keep silent. A processor receives a message in a given step if and only if it keeps silent and precisely one of its neighbors transmits in this step. If none of its neighbors transmits, it hears nothing. If more than one neighbor (including itself) transmits in a given step, then none of the messages is received. In this case we say that a *collision* occurred. It is assumed that the effect at processor $u$ of more than

*Supported by a grant from the United States âĂŞ Israel Binational Science Foundation (BSF) and the United States National Science Foundation (NSF).
†Supported by the IBM Herman Goldstine Postdoctoral Fellowship.


*SPAA '18, July 16–18, 2018, Vienna, Austria*

ACM ISBN 978-1-4503-5799-9/18/07...$15.00
https://doi.org/10.1145/3210377.3210396

one of its neighbors transmitting is the same as of no neighbor transmitting, i.e., a node cannot distinguish a collision from silence.

The usual definition of expanders is not enough to ensure fast message propagation in radio networks. Consider, for example, a radio network $C^+$ consisting of a complete graph $C$ with one more vertex $s_0$, the source, connected to two vertices $x$ and $y$ from $C$. Obviously this is a good expander, but in this case, after the first step of broadcast, if all the vertices that received the message (i.e., the three vertices $s_0$, $x$ and $y$) transmit it simultaneously to all their neighbors, then no one will hear it. This motivates considering another definition of expanders, namely, *unique neighbor expanders* (or unique expanders, in short)[2].

**Unique neighbor expanders:** Let $G = (V, E)$ be an undirected graph. We say that $G$ is an $(\alpha_u, \beta_u)$-*unique neighbor expander* if for every $S \subseteq V$ s.t. $|S| \leq \alpha_u \cdot |V|$, there are at least $\beta_u \cdot |S|$ vertices in $V \backslash S$ that are adjacent in $G$ to exactly one vertex in $S$.

Clearly, if $G$ is a unique expander with good parameters, then broadcasting on it can be fast (again, by requiring all the vertices that received the message to send it to all their neighbors). Unfortunately, it seems that unique neighbor expansion might be hard to come by. For example, while the graph $C^+$ described above is a good (ordinary) expander, it is clearly not a good unique expander, as can be realized by considering the set $S = \{x, y, s_0\}$. (In general, ordinary expanders might have rather small unique neighbor expansion, as will be shown soon.) In addition, explicit constructions of unique expanders are rather scarce and known only for a limited set of parameters [2, 7].

The key observation triggering the current paper is that the property required from unique expanders might be *stronger* than necessary. This is because there is no reason to require *all* the vertices that received the message to send it. Rather, it may be enough to pick a *subset* $X$ of this set, that has a large set of unique neighbors, and require only the vertices of $X$ to transmit. This may be an attractive alternative since such a property may be easier to guarantee than unique neighbor expansion, and therefore may be achievable with better parameters $\alpha$ and $\beta$. (Note, e.g., that this property holds for our example graph $C^+$.) This observation thus motivates our definition for a new variant of expanders.

**Wireless expanders:** Let $G = (V, E)$ be an undirected graph. We say that $G$ is an $(\alpha_w, \beta_w)$-*wireless expander* if for every $S \subseteq V$ s.t. $|S| \leq \alpha_w \cdot |V|$, there exists a subset $S' \subseteq S$ s.t. there are at least $\beta_w \cdot |S|$ vertices in $V \backslash S$ that are adjacent to exactly one vertex in $S'$.

In this paper we are interested in investigating the properties of wireless expanders and the relationships between these graphs and the classes of ordinary expanders and unique neighbor expanders. We ask the following questions: by how much does the relaxed definition of wireless expanders (compared to unique neighbor expanders) help us in providing expanders with better parameters that are suitable for radio network communication? More specifically, given an $(\alpha, \beta)$-expander, can we prove that it is also an $(\alpha_w, \beta_w)$-wireless expander with $\alpha_w = f(\alpha, \beta)$ and $\beta_w = g(\alpha, \beta)$, for some functions $f$ and $g$?

## 1.2 Our Contribution

We present several results relating the parameters of the different notions of expanders. We begin by investigating the relationships between ordinary expanders and the more strict notion of unique neighbor expanders.

- Let $G = (V, E)$ be a $d$-regular graph that is an $(\alpha_u, \beta_u)$-unique neighbor expander, and let $\lambda = \lambda_2$ denote the second largest eigenvalue of its adjacency matrix, given by $a_{uv} = 1$ if $(u, v) \in E$ and $a_{uv} = 0$ otherwise. Then $G$ is an $(\alpha, \beta)$-expander with $\alpha = \alpha_u$ and $\beta \geq (1 - 1/d) \cdot \beta_u + (d - \lambda)/d \cdot (1 - \alpha_u)$.
- Suppose $G = (V, E)$ is an $(\alpha, \beta)$-expander with maximum degree $\Delta$. Then it is also an $(\alpha_u, \beta_u)$-unique expander with $\alpha_u = \alpha$, and $\beta_u \geq 2\beta - \Delta$. On the other hand, we show that there is an $(\alpha, \beta)$ bipartite expander whose unique expansion is $\beta_u \leq 2\beta - \Delta$.

We then turn to consider our new relaxed notion of wireless expander. Our key contribution is in providing nearly tight characterization for the relation between ordinary expanders and wireless expanders. On the positive side, using the probabilistic method, we show:

Theorem 1.1 (Positive Result). *For every $\Delta \geq 1, \beta \geq 1/\Delta$, every $(\alpha, \beta)$-expander $G$ with maximum degree $\Delta$ is a also an $(\alpha_w, \beta_w)$-wireless expander with $\alpha_w \geq \alpha$ and*

$$\beta_w = \Omega(\beta / \log(2 \cdot \min\{\Delta/\beta, \Delta \cdot \beta\})).$$

Our probabilistic argument has some similarity to the known *decay* method [6], which is a standard technique for coping with collisions in radio networks. Roughly speaking, in the decay protocol of [6], time is divided into phases of $\log n$ rounds and in the $i^{th}$ round of each phase, each node that holds a message transmits it with probability $2^{-i}$. Hence, each node that has a neighbor that holds a message, receives it within $O(\log n)$ phases. We use the idea of the decay method to show the existence of a subset $S' \subseteq S$ with a large unique neighborhood in $\Gamma(S)$.

An important feature of our argument is that it bounds the deviation of the wireless expansion from the ordinary expansion as a function of the *average-degree* rather than the maximum degree. As $\beta$ gets closer to $\Delta$ or to $1/\Delta$, this finer dependence leads to significantly better results than what could be achieved using the standard decay argument; our argument is also arguably simpler than the standard decay argument. As a technical note, we use the probabilistic method to prove a lower bound of $\Omega(\beta/\log(2 \cdot \Delta/\beta))$ on $\beta_w$, and then we push it up to the bound of Theorem 1.1 via a separate *deterministic* argument. As a corollary, for the important family of low *arboricity graphs*, which includes planar graphs and more generally graphs excluding a fixed minor, the wireless expansion matches the ordinary expansion up to a constant factor. (Indeed, the arboricity is at least $\min\{\Delta/\beta, \Delta \cdot \beta\}$; see Section 2.1 for the definition of arboricity.) In particular, this shows that radio broadcast in low arboricity graphs can be done much more efficiently than what was previously known.

Beyond the probabilistic argument, we also provide explicit deterministic arguments that obtain better parameters (by a constant factor); these are deferred to Appendix A of the full version [5].

We also show that asymptotically, no tighter connection can be established:

Theorem 1.2 (Negative Result). *There exists an $(\alpha, \beta)$-expander with maximum degree $\Delta$, whose wireless expansion is $\beta_w = O(\beta/\log(2 \cdot \min\{\Delta/\beta, \Delta \cdot \beta\})$.*

The explicit construction of this bad graph example is perhaps the most technically challenging result of this paper. Our explicit construction has interesting connections to related constructions that have been studied in the context of broadcast in radio networks [3, 12]. For instance, our "core graph" from Section 4.3.1 is reminiscent of a fundamental construction from [3]. However, while the construction of [3] is implicit (using the probabilistic method), our construction is explicit and can be viewed in some sense as the deterministic counterpart of [3]; moreover, our construction is arguably much simpler than that of [3]. We view this explicit construction as the technical highlight of our work, and anticipate that it will find further applications.

An additional application of both our positive and negative results is to the *Spokesman Election problem* introduced in the seminal paper of [8], where given a bipartite graph $G = (S, N, E)$, the goal is to compute a subset $S' \subseteq S$ with the maximum number of unique neighbors $\Gamma^1(S')$ in $N$. More specifically, we provide tight bounds for this problem, which apply to any expansion and average degree parameters, whereas the previous result of [8] applies only to one specific (very large) expansion parameter and only with respect to the maximum degree (rather than the average degree, which is a finer measure). In Section 4.2.1, we provide a detailed comparison to the bounds obtained by [8].

Finally, another application of our negative result, and of our explicit core graph in particular, is in the context of broadcast lower bounds in radio networks. In their seminal paper, Kushilevitz and Mansour [12] proved that there exist networks in which the expected time to broadcast a message is $\Omega(D\log(n/D))$, where $D$ is the network diameter and $n$ is the number of vertices, and this lower bound is tight for any $D = \Omega(\log n)$ due to a highly non-trivial upper bound by Czumaj and Rytter [10]. Since the upper bound of [10] holds with high probability, it implies that the lower bound $\Omega(D\log(n/D))$ of [12] also holds with high probability. Newport [13] presented an interesting alternative proof to the one by Kushilevitz and Mansour. Although short and elegant, Newport's proof relies on two fundamental results in this area, due to Alon et al. [1] and Alon et al. [3] – Lemma 3.1 in [13] – whose proof is intricate. Also, as with Kushilevitz and Mansour's proof, Newport only proves an *expected* lower bound on the broadcast time, with the understanding that a high probability bound follows from [10]. By unwinding the ingredients of Newport's proof, the resulting proof (especially for a high probability bound on the broadcast time) is long and intricate. Using the properties of our explicit core graph construction, we derive a simple and self-contained proof for the same lower bound, arguably much simpler than that of [12, 13]. An important advantage of our proof over [12, 13] is that it gives a high probability bound on the broadcast time *directly*, i.e., without having to take a detour through the upper bound of [10].

Summarizing, besides the mathematical appeal of wireless expanders and their connections to well-studied types of expanders, we demonstrate that they find natural applications in the well-studied area of radio networks. We anticipate that a further study of wireless expanders will reveal additional applications, also outside the scope of radio networks.

### 1.3 Organization

In Sec. 2 we introduce the notation and definitions used throughout. We investigate the relations between ordinary expanders and unique neighbor expanders in Section 3. Sec. 4 is devoted to our new notion of wireless expanders, where we present nearly tight characterization for the relation between ordinary expanders and wireless expanders. We start (Sec. 4.1) with describing our basic framework; the positive and negative results are presented in Sec. 4.2 and Sec. 4.3, respectively. Our results for the Spokesman Election problem [8] are given in Section 4.2.1. Finally, Sec. 5 is devoted to our alternative lower bound proof of $\Omega(D\log(n/D))$ on the broadcast time in radio networks.

## 2 PRELIMINARIES

### 2.1 Graph Notation

For an undirected graph $G = (V, E)$, vertex $v \in V$ and a subset $S \subseteq V$, denote the set of $v$'s neighbors in $G$ by $\Gamma(v) = \{u \mid (u, v) \in E\}$, and let $\Gamma(S) = \bigcup_{v \in S} \Gamma(v)$ be the *neighborhood* of a vertex set $S$ in $G$ (including neighbors that belong to $S$ itself), and $\Gamma^-(S) = \Gamma(S) \setminus S$ be the set of neighbors external to $S$. Also define $\Gamma(v, S) = \Gamma(v) \cap S$ as the neighbors of $v$ in the subset $S$. The *expansion* of $S$ is the ratio $|\Gamma^-(S)|/|S|$. The *unique-neighborhood* of $S$, denoted by $\Gamma^1(S)$, is the set of vertices outside $S$ that have a unique neighbor from $S$. The *unique-neighbor expansion* of $S$ is the ratio $|\Gamma^1(S)|/|S|$. Let $S'$ be an arbitrary subset of $S$. The *$S$-excluding neighborhood* of $S'$, denoted by $\Gamma_S(S')$, is the set of all vertices outside $S$ that have at least one neighbor from $S'$. Similarly, the *$S$-excluding unique-neighborhood* of $S'$, denoted by $\Gamma_S^1(S')$, is the set of all vertices outside $S$ that have a unique neighbor from $S'$. In particular, $\Gamma^1(S) = \Gamma_S^1(S)$. The *wireless expansion* of $S$ is the maximum ratio $|\Gamma_S^1(S')|/|S|$ over all subsets $S'$ of $S$. For two sets $S, T \subset V$, let $e(S, T)$ be the set of edges connecting $S$ and $T$. For vertex $v \in V$, let $\deg(v) = \deg_G(v)$ denote the degree of $v$ in $G$, i.e., the number of $v$'s neighbors, and let $\Delta(G) = \max\{\deg(v) \mid v \in V\}$ be the maximum degree over all the vertices in $G$. For set $S \subset V$ and vertex $v \in V$, let $\deg(v, S) = \deg(v) \cap S$ be the number of $v$'s neighbors that are in $S$. For two vertices $v, u \in V$, let $d(u, v)$ be the distance between $u$ and $v$ (i.e., the length of the shortest path connecting them), and let $D = D(G) = \max\{d(u, v) \mid u, v \in V\}$ be the diameter of the graph, i.e. the maximum distance between any two vertices.

We use the combinatorial definition for (vertex) expansion, which requires that every (not too large) set of vertices of the graph has a relatively large set of neighbors. Specifically, an $n$-vertex graph $G$ is called an $(\alpha, \beta)$ *vertex expander* for positive parameters $\alpha$ and $\beta$, if every subset $S \subseteq V$ s.t. $|S| \leq \alpha n$ has many external neighbors, namely, $|\Gamma^-(S)| \geq \beta \cdot |S|$. The *(ordinary) expansion* $\beta(G)$ of $G$ is defined as the minimum expansion over all vertex sets $S \subseteq V$ of size $|S| \leq \alpha n$, namely, $\beta(G) = \min\{|\Gamma^-(S)|/|S| \mid S \subseteq V, |S| \leq \alpha n\}$. A similar definition appears in the literature for bipartite graph, namely, a bipartite graph $G = (L, R, E)$ with sides $L$ and $R$, such that every edge from $E \subset L \times R$ connects one vertex of $L$ and one vertex of $R$ is called an $(\alpha, \beta)$ bipartite vertex expander if every subset $S \subset L$ s.t. $|S| \leq \alpha|L|$ has at least $\beta|S|$ neighbors in $R$. It is usually assumed that the two sides $L$ and $R$ of the bipartition are of (roughly) the same size.

A graph $G = (V, E)$ has *arboricity* $\eta = \eta(G)$ if

$$\eta = \max_{U \subseteq V} \left\lceil \frac{|E(U)|}{|U| - 1} \right\rceil,$$

where $E(U) = \{(u, v) \in E \mid u, v \in U\}$. Thus the arboricity is the same (up to a factor of 2) as the maximum *average degree* over all induced subgraphs of $G$. It is easy to see that for any $(\alpha, \beta)$-expander with maximum degree $\Delta$, the arboricity is at least $\min\{\Delta/\beta, \Delta \cdot \beta\}$.

## 2.2 Unique Neighbor and Wireless Expanders

Let us now define formally the notions of unique and wireless expanders. Let $G = (V, E)$ be an $n$-vertex undirected graph. We say that $G$ is an $(\alpha_u, \beta_u)$-*unique expander* [2] if for every $S \subseteq V$ s.t. $|S| \leq \alpha_u n$, there are at least $\beta_u \cdot |S|$ vertices in $V \backslash S$ that are adjacent to exactly one vertex in $S$, namely, $|\Gamma^1(S)| \geq \beta_u \cdot |S|$. The *unique-neighbor expansion* $\beta_u(G)$ of $G$ is defined as the minimum unique-neighbor expansion over all vertex sets $S \subseteq V$ with $|S| \leq \alpha_u n$, namely,

$$\beta_u(G) = \min\{|\Gamma^1(S)|/|S| \mid S \subseteq V, |S| \leq \alpha_u n\}.$$

We say that $G$ is an $(\alpha_w, \beta_w)$-*wireless expander* if for every $S \subseteq V$ s.t. $|S| \leq \alpha_w n$, there exists a subset $S' \subseteq S$ s.t. there are at least $\beta_w \cdot |S|$ vertices in $V \backslash S$ that are adjacent in $G$ to exactly one vertex in $S'$, i.e., $|\Gamma^1_S(S')| \geq \beta_w \cdot |S|$. The *wireless expansion* $\beta_w(G)$ of $G$ is defined as the minimum wireless expansion over all sets $S \subseteq V$ with $|S| \leq \alpha_w n$, namely,

$$\beta_w(G) = \min\{\max\{|\Gamma^1_S(S')|/|S| \mid S' \subseteq S\} \mid S \subseteq V, |S| \leq \alpha_w n\}.$$

In our arguments, we usually fix $\alpha$ and study the relations between the $\beta$-values for different notions of expanders. The following connection is easy to verify.

Observation 2.1. *If $\alpha = \alpha_u = \alpha_w$, then $\beta(G) \geq \beta_w(G) \geq \beta_u(G)$.*

# 3 RELATIONS BETWEEN $\beta$ AND $\beta_u$

Let $G = (V, E)$ be a $d$-regular undirected graph and let $A = A_G = (a_{uv})_{u,v \in V}$ be its adjacency matrix given by $a_{uv} = 1$ if $(u, v) \in E$ and $a_{uv} = 0$ otherwise. Since $G$ is $d$-regular, the largest eigenvalue of $A$ is $d$, corresponding to the all-1 eigenvector (as $1/d \cdot A$ is a stochastic matrix). Let $\lambda = \lambda_2$ denote the second largest eigenvalue of $G$.

Lemma 3.1. *If a $d$-regular graph $G = (V, E)$ is an $(\alpha_u, \beta_u)$-unique expander, then it also an $(\alpha, \beta)$-expander with $\alpha = \alpha_u$ and $\beta \geq (1 - 1/d) \cdot \beta_u + (d - \lambda) \cdot (1 - \alpha_u)/d$.*

Proof. Alon and Spencer [4] prove that every partition of the set of vertices $V$ into two disjoint subsets $A$ and $B$ satisfies $|e(A, B)| \geq (d - \lambda) \cdot |A| \cdot |B|/|V|$. In our case (i.e. $A = S$, $B = V \setminus S = \bar{S}$, and $|S| \leq \alpha_u \cdot |V|$) we get that

$$\begin{aligned} |e(S, \bar{S})| &\geq (d - \lambda) \cdot \frac{|S| \cdot |\bar{S}|}{|V|} \\ &\geq (d - \lambda) \cdot \frac{|S| \cdot (|V| - \alpha_u \cdot |V|)}{|V|} \\ &= (d - \lambda) \cdot |S| \cdot (1 - \alpha_u). \end{aligned}$$

Moreover, by the expansion properties, there exists a set $U$ of at least $\beta_u \cdot |S|$ vertices in $\Gamma^-(S)$ that have a unique neighbor in $S$. From uniqueness, we have $e(S, U) = |U| \geq \beta_u|S|$. Thus, there are at least $(d - \lambda) \cdot |S| \cdot (1 - \alpha_u) - |U|$ edges in $e(S, \bar{S})$ that are not connect to the vertices in $U$ (i.e. in $e(S, \bar{S} \setminus U)$). Now, because $G$ is $d$-regular, we get that there exist at least $|U| + ((d - \lambda) \cdot |S| \cdot (1 - \alpha_u) - |U|)/d$ vertices in $\Gamma^-(S)$. Hence, we get

$$\begin{aligned} |\Gamma^-(S)| &\geq |U| + \frac{((d - \lambda) \cdot |S| \cdot (1 - \alpha_u) - |U|)}{d} \\ &= \left(1 - \frac{1}{d}\right) \cdot |U| + \frac{(d - \lambda) \cdot (1 - \alpha_u)}{d} \cdot |S| \\ &\geq \left(1 - \frac{1}{d}\right) \cdot \beta_u|S| + \frac{(d - \lambda) \cdot (1 - \alpha_u)}{d} \cdot |S| \\ &= \left(\left(1 - \frac{1}{d}\right) \cdot \beta_u + \frac{(d - \lambda) \cdot (1 - \alpha_u)}{d}\right) \cdot |S| \end{aligned}$$

thus, $G$ is a $(\alpha, \beta)$-expander with $\alpha \geq \alpha_u$ and $\beta \geq (1 - 1/d) \cdot \beta_u + ((d - \lambda) \cdot (1 - \alpha_u)/d$. □

It is known (and easy to verify) that ordinary expanders whose expansion is close to the (maximum) degree in the graph are also good unique expanders, or formally:

Lemma 3.2. *Suppose $G = (V, E)$ is an $(\alpha, \beta)$-expander with maximum degree $\Delta$. Then it is also a unique $(\alpha_u, \beta_u)$-expander, with $\alpha_u = \alpha$ and $\beta_u \geq 2\beta - \Delta$.*

**Remark.** Substituting $\beta = (1 - \varepsilon)\Delta$ (for $\varepsilon \leq 1/2$), we obtain $\beta_u \geq (1 - 2\varepsilon)\Delta$.

The lower bound $2\beta - \Delta$ on the unique-neighbor expansion $\beta_u$ provided by Lemma 3.2 is meaningful only when $\beta$ is larger than $\Delta/2$. The following example shows that this lower bound $2\beta - \Delta$ is tight.

Lemma 3.3. *For any $\Delta$ and $\beta$ such that $\Delta/2 \leq \beta \leq \Delta$, there is an $(\alpha, \beta)$ bipartite expander $G^{bad} = (S, N, E)$ with maximum degree $\Delta$ whose unique expansion is $\beta_u \leq 2\beta - \Delta$.*

Proof. Construct the graph $G^{bad}$ as follows. Let $S = \{v_1, \ldots, v_s\}$, with $s = |S|$, and suppose that each vertex $v_i \in S$ has exactly $\Delta$ neighbors, all of which are in $N$. (For technical convenience, we define $v_0 = v_s$, $v_1 = v_{s+1}$; that is, the vertices $v_1$ and $v_s$ are not different than the other vertices (they should not be viewed as "endpoints", but rather part of an implicit "cycle"). Moreover, for each $i = 1, \ldots, s$, the vertices $v_i$ and $v_{i+1}$ have exactly $\Delta - \beta$ common neighbors; that is, $|\Gamma(v_i) \cap \Gamma(v_{i+1})| = \Delta - \beta$. More concretely, writing $\Gamma(v_i) = \{v_i^1, \ldots, v_i^\Delta\}$, we have that

$$\Gamma(v_i) \cap \Gamma(v_{i+1}) = \{v_i^{\beta+1}, \ldots, v_i^\Delta\} = \{v_{i+1}^1, \ldots, v_{i+1}^{\Delta-\beta}\}.$$

In other words, the "last" $\Delta - \beta$ neighbors $v_i^{\beta+1}, \ldots, v_i^\Delta$ of $v_i$ are the "first" $\Delta - \beta$ neighbors $v_{i+1}^1, \ldots, v_{i+1}^{\Delta-\beta}$ of $v_{i+1}$, respectively. (See Figure 1 for an illustration.)

This means that for each $i = 1, \ldots, s$, the first (resp., last) $\Delta - \beta$ neighbors of $v_i$ are also neighbors of $v_{i-1}$ (resp, $v_{i+1}$). The remaining $\Delta - 2(\Delta - \beta) = 2\beta - \Delta$ neighbors of $v_i$, however, are uniquely

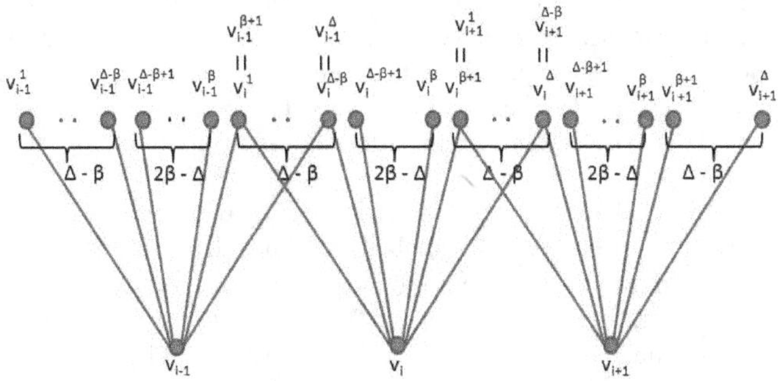

**Figure 1:** An illustration of a worst-case scenario for the unique-neighbor expansion.

covered by $v_i$. It follows that the number of vertices in the neighborhood of $S$ that are uniquely covered by vertices from $S$ is equal to $s(2\beta-\Delta)$. Consequently, the unique neighbor expansion $\beta_u$ is $2\beta-\Delta$, as claimed. Noting that the ordinary expansion is $\beta$ completes the proof of the lemma. □

**Remarks.** (1) The meaning of Lemma 3.3 is that a graph with high (ordinary) expansion may have unique neighbor expansion of zero. For example, in the graph $G^{bad}$ described in the proof of Lemma 3.3, the unique-neighbor expansion is $2\beta - \Delta$, but the wireless expansion is at least $\max\{2\beta - \Delta, \Delta/2\}$. To see that, let $S'$ be a subset of $S$ and suppose $S' = S_1 \cup S_2 \cup \ldots \cup S_k$ such that each $S_i$ is a sequence of consecutive vertices, i.e., using the previous notations, for $S_i$ of size $l$, $S_i = \{v_j, .., v_{j+l}\}$ for some index $1 \le j \le s$. Suppose also that between every two sets $S_i$ and $S_j$ there is at least one vertex that is not in $S'$ (in other words, we can't expand $S_i$ to be a longer sequence in $S'$). Therefore, to compute $\beta_w$, it is enough to compute the expansion parameter for each $S_i = \{v_j, \ldots, v_{j+l}\}$. Consider two options for choosing the set $S'' \subset S_i$. The first choice is to take $S'' = S_i$. Then we get an expansion of $f(l) = (l\Delta - 2(l-1)(\Delta-\beta))/l = ((2-l)\Delta + 2(l-1)\beta)/l$. The second choice is to take into $S''$ every second vertex in the sequence of $S_i$. Then we get an expansion of $g(l) = l\Delta/(2l)$ if $l$ is even, and $g(l) = (l+1)\Delta/(2l)$ if $l$ is odd. (In the case where $S' = S$ we get in the first choice an expansion of $f(l) = l(2\beta - \Delta)/l = 2\beta - \Delta$ and in the second an expansion of $g(l) = (l-1)\Delta/(2l)$). Thus, $\beta_w \ge \min\{\max\{g(l), f(l)\} \mid l > 0\}$. As $f(l)$ and $g(l)$ are both decreasing functions, we get that $\beta_w \ge \max\{\lim_{l\to\infty} g(l), \lim_{l\to\infty} f(l)\} = \max\left\{2\beta - \Delta, \frac{\Delta}{2}\right\}$. This calculation also shows that if $\beta = \Delta/2$, then the unique-neighbor expansion becomes 0, but the wireless expansion becomes $\Delta/2$.

(2) Although the bipartite graph used in the proof of Lemma 3.3 is an ordinary bipartite expander (according to the definition given in Section 2.1), note that the sizes of the two sides $S$ and $N$ differ by a factor of $\beta$. Also, it does not provide an ordinary non-bipartite expander, because the expansion is achieved only on one side, from $S$ towards $N$. Nevertheless, one can plug this "bad" bipartite graph on top of an ordinary $(\alpha, \beta)$-expander with a possibly good unique-neighbor expansion, so that the graph resulting from this tweak is an ordinary $(\alpha, \beta)$-expander with a unique-neighbor expansion bounded by $2\beta - \Delta$. Notice, however, that the maximum degree in the resulting graph, denoted by $\Delta'$, may be as large as the sum of the maximum degrees of the "bad" bipartite graph and the $(\alpha, \beta)$-expander that we started from. For example, if $\Delta' = 2\Delta$, then the unique-neighbor expansion of the resulting graph is bounded by $2\beta-\Delta = 2\beta-\Delta'/2$. Since we apply a similar tweak in Section 4.3 (in the context of wireless expansion rather than unique expansion), we omit the exact details of this rather simple tweak from the extended abstract.

# 4 BOUNDS ON WIRELESS EXPANSION

## 4.1 Our Framework

Consider an arbitrary (ordinary) $(\alpha, \beta)$-expander $G$. As shown in Section 3, the unique-neighbor expansion $\beta_u$ provided by $G$ may be zero even if the ordinary expansion $\beta$ is high. In what follows we demonstrate that the wireless expansion $\beta_w(G)$ of $G$ cannot be much lower than its ordinary expansion $\beta(G)$. Moreover, we prove asymptotically tight bounds on the ratio $\beta(G)/\beta_w(G)$. This yields a strong separation between the unique-neighbor expansion and the wireless expansion, which provides a natural motivation for studying wireless expanders, particularly in applications where we are given a *fixed* expander network (that cannot be changed).

First let us observe that by Obs. 2.1, Lemma 3.2 yields the following bound on $\beta_w$.

LEMMA 4.1. *Suppose $G = (V, E)$ is an $(\alpha, \beta)$-expander with maximum degree $\Delta$. Then it is also a wireless $(\alpha_w, \beta_w)$-expander with $\alpha_w = \alpha$ and $\beta_w \ge 2\beta - \Delta$.*

Throughout what follows, we simplify the discussion by focusing attention to an arbitrary bipartite graph $G_S = (S, N, E_S)$ with sides $S$ and $N$, such that $|N| \ge \beta \cdot |S|$. We assume that no vertex of $G_S$ is isolated, i.e., all vertex degrees are at least 1.

Note that this bipartition can be thought of as representing all edges in the original graph $G$ that connect an arbitrary vertex set $S$ with its neighborhood $N = \Gamma^-(S)$. While in $G$ there might be edges internal to $S$ and/or $N$, ignoring these edges has no effect whatsoever on the expansion bounds.

Our goal is to show the existence of a subset $S'$ of $S$ in the graph $G_S$, whose $S$-excluding unique-neighborhood $\Gamma^1_S(S')$ is not much smaller than the entire neighborhood $N$ of $S$. Of course, this would imply that the wireless expansion of an arbitrary set $S$ in $G$ (of any size) is close to its ordinary expansion, yielding the required result.

## 4.2 Positive Results: Ordinary Expanders are Good Wireless Expanders

Let $\delta_S$ (resp., $\delta_N$) be the average degree of the set $S$ (resp., $N$) in the graph $G_S$. That is, $\delta_S = \sum_{u\in S} \deg(u, N)/|S|$ and $\delta_N = \sum_{u'\in N} \deg(u', S)/|N|$. Clearly, $\delta_N, \delta_S \ge 1$. In this section, we show that $\beta_w$ can be bounded from below as a function of $\min\{\delta_S, \delta_N\}$.

We begin by considering an $(\alpha, \beta)$-expander $G$ for $\beta \ge 1$. We now show:

LEMMA 4.2. *For every $\beta, \Delta \ge 1$, there exists a subset $S^* \subseteq S$, satisfying that*
$|\Gamma^1_S(S^*)| = \Omega(|N|/\log 2\delta_N) = \Omega(\beta/\log 2\delta_N) \cdot |S|$. *Hence, $\beta_w = \Omega(\beta/\log 2(\Delta/\beta))$.*

Proof. Since $\beta \geq 1$, we have $|S| \leq |N|$, $1 \leq \delta_N \leq \delta_S$ and $\delta_N \leq \Delta/\beta$. The proof relies on the probabilistic method. First, consider the set $N'$ of all vertices from $N$ with degree at most $2\delta_N$. Note that $|N'| \geq |N|/2$ and that all vertices of $N'$ have positive degree. We now divide the subset $N'$ into $k = \lfloor \log 2\delta_N \rfloor$ subsets depending on their degree in $S$, where the $i^{th}$ subset $N_i$ consists of all vertices $u \in N'$ with $\deg(u, S) \in [2^i, 2^{i+1})$. Let $N_j$ be the largest subset among these $k$ subsets. We have that $|N_j| \geq |N|/k = \Omega(|N|/\log 2\delta_N) = \Omega(|N|/\log 2(\Delta/\beta))$. We next show that there exists a subset $S^* \subseteq S$ such that $\Gamma^1_S(S^*)$ contains a constant fraction of the vertices of $N_j$.

Consider a random subset $S' \subseteq S$ obtained by sampling each vertex $u \in S$ independently with probability $1/2^j$. For every vertex $u \in N_j$, let $X(u) \in \{0, 1\}$ be the indicator random variable that takes value 1 if $u$ has exactly one neighbor in $S'$. As $\deg(u, S) \in [2^j, 2^{j+1})$, we have that

$$\begin{aligned} \mathbb{E}(X(u)) &= \mathbb{P}(X(u) = 1) = \deg(u, S)/2^j \cdot (1 - 1/2^j)^{\deg(u,S)-1} \\ &\geq (1 - 1/2^j)^{2^{j+1}-1} \geq e^{-3} . \end{aligned}$$

Hence, $\sum_{u \in N_j} \mathbb{E}(X(u)) = \Omega(|N_j|) = \Omega(\beta|S|/\log 2(\Delta/\beta))$. We get that the expected number of vertices in $N$ that are uniquely covered by a random subset $S'$ is $\Omega(\beta|S|/\log 2(\Delta/\beta))$. Hence, there exists a subset $S^* \subseteq S$ with $|\Gamma^1_S(S^*)| = \Omega(\beta/\log 2(\Delta/\beta)) \cdot |S|$. The lemma follows. □

In Appendix A of the full version [5], we provide a sequence of deterministic arguments that obtain better bounds for $\beta_w$ (by constant factors) compared to the probabilistic argument shown above.

We now turn to consider the case $\beta < 1$. In this case the bound on the wireless expansion depends on $\delta_S$, namely, on the average degree in the larger set $S$. We show:

Lemma 4.3. *For every $\Delta \geq 1$ and $\beta \in [1/\Delta, 1)$, there exists a subset $S^* \subseteq S$, satisfying that $|\Gamma^1_S(S^*)| = \Omega(\beta/\log \delta_S) \cdot |S|$. Since $\delta_S \leq \beta \cdot \Delta$, we have $\beta_w = \Omega(\beta/\log 2(\Delta \cdot \beta))$.*

Proof. Let $S' \subseteq S$ be the set of all vertices $u \in S$ with $\deg(u, N) \leq 2\delta_S$, and note that $|S'| \geq |S|/2$. Let $N' = \Gamma^-(S')$ be the set of neighbors of $S'$ in $N$. By the expansion of $G$, we have $|N'| \geq \beta \cdot |S'| \geq \beta|S|/2$. We now claim that there exists a subset $S'' \subseteq S'$ satisfying $\Gamma^-(S'') = N'$ and $|S''| \leq |N'|$. To see this, initially set $S''$ to be empty. Iterate over the vertices of $S'$ and add a vertex $u \in S'$ to $S''$ only if it covers a new vertex of $N'$ (i.e., it has a new neighbor in $N'$ that has not been covered before). Then $|S''| \leq |N'|$ and hence in the induced bipartite graph $G'$ with sides $S''$ and $N'$, the expansion measure $\beta'$, with $\beta' = |N'|/|S''|$, is at least 1. The average degree of a vertex $u \in N'$ in the graph $G'$ is bounded by $|E(G')|/|N'| \leq 2\delta_S \cdot |S''|/|N'| \leq 2\delta_S$. Employing the argument of Lemma 4.2 on the bipartite graph $G'$, we get that there exists a subset $S^* \subseteq S''$ satisfying $|\Gamma^1_{S''}(S^*)| = \Omega(|N'|/\log 4\delta_S) = \Omega(\beta/\log 2\delta_S)|S|$. Since $\delta_S \leq \Delta \cdot \beta$, it follows that $\beta_w = \Omega(\beta/\log 2(\Delta \cdot \beta))$. □

Theorem 1.1 follows from Lemmas 4.2 and 4.3.

*4.2.1 Relation to the Spokesman Election problem [8].* Motivated by broadcasting in multihop radio networks, Chalmtac and Weinstien [8] defined the *spokesmen election problem.* In this problem, given a bipartite graph $G = (S, N, E)$, the goal is to compute a subset $S' \subseteq S$ with the maximum number of unique neighbors $\Gamma^1(S')$ in $N$. This problem was shown in [9] to be NP-hard. In [8], an approximation scheme is presented that computes a subset $S' \subseteq S$ with $|\Gamma^1(S')| \geq |N|/\log|S|$, and this approximation scheme was then used to devise efficient broadcasting algorithms for multihop radio networks.

The bounds provided in Lemmas 4.2 and 4.3 refine and strengthen upon the bound of [8]. Our bounds show that $|\Gamma^1(S')|$ cannot be smaller than $|N|$ by more than a factor that is logarithmic in $2\min\{\delta_N, \delta_S\}$, which depends on the *average degree* in $G$, whereas the bound of 4.3 did not preclude the possibility of $|\Gamma^1(S')|$ being smaller than $|N|$ by a factor of $\log|S|$. Note that $\min\{\delta_N, \delta_S\}$ is always upper bounded by $|S|$, but can be much smaller than it. In particular, $\min\{\delta_N, \delta_S\}$ is always low in low arboricity graphs (even if the maximum degree is huge), regardless of $|S|$.

We remark that our randomized approach of choosing the subset $S' \subseteq S$ is extremely simple, and in particular, it yields a much simpler solution to the Spokesman Election problem than that of [8]. Since the solution to this problem was used in [8] to devise efficient broadcasting algorithms for multihop radio networks, our solution can be used to obtain simpler broadcasting algorithms for multihop radio networks than those of [8].

In the next section (Section 4.3), we show that our positive results for $(\alpha, \beta)$-expanders are essentially the best that one can hope for, by providing a "bad" expander example. A bad graph expander example for the related Spokesman Election problem was given in [8], but our graph example is stronger than that of [8] in several ways, and is based on completely different ideas. The graph example of [8] is tailored for the somewhat degenerate case where $|N| = \Omega(|S|!)$, whence $N$ is exponentially larger than $S$, thus the expansion of the bad graph (and the degree) is huge. In addition, in their example, one cannot uniquely cover more than $|N|/\log(|S|) = |N|/\log\log|N|$ vertices of $N$, leaving a big gap between their positive and negative results. Our bad graph example, in contrast, works for any expansion parameter $\beta$. Moreover, similarly to our positive result, the bounds implied by our negative result depend on the average degree of the graph rather than the maximum degree or the size of $S$. In particular, by taking $\beta$ to be constant and $\Delta$ to be sufficiently large, our graph example shows that one cannot cover more than $|N|/\log|N|$ vertices of $N$, which not only matches our positive result, but also closes the gap left by [8].

## 4.3 Negative Results: Worst-Case Expanders

In this section we present a "bad graph " expander construction. The description of our construction is given in three stages. First, in Section 4.3.1 we construct a bipartite graph $G_S = (S, N, E_S)$ with sides $S$ and $N$ where $|N| = |S|\log 2|S|$ (assuming for simplicity that $|S|$ is an integer power of 2) that satisfies two somewhat contradictory requirements: On the one hand, for every subset $S'$ of $S$, $|\Gamma(S')| \geq \log 2|S| \cdot |S'|$. Hence the ordinary expansion of $G_S$, denoted by $\beta$, is at least $\log 2|S|$. On the other hand, for every subset $S'$ of $S$, $|\Gamma^1_S(S')| \leq (2/\log 2|S|) \cdot |N|$. Hence the wireless expansion of $G_S$, denoted $\beta_w$, satisfies $\beta_w \leq \beta(2/\log 2|S|)$. Although this graph is an ordinary bipartite expander (according to the definition given in Section 2.1), note that the size of $N$ is greater than that of $S$ by a factor of $\log 2|S|$. Also, it does not provide an ordinary non-bipartite expander, because the expansion is achieved only on one side, from $S$ towards $N$. Nevertheless, it provides the core of our worst-case expander, and is henceforth referred to as the *core graph.* Next, in Section 4.3.2 we describe a generalized core graph $G_S^* = (S^*, N^*, E_S^*)$ with an arbitrary expansion $\beta^*$, while preserving the same upper bound on the wireless expansion. Finally, in Section 4.3.3 we plug the generalized core graph on top of an ordinary expander $G(V, E)$ with a possibly good wireless expansion, such that $N^* \subseteq V$ and $S^* \cap V = \emptyset$, and demonstrate that the resulting graph $\tilde{G} = (V \cup S^*, E \cup E_S^*)$ is an ordinary expander with a similar expansion but a poor wireless expansion. While the generalized core graph is bipartite, the ordinary expander $G$ that we started from does not have to be bipartite. If the original expander $G$ is bipartite, we can ensure that the expander resulting from our modification will also be bipartite.

*4.3.1 The Core Graph.*

LEMMA 4.4. *For any integer $s \geq 1$, there is a bipartite graph $G_S = (S, N, E_S)$ such that:*

1. *$s := |S|$ and $|N| = s \log 2s$.*
2. *Each vertex in $S$ has degree $2s - 1$.*
3. *The maximum degree $\Delta_N$ of a vertex in $N$ is $s$, and the average degree $\delta_N$ of a vertex in $N$ is at most $2s/\log 2s$.*
4. *For every subset $S'$ of $S$, $|\Gamma(S')| \geq \log 2s \cdot |S'|$. (Hence the ordinary expansion, denoted $\beta$, is at least $\log 2s$.)*
5. *For every subset $S'$ of $S$, $|\Gamma_S^1(S')| \leq 2s = (2/\log 2s) \cdot |N|$. (Hence the wireless expansion, denoted $\beta_w$, satisfies $\beta_w \leq \beta(2/\log 2s)$.)*

PROOF. As mentioned, we assume for simplicity that $s$ is an integer power of 2; dropping this assumption may affect the bounds in the statements of the lemma by at most a small constant. To describe the edge set $E_S$ of $G_S$, consider a perfect binary tree $T_S$ with $s$ leaves (and $s - 1$ internal vertices). We identify each leaf $z$ of $T_S$ with a unique vertex of $S$. Each vertex $v$ of $T_S$ is associated with a set $N_v$ of vertices from $N$; all these vertex sets are pairwise disjoint, and we have $N = \bigcup_{v \in T_S} N_v$. For a vertex $v$ at level $i$ of the tree, $i = 0, 1, \ldots, \log s$, the set $N_v$ contains $s/2^i$ vertices. Thus the sizes of these vertex sets decrease geometrically with the level, starting with the set $N_{rt}$ at the root $rt$ that consists of $s$ vertices, and ending with singletons at the leaves. Denote by $N_i$ the union of the sets $N_v$ over all $i$-level vertices in $T_S$. For all $i = 0, 1, \ldots, \log s$, we have $|N_i| = s$, hence $|N| = s \log 2s$. For a leaf $z$ in $T_S$, let $A(z)$ denote the set of its ancestors in $T_S$ (including $z$ itself), and let $\hat{N}_z = \bigcup_{w \in A(z)} N_w$. Define $E(z) = \{(z, v) \mid v \in \hat{N}_z\}$. Then $E_S = \bigcup_{z \in S} E(z)$. (See Figure 2 for an illustration.)

OBSERVATION 4.5. *There is an edge between vertex $z \in S$ and vertex $v \in N$ iff the unique vertex $w$ in $T_S$ such that $v \in N_w$ is an ancestor of $z$ in $T_S$.*

Note that the degree of each vertex $z \in S$, namely $|E(z)|$, is equal to $\sum_{i=0}^{\log s} 2^i = 2s - 1$. On the other hand, the degrees of vertices in $N$ are not uniform. For a vertex $v$ in $T_S$, each vertex in $N_v$ is incident on the descendant leaves of $v$. This means that if $v$ is at level $i$ of $T_S$, then all vertices in $N_v$ have degree $2^{\log s - i} = s/2^i$. Hence, the maximum degree $\Delta_N$ of a vertex in $N$ is $s$ and the average degree

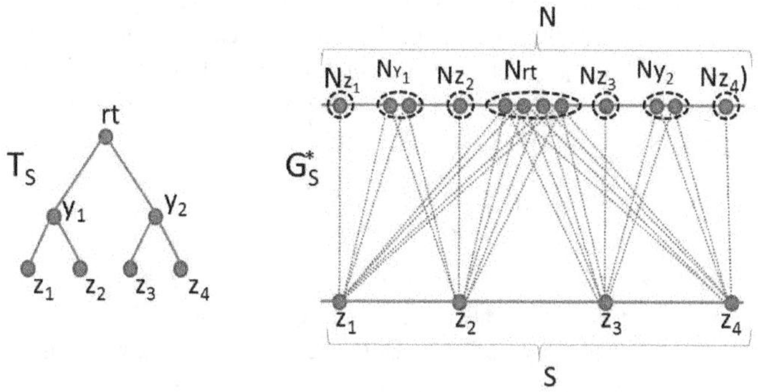


**Figure 2**

$\delta_N$ of a vertex in $N$ is given by

$$\delta_N = \frac{1}{|N|}\left(\sum_{i=0}^{\log s} |N_i|(s/2^i)\right) = \frac{1}{|N|}\left(\sum_{i=0}^{\log s} \frac{s^2}{2^i}\right) \leq \frac{2s^2}{s \log 2s} = \frac{2s}{\log 2s}.$$

Next, we lower bound the expansion $\beta$ of the graph $G_S$. Fix an arbitrary set $S' \subseteq S$ of size $k$, for any $1 \leq k \leq s$, and consider the set of $k$ leaves in $T_S$ identified with $S'$, denoted by $s_1, \ldots, s_k$. Recall that the level of the root $rt$ is 0, the level of its children is 1, etc., the level of the leaves of $T_S$ is $\log s$; in what follows we say that a vertex has *inverse-level* $j$ if its level in $T_S$ is $\log s - j$. For each vertex $v$ at inverse-level $j$ in $T_S$, the associated vertex set $N_v$ has size $2^j$. Next, we distinguish between inverse-levels at most $\lfloor \log k \rfloor$ and higher inverse-levels. For any inverse-level $0 \leq j \leq \lfloor \log k \rfloor$, the number of ancestors of the $k$ leaves $s_1, \ldots, s_k$ in the tree $T_S$ is at least $k/2^j$, hence the union of the corresponding vertex sets is of size at least $k$. (The lower bound is realized when the $k$ leaves are consecutive to each other in $T_S$.) For each inverse-level higher than $\lfloor \log k \rfloor$, the number of ancestors of the $k$ leaves $s_1, \ldots, s_k$ may be as small as 1, but the vertex set associated with such an ancestor is of size at least $k$. It follows that the union of the corresponding vertex sets at each level is lower bounded by $k$, and so the union of the vertex sets of all ancestors of the $k$ leaves $s_1, \ldots, s_k$ over all levels is at least $(\log s + 1) \cdot k$. By Observation 4.5, all the vertices in this union are neighbors of the vertices in $S'$, thereby yielding $|\Gamma(S')| \geq (\log s + 1) \cdot k = \log 2s \cdot |S'|$. It follows that $\beta \geq \log 2s$.

It remains to upper bound the wireless expansion $\beta_w$ of the graph $G_S$. Fix an arbitrary set $S' \subseteq S$, and recall that $\Gamma_S^1(S')$ denotes the set of *all* vertices outside $S$ that have a single neighbor from $S'$. For a vertex $v$ in $T_S$, let $D(v)$ denote the set of its descendants in $T_S$ (including $v$ itself), and let $\check{N}_v = \bigcup_{w \in D(v)} N_w$. We argue that for any vertex $v$ at inverse-level $j$, for $j = 0, 1, \ldots, \log s$, it holds that $|\Gamma_S^1(S') \cap \check{N}_v| \leq 2^{j+1} - 1$. The proof is by induction on $j$. *Basis* $j = 0$. In this case $v$ is a leaf, hence $\check{N}_v = N_v = \{v\}$, and so $|\Gamma_S^1(S') \cap \check{N}_v| \leq 1 = 2^{j+1} - 1$. *Induction step: Assume the correctness of the statement for all smaller values of $j$, and prove it for $j$.* Consider an arbitrary vertex $v$ at level $j$, and denote its left and right children by $v_L$ and $v_R$, respectively. Suppose first that $S'$ contains at least one leaf $z_L$ from the subtree of $v_L$ and at least one leaf $z_R$ from the subtree of $v_R$. By Observation 4.5, every vertex in $N_v$ is incident to both $z_L$ and $z_R$, hence no vertex of $N_v$ belongs to $\Gamma^1_S(S')$. It follows that $\Gamma^1_S(S')\cap\check{N}_v = (\Gamma^1_S(S')\cap\check{N}_{v_L})\cup(\Gamma^1_S(S')\cap\check{N}_{v_R})$. By the induction hypothesis, we conclude that

$$\begin{aligned}|\Gamma^1_S(S')\cap\check{N}_v| &= |\Gamma^1_S(S')\cap\check{N}_{v_L}| + |\Gamma^1_S(S')\cap\check{N}_{v_R}| \\ &\leq 2\cdot(2^j-1) \leq 2^{j+1}-1\,.\end{aligned}$$

We henceforth assume that no leaf in the subtree of either $v_L$ or $v_R$, without loss of generality $v_L$, belongs to $S'$. Hence, by Observation 4.5 again, no vertex of $\check{N}_{v_L}$ belongs to $\Gamma(S') \supseteq \Gamma^1_S(S')$, which gives $\Gamma^1_S(S')\cap\check{N}_v = (\Gamma^1_S(S')\cap N_v)\cup(\Gamma^1_S(S')\cap\check{N}_{v_R})$. Obviously $|(\Gamma^1_S(S')\cap N_v)| \leq |N_v| = 2^j$. By the induction hypothesis, we obtain $|\Gamma^1_S(S')\cap\check{N}_v| = |\Gamma^1_S(S')\cap N_v| + |\Gamma^1_S(S')\cap\check{N}_{v_R}| \leq 2^j + 2^j - 1 = 2^{j+1}-1$. This completes the proof of the induction.

Since $\check{N}_{rt} = N$, applying the induction statement for the root $rt$ of $T_S$ yields

$$|\Gamma^1_S(S')| = |\Gamma^1_S(S')\cap\check{N}_{rt}| \leq 2^{\log s+1} - 1 \leq 2s = (2/\log 2s)\cdot|N|.$$

It follows that $\beta_w \leq \beta(2/\log 2s)$, which completes the proof of the lemma. □

*4.3.2 The Core Graph with Arbitrary Expansion.* Notice that the expansion of the graph provided by Lemma 4.4 is logarithmic in the size of its vertex set and also in the maximum and average degree (both in $S$ and in $N$). In what follows we show how to construct a *generalized core graph* that has an arbitrary expansion.

Lemma 4.6. *For any integer $\Delta^* \geq 1$ and any $\beta^*$ satisfying $(2e)/\Delta^* \leq \beta^* \leq \Delta^*/(2e)$ (where $e$ is the base of the natural logarithm), there exists a bipartite graph $G^*_S = (S^*, N^*, E^*_S)$ with sides $S^*$ and $N^*$ of maximum degree $\Delta^*$, such that*

1. *$|S^*| \leq \Delta^*/2$, $|N^*| = \beta^*\cdot|S^*|$.*
2. *For every subset $S'$ of $S^*$, $|\Gamma(S')| \geq \beta^*\cdot|S'|$. (Thus, ordinary expansion is at least $\beta^*$.)*
3. *For every subset $S'$ of $S^*$, $|\Gamma^1_{S^*}(S')| \leq (4/\log(\min\{\Delta^*/\beta^*, \Delta^*\cdot\beta^*\}))\cdot|N^*|$. (Hence the wireless expansion, denoted $\beta_w$, satisfies $\beta_w \leq \beta^*(4/\log(\min\{\Delta^*/\beta^*, \Delta^*\cdot\beta^*\}))$.)*

To prove Lemma 4.6, we first present the following two lemmas which generalize Lemma 4.4 to get an arbitrary expansion.

Lemma 4.7. *For any integer $s \geq 1$ and any $\beta > \log 2s$, there exists a bipartite graph $\hat{G}_S = (S, \hat{N}, \hat{E}_S)$ such that*

1. *$s := |S|$ and $|\hat{N}| = s\cdot\beta$.*
2. *Each vertex in $S$ has degree $(2s-1)\cdot(\beta/\log 2s)$.*
3. *The maximum degree $\Delta_{\hat{N}}$ of a vertex in $\hat{N}$ is $s$, and the average degree $\delta_{\hat{N}}$ of a vertex in $\hat{N}$ is at most $2s/\log 2s$.*
4. *For every subset $S'$ of $S$, $|\Gamma(S')| \geq \beta\cdot|S'|$. (Hence the ordinary expansion is at least $\beta$.)*
5. *For every subset $S'$ of $S$, $|\Gamma^1_S(S')| \leq 2s\cdot(\beta/\log 2s) = (2/\log 2s)\cdot|\hat{N}|$. (Hence the wireless expansion, denoted $\beta_w$, satisfies $\beta_w \leq \beta(2/\log 2s)$.)*

Proof. We assume for simplicity that $k = \beta/\log 2s$ is an integer, and modify the construction used to prove Lemma 4.4 by creating $k$ copies $v_1, \ldots, v_k$ for each vertex $v$ in $N$. Thus each vertex set $N_v$ is "expanded" by a factor of $k$; denote the expanded vertex set by $\hat{N}_v$. The vertex set $\hat{N}$ of $\hat{G}_S$ is the union of all copies of all vertices in $N$, or in other words, it is the union of all the expanded vertex sets, i.e., $\hat{N} = \bigcup_{v\in T_S}\hat{N}_v$. The edge set $\hat{E}_S$ of $\hat{G}_S$ is obtained by translating each edge $(v, u)$ in the original graph $G_S$, where $v \in N$, into the $k$ edges $(v_1, u), \ldots, (v_k, u)$ in $\hat{G}_S$. Other than this modification, the construction remains intact. Note that $S$ remains unchanged, and the degree of vertices in $\hat{N}$ is the same as the degree of vertices in $N$ in the original graph $G_S$ (both the maximum and average degree). On the other hand, we now have $|\hat{N}| = (s\log 2s)\cdot(\beta/\log 2s) = s\cdot\beta$. Moreover, the expansion increases from at least $\log 2s$ to at least $\beta$, and the degree of vertices in $S$ increases from $2s-1$ to $(2s-1)\cdot(\beta/\log 2s)$. Finally, note that for every subset $S'$ of $S$, $|\Gamma^1_S(S')|$ increases by a factor of $\beta/\log 2s$, hence $|\Gamma^1_S(S')|$ is at most $2s\cdot(\beta/\log 2s) = (2/\log 2s)\cdot|\hat{N}|$, thus the wireless expansion $\beta_w$ satisfies $\beta_w \leq \beta(2/\log 2s)$. □

Lemma 4.8. *For any integer $s \geq 1$ and any $\beta \leq \log 2s$, there exists a bipartite graph $\check{G}_S = (\check{S}, N, \check{E}_S)$ with sides $\check{S}$ and $N$, such that*

1. *$|\check{S}| = s\cdot(\log 2s/\beta)$ and $|N| = s\log 2s$.*
2. *Each vertex in $\check{S}$ has degree $2s-1$.*
3. *The maximum degree $\Delta_N$ of a vertex in $N$ is $s\cdot(\log 2s/\beta)$, and the average degree $\delta_N$ of a vertex in $N$ is at most $2s/\beta$.*
4. *For every subset $S'$ of $\check{S}$, $|\Gamma(S')| \geq \beta\cdot|S'|$. (Hence the ordinary expansion is at least $\beta$.)*
5. *For every subset $S'$ of $\check{S}$, $|\Gamma^1_{\check{S}}(S')| \leq 2s = (2/\log 2s)\cdot|N|$. (Hence the wireless expansion, denoted $\beta_w$, satisfies $\beta_w \leq \beta(2/\log 2s)$.)*

Proof. We assume for simplicity that $k = \log 2s/\beta$ is an integer, and modify the construction used to prove Lemma 4.4 by creating $k$ copies $v_1, \ldots, v_k$ for each vertex $v$ in $S$. The vertex set $\check{S}$ of $\check{G}_S$ is the union of all copies of all vertices in $S$, and the edge set $\check{E}_S$ is obtained by translating each edge $(v, u)$ in the original graph $G_S$, where $v \in S$, into the $k$ edges $(v_1, u), \ldots, (v_k, u)$ in $\check{G}_S$. Other than this modification, the construction remains intact. Note that $N$ remains unchanged, and the degree of vertices in $\check{S}$ is the same as the degree of vertices in $S$ in the original graph $G_S$ (both the maximum and average degree). On the other hand, we now have $|\check{S}| = s\cdot(\log 2s/\beta)$. Moreover, the expansion decreases from at least $\log 2s$ to at least $\beta$, and the degree of vertices in $N$ increases by a factor of $\log 2s/\beta$. Finally, note that for every subset $S'$ of $\check{S}$, $|\Gamma^1_{\check{S}}(S')|$ remains at most $2s = (2/\log 2s)\cdot|N|$, thus the bound on the wireless expansion $\beta_w$ remains unchanged, and we have $\beta_w \leq \beta(2/\log 2s)$. □

We are now ready to complete to proof of Lemma 4.6.

Lemma 4.6. Since $\beta^* \leq \Delta^*/(2e)$, we may write $\Delta^* = 2s\cdot(\beta^*/\log 2s)$, for $s \geq e$. Suppose first that $\beta^* > \log 2s$. In this case we take $G^*_S$ to be the graph provided by Lemma 4.7 for $\lceil s\rceil$ and $\beta^* = \beta$; we assume for simplicity that $s$ is an integer, but this assumption has a negligible effect. The maximum degree in the graph is $(2s-1)\cdot(\beta^*/\log 2s)$, which is bounded by $\Delta^* := 2s\cdot(\beta^*/\log 2s)$. This in particular yields $\Delta^* \geq 2s$, and so $|S^*| = s \leq \Delta^*/2$. We also have $|N^*| = \beta^*\cdot|S^*|$. The second assertion follows immediately from Lemma 4.7(4). It remains to prove the third assertion. Lemma 4.7(5) implies that for every subset $S'$ of $S^*$, $|\Gamma^1_{S^*}(S')| \leq 2s \cdot (\beta^*/\log 2s) = (2/\log 2s) \cdot |N^*|$. Observe that

$$\min\{\Delta^*/\beta^*, \Delta^* \cdot \beta^*\} \;=\; \Delta^*/\beta^* \;=\; 2s/\log 2s \;\leq\; 2s.$$

Hence $2/\log 2s \leq 2/\log(\min\{\Delta^*/\beta^*, \Delta^* \cdot \beta^*\})$, which implies that

$$\begin{aligned}|\Gamma^1_{S^*}(S')| &\leq (2/\log 2s) \cdot |N^*| \\ &\leq (2/\log(\min\{\Delta^*/\beta^*, \Delta^* \cdot \beta^*\})) \cdot |N^*|\,.\end{aligned}$$

We henceforth assume that $\beta^* \leq \log 2s$. Since $\beta^* \geq (2e)/\Delta^*$, we may write $\Delta^* = 2s' \cdot (\log 2s'/\beta^*)$, for $s' \geq e/2$. Next, we argue that $\beta^* \leq \log 2s'$. Since $\beta^* \leq \log 2s$ and as $\Delta^*$ is equal to both $2s \cdot (\beta^*/\log 2s)$ and $2s' \cdot (\log 2s'/\beta^*)$, it follows that

$$((2s')/(2s))\log(2s')\log(2s) \;=\; (\beta^*)^2 \;\leq\; \log^2(2s).$$

Thus $(2s')\cdot\log(2s') \leq (2s)\cdot\log(2s)$, and so $s' \leq s$. Next, we prove that $(2s')/\log(2s') \leq (2s)/\log(2s)$ by taking logarithms for both hand sides and noting that the function $f(x) = x - \log x$ is monotone increasing for $x > \log e$ and that $s \geq s' \geq e/2$. Rearranging, we get $(\beta^*)^2 = ((2s')/(2s))\log(2s')\log(2s) \leq \log^2(2s')$, thus $\beta^* \leq \log 2s'$.

In this case we take $G^*_S$ to be the graph provided by Lemma 4.8 for $\lceil s' \rceil$ and $\beta^* = \beta$; we again assume for simplicity that $s$ is an integer, but this assumption has a negligible effect. The maximum degree in the graph is $\max\{2s'-1, s'\cdot(\log 2s'/\beta^*)\}$, which is bounded by $\Delta^* := 2s'\cdot(\log 2s'/\beta^*)$. Note that $|S^*| = s'\cdot(\log 2s'/\beta^*) = \Delta^*/2$ and $|N^*| = s'\log 2s' = \beta^* \cdot |S^*|$. The second assertion follows immediately from Lemma 4.8(4). It remains to prove the third assertion. Lemma 4.8(5) implies that for every subset $S'$ of $S^*$, $|\Gamma^1_{S^*}(S')| \leq 2s' = (2/\log 2s') \cdot |N^*|$. Observe that

$$\min\{\Delta^*/\beta^*, \Delta^* \cdot \beta^*\} \;\leq\; \Delta^* \cdot \beta^* \;=\; 2s' \cdot \log 2s'.$$

Hence

$$\begin{aligned}2/\log 2s' &= 4/\log((2s')^2) \leq 4/\log(2s' \cdot \log 2s') \\ &\leq 4/\log(\min\{\Delta^*/\beta^*, \Delta^* \cdot \beta^*\}),\end{aligned}$$

which implies that

$$\begin{aligned}|\Gamma^1_{S^*}(S')| &\leq (2/\log 2s') \cdot |N^*| \\ &\leq (4/\log(\min\{\Delta^*/\beta^*, \Delta^* \cdot \beta^*\})) \cdot |N^*|.\end{aligned}$$

□

*4.3.3 Worst-Case Expanders.* Let $G$ be an arbitrary $(\alpha, \beta)$-expander on $n$ vertices with maximum degree $\Delta$, and let $0 < \epsilon < 1/2$ be a "blow-up" parameter. That is, $\epsilon$ will determine the extent by which the parameters of interest blow up due to the modification that we perform on the original graph $G$ to obtain poor wireless expansion. There is a tradeoff between the wireless expansion and the other parameters: The stronger our upper bound on the wireless expansion is, the larger the blow-up in the other parameters becomes.

For technical reasons, we require that $\Delta \cdot \beta \geq 1/(1-\epsilon^2)$. We start by constructing the generalized core graph $G^*_S = (S^*, N^*, E^*_S)$ provided by Lemma 4.6 for $\Delta^* = \epsilon \cdot \Delta$ and expansion $\beta^* = \beta/\epsilon$, thus yielding $|S^*| \leq \Delta^*/2 = \epsilon(\Delta/2)$ and $|N^*| = \beta^* \cdot |S^*| = (\beta/\epsilon) \cdot |S^*|$; in the proof of Claim 4.10 we show that $(2e)/\Delta^* \leq \beta^* \leq \Delta^*/(2e)$, as required in Lemma 4.6. Our worst-case expander $\tilde{G}$ is obtained by plugging $G^*_S$ on top of $G$. The vertices of $S^*$ are not part of the original vertex set of $G$, but are rather new vertices added to it. The vertices of $N^*$ are chosen arbitrarily from $V(G)$.

**Remark.** If $G$ is a bipartite expander, expanding from the left side $L$ to the right side $R$, and if we want $\tilde{G}$ to remain bipartite and to expand from $\tilde{L}$ to $\tilde{R}$, then $\tilde{L}$ will be defined as the union of $L$ and $S^*$, and $\tilde{R}$ will be defined as the union of $R$ and a dummy vertex set of the same size as $S^*$, to guarantee that $|\tilde{L}| = |\tilde{R}|$.

In what follows we analyze the properties of $\tilde{G}$. Denoting the number of vertices in $\tilde{G}$ by $\tilde{n}$, we have $n \leq \tilde{n} \leq n + 2|S^*| \leq n + 2\epsilon(\Delta/2) \leq (1+\epsilon) \cdot n$. Write $\tilde{\Delta} = (1+\epsilon) \cdot \Delta$, and note that the maximum degree in $\tilde{G}$ is bounded by $\Delta + \Delta^* \leq \Delta + \epsilon \cdot \Delta = \tilde{\Delta}$.

Claim 4.9. *$\tilde{G}$ is an ordinary $(\tilde{\alpha}, \tilde{\beta})$-expander, where $\tilde{\beta} = (1-\epsilon) \cdot \beta$, $\tilde{\alpha} = (1-\epsilon) \cdot \alpha$.*

Proof. Since $\tilde{n} < (1+\epsilon) \cdot n$ and as $\tilde{\alpha} = (1-\epsilon) \cdot \alpha$, it follows that $\tilde{\alpha} \cdot \tilde{n} \leq (1-\epsilon)\alpha \cdot (1+\epsilon) \cdot n = (1-\epsilon^2)\alpha \cdot n < \alpha \cdot n$. Consider an arbitrary set $X$ of at most $\tilde{\alpha} \cdot \tilde{n} \leq \alpha \cdot n$ vertices from $\tilde{G}$. By Lemma 4.6(2), the expansion in $G^*_S$ is at least $\beta^* = \beta/\epsilon$, hence $|\Gamma^-(X \cap S^*)| \geq (\beta/\epsilon) \cdot |X \cap S^*|$. If $|X \cap S^*| \geq \epsilon \cdot |X|$, then we have $|\Gamma^-(X)| \geq |\Gamma^-(X \cap S^*)| \geq (\beta/\epsilon) \cdot |X \cap S^*| \geq (\beta/\epsilon) \cdot (\epsilon \cdot |X|) = \beta \cdot |X| > \tilde{\beta} \cdot |X|$. Otherwise, $|X \setminus S^*| \geq (1-\epsilon) \cdot |X|$, and as the expansion in $G$ is at least $\beta$, we have $|\Gamma^-(X)| \geq |\Gamma^-(X \setminus S^*)| \geq \beta \cdot |X \setminus S^*| \geq \beta \cdot (1-\epsilon) \cdot |X| = \tilde{\beta} \cdot |X|$. □

Recall that $\Delta \cdot \beta \geq 1/(1-\epsilon^2)$, and note that $\tilde{\Delta} \cdot \tilde{\beta} = (1+\epsilon)\Delta \cdot (1-\epsilon)\beta \geq 1$. We also have that $\tilde{\Delta}/\tilde{\beta} > \Delta/\beta \geq 1$. Hence the term $\log(\min\{\tilde{\Delta}/\tilde{\beta}, \tilde{\Delta} \cdot \tilde{\beta}\})$ is non-negative, and the upper bound $O(\tilde{\beta}/(\epsilon^3 \cdot \log(\min\{\tilde{\Delta}/\tilde{\beta}, \tilde{\Delta} \cdot \tilde{\beta}\})))$ in the following claim is well-defined.

Claim 4.10. *The wireless expansion $\tilde{\beta}_w$ of $\tilde{G}$ satisfies $\tilde{\beta}_w = O(\tilde{\beta}/(\epsilon^3 \cdot \log(\min\{\tilde{\Delta}/\tilde{\beta}, \tilde{\Delta} \cdot \tilde{\beta}\})))$.*

Proof. Note that $\tilde{\beta}_w$ is trivially upper bounded by $\beta$, thus the claim holds vacuously whenever $\epsilon^3 \cdot \log(\min\{\tilde{\Delta}/\tilde{\beta}, \tilde{\Delta} \cdot \tilde{\beta}\}) < 2$. We may henceforth assume that $\epsilon^3 \cdot \log(\min\{\tilde{\Delta}/\tilde{\beta}, \tilde{\Delta} \cdot \tilde{\beta}\}) \geq 2$, which implies that both $\tilde{\Delta}/\tilde{\beta}$ and $\tilde{\Delta} \cdot \tilde{\beta}$ are at least $2^{2/\epsilon^3}$. Since $\epsilon < 1/2$, it follows that

$$\Delta^* \cdot \beta^* \;=\; \Delta \cdot \beta \;\geq\; (\tilde{\Delta}/(1+\epsilon)) \cdot (\tilde{\beta}/(1-\epsilon)) \;\geq\; \tilde{\Delta} \cdot \tilde{\beta} \;\geq\; 2^{2/\epsilon^3} \;\geq\; 2e$$

and

$$\begin{aligned}\Delta^*/\beta^* &= \epsilon^2(\Delta/\beta) \geq \epsilon^2(\tilde{\Delta}/(1+\epsilon))/(\tilde{\beta}/(1-\epsilon)) \\ &= \epsilon^2((1-\epsilon)/(1+\epsilon)) \cdot (\tilde{\Delta}/\tilde{\beta}) \\ &\geq \epsilon^2((1-\epsilon)/(1+\epsilon)) \cdot 2^{2/\epsilon^3} \;\geq\; 2e.\end{aligned}$$

In particular, we have $(2e)/\Delta^* \leq \beta^* \leq \Delta^*/(2e)$, as required in Lemma 4.6. Since all edges adjacent to the vertices of $S^*$ belong to the core graph $G^*_S$ with parameters $\Delta^*$ and $\beta^*$, Lemma 4.6(3) implies that for every subset $S'$ of $S^*$,

$$\begin{aligned}|\Gamma^1_{S^*}(S')| &\leq (4/\log(\min\{\Delta^*/\beta^*, \Delta^* \cdot \beta^*\})) \cdot |N^*| \\ &\leq (4(1+\epsilon)/(\epsilon^2(1-\epsilon) \cdot \log(\min\{\tilde{\Delta}/\tilde{\beta}, \tilde{\Delta} \cdot \tilde{\beta}\}))) \cdot |N^*| \\ &\leq (12/(\epsilon^2 \cdot \log(\min\{\tilde{\Delta}/\tilde{\beta}, \tilde{\Delta} \cdot \tilde{\beta}\}))) \cdot |N^*| \\ &= (12/(\epsilon^3 \cdot \log(\min\{\tilde{\Delta}/\tilde{\beta}, \tilde{\Delta} \cdot \tilde{\beta}\}))) \cdot \beta \cdot |S^*| \\ &\leq (24/(\epsilon^3 \cdot \log(\min\{\tilde{\Delta}/\tilde{\beta}, \tilde{\Delta} \cdot \tilde{\beta}\}))) \cdot \tilde{\beta} \cdot |S^*|.\end{aligned}$$

(It is easily verified that the third and last inequalities hold for $\epsilon < 1/2$.) The bottom-line constant 24 can be improved; we did not try to optimize it. □

We derive the following corollary, which implies the existence of expanders with worst possible wireless expansion. The bound on the wireless expansion is tight in the entire range of parameters, disregarding constants and dependencies on $\epsilon$.

Corollary 4.11. *For any $n, \Delta, \beta$ and $0 < \epsilon < 1/2$ such that $\Delta \cdot \beta \geq 1/(1-\epsilon^2)$, if there exists an ordinary $(\alpha, \beta)$-expander $G$ on $n$ vertices with maximum degree $\Delta$, then there exists an $(\tilde{\alpha}, \tilde{\beta})$-expander $\tilde{G}$ on $\tilde{n}$ vertices with maximum degree $\tilde{\Delta}$ and wireless expansion $\tilde{\beta}_w$, where: (1) $\Delta \leq \tilde{\Delta} \leq (1+\epsilon) \cdot \Delta$; (2) $n \leq \tilde{n} \leq (1+\epsilon) \cdot n$; (3) $\tilde{\beta} = (1-\epsilon) \cdot \beta$; (4) $\tilde{\alpha} = (1-\epsilon) \cdot \alpha$; and (5) $\tilde{\beta}_w = O(\tilde{\beta}/(\epsilon^3 \cdot \log(\min\{\tilde{\Delta}/\tilde{\beta}, \tilde{\Delta} \cdot \tilde{\beta}\})))$.*

One may use Corollary 4.11 in conjunction with known constructions of explicit expanders (such as Ramanujan graphs), which achieve near-optimal expansion for any degree parameter. Taking $\epsilon$ to be a sufficiently small constant thus completes the proof of Theorem 1.2.

# 5 A TIGHT LOWER BOUND ON THE BROADCAST TIME IN RADIO NETWORKS

In this section we provide a simple proof for obtaining a tight lower bound of $\Omega(D \log(n/D))$ on the broadcast time in radio networks, which holds both in expectation and with high probability.

Consider our core bipartite graph $G_S = (S, N, E_S)$ from Lemma 4.4, with sides $S$ and $N$, where $s = |S|$ and $|N| = s \log 2s$. Suppose that we connect an additional vertex $rt$ to all vertices of $S$ and initiate a (radio) broadcast at $rt$ in the resulting graph. By Lemma 4.4(5), one cannot uniquely cover more than $2s$ vertices (i.e., a $(2/(\log 2s))$-fraction) of $N$ using any subset $S' \subseteq S$. It follows that at any round after the first, the broadcast may reach at most $2s$ new vertices of $N$, which yields the following corollary.

Corollary 5.1. *The number of rounds needed for the broadcast to reach a $(2i/(\log 2s))$-fraction of $N$ is at least $1 + i$, for any $0 \leq i \leq ((\log 2s)/2)$.*

Next, we construct a graph $G$ of diameter $\Theta(D)$, for an arbitrary parameter $D = \Omega(\log n)$, in which the number of rounds needed to complete a broadcast is $\Omega(D \log(n/D))$.

The core graph $G_S$ has $|S|+|N| = s(1+\log 2s) = s(\log 4s)$ vertices. We take $D/2$ copies of this graph, denoted by $G_S^1, G_S^2, \ldots, G_S^{D/2}$, each containing roughly $n/D$ vertices. Thus we take $s$ so that $n/D \approx s(\log 4s)$, and so $\log s = \Theta(\log(n/D))$. Denote the sides of $G_S^i$ by $S^i$ and $N^i$. We connect the root $rt = rt^0$ to all vertices of $S^1$, and for each $1 \leq i \leq D/2$, we randomly sample a vertex from $N^i$, denoted by $rt^i$, and connect it (unless $i = D/2$) to all vertices of $S^{i+1}$. This completes the construction of the graph $G$. It is easy to verify that the diameter of $G$ is $\Theta(D)$, and to be more accurate, the diameter is $D + 2$. In what follows we assume that none of the processors associated with the vertices of the graph initially have any topological information on the graph (except for its size and diameter). This rather standard assumption was also required in the proof of Kushilevitz and Mansour [12].

Consider a broadcast initiated at $rt$. We make the following immediate observation.

Observation 5.2. *The message must reach $rt^{i-1}$ before reaching $rt^i$, for $1 \leq i \leq D/2$.*

Denote by $R^i$ the random variable for the number of rounds needed for the message to be sent from $rt^{i-1}$ to $rt^i$, for each $i$, and let $R$ be the random variable for the number of rounds needed to send the message from $rt$ to $rt^{D/2}$. We thus have $R = R^1 + R^2 + \ldots + R^{D/2}$.

By Corollary 5.1, the number of rounds needed for the broadcast message to reach half of the vertices of $N^1$ (from $rt = rt^0$) is at least $((\log 2s)/4) + 1 = \Theta(\log(n/D))$. Since $rt^1$ was sampled randomly from all vertices $N^1$ and as none of the processors have any topological information on the graph, $rt^1$ received this message within this many rounds with probability at most $1/2$, hence $R^1 = \Omega(\log(n/D))$ with constant probability. By Observation 5.2, the only way for the message to reach any vertex of $S^2$, and later $rt^2$, is via $rt^1$, hence we can repeat this argument, and carry it out inductively. Since the $D/2$ variables $R^1, R^2, \ldots, R^{D/2}$ are independently and identically distributed, and as $D = \Omega(\log n)$ (where the constant hiding in the $\Omega$-notation is sufficiently large), a Chernoff bound implies that $\mathbb{P}(R = \Omega(D \log(n/D))) \geq 1 - n^{-c}$, where $c$ is a constant as big as needed. For the expectation bound, note that $\mathbb{E}(R^i) > (\log 2s)/4 = \Omega(\log(n/D))$ by Corollary 5.1, for each $i$, and by linearity of expectation we obtain $\mathbb{E}(R) = \mathbb{E}(R^1) + \mathbb{E}(R^2) + \ldots + \mathbb{E}(R^{D/2}) = \Omega(D \log(n/D))$. (The assumption that $D = \Omega(\log n)$ is used for deriving the high probability bound but not the expectation bound.)

*Acknowledgments.* We are grateful to Mohsen Ghaffari for the useful discussions on the probabilistic arguments of Sec. 4.2.

# REFERENCES

[1] Noga Alon, Amotz Bar-Noy, Nathan Linial, and David Peleg. 1991. A Lower Bound for Radio Broadcast. *J. Comput. Syst. Sci.* 43, 2 (1991), 290–298.
[2] Noga Alon and Michael R. Capalbo. 2002. Explicit Unique-Neighbor Expanders. In *Proc. 43rd FOCS*. 73–82.
[3] Noga Alon, Mohsen Ghaffari, Bernhard Haeupler, and Majid Khabbazian. 2014. Broadcast throughput in radio networks: routing vs. network coding. In *Proceedings of the twenty-fifth annual ACM-SIAM symposium on Discrete algorithms*. SIAM, 1831–1843.
[4] Noga Alon and Joel Spencer. 1992. *The Probabilistic Method.* John Wiley.
[5] Shirel Attali, Merav Parter, David Peleg, and Shay Solomon. 2018. Wireless Expanders. *CoRR* abs/1802.07177 (2018).
[6] Reuven Bar-Yehuda, Oded Goldreich, and Alon Itai. 1987. On the Time-Complexity of Broadcast in Radio Networks: An Exponential Gap Between Determinism and Randomization. In *Proceedings of the Sixth Annual ACM Symposium on Principles of Distributed Computing, Vancouver, British Columbia, Canada, August 10-12, 1987.* 98–108.
[7] Oren Becker. 2016. Symmetric unique neighbor expanders and good LDPC codes. *Discrete Applied Mathematics* 211 (2016), 211–216.
[8] Imrich Chlamtac. 1991. The wave expansion approach to broadcasting in multihop radio networks. *IEEE Transactions on Communications* 39, 3 (1991), 426–433.
[9] Imrich Chlamtac and Shay Kutten. 1985. On broadcasting in radio networks–problem analysis and protocol design. *IEEE Transactions on Communications* 33, 12 (1985), 1240–1246.
[10] Artur Czumaj and Wojciech Rytter. 2006. Broadcasting algorithms in radio networks with unknown topology. *J. Algorithms* 60, 2 (2006), 115–143.
[11] Shlomo Hoory, Nathan Linial, and Avi Wigderson. 2006. Expander graphs and their applications. *Bull. Amer. Math. Soc.* 43, 4 (2006), 439–561.
[12] Eyal Kushilevitz and Yishay Mansour. 1998. An Ω(D\log(N/D)) lower bound for broadcast in radio networks. *SIAM journal on Computing* 27, 3 (1998), 702–712.
[13] Calvin C. Newport. 2014. Radio Network Lower Bounds Made Easy. In *Distributed Computing - 28th International Symposium, DISC 2014, Austin, TX, USA, October 12-15, 2014. Proceedings.* 258–272.

# Trees for Vertex Cuts, Hypergraph Cuts and Minimum Hypergraph Bisection

Harald Räcke
Department of Informatics,
Technische Universität München
raecke@in.tum.de

Roy Schwartz
Computer Science Department,
Technion, Israel.
schwartz@cs.technion.ac.il

Richard Stotz
Department of Informatics,
Technische Universität München
stotz@in.tum.de

## ABSTRACT

In the Minimum Hypergraph Bisection problem, the vertex set of a hypergraph has to be partitioned into two parts of equal size so that the number of hyperedges intersecting both parts is minimized. This problem is a natural generalization of the well-studied Minimum Bisection problem in graphs.

In this paper we present a sharp distinction between Minimum Bisection in hypergraphs and graphs. Whereas it is well-known that all bi-criteria approximation algorithms for Minimum Bisection in graphs can be extended to hypergraphs with the exact same guarantees, in this paper we prove that this is not the case when considering true (i.e., non bi-criteria) approximation algorithms. Specifically, we show that Minimum Bisection in Hypergraphs admits an $\tilde{O}(\sqrt{n})$ approximation algorithm (and highlight several special cases where a better approximation ratio is possible). Additionally, we show that the problem is at least as hard as the Densest $k$-Subgraph problem. Assuming the Dense vs. Random Conjecture [4], no approximation ratio better than $O(n^{1/4-\varepsilon})$ is possible. In particular, Minimum Hypergraph Bisection is much harder to approximate than Minimum Bisection in graphs, for which a logarithmic approximation algorithms exist [17].

We also consider the problem of constructing trees that are cut sparsifiers for hypergraph and vertex cuts. While similar trees lie at the heart of powerful algorithms for Minimum Bisection in graphs, we prove that this is not the case for hypergraphs. We give upper and lower bounds to the quality of such trees. Our bounds show that this tree cut sparsifying approach cannot improve the general approximation ratio of Minimum Hypergraph Bisection and Minimum Vertex Bisection.

**ACM Reference Format:**
Harald Räcke, Roy Schwartz, and Richard Stotz. 2018. Trees for Vertex Cuts, Hypergraph Cuts and Minimum Hypergraph Bisection. In *SPAA '18: 30th ACM Symposium on Parallelism in Algorithms and Architectures, July 16–18, 2018, Vienna, Austria.* ACM, New York, NY, USA, 10 pages. https://doi.org/10.1145/3210377.3210398


ACM ISBN 978-1-4503-5799-9/18/07...$15.00
https://doi.org/10.1145/3210377.3210398

## 1 INTRODUCTION

One major approach for load balancing in large scale scientific computing is to model the problem as a combinatorial graph partitioning problem ([10]). The computation is modeled as a graph, where the nodes represent processes or data and edges represent communication requirements between processes or data objects. The goal is then to partition the graph into roughly equal parts while minimizing the number of edges (the required communication) between different parts. The number of parts should, of course, correspond to the number of processors/cores available on the parallel machine on which the computation should be executed.

Hypergraph partitioning (see e.g. [20]) is an extension of this basic idea where the communication is not modeled by ordinary edges (point-to-point communication) but by hyperedges, instead. This allows to model the communication more accurately but may make solving the underlying partitioning problem more difficult. We refer the reader to the survey [15] (and the references therein) for applications of hypergraph partitioning to the areas of parallel scientific computing, load balancing and congestion minimization.

There exists many different variants of these partitioning problems. As all of these variants are NP-hard they are usually solved by heuristic approaches. From a theoretical perspective many graph partitioning problems are reasonably well understood. Most variants allow either true polylogarithmic approximations (see e.g. [2, 12, 17]) or bi-criteria approximations ([1, 3, 8, 11, 19]). Some of these approaches can also be transferred to hypergraphs. See e.g. [13], which gives polylogarithmic approximation guarantees for *Sparsest Cut, Small Set Expansion,* and *$\rho$-Separator* on hypergraphs.

However, in this paper we show a sharp distinction between Minimum Bisection in hypergraphs and graphs. In this problem the vertex set of a (hyper-)graph has to be partitioned into two parts of equal size so that the number of (hyper-)edges intersecting both parts is minimized. This corresponds to a load balancing problem for two processors.

While the graph version of this problem admits a true $O(\log n)$-approximation [17], and there exist $(O(1), \sqrt{\log n})$ bicriteria approximations[1] for both graphs and hypergraphs, we show that a true approximation with a guarantee of $O(n^{1/4-\epsilon})$ for hypergraphs is unlikely. This hardness is based on the *Hypergraph Dense vs Random Conjecture.* The Dense vs Random Conjecture for ordinary graphs originates from the study of approximation algorithms for the Densest $k$-subgraph problem. A hypergraph version of this conjecture was introduced by Chlamtáč et al. [5] and was used to

[1]In a bicriteria approximation the algorithm is allowed to return a partition, where the smaller side contains just $\Omega(n)$ vertices instead of exactly $n/2$ vertices. An $(O(1), \sqrt{\log n})$-approximation means that the cost of the (not completely balanced) partition is at most a factor $O(\sqrt{\log n})$ larger than the cost of an optimum bisection.

| | Unweighted Vertex | Weighted Vertex | Hypergraph |
|---|---|---|---|
| Cut Tree Quality U.B. | $O(\sqrt{n}\log^{3/4} n)$ | $O(\sqrt{nw_{\mathrm{avg}}}\log^{3/4} n)$ | $O(\sqrt{nd_{\mathrm{avg}}}\log^{3/4} n)$ |
| Cut Tree Quality L.B. | $\Omega(n^{1/3})$ | $\Omega(\sqrt{n})$ | $\Omega(\sqrt{n})$ |
| Bisection U.B. | | | $O(\sqrt{n}\log^{1.25} n)$ <br> $O(h_{\max} \cdot \log n)$ |
| Bisection L.B. | $\Omega(n^{1/8})$ | $\Omega(n^{1/8})$ | $\Omega(n^{1/4-\varepsilon})$ |

**Table 1: Summary of our results for the Minimum Bisection problem, and the approximation of cuts by trees. Here $h_{\max}$ denotes the maximum size of a hyperedge, and $w_{\mathrm{avg}}$ and $d_{\mathrm{avg}}$ denote the average weight and degree, respectively, of a vertex in the graph.**

prove hardness for the *Minimizing the Union* problem in which one has to select $k$ subsets of vertices such that the size of their union is as small as possible. We also show a direct reduction of the Densest $k$-subgraph problem to Hypergraph Bisection. This shows that no $n^{\mathrm{poly}(\log\log n)}$ approximation algorithm exists while only assuming ETH, the hypothesis that 3SAT requires exponential time. [14] We also consider the special case when all hyperedges have roughly the same size $\Theta(n^{\alpha})$. For this case we show that the Dense vs Random Conjecture implies a lower bound of $\Omega(n^{\min\{\alpha/2,\alpha(1-\alpha)\}})$ on the approximation ratio.

We complement these lower bounds with an approximation algorithm that obtains an upper bound of $\tilde{O}(\sqrt{n})$ for general hypergraphs, and an upper bound of $\tilde{O}(n^{\min\{\alpha,1-\alpha\}})$ on quasi-uniform hypergraphs with hyperedge size $\Theta(n^{\alpha})$. The largest gap between our upper bound and the lower bound occurs for hyperedges of size $\sqrt{n}$.

In a second part we explore to what extent the techniques that underly many graph partitioning results can be transferred to hypergraphs. The results about Minimum Bisection [17], Min-Max Graph Partitioning [19], and Balanced Graph Partitioning [8] are based on a technique that approximates the whole cut-structure of a graph by a tree. Then the respective graph partitioning problem is just solved or approximated on a tree, and one obtains a solution with provable performance guarantees on the original graph. We show that hypergraphs and vertex cuts cannot be represented by a tree-structure with a good approximation guarantee even when allowing vertex cuts in the tree.

In particular we show that this technique cannot obtain a better approximation guarantee than $\Omega(\sqrt{n})$. It is important to note that our lower bounds apply to a *single* tree, as opposed to the more powerful notion of a distribution over trees used for graphs (*e.g.*, see [17]). However, we note that there are previous works that approximate the cut structure of graphs by a tree that are able to obtain a *single* tree that achieves a polylogarithmic guarantee (see [9, 16]). Thus, the comparison between graphs and hypergraphs (as well as vertex cuts) when restricted to a single tree is valid, and our lower bounds (even though restricted to a single tree) exhibit a sharp separation between graphs and hypergraphs. On the positive side we show that one can e.g. find a tree approximation for hypergraph cuts with an approximation guarantee of $\tilde{O}(\sqrt{nd_{\mathrm{avg}}})$, where $d_{\mathrm{avg}}$ denotes the average degree of a vertex in the hypergraph. Table 1 gives an overview of our results. Note that the hardness result for vertex bisection will be included in the full version.

## 1.1 Preliminaries and Definitions

Given a weighted (hyper-)graph $G = (V, E)$ and disjoint sets $A, B \subset V$, an $(A, B)$ *edge cut* is a set of (hyper-)edges whose removal disconnects $A$ and $B$. We use $\delta_G(A, B)$ to denote the total weight of edges in an $(A, B)$ edge cut of minimum weight. We write $\delta_G(A)$ for $\delta_G(A, V \setminus A)$ and drop the subscript, if the graph is clear from the context.

A *vertex cut* separating two disjoint sets of vertices $A$ and $B$ is a set $X \subseteq V$ so that any path between $A$ and $B$ uses a vertex from $X$. The vertex cut may include vertices from both $A$ and $B$. The total weight of the minimum-weight vertex cut between $A$ and $B$ in $G$ is written $\gamma_G(A, B)$. Again, we may drop the subscript if no confusion is possible.

A *vertex separator* $(A, B, X)$ is a set $X \subseteq V$ that separates $G$ into two disconnected pieces $A$ and $B$. Its *sparsity* is defined by

$$\frac{w(X)}{\min\{w(A), w(B)\} + w(X)} ,$$

where for a vertex set $S \subseteq V$, $w(S)$ describes the total weight of vertices in $S$. We assume that the weight-function is normalized so that the minimum weight of a vertex is 1.

The vertex separator of minimum sparsity is called *min-ratio cut* of $G$. Finding the optimal min-ratio cut is NP-complete; Feige et al. [6] give an $O(\sqrt{\log n})$ approximation algorithm for finding the optimal min-ratio cut.

An *edge cut tree* $T = (V_T, E_T)$ of a (hyper)-graph $G = (V, E)$ is a tree with $V \subseteq V_T$; typically, the vertices of $G$ are leaves of the tree. The cut tree is *dominating* if for any two disjoint sets $A, B \subset V$ it holds that $\delta_G(A, B \leq \delta_T(A, B)$, i.e., cuts are larger when measured in the tree. If in addition $\delta_T(A, B) \leq \alpha \cdot \delta_G(A, B)$ holds for all $A, B \subseteq V$ we say that the cut tree has *quality* or *approximation-guarantee* $\alpha$.

Similarly, a *vertex cut tree* $T = (V_T, E_T)$ of a (hyper)-graph $G = (V, E)$ is a tree with $V \subseteq V_T$. The cut tree is dominating and approximates *vertex cuts* with quality $\alpha$, if for any two disjoint sets $A, B \subset V$

$$\gamma_G(A, B) \leq \gamma_T(A, B) \leq \alpha \cdot \gamma_G(A, B) .$$

It approximates *edge cuts* with quality $\alpha$, if for any disjoint sets $A, B \subset V$

$$\delta_G(A, B) \leq \gamma_T(A, B) \leq \alpha \cdot \delta_G(A, B) .$$

## 2 APPROXIMATING MINIMUM HYPERGRAPH BISECTION

The Minimum Hypergraph Bisection Problem asks to select a set $S$ of $|V|/2$ vertices such that the number of hyperedges leaving $S$ is minimized. We first consider the more general problem of removing $k$ vertices from a hypergraph and reduce it to the case of simple graphs, highlighting several special cases. Then we use this procedure in an $\tilde{O}(\sqrt{n})$ approximation algorithm for Minimum Hypergraph Bisection.

### 2.1 Cutting $k$ Vertices from a Hypergraph

This section shows how to efficiently remove $k$ vertices from a hypergraph so that the number of hyperedges in the cut is minimized. This problem is sometimes called *Unbalanced k-cut.*

Given the hypergraph $H$, replace any hyperedge $h$ with a clique on its vertices. Let the weight of each edge in the clique be $1/(|h|-1)$ and call the resulting graph $G'$. The cut cost of $H$ and $G'$ are related via the following inequality, where $h_{\max}$ is the size of the largest hyperedge.

Lemma 1. *For any set $S$ of $k$ vertices, we have $\delta_H(S) \leq \delta_G(S) \leq \min\{k, h_{\max}/2\}\delta_H(S)$.*

Proof. For any hyperedge $h$ in the cut in $H$, there are at least $|h| - 1$ weighted edges in the cut in $G$. As their edge weight is $1/(|h| - 1)$, the first inequality follows.

The number of edges that cross the cut $S$ in $G'$ for a hyperedge $h$ of $G$ is $|h \cap S| \cdot |h \cup S|$. For $h \geq 2k$ this is at most $k(|h| - k)$. Otherwise, it is at most $\lfloor |h|/2 \rfloor \cdot \lceil |h|/2 \rceil \leq |h|^2/4$. In the first case the cut increases by a factor of at most $k(|h| - k)/(|h| - 1) \leq k$, and in the second case by at most $|h|^2/(4(|h| - 1)) \leq |h|/2$ since $|h| \geq 2$. □

Using a convex combination of decomposition trees the optimal unbalanced $k$-cut in a graph can be approximated up to a factor of $O(\log n)$ [17]. Applying this procedure to the graph $G'$ results in an approximation algorithm for finding an unbalanced $k$-cut in a hypergraph.

Proposition 1. *There exists a $\min\{k, h_{\max}/2\} \cdot O(\log n)$ approximation algorithm for finding the unbalanced k-cut in a hypergraph, where $h_{\max}$ is the size of the largest hyperedge.*

If all hyperedges have size at least $k$, no hyperedge can be completely contained in a set of $k$ vertices. In this case, the unbalanced $k$-cut problem becomes the Minimizing $k$-Union problem, studied recently by Chlamtáč et al. [5]. They obtain the following result, where the $\tilde{O}$-notation hides polylogarithmic factors.

Proposition 2 ([5]). *If all hyperedges have at least size k, and $k = n^{1-\alpha}$, then there is an $\tilde{O}(n^{\alpha(1-\alpha)+\varepsilon})$ approximation algorithm for the unbalanced k-cut problem, for every sufficiently small $\varepsilon > 0$.*

### 2.2 Approximation Algorithm for Minimum Hypergraph Bisection

In this section, we adapt an algorithm for graph bisection by Feige et al. [7] to prove the following theorem.

Theorem 1. *There is a polynomial-time $O(\sqrt{n}\log^{5/4} n)$ approximation algorithm for Minimum Hypergraph Bisection.*

Proof. The algorithm first guesses the value OPT of an optimum solution. It then uses an approximation algorithm for Sparsest Cut and recursively cuts pieces from the graph until it does not find a cut of sparsity $\alpha\,\mathrm{OPT}/k$ anymore (in any of the pieces). Here, $\alpha$ denotes the approximation guarantee of the algorithm used (e.g. $\alpha = O(\sqrt{\log n})$ [13]), and $k$ is a parameter to be determined later. Note that this implies that no cut of sparsity below $\mathrm{OPT}/k$ can exist within a piece.

Lemma 2. *The total weight of edges cut in the first phase is at most $\alpha n \log n \cdot \mathrm{OPT}/k$.*

Proof. Every cut $S_i$ of the first phase fulfills the inequality $|\delta(S_i)|/|S_i| \leq \alpha\,\mathrm{OPT}/k$, where $S_i$ denotes the smaller side of the cut. This gives $|\delta(S_i)| \leq \alpha|S_i|\,\mathrm{OPT}/k$.

We can amortize the increase $\delta(S_i)$ of the total cut-cost in the $i$-th step to the vertices on the smaller side. Since during the whole construction a vertex appears on the smaller side of a cut at most $\log n$ times we amortize at most $\alpha \log n \cdot \mathrm{OPT}/k$ against a single vertex. Summing over all vertices gives the lemma. □

Let $G_i$ denote the sub-graphs/pieces returned after the first phase. We fix some optimal bisection represented as a black and white coloring of the vertices. We say a subgraph $G_i$ has *minority color* white, if it contains fewer white vertices than black vertices; otherwiese, its minority color is black. The vertices that have the minority color are called *minority vertices.* The following lemma gives a bound on the number of minority vertices at the end of the first phase.

Lemma 3. *There exist less than k minority vertices by the end of the first phase.*

Proof. Let $r_i$ denote the number of minority vertices in part $G_i$ and let $\mathrm{OPT}_i$ be the number of hyperedges of the (fixed) optimal bisection inside $G_i$. Note that $\sum_i \mathrm{OPT}_i \leq \mathrm{OPT}$, as the graphs $G_i$ are disjoint. As no cut of sparsity below $\mathrm{OPT}/k$ exists, every $i$ must fulfill

$$\frac{\mathrm{OPT}_i}{r_i} \geq \frac{\mathrm{OPT}}{k} .$$

Summing over all $i$ gives

$$\frac{\sum_i \mathrm{OPT}_i}{\mathrm{OPT}} \geq \frac{\sum_i r_i}{k} .$$

As the left-hand side is at most 1, the same holds for the right-hand-side. The total number of minority vertices $\sum_i r_i$ is therefore at most $k$. □

The second phase of the algorithm aims to approximate the optimum cut within each piece $G_i$. For this we "guess" in each subgraph the number of minority vertices $k_i$ and remove so many vertices using the algorithm from Proposition 1. These guesses are made one-by-one within a dynamic program as described in [7]. We can amortize the cost for this step against the cost $\mathrm{OPT}_i$ that the optimum solution has within $G_i$.

For guesses $k_i$ we pay at most

$$O(\log n) \sum_i k_i\,\mathrm{OPT}_i \leq O(\log n) k\,\mathrm{OPT} \tag{1}$$

in this step. A simple dynamic programming approach see e.g. [7] allows to find the optimum "guesses" $k_i$.

We choose $k = \sqrt{\alpha n}$ to balance the approximation factors in Equation 1 and Lemma 2. This gives an overall approximation guarantee of $O(\log n\sqrt{\alpha n}) = O(\log^{5/4} n\sqrt{n})$ as desired. □

If either all hyperedges are large or all hyperedges are small we can obtain the following improved bounds.

THEOREM 2. *If all hyperedges have size at least $\Omega(n^\alpha)$, there exists an $\tilde{O}(n^{1-\alpha})$ approximation algorithm for Minimum Hypergraph Bisection.*

*If all hyperedges have size at most $O(n^\alpha)$, there is an $\tilde{O}(n^\alpha)$-approximation algorithm for Minimum Hypergraph Bisection.*

PROOF. If all hyperedges have at least size $z = \Omega(n^\alpha)$, we choose $k = z$ for the first phase of the algorithm. Then the total number of minority vertices for the second phase is only $z$. This means we can use the algorithm from Proposition 2 for the second phase. The approximation factor of the overall algorithm becomes then $\tilde{O}(n^{1-\alpha}) + \tilde{O}(n^{\alpha(1-\alpha)+\varepsilon}) \in O(n^{1-\alpha})$.

If all hyperedges have size *at most* $O(n^\alpha)$, applying Lemma 1 and a logarithmic approximation algorithm for Minimum Bisection in simple graphs gives an $\tilde{O}(n^\alpha)$ approximation algorithm for Minimum Hypergraph Bisection. □

## 2.3 Hardness Results

In this section, we prove that the existence of an efficient algorithm for Minimum Hypergraph Bisection with approximation ratio $n^{\text{poly}(\log\log n)}$ would violate the Exponential Time Hypothesis (ETH). Under the stronger *Hypergraph Dense vs Random Conjecture*, we show that the approximation ratio of Minimum Hypergraph Bisection cannot be better than $O(n^{1/4-\varepsilon})$.

The Dense vs Random Conjecture originates from the study of strong approximation algorithms for the Densest $k$-Subgraph problem. Let the *log-density* of a (hyper-)graph on $n$ vertices be $\log_n(d_{\text{avg}})$, where $d_{\text{avg}}$ denotes the average vertex degree. For hypergraphs, the conjecture asks to distinguish a random $r$-uniform hypergraph $G = \mathcal{G}_{n,p,r}$ with $p = n^{1+\alpha-r}$ (so $G$ has log-density $\alpha$) and an adversarially chosen hypergraph $G'$ containing a subhypergraph with log-density $\beta$ on $k$ vertices.

CONJECTURE 1 ([5]). *For all constant $r$ and $0 < \beta < r-1$, for all sufficiently small $\varepsilon > 0$, and for all $k$ such that $k^{1+\beta} \le n^{(1+\alpha)/2}$, we cannot solve* HYPERGRAPH DENSE VS RANDOM *with log-density $\alpha$ and planted log-density $\beta$ in polynomial time (w.h.p) when $\beta < \alpha - \varepsilon$.*

Chlamtáč et al. apply the conjecture to show that *Minimizing $k$-Union* (MkU) does not admit an $O(m^{1/4-\varepsilon})$ approximation algorithm. In this problem, we are given a hypergraph $G = (V, E)$ of $n$ vertices and $m$ hyperedges, and an integer $k \le m$. The goal is to select $k$ hyperedges so that their union has minimal size. We extend Chlamtáč et al.'s argument by parameterizing it with the vertex degree of the hypergraph $G$. Later, MkU serves as the starting point for proving the hardness of Minimum Hypergraph Bisection.

We say that an instance of MkU is *quasi $\alpha$-uniform*, if the degree of all vertices is $\Theta(n^\alpha)$ and all hyperedges have constant size $r$. We denote a quasi $\alpha$-uniform instance of MkU with $(G, n, m, \alpha, r)$. The following lemma shows a hardness for quasi $\alpha$-uniform instances of MkU.

LEMMA 4. *Assuming Conjecture 1, there is no polynomial-time $O(m^{\min\{\alpha/(2+2\alpha),\alpha/(1+\alpha)^2\}-\varepsilon})$ approximation algorithm for quasi $\alpha$-uniform Minimizing the Union.*

PROOF. In order to establish the lemma we first show some facts about $\mathcal{G}_{n,p,r}$. The proof of these facts has been deferred to the full version.

CLAIM 1. *A random graph $\mathcal{G}_{n,p,r}$ fulfills the following properties.*

1. *With high probablity $\mathcal{G}_{n,p,r}$ with $p = n^{1+\alpha-r}$ has vertex degree $\Theta(n^\alpha)$.*
2. *Any set of $n$ edges in a $\mathcal{G}_{n,p,r}$ with $p = n^{1+\alpha-r}$ covers at least $\frac{1}{2e}(n/p)^{1/r}$ vertices, with high probability.*
3. *Any set of $n^{(1+\alpha)/2}/r$ edges in a $\mathcal{G}_{n,p,r}$ with $p = n^{1+\alpha-r}$ covers at least $n^{(1+\alpha)/2-\varepsilon}/e$ vertices, with high probability, if $\alpha < 1$, $r$ is sufficiently large and $\varepsilon$ is a small constant.*

The planted subhypergraph of the adversary contains $k^{1+\beta}/r$ many hyperedges as $k^{1+\beta}$ is the sum of all degrees in the induces graph and $r$ is the size of a hyperedge. We choose $\ell = k^{1+\beta}/r$. It follows that in the planted instance the size of a minimum $\ell$ union is at most $k$. Note that the above choice for $\ell$ does not fix $\ell$ but just the relationship between $\ell$ and $k$ because $k$ is a free parameter of the Dense vs. Random instance.

In the following we show that w.h.p. the number of vertices contained in the union of $\ell$ hyperedges in a random instance is considerably larger than $k$. As it is hard to distuingish between random instances and a planted instace the lower bound follows.

Let $\bar{k}$ denote the size of the minimum $\ell$ union in a random instance. We show that $\bar{k}$ is large with high probability. We distinguish two cases according to the value of $\alpha$.

**$\alpha > 1$.** We choose $\ell = n$ (note that this in fact chooses $k$ for the Dense vs. Random instance, because we have set $\ell = k^{1+\beta}/r$ before). We first show that $k^{1+\beta} \le n^{(1+\alpha)}$ as this is a constraint on $k$ that must be fulfilled for Conjecture 1. Indeed, $k^{1+\beta} = r\ell = rn < n^{(1+\alpha)/2}$ for $\alpha > 1$.

Fact 2 implies that with high probability $\bar{k}$ will be at least $\Theta(n/p)^{1/r}$. Let $m$ denote the total number of edges in the random instance. Fact 1 implies that, with high probability, $m = \Theta(n^{1+\alpha})$. We use this fact and rewrite $(n/p)^{1/r}$ with respect to $m$:

$$\begin{aligned}(n/p)^{1/r} &= \Theta\left(\left(m^{1/(1+\alpha)}n^{r-(1+\alpha)}\right)^{1/r}\right)\\ &= \Theta\left(\left(m^{1/(1+\alpha)}m^{r/(1+\alpha)-1}\right)^{1/r}\right)\\ &= \Theta\left(m^{1/(r(1+\alpha))-1/r+1/(1+\alpha)}\right) .\end{aligned}$$

In the first equality, we used that $p = n^{1+\alpha-r}$. As $k = \Theta(n^{1/(1+\beta)}) = \Theta(m^{1/(1+\alpha)(1+\beta)})$ (with $r$ being constant), it follows that

$$\begin{aligned}\bar{k}/k &= \Theta\left(m^{\frac{1}{r(1+\alpha)}-\frac{1}{r}+\frac{1}{1+\alpha}-\frac{1}{(1+\alpha)(1+\beta)}}\right)\\ &> \Theta\left(m^{-\frac{1}{r}+\frac{1}{1+\alpha}-\frac{1}{(1+\alpha)^2}-\varepsilon/4}\right)\\ &= \Theta\left(m^{\alpha/(1+\alpha)^2-\varepsilon}\right) ,\end{aligned}$$

using $\beta = \alpha - \varepsilon$ and $1/r < \varepsilon/2$ sufficiently small.

**$\alpha \le 1$.** We choose $\ell = n^{(1+\alpha)/2}/r$. This choice is valid as $k^{1+\beta} = \ell r \le n^{(1+\alpha)/2}$. Fact 3 implies that with high probability $\bar{k}$ will be at least $\Theta(n^{(1+\alpha)/2-\varepsilon})$, if $r$ is sufficiently large. Again $m = \Theta(n^{1+\alpha})$ by Fact 1, so

$$\bar{k} = \Theta(m^{1/2-\varepsilon/(1+\alpha)}) .$$

On the other hand, $k = \Theta(m^{1/(2(1+\beta))})$, so the gap $\bar{k}/k$ is

$$\begin{aligned}\bar{k}/k &> \Theta(m^{1/2-\varepsilon/(1+\alpha)}) \cdot \Theta(m^{-1/(2(1+\beta))}) \\ &= \Theta(m^{\beta/(2(1+\beta))-\varepsilon/(1+\alpha)}) \\ &\ge \Theta(m^{\alpha/(2(1+\alpha))-\varepsilon'}) ,\end{aligned}$$

using $\beta = \alpha - \varepsilon$ and $\varepsilon'$ sufficiently small.

The combination of both cases directly yields the lemma. □

Theorem 3. *An $f(|V|)$-approximation algorithm for the Minimum Hypergraph Bisection problem on hypergraphs $G = (V, H)$ implies an $O(f(|H'|))$-approximation algorithm for Minimizing k-Union on hypergraphs $G' = (V', H')$.*

Proof. Given an instance of MkU $G' = (V', H')$ with $n = |V'|$ and $m = |H'|$, the reduction constructs the following hypergraph $G = (V, H)$. Essentially, we switch hyperedges and vertices, adding a supervertex incident to every new hyperedge. Formally, the vertex set $V$ consists of a supervertex $w$ and a vertex $v_i$ for each hyperedge $h'_i \in H'$. For $v'_j \in V'$, a hyperedge $h_j$ connects $w$ with all vertices $v_i$ fulfilling $v'_j \in h'_i$. Additionally, there exist $p$ *padding vertices* $u_\ell$, with $p = \max\{m+1-2k, 2k-m-1\}$, where $k$ is the number of hyperedges that must be chosen in the MkU instance. If $k > (m + 1)/2$, the padding vertices are connected with the supervertex $w$ by infinite-cost edges. Otherwise, they are not connected to any vertex.

As every hyperedge in the graph is incident to the supervertex $w$, any bisection $(V_1, V_2)$ of $G$ must have one side without any internal hyperedges (namely the side not containing $w$). Let $V_1$ be this side. Furthermore, let $\bar{n} = |V| = m + 1 + p$ denote the number of vertices in $G$. Note that $\bar{n} \in \Theta(m)$.

First, suppose that $k$ is smaller than $(m + 1)/2$, thus $p = m + 1 - 2k$. Let $(V_1, V_2)$ be the bisection of $G$ obtained by an $f(|V|)$-approximation algorithm. Let $b$ be the cost of the bisection $(V_1, V_2)$. Both $V_1$ and $V_2$ consist of $\bar{n}/2 = m + 1 - k$ vertices. Therefore both of them contain at least $k$ non-padding vertices. These non-padding vertices correspond to sets in the MkU instance. As $V_1$ has no internal hyperedges, the hyperedges incident to vertices of $V_1$ are exactly the ones cut by the bisection. Therefore the corresponding sets of the MkU instance cover $b$ items of the ground set.

Next, observe that the $k$ *optimal* sets for the MkU instance, whose union has cardinality $\text{OPT}_{\text{MkU}}$, correspond to $k$ vertices in the graph $G$. Together with the $p$ padding vertices, they form a bisection of $G$ with cost $\text{OPT}_{\text{MkU}}$. It follows that $b \le f(|V|)\,\text{OPT}_{\text{MkU}}$, i.e., the algorithm has constructed an $f(|V|)$-approximation for the MkU instance. As $|V| = \Theta(|H'|)$, this approximation is also an $O(f(|H'|))$ approximation.

Now suppose that $k > (m + 1)/2$ and therefore $p = 2k - m - 1$. We use a similar argument as above. Observe that an $f(|V|)$-approximate bisection $(V_1, V_2)$ has both $V_1$ and $V_2$ of size $k$. Recall that in this case the padding vertices are connected with the supervertex $w$ by infinite-cost edges. Therefore, with out loss of generality, $V_1$ does not contain any padding vertices. Let $b$ denote the cost of the bisection $(V_1, V_2)$. The vertices of $V_1$ correspond to $k$ sets in the MkU instance, covering $b$ items from the ground set. An optimal solution of the MkU instance with cost $\text{OPT}_{\text{MkU}}$, however, corresponds to a solution to the Hypergraph Bisection instance with cost at most $\text{OPT}_{\text{MkU}}$. It follows as above that $b \le f(|V|)\,\text{OPT}_{\text{MkU}}$, i.e., the algorithm has constructed an $O(f(|E'|))$-approximation for the MkU instance. □

Corollary 1. *Assuming the Dense vs Random Hypothesis, there is no $O(n^{1/4-\varepsilon})$ approximation algorithm for Minimum Hypergraph Bisection, where n denotes the number of vertices of the Hypergraph.*

*Furthermore, there is no $O(n^{\min\{\alpha/2, \alpha(1-\alpha)\}-\varepsilon})$ approximation algorithm for Minimum Hypergraph Bisection on hypergraphs with hyperedge size $\Theta(n^\alpha)$.*

Proof. The reduction performed in the proof of Theorem 3 transforms a quasi $\alpha$-uniform instance $(G', n, m, \alpha, r)$ of MkU into an instance $G = (V, E)$ of Minimum Hypergraph Bisection. The graph $G$ has $\bar{n} = \Theta(m)$ vertices and $\bar{m} = n$ hyperedges. As the instance of MkU is quasi $\alpha$-uniform, every vertex of $G'$ has degree $\Theta(n^\alpha)$, and, given that the size $r$ of the hyperedges is constant, $m = \Theta(n^{1+\alpha}/r) = \Theta(n^{1+\alpha})$. The hyperedges of $G$ therefore have size $\Theta(n^\alpha) = \Theta(m^{\alpha/(1+\alpha)}) = \Theta(\bar{n}^{\alpha/(1+\alpha)})$. With $\gamma = \alpha/(1+\alpha)$, the hyperedges of $G$ thus all have size $\Theta(\bar{n}^\gamma)$.

Lemma 4 implies that quasi $\alpha$-uniform instances of MkU cannot be approximated up to factor $m^{\min\{\alpha/(2+2\alpha), \alpha/(1+\alpha)^2\}-\varepsilon}$. As

$$\frac{\alpha}{(1+\alpha)^2} = \frac{\alpha}{1+\alpha} \cdot \frac{1}{1+\alpha} = \frac{\alpha}{1+\alpha} \cdot \left(1 - \frac{\alpha}{1+\alpha}\right) ,$$

it follows that Minimum Hypergraph Bisection with hyperedge sizes $\Theta(n^\gamma)$ cannot be approximated with factor $\bar{n}^{\min\{\gamma/2, \gamma(1-\gamma)\}}$. □

Using a similar reduction, we show that an $f$-approximation algorithm for the Minimum Hypergraph Bisection problem implies an $f^2$-approximation algorithm for Densest $k$-Subgraph. The Densest $k$-Subgraph is notoriously hard and has recently been shown not to admit approximation algorithms of approximation ratio $n^{\text{poly}(\log\log n)}$ under the Exponential Time Hypothesis [14]. Under the stronger GAP-ETH hypothesis, no subpolynomial approximation ratio is possible.

Theorem 4. *An $f$-approximation algorithm for Minimum Hypergraph Bisection implies an $f^2$-approximation algorithm for Densest $k$-Subgraph.*

Proof. The decision version of Densest $k$-Subgraph asks to return a set of $k$ vertices such that the induced subgraph contains $L$ edges. An $f$-approximation algorithm for a $(k, L)$ instance returns a set of $k$ vertices whose induced subgraph contains $L/f$ edges, if a subgraph inducing $L$ edges exists.

Given an instance $G = (V, E)$ of Densest $k$-Subgraph, guess the number of edges $L$ in the optimal subgraph. Consider the problem of choosing $L$ edges, minimizing the number of edges incident to it. This is an instance of Minimizing $k$-Union.

Following Theorem 3, an $f$-approximation algorithm for Minimum Hypergraph Bisection is an $f$-approximation to the Minimizing $k$-Union problem. Its solution translates into a subset $S \subseteq V$ with $|S| \leq f \cdot k$ and $|E_G(S)| \geq L$.

A random subset $S'$ of $S$ with $k$ vertices induces, in expectation, at least $L/f^2$ edges. This is an $f^2$-approximation to the optimal value $L$. Using the method of conditional expectations, the random selection can be derandomized. □

Corollary 2. *Assuming the Exponential Time Hypothesis, there is no efficient approximation algorithm for Minimum Hypergraph Bisection with approximation ratio* $n^{poly(\log\log n)}$.

Proof. Follows from Theorem 4 and [14]. □

## 3 CUT TREES FOR VERTEX AND HYPERGRAPH CUTS

In this section we explore a more general approach to solving cut problems in hypergraphs. We try to approximate the cut-structure of a hypergraph $G = (V, E)$ by either an edge cut tree or a vertex cut tree. For ordinary graphs this type of approach lies at the heart of the $O(\log n)$-approximation algorithm for minimum bisection.[2]

### 3.1 Constructing vertex cut trees with quality $\tilde{O}(\sqrt{W})$

This section demonstrates the construction of a vertex cut tree of quality $\tilde{O}(\sqrt{W})$, for weighted graphs of total weight $W$. Recall that the minimum weight of a vertex is 1.

*Construction.* The construction of the tree uses an algorithm $\mathcal{A}$ returning an $\alpha$-approximate min-ratio vertex cut. Recall that a polynomial-time algorithm with $\alpha \in O(\sqrt{\log n})$ exists [6].

Use algorithm $\mathcal{A}$ to find the min-ratio vertex cut $(A, B, X)$ in the graph. Let $G_1^X, G_2^X, \ldots$ be the connected components after removing the separator $X$. Repeat the process on each subgraph until no cut of sparsity less than $\alpha f(W)$ can be found, for some function $f$ to be chosen later. This implies that no cut of sparsity less than $f(W)$ exists.

Let $G_1, G_2, \ldots$ denote the subgraphs remaining at the end of this process with $G_i = (V_i, E_i)$ and let $\mathcal{S}$ denote the union of all separators found. The cut tree is constructed by first adding a root vertex $r$ of weight $w(\mathcal{S})$. For any vertex $s \in \mathcal{S}$, the root obtains a child of weight $w(s)$. For any subgraph $G_i$, add a child $t_{G_i}$ of infinite weight to the root. Any vertex $v$ in $V_i$ is added as a leaf of weight $w(v)$ to $t_{G_i}$. A sketch of the construction can be seen in Figure 1.

*Analysis.* The following lemma shows that the tree constructed according to the above algorithm is dominating.

Lemma 5. *For any two disjoint sets $A, B \subseteq V$ we have $\gamma_G(A, B) \leq \gamma_T(A, B)$.*

Proof. Let $X$ be some minimum vertex cut separating $A$ and $B$ in the tree $T$.

Any non-infinite-weight vertex cut in $T$ may only contain leaves and the root. By associating the root with the vertex set $\mathcal{S}$, the

[2]The result by Räcke [17] that gives an $O(\log n)$-approximation for minimum bisection uses an approximation of the graph by a *convex combination* of cut trees. Here we try to approximate the cut-structure by a single tree.

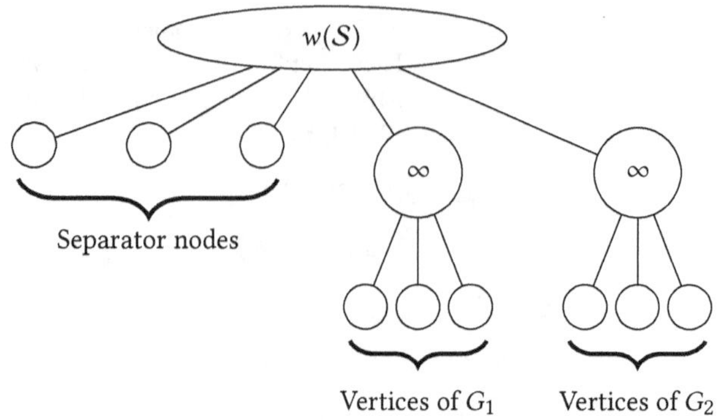


**Figure 1: Construction of the vertex cut tree.**

minimum cut $X$ corresponds to a set $X' \subset V$ of vertices of the graph $G$. Note that $X$ and $X'$ have identical weight. We show that $X'$ separates any pair of vertices $u \in A$ and $v \in B$ in the graph $G$.

The claim is obvious if either $a \in X$ or $b \in X$; suppose $a, b \notin X$. This implies that neither $a$ nor $b$ belong to the set $\mathcal{S}$, defining the root. If $a$ and $b$ belong to the same subgraph $G_i$, then they are not separated by $X$ in the tree, which is a contradiction. If $a$ and $b$ belong to different subtrees $G_i$ and $G_j$, then they can only be separated in the tree, if the root belongs to the cut $X$. This implies that the vertices of $\mathcal{S}$ belong to $X'$. As the vertices of $\mathcal{S}$ separate all subgraphs $G_i$ by construction, it follows that $a$ and $b$ are separated by $X'$. □

Lemma 6. *If $G$ is connected, we have $\gamma_T(A, B) \leq O(\sqrt{\alpha \log n W}) \cdot \gamma_G(A, B)$.*

Proof. In the following we construct a vertex cut $X$ separating $A$ and $B$ in $T$. First, we include the root $r_T$ of $T$ into this cut. We derive a bound on the weight $w(r_T)$ of the root as follows. The weight $w(r_T)$ is the weight of all vertices in the separator $\mathcal{S}$. For any separator $S_i$ found during the construction we have

$$\frac{w(S_i)}{w(A_i) + w(S_i)} \leq \alpha f(W) \ ,$$

where $A_i$ denotes the side of the cut that has the smaller number of vertices (not necessarily the smaller weight). This gives

$$w(S_i) \leq \Big(1 - \alpha f(W)\Big)^{-1} \alpha f(W) \cdot w(A_i) \leq 2\alpha f(W) \cdot w(A_i) \ ,$$

for sufficiently large $n$ if we choose $f$ such that $\alpha f(W) = o(1)$. We can amortize the weight $w(S_i)$ of the separator against the weight $w(A_i)$ of vertices in $A_i$. Since a vertex can be on the smaller side of the cut at most $\log n$ times we get that

$$\begin{aligned} w(\mathcal{S}) = \sum\nolimits_i w(S_i) &\leq 2\alpha \log n \, f(W) \sum\nolimits_i w(A_i) \\ &\leq 2\alpha \log n \, f(W) W \ . \end{aligned}$$

Since the cost of the optimum cut is at least one this gives

$$w(r_T) \leq 2\alpha \log n \, f(W) W \cdot \gamma_G(A, B) \ . \quad (2)$$

In addition to the root $r_T$ we add some leaf vertices from every sub-graph $G_i = (V_i, E_i)$ to the cut $X$. Let $A_i = A \cap V_i$ and $B_i = B \cap V_i$ (note that these sets might be empty). If $w(A_i) \leq w(B_i)$ we add the leaf vertices corresponding to $A_i$; otherwise we add the vertices corresponding to $B_i$. This forms an $(A, B)$-cut: a vertex $a \in A_i$ is separated from $B$-vertices of other sub-graphs $G_i$, because of the root $r_T$, and it is separated from $B$-vertices of its own sub-graph $G_i$ because either $A_i$ or $B_i$ is in the cut. We use $X_i$ to denote the set of vertices that we added in this step for graph $G_i$.

Let $X_i^*$ denote the intersection of the optimal $(A, B)$-cut with the sub-graph $G_i$. Since the sparsity of any cut in $G_i$ is at least $f(W)$ we get that

$$\frac{w(X_i^*)}{w(X_i \cup X_i^*)} \geq f(W) ,$$

because $X_i^*$ is a cut that separates $X_i$ (i.e., either $A_i$ or $B_i$). Consequently, $w(X_i) \leq w(X_i \cup X_i^*) \leq f(W)^{-1} w(X_i^*)$. Summing this over all $i$ gives

$$\sum_i w(X_i) \leq f(W)^{-1} \sum_i w(X_i^*) \leq f(W)^{-1} \gamma_G(A, B) . \quad (3)$$

Combining equations 2 and 3 gives that the cut $X$ that we constructed fulfills

$$w(X) \leq (f(W)^{-1} + 2\alpha \log n f(W) W) \cdot \gamma_G(A, B) .$$

Choosing $f(W) = 1/\sqrt{\alpha \log n W}$ gives the lemma. □

Combining Lemma 5 and Lemma 6 gives the following theorem.

THEOREM 5. *For a graph $G$ with total vertex weight $W$, we can construct an $O(\log^{3/4} n)\sqrt{W}$-approximate vertex cut tree in polynomial time.*

*Application to Hypergraph Bisection.* It is possible to also apply Theorem 5 for approximating hypergraph cuts. In order to do this we construct a vertex weighted graph $G'$ from a given hypergraph $G$, such that vertex cuts in $G'$ correspond to hyperedge cuts in $G$.

Let $G = (V, H)$ be the given hypergraph. We construct a bipartite graph $G' = (V \cup H, E, w)$, as follows. The vertex set $V'$ of $G'$ consists of both the vertices and the hyperedges of $G$. Any vertex $v \in V$ is connected in $G'$ to the hyperedges that it is incident to in $G$ by a simple edge. The weight $w(v)$ is set to $w(v) = \deg_G(v) + 1$, where $\deg_G(v)$ is the degree of $v$ in $G$. The weight of a vertex in $H$ is set to 1.

The following claim shows that edge cuts in $G$ correspond to vertex cuts in $G'$.

LEMMA 7. *For any two sets $A, B \subseteq V$: $\gamma_{G'}(A, B) = \delta_G(A, B)$.*

PROOF. An edge cut in $G$ between $A$ and $B$ induces a vertex cut in $G'$ that also separates $A$ and $B$. This gives $\gamma_{G'}(A, B) \leq \delta_G(A, B)$. On the other hand, a minimum $(A, B)$ vertex cut in $G'$ will not use a vertex $v \in V$ as it would be cheaper to use all hyperedges connected to $v$ instead. Hence, it only consist of hyperedges, which give rise to an $(A, B)$ edge cut in $G$, and therefore $\gamma_{G'}(A, B) \geq \delta_G(A, B)$ holds. □

COROLLARY 3. *There is a $\sqrt{d_{\text{avg}}}$ approximation algorithm for minimum bisection in hypergraphs, where $d_{\text{avg}}$ is the average vertex degree.*

PROOF. We first construct a vertex cut tree $T$ for $G'$. Then we use dynamic programming to compute the minimum vertex cut in $T$ such that one half of the vertices of $V$ are separated from the other half. This induces a bisection in $G'$. Because of the approximation guarantee of the cut tree this is an $O(\log^{3/4} n \cdot \sqrt{nd_{avg}})$-approximation. The full version contains the details of the dynamic programming approach. □

## 3.2 Lower bounds

In this section we show various lower bounds for approximating vertex cuts or hypergraph cuts by cut trees. We first show that in order to get any reasonable approximation guarantee one needs to consider vertex cut trees instead of edge cut trees. This is in strong contrast to ordinary graphs where edge cut trees already give a polylogarithmic approximation guarantee [18].

*3.2.1 Edge Cut Trees for Hyperedge Cuts.*

THEOREM 6. *There exists a hypergraph on $n$ vertices such that the quality of any edge cut tree is $\Omega(n)$.*

PROOF. Consider a hypergraph $G = (V, H)$ with a single hyperedge $e$ spanning all $n$ nodes of the hypergraph. Let $T$ be a dominating edge cut tree of $G$. Each edge in $T$ defines a cut in the hypergraph of weight 1, thus without loss of generality all edges in $T$ have weight 1.

Consider two different vertex sets $\emptyset \neq S_1, S_2 \subset V$ with $|S_1|, |S_2| < n/2$ and let $\bar{X} = V \setminus X$ for any vertex set $X$. Let $F_1, F_2$ be minimum-size sets of tree edges separating $S_1$ from $\bar{S_1}$ and $S_2$ from $\bar{S_2}$, respectively. We show that $F_1$ and $F_2$ cannot be equal.

Assume for a contradiction that $F_1 = F_2 = F$. Removing $F$ from the tree decomposes it into clusters. The vertices of $V$ in a cluster classify it in one of four groups: $S_1 \cap S_2$, $S_1 \cap \bar{S_2}$, $\bar{S_1} \cap S_2$ and $\bar{S_1} \cap \bar{S_2}$. We say that that a cluster is an $(S_1, S_2)$-cluster, if all of its vertices are from $S_1 \cap S_2$; the nomenclature for the other groups is analogous.

We observe that if $F$ contains an edge $e$ linking an $(S_1, S_2)$-cluster to an $(S_1, \bar{S_2})$-cluster, then $F \setminus \{e\}$ still disconnects $S_1$ and $\bar{S_1}$, which is a contradiction to the minimality of $F$. Similarly, no edge $e \in F$ can connect an $(S_1, S_2)$-cluster to an $(\bar{S_1}, S_2)$-cluster, an $(\bar{S_1}, \bar{S_2})$-cluster to an $(\bar{S_1}, S_2)$-cluster, and an $(\bar{S_1}, \bar{S_2})$-cluster to an $(S_1, \bar{S_2})$-cluster.

Define the disjoint sets $A = (S_1 \cap S_2) \cup (\bar{S_1} \cap \bar{S_2})$ and $B = (S_1 \cap \bar{S_2}) \cup (\bar{S_1} \cap S_2)$. Sets $A$ and $B$ cannot be empty as $|S_1|, |S_2| < n/2$ and both are nonempty; also $A = \bar{B}$. We show that $A$ and $B$ are disconnected in $G$, which is a contradiction to fact that $G$ is connected.

On the one hand, $A$ and $B$ must be separated in the tree by removing $F$. To see this, observe that the removal of $F$ disconnects any $x \in S_1 \cap S_2$ must be disconnected from all vertices in $\bar{S_1} \cup \bar{S_2} \supset B$. Similarly, the removal of $F$ disconnects $x \in \bar{S_1} \cap \bar{S_2}$ from all vertices in $S_1 \cup S_2 \supset B$. On the other hand, the clusters containing the vertices of $A$ and the clusters containing the vertices of $B$ are not connected through edges of $F$, as shown above. It follows that $F \setminus F = \emptyset$ disconnects $A$ and $B$ in the tree. This means that $A$ and $B$ are disconnected in $G$, which is a contradiction.

The total number of tree edges can be bounded without loss of generality by $2n$. To see this, note that if a leaf of the tree does not belong to $V$, the edge leading to it is never removed by a minimum cut separating vertex sets of $V$. Furthermore, if any tree vertex not belonging to $V$ has only one child , then it may be merged with its child or parent without affecting the size of any tree cut. The number of vertices not belonging to $V$ is therefore at most $n - 1$

(which is the case if the tree is binary and $V$ lies at the leaves), so the number of tree edges is bounded by $2n-2$.

The number of edge sets containing less than $n/8$ edges is at most

$$\sum_{i=1}^{n/8}\binom{2n}{i} < \sum_{i=1}^{n/8}\binom{2n}{n/8} = \frac{n}{8}\binom{2n}{n/8} < \frac{n}{8}(16e)^{n/8}$$
$$< \frac{n}{8}2^{3n/4} < 2^{3n/4+\log n} \ .$$

The number of vertex sets $S \subset V$, $|S| < n/2$ is larger than $2^{n-2}$. As $2^{3n/4+\log n} < 2^{n-2}$ for $n \geq 32$, it follows that there exist sets $S \subset V$ whose corresponding cut in the tree contains at least $n/8$ edges. The cost of these tree cuts is therefore at least $n/8$, while the cut cost in the graph is 1. It follows that the approximation ratio of the tree is $\Omega(n)$. □

*3.2.2 Vertex Cut Trees for Hyperedge Cuts.* The following theorem gives a lower bound on the quality of vertex cut trees for approximating hyperedge cuts in a hypergraph $G$ over $n$ vertices.

Theorem 7. *There exists a hypergraph on n vertices such that the quality of any vertex-weighted cut tree is $\Omega(\sqrt{n})$.*

Proof. Consider a graph $G = (V, E)$ with a top vertex $v$ connected to $n$ vertices $U = \{u_1, \dots, u_n\}$ with simple edges of weight 1, as well as a hyperedge of weight $\sqrt{n}$ spanning all vertices $u_i$. The graph is shown in Figure 2.

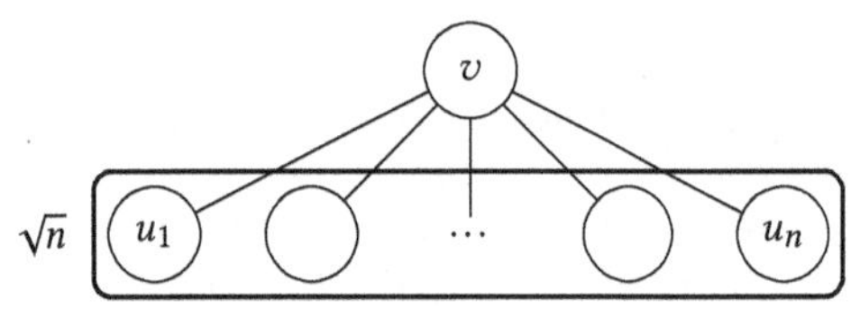


**Figure 2: Bad example for approximating hyperedge cuts via vertex cut trees.**

The cut size of any set $S \subsetneq U$ is $\delta_G(S) = \sqrt{n} + |S|$, as both the hyperedge and all edges connecting $S$ to the top vertex $v$ must be removed. The cut size of any set $S' \cup \{v\}$, $\emptyset \neq S' \subsetneq U$ is $\delta_G(S' \cup \{v\}) = \sqrt{n} + n - |S'|$. It follows that any set $S$ with $1 \leq \ell < n/2$ vertices from $U$ has $\delta_G(S) \geq \sqrt{n} + \ell$.

Let $T$ be a dominating vertex cut tree of $G$. Fix a root of $T$ so that none of its children have more than $n/2$ vertices from $U$ in its subtree. Also fix an arbitrary order among the children of each node. Every node $x$ of this tree with $\ell$ vertices from $U$ in its subtree defines a cut in the graph with both sides having at least $\ell/3$ vertices from $U$ (note that this in particular also holds for the root as we can partition the children into two sets such that both sets contain at least $n/3$ vertices from $U$). As the tree is dominating, node $x$ must have weight at least $\ell/3$.

Suppose without loss of generality that an in-order traversal of the tree visits the vertices of $U$ in the order $u_1, u_2, \dots, u_n$. Let $k = \lfloor\sqrt{n}\rfloor$ and $S = \{u_1, u_{k+1}, \dots, u_{k(k-1)+1}\}$. As $|S| = \Theta(\sqrt{n})$, the cut size in $G$ is $\delta_G(S)$ is $\Theta(\sqrt{n})$. We show that the vertex cut cost in the tree $\gamma_T(S, V \setminus S)$ is $\Omega(n)$.

In the following we refer to the vertices in $S$ as $S$-vertices and to the vertices in $U - S$ as $U$-vertices. Fix a cut $X$ in $T$. We first show that the cut cost of $X$ is large if only few $U$-vertices can reach the root.

Claim 2. *If in a sub-tree $T'$ at least $\ell$ $U$-vertices from $T'$ are separated from the root $r_{T'}$ the cut cost* inside *$T'$ is at least $\ell/3$.*

Proof. Proof by induction over the height of $T'$. The claim clearly holds if $T'$ is just a leaf vertex. If a $U$-vertex is cut away from the root it means that the leaf vertex is in the cut and the cost is at least $\sqrt{n} \geq 1/3$.

For the induction step consider a root vertex $r_{T'}$ with children $c_1, \dots, c_s$, and assume that from the subtree rooted at a child $c_i$ we aim to separate $\ell_i$ $U$-vertices from the root. If we choose $r_{T'}$ into the cut the cost of the cut inside $T'$ is at least $w(r_{T'}) \geq \sum_i \ell_i/3$. Otherwise, we have to pay at least $\ell_i/3$ in each sub-tree by induction hypothesis, which sums up to the same cost. □

This means that the cost of the tree cut for $S$ is at least $\Omega(n)$ if this cut happens to separate at least 50% of the $U$-vertices from the root $r_T$. Now, suppose that the cut separates at most 50% of the $U$-vertices. Observe, that in this case *all* $S$-vertices must be separated from the root. For every $U$-vertex $u$ that is not separated from the root remove the path from $u$ to $r_T$ from $T$. The removed set does not contain any vertices from $X$ and also no $S$-vertices.

The removal partitions the tree into pieces. The key observation is that at least $\Omega(\sqrt{n})$ pieces must contain an element from $S$. To see this observe that if between two (not necessarily consecutive) vertices $s$ and $s'$ from $S$, there exists a vertex from $U - S$ that is connected to $r_T$, then $s$ and $s'$ must lie in different pieces. This holds because the LCA of $s$ and $s'$ must lie on the path from $r_T$ to $u$ and is taken out. The vertices from $U - S$ that can reach the root partition the sequence $u_1, \dots, u_n$ into intervals. In the following we argue that at least $\sqrt{n}/2$ of these intervals contain an element form $S$. Let $k_i$, $i \geq 1$ denote the number of intervals that contain $i$ $S$-vertices. The size of such an interval (number of vertices contained in it) is at least $(i-1) \cdot \sqrt{n}$. Summing the size of all these intervals gives

$$\sum_i k_i(i-1)\sqrt{n} \leq \frac{n+\sqrt{n}}{2} \ , \tag{4}$$

where the inequality follows because the $U$-vertices that can reach the root are not contained in any interval. On the other hand,

$$\sum_i k_i i \geq \sqrt{n} \tag{5}$$

holds, as the left hand side is the total number of $S$-vertices. Combining equations 4 and 5 gives that the total number of intervals that contain an $S$-vertex is $\sum_i k_i \geq (\sqrt{n}-1)/2 = \Omega(\sqrt{n})$.

Since in each piece that contains an element from $S$ we have to select at least one vertex to be in the cut $X$, we have to choose $\Omega(\sqrt{n})$ vertices each with cost $\sqrt{n}$. This gives a total cut-cost of $\Omega(n)$. □

Note that the same result holds for unweighted hypergraphs. To see this, replace the weighted hyperedge with $\lfloor\sqrt{n}\rfloor$ different hyperedges, each spanning the $n$ vertices of the set $U$.

*3.2.3 Vertex Cut Trees for Weighted Vertex Cuts.* We show that the result from the previous section immediately translates to a lower bound for vertex cut trees. The lower bound is based on the graph $G_H = (V_H, E_H)$ shown in Figure 3. Graph $G_H$ is precisely the graph constructed by applying the reduction from Lemma 7 to the hypergraph $G$ from the previous section. The graph $G_H$ consists of a vertex $t$ of weight $\sqrt{n}$ (representing the hyperedge of $G_H$), connected to vertices $u_1, \ldots, u_n$ of weight $\sqrt{n}+1$. Each of the $u_i$ is connected to a vertex $w_i$ of weight 1 (representing the edges of $G_H$). Finally, all $w_i$ are connected to a vertex $v$ of weight $n$. The graph $G_H$ has $N = 2n + 2$ vertices of total weight $2n + n(\sqrt{n} + 1) + \sqrt{n} = \Theta(N\sqrt{N})$.

Graph $G_H$ is precisely the graph constructed by applying the reduction from Lemma 7 to the hypergraph from the previous section.

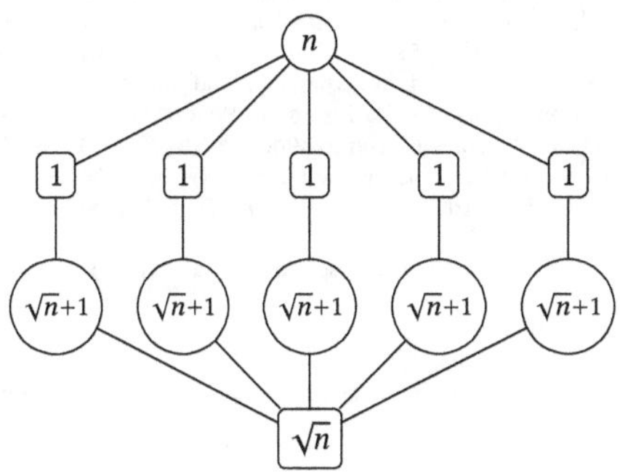


**Figure 3: Bad example for approximating weighted vertex cuts via vertex cut trees.**

Lemma 8. *Any dominating, vertex-weighted cut tree $T$ of $G_H$ has quality $\Omega(\sqrt{N})$.*

Proof. Let $G = (V, E)$ be the hypergraph considered in the previous section, shown in Figure 2. Lemma 7 shows that for any two vertex sets $A, B$ in $G$, the corresponding cut in $G_H$ has identical cost. As the vertex set of $G_H$ is a superset of the vertex set of $G$, any vertex cut tree for $G_H$ is a vertex cut tree for $G$. By Theorem 7, any vertex cut tree for $G$ has quality $\Omega(\sqrt{n})$. As $|V_H| = N = 2n + 2$, it follows that any vertex cut tree for $G_H$ has quality $\Omega(\sqrt{n}) = \Omega(\sqrt{N})$. □

*3.2.4 Vertex-Weighted Cut Trees for unweighted Vertex Cuts.* We modify the construction shown in Figure 3 as follows. For simplicity of exposition, we change the vertex weight of $\sqrt{n}+1$ to $\sqrt{n}$ and assume that $n$ is square. Replace any vertex of weight $w$ with a clique of $w$ vertices and replace the edges between formerly weighted vertices with a full bipartite graph between the respective cliques. Let $U_i$ denote the clique resulting from the vertex $u_i$ in the weighted graph.

We plan to adapt the proof of Theorem 7. This proof is based on the observation that for any tree, there must exist $\sqrt{n}$ vertices $u_i$ that are *spread apart* in the tree and, therefore, separating these vertices in the tree is costly. Applying the same idea to the unweighted case is not straightforward, as the vertices $u_i$ are now cliques $U_i$, whose vertices may not be concentrated in some vertex cut tree.

In the unweighted graph, call the clique vertices $U_i$ *core vertices*; enumerate them so that core vertices of the same clique are consecutive. Given any vertex cut tree, an in-order traversal of the tree induces a *permutation* of the core vertices. We show first show that, for any permutation, there is a choice of core vertices from $\Theta(\sqrt{n})$ cliques, such that the following holds: After applying the permutation, there exist $\Theta(\sqrt{n})$ disjoint intervals of length $n$, in which $\Theta(\sqrt{n})$ chosen core vertices are found. This means that we can choose cliques such that the vertices from these cliques are sufficiently spread apart in the tree.

We formalize the technical observation as follows. Divide the set $L = \{1, \ldots, n\sqrt{n}\}$ into $n$ *clusters* $\{(i-1)\sqrt{n}+1, \ldots, \sqrt{n}\}$ for $i = 1, \ldots, \sqrt{n}$, i.e., a cluster are $\sqrt{n}$ consecutive numbers. Given some permutation $\pi$ of $L$, a *group* is a set $\{\pi((j-1)n+1), \ldots, \pi(jn)\}$ for $j = 1, \ldots, \sqrt{n}$, i.e., the groups are $n$ numbers that are consecutive after applying the permutation.

Lemma 9. *For any permutation $\pi$, there is a choice of $2\sqrt{n}$ clusters, such that there are at least $\sqrt{n}/9$ groups from which $\Theta(\sqrt{n})$ elements have been chosen.*

Proof. Choose $2\sqrt{n}$ clusters uniformly at random and let $Y_j$ be the number of chosen elements in group $j$. With $X_j$ being the indicator variable of the event that $\sqrt{n}/2 \le Y_j \le 7\sqrt{n}/2$, we show that the expected number of groups with $\Theta(\sqrt{n})$ elements, $\mathbb{E}[\sum_{j=1}^{\sqrt{n}} X_j]$ is at least $\sqrt{n}/9$.

The expectation of $Y_j$ is $2\sqrt{n}$. To see this, let $c_{ij}$ be the total number of elements from cluster $i$ whose group is $j$, after applying the permutation $\pi$. Let $C_i$ be the indicator variable of the event that cluster $i$ is chosen; note that $\mathbb{E}[C_i]$ equals $2\sqrt{n}/n = 2/\sqrt{n}$. Furthermore, the total number of elements in group $j$ is $n$, thus, $\sum_{i=1}^{n} c_{ij} = n$. With $Y_j = \sum_{i=1}^{n} c_{ij} C_i$ it follows that $\mathbb{E}[Y_j] = 2n/\sqrt{n} = 2\sqrt{n}$.

We now argue that the variance of $Y_j$ is at most $2n$. With Cov denoting the covariance,

$$\mathrm{Var}[Y_j] = \sum_{i=1}^{n} c_{ij}^2 \,\mathrm{Var}[C_i] + \sum_{1 \le k < \ell \le n} c_{kj} c_{\ell j} \,\mathrm{Cov}[C_k, C_\ell] \ .$$

The variance of indicator variable $C_i$ is $\frac{2}{\sqrt{n}}(1 - \frac{2}{\sqrt{n}}) = (2\sqrt{n} - 4)/n$. The covariance of $C_k$ and $C_\ell$ is $\mathbb{E}[C_k \cdot C_\ell] - \mathbb{E}[C_k]\mathbb{E}[C_\ell]$. The expectation of $C_k \cdot C_\ell$ is the probability that clusters $k$ and $\ell$ are both chosen. As their common choice is less likely as the probability of the two being chosen in an independent choice, $\mathbb{E}[C_k \cdot C_\ell] \le \mathbb{E}[C_k] \cdot \mathbb{E}[C_\ell]$. It follows that the covariance is negative and

$$\mathrm{Var}[Y_j] \le \sum_{i=1}^{n} c_{ij}^2 \,\mathrm{Var}[C_i] < \frac{2}{\sqrt{n}} \sum_{i=1}^{n} c_{ij}^2 \ .$$

The sum $\sum_{i=1}^{n} c_{ij}^2$ is maximized if $\sqrt{n}$ of the terms are at the maximum of $\sqrt{n}$, thus $\sum_{i=1}^{n} c_{ij}^2 \le n\sqrt{n}$. Plugging this fact in the above equation gives that $\mathrm{Var}[Y_j] \le n$.

Chebychev's inequality states with $\mu = \mathbb{E}[Y_j]$ and $\sigma^2 = \mathrm{Var}[Y_j]$ for any $k > 0$

$$\Pr\left[|Y_j - \mu| \le k\right] \ge 1 - \frac{\sigma^2}{k^2} \ .$$

We have $\sigma^2 \leq 2n$, $\mu = 2\sqrt{n}$ and we choose $k = 3\sqrt{n}/2$. It follows that this implies that

$$\Pr\left[\sqrt{n}/2 \leq Y_j \leq 7\sqrt{n}/2\right] \geq 1 - \frac{2n}{(3\sqrt{n}/2)^2} = 1 - \frac{8}{9} = \frac{1}{9} .$$

The expectation of $X_j$ is therefore at least 1/9 and consequently $\mathbb{E}[\sum_{j=1}^{\sqrt{n}} X_j]$ is at least $\sqrt{n}/9$. □

We sketch the proof of the theorem. Note that the strategy is very similar to the proof of Theorem 7, with the modifications highlighted at the beginning of this section.

THEOREM 8. *Any dominating, vertex-weighted cut tree T of G has quality $\Omega(N^{1/3})$, where N is the number of vertices of G.*

PROOF SKETCH. The cut size of any set of $\ell$ cliques $U_i$ is $\sqrt{n}+\ell$, as the clique representing the hyperedge and the vertices representing the simple edges must be removed.

Let $T$ be a dominating vertex cut tree of $G$. Fix a root of $T$ so that none of its children have more than $n\sqrt{n}/2$ core vertices in its subtree. We show that every node $x$ of this tree with $\ell > \sqrt{n}$ core vertices in its subtree must have weight at least $\max\{\sqrt{n}, \ell/3\sqrt{n}\}$. Node $x$ defines a cut in the graph, with both sides having at least $\ell/3$ core vertices. If this cut divides a clique, the cut cost per vertex for this clique is at least one, which implies the theorem. If no cliques are divided, then the cut cost is $\sqrt{n} + \ell/3 > \ell/3\sqrt{n}$, as shown above.

Enumerate the core vertices of the tree via in-order traversal. The vertices $jn+1, \ldots, (j+1)n$ form a *group* in the tree, for $j = 1, \ldots, \sqrt{n}$. Choose $2\sqrt{n}$ cliques $U_i$ so that $\Theta(\sqrt{n})$ groups have $\Theta(\sqrt{n})$ chosen. These vertices form the set $S$. An appropriate choice is possible, as shown by Lemma 9. The cut cost of $S$ in the graph is $\Theta(\sqrt{n})$, as argued above. We prove that the cut cost of $S$ in the tree is $\Omega(n)$.

In the following, call $S$-vertices the vertices in $S$ and $U$-vertices those in $U - S$.

We claim that if in a subtree $T'$ at least $\ell$ $U$-vertices are separated from the root, the cut cost inside $T'$ is at least $\ell/(3\sqrt{n})$. This can be shown by induction as in Claim 2.

Fix a cut $X$ in the tree. If the cut $X$ separates at least $n\sqrt{n} - 3n$ $U$-vertices from the root (so all but $n$ $U$-vertices), then the cut cost is $\Omega(n)$ by the above claim. Now, suppose that the cut separates at most $n$ of the $U$-vertices from the root. For every $U$-vertex that is not separated from the root remove the path from $u$ to the root from $T$. The removed set does not contain any vertices from $X$ and also no $S$-vertices.

The removal partitions the tree into pieces. As $\Theta(\sqrt{n})$ groups contain $\Theta(\sqrt{n})$ $S$-vertices, there exist pieces in all of these groups. However, if an interval has size $z \leq \sqrt{n}$, the cost of the corresponding piece will be at least $z$ (as is the cut cost in the graph). On the other hand, an interval can contain at most $2\sqrt{n}$ $S$-vertices, as the $S$-vertices are $n$ core vertices apart and only $n$ $U$-vertices to fill the intervals exist. It follows that the cost per $S$-vertex is at least 1/2, so the total cost must be $\Omega(n)$.

As the total number of vertices $N$ is $\Theta(n^{3/2})$, the gap between $\gamma_G(S)$ and $\gamma_T(S)$ is $\Omega(\sqrt{n}) = \Omega(N^{1/3})$. □

## 4 ACKNOWLEDGEMENTS

The authors would like to thank the anonymous referees for helpful comments. The work of Roy Schwartz is supported by GIF grant I-2439-407.6/2016 and ISF grant 1336/16.

## REFERENCES


[1] Konstantin Andreev and Harald Räcke. 2004. Balanced Graph Partitions. In *Proc. of the 16th SPAA*. 120–124. https://doi.org/10.1145/1007912.1007931

[2] Sanjeev Arora, Satish Rao, and Umesh Vazirani. 2004. Expander Flows, Geometric Embeddings, and Graph Partitionings. In *Proc. of the 36th STOC*. 222–231. https://doi.org/10.1145/1007352.1007355

[3] Nikhil Bansal, Uriel Feige, Robert Krauthgamer, Konstantin Makarychev, Viswanath Nagarajan, Joseph (Seffi) Naor, and Roy Schwartz. 2011. Min-Max Graph Partitioning and Small Set Expansion. In *Proc. of the 52nd FOCS*. 17–26. https://doi.org/10.1109/FOCS.2011.79

[4] Eden Chlamtáč, Michael Dinitz, and Robert Krauthgamer. 2012. Everywhere-Sparse Spanners via Dense Subgraphs. In *Proc. of the 53th FOCS*. 758–767. https://doi.org/10.1109/FOCS.2012.61

[5] Eden Chlamtáč, Michael Dinitz, and Yury Makarychev. 2017. Minimizing the Union: Tight Approximations for Small Set Bipartite Vertex Expansion. In *Proc. of the 28th SODA*. SIAM, 881–899. https://doi.org/10.1137/1.9781611974782.56

[6] Uriel Feige, MohammadTaghi Hajiaghayi, and James R. Lee. 2008. Improved Approximation Algorithms for Minimum Weight Vertex Separators. *SIAM J. Comput.* 38, 2 (2008), 629–657. https://doi.org/10.1137/05064299X

[7] Uriel Feige, Robert Krauthgamer, and Kobbi Nissim. 2000. Approximating the Minimum Bisection Size. In *Proc. of the 32nd STOC*. 530–536. https://doi.org/10.1145/335305.335370

[8] Andreas E. Feldmann and Luca Foschini. 2012. Balanced Partitions of Trees and Applications. In *Proc. of the 29th STACS*. 100–111. https://doi.org/10.4230/LIPIcs.STACS.2012.100

[9] Chris Harrelson, Kirsten Hildrum, and Satish B. Rao. 2003. A Polynomial-time Tree Decomposition to Minimize Congestion. In *Proc. of the 15th SPAA*. 34–43. https://doi.org/10.1145/777412.777419

[10] Bruce Hendrickson and Tamara G. Kolda. 2000. Graph Partitioning Models for Parallel Computing. *Parallel Comput.* 26, 12 (Nov. 2000), 1519–1534. https://doi.org/10.1016/S0167-8191(00)00048-X

[11] Robert Krauthgamer, Joseph (Seffi) Naor, and Roy Schwartz. 2009. Partitioning Graphs into Balanced Components. In *Proc. of the 20th SODA*. SIAM, 942–949. arXiv:soda:1496770.1496872

[12] Frank Thomson Leighton and Satish B. Rao. 1999. Multicommodity Max-Flow Min-Cut Theorems and Their Use in Designing Approximation Algorithms. *J. ACM* 46, 6 (1999), 787–832. https://doi.org/10.1145/331524.331526

[13] Anand Louis and Yury Makarychev. 2014. Approximation Algorithms for Hypergraph Small Set Expansion and Small Set Vertex Expansion. In *Proc. of the 17th APPROX/RANDOM*. 339–355. https://doi.org/10.4230/LIPIcs.APPROX-RANDOM.2014.339

[14] Pasin Manurangsi. 2017. Almost-Polynomial Ratio ETH-Hardness of Approximating Densest k-Subgraph. In *Proc. of the 49th STOC*. 954–961. https://doi.org/10.1145/3055399.3055412

[15] David A. Papa and Igor L. Markov. 2007. Hypergraph Partitioning and Clustering. In *In Approximation Algorithms and Metaheuristics*. https://doi.org/10.1201/9781420010749.ch61

[16] Harald Räcke. 2002. Minimizing Congestion in General Networks. In *Proc. of the 43th FOCS*. 43–52. https://doi.org/10.1109/SFCS.2002.1181881

[17] Harald Räcke. 2008. Optimal Hierarchical Decompositions for Congestion Minimization in Networks. In *Proc. of the 40th STOC*. 255–264. https://doi.org/10.1145/1374376.1374415

[18] Harald Räcke and Chintan Shah. 2014. Improved Guarantees for Tree Cut Sparsifiers. In *Proc. of the 22nd ESA*. 774–785. https://doi.org/10.1007/978-3-662-44777-2_64

[19] Harald Räcke and Richard Stotz. 2016. Improved Approximation Algorithms for Balanced Partitioning Problems. In *Proc. of the 33rd STACS*. 58:1–58:14. https://doi.org/10.4230/LIPIcs.STACS.2016.58

[20] S. Rajamanickam and E. G. Boman. 2013. Parallel Graph Partitioning with Zoltan: Is hypergraph partitioning worth it? In *Graph Partitioning and Graph Clustering*, D. A. Bader, H. Meyerhenke, P. Sanders, and D. Wagner (Eds.). AMS Contemporary Mathematics, Vol. 588. AMS, 37–52. https://doi.org/10.1090/conm/588

# Dynamic Representations of Sparse Distributed Networks: A Locality-Sensitive Approach

Haim Kaplan*
Tel Aviv University
Tel Aviv, Israel
haimk@post.tau.ac.il

Shay Solomon†
IBM Research, T. J. Watson Research Center
Yorktown Heights, New York
solo.shay@gmail.com

## ABSTRACT

In 1999, Brodal and Fagerberg (BF) gave an algorithm for maintaining a low outdegree orientation of a dynamic uniformly sparse graph. Specifically, for a dynamic graph on $n$-vertices, with arboricity bounded by $\alpha$ at all times, the BF algorithm supports edge updates in $O(\log n)$ amortized update time, while keeping the maximum outdegree in the graph bounded by $O(\alpha)$. Such an orientation provides a basic data structure for uniformly sparse graphs, which found applications to a plethora of dynamic graph algorithms.

A significant weakness of the BF algorithm is the possible *temporary* blowup of the maximum outdegree, following edge insertions. Although BF eventually reduces all outdegrees to $O(\alpha)$, some vertices may reach an outdegree of $\Omega(n)$ during the process, hence local memory usage at the vertices–an important quality measure in distributed systems–cannot be bounded. We show how to modify the BF algorithm to guarantee that the outdegrees of all vertices are bounded by $O(\alpha)$ at all times, without hurting any of its other properties, and present an efficient distributed implementation of the modified algorithm. This provides the *first* representation of distributed networks in which the local memory usage at vertices is bounded by the arboricity (which is essentially the average degree of the densest subgraph) rather than the maximum degree.

For settings where there is no local memory constraints, one may take the temporary outdegree blowup to the extreme and allow a permanent outdegree blowup. This allows us to address the second significant weakness of the BF algorithm – its inherently *global* nature: An insertion of an edge $(u, v)$ may trigger changes in the orientations of edges that are arbitrarily far away from $u$ and $v$. We suggest an alternative *local* scheme, which does not guarantee any outdegree bound on the vertices, yet is just as efficient as the BF scheme for some applications. For example, we obtain a local dynamic algorithm for maintaining a maximal matching with sub-logarithmic update time in uniformly sparse networks, providing an exponential improvement over the state-of-the-art in this context.

## CCS CONCEPTS

• **Theory of computation → Dynamic graph algorithms**; • **Computing methodologies → Distributed algorithms**;

## KEYWORDS

arboricity; dynamic network; local algorithm; local memory

**ACM Reference Format:**
Haim Kaplan and Shay Solomon. 2018. Dynamic Representations of Sparse Distributed Networks: A Locality-Sensitive Approach. In *SPAA '18: 30th ACM Symposium on Parallelism in Algorithms and Architectures, July 16–18, 2018, Vienna, Austria.* ACM, New York, NY, USA, 10 pages. https://doi.org/10.1145/3210377.3210397

## 1 INTRODUCTION

### 1.1 Quality measures in distributed computing

The $\mathcal{LOCAL}$ and the $\mathcal{CONGEST}$ models are perhaps the two most fundamental communication models in distributed computing (see [22]), the former is the standard model capturing the essence of spatial locality, and the latter also takes into account congestion limitations. In these models it is assumed that initially all the processors wake up simultaneously, and that computation proceeds in fault-free synchronous rounds during which every processor exchanges messages with its direct neighbors in the network. In the $\mathcal{LOCAL}$ model these messages are of unbounded size, whereas in the $\mathcal{CONGEST}$ model each message contains $O(\log n)$ bits. An efficient distributed algorithm allows the nodes to communicate with their direct neighbors for a small number of rounds, after which they need to produce their outputs, which are required to form a valid global solution. A task is called *local* if the number of rounds needed for solving it is constant. The locality of many distributed tasks have been studied in the past two decades, with the emerging conclusion that truly local tasks are rather scarce.

Another important locality measure is the local *memory usage* at a processor. The standard premise is that each processor may communicate with *all* its neighbors by sending and receiving messages. To this end, the local memory usage at a processor should be proportional to its degree. Reducing the local memory at processors to be independent of their degree could be of fundamental importance for various applications. In fact, the processors in a distributed network are in many cases *identical*, thus the local memory at low degree processors is not proportional to their degree

*Research was partially supported by the Israel Science Foundation grant no. 1841-14, the Blavatnik Fund, and the German-Israeli Foundation for Scientific Research and Development (GIF) grant no. 1367/2017.
†Supported by the IBM Herman Goldstine Postdoctoral Fellowship.


*SPAA '18, July 16–18, 2018, Vienna, Austria*

ACM ISBN 978-1-4503-5799-9/18/07...$15.00
https://doi.org/10.1145/3210377.3210397

but rather to the *maximum degree* in the network. Moreover, in sparse networks (such as planar networks), the maximum degree may be $n-1$ while the average degree is constant, so the global memory (over all processors) will be blown up by a factor of $n$ if all processors are identical. (In dynamic networks, on which we focus here, this factor $n$ blow-up may occur even if the processors are not identical.) Low-degree spanners have been used to reduce local memory usage at processors, which found many applications, such as to efficient broadcast protocols, data gathering and dissemination tasks in overlay networks, compact routing schemes, network synchronization, computing global functions [4–6, 22, 24]. However, for the vast majority of distributed tasks, such as maximum independent set and coloring, the global solution must consider *all edges* of the network and not just the spanner edges.

The total number of messages needed for solving a distributed task is another important quality measure in distributed computing.

## 1.2 The dynamic distributed setting

The dynamic distributed model is defined as follows. Starting with the empty graph $G_0 = (V, E_0 = \{\emptyset\})$ over an initial vertex set $V$, in every round $t > 0$, the adversary chooses a vertex or an edge to be either inserted to or deleted from $G_{t-1}$, resulting in $G_t$. (As a result of a vertex deletion, all its incident edges are deleted. A vertex is inserted without incident edges.) Upon the insertion or deletion of a vertex $v$ or an edge $e = (u, v)$, an update procedure is invoked, which should restore the validity of the solution being maintained. For example, if we maintain a maximal matching, then following the deletion of a matched edge the matching is no longer maximal, and the update procedure should restore maximality. We shall consider the most natural model in this setting, hereafter the *local wakeup model* (see [3, 10, 21, 23]), where only the affected vertices wake up (following an update to a vertex $v$, only $v$ wakes up; following an edge update $(u, v)$, both $u$ and $v$ wake up). The update procedure proceeds in fault-free synchronous rounds during which every processor exchanges messages with its neighbors, just as in the static setting, until finishing its execution.

In the distributed dynamic setting, the *amortized update time* and *amortized message complexity* bound the *average* number of communication rounds and messages sent, respectively, needed to update the solution per update operation, over a *worst-case* sequence of updates. The *worst-case update time* and *worst-case message complexity* is the maximum number of communication rounds and messages sent, again over a worst-case sequence of updates.

We assume that the topological changes occur serially and are sufficiently spaced so that the protocol has enough time to complete its operation before the occurrence of the next change. The same assumption was made also in previous works (see [3, 10, 21, 23]).

## 1.3 Representations of sparse networks via dynamic edge orientations

*1.3.1 Centralized networks.* A graph $G = (V, E)$ has *arboricity* $\alpha$ if $\alpha = \max_{U \subseteq V} \left\lceil \frac{|E(U)|}{|U|-1} \right\rceil$, where $E(U) = \{(u, v) \in E \mid u, v \in U\}$. Thus the arboricity is close to the maximum *density* $|E(U)|/|U|$ over all induced subgraphs of $G$. While a graph of bounded arboricity is *uniformly sparse*, a graph of bounded density (i.e., a sparse graph) may contain a dense subgraph (e.g., on $\sqrt{m}$ of the vertices), and therefore may have large arboricity. The family of bounded arboricity graphs contains planar and bounded genus graphs, bounded tree-width graphs, and in general all graphs excluding fixed minors.

A fundamental question in data structures is to devise efficient representations of graphs supporting *adjacency queries*: Given two vertices $u$ and $v$, is there an edge between them in the $n$-vertex graph $G = (V, E)$? Using an adjacency matrix (of size $\Theta(n^2)$) one can support such queries in $O(1)$ time. In sparse graphs, however, a quadratic-space data structure seems very wasteful. If one uses adjacency lists instead, the space is reduced to $O(|E|)$, but then adjacency queries may require $\Theta(n)$ time. By maintaining these adjacency lists sorted, the worst-case query time can be reduced to $O(\log n)$, but no further than that, even in sparse graphs. Another approach is to use hashing, which guarantees linear space and constant query time, but alas it requires randomization, otherwise the construction time is super-linear. While some of these data structures have linear (in the graph size) space usage, none of them can bound the *local* space usage (per vertex).

In a pioneering paper from 1999, Brodal and Fagerberg (BF) [9] devised a data structure for adjacency queries in uniformly sparse graphs that is based on *edge orientations*. Specifically, an *arboricity $\alpha$ preserving sequence* is a sequence of edge insertions and deletions starting from an empty graph, in which the arboricity of the dynamic graph is bounded by $\alpha$ at all times. For any arboricity $\alpha$ preserving sequence, the BF algorithm has an amortized update time of $O(\log n)$, while keeping the maximum outdegree in the graph bounded by $\Delta = O(\alpha)$. (The BF algorithm can, in fact, handle vertex updates within the same asymptotic bounds, where $n$ stands for the current number of vertices.) Such an edge orientation, which is called a $\Delta$*-orientation*, allows to support adjacency queries in $O(\alpha)$ worst-case time, thus providing a significant improvement over the known data structures in graphs of sufficiently low arboricity.

BF also showed that the amortized time of their algorithm is asymptotically optimal. Specifically, let $\alpha$, $\delta$ and $\Delta$ be three arbitrary integers satisfying $\alpha \geq 1, \delta = \Omega(\alpha), \Delta = \Omega(\delta)$, and suppose one can maintain a $\delta$-orientation for some sequence of $t$ edge updates while doing $f$ edge flips, starting with the empty graph. (We omit the constants hidden in the $\Omega$ notation above and the $O$ notation to follow.) Then the BF algorithm on this update sequence with an outdegree parameter $\Delta$ maintains a $\Delta$-orientation with a total runtime (and thus number of edge flips) of $O(t + f)$.

Recently, there has been a growing interest in the edge orientation problem. See App. A in the full version [15] for additional results on this problem and some of its applications.

*1.3.2 Distributed networks.* There is a close connection between low outdegree orientations and the forest decomposition problem, where one aims to decompose the edges of a graph $G$ into a small number of (rooted) forests. A decomposition of a graph into $\ell$ forests immediately yields an $\ell$-orientation. The other direction is also true [21]: An $\ell$-orientation yields a decomposition into at most $2\ell$ forests. Also, a dynamic maintenance of the former can be translated into a dynamic maintenance of the latter with a constant overhead in the update time, in both centralized and distributed settings [21].

[7] studied the forest-decomposition problem in the distributed static setting. They showed that for a network $G$ with arboricity $a(G)$ and any $q > 2$, there exists a distributed algorithm that computes a decomposition of $G$ into at most $((2 + q) \cdot a(G))$ forests (and

hence also a $((2+q)\cdot a(G))$-orientation) in $O(\frac{\log n}{\log q})$ rounds. (This result was refined recently by [13].) [7] also showed that given such a forest decomposition (or an edge orientation), one can compute an $O(q\cdot a(G)^2)$-vertex coloring for $G$ in $O(\log^* n)$ more rounds. Using this coloring an MIS can be computed in $O(q\cdot a(G)^2)$ rounds. More generally, low outdegree orientations lead to sublinear-time algorithms for vertex and edge coloring, MIS, and maximal matching in distributed networks of bounded arboricity. (See Chapters 4 and 11.3 in [8] for more details.)

For the dynamic distributed model, [21] devised a distributed algorithm for maintaining $O(\alpha+\log^* n)$-orientation in $O(\log^* n)$ amortized update time. They then used this orientation to maintain within the same time a decomposition into $O(\alpha+\log^* n)$ forests and also an adjacency labeling scheme with label size $O(\alpha+\log^* n)$. They used the same approach to get distributed algorithms for maintaining $O(\alpha\cdot\log^* n)$-coloring and other related structures with the same $O(\log^* n)$ update time. Although the distributed algorithm of [21] has a low amortized update time, it incurs a polynomial (in the network size) bound on three important parameters: (1) the amortized message complexity, (2) the local memory usage at processors, and (3) the messages size. In particular, the algorithm of [21] cannot be implemented in the $\mathcal{CONGEST}$ model.

While the distributed algorithms of [7] can be implemented in the $\mathcal{CONGEST}$ model, they are static, and as such, their message complexity must be at least linear in the size of the network. Moreover, unless there is some underlying representation of the network, for an algorithm to solve any nontrivial task from scratch, any processor must communicate with each of its neighbors at least once. Hence the local memory usage at processors, which should be at least linear in the maximum degree for some processors, may be larger than the arboricity bound $\alpha$ by a factor of $n/\alpha$.

**A fundamental question.** Can one use $O(\alpha)$-orientations to obtain a representation of a dynamic distributed network with a local memory usage of $O(\alpha)$? We first argue that a distributed implementation of the BF algorithm cannot achieve this. Indeed, a significant weakness of the BF algorithm is the possible *temporary* blowup of the maximum outdegree, following edge insertions. More specifically, following an insertion of edge $(u,v)$ that is oriented from $u$ to $v$, the outdegree of $u$ may exceed the threshold $\Delta$. To restore a valid $\Delta$-orientation, the BF algorithm *resets* $u$, thereby flipping all its outgoing edges. As a result, the former *out-neighbors (outgoing neighbors)* of $u$ increase their outdegree. All such neighbors whose outdegree now exceeds $\Delta$ are then handled in the same way, one after the other, and this process is repeated until all vertex outdegrees are $\leq\Delta$. BF used an elegant potential function argument to show that this process not only terminates, but also leads to an asymptotically optimal algorithm (as mentioned before). Although BF eventually reduces all outdegrees to $\leq\Delta$, some of these outdegrees may blow up throughout the reset cascade to $\Omega(n)$.

To implement the BF algorithm with local memory usage of $O(\alpha)$, the orientation should remain a $\Delta$ (or close to $\Delta$)-orientation throughout the reset cascade. We show that this is not the case unless the graph is of arboricity 1. Specifically, we show that for dynamic forests ($\alpha=1$), the BF algorithm never increases the outdegree of a vertex beyond $\Delta+1$, but there exist graphs of arboricity 2 for which the BF algorithm blows up the outdegree of some vertices to $\Omega(n)$! Hence, a distributed implementation of the BF algorithm requires a huge local memory usage. The algorithms of [14, 16], with a worst-case update time, never increase the outdegree of a vertex beyond the specified threshold. However, the tradeoffs between the outdegree and update time provided by these algorithms are significantly inferior to the BF tradeoff. In particular, for constant arboricity graphs, we want the outdegree to remain constant at all times, yet the algorithms of [14, 16] cannot provide outdegree better than $\Omega(\log n/\log\log n)$. (See App. A in [15] for more details.) We remark that the reset cascade of the BF algorithm is inherently sequential and centralized, and it is unclear if it can be distributed efficiently even regardless of local memory constraints. A similar issue arises with the worst-case update time algorithms of [14, 16].

Question 1. *Is there an algorithm with the same optimal (up to constants) tradeoff of BF between the outdegree $\Delta$ and the amortized cost, which guarantees that the outdegree of all vertices is always $O(\Delta)$? Furthermore, can this algorithm be distributed efficiently with a local memory usage of $O(\Delta)$?*

**Our contribution.** Our first attempt towards answering Question 1 is by making a natural modification to the BF algorithm: Instead of resetting vertices of outdegree larger than $\Delta$ at an arbitrary order, we always choose to reset next, the vertex of largest outdegree among all vertices of outdegree larger than $\Delta$. We show that with this modification the BF algorithm keeps the outdegrees $O(\Delta\log(n/\Delta))$ at all times. We complement this upper bound with a matching lower bound, showing that the BF algorithm together with this modification can indeed generate vertices of outdegree $\Omega(\Delta\log(n/\Delta))$ during the reset cascade, and this can happen even in graphs of arboricity 2. This modification does not resolve Question 1, as the outdegree may blow-up by a logarithmic factor during the cascade, and more importantly, it seems unlikely that the algorithm with this modification can be distributed efficiently.

To resolve Question 1 we first give a new *centralized* algorithm, which is inherently different than the BF algorithm, and keeps the outdegree bounded by $O(\Delta)$ at all times. In contrast to the BF algorithm, our algorithm does not apply a cascade of reset operations on vertices whose outdegree exceeds $\Delta$ following an insertion. Note that any reset operation on some vertex "helps" that particular vertex but "hurts" its out-neighbors. Instead, our algorithm first collects a set of vertices of relative high outdegree that would "benefit" from being reset. Then it works on the graph $G^*$ induced by the outgoing edges of these vertices in a somewhat opposite manner to the BF algorithm. More specifically, it applies a cascade of "anti-reset" operations on vertices of outdegree significantly smaller than $\Delta$, where an anti-reset on a vertex flips all its incoming edges to be outgoing of it. In other words, vertices in our algorithm are being helpful to their neighbors rather than hurtful as before. The cascade of "anti-reset" operations leads to a low outdegree orientation within the subgraph $G^*$, but it also makes sure that the outdegree of all vertices would never exceed $\Delta+1$ in the entire graph throughout the process. We show that our algorithm has the same (up to a constant factor) tradeoff of BF between the outdegree and amortized cost. This is nontrivial, since the potential function argument of BF relies heavily on the gain of *any* reset operation to the potential value. Roughly speaking, that argument compares the current orientation to an optimal orientation, where all edges but $\approx \alpha$ must be incoming to any vertex, and so the potential must be reduced after resetting a vertex of outdegree sufficiently larger than $\alpha$. This argument, alas, does not carry over to anti-resets. The argument that we provide is based on a global consideration (of the total potential gain over all anti-resets) rather than on a local consideration (of each reset). We also demonstrate that this approach of replacing resets with anti-resets facilitates efficient distributed implementation, as we can perform all the anti-resets in parallel, without worrying about the neighbors' outdegrees.

In this way we resolve Question 1 in the affirmative, providing a distributed algorithm for maintaining $\Delta$-orientation with the optimal (up to constants, w.r.t. $\Delta$) amortized cost, with a local memory usage of $O(\Delta)$, for any $\Delta = \Omega(\alpha)$. Moreover, the amortized cost bounds not just the amortized update time of our algorithm but also its amortized message complexity. Our algorithm uses short messages, and can thus be implemented in the $\mathcal{LOCAL}$ model. As immediate consequences, we can maintain forest decomposition and adjacency labeling schemes with the same bounds as above, thereby significantly improving [21].

A low outdegree orientation does not provide information on the incoming neighbors of a vertex. Hence, although it finds applications as discussed above, it cannot be viewed as a complete representation of the network. To obtain a complete representation, we distribute the information on the incoming neighbors of each vertex $v$ within the local memory of these neighbors. In this way we can guarantee that the local memory usage remains $O(\Delta)$, yet each vertex can scan its incoming neighbors upon need. On the negative side, this scan of incoming neighbors is carried out sequentially rather than in parallel. Nevertheless, in some applications, we only need to scan a few incoming neighbors. As a first application of our network representation, we obtain a distributed algorithm for maintaining a maximal matching with $O(\log n)$ amortized update time and message complexities, with $O(\alpha)$ local memory usage. (A maximal matching can be maintained via a trivial distributed algorithm with $O(1)$ worst-case update time, even in general networks, but its amortized message complexity and local memory usage are $\Omega(n)$, even in forests.) To enhance the applicability of our network representation, we demonstrate that the *bounded degree sparsifiers* of [26] can be maintained dynamically in a distributed network using low local memory usage. Using these sparsifiers, we obtain efficient distributed algorithms for maintaining approximate matching and vertex cover with low amortized update time and message complexities and with low local memory usage (see Section 2).

This result provides the first efficient representation of uniformly sparse distributed networks with low local memory usage. Besides the aforementioned applications, such a representation may be used more broadly in applications currently suitable only for low degree networks, where local memory is very limited.

## 1.4 The algorithm of BF is global

When dealing with networks of huge scale, it is often important to devise algorithms that are intrinsically *local*. *Local algorithms* have been extensively studied, from various perspectives. (See e.g. [1, 11, 12, 18, 19, 25, 27] and the references therein.) A local algorithm in a dynamic network performs an operation at a vertex $v$ while affecting only $v$ and its immediate neighbors (or more generally vertices in a small ball around $v$). Local algorithms are motivated by environments, both centralized and distributed, in which it is undesirable, and sometimes even impossible, for a change at a particular vertex of the network to affect remote locations unrelated to the change. In the context of I/O efficiency, local algorithms may have better cache performance.

The second drawback of the BF algorithm that we address is the fact that it is not local. A single edge insertion $e = (u, v)$ that increases the outdegree of a vertex beyond $\Delta$ may trigger edge flips that are at distance $\Theta(\log_\Delta n)$ from $u$ and $v$, as shown in Figure 1 of [15] for $\Delta = 2$. In fact, for the example of that figure, *any* algorithm that maintains a $\Delta$-orientation must flip edges that are at distance $\Theta(\log_\Delta n)$ from $u$ and $v$. (There are degenerate examples showing that the BF algorithm sometimes flips edges at distance $\Theta(n)$ from $u$ and $v$.) Consequently, to achieve locality, we must relax the outdegree condition inherent to the edge orientation problem.

**Our contribution.** We propose an alternative *local* scheme that performs a sequence of edge insertions, deletions, and adjacency queries in total time that is asymptotically no worse than that of BF. The scheme is natural and works as follows. Upon a query and/or an update at a vertex $v$ we reset $v$. That is we make $v$'s outgoing edges incoming. (We suggest two versions, one aggressive that always flips $v$'s outgoing edges, and another that flips these edges only if the outdegree of $v$ is larger than $\Delta$.) More specifically, whenever the application of interest has to traverse $v$'s outgoing neighbors it also flips them (thereby intuitively paying for the traversal). Thus, we get locality at the cost of giving away the worst case upper bound on the outdegrees of the vertices. We call this scheme the *flipping game*. We use the flipping game to get local algorithms for adjacency queries and dynamic maximal matching. These two applications can, in fact, be casted as special cases of a generic paradigm, described in detail in Section 3.1 of the full version [15].

The only known local algorithm for maintaining maximal matching has update time of $O(\sqrt{m})$ where $m$ is the number of edges in the graph [20], and this guarantee does not improve for graphs with bounded arboricity. (Even in dynamic forests, the fastest known local algorithm has amortized update time $O(\sqrt{n})$.) Using the flipping game we get a local algorithm with amortized update time of $O(\sqrt{\log n})$ for low arboricity graphs.

The fastest local deterministic data structure for supporting adjacency queries requires a logarithmic query time, again even for dynamic forests. Using the flipping game we get a deterministic local data structure for adjacency queries supporting queries and updates in $O(\log \log n)$ amortized time in low arboricity graphs, providing an exponential improvement over the state-of-the-art.

To prove these bounds, we upper bound the number of flips made by the flipping game in terms of the number of flips made by the BF algorithm for maintaining a $\Delta$-orientation. We remark that the flipping game can be easily and efficiently distributed. This gives rise to a local distributed algorithm for maintaining a maximal matching in a distributed network of low arboricity, with amortized update time and message complexities of $O(\sqrt{\log n})$. (Applying the distributed algorithm of [21] instead of the flipping game yields a global algorithm with amortized message complexity $\Omega(n)$.)

# 2 EFFICIENT REPRESENTATIONS FOR SPARSE NETWORKS

## 2.1 Low outdegree orientations with low local memory usage

Let $\Delta$ denote the outdegree threshold in the BF algorithm. We present here a new algorithm for maintaining a $\Delta$-orientation in dynamic graphs of bounded arboricity $\alpha$. Our algorithm achieves the same (up to a constant factor) parameters as the BF algorithm, yet it guarantees that the outdegree of all vertices is bounded by the required threshold (i.e., $\Delta + 1$) at all times. We first (Section 2.1.1) describe the algorithm in a centralized setting, and then (Section 2.1.2) present a distributed implementation. In Section 2.1.3 of [15] we show that the BF algorithm indeed blows up the outdegree of vertices, even after applying to it several natural adjustments.

*2.1.1 A new centralized algorithm that controls the outdegrees.* Our algorithm handles edge deletions and insertions in the same way as the BF algorithm, until the outdegree of some vertex $u$ exceeds $\Delta$. At this stage our algorithm does not apply a reset cascade, but rather aims at finding all the vertices that would "benefit" from flipping their edges (in terms of reducing the value of a global potential function, details follow), and then applies a cascade of *anti-resets*, where vertices of sufficiently low outdegree flip their incoming edges to be outgoing of them (rather than the other way around. as in the BF algorithm).

Specifically, the algorithm starts by exploring the directed neighborhood $N_u$ outgoing of $u$, stopping at vertices of outdegree at most $\Delta' = \Delta - 2\alpha$. That is, for each vertex of outdegree greater than $\Delta'$ that we reach starting from $u$, hereafter an *internal vertex*, we explore all its out-neighbors. For each vertex of outdegree at most $\Delta'$ that we reach, hereafter a *boundary vertex*, we do not do anything. (Thus internal vertices of $N_u$ have outdegree greater than $\Delta'$ and all their out-neighbors belong to $N_u$, whereas boundary vertices have outdegree at most $\Delta'$ and their out-neighbors may belong to $N_u$ due to other internal vertices, but not due to the boundary vertices themselves.) Denote by $I_u$ and $B_u$ the sets of internal and boundary vertices of $N_u$, respectively. The algorithm constructs the digraph $\overrightarrow{G_u} = (N_u, \overrightarrow{E_u})$, where $\overrightarrow{E_u}$ consists of all the outgoing edges of the internal vertices of $N_u$. This can be carried out in time linear in the size of $\overrightarrow{G_u}$. Having constructed the digraph $\overrightarrow{G_u} = (N_u, \overrightarrow{E_u})$, the algorithm proceeds by computing a new orientation of $\overrightarrow{G_u}$ in which the outdegree of all vertices is bounded by $2\alpha$ as follows. Initially we color (i.e., mark) all edges of $\overrightarrow{G_u}$. Observe that at least one vertex of $\overrightarrow{G_u}$ is adjacent to at most $2\alpha$ colored edges; we maintain a list $L_{2\alpha}$ of all vertices adjacent to at most $2\alpha$ colored edges. We pick an arbitrary vertex in $L_{2\alpha}$, perform an anti-reset on it (flipping all its incoming edges to be outgoing of it), and then uncolor all its at most $2\alpha$ adjacent colored edges and update $L_{2\alpha}$ accordingly. This process is repeated until no edge of $\overrightarrow{G_u}$ is colored, at which stage we have a valid $2\alpha$-orientation for $\overrightarrow{G_u}$. Note that until a vertex performs an anti-reset, its outdegree may only decrease. Whenever a vertex performs an anti-reset, its outdegree may increase, but to at most $2\alpha$, which means that a vertex never increases its outdegree beyond the maximum between $2\alpha$ and its initial out-degree.

Since each boundary vertex had at most $\Delta'$ out-neighbors in the entire graph, its new outdegree will be at most $\Delta' + 2\alpha = \Delta$, and this also bounds its outdegree at any time during the process. Moreover, since all outgoing edges of each internal vertex of $N_u$ are taken to $\overrightarrow{G_u}$, the outdegree of each internal vertex never exceeds $\Delta + 1$. This process of computing a valid $2\alpha$-orientation while never blowing up the outdegree, hereafter the *anti-reset cascade procedure*, is inspired by the static algorithm of [2], with the inherent difference that it works on a carefully chosen (possibly small) subgraph $\overrightarrow{G_u}$, whereas the reset cascade procedure underlying the BF algorithm does not work on a precomputed subgraph, but rather on a subgraph that grows "on the fly" with the resets. While it is easy to see that our procedure runs in linear time on any chosen subgraph (as with the BF algorithm), the challenge is to show that the total cost of these procedures over all chosen subgraphs throuhgout the execution of our algorithm is aymptotically the same as that of the BF algorithm.

Lemma 2.1. *The total runtime of our algorithm is linear in the total number of edge flips made, assuming $\Delta \geq 5\alpha$.*

Proof. Edge insertions and deletions are handled in constant time, until the outdegree of some vertex $u$ exceeds $\Delta$. At this stage a digraph $\overrightarrow{G_u}$ as described above is constructed, along with the aforementioned list $L_{2\alpha}$, within time linear in the size of $\overrightarrow{G_u}$. Then edges of $\overrightarrow{G_u}$ are flipped by the anti-reset cascade procedure, so that each edge is flipped at most once. By maintaining the list $L_{2\alpha}$ throughout the anti-reset cascade procedure, we can easily implement this procedure in time linear in the size of $\overrightarrow{G_u}$. Note also that the size of $\overrightarrow{G_u}$ is given by the sum of outdegrees over the internal vertices of $N_u$. To complete the proof, we argue that a constant fraction of the outgoing edges of each internal vertex of $N_u$ are flipped during the anti-reset cascade procedure. To see this, note that the outdegree of each internal vertex of $N_u$ reduces during this procedure from more than $\Delta' = \Delta - 2\alpha$ to at most $2\alpha$. Recalling that the outdegrees of vertices are bounded by $\Delta + 1$ at all times, at least $\Delta + 1 - 4\alpha$ out of at most $\Delta + 1$ outgoing edges (which is at least a $\frac{1}{5}$-fraction assuming $\Delta \geq 5\alpha$) of each internal vertex must have been flipped during the procedure. □

Although our algorithm and the BF algorithm are inherently different, we use a potential function argument similar to the one in [9] to bound the number of flips made by our algorithm, which by Lemma 2.1 also bounds its total runtime (up to a constant factor). The key insight is that we can apply a potential function argument *globally*, i.e., for all the anti-resets together, rather than to each one of them separately as was done for resets by [9].

Suppose one can maintain a $\delta$-orientation for some sequence of $t$ edge updates while doing $f$ edge flips, starting with the empty graph. As in [9], we define an edge to be *good* if its orientation in our algorithm is the same as in the $\delta$-orientation and *bad* otherwise. We define the potential $\Psi$ to be the number of bad edges in the current graph. Initially $\Psi = 0$. Each insertion or a flip performed by the $\delta$-orientation increases $\Psi$ by at most one, while edge deletions may only decrease $\Psi$. All edge flips made by our algorithm are due to the anti-reset cascade procedures. Consider some digraph $\overrightarrow{G_u}$ on which an anti-reset cascade procedure is applied throughout the execution of our algorithm, and note that all the edges of $\overrightarrow{G_u}$ are outgoing of internal vertices of $N_u$ before the procedure starts. Let $v$ be an arbitrary internal vertex of $N_u$, and note that its outdegree before the procedure starts is greater than $\Delta'$. Moreover, by the definition of a $\delta$-orientation, at most $\delta$ of $v$'s outgoing edges at that moment are good. As a result of the procedure, these $\delta$ edges may become bad. However, since $v$'s outdegree reduces to at most $2\alpha$ at the end, at least $\Delta' + 1 - 2\alpha - \delta$ edges were bad and become good. It follows that $\Psi$ is decreased by at least $\Delta' + 1 - 2\alpha - 2\delta$ per each internal vertex. Consequently, the total number of vertices that serve as internal vertices of some digraph $\overrightarrow{G_u}$ throughout the execution of our algorithm is at most $(t + f)/(\Delta' + 1 - 2\alpha - 2\delta)$. Since the outdegree of all vertices is bounded by $\Delta + 1$ at all times, the total number of edge flips made by our algorithm is bounded by $(t+f)(\Delta+1)/(\Delta'+1-2\alpha-2\delta)$. Assuming $\Delta \geq 6\alpha + 3\delta$, it follows that $(t + f)(\Delta + 1)/(\Delta' + 1 - 2\alpha - 2\delta) \leq 3(t + f)$.

*2.1.2 A distributed implementation with low local memory usage.* Consider a vertex $u$ whose outdegree exceeds $\Delta$. The centralized algorithm starts by exploring the directed neighborhood $N_u$ and coloring all edges of the digraph $\overrightarrow{G_u} = (N_u, \overrightarrow{E_u})$ as described above. We can distribute this step using broadcast and convergecast in a straightforward way. However, we also need to make sure that the local memory usage at processors is bounded by $O(\Delta)$. To this end, every internal processor (with outdegree larger than $\Delta'$) will be responsible for coloring its outgoing edges. Throughout this broadcast we also compute the directed BFS tree $T_u$ on $N_u$, so that each processor will hold information about its parent in $T_u$, using which we can easily carry out the subsequent convergecast. The number of rounds will be linear in the depth $h$ of $T_u$, whereas the number of messages will be linear in the size of $\overrightarrow{G_u}$.

The centralized algorithm proceeds by running the anti-reset cascade procedure. This procedure is inspired by the static algorithm of [2], for which an efficient distributed implementation was given in [7]. We cannot use the distributed algorithm of [7], however, since it lets processors communicate with all their neighbors, hence the local memory usage will depend on the maximum degree in the network, which can be much larger than $O(\Delta)$. (Recall that here $\Delta$ stands for the out-degree threshold, which is linear in the arboricity $\alpha$, and may be $n/\alpha$ times smaller than the maximum degree.)

The distributed algorithm that we propose is a variant of [7], and works as follows. First, we change the threshold $\Delta'$ of the centralized algorithm from $\Delta - 2\alpha$ to $\Delta - 5\alpha$. To compensate for the decrease in the value of $\Delta'$, we increase $\Delta$ by a constant factor. (By letting $\Delta$ increase by a constant factor, the above potential function argument will carry over smoothly.) In each round $i = 1, 2, \ldots, \log|N_u|$, all the colored processors send messages on each of their colored outgoing edges. Every colored processor that receives at least one message checks if the number of its colored outgoing edges plus the number of messages it received is bounded by $5\alpha$. If so, it flips all the edges along which it received messages to be outgoing of it, and then uncolors itself and all its outgoing edges.

This distributed anti-reset cascade procedure implicitly assumes that all processors of $\overrightarrow{G_u}$ wake up simultaneously, and the entire subgraph $\overrightarrow{G_u}$ (both edges and processors) is colored at this moment. To justify this assumption, before initiating this procedure, we perform a broadcast along $T_u$, in which each processor at directed distance $i$ from the root receives message $h-i$. A processor receiving message $h - i$ will wake up in exactly $h - i$ rounds from the time it received the message to color itself and its outgoing edges, and then participate in the distributed anti-reset cascade procedure.

We next analyze this procedure. In each round $i = 1, 2, \ldots, \log|N_u|$, at least 3/5 of the colored processors are adjacent to at most $5\alpha$ colored edges, since the subgraph induced by the colored edges has arboricity at most $\alpha$. This means that the number of colored vertices reduces by a factor of $5/2 > 2$ in each round, hence after the last round all edges have been uncolored, and we obtain a $5\alpha$-orientation for $\overrightarrow{G_u}$. Moreover, we argue that the number of edges being uncolored in each round is no smaller than the number of edges that remain colored. To see this, fix an arbitrary round $i$, consider the graph $G_i$ induced by the colored edges at the beginning of the round, and denote by $V_i'$ and $V_i''$ the set of vertices that get uncolored and remain colored at the end of round $i$, respectively. Since no vertex in $V_i''$ get uncolored in round $i$, the degree of each vertex of $V_i''$ is at least $5\alpha$ in $G_i$. However, the subgraph $G_i''$ of $G_i$ induced by the vertex set $V_i''$ has arboricity at most $\alpha$, hence at least half of the vertices of $V_i''$ have at most $4\alpha$ neighbors in $V_i''$, which means their remaining $\geq \alpha$ neighbors are in $V_i'$. The assertion now follows since the number of edges in $G_i''$, or the number of edges that remain colored, is at most $\alpha \cdot |V_i''|$, whereas the number of edges that got uncolored is at least $\alpha \cdot |V_i''|$. Consequently, the number of messages sent in each round decays geometrically, hence the total number of messages sent is linear in the size of $\overrightarrow{G_u}$. Note also that this procedure terminates within $\log|N_u|$ rounds, which does not exceed the number of messages sent.

THEOREM 2.2. *For any $\alpha \geq 1$ and $\Delta = \Omega(\alpha)$ and any arboricity $\alpha$ preserving sequence of edge and vertex updates starting from empty graph, there is a distributed algorithm for maintaining a $\Delta$-orientation (in the $\mathcal{CONGEST}$ model) with an optimal (up to a constant) amortized message complexity, and the same (or better) amortized update time. The local memory usage at all vertices is $O(\Delta)$ at all times, which is also optimal. For $\Delta = O(\alpha)$, we obtain $O(\alpha)$-orientation with $O(\log n)$ amortized update time and message complexities, with $O(\alpha)$ local memory usage.*

## 2.2 Efficient representations of sparse distributed networks, with applications

In this section we describe a natural representation of sparse distributed networks, along with some applications.

*2.2.1 Forest decomposition and adjacency queries.* For a distributed network with arboricity $\alpha$, Theorem 2.2 provides a distributed algorithm (in the $\mathcal{CONGEST}$ model) for maintaining a low outdegree orientation with low local memory usage. Such an orientation can be viewed as a representation of the network, and it finds two natural applications. First, due to the equivalence between the edge orientation and the forest decomposition problems shown in [21], we obtain a distributed algorithm for maintaining a decomposition into $O(\Delta)$ forests within an optimal (up to a constant) amortized message complexity, and the same (or better) amortized update time, with $O(\Delta)$ local space, for any $\alpha \geq 1$ and $\Delta = \Omega(\alpha)$.

We can then use this forest decomposition to maintain efficient distributed *adjacency labeling schemes.* An adjacency labeling scheme assigns an (ideally short) label to each vertex, allowing one to infer if any two vertices $u$ and $v$ are neighbors directly from their labels. For an adjacency representation scheme to be useful, it should be capable of reflecting online the current up-to-date picture in a dynamic setting. Moreover, the algorithm for generating and revising the labels must be distributed. Given an $f$-forest-decomposition for $G$, the label of each vertex $v$ can be given by $\texttt{Label}(v) = (\texttt{ID}(v), \texttt{ID}(w_1), \ldots, \texttt{ID}(w_f))$ where $w_i$ is the parent of $v$ in the $i$th forest. We derive the following result.

Theorem 2.3. *For any $\alpha \geq 1$ and any arboricity $\alpha$ preserving sequence of updates, there is a distributed algorithm (in the $\mathcal{CONGEST}$ model) for maintaining an adjacency labeling scheme with label size of $O(\alpha \cdot \log n)$ bits with $O(\log n)$ amortized message complexity and update time, with $O(\alpha)$ local memory usage.*

*2.2.2 A complete representation.* A low outdegree orientation may not quality as a complete representation of the network, since a processor cannot access its incoming neighbors, and in particular it cannot communicate with them. Next, we describe a complete representation of a distributed network.

Consider a processor $v$ with $k$ incoming neighbors $v_1, \ldots, v_k$. For each $i$, we will make sure that $v_i$ holds information on $v_{i-1}$ and $v_{i+1}$, with $v_0 = v_{k+1} = \text{NULL}$, and $v$ will hold information on an arbitrary processor among these, say $v_k$. (This information that we hold per neighbor $v_i$ of $v$ should be enough for $v$ to communicate with $v_i$ directly.) Since the network may change dynamically, we need to update the "extra" local information that we hold at processors efficiently. We refer to the processors $v_1, \ldots, v_k$ as *siblings,* and $v$ is referred to as their *parent.* For each $i$, $1 \leq i \leq k$, $v_{i-1}$ and $v_{i+1}$ are referred to as the *left sibling* and *right sibling* of $v_i$, respectively. (The left and right siblings of $v_1$ and $v_k$, respectively, are defined as NULL.) Note that each processor holds information on two of its siblings, per any parent. Since the number of parents of any processor $v$ is given by its outdegree, the information regarding all siblings of $v$ over all of its parents is linear in its outdegree. In addition, any processor $v$ holds information on a single incoming neighbor $v_k$, as described above. Together with all its outgoing neighbors, the total information at a processor is linear in its outdegree. Since the outdegree of the underlying edge orientation is (close to) linear in the arboricity of the network, we can make sure that the local information at processors is (close to) linear in the arboricity, yielding the required bound on the local memory usage.

Following an insertion of edge $(u, v)$ that is oriented from $u$ to $v$, $u$ will hold information on $v$ (by the underlying edge orientation). We also make sure that $v$ will hold information on $u$ by designating $u$ as $v_{k+1}$, i.e., $u = v_{k+1}$ takes the role of $v_k$. Subsequently, $v$ sends a message with information on $v_{k+1}$ to $v_k$ and another message with information on $v_k$ to $v_{k+1}$, so that $v_k$ (respectively, $v_{k+1}$) will hold information on $v_{k+1}$ (resp., $v_k$) as its new right (resp., left) sibling. Following a deletion of edge $(u, v)$ that is oriented from $u$ to $v$, with $v$ being the parent of $u = v_i$ for some index $i$, $v_i$ sends a message with information on both $v_{i-1}$ and $v_{i+1}$ to $v$. Subsequently, $v$ sends two messages (in parallel), one to $v_{i-1}$ and another to $v_{i+1}$, informing $v_{i-1}$ (respectively, $v_{i+1}$) that its right (resp., left) sibling has changed from $v_i$ to $v_{i+1}$ (resp., $v_{i-1}$). Note that we send a message along the deleted edge $(v, v_i)$ in order to update the representation following an edge deletion, i.e., we support a *graceful* edge deletion but not an *abrupt* one. (In the former, the deleted edge may be used for exchanging messages between its endpoints, and retires only once the representation has been updated. In the latter, while the endpoints of the deleted edge discover that the edge has retired, it cannot be used for any communication.) A similar update is triggered by edge flips and vertex updates, where we only support a graceful deletion of vertices.

**Some applications.** The drawback of such a representation is that a processor cannot communicate with its in-neighbors *in parallel.* For $v$ to be able to send a message to an in-neighbor $v_i$, it first needs to retrieve the information on $v_i$ required for communicating with it. To this end, $v$ has to *sequentially* scan and communicate with all its in-neighbors $v_k, v_{k-1}, \ldots, v_{i+1}$, starting at $v_k$ (on which $v$ holds information) and finishing at $v_i$. For some applications, however, such a sequential scan of the in-neighbors is not needed.

For the sake of conciseness, in what follows we focus on edge updates and flips. Vertex updates can be handled in a similar way.

As a first application, consider the problem of maintaining a maximal matching in a distributed network that changes dynamically. Instead of maintaining the information on the in-neighbors as described above, we will maintain information only on the *free* in-neighbors. More specifically, information on the free in-neighbors is being distributed among them in the manner described above. Whenever a processor changes status from free to matched, or vice versa, it notifies all its out-neighbors about that. (Recall that each processor has complete information on all its out-neighbors, and can communicate with all of them in parallel. Interestingly, there is no need to exploit parallelism here.) Any processor that receives such information makes sure to update the relevant local information regarding its free in-neighbors, which is distributed into the relevant neighbors, following along similar lines to the above. The rest of the algorithm now proceeds as in the centralized setting [20]. Specifically, following an edge insertion, we match the two endpoints if they are free, and otherwise there is nothing special to do (besides updating the underlying representation). Following a deletion of an unmatched edge, there is again nothing special to do. Finally, following a deletion of a matched edge $(u, v)$, $u$ and $v$ exchange messages with their out-neighbors, attempting to find a free neighbor among them. Let us focus on $u$ ($v$ is handled in the same way). If none of $u$'s out-neighbors is free, $u$ needs to check whether it has a free in-neighbor. Since we made sure to (distributively) maintain information on the free in-neighbors of each vertex, including $u$, and as there is no need to perform a sequential scan over these neighbors of $u$ (the first one, if any, will do), we conclude that the amortized message complexity of the algorithm, and thus the amortized update time, is dominated (up to constant factors) by the maximum among the outdegree bound of the underlying orientation and the cost of maintaining that orientation.

Theorem 2.4. *For any $\alpha \geq 1$ and any arboricity $\alpha$ preserving sequence of edge and vertex updates starting from an empty graph, there is a distributed algorithm (in the $\mathcal{CONGEST}$ model) for maintaining a maximal matching with an amortized update time and message complexities of $O(\alpha + \log n)$. The local memory usage is $O(\alpha)$.*

As a broader application, we revisit the *bounded degree sparsifiers* introduced recently in [26]. Informally, a bounded degree $(1+\epsilon)$-sparsifier for a graph $G = (V, E)$, a degree parameter $\Delta$ and a slack parameter $\epsilon > 0$ is a *subgraph* $H$ of $G$ with maximum degree bounded by $\Delta$ that preserves certain quantitative properties of the original graph up to a (multiplicative) factor of $1+\epsilon$. For the maximum matching problem, such a sparsifier $H$ should preserve the size of the maximum matching of $G$ up to a factor of $1+\epsilon$. It was shown in [26] that one can *locally* compute a $(1+\epsilon)$-maximum matching sparsifier of degree $O(\alpha/\epsilon)$, for any network of arboricity bounded by $\alpha$. All the sparsifiers of [26] adhere to a rather strict notion of locality, which makes them applicable to several settings. In particular, for distributed networks, all the sparsifiers of [26] can be computed in a single round of communication. The definition of a sparsifier for the minimum vertex problem is more involved, and we omit it here for conciseness (refer to [26] for the formal definition), but the bottom-line is the same: For any distributed network of arboricity bounded by $\alpha$, one can compute a $(1+\epsilon)$-minimum vertex cover sparsifier of degree $O(\alpha/\epsilon)$ in a single round.

Similarly to the maintenance of a maximal matching, maintaining these bounded degree sparsifiers dynamically do not require a sequential scan of the in-neighbors of a processor. Indeed, these sparsifiers have s degree bound of $\Delta = O(\alpha/\epsilon)$ by definition, hence each processor can hold complete information on all its adjacent edges that belong to the sparsifier, or equivalently, on all its corresponding neighbors. Following a deletion of an edge from the graph, we first update the underlying representation. If the edge does not belong to the sparsifier, there is nothing special to do. Otherwise, we remove it from the sparsifier and check if another edge needs to be added to the sparsifier instead. In any case we update the endpoints of the affected edges accordingly. It is straightforward to implement this update efficiently using the underlying representation. Following an edge insertion, we may need to add it to the sparsifier, but this too involves a straightforward update. In this way we can maintain bounded degree $(1+\epsilon)$-sparsifiers for maximum matching and minimum vertex cover using a local memory at processors that is (close to) linear in the network arboricity.

Subsequently, we can naively run static distributed algorithms for approximate maximum matching and minimum vertex cover on top of the bounded degree sparsifiers, following every update step. Due to the degree bound of the sparsifiers, in this way we adhere to the local memory constraints at processors. To be able to run the distributed algorithm (following every update step), alas, we need to assume that all processors wake up prior to each such run, which does not apply to the local wakeup model. Instead of running a static distributed algorithm from scratch on the sparsifiers following every update step, we shall apply more efficient dynamic algorithms on top of the sparsifiers.

[23] devised distributed algorithms for maintaining, in networks of degree bounded by $\Delta$, $(1+\epsilon)$-approximate and $(3/2)$-approximate maximum matching with update time $O(1/\epsilon)$ and message complexities $(\Delta)^{O(1/\epsilon)}$ and $O(\Delta)$, respectively. (In fact, the bounds on the update time and message complexities hold in the worst-case. Moreover, these algorithms extend to bounded arboricity graphs; refer to Corollary 3.1 in [23].) Running these dynamic algorithms on top of the bounded degree $(1+\epsilon)$-maximum matching sparsifier that we maintain dynamically, we obtain the following result.

THEOREM 2.5. *For any $\alpha \geq 1$, any arboricity $\alpha$ preserving sequence of edge and vertex updates starting from an empty graph and any $\epsilon > 0$, there are distributed algorithms for maintaining $(1+\epsilon)$-approximate and $(3/2+\epsilon)$-approximate maximum matching with amortized update time $O(1/\epsilon + \log n)$ and amortized message complexities of $(\alpha/\epsilon)^{O(1/\epsilon)} + O(\log n)$ and $O(\alpha/\epsilon + \log n)$, respectively. The local memory usage is $O(\alpha/\epsilon)$.*

There is a straightforward distributed algorithm for maintaining a maximal matching, in networks of degree bounded by $\Delta$, with update time $O(1)$ and message complexity $O(\Delta)$. Such an algorithm can be used to maintain a 2-approximate minimum vertex cover within the same bounds. Running this dynamic algorithm on top of the bounded degree $(1+\epsilon)$-minimum vertex cover sparsifier that we maintain dynamically, we obtain the following result.

THEOREM 2.6. *For any $\alpha \geq 1$, any arboricity $\alpha$ preserving sequence of edge and vertex updates starting from an empty graph and any $\epsilon > 0$, there is a distributed algorithm for maintaining a $(2+\epsilon)$-approximate minimum vertex cover with an amortized update time of $O(\log n)$ and an amortized message complexity of $O(\alpha/\epsilon + \log n)$. The local memory usage is $O(\alpha/\epsilon)$.*

## 3 THE FLIPPING GAME

This section is devoted to the flipping game and its applications. In Section 3.1 we show a reduction from the edge orientation problem to the flipping game, and in Section 3.2 we show a reduction in the other direction, thus obtaining an equivalence. Some applications of the flipping game are given in Section 3.3. As mentioned, a generic paradigm for this game appears in Section 3.1 of [15].

### 3.1 A reduction from the edge orientation problem to the flipping game

We can easily simulate the BF algorithm using the reset operations of the flipping game. The next lemma shows that for an appropriate outdegree threshold the amortized time per edge update of the simulation is essentially the same as the amortized time per operation (update or reset) of the flipping game. Thus the amortized bound of the flipping game is essentially as large as that of the BF algorithm.

LEMMA 3.1. *Consider an arbitrary sequence of $t$ edge updates, and suppose that the flipping game (either the basic game or the $\Delta$-flipping game) on this update sequence with any $r$ resets performs at most $k(t+r)$ edge flips, for any parameter $r$. Then for any $\Delta \geq k$, the BF algorithm with outdegree threshold $\Delta$, performs at most $(kt)/(1-k/(\Delta+1))$ edge flips.*

PROOF. We simulate the BF algorithm using the flipping game by resetting every vertex whose outgoing edges are flipped by the reset cascade of the BF algorithm. Let $r$ be the total number of resets that the simulation performs and let $f$ be the total number of edge flips. Since each reset of the simulation flips at least $\Delta+1$ edges, $r \leq f/(\Delta+1)$. By our assumption on the flipping game we have $f \leq k(t+r)$. The lemma follows by substituting the upper bound on $r$ into this inequality and rearranging. □

For example, if we set $\Delta = 2k - 1$, the amortized update time of the simulation (per edge update), and hence of the BF algorithm, is at most $2k$. This shows that we only lose a factor of 2 when amortizing over the edge updates rather than over both the edge updates and the reset operations.

## 3.2 A reduction from the flipping game to the edge orientation problem

LEMMA 3.2. *Suppose we can maintain a $\Delta$-orientation for some sequence of $t$ edge updates while doing $f$ edge flips, starting with the empty graph. Then the flipping game on this update sequence with any $r$ resets performs at most $t + f + 2\Delta r$ edge flips, for any $r$.*

PROOF. We charge the edge flips performed by reset operations of the flipping game to edge flips performed to maintain the $\Delta$-orientation. Following a reset on $v$, we place two tokens on every edge that is outgoing of $v$ in the $\Delta$-orientation. When the $\Delta$-orientation flips an edge $e$ we place a token on $e$. When an edge $e$ is inserted to the graph we place a token on $e$. The total number of tokens placed on edges is $t + f + 2\Delta r$. We claim that the number of tokens placed on $e$ is at most the number of times $e = (u, v)$ flips in the flipping game (so these tokens "pay" for these flips). Consider a maximal sequence $\sigma$ of flips of $e$ that occur while the orientation of $e$ in the $\Delta$-orientation does not change. Assume without loss of generality that $e$ is oriented from $u$ to $v$ by the $\Delta$-orientation during $\sigma$. Let $x$ be the number of flips in $\sigma$. During the time span of $\sigma$ both $u$ and $v$ were reset at least $\lfloor x/2 \rfloor$ times. Each such reset of $u$ places 2 tokens on $e$. The total number of these tokens is at least $x - 1$. The flip of $e$ performed by the $\Delta$-orientation or its insertion just before $\sigma$ starts contributes an additional token. □

The number of edge flips per edge update performed for maintaining the $\Delta$-orientation is $f/t$ whereas the number of edge flips per operation of the flipping game is $(t + 2f + 2\Delta r)/(t + r) = O(\max\{\Delta, f/t\})$. Thus the flipping game does not depend on $\Delta$ but its amortized time bound does depend on $\Delta$. To remove the dependency of the amortized time of the flipping game on the outdegree threshold $\Delta$, we modify the game slightly and make it aware of $\Delta$ as follows. We define the *$\Delta$-flipping game* in which when we reset a vertex we flip all its outgoing edges only if there are more than $\Delta$ such edges. By setting $\Delta' = 3\Delta - 1$, we get that the total number of flips of the $\Delta'$-flipping game is at most $3(t + f)$. This bound is the same, up to a constant, as for maintaining the $\Delta$-orientation, even though we also performed $r$ reset operations.

LEMMA 3.3. *Suppose we can maintain a $\Delta$-orientation for some sequence of $t$ edge updates while doing $f$ edge flips, starting with the empty graph. Then the $\Delta'$-flipping game on this update sequence with any $r$ resets performs at most $(t + f)(\Delta' + 1)/(\Delta' + 1 - 2\Delta)$ edge flips, for any parameters $r$ and $\Delta' \geq 2\Delta$.*

PROOF. Our proof uses a potential function argument similar to the one used in Lemma 1 of [9]. We define an edge to be *good* if its orientation in the flipping game is the same as in the $\Delta$-orientation and *bad* otherwise. We define the potential $\Psi$ to be the number of bad edges in the current graph. Initially $\Psi = 0$. Each insertion or a flip performed by the $\Delta$-orientation increases $\Psi$ by at most one, while edge deletions may only decrease $\Psi$.

Consider a reset of some vertex $v$ of outdegree greater than $\Delta'$. By the definition of a $\Delta$-orientation at most $\Delta$ of $v$'s outgoing edges are good. As a result of the flip these $\Delta$ edges may become bad, but at least $\Delta' + 1 - \Delta$ edges were bad and become good. It follows that as a result of the reset $\Psi$ decreases by at least $\Delta' + 1 - 2\Delta$. This implies that the total number of reset operations on vertices with outdegree greater than $\Delta'$ is at most $(t + f)/(\Delta' + 1 - 2\Delta)$. The total number of times a good edge becomes bad due to the resets is bounded by $\Delta(t + f)/(\Delta' + 1 - 2\Delta)$, from which we conclude that the total number of times a bad edge becomes good due to the resets is bounded by $t + f + \Delta(t + f)/(\Delta' + 1 - 2\Delta)$. Summarizing, the total number of flips made by the flipping game is bounded by $(t + f)(1 + 2\Delta/(\Delta' + 1 - 2\Delta)) = (t + f)(\Delta' + 1)/(\Delta' + 1 - 2\Delta)$. □

## 3.3 Applications

As discussed in the introduction, by using the flipping game instead of the BF algorithm, we obtain *local* algorithms for several dynamic graph problems. In this section we describe two such applications.

**Dynamic maximal matching.** The goal here is to maintain a maximal matching $M$ in a graph $G$ that undergoes edge insertions and deletions. Edge insertions and deletions of edges not in $M$ can be handled trivially in constant time. The problematic operation is deletions of edges in $M$. Following an edge deletion $(u, v) \in M$ both $u$ and $v$ become free, and if either $u$ or $v$ has a free neighbor then $M \setminus \{(u, v)\}$ is not maximal anymore, and we must add edges from $u$ and $v$ to one of their free neighbors to restore maximality.

Neiman and Solomon [20] reduced this problem to the edge orientation problem as follows. We maintain an edge orientation of $G$, and each vertex $v$ maintains its free incoming neighbors. Following an edge deletion $(u, v) \in M$, $u$ and $v$ perform the following operations. (We restrict attention to $u$ and describe what it does; $v$ performs the same operations.) First $u$ notifies its out-neighbors that it is free. Then it checks whether its list of free in-neighbors is not empty. If $u$ has a free in-neighbor $x$ then we add the edge $(u, x)$ to $M$ and both $x$ and $u$ notify their out-neighbors that they are now matched. Otherwise $u$ scans its out-neighbors for a free vertex. If $u$ finds a free out-neighbor $x$ then we add $(x, u)$ to $M$ and both $x$ and $u$ notify their out-neighbors that they are matched.

This reduction implies that from an algorithm that maintains a $\Delta$-orientation with an update time of $T$ (either amortized or worst-case), we can get a dynamic algorithm for maximal matching with an update time of $O(\Delta + T)$ (again, either amortized or worst-case).

The result of [14] shows that in a graph with arboricity bounded by $\alpha$ the BF algorithm maintains an $O(\beta\alpha)$-orientation in amortized update time of $T = O(\log(n/(\beta\alpha))/\beta)$ for any parameter $\beta \geq 1$. (Refer to App. A in the full version [15] for more details.) Using this tradeoff in the particular case of $\Delta \approx T$ (where $\Delta = \Theta(\beta\alpha)$), we get a dynamic algorithm for maximal matching with $O(\alpha + \sqrt{\alpha \log n})$ amortized update time. The drawback of the resulting algorithm is that it is not local. Indeed, this is because any algorithm for maintaining $\Delta$-orientation is inherently non-local.

To get a local algorithm for dynamic maximal matching we use our (inherently local) flipping game. As before, we maintain an orientation and each vertex maintains its free in-neighbors. But now, when a vertex $v$ scans its out-neighbors (either when $v$ changes its state from matched to unmatched or vice versa, or when $v$ looks for a free out-neighbor), then we also *reset* $v$, thereby flipping all its outgoing edges. The total running time of the resulting local algorithm for dynamic maximum matching is linear in the number of edge flips made by the underlying flipping game.

To bound the number of edge flips made by the flipping game, note that we reset at most a constant number of vertices per edge update. By Lemma 3.2, combined with the result of [14] for the case $\Delta \approx T$, we conclude that the amortized number of flips made by the flipping game is $O(\alpha + \sqrt{\alpha \log n})$.

The flipping game can be easily distributed. Resetting a vertex requires one communication round, and the message complexity is asymptotically the same as the runtime in the centralized setting.

Theorem 3.4. *For any arboricity $\alpha$ preserving sequence, there is a* local *algorithm for maintaining a maximal matching on the corresponding dynamic $n$-vertex graph $G$ with an amortized update time of $O(\alpha + \sqrt{\alpha \log n})$. The space usage of the algorithm is linear in the graph size. Moreover, there is a distributed algorithm for maintaining a maximal matching with an amortized message complexity of $O(\alpha + \sqrt{\alpha \log n})$ and a constant worst-case update time.*

**Adjacency queries.** In this application we want to maintain a deterministic linear space data structure that allows efficient adjacency queries in a dynamic graph. (If we use dynamic perfect hash tables to represent adjacency lists then the data structure is of linear size but randomized.) Although the problem of supporting adjacency queries is inherently local, the state-of-the-art deterministic solution (described next) relies on the inherently non-local task of maintaining a low outdegree orientation.

The BF algorithm with outdegree threshold $O(\alpha)$ has an amortized update time of $O(\log n)$. Such an orientation allows to support adjacency queries in $O(\alpha)$ worst-case time, since to decide if the graph contains the edge $(u, v)$, it suffices to search $u$ among the out-neighbors of $v$, and $v$ among the out-neighbors of $u$. Later Kowalik [17] proved that for outdegree threshold $O(\alpha \log n)$, the amortized update time of the BF algorithm is constant. Kowalik noted that if the out-neighbors of each vertex are stored in a balanced search tree, then the amortized update time increases from $O(1)$ to $O(\log \alpha + \log \log n)$ (each edge flip requires an insertion to and a deletion from a balanced search tree, and similarly for edge insertions) but the worst-case query time becomes $O(\log \alpha + \log \log n)$. When the arboricity bound is polylogarithmic in $n$, these bounds are $O(\log \log n)$, and using more sophisticated data structures, one can improve this bound to $O(\log \log \log n)$ under the RAM model.

Next, we describe a local data structure for supporting adjacency queries. To this end we use the $\Delta$-flipping game, for $\Delta = O(\alpha \log n)$. Specifically, to perform an adjacency query with $(u, v)$, we start by resetting $u$ and $v$, thereby flipping the out-neighbors of $u$ (resp. $v$) if it has more than $\Delta$ out-neighbors. Following these resets, $u$ and $v$ have at most $\Delta$ out-neighbors and we answer the query by scanning these lists of out-neighbors as before. In order to speed up the query further we keep the out-neighbors of each vertex $v$ with at most $\Delta$ out-neighbors in a balanced search tree as described above. To cope with edge deletions, which is the only way outdegrees may *gradually* decrease (as opposed to instantly drop to zero following a reset), we start building the tree at $v$ when $v$'s outdegree drops below $2\Delta$ and once we have the tree ready we maintain it as long as the outdegree of $v$ is below $2\Delta$; this guarantees that we always have a tree ready when the outdegree is at most $\Delta$, while keeping the cost of constructing the trees in check.

By Lemma 3.3 combined with the result of [17], the amortized number of edge flips made by the $\Delta$-flipping game is constant. Hence both adjacency queries and edge updates take $O(\log \alpha + \log \log n)$ amortized time. So our $\Delta$-flipping game provides a local data structure for adjacency queries at the cost of having an amortized guarantee for the query time rather than a worst-case guarantee.

Theorem 3.5. *For any arboricity $\alpha$ preserving sequence, there is a (deterministic)* local *algorithm for supporting adjacency queries in the corresponding dynamic $n$-vertex graph $G$ with an amortized update and query times of $O(\log \alpha + \log \log n)$. The space usage of the algorithm is linear in the graph size.*

## REFERENCES


[1] Noga Alon, Ronitt Rubinfeld, Shai Vardi, and Ning Xie. 2012. Space-efficient local computation algorithms. In *Proc. 23rd SODA.* 1132–1139.

[2] Srinivasa Rao Arikati, Anil Maheshwari, and Christos D. Zaroliagis. 1997. Efficient Computation of Implicit Representations of Sparse Graphs. *Discrete Applied Mathematics* 78, 1-3 (1997), 1–16.

[3] S. Assadi, K. Onak, B. Schieber, and S. Solomon. 2018 (to appear). Fully Dynamic Maximal Independent Set with Sublinear Update Time. In *Proc. of 50th STOC.*

[4] Baruch Awerbuch. 1985. Communication-Time Trade-Offs in Network Synchronization. In *Proc. of 4th PODC.* 272–276.

[5] B. Awerbuch, A. Baratz, and D. Peleg. 1990. Cost-sensitive analysis of communication protocols. In *Proc. of 9th PODC.* 177–187.

[6] B. Awerbuch, A. Baratz, and D. Peleg. Oct., 1992. Efficient Broadcast and Light-Weight Spanners. *Technical Report CS92-22, Weizmann Institute* (Oct., 1992).

[7] Leonid Barenboim and Michael Elkin. 2010. Sublogarithmic distributed MIS algorithm for sparse graphs using Nash-Williams decomposition. *Distributed Computing* 22, 5-6 (2010), 363–379.

[8] Leonid Barenboim and Michael Elkin. 2013. *Distributed Graph Coloring: Fundamentals and Recent Developments.* Morgan & Claypool Publishers.

[9] G. S. Brodal and R. Fagerberg. 1999. Dynamic Representation of Sparse Graphs. In *Proc. of 6th WADS.* 342–351.

[10] Keren Censor-Hillel, Elad Haramaty, and Zohar S. Karnin. 2016. Optimal Dynamic Distributed MIS. In *Proc. of PODC.* 217–226.

[11] Guy Even, Moti Medina, and Dana Ron. 2014. Best of Two Local Models: Local Centralized and Local Distributed Algorithms. *CoRR* abs/1402.3796 (2014).

[12] Guy Even, Moti Medina, and Dana Ron. 2015. Distributed Maximum Matching in Bounded Degree Graphs. In *Proc. 16th ICDCN.* 18.

[13] Mohsen Ghaffari and Hsin-Hao Su. 2017. Distributed Degree Splitting, Edge Coloring, and Orientations. In *Proc. of 28th SODA.* 2505–2523.

[14] Meng He, Ganggui Tang, and Norbert Zeh. 2014. Orienting Dynamic Graphs, with Applications to Maximal Matchings and Adjacency Queries. In *Proc. 25th ISAAC.* 128–140.

[15] Haim Kaplan and Shay Solomon. 2018. Representations of Sparse Distributed Networks: A Locality-Sensitive Approach. *CoRR* abs/1802.09515 (2018).

[16] Tsvi Kopelowitz, Robert Krauthgamer, Ely Porat, and Shay Solomon. 2014. Orienting Fully Dynamic Graphs with Worst-Case Time Bounds. In *Proc. of 41st ICALP.* 532–543.

[17] Lukasz Kowalik. 2007. Adjacency queries in dynamic sparse graphs. *Inf. Process. Lett.* 102, 5 (2007), 191–195.

[18] Z. Lotker, B. Patt-Shamir, and S. Pettie. 2008. Improved distributed approximate matching. In *Proc. 20th SPAA.* 129–136.

[19] Y. Mansour and S. Vardi. 2013. A Local Computation Approximation Scheme to Maximum Matching. In *Proc. 16th APPROX.* 260–273.

[20] Ofer Neiman and Shay Solomon. 2013. Simple deterministic algorithms for fully dynamic maximal matching. In *Proc. of 45th STOC.* 745–754.

[21] Merav Parter, David Peleg, and Shay Solomon. 2016. Local-on-Average Distributed Tasks. In *Proc. 27th SODA.* 220–239.

[22] D. Peleg. 2000. *Distributed computing: a locality-sensitive approach.* SIAM.

[23] David Peleg and Shay Solomon. 2016. Dynamic $(1 + \epsilon)$-Approximate Matchings: A Density-Sensitive Approach. In *Proc. of 27th SODA.* 712–729.

[24] David Peleg and Jeffrey D. Ullman. 1989. An Optimal Synchronizer for the Hypercube. *SIAM J. Comput.* 18, 4 (1989), 740–747.

[25] R. Rubinfeld, G. Tamir, S. Vardi, and N. Xie. 2011. Fast Local Computation Algorithms. In *Proc. 2nd ICS.* 223–238.

[26] Shay Solomon. 2018. Local Algorithms for Bounded Degree Sparsifiers in Sparse Graphs. In *Proc. of 9th ITCS.* 52:1–52:19.

[27] Jukka Suomela. 2013. Survey of local algorithms. *ACM Comput. Surv.* 45, 2 (2013), 24.

# Greedy and Local Ratio Algorithms in the MapReduce Model

Extended Abstract

Nicholas J. A. Harvey
University of British Columbia
Vancouver, Canada
nickhar@cs.ubc.ca

Christopher Liaw
University of British Columbia
Vancouver, Canada
cvliaw@cs.ubc.ca

Paul Liu
Stanford University
Stanford, California, Canada
paulliu@stanford.edu

## Abstract

MapReduce has become the *de facto* standard model for designing distributed algorithms to process big data on a cluster. There has been considerable research on designing efficient MapReduce algorithms for clustering, graph optimization, and submodular optimization problems. We develop new techniques for designing greedy and local ratio algorithms in this setting. Our randomized local ratio technique gives 2-approximations for weighted vertex cover and weighted matching, and an $f$-approximation for weighted set cover, all in a constant number of MapReduce rounds. Our randomized greedy technique gives algorithms for maximal independent set, maximal clique, and a $(1 + \varepsilon) \ln \Delta$-approximation for weighted set cover. We also give greedy algorithms for vertex colouring with $(1 + o(1))\Delta$ colours and edge colouring with $(1 + o(1))\Delta$ colours.

## CCS Concepts

• **Theory of computation** → **MapReduce algorithms**; *Packing and covering problems*; • **Mathematics of computing** → Graph coloring;

## Keywords

local ratio, vertex cover, weighted matching, mapreduce, graph colouring

**ACM Reference Format:**
Nicholas J. A. Harvey, Christopher Liaw, and Paul Liu. 2018. Greedy and Local Ratio Algorithms in the MapReduce Model: Extended Abstract. In *SPAA '18: 30th ACM Symposium on Parallelism in Algorithms and Architectures, July 16–18, 2018, Vienna, Austria.* ACM, New York, NY, USA, 10 pages. https://doi.org/10.1145/3210377.3210386

## 1 Introduction

A wealth of algorithmic challenges arise in processing the large data sets common in social networks, machine learning, and data mining. The tasks to be performed on these data sets commonly involve graph optimization, clustering, selecting representative subsets, etc. – tasks whose theory is well-understood in a sequential model of computation.


*SPAA '18, July 16–18, 2018, Vienna, Austria*

ACM ISBN 978-1-4503-5799-9/18/07...$15.00
https://doi.org/10.1145/3210377.3210386

The modern engineering reality is that these large data sets are distributed across clusters or data centers, for reasons including bandwidth and memory limitations, and fault tolerance. New programming models and infrastructure, such as MapReduce and Spark, have been developed to process this data efficiently. The MapReduce model is attractive to theoreticians as it is clean, simple, and has rigorous foundations in the work of Valiant [41] and Karloff et al. [25]. Designing MapReduce algorithms often involves concepts arising in parallel, distributed, and streaming algorithms, so it is necessary to understand classic optimization problems in a new light.

In the formalization of the MapReduce model [25], the data for a given problem is partitioned across many machines, where each machine has memory sublinear in the input size. Computation proceeds in a sequence of rounds: in each round, a machine performs a polynomial-time computation on its local data. Between rounds, each machine simultaneously sends data to all other machines, the size of which is restricted only by the sender's and recipients' memory capacity. The primary efficiency consideration in this model is the number of rounds, although it is also desirable to constrain other metrics, such as the memory overhead, the amount of data communicated, and the processing time.

Greedy approximation algorithms have been a popular choice for adapting to the MapReduce model, in the hopes that their simple structure suits the restrictions of the model. Unfortunately, many greedy algorithms also seem to be inherently sequential, a property which is rather incompatible with the parallel nature of MapReduce computations. This phenomenon is, of course, well known to parallel and distributed algorithm researchers, as it was the impetus for Valiant's [40] and Cook's [13] encouragement to study the maximal independent set problem in a parallel setting. Primal-dual approximation algorithms have received comparably less use in the MapReduce setting, perhaps because they seem even more sequential than greedy algorithms.

### 1.1 Techniques and Contributions

We develop two new techniques for designing MapReduce algorithms. The first is a "randomized local ratio" technique, which combines the local ratio method [6] with judicious random sampling in order to enable parallelization. At a high level, the technique choses an i.i.d. random sample of elements, then runs an ordinary local ratio algorithm on this sample. The crux is to show that the weight adjustments performed by the local ratio algorithm cause a significant fraction of the non-sampled elements to be eliminated. Repeating this several times allows us to execute the local ratio method with no loss in the approximation ratio. We use this technique to give a 2-approximation for min-weight vertex cover (Section 2) and a 2-approximation for max-weight matching (Section 5). The vertex cover result is a special case of our $f$-approximation for min-weight set cover, where $f$ is the largest frequency of any element. Additional subtleties arise in applying this technique to the max-weight $b$-matching problem ($b \geq 2$), for which we obtain a $(3-\frac{2}{b}+\varepsilon)$-approximation (in the full version of the paper). Adapting these randomized local ratio algorithms to the MapReduce setting is straightforward: all machines participate in the random sampling, and a single central machine executes the local ratio algorithm. It is worth emphasizing that these algorithms are very simple and could easily be implemented in practice.

Our second technique we call the "hungry-greedy" technique. Whereas randomized local ratio uses i.i.d. sampling, hungry-greedy first samples "heavy" elements, not to maximize an objective function, but to disqualify a large fraction of elements from the solution. Doing so allows us to rapidly shrink the problem size, and thereby execute the greedy method in just a few rounds. We emphasize that the hungry-greedy technique is applicable even to problems without an objective function or an *a priori* ordering on the greedy choices. We use this technique to give efficient algorithms for maximal independent set (Section 3), maximal clique (in the full version of the paper), and a $(1+\varepsilon)\ln\Delta$ approximation to weighted set cover (Section 4).

At first glance one may think that the maximal clique result follows by a trivial reduction from the independent set result, but this is not the case. The formalization of the MapReduce model requires that computations be performed in linear space, so it is not possible to complement a sparse graph. Other problems that are widely studied in the distributed computing literature and can usually be solved by a trivial reduction to maximal independent set include vertex colouring with $\Delta + 1$ colours and edge colouring with $2\Delta - 1$ colours; see the monograph of Barenboim and Elkin [8]. Again, these reductions are not possible in the MapReduce model due to space restrictions. We make progress on these problems by giving algorithms for $(1 + o(1))\Delta$ vertex colouring and $(1 + o(1))\Delta$ edge colouring (Section 6).

## 1.2 Related work

Within the theory community, part of the appeal of the MapReduce model is the connection to several established topics, including distributed algorithms, PRAM algorithms, streaming algorithms, submodular optimization and composable coresets.

One of the earliest papers on MapReduce algorithms is due to Lattanzi et al. [27], in which the filtering technique is introduced. Filtering involves choosing a random sample, from which a partial solution is constructed and used to eliminate candidate elements from the final solution; the process is repeated until all elements are exhausted. This technique has been quite influential, and many subsequent papers can be viewed as employing a similar methodology. Indeed, our randomized local ratio technique can be viewed as a descendant of the filtering technique in which the local ratio weights are used to eliminate elements. The original filtering technique yielded 2-approximations for unweighted matching and vertex cover, and was combined with layering ideas to give an 8-approximation for weighted matching [27]. These layering ideas were improved by Crouch and Stubbs [14] and Grigorescu et al. [21] to give a $(3.5+\varepsilon)$-approximation for weighted matching in the semi-streaming and MapReduce models. In addition, it is also known that any $c$-approximation to maximum weighted matching can be automatically converted to a $(2+\varepsilon)$-approximation algorithm by using the former as a blockbox [30].

Recently Paz and Schwartzman [37] gave a $(2+\varepsilon)$-approximation for weighted matching in the semi-streaming model, using the local ratio method with clever pruning techniques to bound the recursion depth. This result was slightly improved and substantially simplified by Ghaffari [18]. Unfortunately, this work does not apply to the MapReduce setting: it is very space-efficient, but not distributed. Our randomized local ratio technique is inspired by this work, but different. Whereas [18, 37] are deterministic and process the input in a streaming fashion, our technique achieves its space efficiency through random sampling and requires several rounds to process the entire input.

Submodular optimization has also been a fruitful avenue for MapReduce algorithms. Kumar et al. [26] gave a general framework for maximizing monotone submodular functions over hereditary constraints in the MapReduce setting while losing only $\varepsilon$ in the approximation ratio. Their Sample-and-Prune and $\varepsilon$-Greedy techniques are vaguely related to our hungry-greedy technique, but nevertheless different as our technique does not maximize an objective. Barbosa et al. [16] develop a different framework that achieves the same approximation ratio while using fewer MapReduce rounds; it also supports the continuous greedy algorithm and non-monotone functions. A specific result relevant to our work is a $\frac{1}{3+\varepsilon}$-approximation for weighted matching in bipartite graphs [26] in $O(\log(\frac{w_{\max}}{w_{\min}})/\mu\varepsilon)$ rounds and $O(nm^{\mu})$ space per machine. The results of Barbosa et al. seem to improve this to $O(1/\varepsilon)$ rounds and $O(\sqrt{nm})$ space per machine.

Another problem related to submodular maximization is the submodular set cover problem [43], which generalizes the weighted set cover problem, and has been studied* in the MapReduce model by Mirzasoleiman et al. [34, 35]. Both of our techniques are applicable to weighted set cover. Our randomized local ratio technique matches the classic $f$-approximation [7], where $f$ is the largest frequency of an element. Our hungry-greedy technique gives a $(1+\varepsilon)\ln\Delta$ approximation, nearly matching the optimal $\ln\Delta$-approximation for polynomial-time algorithms [12]. It is worth noting that our $f$-approximation is intended (as with vertex cover) for the scenario that $n \ll m$, whereas our second algorithm assumes $m \ll n$. Our latter result has several advantages over the work of Mirzasoleiman et al.: we handle the weighted case, improve the $\ln m$ in the approximation ratio to $\ln\Delta$, our space usage is controllable by an arbitrary parameter $\mu$, and use significantly less space when $m \ll n$.

The classical PRAM model admits algorithms for many of the problems we consider. There are general simulations of EREW PRAMs [25] and CREW PRAMs [20] by MapReduce algorithms,

* The set cover problem was studied earlier in the MapReduce setting by Stergiou and Tsioutsiouliklis [39], although their work appears not to have rigorous guarantees regarding concurrent access to shared state.

**Figure 1: Results for MapReduce algorithms. For graph algorithms, the number of vertices is $n$, the number of edges is assumed to be $n^{1+c}$, and the maximum degree is $\Delta$. For set cover, the number of sets is $n$, the size of the ground set is $m$, the size of the largest set is $\Delta$, and the largest number of sets containing any element is $f$, the maximum (resp. minimum) weight is $w_{\max}$ (resp. $w_{\min}$). For Theorem 2.4 it is assumed that $m = n^{1+c}$. The space per machine is typically $n^{1+\mu}$, which for most results (except [1]) need not be constant; taking $\mu = 1/\log n$ one can often get $O(n)$ space and $O(\log n)$ rounds. For Theorem 4.5, $n$ can depend arbitrarily on $m$.**

| Problem | Weighted? | Approximation | MapReduce Rounds | Space per machine | Reference |
|---|---|---|---|---|---|
| Vertex Cover | | 2 | $O(c/\mu)$ | $O(n^{1+\mu})$ | [26] |
| | Y | $O(\log^2 n)$ | 2 | $\tilde{O}(n^{1.5})$ | [4] |
| | Y | 2 | $O(c/\mu)$ | $O(n^{1+\mu})$ | Theorem 2.4 |
| Set Cover | | $O(\log m)$ | $O(\log(m)\|OPT\|)$ | not analyzed | [34] |
| | | $(1+\varepsilon)\ln m$ | $O\big(\log(\frac{n}{\|OPT\|})\log(\Delta)/\varepsilon + \log m\big)$ | $O(\sqrt{n\|OPT\|}\Delta)$ | [35] |
| | Y | $f$ | $O((c/\mu)^2)$ | $O(f \cdot n^{1+\mu})$ | Theorem 2.4 |
| | Y | $(1+\varepsilon)\ln\Delta$ | $O\left(\frac{\log\left(\frac{w_{\max}}{w_{\min}}\Delta\right)}{\mu^2\varepsilon}\right)$ if $n = \text{poly}(m)$ | $O(m^{1+\mu})$ | Theorem 4.5 |
| Maximal Indep. Set | | | $O(c/\mu)$ | $O(n^{1+\mu})$ | Theorem ?? |
| Maximal Clique | | | $O(1/\mu)$ | $O(n^{1+\mu})$ | Corollary ?? |
| Matching | | 2 | $O(c/\mu)$ | $O(n^{1+\mu})$ | [26] |
| | Y | 8 | $O(c/\mu)$ | $O(n^{1+\mu})$ | [26] |
| | Y | $4+\varepsilon$ | $O(c/\mu)$ | $O(n^{1+\mu})$ | [14] |
| | Y | $3.5+\varepsilon$ | $O(c/\mu)$ | $O(n^{1+\mu})$ | [21] |
| | Y | $2+\varepsilon$ | $O((c/\mu)\log(1/\varepsilon))$ | $O(n^{1+\mu})$ | [30] |
| | Y | $1+\varepsilon$ | $O(1/\mu\varepsilon)$ | $O(n^{1+\mu})$ | [1] |
| | Y | $O(1)$ | 2 | $\tilde{O}(n^{1.5})$ | [4] |
| | | $2+\varepsilon$ | $O((\log\log n)^2\log(1/\varepsilon))$ | $O(n)$ | [15] |
| | | $1+\varepsilon$ | $(1/\varepsilon)^{O(1/\varepsilon)}\log\log n$ | $\tilde{O}(n)$ | [3] |
| | Y | 2 | $O(c/\mu)$ | $O(n^{1+\mu})$ | Theorem 5.6 |
| Vertex Colouring | | $(1+o(1))\Delta$ colours | $O(1)$ | $O(n^{1+\mu})$ | Theorem 6.5 |
| Edge Colouring | | $(1+o(1))\Delta$ colours | $O(1)$ | $O(n^{1+\mu})$ | Theorem 6.7 |

although these lead to polylog($n$)-rounds algorithms, which does not meet the MapReduce gold standard of $O(1)$ rounds.

Composable core-sets have recently emerged as a useful primitive for the design of distributed approximation algorithms; see, e.g., [5, 23, 33] and the references therein. The idea is to partition the data, compute on each part a representative subset called a core-set, then solve the problem on the union of the core-sets. Relevant to this is the work of Assadi et al. [3] (extending work by Assadi and Khanna [4]), which designs $3/2+\varepsilon$ (resp. $3+\varepsilon$) approximate core-sets for unweighted matching (resp. vertex cover). They obtain 2-round MapReduce algorithms as a corollary. Combining with the technique of Crouch and Stubbs [14], these can be extended to $O(1)$ (resp. $O(\log n)$) approximations for weighted variants of the problem.

Primal-dual algorithms have previously been studied in the MapReduce model, notably in the work of Ahn and Guha [1]. They develop sophisticated multiplicative-weight-type techniques to approximately solve the matching (and $b$-matching) LP in very few iterations. Their technique gives a $(1+\varepsilon)$-approximation in $O(1/\mu\varepsilon)$ MapReduce rounds while using only $O(n^{1+\mu})$ space per machine. While their algorithm achieves a superior approximation factor to ours, it is also highly technical. Our algorithm is concise, simple, and could plausibly be the end-of-the-road for filtering-type techniques for the matching problem.

Very recently there have been some exciting developments in MapReduce algorithms. Im et al. [22] have given a general dynamic programming framework that seems very promising for designing more approximation algorithms. Czumaj et al. [15] introduced a round compression technique for MapReduce and applied it to matching to obtain a linear space MapReduce algorithm which gives a $(2+\varepsilon)$-approximation algorithm for unweighted matching in only $O((\log\log n)^2\log(1/\varepsilon))$ rounds. For unweighted matching, Assadi et al. [3] built on this work and gave a $(2+\varepsilon)$-approximation algorithm in $O((\log\log n)\log(1/\varepsilon))$ rounds with $\tilde{O}(n)$ space and a $(1+\varepsilon)$-approximation algorithm in $(1/\varepsilon)^{O(1/\varepsilon)}\log\log n$ rounds with $\tilde{O}(n)$ space. Round compression has also been used to give a $O(\log n)$ approximation for unweighted vertex cover using $O(\log\log n)$ MapReduce rounds [2].

## 1.3 The MapReduce Model

In this paper we adopt the MapReduce model as formalized by Karloff et al. [25]; see also [19]. In their setting, there is an input of size $N$ distributed across $O(N^{\delta})$ machines, each with $O(N^{1-\delta})$ memory. This models the property that modern big data sets must be stored across a cluster of machines. Computation proceeds in a sequence of rounds. In each round, each machine receives input of size $O(N^{1-\delta})$; it performs a computation on that input; then it produces a sequence of output messages, each of which is to be delivered to another machine at the start of the next round. The total size of these output messages must also be $O(N^{1-\delta})$. In between rounds, the output messages are delivered to their recipients as input.

The data format and computation performed is not completely arbitrary. Data is stored as a sequence of key-value pairs, and the computation is performed by the eponymous *map* and *reduce* functions that operate on such sequences. The requirements of these functions are not particularly relevant to our work, so we refer the interested reader to standard textbooks [29] or the work of Karloff et al. [25].

For graph algorithms, we will assume that the space per machine is bounded as a function of $n$, the number of vertices, whereas the input size is $O(N)$ where $N = m$ is the number of edges. As in Lattanzi et al. [27], we will typically assume that the space per machine is $O(n^{1+\mu})$ and the graph has $m = n^{1+c}$ edges, $c > \mu$. This conforms to the requirements of Karloff et al. with $\delta = \frac{c-\mu}{1+c}$.

The memory constraints of graph problems in the MapReduce model stem from the early work of Karloff et al. [25] and Leskovec et al. [28]. In these papers, graph problems with $n$ nodes and $n^{1+c}$ edges were examined. Specifically, Leskovec et al. [28] found that real world graph problems were often not sparse, but had $n^{1+c}$ edges where $c$ varied between 0.08 and larger than 0.5. In practice, MapReduce algorithms also require $\Omega(n)$ memory per machine. One such example is the diameter estimation algorithm of Kang et al. [24], in which $O((n + m)/M)$ memory is required per machine, where $M$ is the number of machines in total.

**Related models.** There have been a series of refinements to the original MRC model of Karloff et al. [25], the most prominent of which is the massive parallel computation (MPC) model developed by Beame et al. [9]. The main difference with the MPC model is that the space requirements are more stringent than in MRC. Given an input of size $N$ and $M$ machines, each machine is only allowed to have at most $S = O(N/M)$ space. In each round, each machine can send $O(S)$ words to other machines. The majority of our algorithms apply in the MPC model as well as the MRC model. The only exceptions are our set cover and $b$-matching algorithms, where our space bound depends on structural parameters of the input.

### 1.4 Organization

In Sections 2 and 3, we develop our "randomized local ratio" and "hungry-greedy" techniques through the weighted set cover and maximal independent set problems respectively. We then apply these techniques to specific problems in the subsequent sections. Our randomized local ratio technique is applied to maximum weight matching (Section 5) and our hungry-greedy technique is applied to maximal independent set (Section 3) as well as an alternate approximation of weighted set cover (Section 4). Algorithms for vertex and edge colouring that may be of independent interest are given in Section 6.

## 2 $f$-approximation for weighted set cover

For notational convenience, let $[n] = \{1, \ldots, n\}$, $S(X) = \bigcup_{i \in X} S_i$ and $w(X) = \sum_{i \in X} w_i$ for all $X \subseteq [n]$. In the weighted set cover problem, we are given $n$ sets $S_1, \ldots, S_n \subseteq [m]$ with weights $w_1, \ldots, w_n \in \mathbb{R}_{>0}$. The goal is to find a subset $X$ such that $w(X)$ is minimal amongst all $X$ with $S(X) = [m]$.

Let $OPT$ denote a fixed set $X$ achieving the minimum. The frequency of element $j \in U$ is defined to be $|\{ i : j \in S_i \}|$. Let $f$ denote the maximum frequency of any element.

THEOREM 2.1 (BAR-YEHUDA AND EVEN [7]). *The following algorithm gives an $f$-approximation to weighted set cover.*

**Sequential local ratio algorithm for minimum weight set cover**

Arbitrarily select an element $j \in U$ such that the minimum weight of all sets containing $j$ is strictly positive, then reduce all those weights by that minimum value. Remove all sets with zero weight, and add them to the cover. Repeat so long as uncovered elements remain.

More explicitly, the weight reduction step works as follows. If element $j \in U$ was selected, then we compute $\epsilon = \min_{i \in [n] : j \in S_i} w_i$ then perform the update $w_i \leftarrow w_i - \epsilon$ for all $i$ with $j \in S_i$.

### 2.1 Randomized local ratio

The local ratio method described above is not terribly parallelizable, as it processes elements sequentially. Nor is it terribly space-efficient, as it might require processing every element in $[m]$. However, it does have the virtue that elements can be processed in a fairly arbitrary order. Our randomized local ratio technique takes advantage of that flexibility and combines the local ratio algorithm with random sampling. There are essentially two components to our randomized local ratio technique: (1) we can cover a large fraction of the remaining sets with just a random sample of elements, and (2) this random sample will be comparable in weight to the optimal solution since the processing order of local ratio is fairly arbitrary. Intuitively, property (1) ensures that the algorithm runs in a few number of rounds, and property (2) ensures a good approximation ratio. These two ideas will come up frequently in the algorithms we present in this paper.

In Algorithm 1, the size of each sample $U'$ is $O(\eta)$ w.h.p., and $\eta$ will be taken to be $n^{1+\mu}$, the space available on each machine.

**Algorithm 1** An $f$-approximation for minimum weight set cover. The lines highlighted in blue are run sequentially on a central machine, and all other lines are run in parallel across all machines.

```
1: procedure ApproxSC(S_1, ..., S_n ⊆ U = [m])
2:     U_1 ← U, r ← 1
3:     while U_r ≠ ∅ do
4:         ▷: U_r is the set of all j ∈ [m] such that min_{i : j∈S_i} w_i > 0
5:         Compute U' by sampling each element of U_r independently with probability p = min(1, 2η/|U_r|)
6:         if |U'| > 6η then fail
7:         Run the local ratio algorithm for set cover on the sets S_1 ∩ U', ..., S_n ∩ U'
8:         Let C ⊆ [n] be the indices of all sets with zero weight
9:         U_{r+1} ← U_r \ S(C)
10:        r ← r + 1
11:    return the indices C of all sets with zero weight
```

Our analysis uses the following useful fact, relating to the filtering technique of Lattanzi et al. [27].

LEMMA 2.2. *Let $U_{r+1}$ be the set computed on line Line 9 of Algorithm 1. If $p = 1$ then $U_{r+1} = \emptyset$, otherwise $|U_{r+1}| < 2n/p$ with probability at least $1 - e^{-n}$.*

Proof. If $p = 1$ then $U' = U_r$, so the local ratio method produces $C$ covering all of $U_r$, and so $U_{r+1} = \emptyset$. So assume $p < 1$.

For each $X \subseteq [n]$, let $\overline{S(X)}$ be the elements left uncovered by $X$. Let $\mathcal{E}_X$ be the event that $U' \cap \overline{S(X)} = \emptyset$. Say that $X$ is large if $|\overline{S(X)}| \geq 2n/p =: \tau$. For large $X$, $\Pr[\mathcal{E}_X] \leq (1-p)^\tau \leq e^{-p\tau} = e^{-2n}$. By a union bound, the probability that all large $\mathcal{E}_X$ fail to occur is at least $1 - e^{-n}$. Since the local ratio method produces a set $C$ for which $U' \cap \overline{S(C)} = \emptyset$, with high probability it must be that $|C|$ is not large. □

Theorem 2.3. *Suppose that $m \leq n^{1+c}$. Let $\eta = n^{1+\mu}$, for any $\mu > 0$. Then Algorithm 1 terminates within $\lceil c/\mu \rceil$ iterations and returns an $f$-approximate set cover, w.h.p.*

Proof. *Correctness:* Observe that the sequential local ratio algorithm for set cover can pick elements in an arbitrary order. Algorithm 1 is an instantiation of that algorithm that uses random sampling to partially determine the order in which elements are picked. It immediately follows that Algorithm 1 outputs an $f$-approximation to the minimum set cover, assuming it does not fail. By a standard Chernoff bound, an iteration fails with probability at most $\exp(-n^{1+\mu}) \leq \exp(-n)$.

*Efficiency:* By Lemma 2.2, while $p < 1$ we have $|U_{r+1}| \leq 2n/p = 2n|U_r|/\eta = 2|U_r|/n^\mu \leq 2n^{1+c-r\mu}$, whp. By iteration $r = \lceil c/\mu \rceil - 1$, we will have $|U_r| \leq 2n^{1+c} = 2\eta$ and so $p = 1$. After one more iteration the algorithm will terminate, again by Lemma 2.2. □

## 2.2 MapReduce implementation

Theorem 2.4. *There is a MapReduce algorithm that computes an $f$-approximation for the minimum weight set cover where each machine has memory $O(f \cdot n^{1+\mu})$. The number of rounds is $O(c/\mu)$ in the case $f = 2$ (i.e., vertex cover) and $O((c/\mu)^2)$ in the case $f > 2$.*

Proof. Instead of representing the input as the sets $S_1, \ldots, S_n$, we instead assume that it is represented as the "dual" set system $T_1, \ldots, T_m$ where $T_j = \{\ i : j \in S_i\ \}$. By definition of frequency, we have $|T_j| \leq f$.

Each element $j \in [m]$ will be assigned arbitrarily to one of the machines, with $n^{1+\mu}$ elements per machine, so $M := m/n^{1+\mu} = n^{c-\mu}$ machines are required. Element $j$ will store on its machine the set $T_j$ and a bit indicating if $j \in U_r$. Thus, the space per machine is $O(f \cdot n^{1+\mu})$.

The main centralized step is the local ratio computation (lines 7-8). The centralized machine receives as input the sets $T_j$ for all $j \in U'$. As $|U'| \leq 6\eta$, the input received by the central machine is $O(f\eta) = O(fn^{1+\mu})$ words. After executing the local ratio algorithm, the centralized machine then computes $C$.

There are two key steps requiring parallel computation: the sampling step (line 5) and the computation of $U_{r+1}$ (line 9). After the central machine computes $C$, it must send $C$ to all other machines. Sending this directly could require $|C| \cdot M = \Omega(n^{1+c-\mu})$ bits of output, which could exceed the machine's space of $O(n^{1+\mu})$. Instead, we can form a broadcast tree over all machines with degree $n^\mu$ and depth $c/\mu$, allowing us to send $C$ to all machines in $O(c/\mu)$ MapReduce rounds. Since each machine knows $C$, each element $j$ can determine if $j \in U_{r+1}$ by determining if $T_j \cap C \neq \emptyset$. The same broadcast tree can be used to compute $|U_{r+1}|$ and send that to all machines. Since each element $j$ knows if $j \in U_r$ and knows $|U_r|$, it can independently perform the sampling step.

In the case $f = 2$ (i.e., vertex cover), this can be improved. Each set $S_i$ (i.e., vertex) will also be assigned to one of the $M$ machines, randomly chosen. By a Chernoff bound (using that $|S_i| \leq n$) the space required per machine is $O(f \cdot n^{1+\mu})$ w.h.p. After computing $C$, the central machine sends a bit to each set $S_i$ indicating whether $i \in C$ or not. Each set $S_i$ then forwards that bit to each element $j \in S_i$. Thus $j$ can determine whether $j \in U_{r+1}$. Each machine can send to a central location the number of edges on that machine that lie in $U_{r+1}$, so the central machine can compute $|U_{r+1}|$ and send it back to all machines. □

# 3 Maximal independent set

As a warm-up to the "hungry-greedy" technique, we first present an algorithm to find a maximal independent set (MIS) in a constant number of MapReduce rounds. In order to clearly explain the concepts, this section presents a simple algorithm using $O(1/\mu^2)$ rounds. In the full version of the paper, we show how to further parallelize this algorithm so that it takes $O(c/\mu)$ rounds.

The algorithm, shown in Algorithm 2, proceeds in phases where each phase takes $O(1/\mu)$ rounds. In phase $i \geq 1$, we reduce the maximum degree from $n^{1-(i-1)\alpha}$ to $n^{1-i\alpha}$. We will choose $\alpha = \mu/2$ so that after $O(1/\mu)$ phases, the maximum degree will be at most $n^\mu$. Following this, we can finish the algorithm in one more round by placing the entire graph onto a central machine.

For a vertex $v$, we define $N(v)$ as the neighbours of $v$ and $N^+(v) = N(v) \cup \{v\}$. For a set $I \subseteq V$, we define $N^+(I) = \cup_{v \in I} N^+(v)$ and $N_I(v) = N(v) \setminus N^+(I)$. In other words, $N_I(v)$ is the set of neighbours of $v$ which are not in $I$ and not adjacent to a vertex in $I$. Finally let $d_I(v) = |N_I(v)|$ if $v \notin N^+(I)$, otherwise $d_I(v) = 0$.

**Algorithm 2** A simple algorithm for maximal independent set. The lines highlighted in blue are run sequentially on a central machine, and all other lines are run in parallel across all machines.

**procedure** MIS1($G = (V, E)$)
  $I \leftarrow \emptyset$ ▷ $I$ is the current independent set
  **for** $i = 1, \ldots, 1/\alpha$ **do**
    ▷: $d_I(v) \leq n^{1-(i-1)\alpha}$ for all $v \in V$
    $V_H \leftarrow \{v : d_I(v) \geq n^{1-i\alpha}\}$ ▷ Heavy vertices
    **while** $|V_H| \geq n^{i\alpha}$ **do**
      Draw $n^{i\alpha}$ groups of $n^{\mu/2}$ vertices from $V_H$, say $X_1, \ldots, X_{n^{i\alpha}}$
      **for** $j = 1, \ldots, n^{i\alpha}$ **do**
        **if** $\exists v_j \in X_j$ such that $d_I(v_j) \geq n^{1-i\alpha}$ **then**
          $I \leftarrow I \cup \{v_j\}$
      $V_H \leftarrow \{v : d_I(v) \geq n^{1-i\alpha}\}$ ▷ Update heavy vertices
    Find maximal independent set in $V_H$ and add it to $I$ ▷ $|V_H| < n^{i\alpha}$
  **return** $I$

Remark 3.1. *In the algorithm, a vertex can lose its label as a heavy vertex during the for loop. This is intentional as when we add a vertex to $I$, we want to make sure we make substantial progress. Moreover,* *since a vertex sends all its neighbours, it is easy to tell whether a vertex is heavy and to update $N^+(I)$.*

Lemma 3.2. *Let $V_H$ be the set of heavy vertices at the beginning of the inner for loop (line 9) and $V'_H$ be the set of heavy vertices after the for loop. Then $|V'_H| \le |V_H|/n^{\mu/4}$ w.h.p.*

Proof. Observe that the first group $\mathcal{X}_1$ of vertices will definitely contain a heavy vertex so it will remove at least $n^{1-i\alpha}$ vertices from the graph.* Now suppose we are currently processing group $\mathcal{X}_j$. If the number of heavy vertices is at most $|V_H|/n^{\mu/4}$ at this point then we are done. So suppose the number of heavy vertices is at least $|V_H|/n^{\mu/4}$. Since we sample the vertices uniformly at random, the group $\mathcal{X}_j$ contains a heavy vertex with probability at least $1 - \left(1 - 1/n^{\mu/4}\right)^{n^{\mu/2}} \ge 1 - \exp\left(-n^{\mu/4}\right)$. At this point, we add another heavy vertex to $I$ and remove it and all its neighbours.

The above process can happen at most $n^{i\alpha}$ times before the number of heavy vertices is at most $|V_H|/n^{\mu/4}$. This is because if it happens $n^{i\alpha}$ times then no vertices remain. Hence, by taking a union bound over all groups, we have that $|V'_H| \le |V_H|/n^{\mu/4}$ with probability at least $1 - n \cdot \exp\left(-n^{\mu/4}\right)$. □

Theorem 3.3. *There is a MapReduce algorithm to find a maximal independent set in $O(1/\mu^2)$ rounds and $O(n^{1+\mu})$ space per machine, w.h.p.*

Proof sketch. As before, there are $M := n^{c-\mu}$ machines. Each vertex and its adjacency list is assigned to one of the $M$ machines, randomly chosen. By a Chernoff bound, the space required per machine is $O(n^{1+\mu})$ whp. Each vertex $v$ will maintain its value of $d_I(v)$, allowing it to determine if $v \in V_H$. Thus, the sampling step (line 7) can be performed in parallel.

A central machine maintains and updates the sets $I$ and $N(I)$. It receives as input the sets of vertices $\mathcal{X}_1, \ldots, \mathcal{X}_{n^{i\alpha}}$ and their lists of alive neighbours, so the total input size is proportional to

$$\sum_{j=1}^{n^{i\alpha}} \sum_{v \in \mathcal{X}_j} d_I(v) \le n^{i\alpha} \cdot n^{\mu/2} \cdot n^{1-(i-1)\alpha} = n^{1+\mu/2+\alpha}.$$

After executing the for-loop, the central machine can use these lists of neighbours to also compute $N^+(I)$.

The next step requiring parallelization is line 11. To execute this, the central machine sends a bit to each vertex $v$ indicating if $v \in N^+(I)$. Then, every $v \notin N^+(I)$ asks each neighbour $w \in N(v)$ if $w \in N^+(I)$. The results of these queries allow $v$ to compute $d_I(v)$.

By Lemma 3.2, the while loop takes $O(1/\mu)$ rounds, so the entire algorithm takes $O(1/\mu^2)$ rounds. □

**Maximal clique.** One might initially assume that, by complementing the graph, our algorithm for MIS implies an algorithm for maximal clique by complementing the graph. However, it may not be to store the complemented graph. Nevertheless, in the full version of the paper, we show that it is possible to adapt Algorithm 2 so that it will compute a maximal clique.

*We will say $v$ is removed from the graph if it is added to $N^+(I)$.

## 4 $(1+\varepsilon)\ln\Delta$-approximation for weighted set cover

For convenience, we reuse the same notation from Section 2. The standard greedy algorithm for weighted set cover is as follows. We maintain a set $C$ of *covered* elements (initially $C = \emptyset$). In each iteration, we find the set $S_i$ which maximizes $|S_i \setminus C|/w_i$. We add $S_i$ to our solution and add the elements of $S_i$ to $C$. It is known [13] that this algorithm has approximation ratio $H_\Delta$ where $\Delta = \max_\ell |S_\ell|$ and $H_k = \sum_{i=1}^k \frac{1}{k}$.

Unfortunately, implementing this greedy algorithm is tricky in MapReduce but, following Kumar et al. [26], we can implement the *$\varepsilon$-greedy algorithm*, which differs from the standard greedy method as follows. Instead of choosing the set $S_i$ to maximize $|S_i \setminus C|/w_i$, we choose $S_i$ such that $|S_i \setminus C|/w_i \ge \frac{1}{1+\varepsilon}\max_j\{|S_j \setminus C|/w_j\}$. The standard dual fitting argument [13, 42] can be easily modified to prove that this gives a $(1+\varepsilon)H_\Delta$-approximate solution.

Our algorithm for set cover is also inspired by some of the PRAM algorithms for set cover (see, for example, [10, 11, 17, 38]). Indeed, we use a similar bucketing approach as [10, 11, 17, 38] which we now describe. Let $L = \max_\ell\{|S_\ell|/w_\ell\}$. We first consider only the "bucket" of sets that have a cost ratio of at least $L/(1+\varepsilon)$ and continue to add sets from this bucket to the cover until the bucket is empty (after which we decrease $L$ by $1+\varepsilon$ and repeat). However, note that once we add a set from the bucket to the cover, some of the sets in the bucket may no longer have a sufficiently cost ratio to remain in the bucket; in this case, we need to remove them from the bucket.

It is shown in [11] (improving on [10]) that exhausting a bucket can be done in $O(\log^2 n)$ time in the PRAM model; this can be easily translated to a $O(\log^2(n)/(\mu\log(m)))$-round algorithm in the MapReduce model. Our main contribution is to show that, in MapReduce, one can exhaust a bucket in $O(\log^2(n)/(\mu^2\log^2(m)))$ rounds. In particular, when $n = \mathrm{poly}(m)$ and $\mu$ is a constant, the number of rounds decreases from $O(\log n)$ to $O(1)$.

The high level idea of our parallel algorithm for approximate minimum set cover is as follows. Let $C$ denote the current elements in the partial solution constructed so far (initially $C = \emptyset$). At this point, the algorithm considers only considers sets, $S_\ell$, which are almost optimal, i.e. $|S_\ell \setminus C|/w_\ell \ge L(1+\varepsilon)$, where initially, $L = \max_\ell\{|S_\ell|/w_\ell\}$ but is decreased as the algorithm runs. We then partition these sets into $1/\alpha$ groups where group $i$ consists of sets whose cardinatliy is in $[m^{1-(i+1)\alpha}, m^{1-i\alpha})$. From each group $i$, we then sample $m^{1-(i+1)\alpha}$ collections of $m^{\mu/2}$ sets. Starting from the group 1, we will see that either every collection contains an almost optimal set or we have made a large amount of progress. It will also turn out that we can decrease a certain potential function by a large amount in each iteration so within a few iterations, there will be no more profitable sets. If we have not covered the universe at this point then we decrease $L$ by $(1+\varepsilon)$ and repeat this process.

We now begin with a more formal treatment of the algorithm for minimum weight set cover. We will assume that each machine has $O(m^{1+\mu}\log(n))$ space and $\sum_{i=1}^n |S_i| \ge m^{1+c}$ so that the memory is sublinear in the input size. The pseudocode for the algorithm is given in Algorithm 3.

In Section 4.1, we will describe the MapReduce implementation of this algorithm. Of particular note is that the second while loop can be implemented in a small number of MapReduce rounds. Our

**Algorithm 3** A $(1+\varepsilon)\ln\Delta$-approximation for minimum weight set cover. Blue lines are centralized.

1: **procedure** APPROXSC($S_1, \ldots, S_n \subseteq U = [m]$, $w_1, \ldots, w_n \in \mathbb{R}_{>0}$)
2: $L \leftarrow \max_\ell \left\{ \frac{|S_\ell|}{w_\ell} \right\}$
3: $\mathcal{S} \leftarrow \emptyset$
4: $C \leftarrow \emptyset$ ▷ $C \subseteq [m]$ maintains set of *covered* elements
5: **while** $C \neq [m]$ **do**
6: $k \leftarrow 1$
7: **while** $\exists \ell$ s.t. $|S_\ell \setminus C_k|/w_\ell \geq L/(1+\varepsilon)$ **do**
8: $C_k \leftarrow C$ ▷ Maintain temporary set of covered elements; used only for proof.
9: Let $\mathcal{S}_{k,i} = \{S_\ell : m^{1-i\alpha} \leq |S_\ell \setminus C_k| < m^{1-(i-1)\alpha}$ and $|S_\ell \setminus C_k|/w_k \geq L/(1+\varepsilon)\}$
10: **for** $i = 1, \ldots, 1/\alpha$ **do**
11: **for** $j = 1, \ldots, 2m^{(i+1)\alpha}$ **do**
12: Include each $S_\ell \in \mathcal{S}_{k,i}$ into group $\mathcal{X}_{i,j}$ with probability $\min\{1, m^{\mu/2}/|\mathcal{S}_{k,i}|\}$
13: **if** $|\mathcal{X}_{i,j}| \leq 4m^{\mu/2}$ **then**
14: Send each $\mathcal{X}_{i,j}$ to the central machine.
15: **else** ▷ At least one $\mathcal{X}_{i,j}$ is too big so fail and continue to next iteration.
16: $k \leftarrow k+1$
17: **continue**
18: **for** $i = 1, \ldots, 1/\alpha$ **do**
19: **for** $j = 1, \ldots, 2m^{(i+1)\alpha}$ **do**
20: **if** $\exists S_\ell \in \mathcal{X}_{i,j}$ such that $|S_\ell \setminus C| \geq m^{1-(i+1)\alpha}/2$ **then**
21: $\mathcal{S} \leftarrow \mathcal{S} \cup \{S_\ell\}$
22: $C \leftarrow C \cup S_\ell$
23: $k \leftarrow k+1$
24: $L \leftarrow L/(1+\varepsilon)$
25: **return** $\mathcal{S}$

goal in this section is to show that the number of times the while loop is executed is small.

To that end, let us fix $L$ and analyze the number of iterations of the second while loop starting at Line 7. To do this, it will be convenient to introduce the potential function

$$\Phi_k := \sum_{\ell \in [n]: \frac{|S_\ell \setminus C_k|}{w_\ell} \geq \frac{L}{1+\varepsilon}} |S_\ell \setminus C_k|.$$

Observe that we have the trivial upper bound $\Phi_k \leq nm$. Moreover, $\Phi_k = 0$ if and only if we finished with the second while loop by iteration $k$.

Using a straightforward Chernoff bound, we can show that each iteration has a small proabilility of failure, i.e. in each iteration, we make it into line 16 with very small probability.

CLAIM 4.1. *Fix an iteration $k$. We have $|\mathcal{X}_{i,j}| \leq 4m^{\mu/2}$ for all $i, j$ with probability at least $1 - \frac{m}{\alpha}\exp\left(-m^{\mu/2}\right)$.*

Let us now fix $\alpha = \mu/8$. In the full paper, we show that the potential function decreases by a polynomial factor in each iteration. In particular, we have the following lemma.

LEMMA 4.2. *Fix an iteration $k$. Then $\Phi_{k+1} \leq \Phi_k/m^{\mu/8}$ with probability at least $1 - \frac{16m}{\mu}\exp\left(-m^{\mu/4}/2\right)$.*

Using this lemma will allow us to prove the following lemma.

LEMMA 4.3. *Let $K = \inf\{k > 0 : \Phi_k = 0\}$. Then $K \leq \frac{18\log\Phi_0}{\mu\log m}$ with probability $\geq 1 - \frac{32m}{\mu}\exp\left(-m^{\mu/4}/2\right)$.*

The proofs of the previous two lemmas can be found in the full version of the paper. We are now ready to prove the main theorem in this section. Define $\Phi = \sum_{\ell\in[n]} |S_\ell|$.

THEOREM 4.4. *Algorithm 3 returns $(1+\varepsilon)H_\Delta$-approximate minimum set cover. Moreover, the inner loop is executed at most*

$$O\left(\frac{\ln(\Phi)\log_{1+\varepsilon}(\Delta w_{\max}/w_{\min})}{\mu\ln m}\right)$$

*times with probability at least*

$$1 - \frac{64m}{\mu}\exp\left(-m^{\mu/4}/2\right).$$

PROOF. The correctness follows because the algorithm implements the $\varepsilon$-greedy algorithm for set cover.

Let $M = \max_\ell \left\{\frac{|S_\ell|}{w_\ell}\right\}$. We can prove the running time as follows. Let $K = \frac{18\log\Phi}{\mu\log m}$ and consider splitting up the iterations of the inner while loop into blocks of size $K$. By block $t$, we will refer to iterations $tK, \ldots, (t+1)K - 1$ of the inner while loop. We say that a block $t$ is good if $L$ has decreased at least once during that block. If the algorithm has already completed by that point, we will instead just flip a coin which comes up heads with probability at least $1 - \frac{32m}{\mu}\exp\left(-m^{\mu/4}/2\right)$. If it comes up heads we will call that block good. Otherwise, we call the block bad.

Note that after $\log_{1+\varepsilon}(Mw_{\max})$ good blocks, we are guaranteed that the algorithm has terminated. If we consider $2\log_{1+\varepsilon}(Mw_{\max})$ blocks then it suffices that at most $\log_{1+\varepsilon}(Mw_{\max})$ blocks are bad. The expected number of bad blocks is $\frac{32m}{\alpha}\exp\left(-m^{\mu/4}/2\right)$ so applying Markov's Inequality shows that after $O\left(\frac{\ln(\Phi)\log_{1+\varepsilon}(Mw_{\max})}{\mu\ln m}\right)$ iterations, the algorithm has terminated with probability at least $1 - \frac{64m}{\alpha}\exp\left(-m^{\mu/4}/2\right)$. Using the trivial bound $M \leq \Delta/w_{\min}$ and replacing $\alpha$ with $\mu/8$ completes the proof. □

## 4.1 MapReduce Implementation

It is straightforward to implement most steps in Algorithm 3 in MapReduce. However, we will highlight two nontrivial step here. The first is how to propagate information such as the set of covered elements $C$ to all the machines. To do this, it is convenient to imagine all the machines as arranged in an $O(m^\mu)$-ary tree where the root of the tree is the central machine. Then the central machine can pass $C$ down to its children. These machines then pass down to their children and so on. By doing this, all machines will know $C$ in $O\left(\frac{\ln n}{\mu\ln m}\right)$ MapReduce rounds.

The machines can also determine $|\mathcal{S}_{k,i}|$ in a similar manner but starting at the leaves of tree. Here, each machine will compute the number of sets that are in $\mathcal{S}_{k,i}$ and send that quantity to its parents.

The parents then sum up the input and their own contribution to $|\mathcal{S}_{k,i}|$ which they send to their own parents. Eventually the root is able to compute $|\mathcal{S}_{k,i}|$ and then propagates the number back down to the leaves as done above. This again takes $O\left(\frac{\ln n}{\mu \ln m}\right)$ rounds in MapReduce.

We can also use a similar strategy to check that $|\mathcal{X}_{i,j}|$ is small in Line 16 of Algorithm 3. We thus have the following theorem.

THEOREM 4.5. *There is a MapReduce algorithm that returns a* $(1+\varepsilon)H_\Delta$*-approximate minimum set cover which uses memory* $O(m^{1+\mu}\log n)$ *and runs in* $O\left(\frac{\ln(\Phi)\log_{1+\varepsilon}(\Delta w_{\max}/w_{\min})\ln(n)}{\mu^2\ln^2(m)}\right)$ *with probability at least* $1 - O\left(\frac{m}{\mu}\right)\exp\left(-m^{\mu/4}/2\right)$.

Using the bound $\Phi \leq nm$ yields the bound given in Figure 1.

REMARK 4.6. *Lemma 2.5 in [10] gives a simple way to preprocess the input so that* $w_{\max}/w_{\min} \leq mn/\varepsilon$ *as follows. First, define* $\gamma = \max_{i\in[m]}\min_{S\ni i} w(S)$. *This is a lower bound on the cost of any cover. First, we add every set with cost at most* $\gamma\varepsilon/n$ *to the cover; this constributes a cost of at most* $\gamma\varepsilon \leq \varepsilon \cdot OPT$. *Next, we remove any set with cost more than* $m\gamma$ *since* $OPT \leq m\gamma$. *All these steps can be done using a broadcast tree in* $O(\log(n)/(\mu\log(m)))$ *rounds of MapReduce.*

## 5 Maximum weight matching

We have a graph $G = (V, E, w)$ but now $w\colon E \to \mathbb{R}$ is a weight function on the edges. A matching in a graph is a subset $M \subseteq E$ such that $e_1 \cap e_2 = \emptyset$ for any distinct $e_1, e_2 \in M$. The maximum weight matching in a graph is a matching $M$ that maximizes $\sum_{e\in M} w_e$.

### 5.1 The local ratio method

**Sequential local ratio algorithm for maximum weight matching**

Arbitrarily select an edge $e$ with positive weight and reduce its weight from itself and its neighboring edges. Push $e$ onto a stack and repeat this procedure until there are no positive weight edges remaining. At the end, unwind the stack adding edges greedily to the matching.

If the edge $e = (u, v)$ was selected, then the weight reduction makes the updates $w_{e'} \leftarrow w_{e'} - w_e$ for any edge $e'$ such that $e' \cap e \neq \emptyset$. In contrast to the minimum vertex cover algorithm, weights in the graph can be reduced to negative weights.

THEOREM 5.1 (PAZ-SCHWARTZMAN [37]). *The above algorithm returns a matching which is at least half the optimum value.*

### 5.2 Randomized local ratio

As in Section 2.1, we apply our randomized local ratio technique to make the algorithm above amenable to parallelization. For intuition, consider a fixed a vertex $v$ and suppose we sample approximately $n^\mu$ of its edges uniformly at random. If $e$ is the heaviest sampled edge then there are only about $d(v)/n^\mu$ edges incident to $v$ that are heavier than $e$. Hence, in the local ratio algorithm, if we choose $e$ as the edge to reduce then this effectively decreases the degree of $v$ by a factor of $n^{-\mu}$.

The following claim follows by a simple Chernoff bound.

**Algorithm 4** 2-approximation for maximum weight matching. Blue lines are centralized.

1: **procedure** ApproxMaxMatching($G = (V, E)$)
2: $E_1 \leftarrow E$, $d_1(v) \leftarrow d(v)$, $i \leftarrow 1$
3: $S \leftarrow \emptyset$ ▷ Initialize an empty stack.
4: **while** $E_i \neq \emptyset$ **do**
5: **for** each vertex $v \in V$ **do**
6: **if** $|E_i| < 4\eta$ **then**
7: Let $E'_v$ be all edges in $E_i$ incident to $v$
8: **else**
9: Construct $E'_v \subseteq E_i \cap \delta(v)$ by sampling i.i.d. with probability $p = \min\left\{\frac{\eta}{|E_i|}, 1\right\}$
10: **if** $\sum_v |E'_v| > 8\eta$ **then**
11: **Fail**
12: **for** each vertex $v \in V$ **do**
13: Let $e \in E'_v$ be the heaviest edge and apply weight reduction to $e$
14: Push $e$ onto the stack $S$
15: Let $E_{i+1}$ be the subset of $E_i$ with positive weights
16: ▷: Let $d_{i+1}(v)$ denote $|\{e \in E_{i+1} : v \in e\}|$
17: $i \leftarrow i + 1$
18: Unwind $S$, adding edges greedily to the matching $M$
19: **return** $M$

CLAIM 5.2. *For* $i \geq 1$ *and conditioned on iteration* $i-1$ *not failing, iteration* $i$ *fails with probability at most* $\exp(-\eta)$.

LEMMA 5.3. *Suppose* $\eta = n^{1+\mu}$ *for some constant* $\mu > 0$ *and* $|E| = n^{1+c}$ *for some* $c > \mu$. *Then, with probability at least* $1 - (n+1)\cdot\exp(-n^\mu)$:

- *the first iteration does not fail; and*
- $d_2(v) \leq n^c$ *for all* $v \in V$, *where* $d_2$ *is as defined in Line 16 of Algorithm 4.*

PROOF. Let $k_v$ be the number of edges incident to $v$ with positive weight when we reach $v$ in the for loop in Line 13. If $k_v \leq n^c$ then we are done so suppose $k_v > n^c$. The probability that we do not sample any of the heaviest $n^c$ edges that are currently incident to $v$ is at most $\left(1 - \frac{n^{1+\mu}}{|E|}\right)^{n^c} \leq \exp\left(-\frac{n^{1+\mu+c}}{|E|}\right) \leq \exp(-n^\mu)$. Combining with Claim 5.2 and taking a union bound completes the proof. □

In the subsequent analysis, we will assume that $\mu$ is a positive constant. (Actually, it suffices to take $\mu = \omega(\log\log n/\log n)$.)

LEMMA 5.4. *Suppose* $\eta = n^{1+\mu}$ *for any constant* $\mu > 0$. *Let* $\Delta_i = \max_v d_i(v)$. *For* $i > 2$ *and conditioning on the past* $i-1$ *iterations not failing, with probability at least* $1 - (n+1)\cdot\exp(-n^{\mu/2})$:

- *iteration* $i$ *does not fail; and*
- $\Delta_{i+1} \leq \Delta_i/n^{\mu/4}$.

PROOF. Let $k_v$ be the number of edges incident to $v$ with positive weight when we reach $v$ in the for loop in Line 13. If $k_v \leq \Delta_i/n^{\mu/4}$ then we are done so suppose $k_v > \Delta_i/n^{\mu/4}$. The probability that we do not sample any of the heaviest $k_v/n^{\mu/4}$ edges that are currently incident to $v$ is at most $\left(1 - \frac{n^{1+\mu}}{|E|}\right)^{k_v/n^{\mu/4}} \leq \exp\left(-\frac{n^{1+\mu/2}\Delta_i}{|E|}\right) \leq \exp(-n^{\mu/2})$. Hence, we have $d_{i+1}(v) \leq k_v/n^{\mu/4} \leq d_i(v)/n^{\mu/4}$ with probability at least $1-\exp(-n^{\mu/2}) = 1-\exp(-\omega(\log n))$. Combining with Claim 5.2 and taking a union bound completes the proof. □

THEOREM 5.5. *Suppose $\eta = O(n^{1+\mu})$ for any constant $\mu > 0$. With probability $1 - O(cn/\mu)\exp(-n^{\mu})$, Algorithm 4 terminates in $O(c/\mu)$ iterations and returns a 2-approximate maximum matching.*

PROOF. By Lemma 5.3, the first iteration does not fail and $d_2(v) \leq n^c$ for all $v \in V$. By Lemma 5.4, after at most $O(c/\mu)$ iterations, the algorithm has not failed and the total number of edges with positive weight remaining is at most $8n^{1+\mu}$. At this point, the algorithm completes its last iteration of weight reduction then unwinds the stack and returns a matching. The correctness of the algorithm follows from Theorem 5.1. □

By slightly modifying the analysis, we can also handle the case where $\mu = 0$. In the full version of the paper, we show that it is not difficult to adapt the algorithm to the MapReduce model. This gives the following theorem.

THEOREM 5.6. *There is a MapReduce algorithm that computes a 2-approximation to the maximum weight matching using $O(n^{1+\mu})$ space per machine and $O(c/\mu)$ rounds (when $\mu = \omega(\log\log n/\log n)$) or $O(\log n)$ rounds (when $\mu = 0$).*

## 6 Vertex and edge colouring

In this section, we show how to colour a graph with maximum degree $\Delta$ using $(1 + o(1))\Delta$ colours in a constant number of rounds. As is the case with MIS, $(\Delta + 1)$-vertex colouring is one of the most fundamental problems of distributed computing. In the CREW PRAM model, both MIS and $(\Delta + 1)$-vertex colouring have algorithms that can be easily translated to $O(\log n)$-round algorithms in the MapReduce model. Luby's randomized algorithms for both MIS [31] and $(\Delta + 1)$-vertex colouring [32] have clean MapReduce implementations by using one machine per processor in the CREW PRAM algorithm. Within the CREW PRAM and LOCAL model, both MIS and $(\Delta + 1)$-vertex colouring have well established lower bounds. However, we are unaware of non-trivial (i.e. non-constant) lower bounds on round complexity in the MapReduce model.

Although our algorithm does not use the randomized local ratio or the hungry-greedy paradigm developed in the previous sections, we feel that it is of independent interest as it is the first constant round algorithm for $\Delta + o(\Delta)$-vertex colouring within the MapReduce model that we are aware of.

Recall that the number of edges is $n^{1+c}$, so $\Delta \geq n^c$ since the maximum degree is at least the average degree. Our algorithm is very simple; first we randomly partition the vertex set into $\kappa := n^{(c-\mu)/2}$ groups. Within each group, the maximum degree is $(1 + o(1))\Delta/\kappa$ with high probability, so $(1 + o(1))\Delta/\kappa + 1$ colours suffices to colour each group. The colour of a vertex is determined by the group that it is in and its colour within each group. Hence, this gives a colouring with $(1+o(1))\Delta$ colours. Furthermore, we show that the subgraph induced by each group has a small number of edges. As a corollary we get a MapReduce algorithm for $(1 + o(1))\Delta$-colouring.

LEMMA 6.1. *For all $\mu > 0$ and $\kappa = n^{(c-\mu)/2}$ then we have $\Delta_i \leq (1 + n^{-\mu/2}\sqrt{6\ln n})\Delta/\kappa$ for all $i$ with probability at least $1 - 1/n$.*

**Algorithm 5** $(1 + o(1))\Delta$-vertex colouring

```
procedure VertexColouring(Graph G = (V, E))
    Randomly partition V into κ groups, V_1, ..., V_κ
    Define E_i = E[V_i] and G_i = (V_i, E_i)
    if ∃i such that |E_i| > 13n^{1+μ} then
        Fail
    for every vertex v in parallel do
        if v ∈ V_i then send N(v) ∩ V_i to central machine i
    for every central machine i in parallel do
        Let Δ_i be max degree of G_i
        Colour G_i using the standard (Δ_i + 1)-vertex colouring algorithm
        for every v ∈ V_i do
            Let c_i(v) be colour of v ∈ V_i in this colouring
            Output (i, c_i(v)) as colour for v.
```

PROOF. For a single vertex $v$ of degree $d$, the probability that $v$ has degree greater than $(1 + \varepsilon)\Delta/\kappa$ (in the subgraph induced by its group) is at most $\exp\left(-\varepsilon^2 \frac{\Delta}{3\kappa}\right)$ by a standard Chernoff bound. Since $\Delta/\kappa \geq n^{c/2+\mu/2} \geq n^{\mu}$, we may take $\varepsilon = n^{-\mu/2}\sqrt{6\ln n}$ in which case the probability that a vertex $v$ has degree greater than $(1 + \varepsilon)\Delta/\kappa$ is at most $1/n^2$. Taking a union bound then yields the lemma. □

COROLLARY 6.2. *Algorithm 5 returns a $\left(1 + n^{-\mu/2}\sqrt{6\ln n} + n^{-\mu}\right)\Delta$-colouring of $G$ with high probability.*

For the next lemma, we will need the following theorem.

THEOREM 6.3 (HAJNAL-SZEMERÉDI). *Every graph with $n$ vertices and maximum degree bounded by $k - 1$ can be coloured using $k$ colours so that each colour class has at least $\lfloor n/k \rfloor \geq n/(2k)$ vertices.*

LEMMA 6.4. *We have $|E_i| \leq 13n^{1+\mu}$ with probability at least $1 - n^2 \cdot \exp(-n^{\mu})$.*

PROOF. By the Hajnal-Szemerédi Theorem (Theorem 6.3) applied to the line graph of $G$, we may partition the edges into $2\Delta$ sets $F_1, \ldots, F_{2\Delta}$ such that the following holds for all $j \in [2\Delta]$:

- $|F_j| \geq n^{1+c}/(4\Delta)$; and
- if $e, e' \in F_j$ and $e \neq e'$ then $e \cap e' = \emptyset$.

For analysis, fix $E_i$ and an edge class $F_j$. For each $e \in F_j$, let $X_{j,e}$ be the indicator random variable which is 1 if edge $e$ ends up in $E_i$. Then $\mathbb{E}\sum_{e\in F_j} X_{j,e} = |F_j|/\kappa^2$. Since any distinct $e, e' \in F_j$ do not share a common vertex, it follows that $\{X_{j,e}\}_{e\in F_j}$ are mutually independent random variables. Therefore, we may apply a Chernoff bound to get

$$\Pr\left[\sum_{e\in F_j} X_{j,e} > 13|F_j|/\kappa^2\right] \leq \exp\left(-12\frac{|F_j|}{3\kappa^2}\right)$$
$$\leq \exp\left(-\frac{n^{1+c}}{\Delta\kappa^2}\right) \leq \exp\left(-\frac{n^c}{\kappa^2}\right) = \exp\left(-n^{\mu}\right).$$

Taking a union bound over all $i$ and $j$ gives the claim. □

THEOREM 6.5. *If $\mu = \omega(\log\log n/\log n)$ and the memory on each machine is $O(n^{1+\mu})$ then there is a MapReduce algorithm for $(1 + o(1))\Delta$-colouring which succeeds with high probability.*

REMARK 6.6. *$(1 + o(1))\Delta$-edge colouring can be achieved with almost the same algorithm, partitioning the edges into groups instead of vertices and colouring the groups with the algorithm of Misra and Gries [36].*

THEOREM 6.7. *There are constant-round MapReduce algorithms for $(1 + o(1))\Delta$-vertex colouring and $(1 + o(1))\Delta$-edge colouring that succeed w.h.p.*

## References


[1] Kook Jin Ahn and Sudipto Guha. 2015. Access to Data and Number of Iterations: Dual Primal Algorithms for Maximum Matching under Resource Constraints. In *Proceedings of the 27th ACM symposium on Parallelism in Algorithms and Architectures (SPAA)*. 202–211.

[2] Sepehr Assadi. 2017. Simple Round Compression for Parallel Vertex Cover. *arXiv preprint arXiv:1709.04599* (2017).

[3] Sepehr Assadi, MohammadHossein Bateni, Aaron Bernstein, Vahab Mirrokni, and Cliff Stein. 2017. Coresets Meet EDCS: Algorithms for Matching and Vertex Cover on Massive Graphs. *arXiv preprint arXiv:1711.03076* (2017).

[4] Sepehr Assadi and Sanjeev Khanna. 2017. Randomized Composable Coresets for Matching and Vertex Cover. In *ACM Symposium on Parallelism in Algorithms and Architectures (SPAA)*.

[5] Maria-Florina Balcan, Steven Ehrlich, and Yingyu Liang. 2013. Distributed $k$-means and $k$-median clustering on general communication topologies. In *Advances in Neural Information Processing Systems (NIPS)*. 1995–2003.

[6] Reuven Bar-Yehuda, Keren Bendel, Ari Freund, and Dror Rawitz. 2004. Local ratio: A unified framework for approximation algorithms in memoriam: Shimon Even 1935-2004. *ACM Comput. Surv.* 36, 4 (2004), 422–463. https://doi.org/10.1145/1041680.1041683

[7] Reuven Bar-Yehuda and Shimon Even. 1985. A Local-Ratio Theorem for Approximating the Weighted Vertex Cover Problem. *Annals of Discrete Mathematics* 25 (1985), 27–45. https://doi.org/10.1016/S0304-0208(08)73101-3

[8] Leonid Barenboim and Michael Elkin. 2017. *Distributed Graph Coloring.* Morgan & Claypool. Draft manuscript.

[9] Paul Beame, Paraschos Koutris, and Dan Suciu. 2013. Communication Steps for Parallel Query Processing. In *Proceedings of the 32Nd ACM SIGMOD-SIGACT-SIGAI Symposium on Principles of Database Systems (PODS '13)*. ACM, New York, NY, USA, 273–284. https://doi.org/10.1145/2463664.2465224

[10] Bonnie Berger, John Rompel, and Peter W. Shor. 1994. Efficient NC algorithms for set cover with applications to learning and geometry. *J. Comput. System Sci.* 49, 3 (1994), 454 – 477. https://doi.org/10.1016/S0022-0000(05)80068-6 30th IEEE Conference on Foundations of Computer Science.

[11] Guy E. Blelloch, Richard Peng, and Kanat Tangwongsan. 2011. Linear-work Greedy Parallel Approximate Set Cover and Variants. In *Proceedings of the Twenty-third Annual ACM Symposium on Parallelism in Algorithms and Architectures (SPAA '11)*. ACM, New York, NY, USA, 23–32. https://doi.org/10.1145/1989493.1989497

[12] Vasek Chvatal. 1979. A greedy heuristic for the set covering problem. *Mathematics of Operations Research* 4, 3 (Aug. 1979), 233–235.

[13] Stephen A. Cook. 1983. An overview of computational complexity. *Commun. ACM* 26, 6 (June 1983), 400–408.

[14] Michael Crouch and Daniel S. Stubbs. 2014. Improved Streaming Algorithms for Weighted Matching, via Unweighted Matching. In *International Workshop on Approximation Algorithms for Combinatorial Optimization Problems (APPROX)*. 96–104. https://doi.org/10.4230/LIPIcs.APPROX-RANDOM.2014.96

[15] Artur Czumaj, Jakub Łącki, Aleksander Mądry, Slobodan Mitrović, Krzysztof Onak, and Piotr Sankowski. 2017. Round Compression for Parallel Matching Algorithms. (2017). http://arxiv.org/abs/1707.03478

[16] Rafael da Ponte Barbosa, Alina Ene, Huy L. Nguyen, and Justin Ward. 2016. A New Framework for Distributed Submodular Maximization. In *Proceedings of the IEEE 57th Annual Symposium on Foundations of Computer Science.*

[17] Laxman Dhulipala, Guy Blelloch, and Julian Shun. 2017. Julienne: A Framework for Parallel Graph Algorithms Using Work-efficient Bucketing. In *Proceedings of the 29th ACM Symposium on Parallelism in Algorithms and Architectures (SPAA '17)*. ACM, New York, NY, USA, 293–304. https://doi.org/10.1145/3087556.3087580

[18] Mohsen Ghaffari. 2017. Space-Optimal Semi-Streaming for $(2 + \epsilon)$-Approximate Matching. (2017). http://arxiv.org/abs/1701.03730

[19] Michael T. Goodrich. 2010. Simulating Parallel Algorithms in the MapReduce Framework with Applications to Parallel Computational Geometry. (2010). http://arxiv.org/abs/1004.4708

[20] Michael T. Goodrich, Nodari Sitchinava, and Qin Zhang. 2011. Sorting, Searching, and Simulation in the MapReduce Framework. In *22nd International Symposium on Algorithms and Computation (ISAAC).*

[21] Elena Grigorescu, Morteza Monemizadeh, and Samson Zhou. 2016. Streaming Weighted Matchings: Optimal Meets Greedy. (2016). http://arxiv.org/abs/1608.01487

[22] Sungjin Im, Benjamin Moseley, and Xiaorui Sun. 2017. Efficient Massively Parallel Methods for Dynamic Programming. In *ACM Symposium on Theory of Computing (STOC).*

[23] Piotr Indyk, Sepideh Mahabadi, Mohammad Mahdian, and Vahab S. Mirrokni. 2014. Composable Core-sets for Diversity and Coverage Maximization. In *Symposium on Principles of Database Systems (PODS).*

[24] U. Kang, Charalampos E. Tsourakakis, Ana Paula Appel, Christos Faloutsos, and Jure Leskovec. 2011. HADI: Mining Radii of Large Graphs. *TKDD* 5, 2 (2011), 8:1–8:24. https://doi.org/10.1145/1921632.1921634

[25] Howard J. Karloff, Siddharth Suri, and Sergei Vassilvitskii. 2010. A Model of Computation for MapReduce. In *Proceedings of the Twenty-First Annual ACM-SIAM Symposium on Discrete Algorithms (SODA)*. 938–948. https://doi.org/10.1137/1.9781611973075.76

[26] Ravi Kumar, Benjamin Moseley, Sergei Vassilvitskii, and Andrea Vattani. 2015. Fast Greedy Algorithms in MapReduce and Streaming. *TOPC* 2, 3 (2015), 14:1–14:22. https://doi.org/10.1145/2809814

[27] Silvio Lattanzi, Benjamin Moseley, Siddharth Suri, and Sergei Vassilvitskii. 2011. Filtering: a method for solving graph problems in MapReduce. In *Proceedings of the 23rd Annual ACM Symposium on Parallelism in Algorithms and Architectures (SPAA)*. 85–94. https://doi.org/10.1145/1989493.1989505

[28] Jure Leskovec, Jon M. Kleinberg, and Christos Faloutsos. 2005. Graphs over time: densification laws, shrinking diameters and possible explanations. In *Proceedings of the Eleventh ACM SIGKDD International Conference on Knowledge Discovery and Data Mining, Chicago, Illinois, USA, August 21-24, 2005.* 177–187. https://doi.org/10.1145/1081870.1081893

[29] Jure Leskovec, Anand Rajaraman, and Jeff Ullman. 2014. *Mining of Massive Datasets.* Cambridge University Press.

[30] Zvi Lotker, Boaz Patt-Shamir, and Seth Pettie. 2015. Improved Distributed Approximate Matching. *J. ACM* 62, 5 (2015), 38:1–38:17. https://doi.org/10.1145/2786753

[31] Michael Luby. 1986. A Simple Parallel Algorithm for the Maximal Independent Set Problem. *SIAM J. Comput.* 15, 4 (1986), 1036–1053. https://doi.org/10.1137/0215074

[32] Michael Luby. 1993. Removing Randomness in Parallel Computation without a Processor Penalty. *J. Comput. Syst. Sci.* 47, 2 (1993), 250–286. https://doi.org/10.1016/0022-0000(93)90033-S

[33] Vahab S. Mirrokni and Morteza Zadimoghaddam. 2015. Randomized Composable Core-sets for Distributed Submodular Maximization. In *ACM Symposium on Theory of Computing (STOC)*. 153–162.

[34] Baharan Mirzasoleiman, Amin Karbasi, Ashwinkumar Badanidiyuru, and Andreas Krause. 2015. Distributed Submodular Cover: Succinctly Summarizing Massive Data. In *Neural Information Processing Systems (NIPS).*

[35] Baharan Mirzasoleiman, Morteza Zadimoghaddam, and Andreas Krause. 2016. Fast Distributed Submodular Cover: Public-Private Data Summarization. In *Neural Information Processing Systems (NIPS).*

[36] J. Misra and David Gries. 1992. A Constructive Proof of Vizing's Theorem. *Inf. Process. Lett.* 41, 3 (March 1992), 131–133. https://doi.org/10.1016/0020-0190(92)90041-S

[37] Ami Paz and Gregory Schwartzman. 2017. A $(2+\epsilon)$-Approximation for Maximum Weight Matching in the Semi-Streaming Model. In *Proceedings of the Twenty-Eighth Annual ACM-SIAM Symposium on Discrete Algorithms (SODA)*. 2153–2161. https://doi.org/10.1137/1.9781611974782.140

[38] Sridhar Rajagopalan and Vijay V. Vazirani. 1998. Primal-Dual RNC Approximation Algorithms for Set Cover and Covering Integer Programs. *SIAM J. Comput.* 28, 2 (1998), 525–540. https://doi.org/10.1137/S0097539793260763 arXiv:https://doi.org/10.1137/S0097539793260763

[39] Stergios Stergiou and Kostas Tsioutsiouliklis. 2015. Set Cover at Web Scale. In *ACM SIGKDD International Conference on Knowledge Discovery and Data Mining (KDD).*

[40] Leslie G. Valiant. 1982. Parallel Computation. In *Proceedings of the 7th IBM Symposium on Mathematical Foundations of Computer Science.*

[41] Leslie G. Valiant. 1990. A bridging model for parallel computation. *Commun. ACM* 33, 8 (Aug. 1990), 103–111.

[42] Vijay V. Vazirani. 2001. *Approximation Algorithms.* Springer-Verlag New York, Inc., New York, NY, USA.

[43] Laurence A. Wolsey. 1982. An analysis of the greedy algorithm for the submodular set covering problem. *Combinatorica* 2, 4 (1982), 385–393.

# Keynote Talk: The Resurgence of Software Performance Engineering

Charles E. Leiserson
MIT Computer Science and Artificial Intelligence Laboratory
Cambridge, MA, USA
cel@mit.edu

## ABSTRACT

Today, most application developers write code without much regard for how quickly it will run. Moreover, once the code is written, it is rare for it to be reengineered to run faster. But two technology trends of historic proportions are instigating a resurgence in software performance engineering, the art of making code run fast. The first is the emergence of cloud computing, where the economics of renting computation, as opposed to buying it, heightens the utility of application speed. The second is the end of Moore's Law, the 50-year technology trend which has, until recently, relentlessly doubled the number of transistors on a semiconductor chip every two years. The end of Moore's Law will cause industry to look beyond semiconductor manufacturers for computing performance. As a result of these two trends, application programmers will increasingly find themselves turning to software performance engineering in order to develop innovative products and applications.

## CCS CONCEPTS

• **General and reference → Surveys and overviews;**

## KEYWORDS

Cloud computing; Moore's Law; software performance engineering

**ACM Reference Format:**

Charles E. Leiserson. 2018. Keynote Talk: The Resurgence of Software Performance Engineering. In *SPAA '18: 30th ACM Symposium on Parallelism in Algorithms and Architectures, July 16–18, 2018, Vienna, Austria.* ACM, New York, NY, USA, 1 page. https://doi.org/10.1145/3210377.3210378

## BIOGRAPHY

Charles E. Leiserson received his B.S. from Yale University in 1975 and his Ph.D. from Carnegie Mellon University in 1981. He joined the faculty of MIT in 1981, where he is now the Edwin Sibley Webster Professor in MIT's Department of Electrical Engineering and Computer Science. He is Associate Director and Chief Operating Officer of the MIT Computer Science and Artificial Intelligence Laboratory, the largest on-campus laboratory at MIT, where he also leads the Supertech research group. He is a Margaret MacVicar Faculty Fellow, the highest recognition at MIT for undergraduate teaching. He is a Fellow of four professional societies — AAAS, ACM, IEEE, and SIAM — and he is a member of the National Academy of Engineering. He has received many Best Paper awards at prestigious conferences, as well as the ACM-IEEE Computer Society Ken Kennedy Award, the IEEE Computer Society Taylor L. Booth Education Award, ACM Paris Kanellakis Theory and Practice Award, and the ACM and Hertz Foundation Doctoral Dissertation Awards.

Professor Leiserson's current research centers on software performance engineering: making computer programs run fast. His contributions include the Cilk multithreaded programming technology, which is available in many compilers today. He founded Cilk Arts, Inc., an MIT spinoff which was acquired by Intel Corporation. On leave from MIT as Director of System Architecture at Akamai Technologies, he led the engineering team that developed Akamai's worldwide content-distribution network comprising tens of thousands of servers. He designed and led the implementation of the network architecture for Thinking Machine Corporation's Connection Machine CM-5, the world's most powerful supercomputer in the early 1990's, which incorporated the "universal" fat-tree interconnection network he conceived at MIT. He led the development of several Cilk-based parallel chess-playing programs, including ★Socrates and Cilkchess, winning numerous prizes in international competition. He coauthored the first paper on systolic architectures, invented the retiming method of digital-circuit optimization, and introduced the notion of cache-oblivious algorithms. He is well known as coauthor of *Introduction to Algorithms* (MIT Press), the leading textbook on computer algorithms, which has sold almost 800,000 copies and is one of the most cited publications in computer science. His annual workshop on *Leadership Skills for Engineering and Science Faculty* has educated hundreds of faculty at MIT and around the world in the human issues involved in leading technical teams in academia. Professor Leiserson has supervised over two dozen Ph.D. students and more than 60 Master's and Bachelor's students.

This research was supported in part by NSF Grants 1314547 and 1533644.


*SPAA '18, July 16–18, 2018, Vienna, Austria*

ACM ISBN 978-1-4503-5799-9/18/07.
https://doi.org/10.1145/3210377.3210378

# A 3D Parallel Algorithm for QR Decomposition

Grey Ballard
Wake Forest University
Winston Salem, NC, USA
ballard@wfu.edu

James Demmel
University of California
Berkeley, CA, USA
demmel@berkeley.edu

Laura Grigori
INRIA Paris-Rocquencourt
Paris, France
laura.grigori@inria.fr

Mathias Jacquelin
Lawrence Berkeley Natl. Lab.
Berkeley, CA, USA
mjacquelin@lbl.gov

Nicholas Knight
New York University
New York, NY, USA
nknight@nyu.edu

## ABSTRACT

Interprocessor communication often dominates the runtime of large matrix computations. We present a parallel algorithm for computing QR decompositions whose bandwidth cost (communication volume) can be decreased at the cost of increasing its latency cost (number of messages). By varying a parameter to navigate the bandwidth/latency tradeoff, we can tune this algorithm for machines with different communication costs.

## CCS CONCEPTS

• **Theory of computation → Massively parallel algorithms**;

## KEYWORDS

communication-avoiding algorithms; bandwidth-latency tradeoffs; communication-memory tradeoffs

**ACM Reference Format:**

Grey Ballard, James Demmel, Laura Grigori, Mathias Jacquelin, and Nicholas Knight. 2018. A 3D Parallel Algorithm for QR Decomposition. In *SPAA '18: 30th ACM Symposium on Parallelism in Algorithms and Architectures, July 16–18, 2018, Vienna, Austria.* ACM, New York, NY, USA, 11 pages. https://doi.org/10.1145/3210377.3210415

## 1 INTRODUCTION

A common task in numerical linear algebra, especially when solving least-squares and eigenvalue problems, is *QR-decomposing* a matrix into a unitary Q-factor times an upper trapezoidal R-factor. We present a QR decomposition algorithm, 3D-CAQR-EG, whose bandwidth and latency costs trade off.

We model the cost of a parallel algorithm in terms of the number of arithmetic operations, the number of words moved between processors, and the number of messages in which these words are moved. These three quantities, measured along critical paths in a schedule, characterize the algorithm's arithmetic cost, bandwidth cost, and latency cost, respectively.



*SPAA '18, July 16–18, 2018, Vienna, Austria*

ACM ISBN 978-1-4503-5799-9/18/07...$15.00
https://doi.org/10.1145/3210377.3210415

THEOREM 1. *An $m \times n$ matrix, $m \geq n$, can be QR-decomposed on $P$ processors with these asymptotic costs:*

| # operations | # words | # messages |
|---|---|---|
| $mn^2/P$ | $n^2/(nP/m)^\delta$ | $(nP/m)^\delta (\log P)^2$ |

(1)

*where $\delta$ can be chosen from* $[1/2,\ 2/3]$, *assuming*

$$P \,/\, (\log P)^4 = \Omega(m \,/\, n), \quad \text{and}$$
$$P \cdot (\log P)^2 = O\left(m^{\frac{\delta}{1+\delta}} \cdot n^{\frac{1-\delta}{1+\delta}}\right). \tag{2}$$

This arithmetic cost is optimal [10], assuming conventional algorithms. For the smallest $\delta = 1/2$, the latency cost is optimal, and for the largest $\delta = 2/3$, the bandwidth cost is optimal [2]. (Optimality is precisely defined in References [2, 10].) However, these bandwidth and latency lower bounds are not attained simultaneously: the bandwidth-latency product is $O(n^2(\log P)^2)$. Similar tradeoffs have been observed in LU-decomposition [22], (Householder) tridiagonalization [20], and triangular substitution [27]. Motivated by lower bounds for Cholesky decomposition and triangular substitution [21], we conjecture that the bandwidth-latency product is $\Omega(n^2)$ for QR-decomposition algorithms in our framework, meaning the tradeoff is inevitable.

Our main contribution is the presentation and analysis of 3D-CAQR-EG, which extends Elmroth-Gustavson's recursive algorithm [11] to the distributed-memory setting and uses communication-efficient subroutines. The inductive cases feature *3D matrix multiplication* (3DMM) [1], which incurs a smaller bandwidth cost than conventional (2D) approaches. The base cases feature a new variant of *communication-avoiding QR* (CAQR) [10]. CAQR incurs a smaller latency cost than conventional (Householder) QR. Our variant further improves the bandwidth cost. A similar approach is known for LU-decomposition [22]. The name '3D-CAQR-EG' reflects this lineage.

For sufficiently tall-and-skinny matrices, it's best to directly call 3D-CAQR-EG's base-case subroutine, 1D-CAQR-EG.

THEOREM 2. *An $m \times n$ matrix can be QR-decomposed on $P \geq m/n \geq 1$ processors with these asymptotic costs:*

| # operations | # words | # messages |
|---|---|---|
| $mn^2/P$ | $n^2$ | $(\log P)^2$ |

(3)

*assuming* $P \cdot (\log P)^2 = O(n^2)$.

The rest of this work is organized as follows. We start by summarizing relevant mathematical background on computing QR decompositions (Section 2). We then introduce our parallel machine model, formalizing how we quantify the costs of communication and computation (Section 3). Next we review the communication-efficient subroutines mentioned above, 3DMM (Section 4) and CAQR (Section 5). With this background in place, we present and analyze the new algorithms, 1D-CAQR-EG (Section 6) and 3D-CAQR-EG (Section 7), proving Theorems 1 and 2, in reverse order. We conclude by discussing limitations and extensions and comparing with related work (Section 8).

## 2 QR DECOMPOSITION

Many applications demand the QR-decomposition of large, dense matrices; let's highlight three. First, QR-decompositions are widely used in computational statistics, e.g., performing regressions and principal-component analyses; Reference [9] features a c. 80M×1K image problem. Second, they are widely used within iterative solvers for orthogonalization; Reference [28] solves a c. 1M×100 problem from GMRES. Third, they are the dominant subroutine in (stable) iterative schemes for matrix functions; Reference [15] includes a 40K×20K problem. In Section 2 we summarize the relevant background concerning computing QR decompositions.

After formalizing the problem in Section 2.1, we present a recursive template algorithm, called REC-QR (Algorithm 1 in Section 2.2), which includes many well-known algorithms as special cases. We then specialize REC-QR to utilize compact matrix representations (Section 2.3) and a simpler recursive splitting strategy (Section 2.4). The result of these specializations, called QR-EG (Algorithm 2), serves as a template for our two new algorithms, 1D-CAQR-EG and 3D-CAQR-EG.

### 2.1 QR Preliminaries

A *QR decomposition* of a matrix $\mathbf{A}$ is a matrix pair $(\mathbf{Q}, \mathbf{R})$ such that $\mathbf{A} = \mathbf{QR}$, the *Q-factor* $\mathbf{Q}$ is unitary, meaning $\mathbf{Q}^H\mathbf{Q} = \mathbf{Q}\mathbf{Q}^H = \mathbf{I}$, and the *R-factor* $\mathbf{R}$ is upper trapezoidal, meaning all entries below its main diagonal equal zero. To specialize for real-valued $\mathbf{A}$, simply substitute $(\cdot)^T$ for $(\cdot)^H$ and 'orthogonal' for 'unitary'.

We will always assume that $\mathbf{A}$ has at least as many rows as columns. (This implies that $\mathbf{R}$ has the same dimensions as $\mathbf{A}$ and is upper triangular.) When $\mathbf{A}$ has more columns than rows, we can obtain a QR decomposition by splitting $\mathbf{A} = \begin{bmatrix}\mathbf{A}_1 & \mathbf{A}_2\end{bmatrix}$ with square $\mathbf{A}_1$, decomposing $\mathbf{A}_1 = \mathbf{QR}_1$, and computing $\mathbf{R} = \begin{bmatrix}\mathbf{R}_1 & \mathbf{Q}^H\mathbf{A}_2\end{bmatrix}$.

### 2.2 Recursive QR Decomposition

We consider QR decomposition algorithms based on REC-QR (Algorithm 1), which split $\mathbf{A}$ vertically (Line 4), QR-decompose the left panel (Line 5), update the right panel (Line 6), QR-decompose the lower part of the (updated) right panel (Line 7), and then assemble a QR decomposition from the smaller ones (Lines 8 and 9).

**Algorithm 1** $(\mathbf{Q}, \mathbf{R})$ = REC-QR $(\mathbf{A})$

1: **if** BASE-CONDITION **then**
2: $(\mathbf{Q}, \mathbf{R})$ = BASE-QR $(\mathbf{A})$.
3: **else**
4: SPLIT $\mathbf{A} = \begin{bmatrix}\mathbf{A}_{11} & \mathbf{A}_{12}\\ \mathbf{A}_{21} & \mathbf{A}_{22}\end{bmatrix}$ with $\mathbf{A}_{11}$ square.
5: $(\mathbf{Q}_\mathrm{L}, \mathbf{R}_\mathrm{L})$ = REC-QR $\left(\begin{bmatrix}\mathbf{A}_{11}\\ \mathbf{A}_{21}\end{bmatrix}\right)$.
6: $\begin{bmatrix}\mathbf{B}_{12}\\ \mathbf{B}_{22}\end{bmatrix} = \mathbf{Q}_\mathrm{L}^H \cdot \begin{bmatrix}\mathbf{A}_{12}\\ \mathbf{A}_{22}\end{bmatrix}$.
7: $(\mathbf{Q}_\mathrm{R}, \mathbf{R}_\mathrm{R})$ = REC-QR $(\mathbf{B}_{22})$.
8: $\mathbf{Q} = \mathbf{Q}_\mathrm{L} \cdot \begin{bmatrix}\mathbf{I} & \mathbf{0}\\ \mathbf{0} & \mathbf{Q}_\mathrm{R}\end{bmatrix}$.
9: $\mathbf{R} = \begin{bmatrix}\mathbf{R}_\mathrm{L} & \begin{bmatrix}\mathbf{B}_{12}\\ \mathbf{R}_\mathrm{R}\end{bmatrix}\end{bmatrix}$.
10: **end if**

We call REC-QR a 'template' because it leaves several details unspecified. To instantiate this template and obtain an algorithm, we must pick a base-case condition (BASE-CONDITION, Line 1), a base-case QR-decomposition subroutine (BASE-QR, Line 2), and a splitting strategy (SPLIT, Line 4). Additionally, we must specify how the operations are scheduled and how the data are distributed.

### 2.3 Compact Representations

In practice, a QR decomposition $(\mathbf{Q}, \mathbf{R})$ of an $m \times n$ matrix ($m \geq n$) is typically not represented as a pair of explicit matrices. In Section 2.3 we specialize REC-QR to represent $\mathbf{Q}$ and $\mathbf{R}$ more compactly.

Since an R-factor is upper triangular, it is identifiable by just its superdiagonal entries. Subsequently, the symbol $\mathbf{R}$ may either denote (1) the actual R-factor, an $m \times n$ upper-triangular matrix; (2) the leading $n$ rows of the R-factor, an $n \times n$ upper-triangular matrix; or (3) the upper triangle of the R-factor, a data structure of size $n(n + 1)/2$. When presenting algorithms, we will prefer convention (2); to obtain an $n \times n$ upper-triangular $\mathbf{R}$ from REC-QR, we agree that BASE-QR (Line 2) returns such an $\mathbf{R}$, and we rewrite the R-factor assembly (Line 9) as

$$\mathbf{R} = \begin{bmatrix}\mathbf{R}_\mathrm{L} & \mathbf{B}_{12}\\ \mathbf{0} & \mathbf{R}_\mathrm{R}\end{bmatrix}.$$

Any unitary matrix $\mathbf{Q}$ can be written as $\mathbf{Q} = \mathbf{I} - \mathbf{VTV}^H$: the matrix pair $(\mathbf{V}, \mathbf{T})$ is called a *basis-kernel representation* [23] of $\mathbf{Q}$. If $\mathbf{Q}$ is the Q-factor of a QR decomposition of an $m \times n$ matrix ($m \geq n$), then there exists such a representation where the *basis* $\mathbf{V}$ is $m \times n$ and the *kernel* $\mathbf{T}$ is $n \times n$.

Modifying REC-QR for basis-kernel representations, Line 6 becomes

$$\begin{bmatrix}\mathbf{B}_{12}\\ \mathbf{B}_{22}\end{bmatrix} = \begin{bmatrix}\mathbf{A}_{12}\\ \mathbf{A}_{22}\end{bmatrix} - \mathbf{V}_\mathrm{L}\mathbf{T}_\mathrm{L}^H\mathbf{V}_\mathrm{L}^H \begin{bmatrix}\mathbf{A}_{12}\\ \mathbf{A}_{22}\end{bmatrix}, \quad (4)$$

and Line 8 becomes

$$\mathrm{V} = \begin{bmatrix} \mathrm{V_L} & \begin{bmatrix} 0 \\ \mathrm{V_R} \end{bmatrix} \end{bmatrix}$$
$$\mathrm{T} = \begin{bmatrix} \mathrm{T_L} & -\mathrm{T_L} \mathrm{V_L^H} \begin{bmatrix} 0 \\ \mathrm{V_R} \end{bmatrix} \mathrm{T_R} \\ 0 & \mathrm{T_R} \end{bmatrix}, \tag{5}$$

where $(\mathrm{V_L}, \mathrm{T_L})$ and $(\mathrm{V_R}, \mathrm{T_R})$ represent $\mathrm{Q_L}$ and $\mathrm{Q_R}$.

To simplify the presentation without affecting our asymptotic conclusions, we will not exploit the block-lower-trapezoidal and block-upper-triangular structures of the bases and kernels. With this understanding, it minimizes arithmetic to evaluate the quadruple matrix product in Equation (4) from right to left, and the quadruple product in Equation (5) from inside-out (two possibilities).

When $m$ is close to $n$, a general basis-kernel representation may require more storage than the explicit $(m \times m)$ Q-factor. The QR decomposition algorithms in (Sca)LAPACK use a variant [17] of *compact WY representation* [19], which we call *Householder representation* in this work. In Householder representation, V is unit lower trapezoidal and T is upper triangular. These properties enable an in-place implementation, where V's strict lower trapezoid and R's upper triangle overwrite A and where T need not be stored, since in this case

$$\mathrm{T} = \left(\mathrm{triu}(\mathrm{V}^H\mathrm{V}, -1) + \mathrm{diag}(\mathrm{diag}(\mathrm{V}^H\mathrm{V}))/2\right)^{-1},$$

using the MATLAB operations 'triu' and 'diag'.

Our algorithms will construct, store, and apply Q-factors in Householder representation. This choice is motivated by our practical goal of integration into the ScaLAPACK library [6]; from a theoretical standpoint, any basis-kernel representation (with $m \times n$ basis) would yield the same asymptotic costs.

## 2.4 Elmroth-Gustavson's Approach

The recursive framework of REC-QR is quite general. We will obtain our desired algorithmic costs by following an approach of Elmroth-Gustavson [11] (see LAPACK's `_geqrt3`), in which we split A vertically (roughly) in half, until the number of columns drops below a given threshold $b \geq 1$. The recursive calls define a binary tree whose $\lceil \log_2(n/b) \rceil$ levels are complete except possibly the last. (We always suppose $b \leq n$; when $b \geq n$, the tree has just one node.) We call this specialized template QR-EG (Algorithm 2); QR-EG utilizes the compact representations as explained in Section 2.3.

We mention that [11] actually proposes a hybrid of the stated approach and an iterative approach, switching between the two for a constant-factor improvement in the arithmetic cost. (It still fits in the REC-QR framework.) While our algorithms can also benefit from this optimization, we omit further discussion in the present work since it does not affect our asymptotic conclusions.

**Algorithm 2** (V, T, R) = QR-EG (A, $b$)

**if** $n \leq b$ **then**
  (V, T, R) = BASE-QR (A).
**else**
  SPLIT $\mathrm{A} = \begin{bmatrix} \mathrm{A_{11}} & \mathrm{A_{12}} \\ \mathrm{A_{21}} & \mathrm{A_{22}} \end{bmatrix}$ so $\mathrm{A_{11}}$ is $\lfloor n/2 \rfloor \times \lfloor n/2 \rfloor$.
  $(\mathrm{V_L}, \mathrm{T_L}, \mathrm{R_L}) = $ QR-EG $\left(\begin{bmatrix} \mathrm{A_{11}} \\ \mathrm{A_{21}} \end{bmatrix}, b\right)$.
  $\mathrm{M_1} = \mathrm{V_L^H} \cdot \begin{bmatrix} \mathrm{A_{12}} \\ \mathrm{A_{22}} \end{bmatrix}$.
  $\mathrm{M_2} = \mathrm{T_L^H} \cdot \mathrm{M_1}$.
  $\begin{bmatrix} \mathrm{B_{12}} \\ \mathrm{B_{22}} \end{bmatrix} = \begin{bmatrix} \mathrm{A_{12}} \\ \mathrm{A_{22}} \end{bmatrix} - \mathrm{V_L} \cdot \mathrm{M_2}$.
  $(\mathrm{V_R}, \mathrm{T_R}, \mathrm{R_R}) = $ QR-EG $(\mathrm{B_{22}}, b)$.
  $\mathrm{V} = \begin{bmatrix} \mathrm{V_L} & \begin{bmatrix} 0 \\ \mathrm{V_R} \end{bmatrix} \end{bmatrix}$.
  $\mathrm{M_3} = \mathrm{V_L^H} \cdot \begin{bmatrix} 0 \\ \mathrm{V_R} \end{bmatrix}$.
  $\mathrm{M_4} = \mathrm{M_3} \cdot \mathrm{T_R}$.
  $\mathrm{T} = \begin{bmatrix} \mathrm{T_L} & -\mathrm{T_L} \cdot \mathrm{M_4} \\ 0 & \mathrm{T_R} \end{bmatrix}$.
  $\mathrm{R} = \begin{bmatrix} \mathrm{R_L} & \mathrm{B_{12}} \\ 0 & \mathrm{R_R} \end{bmatrix}$.
**end if**

## 3 COMPUTATION MODEL

We model a parallel machine as a set of $P$ interconnected processors, each with unbounded local memory. Processors operate on local data and communicate with other processors by sending and receiving messages. A processor can perform at most one task (operation/send/receive) at a time. A (data) word means a complex number; operations are the usual field actions, plus complex conjugation and real square roots. Messages are point-to-point and asynchronous. Each operation takes time $\gamma$, while sending or receiving a message of $w$ words takes time $\alpha + w\beta$, $\alpha$ being the latency and $\beta$ the inverse of the bandwidth.

We model an execution as a DAG whose vertices are tasks and whose edges define $P$ paths, one for each processor's task sequence, plus an inter-path edge for each send/receive pair. Weighting vertices by their tasks' durations, we define runtime as the maximum weight of any path. Therefore, if every path includes at most $F$ operations and at most $S$ messages, containing at most $W$ words in total, the runtime is bounded,

$$\text{runtime} \leq \gamma \cdot F + \beta \cdot W + \alpha \cdot S.$$

When multiple processors send/receive messages simultaneously, it can be more efficient to split the messages into more messages of smaller sizes, to coalesce them into fewer, larger messages, or to route them through intermediate processors. These lower-level implementation details are often irrelevant to our asymptotic analyses, motivating us to express our algorithms' communication patterns abstractly, in terms of collectives.

In the rest of Section 3 we define the eight different collectives appearing in this work, collecting in Table 1 their costs.

| | # operations | # words | # messages |
|---|---|---|---|
| SCATTER | 0 | $(P-1)B$ | $\log P$ |
| GATHER | 0 | $(P-1)B$ | $\log P$ |
| BROADCAST | 0 | $\min(B\log P,\, B+P)$ | $\log P$ |
| REDUCE | $\min(B\log P,\, B+P)$ | $\min(B\log P,\, B+P)$ | $\log P$ |
| ALL-GATHER | 0 | $(P-1)B$ | $\log P$ |
| ALL-REDUCE | $\min(B\log P,\, B+P)$ | $\min(B\log P,\, B+P)$ | $\log P$ |
| ALL-TO-ALL | 0 | $\min(BP\log P,\, (B_*+P^2)\log P)$ | $\log P$ |
| REDUCE-SCATTER | $(P-1)B$ | $(P-1)B$ | $\log P$ |

**Table 1:** Asymptotic costs of the collectives defined in Section 3. $P$ is the number of processors involved, $B = \max_{p,q} B_{pq}$ is the largest block-size, and $B_* = \max\left(\max_q \sum_p B_{pq},\ \max_p \sum_q B_{pq}\right)$ is the maximum number of words any processor holds before/after. Any $P$ can be replaced by $|\{p,q : B_{pq} > 0\}|$ for a possibly smaller (valid) bound.

A general scenario, called an ALL-TO-ALL, is when every processor $p$ initially owns a block of data, containing $B_{pq}$ words, destined for every processor $q$, including itself. All other collectives we use can be interpreted as special cases of an ALL-TO-ALL. Four of these distinguish a 'root' processor $r$: SCATTER, where only $r$'s outgoing blocks are nonempty; GATHER, where only $r$'s incoming blocks are nonempty; BROADCAST, a SCATTER where $r$'s outgoing blocks are identical; and REDUCE, a GATHER where $r$'s incoming blocks have same size and are added entrywise. Four others, including ALL-TO-ALL, can be constructed from the first four: ALL-GATHER, $P$ GATHERS with same outgoing blocks but different roots; ALL-REDUCE, $P$ REDUCEs with same outgoing blocks but different roots; ALL-TO-ALL, $P$ GATHERS with different outgoing blocks and different roots; and REDUCE-SCATTER, $P$ REDUCEs with different outgoing blocks and different roots. (Since the three 'REDUCE' collectives perform arithmetic, they are technically not ALL-TO-ALLs.)

LEMMA 1. *There exist algorithms for the eight collectives satisfying the upper bounds in Table 1.*

PROOF. For all but ALL-TO-ALL we use a *binomial-tree* and possibly a *bidirectional-exchange algorithm*: see, e.g., [8, 24]. In particular, for (ALL-)GATHER and (REDUCE-)SCATTER we use binary tree algorithms, and for BROADCAST and (ALL-)REDUCE we use whichever of the two minimizes all three costs, asymptotically. For ALL-TO-ALL we use the *(radix-2) index algorithm* [7], possibly performed twice using the load-balancing approach of [13]. (For a more detailed proof, see [3, Appendix A].) □

Note that when the number of processors is not too large w.r.t. the block size, the bidirectional-exchange algorithm for BROADCAST, built from SCATTER+ALL-GATHER, is asymptotically cheaper than the corresponding binary tree algorithm in terms of bandwidth. Similarly, the bidirectional-exchange algorithm for (ALL-)REDUCE), built from REDUCE-SCATTER+(ALL-)GATHER, improves both arithmetic and bandwidth.

## 4 3D MATRIX MULTIPLICATION

The key to reducing 3D-CAQR-EG's bandwidth cost below that of previous approaches is *3D matrix multiplication* (3DMM) [1]. Here, *3D* refers to the parallelization of the operations and distribution of data over a three-dimensional (logical) processor grid. 1D-CAQR-EG will also exploit two special cases, 1DMM, performed on a one-dimensional grid, and MM, performed locally on one processor.

For concreteness, consider multiplying an $I \times K$ matrix $\mathbf{A}$ with a $K \times J$ matrix $\mathbf{B}$ to obtain an $I \times J$ matrix $\mathbf{C}$, via the usual (entrywise) formula:

$$\text{for all } (i,j) \in [I] \times [J], \quad \mathbf{C}_{ij} = \sum_{k \in [K]} \mathbf{A}_{ik}\mathbf{B}_{kj}. \tag{6}$$

We identify each of the $IJK$ (scalar) multiplications with a point $(i,j,k)$ in three-dimensional Euclidean space, so the set of multiplications defines a discrete $I \times J \times K$ brick. We point the reader to [5, 18] for further discussions of this geometric terminology.

LEMMA 2. *Suppose input matrices* $\mathbf{A}$ *and* $\mathbf{B}$ *are initially owned by processor* $p$, *and output matrix* $\mathbf{C}$ *is to be finally owned also by processor* $p$. $\mathbf{C} = \mathbf{A} \cdot \mathbf{B}$ *can be computed with runtime*

$$\gamma \cdot O(IJK). \tag{7}$$

PROOF. Directly evaluating the sums-of-products in Equation (6) takes $IJK$ multiplications and $IJ(K-1)$ additions; no communication is necessary. □

LEMMA 3. *Suppose* $I$, $J$, $K$, *and* $P$ *satisfy*

$$P = O\left(\frac{IJK}{\max(I,J,K)}\right) \quad \text{and} \quad P = O(\max(I,J,K)).$$

*If* $K = \max(I,J,K)$, *suppose that matrices* $\mathbf{A}^T$ *and* $\mathbf{B}$ *are initially distributed in matching row-wise layouts where each processor owns* $O(K/P)$ *rows, and that matrix* $\mathbf{C}$ *is to be finally owned by a single processor* $r$. *Alternatively, if* $I = \max(I,J,K)$, *suppose that matrices* $\mathbf{A}$ *and* $\mathbf{C}$ *are initially/finally distributed in matching row-wise layouts where each processor owns* $O(I/P)$ *rows, and that matrix* $\mathbf{B}$ *is initially owned by a single processor* $r$. $\mathbf{C} = \mathbf{A} \cdot \mathbf{B}$ *can be computed with runtime*

$$\gamma \cdot O\left(\frac{IJK}{P}\right) + \beta \cdot O\left(\frac{IJK}{\max(I,J,K)}\right) + \alpha \cdot O(\log P), \tag{8}$$

a

PROOF. In the first case, each processor performs a local MM and then all processors REDUCE to processor $r$. In the second case, processor $r$ BROADCASTS $\mathbf{B}$ to all processors and then each processor performs a local MM. The hypotheses guarantee that $P$ is not too large for these collectives can leverage the bidirectional-exchange algorithms. (For a more detailed proof, see [3, Appendix B].) □

The bound of Equation (8) also holds in a third case, when $J = \max(I, J, K)$ and the distributions are symmetric to the second case, but we will not need this result.

LEMMA 4. *Suppose $I$, $J$, $K$, and $P$ satisfy*

$$c \cdot \frac{IJK}{\min(I,J,K)^3} \le P \le IJK.$$

*There exists a data distribution of $\mathbf{A}$, $\mathbf{B}$, and $\mathbf{C}$ such that each processor initially owns at most $O((I+J)K/P)$ entries of $\mathbf{A}$ and $\mathbf{B}$, and finally at most $O(IJ/P)$ entries of $\mathbf{C}$, where $\mathbf{C} = \mathbf{A} \cdot \mathbf{B}$ can be computed with runtime*

$$\gamma \cdot O\left(\frac{IJK}{P}\right) + \beta \cdot O\left(\left(\frac{IJK}{P}\right)^{2/3}\right) + \alpha \cdot O(\log P). \quad (9)$$

PROOF. Pick $Q = \lfloor I/\rho \rfloor$, $R = \lfloor J/\rho \rfloor$, and $S = \lfloor K/\rho \rfloor$, where $\rho = (IJK/P)^{1/3}$. Under the hypotheses, $Q, R, S$ are positive integers with $QRS \le P$, thus define a valid $Q \times R \times S$ processor grid. Moreover, $QRS = \Omega(P)$. Pick partitions $\{\mathcal{I}_q\}_q$, $\{\mathcal{J}_r\}_r$, and $\{\mathcal{K}_s\}_s$ of $[I]$, $[J]$, and $[K]$ which are *balanced*, meaning their parts differ in size by at most one. Pick a partition $\{\mathcal{A}_{q,r,s}\}_{q,r,s}$ of $[I] \times [K]$ to be a union of balanced $R$-way partitions of the sets $\mathcal{I}_q \times \mathcal{K}_s$ ($(q,s) \in [Q] \times [S]$), and similarly for partitions $\{\mathcal{B}_{q,r,s}\}_{q,r,s}$ and $\{\mathcal{C}_{q,r,s}\}_{q,r,s}$ of $[K] \times [J]$ and $[I] \times [J]$. Distribute entries $\mathcal{A}_{q,r,s}$ of $\mathbf{A}$ to each grid processor $(q,r,s)$, and similarly for $\mathbf{B}$ and $\mathbf{C}$: this distribution satisfies the balance constraint in the theorem statement. The algorithm proceeds with ALL-GATHERS of blocks of $\mathbf{A}$ and $\mathbf{B}$ along processor grid fibers in the $Q$- and $R$-directions. then local MMS, then finally REDUCE-SCATTERS of blocks of $\mathbf{C}$ along processor grid fibers in the $S$-direction. (For a more detailed proof, see [3, Appendix B].) □

We denote by MM, 1DMM, or 3DMM an algorithm that satisfies Lemma 2, Lemma 3, or Lemma 4, resp.

# 5 COMMUNICATION-AVOIDING QR

Our new algorithms 1D-CAQR-EG and 3D-CAQR-EG are closely related to *communication-avoiding QR (CAQR)* and *tall-skinny QR (TSQR)* [10]: we explore this relationship in Section 8. For now we remark that 3D-CAQR-EG specializes QR-EG to use 1D-CAQR-EG as a base-case, and that 1D-CAQR-EG specializes QR-EG to use TSQR (the variant in [4]) as a base-case.

On input, the $m \times n$ matrix $\mathbf{A}$ is partitioned across the $P$ processors so that each processor $p$ owns $m_p \ge n$ rows, not necessarily contiguous. Thus we require $\mathbf{A}$ be sufficiently tall and skinny: $m/n \ge P$. A single processor $r$, which owns $\mathbf{A}$'s $n$ leading rows, is designated as the *root processor*.

On output, the Q-factor is stored in Householder representation ($\mathbf{V}$, $\mathbf{T}$), where $\mathbf{V}$ has the same distribution as $\mathbf{A}$. Both $\mathbf{T}$ and the R-factor are returned only on the root processor.

LEMMA 5. *TSQR's runtime is*

$$\gamma \cdot O\left(\max_p m_p n^2 + n^3 \log P\right) + \beta \cdot O\left(n^2 \log P\right) + \alpha \cdot O(\log P)$$

PROOF. It is crucial to use the TSQR variant in [4]. (See [3, Appendix C] for detailed proof.) □

Recall from Section 3 that when the block-size is sufficiently large, REDUCE and BROADCAST can be performed more efficiently, by REDUCE-SCATTER+GATHER and SCATTER+ALL-GATHER, resp. Unfortunately, TSQR's REDUCE- and BROADCAST-like collectives preclude these optimizations. Next in Section 6, we will show how similar savings are achievable.

# 6 1D-CAQR-EG

We now present a new algorithm, 1D-CAQR-EG, an instantiation of the template QR-EG (Algorithm 2). 1D-CAQR-EG effectively reduces TSQR's bandwidth cost by a logarithmic factor, at the expense of increasing its latency cost by a comparable factor.

The input/output data distributions are the same as for TSQR, so we continue notation from Section 5. We specify 1D-CAQR-EG by stepping line-by-line through QR-EG — base case in Section 6.1 and inductive case in Section 6.2 — then prove Theorem 2 in Section 6.3.

## 6.1 Base Case

1D-CAQR-EG's base-case QR decomposition subroutine (Line 2) is TSQR (Section 5), using the same root processor. Note that $\mathbf{A}$'s distribution satisfies TSQR's requirements, and $\mathbf{V}$, $\mathbf{T}$, and $\mathbf{R}$ are returned distributed as required by 1D-CAQR-EG.

## 6.2 Inductive Case

Let us walk through the inductive case line-by-line. All algorithmic costs are incurred in the two recursive calls (Lines 5 and 9) and the six matrix multiplications (Lines 6 to 8 and 11 to 13).

**(Line 4):** the splitting involves no computation nor communication.

**(Line 5):** the left recursive call is valid since $\begin{bmatrix} \mathbf{A}_{11} \\ \mathbf{A}_{21} \end{bmatrix}$ still satisfies the data distribution requirements (only $n$ decreases).

**(Line 6):** this is a 3DMM with matrix dimensions $I = \lfloor n/2 \rfloor$, $J = \lceil n/2 \rceil$, and $K = m$. We choose a (1D) processor grid with $Q = R = 1$ and $S = P$, thus $T = 0$ and the partitions $\{\mathcal{I}_q\}_q = \{[I]\}$ and $\{\mathcal{J}_r\}_r = \{[J]\}$ are trivial. We pick the partition $\{\mathcal{K}_s\}_s$ to match the distribution of $\mathbf{A}$'s rows, and pick $\{\mathcal{A}_{q,r,s}\}_{q,r,s} = \{[I] \times \mathcal{K}_s\}_s$ and $\{\mathcal{B}_{q,r,s}\}_{q,r,s} = \{\mathcal{K}_s \times [J]\}_s$. Additionally, we set $C_{q,r,s} = \emptyset$ for all $(q,r,s)$ but the root processor.

**(Line 7):** this is an MM on the root processor with matrix dimensions $I = K = \lfloor n/2 \rfloor$ and $J = \lceil n/2 \rceil$.

**(Line 8):** this is a 3DMM with matrix dimensions $I = m$, $J = \lceil n/2 \rceil$, and $K = \lfloor n/2 \rfloor$, followed by a matrix subtraction. We choose a (1D) processor grid with $Q = P$ and $R = S = 1$, thus $T = 0$ and the partitions $\{\mathcal{J}_r\}_r = \{[J]\}$ and $\{\mathcal{K}_s\}_s = \{[K]\}$ are trivial. We pick the partition $\{\mathcal{I}_r\}_r$ to match the distribution of **A**'s rows, and pick $\{\mathcal{A}_{q,r,s}\}_{q,r,s} = \{\mathcal{I}_r \times [K]\}_r$ and $\{C_{q,r,s}\}_{q,r,s} = \{\mathcal{I}_r \times [J]\}_r$. Additionally, we set $\mathcal{B}_{q,r,s} = \emptyset$ for all $(q, r, s)$ but the root processor. The row-wise distribution $\{C_{q,r,s}\}_{q,r,s}$ enables the subsequent matrix subtraction to be performed without further communication.

**(Line 9):** the second recursive call is valid since $\mathbf{B}_{22}$ still satisfies the data distribution requirements: the number of rows owned by the root processor decreases by the same amount that $n$ does, while all other processors keep the same number.

**(Line 10):** each processor assembles its local rows of **V**: no computation nor communication is required.

**(Line 11):** this is a 3DMM with matrix dimensions $I = \lfloor n/2 \rfloor$, $J = \lceil n/2 \rceil$, and $K = m - \lfloor n/2 \rfloor$; we choose a processor grid and partitions as in Line 6.

**(Line 12):** this is an MM on the root processor with the same dimensions as Line 7.

**(Line 13):** this is an MM on the root processor with the same dimensions as Lines 7 and 12.

**(Line 14):** each processor assembles its local rows of **R**: no computation nor communication is required.

Verify that **V**, **T**, and **R** are distributed as desired.

## 6.3 Concluding the Analysis

1D-CAQR-EG is valid for any $P, m, n, b \geq 1$ such that $P \leq m/n$, and there is no loss of generality to suppose $b \leq n$. When $b = n$, 1D-CAQR-EG reduces to TSQR. As we will see, picking $b < n$ allows us to reduce 1D-CAQR-EG's arithmetic and bandwidth costs — while increasing its latency cost — to appear as if we had used bidirectional exchange REDUCE and BROADCAST algorithms (Section 3) within TSQR, despite the fact that these algorithms are inapplicable, as we lamented at the end of Section 5. We will navigate the tradeoff with a nonnegative parameter $\epsilon$, taking

$$b = \Theta\left(n/(\log P)^{\epsilon}\right). \tag{10}$$

We will show that taking $\epsilon = 1$ yields Theorem 2.

LEMMA 6. *If* $P = O(b^2)$, 1D-CAQR-EG *has runtime*

$$\gamma \cdot \left(\frac{mn^2}{P} + nb^2 \log P\right) + \beta \cdot O\left(n^2 + nb \log P\right) + \alpha \cdot O\left(\frac{n}{b} \log P\right). \tag{11}$$

PROOF. Let us derive an upper bound $T(m, n)$ on the runtime of an 1D-CAQR-EG invocation. (The unchanging parameters $P, b$ are implicit.) We will now assume a balanced data distribution, meaning the numbers of rows any two processors owns differ by at most one.

When $P = 1$, the runtime of 1D-CAQR-EG for any $b$ is just $\gamma \cdot O\left(mn^2\right)$, which satisfies the conclusion, so we may assume $P > 1$ hereafter.

In the base case ($n \leq b$), the algorithmic cost is the 3D-CAQR-EG call, so by Lemma 5 we conclude that

$$T(m, n) = \gamma \cdot O\left(\frac{mn^2}{P} + n^3 \log P\right) + \beta \cdot O\left(n^2 \log P\right) + \alpha \cdot O\left(\log P\right).$$

In the inductive case, the algorithmic cost is due to the two recursive calls, the three 1DMM calls (Lines 6, 8 and 11, performed on 1D processor grids, and the three (local) MM calls (Lines 7, 12 and 13), performed by the root.

The local MMs have runtime $\gamma \cdot O\left(n^3\right)$.

To apply Lemma 3 to the 3DMM calls, let us now suppose that $P = O\left(n^2\right)$ and $P = O(m)$, Actually, only the first assumption is new: we already know that $P \leq m/n$ for the initial $m, n$, and when $P > 1$ we see that in any recursive call the current $m$ is within a factor of two of the initial $m$, hence $P = O(m)$ in any recursive call. Confirming that the data distributions chosen in Section 6.2 match those in the proof of Lemma 3, the 1DMMs' runtime is

$$\gamma \cdot O\left(\frac{mn^2}{P}\right) + \beta \cdot O\left(n^2\right) + \alpha \cdot O\left(\log P\right).$$

Overall, we have found that

$$T(m, n) = T(m, \lfloor n/2) + T(m - \lfloor n/2 \rfloor, \lceil n/2 \rceil) + \gamma \cdot O\left(\frac{mn^2}{P}\right) + \beta \cdot O\left(n^2\right) + \alpha \cdot O\left(\log P\right).$$

By induction we may take $T(m, n)$ to be nondecreasing in both $m$ and $n$. The former property justifies replacing $m - \lfloor n/2 \rfloor$ by $m$ in the second recursive call. Hence, we will take $m$ to be its initial value in the analysis of every recursive call.

Supposing $n = b2^L$ for a nonnegative integer $L$, $T(m, n)$ is bounded by Equation (11).

Now observe that $n = b2^{L+1}$ reproduces the asymptotic bound Equation (11), and since $T(m, n)$ is nondecreasing in $n$, this bound also holds when $b2^L < n < b2^{L+1}$.

Requiring $P = O(b^2)$ suffices to ensure that $P = O(n^2)$ at every inductive case. □

PROOF OF THEOREM 2. Let us substitute Equation (10) into Equation (11):

$$\gamma \cdot \left(\frac{mn^2}{P}\left(1 + \frac{nP}{m}(\log P)^{1-2\epsilon}\right)\right) + \beta \cdot O\left(n^2\left(1 + (\log P)^{1-\epsilon}\right)\right) + \alpha \cdot O\left((\log P)^{1+\epsilon}\right),$$

thence the hypothesis is $P(\log P)^{2\epsilon} = O\left(n^2\right)$. We conclude by taking $\epsilon = 1$. □

This argument extends to any $\epsilon \geq 0$, assuming $P(\log P)^{2\epsilon} = O(n^2)$, but the asymptotic tradeoff vanishes when $\epsilon > 1$. For

$1/2 \le \epsilon \le 1$ the tradeoff is only between bandwidth and latency. A sensible interpretation of the case $\epsilon < 0$ is $b = n$, meaning TSQR is invoked immediately. In this case, the costs are given directly by Lemma 5.

## 7 3D-CAQR-EG

We now present our second new algorithm, 3D-CAQR-EG, another instantiation of the template QR-EG (Algorithm 2).

On input, the $m \times n$ matrix **A** ($m \ge n$) is partitioned across the $P$ processors row-cyclically: thus, each processor owns at most $\lceil m/P \rceil$ rows.

On output, the Q-factor is stored in Householder representation (**V**, **T**), where **V** has the same distribution as **A**. Both **T** and the R-factor have the same distribution, matching the top $n \times n$ submatrix of **A**.

After walking through 3D-CAQR-EG in a similar fashion as we did for 1D-CAQR-EG in Section 6, we collect the results to prove Theorem 1.

In the following, $T_{\text{3D-CAQR-EG}}$ denotes an upper bound on the runtime of 3D-CAQR-EG, a function of $P, m, n, b$.

### 7.1 Base Case

Recall that $b$ denotes the recursive threshold for 3D-CAQR-EG. 3D-CAQR-EG's base-case QR decomposition subroutine (Line 2) is 1D-CAQR-EG, with a fixed recursive threshold $b^*$.

To satisfy 1D-CAQR-EG's data distribution requirements, we convert **A** from row-cyclic to block-row layout, distributed over

$$P^* = \min(P, \lfloor m/n \rfloor)$$

processors, ensuring each owns at least $n$ rows and one owns the top $n$ rows (and perhaps others).

Initially, $P' = \min(m, P)$ processors own rows of **A**. (Clearly $P' \le P$ with equality just in case $P \le m$; note further that $P^* \le P'$ with equality just in case $P \le m/n$.) Number these processors from 0 to $P'-1$ according to the cyclic layout of **A**, so that processor 0 owns the top row of $A$. Deal these processors among $P^*$ groups, so processor 0 goes into group 0, processor 1 goes into group 1, and so on. Represent each group by its lowest-numbered processor and within each group, GATHER **A**'s rows to the representative. Since each group contains at most $\lceil P'/P^* \rceil$ processors and each processor initially owns at most $\lceil m/P' \rceil$ rows of **A**, the largest block-size in any GATHER is at most $\lceil m/P' \rceil n$.

Each of the $P^*$ representatives (including processor 0) now owns at least $\lfloor m/P^* \rfloor \ge n$ rows of **A**, satisfying the first part of 1D-CAQR-EG's data distribution requirements: it remains to ensure processor 0 owns the top $n$ rows of **A**. These rows are currently owned by the first $P'' = \min(P^*, n)$ representatives. (Clearly $P'' \le P^*$ with equality just in case $P \le n$.) We next perform a GATHER over the representatives of groups 0 through $P''-1$, taking processor 0 to be the root so that afterwards it owns the top $n$ rows of **A** (and perhaps others). We also perform a SCATTER with the opposite communication pattern so that the overall number of rows per representative is unchanged. The largest block-size in both the GATHER and the SCATTER is at most $\lceil n/P'' \rceil n$.

We can now invoke 1D-CAQR-EG, with parameters $P^*, b^*$. After it returns, we redistribute **V**, **T**, and **R** by reversing the preceding GATHERS/SCATTERS, so that **V** is (resp., **T** and **R** are) distributed over all $P$ processors like **A** was (resp., **A**'s first $n$ rows were) initially.

### 7.2 Inductive Case

Let us walk through the inductive case line-by-line, as we did for 1D-CAQR-EG. All algorithmic costs are incurred in the two recursive calls (Lines 5 and 9) and the six matrix multiplications (Lines 6 to 8 and 11 to 13).

**(Line 4):** the splitting involves no computation nor communication.

**(Line 5):** the left recursive call is valid since $\begin{bmatrix} \mathbf{A}_{11} \\ \mathbf{A}_{21} \end{bmatrix}$ still satisfies the data distribution requirements (only $n$ decreases).

**(Line 6):** this is a 3DMM with matrix dimensions $I = \lfloor n/2 \rfloor$, $J = \lceil n/2 \rceil$, and $K = m$. We do not yet specify the processor grid, but we do suppose that 3D-CAQR-EG uses a balanced parallelization and data distribution as in the proof of Lemma 4: this is possible for any processor grid.

To match this data distribution, we perform an ALL-TO-ALL before and after the 3DMM invocation, each time using the two-phase approach [7]. The first ALL-TO-ALL redistributes the input matrices from column- and row-cyclic to 3DMM layout (the left factor is row-cyclic, transposed); the maximum number of input matrix entries any processor owns before or after this collective is at most

$$\max\left( I\left\lceil \frac{K}{P} \right\rceil + \left\lceil \frac{K}{P} \right\rceil J, \left\lceil \frac{\left\lceil \frac{I}{Q} \right\rceil \left\lceil \frac{K}{S} \right\rceil}{R} \right\rceil + \left\lceil \frac{\left\lceil \frac{J}{R} \right\rceil \left\lceil \frac{K}{S} \right\rceil}{Q} \right\rceil \right),$$

where the processor grid is $Q \times R \times S$. The second ALL-TO-ALL converts the output matrix from 3DMM layout to row-cyclic layout; the maximum number of output matrix entries any processor owns before or after this collective is at most

$$\max\left( \left\lceil \frac{\left\lceil \frac{I}{Q} \right\rceil \left\lceil \frac{J}{R} \right\rceil}{S} \right\rceil, \left\lceil \frac{I}{P} \right\rceil J \right).$$

**(Line 7):** this is a 3DMM with matrix dimensions $I = K = \lfloor n/2 \rfloor$ and $J = \lceil n/2 \rceil$. We pick a 3D processor grid and partitions satisfying the same constraints as for Line 6, and perform similar ALL-TO-ALLs before and after, so we can reuse the preceding analysis, substituting $I$, $J$, and $K$.

**(Line 8):** this is a 3DMM with matrix dimensions $I = m$, $J = \lceil n/2 \rceil$, and $K = \lfloor n/2 \rfloor$, followed by a matrix subtraction. We proceed similarly to Lines 6 and 7, except that the left factor is initially in row-cyclic layout, so the first summand in the first term of the maximum becomes $\lceil I/P \rceil K$ (vs. $I\lceil K/P \rceil$).

**(Line 9):** the second recursive call is valid since $\mathbf{B}_{22}$ still satisfies the data distribution requirements: in particular, unlike 1D-CAQR-EG there is no requirement that a fixed processor owns the first $n$ rows or that every processor owns at least $n$ rows.

**(Line 10):** each processor assembles its local rows of $\mathbf{V}$: no computation nor communication is required.

**(Line 11):** this is a 3DMM with matrix dimensions $I = \lfloor n/2 \rfloor$, $J = \lceil n/2 \rceil$, and $K = m - \lfloor n/2 \rfloor$; we choose a processor grid, partitions, and ALL-TO-ALLS as in Line 6.

**(Line 12):** this is a 3DMM with the same dimensions, processor grid, partitions, and ALL-TO-ALLS as Line 7.

**(Line 13):** this is a 3DMM with the same dimensions, processor grid, partitions, and ALL-TO-ALLS as Lines 7 and 12.

**(Line 14):** each processor assembles its local rows of $\mathbf{R}$: no computation nor communication is required.

Verify that $\mathbf{V}$, $\mathbf{T}$, and $\mathbf{R}$ are distributed as desired.

## 7.3 Concluding the Analysis

3D-CAQR-EG is valid for any $P, m, n, b, b^* \geq 1$, and there is no loss of generality to suppose $b^* \leq b \leq n$. Taking $b = n$ simplifies 3D-CAQR-EG to 1D-CAQR-EG with parameters $P^*, b^*$ and additional data redistributions. As in the case of 1D-CAQR-EG, picking $b < n$ allows us to reduce 3D-CAQR-EG's arithmetic and bandwidth costs, while increasing its latency cost.

We will navigate this tradeoff with two nonnegative parameters $\delta, \epsilon$, taking

$$b = \Theta\left(n/(nP/m)^{\delta}\right), \qquad b^* = \Theta\left(b/(\log P)^{\epsilon}\right). \tag{12}$$

We prove Theorem 1 with $\delta \in [1/2, 2/3]$ and $\epsilon = 1$.

LEMMA 7. *If $P = O(b^2)$ and $P^* = O(b^{*2})$, 3D-CAQR-EG has runtime*

$$\begin{aligned} T(m,n) = \gamma \cdot &\left(\frac{mn^2}{P} + nb^{*2}\log P\right) \\ &+ \beta \cdot O\left(\frac{mn}{P} + nb + nb^*\log P + \left(\frac{mn^2}{P}\right)^{2/3}\right. \\ &\left. + \left(\left(\frac{mn}{P} + n\right)\log\frac{n}{b} + \frac{nP^2}{b}\right)\log P\right) \\ &+ \alpha \cdot O\left(\frac{n}{b^*}\log P\right). \end{aligned} \tag{13}$$

PROOF. Let us derive an upper bound $T(m, n)$ on the runtime of a 3D-CAQR-EG invocation. (The unchanging parameters $P, b, b^*$ are implicit.)

When $P = 1$, the runtime of 3D-CAQR-EG is just $\gamma \cdot O\left(mn^2\right)$, which satisfies the conclusion, so we may assume $P > 1$ hereafter.

In a base case ($n \leq b$), the algorithmic costs are due to the 1D-CAQR-EG invocation and the four communication phases.

The first communication phase, involving $P^*$ independent GATHERS, has runtime bounded by

$$\begin{aligned} &\beta \cdot O\left((\lceil P'/P^* \rceil - 1)\lceil m/P' \rceil n\right) + \alpha \cdot O\left(\log\lceil P'/P^* \rceil\right) \\ &\qquad = \beta \cdot O\left(mn/P + n^2\right) + \alpha \cdot O(\log P), \end{aligned}$$

and the same bound applies for the last phase (matching SCATTERS). (Recall that $P^* = \min(P, \lfloor m/n \rfloor)$ and $P' = \min(P, m)$.) The fact that no communication happens when $m \geq nP$ (and thus $P^* = P$) is evident in the first bound but not the second.

The second communication phase, a simultaneous GATHER/SCATTER, has runtime bounded by

$$\begin{aligned} &\beta \cdot O((P'' - 1)\lceil n/P'' \rceil n) + \alpha \cdot O\left(\log P''\right) \\ &\qquad = \beta \cdot O\left(n^2\right) + \alpha \cdot O(\log P), \end{aligned}$$

and the same bound applies for the third phase (matching SCATTER/GATHER). (Recall that $P'' = \min(P^*, n)$.)

A runtime bound for the 1D-CAQR-EG invocation is given by Theorem 2, supposing now that $P^* = O(b^{*2})$. Actually we use the more refined bound of Equation (11), substituting $P^*, b^*$ for $P, b$.

Altogether, in a base case,

$$\begin{aligned} T(m,n) = \gamma \cdot O&\left(\frac{mn^2}{P} + nb^{*2}\log P\right) \\ &+ \beta \cdot O\left(\frac{mn}{P} + n^2 + nb^*\log P\right) + \alpha \cdot O\left(\frac{n}{b^*}\log P\right) \end{aligned}$$

In the inductive case ($n > b$), the algorithmic cost is due to the two recursive calls, the six 3DMMS, performed on 3D processor grids, and the twelve ALL-TO-ALLS, performed before and after each 3DMM.

To apply Lemma 4 to the 3DMMS, let us now suppose that $P \geq (3c)^{3/4}$ for some $c > 1$ and $b \geq 2P^{1/3}$: since $m \geq n$ at every recursive call and since $n \geq b + 1$ in the inductive case, $c \cdot IJK/\min(I, J, K)^3 \leq P \leq IJK$ for each 3DMM. Thus the 3DMMS' overall runtime is

$$\gamma \cdot O\left(\frac{mn^2}{P}\right) + \beta \cdot O\left(\left(\frac{mn^2}{P}\right)^{2/3}\right) + \alpha \cdot O(\log P).$$

Moreover, the inequalities derived at the start of Lemma 4's proof also yield the following upper bound on the overall runtime of the ALL-TO-ALLS,

$$\beta \cdot O\left(\left(\frac{mn}{P} + n + P^2\right)\log P\right) + \alpha \cdot O(\log P).$$

Overall, we have found that

$$\begin{aligned} T(m,n) &= T(m, \lfloor n/2 \rfloor) + T(m - \lfloor n/2 \rfloor, \lceil n/2 \rceil) \\ &\quad + \gamma \cdot O\left(\frac{mn^2}{P}\right) + \beta \cdot O\left(\left(\frac{mn^2}{P}\right)^{2/3}\right. \\ &\quad \left. + \left(\frac{mn}{P} + n + P^2\right)\log P\right) + \alpha \cdot O(\log P). \end{aligned}$$

By induction we may take $T(m, n)$ to be nondecreasing in both $m$ and $n$. The former property justifies replacing $m - \lfloor n/2 \rfloor$ by $m$ in the second recursive call. Hence, we will take $m$ to be its initial value in the analysis of every recursive call.

Supposing $n = b2^L$ for a nonnegative integer $L$, $T(m, n)$ is bounded by Equation (13). Now observe that $n = b2^{L+1}$ reproduces the asymptotic bound of Equation (13), which thus

a

holds when $b2^L < n < b2^{L+1}$ since $T(m, n)$ is nondecreasing in $n$.

In conclusion, 3D-CAQR-EG's runtime $T(m, n)$ satisfies Equation (13) if $P \geq 3$, $b \geq 2P^{1/3}$, $P = O(b^2)$, and $P^* = O(b^{*2})$. □

Proof of Theorem 1. Consider picking $b, b^*$ as in Equation (12). The constraints relating $P$ and $b$ are satisfiable if

$$P = O\left(m^{\frac{2\delta}{1+2\delta}} \cdot n^{\frac{2-2\delta}{1+2\delta}}\right), \tag{14}$$

and the constraint relating $P^*$ and $b^*$ is satisfiable if

$$P \cdot (\log P)^{\frac{2\epsilon}{1+2\delta}} = O\left(m^{\frac{2\delta}{1+2\delta}} \cdot n^{\frac{2-2\delta}{1+2\delta}}\right), \tag{15}$$

a stronger condition than Equation (14).

Substituting Equation (10) into Equation (11),

$$\gamma \cdot \left(\frac{mn^2}{P}\left(1 + \left(\frac{nP}{m}\right)^{1-2\delta}(\log P)^{1-2\epsilon}\right)\right)$$
$$+ \beta \cdot O\left(\frac{n^2}{\left(\frac{nP}{m}\right)^{\delta}}\left(1 + (\log P)^{1-\epsilon}\right) + W\right)$$
$$+ \alpha \cdot O\left((nP/m)^{\delta}(\log P)^{1+\epsilon}\right),$$

where $W$ denotes the sum of three terms associated with the ALL-TO-ALLS,

$$\frac{mn}{P}\log\frac{nP}{m}\log P,\ \ n\log\frac{nP}{m}\log P,\ \ P^2\left(\frac{nP}{m}\right)^{\delta}\log P,$$

plus a term $n^2/(nP/m)^{2/3}$ associated with the 3DMMS. We obtain the stated arithmetic and latency costs by taking $\delta \geq 1/2$ and $\epsilon = 1$. To suppress the bandwidth term $W$, it suffices to require that there exists $\delta' \in (0, 1-\delta)$, hence $\delta < 1$, such that

$$\begin{aligned} P \,/\, (\log P)^{\frac{\epsilon}{1-\delta-\delta'}} &= \Omega(m \,/\, n), \\ P \cdot (\log P)^{\frac{\epsilon}{\delta+\delta'}} &= O\left(m \cdot n^{\frac{1-\delta-\delta'}{\delta+\delta'}}\right), \\ P \cdot (\log P)^{\frac{\epsilon}{2+2\delta}} &= O\left(m^{\frac{\delta}{1+\delta}} \cdot n^{\frac{1-\delta}{1+\delta}}\right). \end{aligned} \tag{16}$$

The 3DMMS' bandwidth cost cannot be reduced, but it is lower-order if $\delta \leq 2/3$.

The hypotheses of Theorem 1, $\delta \in [1/2, 2/3]$ (and tacitly $\epsilon = 1$) and Equation (2), imply Equations (14) to (16). □

This argument extends to a larger range of nonnegative $\delta, \epsilon$. Assuming fixed $\epsilon$, for $\delta > 2/3$ the 3DMM invocations dominate the bandwidth cost, whose bound remains as if $\delta = 2/3$, no longer a tradeoff, at least asymptotically. In the case $0 \leq \delta < 1/2$, the additive term in the arithmetic cost, due to the small (mostly) triangular matrix operations on TSQR's critical path, possibly dominates. (A sensible interpretation of the case $\delta \leq 0$ is $b = n$, in which case 1D-CAQR-EG is invoked immediately.) Assuming fixed $\delta$, the tradeoffs due to varying $\epsilon \in [0, 1]$ are just as in the proof of Theorem 2, except now the factor in the arithmetic cost is suppressed by increasing $\delta$.

# 8 DISCUSSION

We have presented two new algorithms, 1D-CAQR-EG and 3D-CAQR-EG (Sections 6 and 7), for computing QR decompositions on distributed-memory parallel machines. Our analysis (e.g., Equations (11) and (13)) demonstrates tradeoffs between arithmetic, bandwidth, and latency costs, governed by the choice of one (1D-CAQR-EG) or two (3D-CAQR-EG) block sizes. We navigated these tradeoffs in Theorems 1 and 2 by asymptotically minimizing arithmetic, as well as bandwidth in Theorem 2.

## 8.1 Comparison With Similar Algorithms

Here we compare the two new algorithms with four other instances of the REC-QR framework, deriving Tables 2 and 3. Let us review the other algorithms.

An early and well-known instance of REC-QR (Algorithm 1) was proposed by Householder [14]. It features a splitting strategy (Line 4) where $A_{11}$ is $b \times b$ (*right-looking*) or $n-b \times n-b$ (*left-looking*); a base case threshold (Line 1) asserting $n \leq b$; and a base case subroutine (Line 2) generating a product of $b$ Householder reflectors. Householder's proposal was right-looking and *unblocked*, meaning $b = 1$ (vs. *blocked*, $b > 1$).

Let 1D-HOUSE and 2D-HOUSE denote the un/blocked right-looking variants, specialized to use compact representations (Section 2.3); their costs are summarized in the first rows of Tables 2 and 3. 2D-HOUSE invokes 1D-HOUSE as its base case. For 1D-HOUSE we use a 1D processor grid and for 2D-HOUSE we use a 2D processor grid. For 1D-HOUSE we distribute matrices similar to 1D-CAQR-EG and for 2D-HOUSE we distribute matrices (2D-) block-cyclically with $b \times b$ blocks: the distribution block size matches the algorithmic block size. We parallelize 1D-HOUSE and the base case of 2D-HOUSE to match the distribution of A, analogous to 1D-CAQR-EG. We parallelize 2D-HOUSE's inductive-case matrix multiplications to match the output matrix distribution (a 2D parallelization). In the case of 1D-HOUSE we assume $P = O(m)$. In the case of 2D-HOUSE, we choose an $r \times c$ processor grid with $c = \Theta((nP/m)^{1/2})$ and $r = \Theta(P/c)$, and we choose $b = \Theta(1)$. Assuming $P = \Omega(m/n)$ and $P \cdot (\log P)^2 = O(m \cdot n)$, these choices are valid and simultaneously minimize all three costs, asymptotically.

CAQR [10] modifies 2D-HOUSE to invoke TSQR (Section 5) in the base case. Our algorithms make crucial use of the TSQR enhancements in [4]; additionally, we use that paper's improved CAQR in the following comparison. We parallelize and distribute data for TSQR as discussed in Section 5, and for CAQR's inductive case as we did for 2D-HOUSE's. TSQR and CAQR's costs are summarized in the second rows of Tables 2 and 3. In the case of TSQR we assume $P \leq m/n$. In the case of CAQR we use the same $r \times c$ grid as for 2D-HOUSE but now pick $b = \Theta(n/(nP/m)^{1/2})$. Assuming $P/(\log P)^2 = \Omega(m/n)$ and $P \cdot (\log P)^2 = O(m \cdot n)$, these choices are valid and simultaneously minimize all three costs, asymptotically.

The costs of the new algorithms, 1D-CAQR-EG and 3D-CAQR-EG appear in the third rows of Tables 2 and 3. To make the comparison between TSQR and 1D-CAQR-EG more clear, for the latter we use $b = \Theta(n/(\log P)^{\epsilon})$ in Theorem 2's proof, allowing

| *algorithm* | *# operations* | *# words* | *# messages* |
|---|---|---|---|
| 2D-HOUSE | $mn^2/P$ | $n^2/(nP/m)^{1/2}$ | $n \log P$ |
| CAQR | $mn^2/P$ | $n^2/(nP/m)^{1/2}$ | $(nP/m)^{1/2}(\log P)^2$ |
| 3D-CAQR-EG | $mn^2/P$ | $n^2/(nP/m)^{\delta}$ | $(nP/m)^{\delta}(\log P)^2$ |

**Table 2:** Comparison of approaches for square-ish matrices ($m/n = O(P)$). The algorithms and the assumptions that support these bounds are explained in Section 8.1. (In line 3, $\delta$ varies from 1/2 to 2/3.)

| *algorithm* | *# operations* | *# words* | *# messages* |
|---|---|---|---|
| 1D-HOUSE | $mn^2/P$ | $n^2 \log P$ | $n \log P$ |
| TSQR | $mn^2/P + n^3 \log P$ | $n^2 \log P$ | $\log P$ |
| 1D-CAQR-EG | $mn^2/P + n^3(\log P)^{1-2\epsilon}$ | $n^2(\log P)^{1-\epsilon}$ | $(\log P)^{1+\epsilon}$ |

**Table 3:** Comparison of approaches for tall/skinny matrices ($m/n = \Omega(P)$). The algorithms and the assumptions that support these bounds are explained in Section 8.1. (In line 3, $\epsilon$ varies from 0 to 1.)

the parameter $\epsilon$ to vary over $[0, 1]$, justified by the stronger constraint $P(\log P)^{2\epsilon} = O(n^2)$. For 3D-CAQR-EG we follow Theorem 1's proof and hypotheses.

## 8.2 Elimination By Blocks

Tiskin [25], working in the BSP model [26], proposed an algorithm outside of the REC-QR framework which demonstrates a similar bandwidth/latency tradeoff as 3D-CAQR-EG. Tiskin's algorithm was designed only for square matrices, but it has been extended to rectangular matrices, using the original algorithm as a black box [20]. This extension achieves BSP bandwidth cost $O\left(n^2/(nP/m)^{\delta}\right)$ and BSP synchronization cost $O\left((nP/m)^{\delta}(\log P)^2\right)$. Despite the fact that, in BSP, 3D-CAQR-EG achieves these same communication costs, we still believe 3D-CAQR-EG is a valuable contribution for multiple reasons. Defining a data distribution is a nontrivial and crucial step in developing a distributed-memory implementation using, e.g., MPI. The aforementioned BSP algorithms do not (and need not) explicitly specify their data distributions. Second, our algorithms are based on Householder's algorithm and use Householder representation. Thus, they are readily assembled from robust, tuned subroutines in standard libraries like (P)BLAS and (Sca)LAPACK. Additionally, all interprocessor communication in our algorithms is expressed in terms of standard MPI collectives. Lastly, we feel that Tiskin's recursive scheme, based on a slope-2 wavefront and 'pseudopanels', is much more demanding from an implementation perspective than Elmroth-Gustavson's (QR-EG). To our knowledge no one has implemented Tiskin's algorithm.

## 8.3 Lower Bounds

The algorithms discussed in Section 8.1 are all subject to an arithmetic lower bound of $\Omega(mn^2/P)$ [10].

In the tall-skinny case, we have bandwidth and latency bounds $\Omega(n^2)$ and $\Omega(\log P)$ [2, 8]. 1D-HOUSE attains the arithmetic lower bound, but misses the bandwidth and latency lower bounds by $\Theta(\log P)$ and $\Theta(n)$. TSQR attains the arithmetic lower bound assuming $P \log P = \Omega(m/n)$, but misses the bandwidth and latency lower bounds both by $\Theta(\log P)$. 1D-CAQR-EG attains the latency lower bound when $\epsilon = 0$, the arithmetic lower bound when $\epsilon \leq 1/2$, and the bandwidth lower bound when $\epsilon \geq 1$.

In the (close to) square case, we have bandwidth and latency bounds $\Omega(n^2/(nP/m)^{2/3}$ and $\Omega((nP/m)^{1/2})$ [2]. We restrict parameters so that both CAQR and 3D-CAQR-EG attain the arithmetic lower bound. 2D-HOUSE and CAQR exceed the bandwidth lower bound both by a factor of $\Theta((nP/m)^{1/6})$ and they exceed the latency lower bound by factors of $\Theta\left(n/(nP/m)^{1/2}\log P\right)$ and $\Theta\left((nP/m)^{1/6}(\log P)^2\right)$, resp. 3D-CAQR-EG attains the bandwidth lower bound when $\delta = 2/3$, and exceeds the latency lower bound by just $\Theta((\log P)^2)$ when $\delta = 1/2$.

We did not prove that 3D-CAQR-EG's bandwidth-latency product is optimal — i.e., that the tradeoff is inevitable — although we conjecture this to be the case. Our intuition is based on bandwidth/latency tradeoffs observed in computations whose dependence graphs have similar structure [16, 21].

## 8.4 Limitations and Extensions

Our main upper bound Theorem 1 is substantially limited by its restrictions on permissible parallelism: see Equation (2). 3D-CAQR-EG's ALL-TO-ALLs are responsible for these constraints: if we supposed the ALL-TO-ALLs had zero cost, Equation (2) could be weakened to Equation (15). We make three remarks about improving this aspect of our work.

First, the bound used is worst-case; our knowledge of (and control over) data distribution could lead to stronger bounds. Second, it may be that the index algorithm is suboptimal for the data distribution, e.g., many $B_{pq} = 0$ and a specialized algorithm would perform less communication, or at least yield sharper cost bounds. Third and more generally, we should optimize for the data distribution before and after each subroutine. The constraints are the balance assumptions to invoke Lemma 4 and 1D-CAQR-EG. This is a hard problem.

a

We have also omitted a number of practical optimizations that do not affect our asymptotic analysis. For example, recall from Section 2.3 that T can be reconstructed from V. If the full T is not desired, by replacing the top level of recursion with a right-looking iterative QR-EG variant, we can avoid ever computing superdiagonal blocks of T; this does, however, restrict the available parallelism [11].

The constants hidden in our asymptotic analysis are practically important, and parameter choices for particular machines warrant further study. For parallel dense linear algebra, the typical behavior of a strong-scaling regime (increasing $P$ for a fixed problem) is for arithmetic cost to dominate for small $P$, initially scaling nearly perfectly. However, for larger $P$, local computation is reduced and the bandwidth cost increasingly dominates runtime. This is the scenario when the new tuning parameter $\delta$ will be most useful, reducing the bandwidth cost and extending strong scaling.

Elmroth-Gustavson's recursive approach extends from QR-decomposition to other matrix computations like Cholesky decompositions and solving triangular matrix equations [12]. We see no major obstacles to obtaining the corresponding extensions of Theorems 1 and 2.

## ACKNOWLEDGMENTS

G. Ballard was supported by the National Science Foundation (NSF) Grant No. ACI-1642385. The work of L. Grigori was supported by the NLAFET project as part of the European Union's Horizon 2020 research and innovation program under grant 671633. Support for M. Jacquelin was provided in part through the Scientific Discovery through Advanced Computing (SciDAC) program funded by the US Department of Energy (DOE), Office of Science, Advanced Scientific Computing Research under Contract No. DE-AC02-05CH11231.

## REFERENCES

[1] R. Agarwal, S. Balle, F. Gustavson, M. Joshi, and P. Palkar. 1995. A Three-Dimensional Approach to Parallel Matrix Multiplication. *IBM Journal of Research and Development* 39, 5 (1995), 575–582. https://doi.org/10.1147/rd.395.0575

[2] G. Ballard, E. Carson, J. Demmel, M. Hoemmen, N. Knight, and O. Schwartz. 2014. Communication lower bounds and optimal algorithms for numerical linear algebra. *Acta Numerica* 23 (2014), 1–155. http://journals.cambridge.org/article_S0962492914000038

[3] G. Ballard, J. Demmel, L. Grigori, M. Jacquelin, and N. Knight. 2018. *A 3D Parallel Algorithm for QR Decomposition.* Technical Report 1805.05278. arXiv. https://arxiv.org/abs/1805.05278

[4] G. Ballard, J. Demmel, L. Grigori, M. Jacquelin, N. Knight, and H. D. Nguyen. 2015. Reconstructing Householder Vectors from Tall-Skinny QR. *J. Parallel and Distrib. Comput.* 85 (2015), 3–31. https://doi.org/10.1016/j.jpdc.2015.06.003

[5] G. Ballard, A. Druinsky, N. Knight, and O. Schwartz. 2016. Hypergraph partitioning for sparse matrix-matrix multiplication. *ACM Transactions on Parallel Computing* 3, 3 (2016), 18. http://doi.acm.org/10.1145/3015144

[6] L. S. Blackford, J. Choi, A. Cleary, E. D'Azevedo, J. Demmel, I. Dhillon, J. Dongarra, S. Hammarling, G. Henry, A. Petitet, K. Stanley, D. Walker, and R. C. Whaley. 1997. *ScaLAPACK Users' Guide.* SIAM, Philadelphia, PA, USA. Also available from http://www.netlib.org/scalapack/.

[7] J. Bruck, C.-T. Ho, S. Kipnis, E. Upfal, and D. Weathersby. 1997. Efficient algorithms for all-to-all communications in multiport message-passing systems. *IEEE Transactions on Parallel and Distributed Systems* 8, 11 (1997), 1143–1156. https://doi.org/10.1109/71.642949

[8] E. Chan, M. Heimlich, A. Purkayastha, and R. van de Geijn. 2007. Collective communication: theory, practice, and experience. *Concurrency and Computation: Practice and Experience* 19, 13 (2007), 1749–1783. https://doi.org/10.1002/cpe.1206

[9] P. Constantine and D. Gleich. 2011. Tall and Skinny QR Factorizations in MapReduce Architectures. In *Proceedings of the Second International Workshop on MapReduce and Its Applications (MapReduce '11).* ACM, New York, NY, USA, 43–50. https://doi.org/10.1145/1996092.1996103

[10] J. Demmel, L. Grigori, M. Hoemmen, and J. Langou. 2012. Communication-optimal Parallel and Sequential QR and LU Factorizations. *SIAM Journal on Scientific Computing* 34, 1 (2012), A206–A239. https://doi.org/10.1137/080731992

[11] E. Elmroth and F. Gustavson. 2000. Applying recursion to serial and parallel QR factorization leads to better performance. *IBM Journal of Research and Development* 44, 4 (2000), 605–624. https://doi.org/10.1147/rd.444.0605

[12] E. Elmroth, F. Gustavson, I. Jonsson, and B. Kågström. 2004. Recursive blocked algorithms and hybrid data structures for dense matrix library software. *SIAM Rev.* 46, 1 (2004), 3–45. http://epubs.siam.org/sam-bin/dbq/article/42869

[13] D. Helman, D. Bader, and J. JáJá. 1996. Parallel algorithms for personalized communication and sorting with an experimental study. In *ACM Symposium on Parallel Algorithms and Architectures.* ACM, ACM, New York, NY, USA, 211–222. http://doi.acm.org/10.1145/237502.237558

[14] A. Householder. 1958. Unitary triangularization of a nonsymmetric matrix. *J. ACM* 5, 4 (1958), 339–342. http://doi.acm.org/10.1145/320941.320947

[15] Y. Nakatsukasa and R. Freund. 2016. Computing fundamental matrix decompositions accurately via the matrix sign function in two iterations: The power of Zolotarev's functions. *SIAM Rev.* 58, 3 (2016), 461–493. https://doi.org/10.1137/140990334

[16] C. Papadimitriou and J. Ullman. 1987. A communication-time tradeoff. *SIAM J. Comput.* 16, 4 (1987), 639–646. https://doi.org/10.1137/0216044

[17] C. Puglisi. 1992. Modification of the Householder method based on the compact WY representation. *SIAM J. Sci. Statist. Comput.* 13, 3 (1992), 723–726. https://doi.org/10.1137/0913042

[18] M. Schatz, R. Van de Geijn, and J. Poulson. 2016. Parallel matrix multiplication: A systematic journey. *SIAM Journal on Scientific Computing* 38, 6 (2016), C748–C781. https://doi.org/10.1137/140993478

[19] R. Schreiber and C. Van Loan. 1989. A storage-efficient WY representation for products of Householder transformations. *SIAM J. Sci. Statist. Comput.* 10, 1 (1989), 53–57. http://epubs.siam.org/doi/abs/10.1137/0910005

[20] E. Solomonik, G. Ballard, J. Demmel, and T. Hoefler. 2017. A Communication-Avoiding Parallel Algorithm for the Symmetric Eigenvalue Problem. In *Proceedings of the 29th ACM Symposium on Parallelism in Algorithms and Architectures (SPAA '17).* ACM, New York, NY, USA, 111–121. https://doi.org/10.1145/3087556.3087561

[21] E. Solomonik, E. Carson, N. Knight, and J. Demmel. 2016. Trade-Offs Between Synchronization, Communication, and Computation in Parallel Linear Algebra Computations. *ACM Transactions on Parallel Computing* 3, 1 (2016), 3. http://doi.acm.org/10.1145/2897188

[22] E. Solomonik and J. Demmel. 2011. Communication-optimal Parallel 2.5D Matrix Multiplication and LU Factorization Algorithms. In *Proceedings of the 17th International Conference on Parallel Processing (Euro-Par'11).* Springer-Verlag, Berlin, Heidelberg, 90–109. http://dl.acm.org/citation.cfm?id=2033408.2033420

[23] X. Sun and C. Bischof. 1995. A basis-kernel representation of orthogonal matrices. *SIAM journal on matrix analysis and applications* 16, 4 (1995), 1184–1196. http://epubs.siam.org/doi/abs/10.1137/S0895479894276369

[24] R. Thakur, R. Rabenseifner, and W. Gropp. 2005. Optimization of Collective Communication Operations in MPICH. *International Journal of High Performance Computing Applications* 19, 1 (2005), 49–66. https://doi.org/10.1177/1094342005051521

[25] A. Tiskin. 2007. Communication-efficient parallel generic pairwise elimination. *Future Generation Computer Systems* 23, 2 (2007), 179–188. https://doi.org/10.1016/j.future.2006.04.017

[26] Leslie G Valiant. 1990. A bridging model for parallel computation. *Commun. ACM* 33, 8 (1990), 103–111. http://doi.acm.org/10.1145/79173.79181

[27] T. Wicky, E. Solomonik, and T. Hoefler. 2017. Communication-avoiding parallel algorithms for solving triangular systems of linear equations. In *International Parallel and Distributed Processing Symposium.* IEEE, IEEE Computer Society, Washington, DC, USA, 678–687. https://doi.org/10.1109/IPDPS.2017.104

[28] I. Yamazaki, H. Anzt, S. Tomov, M. Hoemmen, and J. Dongarra. 2014. Improving the Performance of CA-GMRES on Multicores with Multiple GPUs. In *International Parallel and Distributed Processing Symposium.* IEEE Computer Society, Washington, DC, USA, 382–391. https://doi.org/10.1109/IPDPS.2014.48

# Constant-Depth and Subcubic-Size Threshold Circuits for Matrix Multiplication

Ojas Parekh
Sandia National Laboratories
Albuquerque, NM, USA
odparek@sandia.gov

Cynthia A. Phillips
Sandia National Laboratories
Albuquerque, NM, USA
caphill@sandia.gov

Conrad D. James
Sandia National Laboratories
Albuquerque, NM, USA
cdjame@sandia.gov

James B. Aimone
Sandia National Laboratories
Albuquerque, NM, USA
jbaimon@sandia.gov

## ABSTRACT

Boolean circuits of McCulloch-Pitts threshold gates are a classic model of neural computation studied heavily in the late 20th century as a model of general computation. Recent advances in large-scale neural computing hardware has made their practical implementation a near-term possibility. We describe a theoretical approach for multiplying two $N$ by $N$ matrices that integrates threshold gate logic with conventional fast matrix multiplication algorithms, that perform $O(N^{\omega})$ arithmetic operations for a positive constant $\omega < 3$. Our approach converts such a fast matrix multiplication algorithm into a constant-depth threshold circuit with approximately $O(N^{\omega})$ gates. Prior to our work, it was not known whether the $\Theta(N^3)$-gate barrier for matrix multiplication was surmountable by constant-depth threshold circuits.

Dense matrix multiplication is a core operation in convolutional neural network training. Performing this work on a neural architecture instead of off-loading it to a GPU may be an appealing option.

## KEYWORDS

threshold circuits; matrix multiplication; triangle counting; numerical algorithms; neural-inspired algorithms; neuromorphic computing; neural networks

**ACM Reference Format:**

Ojas Parekh, Cynthia A. Phillips, Conrad D. James, and James B. Aimone. 2018. Constant-Depth and Subcubic-Size Threshold Circuits for Matrix Multiplication. In *SPAA '18: 30th ACM Symposium on Parallelism in Algorithms and Architectures, July 16–18, 2018, Vienna, Austria.* ACM, New York, NY, USA, 10 pages. https://doi.org/10.1145/3210377.3210410

## 1 INTRODUCTION

Neuromorphic computing devices (NCDs) are composed of massively parallel networks of artificial neurons that compute boolean functions, akin to conventional logic gates but with relatively larger fan-in. The simplicity of each neuron affords NCDs immense energy efficiency and scalability, circumventing some of the data movement and energy bottlenecks associated with traditional HPC [17]. Within the last few years, large-scale commercial NCD platforms, such as SpiNNaker, IBM's True North, and Intel's Loihi, have emerged and currently offer up to hundreds of millions of neurons, with systems with billions of neurons a near-term likelihood [5, 17, 23]. Such NCDs were envisioned, for example, to accelerate deep learning; however, a specific application for which NCDs offer a clear and rigorously established advantage over conventional parallel computing remains elusive. Developing theoretical models for NCDs and identifying potential advantages and tradeoffs over other parallel models of computation remain largely open problems. We consider a well-known theoretical model that captures some of the features offered by NCDs, and we demonstrate resource-efficient constant-time algorithms for a fundamental problem, matrix multiplication.

We study the computational power of boolean circuits where the fundamental gates have unbounded fan-in and compute a linear threshold function[1]. Such circuits are rooted in the classical McCulloch-Pitts neuronal model [12], with linear threshold functions serving as plausible models of spiking neurons. A boolean *threshold gate* with $m$ binary inputs $y_1, y_2, \ldots, y_m$ computes a *linear threshold function*, outputting 1 if and only if $\sum_{i=1}^{m} w_i y_i \geq t$, where the integer weights $w_i$ and integer threshold $t$ are constants associated with the gate. Rational $w_i$ and $t$ may be represented, for example, by multiplying such $w_i$ and $t$ with a sufficiently large number. There are several natural measures of complexity associated with boolean circuits, including *size*: the total number of gates, *depth*: the length of the longest directed path from an input node to an output node, *edges*: the total number of connections between gates, and *fan-in*: the maximum number of inputs to any gate.

Threshold gates are the most basic model for an artificial neuron, and as such, all currently available neuromorphic computing architectures provide a hardware implementation of threshold circuits. We consider threshold circuits with constant depth and polynomial size with respect to the total number of inputs; this class of circuits is called $TC^0$. Such circuits represent a plausible model of constant-time parallel computing. This is a notion of perfect parallelizability, faster than the polylogarithmic time allowed in the complexity class


*SPAA'18, July 16–18, 2018, Vienna, Austria*

ACM ISBN 978-1-4503-5799-9/18/07...$15.00
https://doi.org/10.1145/3210377.3210410

[1] As we explain below, for convolutional neural networks, we can restrict the fan-in to a constant, or whatever practical fan-in the architecture supports.

*NC*. $TC^0$ circuits can compute a variety of functions including integer arithmetic, sorting, and matrix multiplication [19, 21]. There is also a $TC^0$ threshold-gate circuit of sublinear size to compute the parity of $n$ bits [20]. In contrast, any constant-depth circuit with NOT gates and unbounded-fan-in AND and OR gates requires a superpolynomial number of gates [7, 26].

Understanding the power and limitations of $TC^0$ circuits has been a major research challenge over the last couple of decades. The 1990's saw a flurry of results showing what $TC^0$ circuits could do [19, 21], while more recent results have focused on lower bounds showing what $TC^0$ circuits cannot do [9]. $TC^0$ has been studied as a theoretical model. Its practicality is an open question. Currently, large-scale electronic circuits with high fan-in may be difficult to implement. However, neural-inspired architectures may offer hope.

The adult human brain contains about 100 billion neurons, with maximum fan-in 10,000 or larger some regions, operating at under 50 watts [1]. Though impressive, this figure represents a single class of instance size, so one might wonder how a synthetic system based on the physical limitations governing a brain might scale asymptotically. We are not aware of any generative brain models for which this has been analyzed. However, a fan-in that grows with the total system size seems plausible for a 3-dimensional circuit such as the brain. Although large fan-in is a critical resource in designing $TC^0$ algorithms, in practical neuromorphic devices resource requirements may grow as a function of fan-in. For example, the available numerical precision or dynamic range may decrease as fan-in increases, resulting in an overall increase in energy expenditure or execution time. Thus constant depth, in the $TC^0$ sense, may not practically equate to constant time. However, ideal theoretical algorithms may still guide the development of resource-efficient practical algorithms as neuromorphic architectures become more prevalent.

While neuromorphic computing has long focused on the use of analog computation to emulate neuronal dynamics [8], recent years have seen rapid development of novel digital CMOS neural hardware platforms which can scale to very large numbers of neurons [10, 13]. While initially designed for large biologically inspired circuits, these architectures are attracting attention as an alternative to conventional CMOS architectures for accelerating machine learning algorithms such as deep artificial neural networks [6]. Many of these neural architectures, such as TrueNorth and the SpiNNaker platform, achieve considerable benefits in energy and speed by using large numbers of simple digital spiking neurons instead of a relatively smaller number of powerful multi-purpose processors. These systems are almost configurable threshold gate circuits, except that they are capable of extended temporal dynamics. Scientific computing is an application domain for which neural architectures are often quickly dismissed. There is a perception that human cognition is better for data-centric functions, such as image recognition, and for abstract decision making than for precise numerical calculations, particularly at large scale. While biologically-inspired neural algorithms are often probabilistic or approximate, the neuronal-level computations in large scale neural architectures are sufficiently precise for numerical computation.

We consider a fundamental scientific-computing-inspired problem: can one produce constant-depth threshold circuits that compute the product of two $N \times N$ matrices using $O(N^{3-\varepsilon})$ gates for constant $\varepsilon > 0$? For matrices with relatively large entries (say $\Omega(N)$ bits), this goal seems out of reach as we would need to output $\Omega(N^3)$ bits in the worst case. However, prior to our work, it was not known if this was possible even for *binary* matrices, those with entries that are all either 0 or 1.

We show how to multiply two $N \times N$ integer matrices with $O(\log N)$-bit entries using $O(N^{3-\varepsilon})$ gates in constant depth. The näive algorithm based on the definition of matrix multiplication requires $\Theta(N^3)$ arithmetic operations. Our results are based on classical breakthroughs for fast matrix multiplication [22]: multiplying two $N \times N$ matrices using $O(N^{\omega})$ arithmetic operations, for a positive constant $\omega < 3$, that depends on the particular fast matrix multiplication being employed. These techniques can be extended, in a relatively straightforward manner, to yield $O(\log N)$-time conventional parallel algorithms (for architectures such as PRAMs) with $O(N^{\omega})$ total work. In contrast, we give a constant-time algorithm, in the threshold circuit model, with approximately $O(N^{\omega})$ total gates, which is a reasonable measure of total work.

One of our motivations for neural-circuit-based matrix multiplication is convolutional neural networks for deep learning. See Section 5 for more details. Deep learning is a major driver for neural-inspired architectures. A current vision for using these architectures for deep learning requires the matrix multiplication to be moved off-system to a GPU. If circuit-based matrix multiplication can be made practical, perhaps this computation can be left on-chip, avoiding energy-intensive and slow I/O.

We also consider the somewhat simpler problem of determining whether the trace of $A^3$ is at least $\tau$, for an $N \times N$ integer matrix $A$ with entries of size $O(\log N)$ bits. This case illustrates the fundamental ideas of our approach and has applications in social network analysis, particularly to triangle counting. The problem we solve allows one to answer: "Does a graph $G$ have at least $\tau$ triangles?" The user may select a relevant value of $\tau$. See Section 5 for more details on triangles, social network analysis, and picking $\tau$.

There is a simple depth-2 threshold circuit to solve this problem for a graph $G = (V, E)$. The circuit has an input variable, $x_{ij}$ for $i, j \in V$ with $i < j$; the variable $x_{ij}$ is 1 if $ij \in E$ and 0 otherwise. The first layer of the circuit consists of a gate, $g_{ijk}$ for each triple $i, j, k \in V$ with $i < j < k$. The gate $g_{ijk}$ computes the value of the linear threshold function $x_{ij} + x_{ik} + x_{jk} \geq 3$ as an output $y_{ijk}$. That is, the gate fires ($y_{ijk} = 1$) if and only if all edges in the triangle on $i$, $j$, and $k$ are in the graph. The second layer consists of a single output gate that computes the linear threshold function $\sum_{i,j,k \in V : i<j<k} y_{ijk} \geq \tau$; this gate fires if and only if the number of triangles in $G$ is at least $\tau$. The circuit has $\binom{N}{3} + 1 = \Theta(N^3)$ gates.

We ask (and answer) whether it is possible to beat the size of this threshold circuit in constant depth. This is akin to asking if it is possible to beat the näive matrix multiplication algorithm with an algorithm that performs $O(N^{\omega})$ operations for $\omega < 3$. In fact the above threshold circuit is a specialization of the näive matrix multiplication algorithm.

The analysis of our new threshold circuits is more involved than analyzing conventional fast matrix multiplication methods. We must explicitly consider sparsity (see Definition 2.1), a measure of how many times a matrix element or intermediate result is part of a computation during the fast multiplication. Thus, while we use existing fast matrix multiplication techniques to achieve our results, we use them in a new context. Our performance results exploit different features of fast matrix multiplication techniques than those traditionally used.

## Results and contributions

Consider a fast recursive or divide-and-conquer matrix multiplication algorithm like Strassen's, with run-time complexity $O(N^{\omega})$. We consistently use $\omega$ as the exponent in the runtime complexity of a base non-circuit fast matrix multiplication algorithm. Our results leverage such a fast matrix multiplication to construct a constant-depth threshold circuit with $\widetilde{O}(N^{\omega+\varepsilon})$-gates, where $\varepsilon$ depends on the depth of the circuit.

Our main result is an $O(d)$-depth, $\widetilde{O}(N^{\omega+O(\gamma^d)})$-gate threshold circuit for multiplying two $N \times N$ integer matrices with $O(\log N)$-bit entries, for a positive integer $d$ and constant $\gamma < 1$. Specifically, for a given integer $d$, the depth is $4d+1$. The constant $d$ is a multiplicative factor hidden in the $\widetilde{O}$ for the number of gates. Section 4.3 gives a more detailed discussion of the value of $\gamma$. For Strassen's algorithm it is about $0.491$. The constant multiplier of $\gamma^d$ is about $1.581$ for Strassen's algorithm. Thus for $d > 3$, this circuit will have $O(N^{3-\varepsilon})$ gates for positive constant $\varepsilon > 0$. We also give a $O(\log\log N)$-depth, $\widetilde{O}(N^{\omega})$-gate circuit for this task.

We present a simplified circuit of the same gate complexity and slightly lower depth $(2d + 2)$ for computing the trace of $A^3$, for an $N \times N$ integer matrix $A$. This gives triangle counts for a graph $G$ with adjacency matrix $A$ (see Section 2.3). Our circuits implement limited-depth versions of fast divide-and-conquer matrix multiplication, and our techniques should extend to other types of algebraic divide-and-conquer algorithms.

Our contributions are:

- This work revives and redirects research on designing algorithms for a classical theoretical model of parallel computation to a data science problem on an emerging class of neural-inspired parallel architectures. We show that threshold circuits, comprised of threshold gates that model neurons, might be applicable to linear-algebra computations for deep learning on new neuromorphic hardware.
- We give $O(\log\log n)$-depth and $\widetilde{O}(N^{\omega})$-gate threshold circuits for computing the product of two $N \times N$ matrices with $O(\log N)$-bit entries, where $N^{\omega}$ is the complexity of a fast conventional matrix multiplication algorithm like Strassen's.
- We give constant-depth threshold circuits with $\widetilde{O}(N^{\omega+\varepsilon})$ gates, where $\varepsilon$ is exponentially small in the depth of the circuit.
- Our circuits are elementary and are composed entirely of copies of a relatively simple depth-2 threshold circuit that performs addition. We hope this will facilitate implementation of our approach in neural-inspired hardware.

# 2 PRELIMINARIES AND PROBLEM STATEMENT

## 2.1 Fast matrix multiplication algorithms

Strassen developed the first matrix multiplication algorithm requiring $O(N^{3-\varepsilon})$ multiplications [22]. Strassen observed that one can compute the matrix product, $C = AB$ for $2 \times 2$ matrices $A$ and $B$ using 7 multiplications rather than the 8 multiplications required by the näive algorithm. The reduction in multiplications comes at the expense of additional additions and subtractions.

$$
\begin{aligned}
M_1 &= A_{11}(B_{12} - B_{22}) \\
M_2 &= (A_{21} + A_{22})B_{11} \\
M_3 &= (A_{11} + A_{22})(B_{11} + B_{22}) \\
M_4 &= A_{22}(B_{21} - B_{11}) \\
M_5 &= (A_{11} + A_{12})B_{22} \\
M_6 &= (A_{21} - A_{11})(B_{11} + B_{12}) \\
M_7 &= (A_{12} - A_{22})(B_{21} + B_{22}).
\end{aligned}
\qquad
\begin{aligned}
C_{11} &= M_3 + M_4 - M_5 + M_7 \\
C_{12} &= M_1 + M_5 \\
C_{21} &= M_2 + M_4 \\
C_{22} &= M_1 - M_2 + M_3 + M_6.
\end{aligned}
$$

Figure 1: Strassen's algorithm for multiplying two $2 \times 2$ matrices $A$ and $B$. The 7 multiplications computed in Strassen's algorithm are represented by $M_1, \ldots, M_7$. Each $M_i$ is the product of weighted sums of entries of matrices $A$ and $B$. The entries of product matrix $C$ are then computed from the $M_i$ using only addition and subtraction. One can verify by substitution and expansion that the entries of $C$ are set to the proper expressions involving entries of $A$ and $B$.

Figure 1 gives Strassen's algorithm for $2 \times 2$ matrices. The algorithm is generalized to $N \times N$ matrices $A$ and $B$, where $N = 2^l$ for some positive integer $l$, as follows. We partition $A$ and $B$ into 4 blocks, each of size $N/2 \times N/2$, and let $A_{ij}$ and $B_{ij}$ refer to these blocks, for $i, j \in \{1, 2\}$. The above equations remain correct. However, each $M_i$ now represents a multiplication of two $N/2 \times N/2$ matrices. We can recursively apply the above procedure to perform each of these multiplications until the blocks are individual matrix elements or, for more practical applications, sufficiently small. For each of the $l = \log_2 N$ levels of recursion, we invoke 7 recursive matrix multiplications, resulting in a total of $7^{\log_2 N} = N^{\log_2 7} \approx N^{2.81}$ scalar multiplications. The recurrence relation for the total number of arithmetic operations is $T(N) = 7 \cdot T(N/2) + 18 \cdot (N/2)^2$ and $T(1) = O(1)$. The $18 \cdot (N/2)^2$ term arises from the 18 additions or subtractions on $N/2 \times N/2$ blocks in the expressions above. This recurrence shows the total number of scalar additions or subtractions is also $O(N^{\log_2 7})$.

Although Strassen's seminal approach was based on a fast matrix multiplication algorithm for $2 \times 2$ matrices, subsequent work has yielded improved algorithms by employing a fast matrix multiplication algorithm involving larger square matrices as well as more sophisticated techniques. The currently best known algorithm requires $O(N^{2.373})$ operations [11]. For the sake of exposition, we view fast matrix multiplication algorithms as recursive divide-and-conquer approaches, yet our techniques extend to the more general tensor perspective of fast matrix multiplication. See the survey by Bläser [4] for a detailed introduction to and history of this area, including the connection between the (border) rank of the matrix multiplication tensor and fast matrix multiplication algorithms.

## 2.2 Technical challenges

The divide-and-conquer Strassen's algorithm has a natural $O(\log N)$-time parallel (PRAM) implementation with a total work of $O(N^{\log_2 7})$

arithmetic operations. The main question we consider is whether Strassen's approach and subsequent improvements of it can yield a *constant-time* algorithm implemented using threshold circuits with $O(N^{3-\varepsilon})$ gates, where the latter is a measure of total work. The recursive ($O(\log N)$-depth) implementation of Strassen's algorithm only performs scalar multiplications during the base case. However, it performs matrix additions and subtractions at each level before and after the recursion, reusing computed results.

If we attempt to implement Strassen's approach without recursion and the consequent reuse of computed results, we must first compute $N^{\log_2 7}$ scalars that are linear combinations of entries of $A$ and another $N^{\log_2 7}$ scalars representing linear combinations of entries of $B$. The main technical hurdle is that such linear combinations involve up to $N$ entries of $A$ or $B$, and we seek to compute $O(N^{\log_2 7})$ of these sums with constant-depth threshold circuits. A näive implementation would require $\Omega(N^{1+\log_2 7})$ gates.

We overcome this hurdle by selecting a constant or $O(\log\log N)$ number of levels of recursion out of the $O(\log N)$ levels suggested by the standard implementation of Strassen's approach. We make the notion of selecting a level of recursion precise in Section 4. This allows us enough reuse of computed results within the confines of a constant-depth or $O(\log\log N)$-depth circuit to achieve our results. We note that we must carefully select the levels of recursion employed; for instance, simply selecting every $k$th level does not achieve our best results.

### 2.3 Problem statement

We develop threshold circuits to compute the matrix product $C = AB$ of two $N \times N$ integer matrices $A$ and $B$. Our results assume the entries of $A$ and $B$ require at most $O(\log N)$ bits. We also consider a related problem: given an integer matrix $A$ as above and an integer $\tau$, determine whether the matrix trace of $A^3$ is at least $\tau$. This problem is solved by a simpler threshold circuit than for computing matrix product and serves to illustrate our main ideas. It also has applications to triangle counting in graphs as we describe below.

Let $A$ be the $N\times N$ symmetric adjacency matrix of a simple graph $G = (V, E)$ with $N$ nodes: for $i, j \in V$, $A_{ij} = A_{ji} = 1$ if $ij \in E$, and $A_{ij} = A_{ji} = 0$ otherwise. Since there are no self-loops in the graph, we have $A_{ii} = 0$ for all nodes $i$. Consider the square of the adjacency matrix, $C = A^2$. For $i, j \in V$ with $i \neq j$, $C_{ij} = \sum_{k\in V} A_{ik}A_{kj} = |\{k \in V \mid ik \in E \text{ and } kj \in E \text{ and } k \neq i, j\}|$, which is the number of paths of length 2 between $i$ and $j$. If there is an edge between the nodes $i$ and $j$, then each path of length 2 between them, along with the edge $ij$, forms a triangle in $G$. Moreover, every triangle containing $i$ and $j$ arises in this way. Suppose $G$ has $\Delta$ triangles. Then,

$$3\Delta = \sum_{i,j\in V: i<j} A_{ij}C_{ij}, \qquad (1)$$

since the sum counts each triangle once for each of its edges. Thus one can count the triangles in $G$ by summing some of the entries of $A^2$. An equivalent computation is the trace of $A^3$, trace$(A^3)$, which, from (1), is equal to $6\Delta$. This counts the loop from each vertex in each direction.

We employ a threshold circuit implementation of fast matrix multiplication algorithms to compute this sum in constant depth using $O(N^{3-\varepsilon})$ gates. In fact the exponent of our gate count can be made arbitrarily close to the exponent of the arithmetic operation count for the best possible fast matrix multiplication algorithm.

We explain our notion of a fast matrix multiplication algorithm. We assume we are given an algorithm for multiplying two $T \times T$ matrices using a total of $r$ multiplications (for Strassen's algorithm, $T = 2$ and $r = 7$). We assume $N = T^l$ for some positive integer $l$. As outlined in Section 2.1, this yields a recursive algorithm for computing the product of two $N \times N$ matrices, $C = AB$, using a total of $r^l = r^{\log_T N} = N^{\log_T r}$ scalar multiplications.

As with Strassen's algorithm, we assume we are given a list of $r$ expressions for each of the multiplications, $M_1, \ldots, M_r$; we view each $M_i$ as an expression involving the $T^2$ different $N/T \times N/T$ blocks of $A$ and $B$. In particular each $M_i$ is a product of a $\{-1, 1\}$-weighted sum of blocks of $A$ with a $\{-1, 1\}$-weighted sum of blocks of $B$. We also assume the fast matrix multiplication algorithm provides a list of $T^2$ expressions, each representing a $N/T \times N/T$ block of $C$ as a $\{-1, 1\}$-weighted sum of the $M_i$. More general fast matrix multiplication algorithms may allow the $M_i$ to be products of linear combinations with rational weights beyond $\{-1, 1\}$ (likewise for the entries of $C$). Although we do not present details here, our techniques can be extended for such fast matrix multiplication algorithms (these weights correspond to the $w_i$ in Lemma 3.2 in Section 3).

For $1 \leq i \leq r$, let $a_i$ be the number of distinct blocks of $A$ that appear in the expression $M_i$, and let $b_i$ be defined analogously with respect to $B$. We let $c_i$ be the number of expressions for blocks of $C$ in which $M_i$ appears.

*Definition 2.1.* We let

$$s_A = \sum_{1\leq i\leq r} a_i,\ s_B = \sum_{1\leq i\leq r} b_i, \text{ and } s_C = \sum_{1\leq i\leq r} c_i.$$

We define the *sparsity* of a fast matrix multiplication algorithm as $s = \max\{s_A, s_B, s_C\}$.

Sparsity will be an essential ingredient of our analysis, and we better motivate it in Section 4.3. Others [2, 3] consider sparsity in analyzing and improving the numerical stability of fast matrix multiplication algorithms, though they do not refer to it by the same name.

We use the following notation in proofs of circuit quality. We define bits$(m)$ as the minimum number of bits required to express the nonnegative integer $m$ in binary, i.e. the least integer $l$ such that $m < 2^l$.

## 3 BASIC $TC^0$ ARITHMETIC CIRCUITS

We first develop the fundamental $TC^0$ arithmetic circuits on which our results rely. Our circuits are designed with neuromorphic implementation in mind, and we try to favor simple constructions over those that offer the least depth or gate count. The bulk of the computation performed by our circuits is computing the bits of integer-weighted sums of nonnegative integers, $\sum_i w_i x_i$, where the nonnegative $x_i$ depend upon the inputs to the circuit but the weights $w_i$ are constants associated with the circuit.

Our first circuit follows from a classical technique to compute symmetric functions in $TC^0$ by Muroga from 1959 [14, 15]; it is also a special case of a more general result by Siu et al. [20]. We include a proof to demonstrate the simplicity of the construction.

Lemma 3.1. *Let $s = \sum_i w_i x_i$ be an integer-weighted sum of bits, $x_i \in \{0, 1\}$. We assume $s \geq 0$ and fix an integer $l$ such that $s \in [0, 2^l)$. For $1 \leq k \leq l$, the $k$th most significant bit of $s$ can be computed by a depth-2 threshold circuit using $2^k + 1$ gates.*

Proof. We define bool($P$), for a predicate $P$, to be 1 if predicate $P$ is true and 0 otherwise.

The $k$th most significant bit of $s$ is 1 precisely when $s$ lies in one of the intervals $[i2^{l-k}, (i+1)2^{l-k})$ for some odd integer $1 \leq i < 2^k$. The interval enumerates over all combinations of bits less signicant than the $k$th and the odd multipliers $i$ enumerate over all combinations of bits more significant than $k$. The first layer of our circuit computes the function $y_i := \text{bool}(s \geq i2^{l-k})$, for $1 \leq i \leq 2^k$. The output of the circuit is $\text{bool}(\sum_{i \text{ odd}}(y_i - y_{i+1}) \geq 1)$, since $y_i - y_{i+1}$ is 1 if $s \in [i2^{l-k}, (i+1)2^{l-k})$ and is 0 otherwise. □

The circuit construction for the above lemma requires an integer $l$ such that the sum $s$ is guaranteed to be in $[0, 2^l)$. Note that if $s \notin [0, 2^l)$, the circuit for any $k$ outputs 0. We build upon the above to obtain our primary addition circuit. The next lemma is a generalized and strengthened version of Siu et al.'s Lemma 3.1 in [20] for the depth-2 case.

Lemma 3.2. *Let $s = \sum_i w_i z_i$ be an integer-weighted sum of $n$ nonnegative numbers $z_i$, each with at most $b$ bits. We assume $s \geq 0$ and let $w = \max_i |w_i|$. The sum $s$ can be computed by a depth-2 threshold circuit with $O(wbn)$ gates.*

Proof. The sum $s$ requires at most $\text{bits}(nw(2^b - 1)) \leq \text{bits}(n) + \text{bits}(w) + b$ bits. (Recall the defintion of bits() in Section 2.3).

First we compute the $j$th (least significant) bit of $s$, for $1 \leq j \leq b$. Let $s_j = \sum_i w_i \tilde{z}_i$, where $\tilde{z}_i$ is obtained from $z_i$ by ignoring all but the least significant $j$ bits. Note that $s_j$ requires at most $\text{bits}(n) + \text{bits}(w) + j$ bits and that $s$ and $s_j$ have the same least significant $j$ bits. Furthermore, since we are given the bits of each $\tilde{z}_i$, we may treat $s_j$ as an integer-weighted sum of bits, where each weight is a product of some $w_i$ with a power of 2. Thus we may compute the $jth$ bit of $s_j$ by appealing to Lemma 3.1 on $s_j$ with $k = \text{bits}(n) + \text{bits}(w) + 1$. To see this recall that $k$ represents the $k$th most significant bit. The $j$th least significant bit of $s_j$ is the $(\text{bits}(s_j) - j + 1) = n + w + j - j + 1$ most significant bit. This circuit requires $2^k + 1 = 2 \cdot 2^{\text{bits}(n)} \cdot 2^{\text{bits}(w)} + 1 = O(wn)$ gates, hence $O(bwn)$ gates suffice to compute the $b$ least significant bits of $s$.

Appealing to Lemma 3.1 to compute each of the remaining $a = \text{bits}(n) + \text{bits}(w)$ most significant bits of $s$ requires $O(\sum_{k=1}^{a} 2^k) = O(2^a) = O(wn)$ gates. This is improved in practice by observing that the functions $y_i$ computed for $k = \text{bits}(n) + \text{bits}(w)$ in the proof of Lemma 3.1 include those required for all the most significant $\text{bits}(n) + \text{bits}(w)$ bits of $s$. □

We need to compute products of numbers as well. However, the products we compute are only used as inputs to other threshold gates, and we do not need an explicit base-2 representation of the bits of these products. A more generic representation suffices: a *representation* of an integer $x$ is an integer-weighted sum of binary variables, $x = \sum_{1 \leq i \leq d} w_i x_i$ with $x_i \in \{0, 1\}$ and $d$ polynomial in bits($x$).

Lemma 3.3. *A representation of the product of three $m$-bit nonnegative integers can be computed by a depth-1 threshold circuit with $m^3$ gates.*

Proof. We compute a representation of the product of $x = \sum_{1 \leq i \leq m} 2^{i-1} x_i$, $y = \sum_{1 \leq j \leq m} 2^{j-1} y_j$, and $z = \sum_{1 \leq k \leq m} 2^{k-1} z_k$, with $x_i, y_j, z_k \in \{0, 1\}$. Thus $xyz = \sum_{1 \leq i,j,k \leq m} 2^{i+j+k-3} x_i y_j z_k$, which is a representation for $xyz$. This representation differs from the standard binary representation in that $2^{i+j+k-3}$ can represent the same power of 2 for different values of $i, j$, and $k$. We use $m^3$ gates in a single layer with predicates $x_i + y_j + z_k \geq 3$ to compute $x_i y_j z_k \in \{0, 1\}$ for $1 \leq i, j, k \leq m$. □

Our results require only the above relatively simple arithmetic circuits. This facilitates practical implementation.

*Negative numbers.* The above lemmas give circuits to compute products and weighted sums of nonnegative integers. However, they can be extended to handle negative integers. We represent each integer $x$ as $x = x^+ - x^-$, where $x^+$ and $x^-$ are each nonnegative. Other more efficient representations are possible, but we select this one as it makes for a relatively simple presentation and implementation at the cost of a constant-factor overhead in gate and wire count.

The workhorse subroutine of our circuits, captured by Lemma 3.2, is computing the bits of integer-weighted sums of nonnegative integers, $s = \sum_i w_i x_i$, where the $x_i = x_i^+ - x_i^-$ depend upon the inputs to the circuit but the $w_i$ are constant with respect to the inputs. Let $W^+$ be the set of indices with $w_i > 0$, and let $W^-$ be those indices with $w_i < 0$. We define $s^+ = \sum_{i \in W^+} w_i x_i^+ + \sum_{i \in W^-}(-w_i) x_i^-$ to be the positive terms in sum $s$, and we define $s^- = \sum_{i \in W^+} w_i x_i^- + \sum_{i \in W^-}(-w_i) x_i^+$ to be the negation of the negative terms in sum $s$. We have $s = s^+ - s^-$ and $s^+, s^- \geq 0$. Moreover, each of $s^+$ and $s^-$ is an integer-weighted sum of nonnegative integers, hence the bits of each of $s^+$ and $s^-$ may be computed using two separate instances of the circuit of Lemma 3.2. Each of these circuit instances only depends on the $x_i^+$ and $x_i^-$ hence we may apply them in parallel without increasing the depth of the resulting overall circuit.

Computing products also incurs extra constant overhead. The representation of the product of three numbers, $xyz$ described in the proof of Lemma 3.3 becomes $xyz = \sum_{1 \leq i,j,k \leq m} 2^{i+j+k-3}(x_i^+ - x_i^-)(y_j^+ - y_j^-)(z_k^+ - z_k^-)$. Thus $\sum_{1 \leq i,j,k \leq m}[2^{i+j+k-3}(x_i^+ y_j^+ z_k^+ + x_i^+ y_j^- z_k^- + x_i^- y_j^+ z_k^- + x_i^- y_j^- z_k^+) + (-2^{i+j+k-3})(x_i^+ y_j^+ z_k^- + x_i^+ y_j^- z_k^+ + x_i^- y_j^+ z_k^+ + x_i^- y_j^- z_k^-)]$ is also a representation of $xyz$ that requires eight times as many gates to compute, which is still $O(m^3)$.

For ease of exposition, we proceed as if we were only computing positive quantities. From this point on, we assume that a number $x$ requires at most $b$ bits, by which we mean that each of $x^+$ and $x^-$ requires at most $b$ bits.

# 4 SUBCUBIC $TC^0$ CIRCUITS FOR TRACE AND MATRIX MULTIPLICATION

## 4.1 Overview

Our circuits for matrix trace and matrix multiplication implement a given conventional fast matrix multiplication algorithm in both a depth-efficient and gate-efficient manner. We assume we are given

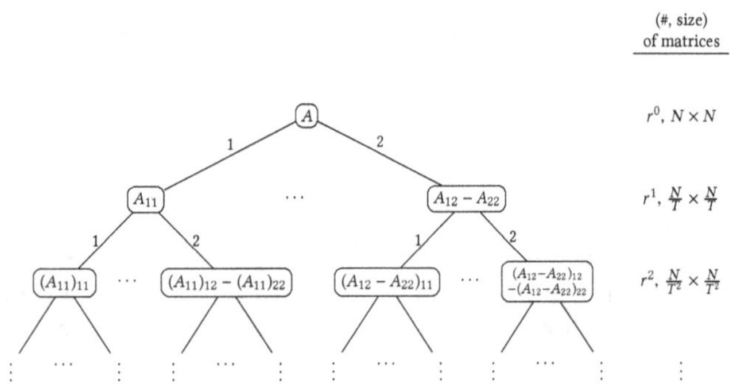


Figure 2: The $r$-ary tree $\mathcal{T}_A$ for Strassen's Algorithm ($r = 7, T = 2$). For $K \times K$ matrices $U$ and $V$, the notation $U_{ij}$ or $(U)_{ij}$ refers to the $(i, j)$th $\frac{K}{T} \times \frac{K}{T}$ block of $U$. Observe that $(U + V)_{ij} = U_{ij} + V_{ij}$. Each node has children corresponding to the $r$ multiplication expressions $M_i$ (see Figure 1). An edge associated with $M_i$ is labeled with the number of terms of $A$ that appear in $M_i$. Each node $u$ on level $h$, starting with the root as level 0, corresponds to a matrix that is a weighted sum of $\frac{N}{T^h} \times \frac{N}{T^h}$ blocks of $A$. The number of blocks of $A$ appearing in such a sum is the product of the edge labels on the path from $u$ to the root of the tree. For example, $(A_{12} - A_{22})_{12} - (A_{12} - A_{22})_{22} = (A_{12})_{12} - (A_{22})_{12} - (A_{12})_{22} + (A_{22})_{22}$ is a weighted sum of 4 $\frac{N}{T^2} \times \frac{N}{T^2}$ blocks of $A$. The $N^{\log_T r}$ leaves of $\mathcal{T}_A$ correspond to scalars that are weighted sums of entries of $A$.

$N \times N$ integer matrices $A$ and $B$ with entries of size $O(\log N)$. We consider two problems: (1) determining whether trace$(A^3) \geq \tau$, for an integer $\tau$, and (2) computing the bits of the matrix product $C = AB$. We consider the first problem in this section, and the second problem in the next section.

We define trees $\mathcal{T}_A$ and $\mathcal{T}_B$ for the input matrices $A$ and $B$, respectively, based on the recursive or divide-and-conquer structure of the fast matrix multiplication algorithm. The nodes in $\mathcal{T}_A$ represent weighted sums of blocks of $A$ and likewise for $\mathcal{T}_B$. The root of $\mathcal{T}_A$ represents the matrix $A$, while the leaves represent weighted sums of its entries. See Figure 2 for a detailed explanation.

In a conventional PRAM implementation of a fast matrix multiplication algorithm, all the matrices at each level of $\mathcal{T}_A$ and $\mathcal{T}_B$ are computed, and the results are reused. Since there are $O(\log N)$ levels, we cannot hope to compute all the matrices at each level in a constant-depth circuit. We give constant-depth threshold circuits that computes all nodes on only a constant number of levels of $\mathcal{T}_A$ and $\mathcal{T}_B$ while using a number of gates arbitrarily close to the total work performed by the fast matrix multiplication algorithm.

Our circuit computes the same $O(N^w)$ scalar products as the underlying fast matrix multiplication algorithm. These scalars correspond to the leaves of $\mathcal{T}_A$ and those of $\mathcal{T}_B$ respectively. Our algorithm processes these trees in a top-down fashion to compute the scalars, corresponding to the leaves. We then appeal to Lemma 3.3 to compute the product of each scalar corresponding to a leaf of $\mathcal{T}_A$ with the corresponding leaf of $\mathcal{T}_B$. For both the problems we solve, we will need to consider another tree with similar structure to $\mathcal{T}_A$ and $\mathcal{T}_B$; however, these trees will be used in different ways.

We assume, as in Section 2.3, that we have a fast matrix multiplication algorithm that multiplies two $T \times T$ matrices using $r$ multiplications. We describe an improved $TC^0$ circuit for computing the values at the leaves of $\mathcal{T}_A$. Our results extend naturally to computing the leaves of $\mathcal{T}_B$. Level $h$ of $\mathcal{T}_A$ contains $r^h$ nodes, each corresponding to an $N/T^h \times N/T^h$ matrix. Moreover, each entry of each matrix at level $h$ is the $\{-1, 1\}$-weighted sum of at most $T^{2h}$ entries of the root matrix, $A$. Hence if each entry of the integer matrix $A$ requires at most $b$ bits, the number of bits required for each entry of a matrix at level $h$ is at most

$$\text{bits}((2^b - 1)T^{2h}) \leq b + \text{bits}(T^{2h}) = b + O(h \log T). \quad (2)$$

For our results we assume $b = O(\log N)$ bits. Moreover, $T$ is a constant associated with the fast matrix multiplication selected, and $h \leq \log_T N$, hence the scalar values at the leaves of $\mathcal{T}_A$ require $O(\log N)$ bits.

We give a subcubic $TC^0$ circuit for computing the matrix product $C = AB$ in the next section, but first, we illustrate our main ideas by showing how to check trace$(A^3) \geq \tau$. As mentioned in Section 2.3, this allows us, for example, to count triangles in a graph. The bulk of our work lies in showing how to compute the $N^{\log_T r}$ scalar products prescribed by the fast matrix multiplication algorithm. Each such scalar product is between a weighted sum of entries of $A$ and a weighted sum of entries of $B$. We next show how to compute these weighted sums for $A$ with a circuit that computes a constant number of levels of $\mathcal{T}_A$. An analogous construction works for $B$.

## 4.2 Approach

Our main goal in the following sections is to give $O(\log\log N)$-depth, $\widetilde{O}(N^{\omega})$-gate and $O(d)$-depth, $\widetilde{O}(N^{\omega+O(\gamma^d)})$-gate threshold circuits for multiplying two $N \times N$ integer matrices with $O(\log N)$-bit entries, for a positive integer $d$ and constant $\gamma < 1$.

We first motivate our approach by attempting to construct a constant-depth and $O(N^{3-\epsilon})$-gate threshold circuit for matrix multiplication using Strassen's algorithm as a guide. As described in the previous section and Figure 2, our immediate goal is to compute the scalars associated with the leaves of $\mathcal{T}_A$ (and $\mathcal{T}_B$) for Strassen's algorithm by selecting a constant number of levels of $\mathcal{T}_A$ to compute. The most natural approach is perhaps to directly compute the leaves, at level $\log_2 N$, without computing any other level. The leaves of $\mathcal{T}_A$ correspond to $\{-1, 1\}$-weighted sums of at most $N$ entries of $A$. By recalling (2) and invoking Lemma 3.2, we can compute each such sum in depth 2 using $O(N \log N)$ gates. However, we must compute $O(N^{\log_2 7})$ such sums, yielding a total of $\widetilde{O}(N^{1+\log_2 7}) \approx \widetilde{O}(N^{3.81})$ gates. This can be improved to $\approx \widetilde{O}(N^{3.58})$ by observing that not all sums have the same number of summands; however, this still fails to achieve our goal.

We can improve the approach by employing addition circuits of depth greater than 2 due to Siu et al. [20] (Corollary 2). This allows computation of the desired sums in depth $O(d)$ using $O(dN^{1/d})$ gates, yielding the following result.

THEOREM 4.1. *Suppose we are given $N \times N$ integer matrices $A$ and $B$ with entries of size $O(\log N)$ bits. There is a threshold circuit of depth $O(d)$ that computes the matrix product $AB$ using $\widetilde{O}(dN^{\omega+1/d})$ gates.*

We do not include a full proof of this theorem as our main results give superior results, both in terms of gate count and the simplicity of the resulting circuits. The results of the following sections show how to more carefully select a constant number of levels of $\mathcal{T}_A$ and $\mathcal{T}_B$ in order to improve the exponent in the gate count from $\omega + 1/d$ to $\omega + O(\gamma^d)$ for a constant $\gamma < 1$.

### 4.3 Matrix trace

We select $t$ levels, $0 = h_0 < h_1 < h_2 < \cdots < h_t$ of the tree $\mathcal{T}_A$. Our $TC^0$ circuit computes all of the matrices at these $t$ levels of $\mathcal{T}_A$. Our goal is to compute the scalars corresponding to the leaves of $\mathcal{T}_A$, hence $h_t = \log_T N$. The benefit of computing level $h_i$ is that each entry of each matrix at level $h_{i+1}$ is then a $\{-1, 1\}$-weighted sum of at most $T^{2(h_{i+1}-h_i)}$ matrices at level $h_i$.

Our results rely on parameters associated with our fast matrix multiplication algorithm. Recall $s_A$ from Definition 2.1. We define $\alpha = r/s_A$ and $\beta = s_A/T^2$, and we have that $0 < \alpha \le 1$ and $\beta \ge 1$ (for Strassen's algorithm, $\alpha = 7/12$ and $\beta = 3$).

Lemma 4.2. *For $1 \le i \le t$, if the matrices at level $h_{i-1}$ of $\mathcal{T}_A$ have been computed, then the matrices at level $h_i$ can be computed in depth 2 using $O((b + h_{i-1})\alpha^{h_{i-1}}\beta^{h_i}N^2)$ gates.*

Proof. The $r^{h_i}$ nodes at level $h_i$ of $\mathcal{T}_A$ each correspond to an $N/T^{h_i} \times N/T^{h_i}$ matrix. We set $\delta_i = h_i - h_{i-1}$ for convenience. We can associate each node $u$ at level $h_i$ with the unique subtree rooted at level $h_{i-1}$ that contains it. The $N/T^{h_i} \times N/T^{h_i}$ matrix corresponding to $u$ is a sum of at most $T^{2\delta_i}$ blocks of the $N/T^{h_{i-1}} \times N/T^{h_{i-1}}$ matrix associated with the root of the subtree containing $u$.

We seek a better bound on the number of such blocks we must sum to obtain the matrix associated with $u$. Let size($u$) represent this quantity, and let root($u$) be the node at level $h_{i-1}$ on the path from $u$ to the root of $\mathcal{T}_A$. Recall that each edge of $\mathcal{T}_A$ corresponds to one of the fast matrix multiplication expressions $M_i$ and that $a_i$ is the number of distinct blocks of $A$ that appear in $M_i$ (defined in Section 2.3). The quantity size($u$) is the product of the $a_i$ associated with the edges on the path from $u$ to root($u$) (see Figure 2). Thus for each node $v$ at level $h_{i-1}$, we have:

$$\sum_{\{u \mid \mathrm{root}(u)=v\}} \mathrm{size}(u) = \sum_{m_1+\cdots+m_r=\delta_i} \binom{\delta_i}{m_1,\ldots,m_r} \prod_{1\le j\le r} a_j^{m_j} = s_A^{\delta_i}, \tag{3}$$

where the last equality follows from the multinomial theorem. We now bound the number of gates required to compute the matrices at level $h_i$. Since we assume the matrices at level $h_{i-1}$ have been computed, by Lemma 3.2, each entry of the matrix associated with node $u$ at level $h_i$ can be computed using $O((b + h_{i-1})\mathrm{size}(u))$ gates in depth 2. We charge the gate count for $u$ to root($u$), and by (3) and (2), we have that the number of gates charged to each node at level $h_{i-1}$ is

$$O((b + h_{i-1})s_A^{h_i - h_{i-1}}N^2/T^{2h_i}),$$

hence the total number of gates required for level $h_i$ is

$$O((b + h_{i-1})r^{h_{i-1}}s_A^{h_i-h_{i-1}}N^2/T^{2h_i}) = O((b + h_{i-1})(r/s_A)^{h_{i-1}}(s_A/T^2)^{h_i}N^2),$$

as desired. □

Next we show how to set the $h_i$ so that the number of gates required at each level is approximately balanced. This yields a total gate count that is, at worst, within a factor of $t$ of the gate count for an optimal setting of the $h_i$. We must assume the number of multiplications our fast $T \times T$ matrix multiplication algorithm requires is greater than $T^2$. The results, as stated and proven below, do not hold if we have an optimal fast matrix multiplication algorithm where the number of multiplications, $r = T^2$. We set $\gamma = \log_\beta(1/\alpha)$. Note that $0 < \gamma < 1$ since $r > T^2$ is equivalent to $\alpha\beta > 1$ (for Strassen's algorithm, $\gamma \approx 0.491$).

Lemma 4.3. *Let $h_i = \lceil (1 - \gamma^i)\rho \rceil$, for some $\rho > 0$. Then all the matrices at levels $h_1, \ldots, h_t$ of $\mathcal{T}_A$ can be computed in depth $2t$ using $O(t(\alpha\beta)^\rho(b + \log N)N^2)$ gates.*

Proof. We have $h_i \le \log_T N$ for all $0 \le i \le t$ since the latter is the height of $\mathcal{T}_A$. By Lemma 4.2, level $h_i$ can be computed in depth 2 using $O((b + \log N)\alpha^{h_{i-1}}\beta^{h_i}N^2)$ gates.

Let $\tilde{h}_i = (1 - \gamma^i)\rho$. Observe that

$$\sum_{1\le i\le t} \alpha^{h_{i-1}}\beta^{h_i} < \beta \sum_{1\le i\le t} \alpha^{\tilde{h}_{i-1}}\beta^{\tilde{h}_i},$$

hence it suffices to bound $\sum_{1\le i\le t} \alpha^{\tilde{h}_{i-1}}\beta^{\tilde{h}_i}$. The terms in this sum are all equal:

$$\alpha^{\tilde{h}_{i-1}}\beta^{\tilde{h}_i} = \left(\frac{\alpha\beta}{\alpha^{\gamma^{i-1}}\beta^{\gamma^i}}\right)^\rho = \left(\frac{\alpha\beta}{\alpha^{\gamma^{i-1}}(\beta^\gamma)^{\gamma^{i-1}}}\right)^\rho = (\alpha\beta)^\rho,$$

so that $\sum_{1\le i\le t} \alpha^{h_{i-1}}\beta^{h_i} = O(t(\alpha\beta)^\rho)$, from which the claim follows. □

The above lemma establishes a tradeoff in the following sense. The value $\rho$ impacts the total number of gates. However, we require that $h_t = \log_T N$, which imposes constraints on $t$ and, consequently, the depth of the circuit. The larger $\rho$, the smaller $t$ needs to be in order for $h_t = \log_T N$.

The natural strategy of taking $h_i = \lceil i \log_T N/t \rceil$ yields a weaker result, comparable to Theorem 4.1. We now establish our main theorems by better quantifying the tradeoff between $\rho$ and $t$. For these theorems we assume we are given a fast matrix multiplication algorithm and take $\omega = \log_T r$.

Theorem 4.4. *Suppose we are given an integer $\tau$ and an $N \times N$ integer matrix $A$ with entries of size $O(\log N)$ bits. There is a threshold circuit of depth $O(\log\log N)$ that determines whether trace($A^3$) $\ge \tau$ using $\tilde{O}(N^\omega)$ gates.*

Proof. We appeal to Lemma 4.3, setting $\rho = \log_T N$. The gate bound follows from $(\alpha\beta)^\rho = (r/T^2)^{\log_T N} = N^{\omega-2}$. To bound the depth, we set $t = \lfloor \log_{1/\gamma} \log_T N \rfloor + 1 > \log_{1/\gamma} \log_T N$. This implies:

$$\log_T N - (1 - \gamma^t)\log_T N < \log_T N - (1 - 1/\log_T N)\log_T N = 1.$$

Thus $h_t = \lceil (1 - \gamma^t)\log_T N \rceil = \log_T N$ as desired.

This shows that we can compute the values corresponding to the leaves of $\mathcal{T}_A$ and $\mathcal{T}_B$ in the stated gate and depth bounds. One may see that each entry $C_{ij}$ is a weighted sum of products, $\sum_{k\in I_{ij}} w_{ijk}p_k$, where each $p_k$ corresponds to a product between a leaf of $\mathcal{T}_A$ and the corresponding leaf of $\mathcal{T}_B$ with each weight $w_{ijk} \in \{-1, 1\}$. We seek to compute

$$\frac{\text{trace}(A^3)}{2} = \sum_{i<j} A_{ij}C_{ij} = \sum_{i<j} A_{ij}\left(\sum_{k\in I_{ij}} w_{ijk}p_k\right) \quad (4)$$

$$= \sum_k p_k \left(\sum_{i<j:k\in I_{ij}} w_{ijk}A_{ij}\right).$$

Thus for each product, $p_k$, we want to multiply it with a $\{-1, 1\}$-weighted sum over entries of $A$. We may compute these weighted sums independently and in parallel with those for $A$ and $B$ using the same techniques. Thus we seek to compute $N^\omega$ products of 3 $O(\log N)$-bit numbers, and we appeal to Lemma 3.3 to accomplish this in depth 1 using a total of $\widetilde{O}(N^\omega)$ gates. A final output gate sums the representations of the products computed by Lemma 3.3 and compares with the threshold $\tau$. □

We now prove our main theorem by exhibiting a more refined tradeoff between $\rho$ and $t$.

Theorem 4.5. *Suppose we are given an integer $\tau$, an $N \times N$ integer matrix $A$ with entries of size $O(\log N)$ bits, and a positive integer $d$. There is a threshold circuit of depth at most $2d + 5$ that determines whether trace$(A^3) \geq \tau$ using $\widetilde{O}(dN^{\omega + c\gamma^d})$ gates, where $c > 0$ and $\gamma < 1$ are constants with respect to $N$ and $d$ that depend on the parameters of the fast matrix multiplication algorithm employed.*

Proof. As for the previous theorem, we appeal to Lemma 4.3, this time setting $\rho = \log_T N + \varepsilon \log_{\alpha\beta} N$, for a constant $\varepsilon > 0$ whose value is given below. We have $(\alpha\beta)^\rho = (r/T^2)^{\log_T N} N^\varepsilon = N^{\omega - 2 + \varepsilon}$.

We set $\varepsilon = \gamma^d \log_T(\alpha\beta)/(1-\gamma) > \gamma^d \log_T(\alpha\beta)/(1-\gamma^d)$. This implies:

$$\begin{aligned}
&\log_T N - (1-\gamma^d)(\log_T N + \varepsilon \log_{\alpha\beta} N) \\
&< \log_T N - (1-\gamma^d)(\log_T N + (\gamma^d/(1-\gamma^d))\log_T(\alpha\beta)\log_{\alpha\beta} N) \\
&= \log_T N - (1-\gamma^d)\log_T N - \gamma^d \log_T N \\
&= 0,
\end{aligned}$$

hence we may take $t < d$ in Lemma 4.3 in order to have $h_t = \log_T N$. The theorem follows from the argument used in the proof of Theorem 4.4 and taking $c = \log_T(\alpha\beta)/(1-\gamma)$ (for Strassen's algorithm, $c \approx 1.585$) . □

## 4.4 Matrix product

Now we describe how to compute the entries of the matrix product $C = AB$, where we assume the entries of the $N \times N$ matrices $A$ and $B$ require $O(\log N)$ bits. We define a tree $\mathcal{T}_{AB}$ with the same structure as $\mathcal{T}_A$ and $\mathcal{T}_B$. Each node of $\mathcal{T}_{AB}$ represents the product of the matrices of the corresponding nodes of $\mathcal{T}_A$ and $\mathcal{T}_B$. Hence the root of $\mathcal{T}_{AB}$ represents the matrix $C = AB$, and the leaves represent the $N^{\log_T r}$ scalar products computed by our fast matrix multiplication algorithm. We compute the root of $\mathcal{T}_{AB}$ in a bottom-up manner assuming that we are only computing the nodes at levels $\log_T N = h_t > h_{t-1} > \ldots > h_1 > h_0 = 0$.

We let $\alpha_C = r/s_C$ and $\beta_C = s_C/T^2$ be parameters that are a function of the fast matrix multiplication algorithm employed. Recall that from (2) we have that the scalars at the leaves of $\mathcal{T}_A$ and $\mathcal{T}_B$ each require $O(\log N)$ bits. Therefore the products of these scalars represented by the leaves of $\mathcal{T}_{AB}$ also require $O(\log N)$ bits.

We show that $\mathcal{T}_{AB}$ can be computed in a bottom-up manner with depth and gate bounds comparable to those we obtained for computing the leaves of $\mathcal{T}_A$ and $\mathcal{T}_B$ in the previous section. We will need a lemma analogous to Lemma 4.2.

Lemma 4.6. *For $1 \leq i \leq t$, if the matrices at level $h_i$ of $\mathcal{T}_{AB}$ have been computed, then the matrices at level $h_{i-1}$ can be computed in depth 2 using $\widetilde{O}(\alpha_C^{h_{i-1}}\beta_C^{h_i}N^2)$ gates.*

Proof: See the appendix.

Using the above lemma, the proof of Lemma 4.3 yields the following.

Lemma 4.7. *Let $h_i = \lceil (1-\gamma^i)\rho \rceil$, for some $\rho > 0$. Then all the matrices at levels $h_1, \ldots, h_t$ of $\mathcal{T}_{AB}$ can be computed in depth $2t$ using $\widetilde{O}(t(\alpha\beta)^\rho N^2)$ gates.*

Armed with the above lemmas, we obtain our main results in similar fashion to those for the trace of $A^3$. The structure of our circuit is that we compute the scalars corresponding to the leaves of $\mathcal{T}_A$ and $\mathcal{T}_B$ as described in the previous section. We then use Lemma 3.3 to compute the scalar products between corresponding leaves of $\mathcal{T}_A$ and $\mathcal{T}_B$ in depth 1. We finally apply the procedure outline above to compute the root of $\mathcal{T}_{AB}$, representing the matrix product $AB$, in a bottom-up manner. This essentially doubles the depth of the circuits we obtain compared to the corresponding circuits for the trace of $A^3$.

Theorem 4.8. *Suppose we are given $N \times N$ integer matrices $A$ and $B$ with entries of size $O(\log N)$ bits. There is a threshold circuit of depth $O(\log \log N)$ that computes the matrix product $AB$ using $\widetilde{O}(N^\omega)$ gates.*

Theorem 4.9. *Suppose we are given $N \times N$ integer matrices $A$ and $B$ with entries of size $O(\log N)$ bits, and a positive integer $d$. There is a threshold circuit of depth at most $4d + 1$ that computes the matrix product $AB$ using $\widetilde{O}(dN^{\omega + c\gamma^d})$ gates, where $c > 0$ and $\gamma < 1$ are constants with respect to $N$ and $d$ that depend on the parameters of the fast matrix multiplication algorithm employed.*

# 5 MATRIX-MULTIPLICATION APPLICATION BACKGROUND

In this section, we provide more background on the relevance of dense matrix multiplication to deep learning. We also discuss the relevance of matrix multiplication to triangle counting in graphs and triangle counting's relevance to social network analysis.

*Deep Learning.* As mentioned in Section 1, our primary motivation for neural-circuit-based matrix multiplication is convolutional neural networks for deep learning. See Warden's clear explanation of the role of matrix multiplication in convolution steps for neural networks [25], which we summarize here. For more details see the Stanford course notes at http://cs231n.github.io. These networks assume the input is a two-dimensional image, with an $n \times n$ grid of pixels, each with $\ell$ channels. The neural networks usually refer to the number of channels as depth, but in this paper, "depth" refers to the number of layers in our circuit. Typically the number of channels $\ell$ is a constant, but not necessarily just the three classic color channels (red, green, blue). In a convolutional step, we apply a set of $K$ *kernels* to the image. Each kernel looks for a particular subpattern such as a horizontal edge or a splash of red. The kernel considers a small constant $q \times q$ submatrix of pixels (with $\ell$ channels) at a time and is applied across the whole image based on a stride. This recognizes the pattern no matter where it is in the image. For example, if the stride is four, then the kernel is applied to every fourth column and every fourth row. A place where the kernel is applied is called a *patch*. For each patch, for each kernel, a dot product scores the extent to which the patch matches the kernel. Computing all the kernels simultaneously is a matrix multiplication. The first matrix is $P \times Q$, where $P = O(n^2)$ is the number of patches and $Q = q \times q \times \ell$ is the number of elements in a kernel. The second matrix is $Q \times K$. This gives a $P \times K$ output matrix, giving the score for each patch for each kernel.

Let $N$ be the largest matrix dimension and suppose we use a fast matrix multiplication algorithm that can multiply two $N \times N$ matrices in time $O(N^\omega)$. Our circuit requires fan-in as large as $O(N^\omega)$. These are gates at the end that compute the final output matrix entries. Two of the relevant matrix dimensions for convolutional neural networks, $K$ and $Q$, are generally constants. The third dimension $P$ is not. However, if the particular architecture can only support fan in $x$, we can break the matrix multiplication into independent pieces, each with at most $\sqrt[\omega]{x}$ rows in the first matrix. These can run in parallel, so they have the same depth, given a large enough architecture. Thus the unbounded fan-in in our algorithm is not neccesarily a practical limitation for our motivating application.

*Social Network Analysis.* Social networks of current interest are too large for our circuit methods to be practical for neuromorphic architectures in the near future. Also social network adjacency matrices are sparse, unlike the dense small matrices for convolutional neural networks we described above. Nevertheless, we briefly review the motivation for matrix multiplication in this setting. One application is computing the clustering coefficient of an $N$-node graph (or subgraph). The global clustering coefficient is the ratio of the number of triangles in the graph to the number of *wedges* (length-2 paths) in the graph. A degree-$\delta$ node is at the center of $\binom{\delta}{2}$ wedges. The global clustering coefficient is the fraction of total wedges in the graph that close into triangles. These triangles are common in social networks, where the central node of a wedge may introduce two neighbors. Social-network-analysis researchers believe a high global clustering coefficient (also called transitivity) means the graph has community structure. For example, Seshadri, Kolda and Pinar [18] assumed constant global clustering coefficients when proving a structural property of social networks they used for their BTER (Block Two-Level Erdös-Renyi) generative model. Orman, Labatut and Cherifi [16] empirically studied the relationship between community structure and clustering coefficient. They found that high clustering coefficients did imply community structure, although low clustering coefficients did not preclude it.

This paper considered the question: "Does a graph $G$ have at least $\tau$ triangles?" The user can pick a value of $\tau$ that represents reasonable community structure for their particular kind of graph. Usually they compute the total number of wedges $D$ in $O(N)$ time and set $\tau$ to some function of $D$ (perhaps just scaling by a constant).

# 6 OPEN PROBLEMS

The main open problem is whether we can do matrix multiplication with $\widetilde{O}(N^\omega)$ gates in constant depth. Theorem 4.4 shows this can be done in $O(\log \log N)$ depth. Another open question is lower bounds: What is the minimum depth of a threshold circuit for computing matrix products using $O(N^{3-\varepsilon})$ gates? Can one show that a constant-depth threshold circuit using $\widetilde{O}(N^\omega)$ gates yields an $O(\log N)$ PRAM algorithm with $O(N^\omega)$ work?

One may show that our circuits are $L$-uniform. Can a stronger uniformity condition be imposed?

One advantage of neural networks is their low energy relative to CMOS-based electronics. One possible energy model for threshold gates is to charge a gate only if it fires [24]. That is, charge a gate one unit of energy for sending a signal if and only if the weighted sum of the inputs exceeds the threshold. What is the energy complexity of the kinds of matrix-multiplication circuits we consider?

# ACKNOWLEDGEMENTS

This research was supported by the Laboratory Directed Research and Development program at Sandia National Laboratories, a multimission laboratory managed and operated by National Technology and Engineering Solutions of Sandia, LLC., a wholly owned subsidiary of Honeywell International, Inc., for the U.S. Department of Energy's National Nuclear Security Administration under contract DE-NA0003525.

# REFERENCES

[1] Frederico A. C. Azevedo, Ludmila R. B. Carvalho, Lea T. Grinberg, José Marcelo Farfel, Renata E. L. Ferretti, Renata E. P. Leite, Wilson Jacob Filho, Roberto Lent, and Suzana Herculano-Houzel. 2009. Equal numbers of neuronal and nonneuronal cells make the human brain an isometrically scaled-up primate brain. *The Journal of Comparative Neurology* 513, 5 (April 2009), 532–541. https://doi.org/10.1002/cne.21974

[2] Grey Ballard, Austin R. Benson, Alex Druinsky, Benjamin Lipshitz, and Oded Schwartz. 2016. Improving the Numerical Stability of Fast Matrix Multiplication. *SIAM J. Matrix Anal. Appl.* 37, 4 (Jan. 2016), 1382–1418. https://doi.org/10.1137/15M1032168

[3] Dario Bini and Grazia Lotti. 1980. Stability of fast algorithms for matrix multiplication. *Numer. Math.* 36 (1980), 63–72.

[4] Markus Bläser. 2013. *Fast Matrix Multiplication.* Number 5 in Graduate Surveys. Theory of Computing Library. http://theoryofcomputing.org/articles/gs005/

[5] M. Davies, N. Srinivasa, T. H. Lin, G. Chinya, Y. Cao, S. H. Choday, G. Dimou, P. Joshi, N. Imam, S. Jain, Y. Liao, C. K. Lin, A. Lines, R. Liu, D. Mathaikutty, S. McCoy, A. Paul, J. Tse, G. Venkataramanan, Y. H. Weng, A. Wild, Y. Yang, and H. Wang. 2018. Loihi: A Neuromorphic Manycore Processor with On-Chip Learning. *IEEE Micro* 38, 1 (Jan. 2018), 82–99. https://doi.org/10.1109/MM.2018.112130359

[6] Steve K Esser, Rathinakumar Appuswamy, Paul Merolla, John V Arthur, and Dharmendra S Modha. 2015. Backpropagation for energy-efficient neuromorphic computing. In *Advances in Neural Information Processing Systems.* 1117–1125.

[7] Merrick Furst, James B. Saxe, and Michael Sipser. 1984. Parity, circuits, and the polynomial-time hierarchy. *Mathematical systems theory* 17, 1 (Dec. 1984), 13–27. https://doi.org/10.1007/BF01744431

[8] Giacomo Indiveri, Bernabe Linares-Barranco, Tara Julia Hamilton, André van Schaik, Ralph Etienne-Cummings, Tobi Delbruck, Shih-Chii Liu, Piotr Dudek, Philipp Häfliger, Sylvie Renaud, Johannes Schemmel, Gert Cauwenberghs, John Arthur, Kai Hynna, Fopefolu Folowosele, Sylvain Saïghi, Teresa Serrano-Gotarredona, Jayawan Wijekoon, Yingxue Wang, and Kwabena Boahen. 2011. Neuromorphic silicon neuron circuits. *Frontiers in Neuroscience* 5, 73 (2011). https://doi.org/10.3389/fnins.2011.00073

[9] Daniel M. Kane and Ryan Williams. 2015. Super-Linear Gate and Super-Quadratic Wire Lower Bounds for Depth-Two and Depth-Three Threshold Circuits. *arXiv:1511.07860 [cs]* (Nov. 2015). http://arxiv.org/abs/1511.07860 arXiv: 1511.07860.

[10] Muhammad Mukaram Khan, David R Lester, Luis A Plana, A Rast, Xin Jin, Eustace Painkras, and Stephen B Furber. 2008. SpiNNaker: mapping neural networks onto a massively-parallel chip multiprocessor. In *Neural Networks, 2008. IJCNN 2008.(IEEE World Congress on Computational Intelligence). IEEE International Joint Conference on*. IEEE, 2849–2856.

[11] François Le Gall. 2014. Powers of Tensors and Fast Matrix Multiplication. In *Proceedings of the 39th International Symposium on Symbolic and Algebraic Computation (ISSAC '14)*. ACM, New York, NY, USA, 296–303. https://doi.org/10.1145/2608628.2608664

[12] Warren S. McCulloch and Walter Pitts. 1943. A logical calculus of the ideas immanent in nervous activity. *The bulletin of mathematical biophysics* 5, 4 (Dec. 1943), 115–133. https://doi.org/10.1007/BF02478259

[13] Paul A Merolla, John V Arthur, Rodrigo Alvarez-Icaza, Andrew S Cassidy, Jun Sawada, Filipp Akopyan, Bryan L Jackson, Nabil Imam, Chen Guo, Yutaka Nakamura, et al. 2014. A million spiking-neuron integrated circuit with a scalable communication network and interface. *Science* 345, 6197 (2014), 668–673.

[14] Robert C. Minnick. 1961. Linear-Input Logic. *IRE Trans. Electronic Computers* 10, 1 (1961), 6–16. https://doi.org/10.1109/TEC.1961.5219146

[15] Saburo Muroga. 1959. The principle of majority decision logical elements and the complexity of their circuits. In *IFIP Congress*. 400–406.

[16] Günce Keziban Orman, Vincent Labatut, and Hocine Cherifi. 2013. An empirical study of the relation between community structure and transivity. *Studies in Computational Intelligence* 424 (2013), 99–110.

[17] Catherine D. Schuman, Thomas E. Potok, Robert M. Patton, J. Douglas Birdwell, Mark E. Dean, Garrett S. Rose, and James S. Plank. 2017. A Survey of Neuromorphic Computing and Neural Networks in Hardware. (May 2017). https://arxiv.org/abs/1705.06963

[18] C Seshadhri, Tamara G. Kolda, and Ali Pinar. 2012. Community structure and scale-free collections of Erdös-Rényi graphs. *Physical Review E* 85, 056109 (2012).

[19] Jiří Šíma and Pekka Orponen. 2003. General-Purpose Computation with Neural Networks: A Survey of Complexity Theoretic Results. *Neural Computation* 15, 12 (Dec. 2003), 2727–2778. https://doi.org/10.1162/089976603322518731

[20] Kai-Yeung Siu, Vwani Roychowdhury, and Thomas Kailath. 1991. Depth-size tradeoffs for neural computation. *IEEE Trans. Comput.* 40, 12 (Dec. 1991), 1402–1412. https://doi.org/10.1109/12.106225

[21] Kai-Yeung Siu, Vwani Roychowdhury, and Thomas Kailath. 1995. *Discrete Neural Computation: A Theoretical Foundation*. Prentice-Hall, Inc., Upper Saddle River, NJ, USA.

[22] Volker Strassen. 1969. Gaussian elimination is not optimal. *Numer. Math.* 13, 4 (Aug 1969), 354–356.

[23] I. Sugiarto, G. Liu, S. Davidson, L. A. Plana, and S. B. Furber. 2016. High performance computing on SpiNNaker neuromorphic platform: A case study for energy efficient image processing. In *2016 IEEE 35th International Performance Computing and Communications Conference (IPCCC)*. 1–8. https://doi.org/10.1109/PCCC.2016.7820645

[24] Kei Uchizawa, Rodney Douglas, and Wolfgang Maass. 2006. Energy Complexity and Entropy of Threshold Circuits. In *Automata, Languages and Programming (Lecture Notes in Computer Science)*. Springer, Berlin, Heidelberg, 631–642. https://doi.org/10.1007/11786986_55

[25] Pete Warden. 2015. Why GEMM is at the heart of deep learning. https://petewarden.com/2015/04/20/why-gemm-is-at-the-heart-of-deep-learning/. online, accessed February 9, 2017.

[26] Andrew C. C. Yao. 1985. Separating the polynomial-time hierarchy by oracles. In *, 26th Annual Symposium on Foundations of Computer Science, 1985*. 1–10. https://doi.org/10.1109/SFCS.1985.49


# APPENDIX

## Proof of Lemma 4.6:

Our proof uses a similar analysis to that of Lemma 4.2. We need new parameters derived from our fast matrix multiplication algorithm. For $1 \le j \le T^2$, we use $j$ to index the $T^2$ expressions for entries of $C$. We define $c'_j$ as the number of $M_i$ terms that appear in the $j$th expression for an entry of $C$. For Strassen's algorithm (Figure 1), we have $c'_1 = 4$, $c'_2 = 2$, $c'_3 = 2$, and $c'_4 = 4$. Recall the sparsity parameter $s_C$ from Definition 2.1, and observe that $s_C = \sum_{1 \le j \le T^2} c'_j$.

We assume the matrix products at level $h_i$ of $\mathcal{T}_{AB}$ have been computed and compute a node $u$ at level $h_{i-1}$. We again define $\delta_i = h_i - h_{i-1}$ for convenience. As an example, suppose we were using the scalars corresponding to the leaves of $\mathcal{T}_{AB}$, at level $h_t$, to construct a $T \times T$ matrix at level $h_t - 1$. Each of the $T^2$ entries of this matrix consists of a $\{-1, 1\}$-weighted sum of the scalars at level $h_t$.

More generally, the matrix corresponding to node $u$ at level $h_{i-1}$ is composed of $T^{2\delta_i}$ blocks that are each $\{-1, 1\}$-weighted sums of matrices of size $N/T^{h_i} \times N/T^{h_i}$ from level $h_i$. We seek to bound the number of terms in each such sum. Let $u_l$ for $1 \le l \le T^{2\delta_i}$ correspond to the blocks of the matrix at node $u$, and let size$(u_l)$ be the number of terms in the weighted sum of matrices from level $h_i$ that is equal to the block $u_l$. Using an approach similar to that from the proof of Lemma 4.2, we have:

$$\begin{aligned} \sum_{1 \le l \le T^{2\delta_i}} \text{size}(u_l) &= \sum_{m_1 + \cdots + m_{T^2} = \delta_i} \binom{\delta_i}{m_1, \ldots, m_{T^2}} \prod_{1 \le j \le T^2} (c'_j)^{m_j} \\ &= \left( \sum_{1 \le j \le T^2} c'_j \right)^{\delta_i} = s_C^{\delta_i}, \end{aligned} \tag{5}$$

where, as in the proof of Lemma 4.2, the penultimate equality follows from the multinomial theorem.

Each block $u_l$ is of size $N/T^{h_i} \times N/T^{h_i}$, and by the discussion preceding this lemma and (2), we have that each entry of a block $u_l$ requires $O(\log N)$ bits. Thus, by Lemma 3.2, we may compute all of the blocks $u_l$ of $u$ in depth 2 with a gate count of:

$$\begin{aligned} &\sum_{1 \le l \le T^{2\delta_i}} O(N^2/T^{2h_i} \log N \text{size}(u_l)) \\ &= O(N^2/T^{2h_i} \log N \sum_{1 \le l \le T^{2\delta_i}} \text{size}(u_l)) \\ &= O(N^2/T^{2h_i} \log N s_C^{\delta_i}), \end{aligned} \tag{6}$$

where the last equality follows from the above equation. Since there are $r^{h_{i-1}}$ nodes in total on level $h_{i-1}$, we may compute all the matrices on level $h_{i-1}$ with a total gate count of,

$$\begin{aligned} O(r^{h_{i-1}} s_C^{h_i - h_{i-1}} N^2/T^{2h_i} \log N) &= O((r/s_C)^{h_{i-1}} (s_C/T^2)^{h_i} N^2 \log N) \\ &= \widetilde{O}(\alpha_C^{h_{i-1}} \beta_C^{h_i} N^2). \end{aligned}$$

□

# Integrated Model, Batch, and Domain Parallelism in Training Neural Networks

Amir Gholami
EECS Department, UC Berkeley
amirgh@eecs.berkeley.edu

Ariful Azad
CRD, Lawrence Berkeley Lab
azad@lbl.gov

Peter Jin
EECS Department, UC Berkeley
phj@eecs.berkeley.edu

Kurt Keutzer
EECS Department, UC Berkeley
keutzer@eecs.berkeley.edu

Aydın Buluç
CRD, Lawrence Berkeley Lab
abuluc@lbl.gov

## ABSTRACT

We propose a new integrated method of exploiting model, batch and domain parallelism for the training of deep neural networks (DNNs) on large distributed-memory computers using minibatch stochastic gradient descent (SGD). Our goal is to find an efficient parallelization strategy for a fixed batch size using $P$ processes. Our method is inspired by the communication-avoiding algorithms in numerical linear algebra. We see $P$ processes as logically divided into a $P_r \times P_c$ grid where the $P_r$ dimension is implicitly responsible for model/domain parallelism and the $P_c$ dimension is implicitly responsible for batch parallelism. In practice, the integrated matrix-based parallel algorithm encapsulates these types of parallelism automatically. We analyze the communication complexity and analytically demonstrate that the lowest communication costs are often achieved neither with pure model nor with pure data parallelism. We also show how the domain parallel approach can help in extending the theoretical scaling limit of the typical batch parallel method.

**ACM Reference Format:**
Amir Gholami, Ariful Azad, Peter Jin, Kurt Keutzer, and Aydın Buluç. 2018. Integrated Model, Batch, and Domain Parallelism in Training Neural Networks. In *SPAA '18: SPAA '18: 30th ACM Symposium on Parallelism in Algorithms and Architectures, July 16–18, 2018, Vienna, Austria.* ACM, New York, NY, USA, 10 pages. https://doi.org/10.1145/3210377.3210394

## 1 INTRODUCTION AND BACKGROUND

Neural Networks (NNs) have proved to be very effective in diverse applications ranging from semantic segmentation [17, 27] and detection [20, 26] to medical image segmentation [10, 18]. In most cases the hardware limits have been reached for most of the kernels, and the next milestone is in distributed computing. This is becoming increasingly important with renewed attention to super resolution machine learning [14], as well as significant increase in the training dataset in cases such as autonomous driving. Effective use of these datasets in a reasonable time is not possible without a scalable parallel method.

Given $N$ empirical samples, the DNN training procedure seeks to find the model parameters, $w$, such that the forward pass on sample inputs would produce outputs that are *similar* to ground truth outputs and that it generalizes well for unseen test samples. The weights are initialized randomly and SGD algorithm updates them iteratively as: $w^{n+1} = w^n - \eta \nabla f_i$, where $i$ is an index chosen randomly (with replacement) from $[1, N]$, $\eta$ is the learning rate, and $f$ is the loss function. In practice, one can use a mini-batch SGD by drawing a set of indices $i \in$ Batch at each iteration, chosen randomly from $[1, N]$ and update the parameters as follows:

$$w^{n+1} = w^n - \eta \frac{1}{B} \sum_{i \in \text{Batch}} \nabla f_i, \tag{1}$$

where $B$ is the mini-batch size. This whole SGD-based training requires a "forward pass" where the network's output and the corresponding loss functional is computed given the current model parameters, and a "backward pass" (commonly referred to as *back-propagation* or simply *backprop*) where the gradient of the loss is computed with respect to the model parameters, $w$.

The forward phase of DNN training is a sequential combination of affine transformation $Y_i = W_i X_i$, followed by nonlinear transforms $X_{i+1} = f(Y_i)$ . Each column of $X_i \in \mathbb{R}^{d_{i-1} \times B}$ holds input activations for one sample and similarly each column of $Y_i \in \mathbb{R}^{d_i \times B}$ holds output activations for one sample. Notice that $X_{i+1}$ and $Y_i$ have the same shape. The matrix $W_i \in \mathbb{R}^{d_i \times d_{i-1}}$ holds the weights of the neural network between the $i$th and $(i-1)$th layer. The number of neurons in the $i$th DNN layer is denoted by $d_i$.

Forward phase is followed by backpropagation that can also be written in matrix form as $\Delta_{X_i} = W_i^T \Delta_{Y_i}$. Here, $\Delta_{X_i}$ and $\Delta_{Y_i}$ are the gradients of the loss function, with respect to input and output activations, respectively. Finally, the gradient of the loss function with respect to model weights is calculated using $\Delta_{W_i} = \Delta_{Y_i} X_i^T$. Consequently, DNN training requires 3 *matrix multiplications*, including gradient computations.[1] The derivations of the forward pass and the backpropagation are shown in detail in the extended version of this paper [8]).

A single pass over the whole data (also called an *epoch*) requires $N/B$ iterations. It takes many iterations until the training error is sufficiently small. Consequently, DNN training is computationally expensive. To accelerate training, one can change the training algorithm with an aim to reduce the number of epochs, or make each

[1]Note that our approach does not require each individual convolution to be computed using matrix multiplication, but we view it as this way for simplicity and connection to high performance computing literature.


*SPAA '18, July 16–18, 2018, Vienna, Austria*

ACM ISBN 978-1-4503-5799-9/18/07...$15.00
https://doi.org/10.1145/3210377.3210394

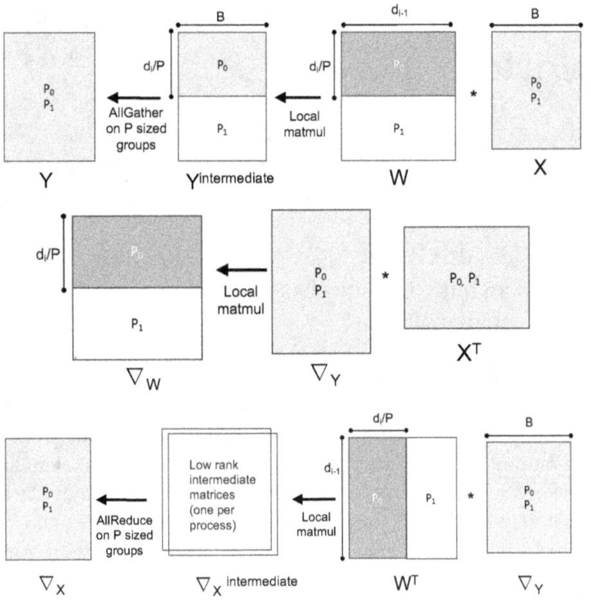


**Figure 1:** *Illustration of matrix multiplications for the pure model parallel training using $P = 2$ (top: forward pass, middle/bottom: weight gradient computation).*

epoch run faster through distributed training. We are focusing on the latter.

Two well-known techniques for distributed SGD based DNN training are *model parallelism* and *data parallelism.* In simplest terms, model parallelism is the partitioning of the weights of the neural network to processes. Data parallelism corresponds to partitioning of the input data to processes. The existing literature merely considers data parallelism to be the assignment of groups of whole data points, such as images, to individual processes. However, one can instead assign fractions of data points to processes as well. For example, training a convolutional neural network (CNN) on two processes with domain parallelism can assign all the top halves of the images to the first processor and all the bottom halves of the images to the second processor [? ]. Consequently, there are two subtypes of data parallelism: *batch parallelism,* which is the commonly studied option in literature, is the assignment of groups of data points in whole to processes and *domain parallelism* is the subdivision of individual data points to processes.

This paper presents a new method for integrated model, batch, and domain parallelism. There are existing approaches that exploit both model and batch parallelism but they often only provide adhoc solutions to hard engineering constraints such as the model no longer fitting into a single GPU or the mini batch sizes hitting a convergence limit. Our method, by contrast, is amenable to precise communication analysis and covers the whole spectrum between pure data parallelism (which includes batch parallelism as a special case) and pure model parallelism. It often finds favorable performance regimes that are better than pure batch parallelism and pure model parallelism, even in the absence of tailored constraints.

*Limitations.* We find it useful and necessary to describe the limitations in our analysis. For the communication complexity we assume that all the compute nodes are connected and thus do not consider the topology of the interconnect, and we also do not consider network conflicts in our model [3]. However, the effects of this can be approximated by adjusting the latency and bandwidth terms accordingly, as a detailed analysis will become network specific.

While the presented simulated results are based on AlexNet, the mathematical analysis we present for the integrated framework is generally applicable to any neural network. For instance, cases with Recurrent Neural Networks mainly consist of fully connected layers and our analysis naturally extends to those cases. Moreover, we empirically measure the computation time. A more detailed analysis of the computation time would require a hardware specific execution model which is outside the scope of this work. Finally, we present simulation results based on the complexity analysis. Those simulation results assume idealized network behavior (i.e. perfect utilization of bandwidth, no additional software overheads, and perfect overlap of communication and computation when considered), and hence provide an upper bound on achievable performance.

## 2 PARALLELISM IN DNN TRAINING

Deep Neural Networks are typically trained using first-order methods, i.e. those that rely on first order derivatives. SGD is the canonical example of first-order methods used in DNN training. Regardless of the specific approach, all methods calculate activations using forward propagation and calculate derivatives using backprop. Consequently, our results generalize to other first-order methods even though we will describe it using SGD for simplicity.

The SGD iterations have a sequential dependency. One possibility to break this barrier for parallel training is the family of asynchronous SGD methods [4, 7, 12, 19, 21, 30]. Here, this dependency is broken and each process is allowed to use *stale* parameters and update either its weights or that of a parameter server. However, these approaches often do not converge to the same performance as in the synchronous SGD cases. Here, we focus only on the latter which obeys the sequential consistency of the original algorithm. However, the framework that we present can be used to accelerate asynchronous methods as well.

In terms of terminology, we use the word "process" to refer to the program running on a compute node. It is often the case that a compute node has many processing elements (or cores); thus one can map multiple processes, each with its own local private memory, to a compute node. The exact nature of process to compute node mapping is immaterial to our analysis.

### 2.1 Layers of Deep Neural Networks

Deep Neural Networks are composed of many layers. Typically each layer is either a convolutional layer, a fully connected layer, activation layer, or a dropout layer. A convolutional layer is composed of a number of filters (also called kernels), applied in a sliding window fashion with a stride length $s$ over the whole input sample. The application of each filter in a convolutional layer results in a distinct *channel* in the output layer. Hence, we will use $X_C^i$ to denote the number of channels in the $i$th layer. The number of input channels in the first layer is equal to the number of channels in the input data (usually three channels for RGB). A convolutional filter in the $i$th layer takes a tensor input $k_h^i \times k_w^i \times X_C^i$ and creates a single

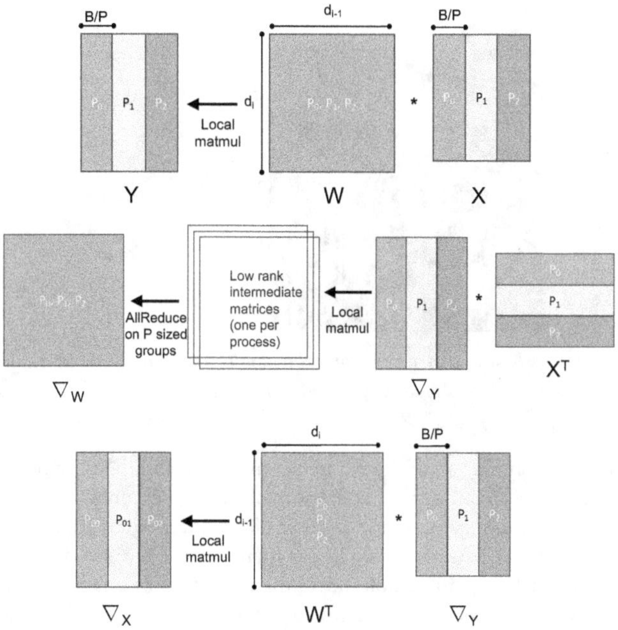


**Figure 2:** *Illustration of matrix multiplications for the pure batch parallel training using $P = 3$ (top: forward pass, middle/bottom: weight gradient computation).*

scalar value (Here $k_h^i$, $k_w^i$ are the kernel convolution kernel's size). There are $Y_C^i$ such different filters in the $i$th convolutional layer. Consequently an input of dimensions $X_H^i$, $X_W^i$, $X_C^i$ is transformed into an output of dimensions $Y_W^i$, $Y_H^i$, $Y_C^i$ where

$$Y_W^i = \left\lceil \frac{X_W^i - k_w}{s} \right\rceil, Y_H^i = \left\lceil \frac{X_H^i - k_h}{s} \right\rceil.$$

With proper padding, it simplifies to $Y_W^i = \lceil X_W^i / s \rceil$ and $Y_H^i = \lceil X_H^i / s \rceil$.

The number of distinct parameters between two convolutional layers is equal to the number of nonzeros in $W$ if they are represented compactly without redundancy. Hence,

$$\begin{aligned} |W_i| &= (k_h k_w X_C^i) Y_C^i, \\ d_{i-1} &= X_H^i X_W^i X_C^i, \\ d_i &= Y_H^i Y_W^i Y_C^i = \lceil X_W^i / s \rceil \lceil X_H^i / s \rceil Y_C^i. \end{aligned} \tag{2}$$

The number of parameters between two fully-connected layers, or between a convolutional layer and a fully-connected layer is simply $|W_i| = d_i d_{i-1}$. Dropout is sometimes applied to fully-connected layers and has the effect of pruning a certain percentage of both the input and output activations.

## 2.2 Communication Cost Analysis of Pure Batch, Pure Model, and Pure Domain-Parallel Approaches

Two possibilities for parallel computations in synchronous SGD is model and data parallel. The latter can be subdivided into batch parallelism and domain parallelism as explained in the previous section.

**Communication costs of pure model parallelism.** In the model parallel case, the computation of the loss in the forward pass can be computed by distributing the model parameters $W$ as shown in Fig. 1.

Consider a convolutional layer without loss of generality: each process performs a subset of the convolutions on the input activations and computes a subset of the output activations. For instance, assume one of the layers consists of $Y_C$ $k_h \times k_w \times X_C$ convolutions, where $k_h$, $k_w$ is the size of each convolution filter and $X_C$, $Y_C$ are the sizes of input and output channels. In the model parallel case, the kernels are distributed so that each process gets $Y_C/P$ filters and computes the corresponding $Y_C/P$ channels of the output activation. As computations of the other layers would require access to all of the previous activations, one needs to perform an all-gather operation *per layer*. Backpropagation also requires an all-reduce communication during $\Delta_X$ calculation. The appendix of our expanded preprint include a detailed derivation of backpropagation [8]. This yields the following communication complexity for the model parallel case:

$$\begin{aligned} T_{comm}(model) = &\sum_{i=1}^{L} \left( \alpha \lceil \log(P) \rceil + \beta B \frac{P-1}{P} d_i \right) \\ &+ 2 \sum_{i=2}^{L} \left( \alpha \lceil \log(P) \rceil + \beta B \frac{P-1}{P} d_{i-1} \right), \end{aligned} \tag{3}$$

where $P$ is the number of processes, $L$ is the number of DNN layers, $\alpha$ is the network latency, and $\beta$ is the inverse bandwidth. The first sum considers the cost for all-gather required after every layer, and the second sum considers the all-reduce cost for backpropagating activation gradients. Note that the second sum starts from $i = 2$ as we do not need to backpropagate the gradient beyond the first layer. This analysis assumes the use of Bruck's algorithm for all-gather and ring algorithm for all-reduce [24]. We note that the complexity depends on the mini-batch size. The model parallel approach was partially used in AlexNet [16], where the model was split into two GPUs. The original GoogLeNet work also exploited a certain amount of model parallelism [23]. Distributed DNN training engines that rely solely on model parallelism also exist [5], especially for low-latency high-bandwidth systems.

The other possibility for distributing the SGD computation is data parallelism. This can be performed either by distributing the data over the batch size, or partition each individual image. We refer to the latter as *domain parallelism*, which will be discussed further below.

**Communication costs of pure batch parallelism.** For the batch parallel case, the reduction for the gradient computation over the mini-batch sum (1) can be computed independently by each process. This approach is known as *batch parallel* method, where each process computes a partial sum, followed by an all-reduce to compute the mini-batch gradient. This communication cost is due to the reduction that is needed to form $\Delta_W = \Delta_Y X^T$ product. The communication complexity for the batch parallel approach using ring algorithm for all-reduce [24] is:

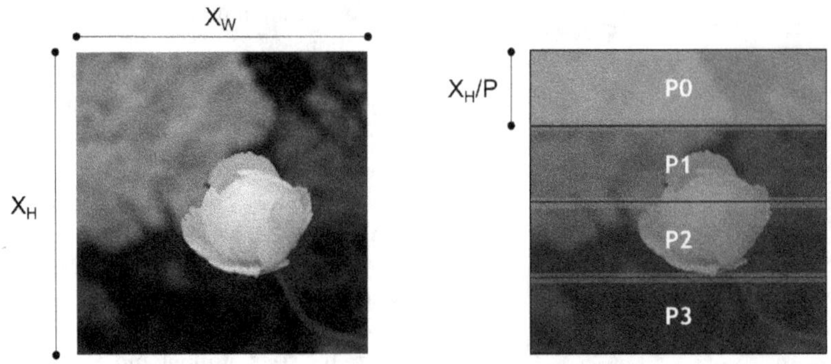


**Figure 3:** *Illustration of domain parallel approach for $P = 4$. For NCHW format, it is best to distribute along the height to avoid non-contiguous memory accesses. NCHW format corresponds to the data layout in the memory, where the data runs fastest in width, height, channel size, and then across batch size.*

$$T_{comm}(batch) = 2\sum_{i=0}^{L}\left(\alpha\lceil\log(P)\rceil + \beta\frac{P-1}{P}|W_i|\right), \quad (4)$$

where $|W_i|$ is the total number of model parameters in the $i$th layer. Here, the factor of 2 is merely due to the all-reduce algorithm [24]. Note that for $P \gg 1$ the bandwidth costs are independent of $P$ and unlike the model parallel case does not depend on the batch size. Most of the current work on distributed training uses batch parallel to scale training [9, 29]. The DistBelief paper [7] provides easy-to-understand descriptions of model and batch parallelism.

For a convolutional layer, based on Equation 2, the ratio of communication volume between pure model and batch parallelism becomes

$$\frac{T_{comm-volume}(batch)}{T_{comm-volume}(model)} = \frac{2|W_i|}{3Bd_i} = \frac{(2k_hk_wX_C^i)Y_C^i}{3BY_H^iY_W^iY_C^i} = \frac{2k_hk_wX_C^i}{3BY_H^iY_W^i} \quad (5)$$

Consequently, whenever $B > (2k_hk_wX_C^i/3Y_H^iY_W^i)$, pure batch parallelism is favorable to pure model parallelism. Surprisingly, it is not a foregone conclusion that batch parallelism is always favorable to model parallelism for convolutional layers. For several convolutional layers that are used in practice (such as those found in AlexNet with 3x3 filters on 13x13x384 activations), model parallelism has lower communication volume than batch parallelism for $B \leq 12$.

If one were to switch from a data parallel distribution shown in Figure 2 to a model parallel distribution shown in Figure 1, the only added communication cost is the redistribution of $X$ to processes using an all-gather operation, with an associated cost of

$$T_{comm}(\text{redistribute batch to model}) = \alpha\lceil\log(P)\rceil + \beta B\frac{P-1}{P}d_i. \quad (6)$$

It is important to note that this redistribution cost is asymptotically free because the subsequent model parallel step has communication cost that is three times of the cost of the redistribution.

**Communication costs of pure domain parallelism.** A third possibility for parallelization is domain parallel [? ], where one can decompose the input activation map as shown in Fig. 3. Here each process contains all of the model parameters (as in the pure batch parallel case), but performs the convolutions only on a subset of the input image, and writes a subset of the output activations. For convolutions with filter size larger than one, we have to perform a halo exchange to communicate the boundary points. This can be performed as a non-blocking, pair-wise exchange while the convolution is being applied to the rest of the image. This means that the convolutions that do not require this boundary data could be computed while the communication is being performed. The cost of the communication in this case will be:

$$\begin{aligned} T_{comm}(domain) = &\sum_{i=0}^{L}\left(\alpha + \beta BX_W^iX_C^i\lfloor k_h^i/2\rfloor\right) \\ &+\sum_{i=0}^{L}\left(\alpha + \beta BY_W^iY_C^i\lfloor k_w^i/2\rfloor\right) \\ &+2\sum_{i=0}^{L}\left(\alpha\lceil\log(P)\rceil + \beta\frac{P-1}{P}|W_i|\right), \end{aligned} \quad (7)$$

where $X_W^i$, $X_H^i$, $X_C^i$, $Y_W^i$, $Y_H^i$, $Y_C^i$ are the input/output activation's width, height, and channel size in the $i$th layer, and $k_h^i$, $k_w^i$ is the corresponding convolution size of that layer. Note that for a $1 \times 1$ convolution no communication is needed. For layers with large input activation size and large number of convolution filters, this approach can reduce the computation time with good strong scaling efficiency. However, it is not effective for small image sizes and not applicable to fully connected layers.

Model parallelism, as published in literature, corresponds to performing a 1D distribution of the matrix $W_i$, replicating $X_i$ and gathering $Y_i$ multivectors after multiplication. The $k$th processor can perform its local matrix multiplication of the form $W_i(k,:)X_i$ without any communication, but in order to fully assemble $Y_i$, each processor needs to gather other components from other processes. Even if input/output multivectors were also distributed, the communication bounds stay the same, because while this communication time would not be necessary for the output $Y_i$, it would be needed for gathering $X_i$ before the local multiplication.

By contrast, in data parallelism, every process starts with the same parameters, which get updated by the same gradient. In fact, the forward pass of batch parallel training needs no communication.

The communication in this case happens during backpropagation, where a collective all-reduce operation is needed to compute the total sum of the partial gradients. The parallel matrix multiplications in the batch parallel case are illustrated in Figure 2, where the input activations $X_i$ and the output activations $Y_i$ are distributed 1D columnwise to processes.

## 2.3 Integrated Model and Batch Parallelism

We first discuss the integrated model and batch parallelism and then discuss the full integration with domain parallelism which extends the scalability limit of the pure batch method. Batch parallelism has a favorable communication complexity, but there is an inherent limit on increasing the batch size. Furthermore, small batch size training is not efficient in terms of hardware utilization and ultimately training time. This is due to the fact that small matrix-matrix operations (aka level-3 BLAS operations) cannot use all the hardware resources, in terms of cores or vectorized units. This is empirically shown in Fig. 4, where we report one epoch training time of AlexNet for different batch sizes measured on a single Intel Knights Landing (KNL) processor. The fastest training time is achieved with a batch size of 256. With the batch parallel approach one has no choice but to reduce per process batch size for scaling before hitting the limit of 1 batch per process.

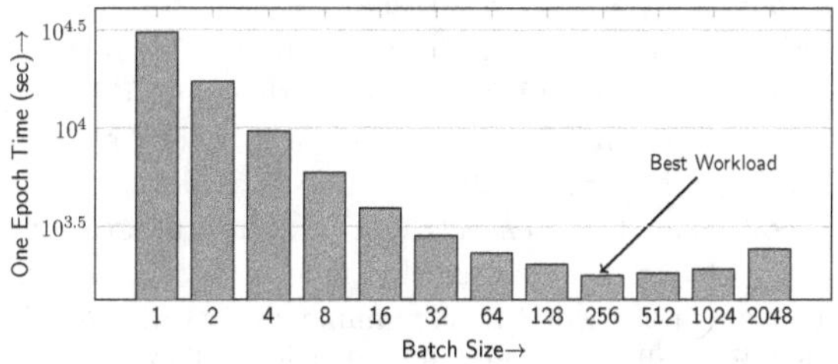


**Figure 4:** *One epoch training time of AlexNet computed on a single KNL. Increasing batch size up to 256, reduces the time due to better use of hardware resources and fewer SGD updates.*

Our *integrated batch and model parallel approach* allows us to reduce the communication overhead of the pure batch parallel case. Here, we consider replicating a subset of $W_i$ as opposed to all of it, a concept that has been explored under the name of 1.5D algorithms for matrix multiplication [15]. We think of our process grid logically partitioned as $P = P_r \times P_c$. Each process holds $(1/P_r)$th piece of $W_i$, effectively replicating $W_i$ matrix $P_c$ times (as opposed to $P$ times in batch parallelism). Conversely, data matrices are replicated $P_r$ times and each process holds $(1/P_c)$th piece of $X_i$ and $Y_i$. Communication cost of this 1.5D algorithm, which is illustrated in Figure 5, is:

$$\begin{aligned} T_{comm} &= \sum_{i=1}^{L} \left( \alpha \lceil \log(P_r) \rceil + \beta \frac{B}{P_c} \frac{P_r - 1}{P_r} d_i \right) \\ &+2 \sum_{i=2}^{L} \left( \alpha \lceil \log(P_r) \rceil + \beta \frac{B}{P_c} \frac{P_r - 1}{P_r} d_{i-1} \right) \\ &+2 \sum_{i=0}^{L} \left( \alpha \lceil \log(P_c) \rceil + \beta \frac{P_c - 1}{P_c} \frac{|W_i|}{P_r} \right). \end{aligned} \tag{8}$$

Note that unlike in Eq. 4, the all-reduce communication volume is now reduced by a factor of $P_r$. This provides a theoretically sound integration of batch and model parallelism. It can be especially valuable for networks with many fully connected layers. Furthermore, this algorithm automatically selects the best configuration to distribute the model and batch parallel work given a fixed batch size on $P$ processes. The closest approach to ours is the hybrid model/batch parallel approach described by Das et al. [6], but that paper does not describe the details of the partitioning of the data and the model to the processes. In addition, the authors claim that using any other dimension to extract parallelism would always be sub-optimal, which we show not be true in general by using domain parallelism.

Similar to the analysis of pure model and pure batch cases, the cost of redistribution is asymptotically amortized in this integrated batch and model parallel case as well. In particular, if one were to switch process grids in between layers, say from a pure batch case ($1 \times P$ grid) to a balanced case ($\sqrt{p} \times \sqrt{p}$) grid, the communication costs would asymptotically stay constant.

For the curious reader familiar with the theory of parallel matrix multiplication, we would like to clarify why we consider our approach a 1.5D algorithm, as opposed to a 2D algorithm such as Cannon's algorithm [2] or SUMMA [25]. 2D matrix multiplication algorithms are optimal in terms of their memory usage; that is, each processor only holds $(1/p)$th of the total memory needed to store all three matrices (2 inputs and 1 output). In other words, there is no replication. The class of .5D algorithms (of which 1.5D algorithm is a member), by contrast, are not optimal in terms of memory consumption. At least one matrix is replicated multiple times, which often results in an asymptotic reduction in communication costs [1]. This is indeed the case for the algorithm described in Figure 5.

## 2.4 Integrated Model, Batch and Domain Parallelism

The pure batch parallel method has a theoretical strong scaling limit of $B$. In the limit each process gets a batch size of one (i.e. it reads a single data). It is possible to extend this limit with the integrated model and batch parallel approach discussed above. But this approach is sub-optimal for early layers of the network, as the all-gather communication volume is very high there (Eq. 8). This is due to the fact that this communication volume depends on the size of the activation map (i.e. $Y_i$) which is prohibitively large in the beginning layers.

However, as we show below the domain parallel approach has a favorable communication complexity for early layers of a neural network where the input activation size is large. For these layers it is favorable to use domain parallelism instead of model parallelism, as it leads to a smaller communication volume that can actually be overlapped with part of the computation in both forward and backward pass. Note that in model parallel one has to perform a blocking all-gather operation which is detrimental for performance. Moreover, the domain parallel approach does not require any communication for $1 \times 1$ convolutions which are actually becoming a dominant portion of the network in recent architectures [11]. However, for fully connected layers the halo exchange region will

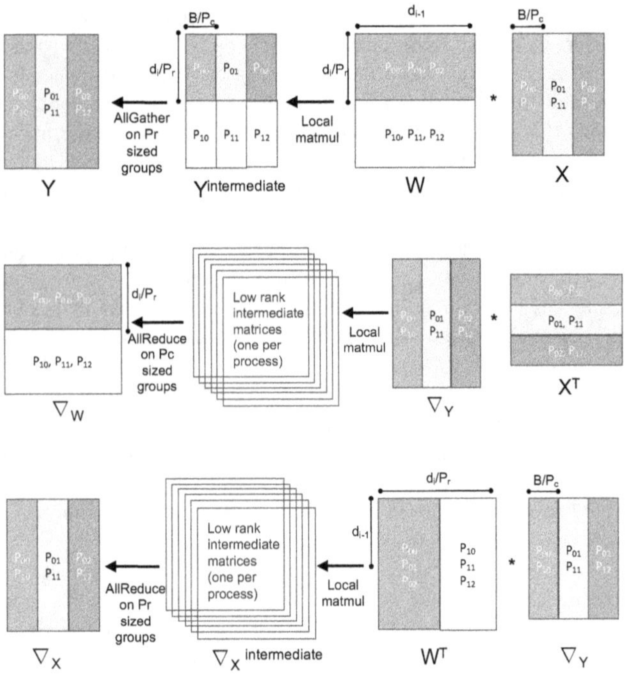


**Figure 5:** *1.5D matrix multiply illustration for integrated parallel DNN training (top: forward pass, middle/bottom: weight gradient computation) using a $2 \times 3$ process grid indexed as $P_{ij}$.*

consist of all of the input activations. To avoid that large communication cost we can actually integrate all the three parallelism methods. The communication complexity for integrating all the three methods would then become:

$$
\begin{aligned}
T_{comm} = & \sum_{i \in L_M} \left( \alpha \lceil \log(P_r) \rceil + \beta \frac{B}{P_c} \frac{P_r - 1}{P_r} d_i \right) + \\
& 2 \sum_{i \in L_M} \left( \alpha \lceil \log(P_r) \rceil + \beta \frac{B}{P_c} \frac{P_r - 1}{P_r} d_{i-1} \right) + \\
& 2 \sum_{i \in L_M} \left( \alpha \lceil \log(P_c) \rceil + \beta \frac{P_c - 1}{P_c} \frac{|W_i|}{P_r} \right) + \\
& \sum_{i \in L_D} \left( \alpha + \beta \frac{B}{P_c} X_W^i X_C^i \lfloor k_h^i / 2 \rfloor \right) + \\
& \sum_{i \in L_D} \left( \alpha + \beta \frac{B}{P_c} X_W^{i+1} X_C^{i+1} \lfloor k_w^i / 2 \rfloor \right) + \\
& 2 \sum_{i \in L_D} \left( \alpha \lceil \log(P) \rceil + \beta \frac{P - 1}{P} |W_i| \right),
\end{aligned} \tag{9}
$$

where $L_M$ and $L_D$ refer to the list of layers where the $P_r$ groups are used to partition either the model or the domain. Note that for $L_M = L$, $L_D = 0$, we get the integrated model and batch parallel complexity as expected.

The choice of whether to partition the model or the domain can be made by computing the communication complexity. Generally, it is better to use domain parallelism for the initial layers of the network, since the activation size is large. However, the domain parallel approach loses its communication advantage for fully connected layers (for which $k_h = X_H$, $k_w = X_W$).

| | Fixed options | Relevant parameters |
|---|---|---|
| Network architecture | AlexNet [16] parameters: 61M | 5 convolutional and 3 fully connected layers |
| Training images | ImageNet LSVRC-2012 contest | training images: 1.2M Number of categories: 1000 |
| Computing platform | NERSC's Cori2 | Processor: Intel KNL latency: $\alpha = 2\mu$ s inverse bw: $1/\beta$ = 6GB/s |

**Table 1:** *Fixed parameters used to simulate the cost of training neural networks using integrated batch and model parallel approach. We only change the mini-batch size and the number and configurations of processes in the presented results.*

# 3 SIMULATED PERFORMANCE IN TRAINING ALEXNET

**Simulation setup.** We analytically explore the spectrum of both the integrated batch and model parallel approach, as well as the full integration with domain parallelism by simulating Eq. 8 and Eq. 9. To limit the number of variables, we fix a network (AlexNet), a training set of images (ImageNet LSVRC-2012 contest), and a computing platform (NERSC's Cori supercomputer). These fixed options, described in Table 1, are chosen just to develop a proof-of-concept of our integrated batch and model parallel approach.

We considered two scenarios: (a) $B \geq P$: here the relevant integration is between model and batch parallel approaches and domain parallelism is not used as its communication overhead is higher than batch parallel (Eq. 7) (b) $B < P$: This is the case where we reach the maximum scaling limit of the batch parallel method, and use domain parallelism to scale beyond this (Eq. 9). For the first scenario, we considered two cases. At first, the same process grid is used for all layers of the network, which means that if $P_r > 1$ then some amount of model parallelism will be used even in convolutional layers. Then we considered the improved case where we force $P_r = 1, P_c = P$ for the convolutional layers and use varying $P_r \times P_c$ grids for the fully connected layers.

We compute the communication time for a single iteration with various choices of the mini-batch size $B$, the number of processes, and the configuration of process grid $P_r \times P_c$. Using this data, we then compute the communication time for a complete epoch by multiplying the communication time form Eq. 4 by $N/B$. A typical simulation of the Neural Network would require many epochs of training (100 epochs in the case of AlexNet [16]).

Furthermore, we also consider the computational time by empirically measuring the time needed for an SGD iteration for AlexNet on a single KNL using Intel Caffe as shown in Fig. 4. We use this data for cases with the same computational workload to compute the total run time.

**Strong scaling with a fixed mini-batch size.** At first, we present the strong scaling results for integrated model and batch. We initially apply the integrated method in a way that the same process grid is used for all layers of the network, which means that

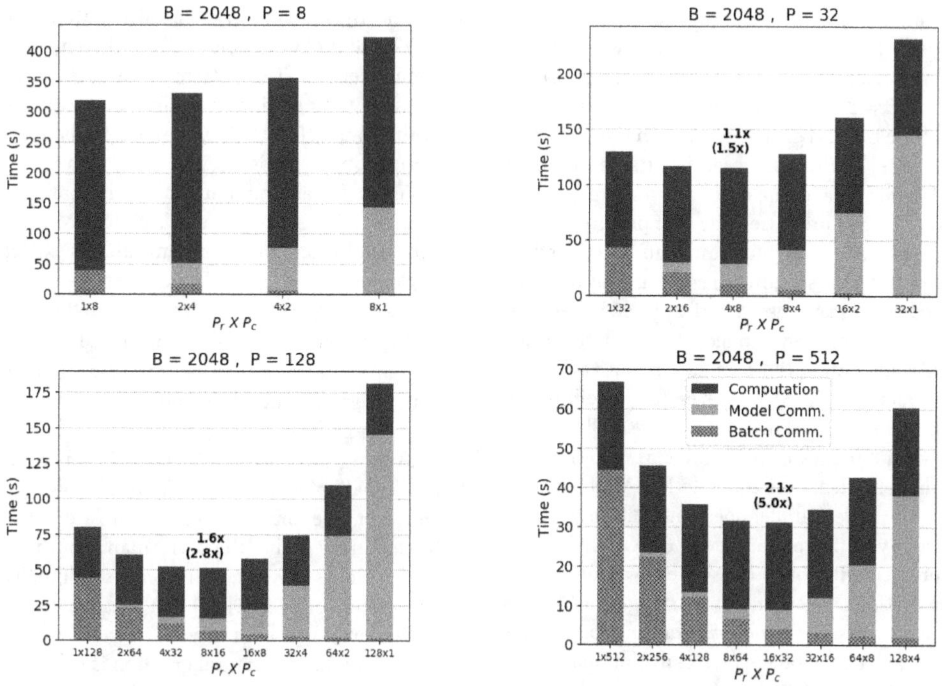


**Figure 6:** *Strong scaling analysis of integrated model and batch parallel approach using the simulated results. The orange bar shows the total communication time, with the cross hatched portion representing the time spent in batch parallel communication (i.e. the ring all-reduce during backprop). Here we use the same process grid for all layers, which means some amount of model parallelism is used for both convolutional and FC layers when $P_r > 1$. The speedup for the total time compared to pure batch parallel is shown in bold text on top of the best bar chart. We also report the corresponding speedup for communication time in parenthesis. In strong scaling, we keep the global batch size fixed, and increase the number of processes to reduce the training time.*

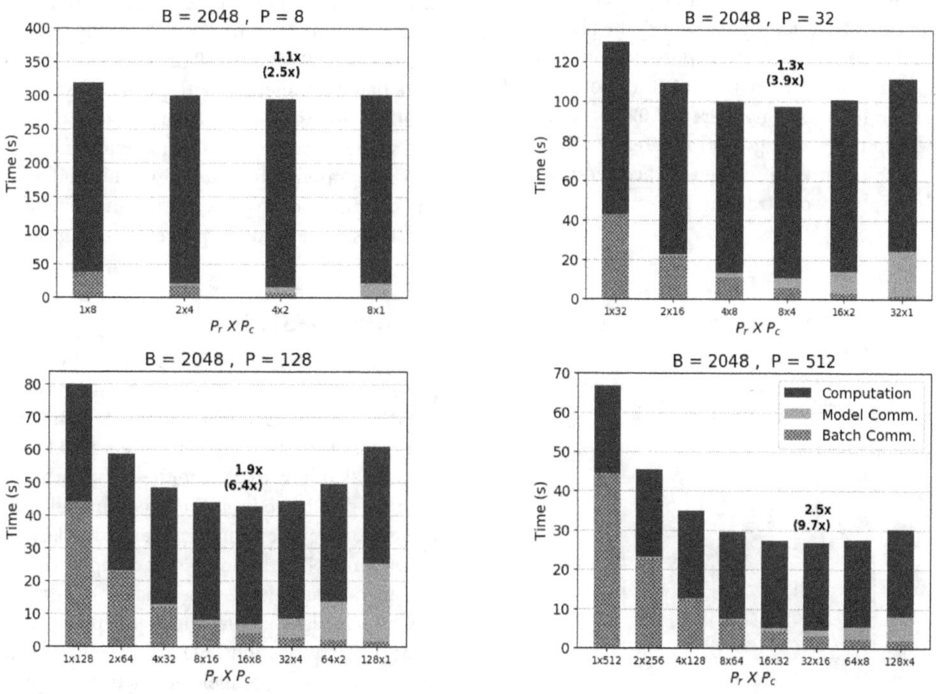


**Figure 7:** *Strong scaling analysis of integrated model and batch parallel approach using the simulated results. Model parallelism is used in FC layers only. Notice the significant improvement in best time compared to Fig. 6 which uses model parallelism in both convolutional and FC layers.*

if $P_r > 1$ then some amount of model parallelism will be used even in convolutional layers. The results are shown Fig. 6 where the training was performed using $P = 8$ to $P = 512$ processes with a fixed mini-batch size of $B = 2,048$. In each subfigure in Fig. 6, only the configurations of the process grid vary. We can see that even in the naive format, better performance can be attained with an integrated batch and model parallelism, especially for larger values of $P$. For example, on $P = 512$ processes, the best performance is observed with $16 \times 32$ process grid which results in $2.1\times$ speed up in the overall runtime and $5.0\times$ speedup in communication ( Figure 6-d). The improved performance is primarily driven by reduced communication needed by the integrated model and batch parallel approach (notice the reduction of the communication volume of the parameters by $P_r$ factor in Eq. 8). However, the benefit of the integrated approach is not realized on a relatively small number processors, such as with 8 processes in Figure 6(a). The first reason is that here the main bottleneck is computation. Moreover, the communication time for model parallel does not scale down since per process batch size is very large (note the $B/P_c$ term in Eq.8).

Next, we considered the improved case where we force $P_r = 1, P_c = P$ for the convolutional layers and use varying $P_r \times P_c$ grids for the fully connected layers. For the configurations considered, this results in using pure batch parallelism in convolutional layers and both model and batch parallelism in FC layers as shown in Figure 7. Making the convolutional layer pure batch parallel can reduce the communication significantly, as evident by comparing Fig. 7 and Fig. 6. For instance, the case with $B = 2048$, $P = 512$ results in $2.5\times$ speedup in overall runtime and $9.7\times$ speedup in communication time (Figure 7-d). We also show how the results would change if we consider a perfect overlap between communication and computation as shown in Fig. 8. This overlapping can only be performed with the backpropagation phase, where the all-reduce communication can happen while the transpose convolution of next layers are being performed (which accounts for two-thirds of the communication). Even in this setting there is $2.0\times$ speedup. We believe that this speed up is actually going to increase, given the new domain specific architectures optimized for accelerating the computation part of neural network training/inference.

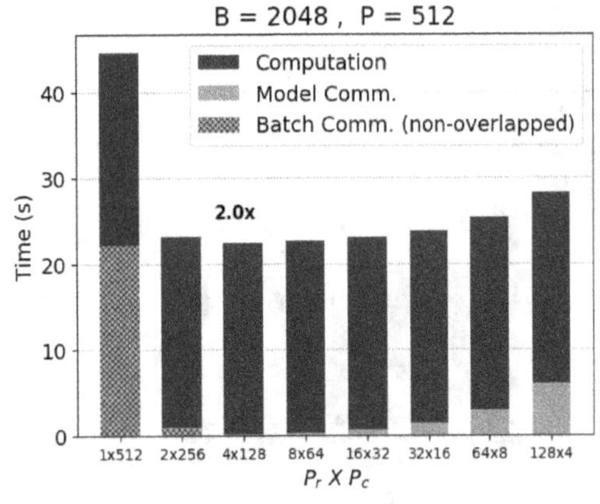


**Figure 8:** *Here we show results for perfect overlapping of communication with backpropagation part of the computations.*

**Scaling with a variable mini-batch size.** We now consider weak scaling by varying the mini-batch size and the process grid simultaneously. Two extreme cases are shown in Fig. 9 (a comprehensive weak scaling result is presented in the extended version of this paper [8]). Here we use model/batch parallel based on the complexity analysis of Eq. 8 (similar to the strong scaling shown in Fig. 7). In each subfigure, only the configurations of the process grid vary for a fixed $P$ and $B$. Since we are simulating the ideal communication time, communication is expected to scale perfectly as can be seen in Fig. 9. We do observe a small decrease in the communication speedup ($10.3\times$ vs $9.4\times$ in the left and right subfigures in Fig. 9) due to the $\frac{P_c-1}{P_c}$ term in all-reduce during backpropagation. Similar to the strong scaling results, we observe that the integrated approach can reduce the communication significantly as we change the mini-batch size.

**Scaling beyond batch size.** The pure batch parallel method has a scaling limit to the maximum batch size that one can use. However, one cannot increase batch size indefinitely as it is known to be detrimental to the performance of the Neural Network [13]. Recent works have tried to increase this limit by changing the hyper-parameters of SGD [9, 28], but these methods also hit a limit and have been only shown to work for certain applications in ImageNet classification. So a natural question is how do we scale beyond this theoretical limit with pure batch parallelism? One could use the integrated approach and scale the model part for all layers, but as shown above this results in sub-optimal communication time. A better approach is to use an integrated batch, domain, and model parallel where for the initial layers we use domain parallel instead of the model. Note that the domain parallel approach requires a much smaller communication as compared to model parallel, and actually requires no communication for $1 \times 1$ convolutions (Eq. 7). To illustrate this, we show the scaling results for $B = 512$ up to $P = 4096$ in Fig. 10. In Fig. 10(a), convolutional layers use pure batch parallelism with per-process batch size set to one. By contrast, in Fig. 10(c-d), each image is partitioned into 2,4, and 8 parts where each process works with one part of the image. Using this integrated batch, domain, and model parallel approach, we can continue scaling beyond the theoretical limit with pure batch parallelism (beyond 512 processes in Fig. 10).

## 4 DISCUSSION

One disadvantage of batch parallelism over model and domain parallelism is that it tends to change the convergence characteristics of DNN training algorithms as larger minibatches beyond a certain point can hurt accuracy. Our integrated framework also provides guidance on how to choose the right parallelization parameters if the user decides to limit the maximum allowable batch parallelism in light of accuracy concerns related to large batch sizes.

Due to DNN training being computational intensive, memory considerations have been secondary to performance. Solutions that exploit pure data parallelism often replicate the whole model in each node. By contrast, the 1.5D matrix-multiplication algorithms used by our integrated parallel approach cut down the model replication cost by a factor of $p_r$, at the cost of an increase in data replication by a factor of $p_c$. Like our communication costs, our memory costs

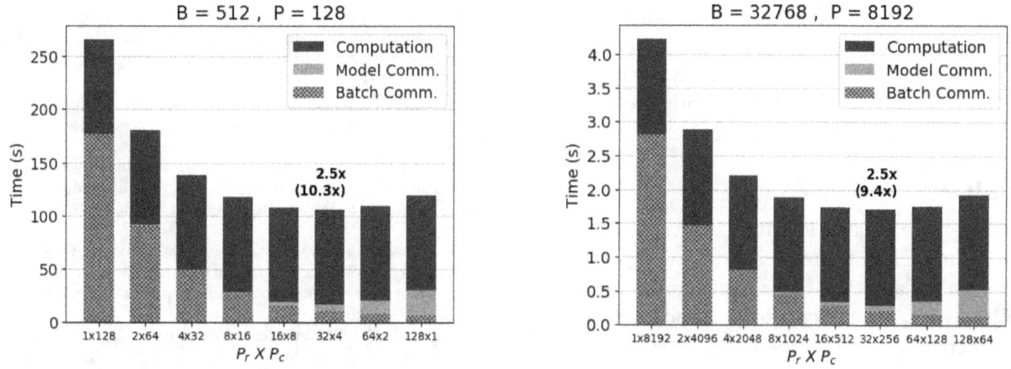


**Figure 9:** *We present weak scaling results for the communication and computation complexity when training AlexNet. Model parallelism is used in FC layers only. We follow the notations used in Figure 6.*

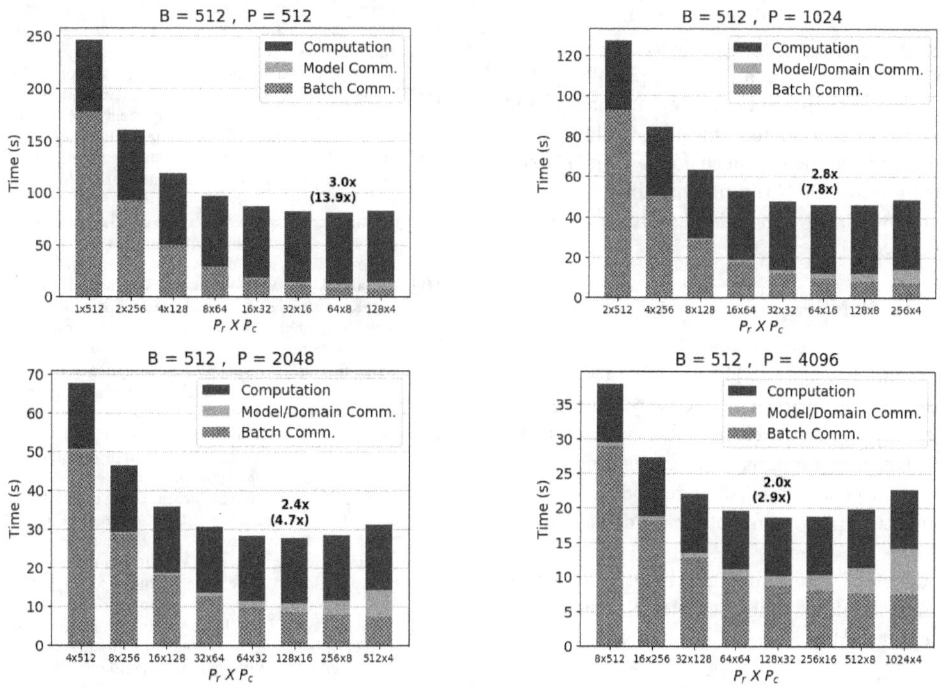


**Figure 10:** *Illustration of how domain parallel can extend strong scaling limit of pure batch parallelism.*

are simply a linear combination of the memory costs of these two extremes of pure data and pure model parallelism.

We also considered the alternative of using 2D matrix multiplication algorithms instead of the 1.5D algorithm. The popular stationary-C variant of the 2D SUMMA algorithm [25] is symmetrical in nature; in the sense that it communicates equal proportions of both input matrices for an operation $C = AB$. When matrices $A$ and $B$ are of comparable sizes, this is a good fit. Often in deep learning, one of the matrices is bigger than the other. For such situations, there are other less-common variants of SUMMA that keep another matrix stationary [22]. These algorithms are more complicated that our 1.5D algorithm, and communicate more data either asymptotically or by higher constants.

Consider stationary-A SUMMA, which is the best fit for the forward propagation $Y = WX$ among all 2D algorithm variants. This algorithm has 4 communication steps compared to a single step in our algorithm. For simplicity assume that $d_i = d_{i-1}$. Also assume that $p_r$ and $p_c$ are large enough such that $(p_r - 1)/p_r \approx (p_c - 1)/p_c \approx 1$. When $|W_i| > Bd_i$, it communicates $2B\,d_i/p_r + B\,d_i/p_c$ words, compared to our 1.5D algorithm's $B\,d_i/p_c$ words. In that sense, its communication costs approach 1.5D when $p_r \gg p_c$ but never surpass it. When $|W_i| < Bd_i$, all possible 2D algorithms become asymptotically slower because they have to communicate two matrices and no matter which two they choose, the costs become higher than solely communicating the single smaller matrix. By contrast, our 1.5D algorithm communicates only that single matrix. Hence, there is no regime where 2D becomes strictly favorable in terms of communication volume. The main advantage of 2D algorithms over 1.5D algorithm is that their memory consumption is optimal in the sense that they do not perform any asymptotic data replication. Memory consumption optimality might be a legitimate concern depending on the platform and the DNN model size.

## 5 CONCLUSION

We presented an integrated parallel algorithm that exploits model, batch, and domain parallelism in training deep neural networks (DNNs). We discussed the associated communication complexity by analyzing both forward and backwards pass, and showed that theoretically the integrated parallel approach can achieve better run time. Furthermore, the integrated parallel approach increases the scalability limit of the pure batch parallel method that is commonly used, by decomposing both along the weight matrix as well as the domain. This approach allows optimal selection of per process batch size and model size which results in better throughput as compared to pure batch/model parallel algorithms.

Our analysis toolset is primarily comprised of parallel matrix algorithms. In particular, the analysis of our integrated model and batch parallel approach relies on a communication-avoiding 1.5D matrix multiplication algorithm. This explicit connection between parallel matrix algorithms and DNN training has the potential to enable the discovery of new classes of parallel algorithms and lower bounds for training DNNs.

## 6 ACKNOWLEGMENTS

This manuscript has been authored by an author at Lawrence Berkeley National Laboratory under Contract No. DE-AC02-05CH11231 with the U.S. Department of Energy. The U.S. Government retains, and the publisher, by accepting the article for publication, acknowledges, that the U.S. Government retains a non-exclusive, paid-up, irrevocable, world-wide license to publish or reproduce the published form of this manuscript, or allow others to do so, for U.S. Government purposes.

This work was supported by the Laboratory Directed Research and Development Program of Lawrence Berkeley National Laboratory under U.S. Department of Energy Contract No. DE-AC02-05CH11231.

The authors would also like to acknowledge generous support from Intel's VLAB team for providing access to KNLs.

## REFERENCES

[1] Grey Ballard, James Demmel, Olga Holtz, and Oded Schwartz. Minimizing communication in numerical linear algebra. *SIAM Journal on Matrix Analysis and Applications*, 32(3):866–901, 2011.

[2] Lynn Elliot Cannon. *A cellular computer to implement the Kalman filter algorithm.* PhD thesis, Montana State University, 1969.

[3] Ernie Chan, Marcel Heimlich, Avi Purkayastha, and Robert Van De Geijn. Collective communication: theory, practice, and experience. *Concurrency and Computation: Practice and Experience*, 19(13):1749–1783, 2007.

[4] Trishul M Chilimbi, Yutaka Suzue, Johnson Apacible, and Karthik Kalyanaraman. Project adam: Building an efficient and scalable deep learning training system. In *OSDI*, volume 14, pages 571–582, 2014.

[5] Adam Coates, Brody Huval, Tao Wang, David Wu, Bryan Catanzaro, and Ng Andrew. Deep learning with COTS HPC systems. In *International Conference on Machine Learning*, pages 1337–1345, 2013.

[6] Dipankar Das, Sasikanth Avancha, Dheevatsa Mudigere, Karthikeyan Vaidynathan, Srinivas Sridharan, Dhiraj Kalamkar, Bharat Kaul, and Pradeep Dubey. Distributed deep learning using synchronous stochastic gradient descent. *arXiv preprint arXiv:1602.06709*, 2016.

[7] Jeffrey Dean, Greg Corrado, Rajat Monga, Kai Chen, Matthieu Devin, Mark Mao, Andrew Senior, Paul Tucker, Ke Yang, Quoc V Le, et al. Large scale distributed deep networks. In *Advances in neural information processing systems*, pages 1223–1231, 2012.

[8] Amir Gholami, Ariful Azad, Kurt Keutzer, and Aydin Buluc. Integrated model and data parallelism in training neural networks. *arXiv preprint arXiv:1712.04432*, 2017.

[9] Priya Goyal, Piotr Dollár, Ross Girshick, Pieter Noordhuis, Lukasz Wesolowski, Aapo Kyrola, Andrew Tulloch, Yangqing Jia, and Kaiming He. Accurate, large minibatch SGD: Training ImageNet in 1 hour. *arXiv preprint arXiv:1706.02677*, 2017.

[10] Mohammad Havaei, Axel Davy, David Warde-Farley, Antoine Biard, Aaron Courville, Yoshua Bengio, Chris Pal, Pierre-Marc Jodoin, and Hugo Larochelle. Brain tumor segmentation with deep neural networks. *Medical image analysis*, 35:18–31, 2017.

[11] Kaiming He, Xiangyu Zhang, Shaoqing Ren, and Jian Sun. Deep residual learning for image recognition. In *Proceedings of the IEEE conference on computer vision and pattern recognition*, pages 770–778, 2016.

[12] Peter H Jin, Qiaochu Yuan, Forrest Iandola, and Kurt Keutzer. How to scale distributed deep learning? *arXiv preprint arXiv:1611.04581*, 2016.

[13] Nitish Shirish Keskar, Dheevatsa Mudigere, Jorge Nocedal, Mikhail Smelyanskiy, and Ping Tak Peter Tang. On large-batch training for deep learning: Generalization gap and sharp minima. *arXiv preprint arXiv:1609.04836*, 2016.

[14] Jiwon Kim, Jung Kwon Lee, and Kyoung Mu Lee. Accurate image super-resolution using very deep convolutional networks. In *Proceedings of the IEEE Conference on Computer Vision and Pattern Recognition*, pages 1646–1654, 2016.

[15] Penporn Koanantakool, Ariful Azad, Aydın Buluç, Dmitriy Morozov, Sang-Yun Oh, Leonid Oliker, and Katherine Yelick. Communication-avoiding parallel sparse-dense matrix-matrix multiplication. In *Proceedings of the IPDPS*, 2016.

[16] Alex Krizhevsky, Ilya Sutskever, and Geoffrey E Hinton. Imagenet classification with deep convolutional neural networks. In *Advances in neural information processing systems*, pages 1097–1105, 2012.

[17] Jonathan Long, Evan Shelhamer, and Trevor Darrell. Fully convolutional networks for semantic segmentation. In *Proceedings of the IEEE Conference on Computer Vision and Pattern Recognition*, pages 3431–3440, 2015.

[18] A. Mang, S. Tharakan A. Gholami, N. Himthani, S. Subramanian, J. Levitt, M. Azmat, K. Scheufele, M. Mehl, C. Davatzikos, B. Barth, and G. Biros. SIBIA-GlS: Scalable biophysics-based image analysis for glioma segmentation. *The multimodal brain tumor image segmentation benchmark (BRATS), MICCAI*, 2017.

[19] Benjamin Recht, Christopher Re, Stephen Wright, and Feng Niu. Hogwild: A lock-free approach to parallelizing stochastic gradient descent. In *Advances in neural information processing systems*, pages 693–701, 2011.

[20] Shaoqing Ren, Kaiming He, Ross Girshick, and Jian Sun. Faster R-CNN: Towards real-time object detection with region proposal networks. In *Advances in neural information processing systems*, pages 91–99, 2015.

[21] RO Rogers and David B Skillicorn. Using the BSP cost model to optimise parallel neural network training. *Future Generation Computer Systems*, 14(5):409–424, 1998.

[22] Martin D Schatz, Robert A Van de Geijn, and Jack Poulson. Parallel matrix multiplication: A systematic journey. *SIAM Journal on Scientific Computing*, 38(6):C748–C781, 2016.

[23] Christian Szegedy, Wei Liu, Yangqing Jia, Pierre Sermanet, Scott Reed, Dragomir Anguelov, Dumitru Erhan, Vincent Vanhoucke, and Andrew Rabinovich. Going deeper with convolutions. In *Proceedings of the IEEE conference on computer vision and pattern recognition*, pages 1–9, 2015.

[24] Rajeev Thakur, Rolf Rabenseifner, and William Gropp. Optimization of collective communication operations in MPICH. *The International Journal of High Performance Computing Applications*, 19(1):49–66, 2005.

[25] Robert A Van De Geijn and Jerrell Watts. SUMMA: Scalable universal matrix multiplication algorithm. *Concurrency-Practice and Experience*, 9(4):255–274, 1997.

[26] Bichen Wu, Forrest Iandola, Peter H Jin, and Kurt Keutzer. Squeezedet: Unified, small, low power fully convolutional neural networks for real-time object detection for autonomous driving. *arXiv preprint arXiv:1612.01051*, 2016.

[27] Bichen Wu, Alvin Wan, Xiangyu Yue, and Kurt Keutzer. Squeezeseg: Convolutional neural nets with recurrent crf for real-time road-object segmentation from 3d lidar point cloud. In *In Review*, 2017.

[28] Yang You, Igor Gitman, and Boris Ginsburg. Scaling SGD batch size to 32k for ImageNet training. *arXiv preprint arXiv:1708.03888*, 2017.

[29] Yang You, Zhao Zhang, C Hsieh, James Demmel, and Kurt Keutzer. ImageNet training in minutes. *CoRR, abs/1709.05011*, 2017.

[30] Sixin Zhang, Anna E Choromanska, and Yann LeCun. Deep learning with elastic averaging SGD. In *Advances in Neural Information Processing Systems*, pages 685–693, 2015.

# Brief Announcement: On Approximating PageRank Locally with Sublinear Query Complexity

Marco Bressan
Sapienza Università di Roma
Roma, Italy
bressan@di.uniroma1.it

Enoch Peserico
Università degli Studi di Padova
Padova, Italy
enoch@dei.unipd.it

Luca Pretto
Università degli Studi di Padova
Padova, Italy
pretto@dei.unipd.it

## ABSTRACT

Can one compute the PageRank score of a single, arbitrary node in a graph, exploring only a vanishing fraction of the graph? We provide a positive answer to this extensively researched open question. We develop the first algorithm that, for any $n$-node graph, returns a multiplicative $(1\pm\epsilon)$-approximation of the score of any given node with probability $(1-\delta)$, using at most $O(n^{2/3}\ln(n)^{1/3}\ln(1/\delta)^{2/3}\epsilon^{-2/3}) = \tilde{O}(n^{2/3})$ queries which return either a node chosen uniformly at random, or the list of neighbours of a given node. Alternatively, we show that the same guarantees can be attained by fetching at most $O(E^{4/5}d^{-3/5}\ln(n)^{1/5}\ln(1/\delta)^{3/5}\epsilon^{-6/5}) = \tilde{O}(E^{4/5})$ arcs, where $E$ is the total number of arcs in the graph and $d$ is its average degree.

## KEYWORDS

PageRank, query complexity, local computation, sublinear algorithms, random walks

**ACM Reference Format:**
Marco Bressan, Enoch Peserico, and Luca Pretto. 2018. Brief Announcement: On Approximating PageRank Locally with Sublinear Query Complexity. In *SPAA '18: 30th ACM Symposium on Parallelism in Algorithms and Architectures, July 16–18, 2018, Vienna, Austria.* ACM, New York, NY, USA, 3 pages. https://doi.org/10.1145/3210377.3210664

## 1 INTRODUCTION

We investigate the query complexity of approximating the PageRank score of a given node in a graph. Our goal is to minimize the portion of the graph we need to fetch in order to give rigorous approximation guarantees.

This problem has several motivations. On the one hand, computing graph centralities efficiently is an essential part of modern network analysis; but the applicability of classic approaches that manipulate the entire graph (e.g. matrix-vector products) is seriously limited by the size and access restrictions of real-world graphs (e.g. web and social networks). In fact, unless one is granted heavy computational resources, even *reading* the entire graph may be infeasible, and one shall accept to see only a tiny portion of it. On the other hand, one usually does not need the exact scores of all nodes in the graph. Indeed, a sufficiently good approximation (for example, with a relative error of 5% with probability 95%) is often enough; and, in many cases, one is interested in just a small subset of target nodes (for example, 100 specific users of a social network). It is thus natural to ask how much of the input graph one must explore in order to approximate the score of a given target node. More precisely, suppose the input graph can be accessed only via *queries* that allow one to retrieve nodes and/or arcs. We ask:

> Given a node $v$ in a graph $G$, and any $\epsilon, \delta > 0$, how many queries are necessary to approximate the centrality score $P(v)$ of $v$ within a factor $(1 \pm \epsilon)$ with probability at least $1 - \delta$?

We investigate this problem for the score given by PageRank [12], a classic centrality measure employed in an ever-growing number of applications [17] and named one of the top 10 algorithms in data mining [25]. With its rich structure, PageRank embodies different well-known mathematical objects – it is the limit distribution of a Markov chain, and the solution of a linear system – and is thus a natural "entry point" for related problems as well [10, 20].

We tackle the problem under the two most common query models. In the first model, one can retrieve all incoming and outgoing arcs of any given node with a single query. This is the model of [7], which is standard in social network mining [2, 4, 6, 14], and that we call the *node-centric* model. In the second model, with a single query one can retrieve the indegree or outdegree of a node, or one of its incoming or outgoing arcs. This is the model of [18], which is standard in query complexity and property testing, and that we call the *edge-centric* model. Note that, if $G$ has $n$ nodes and $E$ arcs, the problem can be trivially solved with $O(n)$ queries in the first model or $O(E)$ queries in the second: just fetch the entire graph $G$, and compute $P(v)$ with any standard offline algorithm. Perhaps surprisingly, however, so far no algorithm has been found that uses less than $O(n)$ or $O(E)$ queries for any choice of $G$ and $v$, despite extensive past research [1, 4–6, 11, 13, 16, 19, 21–23]. In other words, all existing algorithms may need to read essentially the entire graph to provide the aforementioned guarantees.

In this paper we show that exploring a *vanishing* fraction of the graph is *always* sufficient: we design algorithms that use only $\tilde{O}(n^{2/3})$ queries (in the node-centric model) or $\tilde{O}(E^{4/5})$ queries (in the edge-centric model) and, with probability at least $(1-\delta)$, return a multiplicative $(1 \pm \epsilon)$-approximation of $P(v)$. The bounds hold for any choice of $G$ and $v$ (and, of course, of $\epsilon$ and $\delta$); they can be tightened further if the graph's outdegrees are sufficiently small. Our algorithms leverage a combination of local graph exploration and global sketching of PageRank scores. Although developed for PageRank, our techniques are modular and may be of help for related problems.

**Organization of the paper.** The next two subsections respectively introduce notation and definitions, and briefly review related


ACM ISBN 978-1-4503-5799-9/18/07.
https://doi.org/10.1145/3210377.3210664

work. Section 2 states all our results formally. Section 3 sketches the main ideas behind our algorithms. Section 4 provides concluding remarks. Part of our results is ongoing research, and the related proofs will be provided in the full version of the paper.

### 1.1 PageRank and its local approximation

The PageRank [12] score of a node is defined recursively in terms of the PageRank scores of its parents in the graph. Formally, let $\mathbf{M} \in \mathbb{R}^{n \times n}$ be the normalized adjacency matrix of $G$, so that if $u$ has no children then $M_{u,v} = n^{-1}$ for all $v \in G$, and if $u$ has $m > 0$ children then $M_{u,v} = m^{-1}$ if $v$ is a child of $u$ and $M_{u,v} = 0$ otherwise. The PageRank score vector $\mathbf{p}$ is the unique stochastic row vector that satisfies the recursive equation:

$$\mathbf{p} = \alpha \mathbf{p}\mathbf{M} + \frac{(1-\alpha)}{n}\mathbf{1} \quad (1)$$

where $\alpha \in [0, 1)$ is a parameter called damping factor and $\mathbf{1} \in \mathbb{R}^n$ is the row vector whose entries all equal 1. The $u$-th entry of $\mathbf{p}$ is the PageRank score $P(u)$ of $u$. Note that $\frac{1-\alpha}{n} \leq P(u) \leq 1$.

In this work we ask to approximate a single ("local") component $P(v)$ of $\mathbf{p}$, and thus *locally* is used in the sense of local computation algorithms [24]. Formally, our algorithm receives in input the target node $v$ and the approximation parameters $\epsilon, \delta$. It must then output a value $p(v)$ that satisfies $(1-\epsilon)P(v) \leq p(v) \leq (1+\epsilon)P(v)$ with probability at least $1-\delta$. The algorithm has no prior information about $G$, and must explore $G$ by issuing a sequence of *query* invocations. The total number of invocations gives the *query complexity* of the algorithm. We consider two (alternative) query models, both in wide use.

**The node-centric model.** The available queries are:

- *Jump()*, that returns a node picked uniformly at random in $G$
- *Neigh(u)*, that returns the incoming and outgoing arcs of $u$

In a nutshell, a *Neigh(u)* query returns the row and column of $u$ in the adjacency matrix of $G$. In some cases [5, 6, 15, 19] *Neigh(u)* is replaced by the weaker query *Crawl(u)*, which returns a child of $u$ chosen uniformly at random. This model was introduced in [7], and is widely adopted in web and social graph mining [2, 4, 6, 14].

**The edge-centric model.** The available queries are:

- *Jump()*, that returns a node chosen uniformly at random in $G$
- *InDeg(u)* and *OutDeg(u)*, that return respectively the indegree and outdegree of $u$
- *Parent(u, i)* and *Child(u, i)*, that return respectively the $i$-th parent and $i$-th child of $u$, or NIL if $i$ is out of range

This is the model of [18]. It is the standard access model for sparse graphs in query complexity and related fields.

### 1.2 State of the art

The table below summarizes the query complexity upper bounds in the literature; no previous algorithm breaks the $O(n)$ query complexity barrier in the node-centric model. In some cases the bounds are an adaptation of the original ones to the node-centric model. One could alternatively look at the edge-centric model – again, previous literature in the general case cannot break the linear, $O(E)$ barrier.

Query complexity lower bounds are known, too. With *Neigh(·)* alone, any algorithm needs $\Omega(n)$ queries; with *Jump()* + *Crawl(·)*, $\Omega(1/P(v)) = \Omega(n)$ queries are also needed [5, 6]. With *Jump()* + *Neigh(·)*, deterministic and Las Vegas algorithms need $\Omega(n)$ queries [8] – so to break the linear *Jump()* + *Neigh(·)* query complexity barrier, one must resort to a Monte Carlo algorithm.

| reference | query model | upper bound |
|---|---|---|
| [1][13] | *Neigh(·)* | $O(n)$ |
| [3][21][23] | *Jump()* + *Neigh(·)* | $O(n)$ |
| [5][6][15][19] | *Jump()* + *Crawl(·)* | $O(1/P(v)) = O(n)$ |

## 2 OUR RESULTS

The following two subsections present our results for the two query models described in Subsection 1.1.

### 2.1 Node-centric model

Our main result is the following:

THEOREM 2.1. *$O(n^{2/3}\ln(n)^{1/3}\ln(1/\delta)^{2/3}\epsilon^{-2/3})$ queries suffice to obtain with probability $(1-\delta)$ a $(1\pm\epsilon)$-approximation of $P(v)$.*

The bound can be tightened if the maximum outdegree $\Delta$ of $G$ is sufficiently small – for instance, in social network graphs, while the maximum indegree can be extremely large, $\Delta$ is often much smaller. Formally, we prove:

THEOREM 2.2. *$O(n^{1/2}\Delta^{1/2}\ln(1/\delta)^{1/2}\epsilon^{-1})$ queries suffice to obtain with probability $(1-\delta)$ a $(1\pm\epsilon)$-approximation of $P(v)$.*

These are the first general sublinear-query-complexity upper bounds for the local approximation of PageRank under the model of [7]. Moreover, we can show they are both essentially optimal:

THEOREM 2.3. *Approximating $P(v)$ within constant factors with constant probability requires $\Omega\big(\min(n^{2/3}, n^{1/2}\Delta^{1/2})\big)$* Jump() *and* Neigh(·) *queries in the worst case.*

To improve on the bounds of Theorems 2.1 and 2.2, then, one must necessarily look at special classes of graphs $G$ or target nodes $v$. A complete proof of these results can be found in [9].

### 2.2 Edge-centric model

Let $d = E/n$ be the average degree of $G$. We prove:

THEOREM 2.4. *$O(E^{4/5}d^{-3/5}\ln(n)^{1/5}\ln(1/\delta)^{3/5}\epsilon^{-6/5})$ queries suffice to obtain with probability $(1-\delta)$ a $(1\pm\epsilon)$-approximation of $P(v)$.*

Like in the node-centric model, we give an alternative bound that is tighter when $\Delta$ is small enough (for instance when $\Delta = O(d^2)$):

THEOREM 2.5. *$O(E^{2/3}\Delta^{1/3}d^{-2/3}\ln(n)^{1/3}\ln(1/\delta)^{2/3}\epsilon^{-4/3})$ queries suffice to obtain with probability $(1-\delta)$ a $(1\pm\epsilon)$-approximation of $P(v)$.*

In a nutshell, Theorems 2.4 and 2.5 guarantee one can always compute $P(v)$ by fetching just a vanishing fraction of the arcs of $G$. Whether these bounds can be tightened is an open question.

## 3 MAIN IDEAS AND TECHNIQUES

We outline the main ideas and techniques behind our algorithms. The goal is to build a low-variance estimator for $P(v)$ through an appropriate exploration of $G$; the main challenge is that we must do so "blindfolded" since we do not know $G$ in advance.

We start with the algorithm for the node-centric model.

**1. Random-walk sampling.** As a basic primitive we need to sample the nodes $u \in G$ with probability equal to their score $P(u)$. The goal is to associate to every $u \in G$ an indicator random variable $\chi_u$ with expectation $\mathbb{E}[\chi_u] = P(u)$. It is known this sampling can be done via random walks using an expected $O(1)$ queries per sample. Note that estimating $P(v)$ by repeatedly sampling $\chi_v$ requires $\Omega(n)$ queries in general, since $P(v) = O(1/n)$ for most nodes.

**2. Subgraph estimators.** Starting from $v$, we explore a sequence $G_0, \ldots, G_k$ of progressively larger subgraphs of ancestors of $v$. To do this, at the $i$-th step we pick some ancestor $u_i$, we *expand* it by fetching its parents with one *Neigh*$(\cdot)$ call, and add it to $G_{i-1}$. From each $G_i$ we define a distinct estimator $p_{G_i}(v)$, that is, a linear combination of several $\chi_u$ such that $\mathbb{E}[p_{G_i}(v)] = P(v)$.

**3. Weighted estimators.** For $p_{G_i}(v)$ to be an efficient estimator, it must be concentrated around its mean. This happens when the coefficients of the $\chi_u$ are all roughly equal. Unfortunately, those coefficients depend on the structure of $G_i$ and can be arbitrarily unbalanced. To bypass this problem we introduce the *weighted estimator* $p_k(v)$, which is the weighted average of $p_{G_0}(v), \ldots, p_{G_k}(v)$ via nonnegative weights $\beta_0, \ldots, \beta_k$ such that $\sum_{i=0}^{k} \beta_i = 1$.

**4. Building a "perfect" estimator.** We can then show that, if we know the outdegrees of the graph, we can select $G_0, \ldots, G_k$ and $\beta_0, \ldots, \beta_k$ so that, in $p_k(v)$, the coefficients of the $\chi_u$ are all identical. This means $p_k(v)$ is essentially the sum of $k$ independent binary random variables. Via Chernoff-Hoeffding bounds we then show that, by setting $k = O(n^{1/2})$ and taking $O(n^{1/2})$ samples of $p_k(v)$, which requires $O(n^{1/2})$ queries, we get our estimate of $P(v)$.

**5. Working with unknown outdegrees.** We then remove the assumption of knowing the outdegrees of the graph. We prove that, if instead of the exact outdegrees we use an additive $\gamma$-approximation, the query complexity of estimating $P(v)$ grows to $O(n^{1/2}\gamma^{1/2})$. With $\gamma = \Delta$ this leads to Theorem 2.2. We then show one can obtain the additive $\gamma$-approximation using $\tilde{O}(n/\gamma)$ queries, and by setting $\gamma = \tilde{O}(n^{1/3})$ we get the $\tilde{O}(n^{2/3})$ bound of Theorem 2.1.

We then adapt our algorithm to the edge-centric model.

**6. Adapting the algorithm.** The key adaptation is in the expansion of $u_i$ (see above), which under this model requires $\Theta(in(u_i))$ queries. Thus, to build $p_k(v)$ we use $\Theta(\sum_{i=0}^{k} in(u_i))$ queries. For the same cost we can also learn the outdegrees of the parents of $u_i$, which means we do not need the outdegree sketching scheme.

**7. Avoiding heavy nodes.** We should then avoid expanding nodes of high indegree. In fact, we avoid expanding nodes of high score, since a node with high $P(u)$ might have a large $in(u)$. The reason is that we can easily find such "heavy" nodes via the random-walk sampling. We adapt the construction of $p_k(v)$ so to never expand heavy nodes, while keeping the concentration guarantees.

**8. Indegree inequalities.** Finally, we bound $in(u_i)$ as a function of $E, d, \Delta$. To do this we develop two different bounds for $in(u)$ as a function of $E, d, \Delta$ and of $P(u)$, and then we use the fact that $P(u_i)$ is small for every $u_i$ we expand. By applying these bounds to $\sum_{i=0}^{k} in(u_i)$ and picking an appropriate $k$ we obtain Theorem 2.4 and Theorem 2.5.

## 4 CONCLUSIONS

We have shown that one can approximate the PageRank score of a node in a graph, with rigorous guarantees, by accessing only a sublinear portion of the graph – in terms of both nodes and arcs. The techniques yielding our results are modular, and they may prove useful in related problems; an interesting direction is that of local approximation for systems of linear equations.

## ACKNOWLEDGMENTS

Marco Bressan is supported in part by the ERC Starting Grant DMAP 680153 and by the MIUR SIR Grant RBSI14Q743. Enoch Peserico is supported in part by Univ. Padova Project CAEPAE.

## REFERENCES


[1] Reid Andersen, Christian Borgs, Jennifer T. Chayes, John Hopcroft, Vahab Mirrokni, and Shang-Hua Teng. 2008. Local Computation of PageRank Contributions. *Internet Mathematics* 5, 1–2 (2008), 23–45.

[2] Bahman Bahmani, Ravi Kumar, Mohammad Mahdian, and Eli Upfal. 2012. PageRank on an evolving graph. In *Proc. of ACM KDD*. 24–32.

[3] Siddhartha Banerjee and Peter Lofgren. 2015. Fast Bidirectional Probability Estimation in Markov Models. In *Proc. of NIPS*. 1423–1431.

[4] Ziv Bar-Yossef and Li-Tal Mashiach. 2008. Local Approximation of PageRank and Reverse PageRank. In *Proc. of ACM CIKM*. 279–288.

[5] Christian Borgs, Michael Brautbar, Jennifer T. Chayes, and Shang-Hua Teng. 2014. Multiscale Matrix Sampling and Sublinear-Time PageRank Computation. *Internet Mathematics* 10, 1-2 (2014), 20–48.

[6] Christian Borgs, Michael Brautbar, Jennifer T. Chayes, and Shang-Hua Teng. 2012. A Sublinear Time Algorithm for PageRank Computations. In *Proc. of WAW*. 41–53.

[7] Mickey Brautbar and Michael Kearns. 2010. Local Algorithms for Finding Interesting Individuals in Large Networks. In *Proc. of ICS*. 188–199.

[8] Marco Bressan, Enoch Peserico, and Luca Pretto. 2013. The power of local information in PageRank. In *Proc. of WWW (Companion Volume)*. 179–180.

[9] Marco Bressan, Enoch Peserico, and Luca Pretto. 2018. Approximating PageRank locally with sublinear query complexity. *CoRR* abs:1404.1864 (2018).

[10] Marco Bressan, Enoch Peserico, and Luca Pretto. 2018. On approximating the stationary distribution of time-reversible Markov chains. In *Proc. of STACS*. 18:1–18:14.

[11] Marco Bressan and Luca Pretto. 2011. Local Computation of PageRank: the Ranking Side. In *Proc. of ACM CIKM*. 631–640.

[12] Sergey Brin and Lawrence Page. 1998. The anatomy of a large scale hypertextual Web search engine. In *Proc. of WWW*.

[13] Yen-Yu Chen, Qingqing Gan, and Torsten Suel. 2004. Local Methods for Estimating PageRank Values. In *Proc. of ACM CIKM*. 381–389.

[14] Flavio Chierichetti, Anirban Dasgupta, Ravi Kumar, Silvio Lattanzi, and Tamás Sarlós. 2016. On Sampling Nodes in a Network. In *Proc. of WWW*. 471–481.

[15] Dániel Fogaras and Balázs Rácz. 2004. Towards Scaling Fully Personalized PageRank. In *Proc. of WAW*. 105–117.

[16] David Gleich and Marzia Polito. 2007. Approximating Personalized PageRank with Minimal Use of Web Graph Data. *Internet Mathematics* 3, 3 (2007), 257–294.

[17] David F. Gleich. 2015. PageRank Beyond the Web. *SIAM Rev.* 57, 3 (2015), 321–363.

[18] Oded Goldreich, Shari Goldwasser, and Dana Ron. 1998. Property Testing and Its Connection to Learning and Approximation. *J. ACM* 45, 4 (1998), 653–750.

[19] Christina E Lee, Asuman Ozdaglar, and Devavrat Shah. 2013. Computing the Stationary Distribution Locally. In *Proc. of NIPS*. 1376–1384.

[20] Christina E. Lee, Asuman E. Ozdaglar, and Devavrat Shah. 2014. Solving Systems of Linear Equations: Locally and Asynchronously. *CoRR* abs/1411.2647 (2014).

[21] Peter Lofgren, Siddhartha Banerjee, and Ashish Goel. 2015. Bidirectional PageRank Estimation: From Average-Case to Worst-Case. In *Proc. of WAW*. 164–176.

[22] Peter Lofgren, Siddhartha Banerjee, and Ashish Goel. 2016. Personalized PageRank Estimation and Search: A Bidirectional Approach. In *Proc. of ACM WSDM*. 163–172.

[23] Peter Lofgren, Siddhartha Banerjee, Ashish Goel, and C. Seshadhri. 2014. FAST-PPR: Scaling Personalized PageRank Estimation for Large Graphs. In *Proc. of ACM KDD*. 1436–1445.

[24] Ronitt Rubinfeld, Gil Tamir, Shai Vardi, and Ning Xie. 2011. Fast Local Computation Algorithms. In *Proc. of ICS*. 223–238.

[25] Xindong Wu, Vipin Kumar, J. Ross Quinlan, Joydeep Ghosh, Qiang Yang, Hiroshi Motoda, Geoffrey J. McLachlan, Angus Ng, Bing Liu, Philip S. Yu, Zhi-Hua Zhou, Michael Steinbach, David J. Hand, and Dan Steinberg. 2007. Top 10 algorithms in data mining. *Knowl. Inf. Syst.* 14 (2007), 1–37. Issue 1.

# Brief Announcement: Coloring-based Task Mapping for Dragonfly Systems

Ink Chinavinijkul
Knox College
Galesburg, IL, USA
cchinavinijkul@knox.edu

Jacob Newcomb
Knox College
Galesburg, IL, USA
jlnewcomb@knox.edu

Lingzhi Xi
Knox College
Galesburg, IL, USA
lxi@knox.edu

David P. Bunde
Knox College
Galesburg, IL, USA
dbunde@knox.edu

## ABSTRACT

Task mapping is the assignment of job tasks to nodes. Traditionally, the goal of task mapping is to maximize locality, reducing the number of network hops needed to deliver messages as a way of reducing bandwidth consumption. We show that on a Dragonfly topology, such a strategy can be counterproductive because, while traffic is reduced, it is also concentrated on only a few global links, creating hot spots. We formulate the balanced adjacency coloring problem to design mappings that evenly spread network traffic, give optimal algorithms to solve it for a number of cases, and use simulations to show that mappings based on these algorithms can reduce the communication time of a stencil job by up to 20%.

## CCS CONCEPTS

• **Computing methodologies → Parallel algorithms**;

## KEYWORDS

Dragonfly topology; task mapping; stencil communication; balanced adjacency coloring

**ACM Reference Format:**

Ink Chinavinijkul, Jacob Newcomb, Lingzhi Xi, and David P. Bunde. 2018. Brief Announcement: Coloring-based Task Mapping for Dragonfly Systems. In *SPAA '18: 30th ACM Symposium on Parallelism in Algorithms and Architectures, July 16–18, 2018, Vienna, Austria.* ACM, New York, NY, USA, 3 pages. https://doi.org/10.1145/3210377.3210665

## 1 INTRODUCTION

This paper looks at task mapping for stencil jobs on Dragonfly systems. Dragonfly [7] is a hierarchical network topology based on a tuple of parameters $(p, a, h)$. To construct a Dragonfly system, $p$ compute nodes are connected to each network switch. The switches are organized into groups of size $a$, with all switches in a group connected by *local links*. In addition, each switch also has $h$ *global links* to other groups, arranged to give a single global link between each pair of groups. A big selling point for Dragonfly is its constant network diameter; each pair of switches is separated by at most three hops, one local link within the group of the source switch, one global link to the group of the destination switch, and then a final local link to the destination switch.

A stencil job is one using a nearest neighbor communication pattern in which tasks correspond to cells of a 2D or 3D grid and each task communicates with the adjacent tasks, those with whom it shares an edge in 2D or a face in 3D. This is an important communication pattern for scientific computations, with each task simulating its geographic region and periodically exchanging boundary conditions with its neighbors.

*Task mapping* is the assignment of job tasks to nodes. It is performed after the job is started, meaning that the job has already been assigned specific nodes. For jobs running MPI, task mapping is the assignment of roles to MPI ranks. Task mapping has been shown to significantly effect stencil job performance on a mesh topology [3]. Several researchers have previously considered its effect for stencil jobs on Dragonfly systems [1, 2, 5, 6, 8]. Several of these, starting with Bhatele et al. [1], utilize *blocking*, which maps a contiguous group of cells to the nodes of each switch and/or group. Blocking increases the proportion of communication that stays within a switch or group. Unfortunately, it can interact poorly with the hierarchical structure of Dragonfly. For example, consider the blocked mapping shown in Figure 1(a), in which a mesh is divided into $2 \times 5$ blocks, each assigned to a single group (numbers shown). With this mapping, group 1 needs to exchange 5 cells of boundary information in the horizontal direction with group 2, 2 cells worth in the vertical direction with group 6, and nothing with any other group. If the network uses shortest path routing, this causes a large network load imbalance, which would worsen with mesh size.

The network imbalance of blocking led some to advocate for random mapping of cells to nodes [1], but this has been shown to lose about half the potential throughput in several cases [6]. Instead, we propose a type of coloring called *balanced adjacency coloring* that balances the number of times each pair of colors is adjacent. A mapping based on this coloring is shown in Figure 1(b). Every pair of groups is adjacent 4 times, giving perfect network load balance.

A possible alternative to clever task mapping is improved routing. The strategy of always using the local-global-local link pattern is called *minimal routing*. As observed above, this can lead to hotspots on global links. One solution, called Valiant routing [7], routes each


*SPAA '18, July 16–18, 2018, Vienna, Austria*

ACM ISBN 978-1-4503-5799-9/18/07.
https://doi.org/10.1145/3210377.3210665

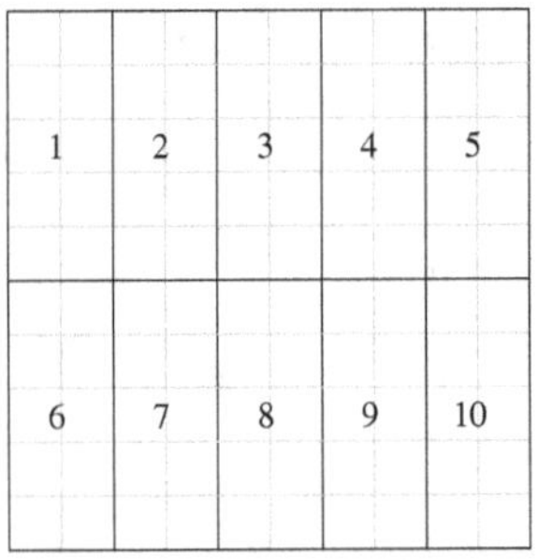


(a)

| 1 | 2 | 3 | 4 | 5 | 6 | 7 | 8 | 9 | 10 |
|---|---|---|---|---|---|---|---|---|---|
| 3 | 1 | 5 | 2 | 7 | 4 | 9 | 6 | 10 | 8 |
| 2 | 4 | 1 | 6 | 3 | 8 | 5 | 10 | 7 | 9 |
| 5 | 3 | 7 | 1 | 9 | 2 | 10 | 4 | 8 | 6 |
| 4 | 6 | 2 | 8 | 1 | 10 | 3 | 9 | 5 | 7 |
| 7 | 5 | 9 | 3 | 10 | 1 | 8 | 2 | 6 | 4 |
| 6 | 8 | 4 | 10 | 2 | 9 | 1 | 7 | 3 | 5 |
| 9 | 7 | 10 | 5 | 8 | 3 | 6 | 1 | 4 | 2 |
| 8 | 10 | 6 | 9 | 4 | 7 | 2 | 5 | 1 | 3 |
| 10 | 9 | 8 | 7 | 6 | 5 | 4 | 3 | 2 | 1 |

(b)

**Figure 1: Two mappings (group numbers shown). (a) Blocking. (b) Balanced adjacency coloring.**

| 1 | 2 | 3 | 4 | 5 | 6 | 7 | 8 |
|---|---|---|---|---|---|---|---|
| 3 | 1 | 5 | 2 | 7 | 4 | 8 | 6 |
| 2 | 4 | 1 | 6 | 3 | 8 | 5 | 7 |
| 5 | 3 | 7 | 1 | 8 | 2 | 6 | 4 |
| 4 | 6 | 2 | 8 | 1 | 7 | 3 | 5 |
| 7 | 5 | 8 | 3 | 6 | 1 | 4 | 2 |
| 6 | 8 | 4 | 7 | 2 | 5 | 1 | 3 |
| 8 | 7 | 6 | 5 | 4 | 3 | 2 | 1 |

(a)

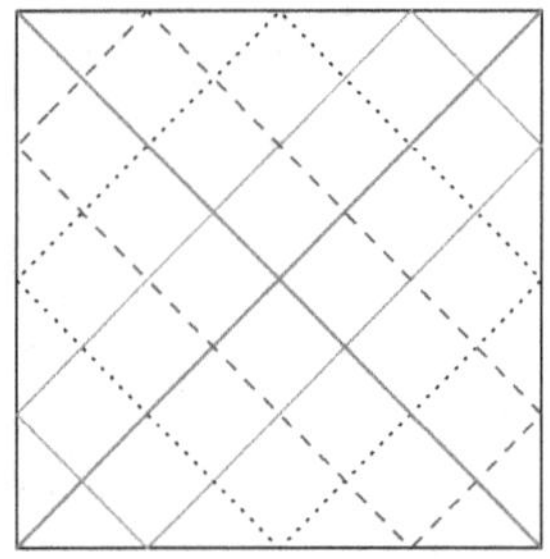

(b)

**Figure 2: An $8 \times 8$ balanced adjacency coloring. (a) Coloring itself. (b) Lines and cycles generating it.**

message by way of a randomly-chosen intermediate group. This increases the maximum distance between switches to five hops: local link, global link to intermediate group, local link within intermediate group, global link to destination group, and local link. Although it uses longer paths, Valiant routing spreads traffic more evenly among the links. Work on routing continues (e.g. [4]), with most of the focus on *adaptive routing*, which adjusts the routing based on the congestion level. We use UGAL-L [7] as a representative of adaptive routing; it chooses between minimal and Valiant routing on a per-packet basis using an estimate of network latency. Our results show that balanced mapping achieves better performance than good routing on top of a baseline mapping.

Also related is work of Zhang et al. [9] on allocation, the assignment of nodes to jobs. Their algorithm strives to localize small jobs, but to spread out large jobs to balance the global link load. The goal is thus similar to ours, but their algorithm does not apply in this work, which concerns jobs occupying the entire machine.

## 2 BALANCED ADJACENCY COLORING

We define a *balanced adjacency coloring* of an $n \times m$ mesh as a coloring using $k$ colors with the following properties:

(1) Every color is used either $\lfloor nm/k \rfloor$ or $\lceil nm/k \rceil$ times.
(2) Each pair of colors is adjacent $\lfloor A/\binom{k}{2} \rfloor$ or $\lceil A/\binom{k}{2} \rceil$ times, where $A$ is the number of adjacent cells with distinct colors.

The conditions balance the group workload and the load on global links, respectively.

Chakaravarthy et al. [2] also proposed a coloring problem to capture task mapping in a Dragonfly system, but they required that all neighbors of each color be distinct. Balanced adjacency coloring is a generalization of their notion. Their algorithms are fairly restricted, but incomparable with the results of this paper.

Our main algorithm colors an $n \times n$ mesh with $n$ colors. Initially, assume $n$ is even. The algorithm begins with a permutation of the colors on one row, which we call the *reference row*.

To extend the coloring of the reference row to the rest of the mesh, we consider a collection of lines and cycles in a visualization of the mesh with square unit cells as shown in Figure 2(b). The two lines are created by joining opposite corners. Each cycle has a starting point $(x, n)$ satisfying $1 < x < n$ with $x$ even. It proceeds at slope -1 to the mesh's right edge ($x = n$). Each time an edge of the mesh is encountered, change the slope as if it is reflecting off that edge. We say a mesh cell is *on* a line or cycle if the line or cycle passes through the cell's geometric center.

It is not hard to show that every mesh cell is on one line or cycle. To assign colors based on the lines and cycles, we copy colors of the reference row along them. The reference row has one cell on each line and we copy the color of this cell to all the line's cells. The reference row has two cells on each cycle and we alternate these colors around the cycle. Following this process using the lines and cycles in Figure 2(b) gives the coloring in Figure 2(a).

This algorithm uses every color $n$ times, either because it occupies an entire diagonal or because it alternates around a cycle which is twice as long. The remaining step to show we have a balanced adjacency coloring is to count color adjacencies:

Lemma 1. *Each pair of colors is adjacent 4 times in the coloring.*

Proof. We count the adjacencies within and between the lines and cycles. Lines contain no adjacent cells. This is true of cycles except at the 4 mesh boundaries, when they reflect and cross adjacent cells, each making one adjacency between the cycle's colors.

The two lines intersect once. Since lines contain only a single color, each diagonally-opposite pair of cells around the intersection point have a shared color. These pairs of cells make four adjacencies.

Consider a line-cycle intersection. The diagonally-opposite cells along the line share its color. Since colors alternate on the cycle, each of the other cells has a distinct color of the cycle. Each of these is adjacent with the line's color twice. The line and cycle intersect twice, doubling the number of adjacencies to four.

In a cycle-cycle intersection, diagonally-opposite cells are split between the cycle's colors. Thus, the intersection forms 1 adjacency for each pair of colors in different cycles. Each pair of cycles has 4 intersections, creating 4 adjacencies between their colors. □

*Generalizations.* The algorithm when $n$ is odd is the same as the even case except only one line is used. It also generalizes to algorithms for an $n \times n$ mesh using $2n$ colors (use 4 colors per cycle and two per line) and an $n \times n \times n$ cube (color 2D slices).

## 3 MAPPINGS

The obvious way to turn a balanced adjacency coloring into a mapping is to assign each mesh cell to a node in the group indicated

| Mesh | Groups used | System $(p, a, h)$ | System nodes |
|---|---|---|---|
| 8×8 | 8 | (2, 4, 2) | 72 |
| 32×32 | 32 | (4, 8, 4) | 1,056 |
| 72×72 | 72 | (6, 12, 6) | 5,256 |
| 128×128 | 128 | (8, 16, 8) | 16,512 |
| 200×200 | 200 | (10, 20, 10) | 40,200 |

**Figure 3: Description of simulated systems and jobs.**

by its color. This puts all communication over global links and performs poorly. Thus, our algorithm uses a small amount of blocking. Specifically, we divide the job into $2 \times 2$ submeshes to form a $(n/2) \times (n/2)$ mesh of task units, each containing 4 tasks. The mesh of task units is then colored using the generalization that uses twice as many colors as the mesh dimensions. These colors are used to assign the task units to groups. We call this algorithm *Blocking Balanced Adjacency Coloring* (B-BAC) because it uses some blocking to increase traffic within groups but primarily follows the coloring.

As a baseline, we use the Blocked Supernodes Mapping (BSM) by Bhatele et al. [1]. It maximizes locality by assigning a contiguous block for each group and contiguous subblocks for each switch.

We compare the mappings with simulations of a *capability workload*, where a single job runs on most of the machine. This is an important workload for the largest systems, whose construction is justified by the need to run huge jobs. We tested a range of job and system sizes, shown in Figure 3. All jobs are square and use all but one group of a system. All systems have $2p = a = 2h$ for balance.

We used a packet-level simulator, with local and global link latencies of 100, virtual channel buffer sizes of 256, and ISLIP for buffer allocation with an internal speedup of 1.5. We assume a communication-intensive job, with boundary exchanges sending 30 packets each way. Each task sends to its neighbors, waits for their message, computes for 5 time units, and repeats for 10 rounds.

Figure 4 shows the simulation results comparing the blocking-based baseline strategy with B-BAC. Looking just at the results for minimal routing (first two bars for each mesh size), we see that B-BAC is very slightly worse than the baseline for the smallest size (less than 0.02%), but then consistently better, with a percent improvement generally in the mid-teens (16%, 8%, 14%, 17.5% respectively). Looking at the results for UGAL-L routing (last two bars for each size), B-BAC is worse for the two smaller sizes (by 1.5% and 4%), but better at the larger sizes (by 5%, 7%, and 20%). For both routing algorithms, B-BAC wins at larger job sizes.

Of particular note is that B-BAC with minimal routing outperforms both mappings with adaptive routing in nearly all cases. In fact, for a given mapping, UGAL-L routing is nearly always worse than minimal routing. This is initially surprising since UGAL-L is adaptive and can always revert to minimal routing. In intense communication patterns such as ours, however, the penalty for extra hops can be particularly high since they consume extra bandwidth. With B-BAC mapping, nearly all global links are equally loaded so Valiant routes are nearly always bad. The baseline strategy has many unused global links, but the results show that adaptive routing cannot compensate for the initial poor link load balance.

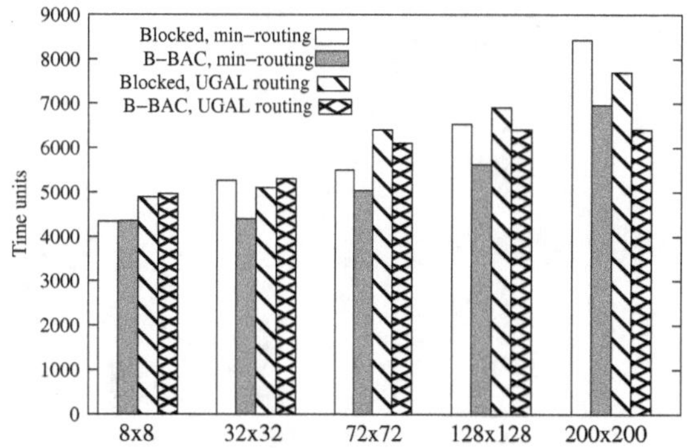


**Figure 4: Simulated job times for different mesh sizes. Compares blocking-based mapping and coloring-based (B-BAC) for minimal and UGAL-L routing.**

## 4 DISCUSSION

Our results show the potential of spreading the network traffic more fairly, even at the cost of increasing the total amount of global traffic. Going forward, one idea is to block at the switch level so that all nodes of a switch are working on a single mesh submesh. We used $2 \times 2$ submeshes since non-square submeshes make the traffic sent between neighbors depend on the direction due to the different number of cells along each boundary. This could be overcome with a weighted coloring. Another goal is to find colorings for non-square meshes and graphs representing other communication patterns.

## ACKNOWLEDGMENTS

This work was partially supported by the National Science Foundation under grant CNS-1423413 and the Paul K. and Evalyn Richter Memorial Funds.

## REFERENCES

[1] A. Bhatele, N. Jain, W.D. Gropp, and L.V. Kale. 2011. Avoiding hot-spots on two-level direct networks. In *Proc. Conf. High Performance Computing, Networking, Storage and Analysis (SC)*.

[2] V.T. Chakaravarthy, M. Kedia, Y. Sabharwal, N.P.K. Katta, R. Rajamony, and A. Ramanan. 2012. Mapping Strategies for the PERCS Architecture. In *Proc. 19th Intern. Conf. High Performance Computing (HiPC)*.

[3] M. Deveci, S. Rajamanickam, V.J. Leung, K.T. Pedretti, S.L. Olivier, D.P. Bunde, Ü.V. Çatalyürek, and K.D. Devine. 2014. Exploiting Geometric Partitioning in Task Mapping for Parallel Computers. In *Proc. 28th IEEE Intern. Parallel and Distributed Processing Symp. (IPDPS)*.

[4] P. Faizian, M.A. Mollah, Z. Tong, X. Yuan, and M. Lang. 2017. A Comparative Study of SDN and Adaptive Routing on Dragonfly Networks. In *Proc. Conf. High Performance Computing, Networking, Storage and Analysis (SC)*.

[5] N. Jain, A. Bhatele, X. Ni, N.J. Wright, and L.V. Kale. 2014. Maximizing throughput on a dragonfly network. In *Proc. Conf. High Performance Computing, Networking, Storage and Analysis (SC)*.

[6] A. Jokanovic, B. Prisacari, G. Rodriguez, and C. Minkenberg. 2013. Randomizing task placement does not randomize traffic (enough). In *Proc. 2013 Interconnection Network Architecture: On-Chip, Multi-Chip (IMA-OCMC)*. 9–12.

[7] J. Kim, W. Dally, S. Scott, and D. Abts. 2008. Technology-Driven, Highly-Scalable Dragonfly Topology. In *Proc. 35th Ann. Intern. Symp. Comput. Arch. (ISCA)*. 77–78.

[8] B. Prisacari, G. Rodriguez, P. Heidelberger, D. Chen, C. Minkenberg, and T. Hoefler. 2014. Efficient Task Placement and Routing in Dragonfly Networks. In *Proc. 23rd ACM Intern. Symp. High-Performance Parallel and Distributed Computing (HPDC)*.

[9] Y. Zhang, O. Tuncer, F. Kaplan, K. Olcoz, V.J. Leung, and A.K. Coskun. 2018. Level-Spread: A new job allocation policy for Dragonfly networks. In *Proc. 32nd IEEE Intern. Parallel and Distributed Processing Symp. (IPDPS)*.

# Brief Announcement: Parallel Transitive Closure Within 3D Crosspoint Memory

Alvaro Velasquez
Department of Computer Science
University of Central Florida
velasquez@cs.ucf.edu

Sumit Kumar Jha
Department of Computer Science
University of Central Florida
jha@cs.ucf.edu

## ABSTRACT

The infamous memory-processor bottleneck has motivated the search for logic-in-memory architectures. In this paper, we demonstrate how the transitive closure problem can be solved through in-memory computing within a 3D crosspoint memory. The proposed architecture requires only two layers of 1-diode 1-resistor (1D1R) interconnects and external feedback loops.

**ACM Reference Format:**
Alvaro Velasquez and Sumit Kumar Jha. 2018. Brief Announcement: Parallel Transitive Closure Within 3D Crosspoint Memory. In *SPAA '18: 30th ACM Symposium on Parallelism in Algorithms and Architectures, July 16–18, 2018, Vienna, Austria.* ACM, New York, NY, USA, 4 pages. https://doi.org/10.1145/3210377.3210657

## 1 INTRODUCTION

Performance in traditional von Neumann architectures is increasingly being hindered due to the memory wall [1] that arises when the memory and the processing units are segregated. Indeed, a study by NVIDIA [2] demonstrated that a 64-bit arithmetic operation consumes 20 pJ of energy as opposed to the 16 nJ consumed during DRAM read/write operations. This significant gap in energy is due to the distance that must be traversed in order to fetch data from memory. Due to these overheads, there has been a push towards in-memory computing in recent years.

In this paper, we focus on an in-memory solution to the transitive closure problem, which has been studied extensively within graph theory and has ubiquitous applications in many different areas. In the theoretical domain, a classic result of Skyum and Valiant demonstrates how problems computable by circuits of polynomial size can be reduced to the transitive closure operation via projections [3]. In more applied domains, this problem underpins many important procedures, such as resolving database queries [4], parsing grammars [5], determining data dependencies at compilation [6], as well as formal verification algorithms such as model checking [7]. Inspired by these applications and motivated by the memory wall problem, we investigate how the inherently parallel flow of information in 3D crosspoint memories can be used to perform graph transitive closure in an efficient manner. In particular, we solve the transitive closure problem through repeated Boolean matrix multiplication within memory. The method proposed may be suitable for memories similar to Intel's recently unveiled 3D XPoint$^{TM}$ memory architecture [8] – a 3-dimensional crosspoint architecture with two layers of non-volatile memory cells which is orders of magnitude faster than traditional solid-state drives [9]. This technology can already be found on the market in the form of Intel's Optane$^{TM}$ drives [10].


ACM ISBN 978-1-4503-5799-9/18/07...$15.00
https://doi.org/10.1145/3210377.3210657

## 2 3D CROSSPOINT DYNAMICS

Due to advancements in memristor and phase-change memory technologies, as well as concerns over the memory-processor bottleneck, the field of in-memory computing in 2-dimensional memories has garnered much interest in recent years. Many of the proposed digital computing architectures are derived from memristor implication logic [11] and paths-based logic [12] [13]. However, computation within 3D memories has gone largely unexplored.

The computational fabric we adopt in this paper is a 3D crosspoint memory with two layers of cells stacked vertically. These memories consist of sets of parallel wires, with each wire from one set placed perpendicularly to every wire in another set. At every junction of wires, there is a memory cell acting as a switch between the two wires and exhibiting a low-resistance state (LRS) and a high-resistance state (HRS). This is a generalization of modern memristor-based systems and phase change memories, wherein the memory cells have charge-dependent [14] and temperature-dependent [15] resistances, respectively. A selector element is used with each memory cell. This typically consists of a diode, leading to 1-diode 1-resistor (1D1R) structures.

In our approach, the top and bottom rows or nanowires of the crosspoint memory are connected to each other using individual external connections as shown in Fig. 1 (*Top*). It is mainly in this respect that the proposed architecture differs from existing 3D memories, such as Intel's 3D XPoint$^{TM}$. Definition 2.1 presents an abstraction of the 3D crosspoint architecture.

*Definition 2.1.* An $n \times n$ 3D crosspoint memory with two externally interconnected layers is a 4-tuple $\mathbb{C} = (M^1, M^2, R, C)$, where

- $M^k = \begin{pmatrix} m^k_{11} & m^k_{12} & \dots & m^k_{1n} \\ \vdots & \vdots & \ddots & \vdots \\ m^k_{n1} & m^k_{n2} & \dots & m^k_{nn} \end{pmatrix}$ is a Boolean matrix representing the interconnects with $n$ rows and $n$ columns. Each $m^k_{ij} \in \{0, 1\}$ denotes the state of the device connecting row $i$ with column $j$ in layer $k \in \{1, 2\}$. $m^k_{ij} = 1$ denotes a 1D1R device in the low-resistance state (LRS) state and $m^k_{ij} = 0$ denotes the same device in a high-resistance state (HRS).

- $R = \{r_1, \ldots, r_n\}$ is a vector of row nanowire values and $r_i \in \{0, 1\}$ provides the same input voltage to every component $m^1_{i1}, \ldots, m^1_{in}$ in the first layer. External feedback loops connect the bottommost row nanowires with the corresponding topmost nanowires. Hence, it is enough to model both the topmost and bottommost rows or nanowires using the same vector of values. See Fig. 1 for an illustrative example.
- $C = \{c_1, \ldots, c_n\}$ is a vector of column nanowire values and $c_j \in \{0, 1\}$ provides the same input to every component $m^2_{1j}, \ldots, m^2_{nj}$ in the second layer of the 3D crosspoint memory.

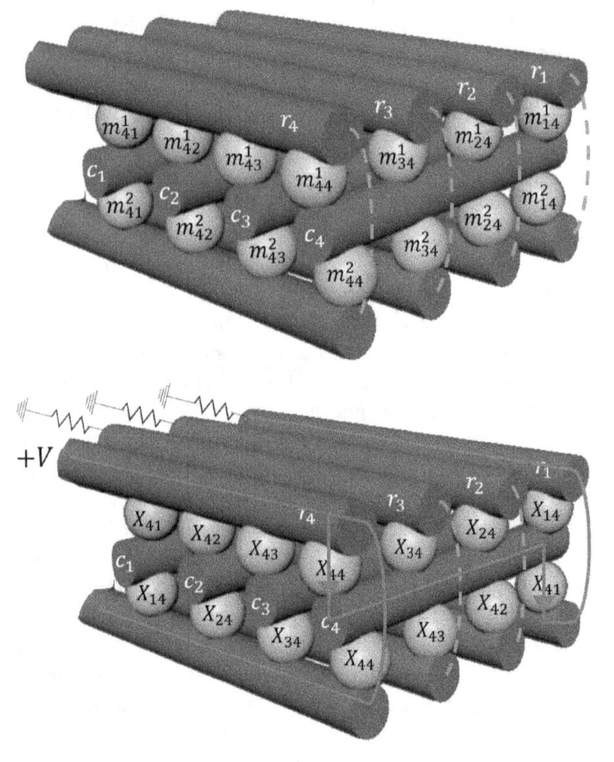

**Figure 1: (*Top*) Illustration of a 3D crosspoint memory $\mathbb{C} = (M^1, M^2, R, C)$ with two layers of interconnects and external feedback loops. The dashed arcs denote an external interconnection between the corresponding bottom and top nanowires. (*Bottom*) Given $X = ((1,0,0,0),(0,1,0,0),(0,0,1,0),(1,0,0,1))$, we configure the crosspoint memory in accordance with Theorem 3.1 so that $M^1 = X$ and $M^2 = X^T$. In order to compute the $4^{\text{th}}$ row vector of the transitive closure of $X$, a voltage bias is applied to $r_4$ and $r_1, r_2, r_3$ are grounded. Note that the voltage readings obtained from $(r_1, r_2, r_3, r_4)$ will correspond to $(1, 0, 0, 1)$, as expected.**

In Definition 2.1, a nanowire value of 1 denotes a high voltage value (with respect to ground) and 0 denotes a negligible voltage value. The LRS state is analogous to a closed switch, i.e. a component that allows current to flow from one terminal to the next. Conversely, the HRS state functions as an open switch; namely, it impedes the flow of current. Since each 1D1R component contains a diode, current will only flow in one direction when said component is in the LRS state. Without loss of generality, we assume that $m^1_{ij}$ and $m^2_{ij}$ allow current to flow from wire $r_i$ to $c_j$ and $c_j$ to $r_i$, respectively. For the remainder of this paper, we use the terms interconnect, component, and device interchangeably.

Suppose we have a 3D crosspoint memory $\mathbb{C} = (M^1, M^2, R, C)$. In order to induce a flow of current through the memory, a voltage bias is applied to some row wire $r_i$ and other wire(s) are grounded. The trajectory of current will depend on the configuration of the interconnect matrices $M^1$, $M^2$. Due to the unidirectional flow of current imposed by 1D1R interconnects, current will flow from wire $r_i$ to $c_j$ if $m^1_{ij}$ is in the LRS state and wire $r_i$ has a high voltage with respect to ground (i.e. $m^1_{ij} = 1$ and $r_i = 1$). Similarly, current will flow from $c_j$ to $r_i$ when $m^2_{ij} = 1$ and $c_j = 1$. We can thus define the outputs of components $m^1_{ij}$ and $m^2_{ij}$ by $r_i \wedge m^1_{ij}$ and $c_j \wedge m^2_{ij}$, respectively. We can now define the values of $r_i$ and $c_j$ by equations (1) and (2), where $\mathcal{I}_i = 1$ if a voltage source is applied to wire $r_i$ and $\mathcal{I}_i = 0$ denotes a grounded wire.

$$c_j = \bigvee_{i=1}^{n} \left( r_i \wedge m^1_{ij} \right) \tag{1}$$

$$r_i = \mathcal{I}_i \vee \bigvee_{j=1}^{n} \left( c_j \wedge m^2_{ij} \right) \tag{2}$$

To capture the dynamics of the feedback loop connecting the top and bottom row wires, we model the flow of information in the crosspoint memory through a discrete notion of time. Let $r_{i,t}$ and $c_{j,t}$ denote the state of wires $r_i$ and $c_j$ during the $t^{\text{th}}$ iteration of the feedback loop. At time $t = 0$, we have $r_{i,0} = \mathcal{I}_i = 1$ if a voltage source is applied to wire $r_i$ and $r_{i,0} = \mathcal{I}_i = 0$ if the wire is grounded. The values of the wires then evolve from $t = 1$ onwards according to equations (3) and (4).

$$c_{j,t} = \bigvee_{i=1}^{n} \left( r_{i,t-1} \wedge m^1_{ij} \right) \tag{3}$$

$$r_{i,t} = \bigvee_{j=1}^{n} \left( c_{j,t} \wedge m^2_{ij} \right) \tag{4}$$

Equation (3) suggests that column $j$ has a flow of current at time $t$ if and only if a row nanowire $r_i$ has a flow at time $t-1$ and the corresponding component $m^1_{ij}$ is in the LRS state in the first layer of the memory. Similarly, equation (4) describes the fact that row $r_i$ has a new flow of current at time $t$ if and only if a column nanowire $c_j$ has a flow at time $t$ and the corresponding component $m^2_{ij}$ is in the LRS state in the second layer. While the state of the flows in the nanowires changes as time evolves, the states of the interconnects are set at time $t = 0$ and do not evolve. Essentially, the interconnects store the data values in the crosspoint memory while the interconnecting nanowires enable the desired computation in our approach.

## 3 TRANSITIVE CLOSURE

We solve the transitive closure problem through repeated Boolean matrix multiplication using in-memory computing. The mapping proposed may be suitable for memories similar to Intel's recently unveiled 3D XPoint™ memory architecture [8], provided that feedback loops are added externally (see Fig. 1). Given a graph $G = (V, E)$, where $V$ is the set of vertices in the graph and $E \in \{0,1\}^{|V|\times|V|}$ is its adjacency matrix, the transitive closure of $G$ consists of the matrix $X^*$, where $X^*_{ij} = 1$ if $i = j$ or there is a path from $v_i$ to $v_j$ in $G$, and 0 otherwise.

Let $X^{(k)}$ denote the $k$-reachability matrix specifying which nodes are reachable by a path of at most $k$ edges. We assume that every node has a path of length 0 to itself, thus $X^{(0)} = I$, where $I$ denotes the identity matrix. $X^{(k)}$ can be defined recursively as $X^{(k)} = (I \vee E)^k = X^{(k-1)}X^{(1)}$. Since the maximum length of a path in $G$ is $|V| - 1$, we have $X^* = X^{|V|-1} = (I \vee E)^{|V|-1}$.

The preceding argument implies that the transitive closure of a graph can be computed using repeated matrix multiplication. While efforts have been made to multiply two Boolean matrices within memory [16], only a single matrix could be stored in memory. An attempt to multiply a set of Boolean matrices within memory has also been presented in [17]. However, the method proposed therein requires a layer of interconnects for each matrix to be multiplied. Thus, given an arbitrary graph $G = (V, E)$, the number of layers required is $O(|V|)$ as opposed to the two layers required by our approach. This is significant not just from a complexity standpoint, but from a practical perspective as well.

Theorem 3.1 below demonstrates how repeated Boolean matrix multiplication can be efficiently computed in an $n \times n$ 3D crosspoint memory with feedback loops. The values of the bits stored at the crosspoints are fixed during initialization and do not change for the entirety of the procedure. See Fig. 1 (*Bottom*) for a simple example.

Theorem 3.1. *Let $\mathbb{C} = (M^1, M^2, R, C)$ be an $n \times n$ 3D crosspoint memory, $X$ denote a Boolean matrix, $I$ be the $n \times n$ identity matrix, and $\gamma \in \{1, \ldots, n\}$ be a row index. If $M^1 = X$, $M^2 = X^T$ and $(r_{10}, \ldots, r_{n0}) = (I_{\gamma 1}, \ldots, I_{\gamma n})$, then $r_{it} = (X^{2t})_{\gamma i}$ and $c_{jt} = (X^{2t-1})_{\gamma j}$ at any given time index $t$.*

Proof. The proof is by induction on $t$. When $t = 1$,

$$r_{i1} = \bigvee_{j=1}^{n}\left(c_{j1} \wedge m^2_{ij}\right) = \bigvee_{j=1}^{n}\left(\bigvee_{k=1}^{n}\left(r_{k0} \wedge m^1_{kj}\right) \wedge m^2_{ij}\right) = \bigvee_{j=1}^{n}\left(m^1_{\gamma j} \wedge m^2_{ij}\right) = \bigvee_{j=1}^{n}\left(X_{\gamma j} \wedge X_{ji}\right) = \left(X^2\right)_{\gamma i}$$

Assume that $r_{it} = \left(X^{2t}\right)_{\gamma i}$. We compute $r_{i,t+1}$ as follows.

$$\begin{aligned} r_{i,t+1} &= \bigvee_{j=1}^{n}\left(c_{j,t+1} \wedge m^2_{ij}\right) = \bigvee_{j=1}^{n}\left(\bigvee_{k=1}^{n}\left(r_{kt} \wedge m^1_{kj}\right) \wedge m^2_{ij}\right) \\ &= \bigvee_{j=1}^{n}\left(\bigvee_{k=1}^{n}\left(\left(X^{2t}\right)_{\gamma k} \wedge X_{kj}\right) \wedge X_{ji}\right) \\ &= \bigvee_{j=1}^{n}\left(\left(X^{2t+1}\right)_{\gamma j} \wedge X_{ji}\right) = \left(X^{2t+2}\right)_{\gamma i} \end{aligned}$$

The proof of $c_{jt} = (X^{2t-1})_{\gamma j}$ is similar and therefore omitted. □

From Theorem 3.1, we arrive at the transitive closure of a graph $G$ using an in-memory computing architecture that can implement only repeated Boolean matrix multiplication. Repeating this procedure for each $\gamma \in \{1, \ldots, n\}$ yields the $n$ vectors of the transitive closure matrix $X^*$. We illustrate this with the simple example below, where the matrices $X^{(1)}, \ldots, X^{(4)}$ are reachability matrices. Clearly, the transitive closure matrix is $X^* = X^{(4)}$. A visualization of how $X^*$ is computed in a $5 \times 5$ crosspoint memory can be seen in Fig. 2.

$$X^{(1)} = \begin{pmatrix} 1 & 1 & 0 & 0 & 0 \\ 0 & 1 & 1 & 0 & 0 \\ 0 & 0 & 1 & 1 & 0 \\ 0 & 0 & 0 & 1 & 1 \\ 0 & 0 & 0 & 0 & 1 \end{pmatrix}, \quad X^{(2)} = \begin{pmatrix} 1 & 1 & 1 & 0 & 0 \\ 0 & 1 & 1 & 1 & 0 \\ 0 & 0 & 1 & 1 & 1 \\ 0 & 0 & 0 & 1 & 1 \\ 0 & 0 & 0 & 0 & 1 \end{pmatrix}$$

$$X^{(3)} = \begin{pmatrix} 1 & 1 & 1 & 1 & 0 \\ 0 & 1 & 1 & 1 & 1 \\ 0 & 0 & 1 & 1 & 1 \\ 0 & 0 & 0 & 1 & 1 \\ 0 & 0 & 0 & 0 & 1 \end{pmatrix}, \quad X^{(4)} = \begin{pmatrix} 1 & 1 & 1 & 1 & 1 \\ 0 & 1 & 1 & 1 & 1 \\ 0 & 0 & 1 & 1 & 1 \\ 0 & 0 & 0 & 1 & 1 \\ 0 & 0 & 0 & 0 & 1 \end{pmatrix}$$

It follows from Theorem 3.1 that, given a 3D crosspoint memory $\mathbb{C} = (M^1, M^2, R, C)$, $(r_1, \ldots, r_n)$ and $(c_1, \ldots, c_n)$ will converge on $(X^*_{\gamma 1}, \ldots, X^*_{\gamma n})$ when the wire vector $(r_{10}, \ldots, r_{n0})$ is configured according to $(I_{\gamma 1}, \ldots, I_{\gamma n})$. This convergence holds independently of timing errors, as is evidenced by equation (5), which is an expansion of (4). This provides a definition for $r_{it}$ that is independent of time.

$$\begin{aligned} r_{it} &= \bigvee_{j_1=1}^{n}\left(\bigvee_{i_1=1}^{n} \cdots \left(\bigvee_{j_t=1}^{n}\left(\bigvee_{i_t=1}^{n}\left(r_{i_t,0} \wedge m^1_{i_t j_t}\right) \cdots\right)\right)\right) \\ &= \bigvee_{j_1=1}^{n}\bigvee_{i_1=1}^{n} \cdots \bigvee_{j_t=1}^{n}\left(m^1_{\gamma j_t} \wedge \cdots \wedge m^1_{i_1 j_1} \wedge m^2_{i j_1}\right) \end{aligned} \tag{5}$$

Note from (5) that $r_{it}$ holds if and only if there is some sequence of interconnects in the LRS state. This assertion is independent of differing delays in wires or interconnects. That is, wire $r_i$ will eventually have a high voltage with respect to ground as long as the right sequence of interconnects is in the LRS state. It follows that delays arising from process variations or external factors can be accounted for by increasing the time interval before reading the outputs of the system. Thus, no additional complexity or circuitry need be introduced in order to deal with such timing errors.

## 4 COMPLEXITY

Given a graph $G = (V, E)$ with $|V| = n$ and a crossbar $\mathbb{C} = (M^1, M^2, R, C)$, the mapping proposed in Theorem 3.1 uses $O(n^2)$ devices. Since the maximum length of a path is $n - 1$, we need only compute $(I \vee E)^{n-1}$. It follows from Theorem 3.1 that, if $M^1 = (I \vee E)$ and $M^2 = (I \vee E)^T$, then $c_{j,n/2} = (I \vee E)^{2(n/2)-1}_{\gamma j} = (I \vee E)^{n-1}_{\gamma j}$. In the case of transitive closure, this computation must be done for every $\gamma \in \{1, \ldots, n\}$. Thus we have a time complexity of $O(n^2)$ for the transitive closure problem. The complexity becomes $O(n \cdot \text{diam}(G))$ if the diameter of the graph is known. The single-source variant of this problem can be solved in $O(n)$ operations since we only need to compute values for exactly one $\gamma \in \{1, \ldots, n\}$ corresponding to the source vertex. As a point of comparison, the in-memory approach in [17] achieves the same runtimes of $O(n)$ and $O(n^2)$

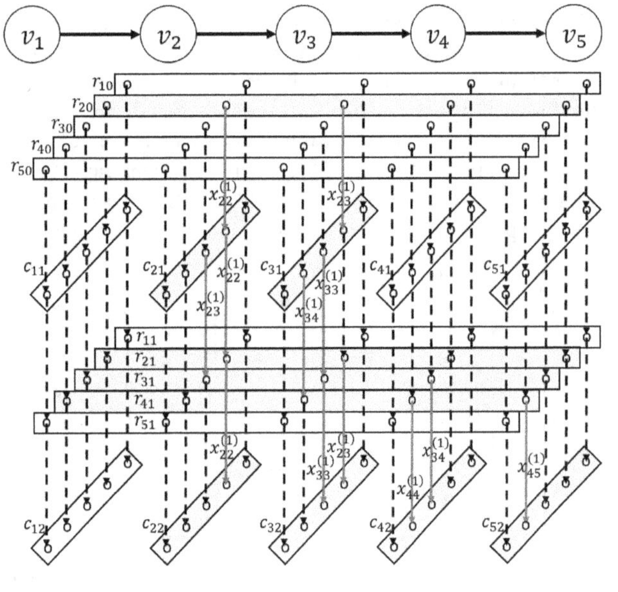


**Figure 2: Procedure for computing the transitive closure $X^*$ of directed graph $G = ((v_1, v_2, v_3, v_4, v_5), E)$ *(Top)*. The two-layer crosspoint memory with feedback loop $\mathbb{C} = (M^1, M^2, (r_1, r_2, r_3, r_4, r_5), (c_1, c_2, c_3, c_4, c_5))$ *(Bottom)* is unrolled in order to help visualize the computation. Dashed lines represent interconnections between row and column wires, yellow bars denote a wire with a truth value of 1, and solid red lines correspond to interconnects redirecting the flow of current from one wire to another. In this case, we are computing the second row vector $(X^*_{21}, \ldots, X^*_{25})$ of $X^*$ by setting $(r_{10}, r_{20}, r_{30}, r_{40}, r_{50}) = (0, 1, 0, 0, 0)$. Note that $(c_{12}, c_{22}, c_{32}, c_{42}, c_{52}) = (X^*_{21}, X^*_{22}, X^*_{23}, X^*_{24}, X^*_{25})$.**

for single-source reachability and transitive closure, but requires $O(n^3)$ components as opposed to the $O(n^2)$ memory cells used by our method.

It is worth noting that the runtime complexity of our approach, and of the transitive closure operation in general, can be reduced significantly if the underlying graph structure is exploited. Take, for example, the scale-free graphs created by the popular procedure wherein a node is connected to an existing node with a probability that is proportional to the node degree. Simulations [18] and heuristic studies [19] have demonstrated that the diameter of such graphs is approximately $\log n$, where $n$ is the number of nodes. This result also holds for small-world networks [20]. A simple modification to the graph construction model in [21] can significantly change the diameter of the resulting graphs. Indeed, it has been shown that, when a node is randomly connected to two or more existing nodes using degree-proportional probability, the resulting graph has a diameter of asymptotically $\frac{\log n}{\log \log n}$ [22]. For the two cases mentioned, our approach has an expected runtime of $O(n \log n)$ and $O(\frac{n \log n}{\log \log n})$, respectively, using $O(n^2)$ components.

## 5 CONCLUSIONS

We have presented a new in-memory computing design for obtaining the transitive closure of a graph using a 3D crosspoint memory with two layers of interconnects. Our proposed design only requires the addition of external feedback loops to already existing 3D memories.

## ACKNOWLEDGEMENT

The authors would like to thank the US Air Force for support provided through the AFOSR Young Investigator Award to Sumit Jha and the National Science Foundation for support provided to Alvaro Velasquez through the NSF Graduate Research Fellowship. This material is based upon work supported by the Air Force Office of Scientific Research under award number FA9550-16-1-0255.

## REFERENCES


[1] Andreas Nowatzyk, Fong Pong, and Ashley Saulsbury. Missing the memory wall: The case for processor/memory integration. In *Computer Architecture, 1996 23rd Annual International Symposium on*, pages 90–90. IEEE, 1996.

[2] Bill Dally. Challenges for future computing systems. https://www.hipeac.net/events/activities/7151/challenges-for-future-computing-systems/, January 19 2015. HiPEAC 2015 Keynote speech.

[3] Sven Skyum and Leslie G Valiant. A complexity theory based on boolean algebra. *Journal of the ACM (JACM)*, 32(2):484–502, 1985.

[4] Juan L Reutter, Miguel Romero, and Moshe Y Vardi. Regular queries on graph databases. In *18th International Conference on Database Theory (ICDT 2015)*, volume 31, pages 177–194. Schloss Dagstuhl-Leibniz-Zentrum fuer Informatik, 2015.

[5] Leslie G Valiant. General context-free recognition in less than cubic time. *Journal of computer and system sciences*, 10(2):308–315, 1975.

[6] Dick Grune, Kees Van Reeuwijk, Henri E Bal, Ceriel JH Jacobs, and Koen Langendoen. *Modern compiler design*. Springer Science & Business Media, 2012.

[7] Ahmed Bouajjani, Bengt Jonsson, Marcus Nilsson, and Tayssir Touili. Regular model checking. In *Computer Aided Verification*, pages 403–418. Springer, 2000.

[8] Intel PR. Intel and micron produce breakthrough memory technology. `http://newsroom.intel.com/community/intel_newsroom/blog/2015/07/28/intel-and-micron-produce-breakthrough-memory-technology`. Accessed: 28 July, 2015.

[9] Katherine Bourzac. Has intel created a universal memory technology?[news]. *IEEE Spectrum*, 54(5):9–10, 2017.

[10] Frank T Hady, Annie Foong, Bryan Veal, and Dan Williams. Platform storage performance with 3d xpoint technology. *Proceedings of the IEEE*, 2017.

[11] P Kuekes. Material implication: digital logic with memristors. In *Memristor and memristive systems symposium*, volume 21, 2008.

[12] Alvaro Velasquez and Sumit Kumar Jha. Automated synthesis of crossbars for nanoscale computing using formal methods. In *Nanoscale Architectures (NANOARCH), 2015 IEEE/ACM International Symposium on*, pages 130–136. IEEE, 2015.

[13] Alvaro Velasquez and Sumit Kumar Jha. Fault-tolerant in-memory crossbar computing using quantified constraint solving. In *Computer Design (ICCD), 2015 33rd IEEE International Conference on*, pages 101–108. IEEE, 2015.

[14] R Williams. How we found the missing memristor. *Spectrum, IEEE*, 45(12):28–35, 2008.

[15] H-S Philip Wong, Simone Raoux, SangBum Kim, Jiale Liang, John P Reifenberg, Bipin Rajendran, Mehdi Asheghi, and Kenneth E Goodson. Phase change memory. *Proceedings of the IEEE*, 98(12):2201–2227, 2010.

[16] Alvaro Velasquez and Sumit Kumar Jha. Parallel boolean matrix multiplication in linear time using rectifying memristors. In *Circuits and Systems (ISCAS), 2016 IEEE International Symposium on*, pages 1874–1877. IEEE, 2016.

[17] Alvaro Velasquez and Sumit Kumar Jha. Computation of boolean matrix chain products in 3d reram. In *Circuits and Systems (ISCAS), 2017 IEEE International Symposium on*, pages 1–4. IEEE, 2017.

[18] Réka Albert, Hawoong Jeong, and Albert-László Barabási. Internet: Diameter of the world-wide web. *nature*, 401(6749):130, 1999.

[19] Mark EJ Newman, Steven H Strogatz, and Duncan J Watts. Random graphs with arbitrary degree distributions and their applications. *Physical review E*, 64(2):026118, 2001.

[20] Luıs A Nunes Amaral, Antonio Scala, Marc Barthelemy, and H Eugene Stanley. Classes of small-world networks. *Proceedings of the national academy of sciences*, 97(21):11149–11152, 2000.

[21] Albert-László Barabási and Réka Albert. Emergence of scaling in random networks. *science*, 286(5439):509–512, 1999.

[22] Béla Bollobás and Oliver Riordan. The diameter of a scale-free random graph. *Combinatorica*, 24(1):5–34, 2004.

# BQ: A Lock-Free Queue with Batching*

Gal Milman
Technion, Israel
galy@cs.technion.ac.il

Alex Kogan
Oracle Labs, USA
alex.kogan@oracle.com

Yossi Lev
Oracle Labs, USA
levyossi@icloud.com

Victor Luchangco
Oracle Labs, USA
vluchangco@gmail.com

Erez Petrank
Technion, Israel
erez@cs.technion.ac.il

## ABSTRACT

Concurrent data structures provide fundamental building blocks for concurrent programming. Standard concurrent data structures may be extended by allowing a sequence of operations to be submitted as a batch for later execution. A sequence of such operations can then be executed more efficiently than the standard execution of one operation at a time. In this paper we develop a novel algorithmic extension to the prevalent FIFO queue data structure that exploits such batching scenarios. An implementation in C++ on a multicore demonstrates a significant performance improvement of up to 16x (depending on batch lengths), compared to previous queue implementations.

## KEYWORDS

Concurrent Algorithms; Concurrent Data Structures; Lock-Freedom; Linearizability; FIFO Queue

**ACM Reference Format:**
Gal Milman, Alex Kogan, Yossi Lev, Victor Luchangco, and Erez Petrank. 2018. BQ: A Lock-Free Queue with Batching. In *SPAA '18: 30th ACM Symposium on Parallelism in Algorithms and Architectures, July 16–18, 2018, Vienna, Austria.* ACM, New York, NY, USA, 11 pages. https://doi.org/10.1145/3210377.3210388

## 1 INTRODUCTION

The era of multi-core architectures has been having a huge impact on software development: exploiting concurrency has become the main challenge of today's programming. Concurrent data structures provide the basic blocks for concurrent programming; hence it is crucial that they are efficient and scalable. In this paper we consider a setting in which threads sometimes execute a *sequence* of operations on a shared concurrent data structure (rather than a single operation each time). This scenario occurs either because the threads are willing to delay execution of operations in order to improve performance, or because they deliberately want operations to be executed later.

*This work was supported by the Israel Science Foundation grant No. 274/14


*SPAA '18, July 16–18, 2018, Vienna, Austria*

ACM ISBN 978-1-4503-5799-9/18/07...$15.00
https://doi.org/10.1145/3210377.3210388

As an example, consider a server thread that serves requests of remote clients. Such a thread may accumulate several relevant operations required by some client, generate a sequence of these operations, submit them for execution on shared data, finish handling them, and then proceed to handle other clients whose operations can be accumulated similarly.

Kogan and Herlihy [17] formulated batching of operations in a concurrent setting using the *future* programming construct. *Batching* means grouping a sequence of standard operations to a single *batch operation*, which applies them together to the shared object. They formalized correctness (linearization) guarantees and demonstrated the advantages of batching even when using naive batching strategies.

In this paper we present a novel extension to the concurrent lock-free queue by Michael and Scott [22] (henceforth MSQ) that can handle a sequence of operations in a batch. Our queue extension, denoted BQ (which stands for Batching Queue), provides faster execution for operation sequences. Kogan and Herlihy suggested to apply each sequence of operations of the same type to the shared queue at once. Specifically, they execute each subsequence of enqueues-only together by appending adequate nodes at the end of the queue, and each subsequence of dequeues-only by unlinking several nodes from the head of the queue. The advantage of this method degrades when operations in the batch switch frequently between enqueues and dequeues, which is the case with general sequences. We present an algorithm that handles any batch of enqueues and dequeues locally and applies it at once to the shared queue to reduce contention. Using novel observations on the effect of a mixed sequence on the shared queue, we achieve a fast application of the sequence on the shared queue with low synchronization.

Concurrent queues are typically not scalable because they have two points of contention: the head and the tail. However, batching of operations provides an excellent opportunity to combine operations locally and improve scalability. Such local computation reduces the number of accesses to the shared structure, which yields an overall reduced contention. As shown in the measurements, BQ improves the performance and scalability over MSQ and over the simpler batching method of Kogan and Herlihy.

We also extend Kogan and Herlihy's formal treatment of systems that only execute batch operations, to allow simultaneous execution of standard (single) operations, while still satisfying an extended form of linearizability that we present.

BQ is lock-free. It uses only compare-and-swap (CAS) atomic operations (which can easily be replaced with *LL*/*SC* instructions) and can thus be ported to other existing platforms. The original

MSQ we build upon is widely known as a well-performing queue for general hardware and is included as part of the Java$^{TM}$ Concurrency Package [20]. Measurements for BQ demonstrate a significant performance improvement of up to 16x compared to MSQ when threads employ batch operations to update the queue.

Batching provides a performance improvement for operations that the user agrees to delay. Additionally, BQ guarantees that deferred operations of a certain thread will not take effect until that thread performs a non-deferred operation or explicitly requests an evaluation of previous future operations. This is useful when the user wishes to call several operations and knowingly delay their execution to a chosen time.

The rest of the paper is organized as follows: Section 2 introduces the model we work with and surveys the work we build on. In Section 3 we define linearizability and its extensions to objects with batch operations. Having set the terminology, we discuss related work in Section 4. Section 5 presents an overview of the BQ algorithm, whose implementation details are described in Section 6. The algorithm's correctness is laid out briefly in Section 7. Section 8 describes measurement results. Further results, lock-freedom arguments, supplementary implementation details and the memory management mechanism are deferred to [23] (the full version of this paper).

## 2 PRELIMINARIES

*Model.* We consider a standard shared memory setting, with a set of threads accessing the shared memory using the atomic primitives `Read`, `Write` and `CAS`. A `CAS` primitive is defined by a triplet consisting of a target memory address, an expected value, and a new value. A `CAS` operation compares the value stored in the target address to the expected value. If they are equal, the value in the target address is replaced with the new value, and the Boolean value true is returned. In such a case we say that the `CAS` is successful. Otherwise, the shared memory remains unchanged, and false is returned.

*Future.* A *future* is an object returned by an operation whose execution might be delayed. The user may call an *Evaluate* method to ensure the operation's execution and get its result.

*MS-Queue.* BQ extends MSQ to support future operations. MSQ is a lock-free algorithm for a FIFO queue, which supports *Enqueue* and *Dequeue* operations. It implements the queue as a singly-linked list with *head* and *tail* pointers. *head* points to the first node of the list, which functions as a dummy node. The following nodes, starting with the node pointed to by the dummy node's *next* pointer and ending with the node whose *next* pointer's value is `NULL`, contain the queue's items. The queue is initialized as a list containing a single (dummy) node, to which both *head* and *tail* point. This setup represents an empty queue.

Dequeuing is implemented as follows: If *head->next* is `NULL`, the queue is empty, and hence the dequeue operation returns without extracting an item from the queue. Otherwise, an attempt is made to update *head* to point to its successive node in the list, using `CAS`. On the occasion that the `CAS` fails, the dequeue operation starts over.

Enqueuing requires two `CAS` operations. Initially, a node with the item to enqueue is created. Then, an attempt to set *tail->next* to the address of the new node is made using a first `CAS`. The `CAS` fails if the current value of *tail->next* is not `NULL`. In such a case, *tail* is promoted to the current value of *tail->next* using an assisting `CAS`, in order to help an obstructing enqueue operation complete. Then, a new attempt to perform the first `CAS` starts. After the first `CAS` succeeds, a second `CAS` is applied to update *tail* to point to the new node. There is no need to retry this `CAS`, since it fails only if another thread has already performed the required update, trying to help our operation complete in order to next apply its own operation.

*Lock-Freedom.* A concurrent object implementation is *lock-free* [12] if each time a thread executes an operation on the object, some thread (not necessarily the same one) completes an operation on the object within a finite number of steps. Thus, lock-freedom guarantees system-wide progress. Our implementation is lock-free.

## 3 LINEARIZABILITY AND FUTURES

We describe the original linearizability [14], defined for a setting of no future operations, and generalize it for a setting with future operations. Some basic terms are required first: A *method call* is described by two events – its *invocation*, which refers to the call to the method, and its *response*, which refers to the return from the method. Each object has a *sequential specification*, which describes its behavior in sequential executions, where method calls do not overlap.

### 3.1 Linearizability

An execution is considered *linearizable* [14] if each method call appears to take effect at once, between its invocation and its response events, in a way that satisfies the sequential specification of the objects.

### 3.2 Medium Futures Linearizability (MF-Linearizability)

Medium futures linearizability is defined by Kogan and Herlihy [17] as an extension of linearizability to futures, which we adopt and extend. For each future operation, we look at two associated method calls: the future one, which creates a future and returns it, and *Evaluate*, which is called with the future returned by the first method call and ensures the operation's execution. MF-linearizability requires the following:

1. Each operation takes effect at some instant between the invocation of its first related method (which produces the future) and the response of its second related method (which evaluates the future).
2. Two operations issued by the same thread to the same object take effect in the order of their first method calls (i.e. their future method calls).

### 3.3 Extended Medium Futures Linearizability (EMF-Linearizability)

We extend the MF-linearizability definition to cover a data structure which supplies standard (single) operations in addition to future-returning operations (the original paper did not refer to single operations). We do so by reduction to MF-linearizability: informally, we transform an execution that possibly contains single calls into one that contains only future-returning operations, by replacing each single operation call with an adequate future call followed by an *Evaluate* call.

Next, we define *extended medium futures linearizability* (*EMF-linearizability*) formally.

*Definition 3.1.* Let $H$ be a history, consisting of operation invocation and response events. We construct a new history $H_f$, denoted the *future history*, as follows. The invocations and responses of all future dequeue, future enqueue and *Evaluate* calls are copied to $H_f$ unchanged. Each dequeue call $op$ in $H$ is rewritten in $H_f$: its invocation is replaced with an invocation and an immediate response of a future dequeue call, and its response is replaced with an invocation and an immediate response of an *Evaluate* call that evaluates this future dequeue. Enqueue calls are rewritten similarly.

*Definition 3.2.* A history $H$ is *EMF-linearizable* if its future history $H_f$ is MF-linearizable.

### 3.4 Atomic Execution

We define *atomic execution*, a property of an object with future methods regarding its linearization. We then describe its implication for EMF-linearizable objects and its benefit. We begin with an auxiliary term regarding future operations on shared objects:

*Definition 3.3.* A *pending operation* is a future operation that has not yet been applied to the shared object.

*Definition 3.4.* Let $ob$ be an object with future methods and $t$ be a thread. $ob$ satisfies *atomic execution* if:

(1) Pending operations of $t$ on $ob$ are applied only during the following calls on $ob$ by $t$: either a single operation call, or an *Evaluate* call for one of $t$'s pending operations.
(2) Let $op$ be a call in $t$ during which some pending operations of $t$, denoted $op_1, ..., op_n$, are applied. Then $op_1, ..., op_n$ must be linearized successively in their original invocation order, without any other operation on $ob$ linearized between them. Moreover, if $op$ is a single operation (i.e., not an *Evaluate* or a future operation), then $op_1, ..., op_n$ and also $op$ must be linearized successively in their original invocation order, without any other operation on $ob$ linearized between them.

If $ob$ is EMF-linearizable, then when a single method $op$ is called by a thread $t$, all pending operations of $t$ must take effect prior to $op$ to satisfy EMF-linearizability. Atomic execution dictates that they are executed at once together with $op$.

Similarly, when $t$ calls the *Evaluate* method for some pending operation $op$, all $t$'s pending operations preceding $op$ must take effect prior to $op$ to satisfy EMF-linearizability. Additional pending operations by $t$ may be applied as well. Atomic execution dictates that all these operations are executed at once.

An example of a potential benefit of atomic execution is that it can achieve locality for a producers-consumers system, where consumer servers handle requests of remote producer clients. In such scenario, the clients enqueue their requests, possibly several at a time, to a shared queue. Each server consumes requests regularly by performing a batch operation consisting of a certain number of dequeues. Both clients and servers perform batch operations by calling several future operations, followed by an *Evaluate* operation of the last future operation.

Serving requests of the same client consecutively may allow for more efficient processing due to locality of the client's data. A queue that supports batching and satisfies atomic execution would enable the servers to exploit locality and successively serve several requests by the same client, which he applied in the same batch-of-enqueues operation. This is thanks to the atomic execution's guarantee that both a batch-of-enqueues operation by a client and a batch-of-dequeues operation by a server take effect instantaneously.

## 4 RELATED WORK

Various papers introduce lock-free linearizable FIFO queues, which use different strategies to outperform MSQ.

Tsigas et al. [27] present a queue that allows the head and tail to lag at most $m$ nodes behind the actual head and tail of the queue, so that the amortized number of CAS executions per operation is $1 + 1/m$. Their algorithm is limited to bounded queues due to their static allocation. Additional cyclic array queues are described in [3, 6, 26]. Moir et al. [24] present a queue that uses elimination as a back-off strategy to increase scalability: pairs of concurrent enqueue and dequeue method calls may exchange values without accessing the shared queue. However, in order to keep the FIFO queue semantics, the enqueue method can be eliminated only after all items of preceding enqueue operations have been dequeued, which makes the algorithm practical only for nearly empty or highly overloaded queues. Hoffman et al. [15] present the baskets queue, which increases scalability by allowing concurrent enqueue operations to insert nodes at adjacent positions at the end of the linked list, regarded as baskets. Such insertion, however, is done only after a failed initial attempt to append the node to the tail. Thus, the contention on the tail is only partially diminished, and there is also contention on the baskets.

Ladan-Mozes et al. [19] present an optimistic queue, which replaces one of the two CAS operations performed during an enqueue operation with simple stores. Like the original MSQ, this algorithm does not scale, due to synchronization on the head and tail variables that allows only one enqueue operation and one dequeue operation to be applied concurrently. Gidenstam et al. [7] present a cache-aware queue that stores the items in fixed-size blocks, connected in a linked list. This allows for a lazy update of the head and tail, only once per block. Nevertheless, at least one CAS per operation is still required, making the queue non-scalable under high contention. Morrison et al. [25] present a queue based on a linked list of ring queue nodes. To reduce contention, it relies on the fetch-and-add primitive to spread threads among items in the queue and let them operate in parallel. Yang et al. [28] utilize fetch-and-add as well, to form a wait-free queue. Queues that improve scalability by relaxing the sequential specification of the queue appear in [1, 10, 16]. For example, Basin et al. [1] suggest to trade fairness for lower contention by relaxing the FIFO semantics of the queue. The extension of linearizability BQ adheres to could be viewed as a relaxation, but a stricter one, as it forces FIFO semantics and preserves process order.

Previous works [e.g., 4, 5, 8, 9, 11, 13, 18] present concurrent constructs that combine multiple operations into a single operation on the shared object. We chose to combine operations and apply them as batches, in order to increase scalability. The paper of Kogan and Herlihy [17] is the closest to this work. They propose alternative definitions for linearizability of executions with batches, including MF-linearizability, which we use. They describe very simple implementations of stacks, queues and linked lists that demonstrate the benefits of using futures. In this work we propose a novel implementation of the queue that obtains better scalability and performance. Moreover, BQ satisfies atomic execution, while Kogan and Herlihy's simple queue does not.

# 5 ALGORITHM OVERVIEW

We present BQ, an extension to MSQ, which supports deferred operations and satisfies EMF-linearizability. Unlike standard operations, deferred operations need not be applied to the shared queue before their responses occur. When a future method is called, its details are recorded locally together with previous deferred operations that were called by the same thread. A *Future* object is returned to the caller, who may evaluate it later.

Deferred operations allow to apply pending operations in batches: BQ delays their execution until the user explicitly evaluates a future of one of them or calls a standard method. When that happens, all pending operations of the same thread are gathered to a single batch operation. This operation is then applied to the shared queue. Afterwards, the batch execution is finalized by locally filling the futures' return values. This mechanism reduces synchronization overhead by allowing fewer accesses to the shared queue, as well as less processing in the shared queue – thanks to the preparations performed locally by the initiating thread during the run of each future operation, and the local pairing of applied futures with results following the batch execution.

## 5.1 Batch Execution

Whenever a deferred enqueue operation is called, the executing thread appends its item to a local list. This way, when the thread has to perform a batch operation, the list of nodes to be linked to the shared queue's list is already prepared.

The key to applying all operations of a batch at once to the shared queue, is to set up a moment in which the state of the queue is "frozen". Namely, we establish a moment in which we hold both ends of the queue, so that we know its head and tail, and its size right before the batch takes effect. This way we can unambiguously determine the queue's shape after applying the batch, including its new head and tail. We achieve a hold of the queue's ends by executing a batch operation in stages, according to the following scheme.

The thread first creates an announcement describing the required batch operation. An announcement is an auxiliary object used to announce an ongoing batch operation, so that other threads will not interfere with it but rather help it complete. Then, the thread modifies the shared queue's head to point to the created announcement. This marks the head so that further attempted dequeues will help the batch execution to be completed before executing their own operations. Now we hold one end of the queue.

Next, the initiating thread or an assisting thread links the list of items, which the initiating thread has prepared in advance, after the shared queue's tail. This determines the tail location after which the batch's items are enqueued. Thus, now we hold both ends of the queue, as required. We then update the shared queue's tail to point to the last linked node.

As a last step that would uninstall the announcement and finish the batch execution, we update the shared queue's head. It is possible that during the execution of the required enqueues and dequeues the queue becomes empty and that some of the dequeues operate on an empty queue and return `NULL`. We make a combinatorial observation that helps quickly determine the number of non-successful dequeues. This number is used to determine the node to which the queue's head points following the batch execution. By applying this fast calculation, we execute the batch with minimal interference with the shared queue, thus reducing contention. This computation is described in Section 5.2 below.

The entire algorithm, including the process of setting futures' results, is discussed in detail in Subsection 6.2.

## 5.2 A Key Combinatorial Property of Batches on Queues

Let us state combinatorial observations that help us execute the local batch quickly on the queue. The enqueued items in the batch are kept as a linked-list so that they can be attached at the end of the list in a single `CAS`. This list is added to the tail of the queue and then $\#successfulDequeues$ dequeues are executed by pushing the head $\#successfulDequeues$ nodes further in the shared linked-list representing the queue, and then dequeued items are privately matched with the batch dequeue operations. In the simplest scenario, $\#successfulDequeues$ equals the number of future dequeues in the batch. The problem is that some dequeues may operate on an empty queue and thus, must return a `NULL` value. The following discussion explains how the adequate $\#successfulDequeues$ can be computed.

*Definition 5.1.* We call a future dequeue *a failing dequeue* with respect to a given state of the shared queue, if the application of the batch that contains it (as well as the other local pending operations) on this shared queue makes this dequeue operate on an empty shared queue. A future dequeue that is not failing is called a *successful dequeue*.

Note that a failing dequeue does not modify the queue, and its future's result is `NULL`.

We start by analyzing the execution of a batch on an empty queue (which can be analyzed independently of the current shape of the shared queue) and then we show that this analysis can be extended to a general shared queue, simply by plugging the shared queue size.

*Definition 5.2.* An *excess dequeue* is a future dequeue operation that is a failing dequeue with respect to an empty queue.

For example, if the sequence of pending operations in some thread is EDDEEDDDEDDEE, where E and D represent enqueue and dequeue operations respectively, then the thread has three excess dequeues (the second, fifth and seventh).

An excess dequeue is a special case of a failing dequeue. We start by computing how many excess dequeues there are in a batch.

Lemma 5.3. *Let B be a batch of queue operations. The number of excess dequeues in this batch equals the maximum over all prefixes of this batch, of the number of dequeues in the prefix minus the number of enqueues in this prefix.*

Proof. First, we note that if, for some prefix $p$ of the batch operations, the number of dequeues minus the number of enqueues is $k$, then the overall number of excess dequeues must be at least $k$. This is simply because when executing the prefix $p$ on the empty queue, the number of items that enter the queue is at most *#enqueues*, the number of enqueues in the prefix. On the other hand, *#dequeues*, the number of dequeues that are executed in this prefix, is larger by $k$. So at least $k$ dequeues must operate on an empty queue (returning NULL).

On the other hand, we show by induction on the number of excess dequeues that in the prefix that ends in the $\ell^{th}$ excess dequeue, $\#dequeues - \#enqueues \geq \ell$. We inspect the execution of the prefix on an empty queue. The base of the induction follows from the fact that the first excess dequeue must happen when the number of dequeues so far exceeds the number of enqueues. (Otherwise, there is an item to dequeue.) For the induction step we look at the prefix of the batch that ends in the $\ell - 1^{st}$ excess dequeue. By the induction hypothesis, for that prefix $\#dequeues - \#enqueues \geq \ell - 1$. Also, the queue must be empty after (any excess dequeue and in particular after) the $\ell - 1^{st}$ excess dequeue. So the subsequence of operations between the $\ell - 1^{st}$ excess dequeue and the $\ell^{th}$ excess dequeue operates on an empty queue and has an excess dequeue at the end, which means that for this subsequence $\#dequeues - \#enqueues \geq 1$ (like in the base case of the induction), and we are done. □

Now we proceed to discuss a batch applied to a queue of any size.

Claim 5.4. *Let n be the size of the queue right before a given batch is operated on it. The number of failing dequeues in the batch with respect to a queue of size n equals to the maximum value of* $(\#dequeues - \#enqueues - n)$ *over all prefixes of the batch's operation sequence, or* 0 *if this maximum is negative.*

The claim can be proven by adjusting the proof of Lemma 5.3 to failing dequeues instead of excess dequeues, and to a queue of general size $n$ rather than 0. Note that the first $n$ excess dequeues are not failing dequeues because they can dequeue the $n$ items in the original queue. Any additional excess dequeues will become failing dequeues.

Claim 5.4 and Lemma 5.3 yield the following corollary:

Corollary 5.5. *Let n be the size of the queue right before a given batch is operated on it. The number of failing dequeues in the batch equals to* $\max\{\#excessDequeues - n, 0\}$.

It immediately follows that the number of successful dequeues in a batch with respect to a queue of size $n$ equals:
$\#successfulDequeues = \#dequeues - \max\{\#excessDequeues - n, 0\}$

*5.2.1 Using The Combinatorial Property in BQ.* In order to optimize the calculation of the new head after a batch is applied, each thread maintains three local counters: the quantities of *FutureEnqueue* and *FutureDequeue* operations that have been called but not yet executed on the shared queue, and the number of excess dequeues. The thread updates these counters on each of its future operation calls. When a thread executes a batch operation, it includes its local counters in the batch's announcement, to allow any helping thread to complete the batch execution.

In addition, we let the shared queue's head and tail contain not only a pointer, but also a successful dequeue and enqueue counters respectively. When applying a batch, they are updated using the announcement's counts. The difference between the queue's enqueue and dequeue counts prior to a batch execution yields the queue's size $n$ in its "frozen" state right before linking the batch's items.

These counters in the batch's announcement and in the head and tail are used to quickly calculate the number of successful dequeues according to Corollary 5.5. This number helps discovering the new head – by iterating over *#successfulDequeues* nodes, and avoids a heavier simulation of the batch enqueues and dequeues one by one to discover the shape of the resulting shared queue.

Indeed, to determine the result of each future dequeue in the batch, the thread that initiated the batch operation will need to simulate these future operations according to their order. Nevertheless, it will conduct this simulation after the announcement is removed from the shared queue, without delaying other threads that access the shared queue.

## 6 ALGORITHM DETAILS

We now turn to the details of the algorithm. In Section 6.1 we elaborate on the principal underlying data structures, in Subsection 6.2 we describe the algorithm, and in Subsection 6.3 we refer to memory management.

### 6.1 Underlying Data Structures

Table 1 depicts the auxiliary data structures, out of which the *Future* structure is the only one exposed to the user of the *Queue* object, while all others are internal to the queue's implementation.

*6.1.1 Queue.* Similarly to MSQ, the shared queue is represented as a linked list of nodes in which the first node is a dummy node, and all nodes thereafter contain the values in the queue in the order they were enqueued. We maintain pointers to the first and last nodes of this list, denoted *SQHead* and *SQTail* respectively (which stand for *Shared Queue's Head and Tail*).

Batch operations require the size of the queue for a fast calculation of the new head after applying the batch's operations. To this end, *Queue* maintains counters of the number of enqueues and the number of successful dequeues applied so far. These are kept size-by-side with the tail and head pointers respectively, and are updated atomically with the respective pointers using a double-width CAS. This is implemented using a Pointer and Count object (*PtrCnt*, that can be atomically modified) for the head and tail of the shared queue.

Batch operations that enqueue at least one item install an announcement in the head. *SQHead* can either hold the aforesaid *PtrCnt* object with a pointer to the head of the queue, or a pointer to an *Ann* object, described next. Therefore, *SQHead* is a Pointer

**Table 1: Underlying Data Structures**

| | |
|---|---|
| **struct** Future | {result: Item*, isDone: **Boolean**} |
| **struct** Node | {item: Item*, next: Node*} |
| **struct** BatchRequest | {firstEnq: Node*,<br>lastEnq: Node*,<br>enqsNum: **unsigned int**,<br>deqsNum: **unsigned int**,<br>excessDeqsNum: **unsigned int**} |
| **struct** PtrCnt | {node: Node*,<br>cnt: **unsigned int**} |
| **struct** Ann | {batchReq: BatchRequest,<br>oldHead: PtrCnt,<br>oldTail: PtrCnt} |
| **union** PtrCntOrAnn | {ptrCnt: PtrCnt,<br>**struct** {tag: **unsigned int**,<br>ann: Ann*}} |
| **struct** FutureOp | {type: {ENQ, DEQ},<br>future: Future*} |
| **struct** ThreadData | {opsQueue: Queue of FutureOp,<br>enqsHead: Node*,<br>enqsTail: Node*,<br>enqsNum: **unsigned int**,<br>deqsNum: **unsigned int**,<br>excessDeqsNum: **unsigned int**} |

and Count or Announcement object (*PtrCntOrAnn*), which is a 16-byte union that may consist of either *PtrCnt* or an 8-byte tag and an 8-byte *Ann* pointer. Whenever it contains an *Ann*, the tag is set to 1. Otherwise, *SQHead* contains a *PtrCnt* (the tag overlaps *PtrCnt.node*, whose least significant bit is 0 since it stores either NULL or an aligned address).

For brevity, we will mostly avoid specific mention of the counter; however, when we refer to an update of the head's pointer, it means that the head's counter is updated as well, and likewise for the tail.

It is possible to avoid the double-width CAS in platforms that do not support such an operation. This can be accomplished by replacing the *PtrCnt* object with a pointer to a node, replacing the *PtrCntOrAnn* object with a pointer to either a node or an announcement (with a least significant bit mark indicating the type of the pointed object), and have the *Node* object contain a counter. We describe this variation of BQ in [23]. Measurements demonstrate that this variation does not incur a significant performance degradation.

*Thread-Local Data.* A *threadData* array holds local data for each thread. First, the pending operations details are kept, in the order they were called, in an operation queue *opsQueue*, implemented as a simple local non-thread-safe queue. It contains *FutureOp* items. Second, the items of the pending enqueue operations are kept in a linked list in the order they were enqueued by *FutureEnqueue* calls. This list is referenced by *enqsHead* and *enqsTail* (with no dummy nodes here). Lastly, each thread keeps record of the number of *FutureEnqueue* and *FutureDequeue* operations that have been called but not yet applied, and the number of excess dequeues.

Each thread can access its local data in *threadData* using its thread ID as an index. In the pseudo-code, *threadData[threadId]* is abbreviated to *threadData* for brevity.

*6.1.2 Future.* A *Future* contains a *result*, which holds the return value of the deferred operation that generated the future (for dequeues only, as enqueue operations have no return value) and an *isDone* Boolean value, which is true only if the deferred computation has been completed. When *isDone* is false, the contents of *result* may be arbitrary.

*6.1.3 BatchRequest.* *BatchRequest* is prepared by a thread that initiates a batch, and consists of the details of the batch's pending operations: *firstEnq* and *lastEnq* are pointers to the first and last nodes of a linked list containing the pending items to be enqueued; *enqsNum*, *deqsNum*, and *excessDeqsNum* are, respectively, the numbers of enqueues, dequeues and excess dequeues in the batch.

*6.1.4 Announcement.* An *Ann* object represents an announcement. It contains a *BatchRequest* instance, with all the details required to execute the batch operation it stands for. Thus, any operation that encounters an announcement may help the related batch operation complete before proceeding with its own operation.

In addition to information regarding the batch of operations to execute, *Ann* includes *oldHead*, the value of the head pointer (and dequeue counter) before the announcement was installed, and *oldTail*, an entry for the tail pointer (and enqueue counter) of the queue right before the batch is applied (i.e., a pointer to the node to which the batch's list of items is linked).

## 6.2 Algorithm Implementation

We detail the algorithm implementation, accompanied by pseudo-code. First we describe the core operations, performed on the shared queue. Then we outline the enclosing methods, which call the core methods and commit complementary local computations. Finally we refer to the special case of a dequeues-only batch operation.

*6.2.1 Internal Methods Operating on the Shared Queue.* The following methods are used internally to apply operations to the shared queue: *EnqueueToShared*, *DequeueFromShared* and *ExecuteBatch*. To help a concurrent batch execution and obtain the new head, they call the *HelpAnnAndGetHead* auxiliary method. To carry out a batch, the *ExecuteAnn* auxiliary method is called. Its caller may be either the batch's initiating thread, or a helping thread that encountered an announcement when trying to commit its own operation.

Let us elaborate on each of these methods.

*EnqueueToShared.* *EnqueueToShared* appends an item after the tail of the shared queue, using two CAS operations, in a similar manner to MSQ's *Enqueue*: it first updates *SQTail.node->next* to point to a node consisting of the new item, and then updates *SQTail* to point to this node. An obstructing operation might enqueue its items concurrently, causing the first CAS (in Line 5) to fail. In this case, *EnqueueToShared* would try to help complete the obstructing operation, before starting a new attempt to enqueue its own item. This assistance is performed in Lines 9-13. Herein lies the distinction between *EnqueueToShared* in BQ and *Enqueue* in MSQ: In MSQ, the first CAS might fail only due to an obstructing enqueue operation, and thus only the equivalent to Line 13 of BQ is executed. In BQ, on the other hand, the obstructing operation may be either a standard enqueue operation or a batch operation.

**Listing 1: EnqueueToShared**

```
EnqueueToShared(item)
   newNode = new Node(item, NULL)
   while (true)
      tailAndCnt = SQTail
      if (CAS(&tailAndCnt.node->next, NULL, newNode))
         // newNode is linked to the tail
         CAS(&SQTail, tailAndCnt, ⟨newNode, tailAndCnt.cnt
              + 1⟩)
         break
      head = SQHead
      if head consists of Ann: // (head.tag & 1 != 0)
         ExecuteAnn(head.ann)
      else
         CAS(&SQTail, tailAndCnt, ⟨tailAndCnt.node->next,
              tail.cnt + 1⟩)
```

*DequeueFromShared.* If the queue is not empty when the dequeue operation takes effect, *DequeueFromShared* extracts an item from the head of the shared queue and returns it; otherwise it returns NULL. The only addition to the MSQ's *Dequeue* is helping pending batch operations complete first by calling the *HelpAnnAndGetHead* method.

**Listing 2: DequeueFromShared**

```
Item* DequeueFromShared()
   while (true)
      headAndCnt = HelpAnnAndGetHead()
      headNextNode = headAndCnt.node->next
      if (headNextNode == NULL)
         return NULL
      if (CAS(&SQHead, headAndCnt, ⟨headNextNode,
            headAndCnt.cnt + 1⟩))
         return headNextNode->item
```

*HelpAnnAndGetHead.* This auxiliary method assists announcements in execution, as long as there is an announcement installed in *SQHead*.

**Listing 3: HelpAnnAndGetHead**

```
PtrCnt HelpAnnAndGetHead()
   while (true)
      head = SQHead
      if head consists of PtrCnt: // (head.tag & 1 == 0)
         return head.ptrCnt
      ExecuteAnn(head.ann)
```

*ExecuteBatch. ExecuteBatch* is responsible for executing the batch. Before it starts doing so, it checks whether there is a colliding ongoing batch operation whose announcement is installed in *SQHead*. If so, *ExecuteBatch* helps it complete (Line 31). Afterwards, it stores the current head in *ann* (Line 32), installs *ann* in *SQHead* (Line 33) and calls *ExecuteAnn* to carry out the batch. The batch execution's steps are illustrated in Figure 1.

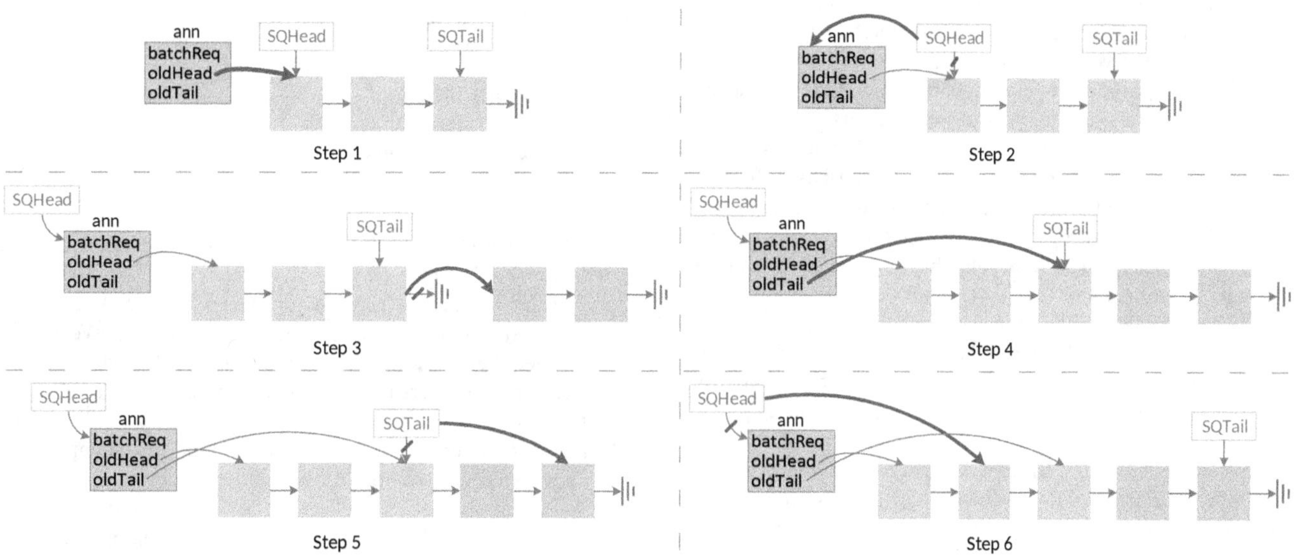


**Figure 1: Steps of the Batch Execution**

(1) Setting *ann->oldHead* to the head of the queue right before committing the batch.
(2) Installing *ann* in *SQHead*.
(3) Linking the batch's items to *SQTail.node->next*.
(4) Setting *oldTail* field in the installed announcement *ann*.
(5) Promoting *SQTail* to point to the last node enqueued by the batch operation (and increasing its enqueue count by the number of enqueues).
(6) Setting *SQHead* to point to the last node dequeued by the batch operation in place of *ann* (and increasing its dequeue count by the number of successful dequeues).

**Listing 4: ExecuteBatch**

```
28 Node* ExecuteBatch(batchRequest)
29     ann = new Ann(batchRequest)
30     while (true)
31         oldHeadAndCnt = HelpAnnAndGetHead()
32         ann->oldHead = oldHeadAndCnt // Step 1 in Figure 1
33         if (CAS(&SQHead, oldHeadAndCnt, ann)) // Step 2 in
               Figure 1
34             break
35     ExecuteAnn(ann)
36     return oldHeadAndCnt.node
```

*ExecuteAnn.* *ExecuteAnn* is called with *ann* after *ann* has been installed in *SQHead*. *ann*'s *oldHead* field consists of the value of *SQHead* right before *ann*'s installation. *ExecuteAnn* carries out *anns*'s batch. If any of the execution steps has already been executed by another thread, *ExecuteAnn* moves on to the next step. Specifically, if *ann* will have been removed from *SQHead* by the time *ExecuteAnn* is executed, *ann*'s execution will have been completed, and all the steps of this run of *ExecuteAnn* would fail and have no effect.

*ExecuteAnn* first makes sure that *ann*'s enqueued items are linked to the queue, in the while loop in Line 39. If they have already been linked to the queue, and the old tail after which they were linked has also been recorded in *ann*, it follows that another thread has completed the linking, and thus we break out of the loop in Line 43. Otherwise, we try to link the items by performing a CAS operation on the next pointer of the node pointed to by the tail in Line 44. In Line 45 we check whether the items were linked after *tail*, regardless of which thread linked them. If so, we record *tail*, to which the items were linked, in *ann*. Otherwise, we try to help the obstructing enqueue operation complete in Line 50, and start over with a new attempt to link the batch's items.

The next step is *SQTail*'s update in Line 52. There is no need to retry it, since it fails only if another thread has written the same value on behalf of the same batch operation. Lastly, we call *UpdateHead* to update *SQHead* to point to the last node dequeued by the batch. This update uninstalls the announcement and completes its handling.

The *UpdateHead* method calculates *successfulDeqsNum* as described in Corollary 5.5. It then determines the new head according to the following optimization: If the number of the batch's successful dequeues is at least the size of the queue before applying the batch, which implies that the new dummy node is one of the batch's enqueued nodes, the new head is determined by passing over *successfulDeqsNum* – *oldQueueSize* nodes, starting with the node pointed to by the old tail. Otherwise, it is determined by passing over *successfulDeqsNum* nodes, starting with the old dummy node. Finally, *UpdateHead* updates *SQHead* (and as in *SQTail*'s update, there is no need to retry the CAS).

**Listing 5: ExecuteAnn**

```
37 ExecuteAnn(ann)
38     // Link items to tail and update ann
39     while (true)
40         tailAndCnt = SQTail
41         annOldTailAndCnt = ann->oldTail
42         if (annOldTailAndCnt.node != NULL)
43             break
44         CAS(&tailAndCnt.node->next, NULL, ann->batchReq.
               firstEnq) // Step 3 in Figure 1
45         if (tailAndCnt.node->next == ann->batchReq.firstEnq)
46             // Step 4 in Figure 1:
47             ann->oldTail = annOldTailAndCnt = tailAndCnt
48             break
49         else
50             CAS(&SQTail, tailAndCnt, ⟨tailAndCnt.node->next,
                   tailAndCnt.cnt + 1⟩)
51     newTailAndCnt = ⟨ann->batchReq.lastEnq, annOldTailAndCnt.
           cnt + ann->batchReq.enqsNum⟩
52     CAS(&SQTail, annOldTailAndCnt, newTailAndCnt) // Step 5
           in Figure 1
53     UpdateHead(ann)
54
55 UpdateHead(ann)
56     oldQueueSize = ann->oldTail.cnt - ann->oldHead.cnt
57     successfulDeqsNum = ann->batchReq.deqsNum
58     if (ann->batchReq.excessDeqsNum > oldQueueSize)
59         successfulDeqsNum -= ann->batchReq.excessDeqsNum -
               oldQueueSize
60     if (successfulDeqsNum == 0)
61         CAS(&SQHead, ann, ann->oldHead) // Step 6 in Figure 1
62         return
63     if (oldQueueSize > successfulDeqsNum)
64         newHeadNode = GetNthNode(ann->oldHead.node,
               successfulDeqsNum)
65     else
66         newHeadNode = GetNthNode(ann->oldTail.node,
               successfulDeqsNum - oldQueueSize)
67     CAS(&SQHead, ann, ⟨newHeadNode, ann->oldHead.cnt +
           successfulDeqsNum⟩) // Step 6 in Figure 1
68
69 Node* GetNthNode(node, n)
70     repeat n times:
71         node = node->next
72     return node
```

*6.2.2 Interface Methods.* The queue's interface methods exposed to the user are *Enqueue*, *Dequeue*, *FutureEnqueue*, *FutureDequeue* and *Evaluate*. These methods wrap the methods that access the shared queue, which are detailed in Subsection 6.2.1. We will describe them here, but present their pseudo-code (which is straight forward) in [23]. Thereafter, we will elaborate on the *PairFuturesWithResults* auxiliary method, which is called by *Evaluate*, and locally sets the futures' results to complete the batch operation.

*Enqueue* checks whether the thread-local operation queue *opsQueue* is empty. If it is, it directly calls *EnqueueToShared*. Otherwise, to satisfy EMF-linearizability, the pending operations in *opsQueue* must be applied before the current *Enqueue* is applied. Hence, *Enqueue* calls *FutureEnqueue* with the required item, which in turn returns a future. It then calls *Evaluate* with that future. This results in committing all preceding pending operations, as well as committing the current operation. The implementation of *Dequeue* is similar. If *Dequeue* succeeds, it returns the dequeued item, otherwise (the queue is empty when the operation takes effect) it returns NULL.

*FutureEnqueue* enqueues a *FutureOp* object representing an enqueue operation to the thread's *opsQueue*. A pointer to the *Future* object encapsulated in the created *FutureOp* will be returned by the method, so that the caller could later pass it to the *Evaluate* method. In addition, *FutureEnqueue* updates the numbers of pending enqueue operations. *FutureDequeue* operates similarly, but updates the numbers of pending dequeue operations and excess dequeues. *FutureEnqueue* also adds the item to be enqueued to thread's list of items pending to be enqueued. This list will be appended directly to the end of the shared queue's list of nodes when a batch operation is executed by this thread. This is the reason why these items are stored in a linked list of nodes rather than directly in *opsQueue*.

*Evaluate* receives a future and ensures it is applied when the method returns. If the future has already been applied from the outset, its result is immediately returned. Otherwise, all locally-pending operations found in *threadData.opsQueue* are applied to the shared queue at once by calling *ExecuteBatch*. After the batch operation's execution completes, while new operations may be applied to the shared queue by other threads, *PairFuturesWithResults* (described next) is called to pair the operation results to the appropriate futures of operations in *opsQueue*.

*ExecuteBatch* and then *PairFuturesWithResults* are called only if *opsQueue* consists of at least one enqueue operation. If all pending operations are dequeues, we pursue a different course of action, on which we elaborate in Subsection 6.2.3.

*PairFuturesWithResults.* *PairFuturesWithResults* receives the old head. It simulates the pending operations one by one according to their original order, which is recorded in the thread's *opsQueue*. Namely, it simulates updates of the head and tail of the shared queue. This is done by advancing *nextEnqNode* (which represents the value of *tail->next* in the current moment of the simulation) on each enqueue, and by advancing *currentHead* on dequeues that occur when the queue in its current state is not empty. The simulation is run in order to set results for future objects related to the pending operations and mark them as done.

**Listing 6: PairFuturesWithResults**

```
PairFuturesWithResults(oldHeadNode)
   nextEnqNode = threadData.enqsHead
   currentHead = oldHeadNode
   noMoreSuccessfulDeqs = false
   while threadData.opsQueue is not empty:
      op = threadData.opsQueue.Dequeue()
      if (op.type == ENQ)
         nextEnqNode = nextEnqNode->next
      else // op.type == DEQ
         if (noMoreSuccessfulDeqs ||
            currentHead->next == nextEnqNode)
            // The queue is currently empty
            op.future->result = NULL
         else
            currentHead = currentHead->next
            if (currentHead == threadData.enqsTail)
               noMoreSuccessfulDeqs = true
            op.future->result = currentHead->item
      op.future->isDone = true
```

*6.2.3 Dequeues-Only Batch.* The batch execution scheme outlined in Subsection 5.1 and detailed in Subsection 6.2.1 does not work if the batch operation consists solely of dequeue operations. In such scenario, the *Evaluate* method calls *ExecuteDeqsBatch* to apply the batch operation. The *ExecuteDeqsBatch* method first assists a colliding ongoing batch operation if there is any (in Line 94). It then calculates the new head and the number of successful dequeues by traversing over the items to be dequeued in the loop in Line 97. If there is at least one successful dequeue, the dequeues take effect at once using a single CAS operation in Line 105. The CAS pushes the shared queue's head *successfulDeqsNum* nodes forward.

Then *Evaluate* calls *PairDeqFuturesWithResults* to pair the successfully-dequeued-items to futures of the appropriate operations in *opsQueue*. The remaining future dequeues are unsuccessful, thus their results are set to NULL.

**Listing 7: ExecuteDeqsBatch**

```
92  ⟨unsigned int, Node*⟩ ExecuteDeqsBatch()
93     while (true)
94        oldHeadAndCnt = HelpAnnAndGetHead()
95        newHeadNode = oldHeadAndCnt.node
96        successfullDeqsNum = 0
97        repeat threadData.deqsNum times:
98           headNextNode = newHeadNode->next
99           if (headNextNode == NULL)
100             break
101          ++successfullDeqsNum
102          newHeadNode = headNextNode
103       if (successfullDeqsNum == 0)
104          break
105       if (CAS(&SQHead, oldHeadAndCnt, ⟨newHeadNode,
             oldHeadAndCnt.cnt + successfullDeqsNum⟩))
106          break
107    return ⟨successfullDeqsNum, oldHeadAndCnt.node⟩
```

**Listing 8: PairDeqFuturesWithResults**

```
PairDeqFuturesWithResults(oldHeadNode, successfulDeqsNum)
   currentHead = oldHeadNode
   repeat successfulDeqsNum times:
      currentHead = currentHead->next
      op = threadData.opsQueue.Dequeue()
      op.future->result = currentHead->item
      op.future->isDone = true
   repeat threadData.deqsNum - successfulDeqsNum times:
      op = threadData.opsQueue.Dequeue()
      op.future->result = NULL
      op.future->isDone = true
```

## 6.3 Memory Management

We utilized the optimistic access scheme [2], which extends the hazard pointers scheme [21], as a lock-free manual memory management mechanism for BQ. Due to space limitations, all related details appear in [23]. All measurements include use of memory reclamation.

# 7 CORRECTNESS

In this section we argue about the correctness of the algorithm. We start with an abstraction of the queue in Subsection 7.1, and then specify the linearization points in Subsection 7.2. We argue about lock-freedom in [23].

### 7.1 The Abstract State of the Queue

The abstract state of the queue is the sequence of items contained in the underlying list's nodes, starting with the item in the second node (i.e., the node succeeding the dummy node pointed to by the abstract head) if any, and ending with the node whose next pointer is NULL. The queue is empty iff the next pointer of the node pointed to by the abstract head is NULL. The tail pointer does not affect the state of the abstract queue.

The fine point is the definition of the abstract head of the queue:

- If no announcement is installed in *SQHead*, the abstract head is the same as *SQHead*.
- If there is an announcement installed in *SQHead*, but the CAS that links its items to the tail (in Line 44 in Listing 5) has not yet been performed successfully, then the abstract head is the same as *SQHead.ann->oldHead*, which is in practice *SQHead*'s value prior to the announcement's installation. Thus, installing an announcement does not change the abstract head.
- If there is an announcement installed in *SQHead*, and the CAS that links its items to the tail has already succeeded, then the abstract head points to the node that is going to be the dummy node after all enqueues and dequeues of the batch operation have taken effect. *SQHead* is going to be set to the same value when the announcement is uninstalled. Thus, removing an announcement does not change the abstract head.

Hence, when a batch operation is announced (i.e., *SQHead* is set to point to the related announcement), the abstract state of the queue does not change. It remains the sequence of items currently contained in the nodes of the shared queue's list, starting with the node succeeding the node pointed to by the previous *SQHead*. The moment the CAS that links the batch's enqueued items to the tail (in Line 44 in Listing 5) succeeds, the abstract queue's head is changed to point to the node to which *SQHead* will point after completing the announcement handling. Therefore, the whole batch, including both its enqueues and dequeues, takes effect instantaneously. From that moment, until another operation takes effect, the abstract state of the queue is the sequence of items in the list starting with the node succeeding the new dummy node, including the batch's linked items.

### 7.2 Linearization Points

From the above definitions of the abstract head and the abstract state of the queue, we derive linearization points for all operation types. These linearization points are detailed next.

A successful dequeue operation takes effect when it modifies the head pointer (and counter). An unsuccessful dequeue operation is linearized when it reads the next pointer of the dummy node (whose value is revealed to be NULL). All dequeues of a batch operation that contains only dequeue operations are linearized one after another, in the moment of reading the next pointer in Line 98 (of Method *ExecuteDeqsBatch* in Listing 7) for the last time before *ExecuteDeqsBatch* returns. This reading ends the list traversal performed to calculate the new head, either due to encountering the end of the list (as detected in Line 99), or due to completing a traversal of *deqsNum* items.

An enqueue operation takes effect when the next pointer of the last node in the list is modified from NULL to point to a new node. Similarly, all enqueues and dequeues of a batch operation that enqueues at least one item take effect one after another when the next pointer of the last node is modified from NULL to point to the first node of the batch. This modification may be carried out by a helping thread rather than the thread that invoked the operation.

To satisfy EMF-linearizability, the future history $H_f$, constructed from the original history $H$ (as described in Definition 3.1), should be MF-linearizable. Thus far, we described linearization points relating to $H$. We set the same linearization points in $H_f$: the linearization point in $H_f$ is the same as in $H$ for a future operation call, and for a single operation call – we set the linearization point of the appropriate future call to the same moment as the linearization of the single call in $H$. Note that since the linearization points described for single operations occur during their method calls in $H$, they occur between the adequate future call's invocation and *Evaluate* call's response in $H_f$, which complies with MF-linearizability.

## 8 PERFORMANCE

We compared the proposed BQ to two queue algorithms: the original MSQ that executes one operation at a time, and the queue by Kogan and Herlihy [17] that satisfies MF-linearizability, hence denoted KHQ. KHQ executes pending operations in batches of homogeneous operations: it executes each subsequence of enqueues-only together by linking nodes to the end of the queue, and each subsequence of dequeues-only by unlinking nodes from the head of the queue.

We implemented the shared parts of the different queue versions identically to filter any unrelated performance difference. All queues use the optimistic access scheme for memory management. The implementations were coded in C++ and compiled using the GCC compiler version 6.3.0 with a $-O3$ optimization level.

We conducted our experiments on a machine running Linux (Ubuntu 16.04) equipped with 4 AMD Opteron(TM) 6376 2.3GHz processors. Each processor has 16 cores, resulting in 64 threads overall. The number of threads in each experiment varied from 1 to 128. Each thread was attached to a different core, except for the experiment that ran 128 threads, in which two threads were attached to each core. The machine used 64GB RAM, an L1 data cache of 16KB per core, an L2 cache of 2MB for every two cores, and an L3 cache of 6MB for every 8 cores.

In each experiment testing BQ or KHQ, our workload performed batch operations with a fixed number of future operations for that experiment. Our workload for MSQ performed standard operations only. In the workloads of all queues, we randomly determined whether each operation (standard or future) would be an enqueue or a dequeue.

Each data point $[x, y]$ in the graphs in Figure 2 represents the average result of 10 experiments. In each experiment, $x$ threads performed operations concurrently for two seconds. The graphs depict the throughput in each case, i.e., the number of operations (*Enqueue* / *Dequeue* / *FutureEnqueue* / *FutureDequeue*) applied to the shared queue per second by the threads altogether, measured in million operations per second. The BQ curve appears along with the MSQ and KHQ curves for different batch sizes.

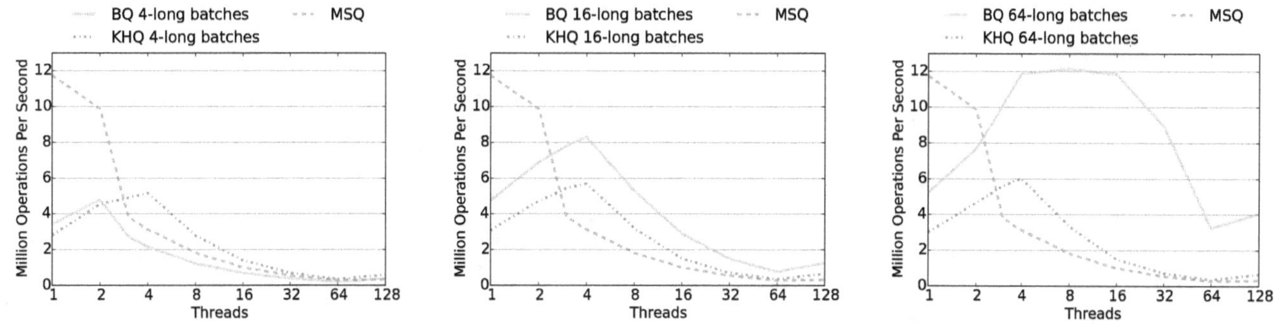


**Figure 2: Throughput for 4, 16 and 64 long batches respectively**

BQ demonstrates a significant performance improvement over both competitors for batches of more than 10 operations. Indeed, for batches containing 4 operations, MSQ and KHQ are preferable. The overhead of executing a batch operation makes small batches less worthwhile. However, for longer batches, and when at least 3 threads operate on the queue, BQ performs better.

BQ exploits parallelism better as execution of operations in batches reduces contention substantially: instead of accessing the shared queue for every operation, each thread interacts with the shared queue throughout the execution of a single batch operation. Later, it performs local work to pair futures applied by the batch operation with results. BQ performs better than KHQ as well, since it applies each batch at once to the shared queue, while KHQ applies each batch operation using several homogeneous batch executions. Therefore, BQ is an excellent choice for a lock-free queue when future operations can be employed.

The throughput of MSQ decreases as the number of threads increases, since the contention makes it impossible to exploit parallelism. On the other hand, when using batches of size 16 or more, 3 threads achieve better throughput in BQ than 2, and 4 perform better than 3, demonstrating improved scalability.

The more operations a batch contains, the greater the performance gap between BQ and the other queues becomes. BQ performs better as batch size increases since the reduction in contention more than compensates for the greater overhead. The performance improvement from batches containing 4 operations to ones containing 16, and from these to 64-long batches, is shown in Figure 2. Additional measurements we conducted demonstrate further improvement for 256-long batches in comparison to 64-long batches, especially for executions with many threads.

## REFERENCES


[1] Dmitry Basin, Rui Fan, Idit Keidar, Ofer Kiselov, and Dmitri Perelman. 2011. Café: Scalable task pools with adjustable fairness and contention. In *DISC*.

[2] Nachshon Cohen and Erez Petrank. 2015. Efficient memory management for lock-free data structures with optimistic access. In *SPAA*.

[3] Robert Colvin and Lindsay Groves. 2005. Formal verification of an array-based nonblocking queue. In *ICECCS*.

[4] Panagiota Fatourou and Nikolaos D. Kallimanis. 2011. A highly-efficient wait-free universal construction. In *SPAA*.

[5] Panagiota Fatourou and Nikolaos D. Kallimanis. 2012. Revisiting the combining synchronization technique. In *PPoPP*.

[6] John Giacomoni, Tipp Moseley, and Manish Vachharajani. 2008. FastForward for efficient pipeline parallelism: a cache-optimized concurrent lock-free queue. In *PPoPP*.

[7] Anders Gidenstam, Håkan Sundell, and Philippas Tsigas. 2010. Cache-aware lock-free queues for multiple producers/consumers and weak memory consistency. In *OPODIS*.

[8] James R. Goodman, Mary K. Vernon, and Philip J. Woest. 1989. Efficient synchronization primitives for large-scale cache-coherent multiprocessors. In *ASPLOS*.

[9] Allan Gottlieb, Boris D. Lubachevsky, and Larry Rudolph. 1983. Basic techniques for the efficient coordination of very large numbers of cooperating sequential processors. *TOPLAS* 5, 2 (1983).

[10] Andreas Haas, Michael Lippautz, Thomas A. Henzinger, Hannes Payer, Ana Sokolova, Christoph M. Kirsch, and Ali Sezgin. 2013. Distributed queues in shared memory: multicore performance and scalability through quantitative relaxation. In *CF*.

[11] Danny Hendler, Itai Incze, Nir Shavit, and Moran Tzafrir. 2010. Flat combining and the synchronization-parallelism tradeoff. In *SPAA*.

[12] Maurice Herlihy. 1991. Wait-free synchronization. *TOPLAS* 13, 1 (1991).

[13] Maurice Herlihy, Beng-Hong Lim, and Nir Shavit. 1995. Scalable concurrent counting. *TOCS* 13, 4 (1995).

[14] Maurice Herlihy and Jeannette M. Wing. 1990. Linearizability: a correctness condition for concurrent objects. *TOPLAS* 12, 3 (1990).

[15] Moshe Hoffman, Ori Shalev, and Nir Shavit. 2007. The baskets queue. *OPODIS* (2007).

[16] Christoph M. Kirsch, Michael Lippautz, and Hannes Payer. 2013. Fast and scalable, lock-free k-FIFO queues. In *PaCT*.

[17] Alex Kogan and Maurice Herlihy. 2014. The future(s) of shared data structures. In *PODC*.

[18] Alex Kogan and Yossi Lev. 2017. Transactional lock elision meets combining. In *PODC*.

[19] Edya Ladan-Mozes and Nir Shavit. 2008. An optimistic approach to lock-free FIFO queues. *Distributed Computing* 20, 5 (2008).

[20] Doug Lea. 2009. The java concurrency package (JSR-166).

[21] Maged M. Michael. 2004. Hazard pointers: safe memory reclamation for lock-free objects. *TPDS* 15, 6 (2004).

[22] Maged M. Michael and Michael L. Scott. 1996. Simple, fast, and practical non-blocking and blocking concurrent queue algorithms. In *PODC*.

[23] Gal Milman, Alex Kogan, Yossi Lev, Victor Luchangco, and Erez Petrank. 2018. BQ: a lock-free queue with batching (full paper). (2018). http://www.cs.technion.ac.il/~erez/Papers/bq-full.pdf

[24] Mark Moir, Daniel Nussbaum, Ori Shalev, and Nir Shavit. 2005. Using elimination to implement scalable and lock-free FIFO queues. In *SPAA*.

[25] Adam Morrison and Yehuda Afek. 2013. Fast concurrent queues for x86 processors. In *PPoPP*.

[26] Niloufar Shafiei. 2009. Non-blocking array-based algorithms for stacks and queues. In *ICDCN*.

[27] Philippas Tsigas and Yi Zhang. 2001. A simple, fast and scalable non-blocking concurrent FIFO queue for shared memory multiprocessor systems. In *SPAA*.

[28] Chaoran Yang and John Mellor-Crummey. 2016. A wait-free queue as fast as fetch-and-add. In *PPoPP*.

# An Efficient Wait-free Resizable Hash Table

Panagiota Fatourou
FORTH ICS & University of Crete,
Department of Computer Science
faturu@csd.uoc.gr

Nikolaos D. Kallimanis
FORTH ICS
nkallima@ics.forth.gr

Thomas Ropars
Univ. Grenoble Alpes
thomas.ropars@univ-grenoble-alpes.fr

## ABSTRACT

This paper presents an efficient wait-free resizable hash table. To achieve high throughput at large core counts, our algorithm is specifically designed to retain the natural parallelism of concurrent hashing, while providing wait-free resizing. An extensive evaluation of our hash table shows that in the common case where resizing actions are rare, our implementation outperforms all existing lock-free hash table implementations while providing a stronger progress guarantee.

**ACM Reference Format:**

Panagiota Fatourou, Nikolaos D. Kallimanis, and Thomas Ropars. 2018. An Efficient Wait-free Resizable Hash Table. In *SPAA '18: 30th ACM Symposium on Parallelism in Algorithms and Architectures, July 16–18, 2018, Vienna, Austria.* ACM, New York, NY, USA, 10 pages. https://doi.org/10.1145/3210377.3210408

## 1 INTRODUCTION

As the core count is increasing in modern processors, designing data structures that provide good performance when a large number of threads access them concurrently is a must [22], but it is also a highly challenging task [10], especially if strong liveness guarantees, such as *wait-freedom*, are to be provided [13]. Wait-freedom is highly desirable as it ensures *progress* for all running threads independently of their speeds or any *crash* failures that other threads may experience. Specifically, wait-freedom ensures that *every* operation on the data structure (executed by a running thread) will complete within a finite number of steps. *Lock-freedom* is a weaker progress condition which guarantees that *at least one* thread makes progress, thus allowing other threads to starve.

A hash table is a data structure commonly used to implement a dictionary of key-value pairs. It provides two *update* operations (Insert and Delete) and a LookUp operation. A hash function is used to associate keys to buckets so that each operation on the hash table takes constant average time [14]. To ensure this property even when the number of stored items varies over time, dynamic hashing aims at dynamically resizing the hash table to adapt the number of buckets to the number of items [4]. Resizing actions (splitting or merging of buckets) are triggered during Insert and Delete operations.



*SPAA '18, July 16–18, 2018, Vienna, Austria*



ACM ISBN 978-1-4503-5799-9/18/07...$15.00
https://doi.org/10.1145/3210377.3210408

It is commonly acknowledged that, in most cases, LookUps are by far the most frequent operations on a hash table [14, 23]. Given that update operations are not frequent, resizing actions are rare events since the number of items to store does not vary much over time. In theory, hashing can be made very efficient in a concurrent environment due to its *natural parallelism* [14]. In most cases, concurrent operations access different parts of the hash table, and thus they can proceed in parallel without any interference with one another. However, the case of dynamic hashing is more complex. Allowing hash table operations to be executed in parallel with resizing actions while ensuring *linearizability* [15], is difficult, especially for algorithms providing strong progress guarantees [19, 21].

This paper presents a new wait-free implementation of a resizable hash table. Our hash table aims at achieving best performance for the most common operations on a hash table, while providing *wait-freedom* progress guarantee. To guide our design, we identify two design rules that are important to achieve high performance at large core counts: (A) LookUp operations should always be allowed to proceed without any synchronization; (B) when no resizing actions are executed, update operations applying to different buckets should be allowed to progress fully in parallel (i.e., without any interference with each other). These rules aim at preserving the natural parallelism of hash tables in the most frequent case where no resizing is required. Rule (A) additionally aims at minimizing the cost of the most frequent operations in all cases.

To implement a hash table that complies with these design rules, we propose an algorithm based on *extendible hashing*, a dynamic hashing technique that considers keys as bit strings [5]. An extendible hash table can be seen as an array (the *directory*) of pointer to fixed-size buckets. In its sequential implementation, every resizing operation is local, e.g., one bucket can be split into two without modifying the other buckets.

Our wait-free extendible hash table relies on the PSim universal construction [7]. PSim provides a general mechanism to implement any concurrent object in a wait-free manner. It exploits the well-known technique [6] of having a thread that executes an operation help other announced operations by applying them, in addition to its own, on a local copy of the simulated object state. Then, it attempts to change a shared reference to the object state to point to this local copy. PSim results in highly-efficient wait-free implementations of data structures that have a single or a small number of points of contention, such as stacks and queues [7]. In this paper, we show how we can use several instances of the PSim algorithm and synchronize them appropriately to get an efficient wait-free implementation of an extendible hash table. To match our design rules, our hash table uses an instance of PSim's algorithm for each bucket. These instances run update operations on each bucket fully independently as long as no resizing actions are required. An additional instance of PSim's algorithm is used to manage resizing actions modifying the state of the hash table. The crux of our algorithm is in the mechanisms used to coordinate the different instances of PSim during resize actions in order to ensure linearizability and wait-freedom, while complying with our design rules.

We evaluate our algorithm experimentally and compare it with that of two state-of-the-art lock-free concurrent hash tables: the lock-free resizable hash table proposed by Liu et al. [19] and the hash table based on a *split-ordered list* proposed by Shalev and Shavit [21]. Experiments run on two Intel processors (48-core Haswell, and 64-core Broadwell) show that in a directory-stable state, i.e., when resizing actions are rare, the performance of our algorithm is highly competitive. When manipulating a small number of items, and when the percentage of LookUps is high, our wait-free algorithm outperforms the most efficient lock-free algorithm by up to 47% on a 64-core machine. When the size of the hash table increases, a modified version of the *lock-free* algorithm presented by Liu et al. [19], that we propose, becomes the most efficient with our algorithm being the second most efficient. The very high performance of our algorithm in directory-stable states comes at the cost of slower resizing actions. However, our experiments demonstrate that the resizing cost is acceptable when it can be amortized over long runs. In this case, our wait-free hash table is as efficient as or more efficient than the best existing lock-free solutions.

The main contributions of this paper are summarized as follows:

- We present a new wait-free resizable hash table based on extendible hashing (Section 4). Its implementation follows two design rules that aim at preserving the natural parallelism of dynamic hashing for the most frequent operations.
- We provide an extensive performance evaluation of the new algorithm at large core counts that shows that, when resizing actions are rare, our wait-free hash table largely outperforms all previous lock-free implementations (in terms of throughput), at the cost of slower resizing (Section 6).

The results of our experiments show evidence that the design rules we identify are of key importance to build efficient non-blocking resizable hash tables.

## 2 RELATED WORK

Hash tables are important data structures in domains ranging from operating systems' kernels [1, 23] to runtime and programming languages [16].

The easiest way to implement a resizable hash table is probably using locks, i.e., in a *blocking* way. One such implementation is the *ConcurrentHashMap* provided in the Java `concurrency.utils` library [18]. It uses a fixed number of locks, each of which guards a subset of the buckets. Resizing can be performed only by a thread that has acquired all locks, thus excluding all other threads from executing operations during a resizing phase. A concurrent *extendible* hashing algorithm based on locks was presented by Ellis [3]. It is based on a two-level locking scheme where a lock on the directory must be grabbed first, before locking a specific bucket.

Non-blocking resizable hash tables are appealing because of their stronger progress guarantees that have been shown to lead to higher performance in several studies [10, 21]. One of the first lock-free non-resizable hash table implementations was described by Michael [20]. It is based on an array of lock-free linked lists. At the same period, Greenwald [11] presented a lock-free resizable hash table that relied on a DCAS (*double-compare-and-swap*) operation. However, DCAS is not supported on most hardware architectures.

The lock-free resizable hash table proposed in [21], which we will call LF-Split, relies on a *split-ordered* list. The items of the hash table are stored in an ordered linked-list and a separate array of pointers pointing to elements in the linked list plays the role of the directory. The items belonging to bucket numbered $i$ are all the items accessible in the linked-list starting from the node pointed to by entry $i$ of the directory and finishing at the node pointed to by the next entry of the directory. Hence, inserting a new element in a bucket simply requires to insert it in the linked list. Splitting a bucket into two only implies adding in the directory a new pointer to an element in the list. Relying on a list to implement the hash table makes resizing operations very efficient. However, LookUp operations might be less efficient than with array-based hash tables because of the cost of pointer chasing paid when iterating over the elements of a bucket [2, 19]. LF-Split complies with neither of the design rules we introduce to optimize directory-stable-state performance. Indeed, rule (A) is violated because when a node is marked for deletion, threads running LookUp operations might have to help removing these nodes from the list. Moreover, a global counter has to be updated when an item is removed or a *new* item is inserted, which breaks rule (B). The experiments presented in Section 6 show that these two facts limit the performance of LF-Split when the directory is stable.

To the best of our knowledge, only two wait-free resizable hash tables have been described thus far [8, 19]. The algorithm of Feldman et al. [8] is based on a multi-level array resulting in pointer chasing and therefore reduced performance for LookUp operations.

Liu et al. have proposed in [19] an array-based resizable lock-free hash table, which we will call LF-Freeze. Buckets are implemented as arrays of items, and the directory is an array of pointers to items. When the directory needs to be resized, the buckets are *frozen*: no update operations are allowed to proceed on these buckets anymore. Splitting the buckets is then lazily done during Insert operations. LF-Freeze respects the two design rules that we have defined. The experimental analysis on large multicore machines that is provided in [19], shows that LF-Freeze outperforms LF-Split [21]. Our algorithm shares some of the design ideas of LF-Freeze. However, it ensures wait-freedom by using instances of the PSim algorithm for ensuring synchronization.

Liu et al. also proposed in [19] a wait-free variant of their lock-free implementation, which we will call WF-Freeze. In this variant, threads should help each other running update operations and resize actions on the buckets. This is done by assigning sequence numbers to all update operations, a technique that is implemented using a globally shared counter (thus violating rule (B)). The experiments in [19] show that WF-Freeze exhibits performance that is by far lower than the performance of LF-Freeze. Our algorithm ensures wait-freedom without using any globally shared counter.

Kogan and Petrank proposed in [17] the *fast-path-slow-path* technique, an approach to get a wait-free variant of a lock-free algorithm with a relatively small performance cost. In their experimental analysis, Liu et al. included a wait-free variant of their lock-free algorithm based on this technique. The resulted algorithm performs much better than WF-Freeze (their brute-force wait-free

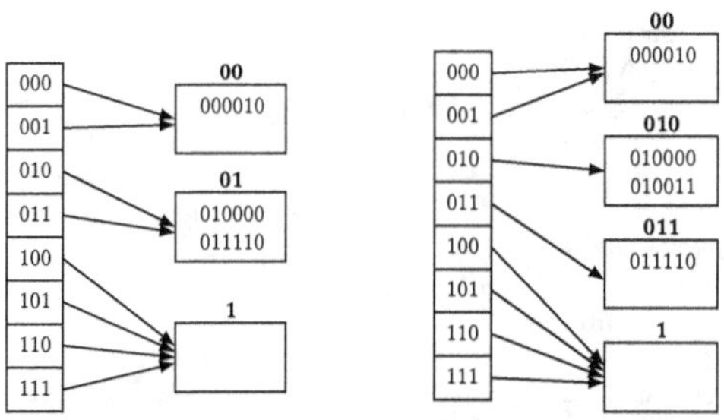


(a) Initial state (b) After inserting 010011

**Figure 1: An extendible hash table. The directory has a depth of 3 and each bucket can store at most 2 items.**

solution), but its performance is lower than that of LF-Freeze (their lock-free algorithm). Our evaluation shows that our brute-force wait-free implementation outperforms LF-Freeze in several cases when the hash table is in a directory-stable state.

## 3 EXTENDIBLE HASHING

An *extendible hash table* is a data structure of two levels. It consists of a set of *buckets*, in each of which a fixed number $b$ of items are stored, and a resizable array, called the *directory*, where each entry stores a pointer to a bucket. Extendible hashing manipulates hash keys as bit strings: the bit strings are used to distribute items to buckets. The directory has $2^D$ entries, where $D$ is a parameter called the *depth* of the directory. Figure 1 describes an extendible hash table with $D = 3$. A prefix corresponding to the $D$ most significant bits of the hash key is used to associate items to directory entries and the buckets they point to. For instance, in Figure 1, key 010000 is associated with the directory entry 010. The depth of the directory is at most as big as the total number of bits in the hash key. The size of the directory is always exponential to its depth.

In practice, the number of buckets does not have to be the same as the number of directory entries: to improve memory efficiency, it is adapted to the number of items to store. In Figure 1a, a single bucket is allocated to store all keys with prefix 1 since there is no such key, and all four directory entries with prefix 1 point to that bucket. The *depth* of this bucket is 1, i.e., it equals the length of the prefix that identifies the hash keys that are to be stored in it.

As illustrated in Figure 1b, a bucket is split in two buckets when it is full (i.e., when it already contains $b$ items) and a newly inserted item must be stored in this bucket. For instance, to insert key 010110, two new buckets 010 and 011 should be created to replace the existing bucket 01. In this case, the directory will not be resized because the bucket with prefix 01 has depth 2 and the two newly created buckets to replace it, have depth 3 which is smaller than or equal to the directory depth. However, to insert another item 010111 in the table of Figure 1b, resizing the directory would be required. The depth of the directory should be increased to 4 to allow storing the pointers of two new buckets 0100 and 0101. We remark that the resizing actions are *local*: to replace a bucket with two new buckets, all the items of the old bucket are stored in the new buckets and no additional elements are stored in them.

## 4 A WAIT-FREE IMPLEMENTATION OF AN EXTENDIBLE HASH TABLE

This section presents the new wait-free implementation of the extendible hash table. We start by describing the main ideas of the algorithm. Then, we present how the hash table works when no resizing occurs. Finally, we provide the details of resizing. Our wait-free algorithm incorporates and builds upon the code of PSim [7] for updating the buckets and the directory.

In our implementation (as well as in the experimental analysis of Section 6), an invocation of INSERT for an already existing key, updates the value associated with the key. This semantics correspond to that of dictionaries provided by popular programming languages such as Java[1] or Python[2]. The description assumes that a wait-free garbage collector is available. (Section 5 provides a discussion on memory reclamation.) We consider a system of $n$ threads.

### 4.1 The algorithm in a nutshell

Figure 2 presents the structure of our hash table and describes how it evolves when update operations are executed. The main challenge when designing a resizable hash table is allowing operations of the hash table to be executed in parallel with resizing actions. To this end, our algorithm uses two levels of indirection between the DState object that implements the directory and the BState objects that store the items of buckets (see Figure 2a). In a BState object, items are stored in a fixed size array (in Figure 2, this size is 2). The data records used to implement our hash table are presented in Figure 3. To distinguish a variable that stores a reference to an object, we add the suffix _p to its type.

To insert a new element into a non-full bucket in a wait-free manner, a thread creates a local copy of the corresponding BState. It applies its operation on this local copy and uses a CompareAndSwap (CAS) operation to attempt to update the BState pointer in the corresponding bucket to point to its local BState object (see Figure 2b). If the corresponding bucket is full, it will be replaced by two new buckets to complete the INSERT. This case is illustrated in Figure 2c. The directory, i.e., the DState object, must be updated to store references to the new buckets. To perform the update on the directory state in a wait-free manner, a thread first creates a local copy of the currently active DState object (pointed to by the shared variable ht). Note that this copy contains pointers to the existing buckets. The thread can then create the new buckets from the full bucket (buckets 00 and 01 from bucket 0 in Figure 2c), update its local DState object accordingly, and finally, try to make its local DState object the active DState object by updating ht using CAS.

The algorithm has to ensure that update operations are not lost if they run concurrently with a resizing action that requires replacing the current DState object. Thus, our algorithm has to handle the following two cases that might arise during the creation of a new DState object: (i) no update should be lost if a pointer to a bucket is replaced with pointers to new buckets in the new DState object, and (ii) no update targeting the non-full buckets should be lost, i.e., the non-full buckets must still be referenced by the new DState object. To prevent the appearance of the first case, our algorithm ensures that (1) a bucket is split only if it is full and (2) no update

[1] Package java.util.AbstractMap
[2] https://docs.python.org/3/library/stdtypes.html#dict

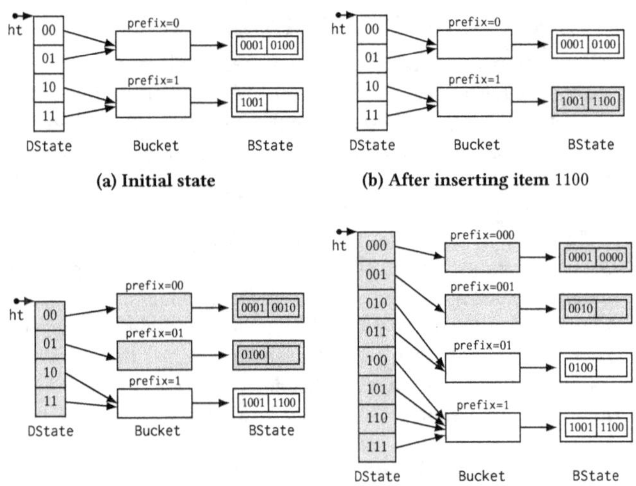


(a) Initial state

(b) After inserting item 1100

(c) After bucket splitting (inserting item 0010)

(d) After directory resizing (inserting item 0000)

**Figure 2: Operations on the wait-free extendible hash table. (The new objects created during an operation are grayed)**

```
struct Operation:
  type : {INS, DEL}
  key : integer
  value : integer
  seqnum : integer

struct Result:
  status : {TRUE, FALSE, FAIL}
  seqnum : integer

struct DState:
  depth : integer
  dir[2^depth] : Bucket_p

struct Bucket:
  prefix : bit-string
  depth : integer
  state : BState_p
  toggle[n] : boolean

struct BState:
  items : set of key-value pairs
  applied[n] : boolean
  results[n] : Result
```

**Figure 3: Data structures definitions (for $n$ threads).**

```
Shared variables :
  ht : DState_p
  help[n] : Operation_p

Persistent private variable :
  opSeqnum_i : integer
```

**Figure 4: Variables for thread $T_i$.**

operation (not even DELETE) is executed on a full bucket. To prevent the second case from occurring, our algorithm employs two levels of indirection between a `DState` object and the `BState` objects. Assume that a `BState` object is updated as shown in Figure 2b, while the `DState` object pointing to this bucket is also updated (as shown Figure 2c). In this case, the new `DState` object will still point to the previously existing `Bucket` objects that are not split (i.e., that are not full). Thus, even if the `BState` reference stored in a `Bucket` changes, it will still be accessible through the new `DState` object.

Resizing the directory is required when its depth becomes smaller than the depth of new buckets that are created during an INSERT operating on a full bucket. In this case, after creating a local copy of the currently active `DState` object (i.e., after copying all pointers to buckets locally), the thread executing the INSERT must create a new `DState` object of larger depth, and copy the existing bucket references into it. Figure 2d illustrates this case.

In the following sections, we provide the details of our algorithm. We discuss how update operations on `DState` and `BState` objects are implemented in a wait-free manner, as well as how they are synchronized to ensure linearizability.

## 4.2 Data structures for the resizable hash table implementation

Recall that the data records used to implement our hash table are presented in Figure 3. Part of the `Bucket` state is stored in a `BState` record. This part is copied by every thread that wants to apply an atomic update on the bucket. Each `Bucket` record, as well as each `BState` record includes a bit vector of size $n$ (called `toggle` and `applied`, respectively) that are used to efficiently track the pending operations on a bucket. A `BState` record also stores an array, called `Result`, that is used to store the results of active operations. (We describe how these fields are used in more detail in the subsequent sections.) The fixed size array[3] used to store the items associated with a `BState` is called *items*. In the following, we use the notation *items[key]* to set or get the value associated with one key. The hash table is represented by a record of type `DState` that is composed of an array of references to elements of type `Bucket` and a variable `depth` storing the depth of the directory.

The shared variables and the private persistent variables for each thread are provided in Figure 4. Each operation initiated by a process $i$ is announced in element $i$ of the shared array *help*. A per-thread sequence number (*opSeqnum*$_i$) is introduced but it will only become useful when discussing resizing in Section 4.4.

## 4.3 The case of no resizing

This section describes how INSERT and LOOKUP work when no resizing is required. Figure 5 provides code for INSERT and LOOKUP. DELETE is implemented in the same way as INSERT.

As described in Section 4.1, to insert an item in a non-full bucket $b$, a thread must update the corresponding `BState`. This is done in `ApplyWFOp()`. Note that the thread executes other pending updates on the bucket (in addition to its own), leveraging the core idea of PSim. Specifically, the thread first announces its operations (lines 40 and 50). Then it tries to apply its operation, as well as all other pending operations for bucket $b$, on a local copy *newb* of the bucket state (lines 52-60). Finally, it executes a CAS to make this updated state the new value of *b.state* (line 61). When a thread executes an operation on behalf of another thread, it stores the result of this operation in *newb.results* so that the other thread can find there the result of its operation (line 47).

[3] The size of the array equals the maximum number of elements a bucket can store. To look for a key, a thread has to iterate over all elements currently stored in the array.

```
33 def Lookup(integer key): (boolean, integer)
34     htl ← ht ★
35     bs ← htl.dir[Prefix(key, htl.depth)].bstate
36     return ((key ∈ bs.items) ? (TRUE, bs.items[key]) : (FALSE, −1))

38 def Insert(integer key, integer value): boolean
39     opSeqnum_i ← opSeqnum_i+1 ★
40     help[i] ← new Operation(INS, key, value, opSeqnum_i)
41     htl ← ht ★
42     ApplyWFOp( htl.dir[ Prefix(key, htl.depth) ] )
43     htl ← ht ★
44     if htl.dir[ Prefix(key, htl.depth) ].state.results[i].seqnum != opSeqnum_i: ★
45         ResizeWF() ★
46     htl ← ht ★
47     return htl.dir[ Prefix(key, htl.depth) ].state.results[i].status

49 def ApplyWFOp(Bucket_p b):
50     Flip(b.toggle, i) # change the value of bit i
51     for k in 1..2:
52         oldb ← b.state
53         newb ← New BState(oldb) # create a copy of object oldb
54         t ← b.toggle
55         for j in [ tid for tid in 1..n if t[tid] != newb.applied[tid] ]:
56             if newb.results[j].seqnum < help[j].seqnum: ★
57                 newb.results[j].status ← ExecOnBucket(newb, help[j])
58                 if newb.results[j].status is not FAIL: ★
59                     newb.results[j].seqnum ← help[j].seqnum ★
60         newb.applied ← t
61         CAS( b.state, oldb, newb)

63 def ExecOnBucket(BState_p b, Operation_p op): status
64     if b.items is full:
65         return FAIL
66     else:
67         exist ← (op.key ∈ b.items)
68         if op.type == INS:
69             b.items[op.key] ← op.value # updates or inserts
70             return !exist
71         else:
72             delete b.items[op.key] # does nothing if key not present
73             return exist
```

**Figure 5: Code of Insert and LookUp operations (lines marked with the ★ symbol are required only to implement resizing).**

To identify pending updates on a bucket, the `toggle` vector of the `Bucket` and the `applied` vector of the corresponding `BState` are used. To announce an update operation *op* on a bucket *b*, a thread $T_i$ flips its bit in *b.toggle* (line 50) in an atomic way. Hence, if a bit *j* has different values in *b.toggle* and *b.state.applied*, then thread $T_j$ has a pending operation. Note that $T_i$ announces *op* in *help*[*i*] before flipping its bit in *b.toggle*.

After $T_i$ has executed the body of the loop on lines 51-61 twice, it is guaranteed that the operation of thread $T_i$ has been executed [7]: If both $T_i$'s CAS operations fail (line 61), it means that another thread $T_j$ has run an iteration of this loop and has executed a successful CAS between $T_i$'s first and second CAS step. Since an iteration executes all pending operations and thread $T_i$ had registered its own operation before executing its first CAS step (line 50), $T_j$ has applied the operation of thread $T_i$. So, after executing it second CAS step, $T_i$ can read the result of its operation in the corresponding entry of the *result* array of the active `BState` (line 47). The function `ExecOnBucket()` (lines 63-73) is called to (sequentially) execute an update operation on a local copy of a bucket state.

Complying with design rule (A), LookUp operations (line 33) do not require any synchronization, i.e., they execute a code that is exactly the same as their sequential code independently of whether the buckets they are directed at are being resized when they are executed. Doing so does not violate linearizability because when a thread makes a copy of the current `BState` to apply an update to it, it copies the set of items as part of this state. Therefore, the bucket states are immutable, allowing to access them safely without synchronization. Performing this copy has a cost for update operations. However, it allows for very efficient LookUp operations which are the most frequent operations performed on a hash table.

To access a bucket (e.g., line 35), a thread first stores a copy of *ht* in local variable *htl* (lines 34, 41, 43, and 46). This is needed because *ht.dir* and *ht.depth* should refer to the same `DState`. This might not be the case without copying the reference stored in *ht* locally, given that *ht* may be concurrently updated by resizing actions.

## 4.4 Resizing the hash table

Figure 6 describes the operations required to resize the hash table, i.e., to split each of the full buckets into two buckets, as well as to increase the size of the directory. We defer the discussion of bucket merging to Section 4.5.

**Updating the directory.** When an Insert operation fails because a bucket is full, the calling thread runs the `ResizeWF()` function (line 45). The algorithm executed by `ResizeWF()` follows the same basic principle as that executed by `ApplyWFOp()`. All threads willing to apply a resize action (here splitting a full bucket) will run two iterations of a loop where they will first make a local copy of the directory (line 119), then apply the required modifications on their local copy, and finally try to make their local copy the active state of the directory using a CAS instruction (line 124). However, there is no need to use bit vectors to determine the actions to be executed on the directory: all such actions will be resizing actions.

Making `ApplyWFOp()` and `ResizeWF()` wait free is not enough to ensure that Insert is wait free. We need to also ensure that a thread calls these functions a bounded number of times to complete an Insert. To this end, special care should be given to *pending resize actions* and pending update operations during resizing. A *pending resize action* is a resize action that must be performed in order for a pending update on a bucket to complete. Specifically, (i) a thread running a resize action has to execute all pending resize actions on the current state of the hash table, and (ii) when creating a new bucket, a thread has to execute all pending update operations on the newly created bucket. We explain the necessity of each of these two special actions in the next two paragraphs.

Consider the case where two threads, $T_1$ and $T_2$, need to execute `ResizeWF()` to complete an Insert operation each, on distinct buckets. Assume that $T_1$ needs to split bucket $b_a$ and $T_2$ needs to split bucket $b_c$ to complete their operations. If $T_1$ tries to update the directory in parallel with $T_2$, without executing the split of bucket $b_c$, there is a chance that only $T_1$ will manage to make its new computed state active using CAS (line 124), requiring $T_2$ to run again its resize action. The second time, a thread $T_3$ could be trying to split a bucket $b_d$ in parallel with $T_2$ splitting $b_c$, and make

```
74  def SplitBucket(Bucket_p b): (Bucket_p, Bucket_p)
75      b0 ← new Bucket(b) # copy of bucket b
76      b0.depth ← b.depth + 1
77      b0.prefix ← b.prefix << 1 # bucket with prefix B1B2B3...0
78      b0.state ← new BState() # new empty BState
79      b0.state.results ← b.state.results #copy if the results array of b
80      b0.state.applied ← b0.toggle
81      b1 ← new Bucket(b0)
82      b1.prefix ← b0.prefix + 1 # bucket with prefix B1B2B3...1
83      for (k,v) in b.state.items: # insert the key-value pairs in new BStates
84          if Prefix(k, b0.depth) == b0.prefix:
85              b0.state.items[k] ← v
86          else:
87              b1.state.items[k] ← v
88      return b0, b1

90  def DirectoryUpdate(DState_p d, Bucket_p blist[]):
91      for b in blist:
92          if b.depth > d.depth: # doubling directory size is required
93              alloc d.dir with size 2^(d.depth+1)
94              copy all Bucket_p from previous dir to new d.dir
95              d.depth ← d.depth + 1
96          #compute the set of directory entries that should point to b
97          entries ← {e for e in 1..2^(d.depth) if Prefix(e, b.depth) = b.prefix}
98          for e in entries: # insert b in all required entries of d.dir
99              d.dir[e] ← b

101 def ApplyPendingResize(DState_p d, Bucket_p bFull):
102     for j in 1..n:
103         if Prefix(help[j].op.key, bFull.depth) == bFull.prefix:
104             if bFull.state.results[j].seqnum < help[j].seqnum:
105                 # help[j] is a pending request that was applying to bFull
106                 # bDest is the destination of help[j] in the current state
107                 bDest = d.dir[ Prefix(help[j].op.key, d.depth) ]
108                 while bDest is full:
109                     (b0,b1) ← SplitBucket(bDest)
110                     DirectoryUpdate(d, (b0, b1))
111                     #update bDest based on the new state of the directory
112                     bDest ← d.dir[ Prefix(help[j].op.key, d.depth) ]
113                 bDest.state.results[j].status ← ExecOnBucket(bDest, help[j])
114                 bDest.state.results[j].seqnum ← help[j].seqnum

116 def ResizeWF():
117     for k in 1..2:
118         oldD ← ht
119         newD ← new DState(oldD) # copy of object oldD
120         for j in 1..n: # iterates over operations in help
121             b ← newD.dir[ Prefix(help[j].op.key, newD.depth) ]
122             if b is full and b.state.results[j].seqnum < help[j].seqnum:
123                 ApplyPendingResize(newD, b)
124         CAS(ht, oldD, newD)
```

**Figure 6: Code for the Resizable Hash Table.**

$T_2$ fail again. As such a scenario could keep happening, a thread that executes `ResizeWF()` executes all pending resize actions in the current state of the directory in order to ensure wait-freedom.

Consider now the following scenario where multiple threads run INSERT on a single bucket that is to be split. Assume that a thread $T_1$ applies an INSERT on a full bucket $b$ and so it calls `ResizeWF()`. At this time, it experiences some delay and in the meantime another thread $T_2$ executes resizing actions and replaces the full bucket $b$ with two new buckets. Thread $T_1$ would now have to apply its INSERT operation on one of the newly created buckets. However, suppose that other threads applied INSERT operations in the meantime, so that this new bucket is full again. In this case, the operation of thread $T_1$ would fail again and $T_1$ would have to execute another resize action using `ResizeWF()`, with the risk that the same thing would happen again. To prevent such a scenario, a thread creating a new bucket executes all pending updates directed to this bucket.

**Executing each operation exactly once.** Since INSERT operations may be executed through two different paths, namely during the execution of `ApplyWFOp()` (line 57) or during the execution of `ApplyPendingResize()` (line 113) which is called by `ResizeWF()` (line 123), we need a way to figure out when an operation has already been executed or is still pending. To this end, we use a per-thread sequence number *opSeqnum*. A thread $T_i$ tags each update operation it executes with a distinct sequence number (line 40). When an operation of $T_i$ has been successfully executed on a bucket $b$, its sequence number is copied into the entry $i$ of the `results` array associated with $b.state$, i.e., `results[i].seqnum` is the sequence number of the last update executed by $T_i$ on $b$.

The sequence number of the operations announced in `help[j]` (for some $j$) targeting a bucket $b$ is compared to the corresponding entry `b.state.results[j].seqnum` to determine whether the operation is pending. This test is made both in `ApplyWFOp()` (line 56) and in `ApplyPendingResize()` (line 104) to decide which operations to execute on the bucket.

Note that in `ApplyWFOp()`, a thread cannot solely rely on the toggle vector of the bucket to decide which operations to execute (line 55). Indeed, since a thread starts an update operation by registering its operation in the `help` array (line 40), there is a chance that its operation would be executed during a resizing action even before it calls `ApplyWFOp()` and flips its bit in the toggle vector (line 50). As such, the only safe way to identify pending updates is using the sequence numbers. The toggle vector associated with each bucket is used to improve performance: It allows to identify very fast potentially pending updates without having to read the whole `help` array in `ApplyWFOp()`.

**Detailed description of the resizing algorithm.** We now describe the `ResizeWF()` function in detail. After making a local copy of the directory state, a thread iterates over the `help` array to find *pending resize actions* (lines 120-122); specifically, the thread looks in `help` for pending update operations that apply to a full bucket. For each pending resize action, the thread calls `ApplyPendingResize()` with the corresponding bucket, *bFull*, as parameter.

In `ApplyPendingResize()`, a thread should run all pending updates that are to be applied to bucket *bFull*. To this end, it iterates over the help array to find the pending operations that apply to *bFull* (lines 102-104). For such an operation, it selects the bucket *bDest* on which the operation should be applied in the current local directory state (line 107). As long as *bDest* is full, it splits *bDest* into two buckets *b0* and *b1* (call to `SplitBucket()` line 109), updates the directory with the two new buckets calling `DirectoryUpdate()` (line 110), and updates *bDest* based on the new state of the directory (line 112). Finally, it executes the pending operation on bucket *bDest* and updates the sequence number in $bDest.state.results$ accordingly (lines 113-114).

We remark that *bDest* can be different from *bFull* when executing line 107. The first operation applied on *bFull* will split *bFull* and replace it by non-full buckets. Hence, for other operations targeting *bFull*, *bDest* should be set to point directly to the appropriate newly created bucket. Note also that buckets might have to be split several times before completing a single INSERT operation (lines 108-112). The reason is that when one full bucket $b$ is split into two new buckets $b0$ and $b1$, there is a chance that all items stored in $b$ should be moved to just one of the two new buckets. For instance, in Figure 1b, when splitting bucket 010, all items will be stored in bucket 0100, which thus should be split again.

Function `SplitBucket()` takes, as a parameter, a reference to a bucket $b$ of depth $D$ with prefix "$B_1B_2 \dots B_D$" and returns references to two new buckets $b_0$ and $b_1$ of depth $D+1$, with prefixes "$B_1B_2 \dots B_D0$" and "$B_1B_2 \dots B_D1$". Key-value pairs stored in the `BState` of $b$ are copied to the `BState` of $b0$ and $b1$ based on their prefix (lines 83-87). We recall that since $b$ is full, the algorithm guaranties that its `BState` is immutable. Note also that $b.state.results$ is copied in $b0$'s and $b1$'s state (line 79) so that the results of operations previously applied to $b$ are also available through $b0$ and $b1$. Finally, for each new bucket, its `applied` vector is initialized to be equal to its `toggle` vector (line 80): since all pending updates on the bucket are executed by the `ApplyPendingResize()` function, and since the bucket is not visible to other threads as long as the `CAS` instruction that updates the active directory has not been executed (line 124), its toggle vector should reflect no pending operations.

`DirectoryUpdate()` inserts in the directory the new buckets generated by `SplitBucket()`. The function doubles the size of the directory if needed, and stores the references of the new buckets in the appropriate entries of the directory. Although we do not detail all steps to be executed to double the size of the directory, the two main steps are: (i) allocating a new array corresponding to the new size of the directory (line 93), and (ii) copying all the bucket references from the previous array to the appropriate entries of the new array (line 94). Note that a new bucket might have to be inserted in more than one entry if the depth of the directory if bigger than the depth of the bucket (lines 97-99).

**Avoiding losing updates.** Our algorithm allows update operations on non-full buckets to run concurrently with resize actions. As pointed in Section 4.1, the two levels of indirection between the `DState` objects and the `BState` objects storing items ensure that updates are not lost in this case. Indeed, when a thread creates a new directory state during resizing, it copies the references of all existing buckets (line 119) in the new state. Since applying an update on a bucket $b$ only modifies the `BState` reference stored in $b.state$ (line 61), the newly created directory state will allow accessing the concurrently updated `BState` objects.

Note that since resizing requires full buckets to be immutable to avoid losing updates when running `SplitBucket()`, DELETE operations must not be executed on a full bucket (lines 64-65).

**Compliance with the design rules.** The described algorithm complies with the two design rules we have previously defined. (A) LOOKUP operations are executed without ever requiring any synchronization. The LOOKUP implementation is equivalent to a sequential implementation. (B) When no resize action is running, an update operation is executed by the instance of PSim of the corresponding bucket (function `ApplyWFOp()`) fully in parallel with operations applying to other buckets. The use of per-thread sequence numbers does not impair execution parallelism.

## 4.5 Merging buckets and shrinking the directory

We now provide a high level description of how our implementation copes with merging and shrinking. Merging buckets and shrinking the directory should both be run through the `ResizeWF()` function. Shrinking the directory can be implemented in the same way as doubling its size is done. Merging buckets is more complex. The basic idea is the same as for splitting: no update operations should be allowed to execute on buckets that can be merged (in order to avoid violating linearizability). However, there are two main differences between merging and splitting: (i) merging is applied to non-full buckets, and (ii) it involves more than one bucket.

To address the first point we use a mechanism to freeze a bucket, similarly to what is proposed in [19]. No update operations can be run on a frozen bucket even if it is not full. Instead, the thread willing to run an update operation on a frozen bucket should help running the merging action first. We have implemented freezing using a flag that is stored in the bucket state. The flag is modified by a thread using `ApplyWFOp()`. To address the second point, we perform merging in two steps: first, a thread tries to freeze all buckets involved in the merging, and then it calls `ResizeWF()` to perform the merging action.

Note that since the merging of buckets is done in several steps, it may fail: a thread may not manage to freeze all buckets involved in the merging action. The first reason why a thread may fail to freeze a bucket is that the bucket might be full. The second reason is that the bucket might be already frozen, e.g., because it is involved in another merging action. This might happen if two threads want to execute conflicting merging actions, for instance, one wants to create a bucket with prefix 001 and the other with prefix 0010. Since the two new buckets have a common prefix, the two merging actions involve overlapping sets of buckets. One of the two threads will not manage to freeze all required buckets for its action to take place. We remark that to avoid having both conflicting merge actions fail, all threads should freeze buckets in the same order. If a merge action fails, some buckets might have to be unfrozen. This operation is done during a directory update through the `ResizeWF()` function. It is determined by the user when merging will be triggered.

## 4.6 Corrrectness and Progress

When no resizing occurs, linearizability is proved following similar arguments as those used to prove PSim correct. When resizing occurs, we prove that: (1) each operation is executed exactly once, and (2) once an update operation has been executed, its modifications cannot be lost due to resizing. Due to lack of space, the full proof of correctness will be provided in the full version of the paper.

LOOKUP operations are obviously wait-free. Each INSERT operation calls at most two functions (`ApplyWFOp()` and `ResizeWF()`) that implement PSim. Since PSim is wait-free, it remains to show that functions called by these two functions execute a bounded number of instructions. PSim creates a copy of the state to manipulate. Hence, the code executed by any instance of PSim is sequential. Note that functions `ExecOnBucket()`, `SplitBucket()` and `DirectoryUpdate()` execute a bounded number of instructions. `ApplyWFOp()` calls `ExecOnBucket()` at most $n$ times. So, the total number of executed instructions is bounded in this case.

The loops at lines 120 and 102 imply that the upper bound on the number of calls to `ApplyPendingResize()` by `ResizeWF()` is $O(n^2)$. The number of instructions run by `ApplyPendingResize()` is bounded by the number of times a bucket should be split in order to apply its pending operations. We conclude that the total number of instructions executed is bounded.

## 5 IMPLEMENTATION

The description provided in Section 4 assumes that a garbage collector (GC) is available. As pointed out in previous studies [2, 10], memory management can have a severe impact on the performance of concurrent data structures. So, we paid special attention to this issue while we were implementing our algorithm. Specifically, we use an epoch-based non-blocking garbage collector [9]. It is based on thread-local counters that are incremented when a thread performs an operation. The value of these counters are checked periodically to decide when some released memory can safely be reused. The frequency at which counters are checked depends on the size of the thread-local batches that are used to store references to elements that have been released: when a batch becomes full, the counters are checked to see if previous batches can be released.

Our implementation has to be able to efficiently allocate bucket states (`BState`) since any update operation requires the allocation of a new `BState` record. We implemented thread-local memory pools (heaps) that are optimized to allocate memory blocks of the size of a `BState` record. We also implemented a mechanism to allow memory that has been released by the GC to be inserted back in these thread-local heaps.

To further improve the performance of our algorithm in practice, we apply an optimization to reduce the size of `BState` objects. Namely, we reduce the size of the *results* array by storing the actual results of the operations in a separate shared array and storing in the `BState` an array of integers corresponding to indices in this shared array. To obtain the result of its executing operation, a thread $i$ should read $results[i]$ in the `BState`, and then access the appropriate element of the shared array. This shared array is divided to non-overlapping blocks, one for each thread, so that each thread writes to its own block (with no need for synchronization).

We implemented the toggle vectors so that bits can be flipped efficiently using atomic `Add` (see [7]). Note also that when the `CAS` of lines 61 is successful, `ApplyWFOp()` can return immediately.

## 6 PERFORMANCE EVALUATION

### 6.1 Evaluated algorithms

We implemented our algorithm and the memory management component in C. The implementation allows activating or deactivating the use of local heaps for memory allocation. Our algorithm is called WF-Ext hereafter.

We compare the performance of WF-Ext with the performance of the lock-free implementations presented by Shalev and Shavit [21] (called LF-Split) and by Liu et al. [19] (called LF-Freeze). LF-Split is the reference implementation of the algorithm by Shalev and Shavit available online[4]. LF-Freeze is the C version of the code provided by the authors[5]. To ensure a fair comparison, we also created modified versions of these algorithms. A modified version is identified with the suffix -U. Specifically, for LF-Split, we removed the global counter, used for resizing decisions, that is accessed at the end of the execution of each update operation. Instead, resizing decisions are taken based on the size of individual buckets. For LF-Freeze, the original version of the authors only stored keys. We modified it to store key-value pairs. Also, in the original version, inserting a key that is already present implies no modification of the hash table. In our modified version, the value should be updated to comply with the semantics of the operations we described in Section 4. Note that this has a big impact on the performance results because with this semantic no INSERT boils down to a LOOKUP (This explains the differences between our graphs and the ones presented in [19]). Starting from these modified versions, we also implemented a version of each algorithm that uses our memory management component (marked with suffix -M). LF-Freeze-M uses fixed-size buckets (instead of varying size buckets) to better leverage our local heaps. In its original implementation, LF-Split relies on the system memory allocator, while LF-Freeze relies on its own epoch-based GC and does not use local heaps.

Our evaluation also includes a simple *blocking* non-resizable hash table (called Lock) where each bucket is protected using a lock and each operation on the bucket has to acquire this lock.

### 6.2 Experimental setup

We have performed experiments in two multiprocessor architectures: a 48-core machine equipped with 4 Intel Haswell-EX E7-4830-v3 processors and a 64-core machine equipped with 4 Intel Broadwell E7-4850-v4 processors. All experiments showed similar performance behavior in both machines. Hence, we only present the results of our experiments on the larger and newer 64-core machine. This machine features 256GB of RAM distributed over 4 NUMA nodes. The operating system is Linux with kernel 4.9.9 and the compiler is gcc 5.4. All codes are compiled at the maximum level of optimization. All tests were run 8 times with a 5-second duration per test. We present the average throughput over all runs.

As discussed in other studies, the underlying memory allocator has a big performance impact. All evaluations were run with two allocators: the *glibc* allocator and the TCMalloc allocator[6]. For each experiment and each algorithm, we display results for the allocator that provides the best throughput. Information about the selected allocator is provided in the legend of the graphs: "G" for the *glibc* allocator and "T" for TCMalloc. We also test the two main NUMA policies for physical memory allocation, that is *local* (named "L" in graphs' legends) and *interleave* (named "I"), and display the best result. The NUMA policy is enforced using the *numactl* program.

Several parameters can be configured for each algorithm, namely, the bucket size, the size of the batches used to store released memory records before running the Garbage Collector (GC), and the size of the thread-local heaps. We performed a wide range of experiments to identify parameters that suits all algorithms. We use these parameters throughout all experiments: buckets of size 8, GC batches of size 256, thread-local heaps of size 8.

Finally, in all experiments, the operations to be executed, as well as their parameter (the key), are randomly selected using the

[4] http://www.memoryhole.net/kyle/2011/06/02/

[5] https://github.com/mfs409/nonblocking/tree/master/tsx_acceleration/chash

[6] http://goog-perftools.sourceforge.net/doc/tcmalloc.html

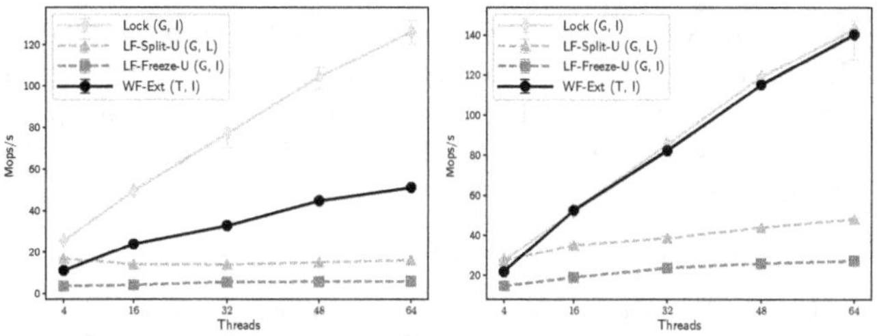


(a) 50% LookUp operations. (b) 90% LookUp operations.

**Figure 7: Directory-stable state throughput in the Intel 64-core machine using $1K$ items. No local heaps.**

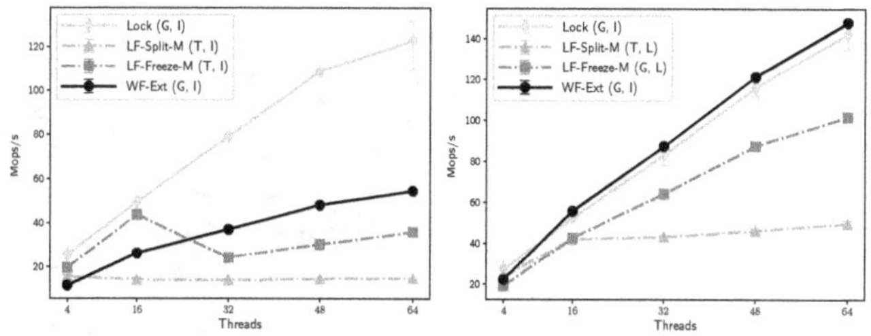


(a) 50% LookUp operations. (b) 90% LookUp operations.

**Figure 8: Directory-stable state throughput in the Intel 64-core machine, using $1K$ keys. With local heaps.**

TinyMT[7] pseudo-random number generator. This generator produces numbers with a uniform distribution.

## 6.3 Directory-stable performance

First, we study the performance of hash tables in the most common scenario, that is, when resizing is rare. More specifically, we evaluate the throughput of the implementations starting from a hash table where we have already inserted key-value pairs corresponding to half of the keys manipulated during the experiment and we run workloads with the same amount of Delete and Insert operations.

Our first test uses $1K$ keys. Figures 7a and 7b correspond to loads with 50% and 90% of LookUp operations, respectively. The rest of the operations are equally divided between Insert and Delete. The figures compare the performance of our wait-free algorithm with the performance of the two modified lock-free algorithms LF-Split-U and LF-Freeze-U, when relying on the underlying system memory allocator (*glibc* malloc or TCMalloc) for memory allocation. We choose to display LF-Split-U because it constantly outperforms the original LF-Split algorithm (which confirms the importance of rule (B)). We choose to display LF-Freeze-U because a comparison with LF-Freeze would not be fair due to the differences in the implementation of Insert (see Section 6.1).

In Figure 7, our hash table outperforms the two lock-free algorithms. The high throughput of our algorithm is mostly due to highly efficient LookUpThis is confirmed by the large improvement observed when increasing the percentage of LookUps to 90%. We attribute the lower performance of the two lock-free algorithms to different factors. Specifically, for LF-Split-U, the reason is twofold: (i) the algorithm does not comply with design rule (A), implying less efficient LookUp operations in this case; (ii) the buckets are implemented as lists of items, which makes item search less efficient than with buckets implemented as arrays. In the case of LF-Freeze-U the main reason we identified for the lower performance is that the bucket size is not fixed. It is adapted to the number of items to store. Since a new bucket should be allocated for each update operation, it creates an unfriendly workload for the memory allocation system.

Figure 8 presents the same experiment as in Figure 7, this time using both our GC and the local heaps for all non-blocking algorithms (-M suffix). This figure shows that even when compared using the exact same memory management component, WF-Ext is more efficient than the lock-free algorithms. In this experiment, with 90% LookUps, our algorithm is up to 47% better than the second best non-blocking algorithm. Still, the performance of LF-Freeze-M shows that using our memory management component and fixed-size buckets greatly improves the performance of LF-Freeze. On the other hand, LF-Split does not benefit from using local heaps.

To assess the performance of our algorithm when storing a larger number of items, Figure 9 presents the same experiment as in Figure 8, this time when keys are selected among $256K$ keys. For the sake of completeness, we present the performance of two versions of each lock-free algorithm. For LF-Split, we present the original version and LF-Split-U (LF-Split-M is not considered because it does not reach the performance of LF-Split-U). For the other algorithm, we present both LF-Freeze-U and LF-Freeze-M.

Compared to the algorithms described in the related work (original algorithms or -U versions), the performance of our algorithm is again by far the best. It even outperforms the lock-based hash-table when the percentage of LookUps is high. The high performance of LF-Freeze-M demonstrates that the algorithm proposed by Liu et al. can benefit from the modifications we suggest to efficiently manage memory allocation. Once memory management issues are solved, LF-Freeze-M outperforms WF-Ext because its update operations are less complex since it implements a weaker progress condition.

The fact that WF-Ext outperforms all lock-free implementations when the hash table has a small number of buckets can be surprising, especially since existing wait-free resizable hash tables are performing much worse than their lock-free counterparts [19]. This result is due to the use of the PSim universal construction [7]. Indeed, PSim performs especially well on contented objects since it employs the technique of *combining* the operations of different threads that are applied to the same object [12].

## 6.4 Resizing efficiency

To evaluate resizing performance, we run a test where the hash table starts with only 2 buckets. Multiple threads start inserting items randomly, and we measure the time it takes for the hash table to reach its final size. To have a more realistic workload, threads also execute LookUp operations on the items with a 50% probability. Figure 10a presents the results. Note that to make the figure readable, we use log scales on both axis.

[7]https://github.com/MersenneTwister-Lab/TinyMT

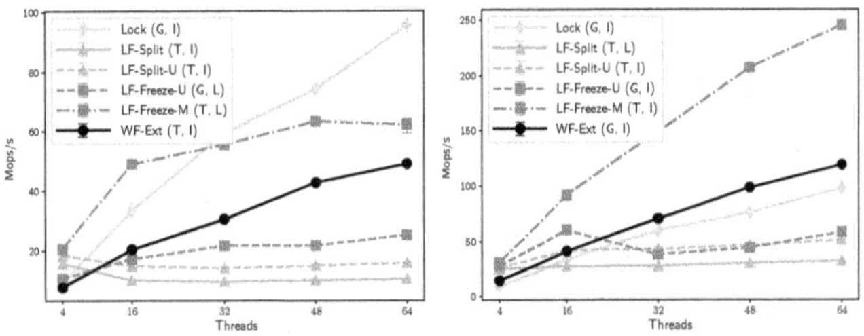


(a) 50% LookUp operations. (b) 90% LookUp operations.

**Figure 9: Directory-stable state throughput in the Intel 64-core machine, using $256K$ keys.**

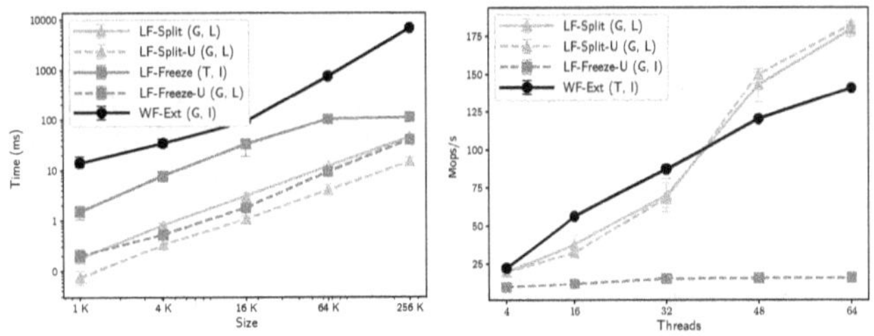


(a) Resizing efficiency (b) Throughput of 5-second runs with 1k items

**Figure 10: Performance with Resizing. Tests with 64 threads**

The figure shows that the resizing performance of our algorithm is much lower than that of evaluated lock-free algorithms. However, the experiment of Figure 10b illustrates that WF-Ext still performs well under resizing, if the cost of resizing is amortized over long runs. In this experiment, we evaluate the throughput on a 5-second run when starting from a hash table with 2 buckets and manipulating $1K$ items in a load with 90% LookUp and 10% Insert operations. In this case, WF-Ext reaches the same throughput as when resizing actions are rare (Figure 8b). Thus, in sufficiently long runs the performance impact of resizing is not significant. We note that LF-Split achieves much better performance than in previous experiments. Indeed, in this test, LookUps for LF-Split are more efficient since no item is ever deleted, confirming the validity of design rule (A).

# 7 CONCLUSION

This paper presents a resizable wait-free hash table based on extendible hashing. The design of our algorithm is based on two design rules that aim at preserving the natural parallelism of concurrent hashing in the most common case, that is, when no resizing action occurs. Leveraging several instances of the PSim universal construction to ensure wait-freedom, our implementation achieves unprecedented performance for a wait-free resizable hash table. More generally, our approach provides a new trade-off in the performance of resizable hash tables. Namely, experiments run on large multicore architectures, show that, at the cost of more expensive resizing actions, our algorithm largely outperforms lock-free hash tables described in related studies when resizing actions are rare, while providing a stronger progress guarantee.

# ACKNOWLEDGMENTS

Part of this work has received funding from the European Union's Horizon 2020 research and innovation programme under grant agreement No 671578. The authors would like to thank Darko Petrović and André Schiper for following the initial stages of this work and providing feedback.

# REFERENCES

[1] S. Boyd-Wickizer, A. T. Clements, Y. Mao, A. Pesterev, M. F. Kaashoek, R. Morris, and N. Zeldovich. An analysis of linux scalability to many cores. In *Proceedings of the 9th USENIX Conference on Operating Systems Design and Implementation*, OSDI'10, pages 1–16, 2010.

[2] T. David, R. Guerraoui, and V. Trigonakis. Asynchronized concurrency: The secret to scaling concurrent search data structures. In *Proceedings of the Twentieth International Conference on Architectural Support for Programming Languages and Operating Systems*, ASPLOS '15, pages 631–644, 2015.

[3] C. S. Ellis. Extendible hashing for concurrent operations and distributed data. In *Proceedings of the 2Nd ACM SIGACT-SIGMOD Symposium on Principles of Database Systems*, pages 106–116, 1983.

[4] R. J. Enbody and H. C. Du. Dynamic hashing schemes. *ACM Computing Surveys*, 20(2), July 1988.

[5] R. Fagin, J. Nievergelt, N. Pippenger, and H. R. Strong. Extendible hashing – a fast access method for dynamic files. *ACM Transactions on Database Systems*, 4(3):315–344, Sept. 1979.

[6] P. Fatourou and N. D. Kallimanis. Revisiting the combining synchronization technique. In *Proceedings of the 17th ACM SIGPLAN symposium on Principles and Practice of Parallel Programming*, 2012.

[7] P. Fatourou and N. D. Kallimanis. Highly-efficient wait-free synchronization. *Theory of Computing Systems*, pages 1–46, 2013.

[8] S. Feldman, P. LaBorde, and D. Dechev. Concurrent multi-level arrays: Wait-free extensible hash maps. In *International Conference on Embedded Computer Systems: Architectures, Modeling, and Simulation*, pages 155–163, 2013.

[9] K. Fraser. *Practical Lock-Freedom*. PhD thesis, University of Cambridge, 2004.

[10] V. Gramoli. More than you ever wanted to know about synchronization: Synchrobench, measuring the impact of the synchronization on concurrent algorithms. In *Proceedings of the 20th ACM SIGPLAN Symposium on Principles and Practice of Parallel Programming*, PPoPP 2015, 2015.

[11] M. Greenwald. Two-handed emulation: How to build non-blocking implementations of complex data-structures using dcas. In *Proceedings of the 21st Annual Symposium on Principles of Distributed Computing*, PODC '02, 2002.

[12] D. Hendler, I. Incze, N. Shavit, and M. Tzafrir. Flat combining and the synchronization-parallelism tradeoff. In *Proceedings of the 22nd ACM symposium on Parallelism in algorithms and architectures*, 2010.

[13] M. Herlihy. Wait-free synchronization. *ACM Transactions on Programming Languages and Systems*, 13(1):124–149, Jan. 1991.

[14] M. Herlihy and N. Shavit. *The Art of Multiprocessor Programming*. Morgan Kaufmann Publishers Inc., 2008.

[15] M. Herlihy and J. Wing. Linearizability: a correctness condition for concurrent objects. *ACM Transactions on Programming Languages and Systems*, 12(3):463–492, July 1990.

[16] L. Jenkins, T. Zhou, and M. Spear. Redesigning Go's Built-In Map to Support Concurrent Operations. In *26th International Conference on Parallel Architectures and Compilation Techniques (PACT)*, 2017.

[17] A. Kogan and E. Petrank. A methodology for creating fast wait-free data structures. In *Proceedings of the 17th ACM SIGPLAN Symposium on Principles and Practice of Parallel Programming*, PPoPP '12, 2012.

[18] D. Lea. Package util.concurrent release 1.3.4 (2003). http://gee.cs.oswego.edu/dl/classes/EDU/oswego/cs/dl/util/concurrent/intro.html.

[19] Y. Liu, K. Zhang, and M. Spear. Dynamic-sized Nonblocking Hash Tables. In *Proceedings of the 2014 ACM Symposium on Principles of Distributed Computing*, PODC '14, 2014.

[20] M. M. Michael. High performance dynamic lock-free hash tables and list-based sets. In *Proceedings of the 14th Annual ACM Symposium on Parallel Algorithms and Architectures*, SPAA '02, 2002.

[21] O. Shalev and N. Shavit. Split-ordered lists: Lock-free extensible hash tables. *Journal of the ACM*, 53(3):379–405, 2006.

[22] N. Shavit. Data structures in the multicore age. *Communications of the ACM*, 54(3):76–84, Mar. 2011.

[23] J. Triplett, P. E. McKenney, and J. Walpole. Resizable, scalable, concurrent hash tables via relativistic programming. In *USENIX Annual Technical Conference*, 2011.

# Lock-free Contention Adapting Search Trees

Kjell Winblad
Uppsala Univeristy
kjell.winblad@it.uu.se

Konstantinos Sagonas
Uppsala Univeristy
konstantinos.sagonas@it.uu.se

Bengt Jonsson
Uppsala Univeristy
bengt.jonsson@it.uu.se

## ABSTRACT

Concurrent key-value stores with range query support are crucial for the scalability and performance of many applications. Existing lock-free data structures of this kind use a fixed synchronization granularity. Using a fixed synchronization granularity in a concurrent key-value store with range query support is problematic as the best performing synchronization granularity depends on a number of factors that are difficult to predict, such as the level of contention and the number of items that are accessed by range queries. We present the first lock-free key-value store with linearizable range query support that dynamically adapts its synchronization granularity. This data structure is called the lock-free contention adapting search tree (LFCA tree). An LFCA tree does local adaptations of its synchronization granularity based on heuristics that take contention and the performance of range queries into account. We show that the operations of LFCA trees are linearizable, that the lookup operation is wait-free, and that the remaining operations (insert, remove and range query) are lock-free. Our experimental evaluation shows that LFCA trees achieve more than twice the throughput of related lock-free data structures in many scenarios. Furthermore, LFCA trees are able to perform substantially better than data structures with a fixed synchronization granularity over a wide range of scenarios due to their ability to adapt to the scenario at hand.

## CCS CONCEPTS

• **Software and its engineering → Concurrent programming structures**; • **Information systems →** *Unidimensional range search*; *Key-value stores*;

## KEYWORDS

concurrent data structures, range queries, lock-freedom, adaptivity, linearizability

**ACM Reference Format:**

Kjell Winblad, Konstantinos Sagonas, and Bengt Jonsson. 2018. Lock-free Contention Adapting Search Trees. In *SPAA '18: 30th ACM Symposium on Parallelism in Algorithms and Architectures, July 16–18, 2018, Vienna, Austria.* ACM, New York, NY, USA, 12 pages. https://doi.org/10.1145/3210377.3210413


ACM ISBN 978-1-4503-5799-9/18/07...$15.00
https://doi.org/10.1145/3210377.3210413

## 1 INTRODUCTION

On multicore machines, concurrent key-value stores (maps) with range query support are crucial for the scalability of applications such as big scale data processing and in-memory databases (e.g., Google's F1 [21] and Yahoo's Flurry [24]). It is thus of no surprise that the multicore revolution has motivated a number of data structures of this type, e.g., [1, 2, 4, 17]. A key-value store represents a set of items (keys), each with an associated value. Sets can be seen as a simplification of key-value stores that do not have any values associated with the items. From here on, we will discuss sets but we note that what applies to sets also applies to key-value stores as sets can trivially be modified to become key-value stores.

Concurrent sets that support both single-item operations (insert, remove and lookup[1]) and multi-item operations (e.g., range query and clone[2]) face the following dilemma: Single-item operations usually benefit from as fine-grained synchronization as possible, as this leads to few conflicts. In contrast, multi-item operations usually benefit from more coarse-grained synchronization, as this leads to less time spent on synchronization-related overhead (e.g., fewer locks need to be acquired). We say that the *conflict time* for an operation is the amount of the time during which the operation can conflict with other concurrent operations. More coarse-grained synchronization can also lead to short conflict times for operations in concurrent sets that internally use and exploit immutable data in a way that we will now explain. We will use the lock-free $k$-ary search tree [4] to illustrate how immutable data can be used to make the conflict time for range queries short. Lock-free $k$-ary search trees store all items inside immutable leaf nodes that can contain $k$ items each. The insert and remove operations of such trees work by replacing leaf nodes. A range query $Q$ in a $k$-ary search tree first collects all the immutable leaf nodes that $Q$ needs. The range query $Q$ ends its conflict time and linearizes once this collection phase finishes. The items that $Q$ needs to return are scanned from the collected leaf nodes after $Q$'s conflict time. This removal of this scanning from the conflict time is possible due to the immutability of the leaf nodes.

An even more extreme way to exploit immutability in range queries is to store all items in a single immutable data structure. Such a data structure, that we call *Im-Tr*, is constructed from a single mutable reference pointing to an immutable balanced search tree $T$. A new instance of $T$ reflecting an update (insert or remove) can be constructed in $O(\log n)$ time (where $n$ is the number of items before the update) as one only needs to "copy" nodes on a path from the root to a leaf to create the new instance [12]. The insert and remove operations of *Im-Tr* change the mutable reference using an atomic

[1] An insert operation inserts an item (replacing an existing item if one with an equal key already exists), the remove operation removes an item with the given key if such an item exists and the lookup operation returns an item with the given key if such an item exists.

[2] A range query operation returns all items with keys within the given range (specified by two keys) and clone makes a clone of the data structure.

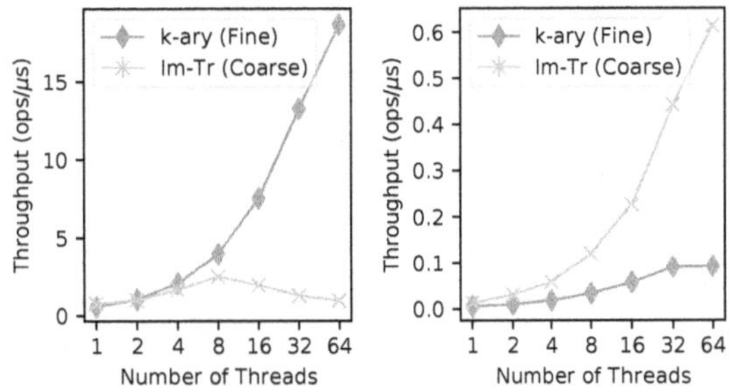


(a) Using small range queries (b) Using large range queries

**Figure 1: Throughput of coarse- vs fine-grained synchronization.**

compare-and-swap (CAS) operation so the reference points to a new immutable instance reflecting the update. Using this scheme, which is also described by Herlihy [9], it is trivial to perform range queries with constant conflict time as they only need to get a snapshot by reading the mutable reference and then perform the range query in the snapshot.

Figure 1[3] illustrates the scalability of a data structure that uses a fixed relatively fine-grained synchronization (the lock-free $k$-ary search tree [4] with the $k$ parameter set to 64) and one that uses coarse-grained synchronization (*Im-Tr*) in two scenarios that only differ in the sizes of the ranges involved in the range queries. As shown in the graphs, fine-grained synchronization achieves superior scalability when the size of ranges in range queries is small (Fig. 1a) as the mutable reference of *Im-Tr* gets heavily contended, while *Im-Tr* with coarse-grained synchronization has superior scalability when range queries are large (Fig. 1b) as the $k$-ary search tree's range queries have long conflict times in this scenario.

As the above example illustrates, having concurrent sets with a fixed synchronization granularity is far from ideal. A natural way to deal with this problem is to design sets that can adapt their synchronization granularity to the workload at hand. In earlier work [17], we have described the first data structure that dynamically changes its synchronization granularity based on heuristics that take both the performance of single-item operations and multi-item operations into account, called the contention adapting search tree (*CA tree* for short). The CA tree is lock-based.

The lock-based CA tree performs well in a variety of scenarios due to its ability to adapt its synchronization granularity to the workload at hand. However, lock-based data structures are prone to a number of problems that are inherent from the use of locks, e.g., waiting, priority inversion, convoying, and lock overhead (memory usage, acquire and release time). The performance of lock-based algorithms is also heavily dependent on the lock implementation itself and on scheduling. For all these reasons, lock-free data structures that guarantee system-wide progress even in the presence of adversary scheduling can be preferable to lock-based ones. Furthermore, it is crucial with a wait-free (i.e., makes progress within a bounded number of steps) lookup operation for applications where lookups are very common, which the lock-based CA tree is lacking.

[3]The benchmark used to produce the graphs in Fig. 1 was executed on an Intel machine with 64 logical cores using the Oracle JVM. With small and large range queries we refer to range queries that on average include about 2.5 items and $25k$ items respectively. Further details about the experiment can be found in Section 7.

This paper presents a lock-free variant of the CA tree, called the *lock-free contention adapting search tree* (*LFCA tree* for short). LFCA trees support lock-free insert, remove and range query operations as well as a wait-free lookup operation. Operations update the data stored in an LFCA tree by swapping immutable leaf nodes pointing to immutable balanced search trees storing the actual items. The granularity of the LFCA tree is adjusted by splitting and joining such leaf nodes that also store a statistics value which is updated based on CAS successes or failures as well as based on the number of leaf nodes range queries need to access.

The technique that the LFCA tree uses for supporting range queries is interesting in its own right as it is applicable to other lock-free data structures such as the lock-free k-ary search tree [4]. A range query operation is performed by replacing the needed leaf nodes with nodes of a special node type that contains the information needed by other threads to help in completing the operation. The previously proposed method for doing range queries in the k-ary search tree [4] is prone to starvation [2, 22].

Overall, we claim that LFCA trees are important concurrent data structures as they provide an unique set of desirable properties:

**Efficient non-blocking operations** Our experimental comparison shows that LFCA trees achieve substantially better throughput than the best of the competing lock-free data structures over a wide range of scenarios. Also, LFCA trees perform better than lock-based CA trees in many scenarios (especially in scenarios with more threads than hardware threads).

**Configuration-less** As an LFCA tree automatically adjusts its structure using heuristics, there is no need for the user to configure the LFCA tree to use a certain synchronization granularity.

**Adaptive** As the synchronization granularity changes with the workload, the data structure can perform very well even when the workload changes during the lifetime of the data structure. As the adaptations of the granularity happen through local changes, the data structure can even adapt to scenarios where the workload is different in different parts of the data structure.

**Flexible** Performance characteristics of an LFCA tree can be changed by providing a different set implementation. We do not experiment with this property, but see no reason why the LFCA tree would be different from the lock-based CA tree in this regard [17].

*Outline:* We start with a high level description of how LFCA trees work and an overview of related work (Section 3) before we describe the algorithm in detail (Section 4) and give a proof sketch (Section 5). An optimization for range queries is described (Section 6) before we experimentally evaluate the LFCA tree (Section 7) and conclude the paper (Section 8).

## 2 A BIRD'S EYE VIEW OF LFCA TREES

A lock-free CA tree consists of *route nodes* (round boxes in Fig. 2a) and *base nodes* (square shaped boxes in Fig. 2a). The route nodes form a binary search tree with the base nodes as leaves. The actual items that are stored in the set represented by an LFCA tree are located in immutable data structures rooted in the base nodes, called *leaf containers*. All operations use the binary search tree property of the route nodes to find the base node(s) whose leaf container(s) should contain the items involved in the operation if they exist. An update operation (insert or remove) is illustrated

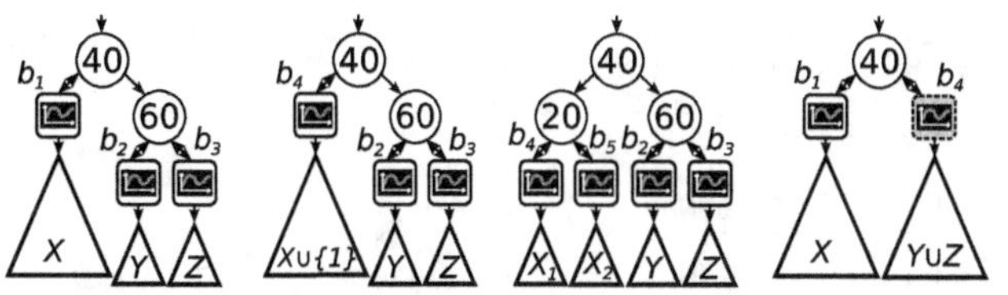
(a) Initial (b) Update: insert (c) Adaptation: split (d) Adaptation: join

**Figure 2: LFCA Trees illustrating various operations.**

by Figs. 2a and 2b. An update operation uses a compare-and-swap (CAS) to attempt to replace a base node $b_1$ with a new base node $b_4$ reflecting the update, until the update succeeds. The update can be made efficient even though the data structure in the base node is immutable, since many immutable balanced tree data structures (e.g., red-black trees and treaps) support creating a new instance with an update in $O(\log n)$ time, where $n$ is the number of items in the data structure [12, 19]. Before an update operation returns it checks whether the statistics value stored in the updated base node indicates that a structural adaptation should happen. The first kind of adaptation, called *split*, is illustrated by Figs. 2a and 2c. A split aims at reducing the contention in the LFCA tree and replaces a base node $b_1$ with a route node linking together two new base nodes ($b_4$ and $b_5$) so that approximately half of the original items are in each of them. The second kind of adaptation, called *join*, is illustrated with Figs. 2a and 2d and aims at optimizing the structure of the LFCA tree for range queries that span multiple base nodes and for situations where the contention is low. A join splices out a base node $b_2$ and its parent and replaces the base node $b_3$ with a new base node $b_4$ containing the items of both $b_2$ and $b_3$. Splits and joins of the base nodes can also be supported efficiently (i.e., in $O(\log n)$ time, where $n$ is the number of items in the involved instances) in many immutable balanced tree data structures (e.g., treaps [19] that are used by our LFCA tree implementation).

## 3 RELATED WORK

There are several data structures with range query support. The *SnapTree* by Bronson *et al.* [3] has an efficient linearizable clone operation that returns a copy of the data structure from which a range query operation can easily be derived. *SnapTree*'s clone operation waits for active update operations to complete and forces subsequent update operations to copy nodes lazily before node modifications, so that the clone is not modified.

The lock-free $k$-ary search tree is an external (i.e. the items are stored in leaf nodes) unbalanced search tree with up to $k$ keys stored in every node [5]. Range queries in $k$-ary search trees are performed by doing a read scan and a validation scan of the immutable leaf nodes containing items in the range [4]. The range query operation needs to retry if the validation scan fails. The $k$-ary search tree is an example of the fixed synchronization granularity approach discussed in the introduction. Another example of this approach based on software transactional memory is the Leaplist [1]. Both the $k$-ary search tree and the Leaplist make use of immutable data structures to reduce the conflict time of range queries in the way explained in the introduction. As they both use arrays as their immutable data structures, updates become very expensive when the parameter that decides both the synchronization granularity and the maximum size of the immutable data structures is set too high. Even though this problem could be fixed by using immutable balanced search trees instead of the arrays, they would still use a fixed synchronization granularity and would thus only perform well in certain scenarios.

Chatterjee has proposed a general method for performing range queries in lock-free ordered set data structures [6] based on an idea for doing snapshots by Petrank and Timnat [14]. Chatterjee's method makes use of a list of so-called range collector objects that all updates and range queries need to access. Unfortunately, the scalability of Chatterjee's method suffers from a global sequential hot spot in the list of range-collector objects that all range queries have to modify in the worst case.

The *KiWi* data structure by Basin *et al.* [2] supports wait-free range queries and lookup operations as well as lock-free update operations. Update operations help range queries by storing additional versions of inserted items when it is needed for the range queries. Similarly to Robertson's data structure [15], *KiWi*'s range queries atomically increment a global version counter which is used by update operations to decide whether storing an additional version for an item is necessary. *KiWi*'s global version number counter is bound to become a scalability bottleneck with a high enough level of parallel range queries. LFCA trees do not suffer from such global scalability bottleneck as their range query operation only need to synchronize with update operations that operate on items in the same range as the range query.

The above non-adaptive set data structures with support for efficient range queries and scalable updates [1, 2, 4, 6, 15, 16] have range queries with a conflict time that depends at least linearly on the number of items covered by the range given to the range query. The CA trees (both the lock-based and the lock-free) can do much better over a wide range of scenarios as the conflict time of their range queries can be constant (i.e., independent of the number of items covered by the range query) and their heuristics work towards getting a good trade-off between range queries conflict time and the scalability of updates.

Even though the fundamental ideas behind the lock-based CA tree [17] and LFCA tree are the same, lock-freedom gives LFCA trees better progress guarantees that are of importance for real-time systems. The lookup operation of LFCA trees is wait-free and can thus perform efficiently regardless of how contended the data structure is, which is crucial for many applications as lookups often dominate the workload. Still, the lock-based CA tree has a few advantages over LFCA tree. The use of locks makes it possible to use mutable sequential data structures to store the items. This can be advantageous in systems where memory management is expensive and when range queries are infrequent, as it reduces the number of memory allocations that are needed. The use of locks also makes it easier to extend the interface of the data structure with more linearizable operations.

The technique for joining base nodes in LFCA trees has some similarities with the replace operation of non-blocking Patricia tries [20]. The replace operation deletes an item and adds another item in a way that appears atomic. Our join is simpler, as a single thread can "mark" the involved nodes in a non-collaborative fashion, since other threads can abort the join without affecting correctness.

Several works have previously explored the idea of dynamically switching between a data structure that uses coarse-grained synchronization to a data structure that use fine-grained synchronization in one transformation step [7, 11, 13]. The drawback of the global mode switching approach proposed in these papers compared to LFCA tree's approach is that the switch between the modes is time-consuming and coarse-grained, whereas the LFCA tree can smoothly transition between different levels of synchronization granularity. Work has also been done to adapt to contention in other types of data structures (e.g., [8]).

## 4 ALGORITHM

Pseudo-code for all the non-trivial parts of the lock-free CA tree can be found in Figs. 3 to 5 and 7. The pseudo-code is derived from a model of the lock-free CA tree implemented in the C programming language with some minor adjustments for readability. This section contains a detailed description of the algorithm and the pseudo-code. In the next section, a detailed proof sketch will be given, showing that the operations are linearizable and have the stated progress guarantees.

*Node types.* A lock-free CA tree is built from instances of the node types that are defined in Fig. 3, lines 14–52. Note that the keyword `with_fields_from` (on lines 26, 32 and 39) is used to add fields from another `struct` definition. All internal route nodes are of type `route_node` (lines 14–20). The route nodes contain a key field (line 15) which is used to direct searches for a specific item in the tree. Together, they form a binary search tree. Leaves are called base nodes (lines 21–42) and have a `data` field (line 22) that points to immutable data structure instances (called *leaf containers*) that contain the items that are in the represented set. That a base node $B$ is of type `normal_base` (lines 21-25) indicates that $B$ is not involved in an ongoing operation. A base node of type `range_base` is a node that currently is or has been involved in a range query. Similarly, a base node of type `join_main` or `join_neighbor` is a node that currently is or has been involved in a join operation.

Data in nodes that can be modified by more than one thread are marked with the modifier `atomic`. These fields can only be accessed by the atomic and sequentially consistent functions `aload` (that loads the value at a given address), `astore` (that stores the given value at the given address) and `CAS` (a compare-and-swap that stores the value of its third parameter at the location of a given address (first parameter) iff the value at the given address is equal to the second parameter and returns true, or returns false otherwise).

*Lookup.* The wait-free lookup operation (lines 135–138) calls the `find_base_node` function (pseudo-code for this and other similar functions appears in an extended version of this paper [23]), which traverses the route nodes using binary search until a base node is found, and then performs the lookup in the corresponding immutable data structure.

*Insert and Remove.* The functions for inserting and removing a single item (Fig. 4, lines 129–134) are performed by the `do_update` function (lines 106–127) with the remove or insert function and the item in question as arguments. The `do_update` function searches for a base node using the given key, and then tries to replace that base node and its leaf container with a new one in which the key

```
1  // Constants
2  #define CONT_CONTRIB      250        // For adaptation
3  #define LOW_CONT_CONTRIB  1          // ...
4  #define RANGE_CONTRIB     100        // ...
5  #define HIGH_CONT         1000       // ...
6  #define LOW_CONT          -1000      // ...
7  #define NOT_FOUND         (node*)1 // Special pointers
8  #define NOT_SET           (treap*)1// ...
9  #define PREPARING         (node*)0 // Used for join
10 #define DONE              (node*)1 // ...
11 #define ABORTED           (node*)2 // ...
12 enum contention_info { contended, uncontened, noinfo }
13 // Data Structures
14 struct route_node {
15   int key;                          // Split key
16   atomic node* left;                // < key
17   atomic node* right;               // >= key
18   atomic bool valid = true;         // Used for join
19   atomic node* join_id = NULL; // ...
20 }
21 struct normal_base {
22   treap* data = NULL;   // Items in the set
23   int stat = 0;         // Statistics variable
24   node* parent = NULL; // Parent node or NULL (root)
25 }
26 struct join_main with_fields_from normal_base {
27   node* neigh1;  // First (not joined) neighbor base
28   atomic node* neigh2 = PREPARING; // Joined n...
29   node* gparent; // Grand parent
30   node* otherb;  // Other branch
31 }
32 struct join_neighbor with_fields_from normal_base {
33   node* main_node   // The main node for the join
34 }
35 struct rs { // Result storage for range queries
36   atomic treap* result = NOT_SET; // The result
37   atomic bool more_than_one_base = false;
38 }
39 struct range_base with_fields_from normal_base {
40   int lo; int hi; // Low and high key
41   rs* storage;
42 }
43 enum node_type {
44   route, normal, join_main, join_neighbor, range
45 }
46 struct node with_fields_from normal_base, range_base,
47                              join_main, join_neighbor{
48   node_type type;
49 }
50 struct lfcat{
51   atomic node* root;
52 }
53 // Help functions
54 bool try_replace(lfcat* m, node* b, node* new_b){
55   if( b->parent == NULL )
56     return CAS(&m->root, b, new_b);
57   else if(aload(&b->parent->left) == b)
58     return CAS(&b->parent->left, b, new_b);
59   else if(aload(&b->parent->right) == b)
60     return CAS(&b->parent->right, b, new_b);
61   else return false;
62 }
63 bool is_replaceable(node* n) {
64   return (n->type == normal ||
65           (n->type == join_main &&
66            aload(&n->neigh2) == ABORTED) ||
67           (n->type == join_neighbor &&
68            (aload(&n->main_node->neigh2) == ABORTED ||
69             aload(&n->main_node->neigh2) == DONE)) ||
70           (n->type == range &&
71            aload(&n->storage->result) != NOT_SET));
72 }
```

**Figure 3: Data structures and help functions.**

```
73  // Help functions
74  void help_if_needed(lfcatree* t, node* n){
75    if(n->type == join_neighbor) n = n->main_node;
76    if(n->type == join_main &&
77       aload(&n->neigh2) == PREPARING){
78      CAS(&n->neigh2, PREPARING, ABORTED);
79    }else if(n->type == join_main &&
80            aload(&n->neigh2) > ABORTED){
81      complete_join(t, n);
82    }else if(n->type == range &&
83            aload(&n->storage->result) == NOT_SET){
84      all_in_range(t, n->lo, n->hi, n->storage);
85    }
86  }
87  int new_stat(node* n, contention_info info){
88    int range_sub = 0;
89    if(n->type == range &&
90       aload(&n->storage->more_than_one_base))
91      range_sub = RANGE_CONTRIB;
92    if (info == contended && n->stat <= HIGH_CONT) {
93      return n->stat + CONT_CONTRIB - range_sub;
94    }else if(info == uncontened && n->stat >= LOW_CONT){
95      return n->stat - LOW_CONT_CONTRIB - range_sub;
96    }else return n->stat;
97  }
98  void adapt_if_needed(lfcatree* t, node* b){
99    if(!is_replaceable(b)) return;
100   else if(new_stat(b, noinfo) > HIGH_CONT)
101     high_contention_adaptation(t, b);
102   else if(new_stat(b, noinfo) < LOW_CONT)
103     low_contention_adaptation(t, b);
104 }
105
106 bool do_update(lfcatree* m,
107                treap*(*u)(treap*,int,bool*), int i){
108   contention_info cont_info = uncontened;
109   while(true){
110     node* base = find_base_node(aload(&m->root), i);
111     if(is_replaceable(base)){
112       bool res;
113       node* newb = new node{
114         type = normal,
115         parent = base->parent,
116         data = u(base->data, i, &res),
117         stat = new_stat(base, cont_info)
118       }
119       if(try_replace(m, base, newb)){
120         adapt_if_needed(m, newb);
121         return res;
122       }
123     }
124     cont_info = contended;
125     help_if_needed(m, base);
126   }
127 }
128 // Public interface
129 bool insert(lfcat* m, int i){
130   return do_update(m, treap_insert, i);
131 }
132 bool remove(lfcat* m, int i){
133   return do_update(m, treap_remove, i);
134 }
135 bool lookup(lfcat* m, int i){
136   node* base = find_base_node(aload(&m->root), i);
137   return treap_lookup(base->data, i);
138 }
139 void query(lfcat* m, int lo, int hi,
140            void (*trav)(int, void*), void* aux){
141   treap* result = all_in_range(m, lo, hi, NULL);
142   treap_query(result, lo, hi, trav, aux);
143 }
```

**Figure 4: Help functions and public interface.**

has been removed or inserted (lines 113–119). The replacement is done using the `try_replace` function, which uses a CAS to attempt to change the pointer of the base node's parent to a new base node with the updated leaf container. If successful, the CAS operation is the linearization point of the operation; if unsuccessful, the whole operation is retried. A replacement attempt is made only if the found base node is replaceable (line 111 and lines 63–72). If the base node is irreplaceable, then it may be involved in another operation; in this case `do_update` will first attempt to help this operation (line 125 and lines 74–86) before proceeding.

Note that the new base node gets a value for its `stat` field which is based on the replaced node's `stat` field and type as well as on whether conflicting operations have been detected (i.e., a base node which was not replaceable has been found or a `try_replace` call has failed; see line 117 and lines 87–97). Once a base node has been successfully replaced, the update operation calls `adapt_if_needed` to adapt the granularity of the data structure if the heuristics suggests that this is beneficial (line 120 and lines 98–104), before returning.

*Range queries.* The range query operation (lines 139–143) first calls `all_in_range` (line 141) to create a snapshot of all base nodes in the requested range and then traverses the snapshot to complete the range query (line 142). The function `all_in_range` (lines 162–215) goes through all base nodes that may contain items in the range in ascending key order, starting with the base node containing the smallest keys, to replace them, using a CAS, by base nodes of another type. The base nodes are found by the functions `find_base_stack` and `find_next_base_stack` in a depth-first traversal of the concerned portion of the tree. This traversal uses a stack `s` to store the search path to the current base node. The replacing base node is of type `range_base` (lines 39–42), which has fields for specifying the range of the ongoing range query (`lo` and `hi`) as well as a `storage` field pointing to a result storage (lines 35–38). This storage has a `result` field, which is initially `NOT_SET` and will be set once the range query has been completed (line 211). A `range_base` node is initially irreplaceable as long as its `result` field is `NOT_SET`; see the `is_replaceable` function (lines 63–72). A range query's linearization point is when all concerned base nodes have been replaced and the `result` field of the result storage has been replaced by the actual result of the query (line 211). The `lo` and `hi` fields of nodes of the `range_base` type are used by operations that try to help an uncompleted range query in order to make an irreplaceable `range_base` node replaceable; see `help_if_needed` (lines 74–86). Thus, range queries achieve atomicity by ensuring that all base nodes containing items in the range are irreplaceable for a short instance, and are able to maintain the non-blocking progress guarantee by enabling other threads to help them.

Once a range query has been completed, a special field in the result storage associated with the range query is set to a value indicating if more than one base node were needed to complete the range query. This information is used by the `new_stat` function (lines 87–97) when calculating a statistics value for a base node. Before `all_in_range` returns, `adapt_if_needed` (lines 98–104) is called (line 213) with a random base node within the range as parameter. This is done to ensure that the structure of the tree stays up-to-date with the collected heuristics.

```
144 node* find_next_base_stack(stack* s) {
145   node* base = pop(s);
146   node* t = top(s);
147   if(t == NULL) return NULL;
148   if(aload(&t->left) == base)
149     return leftmost_and_stack(aload(&t->right), s);
150   int be_greater_than = t->key;
151   while(t != NULL){
152     if(aload(&t->valid) && t->key > be_greater_than)
153       return leftmost_and_stack(aload(&t->right), s);
154     else { pop(s); t = top(s); }
155   }
156   return NULL;
157 }
158 node* new_range_base(node* b, int lo, int hi, rs* s){
159   return new node{... = b, // assign fields from b
160                   lo = lo, hi = hi, storage = s}; }
161 treap*
162 all_in_range(lfcat* t, int lo, int hi, rs* help_s){
163   stack* s = new_stack();
164   stack* backup_s = new_stack();
165   stack* done = new_stack();
166   node* b;
167   rs* my_s;
168  find_first:b = find_base_stack(aload(&t->root),lo,s);
169   if(help_s != NULL){
170     if(b->type != range || help_s != b->storage){
171       return aload(&help_s->result);
172     }else my_s = help_s;
173   }else if(is_replaceable(b)){
174     my_s = new rs;
175     node* n = new_range_base(b, lo, hi, my_s);
176     if(!try_replace(t, b, n)) goto find_first;
177     replace_top(s, n);
178   }else if( b->type == range   && b->hi >= hi){
179     return all_in_range(t, b->lo, b->hi, b->storage);
180   }else{
181     help_if_needed(t, b);
182     goto find_first;
183   }
184   while(true){   // Find remaining base nodes
185     push(done, b);
186     copy_state_to(s, backup_s);
187     if(!empty(b->data) && max(b->data) >= hi) break;
188   find_next_base_node: b = find_next_base_stack(s);
189     if(b == NULL) break;
190     else if(aload(&my_s->result) != NOT_SET){
191       return aload(&my_s->result);
192     }else if(b->type == range && b->storage == my_s){
193       continue;
194     }else if(is_replaceable(b)){
195       node* n = new_range_base(b, lo, hi, my_s);
196       if(try_replace(t, b, n)) {
197         replace_top(s, n); continue;
198       } else {
199         copy_state_to(backup_s, s);
200         goto find_next_base_node;
201       }
202     }else{
203       help_if_needed(t, b);
204       copy_state_to(backup_s, s);
205       goto find_next_base_node;
206     }
207   }
208   treap* res = done->stack_array[0]->data;
209   for(int i = 1; i < done->size; i++)
210     res = treap_join(res, done->stack_array[i]->data);
211   if(CAS(&my_s->result,NOT_SET,res) && done->size > 1)
212     astore(&my_s->more_than_one_base, true);
213   adapt_if_needed(t, done->array[r() % done->size]);
214   return aload(&my_s->result);
215 }
```

**Figure 5: Helper function for the range query operation.**

*Adaptations.* The granularity of the immutable parts of a LFCA tree can be changed with two different types of adaptations. The first one, called *high-contention adaptation* (or *split*), splits the items in a base node into two new base nodes, in order to decrease the contention in a part of the tree where the contention has been high. The second type, called *low-contention adaptation* (or *join*), joins the content of two base nodes into a new base node, in order to improve the performance of range queries. Joins can potentially also improve the performance of the LFCA tree for uncontended single-item operations as a join can make the search paths to items shorter (because the part of the tree consisting of route nodes may be unbalanced), but joins may also make updates slightly more expensive (due to increased amount of memory allocation and coping when creating new instances of the leaf containers). An adaptation is issued by the function adapt_if_needed (lines 98–104) that is executed by the update operations (line 120) and by range queries (line 213). Whether an adaptation should occur and what kind of adaptation it should be is decided based on a statistics value calculated by the new_stat function (lines 87–97). High-contention or low-contention adaptation is issued if this statistics value is above (line 100) or below (line 102) a threshold, respectively. The new_stat function calculates the statistics value based on its two parameters: a base node and a parameter that is encoding information about detected contention. The core idea behind the heuristics is to make the synchronization more fine-grained in parts of the data structure where contention has been common and to make it more coarse-grained in parts where contention has been uncommon or where range queries often need to access more than one base node.

If no contention information is given to the new_stat function (as is the case when this function is called by adapt_if_needed), then the value is the value of the stat field in the base node subtracted by $x$, where $x$ is a positive constant if it is a base node of type range whose corresponding range query was completed by reading more than one base node (lines 89–91). When update operations call new_stat to get the value that will be used for the stat field of the new base node that the update operation creates they also pass information whether contention was detected (cf. line 117). This information is used to increase the statistics value if contention has been detected (line 93), and decrease the statistics value otherwise (line 95). The constant that is used to increase the statistics value when contention is detected is larger than the constant that decreases the statistics value when no contention has been detected so that adaptations happen quickly when contention is common and to avoid frequent adaptations back-and-forth. The constants used in our heuristics can be found in lines 2 to 6.

*High-contention adaptation.* The function for high-contention adaptation (lines 277–287) splits the content of a base node b into two new base nodes that are linked together with a route node r. The function attempts to replace the base node b with r using a CAS operation (line 286). This replacement is atomic to other operations and does not change the contents of the tree.

*Low-contention adaptation.* The function for low-contention adaptation (lines 268–276) intuitively replaces two neighboring base nodes b and n0 by a new node n2, which contains the union of the items in b and n0. It splices out b and its parent route node from

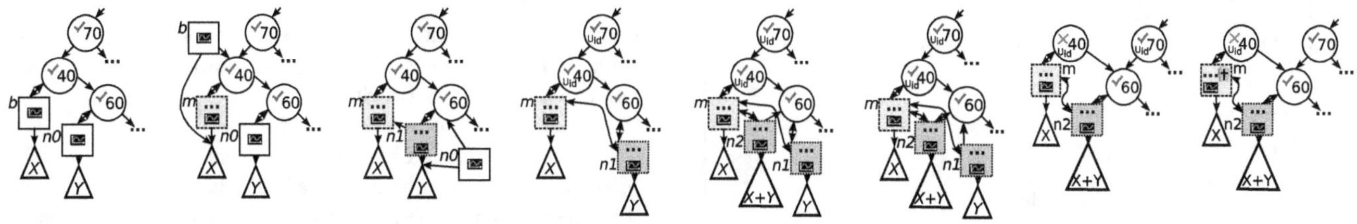

(a) Before join (b) Replace b (c) Replace n0 (d) Store join info (e) Secure join (f) Replace n1 (g) Splice out 40 (h) Let m die

**Figure 6: Figures showing the main steps of the low-contention join operation.**

the tree and replaces `n0` by `n2`. Figure 6 illustrates the major steps which are done by a successful low-contention adaptation.

A successful low-contention adaptation (lines 268–276) is done in two phases. The first phase, illustrated in Figs. 6a to 6e and performed by `secure_join_left` in lines 216–250 (or the corresponding function for the right case), "marks" the part of the tree that will be involved in the join, to prevent other threads from changing it while the join is ongoing. Other threads cannot help complete this phase, but system-wide-progress is guaranteed as other threads can interrupt this phase by killing the join (line 78). The second phase (Figs. 6f to 6h), which is performed by `complete_join` (lines 251–267), is executed only if the first phase was successful (line 272). Other threads can help the join to complete this second phase (line 81). The second phase completes the join by splicing out `b` and its parent and replaces `n1` by `n2`.

We will describe how the low-contention adaptation works by going through a successful join of the base node `b` in Fig. 6a. As `b` is the left child of its parent, `secure_join_left` is called (line 270). Lines 217–222 find the neighbor `n0` of `b` (the leftmost leaf of `b`'s parent's right branch) and replaces `b` with a new base node `m` of type `join_main` (Fig. 6b). Note that the join would have aborted if `n0` would have been irreplaceable or if the replacement of `b` would have failed (which would have meant that `b` was no longer in the tree). Next, `n0` is replaced with a new base node `n1` of type `join_neighbor`, which is linked to `m` with the field `main_node` (line 227 and Fig. 6c). Both `m` and `n1` are now irreplaceable (lines 63–72). The only way for other threads to make them replaceable at this point is to set the field `neigh2` of `m` to `ABORTED`. On lines 228–233, the `join_id` field of both the parent and the grandparent of `m` is set to the reference `m` to make sure that they are not modified by any other join operation. Using the reference `m`, which is a unique identifier for the join operation, to mark the route nodes involved in the join makes it easy for threads to collaboratively change this field in the second phase. In lines 234–236, more information that is needed by `complete_join` to finish the operation is stored in `m` (cf. Fig. 6d). The final step of the first phase is done in lines 237-243 (cf. Fig. 6e). These lines attempt to set `m`'s field `neigh2` to a base node `n2` which can replace both `m` and `n1` using a `CAS` operation. If this `CAS` is successful, we know that the following are true directly after the change:

- Both `m` and `n1` must have been irreplaceable at the time of the change, as this means that the field `neigh2` has not been set to `ABORTED` by any other thread.
- The node referenced by `m`'s `parent` field is the parent of `m`, the node referenced by `m` `gparent` field is the grandparent of `m`, and `m`'s field `otherb` is set to the sibling of `m`. This follows from the observations that (i) the only type of change that can happen to a path from the root of the tree to a base node that is inside the tree is that a route node gets spliced out which can only happen if both the spliced out node and its parent has their `join_id` fields set to something different from `NULL`, (ii) the `join_id` field of the spliced out node is never set to `NULL` again, and (iii) no other threads can change the `join_id` field of parent and gparent while the `neigh2` field of `m` is set to `PREPARING`.

Once the `neigh2` field of `m` has been successfully set to the new base node, the first phase of the operation is finished and the second phase can start. Note that the changes done by the operation would have been rolled back on lines 245–248 if some `CAS` operations had failed.

As mentioned, the second phase of a low-contention adaptation is done by `complete_join` (lines 251–267). Multiple threads can execute this function with the same base node of type `join_main` as input parameter. This happens when another thread needs to change a base node of type `join_main` or `join_neighbor` and the join associated with the base node has finished the first phase but not yet the second (which means that the base node is irreplaceable; see lines 63–72). That other thread will call the `help_if_needed` function that in turn will call `complete_join` (line 81). The first modification that is done by the second phase is to replace the base node `n1` with the base node `n2` that is referenced to by the field `neigh2` in `m` which was set in the first phase (cf. Fig. 6f). Note that any thread that executes `complete_join` with the base node `m` as parameter can perform this step as it is done with a `CAS` operation (line 254 and the `try_replace` function). The next change is to set the `valid` flag of the parent to false (line 255). The sole purpose of this is so that the range query operation can avoid traversing branches that are no longer relevant for the range query (line 152). On lines 256–257, it is determined what will be the replacement of `m`'s parent. If `m` and `n2` share the same parent (in this case `b->otherb`, which is set on line 235, will be equal to `n1`, a.k.a. `b->neigh1`) the replacement will be `n2`, otherwise the replacement will be the branch of the parent that does not lead to `m` (this case is illustrated in Fig. 6f). The parent of `m` and `m` itself is spliced out from the tree on lines 258–265 (cf. Fig. 6g). Note that only one thread can succeed with the splice out as it is done with a `CAS` operation. Likewise, only one thread can succeed in resetting the `join_id` of the grandparent of `m` (line 262). The only remaining step after these lines have executed is to set the `neigh2` field of `m` to `DONE`, which is done on line 266 (cf. Fig. 6h). This is done to indicate that the join has completed and to make `n2` replaceable.

```
node* secure_join_left(lfcatree* t, node* b){
  node* n0 = leftmost(aload(&b->parent->right));
  if(!is_replaceable(n0)) return NULL;
  node* m = new node{
    ... = b, // assign fields from b
    type = join_main};
  if(!CAS(&b->parent->left, b, m)) return NULL;
  node* n1 = new node{
    ...         = n0, // assign fields from n0
    type        = join_neighbor,
    main_node = m};
  if(!try_replace(t, n0, n1)) goto fail0;
  if(!CAS(&m->parent->join_id, NULL, m))
    goto fail0;
  node* gparent = parent_of(t, m->parent);
  if(gparent == NOT_FOUND ||
     (gparent != NULL &&
      !CAS(&gparent->join_id,NULL,m))) goto fail1;
  m->gparent = gparent;
  m->otherb = aload(&m->parent->right);
  m->neigh1 = n1;
  node* joinedp = m->otherb==n1 ? gparent: n1->parent;
  if(CAS(&m->neigh2, PREPARING,
         new node{... = n1, // assign fields from n1
                  type = join_neighbor,
                  parent = joinedp,
                  main_node = m,
                  data = treap_join(m, n1)}))
    return m;
  if(gparent == NULL) goto fail1;
  astore(&gparent->join_id, NULL);
 fail1: astore(&m->parent->join_id, NULL);
 fail0: astore(&m->neigh2, ABORTED);
  return NULL;
}
void complete_join(lfcatree* t, node* m){
  node* n2 = aload(&m->neigh2);
  if(n2 == DONE) return;
  try_replace(t, m->neigh1, n2);
  astore(&m->parent->valid, false);
  node* replacement =
    m->otherb == m->neigh1 ? n2 : m->otherb;
  if (m->gparent == NULL){
    CAS(&t->root, m->parent, replacement);
  }else if(aload(&m->gparent->left) == m->parent){
    CAS(&m->gparent->left, m->parent, replacement);
    CAS(&m->gparent->join_id, m, NULL);
  }else if(aload(&m->gparent->right) == m->parent){
    ... // Symmetric case
  }
  astore(&m->neigh2, DONE);
}
void low_contention_adaptation(lfcatree* t, node* b){
  if(b->parent == NULL) return;
  if(aload(&b->parent->left) == b){
    node* m = secure_join_left(t, b);
    if (m != NULL) complete_join(t, m);
  }else if (aload(&b->parent->right) == b){
    ... // Symmetric case
  }
}
void high_contention_adaptation(lfcatree* m, node* b){
  if(less_than_two_items(b->data)) return;
  node* r = new node{
   type  = route,
   key   = split_key(b->data),
   left  = new node{type = normal, parent= r, stat= 0,
                    data = split_left(b->data)}),
   right = ..., // Symmetric case
   valid = true};
  try_replace(m, b, r);
}
```

**Figure 7: Low and high contention adaptation.**

# 5 CORRECTNESS

In this section, we outline the main steps for proving that the algorithm is correct (in the sense of being a linearizable [10] implementation of a set of items which also supports range queries), and has the stated progress guarantees. We first provide global invariants, thereafter argue for linearizability, and finally for progress.

We define a route or base node to be *reachable* if it can be reached from the root of the tree by following `left` and `right` pointers. We define the *contents* of the tree as the union of all items in the leaf containers of reachable base nodes. The contents serve as the abstract state of the LFCA tree in our argument for linearizability. Finally, we define a base node to be *replaceable* if the `is_replaceable` function returns true when applied to it. The LFCA tree satisfies the following invariants and properties.

(1) The reachable route nodes and items in leaf containers of reachable base nodes are organized as a binary search tree. There is one exception to this, illustrated by Fig. 6f of a join operation, when the leaf container of node `m` is included in the leaf container of node `n2`. More precisely, this happens if a reachable route node `n` (corresponding to the parent of `m` in Fig. 6f) is such that `n->left` is a base node `m` of type `join_main` and *m*->`neigh2` is a pointer to a reachable node; if so, then the items in the leaf container of `m` are exactly the set of items in the leaf container of `m->neigh2` which are smaller than `n->key`. There is also a symmetric case when `n->right` is a base node of type `join_main`. Note that in these cases, the search `find_base_node` will reach the elements in `m`'s leaf container only via `n`, and after `n` is spliced out, the same elements will be found in the leaf container of `m->neigh2`. In both cases, the tree appears like a valid binary search tree.

(2) A replaceable base node can not become irreplaceable (but can be replaced by an irreplaceable node).

(3) A replaceable base node `n` is reachable iff `n` is obtained either as `n->parent->left` or as `n->parent->right`. A reachable node that has become non-reachable cannot become reachable again. The parent of a reachable and replaceable base node never changes.

Having established these properties of the LFCA tree, we can now proceed to establishing linearizability of operations.

**update** An update operation replaces a replaceable base node using a CAS operation, which succeeds only if the node is pointed to by the `left` or `right` pointer of its parent route node. By invariant (2) and (3), this ensures that the replaced node is reachable when the CAS succeeds. We let the linearization point of an update operation coincide with the successful CAS. Since the operation replaces a reachable node, the corresponding operation replaces a leaf container that is included in the contents of the tree just before the linearization point. To make sure that the operation indeed changes the contents of the tree in the intended way, we should make sure that it does not replace a node that is of type `join_main` or `join_neighbor`, in a situation where it participates in an uncompleted join and can have duplicated elements in another leaf container. This follows by noting that such a node is not replaceable, and therefore cannot be subject to an update operation.

**lookup** By invariant (3), only joins can make reachable base nodes non-reachable by making a route node non-reachable. Thus by invariant (1), a lookup operation always reaches a base node that was reachable and reflects the presence of the item searched for either at the point (i) when the route node that it currently "visits" is spliced out during a join operation (at lines 258–265), or if this does not happen (ii) when it reads the pointer to its destination base node. Thus, one of the above points can serve as linearization point.

**range query** A range query visits reachable nodes in its scope in increasing item order. For each node, it checks that the node is replaceable, and if so replaces it by a node of type `range_base`, thereby making it irreplaceable (unless the range query has been completed by another thread, in which case such a replacement has no effect). By the limitations on how nodes can be replaced, this guarantees to visit and replace a contiguous sequence of base nodes in the scope of the range query. After completing these replacements, the concerned base nodes are irreplaceable and the operation linearizes, whereafter the base nodes become replaceable.

Let us also show that a join preserves the contents of the tree. A join replaces two reachable (i.e., located in reachable base nodes) leaf containers by a new one. The new leaf container is replacing one of the old leaf containers using a successful CAS (line 254), whereafter the remaining old leaf container is spliced out at lines 258–265. Since the corresponding base nodes are irreplaceable when the replacements happen, and in addition the parent and grandparent of the `join_main` node are marked, no other operation can interfere with invariant (1), viz. that the new joined base node contains the union of the elements in the replaced base nodes.

Let us next consider progress properties of the involved operations. We first note that the lookup operation is wait-free. This follows by observing that it traverses the nodes of the tree without any possibility of being blocked. Progress is achieved at each pointer traversal, as the search space is decreased.

We then note that update operations are lock-free, since they reach the base node to be replaced without being blocked. The update may need to retry, either due to a failed CAS, or because the concerned base node is irreplaceable, because of interference from some other operation. At all such places the operation causing the interference must have made progress. Furthermore, when an operation can not proceed directly due to irreplaceable base nodes, then the operation can always make them replaceable by helping or (in case of a non-secured join) aborting the interfering operation. Range query operations are also lock-free, for analogous reasons.

## 6 OPTIMIZATION FOR RANGE QUERIES

If possible, it can be advantageous for range queries to avoid writing to shared memory as this induces less cache-coherence traffic. Therefore, we have applied an optimization to our LFCA tree implementation that optimistically tries to perform a range query without writing to shared memory. If this optimistic attempt fails, the range query is performed using the algorithm described in Section 4. The optimistic attempt consists of a test scan and then a validation scan of the base nodes needed for the range query. If nothing has changed between the test and the validation scan, one can be certain that all base nodes in the scans were present at some point and the optimistic attempt can succeed. This scheme is essentially the same as the one described for doing range queries in the $k$-ary data structure [4]. We refer to that paper for how to prove this scheme correct.

## 7 EVALUATION

We will now experimentally evaluate LFCA trees. Our implementation uses an immutable treap for the leaf containers and employs the optimization described in Section 6. To facilitate cache friendly range queries, the treap implementation stores all items in fat leaf nodes containing arrays that can store up to 64 items. The LFCA tree is compared to recent proposals for performing linearizable range queries in ordered sets: *SnapTree* [3], $k$-ary [4], Chatterjee's method applied to a lock-free skiplist [6] (*ChatterjeeSL*) and *KiWi* [2]. We also include the lock-based CA tree [22] in the comparison; it uses the same immutable treap as the LFCA tree in its leaf containers, and is optimized to take advantage of the immutability of the leaf containers so that range queries and lookups do not read the items in the leaf containers while holding locks. Finally, the lock-free ConcurrentSkipListMap from the Java library, which only supports non-linearizable range queries (*NonAtomicSL*), and the coarse-grained data structure (*Imm-Tr-Coarse*) that we described in the introduction are also included. All data structures are in Java as implemented by their respective authors. The maximum number of items in the nodes is set to 64 for $k$-ary, *Im-Tr-CA* and *SL-CA* as this value has previously been shown to give good results [4]. *KiWi*'s constants are set as described in the *KiWi* paper [2].

The benchmarks were run on a machine with four Intel(R) Xeon(R) E5-4650 CPUs (2.70GHz each with eight cores and hyperthreading, giving a total of 32 actual and 64 logical cores), turbo boost turned off, 128GB of RAM, running Linux 4.9.0-4-amd64 and Oracle JVM 1.8.0_151 (with the JVM flags -Xmx8g -Xms8g -server -d64 -XX:+UseCondCardMark). Each data point comes from the average of three measurements runs of 10 seconds each that were preceded by three warm up runs, also of 10 seconds each, whose purpose is to give the JiT compiler enough time to compile the code.

The keys for the operations lookup, insert and remove as well as the starting keys for range queries are randomly generated integers from a range of size $S$. The data structure is pre-filled before the start of each benchmark run so that it contains $S/2$ random integers. We use $S = 10^6$ in all experiments presented in this section, which corresponds to a set of size approximately $5 \times 10^5$. (Results for $S = 10^5$ and $S = 10^7$ can be found in the extended version of this paper [23].) Range queries calculate the sum of the items in the range and the number of items in the range. As a sanity check, the average number of items that are traversed per range query is calculated and checked against the expected value.

The benchmark scenarios measure throughput of a mix of operations performed by $N$ threads. In figure captions, the scenarios are described by strings of the form w:$A$% r:$B$% q:$C$%-$R$, meaning that the benchmark performs $(A/2)$% insert, $(A/2)$% remove, $B$% lookup operations and $C$% range queries of maximum range size $R$. The range sizes are randomly set to values between 1 and $R$.

We start with three scenarios without range queries; cf. Fig. 8. As the machine only has 64 hardware threads, thread counts above 64 show how the data structures perform when there are more threads than hardware can execute in parallel. Both the lock-based and the

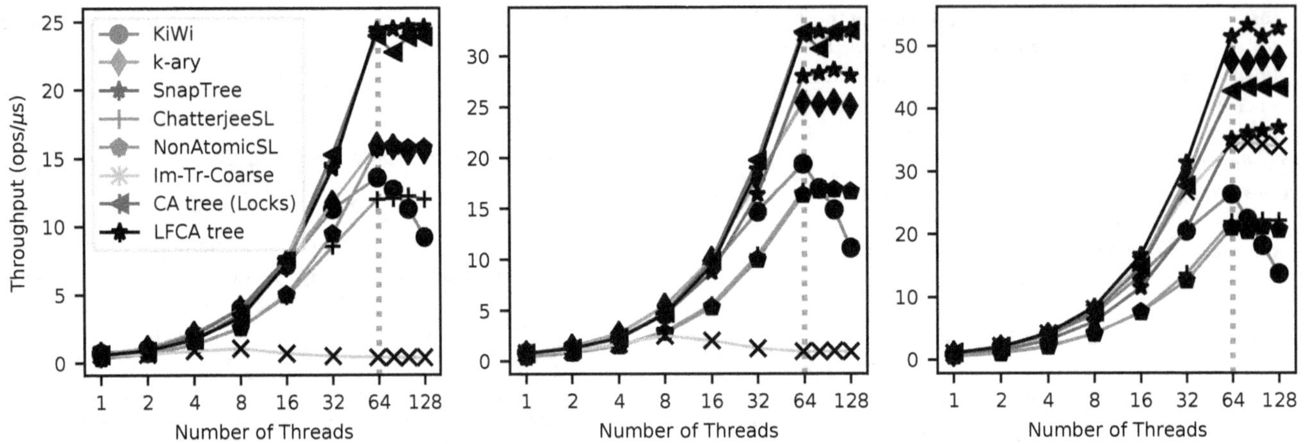


(a) w:50% r:50% (b) w:20% r:80% (c) w:1% r:99%

**Figure 8: Single-item operations only. Throughput (operations/μs) on the y-axis and thread count on the x-axis. The sub-figures are ordered in increasing amount of lookups. (Note that the SnapTree is hidden behind the CA trees in Fig. 8a).**

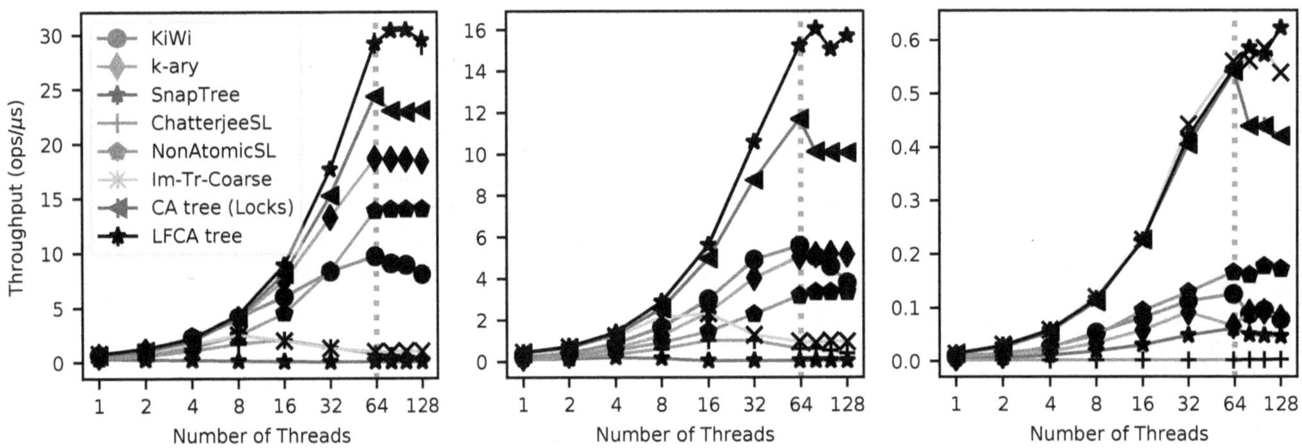


(a) w:20% r:55% q:25%-10 (b) w:20% r:55% q:25%-1000 (c) w:20% r:55% q:25%-100000

**Figure 9: Range queries and single-item operations. Throughput (operations/μs) on the y-axis and thread count on the x-axis. The sub-figures are ordered in increasing range query size**

lock-free CA tree compare well with the competing data structures both when we have 50% updates and 50% lookups (Fig. 8a) and in the read-heavy scenarios with up to 99% lookups (Figs. 8b and 8c). This shows that the LFCA tree can be a good choice even without range queries. The LFCA tree performs substantially better than the lock-based CA tree at 64 threads and beyond in the read-heavy scenario, which is likely due to LFCA tree's wait-free lookup operation.

Let us now consider scenarios that also contain range queries; cf. Fig. 9. These scenarios show the key strength of the CA trees. Namely, their ability to change the sizes of their immutable parts to fit the workload at hand. Figure 9a shows that the LFCA tree performs better than all the other data structures in a scenario with relatively small range queries of maximum size 10. In the scenario with moderately-sized range queries of maximum size 1000 (Fig. 9b), the LFCA tree outperforms all the other data structures with an even wider margin even though the lock-based CA tree also performs very well there. Data structures clearly benefit from fine-grained synchronization in the scenarios with range queries up to a maximum size of 1000 (e.g., *Im-Tr-Coarse* scales relatively poorly in the scenarios of Figs. 9a and 9b). In contrast, in the scenario with large range queries (Fig. 9c), it seems like the combination of immutable data and coarse-grained synchronization is the best as *Im-Tr-Coarse*'s performance is on par with LFCA trees's performance. Therefore, it seems like the LFCA tree can perform extremely well across a wide variety of workloads (only single-key operations, small range queries and large ones) due to its ability to adapt its structure to fit the workload. The performance drop that can be observed for the lock-based CA tree after 64 threads is probably due to lock-related problems that become more apparent when thread preemption becomes more common (e.g., threads may need to wait for a thread that has got preempted by the OS).

With the benchmark configurations discussed above, the threads spend much more time in range queries than in single-item operations when the range queries are large. Thus, another benchmark is needed to measure the data structures' ability to handle large range queries concurrently with frequent update operations. To

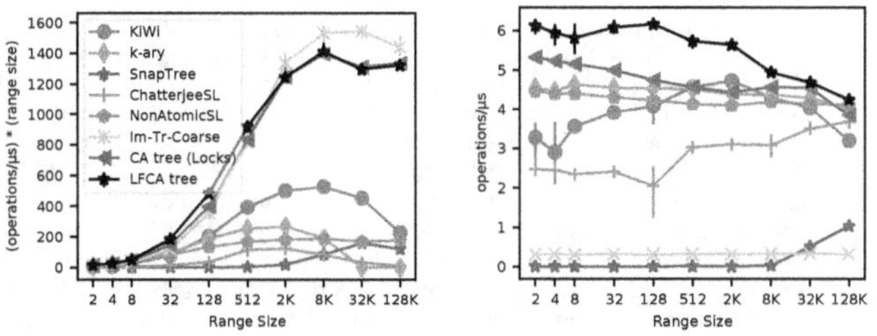


(a) Range queries (parallel updates) (b) Updates (parallel range queries)

**Figure 10: On the left, throughput for the 16 range query threads, and on the right, throughput for the threads doing only inserts and removes.**

this end, we use a similar benchmark to the one developed by the *KiWi* authors. In this benchmark, half the threads (16) do update operations (insert and remove with equal probability) while the other half (also 16) do range queries with a range of fixed size. In the results for the benchmarks, the throughput for updates (Fig. 10b) is presented separately from the range query throughput (Fig. 10a) so that one can study the performance of these operations separately. Note that in the graphs that show the range query throughput, the number of operations per $\mu s$ is shown multiplied by the range query size on the y-axis to make the graphs more readable. The range query size used in the experiment is shown on the x-axis.

Taking both the performance of the range queries and updates into account, it is clear that the LFCA tree is the best data structure for all range query sizes. It is tightly followed by the lock-based CA tree. Looking only at the throughput for the update operations, *k*-ary, *NonAtomicSL* and *KiWi* can also keep up quite well (at least with some range query sizes). However, when also taking range queries into account, these data structures are all far behind LFCA tree for all range query sizes above 128. In short, *k*-ary, *NonAtomicSL* and *KiWi* can perform well only in a few scenarios that fit their synchronization granularity and the sizes of their immutable parts, while the CA trees can perform well in a wider range of scenarios thanks to their ability to adapt.

We now take a look at the statistics shown in Tables 1 and 2. They show the base node count (measured after the experiments), the average number of traversed base nodes per range query and the number of splits and joins per millisecond for the scenarios that are shown in Figs. 9b and 10, respectively. These statistics indicate that the heuristics works as intended. That is, larger range queries result in fewer base nodes and more threads result in more base nodes. Looking at the number of base nodes traversed per range query, it is also clear that range queries spend a relatively short time traversing shared mutable data (compared to the non-adaptive data structures in the comparison) even for large range queries. This explains how the LFCA tree can perform so much better than the non-adaptive data structures which is compared against.

The five parts of Fig. 11 show results from a time series experiment that was run in order to illustrate into how an LFCA tree adapts its structure when the workload suddenly changes and how this adaptation affects its performance. The top part of the figure shows the number of route nodes, and the bottom part the throughput which is achieved at different time points. At time zero, the LFCA tree contains only one base node with 500$K$ items. The experiment begins with the workload w:20% r:55% q:25%-1000, which

**Table 1: Statistics for the LFCA tree in the scenarios of Fig. 9b (w:20% r:55% q:25%-1000).**

| Threads | 1 | 2 | 4 | 8 | 16 | 32 | 64 |
|---|---|---|---|---|---|---|---|
| # route nodes | 0 | 53 | 130 | 270 | 440 | 740 | 980 |
| # traversed base nodes / # range queries | 1.0 | 1.0 | 1.0 | 1.0 | 1.0 | 1.1 | 1.1 |
| # splits / milliseconds | 0 | 0.024 | 0.048 | 0.1 | 0.23 | 0.53 | 1.0 |
| # joins / milliseconds | 0 | 0.019 | 0.036 | 0.078 | 0.19 | 0.46 | 0.91 |

**Table 2: Statistics for the LFCA tree in the scenarios of Fig. 10. 16 threads doing range queries and 16 threads doing updates.**

| Range Size | 2 | 128 | 512 | 2K | 8K | 32K | 128K |
|---|---|---|---|---|---|---|---|
| # route nodes | 2.9K | 2.3K | 2.1K | 1.3K | 680 | 370 | 330 |
| # traversed base nodes / # range queries | 1.0 | 1.0 | 1.3 | 2.6 | 5.5 | 12 | 42 |
| # splits / milliseconds | 1.1 | 1.3 | 1.5 | 2.4 | 5.0 | 10 | 13 |
| # joins / milliseconds | 0.79 | 1.0 | 1.3 | 2.3 | 4.9 | 10 | 13 |

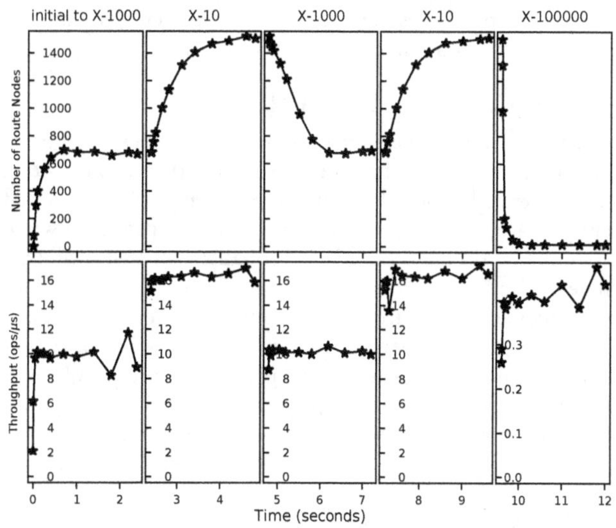


**Figure 11: Time series illustrating sudden changes in the workloads. Number of route nodes in the top and throughput in the bottom. Only the maximum size of the range queries changes between the figures. X = 20% r:55% q:25%.**

is executed using 30 threads for 2.4 seconds. Every 2.4 seconds the maximum range query size changes: besides the initial value (1000) it also takes the values 10, 1000, 10 and 100000 (cf. the values at the top line of Fig. 11). From the time series, we can see that, after each workload change, the rate of change for the number of route nodes gradually decreases until the number of route nodes stabilizes around a certain value. In the parts titled "initial to X-1000" and "X-100000", one can also see a positive change in throughput when the number of route nodes increases/decreases quickly. The change in throughput while the number of route nodes changes quickly is not as big in the three middle parts ("X-10", "X-1000" and "X-10"), which is not strange considering that the synchronization granularity changes relatively less in these parts.

The benchmark set up for the time series experiment is a bit involved in order to obtain numbers that are not disturbed by taking measurements during very short periods of time. It goes as follows. For every time point shown with a dot in the graphs, average measurements from five experiment runs in different JVM instances were collected. Each such run consists of 35 warm up runs and 10 measurement runs (that we take the average measurements from). A warm up or a measurement run does the following after the LFCA tree has been filled with $500K$ items: It performs a triggering run (skipped in the first workload of the time series) of 2.2 seconds that applies the workload $W$ (where $W$ is the previous workload in the time series), before the actual warm up/measurement run is executed for $t$ seconds ($t$ is always 2 seconds for the warm up runs), after which the number of route nodes and the number of performed operations by the threads are collected. For example, a run to collect measurements for time point 3.4 seconds performs a triggering run with the workload w:20% r:55% q:25%-1000 and then a measurement run with the workload w:20% r:55% q:25%-10 (running for 1 second). The throughput for a time point $t_n$ is calculated as $\frac{o(t_n)-o(t_{n-1})}{(t_n-t_{n-1})}$, where $t_{n-1}$ denotes the previous time point in the time series and $o(t)$ denotes the average number of performed operations measured for time point $t$.

# 8 CONCLUDING REMARKS

We have given a detailed description and correctness arguments for the LFCA tree, the first lock-free data structure supporting range queries that adapts its structure based on heuristics that take detected contention and information about range queries into account. LFCA trees make use of information gathered at runtime to get a good trade-off between the performance of operations that generally benefit from coarse-grained synchronization and those that generally benefit from fine-grained synchronization. Our experimental evaluation, in the previous section as well as in its extended version of this paper [23], shows that this has real benefits in practice, as the LFCA tree can maintain exceptionally good performance across a wide range of scenarios.

# DATA AVAILABILITY STATEMENT

The source code for the LFCA tree as well as the code for the benchmarks are available online [18].

# ACKNOWLEDGMENTS

This work was carried out within the Linnaeus centre of excellence UPMARC (Uppsala Programming for Multicore Architectures Research Center), and was partly supported by grants from the Swedish Research Council.

# REFERENCES

[1] Hillel Avni, Nir Shavit, and Adi Suissa. 2013. Leaplist: Lessons Learned in Designing TM-supported Range Queries. In *Proceedings of the 2013 ACM Symposium on Principles of Distributed Computing (PODC '13)*. ACM, New York, NY, USA, 299–308. https://doi.org/10.1145/2484239.2484254

[2] Dmitry Basin, Edward Bortnikov, Anastasia Braginsky, Guy Golan-Gueta, Eshcar Hillel, Idit Keidar, and Moshe Sulamy. 2017. KiWi: A Key-Value Map for Scalable Real-Time Analytics. In *Proceedings of the 22Nd ACM SIGPLAN Symposium on Principles and Practice of Parallel Programming (PPoPP '17)*. ACM, New York, NY, USA, 357–369. https://doi.org/10.1145/3018743.3018761

[3] Nathan G. Bronson, Jared Casper, Hassan Chafi, and Kunle Olukotun. 2010. A practical concurrent binary search tree. In *Proceedings of the 15th ACM SIGPLAN Symposium on Principles and Practice of Parallel Programming (PPoPP '10)*. ACM, New York, NY, USA, 257–268. https://doi.org/10.1145/1693453.1693488

[4] Trevor Brown and Hillel Avni. 2012. Range Queries in Non-blocking k-ary Search Trees. In *Principles of Distributed Systems: 16th International Conference, OPODIS 2012. Proceedings*, Roberto Baldoni, Paola Flocchini, and Ravindran Binoy (Eds.). Springer, 31–45. https://doi.org/10.1007/978-3-642-35476-2_3

[5] Trevor Brown and Joanna Helga. 2011. Non-blocking k-ary Search Trees. In *Principles of Distributed Systems: 15th International Conference, OPODIS 2011. Proceedings*, Antonio Fernàndez Anta, Giuseppe Lipari, and Matthieu Roy (Eds.). Springer, 207–221. https://doi.org/10.1007/978-3-642-25873-2_15

[6] Bapi Chatterjee. 2017. Lock-free Linearizable 1-Dimensional Range Queries. In *Proceedings of the 18th International Conference on Distributed Computing and Networking (ICDCN '17)*. ACM, New York, NY, USA, Article 9, 10 pages. https://doi.org/10.1145/3007748.3007771

[7] Chao-Hong Chen, Vikraman Choudhury, and Ryan R. Newton. 2017. Adaptive Lock-free Data Structures in Haskell: A General Method for Concurrent Implementation Swapping. In *Proceedings of the 10th ACM SIGPLAN International Symposium on Haskell (Haskell 2017)*. ACM, New York, NY, USA, 197–211. https://doi.org/10.1145/3122955.3122973

[8] Phuong Hoai Ha, Marina Papatriantafilou, and Philippas Tsigas. 2007. Self-tuning reactive diffracting trees. *J. Parallel and Distrib. Comput.* 67, 6 (2007), 674–694. https://doi.org/10.1016/j.jpdc.2007.01.011

[9] M. Herlihy. 1990. A Methodology for Implementing Highly Concurrent Data Structures. In *Proceedings of the Second ACM SIGPLAN Symposium on Principles & Practice of Parallel Programming (PPoPP '90)*. ACM, New York, NY, USA, 197–206. https://doi.org/10.1145/99163.99185

[10] Maurice P. Herlihy and Jeannette M. Wing. 1990. Linearizability: A Correctness Condition for Concurrent Objects. *ACM Trans. Program. Lang. Syst.* 12, 3 (July 1990), 463–492. https://doi.org/10.1145/78969.78972

[11] Ryan R. Newton, Peter P. Fogg, and Ali Varamesh. 2015. Adaptive Lock-free Maps: Purely-functional to Scalable. In *Proceedings of the 20th ACM SIGPLAN International Conference on Functional Programming (ICFP 2015)*. ACM, New York, NY, USA, 218–229. https://doi.org/10.1145/2784731.2784734

[12] Chris Okasaki. 1999. *Purely functional data structures*. Cambridge Univ. Press.

[13] Erik Österlund and Welf Löwe. 2014. Concurrent Transformation Components Using Contention Context Sensors. In *Proceedings of the 29th ACM/IEEE International Conference on Automated Software Engineering (ASE '14)*. ACM, New York, NY, USA, 223–234. https://doi.org/10.1145/2642937.2642995

[14] Erez Petrank and Shahar Timnat. 2013. Lock-Free Data-Structure Iterators. In *Proceedings of the 27th International Symposium on Distributed Computing - Volume 8205 (DISC 2013)*. Springer-Verlag New York, Inc., New York, NY, USA, 224–238. https://doi.org/10.1007/978-3-642-41527-2_16

[15] Callum Robertson. 2014. *Implementing Contention-Friendly Range Queries in Non-Blocking Key-Value Stores*. Bachelor Thesis. The University of Sydney.

[16] Konstantinos Sagonas and Kjell Winblad. 2016. Efficient Support for Range Queries and Range Updates Using Contention Adapting Search Trees. In *Languages and Compilers for Parallel Computing - 28th International Workshop, LCPC (LNCS)*, Xipeng Shen, Frank Mueller, and James Tuck (Eds.), Vol. 9519. Springer, 37–53. https://doi.org/10.1007/978-3-319-29778-1_3

[17] Konstantinos Sagonas and Kjell Winblad. 2017. A contention adapting approach to concurrent ordered sets. *J. Parallel and Distrib. Comput.* (2017). https://doi.org/10.1016/j.jpdc.2017.11.007

[18] Konstantinos Sagonas and Kjell Winblad. 2018. Contention Adapting Search Trees. (2018). http://www.it.uu.se/research/group/languages/software/ca_tree.

[19] R. Seidel and C. R. Aragon. 1996. Randomized search trees. *Algorithmica* 16, 4 (01 Oct. 1996), 464–497. https://doi.org/10.1007/BF01940876

[20] N. Shafiei. 2013. Non-blocking Patricia Tries with Replace Operations. In *2013 IEEE 33rd International Conference on Distributed Computing Systems*. 216–225. https://doi.org/10.1109/ICDCS.2013.43

[21] Jeff Shute, Radek Vingralek, Bart Samwel, Ben Handy, Chad Whipkey, Eric Rollins, Mircea Oancea, Kyle Littlefield, David Menestrina, Stephan Ellner, John Cieslewicz, Ian Rae, Traian Stancescu, and Himani Apte. 2013. F1: A Distributed SQL Database That Scales. *Proceedings of the VLDB Endowment* 6, 11 (Aug. 2013), 1068–1079. https://doi.org/10.14778/2536222.2536232

[22] Kjell Winblad. 2017. Faster Concurrent Range Queries with Contention Adapting Search Trees Using Immutable Data. In *2017 Imperial College Computing Student Workshop (ICCSW 2017) (OpenAccess Series in Informatics (OASIcs))*. Schloss Dagstuhl–Leibniz-Zentrum fuer Informatik, Dagstuhl, Germany.

[23] Kjell Winblad, Konstantinos Sagonas, and Bengt Jonsson. 2018. Lock-free Contention Adapting Search Trees. (2018). Extended version of this paper available at http://www.it.uu.se/research/group/languages/software/ca_tree.

[24] Yahoo! Developer Network. 2017. Flurry analytics. (2017). https://developer.yahoo.com/flurry/docs/analytics/ Accessed: 2017-07-26.

# Distributionally Linearizable Data Structures

Dan Alistarh
IST Austria

Trevor Brown
IST Austria

Justin Kopinsky
MIT

Jerry Z. Li
MIT

Giorgi Nadiradze
ETH Zurich

## ABSTRACT

Relaxed concurrent data structures have become increasingly popular, due to their scalability in graph processing and machine learning applications ([14, 24]).

Despite considerable interest, there exist families of natural, high performing *randomized* relaxed concurrent data structures, such as the popular MultiQueue [27] pattern for implementing relaxed priority queue data structures, for which no guarantees are known in the concurrent setting [4].

Our main contribution is in showing for thefi rst time that, under a set of analytic assumptions, a family of relaxed concurrent data structures, including variants of MultiQueues, but also a new approximate counting algorithm we call the MultiCounter, provides strong probabilistic guarantees on the degree of relaxation with respect to the sequential specification, *in arbitrary concurrent executions.* We formalize these guarantees via a new correctness condition called *distributional linearizability*, tailored to concurrent implementations with randomized relaxations. Our result is based on a new analysis of an *asynchronous* variant of the classic power-of-two-choices load balancing algorithm, in which placement choices can be based on inconsistent, outdated information (this result may be of independent interest). We validate our results empirically, showing that the MultiCounter algorithm can implement scalable relaxed timestamps.

**ACM Reference Format:**

Dan Alistarh, Trevor Brown, Justin Kopinsky, Jerry Z. Li, and Giorgi Nadiradze. 2018. Distributionally Linearizable Data Structures. In *SPAA '18: 30th ACM Symposium on Parallelism in Algorithms and Architectures, July 16–18, 2018, Vienna, Austria.* ACM, New York, NY, USA, 10 pages. https://doi.org/10.1145/3210377.3210411

## 1 INTRODUCTION

Consider a system of $n$ threads, which share a set of $m$ distinct atomic counters. We wish to implement a *scalable approximate counter*, which we will call a *MultiCounter*, by distributing the contention among these $m$ distinct instances: to *increment* the global counter, a thread selects two atomic counters $i$ and $j$ uniformly at random, reads their values, and (atomically) increments by 1 the value of the one which has *lower value* according to the values it read. To *read* the global counter, the thread returns the value of a randomly chosen counter $i$, multiplied by $m$. [1]

The astute reader will have noticed that this process is similar to the classic two-choice load balancing process [7], in which a sequence of balls are placed into $m$ initially empty bins, and, in each step, a new ball is placed into the less loaded of two randomly chosen bins. Here, the individual atomic counters are the *bins*, and each increment corresponds to a new *ball* being added. This sequential load balancing process is extremely well studied! [23, 26]: a series of deep technical results established that the difference between the most loaded bin and the average is $O(\log \log m)$ in expectation [7, 23], and that this difference remains stable as the process executes for increasingly many steps [10, 25]. We would therefore expect the above relaxed concurrent counter to have relatively low and stable skew among the outputs at consecutive operations, and to scale well, as contention is distributed among the $m$ counters.

However, there are several technical issues when attempting to analyze this natural process in a concurrent setting.

- First, concurrency interacts with classic two-choice load balancing process in non-trivial ways. The key property of the two-choice process which ensures good load balancing is that trials are *biased towards less loaded bins*—equivalently, operations are biased towards incrementing counters of lesser value. However, this property may break due to concurrency: *at the time of the update*, a thread may end up updating the counter of *higher* value among its two choices if the counter of smaller value is updated concurrently since it was read by the thread, thus surpassing the other counter.
- Second, perhaps suprisingly, it is currently unclear how to even *specify* such a concurrent data structure. Despite a significant amount of work on specifying *deterministic relaxed* data structures [1, 15, 17] , none of the existing frameworks cover relaxed *randomized* data structures.
- Finally, assuming such a data structure can be analyzed and specified, it is not clear whether it would be in any way *useful*: many existing applications are built around data structures with deterministic guarantees, and it is not obvious how scalable, relaxed data structures can be leveraged in standard concurrent settings.

One mayfi nd it surprising that analysing such a relatively simple concurrent process is so challenging. Beyond this specific instance, these difficulties reflect wider issues in this area: although these constructs are reasonably popular in practice due to their good scalability, e.g. [8, 24, 27, 31], their properties are non-trivial to pin

[1] This multiplication serves to maintain the same magnitude as the total number of updates to the distributed counter up to a point in time.


*SPAA '18, July 16–18, 2018, Vienna, Austria*

ACM ISBN 978-1-4503-5799-9/18/07...$15.00
https://doi.org/10.1145/3210377.3210411

down [4], and it is as of yet unclear how they interact with the higher-order algorithmic applications they are part of [20].

**Contribution.** In this work, we take a step towards addressing these challenges. Specifically:

- We provide thefi rst analysis of a two-choice load balancing process in an asynchronous setting, where operations may be interleaved, and the interleaving is decided by an adversary. We show that the resulting process is robust to concurrency, and continues to provide strong balancing guarantees in potentially infinite executions, as long as the ratio between the number of bins and the number of threads is above a large constant threshold.
- We introduce a new correctness condition for *randomized relaxed* data structures, called *distributional linearizability*. Intuitively, a concurrent data structure $D$ is distributionally linearizable to a *sequential random process* $R$, defined in terms of a sequential specification $S$, a cost function *cost* measuring the deviation from the sequential specification, and a distribution $\mathcal{P}$ on the values of the cost function, if every execution of $D$ can be mapped onto an execution of the relaxed sequential process $R$, respecting the outputs and the costs incurred, as well as the order of non-overlapping operations.
- We prove that the randomized *MultiCounter* data structure introduced above is distributionally linearizable to a (sequential) variant of the classic two-choice load balancing process. This allows us to formally define the properties of MultiCounters. Moreover, we show that this analytic framework also covers variants of *MultiQueues* [27], a popular family of concurrent data structures implementing relaxed concurrent priority queues. This yields thefi rst analytical guarantees for MultiQueues in concurrent executions.
- We implement the MultiCounters, and show that they can provide a highly scalable approximate timestamping mechanism, with relatively low skew.

**Techniques.** Our main technical contribution is the concurrent analysis of the classic two-choice load balancing process, in an asynchronous setting, where the interleaving of low-level steps is decided by an oblivious adversary. The core of our analysis builds on the elegant potential method of Peres, Talwar and Wieder [25], which we render robust to asynchronous updates based on potentially stale information. To achieve this, we overcome two key technical challenges. Thefi rst is that, given an operation *op*, as more and more other operations execute between the point where it reads and the point where it updates, the more stale its information becomes, and so the probability that *op* makes the "right" choice at the time of update, inserting into the less loaded of its two random choices, *decreases*. Moreover, operations updating with stale information will "stampede" towards lower-weight bins, effectively skewing the distribution. The second technical issue we overcome is that long-running operations, which experience a lot of concurrency, may in fact be adversarially biased towards the wrong choice, inserting into the more loaded of its two choices with non-trivial probability.

In brief, our analysis circumvents this issues by showing that a variant of the two-choice process where up to a constant fraction of updates are corrupted, in the sense that they perform the "wrong" update, will still have similar balance properties as the original process. It is interesting to note that even the *order* in which corrupted updates occur can be controlled by the adversary through increased concurrency, which is not the case in standard analyses [25]. The critical property which we leverage in our analysis is that, while individual operations can be arbitrarily contended (and therefore biased), there is a bound of $n$ on the *average* contention per operation, which in turn bounds the average amount of bias the adversary can induce over a period of time. Our argument formalizes this intuition, and phrases it in terms of the evolution of the potential function.

We show that this result has implications beyond "parallelizing" the classic two-choice process, as we can leverage it to obtain probabilistic bounds on the skew of the MultiCounter. Using the framework of [4], which connected two-choice load balancing with MultiQueue data structures in the sequential case, we can obtain guarantees for this popular data structure pattern in concurrent executions.

## 2 RELATED WORK

**Randomized Load Balancing.** The classic two-choice balanced allocation process was introduced in [7], where the authors show that, under two-choice insertion, the most loaded among $m$ bins is at most $O(\log \log m)$ above the average, both in expectation and with high probability. The literature studying analyses and extensions of this process is extremely vast, hence we direct the reader to [23, 26] for in-depth surveys of these techniques. Considerable effort has been dedicated to understanding guarantees in the "heavily-loaded" case, where the number of insertion steps is unbounded [10, 25], and in the "weighted" case, in which ball weights come from a probability distribution [11, 30]. A tour-de-force by Peres, Talwar, and Wieder [25] gave a potential argument characterizing a general form of the heavily-loaded, weighted process on *graphs*. Our analysis starts from their framework, and modifies it to analyze a concurrent, adversarial process. One significant change from their analysis is that, due to the adversary, changes in the potential are only partly stochastic: most steps might be slightly biased away from the better of the two choices, while a subset of choices might be almost deterministically biased towards the *wrong* choice. Further, the adversary can decide the *order* in which these different steps, with different biases, occur.

Lenzen and Wattenhofer [21] analyzed *parallel* balls-into-bins processes, in which $m$ balls need to be distributed among $m$ bins, under a communication model between the balls and the bins, showing that almost-perfect allocation can be achieved in $O(\log^* m)$ rounds of communication. This setting is quite different from the one we consider here. Similar delayed information models, where outdated information is given to the insertion process were considered by Mitzenmacher [22] and by Berenbrink, Czumaj, Englert, Friedetzky, and Nagel [9]. The former reference proposes a bulletin board model with periodic updates, in which information about the load of the model is updated only periodically (every $T$ seconds), and various allocation mechanisms. The author provides an analysis of this process in the asymptotic case (as $m \to \infty$), supported by simulations. The latter reference [9] considers a similar model where balls arrive in *batches*, and must perform allocations collectively based solely on the information available at the beginning of the batch, without additional communication. The authors prove that the greedy multiple-choice process preserves its strong load balancing properties in this setting: in particular, the gap between min and max remains $O(\log m)$. The key difference between these models and the one we consider is that our model is completely asynchronous, and in fact the interleavings are chosen adversarially. The technique we employ is fundamentally different from those of [9, 22]. In particular, we believe our techniques could be adapted to re-derive the main result of [9], albeit with worse constants.

Recent work by a subset of the authors [4] analyzed the following producer-consumer process: a set of balls labelled $1, 2, \ldots, b$ are inserted sequentially at random into $m$ bins; in parallel, balls are removed from the bins by always picking the lower labelled (higher priority) of two uniform random choices.[2] This process sequentially models a series of popular implementations of concurrent priority queue data structures, e.g. [16, 27]. This process provides the following guarantees: in each step $t$, the expected *rank* of the label removed among labels still present in the system is $O(m)$, and $O(m \log m)$ with high probability in $m$. That is, this sequential process provides a structured probabilistic relaxation of a standard priority queue.

**Relaxed Data Structures.** The process considered in [4] is sequential, whereas the data structures implemented are concurrent. Thus, there was a significant gap between the theoretical guarantees and the practical implementation. Our current work extends to concurrent data structures, closing this gap. Under the oblivious adversary assumption and given our parametrization, we show for thefi rst time that practical data structures such as [4, 16, 27] provide guarantees in real executions.

Designing efficient concurrent/parallel data structures with relaxed semantics was initiated by Karp and Zhang [19], with other significant early work by Deo and Prasad [12] and Sanders [28]. It has recently become an extremely active research area, see e.g. [4, 5, 8, 16, 24, 27, 29, 31] for recent examples. To the best of our knowledge, ours is thefi rst analysis of randomized relaxed concurrent data structures which works under arbitrary oblivious schedulers: previous analyses such as [4, 5, 27] required strong assumptions on the set of allowable interleavings. Dice et al. [13] considered randomized data structures for scalable exact and approximate counting. They consider the efficient parallelization of sequential approximate counting methods, and therefore have a significantly different focus than our work.

## 3 SYSTEM MODEL

**Asynchronous Shared Memory.** We consider a standard asynchronous shared-memory model, e.g. [6], in which $n$ threads (or processes) $P_1, \ldots, P_n$, communicate through shared memory, on which they perform atomic operations such as read, write, compare-and-swap and fetch-and-increment. The fetch-and-increment operation takes no arguments, and returns the value of the register before the increment was performed, incrementing its value by 1.

**The Oblivious Adversarial Scheduler.** Threads follow an algorithm, composed of shared-memory steps and local computation, including random coinfl ips. The order of process steps is controlled by an adversarial entity we call the *scheduler*. Time $t$ is measured in terms of the number of shared-memory steps scheduled by the adversary. The adversary may choose to crash a set of at most $n-1$ processes by not scheduling them for the rest of the execution. A process that is not crashed at a certain step is *correct*, and if it never crashes then it takes an infinite number of steps in the execution. In the following, we assume a standard *oblivious* adversarial scheduler, which decides on the interleaving of thread steps independently of the coinfl ips they produce during the execution.

**Shared Objects.** The algorithms we consider are implementations of shared objects. A shared object $O$ is an abstraction providing a set of *methods*, each given by a sequential specification. In particular, an implementation of a method $M$ for an object $O$ is a set of $n$ algorithms, one for each executing process. When thread $P_i$ invokes method $M$ of object $O$, it follows the corresponding algorithm until it receives a response from the algorithm. Upon receiving the response, the process is immediately assigned another method invocation. In the following, we do not distinguish between a method $M$ and its implementation. A method invocation is *pending* at some point in the execution if has been initiated but has not yet received a response. A pending method invocation is *active* if it is made by a *correct* process (note that the process may still crash in the future). For example, a concurrent counter could implement read and increment methods, with the same semantics as those of the sequential data structure.

**Linearizability.** The standard correctness condition for concurrent implementations is *linearizability* [18]: roughly, a linearizable implementation ensures that each concurrent operation can be seen as executing at a single instant in time, called its linearization point. The mapping from method calls to linearization points induces a global order on the method calls, which is guaranteed to be consistent to a sequential execution in terms of the method outputs; moreover, each linearization point must occur between the start and end time of the corresponding method.

Recent work, e.g. [17], considers deterministic relaxed variants of linearizability, in which operations are allowed to deviate from the sequential specification by a *relaxation* factor. Such relaxations appear to be necessary in the case of data structures such as exact counters or priority queues in order to circumvent strong linear lower bounds on their concurrent complexity [2]. While specifying such data structures in the concurrent case is well-studied [1, 15, 17], less is known about how to specify structured randomized relaxations.

**With High Probability.** We say that an event occurs *with high probability* in a parameter, e.g. $m$, if it occurs with probability at least $1 - 1/m^c$, for some constant $c \geq 1$.

## 4 THE MULTICOUNTER ALGORITHM

**Description.** The algorithm implements an approximate counter by distributing updates among $m$ distinct counters, each of which supports atomic read and increment operations. Please see Algorithm 1 for pseudocode. To read the counter value, a thread simply picks one of the $m$ counters uniformly at random, and returns its value multiplied by $m$. To increment the counter value, the thread picks two counter indices $i$ and $j$ uniformly at random, and reads

[2] Balls in each bin are sorted in increasing order of label, i.e. each bin corresponds to a sequential priority queue.

their current values sequentially. It then proceeds to update (increment) the value of the counter which appeared to have a lower value given its two reads. (In case of a tie, or when the two choices are identical, the tie is broken arbitrarily.)

**Algorithm 1** Pseudocode for the MultiCounter Algorithm.

```
Shared: Counters[m] // Array of integers representing set of m
distinct counters
function Read()
i ← random(1, m)
return m · Counters[i].read()

function Increment()
i ← random(1, m)
j ← random(1, m)
v_i ← Counters[i].read()
v_j ← Counters[j].read()
Counters[arg min(v_i, v_j)].increment()
```

**Relation to Load Balancing.** A *sequential* version of the above process, in which the counter is read or incremented *atomically*, is identical to the classic two-choice balanced allocation process [7], where each counter corresponds to a bin, and each increment corresponds to a new ball being inserted into the less loaded of two randomly chosen bins.

In a concurrent setting, the critical departure from the sequential model is that the values read can be *inconsistent* with respect to a sequential execution: there may be no single point in time when the two counters had the values $v_i$ and $v_j$ observed by the thread; moreover, these values may change between the point where they are read, and the point where the update is performed.

More technically, the sequential variant of the two-choice process has the crucial property that, at each increment step, it is "biased" towards incrementing the counter of lower value. This does not necessarily hold for the concurrent approximate counter: for an operation where a large number of updates occur between the read and the update points, the read information is stale, and therefore the thread's increment choice may be no better than a perfectly random one; in fact, as we shall see in the analysis, it is actually possible for an adversary to engineer cases where the algorithm's choice is biased towards incrementing the counter of *higher value.*

# 5 DISTRIBUTIONAL LINEARIZABILITY

We generalize the classic linearizability correctness condition to cover *randomized relaxed* concurrent data structures, such as the MultiCounter. Intuitively, we will say that a concurrent data structure $D$ is distributionally linearizable to a corresponding *relaxed sequential process* $R$, defined in terms of a sequential specification $S$, a cost function *cost* measuring the deviation from the sequential specification, and a distribution $\mathcal{P}$ on the *cost* function values, such that every execution of $D$ can be mapped onto an execution of the relaxed sequential process $R$, respecting the outputs and the incurred costs, as well as the order of non-overlapping operations. To formalize this definition, we introduce the following machinery, part of which is adopted from [17].

**Data Structures and Labeled Transition Systems.** Let $\Sigma$ be a set of methods including input and output values. A sequential history $s$ is a sequence over $\Sigma$, i.e. an element in $\Sigma^*$. A (sequential) data structure is a sequential specification $S$ which is a prefix-closed set of sequential histories. For example, the sequential specification of a stack consists of all valid sequences for a stack, i.e. in which every push places elements on top of the stack, and every pop removes elements from the top of the stack.

Given a sequential specification $S$, two sequential histories $s, t \in S$ are equivalent, written $s \simeq t$, if they correspond to the same "state:" formally, for any sequence $u \in \Sigma^*$, $su \in S$ iff $tu \in S$. Let $[s]_S$ be the equivalence class of $s \in S$.

DEFINITION5.1. *Let $S$ be a sequential specification. Its corresponding labeled transition sequence (LTS) is an object $LTS(S) = (Q, \Sigma, \rightarrow, q_0)$, with states $Q = \{[s]_S | s \in S\}$, set of labels $\Sigma$, transition relation $\rightarrow \subseteq Q \times \Sigma \times Q$ given by $[s]_S \rightarrow^m [sm]_S$ iff $sm \in S$,* and *initial state* $q_0 = [\epsilon]_S$.

Notice that the sequential specification $S$ can be alternatively defined as the set of all traces of the initial state of $LTS(S)$: formally, for any $u \in \Sigma^*$, we have $u \in S$ iff $q_0 \rightarrow^u$.

**Randomized Quantitative Relaxations.** Let $S \in \Sigma^*$ be a data structure with $LTS(S) = (Q, \Sigma, \rightarrow, q_0)$. To obtain a randomized quantitative relaxation of $S$, we apply the following four steps. The first three steps are identical to deterministic quantitative relaxations [17], whereas the fourth defines the probability distribution on costs:

(1) **Completion**: We start from $LTS(S)$, and construct a completed labeled transition system, with transitions from any state to any other state by any method:

$$LTS_c(S) = (Q, \Sigma, Q \times \Sigma \times Q, q_0).$$

(2) **Cost function:** We add a cost function $cost : Q \times \Sigma \times Q \rightarrow \mathbb{R}$ to the LTS. The transition cost will satisfy

$cost(q, m, q') = 0$ if and only if $q \rightarrow^m q'$ in $LTS(S)$.

A quantitative path is a sequence

$$\kappa = q_1 \rightarrow^{m_1, k_1} q_2 \rightarrow^{m_2, k_2} \dots \rightarrow^{m_n, k_n} q_{n+1}.$$

We call the sequence $\tau = (m_1, k_1), \dots, (m_n, k_n)$ of transitions and costs the quantitative trace of $\kappa$, denoted by $qtr(\kappa)$.

(3) **Path cost function**: Given a quantitative path $\kappa$, its path cost is defined as $pcost : qtr(S) \rightarrow C$. Path costs are monotone with respect to prefix order: if $\tau$ is a prefix of $\tau'$, then $pcost(\tau) \leq pcost(\tau')$.

(4) **Probability distribution**: Given an arbitrary state $[s]$ in $LTS(S)$, we define a probability space $(\Omega, \mathcal{F}, \mathcal{P})$ on the set of possible transitions and their corresponding costs from this state, where the sample space $\Omega$ is the set of all transitions in $Q \times \Sigma \times Q$, the $\sigma$-algebra $\mathcal{F}$ is defined in the straightforward way based on the set of elementary events $\Omega$, and $\mathcal{P}$ is a probability measure $\mathcal{P} : \mathcal{F} \rightarrow [0, 1]$.
Importantly, this allows us to define, for any path, the notion of probability for costs incurred at each step. This probability space is readily extended for arbitraryfi nite paths, where we assume that the cost probabilities at each step are independent of previous steps, i.e., historyless. This process induces

a Markov chain, whose state at each step is given by the state $[s]$ of the corresponding LTS, and whose transitions are LTS transitions, with costs and probabilities as above.

**Distributional Linearizability.** With this in place, we now define distributionally linearizable data structures:

DEFINITION5.2. *Let D be a randomized concurrent data structure, and let R be a randomized quantitative relaxation R of a sequential specification S with respect to a cost function* cost*, and a probability distribution $\mathcal{P}$ on costs. We say that D is distributionally linearizable to R iff for every concurrent schedule $\sigma$, there exists a mapping of completed operations in D under $\sigma$ to transitions in the quantitative path of R, preserving outputs, and respecting the order of non-overlapping operations. This mapping can be used to associate any schedule $\sigma$ to a* distribution of costs *for D under the schedule $\sigma$.*

We now make a few important remarks on this definition.

(1) The main difficulty when formally defining the "costs" incurred by $D$ in a concurrent execution is in dealing with the execution history, and with the impact of pending operations on these costs. The above definition allows us to define costs, given a schedule, only in terms of the sequential process $R$, and bounds the incurred costs in terms of the probability distribution defined in $R$. This definition ensures that the probability distribution on costs incurred at each step only depends on the current state of the sequential process.
(2) The second key question is how to use this definition. One subtle aspect of this definition is that the mapping to the sequential randomized quantitative relaxation is done *per schedule*: intuitively, this is because an adversary might change the schedule, and cause the distribution of costs of the data structure to *change*. Thus, it is often difficult to specify a precise cost distribution, which covers all possible schedules. However, for the data structures we analyze, we will be able to provide *tail bounds* on the cost distributions induced by *all possible schedules.*

The natural next question, which we answer in the following section, is whether non-trivial such data structures exist and can be analyzed.

## 6 ANALYSIS OF THE MULTICOUNTER

We will focus on proving the following result.

THEOREM6.1. *Fix a large constant C. Given an oblivious adversary, m distributed counters and n threads with $m \geq 8Cn$, for anyfi xed schedule, the MultiCounter algorithm is distributionally linearizable to a randomized relaxed sequential counter process, which, at any step t, returns a value that is at most $O(m \log m)$ away from the number of increments applied up to t, both in expectation and with high probability in m.*

We emphasize that the relaxation guarantees are independent of the time $t$ at which the guarantee is examined, and that they would thus hold in infinite executions.

### 6.1 Modeling the Concurrent Process

In the following, we will focus on analyzing executions formed exclusively of increment operations, whose lower-level steps may be interleaved. (Adding read operations at any point during the execution will be immediate.) We model the process as follows. First, we assume a schedule that isfi xed by the adversary. For each thread $P_j$, and non-negative integers $j$, we consider a sequence of increment operations $(op_i^{(j)})$, each of which is defined by its starting time $s_i^{(j)}$, corresponding to the time when itsfi rst read step was scheduled, and completion time $f_i^{(j)}$, corresponding to the time when its update time is scheduled, such that $s_{i+1}^{(j)} > f_i^{(j)}$ for all $i, j$. (Recall that the scheduler defines a global order on individual steps.) At most $n$ operations may be active at a given time, corresponding to the fact that we only have $n$ parallel threads.

For each operation $op_i$, we record its *contention* $\ell_i$ as the number of distinct increment operations scheduled between its start and end time. (Alternatively, we could define this quantity as the number of operations which complete in the time interval $(s_i, f_i)$.) Note that at most $n-1$ distinct operations can be concurrent with $op_i$ at any given time, but the contention for a specific operation is potentially unbounded.

We can rephrase the original process as follows. For each operation $op_i$, the adversary sets the time when it performs thefirst and its second read of counter values / bin weights, as well as its contention $\ell_i$, by scheduling other operations concurrently. The only constraint on the adversary is that not more than $n$ operations can be active at the same time.

Since the adversary is oblivious, we notice that the update process is equivalent to the following: at the time when the update is scheduled, the thread executing the operation generates two uniform random indices $i$ and $j$, and is given values $v_i$ and $v_j$ for the two corresponding counters / bin weights, read at previous (possibly different) points in time. We will stick to the bin weight formulation from now on, with the understanding that the two are equivalent.

The thread will then increment the weight of the bin with the smaller value read (among $v_i$ and $v_j$) by 1. This formulation has the slight advantage that it makes the update process sequential, by moving the random choices to the time when the update is made, using the principle of deferred decisions. Critically, the bin weights on which the update decision is based are potentially stale. We will focus on this simplified variant of the process in the following.

**Discussion.** The key difference between the above process and the classic power-of-two-choices process is the fact that the choice of bin / counter which the thread updates is based on stale, potentially invalid information. Recall that key to the strong balancing properties of the classic process is the fact that it is biased towards inserting in *less loaded* bins; the process which inserts into randomly chosen bins is known to diverge [25]. In particular, notice it is possible that, by the time when the thread performs the update, the order of the bins' load may have changed, i.e. the thread in fact inserts into the *more loaded* bin among its two choices at the time of the update.

Since the oblivious adversary decides its schedule independently of the threads' random choices, it cannot *deterministically* cause a specific update to insert into the more loaded bin. However, it can *significantly bias* an update towards inserting into the more loaded bin:

Assume for example an execution suffix where all $n$ threads read concurrently at some time $t_R$[3] and then proceed to perform updates, one after another. Pick an operation $op$ for which the gap between the two values read $v_i$ and $v_j$ (at the time of the read) is 1, say $v_i = v_j + 1$. So $op$ will increment $v_j$. At the same time, notice that all the other operations which read concurrently with $op$ are biased towards inserting in $v_j$ rather than $v_i$, since its rank (in increasing order of weight) is lower than that of bin $i$. Hence, as the adversary schedules more and more operations between $t_R$ at $op$'s update time, it is increasingly likely to *invert* the relation between $i$ and $j$ by the time of $op$'s update, causing it to insert into the "wrong" bin.

The previous example suggests that the adversary is able to bias some subset of the operations towards picking the wrong bin at the time of the update. Another issue is that operations which experience high contention, for which there are many updates between the read point and the update point, the read values $v_i$ and $v_j$ become meaningless: for example, if the weights of bin $i$ and $j$ become equal at some time $t_0$ between $t_R$ and $op$'s update, then from this point in time these two bins appear completely symmetrical to the algorithm, and $op$'s choice given the information that $v_i > v_j$ at $t_R$ may be no better than uniform random.

One issue which further complicates this last example is that, at $t_0$, there may be a non-zero number of other operations which already made their reads (for instance, at $t_R$), but have not updated yet. Since these operations read at a point where $v_i > v_j$, they are in fact biased towards inserting in $v_j$. So, looking at the event that $op$ updates the *less loaded* of its two random choices at update time, we notice that its probability in this example is *strictly worse* than uniform random choice.

We summarize this somewhat lengthy discussion with two points, which will be useful in our analysis:

(1) As they experience concurrent updates, operations may accrue bias towards inserting into the *more loaded* of their two random choices.
(2) Long-running operations may in fact have a higher probability of inserting into the more loaded bin than into the less loaded one, i.e. may become biased towards making the "wrong" choice at the time of the update.

## 6.2 Notation and Background

**The $(1 + \beta)$ Process.** In the following, it will be useful to consider the following *sequential* relaxation of the two-choice process, introduced by [25], called the $(1 + \beta)$-choice process: We are given $m$ bins, initially empty. In each step $t$, wefl ip a biased coin: with probability $\beta > 0$ we will insert a ball into the less loaded of two randomly chosen bins; otherwise, we insert the ball into a randomly chosen bin. This process is analyzed in [25], which shows that, at any time $t$ in its execution, the gap between the maximum and minimum value of a bin is $O(\log m/\beta)$, with high probability in $m$, irrespective of $t$.

We now introduce some notation, which will be common between our analysis and that of [25]. For simplicity, we will assume that, at the beginning of each step in this sequential process, bins are always ranked in *increasing order of their weight.* If $p_i$ is the probability that we pick the $i$th ranked bin for insertion, and $\beta$ is the two-choice probability, then it is easy to see that the $(1 + \beta)$ process guarantees

$$p_i = (1-\beta)\frac{1}{m} + \beta\left[\frac{2}{m}\left(1 - \frac{i-1}{m}\right) - \frac{1}{m^2}\right].$$

Further, notice that, for any $1 \le k \le m$, we have, ignoring the negligible $O(1/m^2)$ factor, that

$$\sum_{i=1}^{k} p_i \simeq \frac{k}{m}\left(1 + \beta - \frac{k}{m}\beta\right).$$

For any bin $j$ and time $t$, let $x_j(t)$ be the weight of bin $j$ at time $t$. Let $\mu(t) = \sum_{j=1}^{m} x_j(t)/m$ be the average weight at time $t$ over the bins. Let $y_i(t) = x_i(t) - \mu(t)$, and let $\alpha < 1$ be a parameter to be fixed later. Define

$$\Phi(t) = \sum_{j=1}^{n} \exp(\alpha y_i(t)), \text{ and } \Psi(t) = \sum_{j=1}^{n} \exp(-\alpha y_i(t)).$$

Finally, define the potential function

$$\Gamma(t) = \Phi(t) + \Psi(t).$$

The main technical result of [25] can be phrased as:

Theorem6.2. *Let $\alpha$, $\beta$ be parameters as given above, and let $\epsilon = \frac{\beta}{16}$. Then there exists a constant $C(\epsilon) = \text{poly}(\frac{1}{\epsilon})$ such that, for any time $t \ge 0$, we have $\mathbb{E}[\Gamma(t)] \le C(\epsilon)m$.*

In turn, this implies that the maximum gap between the most loaded and the least loaded bin at a step is $O(\log m)$ in expectation and with high probability in $m$.

## 6.3 Main Argument

**Analysis Overview.** Throughout the analysis, we willfi x a large constant $C$ such that $m \ge 8Cn$. The analysis proceeds in the following technical steps.

- We define an operation $op_t$ as $good(\gamma)$ for $\gamma > 0$ if, with probability at least $1/2 + \gamma$, the bin $op_t$ adds to is not accessed by another operation at any point during the execution of $op_t$. We will identify a constant $\gamma > 0$ such that all operations with contention $\le Cn$ are $good(\gamma)$.
- We lower bound the expected decrease in potential caused by a step that is $good(\gamma)$.
- We upper bound the expected increase in potential caused by a step that is not $good(\gamma)$.
- We argue that, for any adversarial strategy, out of any group of $Cn$ consecutive operations, at least $(C-1)n$ have to be $good(\gamma)$. We then upper bound the change in potential over any stretch of $Cn$ operations, showing that it has to stay in $O(m)$.

We will prove the following simple claim as starting point for the analysis:

Lemma6.3. *If for $op_t$ we have that its contention $\ell_t \le Cn$, then the step (operation) $t$ is $good(\frac{1}{5})$.*

[3] Technically, since we count time in terms of shared-memory operations, these reads occur at consecutive times after $t_R$. However, all their read values are identical to the read value at $t_R$, and hence we choose to simplify notation in this way.

PROOF. Let $i$ and $j$ be two random bins chosen by $op_t$, w.l.o.g we assume that $i$ is chosen to add to by $op_t$. Considering that $\ell_t \le Cn$ and for any operation, the probability of accessing bin $i$ is at most $\frac{2}{m}$, we get:

$$Pr[\text{bin } i \text{ untouched}] \ge \left(1 - \frac{2}{m}\right)^{Cn} \ge 2^{-\frac{1}{2}} \ge \frac{7}{10}.$$

where we used inequalities $1 - \frac{x}{2} \ge 2^{-x}$ and $m \ge 8Cn$. □

Next we try to bound the expected decrease in potential if operation $t$ is $good(\gamma)$.

LEMMA6.4. *If $op_t$ is $good(\gamma)$, then :*

$$\mathbb{E}[\Gamma(t+1)|y(t)] \le \Gamma(t)\left(1 - \frac{\alpha\epsilon}{4m}\right) + c, \quad for\ \epsilon = \gamma/6\ and\ c = c(\epsilon) = poly(1/\epsilon). \tag{1}$$

PROOF. First notice that if $op_t$ chooses to delete from bin $i$ after looking at bins $i, j$ and bin $i$ is not accessed by any other operation during execution of $op_t$, then bin $i$ must have been less loaded than bin $j$ for the entire interval between the *second* read of $op_t$ and the write of $op_t$.

Now, we will use Theorem 3.1 from [25], stated below. Assume that we are given a weight vector $y(t)$, in increasing order of weight, and two probability vectors $p = (p_1, p_2, ..., p_m)$ and $q = (q_1, q_2, .., q_m)$, where we assume that probability vectors are sorted in decreasing order. We say that $p$ majorizes $q$ if for any $1 \le k \le m$:

$$\sum_{i=1}^{k} p_i \ge \sum_{i=1}^{k} q_i$$

Let $\mathbb{E}[\Gamma_p(t+1)|y(t)]$ be expected potential function if we choose bin according to probability vector $p$ (that is, $i$-th less loaded bin is chosen with probability $p_i$) and let $\mathbb{E}[\Gamma_q(t+1)|y(t)]$ be expected potential function if we choose bin according to probability vector $q$ (that is, the $i$-th least loaded bin is chosen with probability $q_i$). Then Theorem 3.1 from [25] implies that $\mathbb{E}[\Gamma_p(t+1)|y(t)] \le \mathbb{E}[\Gamma_q(t+1)|y(t)]$, because probability vector $p$ is more biased towards lesser loaded bins than probability vector $q$.

What we need to show is that probability vector of $op_t$ which is $good(\gamma)$ majorizes the probability vector of $1+\beta$ choice process for some $\beta = 2\gamma$. That is, for any $1 \le k$:

$$\sum_{i=1}^{k} p_i \ge \sum_{i=1}^{k} q_i.$$

We do exactly that in the following. Let $q$ be the probability vector for the bin choice of the fully sequential process. As we know, for any $1 \le i \le m$, $q_i = \beta\frac{2(m-i)+1}{m^2} + \frac{1-\beta}{m}$. Recall that if bin $i$ is not accessed by another operation during the execution of $op_t$, then $op_t$ must add to the bin which is the lesser loaded at the time of writing. Thus, if $\rho \ge 1/2 + \gamma$ is the probability that $op_t$ adds to the lesser loaded bin, we have that $p_i = \rho\frac{2(m-i)}{m^2} + \frac{1}{m^2} + (1-\rho)\frac{2(i-1)}{m^2}$.

Then:

$$\begin{aligned}
\sum_{i=1}^{k} p_i &= \sum_{i=1}^{k}\left(\rho\frac{2(m-i)}{m^2} + \frac{1}{m^2} + (1-\rho)\frac{2(i-1)}{m^2}\right) \\
&= \rho\frac{2mk - k(k+1)}{m^2} + \frac{k}{m^2} + (1-\rho)\frac{k(k-1)}{m^2} \\
&= \rho\frac{2mk - 2k^2}{m^2} + \frac{k^2}{m^2} = 2\rho\frac{mk - k^2}{m^2} + \frac{k^2}{m^2}.
\end{aligned}$$

On the other hand:

$$\begin{aligned}
\sum_{i=1}^{k} q_i &= \sum_{i=1}^{k}\left(\frac{1-\beta}{m} + \beta\frac{2(m-i)+1}{m^2}\right) \\
&= \frac{k}{m} + \beta\frac{mk - k^2}{m^2} = \beta\frac{mk - k^2}{m^2} + \frac{mk - k^2}{m^2} + \frac{k^2}{m^2} \\
&= (1+\beta)\frac{mk - k^2}{m^2} + \frac{k^2}{m^2}.
\end{aligned}$$

From the equations above, it is easy to see that for any $k$ and $\beta = 2\gamma$:

$$\sum_{i=1}^{k} p_i \ge \sum_{i=1}^{k} q_i.$$

Theorem 2.9 from [25] gives us that :

$$\mathbb{E}[\Gamma_q(t+1)|y(t)] \le \Gamma(t)\left(1 - \frac{\alpha\epsilon}{4m}\right) + c, \quad \text{for } \epsilon = \beta/12 = \gamma/6 \text{ and } c = c(\epsilon) = poly(1/\epsilon). \tag{2}$$

The fact that $\mathbb{E}[\Gamma(t+1)|y_t] = \mathbb{E}[\Gamma_p(t+1)|y(t)] \le \mathbb{E}[\Gamma_q(t+1)|y(t)]$ gives us the lemma. □

If $op_t$ inserts into the lesser loaded bin with probability at most $\frac{1}{2}$, we assume the worst scenario. That is, we assume that $op_t$ always inserts into the more loaded bin and we try to bound the expected potential increase for that case. For this, again let us assume that the weight vector $y(t)$ is ordered such that $y_1(t) \le y_2(t) \le ... \le y_m(t)$ and let $p_i$, $1 \le i \le m$ be a probability that bin $i$ is chosen. In this case, $p_i = \frac{2i-1}{m^2}$.

We nowfi x some constants: let $\lambda = 1$ and $S = 1$, so that for every $z < \lambda/2$ we have $e^z < 2S$. Also, to be consistent with the above lemma wefix $\epsilon = \beta/12 = \gamma/6$. At this point, we alsofix $\alpha = \min(\frac{\lambda}{2}, \frac{\epsilon}{6S})$. This allows us to prove the following lemma:

LEMMA6.5. *If $op_t$ is a bad operation, then:*

$$\mathbb{E}[\Gamma(t+1)|y(t)] \le \left(1 + \frac{2}{m}\left(\alpha + \frac{\epsilon}{6}\right)\right)\Gamma(t). \tag{3}$$

PROOF. First, we consider what is expected change in $\Phi$. Let $\Phi_i(t) = \exp(\alpha y_i(t))$. We have two cases here. If bin $i$ is chosen, then the change is:

$$\begin{aligned}
\Delta\Phi_i &= \Phi_i(t+1) - \Phi_i(t) = \\
&= \exp\Big(\alpha\Big(y_i(t) + (1-\frac{1}{m})\Big)\Big) - \exp\Big(\alpha y_i(t)\Big) \\
&= \exp\Big(\alpha y_i(t)\Big)\Big(\exp\Big(\alpha(1-\frac{1}{m})\Big) - 1\Big) \\
&\overset{*}{=} \exp\Big(\alpha y_i(t)\Big)\Big(1 + \alpha(1-\frac{1}{m}) + e^{\zeta}\Big(\alpha(1-\frac{1}{m})\Big)^2/2 - 1\Big) \\
&\leq \exp\Big(\alpha y_i(t)\Big)\Big(\alpha(1-\frac{1}{m}) + S\alpha^2\Big).
\end{aligned} \tag{4}$$

where in (∗) we used the Taylor expansion of the exponential around 0 and the fact that since $\zeta \in [0, \alpha(1-\frac{1}{m})]$, we have that $e^{\zeta} < 2$. Using similar arguments we can prove that, when some other bin $j \neq i$ is chosen:

$$\Delta\Phi_i \leq e^{\alpha y_i(t)}\Big(-\frac{\alpha}{m} + S\frac{\alpha^2}{m^2}\Big). \tag{5}$$

Therefore, we get that:

$$\begin{aligned}
\mathbb{E}\Big[\Delta\Phi_i | y(t)\Big] &= p_i\Big(\alpha(1-\frac{1}{m}) + S\alpha^2\Big)e^{\alpha y_i(t)} \\
&+ (1-p_i)\Big(-\frac{\alpha}{m} + S\frac{\alpha^2}{m^2}\Big)e^{\alpha y_i(t)} \\
&\leq e^{\alpha y_i(t)}\Big(p_i\Big(\alpha + S\alpha^2\Big) - \frac{\alpha}{m} + S(\frac{\alpha}{m})^2\Big) \\
&\leq e^{\alpha y_i(t)}\Big(p_i\Big(\alpha + S\alpha^2\Big)\Big) \leq e^{\alpha y_i}\frac{2}{m}\Big(\alpha + \frac{\epsilon}{6}\Big),
\end{aligned} \tag{6}$$

where we used that $p_i \leq \frac{2}{m}$ and $S\alpha \leq \frac{\epsilon}{6}$. This gives us that:

$$\mathbb{E}[\Delta\Phi | y(t)] = \sum_{i=1}^{m}\mathbb{E}[\Delta\Phi_i | y(t)] \leq \frac{2}{m}\Big(\alpha + \frac{\epsilon}{6}\Big)\Phi(t). \tag{7}$$

In a similar way, we can prove that:

$$\mathbb{E}[\Delta\Psi | y(t)] \leq \sum_{i=1}^{m}\Big(p_i\Big(-\alpha + S\alpha^2\Big) + \Big(\frac{\alpha}{m} + S\frac{\alpha^2}{m^2}\Big)\Big)e^{-\alpha y_i}. \tag{8}$$

Since $\alpha S \leq 1$, we get that $\mathbb{E}[\Delta\Psi | y(t)] \leq \frac{2}{m}\alpha\Psi(t)$. Combining this with inequality 7 gives us the Lemma. □

Now we consider $Cn$ consecutive operations and prove that at most $n$ of them can be bad:

Lemma 6.6. *For any $t$, we have that:* $|t' : t \leq t' \leq t + Cn - 1, \ell_{t'} > Cn| < n$.

Proof. We argue by contradiction. Let us assume that the number of bad operations is at least $n$. By the pigeonhole principle, there exist bad operations $op_i$ and $op_j$, $t \leq i < j \leq t + Cn - 1$, which are performed by the same thread. This means that since these operations are not concurrent, we have that $s_j > f_i = i$. Thus, we get a contradiction: $Cn \leq \ell_j = |t' : s_j \leq t' < f_j = j| \leq j - i < Cn$. □

**Endgame.** With all this machinery in place, we proceed to prove the following.

Lemma 6.7. *Given any time $t$, we have*

$$\mathbb{E}[\Gamma(t)] \leq e^2\frac{8c}{\alpha\epsilon}m.$$

Proof. We will proceed by induction on $t$. We willfi rst prove that, if $\Gamma(t) \leq e\frac{8c}{\alpha\epsilon}$, then $\mathbb{E}[\Gamma(t+Cn)|\Gamma(t)] \leq e\frac{8c}{\alpha\epsilon}$.

We have two cases. Thefi rst is if there exists a time $\tau \in [t, t+Cn]$ such that $\Gamma(\tau) \leq \frac{7c}{\alpha\epsilon}m$. Let us now focus on bounding the maximum expected value of $\Gamma(t+3n)$ in this case. First notice that the maximum expected increase of $\Gamma$ because of a good step is an additive $c$ factor. The expected value of $\Gamma$ after a bad step is upper bounded a multiplicative $(1 + \frac{2}{m}(\alpha + \frac{\epsilon}{6}))$ factor. Hence, by Lemma 6.6 and using the fact that $C \geq 3$, the expected maximum value of $\Gamma$ at $t + Cn$ is at most

$$\Big(\frac{7c}{\alpha\epsilon}m + c(C-1)n\Big)\Big(1 + \frac{2}{m}\Big(\alpha + \frac{\epsilon}{6}\Big)\Big)^n \leq e\frac{8c}{\alpha\epsilon}m.$$

The second case is if there exists no such time in $[t, t+Cn]$, meaning that $\Gamma(\tau) > \frac{7c}{\alpha\epsilon}m, \forall\tau \in [t, t+Cn]$. Then, by Lemma 6.4, we have that, at each good step,

$$\mathbb{E}[\Gamma(t+1)|y(t)] \leq \Gamma(t)\Big(1 - \frac{\alpha\epsilon}{12m}\Big). \tag{9}$$

Hence, we can expand the recursion to upper bound the change in $\Gamma$ between $t$ and $t + Cn$ as

$$\mathbb{E}[\Gamma(t+Cn)|y(t)] \leq \Gamma(t)\Big(1 - \frac{\alpha\epsilon}{12m}\Big)^{(C-1)n}\Big(1 + \frac{2}{m}\Big(\alpha + \frac{\epsilon}{6}\Big)\Big)^n. \tag{10}$$

This last expression is upper bounded by $\Gamma(t)$ if $C \geq 1 + 36/\epsilon$, which concludes the proof of ourfi rst claim above. Hence, at the end of each interval of $Cn$ additional operations, the expected potential cannot exceed $e\frac{8c}{\alpha\epsilon}$. To complete the proof, we notice that the value that $\Gamma$ attains *inside* the interval of size $Cn$ occurs if $n$ bad steps occur in succession immediately after its start. However, the maximum value that $\Gamma$ can attain is upper bounded as

$$\mathbb{E}[\Gamma(t+n)|y(t)] \leq \Gamma(t)\Big(1 + \frac{2}{m}\Big(\alpha + \frac{\epsilon}{6}\Big)\Big)^n \leq e^2\frac{8c}{\alpha\epsilon}m. \tag{11}$$

This concludes the proof of the Lemma. □

**The Constant** $C$. A sufficient setting for $C$ for the analysis to hold is $C \geq 1024$, yielding $m \geq 8192n$.

The following claim completes the proof of Theorem 6.1.

Lemma 6.8. *Fix a large constant $C$. Given an oblivious adversary, $m$ distributed counters and $n$ threads with $m \geq 8Cn$, for any time $t$ in the execution of the approximate counter algorithm the counter returns a value that is at most $O(m \log m)$ away from the number of increment operations which completed up to time $t$, in expectation. Moreover, for any $t$ and all $R$ sufficiently large, we have*

$$\Pr\Big[\exists j : \Big|m \cdot x_j(t) - m \cdot \mu_j(t)\Big| > Rm\log m\Big] \leq m^{-\Omega(R)}.$$

Proof. The proof is similar to [25] (the main difficulty was to reach asymptotically the same potential upper bound). We aim to bound *Gap(t)*, the maximum gap between the weight of two bins at a step.

By choosing $C$ sufficiently large, we have that $\alpha^{-1}, \epsilon^{-1} = \Theta(1)$ in Lemma 6.7. Wefi rst prove the bound in expectation. Note that Lemma 6.7 implies that $\mathbb{E}[\Phi(t)] = O(m)$ and $\mathbb{E}[\Psi(t)] = O(m)$ for all $t$. Let $\max(t)$ denote the maximum weight of any bin at time $t$, and let $\min(t)$ be the minimum weight of any bin. Then, we have

$$\begin{aligned}\alpha\,\mathbb{E}[\max(t)-\mu(t)] &= \log\exp\left(\mathbb{E}[\alpha(\max(t)-\mu(t))]\right)\\ &\overset{(a)}{\leq} \log\mathbb{E}[\exp(\alpha(\max(t)-\mu(t)))]\\ &\overset{(b)}{\leq} \log\mathbb{E}[\Phi(t)] \leq O(\log m)\,,\end{aligned}$$

where (a) follows from Jensen's inequality, and (b) follows from the definition of $\Phi$. Similarly, we have $\mathbb{E}[\mu(t)-\min(t)] \leq O(\log m)$. Since the true value of the counter at time $t$ is $m\cdot\mu(t)$, these two statements imply that for all $j$, we have $\mathbb{E}[|m\cdot x_j(t) - m\cdot\mu(t)|] \leq O(m\log m)$, as desired.

We now prove the high probability bound. Observe that if $\max(t) - \mu(t) > R\log m$, then we have $\Gamma(t) \geq \Phi(t) \geq e^{\alpha R\log m}$. Hence,

$$\begin{aligned}\Pr[\max(t)-\mu(t) > R\log m] &\leq \Pr[\Phi(t) \geq e^{\alpha R\log m}]\\ &\leq \frac{O(m)}{e^{\alpha R\log m}}\\ &\leq m^{-O(R)}\,.\end{aligned}$$

Similarly, $\Pr[\mu(t)-\min(t) > R\log m] \leq m^{-\Omega(R)}$.

Combining these two guarantees with a union bound immediately yields the desired guarantee. □

## 6.4 Application to Concurrent Relaxed Queues

We now provide an overview of how to extend the analysis to imply distributional linearizability guarantees in concurrent executions for a variant of the MultiQueue process analyzed by [4]. This process peforms concurrent *Enqueue*() and *Dequeue*() operations on the relaxed concurrent queue. We assume that we are given a set of $m$ linearizable priority queues such that each supports Add$(e,p)$, where $p$ is the priority of the element $e$, and DeleteMin, which deletes the element with the highest priority. We also assume that each processor $i$ has access to the clock which gives an absolute time, and which is consistent amongst all the processors, that is, if processor $i$ reads the clock in the linearization before processor $j$, then processor $i$'s value is smaller. Such an assumption is realistic; recent Intel processors support the RDTSC hardware operation, which provides this functionality for cores on the same socket.

To enqueue, a thread reads the wall clock, chooses a random priority queue, and adds the element to that priority queue with priority given by the time. To dequeue, we choose two random priority queues,fi nd the one having a higher priority element on top, and delete from that priority queue. In case two processes enqueue to the same priority queue concurrently, their clock values will ensure a consistent ordering, handled by the internal implementation of the priority queues.

Following [4], we make the additional assumption that every execution is *prefixed*, intuitively implying that no *Dequeue*() operation ever observes an empty priority queue.

We sketch the analysis of this process for $m = 8Cn$. Initially, as in [4], we couple this process with an exponential process, where if *Dequeue*() removes element with timestamp $t$ from priority queue $i$, the new head element of $i$ has timestamp $t + Exp(1/m)$. Here, $Exp(1/m)$ is an exponentially distributed random variable with mean $m$. Notice that if we divide timestamps by $m$, we have that timestamps increase by 1 in expectation. Next ,we can show that Lemmas 6.4 and 6.5, hold even if instead of incrementing counter(timestamp) by 1, we increment it by a random variable with mean 1 (the proof is given in the full version of the paper [3]). Lemma 6.7 yields that the potential $\Gamma$ defined for the exponential process above (after we divide timestamps by $m$) is linear in expectation. This allows us to use Theorem 4 in [4], which states that in this case expected *rank gap* between the smallest timestamp head element of any queue and the largest timestamp head element of any queue in the original process is at most $O(m\log m)$. A complete proof of this claim is given in the full version of this paper [3].

# 7 EXPERIMENTAL RESULTS

**Setup.** Our experiments were run on an Intel E7-4830 v3 with 12 cores per socket and 2 hyperthreads (HTs) per core, for a total of 24 threads, and 128GB of RAM. In all of our experiments, we pinned threads to avoid unnecessary context switches. Hyperthreading is only used with more than 12 threads. The machine runs Ubuntu 14.04 LTS. All code was compiled with the GNU C++ compiler (G++) 6.3.0 with compilation options `-std=c++11 -mcx16 -O3`.

**Synthetic Benchmarks.** We implemented and benchmarked the MultiCounter algorithm on a multicore machine. To test the behavior under contention, threads continually increment the counter value using the two-choice process. We use no synchronization other than the atomic fetch and increment instruction for the update. Figure 1(a) shows the scalability results, while Figure 1(b) shows the "quality" guarantees of the implementation in terms of values returned by the counter over time, as well as maximum gap between bins over time. Quality is measured in a single-threaded execution, for 64 counters. (Recording quality accurately in a concurrent execution appears complicated, as it is not clear how to order the concurrent read steps.)

# 8 CONCLUSIONS AND FUTURE WORK

We have presented thefi rst concurrent analysis of the two-choice load-balancing process, showing that this classic randomized algorithm is in fact robust to asynchrony under an oblivious adversary. Our analysis extends existing tools, namely [25], in non-trivial ways, in particular by showing that the potential analysis can withstand adversarially corrupted updates. Our results have non-trivial practical applications, as they show that a popular set of randomized concurrent data structures in fact provide strong probabilistic guarantees in arbitrary executions, which we express via a new correctness condition called *distributional linearizability.* This inspires a scalable approximate counting mechanism, trading offcontention and exactness guarantees.

An immediate direction of future work is to reduce the large constant gap between the number of bins $m$ and the number of threads $n$. We did not specifically optimize for this gap in the current version. It is interesting to also ask whether the process will preserve its properties even under high contention, e.g. $m <= n$. The main reason for which we assume that $m \geq 8Cn$ is to withstand adversarial executions in which the adversary schedules whole "blocks" of updates, which effectively reset the distribution of bin loads. Threads acting with stale information after such a block perform choices which are effectively random (or worse than random).

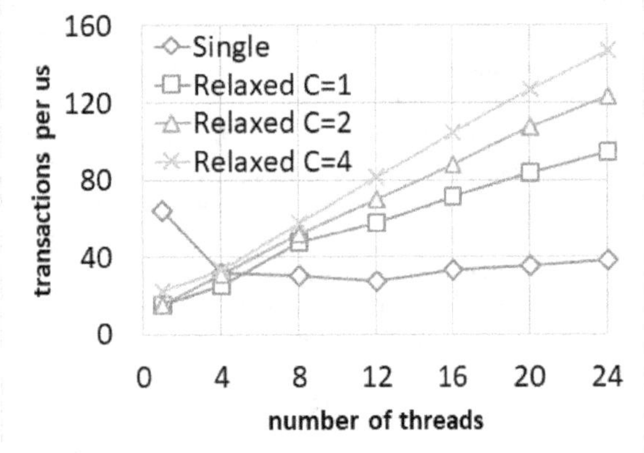


(a) Scalability of the concurrent counter for different values of the ratio $C$ between counters and # threads.

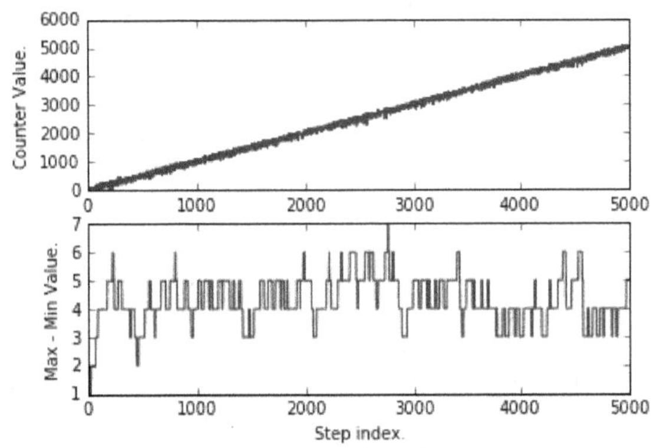


(b) Quality results for the concurrent counter in a single-threaded execution. The $x$ axis is # increments.

**Figure 1: Experimental Results for the Concurrent Counter**

## 9 ACKNOWLEDGMENTS

Giorgi Nadiradze was supported by the Swiss National Fund Ambizione Project PZ00P2 161375. Justin Kopinsky was supported by the NSF under grants IIS-1447786 and CCF-1563880. Jerry Li was supported by NSF CAREER Award CCF-1453261, a Google Faculty Research Award, and an NSF Fellowship. Trevor Brown was funded in part by a post-doctoral fellowship from the Natural Sciences and Engineering Research Council of Canada.

## REFERENCES

[1] Yehuda Afek, Guy Korland, and Eitan Yanovsky. Quasi-linearizability: Relaxed consistency for improved concurrency. In *International Conference on Principles of Distributed Systems*, pages 395–410. Springer, 2010.

[2] Dan Alistarh, James Aspnes, Keren Censor-Hillel, Seth Gilbert, and Rachid Guerraoui. Tight bounds for asynchronous renaming. *J. ACM*, 61(3):18:1–18:51, June 2014.

[3] Dan Alistarh, Trevor Brown, Justin Kopinsky, Jerry Z. Li, and Giorgi Nadiradze. Distributionally linearizable data structures, 2018. arXiv:1804.01018.

[4] Dan Alistarh, Justin Kopinsky, Jerry Li, and Giorgi Nadiradze. The power of choice in priority scheduling. *arXiv preprint arXiv:1706.04178*, 2017. To appear in PODC 2017.

[5] Dan Alistarh, Justin Kopinsky, Jerry Li, and Nir Shavit. The spraylist: A scalable relaxed priority queue. In *20th ACM SIGPLAN Symposium on Principles and Practice of Parallel Programming*, PPoPP 2015, San Francisco, CA, USA, 2015. ACM.

[6] Hagit Attiya and Jennifer Welch. *Distributed computing: fundamentals, simulations, and advanced topics*, volume 19. John Wiley & Sons, 2004.

[7] Yossi Azar, Andrei Z Broder, Anna R Karlin, and Eli Upfal. Balanced allocations. *SIAM journal on computing*, 29(1):180–200, 1999.

[8] Dmitry Basin, Rui Fan, Idit Keidar, Ofer Kiselov, and Dmitri Perelman. CafÉ: Scalable task pools with adjustable fairness and contention. In *Proceedings of the 25th International Conference on Distributed Computing*, DISC'11, pages 475–488, Berlin, Heidelberg, 2011. Springer-Verlag.

[9] Petra Berenbrink, Artur Czumaj, Matthias Englert, Tom Friedetzky, and Lars Nagel. Multiple-choice balanced allocation in (almost) parallel. In *APPROX-RANDOM*, pages 411–422. Springer, 2012.

[10] Petra Berenbrink, Artur Czumaj, Angelika Steger, and Berthold Vöcking. Balanced allocations: The heavily loaded case. In *Proceedings of the Thirty-second Annual ACM Symposium on Theory of Computing*, STOC '00, pages 745–754, New York, NY, USA, 2000. ACM.

[11] Petra Berenbrink, Tom Friedetzky, Zengjian Hu, and Russell Martin. On weighted balls-into-bins games. *Theor. Comput. Sci.*, 409(3):511–520, December 2008.

[12] N. Deo and S. Prasad. Parallel heap: An optimal parallel priority queue. *The Journal of Supercomputing*, 6(1):87–98, March 1992.

[13] Dave Dice, Yossi Lev, and Mark Moir. Scalable statistics counters. In *25th ACM Symposium on Parallelism in Algorithms and Architectures, SPAA '13, Montreal, QC, Canada*, pages 43–52, 2013.

[14] Joseph E Gonzalez, Yucheng Low, Haijie Gu, Danny Bickson, and Carlos Guestrin. Powergraph: distributed graph-parallel computation on natural graphs. In *OSDI*, volume 12, page 2, 2012.

[15] Andreas Haas, Thomas A Henzinger, Andreas Holzer, Christoph M Kirsch, Michael Lippautz, Hannes Payer, Ali Sezgin, Ana Sokolova, and Helmut Veith. Local linearizability. *arXiv preprint arXiv:1502.07118*, 2015.

[16] Andreas Haas, Michael Lippautz, Thomas A. Henzinger, Hannes Payer, Ana Sokolova, Christoph M. Kirsch, and Ali Sezgin. Distributed queues in shared memory: multicore performance and scalability through quantitative relaxation. In *Computing Frontiers Conference, CF'13, Ischia, Italy, May 14 - 16, 2013*, pages 17:1–17:9, 2013.

[17] Thomas A. Henzinger, Christoph M. Kirsch, Hannes Payer, Ali Sezgin, and Ana Sokolova. Quantitative relaxation of concurrent data structures. *SIGPLAN Not.*, 48(1):317–328, January 2013.

[18] Maurice P. Herlihy and Jeannette M. Wing. Linearizability: A correctness condition for concurrent objects. *ACM Trans. Program. Lang. Syst.*, 12(3):463–492, July 1990.

[19] R. M. Karp and Y. Zhang. Parallel algorithms for backtrack search and branch-and-bound. *Journal of the ACM*, 40(3):765–789, 1993.

[20] Andrew Lenharth, Donald Nguyen, and Keshav Pingali. Priority queues are not good concurrent priority schedulers. In *European Conference on Parallel Processing*, pages 209–221. Springer, 2015.

[21] Christoph Lenzen and Roger Wattenhofer. Tight bounds for parallel randomized load balancing. *Distrib. Comput.*, 29(2):127–142, April 2016.

[22] Michael Mitzenmacher. How useful is old information? *IEEE Transactions on Parallel and Distributed Systems*, 11(1):6–20, 2000.

[23] Michael David Mitzenmacher. *The Power of Two Random Choices in Randomized Load Balancing*. PhD thesis, PhD thesis, Graduate Division of the University of California at Berkley, 1996.

[24] Donald Nguyen, Andrew Lenharth, and Keshav Pingali. A lightweight infrastructure for graph analytics. In *Proceedings of the Twenty-Fourth ACM Symposium on Operating Systems Principles*, SOSP '13, pages 456–471, New York, NY, USA, 2013. ACM.

[25] Yuval Peres, Kunal Talwar, and Udi Wieder. Graphical balanced allocations and the 1 + beta-choice process. *Random Struct. Algorithms*, 47(4):760–775, December 2015.

[26] Andrea W Richa, M Mitzenmacher, and R Sitaraman. The power of two random choices: A survey of techniques and results. *Combinatorial Optimization*, 9:255–304, 2001.

[27] Hamza Rihani, Peter Sanders, and Roman Dementiev. Brief announcement: Multiqueues: Simple relaxed concurrent priority queues. In *Proceedings of the 27th ACM Symposium on Parallelism in Algorithms and Architectures*, SPAA '15, pages 80–82, New York, NY, USA, 2015. ACM.

[28] P. Sanders. Randomized priority queues for fast parallel access. *Journal Parallel and Distributed Computing, Special Issue on Parallel and Distributed Data Structures*, 49:86–97, 1998.

[29] Nir Shavit and Itay Lotan. Skiplist-based concurrent priority queues. In *Parallel and Distributed Processing Symposium, 2000. IPDPS 2000. Proceedings. 14th International*, pages 263–268. IEEE, 2000.

[30] Kunal Talwar and Udi Wieder. Balanced allocations: The weighted case. In *Proceedings of the Thirty-ninth Annual ACM Symposium on Theory of Computing*, STOC '07, pages 256–265, New York, NY, USA, 2007. ACM.

[31] Martin Wimmer, Jakob Gruber, Jesper Larsson Träff, and Philippas Tsigas. The lock-free k-lsm relaxed priority queue. In *ACM SIGPLAN Notices*, volume 50, pages 277–278. ACM, 2015.

# Distributed Domination on Graph Classes of Bounded Expansion*

Saeed Akhoondian Amiri
Max-Planck-Institut für Informatik, Saarbrücken, Germany
samiri@mpi-inf.mpg.de

Patrice Ossona de Mendez
CAMS (CNRS UMR 8557), EHESS, Paris, France
pom@ehess.fr

Roman Rabinovich
Technische Universität Berlin, Germany
roman.rabinovich@tu-berlin.de

Sebastian Siebertz
University of Warsaw, Poland
siebertz@mimuw.edu.pl

## ABSTRACT

We provide a new constant factor approximation algorithm for the (connected) distance-$r$ dominating set problem on graph classes of bounded expansion. Classes of bounded expansion include many familiar classes of sparse graphs such as planar graphs and graphs with excluded (topological) minors, and notably, these classes form the most general subgraph closed classes of graphs for which a sequential constant factor approximation algorithm for the distance-$r$ dominating set problem is currently known. Our algorithm can be implemented in the $CONGEST_{BC}$ model of distributed computing and uses $O(r^2 \log n)$ communication rounds.

Our techniques, which may be of independent interest, are based on a distributed computation of sparse neighborhood covers of small radius on bounded expansion classes. We show how to compute an $r$-neighborhood cover of radius $2r$ and overlap $f(r)$ on every class of bounded expansion in $O(r^2 \log n)$ communication rounds for some function $f$.

Finally, we show how to use the greater power of the *LOCAL* model to turn any distance-$r$ dominating set into a constantly larger connected distance-$r$ dominating set in $3r + 1$ rounds on any class of bounded expansion. Combining this algorithm, e.g., with the constant factor approximation algorithm for dominating sets on planar graphs of Lenzen et al. gives a constant factor approximation algorithm for connected dominating sets on planar graphs in a constant number of rounds in the *LOCAL* model, where the approximation ratio is only 6 times larger than that of Lenzen et al.'s algorithm.

## KEYWORDS

Distributed algorithm, Dominating set, Connected dominating set, Bounded expansion

**ACM Reference Format:**
Saeed Akhoondian Amiri, Patrice Ossona de Mendez, Roman Rabinovich, and Sebastian Siebertz. 2018. Distributed Domination on Graph Classes of Bounded Expansion. In *SPAA '18: 30th ACM Symposium on Parallelism in Algorithms and Architectures, July 16–18, 2018, Vienna, Austria.* ACM, New York, NY, USA, 9 pages. https://doi.org/10.1145/3210377.3210383

## 1 INTRODUCTION AND CONTRIBUTIONS

The Dominating Set and Connected Dominating Set problems are two of the most well-studied problems in algorithms and combinatorics [28]. Recall that a subset $D$ of vertices of a graph $G$ is a *dominating set* of $G$ if every vertex of $G$ is either in $D$ or adjacent to a vertex in $D$, and that a dominating set is a *connected dominating set* if it induces a connected subgraph.

The Dominating Set problem, which aims at finding a minimum size dominating set in a graph is NP-complete in general [31], and even so on planar graphs of maximum degree 3 (cf. [GT2] in [23]). The simple greedy algorithm—which at each step adds a vertex dominating the largest number of non-dominated vertices—achieves an approximation ratio [1] of $\ln n - \ln\ln n + \Theta(1)$ on graphs of order $n$ [15, 39], and no better approximation ratio can be achieved in general under standard complexity theoretic assumptions [4, 6, 12, 20, 22, 40, 50].

Recall that a class $C$ (closed under taking subgraphs) has *bounded expansion* if, for every integer $r$, the average degree of all graphs having their $r$-subdivision (that is the graph obtained by replacing each edge by a path of length $r + 1$) in $C$ is bounded by some constant $C(r)$ [42–45]. Not only do many familiar classes of sparse graphs, such as planar graphs and graphs with excluded (topological) minors have bounded expansion, but so do many geometrically defined graphs [27, 47], and experimental evidence that real world complex networks have bounded expansion is given in [19]. Also,

*S.A. Amiri, R. Rabinovich and, partially, S. Siebertz's research was supported by the European Research Council (ERC) under the European Union's Horizon 2020 research and innovation programme (ERC consolidator grant DISTRUCT, agreement No 648527). P. Ossona de Mendez's research was supported by grant ERCCZ LL-1201 and by the European Associated Laboratory "Structures in Combinatorics" (LEA STRUCO), and partially supported by ANR project Stint under reference ANR-13-BS02-0007. The work of S. Siebertz is partially supported by the National Science Centre of Poland via POLONEZ grant agreement UMO-2015/19/P/ST6/03998, which has received funding from the European Union's Horizon 2020 research and innovation programme (Marie Skłodowska-Curie grant agreement No. 665778).


*SPAA '18, July 16–18, 2018, Vienna, Austria*

ACM ISBN 978-1-4503-5799-9/18/07...$15.00
https://doi.org/10.1145/3210377.3210383

[1] Note that these results are for the Set Cover problem, which however reduces to the Dominating Set problem by an approximation preserving reduction and, in fact, the two problems achieve exactly the same approximation ratio [30].

widely used random models of sparse graphs, like the Configuration Model [41] and the Chung–Lu Model [14] with specified asymptotic degree sequences generate graphs that asymptotically almost surely belong to a bounded expansion class determined by the parameters of the model [19].

In [21] it is proved that in linear time one can compute a constant factor approximation on classes with bounded expansion for a generalization of the Dominating Set, the Distance-$r$ Dominating Set problem, which consists in finding in an input graph $G$ a minimum size subset $D$ of vertices, such that every vertex of $G$ is at distance at most $r$ from a vertex in $D$. This problem (also known as the $(k, r)$-center problem) has been extensively studied in the literature.

**Contribution 1.** We present a new approximation algorithm for the Distance-$r$ Dominating Set problem on classes of bounded expansion which improves the approximation ratio achieved by the algorithm of [21]. Our algorithm can be implemented in linear time on any class of bounded expansion. A key feature of our algorithm is that it is tailored to be executed in a distributed setting.

There has been lots of effort to approximate the Dominating Set problem with distributed algorithms, however, similar hardness results also apply to distributed algorithms. It was shown in [34] that in $t$ communication rounds the Dominating Set problem on $n$-vertex graphs of maximum degree $\Delta$ can only be approximated within factor $\Omega(n^{c/t^2})$ and $\Omega(\Delta^{c'/t})$, where $c$ and $c'$ are constants. This implies that, in general, to achieve a constant approximation ratio, every distributed algorithm requires at least $\Omega(\sqrt{\log n})$ and $\Omega(\log \Delta)$ communication rounds. Kuhn et al. [34] also provides an approximation algorithm on general graphs, which achieves a $(1+\varepsilon)\ln\Delta$-approximation in $O(\log(n)/\varepsilon)$ rounds for any $\varepsilon > 0$. Ghaffari et al. [24] provide a polylog-time distributed approximation scheme for covering and packing integer linear programs. In particular, based on their techniques one can compute a $(1+\varepsilon)$-approximation for dominating sets and distance-$r$ dominating sets in $O(poly(\log n/\varepsilon))$ rounds in the *LOCAL* model. Observe however that this result requires learning polylog-neighborhoods and solving the dominating set problem optimally on these neighborhoods. In particular, the algorithm cannot be carried out in the *CONGEST* model (in this number of steps).

For graphs of arboricity $a$ there exists a forest decomposition algorithm achieving a factor $O(a^2)$-approximation in randomized time $O(\log n)$, and a deterministic $O(a \log \Delta)$ approximation algorithm requiring $O(\log \Delta)$ rounds [38]. Given any $\delta > 0$, $(1+\delta)$-approximations of a maximum independent set, of a maximum matching, and of a minimum dominating set can be computed in $O(\log^* n)$ rounds in planar graphs [16], which is asymptotically optimal [37]. A constant factor approximation on planar graphs [36, 57] and on graphs of bounded genus [5] can be computed locally in a constant number of communication rounds. In terms of lower bounds, it was shown that there is no deterministic local algorithm (constant-time distributed graph algorithm) that finds a $(7-\varepsilon)$-approximation of a minimum dominating set on planar graphs, for any positive constant $\varepsilon$ [29].

Observe that the above algorithms for restricted graph classes cannot be directly employed to obtain good approximations for the Distance-$r$ Dominating Set problem, as all structural information which is used in the algorithms may be lost when building the $r$-transitive closure of the graph. The distributed algorithms of [35, 49] find distance-$r$ dominating sets of size $O(n/r)$ in time $O(r \cdot \log^* n)$, without any relation to the size of an optimal distance-$r$ dominating set. In very restrictive settings, e.g., in trees [54] or in star-split graphs [56] better solutions are known.

The Distance-$r$ Dominating Set problem is closely related to the problem of covering local neighborhoods in a graph by connected clusters of small radius. An $r$-neighborhood cover [9] is a set $\mathcal{X}$ of vertex sets $X \subseteq V(G)$ such that for each vertex $v \in V(G)$ there is a set $X \in \mathcal{X}$ with $N_r[v] \subseteq X$. We are interested in covers of small *radius*, that is, $\mathrm{rad}(G[X])$ shall be small for all $X \in \mathcal{X}$ and small *degree*, that is, every vertex $v \in V(G)$ shall lie in only a few clusters.

Sparse covers have many applications such as distance coordinates, routing with succinct routing tables [2, 9], mobile user tracking [9], resource allocation [7], synchronisation in distributed algorithms [8], and many more. Every graph admits an $r$-neighborhood cover of radius at most $2r-1$ and degree at most $2r \cdot n^{1/r}$ [9] and asymptotically, this cannot be improved [53]. Better covers are known to exist, e.g., for planar graphs [13] and for classes that exclude a minor [3]. In particular, the construction of [1] provides $r$-neighborhood covers of radius $O(t^2 r)$ and degree $2^{O(t)} \cdot t!$ for graphs that exclude $K_t$ as a minor. It follows from a construction in [26] that classes of bounded expansion admit $r$-neighborhood covers of radius at most $2r$ and degree at most $f(r)$ for some function $f$.

**Contribution 2.** We show that the algorithm of [26] for constructing sparse $r$-neighborhood covers on classes of bounded expansion can be implemented in the $CONGEST_{BC}$ model of distributed computing in $O(r^2 \log n)$ communication rounds. Based on this construction, we show that our newly proposed algorithm for the Distance-$r$ Dominating Set problem can be implemented in the $CONGEST_{BC}$ model in $O(r^2 \log n)$ communication rounds on any class of graphs of bounded expansion. Our result is based on a routing scheme presented by Nešetřil and Ossona de Mendez in [46], which in turn is based on an iterative application of an algorithm of Barenboim and Elkin [11].

While in a sequential setting one can trivially connect the vertices of a (distance-$r$) dominating set along a spanning tree to obtain a connected (distance-$r$) dominating set of small size, creating such connections is a non-trivial task in the distributed setting. Several algorithms were proposed to compute connected dominating sets in general graphs [17, 18, 34, 51, 52, 58]. We also refer to these papers for applications of connected dominating sets for distributed computing and routing. All lower bounds for the Dominating Set problem hold all the more so for the Connected Dominating Set problem. In particular, none of the above algorithms computes a constant factor approximation of a minimum connected dominating set in a sub-linear number of communication rounds. To our knowledge, there is no distributed algorithm to compute a constant factor approximation to the Connected (Distance-$r$) Dominating Set problem on restricted graph classes.

**Contribution 3.** We show how to extend our algorithm for the Distance-$r$ Dominating Set problem to compute a constant factor approximation for the Connected Distance-$r$ Dominating Set problem. We hence prove that there exists a constant factor approximation algorithm for the Connected Distance-$r$ Dominating Set problem which works in the *CONGEST*$_{BC}$ model in $O(r^2 \log n)$ communication rounds on any class of graphs of bounded expansion.

Finally, we show how to use the greater power of the *LOCAL* model to turn any distance-$r$ dominating set $D$ into a connected distance-$r$ dominating set of size at most $c(r) \cdot |D|$, for some small constant $c(r)$ depending only on $r$ and the class under consideration. This new algorithm can be implemented in $3r + 1$ communication rounds in the *LOCAL* model. In combination with the algorithm of Lenzen et al. [36] we obtain a constant factor approximation algorithm for the Connected Dominating Set problem on planar graphs in a constant number of communication rounds in the *LOCAL* model (the constant $c(1)$ which we need here is 6). A similar result follows for graphs of bounded genus by combining our new algorithm with an algorithm of [5].

## 2 PRELIMINARIES

Graphs. In this paper, we consider *finite, undirected simple graphs.* For a graph $G$, we write $V(G)$ for the *vertex set* of $G$ and $E(G)$ for its *edge set.* A *path of length* $\ell$ in $G$ is a subgraph $P \subseteq G$ with vertex set $V(P) = \{v_1, \ldots, v_{\ell+1}\}$ and edge set $E(P) = \{\{v_i, v_{i+1}\} : 1 \leq i < \ell\}$. The path $P$ *connects its endpoints* $v_1$ and $v_{\ell+1}$. The *distance* between two vertices $u, v \in V(G)$, denoted $\mathrm{dist}(u, v)$, is the minimum length of a path that connects $u$ and $v$ or $\infty$ if no such path exists. For $v \in V(G)$, we write $N_r[v]$ for the *closed r-neighborhood of* $v$, that is $N_r[v] = \{u \in V(G) : \mathrm{dist}(u, v) \leq r\}$. Note that we allow paths of length 0, so $N_r[v]$ always contains $v$ itself. For a set $A \subseteq V(G)$, we write $N_r[A]$ for $\bigcup_{v \in A} N_r[v]$. The radius of a connected graph $G$ is the minimum number $\mathrm{rad}(G)$ such that there is a vertex $v \in V(G)$ with $N_{\mathrm{rad}(G)}[v] = V(G)$.

The *arboricity* of a graph is the minimum number of spanning forests that partition its edge set. The arboricity of a graph is within factor 2 of its degeneracy. For a set $X \subseteq V(G)$ we write $G[X]$ for the subgraph of $G$ *induced* by $X$. For $k \in \mathbb{N}$, $G$ is $k$*-degenerate* if for each $X \subseteq V(G)$ the graph $G[X]$ contains a vertex of degree at most $k$. If an $n$-vertex graph $G$ is $k$-degenerate, then $G$ contains at most $k \cdot n$ edges.

We assume that all graphs are represented by adjacency lists. If $G$ is $k$-degenerate, then in linear time we can order the vertices as $v_1, \ldots, v_n$ such that every vertex $v_i$ has at most $k$ smaller neighbours $v_{j_1}, \ldots, v_{j_k}$, $j_\ell < i$ for $\ell \in \{1, \ldots, k\}$. In the same time complexity we can order all adjacency lists consistently with the order. For the sequential model in Section 3 we assume that the identifiers of the vertices occupy constant space while in the distributed model we assume $\log n$-bit identifiers.

Distance - $r$ dominating sets. For an integer $r$, a *distance-r dominating set* in a graph $G$ is a set $M \subseteq V(G)$ such that $N_r[M] = V(G)$. A distance-1 dominating set is simply called a *dominating set.*

Distributed system model. The clients of a network are modelled as the vertices $V(G)$ of a graph $G$, its communication links are represented by the edges $E(G)$ of the graph. Each client has a unique identifier *(id)* of size $\log n$ where $n := |V(G)|$ is the order of the graph known to every vertex. Communication is synchronous and reliable. In each round, each vertex $v \in V(G)$ may send a (different) message to each of its neighbors $w \in N_1[v]$ (the vertex specifies which message is sent to which neighbor) and receives all messages from its neighbors. In the *LOCAL* model, messages may have arbitrary size, in the *CONGEST* model, messages may have size $O(\log n)$. In the *CONGEST*$_{BC}$ model, every vertex may only broadcast the same message of size $O(\log n)$ to all its neighbors. After sending and receiving messages, every client may perform arbitrary finite computations. The complexity of a distributed algorithm is its number of communication rounds. The network graph also represents the graph problem that we are trying to solve, e.g., the Distance-$r$ Dominating Set instance. At termination, each vertex must output whether it is part of the distance-$r$ dominating set or not, and these outputs must define a valid solution of the problem. We refer to [48] for more background.

Bounded expansion classes. A graph $H$ with vertex set $V(H) = \{v_1, \ldots, v_n\}$ is a *minor* of $G$, written $H \preccurlyeq G$, if there are pairwise disjoint connected subgraphs $H_1, \ldots, H_n \subseteq G$, called *branch sets,* such that if $\{v_i, v_j\} \in E(H)$, then there are vertices $u_i \in V(H_i)$ and $u_j \in V(H_j)$ with $\{u_i, u_j\} \in E(G)$. We call $(H_1, \ldots, H_n)$ a *minor model* of $H$ in G. For $r \in \mathbb{N}$, the graph $H$ is a *depth-r minor* of $G$, denoted $H \preccurlyeq_r G$, if there is a minor model $(H_1, \ldots, H_n)$ of $H$ in $G$ such that each $H_i$ has radius at most $r$. We write $d(H)$ for the *average degree* of $H$, that is, for the number $2|E(H)|/|V(H)|$. A class $C$ of graphs has *bounded expansion* if there is a function $f \colon \mathbb{N} \to \mathbb{N}$ such that for all $r \in \mathbb{N}$ and all graphs $H$ and $G \in C$, if $H \preccurlyeq_r G$, then $d(H) \leq f(r)$. Observe that every $n$-vertex graph from a bounded expansion class is $f(0)$-degenerate and hence has at most $f(0) \cdot n$ many edges (depth-0 minors of $G$ are its subgraphs).

Generalized colouring numbers. Let $G$ be a graph. A *linear order* $L$ of $V(G)$ is a reflexive, anti-symmetric, transitive total binary relation $L \subseteq V(G) \times V(G)$. In the following, we will write $u \leq_L v$ instead of $(u, v) \in L$. We write $\Pi(G)$ for the set of all linear orders on $V(G)$. Let $r \in \mathbb{N}$ and let $u, v \in V(G)$. Vertex $u$ is *weakly r-reachable* from vertex $v$ with respect to a linear order $L \in \Pi(G)$ if there exists a path $P$ of length at most $r$ between $u$ and $v$ such that $u$ is minimum among the vertices of $P$ (with respect to $L$). Let $\mathrm{WReach}_r[G, L, v]$ be the set of vertices that are weakly $r$-reachable from $v$ with respect to $L$. Note that $v \in \mathrm{WReach}_r[G, L, v]$. The *weak r-colouring number* $\mathrm{wcol}_r(G)$ of $G$ is defined as

$$\mathrm{wcol}_r(G) = \min_{L \in \Pi(G)} \max_{v \in V(G)} |\mathrm{WReach}_r[G, L, v]|.$$

The generalized colouring numbers were introduced by Kierstead and Yang in the context of colouring games and marking games on graphs [32], and received much attention as a measure for uniform sparseness in graphs, in particular, they can be used to characterize classes of bounded expansion.

Theorem 2.1 (Zhu [59]). *A class $C$ of graphs has bounded expansion if and only if there is a function $f \colon \mathbb{N} \to \mathbb{N}$ such that $\mathrm{wcol}_r(G) \leq f(r)$ for all $r \in \mathbb{N}$.*

Bounds for several restricted classes such as graphs of bounded tree-width, planar graphs or graphs with excluded (topological) minors, were provided in [25, 33, 55]. The weak colouring numbers can be well approximated in linear time as shown in [21].

Theorem 2.2 (Dvořák [21]). *Let $C$ be a class of bounded expansion. There is a linear time algorithm and a function $d : \mathbb{N} \to \mathbb{N}$ which on input $G \in C$ and $r \in \mathbb{N}$ computes in linear time a linear order of $V(G)$ witnessing that $\mathrm{wcol}_r(G) \le d(r)$.*

The next theorem is implicit in [46, Section 4.4] and shows that we can compute these orders also in the distributed setting.

Theorem 2.3 (Nešetřil and Ossona de Mendez [46]). *Let $C$ be a class of bounded expansion and let $r \in \mathbb{N}$. There is a constant $d(r)$ such that one can compute for every $G \in C$ in $O(r^2 \log n)$ communication rounds in the CONGEST$_{BC}$ model an order of $V(G)$ witnessing that $\mathrm{wcol}_r(G) \le d(r)$.*

The procedure described in Theorem 2.3 uses an algorithm by Barenboim and Elkin [11] which computes an orientation of degenerate graphs. For this, we must assume that all vertices know the order $n$ of the input graph. The order is represented by assigning every vertex a *class-id*, which together with the unique vertex-id induces a total order of $V(G)$. We remark that (though not explicitly stated) this order can be obtained as a by-product of the procedure orient$(z, C)$ described in [46, Section 4.4].

In fact, it suffices if the vertices know a polynomial approximate of $n$ as this changes $\log n$ only by a constant factor. In the following, we will assume that the exact value of $n$ is available to avoid unnecessary complication.

Sparse neighborhood covers. Let $G$ be a graph. For $r \in \mathbb{N}$, an *$r$-neighborhood cover* of $G$ is a set $\mathcal{X}$ of subsets $X \subseteq V(G)$, called the *clusters* of $\mathcal{X}$, such that for each $v \in V(G)$ there is some $X \in \mathcal{X}$ with $N_r(v) \subseteq X$. The *radius* of $\mathcal{X}$ is the maximum radius of the graph induced by a cluster $X \in \mathcal{X}$. Note that in every $r$-neighborhood cover of bounded radius each of the clusters induces a connected subgraph of $G$. The *degree* $d_{\mathcal{X}}(v)$ of a vertex $v \in V(G)$ with respect to $\mathcal{X}$ is the number of clusters that contain $v$. The degree of $\mathcal{X}$ is the maximum degree $d_{\mathcal{X}}(v)$ over all vertices $v \in V(G)$. The generalized colouring numbers can be used to construct sparse neighborhood covers.

We fix a number $r \in \mathbb{N}$ for the remainder of the paper. For a vertex $v \in V(G)$, let $X_v$ be the set of the vertices $w$ such that $v \in \mathrm{WReach}_{2r}[G, L, w]$.

Theorem 2.4 (Grohe et al. [26]). *Let $G$ be a graph and let $c, r \in \mathbb{N}$. Let $L$ be an order witnessing that $\mathrm{wcol}_{2r}(G) \le c$. Then the collection $\mathcal{X} = \{X_v : v \in V(G)\}$ is an $r$-neighborhood cover of $G$ of radius $2r$ and degree $c$.*

Hence, by combining Theorem 2.1 and Theorem 2.4, we obtain $r$-neighborhood covers of radius at most $r$ and degree at most $f(r)$ for every class of bounded expansion. We will show in Section 4 how to compute the $r$-neighborhood covers presented in Theorem 2.4 in a distributed setting.

# 3 APPROXIMATING DOMINATING SETS

Our first result shows how to (sequentially) compute good distance-$r$ dominating sets in any fixed class of bounded expansion. The remainder of this section is devoted to the proof of the following theorem.

Theorem 3.1. *For every class $C$ of bounded expansion there is a function $c\colon \mathbb{N} \to \mathbb{N}$ and a linear time algorithm which on input $G \in C$ and $r \in \mathbb{N}$ computes an order $L \in \Pi(G)$ witnessing $\mathrm{wcol}_{2r}(G) \le c(r)$ and a $c(r)$-approximation of a minimum distance-$r$ dominating set of $G$.*

Our result improves the following result of Dvořák [21] who proved that there exists a $c(r)^2$-approximation, where $c(r)$ is the constant in Theorem 3.1.

Recall the definition of $X_v$ (see Section 2):

$$X_v = \{w \in V(G) \,:\, v \in \mathrm{WReach}_{2r}[G, L, w]\}\,. \tag{1}$$

We define for a fixed vertex $v \in V(G)$,

$$R_v := \{w \in X_v \,:\, v = \min \mathrm{WReach}_r[G, L, w]\}\,.$$

Lemma 3.2. *For all vertices $v \in V(G)$ and for all $w \in R_v$ we have $N_r[w] \subseteq X_v$.*

Proof. Let $w \in R_v$. Observe first that $v$ is the minimum element in $N_r[w]$. Now let $u \in N_r[w]$. Then there is a path of length at most $r$ from $u$ to $w$ with all vertices in $N_r[w]$ and a path of length at most $r$ from $w$ to $v$ again with all vertices in $N_r[w]$. Hence there is a path of length at most $2r$ from $u$ to $v$ with all vertices in $N_r[w]$. As $v$ is minimal in $N_r[w]$, this path witnesses that $v \in \mathrm{WReach}_{2r}[G, L, u]$, and hence by definition of $X_v$ it holds that $u \in X_v$. □

Proof of Theorem 3.1. We claim that the set

$$\begin{aligned} D := \{&\min \mathrm{WReach}_r[G, L, w] \,:\\ &w \in V(G)\} = \{v \in V(G) \,:\, R_v \neq \emptyset\} \end{aligned} \tag{2}$$

is a $c(r)$-approximation of a minimum distance-$r$ dominating set. Obviously, $D$ is a distance-$r$ dominating set of $V(G)$, as every vertex $w$ is dominated by $\min \mathrm{WReach}_r[G, L, w]$. It remains to show that we achieve the claimed approximation ratio.

For $v \in V(G)$, let $X_v$ and $R_v$ be as above. Let $\mathcal{X}$ be the collection $\{X_v : v \in V(G)\}$ as in Theorem 2.4. Then $\mathcal{X}$ is an $r$-neighborhood cover of degree $c(r)$ and by Lemma 3.2, for $w \in R_v$, we have $N_r[w] \subseteq X_v$. Let $M$ be a minimum distance-$r$ dominating set in $G$. As every $w \in V(G)$ can be distance-$r$ dominated only from $N_r[w] \subseteq X_v$, it follows that if $w \in R_v$, then $M \cap X_v \neq \emptyset$.

Hence, as every vertex appears in at most $c(r)$ clusters, it holds that

$$|D| = |\bigcup_{\substack{v \in V(G)\\ R_v \neq \emptyset}} \{v\}| \le \sum_{\substack{v \in V(G)\\ R_v \neq \emptyset}} |M \cap X_v| \le c(r) \cdot |M|.$$

We finally show how to compute $D$ in linear time. We assume that $G$ is stored in memory by $n$ adjacency lists. We first use the linear time approximation algorithm for the weak coloring numbers from Theorem 2.2 to compute an order $L$, which will be represented in a way such that one can iterate through the vertices along $L$ in $O(|V(G)|)$ time and such that a comparison $u <_L w$ for every pair $u, w \in V(G)$ takes $O(1)$ time. Here we assume that vertices are equipped with constant size identifiers representing the order. The algorithm is given as Algorithm 1.

In the first step (Line 1 of Algorithm 1 and Algorithm 2), we ensure in linear time that every adjacency list is sorted increasingly with respect to $L$. Algorithm 2 iterates through the vertices of $G$ in order $L$ starting from the least vertex (such that the next vertex

**Algorithm 1** DomSet($G, L$)

**Input:** Graph $V(G)$; $V(G) = \{v_i : 1 \le i \le n\}$; $v_i <_L v_j$ for $i < j$; $A(v_i)$ is the adjacency list of $v_i$
**Output:** A $c(r)$-approximation of a dominating set of $G$

1: SortLists($L$) ▷ Algorithm 2
2: $D \leftarrow \emptyset$
3: $Dominated \leftarrow \emptyset$
4: **for** $i \leftarrow 1, \dots, n$ **do**
5: $\quad N_i \leftarrow$BFS($v_i, L$) ▷ Algorithm 3
6: $\quad$**if** $N_i \setminus Dominated \neq \emptyset$ **then**
7: $\quad\quad D \leftarrow D \cup \{v_i\}$
8: $\quad\quad Dominated \leftarrow Dominated \cup N_i$
9: **return** $D$

can always be found in constant time) and thus has running time $O(m)$. As graphs of bounded expansion are degenerate, we have $m \in O(n)$.

**Algorithm 2** SortLists($L$)

**Input:** Graph $V(G)$; $V(G) = \{v_i : 1 \le i \le n\}$; $v_i <_L v_j$ for $i < j$; $A(v_i)$ is the adjacency list of $v_i$
**Output:** $A(v_i)$ is increasingly sorted with respect to $L$

1: **for** $i \leftarrow 1, \dots, n$ **do** $B(v_i) \leftarrow A(v_i)$ and $A(v_i) \leftarrow ()$
2: **for** $i \leftarrow 1, \dots, n$ **do**
3: $\quad$**for** $v_j \in B(v_i)$ **do**
4: $\quad\quad$add $v_i$ at the end of $A(v_j)$

Now Algorithm 1 iterates through the vertices of $G$ starting with the least element $v_1$ along $L$. For every $v_i \in V(G)$, it uses Algorithm 3 to compute the set of vertices that are bigger than $v_i$ and are dominated by $v_i$. If such a vertex is not dominated by a vertex smaller than $v_i$, it serves as a vertex $w$ in the definition of $D$ (see (2)). Indeed, $v_i \in \text{WReach}_r[G, L, w]$ because $w$ was found by a breadth-first search from $v$ restricted to vertices greater than $v$ with respect to $L$ and to distances at most $r$. On the other hand, if not $v$ was the minimum vertex in $\text{WReach}_r[G, L, w]$ but, say, $u$, then $w$ would be dominated by $u$ and added to the set *Dominated* in the earlier iteration $j$ for $u = v_j$. Thus $v_i = \min \text{WReach}_r[G, L, w]$ and $v_i$ is added to $D$.

Let us estimate the running time of Algorithm 1. Recall that Line 1 has linear running time. Note that every set $N_i$ computed in Line 5 for a vertex $v_i$ is a subset of $X_{v_i}$ because Algorithm 3 restricts its search to vertices bigger than $v_i$ and to distances at most $r$. That is, if $w \in N_{v_i}$, then $v_i \in \text{WReach}_r[G, L, w] \subseteq \text{WReach}_{2r}[G, L, w]$ and thus $w \in X_{v_i}$. As every graph $G \in C$ is $c(r)$-degenerate, every induced subgraph $H \subseteq G$ has at most $c(r) \cdot |V(H)|$ many edges, also the graph induced by $N_i$. When constructing $N_i$ in Algorithm 3 we will only visit vertices of $N_i$ and, for every $w \in N_i$ at most one vertex in its adjacency list that is not in $N_i$. This can be achieved if Line 6 of Algorithm 3 is implemented as an iteration through $A(w)$ starting from the biggest vertex and stopping if a vertex $u \in A(w)$ with $u <_L w$ is reached (recall that $A(w)$ sorted). Hence this search requires time at most $O((c(r)+1) \cdot |N_{v_i}|) = O(c(r) \cdot |X_{v_i}|)$. As every vertex $w$ appears in at most $c(r)$ clusters $X_v$, we obtain a running time of $\sum_{v \in V(G)} O(c(r) \cdot |X_v|) = O(c(r)^2 \cdot n)$. □

**Algorithm 3** BFS($v, L, r$)

▷ As usual BFS, but restricted to vertices $w >_L v$ and only for $r$ steps.
**Input:** Graph $G$; for $w \in V(G)$, the adjacency list $A(w)$ is increasingly sorted w.r.t. to $L$

1: $Q \leftarrow$ empty queue
2: Enqueue $(v, 0)$ in $Q$
3: **while** $Q \neq \emptyset$ **do**
4: $\quad(w, dist) \leftarrow$ dequeue from $Q$
5: $\quad$**if** $dist < r$ **then**
6: $\quad\quad$**for** $u \in A(w)$ and $u >_L v$ **do**
7: $\quad\quad\quad$**if** $u$ not marked as visited **then**
8: $\quad\quad\quad\quad$mark $u$ as visited
9: $\quad\quad\quad\quad$enqueue $(u, dist + 1)$ in $Q$
10: **return** marked vertices

Note that by Theorem 2.1 the constant $c(r)$ in the theorem exists for every class of bounded expansion. Besides the improved approximation ratio, our algorithm is simpler than that of [21]. In particular, given an order $L \in \Pi(G)$, it can straightforwardly be implemented in a distributed way.

## 4 DISTRIBUTED *R*-NEIGHBORHOOD COVERS AND *R*-DOMINATING SETS

In this section we will show how to compute sparse $r$-neighborhood covers as described in Theorem 2.4 and the Distance-$r$ Dominating Set of Theorem 3.1 in a distributed setting.

In order to compute $r$-neighborhood covers according to Theorem 2.4, we want to compute an order $L$ of $V(G)$ which witnesses that $\text{wcol}_{2r}(G) \le c := c(2r)$. In the distributed setting, that means that every vertex $w$ learns its weak reachability set $\text{WReach}_{2r}[G, L, w]$ and, for each $v \in \text{WReach}_{2r}[G, L, w]$, a path within $X_v$ of length at most $2r$ from $w$ to $v$.

In order to find the distance-$r$ dominating set described in Theorem 3.1, every vertex $w$ will choose as its dominator the vertex $\min \text{WReach}_r[G, L, w]$ and send a message to that vertex along the stored path. Even if all vertices send their messages at once, no vertex will have to forward more than $c$ messages.

First, using Theorem 2.3, we compute for a given input graph $G$ an order $L$ witnessing that $\text{wcol}_{2r}(G) \le c$ using $O(r^2 \log n)$ communication rounds. Note that the number of rounds does not depend on $c$, which influences only the size of messages. The latter is $O(c^2 \cdot r \cdot \log n)$, which implicitly follows from Theorem 2.3 in [46]. We show that every vertex can learn its weak reachability set as well as a routing scheme which preserves short distances. Recall from (1) on Page 4 that $X_v$ is defined as $X_v = \{w \in V(G) : v \in \text{WReach}_{2r}[G, L, w]\}$.

Lemma 4.1. *Let $C$ be a class of bounded expansion and $r \in \mathbb{N}$. There is a constant $c = c(2r)$ such that for every $G \in C$ there is a linear order $L$ on $V(G)$ such that $|\text{WReach}_{2r}[G, L, w]| \le c$ for all $w \in V(G)$ and in $O(r^2 \cdot \log n)$ communication rounds (in CONGEST$_{BC}$) every vertex $w$ can learn $\text{WReach}_{2r}[G, L, w]$ and for each $v \in \text{WReach}_{2r}[G, L, w]$ a path $P_{v,w}$ of length at most $2r$ from $w$ to $v$, which is a shortest path between $v$ and $w$ in the graph induced by $X_v$. In particular, if*

$v = \min \mathrm{WReach}_r[G, L, w]$, *then the path* $P_{v,w}$ *is a shortest path between* $v$ *and* $w$ *in* $G$.

Proof. The pseudocode is given in Algorithm 4. First, using Theorem 2.3, we compute for a given graph $G$ an order $L$ witnessing that $\mathrm{wcol}_{2r}(G) \le c(2r)$ in $O(r^2 \log n)$ communication rounds.

The procedure implicitly uses an algorithm of Barenboim and Elkin [11], which assigns to each vertex $v$ a *class id* $cl(v)$, which together with the unique vertex identifier induces the linear order $L$. For ease of presentation, we write $v_i$ for the vertex at position $i$ in the order $L$ and call $i$ the *super-id* of the vertex.

**Algorithm 4** WReachDist($r$)

**Input (for a vertex $w$):** $n = |V(G)|$, adjacency list of $w$, id of $w$
**Output:** $\mathrm{WReach}_{2r}[G, L, w]$, $\min \mathrm{WReach}_r[G, L, w]$ for a particular linear order $L$ (see text)

in parallel, compute $L$ ▷ by Theorem 2.3
  ▷ when done, every vertex $w$ knows its super-id sid($w$)
in parallel, $\mathcal{P}_w = \{\{\mathrm{sid}(w)\}\}$
**for** $i = 1, \dots, r$ **do**
  in parallel, broadcast $\mathcal{P}_w$, receive new paths in $\mathcal{P}$
  in parallel (for vertex $w$):
  *toSend* $\leftarrow \emptyset$
  **for** $u_1$ first vertex in a path from $\mathcal{P}$ **do**
    **if** $\mathrm{sid}(u_1) < \mathrm{sid}(w)$ **then**
      $P \leftarrow$ shortest path from $\mathcal{P} \cup \mathcal{P}_w$ that starts in $u_1$, break ties using super-ids
    **if** exists $P' \in \mathcal{P}_w$ with $P' = u_1, \dots$ **then**
      remove $P'$ from $\mathcal{P}_w$
    $\mathcal{P}_w \leftarrow \mathcal{P}_w \cup \{P\}$ ▷ let $P = u_1, \dots, u_j$
    *toSend* $\leftarrow$ *toSend* $\cup \{u_1, \dots, u_j, w\}$
  broadcast the set *toSend*

The remaining part of the computation has $2r$ rounds which correspond to $2r$ rounds of a breadth-first search as in Algorithm 3. This time, the search is performed in parallel and we have to make sure that only a logarithmic amount of information is sent by every vertex for the $CONGEST_{BC}$ model. The idea is that every vertex $w$ forwards only information about paths that start in a vertex $v \in \mathrm{WReach}_{2r}[G, L, w]$.

Every vertex $w$ maintains a set $\mathcal{P}_w$ of paths of length at most $2r$ from vertices $v \in \mathrm{WReach}_{2r}[G, L, w]$. For every vertex $v \neq w$ there is at most one path $P_v$ in $\mathcal{P}_w$ that starts in $v$ and certifies that $v \in \mathrm{WReach}_{2r}[G, L, w]$. In the first round, every vertex broadcasts its super-id, which we understand as a path of length 0. A vertex $w$ receives super-ids and stores only those which are smaller than its own super-id.

In a later iteration, every vertex $w$ receives some sets of paths from its neighbors and computes their union $\mathcal{P}$. For every vertex $u_1$, with a super-id greater than the super-id of $w$, all paths from $\mathcal{P}$ starting in $u_1$ are discarded. For every vertex $u_1$ with a smaller super-id, vertex $w$ selects the shortest path starting in $u_1$ among all paths in $\mathcal{P}$ and $\mathcal{P}_w$. (There is at most one path in $\mathcal{P}_w$ that starts in $u_1$.) If there are many such shortest paths, $w$ chooses the lexicographically least one (with respect to the super-ids). Let this path be $P = u_1, \dots, u_j$ for some $j \le 2r$. Then $P$ is stored in $\mathcal{P}_w$ (if there is already a path in $\mathcal{P}_w$ that starts in $u_1$, it is replaced by $P$). If $j < 2r$, then $w$ broadcasts the path $u_1, \dots, u_j, w$.

Observe that every vertex $w$ forwards information about a vertex $v$ only if $v \in \mathrm{WReach}_{2r}[G, L, w]$. Hence, $w$ forwards only at most $c$ paths simultaneously and the whole procedure works in the $CONGEST_{BC}$ model. Observe also that we perform a breadth-first search through the cluster $X_v$ and break ties according to the order by vertex super-ids. This implies our claims on shortest paths. □

We can now combine Theorem 2.4 and Lemma 4.1 to obtain the first main theorem of this section.

Theorem 4.2. *Let $C$ be a class of bounded expansion. There is a distributed algorithm which for every graph $G \in C$ and every $r \in \mathbb{N}$ computes a representation of a sparse $r$-neighborhood cover in the $CONGEST_{BC}$ model in $O(r^2 \cdot \log n)$ communication rounds. More precisely, the algorithm computes an order $L$, represented by $\log n$-sized labels and for every vertex $v$ a routing scheme of length at most $2r$ to every vertex in* $\mathrm{WReach}_{2r}[G, L, v]$.

Also Theorem 3.1 can now be implemented as a distributed algorithm.

Theorem 4.3. *Let $C$ be a class of bounded expansion and let $r \in \mathbb{N}$. There is a constant $c(r)$ and a distributed algorithm which for every graph $G \in C$ computes a $c(r)$-approximation of a minimum distance-$r$ dominating set in the $CONGEST_{BC}$ model in $O(r^2 \cdot \log n)$ communication rounds.*

Proof. Recall that we want to compute the distance-$r$ dominating set

$$D := \{v \in V(G) : v = \min \mathrm{WReach}_r[G, L, w] \text{ for some } w \in V(G)\},$$

that is, every vertex $w$ elects the smallest vertex from its $r$-neighborhood with respect to $L$ to the distance-$r$ dominating set. As $w$ knows $\mathrm{WReach}_r[G, L, w]$ and a routing scheme to these vertices, all vertices can send to the smallest vertex in the list a short message that it should be included in the dominating set. Observe that if a vertex $u$ has to forward the identifier of a vertex $w \in \mathrm{WReach}_r[G, L, v]$ from some other vertex $v$, then also $w \in \mathrm{WReach}_r[G, L, u]$. Hence, no vertex has to forward more than $c(r)$ messages of total size at most $O(c(2r)^2 \cdot r \cdot \log n)$: every vertex $v$ forwards id's of at most $c(2r)$ vertices $w$ from its $\mathrm{WReach}_{2r}[G, L, v]$ together with their rooting schemes (of size at most $2r$) to at most $c(2r)$ vertices in $\mathrm{WReach}_{2r}[G, L, w]$. □

## 5 CONNECTED DOMINATING SETS

In this section we study the Connected Distance-$r$ Dominating Set problem. Our main result in this section is the following theorem.

Theorem 5.1. *Let $C$ be a class of bounded expansion and let $r \in \mathbb{N}$. There is a constant $c$ and a distributed algorithm which for every graph $G \in C$ computes a $c$-approximation of a minimum connected distance-$r$ dominating set in the $CONGEST_{BC}$ model in $O(r^2 \cdot \log n)$ communication rounds.*

The following observation is folklore.

Lemma 5.2. *Let $G$ be a connected graph and let $D$ be a distance-r dominating set of $G$. Let $\mathcal{P}$ be a set of paths in $G$ such that for each pair $u, v \in D$ with $\text{dist}(u, v) \leq 2r+1$ there is a path $P_{u,v} \in \mathcal{P}$ connecting $u$ and $v$. Then the subgraph $H$ induced by $D \cup \bigcup_{P \in \mathcal{P}} V(P)$ is connected.*

Now, we use the local separation properties of the weak colouring numbers to connect the dominating set we computed in Theorem 4.3. The proof of the following lemma is immediate by definition of weak reachability.

Lemma 5.3. *Let $G$ be a graph and let $L$ be a linear order on $V(G)$. Let $u, v \in V(G)$ be such that there exists a path $P$ between $u$ and $v$ of length at most $r$. Let $w$ be the minimal vertex of $P$ with respect to $L$. Then $w \in \text{WReach}_r[G, L, u]$ and $w \in \text{WReach}_r[G, L, v]$.*

From Lemma 5.2 and Lemma 5.3 we obtain the following corollary.

Corollary 5.4. *Let $G$ be a connected graph and let $L$ be a linear order on $V(G)$. Let $D$ be an r-dominating set of $G$. Let $D'$ be a set which is obtained by adding for each $v \in D$ and each $w \in \text{WReach}_{2r+1}[G, L, v]$ the vertex set of a path between $v$ and $w$. Then $D'$ is a connected distance-r dominating set of $G$.*

Proof. Fix a set $\mathcal{P}$ of paths in $G$ such that for each pair $u, v \in D$ with $\text{dist}(u, v) \leq 2r+1$ there is a path $P_{u,v} \in \mathcal{P}$ connecting $u$ and $v$. According to Lemma 5.2, the subgraph $H$ induced by $D \cup \bigcup_{P \in \mathcal{P}} V(P)$ is connected. According to Lemma 5.3, for each path $P_{u,v}$ between $u$ and $v$, there is a vertex $w \in V(P_{u,v})$ is weakly $2r+1$-reachable both from $u$ and from $v$. As $D'$ contains the vertex set of a path between $u$ and $w$ and of a path between $v$ and $w$, it follows that $D'$ is a connected distance-$r$ dominating set of $G$. □

We are now ready to prove the main theorem.

Proof of Theorem 5.1. Instead of computing an order $L$ for $\text{wcol}_{2r}(G)$ as in Theorem 4.3, we compute an order $L$ for $\text{wcol}_{2r+1}(G)$. Assume $|\text{WReach}_{2r+1}[G, L, v]| \leq c'$ for all $v \in V(G)$. We compute an $r$-dominating set $D$ based on the order $L$. Note that in Section 4 we used $L$ computed for parameter $2r$ and now we use $L$ computed for $2r+1$, but for all orders $L$ and all $v \in V(G)$ we have $|\text{WReach}_{2r}[G, L, v]| \leq |\text{WReach}_{2r+1}[G, L, v]|$.

By Theorem 3.1, the set $D$ is at most $c'$ times larger than a minimum distance-$r$ dominating set. As a by-product, see Lemma 4.1, every vertex $v$ learns a path of length at most $2r+1$ to each $w \in \text{WReach}_{2r+1}[G, L, v]$. Now, every vertex broadcasts its set of paths to construct the set $D'$. As in the proof of Theorem 4.3, observe that if a vertex $x$ has to forward a path from $w \in \text{WReach}_r[G, L, v]$ to $v$ for some other vertex $v$, then also $w \in \text{WReach}_r[G, L, x]$. Hence, no vertex has to forward more than $c'$ messages of total size at most $O(c' \cdot r \cdot \log n)$. Clearly, the computed set $D'$ has size at most $c' \cdot (2r+1) \cdot |D|$ and by Corollary 5.4 it is a connected distance-$r$ dominating set. We conclude be defining $c := c'^2 \cdot (2r+1)$. □

We now show how to use the greater power of the *LOCAL* model to compute connected dominating sets with much smaller constants involved. Our theorem is based on the simple observation that in the *LOCAL* model we can construct for every connected graph from an $r$-dominating set $D$ a connected depth-$r$ minor with $|D|$ vertices. This minor (by definition of bounded expansion classes) has only a linear number of edges and we can hence choose a set of short paths realizing the corresponding connections to connect the dominating set.

We want to define a partition of $V(G)$ into balls around vertices from an r-dominating set $D$. For a connected graph $G$ and an injection $id\colon V(G) \to \mathbb{N}$, we define the *lexicographic order* $<_{\text{lex}}$ on the set of paths in $V(G)$ with respect to $id$ as follows. Consider two paths $P_1 = v_1, \ldots, v_k$ and $P_2 = w_1, \ldots, w_\ell$. If $k < \ell$, then $P \leq_{\text{lex}} P_2$. If $k = \ell$, then $P_1 \leq_{\text{lex}} P_2$ if the sequence $id(v_1), \ldots, id(v_k)$ is lexicographically smaller than the sequence $id(w_1), \ldots, id(w_\ell)$ or $P_1 = P_2$. For vertices $v, w \in V(G)$, let $P(v, w)$ be the lexicographically shortest path from $v$ to $w$.

Let $G$ be a connected graph, let $id(v)$ be the unique identifier of $v$ and let $D$ be a distance-$r$ dominating set of $G$. For each $v \in D$ let

$$B(v) := \{w \in V(G) \ : \ P(v, w) \leq_{\text{lex}} P(u, w) \text{ for all } u \in D, u \neq v\}.$$

The *D-partition* $\mathcal{B}(D)$ of $G$ with respect to $id$ is the set $\{B(v) \ : \ v \in D\}$.

Lemma 5.5. *Let $G$ be a connected graph and let $D$ be a distance-r dominating set of $G$. Then $\mathcal{B}(D) = \{B(v) : v \in D\}$ is a partition of $V(G)$ and $G[B(v)]$ has radius at most $r$ for all $v \in D$.*

Proof. As $G$ is connected and $D$ is a distance-$r$ dominating set, $\mathcal{B}$ is a partition of $V(G)$. Furthermore, for each $w \in V(v)$, there is a lexicographically shortest path $P$ of length at most $r$ from $v$ to $w$ in $G$. Assume towards a contradiction that $P$ is not also a path in $B(v)$. Then there is $z \in V(P)$ and $u \in D$ such that $z \in B(u)$. By definition of $B(u)$, the lexicographically shortest path $Q'$ from $u$ to $z$ is smaller than the lexicographically shortest path $Q$ between $v$ and $z$. But then the path $P'$ obtained by replacing the initial part $Q$ of $P$ by $Q'$ is lexicographically smaller than $P$, a contradiction. □

Lemma 5.6. *Let $G$ be a connected graph and let $D$ be a distance-r dominating set of $G$. By contracting the sets $B(v)$ for $v \in D$, we obtain a connected depth-r minor of $G$.*

Proof. It is immediate by definition of depth-$r$ minors and Lemma 5.5 that we construct a depth-$r$ minor $H \preccurlyeq_r G$. Furthermore, as $G$ is connected and as $\mathcal{B}(D)$ is a partition of $V(G)$ by the same lemma, it is easy to see that $H$ is connected. □

Lemma 5.7. *Let $G$ be a connected graph such that for each depth-r minor $H \preccurlyeq_r G$ we have $|E(H)| \leq d \cdot |V(H)|$. Let $D$ be a distance-r dominating set of $G$. We can compute a connected dominating set $D'$ of $G$ of size at most $2r \cdot d \cdot |D|$ in $3r+1$ communication rounds in the LOCAL model.*

Proof. In this proof, we write $H(D)$ for the depth-$r$ minor constructed from a distance-$r$ dominating set $D$ as in Lemma 5.6.

Every vertex $v \in D$ can find its $2r+1$-neighborhood in $2r+1$ communication rounds. With this information, each $v \in D$ can construct $B(v)$, as all possible dominators for $w \in N_r[v]$ must come from $N_{2r}[v]$. Each vertex $v \in D$ (now understood as representing a vertex of $H(D)$) can also learn its neighbors in $H(D)$ (here we need to learn $N_{2r+1}[v]$). Now each vertex $v$ computes the lexicographically shortest path $P_{uv}$ of length at most $2r+1$ for each neighbor $u$ in $H(D)$ (take the ordering induced by vertex id's). Observe that $u$ and $v$ fix the same path $P_{vu}$, hence, the two vertices can report to all vertices on $P_{vu}$ in another $r$ communication rounds that they shall be included in the connected dominating set $D'$.

By Lemma 5.6, the constructed set $D'$ is a connected distance-$r$ dominating set. Furthermore, by assumption, $H(D)$ has at most $d \cdot |D|$ many edges. Each edge is replaced by at most $2r - 1$ vertices in the above construction. Adding the $|D|$ vertices of the original set $D$, we obtain the claimed bounds. □

As a corollary from Lemma 5.5 and Lemma 5.7 we obtain the following theorem.

THEOREM 5.8. *Let $C$ be a class of graphs of bounded expansion and assume that for every graph $G \in C$ we can compute a $c$-approximation $D$ of a minimum distance-$r$ dominating set of $G$ in $t$ rounds in the LOCAL model. Let $f: \mathbb{N} \longrightarrow \mathbb{N}$ denote the edge density function of depth-$r$ minors of $C$. Then there is a distributed algorithm which finds a $2rcf(r)$-approximation for connected distance-$r$ dominating set of $G$ in $O(t + r)$ rounds in the LOCAL model.*

The theorem can be applied, e.g., to extend the algorithm of Lenzen et al. [36] to obtain a connected dominating set on planar graphs in the local model which is only 6 times larger than the dominating set computed for the planar graph (an $n$-vertex planar graph has at most $3n - 6$ edges). Similarly, it applies to the extension of Lenzen et al.'s algorithm by Amiri et al. [5] for graphs of bounded genus or to the randomized $O(a^2)$ approximation of Lenzen and Wattenhofer [38] applied to graphs with excluded minors (here, $a \in O(t \log t)$ if $K_t$ is excluded as a minor).

## 6 CONCLUSION

What are the most general classes of graphs that admit efficient algorithms for certain problems? The ambitious goal to answer this question for the dominating set problem has lead to strong graph theoretic and algorithmic results once it was known that it cannot be solved efficiently in full generality. Lower bounds both in classical complexity and in distributed complexity have motivated the study of more and more general graph classes.

Bounded expansion classes of graphs are very general classes of sparse graphs. In this paper we proposed a new constant factor approximation algorithm for the (CONNECTED) DISTANCE-$r$ DOMINATING SET problem on these classes of graphs. The algorithm improves the previously best known approximation algorithm by Dvořák [21], however, its main feature is that it is tailored to be implemented in a distributed setting.

It was proved in [10] that on the class of graphs with arboricity at most $a$ the size of a minimum dominating set can be approximated by a factor $3a$ by an LP rounding algorithm, but that it is NP-hard to approximate the size of the minimum dominating set to within $a - 1 - \varepsilon$ in this class for every $\varepsilon > 0$. This natural leads to consider that bounded average degree (or bounded arboricity) is a natural requirement for a class of graphs closed under taking subgraphs to allow constant factor approximation for the size of the minimum dominating set. By considering subdivisions, it follows that the property of every graph present as an $r$-subdivision in the class should have average degree at most $C(r)$ — that is of having bounded expansion — is a natural requirement to allow constant factor approximation for the size of the distance-$r$ minimum dominating sets for every $r$.

Our techniques are based on a distributed computation of sparse neighborhood covers of small radius on bounded expansion classes of graphs. Formerly, no distributed algorithms that compute such covers were known and we believe that these techniques are interesting beyond the presented applications of computing (connected) dominating sets. We pose the question whether sparse neighborhood covers can be computed in distributed constant time. This question is open even on more restrictive graph classes, e.g., on planar graphs, where dominating sets can be approximated in constant time.

## REFERENCES


[1] Ittai Abraham, Cyril Gavoille, Anupam Gupta, Ofer Neiman, and Kunal Talwar. 2014. Cops, robbers, and threatening skeletons: padded decomposition for minor-free graphs. In *Symposium on Theory of Computing, STOC 2014*. 79–88.

[2] Ittai Abraham, Cyril Gavoille, and Dahlia Malkhi. 2005. Compact routing for graphs excluding a fixed minor. In *International Symposium on Distributed Computing*. Springer, 442–456.

[3] Ittai Abraham, Cyril Gavoille, Dahlia Malkhi, and Udi Wieder. 2007. Strong-diameter decompositions of minor free graphs. In *Proceedings of the nineteenth annual ACM symposium on Parallel algorithms and architectures*. ACM, 16–24.

[4] Noga Alon, Dana Moshkovitz, and Shmuel Safra. 2006. Algorithmic construction of sets for k-restrictions. *ACM Transactions on Algorithms (TALG)* 2, 2 (2006), 153–177.

[5] Saeed Akhoondian Amiri, Stefan Schmid, and Sebastian Siebertz. 2016. A Local Constant Factor MDS Approximation for Bounded Genus Graphs. In *Proceedings of the 2016 ACM Symposium on Principles of Distributed Computing, PODC 2016*. 227–233.

[6] Sanjeev Arora and Madhu Sudan. 2003. Improved low-degree testing and its applications. *Combinatorica* 23, 3 (2003), 365–426.

[7] Baruch Awerbuch and David Peleg. 1990. *Locality-sensitive resource allocation.* Citeseer.

[8] Baruch Awerbuch and David Peleg. 1990. Network synchronization with polylogarithmic overhead. In *Foundations of Computer Science, 1990. Proceedings., 31st Annual Symposium on*. IEEE, 514–522.

[9] Baruch Awerbuch and David Peleg. 1990. Sparse partitions. In *Foundations of Computer Science, 1990. Proceedings., 31st Annual Symposium on*. IEEE, 503–513.

[10] Nikhil Bansal and Seeun William Umboh. 2017. Tight approximation bounds for dominating set on graphs of bounded arboricity. *Inform. Process. Lett.* 122 (2017), 21–24.

[11] Leonid Barenboim and Michael Elkin. 2010. Sublogarithmic distributed MIS algorithm for sparse graphs using Nash-Williams decomposition. *Distributed Computing* 22, 5-6 (2010), 363–379.

[12] M. Bellare, S. Goldwasser, C. Lund, and A. Russell. 1993. Efficient multi-prover interactive proofs with applications to approximation problems. In *Proc. 25th ACM Symp. on Theory of Computing*, Vol. 113. 131.

[13] Costas Busch, Ryan LaFortune, and Srikanta Tirthapura. 2007. Improved sparse covers for graphs excluding a fixed minor. In *Proceedings of the twenty-sixth annual ACM symposium on Principles of distributed computing*. ACM, 61–70.

[14] Fan Chung and Linyuan Lu. 2002. Connected components in random graphs with given expected degree sequences. *Annals of combinatorics* 6, 2 (2002), 125–145.

[15] Vasek Chvatal. 1979. A greedy heuristic for the set-covering problem. *Mathematics of operations research* 4, 3 (1979), 233–235.

[16] Andrzej Czygrinow, Michal Hańćkowiak, and Wojciech Wawrzyniak. 2008. Fast distributed approximations in planar graphs. In *International Symposium on Distributed Computing*. Springer, 78–92.

[17] Bevan Das and Vaduvur Bharghavan. 1997. Routing in ad-hoc networks using minimum connected dominating sets. In *Communications, 1997. ICC'97 Montreal, Towards the Knowledge Millennium. 1997 IEEE International Conference on*, Vol. 1. IEEE, 376–380.

[18] Bevan Das, Raghupathy Sivakumar, and Vaduvur Bharghavan. 1997. Routing in ad hoc networks using a spine. In *Computer Communications and Networks, 1997. Proceedings., Sixth International Conference on*. IEEE, 34–39.

[19] Erik D Demaine, Felix Reidl, Peter Rossmanith, Fernando Sánchez Villaamil, Somnath Sikdar, and Blair D Sullivan. 2014. Structural sparsity of complex networks: Bounded expansion in random models and real-world graphs. *arXiv preprint arXiv:1406.2587* (2014).

[20] Irit Dinur and David Steurer. 2014. Analytical approach to parallel repetition. In *Proceedings of the 46th Annual ACM Symposium on Theory of Computing*. ACM, 624–633.

[21] Zdeněk Dvořák. 2013. Constant-factor approximation of the domination number in sparse graphs. *European Journal of Combinatorics* 34, 5 (2013), 833–840.

[22] Uriel Feige. 1998. A threshold of ln n for approximating set cover. *Journal of the ACM (JACM)* 45, 4 (1998), 634–652.

[23] Michael R. Garey and David S. Johnson. 1979. Computers and intractability: a guide to the theory of NP-completeness. *WH Free. Co., San Fr* (1979).

[24] Mohsen Ghaffari, Fabian Kuhn, and Yannic Maus. 2017. On the complexity of local distributed graph problems. In *Proceedings of the 49th Annual ACM SIGACT Symposium on Theory of Computing, STOC 2017.* 784–797.

[25] Martin Grohe, Stephan Kreutzer, Roman Rabinovich, Sebastian Siebertz, and Konstantinos Stavropoulos. 2015. Colouring and Covering Nowhere Dense Graphs. In *Graph-Theoretic Concepts in Computer Science - 41st International Workshop, WG 2015.* 325–338.

[26] Martin Grohe, Stephan Kreutzer, and Sebastian Siebertz. 2014. Deciding first-order properties of nowhere dense graphs. In *Proceedings of the 46th Annual ACM Symposium on Theory of Computing.* ACM, 89–98.

[27] Sariel Har-Peled and Kent Quanrud. 2015. Approximation algorithms for polynomial-expansion and low-density graphs. In *Algorithms-ESA 2015.* Springer, 717–728.

[28] Teresa W Haynes, Stephen Hedetniemi, and Peter Slater. 1998. *Fundamentals of domination in graphs.* CRC Press.

[29] Miikka Hilke, Christoph Lenzen, and Jukka Suomela. 2014. Brief announcement: Local approximability of minimum dominating set on planar graphs. In *Proceedings of the 2014 ACM symposium on Principles of distributed computing.* ACM, 344–346.

[30] Viggo Kann. 1992. *On the approximability of NP-complete optimization problems.* Ph.D. Dissertation. Royal Institute of Technology Stockholm.

[31] Richard M Karp. 1972. Reducibility among combinatorial problems. In *Complexity of computer computations.* Springer, 85–103.

[32] Hal A. Kierstead and Daqing Yang. 2003. Orderings on graphs and game coloring number. *Order* 20, 3 (2003), 255–264.

[33] Stephan Kreutzer, Michał Pilipczuk, Roman Rabinovich, and Sebastian Siebertz. 2016. The Generalised Colouring Numbers on Classes of Bounded Expansion. In *41st International Symposium on Mathematical Foundations of Computer Science, MFCS.* 85:1–85:13.

[34] Fabian Kuhn, Thomas Moscibroda, and Roger Wattenhofer. 2016. Local computation: Lower and upper bounds. *Journal of the ACM (JACM)* 63, 2 (2016), 17.

[35] Shay Kutten and David Peleg. 1995. Fast distributed construction of k-dominating sets and applications. In *Proceedings of the fourteenth annual ACM symposium on Principles of distributed computing.* ACM, 238–251.

[36] Christoph Lenzen, Yvonne-Anne Pignolet, and Roger Wattenhofer. 2013. Distributed minimum dominating set approximations in restricted families of graphs. *Distributed computing* 26, 2 (2013), 119–137.

[37] Christoph Lenzen and Roger Wattenhofer. 2008. Leveraging Linial's locality limit. In *International Symposium on Distributed Computing.* Springer, 394–407.

[38] Christoph Lenzen and Roger Wattenhofer. 2010. Minimum dominating set approximation in graphs of bounded arboricity. In *International Symposium on Distributed Computing.* Springer, 510–524.

[39] László Lovász. 1975. On the ratio of optimal integral and fractional covers. *Discrete mathematics* 13, 4 (1975), 383–390.

[40] Carsten Lund and Mihalis Yannakakis. 1994. On the hardness of approximating minimization problems. *Journal of the ACM (JACM)* 41, 5 (1994), 960–981.

[41] Michael Molloy and Bruce Reed. 1995. A critical point for random graphs with a given degree sequence. *Random structures & algorithms* 6, 2-3 (1995), 161–180.

[42] Jaroslav Nešetřil and Patrice Ossona de Mendez. 2008. Grad and classes with bounded expansion I. Decompositions. *European Journal of Combinatorics* 29, 3 (2008), 760–776.

[43] Jaroslav Nešetřil and Patrice Ossona de Mendez. 2008. Grad and classes with bounded expansion II. Algorithmic aspects. *European Journal of Combinatorics* 29, 3 (2008), 777–791.

[44] Jaroslav Nešetřil and Patrice Ossona de Mendez. 2008. Grad and classes with bounded expansion III. Restricted graph homomorphism dualities. *European Journal of Combinatorics* 29, 4 (2008), 1012–1024.

[45] Jaroslav Nešetřil and Patrice Ossona de Mendez. 2012. *Sparsity.* Springer.

[46] Jaroslav Nešetřil and Patrice Ossona de Mendez. 2016. A distributed low tree-depth decomposition algorithm for bounded expansion classes. *Distributed Computing* 29, 1 (2016), 39–49.

[47] Jaroslav Nešetřil, Patrice Ossona de Mendez, and David R. Wood. 2012. Characterizations and Examples of Graph Classes with Bounded Expansion. *European Journal of Combinatorics* 33, 3 (2012), 350–373.

[48] David Peleg. 2000. Distributed computing: a locality sensitive approach. *SIAM Monographs on discrete mathematics and applications* 5 (2000).

[49] Lucia D. Penso and Valmir C. Barbosa. 2004. A distributed algorithm to find k-dominating sets. *Discrete Applied Mathematics* 141, 1 (2004), 243–253.

[50] Ran Raz and Shmuel Safra. 1997. A sub-constant error-probability low-degree test, and a sub-constant error-probability PCP characterization of NP. In *Proceedings of the twenty-ninth annual ACM symposium on Theory of computing.* ACM, 475–484.

[51] R. Sivakumar, B. Das, and V. Bharghavan. 1998. An improved spine-based infrastructure for routing in ad hoc networks. In *IEEE Symposium on Computers and Communications*, Vol. 98.

[52] Ivan Stojmenovic, Mahtab Seddigh, and Jovisa Zunic. 2002. Dominating sets and neighbor elimination-based broadcasting algorithms in wireless networks. *IEEE Transactions on parallel and distributed systems* 13, 1 (2002), 14–25.

[53] Mikkel Thorup and Uri Zwick. 2005. Approximate distance oracles. *Journal of the ACM (JACM)* 52, 1 (2005), 1–24.

[54] Volker Turau and Sven Köhler. 2015. A Distributed Algorithm for Minimum Distance-k Domination in Trees. *Journal of Graph Algorithms and Applications* 19, 1 (2015), 223–242.

[55] Jan van den Heuvel, Patrice Ossona de Mendez, Daniel Quiroz, Roman Rabinovich, and Sebastian Siebertz. 2017. On the generalised colouring numbers of graphs that exclude a fixed minor. *Eur. J. Comb.* 66 (2017), 129–144.

[56] Fu-Hsing Wang, Jou-Ming Chang, Yue-Li Wang, and Sun-Jen Huang. 2003. Distributed algorithms for finding the unique minimum distance dominating set in directed split-stars. *J. Parallel and Distrib. Comput.* 63, 4 (2003), 481–487.

[57] Wojciech Wawrzyniak. 2014. A strengthened analysis of a local algorithm for the minimum dominating set problem in planar graphs. *Inform. Process. Lett.* 114, 3 (2014), 94–98.

[58] Jie Wu and Hailan Li. 1999. On calculating connected dominating set for efficient routing in ad hoc wireless networks. In *Proceedings of the 3rd international workshop on Discrete algorithms and methods for mobile computing and communications.* ACM, 7–14.

[59] Xuding Zhu. 2009. Colouring graphs with bounded generalized colouring number. *Discrete Mathematics* 309, 18 (2009), 5562–5568.

# Possibilities and Impossibilities for Distributed Subgraph Detection

Orr Fischer
Tel-Aviv University
Tel-Aviv, Israel
orrfischer@mail.tau.ac.il

Tzlil Gonen
Tel-Aviv University
Tel-Aviv, Israel
tzlilgon@mail.tau.ac.il

Fabian Kuhn
University of Freiburg
Freiburg, Germany
kuhn@cs.uni-freiburg.de

Rotem Oshman
Tel-Aviv University
Tel-Aviv, Israel
roshman@tau.ac.il

## ABSTRACT

In the distributed subgraph detection problem, we are given a fixed subgraph $H$, and the network must decide whether the network graph contains a copy of $H$ or not. Subgraph detection can be solved in a constant number of rounds if message size is unbounded, but in the CONGEST model, where each message has bounded size, it can have high round complexity. Distributed subgraph detection has received significant attention recently, with new upper and lower bounds, but several fundamental questions remain open.

In this paper we prove new possibility and impossibility results for subgraph detection in the CONGEST model. We show for the first time that some subgraphs require superlinear — in fact, nearly quadratic — running time, even in small-diameter networks. We also study cycle-detection, and show that any even cycle can be detected in sublinear time (in contrast to odd cycles, which require linear time). For the special case of triangle-detection, we show that deterministic algorithms require $\Omega(\log n)$ total communication even in graphs of degree 2, and that one-round randomized algorithms must send $\Omega(\Delta)$ bits in graphs of degree $\Delta$, improving on the recent results of [Abboud et. al.]. Finally, we extend a recent lower bound of [Izumi, Le Gall] on listing all triangles to cliques of any size.

## CCS CONCEPTS

• **Networks** → **Network algorithms**; • **Theory of computation** → **Distributed algorithms**; *Lower bounds and information complexity*;

**ACM Reference Format:**
Orr Fischer, Tzlil Gonen, Fabian Kuhn, and Rotem Oshman. 2018. Possibilities and Impossibilities for Distributed Subgraph Detection. In *SPAA '18: 30th ACM Symposium on Parallelism in Algorithms and Architectures, July 16–18, 2018, Vienna, Austria.* ACM, New York, NY, USA, 10 pages. https://doi.org/10.1145/3210377.3210401


*SPAA '18, July 16–18, 2018, Vienna, Austria*

ACM ISBN 978-1-4503-5799-9/18/07...$15.00
https://doi.org/10.1145/3210377.3210401

## 1 INTRODUCTION

In the *subgraph detection* problem (also called *subgraph freeness*), we are given a constant-size graph $H$, and the goal is to determine whether the network graph contains a copy of $H$ as a subgraph, or not. Subgraph-detection is an extremely local problem: in the LOCAL model of distributed computing, where network nodes can send messages of unrestricted size in each round, the $H$-detection problem for any graph $H$ of size $k$ can be solved in at most $O(k)$ rounds — we simply have each node collect its entire $k$-neighborhood and check if it contains a copy of $H$. However, in the CONGEST model, where the bandwidth on each edge *is* restricted, subgraph detection can be much harder.

Subgraph-freeness in the CONGEST network model has recently received significant attention from the distributed computing community [1, 6, 10, 12–15, 18]. Several linear and sublinear upper and lower bounds have been shown for special cases, including triangles and larger cycles [1, 6, 10, 13]; trees, which can be detected in $O(1)$ rounds [12]; cliques and complete bipartite subgraphs, which can be detected in $O(n)$ rounds [10]; and more complicated classes of graphs, for which in some cases we can prove a lower bound of the form $\Omega(n^{\delta})$, where $\delta < 1$ [15].

In this work we aim to better understand several fundamental questions regarding the subgraph-freeness problem.

### 1.1 Our Results

*Solving $C_{2k}$-detection in sublinear time.* In [10] it was shown that for any odd cycle $C_k$ for $k \geq 5$, the $C_k$-detection problem takes $\tilde{\Omega}(n)$ rounds. It is easy to see that $O(n)$ rounds suffice, so this bound is nearly tight. For *even* cycles, on the other hand, the best known lower bound is $\Omega(\sqrt{n})$ [10, 18], but no sublinear upper bounds were known for $k \geq 6$, so it was unclear whether even cycles require nearly-linear time, or whether they can be detected faster. We show that in fact any even cycle can be detected in sublinear time:

**Theorem 1.1.** *For any fixed $k \geq 2$, $C_{2k}$-detection can be solved in $O(n^{1-1/(k(k-1))})$ rounds.*

(Our algorithm is randomized, but it is easily de-randomized using standard techniques, at the cost of an additional $O(\log n)$ factor in the running time. (See, e.g, [15] for a similar argument.)

*Near-quadratic lower bounds on subgraph-freeness.* A wide variety of subgraphs, such as cycles and cliques, can be detected in a linear number of rounds. A natural question that arises is whether *any* constant-sized subgraph $H$ be detected in $O(n)$ rounds. We show that the answer is negative:

**Theorem 1.2.** *For any $k, n \geq 2$, there is a graph $H_k$ of size $O(k)$ and diameter 3, such that $H_k$-freeness requires $\Omega(n^{2-1/k}/(Bk))$ rounds in the* CONGEST *model, even when the network diameter is 3.*

Our lower bound provides another "natural" problem which has a superlinear lower bound in the CONGEST model; to our knowledge, previously the only examples of such problems were found in [8]. Since the subgraph-freeness problem is also extremely local, we get a separation between the CONGEST and LOCAL models, nearly the largest possible: by Theorem 1.2, if we take $k = \Theta(\log n)$, we get a graph that requires $\widetilde{\Omega}(n^2)$ rounds to detect, but only $O(\log n)$ rounds in the LOCAL model.

We also show a variant of this theorem for a *bipartite* subgraph. We note that any bipartite graph $H$ has Túran number $\text{ex}(n, H) \leq O(n^{2-\Omega(1)})$: any graph on $n$ vertices that does *not* contain a copy of $H$ cannot have more than $O(n^{2-\Omega(1)})$ edges. Therefore, any such graph can be detected in sub-quadratic time, by simply collecting all edges of the network graph. Thus, the $H$-detection problem for bipartite $H$ is a somewhat natural intermediate problem in CONGEST: it is strongly sub-quadratic, yet super-linear.

*Improved lower bounds on triangle-detection.* Recently, [1] showed that for deterministic algorithms, if the bandwidth is $B = 1$ (i.e., one bit per round), then $\Omega(\log^* n)$ rounds are required, even in constant-degree graphs; and if the algorithm only has one round, and *each triangle node* must announce that it is in a triangle, then the bandwidth must be $\Omega(\Delta \log n)$, where $\Delta$ is the maximum degree of the graph.

Here we show:

(a) In any deterministic triangle-detection algorithm, even when the maximum degree is constant, $\Omega(\log n)$ bits must be sent on some edge, if the namespace is of size $\Theta(n)$; and
(b) Randomized one-round triangle-detection requires bandwidth $\Omega(\Delta)$ in graphs of maximum degree $\Delta$.

The first result is shown using a technique similar to [1], but we strengthen the lower bound from $\Omega(\log^* n)$ to $\Omega(\log n)$, which is tight for the lower bound graph. The second result, for randomized algorithms, uses standard information theory instead of the fooling views technique introduced in [1] for their deterministic lower bound. This allows us to both generalize from deterministic to randomized algorithms, and lift the restriction that all three triangle nodes must detect that they are in a triangle (instead, we use the usual definition, where it suffices if one node detects the triangle).

One might wonder what happened to the $\log n$ factor that is present in the deterministic $\Omega(\Delta \log n)$ lower bound from [1] but missing in our $\Omega(\Delta)$ randomized lower bound. It is not clear whether randomized algorithms need to pay this logarithmic factor or not; we leave this question for future work.

*Lower bound on listing $s$-cliques in the Congested Clique.* Finally, we extend a recent lower bound of $\widetilde{\Omega}(n^{1/3})$ rounds on listing all triangles in the graph [16, 20], to a lower bound of $\widetilde{\Omega}(n^{1-2/s})$ for listing all $s$-cliques, for any $s \geq 3$. This lower bound holds even when each node can send $O(\log n)$ bits to each other node in every round. For lack of space, the details of this lower bound are relegated to the full paper. The proof is similar to the one in [16], and the main difference is that we need to prove the following lemma:

**Lemma 1.3.** *For $s \geq 2$, any graph on $m$ edges has at most $O(m^{s/2})$ copies of $K_s$.*

This lemma generalizes a corresponding lemma for triangles from [23], which was used in the lower bound of [16].

For lack of space, many technical details and full proofs are omitted in the body of the paper; they appear in the full paper.

## 1.2 Related Work

The problem of subgraph-freeness (also called *excluded* or *forbidden subgraphs*) has been extensively studied in both the centralized and the distributed worlds. For the general problem of detecting whether a graph $H$ is a subgraph of $G$, where both $H$ and $G$ are part of the input, the best known sequential algorithm is exponential [24]. When $H$ is fixed and only $G$ is the input, the problem becomes solvable in polynomial time.

In the distributed setting, [12] very recently provided a constant-round deterministic algorithm for detecting a fixed tree in the CONGEST model. This paper, as well as several others [4, 6, 14] , also considered more general graphs, but with the exception of trees, they studied the *property testing* relaxation of the problem, where we only need to distinguish a graph that is $H$-free from a graph that is *far* from $H$-free. Here we consider the *exact* version.

Another recent work [16] gave randomized algorithms in the CONGEST model for triangle detection and triangle listing, with round complexity $\widetilde{O}(n^{2/3})$ and $\widetilde{O}(n^{3/4})$, respectively. In [16, 20] a lower bound of $\widetilde{\Omega}(n^{1/3})$ on the round complexity of triangle listing in the congested clique is shown. There is also work on testing triangle-freeness in the congested clique model [7, 9] and in other, less directly related distributed models.

As for lower bounds on $H$-freeness in the CONGEST model, the only ones in the literature (to our knowledge) are for cycles [10] and restricted lower bounds for triangles [1], and the reductions from [15], which construct hard graphs from other hard graphs by replacing their vertices or their edges with other graphs. (In [10] there are lower bounds for other graphs, in a broadcast variant of the CONGEST model where nodes are required to send the *same* message on all their edges.) For any fixed $k > 3$, there is a polynomial lower bound for detecting the $k$-cycle $C_k$ in the CONGEST model: it was first presented by [10], which showed that $\Omega(\text{ex}(n, C_k)/B)$ rounds are required, where $\text{ex}(n, C_k)$ is the largest possible number of edges in a $C_k$-free graph over $n$ vertices. In particular, for odd-length cycles, the lower bound of [10] is nearly linear. Very recently, [18] improved the lower bound for even-length cycles to $\Omega(\sqrt{n}/B)$. All lower bounds mentioned above are linear or sublinear.

In a recent work [8], the first near-quadratic lower bounds (and indeed the first superlinear lower bounds) in CONGEST were shown. The problems addressed in [8] include some NP-hard problems such as minimum vertex cover and graph coloring, as well as a weighted variant of $C_8$-freeness, called *weighted cycle detection*: given a weight $W \in [0, \text{poly}(n)]$, the goal is to determine whether the graph has a cycle of length 8 and weight exactly $W$.

## 2 PRELIMINARIES

*Notation.* We let $V(G), E(G)$ denote the vertex and edge set of graph $G$, respectively. In Section 5, which uses information theory, we use the convention that bold-face letters denote random variables, while normal letters denote concrete (scalar) values.

*The* CONGEST *model.* The CONGEST model is a synchronous network model, where computation proceeds in *rounds*. In each round, each node of the network may send $B$ bits on each of its edges, and these messages are received by neighbors in the current round. Typically, $B$ is taken to be logarithmic in the size $n$ of the network graph.

*Subgraph detection.* We are interested in the *subgraph-detection* problem (also called *subgraph-freeness*), defined as follows:

**Definition 1** (Subgraph detection). *Fix a graph $H$. In the $H$-*detection *problem, the goal is to determine whether the input graph $G = (V, E)$ contains a copy of $H$ as a subgraph or not; that is, whether there are subsets $U \subseteq V, F \subseteq E$ of vertices and edges, respectively, such that $(U, F)$ is isomorphic to $H$.*

We say that a distributed algorithm $A$ *solves $H$-detection with success probability $p$* if whenever $A$ is executed in a graph that contains a copy of $H$, with probability at least $p$ some node rejects; and on the other hand, when $A$ is executed in a graph that is $H$-free, with probability at least $p$ all nodes accept. We typically assume constant $p$, e.g., $p = 2/3$.

*Túran numbers.* For a fixed graph $H$, the *Túran number* of $H$, denoted $\mathrm{ex}(n, H)$, is the maximum number of edges in any $H$-free graph on $n$ vertices.

*Two-party communication complexity.* Our superlinear lower bound is shown by reduction from *two-party communication complexity*: we have two players, Alice and Bob, with private inputs $X, Y$, respectively. The players wish to compute a joint function $f(X, Y)$ of their inputs, and we are interested in the total number of bits they must exchange to do so (see the textbook [19] for more background on communication complexity).

In particular, we are interested in the *set disjointness* function, where the inputs $X, Y$ are interpreted as subsets $X, Y \subseteq [n]$, and the goal of the players is to determine whether $X \cap Y = \emptyset$. The celebrated lower bound of [17, 22] shows that even for randomized communication protocols, the players must exchange $\Omega(n)$ bits to solve set disjointness with constant success probability.

*Information theory.* In Section 5 we use information theory to prove a randomized lower bound on 1-round triangle-detection. The basic concept we need is the *mutual information* between two variables: if $\mathbf{X}, \mathbf{Y}$ are two possibly-dependent random variables, then their mutual information is defined to be $\mathrm{I}(\mathbf{X}; \mathbf{Y}) = \mathrm{H}(\mathbf{X}) - \mathrm{H}(\mathbf{X}|\mathbf{Y})$. Here, $\mathrm{H}(\mathbf{X})$ is the Shannon entropy of $\mathbf{X}$, and $\mathrm{H}(\mathbf{X}|\mathbf{Y}) = \mathrm{E}_y [\mathrm{H}(\mathbf{X}|\mathbf{Y} = y)]$ is the conditional Shannon entropy — the average entropy remaining in $\mathbf{X}$, after the value of $\mathbf{Y} = y$ is revealed. Intuitively, the mutual information $\mathrm{I}(\mathbf{X}; \mathbf{Y})$ measures the *uncertainly loss* of $\mathbf{X}$ when we learn $\mathbf{Y}$. (It is symmetric in $\mathbf{X}, \mathbf{Y}$.)

The *conditional* mutual information of $\mathbf{X}$ and $\mathbf{Y}$ given a third random variable $\mathbf{Z}$ is defined as the loss of conditional entropy: $\mathrm{I}(\mathbf{X}; \mathbf{Y}|\mathbf{Z}) = \mathrm{H}(\mathbf{X}|\mathbf{Z}) - \mathrm{H}(\mathbf{X}|\mathbf{Y}, \mathbf{Z})$. We sometimes abuse notation by writing *events* on the right-hand side instead of random variables, e.g., $\mathrm{I}(\mathbf{X}; \mathbf{Y}|\mathbf{Z} = z)$. When we do this, we are referring to the mutual information between $\mathbf{X}$ and $\mathbf{Y}$ when their joint distribution is conditioned on $\mathbf{Z} = z$.

## 3 SUPERLINEAR LOWER BOUNDS ON SUBGRAPH DETECTION

We begin by proving Theorem 1.2, namely, that some graphs require nearly-quadratic running time to detect.

We give here informal descriptions of the subgraph $H_k$ and the lower bound graph family $\mathcal{G}$ in which we show that $H_k$-detection is hard. The formal constructions can be found in the full paper.

### 3.1 Informal Description of $H_k$

The graph $H_k$ is composed of several "parts" (see Figure 1):

*Cliques.* We put in five cliques, one of each size $s = 6, \ldots, 10$. We pick one special vertex $v_s$ from each clique, and connect $\{s_6, \ldots, s_{10}\}$ in a 5-clique. Each remaining (non-clique) vertex of $H_k$ is connected to exactly one special clique vertex $v_s$, and no other clique vertices.

The cliques serve two purposes. First, they reduce the diameter of $H_k$ to 3: each vertex in $H_k$ is connected to some special clique vertex $v_s$, and all special clique vertices are connected to each other. Second, the cliques serve to "mark" the different parts of $H_k$: each "part" of $H_k$ (except for the cliques themselves) is connected to exactly one $s$-clique for $s \in \{6, \ldots, 10\}$. When we construct the network graph $G$ in which we show the lower bound on $H_k$-freeness, we will make sure $G$ also contains exactly one copy of each $s$-clique for $s = 6, \ldots, 10$, so that any isomorphism mapping $H_k$ into $G$ must map the $s$-clique of $H_k$ onto the $s$-clique in $G$. The "parts" of $G$ will echo the "parts" of $H_k$, and the connections between the cliques and the other vertices will force any isomorphism from $H_k$ into $G$ to respect this logical partition.

*Top and bottom.* The remainder of $H_k$ consists of two identical copies of a graph $H$. We call the two copies "top" and "bottom", respectively. The subgraph $H$ consists of $k$ triangles $\mathsf{Tri}_1, \ldots, \mathsf{Tri}_k$, and two additional "endpoint nodes", which we call A and B. In each triangle $\mathsf{Tri}_i$, we have three vertices denoted $(i, \mathrm{A}), (i, \mathrm{B}), (i, \mathrm{Mid})$. Endpoint A is connected to all triangle vertices in $\{(i, \mathrm{A}) \mid i \in [k]\}$, endpoint B is connected to all triangle vertices in $\{(i, \mathrm{B}) \mid i \in [k]\}$, and the "middle vertices" of the triangles are not connected to either endpoint. (The triangles ensure that a copy of $H$ cannot be embedded in any bipartite graph; we will need this for the lower bound.)

We refer to the triangles as the *body* of $H_k$, and the top and bottom endpoint nodes on both sides (A and B) as *endpoints*. There are no edges between the top and the bottom copy of $H$, except for exactly two edges: the top and bottom A-endpoints are connected by an edge, and the top and bottom B-endpoints are connected by an edge.

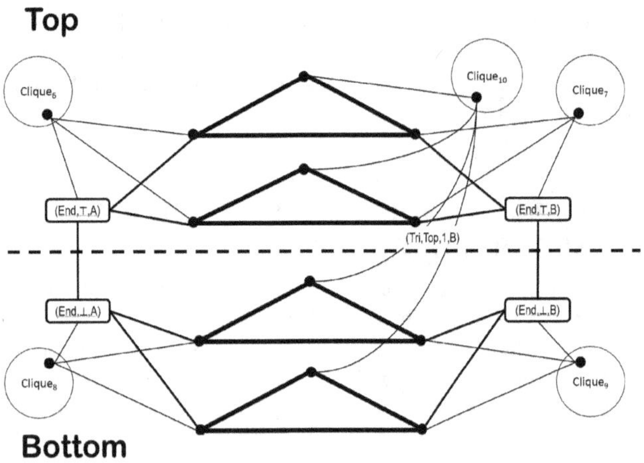


**Figure 1: The graph $H_k$ for $k = 2$. In addition to the edges shown here, the five clique nodes $\{(\mathsf{Clique}_s, 0) \mid 6 \leq s \leq 10\}$ are connected to each other; we omit these edges from the figure for clarity.**

## 3.2 The Lower Bound Family $\mathcal{G}_{k,n}$

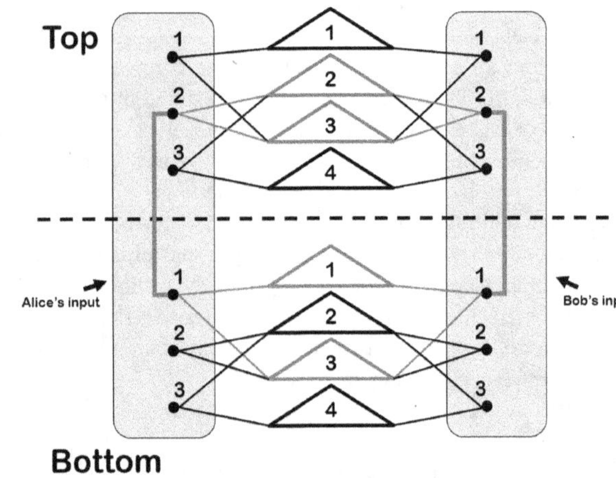


**Figure 2: The graph $G_{X,Y} \in \mathcal{G}_{k,n}$ for $n = 3, k = 2$, so that $m = k\lceil n^{1/k}\rceil = 2 \cdot \lceil 3^{1/2}\rceil = 4$. For clarity, the figure omits the five cliques $\{\mathsf{Clique}'_s \mid 6 \leq s \leq 10\}$ and their edges. The inputs $X, Y$ whose graph $G_{X,Y}$ is depicted here both include $(2, 1)$ (that is $(2, 1) \in X \cap Y$). As a result, a copy of $H_k$ appears in $G_{X,Y}$, highlighted in red.**

Let us now describe the graph family $\mathcal{G}_{k,n}$, in which we show that $H_k$-detection requires $\Omega(n^{2-1/k}/(Bk))$ rounds. (Here, $\Theta(n)$ is the number of vertices in each graph $G \in \mathcal{G}_{k,n}$.)

Our lower bound graph family $\mathcal{G}_{k,n}$ echoes the graph $H_k$: it comprises many "potential copies" of the subgraph $H_k$, each containing all parts of $H_k$ *except* the edges between the top and bottom endpoints. When we reduce from set disjointness, Alice and Bob will use their inputs to decide which endpoints to connect to which other endpoints: Alice will put in top-to-bottom edges between the A-endpoints, and Bob will do the same for the B-endpoints, in such a way that a complete copy of $H_k$ appears iff the players' inputs are not disjoint. The players will then simulate the execution of an $H_k$-detection algorithm on the graph they constructed, with Alice simulating all the A-vertices, Bob simulating all the B-vertices, and both players simulating the "middle" vertices of the triangles.

The naïve way to construct $\mathcal{G}_{k,n}$ would be to take $n$ disjoint copies of $H_k$, each missing the top-bottom endpoint edges, and have the players add the endpoint edges as we described above. This gives us $n^2$ *pairs* of endpoints on each side (A and B), so we can reduce from a disjointness instance of size $n^2$, and achieve our goal of having a copy of $H_k$ appear iff the inputs are not disjoint. However, taking $n$ disjoint copies of $H_k$ would result in a *large cut*, of linear size, between the A-part of the graph and the B-part of the graph. This would make simulating the distributed algorithm too expensive: simulating one round would cost us $O(n \cdot B)$ bits, so the best round lower bound we could hope for would be $\Omega(n^2/(nB)) = \Omega(n/B)$.

To reduce the cut size, we do not take $n$ *fully* disjoint copies of $H_k$. Instead, for top and bottom respectively, we take only $\Theta(kn^{1/k})$ disjoint triangles. Now we can mix-and-match among the $\Theta(kn^{1/k})$ triangles to form a copy of the body of $H$ (which has $k$ triangles). However, we still take $n$ copies of the two endpoints of $H$ (A/B), because we want to work with a disjointness universe of size $n^2$. Now we must connect the $n$ endpoint-copies to the $\Theta(kn^{1/k}) \ll n$ triangles, in such a way that a complete copy of $H_k$ appears iff Alice and Bob connected the same pair $(i, j)$ of endpoint-copies on their respective sides (A and B).

Recall that in $H$ we have $k$ triangles, and the A- and B-endpoints are connected to opposite ends of each triangle, so the degree of each endpoint is $k$. Let us *encode* each index $i \in [n]$ as a subset $P_i$ of $k$ elements from the universe $\lceil kn^{1/k}\rceil$, in such a way that no two indices in $[n]$ have the same encoding. (This is possible, because $\binom{\lceil kn^{1/k}\rceil}{k} \geq n$.) Now, we connect the $i$-th endpoint to the $k$ copies of $H$ in its encoding: the $i$-th endpoint on side A (resp. B) is connected to the A-vertex (resp. B-vertex) of triangle $j$ iff $j \in P_i$. Since the encoding is *unique*, and in $H_k$ each of the top/bottom endpoints is connected to $k$ top/bottom triangles (resp.), a complete copy of $H_k$ can appear iff there is a pair $(i, j) \in [n]^2$, such that Alice connected the $i$-th copy of the top-A endpoint to the $j$-th copy of the bottom-A endpoint, and Bob did the same on his side (B).

The advantage of working with only $\Theta(kn^{1/k})$ triangles is that now the cut size is also $\Theta(kn^{1/k})$: the cut between the players' sides "cuts through" each triangle.

We now describe the construction formally. Let $m = k\lceil n^{1/k}\rceil$. Fix an ordering $Q_1, \ldots, Q_N$ of the subsets of size $k$ of $[m]$, where $N = \binom{m}{k} = \binom{k\lceil n^{1/k}\rceil}{k}$. Note that

$$N = \binom{k\lceil n^{1/k}\rceil}{k} \geq \left(\frac{kn^{1/k}}{k}\right)^k = \frac{k^k n}{k^k} = n.$$

For each $i \in [N]$, let us denote $Q_i = \left\{q_i^1, \ldots, q_i^k\right\}$. (We will only use the first $n$ subsets, $Q_1, \ldots, Q_n$.)

**Definition 2** (The graph family $\mathcal{G}_{k,n}$). *Fix integers $k, n$. A graph $G$ is in the family $\mathcal{G}_{k,n}$ if it has the following structure.*

*First, the graph contains the following "components":*

- *$n$ "potential top endpoints" and "potential bottom endpoints" of $H_k$, denoted $\mathsf{End}' \times [n]$. For $S \in \{\top, \bot\}$ and $P \in \{\mathsf{A}, \mathsf{B}\}$, we denote*

$$\mathsf{End}'_{S,P} = \{(\mathsf{End}', S, P, i) \mid i \in [n]\}.$$

- *$2m$ triangles, indexed by $\{\top, \bot\} \times [m]$. Triangle $(S, i)$ comprises vertices $(\mathsf{Tri}, S, i, P)$ for each $P \in \{\mathsf{A}, \mathsf{B}, \mathsf{Mid}\}$.*
- *Copies of each of the cliques in $H_k$.*

*The graph contains the following edges between the components, and no other edges:*

- *For each "direction" $(S, P) \in \{\top, \bot\} \times \{\mathsf{A}, \mathsf{B}\}$, all vertices in $\mathsf{End}'_{S,P}$ are connected to one fixed vertex of the $c_{S,P}$-clique.*
- *For each "direction" $(S, X) \in \{\top, \bot\} \times \{\mathsf{A}, \mathsf{B}, \mathsf{Mid}\}$, all vertices in $\mathsf{Tri}'_{S,X}$ are connected to one fixed vertex of the $c_{S,P}$-clique.*
- *The fixed vertices of the five cliques are connected to each other.*
- *For each $S \in \{\top, \bot\}$, $P \in \{\mathsf{A}, \mathsf{B}\}$, and $i \in [n]$, the endpoint-copy $(\mathsf{End}', S, P, i)$ is connected to each of the $k$ triangle nodes $(\mathsf{Tri}, S, j, P)$ where $j \in Q_i$.*
- *Finally, for each $P \in \{\mathsf{A}, \mathsf{B}\}$, the graph may contain an arbitrary subset of the edges in $\mathsf{End}'_{\top,P} \times \mathsf{End}'_{\bot,P}$, depending on Alice and Bob's inputs..*

**Property 1.** *Any graph in $\mathcal{G}_{k,n}$ has diameter 3 and size $O(n)$.*

Crucially, the only copies of $H_k$ that can appear in $\mathcal{G}_{k,n}$ have very specific structure: the endpoints of $H_k$ must be mapped onto endpoints in $\mathcal{G}_{k,n}$, respecting the "top/down" partition and also the "directions" A, B. Consequently, we get:

**Lemma 3.1.** *A graph $G \in \mathcal{G}_{k,n}$ contains $H_k$ as a subgraph iff there exist $i_\top, i_\bot \in [n]$ such that $(\mathsf{End}', \top, \mathsf{A}, i_\top), (\mathsf{End}', \bot, \mathsf{A}, i_\bot) \in E(G)$ and $(\mathsf{End}', \top, \mathsf{B}, i_\top), (\mathsf{End}', \bot, \mathsf{B}, i_\bot) \in E(G)$.*

### 3.3 The Lower Bound

To prove that $H_k$-detection requires $\Omega(n^{2-1/k}/(Bk))$ rounds, we give a reduction from 2-party set disjointness on the universe $[n]^2$.

Proof of Theorem 1.2. Fix an algorithm $A$ for which solves $H_k$-freeness in the class $\mathcal{G}_{k,n}$, and let us construct from $A$ a protocol for disjointness. Given inputs $X, Y \subseteq [n]^2$, Alice and Bob construct a graph $G_{X,Y} \in \mathcal{G}_{k,n}$. The only freedom when constructing a graph in $\mathcal{G}_{k,n}$ is the choice of the edges we take from $\mathsf{End}'_{\top,\mathsf{A}} \times \mathsf{End}'_{\bot,\mathsf{A}}$ and from $\mathsf{End}'_{\top,\mathsf{B}} \times \mathsf{End}'_{\bot,\mathsf{B}}$. For this choice the players use their inputs:

- Edge $\{(\mathsf{End}', \top, \mathsf{A}, i), (\mathsf{End}', \bot, \mathsf{A}, j)\}$ is included in $G_{X,Y}$ iff $(i, j) \in X$, and
- Edge $\{(\mathsf{End}', \top, \mathsf{B}, i), (\mathsf{End}', \bot, \mathsf{B}, j)\}$ is included in $G_{X,Y}$ iff $(i, j) \in Y$.

By Lemma 3.1, the graph $G_{X,Y}$ includes a copy of $H_k$ as a subgraph iff $X \cap Y \neq \emptyset$. Thus, to solve their disjointness instance, Alice and Bob simulate the execution of $A$ in $G_{X,Y}$, and output "$X \cap Y = \emptyset$" iff $A$ rejects.

Let us describe the simulation. We partition $V(G_{X,Y})$ into three parts: Alice's part,

$$V_A = \bigcup_{S \in \{\top,\bot\}} \left(\mathsf{End}'_{S,\mathsf{A}} \times [n] \cup \mathsf{Tri}'_{S,\mathsf{A}}\right) \cup \mathsf{Clique}'_6 \cup \mathsf{Clique}'_8,$$

Bob's part,

$$V_B = \bigcup_{S \in \{\top,\bot\}} \left(\mathsf{End}'_{S,\mathsf{B}} \times [n] \cup \mathsf{Tri}'_{S,\mathsf{B}}\right) \cup \mathsf{Clique}'_7 \cup \mathsf{Clique}'_9,$$

, and a shared part, $U$, comprising the remaining vertices, $U = \mathsf{Tri}'_{\top,\mathsf{Mid}} \cup \mathsf{Tri}'_{\bot,\mathsf{Mid}} \cup \mathsf{Clique}'_{10}$. Note that each player knows all edges of $G_{X,Y}$, except those edges that are internal to the other player's part — those are the only edges that depend on the other player's input. For example, Alice knows all edges in $(V_A \cup V_B \cup U) \times (V_A \cup U)$. Thus, the players only need to tell each other about messages crossing the cut between the part only they simulate, and the rest of the graph. By construction of the family $\mathcal{G}_{k,n}$, the cut is of size $O(kn^{1/k})$, so the cost of the simulation is $O(kn^{1/k} \cdot B)$ bits per round. (We omit the details of the simulation here, as they are fairly standard.)

If $A$ runs for $R$ rounds, then the total cost of the simulation is $O(R \cdot kn^{1/k} \cdot B)$. Solving disjointness on $[n]^2$ requires $\Omega(n^2)$ bits. Thus, we must have $R = \Omega\left(n^2 / \left(kn^{1/k} \cdot B\right)\right) = \Omega(n^{2-1/k}/(Bk))$. □

### 3.4 A Superlinear Lower Bound for Bipartite Subgraphs

The superlinear lower bound described above is for a specific graph $H_k$ which is not bipartite: we relied on the fact that the body of $H_k$ contained *triangles*, while the subgraph connecting the top/bottom endpoints on each side is *bipartite*. This ensured that any embedding of $H_k$ into the larger graph $G$ had to "use" the triangles in $G$ "in the role of" the triangles of $H_k$. We also used cliques (also not bipartite, of course) to "mark" the various parts of $H_k$.

Could it be that all bipartite subgraphs *can* be detected in linear time? It turns out that the answer is no: we show that for any $s, k > 1$, there is a bipartite graph $H_{s,k}$ of size $\Theta((s!)^2 \cdot k)$, such that $B$-freeness requires $\Omega(n^{2-1/k-1/s}/(Bk))$ rounds in graphs of size $\Theta(n)$. This construction follows the same approach as the non-bipartite one, but it is much more involved, because we cannot use non-bipartite "components" (e.g., triangles) to constrain an embedding of the subgraph into the graph $G_{X,Y}$ simulated by Alice and Bob. Instead, we rely on the fact that each endpoint in $G_{X,Y}$ has degree $k$. We restrict the edges that Alice and Bob can receive, and construct a bipartite "gadget" that cannot be embedded in $G_{X,Y}$ without using two endpoints from Alice's side and two endpoints from Bob's side, as intended. This gadget replaces the triangles, allowing the reduction to go through (with more effort).

## 4 LOWER BOUND ON DETERMINISTIC TRIANGLE-DETECTION

In this section we show:

**Theorem 4.1.** *Distinguishing a triangle from a 6-cycle deterministically requires $\Omega(\log(N))$ bits of communication in the* CONGEST *model, given a namespace of size $N$.*

As in the proof of the $\Omega(\log^* n)$ lower bound from [1], we rely on the following result from extremal graph theory: let $K^{(r)}(\ell)$ be the complete $r$-uniform $r$-partite hypergraph, where each side has size $\ell$, (Formally, $K^{(r)}(\ell)$ is defined as follows: let $V_1, ..., V_r$ be disjoint vertex sets of size $\ell$ each. Then $K^{(r)}(\ell)$ is the hypergraph with vertex set $\bigcup_{i=1}^{r} V_i$ and edge set $E = \{(v_1, ..., v_r) \mid v_i \in V_i\}$.)

**Theorem 4.2** ([11], Theorem 1). *If $G$ is an $r$-uniform hypergraph that does not contain $K^{(r)}(\ell)$ as a subgraph, then $|E(G)| \leq n^{r-1/(\ell^{r-1})}$.*

For our purposes, we take $r = 3$ and $\ell = 2$, and obtain that if $G$ is 3-regular hypergraph with at least $n^{2.75}$ edges, then $G$ contains the complete 3-uniform 3-partite graph where each side is of size 2.

We make two assumptions about the algorithms we consider: first, we assume that in each round, each node sends at least one bit. If we do not impose this restriction, nodes might communicate information to each other 'for free' by remaining silent in a given round (we do not charge them for *not* sending bits). Second, we assume that the algorithm's messages are self-delimiting, that is, they form a *prefix code*: if $M_1$ and $M_2$ are possible messages the algorithm can send, then $M_1$ is not a prefix of $M_2$ and vice-versa. Any algorithm can be transformed into an algorithm that has this property by at most doubling its total communication cost.

The intuition behind the lower bound is that if the bandwidth is so small that nodes cannot even send their neighbors' identifiers, then for some adversarial choice of identifiers, the algorithm cannot distinguish between a *triangle* and a *hexagon* (a 6-cycle). This idea was used in [1], and its roots go back to the proof of impossibility of Byzantine consensus with 3 processors of which one may be faulty [21].

The approach of [1] was *recursive*, showing that after each bit sent, the adversary can still use many identifiers to "fool" the algorithm. However, if before the $i$-th bit the adversary had $n$ identifiers available, then after the $i$-th bit, [1] shows that it has roughly $\log n$; because of this fast shrinkage rate, the lower bound of [1] is $\Omega(\log^* n)$.

Here we do not take the recursive approach. Instead we argue that there is a *complete transcript t* of all messages sent by the algorithm during its execution, which occurs for many triangles (where each triangle is defined by the choice of identifiers for its nodes). As in [1], we construct a 3-regular hypergraph representing the adversary's choices, with nodes representing identifiers and each edge representing a triangle that yields the transcript $t$. Then we use Theorem 4.2 to argue that the adversary can choose two "compatible" triangles and combine them to form a hexagon, in a way that guarantees that each node's view is consistent with some triangle that generates transcript $t$. Thus, the adversary can make the algorithm reject the hexagon (which it is supposed to accept).

There are several subtle points in the proof: we must set up our construction carefully, to ensure that the algorithm's transcript really does capture "everything there is to know" about the algorithm's execution. In particular, from the transcript we must be able to read off the source and destination of each message. Because we are working with total communication less than $\log N$, we cannot use the naïve solution of assuming w.l.o.g. that this information is contained in the messages themselves, so we are careful about the order of messages when we define the representation of a transcript.

We remark that although the lower bound specifically shows that it is impossible to distinguish two constant-sized shapes (a triangle and a hexagon), it is easy to "pad" the graph to any desired size of at most $n < N/3$ nodes, by, e.g., attaching a fixed line of $\Theta(n)$ nodes to one of the triangle or hexagon nodes.

Proof of Theorem 4.1. Let $A$ be deterministic algorithm that solves the triangle-freeness problem in the CONGEST model given a namespace of size $N = 3n$. We split $N$ into three equal-size disjoint subsets, $N_0, N_1, N_2$, and define $S := N_0 \times N_1 \times N_2$. In the lower bound, we are interested in the class of graphs

$$\mathcal{G}_\triangle := \{\triangle(u_0, u_1, u_2) \mid (u_0, u_1, u_2) \in S\},$$

where $\triangle(u_0, u_1, u_2)$ is the graph consisting of a single triangle on nodes $u_0, u_1, u_2$.

Let $C$ be the worst-case number of bits sent by a node in any execution of $A$. Assume for the sake of contradiction that $C \leq \log(n)/60$.

*Making decision values uniform.* Our first step is to transform $A$ into a modified algorithm $A'$, which has one extra round. In $A'$, nodes first execute $A$, and then in the extra round they send their decision according to $A$ (i.e., whether they decided to accept or reject) to all their neighbors. Finally, each node $v$ accepts iff under $A$, node $v$ and all its neighbors decided to accept.

The communication cost of $A'$ is $C + 1$. The transformation preserves the correctness of $A$, because $A'$ accepts iff all nodes of $A$ accept, and rejects iff some node rejects in $A$. It also has the following property, which will be important for our proof:

**Claim 4.3.** *When $A'$ is executed in a graph that contains exactly one triangle, all nodes of the triangle reject.*

*Transcripts.* Next we formally define the *transcript* generated by a node executing $A'$ in some triangle $\triangle(u, v, w)$. Although it is intuitively obvious "what this should mean", some care is required to ensure that transcripts can be parsed in a unique way, otherwise our proof does not go through.

Consider the graph $\triangle(u_0, u_1, u_2)$ for $(u_0, u_1, u_2) \in S$. (Recall that $S = N_0 \times N_1 \times N_2$.) We define *the transcript of node $u_i$ in $\triangle(u_0, u_1, u_2)$*, denoted $\mathrm{Tr}_{u_0,u_1,u_2}(u_i)$, to be the binary string obtained by first writing all the messages sent by $u_i$ to $u_{(i+1) \bmod 3}$ (in order, round after round), and then writing all the messages sent by $u_i$ to $u_{(i+2) \bmod 3}$.

We define *the transcript of $A'$ in $\triangle(u_0, u_1, u_2)$* to be the concatenation of the nodes' transcripts:

$$\mathrm{Tr}(u_0, u_1, u_2) = \\ = \mathrm{Tr}_{u_0,u_1,u_2}(u_0)\, \mathrm{Tr}_{u_0,u_1,u_2}(u_1)\, \mathrm{Tr}_{u_0,u_1,u_2}(u_2).$$

Note that the nodes' transcripts are written in order of the part of the namespace to which the nodes belong: first the transcript of $u_0$, which is a node from $N_0$, then the transcript of $u_1 \in N_1$ and finally $u_2 \in N_2$.

With this encoding, transcripts can be parsed uniquely: given the binary transcript and three nodes $(u_0, u_1, u_2) \in S$, we know exactly which message was sent by which node in which round. This is the reason we insisted that $A$'s messages be a prefix code, partitioned the namespace into disjoint subsets, and took care to define the order in which messages appear in the transcript.

Since the total number of bits sent by any node to any other node is at most $C + 1$ in any execution of $A'$, and the transcript contains all the messages sent by any node to any other node with no bits added, the length of any transcript generated by $A'$ is at most $6(C + 1)$.

For each binary string $t$ of length $6(C+1)$, define the subset $S_t \subseteq S$ to be the set of all triples in $S$ on which $A'$ produces transcript $t$: $S_t := \{(u_0, u_1, u_2) \in S \mid \mathrm{Tr}(u_0, u_1, u_2) = t\}$.

Now fix $t$ to be the transcript with the largest set $S_t$ (or one of the transcripts maximizing $|S_t|$, if there is more than one). Observe that

$$|S_t| \geq \frac{|S|}{2^{6(C+1)}} = \frac{n^3}{2^{6(C+1)}}.$$

Consider the undirected 3-uniform hypergraph $H$ with $N$ as the vertex set, and edges given by the triplets in $S_t$. Note that although $S_t$ is defined as a set of *ordered* triplets, because $S_t \subseteq N_0 \times N_1 \times N_2$, and $N_0, N_1, N_2$ are mutually disjoint, we may as well think of $S_t$ as a set of unordered triplets.

The number of edges in $H$ is $|E(H)| = |S_t| \geq n^3/2^{(6(C+1))}$. By assumption, $C \leq \log(n)/60 - 1$, so

$$|E(H)| \geq \frac{n^3}{2^{6 \cdot \log(n)/60}} = n^{2.9}.$$

By Theorem 4.2, if $H$ has at least $\Omega(n^{2.75})$ edges, then it must contain a complete 3-partite 3-uniform hypergraph such that each part contains exactly two vertices. Let

$$F = (\{u_0, u_0'\}, \{u_1, u_1'\}, \{u_2, u_2'\})$$

and $E(F)$ be one such hypergraph, with the edge set $E(F)$ containing *every triplet* $\{x, y, z\}$ such that $x \in \{u_0, u_0'\}, y \in \{u_1, u_1'\}, z \in \{u_2, u_2'\}$. Since $E(F) \subseteq E(H) = S_t$, each side of $F$ is a subset of $N_i$ for some $i$; without lose of generality we assume that $u_0, u_0' \in N_0, u_1, u_1' \in N_1$ and $u_2, u_2' \in N_2$.

Now consider the execution of $A'$ on the 6-cycle $Q$ with vertices $u_0, u_1, u_2, u_0', u_1', u_2'$ in this order. Let $\mathrm{Tr}_Q(u)$ denote the transcript generated by node $u$ in the execution of $A'$ in $Q$: if $u \in N_i$, then $\mathrm{Tr}_Q(u)$ is the binary string obtained by first writing all the messages sent by $u$ to its neighbor in $N_{(i+1) \bmod 3}$ (in order, round after round), followed by all the messages sent by $u$ to its neighbor in $N_{(i+2) \bmod 3}$.

**Claim 4.4.** *Let us write $t = t_0 t_1 t_2$, where $t_i = \mathrm{Tr}_{u_0, u_1, u_2}(u_i) = \mathrm{Tr}_{u_0', u_1', u_2'}(u_i')$ for each $i \in \{0, 1, 2\}$. Then for each $i \in \{0, 1, 2\}$ we have $\mathrm{Tr}_Q(u_i) = \mathrm{Tr}_Q(u_i') = t_i$.*

Proof sketch. By induction on rounds. In the step we use the fact that for each node $v$ in $Q$, if $x$ and $y$ are $v$'s neighbors in $Q$, then $\{x, v, y\}$ is an edge of $F$, meaning that the transcript generated by $A'$ in $\Delta(x, v, y)$ is the same transcript $t$ we work with; therefore, $v$'s view in $Q$ stays consistent its view in $\Delta(x, v, y)$. □

Now consider node $u_1$'s view at the end of the execution of $A'$ in $Q$. By the claim above, the messages $u_1$ receives throughout the execution in $Q$ are the same messages it would receive in $\Delta(u_0, u_1, u_2)$. Also, the neighbors of $u_1$ in $Q$ are the same neighbors it has in $\Delta(u_0, u_1, u_2)$. Thus, the state of $u_1$ is the same at the end of the execution in $Q$ and in $\Delta(u_0, u_1, u_2)$. In $\Delta(u_0, u_1, u_2)$ we know that $u_1$ rejects (by Claim 4.3); therefore it also rejects in $Q$, violating the correctness of $A'$ and hence also of $A$. □

# 5 BANDWIDTH LOWER BOUND ON 1-ROUND TRIANGLE-DETECTION

In this section we show:

**Theorem 5.1.** *There exist a constant $\epsilon \in (0, 1)$ such that any protocol solving triangle-detection in one round with error probability at most $\epsilon$ requires bandwidth $B = \Omega(n)$ in graphs of maximum degree $\Theta(n)$.*

To generalize to any degree $\Delta$, we can embed our lower bound construction in a larger graph, and trivially obtain the lower bound of $\Omega(\Delta)$ for maximum degree $\Delta$.

The idea behind the lower bound is to take three "special" nodes, with randomly chosen identifiers, and connect every pair of them with iid probability 1/2, so that a triangle appears w.p. 1/8. The error of the protocol is assumed to be much smaller, $\epsilon \ll 1/8$, so the protocol must reject with good probability in this case. In addition to the three special nodes, we give each of them $\Theta(n)$ non-special neighbors, in such a way that no special node can tell a-priori whether a particular neighbor is another special node or not. This way, the triangle edges are "hidden" among many other edges, which look the same to each special node.

We do not prevent a special node from *learning* the identities of the other two special nodes after it receives their messages, but by this point it is too late for the protocol: because each special node did not know a-priori which edges it should care about, we show that its message does not convey much information about the presence or absence of the potential triangle edges (i.e., the edges between special nodes).

Let us now describe the graph construction more formally, and proceed to sketch the proof of the lower bound.

*The template graph.* In our lower bound, we work with random subgraphs of the following graph $G_T$.

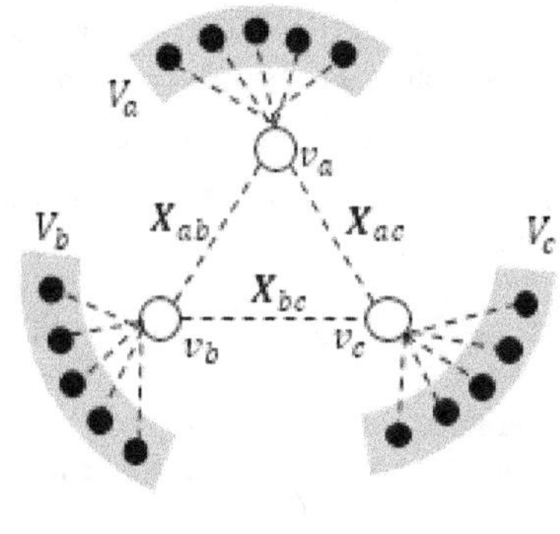


**Figure 3: The template graph $G_T$.**

Let $V_a = \{v_1^a, \ldots, v_n^a\}$, $V_b = \{v_1^b, \ldots, v_n^b\}$, $V_c = \{v_1^c, \ldots, v_n^c\}$ be three disjoint vertex sets with $|A| = |B| = |C| = n$. The vertex set of $G_T$ is $V(G_T) = V_a \cup V_b \cup V_c \cup \{v_a, v_b, v_c\}$, and the edges are the following:

- Nodes $v_a, v_b, v_c$ are connected in a triangle, and
- For each $s \in \{a, b, c\}$, every $u \in V_s$ is connected to $v_s$.

We refer to $v_a, v_b, v_c$ as *special nodes*; they are the only nodes that are part of a triangle in $G_T$. Throughout this proof sketch, we ignore the non-special nodes, because their input gives them no information about the presence of a triangle. (We account for the non-special nodes more formally in the full proof, see the full version for details.)

In a departure from the rest of the paper, here we treat a *graph node* as a separate entity from its *identifier*: we construct a random graph $G$ by taking a random subgraph of $G_T$ as we describe below, and assigning to each node a random identifier. The algorithm executed at node $v \in V(G)$ knows only the identifier assigned to node $v$, and the identifiers of $v$'s neighbors; it does not know $v$. This is merely a technical convenience due to the fact that the graphs we consider are all subgraphs of $G_T$, and does not weaken the lower bound.

*The input distribution.* We define $G$ to be a random subgraph of $G_T$, where each edge of $G_T$ is included with iid probability $1/2$. Identifiers are also assigned at random: for each $v \in V(G_T)$, we choose an identifier $\boldsymbol{id}(v)$ uniformly at random from $[n^3]$.

*Remark.* Since we choose the identifiers independently from $[n^3]$, there is a small but non-zero chance that two vertices get the same identifier. In this case we do not know what the algorithm will do, as it is not obligated to work when identifiers are not unique. However, the probability of this event is so tiny that it does not affect us by much.

For each $s \in \{a, b, c\}$, let $\boldsymbol{u}_s = \boldsymbol{id}(v_s)$ be the identifier assigned to $v_s$.

*Input representation.* It is technically convenient to represent the input to each node as the sequence of identifiers assigned to its neighbors in $G_T$ (i.e., possibly *more* neighbors than it has in $G$), together with a bit-vector indicating for each one whether it is a neighbor in $G$ or not. The algorithm is free to ignore the extra information, so this only strengthens the lower bound. This representation makes it technically easy to view the potential triangle edges as "hidden" among $\Theta(n)$ other iid Bernoulli random variables.

Thus, we give each special node $v_s$ the sequence

$$\boldsymbol{U}_s = \{\boldsymbol{id}(w) \mid \{w, v_s\} \in E(G_T)\}$$

of identifiers of $v_s$'s neighbors in $G_T$, but we apply a random permutation $\boldsymbol{\pi}_s$ to the sequence, so that $v_s$ cannot tell which node in $G_T$ corresponds to which identifier in $G$. In addition, $v_s$ receives the bit-vector $\boldsymbol{X}_s$ indicating for each potential neighbor $w$ in $G_T$ whether the edge $\{v_s, w\}$ is in $G$; the vector $\boldsymbol{X}_s$ is also scrambled using the same permutation $\boldsymbol{\pi}_s$, so that its order matches the order of the identifiers in $\boldsymbol{U}_s$. And finally, $v_s$ receives its own identifier, $\boldsymbol{u}_s$.

For $s \neq t \in \{a, b, c\}$, let $\boldsymbol{i}_s(t)$ be the index in $\boldsymbol{X}_s$ indicating whether the potential triangle edge $\{v_s, v_t\}$ is in $G$ or not. (This is a uniformly random index from $v_s$'s perspective.) We use the following short-hand notation: $\boldsymbol{N}_s = (\boldsymbol{U}_s, \boldsymbol{X}_s, \boldsymbol{u}_s)$ is the input to $v_s$, and $\boldsymbol{X}_{st} = \boldsymbol{X}_s(\boldsymbol{i}_s(t))$ is the bit indicating whether the edge $\{v_s, v_t\}$ is in $G$.

**Observation 5.2.** *$G$ contains a triangle if and only if $\boldsymbol{X}_{ab} \wedge \boldsymbol{X}_{bc} \wedge \boldsymbol{X}_{ac} = 1$.*

Now, fix an algorithm $A$ with distributional error at most $1/1000$ on $\mu$; that is, when we draw $G \sim \mu$, the probability that $A$ outputs the correct answer is at least $999/1000$. (The constant is fairly arbitrary.)

Because a triangle appears with probability $1/8$, and $A$ has overall error at most $1/1000$, it is easy to verify that *conditioned* on the presence of the triangle, $A$ rejects with probability at least $1 - 8/1000 > 99/100$. This means that at least one of the three special vertices, w.l.o.g. $v_a$, rejects w.p. $> 33/100$ in this case. On the other hand, if $\boldsymbol{X}_{ab} = \boldsymbol{X}_{ac} = 1$ but $\boldsymbol{X}_{bc} = 0$, then $v_a$ must accept with probability at least $1 - 8/1000 > 99/100$. So, conditioned on the event $\boldsymbol{X}_{ab} = \boldsymbol{X}_{ac} = 1$, node $v_a$ must *learn* some information about $\boldsymbol{X}_{bc}$, and this is formalized by the following lemma. For two vertices $u, w$, Let $\boldsymbol{M}_{uw}$ denote the messages sent by $u$ to $w$.

**Lemma 5.3.** *If $\Pi$ is a protocol that solves triangle-detection, then either*

$$\mathrm{I}(\boldsymbol{X}_{bc}; \boldsymbol{M}_{ba}, \boldsymbol{M}_{ca} | \boldsymbol{N}_a, \boldsymbol{X}_{ab} = 1, \boldsymbol{X}_{ac} = 1) \geq 0.3,$$

*or a symmetric claim holds for $v_b$ or for $v_c$.*

Proof sketch. Let $\boldsymbol{acc}_a$ be an indicator for the event that $v_a$ accepts. By the data processing inequality, since $v_a$'s decision is a function of its input and the messages it receives,

$$\mathrm{I}(\boldsymbol{X}_{bc}; \boldsymbol{M}_{ba}, \boldsymbol{M}_{ca} | \boldsymbol{N}_a, \boldsymbol{X}_{ab} = 1, \boldsymbol{X}_{ac} = 1) \geq \mathrm{I}(\boldsymbol{X}_{bc}; \boldsymbol{acc}_a | \boldsymbol{N}_a, \boldsymbol{X}_{ab} = 1, \boldsymbol{X}_{ac} = 1),$$

so it suffices to lower-bound the right-hand side.

As we said above, the distribution of $\boldsymbol{acc}_a$ changes noticeably depending on the value of $\boldsymbol{X}_{bc} = 1$: when $\boldsymbol{X}_{bc} = 0$, the probability that $v_a$ accepts is at least $99/100$. However, the *prior* probability that $v_a$ accepts, when $\boldsymbol{X}_{bc} \sim \text{Bernoulli}(1/2)$, is at most $(1/2) \cdot (99/100) + (1/2) \cdot (67/100) < 8/10$. This "change in behavior" translates to a lower bound on mutual information (see the full proof for the details). □

On the other hand, we claim that nodes $v_b$ and $v_c$ cannot convey this much information about $\boldsymbol{X}_{bc}$ to $v_a$.

**Lemma 5.4.** *The information node $v_a$ learns about $\boldsymbol{X}_{bc}$ given its input and the presence of edges $\{v_a, v_b\}, \{v_a, v_c\}$ is at most:*

$$\mathrm{I}(\boldsymbol{X}_{bc}; \boldsymbol{M}_{ba}, \boldsymbol{M}_{ca} | \boldsymbol{N}_a, \boldsymbol{X}_{ab} = 1, \boldsymbol{X}_{ac} = 1) \leq \frac{4(|\boldsymbol{M}_{ca}| + |\boldsymbol{M}_{ba}|)}{n+1} + \frac{2}{n}.$$

*Symmetric claims hold for $v_b$ and $v_c$.*

Proof sketch. First, since $\Pr(\boldsymbol{X}_{ab} = 1, \boldsymbol{X}_{ac} = 1) = 1/4$ and mutual information is non-negative,

$$\mathrm{I}(\boldsymbol{X}_{bc}; \boldsymbol{M}_{ba}, \boldsymbol{M}_{ca} | \boldsymbol{N}_a) \geq (1/4)\,\mathrm{I}(\boldsymbol{X}_{bc}; \boldsymbol{M}_{ba}, \boldsymbol{M}_{ca} | \boldsymbol{N}_a, \boldsymbol{X}_{ab} = 1, \boldsymbol{X}_{ac} = 1).$$

(This can be seen by writing the expectation on $\boldsymbol{N}_a$ as an expectation on $\boldsymbol{X}_{ab}, \boldsymbol{X}_{ac}$ and the rest of $\boldsymbol{N}_a$, and expanding out the expectation on $\boldsymbol{X}_{ab}, \boldsymbol{X}_{ac}$.)

We bound the left-hand side. It expresses the information $v_b$ and $v_c$'s messages *together* convey about $\boldsymbol{X}_{bc}$. However, because the two nodes' inputs are independent given the conditioning and $\boldsymbol{X}_{bc}$, we can actually break it up into the sum of what each message conveys by itself: we show that

$$\mathrm{I}(\boldsymbol{X}_{bc}; \boldsymbol{M}_{ba}, \boldsymbol{M}_{ca} | \boldsymbol{N}_a) \leq \mathrm{I}(\boldsymbol{X}_{bc}; \boldsymbol{M}_{ba} | \boldsymbol{N}_a, \boldsymbol{u}_c) + \mathrm{I}(\boldsymbol{X}_{bc}; \boldsymbol{M}_{ca} | \boldsymbol{N}_a, \boldsymbol{u}_b).$$

We bound each term separately.

Consider the first term, $I(\boldsymbol{X}_{bc};\boldsymbol{M}_{ba}|\boldsymbol{N}_a,\boldsymbol{u}_c)$ (the other term is similar). This term essentially measures the information $v_b$ sends to $a$ about $\boldsymbol{X}_{bc}$, for a "typical" identifier $\boldsymbol{u}_c$. Crucially, when $v_b$ sends its message to $v_a$, it does not *know* the identity of $\boldsymbol{u}_c$; that is, its message is *independent* of the choice of $\boldsymbol{u}_c$, conditioned on its input. Consequently, we can argue that $\boldsymbol{M}_{bc}$ is independent of the index $\boldsymbol{i}_b(c)$ where we hid the bit $\boldsymbol{X}_{bc}$. (This is slightly delicate, because we could have duplicate identifiers; $\boldsymbol{u}_c$ does not uniquely specify $\boldsymbol{i}_b(c)$. We handle this in the proof by conditioning on the high-probability event that there are no duplicate identifiers; hence the additive $O(1/n)$ term in the bound we get.)

Now we have reduced everything to the following question: how much does $v_b$'s message $\boldsymbol{M}_{ba}$ reveal about a *random* coordinate $\boldsymbol{X}_b(\boldsymbol{i})$ of its input, where the index $\boldsymbol{i}$ is uniformly random on $n+1$ locations,[1] and not known to $v_b$ in advance? Using standard arguments, we show that the answer is $O(|\boldsymbol{M}_{ba}|/(n+1))$. The claim follows. □

**Corollary 5.5.** *If* $|\boldsymbol{M}_{ba}|, |\boldsymbol{M}_{ca}| < n/60$ *then*

$$I(\boldsymbol{X}_{bc};\boldsymbol{M}_{ba},\boldsymbol{M}_{ca}|\boldsymbol{N}_a,\boldsymbol{X}_{ab}=1,\boldsymbol{X}_{ac}=1) < 0.1.$$

By combining the two lemmas above, and dealing with the low-probability event that $G$ contains duplicate identifiers, we get Theorem 5.1.

## 6 SUBLINEAR-TIME PROTOCOL FOR $C_{2k}$

In this section we show that for any $k \geq 2$, the $C_{2k}$-subgraph detection problem can be solved in $O(n^{1-1/(k(k-1))})$ rounds. E.g., $C_4$ can be detected in in $O(n^{1/2})$ rounds (which was already known [10]); $C_6$ can be detected in $O(n^{5/6})$ rounds; and so on. Our algorithm combines several techniques: color coding [2], pipelining, and a particular decomposition of low-arboricity graphs (previously used in, e.g., [3]). We also rely on the fact that the Túran number of an even cycle $C_{2k}$ is $\mathrm{ex}(n, C_{2k}) = O(n^{1+1/k})$ (see, e.g., [5]).

Let $M = O(n^{1+1/k})$ be an upper bound on $\mathrm{ex}(n, C_{2k})$. We assume for simplicity that the bandwidth is sufficiently large to send a sequence of $2k$ identifiers in one message. (Note that $k$ is treated as a constant throughout.)

*Phase I: dealing with high-degree nodes.* Our goal in this step is to find a copy of $C_{2k}$ that includes at least one "high-degree node": a node with degree at least $n^\delta$, where $\delta = 1/(k-1)$. If there is such a $C_{2k}$ in the graph, then in this phase at least one node rejects. Otherwise we will search for cycles comprising only low-degree nodes, in the next phase of the algorithm.

We rely on the fact that if $|E(G)| \leq M$, then there cannot be more than $\lceil M/n^\delta \rceil$ nodes with degree at least $n^\delta$. On the other hand, if $|E(G)| > M$, then we may fail, but in this case we know that the graph contains a $2k$-cycle, because it has too many edges (more than $\mathrm{ex}(n, C_{2k})$).

We first color-code the graph, assigning each node $u$ a random color $c(u) \in \{0, \ldots, 2k-1\}$. Then we look for a *properly-colored* copy of $C_{2k}$: a cycle $u_0, \ldots, u_{2k-1}$, where $c(u_i) = i$ for each $i = 0, \ldots, 2k-1$. To search for such cycles, we start a "color-coded" BFS to depth $2k$, from *every node* that has degree at least $n^\delta$ and color 0. A color-coded BFS is like a regular BFS, except that the BFS token is only allowed to move from node $u$ to a neighbor $v$ if $c(v) = c(u)+1$. In this way we "unravel" paths of nodes with colors $0, 1, \ldots, 2k-1$ respectively, until finally the last node, whose color is $2k-1$, sends the BFS token back to node 0, and then node 0 detects the cycle and rejects.

The color-coded BFS is executed in parallel for all nodes, as follows. Each node $u$ maintains a queue of messages it needs to send; initially, if $c(u) = 0$ and $\deg(u) \geq n^\delta$, then $u$ adds the message (ColorBFS, $u$, 0) to its queue, and otherwise $u$'s queue is initially empty.

In each round, every node chooses an arbitrary message from its queue, sends it to all its neighbors, and removes it from its queue. Upon receipt of a message (ColorBFS, $u$, $i$), node $v$ does the following:

- If node $v$ previously received the same message, it discards the new copy.
- If $u = v$ (i.e., node $u$ received its own message back), and $i = 2k-1$, then we have found a $2k$-cycle, and node $u$ rejects.
- If $c(v) \neq i+1$, it discards the message.
- Otherwise, $v$ adds a message (ColorBFS, $u$, $i+1$) to its queue.

Phase I takes $R_1 := \lceil M/n^\delta \rceil + 2k$ rounds. At the end of $R_1$ rounds, if any node has a non-empty message queue, it rejects.

A standard pipelining argument shows:

**Lemma 6.1.** *If* $|E(G)| \leq M$, *then after* $R_1 = \lceil M/n^\delta \rceil + 2k$ *rounds, all nodes have empty queues.*

Intuitively, this is because at most $\lceil M/n^\delta \rceil$ BFS tokens can "stand in the way" of any given token (as this is an upper bound on the number of high-degree nodes), and each token only travels to distance $2k$.

Consequently, at the end of phase I, if $|E(G)| \leq M$ then all BFS instances complete, and we get:

**Corollary 6.2.** *If* $|E(G)| \leq M$, *and* $G$ *contains a copy of* $C_{2k}$ *that includes a node with degree at least* $n^\delta$, *then in phase I, with probability at least* $1/(2k)^{2k}$, *some node rejects.*

What happens if $|E(G)| > M$? In this case we know that the graph *must* contain a $2k$-cycle, but still, we might not find it. However, we are guaranteed that if after $R_1$ rounds some node has a non-empty queue, then the graph has more than $M$ edges, and it contains a $2k$-cycle. Hence:

**Lemma 6.3.** *If in phase I some node rejects, then* $G$ *contains a copy of* $C_{2k}$.

*Phase II: dealing with the remaining graph.* At the end of phase I, any node with degree at least $n^\delta$ removes itself and all its edges from the graph. Now we search for copies of $C_{2k}$ among the remaining nodes.

Let $d = \lceil M/2n \rceil$. Using the decomposition from [3], *if* the graph is $C_{2k}$-free (which we do not know), we can decompose it into $\lceil \log n \rceil$ layers $V_1, \ldots, V_L$, with the property that for each layer $\ell$ and node $v \in V_\ell$, the number of edges going "up" from $v$ to nodes in equal-or-higher layers $V_\ell, V_{\ell+1}, \ldots, V_L$ is at most $d = \lceil M/2n \rceil$. Essentially, we recursively remove from the graph nodes with degree

[1] One location is taken up by the bit $\boldsymbol{X}_{ab}$; since we condition here on $\boldsymbol{u}_a$, as it is part of $v_a$'s input $\boldsymbol{N}_a$, only $n+1$ locations are possible for $\boldsymbol{X}_{bc}$.

sufficiently small in the remaining graph, relying on the fact that if there is no $2k$-cycle, then at each point the average degree cannot exceed $\lceil M/n \rceil$. After $\lceil \log n \rceil$ such steps, if there is some node that has not been assigned to any layer, this node rejects, as we know that there is a $2k$-cycle.

Otherwise we continue as follows: for each $v \in V$, let $\ell(v)$ denote the layer of node $v$. We randomly assign each node $v$ a color $c(v) \in [2k]$. We look only for properly-colored $2k$-cyles $u_0, \ldots, u_{2k-1}$ where $c(u_0) = 0, \ldots, c(u_{2k-1}) = 2k - 1$ and furthermore, $u_0$ is on the highest layer out of all the cycle nodes. (That is, for each $i = 1, \ldots, 2k - 1$ we have $\ell(u_i) \leq \ell(u_0)$.)

For this type of cycle, we have the advantage that from the perspective of nodes $u_1$ and $u_{2k-1}$, the number of neighbors they need to "consider for the role of $u_0$" is bounded by their "up-degree" $d$ — the number of neighbors they have in equal-or-higher layers.

Let us call a sequence $u_0, \ldots, u_i$ a *length-$i$ increasing prefix* if $c(u_0) = 0, c(u_1) = 1, \ldots, c(u_i) = i$, or a *length-$i$ decreasing prefix* if $c(u_0) = 0, c(u_1) = 2k-1, c(u_2) = 2k-2, \ldots, c(u_i) = 2k-i$. Our goal now is to have node $u_k$ (the "midpoint" of the $2k$-cycle) receive a length-$k$ increasing sequence *and* a length-$k$ decreasing sequence, both starting from node $u_0$ (the highest-layer node). Node $u_k$ will then detect the cycle and reject.

We propagate prefixes of increasing length, as follows:

(1) First, each $v$ with $c(v) = 0$ sends the message $(v, \ell(v))$.
(2) Next, each node $v$ colored 1 or $2k - 1$ sends the following: for each message $(u, \ell(u))$ received in the previous round, *if* $\ell(u) \geq \ell(v)$, then $v$ sends out the prefix $(u, v)$. Since node $v$ has at most $d$ neighbors in equal-or-higher layers, this requires at most $d$ rounds.
(3) For each $i \in \{2, \ldots, k-1\}$, nodes colored $i$ (resp. $2k - i$) send all the length-$(i-1)$ increasing (resp. decreasing) prefixes they received, appending their name at the end to form length-$i$ increasing (resp. decreasing) prefixes. This takes at most $d \cdot n^{\delta \cdot (k-2)}$ rounds.
(4) Finally, nodes $v$ colored $k$ collect the length-$k$ increasing and decreasing prefixes they received, and check if there is some node $u_0$ that starts both an increasing and a decreasing prefix ending at $v$. If so, they have found a $2k$-cycle, and they reject.

**Claim 6.4.** *Assume that $|E(G)| \leq M$. Then (a) all nodes are assigned to a layer after $\lceil \log n \rceil$ steps of layer assignment; and (b) if $G$ contains a $2k$-cycle, then with probability at least $1/(2k)^{2k}$ some node rejects in phase II.*

The running time of phase II is $R_2 = \lceil \log n \rceil + (2k) \cdot d \cdot n^{\delta \cdot (k-2)}$. Balancing the running times $R_1, R_2$ of the two phases, we see that when we take $\delta = 1/(k-1)$, both running times are $O(n^{1-1/(k(k-1))})$, as desired.

*Putting everything together.* Phases I and II together give us the following guarantee:

- If $|E(G)| \leq M$, and the graph contains a $2k$-cycle, then with probability at least $1/(2k)^(2k)$ some node rejects.
- If some node rejects, then either $|E(G)| > M$, or the graph contains a $2k$-cycle.

Of course, if $|E(G)| > M$, then we know that the graph *must* contain a $2k$-cycle, even though we did not necessarily detect a specific one. Therefore it is proper that the algorithm reject in this case.

To construct an algorithm that detects a $2k$-cycle with *constant* probability, we simply repeat each phase $O\left(2k^{2k}\right)$ times, each iteration using independently-chosen colors for the nodes.

## 7 ACKNOWLEDGMENTS

We would like to thank Dan Karliner for fruitful discussions, and for pointing out Theorem 4.2 to us.

## REFERENCES

[1] Amir Abboud, Keren Censor-Hillel, Seri Khoury, and Christoph Lenzen. 2017. Fooling Views: A New Lower Bound Technique for Distributed Computations under Congestion. *CoRR* abs/1711.01623 (2017).
[2] Noga Alon, Raphael Yuster, and Uri Zwick. 1995. Color-coding. *J. ACM* 42, 4 (1995), 844–856.
[3] Leonid Barenboim and Michael Elkin. 2008. Sublogarithmic Distributed MIS Algorithm for Sparse Graphs Using Nash-williams Decomposition *(PODC '08)*. 25–34.
[4] Zvika Brakerski and Boaz Patt-Shamir. 2011. Distributed discovery of large near-cliques. *Distributed Computing* 24, 2 (2011), 79–89.
[5] Boris Bukh and Zilin Jiang. 2017. A bound on the number of edges in graphs without an even cycle. *Combinatorics, Probability and Computing* 26, 1 (2017), 1–15.
[6] Keren Censor-Hillel, Eldar Fischer, Gregory Schwartzman, and Yadu Vasudev. 2016. *Fast Distributed Algorithms for Testing Graph Properties.* 43–56.
[7] Keren Censor-Hillel, Petteri Kaski, Janne H. Korhonen, Christoph Lenzen, Ami Paz, and Jukka Suomela. 2015. Algebraic Methods in the Congested Clique. In *Proceedings of the 2015 ACM Symposium on Principles of Distributed Computing, PODC 2015.* 143–152.
[8] Keren Censor-Hillel, Seri Khoury, and Ami Paz. 2017. Quadratic and Near-Quadratic Lower Bounds for the CONGEST Model. In *31st International Symposium on Distributed Computing, DISC 2017, October 16-20, 2017, Vienna, Austria.* 10:1–10:16.
[9] Danny Dolev, Christoph Lenzen, and Shir Peled. 2012. *"Tri, Tri Again": Finding Triangles and Small Subgraphs in a Distributed Setting.* 195–209.
[10] Andrew Drucker, Fabian Kuhn, and Rotem Oshman. 2014. On the Power of the Congested Clique Model. In *Proceedings of the 2014 ACM Symposium on Principles of Distributed Computing (PODC '14).* 367–376.
[11] P. Erdös. 1964. On extremal problems of graphs and generalized graphs. *IJoM* (1964).
[12] Guy Even, Orr Fischer, Pierre Fraigniaud, Tzlil Gonen, Reut Levi, Moti Medina, Pedro Montealegre, Dennis Olivetti, Rotem Oshman, Ivan Rapaport, and Ioan Todinca. 2017. Three Notes on Distributed Property Testing. In *31st International Symposium on Distributed Computing (DISC 2017) (Leibniz International Proceedings in Informatics (LIPIcs))*, Vol. 91. 15:1–15:30.
[13] Pierre Fraigniaud and Dennis Olivetti. 2017. Distributed Detection of Cycles. In *Proceedings of the 29th ACM Symposium on Parallelism in Algorithms and Architectures, SPAA 2017, Washington DC, USA, July 24-26, 2017.* 153–162.
[14] Pierre Fraigniaud, Ivan Rapaport, Ville Salo, and Ioan Todinca. 2016. *Distributed Testing of Excluded Subgraphs.* 342–356.
[15] Tzlil Gonen and Rotem Oshman. 2017. Lower Bounds for Subgraph Detection in the CONGEST Model. To appear in OPODIS 2017.
[16] Taisuke Izumi and François Le Gall. 2017. Triangle Finding and Listing in CONGEST Networks. In *Proceedings of the ACM Symposium on Principles of Distributed Computing (PODC '17).* 381–389.
[17] Bala Kalyanasundaram and Georg Schnitger. 1992. The Probabilistic Communication Complexity of Set Intersection. *SIAM J. Discrete Math.* 5, 4 (1992), 545–557.
[18] Janne H. Korhonen and Joel Rybicki. 2017. Deterministic Subgraph Detection in Broadcast CONGEST. In *21st International Conference on Principles of Distributed Systems, OPODIS 2017, Lisbon, Portugal, December 18-20, 2017.* 4:1–4:16.
[19] Eyal Kushilevitz and Noam Nisan. 1997. *Communication Complexity.* Cambridge University Press.
[20] Gopal Pandurangan, Peter Robinson, and Michele Scquizzato. 2016. Tight Bounds for Distributed Graph Computations. *CoRR* (2016). http://arxiv.org/abs/1602.08481
[21] M. Pease, R. Shostak, and L. Lamport. 1980. Reaching Agreement in the Presence of Faults. *J. ACM* 27, 2 (1980), 228–234.
[22] Alexander A. Razborov. 1992. On the Distributional Complexity of Disjointness. *Theor. Comput. Sci.* 106, 2 (1992), 385–390.
[23] Igor Rivin. 2002. Counting Cycles and Finite Dimensional Lp Norms. *Adv. Appl. Math.* 29, 4 (2002), 647–662.
[24] J. R. Ullmann. 1976. An Algorithm for Subgraph Isomorphism. *J. ACM* 23, 1 (1976), 31–42.

# Towards a Complexity Theory for the Congested Clique*

Janne H. Korhonen
Aalto University
janne.h.korhonen@aalto.fi

Jukka Suomela
Aalto University
jukka.suomela@aalto.fi

## ABSTRACT

The *congested clique* model of distributed computing has been receiving attention as a model for densely connected distributed systems. While there has been significant progress on the side of upper bounds, we have very little in terms of lower bounds for the congested clique; indeed, it is now known that proving explicit congested clique lower bounds is as difficult as proving circuit lower bounds.

In this work, we use various more traditional complexity theory tools to build a clearer picture of the complexity landscape of the congested clique:

- *Nondeterminism and beyond:* We introduce the *nondeterministic congested clique model* (analogous to NP) and show that there is a natural canonical problem family that captures all problems solvable in constant time with nondeterministic algorithms. We further generalise these notions by introducing the *constant-round decision hierarchy* (analogous to the polynomial hierarchy).
- *Non-constructive lower bounds:* We lift the prior non-uniform counting arguments to a general technique for proving non-constructive uniform lower bounds for the congested clique. In particular, we prove a *time hierarchy theorem* for the congested clique, showing that there are decision problems of essentially all complexities, both in the deterministic and nondeterministic settings.
- *Fine-grained complexity:* We map out relationships between various natural problems in the congested clique model, arguing that a reduction-based complexity theory currently gives us a fairly good picture of the complexity landscape of the congested clique.

## CCS CONCEPTS

• **Theory of computation** → **Distributed computing models; Complexity classes; Distributed algorithms;**

## KEYWORDS

distributed computing, congested clique, complexity theory

*A preliminary version presented as a brief announcement at DISC 2017.


*SPAA '18, July 16–18, 2018, Vienna, Austria*

ACM ISBN 978-1-4503-5799-9/18/07...$15.00
https://doi.org/10.1145/3210377.3210391

**ACM Reference format:**
Janne H. Korhonen and Jukka Suomela. 2018. Towards a Complexity Theory for the Congested Clique. In *Proceedings of 30th ACM Symposium on Parallelism in Algorithms and Architectures, Vienna, Austria, July 16–18, 2018 (SPAA '18),* 10 pages.
https://doi.org/10.1145/3210377.3210391

## 1 INTRODUCTION

*The congested clique.* In this work, we study computational complexity questions in the *congested clique* model of distributed computing. The congested clique is essentially a fully-connected specialisation of the classic CONGEST model of distributed computing: There are $n$ nodes that communicate with each other in a fully-connected synchronous network by exchanging messages of size $O(\log n)$. Each node in the network corresponds to a node in an input graph $G$, each node starts with knowledge about their incident edges in $G$, and the task is to solve a graph problem related to $G$.

The congested clique has recently been receiving increasing attention especially on the side of the upper bounds, and the fully-connected network topology enables significantly faster algorithms than what is possible in the CONGEST model. However, on the side of complexity theory, there has been significantly less development. Compared to the LOCAL and CONGEST models, where complexity-theoretic results have generally taken the form of unconditional, explicit lower bounds for concrete problems, such developments have not been forthcoming in the congested clique. Indeed, it was show by Drucker et al. [19] that congested clique lower bounds imply *circuit* lower bounds, and the latter are notoriously difficult to prove – overall, it seems that there are many parallels between computational complexity in the congested clique and *centralised* computational complexity.

*Towards a complexity theory.* We use concepts and techniques from centralised complexity theory to map out the complexity landscape of the congested clique model. First, we focus on *decision problems*:

- We introduce the *nondeterministic* version of the congested clique model. In particular, the class NCLIQUE(1) of problems solvable in constant time with nondeterministic algorithms is a natural analogue of the class NP. We show that there is a natural canonical problem family that captures all NCLIQUE(1) problems.
- We further generalise the notion of nondeterministic congested clique by introducing the *constant-round decision hierarchy*, analogous to the polynomial hierarchy.
- We prove *time hierarchy theorems* for the congested clique, showing that there are decision problems of essentially all complexities both in deterministic and nondeterministic settings.

Furthermore, we study the landscape of natural graph problems in the congested clique using a *fine-grained complexity* approach:

- While we cannot prove explicit lower bounds for the congested clique, we map out the *relative complexity* of problems with polynomial complexity.

## 1.1 Results: time hierarchy

It is known that in the centralised setting, there are problems of almost any deterministic time complexity, due to the time hierarchy theorem [29, 33]. However, in distributed computing, we know that the picture can be quite different; for LCL problems in the LOCAL model, there are known *complexity gaps*, implying that at least in some ranges LCL problems can have only very specific complexities [3, 8, 13, 48]. Thus, it makes sense to ask how the picture looks like in the congested clique: for example, it could be that – similarly to LCL problems in the LOCAL model – there are no problems with complexity $o(\log^* n)$ and $\omega(1)$.

We show that no such gaps occur in the congested clique model. Writing $\mathsf{CLIQUE}(T(n))$ for the set of decision problems that can be solved in $O(T(n))$ rounds, we prove a time hierarchy theorem for the congested clique: for any sensible complexity functions $S$ and $T$ with $S(n) = o(T(n))$, we have that

$$\mathsf{CLIQUE}(S(n)) \subsetneq \mathsf{CLIQUE}(T(n)).$$

The proof of the time hierarchy theorem is based on the earlier circuit counting arguments for a non-uniform version of the congested clique [1, 19]. We show how to lift this result into the uniform setting, allowing us to show the existence of decision problems of essentially arbitrary complexity. Indeed, we use this same technique also for the other separation results in this paper.

## 1.2 Results: nondeterminism and beyond

*Nondeterministic congested clique.* The class NP and NP-complete problems are central in our understanding of centralised complexity theory. We build towards a similar theory for the congested clique by introducing a *nondeterministic congested clique model.* We define the class $\mathsf{NCLIQUE}(T(n))$ as the class of decision problems that have nondeterministic algorithms with running time $O(T(n))$, or equivalently, as the set of decision problems $L$ for which there exists a deterministic algorithm $A$ that runs in $O(T(n))$ rounds and satisfies

$$G \in L \quad \text{if and only if} \quad \exists z\colon A(G, z) = 1,$$

where $z$ is a *labelling* assigning each node $v$ a nondeterministic guess $z_v$; for details, see Section 5.

We show that nondeterminism is only useful up to the number of bits communicated by the algorithm: any nondeterministic algorithm with running time $O(T(n))$ can be converted to a *normal form* where each yes-instance has an accepting labelling with $|z_v| \leq O(T(n)n \log n)$. As an application of this result, we show that $\mathsf{NCLIQUE}(S(n))$ does not contain $\mathsf{CLIQUE}(T(n))$ for any $S(n) = o(T(n))$.

*Constant-round nondeterministic decision.* We argue that the class $\mathsf{NCLIQUE}(1)$, consisting of problems solvable in constant time with nondeterministic algorithms, is a natural analogue of the class NP. The class $\mathsf{NCLIQUE}(1)$ contains most natural decision problems that have been studied in the congested clique, as well as many NP-complete problems such as $k$-colouring and Hamiltonian path. In particular, the question of proving that

$$\mathsf{CLIQUE}(1) \neq \mathsf{NCLIQUE}(1)$$

can be seen as playing a role similar to the P vs. NP question in the centralised setting. Alternatively, $\mathsf{NCLIQUE}(1)$ can be seen as an analogue of the class LCL of locally checkable labellings that has been studied extensively in the context of the LOCAL model; see Section 8.

While we cannot prove a separation between deterministic and nondeterministic constant time, we identify a family of *canonical problems* for $\mathsf{NCLIQUE}(1)$: we show that any $\mathsf{NCLIQUE}(1)$ problem can be formulated as a specific type of *edge labelling problem.* In particular, showing a non-constant lower bound for any edge labelling problem would be sufficient to separate $\mathsf{CLIQUE}(1)$ and $\mathsf{NCLIQUE}(1)$.

*Constant-round decision hierarchy.* We extend the notion of nondeterministic clique by studying a *constant-round decision hierarchy.* This can be seen as analogous to the polynomial hierarchy in the centralised setting; each node can be seen as running an *alternating* Turing machine.

Unlike for nondeterministic algorithms, it turns out that the label size for algorithms on the higher levels of this hierarchy is not bounded by the amount of communication. Thus, we get two very different versions of this hierarchy:

- *Unlimited hierarchy* $(\Sigma_k, \Pi_k)_{k=1}^{\infty}$ with unlimited label size: we show that this version of the hierarchy collapses, as all decision problems are contained on the second level.
- *Logarithmic hierarchy* $(\Sigma_k^{\log}, \Pi_k^{\log})_{k=1}^{\infty}$ with $O(n \log n)$-bit label per node: we show that there are problems that are not contained in this hierarchy.

## 1.3 Results: fine-grained complexity

By the time hierarchy theorem, we know that there are decision problems of all complexities, but it is beyond our current techniques to prove lower bounds for any specific problem, assuming we exclude lower bounds resulting from input or output sizes. However, what we can do is study the relative complexity of natural problems, much in the vein of centralised *fine-grained* complexity. In Section 7, we study the relative complexities of various concrete problems that are thought to have *polynomial* complexity in the congested clique. Specifically, our framework is to compare *problem exponents,* defined for problem $L$ as

$$\delta(L) = \inf\{\delta \in [0, 1] \colon L \text{ can be solved in } O(n^{\delta}) \text{ rounds}\}.$$

By mapping out known relationships in this regime, we argue that despite the lack of explicit lower bounds, our understanding of the landscape of problems of polynomial complexity in the congested clique is in many senses better than e.g. in the CONGEST model.

# 2 RELATED WORK

*Upper bounds for the congested clique.* As noted in the introduction, upper bounds have been extensively studied in the congested clique model. Problems studied in prior work include routing and sorting [43], minimum spanning trees [26, 30, 34, 45], subgraph detection [10, 16], shortest path problems [4, 10], local problems [11, 31, 32] and problems related to matrix multiplication [10, 42].

*Complexity theory for the congested clique.* Prior work on computational complexity in the congested clique is fairly limited; the notable exceptions are the connections to circuit complexity [19] and counting arguments for the non-uniform version of the model [1, 19]. However, lower bounds can be proven if we consider problems with large outputs; for example, lower bounds are known for triangle enumeration [49] or, trivially, a problem where all nodes are required to output the whole input graph. Moreover, for the *broadcast congested clique*, a version of the model where each node sends the same message to each other node every round, lower bounds have been proven using communication complexity arguments [19].

*Complexity theory for* CONGEST. For the CONGEST model, explicit lower bounds are known for many problems, even on graphs with very small diameter [15, 24, 40, 44, 47, 50]. These are generally based on reductions from known lower bounds in communication complexity; however, these reductions tend to boil down to constructing graphs with *bottlenecks*, that is, graphs where large amounts of information have to be transmitted over a small cut. A key motivation for the study of the congested clique model is to understand computation in networks that do not have such bottlenecks.

*Complexity theory for* LOCAL. Perhaps the most active development related to the computational complexity theory of distributed computing is currently taking place in the context of the LOCAL model. There is a lot of very recent work that aims at developing a complete classification of the complexities of LCL problems in the LOCAL model [3, 7, 8, 12, 13, 27]. In this line of research, the focus is on low-degree large-diameter graphs, while in the congested clique model we will study the opposite corner of the distributed computing landscape: high-degree low-diameter graphs.

*Nondeterminism and alternation.* Nondeterministic models of distributed computing have been studied under various names – for example, *proof labeling schemes* [36–39], *nondeterministic local decision* [23], and *locally checkable proofs* [28] can be interpreted as nondeterministic versions of variants of the LOCAL and CONGEST models; we refer to the survey by Feuilloley and Fraigniaud [21] for further discussion. However, there seem to be very few papers that take the next step from nondeterministic machines to alternating machines in the context of distributed computing – we are only aware of Reiter [51], who studies alternating quantifiers in finite state machines, and Feuilloley et al. [22] and Balliu et al. [2], who study alternating quantifiers in the LOCAL model.

## 3 PRELIMINARIES

*The congested clique.* The congested clique is a specialisation of the standard CONGEST model of distributed computing to a fully connected network topology. The network consists of $n$ nodes (i.e. computers) that are connected to all other nodes by edges (i.e. communication links) – that is, the communication graph is a clique.

As an input, we are given an undirected, unweighted graph $G = (V, E)$ with $V = \{1, 2, \ldots, n\}$. Each node of the communication network has a unique identifier $v \in \{1, 2, \ldots, n\}$ and, in addition to it's own unique identifier, has initially knowledge about edges incident to node $v$ in $G$. The nodes collaborate to solve a problem related to the graph $G$.

The computation is done in synchronous rounds, and all nodes run the same deterministic algorithm. Each round, all nodes (1) perform an unlimited amount of local communication, (2) send a possibly different $O(\log n)$-bit message to each other node, and (3) receive the messages sent to them. The time complexity of an algorithm is measured in the number of rounds used.

*Decision problems.* To avoid artefacts resulting from input and output sizes, we restrict our attention for the most part to decision problems on unweighted, undirected graphs. A *decision problem* $L$ is a family of graphs; a graph $G$ is a yes-instance of $L$ if $G \in L$ and a no-instance otherwise. The *complement* $\bar{L}$ of problem $L$ contains all graphs $G$ that are not in $L$.

Note that we do not require decision problems to be closed under isomorphisms, that is, problems can refer to the names of the nodes. However, we are only interested in decision problems that are computable in the centralised sense, and we will implicitly assume that this is the case for any problem considered.

An algorithm $A$ solves problem $L$ if for any graph $G$, each node $i$ produces output $A_i(G) = 1$ if $G \in L$ and $A_i(G) = 0$ if $G \notin L$; we write $A(G) = 1$ to indicate that all nodes produce output 1 (the algorithm *accepts*) and $A(G) = 0$ to indicate that all nodes output 0 (the algorithm *rejects*).

*Input encoding.* We will tacitly assume that the input is provided for node $v \in V$ in the form of a length-$(n-1)$ bit vector $x_v$ indexed by $V \setminus \{v\}$ describing whether each of the potential incident edges is present in the input graph $G = (V, E)$. In particular, any two nodes $u$ and $v$ will share the bit $x_{u,v} = x_{v,u}$.

However, for technical reasons, it is convenient to consider a setting where each node has *private* input bits, so we will implicitly assume that each of these bits is assigned to exactly one node, so that (1) for each possible edge in the graph, exactly one of its endpoints has the bit corresponding to that edge and (2) each node has at least $\lfloor (n-1)/2 \rfloor$ input bits. Note that it takes a single round to move from the latter setting to the former.

*Algorithms.* As noted above, we assume all nodes run the same deterministic algorithm. While the congested clique allows $O(\log n)$ bandwidth per round, where the constant hidden by O-notation can depend on the algorithm, we can always move the constant factors to the running time and assume that all algorithms use exactly $\lceil \log_2 n \rceil$ bits of communication per round.

*Deterministic complexity classes.* For any computable function $T \colon \mathbb{N} \to \mathbb{N}$, we define the complexity class $\mathsf{CLIQUE}(T(n))$ as the family of all graph problems that can be solved in $T(n)$ rounds.

*Counting arguments.* We will now review known results on the *non-uniform* version of the congested clique [1, 19]. Specifically, we consider a setting where the number of nodes $n$ and the communication bandwidth $b$ is fixed beforehand, and we want to compute a function $f \colon \{0, 1\}^{nL} \to \{0, 1\}$, where $L$ is an integer; each node receives $L$ private input bits, and we want all nodes to output the same result $y \in \{0,1\}$. We define an $(n,b,L,t)$-*protocol* $P$ to be an algorithm that works in this setting and computes an output $P(x_1,x_2,\ldots,x_n) \in \{0,1\}$ in $t$ rounds. Since the parameters are fixed, there are only a finite number of different $(n,b,L,T)$-protocols, and this number can be bounded by standard counting arguments:

LEMMA 3.1 ([1]). *The number of different $(n,b,L,t)$-protocols is at most*

$$2^{2bn^2 2^{L+bt(n-1)}} .$$

By contrast, the number of functions $f\colon \{0,1\}^{nL} \to \{0,1\}$ is $2^{2^{nL}}$, so this implies that for sufficiently large $n$, most such functions do not have a $(n,b,L,t)$-protocol when $t < L/b - 1$ [1].

## 4 TIME HIERARCHY

We start by proving the deterministic time hierarchy theorem: there are problems of essentially all complexities in the congested clique model.

THEOREM 4.1. *Let $S,T\colon \mathbb{N} \to \mathbb{N}$ be computable functions such that $S(n) = o(T(n))$ and $T(n) = O(n/\log n)$. Then*

$$\mathsf{CLIQUE}(S(n)) \subsetneq \mathsf{CLIQUE}(T(n)) .$$

PROOF. We prove the theorem by constructing a language

$$L \in \mathsf{CLIQUE}(T(n)) \setminus \mathsf{CLIQUE}(S(n)).$$

For convenience, let us assume that $T(n) < n/(4\log n)$ for all sufficiently large $n$. Now, for all sufficiently large $n$, we define the set of $n$-node graphs that belong to $L$ as follows:

- Fix $L = T(n)\log n \le \lfloor n/2 \rfloor$, and fix a function $f_n\colon \{0,1\}^{nL} \to \{0,1\}$ that does not have a $(n,\log n, L, T(n)/2)$-protocol; by Lemma 3.1, such a function exists. Moreover, we can select $f_n$ to be a first function that satisfies this condition under the lexicographical ordering when interpreting functions $\{0,1\}^{nL} \to \{0,1\}$ as bit vectors of length $2^{nL}$.
- Let $G$ be a graph on $n$ nodes and let $x_v$ be the $L$-bit prefix of the input bit vector that node $v$ receives when $G$ is the input graph. We set $G \in L$ if $f_n(x_1,x_2,\ldots,x_n) = 1$, and $G \notin L$ otherwise.

First, we observe that $L \in \mathsf{CLIQUE}(T(n))$. That is, we can decide if the input graph $G$ belongs to $L$ in time $T(n)$ as follows:

(1) Each node $v$ broadcasts the first $L = T(n)\log n$ bits of its input – that is, the vector $x_v$ – to all other nodes. This takes $T(n)$ rounds.
(2) Each node $v$ uses local computation to find the function $f_n$ as specified above; this can be done by exhaustively enumerating all functions $f\colon \{0,1\}^{nL} \to \{0,1\}$ and all $(n,\log n, L, T(n))$-protocols. Each node then locally computes the value $f_n(x_1,x_2,\ldots,x_n)$ and outputs it.

It remains to show that $L \notin \mathsf{CLIQUE}(S(n))$. Assume for contradiction that there is an algorithm that solves $L$ in time $O(S(n))$. This implies that for any sufficiently large $n$, there is an $(n,\log n, L, O(S(n)))$-protocol $P_n$ for $f_n$. However, we have that $S(n) = o(T(n))$, so by the choice of $f_n$ the protocol $P_n$ cannot exist. □

## 5 NONDETERMINISM

### 5.1 Nondeterministic complexity classes

A *labelling* $z$ of size $k$ is a mapping that assigns each node $v \in V$ a *label* $z_v \in \{0,1\}^*$ of length at most $k$. A *nondeterministic congested clique algorithm* $A$ is an algorithm that takes as an input, in addition to the input graph $G$, a labelling $z$ of size $S(n)$ for some computable function $S\colon \mathbb{N} \to \mathbb{N}$; we say that $S(n)$ is the labelling size of $A$. We can think of $z$ as the sequence of nondeterministic choices made by $A$, or alternatively as a certificate provided by an external prover. We say that $A$ decides the language $L$ if for all graphs $G$,

$$G \in L \quad \text{if and only if} \quad \exists z\colon A(G,z) = 1 ,$$

where $z$ is a labelling of size $S(n)$.

For a computable function $T\colon \mathbb{N} \to \mathbb{N}$, we define the complexity class $\mathsf{NCLIQUE}(T(n))$ as the set of languages $L$ such that there exists a nondeterministic algorithm $A$ with running time of $T(n)$ rounds that decides $L$.

### 5.2 NCLIQUE normal form

While the definition of $\mathsf{NCLIQUE}(T(n))$ allows the algorithms to use an essentially arbitrary amount of nondeterministic bits, we show that nondeterministic bits are only useful, roughly speaking, as long as they can be communicated to other nodes by the algorithm. More precisely, we prove that any nondeterministic algorithm can be converted to a *normal form*:

THEOREM 5.1. *If $L \in \mathsf{NCLIQUE}(T(n))$, then there is a nondeterministic algorithm $B$ that decides $L$ with running time $T(n)$ and labelling size $O(T(n)n\log n)$.*

PROOF. Let $A$ be the algorithm certifying $L \in \mathsf{NCLIQUE}(T(n))$. We say that a *communication transcript* of an execution of $A$ of node $v$ is a bit vector consisting of all messages sent and received by $v$ during the execution of $A$. Clearly, a communication transcript of a node $v$ has length $O(T(n)n\log n)$.

We define an algorithm $B$ that works as follows on input $(G,z)$:

(1) Each node $v \in V$ checks that their label $z_v$ is a valid communication transcript of length $O(T(n)n\log n)$ (if not, reject).
(2) Nodes verify that their labels are consistent with each other; this can be done in $T(n)$ rounds by simply replaying the transcripts and checking that all the received messages agree with the transcript (if not, reject).
(3) Each node $v \in V$ locally tries all possible local labels of size at most $S(n)$, where $S(n)$ is the labelling size of $A$, to see if there is a label $z'_v$ so that the execution of $A$ with local label $z'_v$ and the local input of node $v$ agrees with the transcript $z_v$ and accepts (if not, reject; otherwise accept).

Clearly $B$ runs in $T(n)$ rounds. If there is a labelling $z'$ such that $A(G,z') = 1$, then using the transcripts from this execution of $A$ as the labelling $z$ clearly gives $B(G,z) = 1$. On the other hand, if there is a $z$ such that $B(G,z) = 1$, then there are local labels $z'_v$ for each $v \in V$ such that $A(G,z') = 1$. □

### 5.3 Nondeterministic time hierarchy

As an application of the normal form theorem, we can extend the time hierarchy theorem to the nondeterministic congested clique. In fact, we prove a somewhat stronger statement:

Theorem 5.2. *Let $S, T: \mathbb{N} \to \mathbb{N}$ be computable functions such that $S(n) = o(T(n))$ and $T(n) = O(n/\log n)$. Then there is a decision problem $L$ such that*

$$L \notin \mathsf{NCLIQUE}(S(n)) \quad \text{and} \quad L \in \mathsf{CLIQUE}(T(n)).$$

Proof. We say that a $(n, b, M+L, t)$-protocol is a *nondeterministic protocol* for function $f: \{0,1\}^{nL} \to \{0,1\}$ if for all $x \in \{0,1\}^{nL}$ it holds that $f(x_1, x_2, \dots, x_n) = 1$ if and only if there is $z \in \{0,1\}^{nM}$ such that $P(z_1x_1, z_2x_2, \dots, z_nx_n) = 1$.

Now we construct a decision problem $L \in \mathsf{CLIQUE}(T(n)) \setminus \mathsf{NCLIQUE}(S(n))$ using the same construction as in the proof of Theorem 4.1, with minor modifications as follows. Let $L = T(n)\log n$, and let $M = \frac{1}{4}T(n)n\log n$. We select the functions $f_n: \{0,1\}^{nL} \to \{0,1\}$ in the construction of $L$ with the extra constraint that $f_n$ does not have a nondeterministic $(n, \log n, M+L, T(n)/4)$-protocol; this is possible for sufficiently large $n$, since then

$$\begin{aligned} M + L + T(n)(n-1)\log n &\leq \left(\frac{1}{2} + \frac{1}{n}\right)T(n)n\log n \\ &< \frac{3}{4}T(n)n\log n = \frac{3}{4}nL, \end{aligned}$$

and thus by Lemma 3.1 the number of $(n, \log n, M+L, T(n)/4)$-protocols is $2^{o(2^{nL})}$.

The problem $L$ constructed using the functions $f_n$ is clearly in $\mathsf{CLIQUE}(T(n))$ using the same argument as in the proof of Theorem 4.1. On the other hand, if $L \in \mathsf{NCLIQUE}(S(n))$, then by Theorem 5.1 there is a nondeterministic algorithm for $L$ with running time $O(S(n))$ and labelling size $O(S(n)n\log n)$. But this implies that the functions $f_n$ have nondeterministic $(n, \log n, L + O(S(n)n\log n), O(S(n)))$-protocols, which is not possible for large $n$ by the choice of $f_n$, since we have $S(n) = o(T(n))$. □

Since $\mathsf{CLIQUE}(T(n)) \subseteq \mathsf{NCLIQUE}(T(n))$, we obtain a time hierarchy theorem for the nondeterministic congested clique:

Corollary 5.3. *Let $S, T: \mathbb{N} \to \mathbb{N}$ be computable functions such that $S(n) = o(T(n))$ and $T(n) = O(n/\log n)$. Then*

$$\mathsf{NCLIQUE}(S(n)) \subsetneq \mathsf{NCLIQUE}(T(n)).$$

# 6 CONSTANT-ROUND DECISION

## 6.1 Constant-round nondeterministic clique

The class $\mathsf{NCLIQUE}(1)$ is a natural analogue of class NP in the congested clique; it contains decision versions of most natural problems considered in the congested clique setting. It is also easy to see that $\mathsf{NCLIQUE}(1)$ contains many NP-complete decision problems, such as $k$-colouring and Hamiltonian paths. By Theorem 5.2, we also know that there are problems that can be solved in slightly super-constant time, but are not in $\mathsf{NCLIQUE}(1)$. However, our lower bound techniques are not sufficient to show that

$$\mathsf{CLIQUE}(1) \neq \mathsf{NCLIQUE}(1);$$

in a sense, this is the congested clique analogue of the P vs. NP question.

However, we can interpret Theorem 5.1 to state that there is a *canonical problem family* for $\mathsf{NCLIQUE}(1)$. Specifically, we say that a *neighbourhood constraint* $C$ is a computable mapping that for any number of nodes $n$, any edge $\{u, v\}$, and any edge-neighbourhood $\partial(u)$ of $u$, gives a set $C_{n,u,v,\delta(u)}$ of allowed $O(\log n)$-bit labels for the edge $\{u, v\}$. An *edge labelling problem* is defined by an edge neighbourhood constraint $C$: given a graph $G$, find a labelling $\ell$ of all edges of the clique with labels $\ell(u, v)$ of size $O(\log n)$ so that the labels satisfy the local constraints at all nodes, that is

$$\ell(u,v) \in C_{n,u,v,\partial(u)} \quad \text{and} \quad \ell(u,v) \in C_{n,v,u,\partial(v)}$$

for all $u$ and $v$.

By Theorem 5.1, any problem with $\mathsf{NCLIQUE}(1)$ algorithm $A$ can be interpreted as an edge labelling problem: the edge labels are defined as the set of valid communication transcripts of an accepting run of $A$. This gives us a limited notion of completeness for $\mathsf{NCLIQUE}(1)$:

Theorem 6.1. *We have $\mathsf{NCLIQUE}(1) \subseteq \mathsf{CLIQUE}(T(n))$ if and only if all edge labelling problems can be solved deterministically in $O(T(n))$ rounds.*

In particular, we have $\mathsf{CLIQUE}(1) = \mathsf{NCLIQUE}(1)$ if and only if all edge labelling problems can be solved deterministically in $O(1)$ rounds. However, it seems that identifying a single graph decision problem that is "complete" for $\mathsf{NCLIQUE}(1)$ is difficult; in essence, we would have to work reductions running in *constant time*, which makes the use of any sort of gadget constructions extremely difficult.

## 6.2 Constant-round decision hierarchy

Whereas $\mathsf{NCLIQUE}(1)$ is the congested clique analogue of NP, we can extend this analogue to the polynomial hierarchy by adding more quantifiers, that is, by allowing the nodes to alternate between nondeterministic and co-nondeterministic choices; similar ideas has been studied in the context of local verification [2, 22, 51].

Formally, we say that a *$k$-labelling algorithm $A$ of labelling size $S(n)$* is a constant-round congested clique algorithm that takes as an input $k$ labellings $z_1, z_2, \dots, z_k$ of size at most $S(n)$. We define the class $\Sigma_k$ as the set of languages $L$ for which there exists a $k$-labelling algorithm $A$ of labelling size $S(n)$ such that

$$G \in L \quad \text{if and only if} \quad \exists z_1 \forall z_2 \dots Q z_k \colon A(G, z_1, z_2, \dots, z_k) = 1,$$

where $z_1, z_2, \dots, z_k$ are labellings of size at most $S(n)$ and $Q$ is the universal quantifier if $k$ is even and the existential quantifier if $k$ is odd. Similarly, we define $\Pi_k$ as the set of languages $L$ for which there exists a $k$-labelling algorithm $A$ of labelling size $S(n)$ such that

$$G \in L \quad \text{if and only if} \quad \forall z_1 \exists z_2 \dots Q z_k \colon A(G, z_1, z_2, \dots, z_k) = 1,$$

where $z_1, z_2, \dots, z_k$ are labellings of size at most $S(n)$ and $Q$ is the existential quantifier if $k$ is even and the universal quantifier if $k$ is odd. Finally, we define $\Delta_k = \Sigma_k \cup \Pi_k$.

At the first level of the hierarchy we have the class

$$\Sigma_1 = \mathsf{NCLIQUE}(1);$$

by Theorem 5.1 we know that limiting the labelling size to $O(n\log n)$ gives us the same class as unlimited labelling size. A natural question is then if the same phenomenon happens at the higher levels of the hierarchy?

Turns out this is not the case; we will consider two different versions of the constant-round decision hierarchy:

- *Unlimited hierarchy:* the hierarchy $(\Sigma_k, \Pi_k)_{k=1}^{\infty}$ as defined above, with arbitrary labelling size allowed.
- *Logarithmic hierarchy:* the hierarchy $(\Sigma_k^{\log}, \Pi_k^{\log})_{k=1}^{\infty}$ defined otherwise as above, but the algorithm $A$ is required to have labelling size of $O(n \log n)$ – in other words, $O(\log n)$ bits per edge.

In a sense, these correspond to the different LOCAL model hierarchies studied by Feuilloley et al. [22] (the logarithmic hierachy) and Balliu et al. [2] (the unlimited hierarchy).

*Basic properties.* We first note basic properties of the constant-round hierarchies. Trivially, we have that

$$\Sigma_k \subseteq \Delta_k \subseteq \Sigma_{k+1} \quad \text{and} \quad \Pi_k \subseteq \Delta_k \subseteq \Pi_{k+1},$$

and thus also

$$\Pi_k \subseteq \Sigma_{k+1} \quad \text{and} \quad \Sigma_k \subseteq \Pi_{k+1}.$$

Moreover, if a decision problem $L$ is in $\Sigma_k$, then the complement language $\bar{L}$ is in $\Pi_k$, and vice versa. These observations also hold for the logarithmic version of the constant-round hierarchy.

*Unlimited hierarchy* $(\Sigma_k, \Pi_k)_{k=1}^{\infty}$. For the unlimited hierarchy, we obtain an essentially complete characterisation. By Theorem 5.2, we know there are problems that are not on the first level. Moreover, in a similar manner as happens with the LOCAL hierarchy of Balliu et al. [2], we show that the unlimited hierarchy collapses to the second level:

THEOREM 6.2. *All decision problems $L$ are in $\Sigma_2 = \Pi_2$.*

PROOF. Let $L$ be a decision problem. To see that $L \in \Sigma_2$, consider the following algorithm $A$:

(1) The existential quantifier is used to guess a graph $G'_v$ in each node $v$, using $n^2$ bits per node.
(2) The universal quantifier is used to verify that all guesses $G'_v$ equal the input graph $G$: each node $v$ uses $O(\log n)$ universal bits to pick a single bit from the encoding of $G'_v$ and broadcasts this bit and its index to all other nodes. All nodes $u$ verify that the information broadcast by other nodes is consistent with their guess of $G'_u$ and their local view of $G$ (if not, reject).
(3) Each node $v$ locally checks if $G'_v \in L$ (if this holds for all nodes, accept; otherwise reject).

Clearly, if the input graph $G$ is in $L$, then picking the real input graph $G$ as the existential guess results in $A$ accepting for all universal guesses. On the other hand, if $G \notin L$, then regardless of the existential guess, $A$ will not accept for all universal guesses: if $G'_v = G$ for all $v$, then step (3) will reject, and if $G'_v \neq G$ for some $v$, then there is a universal guess that will lead to step (2) rejecting.

Moreover, the above implies that for any decision problem $L$, we have that $\bar{L} \in \Sigma_2$, and thus $L \in \Pi_2$. It follows that all decision problems are also in $\Pi_2$. □

*Logarithmic hierarchy* $(\Sigma_k^{\log}, \Pi_k^{\log})_{k=1}^{\infty}$. For the logarithmic version of the constant-round hierarchy, the complexity landscape seems to be much richer that in the case of the unlimited hierarchy: any constant number of quantifiers is not enough to replicate the trick of Theorem 6.2 of guessing the whole input at all nodes. Indeed, we show that there are problems that are not on any level of the logarithmic constant-round hierarchy:

THEOREM 6.3. *There is a decision problem $L$ not in $\bigcup_{k=0}^{\infty} \Sigma_k^{\log}$.*

PROOF. Again, we use the same general proof technique as in the proofs of Theorems 4.1 and 5.2. Fix a computable function $T(n) = \omega(n)$; let $L = (T(n))^2 \log n$ and $M = \frac{1}{4}T(n)n \log n$. Otherwise using the same construction for the language $L$ as before, we select the functions $f_n\colon \{0,1\}^{nL} \to \{0,1\}$ so that for any $k \leq T(n)$, there is no $(n, \log n, kM + L, (T(n))^2/4)$-protocol that $\Sigma_k^{\log}$-computes $f_n$; this is possible for sufficiently large $n$, since then

$$kM + L + \frac{1}{4}(T(n))^2(n-1)\log n < \frac{3}{4}(T(n))^2 n \log n = \frac{3}{4}nL,$$

and thus by Lemma 3.1 the number of $(n, \log n, kM + L, (T(n))^2/4)$-protocols is $2^{o(2^{nL})}$.

If $L \in \Sigma_k^{\log}$ for some $k$, then there is a $\Sigma_k$ algorithm for $L$ with running time $O(1)$ and labelling size $O(n \log n)$. But this implies that there is an $(n, \log n, O(kn \log n) + L, O(1))$-protocol that $\Sigma_k$-computes $L$; this is not possible for large $n$ by the choice of $f_n$, since we have $T(n) = \omega(1)$. □

The proof of Theorem 6.3 actually implies that there are problems with only slightly super-constant deterministic complexity that are not on any level of the hierarchy. However, our lower bound technique does not appear to be sufficiently refined to separate different levels of the logarithmic constant-round hierarchy, so it remains open whether the hierarchy has infinitely many levels.

## 7 FINE-GRAINED COMPLEXITY

*Problem exponent.* In the following, we will consider concrete problems that are not necessarily decision problems, and allow more generally problems defined in terms of weighted graphs and matrices. For a problem $L$, we define the *exponent* of $L$ as

$$\delta(L) = \inf\{\delta \in [0,1] : L \text{ can be solved in } O(n^{\delta}) \text{ rounds}\}.$$

The basic idea is that the problem exponent captures the polynomial complexity of the problem, and we can compare the relative complexity of problems by comparing their exponents.

*Relationships between problems.* In Figure 1, we summarise the relationships between prominent problems using this framework. These relations follow from prior work:

- Relationships between $k$-independent set ($k$-IS), maximum independent set (MaxIS) and minimum vertex cover (MinVC) are trivial. The upper bound for $k$-independent set is due to Dolev et al. [16].
- Relationships between 3-independent set detection (i.e. triangle detection), $k$-cycle detection ($k$-CYCLE), subgraph detection and Boolean matrix multiplication (Boolean-MM) as well as between approximate weighted all-pairs shortest paths problem and ring matrix multiplication (Ring MM) follow from the work of Censor-Hillel et al. [10]; they also give the upper bound $\delta(\text{Ring MM}) \leq 1 - 2/\omega$, where $\omega < 2.3728639$ is the matrix multiplication exponent [41].

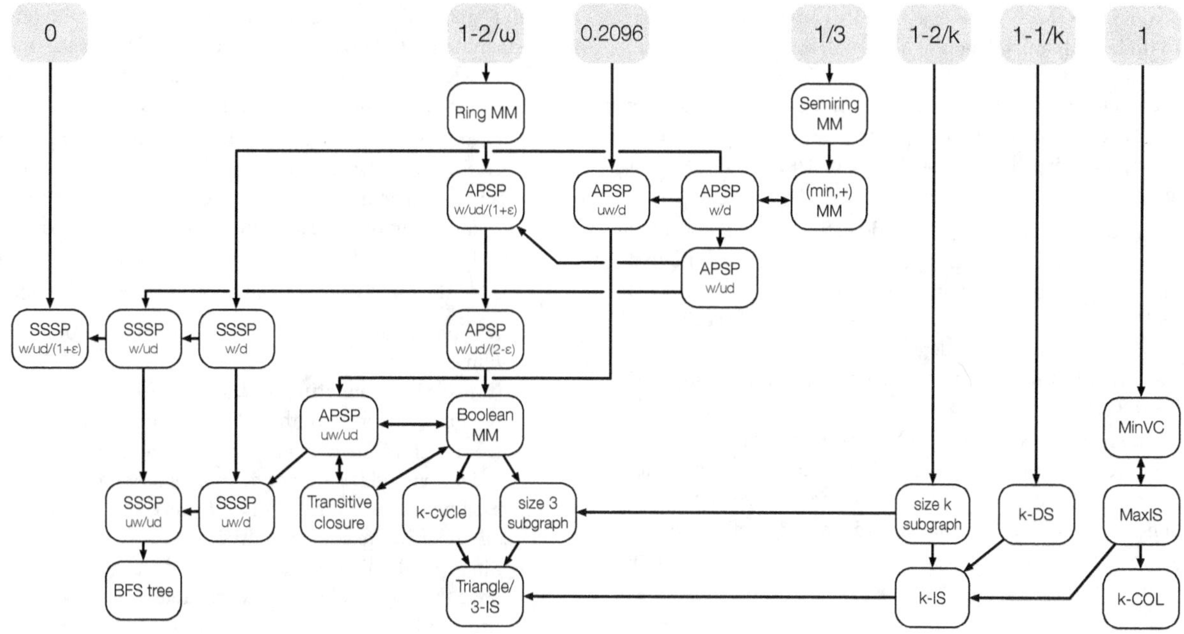


**Figure 1: Relationships between selected problems in the congested clique model. Arrow to $L_1$ from $L_2$ indicates $\delta(L_1) \leq \delta(L_2)$; $k \geq 3$ and $\varepsilon > 0$ are arbitrary constants. For** APSP **and** SSSP, w/uw **indicates weighted and unweighted variants,** d/ud **indicates directed and undirected variants, and a number $\alpha$ indicates $\alpha$-approximate variant. Edge weights and matrix entries are assumed to be encodable in $O(\log n)$ bits in all problems.**

- The relationship between the $k$-colouring problem ($k$-COL) and maximum independent set follows from an easy reduction [46]: replace each vertex $v$ with $k$ copies $v_1, \ldots, v_k$ connected into a clique, and connect $v_i$ and $u_i$ if the edge $\{v, u\}$ is present in the original graph. Clearly, the new graph has independent set of size $n$ if and only if the original graph is $k$-colourable. For constant $k$, the blowup from implementing this reduction is constant.
- The relationship between $(2 - \varepsilon)$-approximate weighted undirected all-pairs shortest paths problem and Boolean matrix multiplication follows from a reduction by Dor et al. [17].
- The relationships between other variants of the all-pairs shortest paths problem (APSP) and single-source shortest paths problem (SSSP) are trivial. The upper bound for unweighted directed APSP is due to Le Gall [42], and the upper bound for approximate SSSP is due to Becker et al. [5].

These are our main new contributions (see Sections 7.1–7.3 for proofs):

- Dominating set of size $k$ ($k$-DS) can be found in $O(n^{1-1/k})$ rounds, showing $\delta(k\text{-DS}) \leq 1 - 1/k$.
- For any fixed constant $k$, if a dominating set of size $k$ can be found in $O(n^{\delta})$ rounds, then an independent set of size $k$ can be found in $O(k^{2\delta+4} n^{\delta})$ rounds, showing $\delta(k\text{-IS}) \leq \delta(k\text{-DS})$.
- A vertex cover of size $k$ ($k$-VC) can be found in $O(k)$ rounds, showing $\delta(k\text{-VC}) = 0$ in our framework.

We note that one challenge involved in this approach is that the congested clique setting requires the use of extremely fine-grained reductions; we are essentially allowed only $n^{o(1)}$ factor blowups in the reductions. By contrast, most known reductions between NP-complete problems have polynomial blowup, making them useless in this setting.

One potentially fruitful perspective is to consider for which pairs of problems we *cannot* prove reductions. For example, the reduction from Boolean matrix multiplication to $(2 - \varepsilon)$-approximate APSP breaks down if we consider 2-approximate APSP instead. Indeed, we know that constant-approximation APSP can be solved faster than the current matrix multiplication upper bound, using the spanner constructions of Censor-Hillel et al. [11], so conjecturing the existence of a faster-than-matrix-multiplication algorithm for 2-approximate APSP does not seem unreasonable. Another similar question is the existence of faster-than-matrix-multiplication algorithms for exact single-source shortest paths problems.

## 7.1 Dominating set upper bound

We now prove the upper bound for finding $k$-dominating sets:

Theorem 7.1. *Dominating set of size k can be found in $O(n^{1-1/k})$ rounds in the congested clique model.*

We employ a slight modification of the Dolev et al. [16] algorithm for finding subgraphs of size $k$. For convenience, let us assume that $n^{1/k}$ is an integer; if not, we use $\lfloor n^{1/k} \rfloor$ instead.

(1) Partition the node set $V$ arbitrarily into sets $S_1, S_2, \ldots, S_{n^{1/k}}$ of size $O(n^{1-1/k})$.
(2) Assign each node $v \in V$ a label $\ell(v) \in [n^{1/k}]^k$, so that each possible label is assigned to some node. Moreover, we will

assume that this is done in a globally consistent manner so all nodes will know labels of all nodes.

(3) For each node $v \in V$, let $S_v = S_{\ell(v)_1} \cup S_{\ell(v)_2} \cup \cdots \cup S_{\ell(v)_k}$. Node $v$ learns all edges incident to nodes in $S_v$, and locally checks if there is a dominating set of size $k$ contained in $S_v$; clearly, knowing all edges incident to nodes in $S_v$ is sufficient for checking this.

It remains to prove that the algorithm detects a dominating set of size $k$ if one exist, and that it runs in $O(kn^{1-1/k})$ rounds. The first part is simple: if there is a dominating set $D = \{v_1, v_2, \ldots, v_k\}$ of size $k$ such that $v_i \in S_{j_i}$, then some node $v \in V$ will receive the label $\ell(v) = (j_1, j_2, \ldots, j_k)$ and detect $D$.

For the running time, we observe first that there are at most $kn^{2-1/k} = O(n^{2-1/k})$ edges incident to nodes in $S_v$ for all $v \in V$, so each node has to receive $O(n^{2-1/k})$ messages in step 3. On the other hand, we note that for each edge $e$, there are $2kn^{1-1/k}$ nodes $v \in V$ that have to learn about the existence of $e$, so each node has to send at most $2kn^{2-1/k}$ messages in step 3. Delivering the messages can thus be done in $O(n^{1-1/k})$ rounds using the routing protocol of Lenzen [43].

## 7.2 From independent set to dominating set

We next prove that finding a $k$-dominating set is at least as hard as finding a $k$-independent set in the congested clique, for any fixed $k$:

THEOREM 7.2. *If a dominating set of size k can be found in $O(n^\delta)$ rounds in the congested clique model, then an independent set of size k can be found in $O(k^{2\delta+4}n^\delta)$ rounds.*

The proof is straightforward; we construct a reduction from $k$-independent set to $k$-dominating set that increases the number of vertices by a linear factor.

*Construction.* Let $G = (V, E)$ be the input graph. We construct a new graph $G' = (V', E')$ such that $G$ has an independent set of size $k$ if and only if $G'$ has a dominating set of size $k$:

- As a base for the construction of $G'$, we start with $k$ copies $K^1, K^2, \ldots, K^k$ of clique on $n$ nodes. We identify the nodes in each clique with the original node set $V$ so that for each node $v \in V$, there is a corresponding node $v^i$ in the clique $K^i$.
- For each pair $(i, j) \in [k]^2$ with $i < j$, we construct a *compatibility gadget* as follows. We add an independent set $I^{i,j}$ on $n$ nodes to $G'$, again identified with the original node set $n$ so that for each node $v \in V$, there is a corresponding node $v^{i,j}$ in the independent set $I^{i,j}$. We connect $I^{i,j}$ to $K^i$ and $K^j$:
  - for each $v \in V$, we add an edge between the node $v^i$ in $K^i$ and $u^{i,j}$ in $I^{i,j}$ for all $u \in V \setminus \{v\}$, and
  - for each $v \in V$, we add an edge between the node $v^j$ in $K^j$ and $u^{i,j}$ in $I^{i,j}$ for all $u \in V \setminus \{v\}$ that are not neighbours of $v$ in the original graph $G$.
- For each clique $K^i$, we add two new *special* nodes $x^i$ and $y^i$ that are connected to all nodes in $K^i$, but not to other nodes.

See Figure 2 for an illustration.

*Properties of the construction.* Clearly, the graph $G'$ has at most $(k^2+k+2)n$ nodes. To see the correspondence between independent sets in $G$ and dominating sets in $G'$, we make the following observations; note that we will tacitly abuse the identification between various nodes in the original graph $G$ and the new graph $G'$.

- Consider an independent set $I = \{v_1, v_2, \ldots, v_k\}$ of size $k$ in $G$, and let $D$ be a node set obtained by picking $v_i^i$ from $K^i$ in $G'$ for all $i = 1, 2, \ldots, k$. Clearly $D$ dominates all nodes in set $K^i$ as well as the two special vertices attached to $K^i$, for all $i$. Furthermore, for each compatibility gadget corresponding to $(i, j)$, the node $v_i^i$ in $K^i$ dominates all nodes in $I^{i,j}$ except $v_i^{i,j}$; since $v_j$ is not a neighbour of $v_i$ in $G$, the node $v_j^j$ in $K^j$ dominates $v_i^{i,j}$ in $I^{i,j}$. Thus $D$ is a dominating set of size $k$ in $G'$.
- Consider a dominating set $D = \{w_1, w_2, \ldots, w_k\}$ of size $k$ in $G'$. First, we observe that $D$ must contain exactly one node from each of the cliques $K^1, K^2, \ldots, K^k$, since otherwise all the special nodes are not dominated; for convenience, let us assume that $w_i$ is in $K^i$ for all $i$. Since $D$ is a dominating set, all nodes in the compatibility gadget $I^{i,j}$ are also dominated. Since $w_i$ dominates all nodes in $I^{i,j}$ except one, we must have that $w_j$ in $K^j$ dominates the remaining node in $I^{i,j}$. But this implies by construction that $w_i$ and $w_j$ correspond to different nodes in $G$, and they are also not neighbours in $G$. Thus, $D$ corresponds to an independent set of size $k$ in $G$.

*Simulation in the congested clique.* It remains to argue that given an input graph $G$ and a dominating set algorithm $A$ with running time $O(n^\delta)$, we can simulate in the congested clique the execution of $A$ on $G'$ in $O(n^\delta)$ rounds. We have each node $v \in V$ simulate the nodes $v^i$ and $v^{i,j}$ for the possible choices of parameters $i$ and $j$; by construction, $v$ can determine all edges incident to those nodes in $G'$ from its local view of $G$. Moreover, we have nodes 1 and 2 simulate the special nodes in $x^i$ and $y^i$, respectively. Thus, each node is simulating at most $O(k^2)$ nodes in $G'$. The running time of $A$ in $G'$ is $O((k^2n)^\delta)$, and the overhead from simulating $O(k^2)$ nodes per each node in $G$ is $O(k^4)$ rounds for each round in $G'$, for total running time $O(k^{2\delta+4}n^\delta)$.

## 7.3 Vertex cover and fixed-parameter tractability

*Vertex cover.* Minimum vertex cover and maximum independent set are known to be essentially the same problem. However, we show that the *parameterised* version of vertex cover is significantly easier than independent set in the congested clique model:

THEOREM 7.3. *Vertex cover of size k can be found in $O(k)$ rounds in the congested clique model.*

We use a very simple idea that also appears in the centralised Buss kernelisation algorithm [9, 14].

LEMMA 7.4. *If $G = (V, E)$ has a vertex cover C of size k, and $v \in V$ is a vertex of degree at least $k + 1$, then $v \in C$.*

PROOF. If $v \notin C$, then all neighbours of $v$ are in $C$, which implies $|C| \geq k + 1$. □

In the congested clique, we exploit this idea as follows. As a preprocessing phase, all nodes of degree at least $k + 1$ join the

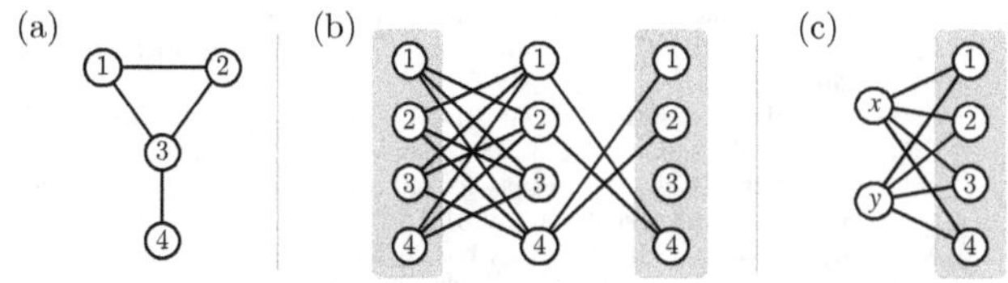


**Figure 2: Gadgets in the reduction from independent set to dominating set. Corresponding nodes in the original graph and the gadgets are labelled with same numbers. (a) The original graph $G$. (b) The compatibility gadget between two cliques, shown in gray. (c) Special nodes attached to a clique.**

vertex cover—denote this set by $C$—and broadcast this information to all nodes; if more than $k$ nodes attempt to join the vertex cover, we know that there is no vertex cover of size $k$. As the main phase, all nodes $v \notin C$ broadcast full information about their incident edges not covered by $C$, and all nodes locally compute a minimum vertex cover for $G[V \setminus C]$. By Lemma 7.4, we know that there is a vertex cover of size $k$ for $G$ if and only if there is a vertex cover of size $k - |C|$ for $G[V \setminus C]$.

The preprocessing phase takes a single round. Since all nodes of degree at least $k + 1$ join $C$ in the preprocessing phase, all nodes active in the main phase have to broadcast information about at most $k$ edges, so the main phase takes at most $k$ rounds.

*Fixed-parameter tractability.* The above result, taken together with prior upper bounds results for parameterised problems such as $k$-independent set and $k$-cycle detection, illustrate that ideas from *fixed-parameter algorithms* [14, 18] can also be applied in the congested clique. Specifically, the following is known in the congested clique model:

- A vertex cover of size $k$ can be found in $O(k)$ rounds – the complexity is dependent polynomially on $k$, and not at all on $n$.
- A $k$-path can be found in $\exp(k)$ rounds [20, 35] and a $k$-cycle in $\exp(k)n^{0.157}$ rounds [10] – the complexity is exponential in $k$, but the complexity in terms of $n$ is independent of $k$.
- An independent set of size $k$ can be found in $O(n^{1-2/k})$ rounds and a dominating set of size $k$ in $O(n^{1-1/k})$ rounds – the complexity in terms of $n$ is dependent on $k$.

Compare this to what we know from the centralised setting:

- Vertex cover, $k$-path and $k$-cycle are all *fixed-parameter tractable* problems: they can be solved in time $\exp(k)\,\mathrm{poly}(n)$. However, vertex cover admits a *polynomial kernel* [9, 14] – intuitively, this means that vertex cover instances can be compressed to size $\mathrm{poly}(k)$ in polynomial time[1] – while the other two do not [6].
- By contrast, parameterised versions of independent set and dominating set are W[1]-hard and W[2]-hard, respectively, which strongly suggests that they are not fixed-parameter tractable, but rather require $n^{\Omega(k)}$ time to be solved [18].

[1]We refer to the recent book by Cygan et al. [14] for the formal definition of a kernel, as well as detailed discussion of the topic.

## 8 CONCLUSIONS

*Nondeterminism.* As a major open question, we highlight the lack of separation between constant-round deterministic and nondeterministic congested clique. It seems reasonable to conjecture that $\mathsf{CLIQUE}(1) \neq \mathsf{NCLIQUE}(1)$, but it is not clear how we should approach proving such separation. Indeed, it would be interesting even if we could prove this conditional on a centralised complexity assumption, such as P ≠ NP.

*NCLIQUE(1) as an LCL analogue.* As we noted before, the class NCLIQUE(1) plays a similar role in the congested clique to the class LCL of locally checkable labellings that been in the focus of recent complexity-theoretic work in the LOCAL model. Note that here we refer to LCL problems in the original sense of Naor and Stockmeyer [48], that is, class LCL consists of search problems such as 2-colouring, sinkless orientation and maximal independent set, where a valid output can be verified in constant rounds. By contrast, work on local decision often uses LCL to refer to the corresponding labelling verification problems, such as verifying a valid colouring of a graph [23, 28].

Similarly to the LCL problems, the class of NCLIQUE(1)-labelling problems on labelled graphs is a natural class of search problems on the congested clique. We define an NCLIQUE(1)-labelling problem $L$ as a set of pairs $(G, z)$, where $G$ is an input graph with edge and node labels of $O(\log n)$ bits, $z$ is an output labelling, and the membership $(G, z) \in L$ is decidable in constant rounds. Given an input graph, the computational task is to output a label $z_v$ for each node $v$ such that $(G, z) \in L$, or reject if such labelling does not exist. This class captures many natural graph problems of interest, but we do not have lower bounds for any problem in this class.

*Randomness.* In this work, we have focused on deterministic and nondeterministic computation; however, there are problems in the congested clique model where the best *randomised* upper bounds are significantly better than the best deterministic upper bounds, e.g. minimum spanning tree [25, 45]. Thus, a possible extension of the present work is to study the randomised complexity landscape of the congested clique. Indeed, the counting arguments of Applebaum et al. [1] extend to randomised protocols. Likewise, Theorem 5.2 implies that there are problems that cannot be solved in $O(S(n))$ rounds with one-sided Monte Carlo algorithms, but can be solved in $O(T(n))$ rounds deterministically for $S(n) = o(T(n))$, as the Monte Carlo algorithm can be converted to a nondeterministic algorithm.

*Acknowledgements.* This work was supported in part by the Academy of Finland, Grant 285721. We thank Alkida Balliu, Parinya Chalermsook, Magnús M. Halldórsson, Juho Hirvonen, Petteri Kaski, Dennis Olivetti and Christopher Purcell for comments and discussions.

## REFERENCES

[1] Benny Applebaum, Dariusz R. Kowalski, Boaz Patt-Shamir, and Adi RosÃl'n. 2016. Clique Here: On the Distributed Complexity in Fully-Connected Networks. *Parallel Processing Letters* 26, 01 (2016), 1650004. https://doi.org/10.1142/S0129626416500043

[2] Alkida Balliu, Gianlorenzo D'Angelo, Pierre Fraigniaud, and Dennis Olivetti. 2017. What Can Be Verified Locally?. In *Proc. 34th Symposium on Theoretical Aspects of Computer Science (STACS 2017)*, Vol. 66. 8:1–8:13. https://doi.org/10.4230/LIPIcs.STACS.2017.8

[3] Alkida Balliu, Juho Hirvonen, Janne H. Korhonen, Tuomo LempiÃd'inen, Dennis Olivetti, and Jukka Suomela. 2018. New Classes of Distributed Time Complexity. In *Proc. 50th Annual ACM Symposium on the Theory of Computing (STOC 2018)*. To appear.

[4] Ruben Becker, Andreas Karrenbauer, Sebastian Krinninger, and Christoph Lenzen. 2016. Near-Optimal Approximate Shortest Paths and Transshipment in Distributed and Streaming Models. (2016). arXiv:1607.05127 [cs.DC].

[5] Ruben Becker, Andreas Karrenbauer, Sebastian Krinninger, and Christoph Lenzen. 2017. Near-Optimal Approximate Shortest Paths and Transshipment in Distributed and Streaming Models. In *Proc. 31st International Symposium on Distributed Computing (DISC 2017)*.

[6] Hans L. Bodlaender, Rodney G. Downey, Michael R. Fellows, and Danny Hermelin. 2009. On problems without polynomial kernels. *J. Comput. System Sci.* 75, 8 (2009), 423–434.

[7] Sebastian Brandt, Orr Fischer, Juho Hirvonen, Barbara Keller, Tuomo Lempiäinen, Joel Rybicki, Jukka Suomela, and Jara Uitto. 2016. A Lower Bound for the Distributed Lovász Local Lemma. In *Proc. 48th Annual Symposium on the Theory of Computing (STOC 2016)*. ACM, 479–488. https://doi.org/10.1145/2897518.2897570

[8] Sebastian Brandt, Juho Hirvonen, Janne H. Korhonen, Tuomo Lempiäinen, Patric R. J. Östergård, Christopher Purcell, Joel Rybicki, Jukka Suomela, and PrzemysÅĆaw Uznański. 2017. LCL problems on grids. In *Proc. 36nd ACM Symposium on Principles of Distributed Computing (PODC 2017)*.

[9] Jonathan F. Buss and Judy Goldsmith. 1993. Nondeterminism Within P. *SIAM Journal of Computing* 22, 3 (1993), 560–572. https://doi.org/10.1137/0222038

[10] Keren Censor-Hillel, Petteri Kaski, Janne H. Korhonen, Christoph Lenzen, Ami Paz, and Jukka Suomela. 2015. Algebraic methods in the congested clique. In *Proc. ACM Symposium on Principles of Distributed Computing (PODC 2015)*. 143–152.

[11] Keren Censor-Hillel, Merav Parter, and Gregory Schwartzman. 2016. Derandomizing Local Distributed Algorithms under Bandwidth Restrictions. (2016). arXiv:1608.01689 [cs.DC].

[12] Yi-Jun Chang, Tsvi Kopelowitz, and Seth Pettie. 2016. An Exponential Separation Between Randomized and Deterministic Complexity in the LOCAL Model. In *Proc. 57th Annual IEEE Symposium on Foundations of Computer Science (FOCS 2016)*. IEEE, 615–624.

[13] Yi-Jun Chang and Seth Pettie. 2017. A Time Hierarchy Theorem for the LOCAL Model. In *Proc. 58th Annual IEEE Symposium on Foundations of Computer Science (FOCS 2017)*.

[14] Marek Cygan, Fedor V. Fomin, ÅĄukasz Kowalik, Daniel Lokshtanov, Daniel Marx, Marcin Pilipczuk, MichaÅĆ Pilipczuk, and Saket Saurabh. 2015. *Parameterized Algorithms*. Springer. https://doi.org/10.1007/978-3-319-21275-3

[15] Atish Das Sarma, Stephan Holzer, Liah Kor, Amos Korman, Danupon Nanongkai, Gopal Pandurangan, David Peleg, and Roger Wattenhofer. 2011. Distributed Verification and Hardness of Distributed Approximation. In *Proc. 43th ACM Symposium on Theory of Computing (STOC 2011)*. 363–372. https://doi.org/10.1145/1993636.1993686

[16] Danny Dolev, Christoph Lenzen, and Shir Peled. 2012. "Tri, Tri Again": Finding Triangles and Small Subgraphs in a Distributed Setting. In *Proc. 26th International Symposium on Distributed Computing (DISC 2012)*. 195–209. https://doi.org/10.1007/978-3-642-33651-5_14

[17] Dorit Dor, Shay Halperin, and Uri Zwick. 2000. All-Pairs Almost Shortest Paths. *SIAM J. Comput.* 29, 5 (2000), 1740–1759. https://doi.org/10.1137/S0097539797327908

[18] Rodney G. Downey and Michael R. Fellows. 2012. *Parameterized complexity*. Springer.

[19] Andrew Drucker, Fabian Kuhn, and Rotem Oshman. 2014. On the Power of the Congested Clique Model. In *Proc. 33rd ACM Symposium on Principles of Distributed Computing (PODC 2014)*. 367–376. https://doi.org/10.1145/2611462.2611493

[20] Guy Even, Orr Fischer, Pierre Fraigniaud, Tzlil Gonen, Reut Levi, Moti Medina, Dennis Olivetti Pedro Montealegre, Rotem Oshman, Ivan Rapaport, and Ioan Todinca. 2017. Three Notes on Distributed Property Testing. In *Proc. 31st International Symposium on Distributed Computing (DISC 2017)*.

[21] Laurent Feuilloley and Pierre Fraigniaud. 2016. Survey of Distributed Decision. *Bulletin of the EATCS* 119 (2016), 41–65. arXiv:1606.04434 [cs.DC].

[22] Laurent Feuilloley, Pierre Fraigniaud, and Juho Hirvonen. 2016. A Hierarchy of Local Decision. In *Proc. 43rd International Colloquium on Automata, Languages, and Programming (ICALP 2016)*, Vol. 55. 118:1–118:15. https://doi.org/10.4230/LIPIcs.ICALP.2016.118

[23] Pierre Fraigniaud, Amos Korman, and David Peleg. 2011. Local Distributed Decision. In *Proc. 52nd Annual Symposium on Foundations of Computer Science (FOCS 2011)*. 708–717. https://doi.org/10.1109/FOCS.2011.17

[24] Silvio Frischknecht, Stephan Holzer, and Roger Wattenhofer. 2012. Networks Cannot Compute their Diameter in Sublinear Time. In *Proc. 23rd Annual ACM-SIAM Symposium on Discrete Algorithms (SODA 2012)*. 1150–1162.

[25] Mohsen Ghaffari, Fabian Kuhn, and Yannic Maus. 2016. On the Complexity of Local Distributed Graph Problems. In *Proc. 49th ACM Symposium on Theory of Computing (STOC 2017)*. arXiv:1611.02663 [cs.DC].

[26] Mohsen Ghaffari and Merav Parter. 2016. MST in Log-Star Rounds of Congested Clique. In *Proc. 35nd ACM Symposium on Principles of Distributed Computing (PODC 2016)*.

[27] Mohsen Ghaffari and Hsin-Hao Su. 2017. Distributed Degree Splitting, Edge Coloring, and Orientations. In *Proc. 28th Annual ACM-SIAM Symposium on Discrete Algorithms (SODA 2017)*. Society for Industrial and Applied Mathematics, 2505–2523. https://doi.org/10.1137/1.9781611974782.166

[28] Mika Göös and Jukka Suomela. 2016. Locally Checkable Proofs in Distributed Computing. *Theory of Computing* 12, 1 (2016), 1–33. https://doi.org/10.4086/toc.2016.v012a019

[29] Juris Hartmanis and Richard E. Stearns. 1965. On the computational complexity of algorithms. *Trans. Amer. Math. Soc.* 117 (1965), 285–306.

[30] James W. Hegeman, Gopal Pandurangan, Sriram V. Pemmaraju, Vivek B. Sardeshmukh, and Michele Scquizzato. 2015. Toward Optimal Bounds in the Congested Clique: Graph Connectivity and MST. In *Proc. 34nd ACM Symposium on Principles of Distributed Computing (PODC 2015)*. 91–100. https://doi.org/10.1145/2767386.2767434

[31] James W. Hegeman and Sriram V. Pemmaraju. 2014. Lessons from the Congested Clique Applied to MapReduce. In *Proc. 21st Colloquium on Structural Information and Communication Complexity (SIROCCO 2014)*. 149–164. https://doi.org/10.1007/978-3-319-09620-9_13

[32] James W. Hegeman, Sriram V. Pemmaraju, and Vivek B. Sardeshmukh. 2014. Near-Constant-Time Distributed Algorithms on a Congested Clique. In *Proc. 28th International Symposium on Distributed Computing (DISC 2014)*. 514–530. https://doi.org/10.1007/978-3-662-45174-8_35

[33] Fred C. Hennie and Richard E. Stearns. 1966. Two-tape simulation of multitape Turing machines. *Journal of the ACM* 13, 4 (1966), 533–546.

[34] Janne H. Korhonen. 2016. Brief Announcement: Deterministic MST sparsification in the congested clique. In *Proc. 30th International Symposium on Distributed Computing (DISC 2016)*.

[35] Janne H. Korhonen and Joel Rybicki. 2017. Deterministic subgraph detection in broadcast CONGEST. In *Proc. 21st Conference on Principles of Distributed Systems (OPODIS 2017)*.

[36] Amos Korman and Shay Kutten. 2006. On Distributed Verification. In *Proc. 8th International Conference on Distributed Computing and Networking (ICDN'06)*. 100–114. https://doi.org/10.1007/11947950_12

[37] Amos Korman and Shay Kutten. 2007. Distributed verification of minimum spanning trees. *Distributed Computing* 20, 4 (2007), 253–266. https://doi.org/10.1007/s00446-007-0025-1

[38] Amos Korman, Shay Kutten, and David Peleg. 2010. Proof labeling schemes. *Distributed Computing* 22, 4 (2010), 215–233. https://doi.org/10.1007/s00446-010-0095-3

[39] Amos Korman, David Peleg, and Yoav Rodeh. 2010. Constructing Labeling Schemes through Universal Matrices. *Algorithmica* 57, 4 (2010), 641–652. https://doi.org/10.1007/s00453-008-9226-7

[40] Shay Kutten and David Peleg. 1998. Fast Distributed Construction of Small $k$-Dominating Sets and Applications. *Journal of Algorithms* 28, 1 (1998), 40–66. https://doi.org/10.1006/jagm.1998.0929

[41] François Le Gall. 2014. Powers of Tensors and Fast Matrix Multiplication. In *Proc. 39th Symposium on Symbolic and Algebraic Computation (ISSAC 2014)*. 296–303. https://doi.org/10.1145/2608628.2608664

[42] François Le Gall. 2016. Further Algebraic Algorithms in the Congested Clique Model and Applications to Graph-Theoretic Problems. In *Proc. 30th International Symposium on Distributed Computing (DISC 2016)*. 57–70.

[43] Christoph Lenzen. 2013. Optimal deterministic routing and sorting on the congested clique. In *Proc. 32nd ACM Symposium on Principles of Distributed Computing (PODC 2013)*. 42–50. https://doi.org/10.1145/2484239.2501983

[44] Christoph Lenzen and David Peleg. 2013. Efficient Distributed Source Detection with Limited Bandwidth. In *Proc. 32nd ACM Symposium on Principles of Distributed Computing (PODC 2013)*. 375–382. https://doi.org/10.1145/2484239.2484262

[45] Zvi Lotker, Boaz Patt-Shamir, Elan Pavlov, and David Peleg. 2005. Minimum-Weight Spanning Tree Construction in $O(\log \log n)$ Communication Rounds. *SIAM J. Comput.* 35, 1 (2005), 120–131. https://doi.org/10.1137/S0097539704441848

[46] Michael Luby. 1986. A Simple Parallel Algorithm for the Maximal Independent Set Problem. *SIAM J. Comput.* 15, 4 (1986), 1036–1053. https://doi.org/10.1137/0215074

[47] Danupon Nanongkai. 2014. Distributed Approximation Algorithms for Weighted Shortest Paths. In *Proc. 46th ACM Symposium on Theory of Computing (STOC 2014)*. 565–573.

[48] Moni Naor and Larry Stockmeyer. 1995. What can be computed locally? *SIAM J. Comput.* 24, 6 (1995), 1259–1277. https://doi.org/10.1137/S0097539793254571

[49] Gopal Pandurangan, Peter Robinson, and Michele Scquizzato. 2016. Tight bounds for distributed graph computations. (2016). arXiv:1602.08481 [cs.DC].

[50] David Peleg and Vitaly Rubinovich. 2000. Near-tight Lower Bound on the Time Complexity of Distributed MST Construction. *SIAM J. Comput.* 30, 5 (2000), 1427–1442. https://doi.org/10.1137/S0097539700369740

[51] Fabian Reiter. 2015. Distributed graph automata. In *Proc. 30th Annual ACM/IEEE Symposium on Logic in Computer Science (LICS 2015)*. IEEE, 192–201.

# Breaking the $\tilde{\Omega}(\sqrt{n})$ Barrier: Fast Consensus under a Late Adversary

Peter Robinson
McMaster University
Hamilton, Ontario, Canada
peter.robinson@mcmaster.ca

Christian Scheideler
Paderborn University
Paderborn, Germany
scheideler@mail.upb.de

Alexander Setzer
Paderborn University
Paderborn, Germany
asetzer@mail.upb.de

## ABSTRACT

We study the consensus problem in a synchronous distributed system of $n$ nodes under an adaptive adversary that has a slightly outdated view of the system and can block all incoming and outgoing communication of a constant fraction of the nodes in each round. Motivated by a result of Ben-Or and Bar-Joseph (1998), showing that any consensus algorithm that is resilient against a linear number of crash faults requires $\tilde{\Omega}(\sqrt{n})$ rounds in an $n$-node network against an *adaptive* adversary, we consider a late adaptive adversary, who has full knowledge of the network state at the beginning of the *previous* round and unlimited computational power, but is oblivious to the current state of the nodes. Our main contributions are randomized distributed algorithms that achieve consensus with high probability among all except a small constant fraction of the nodes (i.e., "almost-everywhere") against a late adaptive adversary who can block up to $\epsilon n$ nodes in each round, for a small constant $\epsilon > 0$. Our first protocol achieves binary almost-everywhere consensus and also guarantees a decision on the majority input value, thus ensuring plurality consensus. We also present an algorithm that achieves the same time complexity for multi-value consensus. Both of our algorithms succeed in $O(\log n)$ rounds with high probability, thus showing an exponential gap to the $\tilde{\Omega}(\sqrt{n})$ lower bound of Ben-Or and Bar-Joseph for strongly adaptive crash-failure adversaries, which can be strengthened to $\Omega(n)$ when allowing the adversary to block nodes instead of permanently crashing them. Our algorithms are scalable to large systems as each node contacts only an (amortized) constant number of peers in each communication round. We show that our algorithms are optimal up to constant (resp. sub-logarithmic) factors by proving that every almost-everywhere consensus protocol takes $\Omega(\log_d n)$ rounds in the worst case, where $d$ is an upper bound on the number of communication requests initiated per node in each round. We complement our theoretical results with an experimental evaluation of the binary almost-everywhere consensus protocol revealing a short convergence time even against an adversary blocking a large fraction of nodes.


*SPAA '18, July 16–18, 2018, Vienna, Austria*

ACM ISBN 978-1-4503-5799-9/18/07...$15.00
https://doi.org/10.1145/3210377.3210399

## KEYWORDS

Randomized Algorithm, Almost-everywhere consensus, probabilistic analysis, adaptive adversary

**ACM Reference Format:**

Peter Robinson, Christian Scheideler, and Alexander Setzer. 2018. Breaking the $\tilde{\Omega}(\sqrt{n})$ Barrier: Fast Consensus under a Late Adversary. In *SPAA '18: SPAA '18: 30th ACM Symposium on Parallelism in Algorithms and Architectures, July 16–18, 2018, Vienna, Austria.* ACM, New York, NY, USA, 10 pages. https://doi.org/10.1145/3210377.3210399

## ACKNOWLEDGMENTS

This work was supported by the LMS/ Computer Science Scheme 7 Grant Ref No.: SC7-1516-11 and by the German Research Foundation (DFG) within the Collaborative Research Center "On-The-Fly Computing" (SFB 901) under Grant No.: GZ SFB 901/02. Peter Robinson acknowledges the support of the Natural Sciences and Engineering Research Council of Canada (NSERC).

## 1 INTRODUCTION

Reaching consensus among the members of a distributed system is a fundamental ingredient for building a reliable distributed system out of unreliable parts (c.f., [7, 31]), with applications ranging from synchronization of processes to distributed commit in databases.

Given that several impossibility results in asynchronous systems [23] and pessimistic lower bounds [19, 22] for synchronous systems have been discovered for deterministic algorithms when nodes can be subjected to failures, much of the recent work on the consensus problem focuses on using randomization to defeat the adversary (see [5] for a comprehensive overview). Early randomized consensus algorithms include the work of Ben-Or [15], which achieves consensus even in the asynchronous setting, where nodes perform steps at different speeds and messages can exhibit delays. For the more severe case of Byzantine failures, where some nodes are directly controlled by an adversary and hence deviate from the protocol, Rabin [36] showed that it is possible to achieve agreement in a constant number of rounds in expectation when nodes have access to a shared common coin. The recent work of [27], which assumes private communication channels between non-corrupted nodes, and [33] achieved a significant reduction of the required message complexity of randomized Byzantine agreement protocols.

Since all of the classic agreement protocols mentioned above require all-to-all communication and hence do not scale well to large systems, one direction of research is to study the consensus problems in systems where the nodes are interconnected by a sparse communication network. Considering that the adversary can isolate (small) regions of a sparse network, achieving agreement among *all* nodes is impossible without strong guarantees on the network's connectivity [22]. However, for many practical applications such as achieving eventual consistency in a peer-to-peer network (e.g., [34]), it is sufficient if a common decision is reached "almost everywhere", i.e., among all but a small fraction of nodes. The *almost-everywhere consensus* problem was first introduced in [21] (called almost-everywhere agreement) as a way to circumvent the classical impossibility results for consensus and Byzantine agreement in sparse communication networks and has been studied under various failure models, such as strongly adaptive and oblivious adversaries. More specifically, [21] provided an almost-everywhere agreement algorithm that can tolerate $O(n/\log n)$ Byzantine faults in a sparse network. Later, [40] improved over these results by presenting a protocol that tolerates a linear number of failures. However, both of these protocols require nodes to use a polynomial number of bits of communication. More recently, almost-everywhere consensus with Byzantine nodes was studied in the context of bounded-degree peer-to-peer networks in the work of [28]. We point out that [21, 28, 40] require nodes to be equipped with a priori knowledge about the network topology that needs to be hard-coded into the distributed algorithm.

Other works consider almost-everywhere consensus in dynamically changing expander network topologies [8, 9] where the nodes can be subjected to churn over time. More specifically, [8] provide an algorithm using logarithmic-size messages in the presence of $\tilde{O}(\sqrt{n})$[1] (obliviously-controlled) churn and Byzantine nodes, while an extension of the algorithm can tolerate a strongly adaptive adversary albeit at the cost of requiring polynomial message sizes. When there are no Byzantine nodes, [9] show that it is possible to tolerate even $O(n)$-churn when the adversary is oblivious. However, none of these algorithms work against a late adversary (defined in Section 1.4) who is adaptive *and* can fail a constant fraction of nodes.

## 1.1 Our Main Results

In this work, we consider the almost-everywhere consensus problem under a "late" adaptive adversary who has a slightly outdated view of the entire system when deciding its next move. Studying late adversaries is reasonable as it is unrealistic to assume that an adversary can make instantaneous decisions based on the global system state, and our results demonstrate that it already makes a huge difference if the adversary is just late by a single communication round.

We present new distributed algorithms for almost-everywhere consensus in a system of $n$ synchronous, completely interconnected nodes that can withstand attacks on a constant fraction of the nodes in each round by a late adversary who has full knowledge of the system state at the start of the previous round. In our protocols, every node sends and receives at most $O(\log n)$ messages per round with high probability[2]. In particular we present the following results under a late adaptive adversary that can block the communication of up to $\epsilon n$ nodes in each round, for a constant $\epsilon > 0$:

(1) In Section 2, we provide an $O(\log n)$-rounds algorithm that achieves almost-everywhere binary consensus with high probability, where each node contacts $O(1)$ other nodes per round. Moreover, the algorithm achieves plurality consensus (w.h.p.).
(2) In Section 3, we present an $O(\log n)$-rounds algorithm that solves almost-everywhere multi-value consensus (w.h.p.). (Instead of the plurality guarantee, this algorithm satisfies the classical validity condition of consensus; see Section 1.4.)
(3) In Section 4 we show a lower bound on the time complexity of any algorithm that achieves almost-everywhere agreement with high probability assuming that each node can communicate with at most $d$ nodes (chosen by the algorithm and not by the adversary), requires $\Omega(\log_d n)$ rounds in the worst case. This implies that our algorithm for binary consensus (cf. Section 2) is asymptotically optimal, whereas the multi-value algorithm (cf. Section 3) is optimal up to sub-logarithmic factors, due to requiring $d = \Theta(\log n)$.
(4) Finally, in Section 5 we present an experimental evaluation of the algorithm from Section 2 with different parameters, suggesting a good practical performance of at most $2\log(n)$ rounds convergence time (on average) of that algorithm and variants of it, even against an adversary who can block a large number of nodes.

**Tightness of the Power of the Adversary.** The work of [11] shows that if a *strongly adaptive* adversary who observes the current system state including the output of the random coinflips can fail up to $t$ of the $n$ nodes in each round, then with high probability the adversary can force any consensus algorithm to run for $\Omega(t/\sqrt{n \log n})$ rounds. This result holds even without restricting the communication of the nodes. In fact, when considering a strongly adaptive adversary who can block a set of nodes, instead of permanently crashing them, it is possible to show that $\Omega(n)$ rounds are necessary. We elaborate on this point in Theorem 6 in the full version of this paper [37].

## 1.2 Technical Contribution

The main challenge that we have to overcome is the fact that the adversary has an almost up-to-date knowledge of the state of the system. The key ingredient in our approach in handling a linear number of adversarial attacks is to limit the extent to which the previous state of a node influences the computations of the algorithms.

For the binary consensus problem, at first glance the median rule presented in [18] seems to be a good candidate to handle a late adversary. It uses a simple "pull" strategy in which each node requests the values from 2 nodes chosen uniformly and independently at random, and selects the median of these two values and its own value as its new value. However, "pull" strategies, which inherently require two communication rounds to compute a new value, do not work against a late adaptive adversary, as a late adversary can anticipate the values received at the end of the response round by the end of the request round. This essentially makes the adversary as powerful as the strongly adaptive one. Another problem is that the value of a node depends on its previous value. In fact, it can be shown that the median rule fails w.h.p. against a late adversary that can just cause $\Omega(\sqrt{n \log n})$ faults. Thus, we converted the median rule into a "push" strategy, in which each node spreads its value

[1]The notation $\tilde{O}(.)$ hides a polylogarithmic factor.
[2]We say an event $E$ holds with high probability (w.h.p.) if $\Pr[E] \geq 1 - n^{-\Omega(1)}$.

in every communication round to other nodes selected uniformly at random, and picks the majority of a random subset of received values for its new value. When using such a procedure, however, the probabilities of the nodes to receive certain values are no longer independent from each other. This requires a much more involved analysis, as we can no longer rely on standard Chernoff bounds and the central limit theorem for showing a drift towards one value and need to use the Paley-Zygmund inequality instead. Also, it can happen that nodes do not receive enough values to compute a new value. In that case, we need an additional undecided state for the nodes to ensure independency from the past node state, which has the effect that the number of nodes with a value may vary from round to round. This, in turn, causes the support of the dominating value to no longer increase in absolute terms but rather only relatively to the number of nodes that are not in an undecided state.

While the algorithm for binary almost-everywhere consensus (Section 2) solely bases its computations on the values received from other nodes, in our algorithm for handling multi-value inputs (Section 3) a node does keep its value unless it is blocked or learns about a larger value. Hence, eventually a consensus is reached on the maximum value in the system. However, as the events of nodes joining the set that is informed about the maximum value are not independent, we use the method of bounded differences and Azuma's Inequality that a consensus is reached even under a late adversary that can block a constant fraction of the nodes.

## 1.3 Other Related Work

As mentioned above, our algorithm for binary consensus is inspired by [18] which considers almost-stable consensus under an adversary that may adaptively change the values of up to $\sqrt{n}$ nodes after each round. The authors derive an $O(\log n + \log k \log\log n)$ runtime bound w.h.p. for an arbitrary number of distinct initial values $k$ and $O(\log n)$ if $k = 2$. The latter bound is tight (even without an adversary) as we show in this work. To achieve their results, the authors use the median rule. In the binary case this is equivalent to taking the majority of the received values, which resembles the 3-majority rule. [14] study the 3-majority rule under an $o(\sqrt{n})$-adaptive adversary, showing that it converges in time polynomial in $k$ and $n$ w.h.p.

Our algorithm in Section 2 guarantees a decision on the majority input value (if any), which was studied in non-adversarial settings by [13]. They present an algorithm with runtime $\Theta(k \log n)$ w.h.p. for $k$ being the number of distinct initial values, which they prove to be tight for a wide range of values of $k$ and the initial bias. For certain values of $k$, the runtime of this algorithm is outperformed by [12] in which each node may contact one neighbor at random in each round. The authors of the latter paper consider what they call the Undecided-State Dynamics (originally introduced in [4] as Third-State dynamics), which makes use of an additional "undecided" value different from all input values. This idea has also been used in [16] and [24] to solve plurality consensus with small memory overhead and an exponential improvement on the runtime compared to [13]. In contrast to these works that do not consider adversaries, our algorithms, which also use undecided values, do so to prevent the adversary from influencing the distribution of values by releasing previously blocked nodes. Note that all consensus protocols mentioned thus far use a "pull" strategy, under which a late adversary is as powerful as a fully adaptive one (as was argued in Section 1.2). Thus none of the analyses of these protocols could be trivially adapted to achieve a consensus under a constant fraction of adversarial nodes in $\tilde{o}(\sqrt{n})$ rounds .

The idea of considering a late adversary who knows a previous state of the system has only been studied in a few papers so far (e.g., [2, 3, 10, 20, 29]). As one of the first attempts, [10] studies how to make an information system resilient against a blocking adversary that has knowledge of the system up to some point in time. In [2] and [3], an adversary is called $\tau$-oblivious if it knows the randomness of the nodes up to round $r - \tau$ to make a decision for round $r$, in which the special case of a 0-oblivious adversary is called a strongly adaptive adversary. The authors of [20] consider a so-called $t$-late adversary that bases its decision in round $r$ on knowledge of the complete state of nodes in round $r - t$ and use this concept to maintain connectivity under an $O(\log\log n)$-late adversary who may cause churn and block nodes. [29] introduces the notion of a $c$-round-delayed adversary which resembles a $c$-oblivious adversary in the notation of [2].

A failure model related to the blocking adversary is the crash-recovery model considered for asynchronous consensus in [1]. We point out that, in contrast to our model, in [1] nodes lose their entire state upon recovery and can only recover state that was written to a stable storage.

[25] presents a protocol that achieves consensus against an oblivious adversary requiring only $O(n)$ message complexity, which is clearly optimal. While the overall communication of their algorithm is small, it requires an asymmetric communication load, as some nodes need to send $\Omega(\sqrt{n})$ messages. Other work that considers consensus in models with restricted communication includes [35], who studies agreement in the radio network model of wireless communication.

## 1.4 Computing Model and Problem Definition

We consider a system of $n$ anonymous, completely interconnected nodes that operate in synchronous rounds. In each round, every node first receives all messages from the previous round (that are not blocked by the adversary), then does some arbitrary finite internal computation, and then sends off messages to other nodes.

**Adversarial Model.** Due to the lower bound results of [8, 11] discussed in Section 1.1, achieving agreement in logarithmic time is out of reach against a strongly adaptive adversary who can block a linear number of nodes per round, even when the amount of communication that a node can perform in each round is unrestricted. This motivates us to consider a *late $\epsilon$-bounded adaptive adversary*, who, at the start of each round $t \geq 2$, can observe the state of the entire system at the beginning of round $t - 1$. Based on that state, the adversary can block any set $B_t$ of $\leq \epsilon n$ nodes, with the effect that none of these nodes can receive or send messages in that round. We point out that, in the very first round, the adversary knows the initial state of the system. However, it does not know the coin flips performed by nodes in this round. Moreover, we assume that nodes know if they are currently blocked. Notice that the adversary is still adaptive in the sense that it can tailor its next attack on the previously observed network state.

Definition 1. *Let $\gamma < \frac{1}{2}$ be a positive constant. We assume that each node $u$ starts with an* input value *chosen by the adversary from a domain of size polynomial in $n$ and, eventually, $u$ irrevocably decides on a value. We say that an algorithm solves* almost-everywhere agreement in $t$ rounds with high probability and loss $\gamma n$, *if the algorithm terminates in $t$ rounds and the following properties hold w.h.p.*

**(Almost-Everywhere Agreement)** *All except at most $\gamma n$ nodes decide on the same value.*

**(Validity)** *If all nodes start with the same input value $x$, then $x$ is the only possible decision.*

In addition to the classic validity definition above, we are also interested in a stronger validity condition:

**(Plurality)** If an almost-everywhere agreement algorithm $\mathcal{A}$ guarantees the stronger validity condition that stipulates $x$ as the only possible decision if the number of nodes having input $x$ exceeds the number of nodes having input $y$ for every other possible value $y \neq x$ by at least $s \geq \gamma n$. In this case, we say that $\mathcal{A}$ *solves almost-everywhere plurality consensus with initial bias s.*

## 2 BINARY CONSENSUS

In this section, we assume that each node $u$ has a local variable $x_u$ that can hold the values 0, 1, or $\perp$ (i.e. "undefined"). A node $u$ is called *undefined* if $x_u = \perp$ and otherwise *defined.* Consider the following protocol for some integers $k, \ell > 0$, where $k \geq \ell$ and $\ell$ odd:

**$(k, \ell)$-majority algorithm.** In each round, every node $u$ acts according to the following rules:

- **reset rule:** If $u$ has received less than $\ell$ values from the previous round, or it is blocked, then it sets $x_u := \perp$ and skips the rest of this round.
- **update rule:** Otherwise, $u$ picks $\ell$ of the received values uniformly at random, sets $x_u$ to the majority value of the $\ell$ values, and sends out $x_u$ to $k$ nodes chosen independently and uniformly at random.

We assume here that if the adversary blocks $u$, then $u$ notices it. (In practice, it may simply not receive enough values, which would also have the effect in our protocol that $x_u$ is set to $\perp$.) In the rest of this section we show:

Theorem 1. *For any initial assignment of values to the nodes with no undefined node and any $\epsilon \leq 1/16$, $O(\log n)$ rounds of the $(6, 3)$-majority rule suffice to ensure that all except a constant fraction of nodes hold the same value (w.h.p) against a late $\epsilon$-bounded blocking adversary.*

On a high-level view, the proof works as follows: Let $X_t$ be the number of nodes with value 0 at the end of round $t$, let $Y_t$ be the number of nodes with value 1 at the end of round $t$, and let $n_t := X_t + Y_t$ be the number of defined nodes at the end of round $t$. First of all, observe that there will be at least $3n/4$ defined nodes at the end of round 1 since the adversary can block at most $n/16$ many nodes. In Lemma 2 we show that this holds after every round. In the remaining part, we assume without loss of generality that $X_t \leq Y_t$ and define the *imbalance* at round $t$ by $\Delta_t = (Y_t - X_t)/2$ (which is non-negative by our assumption). Based on the imbalance $\Delta_t$ we distinguish between three cases. First, we show that if the imbalance $\Delta_t$ exceeds $n_t/4$, i.e., there is a value that at least $3/4$ of the defined nodes have, then this value will be spread to almost every node within $O(\log \log n)$ rounds w.h.p. Second, we show that if $c\sqrt{n_t \ln n_t} \leq \Delta_t < n_t/4$ for a sufficiently large constant $c$, the number of nodes having the dominating value will grow within $O(\log n)$ rounds w.h.p. such that it is held by at least $3/4$ of all defined nodes. While the overall structure of the proof in the first two cases follows [18], here we face additional complications due to dependencies among the random variables. Note that these two cases directly imply that the $(k, \ell)$-majority algorithm solves the plurality consensus problem for initial bias $s \geq \sqrt{n(1+\epsilon)\log(n(1+\epsilon))}$. In the third case, we show that for very low imbalances, with high probability one of the two values will take over a sufficiently large number of the nodes such that the requirements of the second case are fulfilled. Any proofs omitted from this section due to space constraints can be found in the full paper [37].

To begin with the formal analysis, we introduce some results from probability theory.

Definition 2. *Let $X_1, \ldots, X_n$ be binary random variables. We say that $X_1, \ldots, X_n$ are* s-wise independently upper bounded by *$p_1, \ldots, p_n$ if for any subset $S \subset \{1, 2, \ldots, n\}$ with $|S| \leq s$ and any $i \in \{1, 2, \ldots, n\} \setminus S$ it holds that $\Pr[X_i = 1 \mid \bigwedge_{j \in S} X_j = 1] \leq p_i$.*

For these random variables the following variant of the Chernoff bounds can be shown:

Lemma 1. *Let $X_1, \ldots, X_n$ be binary random variables that are $k$-wise independently upper bounded by $p_1, \ldots, p_n$ and $X = \sum_{i=1}^{n} X_i$. Also, let $\mu = \sum_{i=1}^{n} p_i$. Then it holds for all $\delta > 0$ that*

$$\Pr[X \geq (1+\delta)\mu] \leq \left(\frac{e^{\delta}}{(1+\delta)^{1+\delta}}\right)^{\mu} \leq e^{-\delta^2\mu/(2(1+\delta/3))} \leq e^{-\min\{\delta^2, \delta\}\mu/3}$$

*as long as $k \geq (1+\delta)\mu$.*

This lemma directly follows from Theorem 3.52 in [38] which itself is based on results in [39].

Certainly, there will be at least $3n/4$ defined nodes at the end of round 1 since the adversary can block at most $n/16$ many nodes. For all subsequent rounds it holds:

Lemma 2. *For any assignment of values to the nodes with at least $3n/4$ defined nodes at the end of round $t$, there will also be at least $3n/4$ defined nodes at the end of round $t + 1$ w.h.p.*

Proof. Recall that $n_t$ is the number of defined nodes at the end of round $t$. For any non-blocked node $u$ in round $t + 1$ it holds that

$$\Pr[u \text{ receives no value}] = (1 - 1/n)^{6n_t} \leq e^{-6n_t/n} \text{ and}$$

$$\Pr[u \text{ receives one value}] = \binom{6n_t}{1}(1/n) \cdot (1 - 1/n)^{6n_t - 1} \leq \frac{6n_t}{n} \cdot e^{-(6n_t - 1)/n},$$

$$\Pr[u \text{ receives two values}] = \binom{6n_t}{2}(1/n)^2 \cdot (1-1/n)^{6n_t-2} \leq \frac{1}{2}\left(\frac{6n_t}{n}\right)^2 \cdot e^{-(6n_t-2)/n}.$$

Hence,

$$\Pr[u \text{ receives} \leq 2 \text{ values}] \leq \left(1 + \frac{6n_t}{n} + \frac{1}{2}\left(\frac{6n_t}{n}\right)^2\right) \cdot e^{-(6n_t-2)/n}.$$

If $n_t \geq 3n/4$ then $\Pr[u$ receives $\leq 2$ values$] \leq 2/11$ if $n$ is large enough. Since the adversary can block at most $n/16$ nodes, we get $E[\text{number of undefined nodes}] \leq (2/11)(1-1/16)n + n/16 \leq n/4.4$. Unfortunately, the probabilities of the nodes to be undefined are not independent, but they are $n/4$-wise independently upper bounded by $2/11$ as shown by the following claim.

Claim 1. *For any subset $S$ of non-blocked nodes with $|S| \leq n/4$ and any non-blocked node $u \notin S$ it holds that $\Pr[u$ undefined $\mid$ all nodes in $S$ undefined$] \leq 2/11$.*

Proof. Let $s = |S|$. Suppose that exactly $k$ of the $6n_t$ values have been sent to nodes in $S$. Certainly, if all nodes in $S$ are undefined, then $k \leq 2s$. It is easy to check that if $n$ is sufficiently large, then for any $n_t \geq 3n/4$ and any $k \leq 2s$, $(6n_t - k)/(n-s) \geq 6n_t/n$. Moreover, the functions $e^{-x}$, $x \cdot e^{-x}$ and $x^2 \cdot e^{-x}$ are monotonically decreasing for any $x \geq 2$. Hence, given that all nodes in $S$ are undefined, we get:

$\Pr[u$ receives no value$]$

$$= (1-1/(n-s))^{6n_t-k} \leq e^{-(6n_t-k)/(n-s)} \leq e^{-6n_t/n}$$

$\Pr[u$ receives one value$]$

$$= \binom{6n_t-k}{1}(1/(n-s)) \cdot (1-1/(n-s))^{6n_t-k-1}$$
$$\leq \frac{6n_t-k}{n-s} \cdot e^{-(6n_t-k-1)/(n-s)} \leq \frac{6n_t}{n} \cdot e^{-6n_t/n} \cdot e^{1/(n-s)}$$

$\Pr[u$ receives two values$]$

$$= \binom{6n_t-k}{2}(1/(n-s))^2 \cdot (1-1/(n-s))^{6n_t-k-2}$$
$$\leq \frac{1}{2}\left(\frac{6n_t-k}{n-s}\right)^2 \cdot e^{-(6n_t-k-2)/(n-s)}$$
$$\leq \frac{1}{2}\left(\frac{6n_t}{n}\right)^2 \cdot e^{-6n_t/n} \cdot e^{2/(n-s)}$$

Hence, given that all nodes in $S$ are undefined,

$\Pr[u$ receives $\leq 2$ values$]$

$$\leq \left(1 + \frac{6n_t}{n} + \frac{1}{2}\left(\frac{6n_t}{n}\right)^2\right) \cdot e^{-6n_t/n} \cdot e^{2/(n-s)} \leq 2/11$$

as long as $|S| \leq n/4$ and $n$ is sufficiently large. □

Therefore, we can make use of the Chernoff bounds in Lemma 1 to show that the number of undefined nodes is at most $n/4$ w.h.p. This completes the proof of the lemma. □

In the remaining part of the analysis, we carry out the aforementioned case distinction based on the value of $\Delta_t$.

*Case 1: $\Delta_t \geq n_t/4$.*

Lemma 3. *If there is a round $t_0$ with $\Delta_{t_0} \geq n_{t_0}/4$, then there is a round $t_1 = t_0 + O(\log\log n)$ at which we reach an almost-everywhere consensus, w.h.p.*

*Case 2: $c\sqrt{n_t \ln n_t} \leq \Delta_t < n_t/4$ for a sufficiently large constant $c$.*

Lemma 4. *If there is a round $t_0$ with $c\sqrt{n_{t_0} \ln n_{t_0}} \leq \Delta_{t_0} \leq n_{t_0}/4$ for a sufficiently large constant $c$, then there is a round $t_1 = t_0 + O(\log n)$ with $\Delta_{t_1} \geq n_t/4$ w.h.p.*

*Case 3: $|\Delta_t| < c\sqrt{n_t \ln n_t}$.* Up to this point we assumed that $X_t \leq Y_t$ w.l.o.g. because once the difference between the number of 0s and 1s is at least $c\sqrt{n_t \ln n_t}$, the majority value will win w.h.p. However, if $|\Delta_t| < c\sqrt{n_t \ln n_t}$, it may not be clear any more who will win. First, we show that with constant probability it just takes a constant number of rounds until $|\Delta_t| \geq c'\sqrt{n_t}$, and then we use that insight together with insights from Case 2 and a result about Markov chains to argue that within $O(\log n)$ rounds, $|\Delta_t| \geq c\sqrt{n_t \ln n_t}$ w.h.p. Before that, we need two technical lemmas.

We say that a random variable $Z$ *stochastically dominates* a random variable $Z'$, and write $Z \succeq Z'$, if $\Pr[Z \geq x] \geq \Pr[Z' \geq x]$ for any $x$. Recall that $\Delta_t = (Y_t - X_t)/2$, where $X_t$ is the number of 0s and $Y_t$ is the number of 1s. For simplicity we assume that $n_t$ is even so that $\Delta_t$ is an integer.

Lemma 5. *For any two imbalances $\Delta_t$ and $\Delta'_t$ with $\Delta_t \geq \Delta'_t \geq 0$ it holds that $\Delta_{t+1} \succeq \Delta'_{t+1}$.*

The main lemma of this section is the following:

Lemma 6. *For any $|\Delta_t| \geq 0$, $\Pr[|\Delta_{t+1}| \geq \sqrt{n_t/16}] \geq \alpha$ for some constant $\alpha > 0$, provided $n_t$ is large enough.*

To prove this lemma, we use the Paley-Zygmund inequality (Lemma 7) defined as follows:

Lemma 7 (Paley-Zygmund). *If $X \geq 0$ is a random variable with finite variance, then for any $0 \leq \epsilon \leq 1$,*

$$\Pr[X > \epsilon E[X]] \geq (1-\epsilon)^2 \frac{E[X]^2}{E[X^2]}$$

We now sketch the proof of Lemma 6 omitting some technical details (present in the full proof in the full paper [37]).

Proof Sketch. We only need to prove the lemma for $\Delta_t = 0$ because the general case follows from stochastic domination (see Lemma 5).

Since for $\Delta_t = 0$ every defined node $v$ in round $t+1$ has the same probability of having $x_v = 0$ or $x_v = 1$, $E[\Delta_{t+1}] = 0$. For any defined node $v$ in round $t+1$, let the binary random variable $Z_v$ be 1 if and only if $x_v$ is set to 0 in round $t+1$. In this case, given $N_{t+1}$,

$$\Delta_{t+1} = \frac{1}{2}\left(\left(n_{t+1} - \sum_{v \in N_{t+1}} Z_v\right) - \sum_{v \in N_{t+1}} Z_v\right) = n_{t+1}/2 - \sum_{v \in N_{t+1}} Z_v$$

From the definition of the variance it follows that

$$V[\Delta_{t+1} \mid N_{t+1}] = \sum_{v \in N_{t+1}} V[Z_v] + \sum_{v,w \in N_{t+1}, v \neq w} cov(Z_v, Z_w)$$

For any $v \in N_{t+1}$, $V[Z_v] = E[Z_v^2] - E[Z_v]^2$. Furthermore, $E[Z_v] = \Pr[Z_v = 1] = 1/2$ and $E[Z_v^2] = \Pr[Z_v = 1] = 1/2$ as well. Hence, $V[Z_v] = 1/2 - 1/4 = 1/4$. Moreover, $cov(Z_v, Z_w) = E[(Z_v - E[Z_v])(Z_w - E[Z_w])] = E[Z_v \cdot Z_w] - E[Z_v] \cdot E[Z_w]$.

Certainly,
$$\begin{aligned} E[Z_v \cdot Z_w] &= \Pr[Z_v = Z_w = 1] \\ &= \Pr[Z_v = 1] \cdot \Pr[Z_w = 1 \mid Z_v = 1] \\ &= \frac{1}{2} \Pr[Z_w = 1 \mid Z_v = 1] \end{aligned}$$

but obtaining a good estimate of $\Pr[Z_w = 1 \mid Z_v = 1]$ is difficult, so we first note that

$$\Pr[v \text{ sees } (0,0,1)] = \frac{1}{8} + \frac{1}{48n_t} \pm O\left(\frac{1}{n_t^2}\right), \text{ and}$$

$$\Pr[v \text{ sees } (0,0,0)] = \frac{1}{8} - \frac{1}{16n_t} \pm O\left(\frac{1}{n_t^2}\right).$$

Next, we estimate $\Pr[Z_w = 1]$ for the case that $v$ sees $(0,0,1)$ or $(0,0,0)$. This yields:

$$\Pr[Z_w = 1 \mid v \text{ sees } (0,0,1)] = \frac{1}{2} - \frac{1}{8n_t} \pm O\left(\frac{1}{n_t^2}\right), \text{ and}$$

$$\Pr[Z_w = 1 \mid v \text{ sees } (0,0,0)] = \frac{1}{2} - \frac{3}{8n_t} \pm O\left(\frac{1}{n_t^2}\right)$$

Hence, altogether,

$$\begin{aligned} E[Z_v \cdot Z_w] = 3 \cdot &\left(\frac{1}{8} + \frac{1}{48n_t}\right)\left(\frac{1}{2} - \frac{1}{8n_t}\right) \\ &+ \left(\frac{1}{8} - \frac{1}{16n_t}\right)\left(\frac{1}{2} - \frac{3}{8n_t}\right) \pm O\left(\frac{1}{n_t^2}\right) \\ =&\frac{1}{4} - \frac{3}{32n_t} \pm O\left(\frac{1}{n_t^2}\right) \end{aligned}$$

and therefore, $cov(Z_v, Z_w) = -\frac{3}{32n_t} \pm O\left(\frac{1}{n_t^2}\right)$.

Plugging this into the formula for the variance, and using the fact that w.h.p. $n_t \in [3n/4, n]$ and therefore, $n_{t+1}/n_t \in [3/4, 4/3]$, we get

$$\begin{aligned} V[\Delta_{t+1} \mid N_{t+1}] &= \frac{n_{t+1}}{4} - \frac{3n_{t+1}(n_{t+1} - 1)}{32n_t} \pm O\left(\frac{n_{t+1}^2}{n_t^2}\right) \\ &\geq \frac{n_{t+1}}{8} \pm O(1) \end{aligned}$$

Moreover, it follows from the def. of the variance that $V[\Delta_{t+1}] = E[\Delta_{t+1}^2] - E[\Delta_{t+1}]^2$ and since $E[\Delta_{t+1}] = 0$,

$$E[|\Delta_{t+1}|^2] = E[\Delta_{t+1}^2] \geq \frac{n_{t+1}}{8} \pm O(1)$$

Via tedious calculations, we also obtain the following upper bound on $E[|\Delta_{t+1}|^4]$:

$$E[|\Delta_{t+1}|^4] \leq \frac{1}{12} {n_{t+1}}^2 + \frac{5}{216} n_{t+1} + \frac{77}{5184} + \frac{371}{31104 \cdot n_{t+1}} + O\left(\frac{1}{n_{t+1}^2}\right)$$

As an intuition why $E[|\Delta_{t+1}|^4] = O(n_{t+1}^2)$ holds, note that if the $Z_v$'s are independent, then one can make use of the formulas for higher moments of binomial distributions (see, e.g., [26]) to show that $E[|\Delta_{t+1}|^4] = O(n_{t+1}^2)$. In addition to that, as indicated by the negative covariance, seeing a majority of 0s (resp. 1s) in some nodes implies seeing fewer 0s (resp. 1s) for subsequent nodes, so one expects higher moments in our case to be less than in the independent case. In fact, in the independent case, $E[|\Delta_{t+1}|^2] = n_{t+1}/4$.

Hence, it follows from the Payley-Zygmund inequality that $\Pr[|\Delta_{t+1}|^2 \geq \frac{n_{t+1}}{16}] \geq \alpha$ for some constant $\alpha > 0$, which completes the proof. □

Moreover, from the proof of Lemma 4 and the Chernoff bounds in Lemma 1 we get:

Lemma 8. *For any $\delta_t = \Omega(1/\sqrt{n_t})$, $\Pr[\delta_{t+1} \geq (9/8)\delta_t] \geq 1 - \exp\left(-\Theta(\delta_t^2 n_{t+1})\right)$.*

Now we can finish Case 3.

Lemma 9. *If at a round $t_0$ we have $|\Delta_{t_0}| < c\sqrt{n_{t_0} \ln n_{t_0}}$ for the value of $c$ needed by Lemma 4, then there is a round $t_1 = t_0 + O(\log n)$ with $|\Delta_{t_1}| \geq c\sqrt{n_t \ln n_t}$ w.h.p.*

**Deciding on a consensus value.** Note that although the $(k, \ell)$-majority algorithm converges to a common plurality value within $O(\log n)$ rounds, the nodes cannot determine whether an almost-everywhere consensus has already been reached. We address this by executing the **deciding $(k, \ell)$-majority algorithm** in which each node $u$ executes both the reset rule and the update rule of the original $(k, \ell)$-majority algorithm and, additionally, the following rule:

- **decision rule:** If there is some $y \in \{0, 1\}$ so that for the past $\alpha \ln n$ rounds, $x_u \in \{y, \perp\}$ and for at least half of them, $x_u = y$, then $u$ outputs $y$.

Here, $\alpha > 0$ is a constant determined in the proofs of the following two lemmas.

Lemma 10. *For any initial assignment of values to the nodes with no defined node and any $\epsilon \leq 1/16$, there is a constant $\beta > 0$ so that every node that is blocked in at most a fifth of $\beta \ln n$ rounds will output a value within these rounds, w.h.p.*

Note that a 1/16-bounded adversary can cause at most 1/3 of the nodes to be blocked more than 1/5 of the rounds, which implies that at least 2/3 of the nodes will produce an output w.h.p. Finally, we show that it cannot happen that two nodes output different values, so nodes eventually decide such that almost-everywhere consensus holds w.h.p.

Lemma 11. *There is a constant $\alpha > 0$ such that if a node $u$ outputs a value $y \in \{0, 1\}$ in the deciding $(k, \ell)$-majority algorithm, then no node ever outputs a value $z \neq y$ w.h.p.*

Combining Lemma 10 and Lemma 11 with Theorem 1, and observing that Cases 1 and 2 imply the plurality property we have shown the following result:

Theorem 2. *The $(k, \ell)$-majority algorithm together with the decision rule achieves binary almost-everywhere consensus (w.h.p.) in $O(\log n)$ rounds, against a late adversary who can block up to $\epsilon n$ nodes in each round, for $\epsilon < \frac{1}{16}$. Moreover, the decision value will satisfy the plurality property (w.h.p.).*

## 3 MULTI-VALUE CONSENSUS

We now describe an algorithm for the case where nodes start out with arbitrary input values. While the algorithm achieves the same runtime bound as the majority rule algorithm presented in Section 2, we point out that it does not guarantee the plurality property, due to its use of a maximum-rule for spreading a common value.

We first give a high-level overview and present the detailed pseudocode in Algorithm 1. Initially, each node $u$ has a local variable $x_u$ that is set to an input value chosen by the adversary from a fixed domain of size poly($n$). We say that a node is *active in the current round*, if it initiates communication with other nodes and call it *inactive* otherwise. In the first round, each node becomes active with probability $\Theta(\frac{\log n}{n})$ and every active node sends its input value to a set of $\Theta(\log n)$ nodes chosen uniformly at random. Only initially active nodes retain their input value; all other nodes (including the ones that are blocked) reset their value to a default value $\bot$, which is considered to be the minimum value.

From this point onward, the algorithm performs $\Theta(\log n)$ iterations of information spreading: We start an iteration by instructing nodes that have received messages to mark themselves as active. Then, every active node computes its new value as the maximum of the received values including its current value, sends its updated value to 2 nodes $v$ and $w$ chosen uniformly at random. In the next iteration, $v$ and $w$ in turn become active and participate in spreading their newly computed values. After $\Theta(\log n)$ iterations, all nodes decide on their current value.

To understand why the first round requires active nodes to communicate with $\Theta(\log n)$ nodes each, it is instructive to consider the "uniform" algorithm where active nodes always contact 2 peers. Since the adversary can block up to $\epsilon n$ nodes in each round, it has constant probability of blocking *all* nodes that currently hold the maximum value $x^*$, assuming it targets a randomly chosen subset of nodes during the first few rounds. If successful, the adversary can slowdown the spreading of value $x^*$ among the nodes in the network. The end result of this scenario is that a large constant fraction of the nodes never receive $x^*$ and thus end up deciding on some other value $x' < x^*$ instead—a violation of almost-everywhere agreement.

**Algorithm 1** Multi-value consensus against a late adversary

Every node $u$ initalizes $x_u$ with its input value and, with probability $\frac{c_1 \log n}{n}$, joins the *active* nodes; otherwise it marks itself *inactive*. // Note that $c_1, c_2, c_3 > 0$ are constants.
Each active node $u$ sends $x_u$ to a set of $\lceil c_2 \log n \rceil$ uniformly at random chosen nodes.
Every inactive or blocked node $v$ sets $x_v = \bot$; (we define $\bot \leq x$ for all values $x$).
**for** $t = 1, \ldots, \lceil c_3 \log n \rceil$ iterations **do**
  **for** every node $v$ **do**
    $v$ updates $x_v = \max(R \cup \{x_v\})$, where $R$ is the set of newly received values.
    **if** $x_v \neq \bot$ **then** $v$ joins *active* nodes.
    **if** $t < c_3 \log n$ and $v$ is active **then**
      Node $v$ sends $x_v$ to 2 unif. at random chosen nodes.
Every node $u$ decides on $x_u$ and terminates.

THEOREM 3. *Consider the late adversary that can block up to $\epsilon n$ nodes in each round, for $\epsilon \leq \frac{1}{10}$, and suppose that nodes start with input values chosen by the adversary. Then, for any positive constant $\delta < 1$, there is an algorithm that achieves consensus among $(1 - \frac{\epsilon}{\delta})n$ nodes in $O(\log n)$ rounds with high probability, while sending $O(n \log n)$ messages in total.*

We first recall some concentration bounds.

DEFINITION 3 (MARTINGALE [32]). *A sequence of random variables $Z_0, Z_1, \ldots$ is a martingale with respect to the sequence $X_0, X_1, \ldots$ if, for all $t \geq 0$, the following conditions hold:*

*(1) $Z_t$ is a function of $X_0, \ldots, X_t$.*
*(2) $E[Z_t] < \infty$.*
*(3) $E[Z_{t+1} \mid X_0, \ldots, X_t] = Z_t$.*

DEFINITION 4 (LIPSCHITZ CONDITION [32]). *Let $f(X_1, \ldots, X_n)$ be a function to the reals. We say that $f$ satisfies the* Lipschitz condition *with bound $c$ if, for any set of values $x_1, \ldots, x_n$ and $y_i$,*

$$|f(x_1, \ldots, x_{i-1}, x_i, x_{i+1}, \ldots, x_n) - f(x_1, \ldots, x_{i-1}, y_i, x_{i+i}, \ldots, x_n)| \leq c.$$

THEOREM 4 (AZUMA-HOEFFDING INEQUALITY [32]). *Let $X_0, \ldots,$ be a martingale sequence such that for each $k$, $|X_k - X_{k-1}| \leq c_k$. Then, for all $t \geq 0$ and all $\lambda > 0$,*

$$Pr[|X_t - X_0| \geq \lambda] \leq 2 \exp\left(-\frac{\lambda^2}{2\sum_{k=1}^{t} c_k^2}\right).$$

**Proof of Theorem 3.** Since the late adversary can block a constant fraction of nodes, we cannot rely on existing results on information spreading to show almost-everywhere agreement. For round $t$, let $B_t$ be the set of blocked nodes and define $A$ to be the set of active nodes in round 1. Let $x^*$ be the maximum value of all input values of nodes in $A \setminus B_1$ and let $S_0 \subseteq A \setminus B_1$ be the set of non-blocked active nodes[3] starting with $x^*$.

For rounds $t \geq 1$, we define $S_t$ to be the set of nodes whose value is $x^*$ at the end of round $t$ and define $\sigma_t = |S_t|$. The following two lemmas show that $\sigma_t$ grows by a constant factor until it reaches a size of $\Omega(n)$.

LEMMA 12. *$\sigma_1 \geq \Omega(\log n)$.*

LEMMA 13. *Let $r = r(t) = \frac{\sigma_{t-1}}{n}$ and let $\rho < 1$ be a positive constant determined in the proof. There is a constant $\alpha > 0$ such that, for any $t$ where $r < \rho$, we have $\sigma_t \geq \max\{(1+\alpha)\sigma_{t-1}, \Theta(\log n)\}$.*

PROOF. We proceed by induction over $t$. To simplify our analysis, we assume that after having sent it to 2 randomly chosen peers, active nodes "forget" their current value and adopt value $\bot$. Clearly, this assumption can only worsen the runtime of the algorithm. In other words, $\sigma_t$ only accounts for nodes that have received a message with $x^*$ in round $t$.

The base case $t = 1$ follows from Lemma 12. Now consider any round $t > 1$. By the inductive hypothesis, $S_{t-1}$ (i.e. the set of nodes currently holding $x^*$) contains at least $\max\{(1+\alpha)\sigma_{t-2}, \Theta(\log n)\}$ nodes unknown to the adversary. Let $U \subseteq S_{t-1}$ be the subset of non-blocked nodes in round $t$ that hold $x^*$ and let

$$\beta = \tfrac{7}{8}(1 - \epsilon). \tag{1}$$

[3] Recall that the nodes that the adversary blocks are affected *after* they have performed their local computation.

Since $\sigma_{t-1} = |S_{t-1}| \geq c_1 \log n$ for a sufficiently large constant $c_1 > 0$ (see Lemma 12), we can apply a standard Chernoff bound to show that $|U| \geq \beta \cdot \sigma_{t-1}$ with high probability. Let $m = 2|U|$ denote the number of messages sent by nodes in $U$. Since $\epsilon < \frac{1}{2}$, the event $M$, which we define as

$$m \geq (1+\beta)\sigma_{t-1}, \tag{2}$$

happens with high probability.

For the purpose of our analysis, we consider each of the $m$ messages as a *ball* and the possible destinations of these messages as *bins*. Let $X_i$ be the indicator random variable that the $i$-th bin is hit by at least 1 ball. From (2) and the fact that $r = \frac{\sigma_{t-1}}{n}$, we get

$$\Pr[X_i = 1 \mid M] = 1 - \left(1 - \tfrac{1}{n}\right)^m \geq 1 - e^{-(1+\beta)r}. \tag{3}$$

Consider the functions $f(r) = 1 - e^{-(1+\beta)r}$ and $g(r) = \left(1 + \frac{\beta}{10}\right) r$, and their respective derivatives $f'(r) = (1+\beta)e^{-(1+\beta)r}$ and $g'(r) = 1 + \frac{\beta}{10}$. Let

$$\rho = \log\left(\frac{1+\beta}{1+\beta/10}\right) / (1+\beta) > \tfrac{1}{5} \geq 2\epsilon, \tag{4}$$

where we have used the assumption that $\epsilon \leq \frac{1}{10}$ and (1). Since $f(0) = g(0)$ and $f'(r) > g'(r)$ for all $r \in [0, \rho]$, we know that $f$ is bounded from below by $g$. It follows from (3) that $\Pr[X_i = 1 \mid M] \geq \left(1 + \frac{\beta}{10}\right) r$. By definition, $\sigma_t = \sum_{i=1}^n X_i$, hence

$$E[\sigma_t \mid M] \geq \left(1 + \tfrac{\beta}{10}\right) \sigma_{t-1}. \tag{5}$$

As the random variables $X_i$ are not independent, we cannot apply a simple Chernoff Bound argument to obtain a high concentration bound. Instead, we will set up a martingale and use the method of bounded differences (cf. Chap 12 in [32]). Let $Y_i$ be the bin chosen by the $i$-th ball and let $Z = h(Y_1, \ldots, Y_n)$ be the number of nonempty bins. For $1 \leq i \leq n$, we define $Z_i = E[h(Y_1, \ldots, Y_n) \mid Y_1, \ldots, Y_i, M]$, and let $Z_0 = E[h(Y_1, \ldots, Y_n) \mid M]$. To see that the sequence $Z_0, Z_1, \ldots, Z_n$ is a martingale (cf. Def. 3), note that, by definition of $Z_i$, we have

$$\begin{aligned} &E[Z_i \mid Y_1, \ldots, Y_{i-1}, M] \\ &\quad = E[\,E[Z \mid Y_1, \ldots, Y_i, M] \mid Y_1, \ldots, Y_{i-1}, M] \\ &\quad = E[Z \mid Y_1, \ldots, Y_{i-1}, M] = Z_{i-1}. \end{aligned}$$

As changing the destination of any ball can affect the number of nonempty bins by at most 1, we know that the function $h$ satisfies the Lipschitz condition (see Def. 4) with bound 1. Thus we can apply the Azuma-Hoeffding inequality (see Theorem 4) with parameter $\lambda = \sqrt{c'\, \sigma_{t-1} \log n}$, for a sufficiently large constant $c' > 0$, to derive that

$$\begin{aligned} \Pr\left[\sigma_t \leq \left(1 + \tfrac{\beta}{20}\right) \sigma_{t-1} \mid M\right] &\leq \Pr\left[\sigma_t \leq \left(1 + \tfrac{\beta}{10}\right) \sigma_{t-1} - \lambda \mid M\right] \\ &\leq \Pr\left[\sigma_t \leq E[\sigma_t \mid M] - \lambda \mid M\right] \\ &\qquad \text{(by (5))} \\ &\leq 2\exp\left(-\frac{c'\, \sigma_{t-1} \log n}{2m}\right), \\ &\qquad \text{(by Theorem 4)} \end{aligned}$$

which is $n^{-\Omega(1)}$ because of (2). Recalling that event $M$ happens w.h.p., we can remove the conditioning and conclude that

$$\begin{aligned} \Pr\left[\sigma_t \geq \left(1 + \tfrac{\beta}{20}\right) \sigma_{t-1}\right] &\geq \Pr\left[\sigma_t \geq \left(1 + \tfrac{\beta}{20}\right) \sigma_{t-1} \mid M\right] \cdot \Pr[M] \\ &\geq 1 - n^{-\Omega(1)}. \end{aligned}$$

□

Consider iterations $t = 1, \ldots, \Theta(\log n)$ of the algorithm. As long as $r \leq \rho$, Lemma 13 tells us that the current set of nodes that are adopting $x^*$ keeps growing by a constant factor with high probability in each iteration. We can guarantee that this happens (w.h.p.) by taking a union bound over the $\Theta(\log n)$ iterations of the algorithm until $r > \rho$. In the following lemma, we handle the "last mile" of spreading value $x^*$ to (almost) all of the remaining $< (1-\rho)n$ nodes.

Lemma 14. *Let $t_1$ be a round where $r = \frac{\sigma_{t_1}}{n} > \rho$. Then, after additional $\Theta(\log n)$ iterations of the algorithm, all except at most $(1 - \frac{\epsilon}{\delta})n$ nodes adopt value $x^*$ with high probability, where $\delta$ is any constant $< 1$. This holds even if the adversary is strongly adaptive.*

From Lemma 14 it follows that value $x^*$ reaches all but a small constant fraction of the nodes. Since $x^*$ is the maximum value in the network after round 1 (cf. Line 3), the algorithm satisfies almost-everywhere agreement and the validity property as claimed, thus completing the proof of Theorem 3.

## 4 A TIME LOWER BOUND FOR AGREEMENT WITH LIMITED COMMUNICATION

We now study the impact of limited communication on the ability of nodes to solve almost everywhere consensus. In particular, we use the time-tested method of indistinguishable executions to provide a trade-off between the amount of communication available and the time required for termination correctly. We point out that these results hold even if the adversary does not block any nodes. Consequently, this means that increasing the lateness of the adversary cannot improve the time complexity bounds of solving almost-everywhere consensus.

Theorem 5. *Suppose that each node can send a message to up to $d$ nodes in each round. There is no randomized Monte Carlo algorithm that achieves almost-everywhere consensus with probability at least $1 - O(\frac{1}{n})$ among $> (1-\epsilon')n$ nodes and terminates in $o(\log_d n)$ rounds, where $0 < \epsilon' < \frac{1}{2}$. This holds even if no nodes are blocked by the adversary and each node has a unique identifier known to all other nodes.*

Before proving Theorem 5, we consider its impact on the complexity bounds of our algorithms. Since the majority-rule algorithm presented in Section 2 has $d = O(1)$, its time complexity bound is optimal. For the maximum propagation algorithm in Section 3 we have $d = O(\log n)$, thus applying Theorem 5 tells us that the bound is optimal up to a factor of $O(\log\log n)$.

The overall structure of our proof follows the classical results of [17, 19] and a more recent generalization of these techniques to the asynchronous setting presented in [6], with the important difference that here we consider almost everywhere agreement instead of consensus. We first introduce some technical machinery.

We recall that an *execution* of an algorithm is a sequence of rounds that is fully determined by the input value assignment of the nodes and $n$ (infinite) bit strings representing the nodes' private sources of randomness. We use the notation $\alpha \overset{P}{\sim} \alpha'$ to say that executions $\alpha$ and $\alpha'$ are *indistinguishable for a set of nodes* $P$, which means that each $u \in P$ goes through the same sequence of local state transitions in both executions. Intuitively speaking, this means that node $u$ cannot tell the difference between $\alpha$ and $\alpha'$. A necessary and sufficient condition for this is that $u$ observes the same sequence of random bits and messages in both executions, and starts with the same input value. We define an *indistinguishability chain* as a sequence of executions $(\alpha_1, \alpha_2, \dots)$, where there are nonempty sets of nodes $P_1, P_2, \dots$ such that, for all $i$, it holds that $\alpha_i \overset{P_i}{\sim} \alpha_{i+1}$. We refer the reader to Chapter 5 in [7] for a more complete definition.

We are now ready to prove Theorem 5. For the sake of a contradiction, suppose that there is an algorithm $\mathcal{A}$ that terminates in $t = o(\log_d n)$ rounds and achieves almost-everywhere consensus among all except $< \epsilon' n$ nodes with high probability. For parameter

$$k = \frac{(1-\epsilon')n}{d^t}, \tag{6}$$

consider a partitioning of the set $V$ of $n$ nodes into $\{S_1, \dots, S_{\lceil n/k \rceil}\}$ such that $|S_i| \leq k$. For $0 \leq i \leq n/k$, we consider an execution $\alpha_i$ and assign the nodes in $\bigcup_{j=1}^{i} S_j$ input value 1, where we follow the convention that $\bigcup_{j=1}^{0} S_j = \emptyset$. All other nodes start with input value 0 in $\alpha$. This ensures that all nodes start with 0 in $\alpha_0$ whereas all nodes start with 1 in $\alpha_{\lceil n/k \rceil}$. We will now show that $(\alpha_0, \dots, \alpha_{\lceil n/k \rceil})$ forms an indistinguishability chain with respect to large sets of nodes.

Lemma 15. *Suppose that each node is equipped with the same random bits in every $\alpha_i$. For all $0 \leq i \leq \lceil n/k \rceil$, there exists a set $P_i$ of size $\geq \epsilon' n$, such that $\alpha_i \overset{P_i}{\sim} \alpha_{i+1}$ during the first $t = o(\log_d n)$ rounds of the algorithm.*

Proof. Consider any $i$. We observe that the only difference between the initial configurations of $\alpha_i$ and $\alpha_{i+1}$ are the input values for nodes in $S_{i+1}$, and this distinction is known to $|S_{i+1}| \leq k$ distinct nodes initially. Since each node can communicate with at most $d$ other nodes in each round, (6) tells us that the total number of nodes that can be causally influenced (cf. [30]) by any node in $S_{i+1}$ is at most $kd^t \leq (1-\epsilon')n$ during the first $t$ rounds of the algorithm. Thus, there exists a set $P_i$ of at least $\epsilon' n$ nodes for which $\alpha_i$ and $\alpha_{i+1}$ are indistinguishable. □

In the remainder of the proof we use Lemma 15 and adapt the arguments of [6]. Let $F$ be the event that algorithm $\mathcal{A}$ fails by violating almost-everywhere agreement in at least one $\alpha_i$ in the chain. Note that this is the case when two sets of nodes of size $\geq \epsilon' n$ decide on conflicting values in $\alpha_i$.

A crucial consequence of Lemma 15 is that, for each pair $\alpha_i$ and $\alpha_{i+1}$, there is a large set of $\geq \epsilon' n$ nodes that decide on the same value in both executions. By the validity property, we know that the decision is 0 in $\alpha_0$ and 1 in $\alpha_{\lceil n/k \rceil}$. Therefore, considering that $\mathcal{A}$ is a Monte Carlo algorithm that is guaranteed to terminate within $t$ rounds, we have $\Pr[F] = 1$.

Recall that we have assumed in contradiction that algorithm $\mathcal{A}$ succeeds with probability at least $1 - O(\frac{1}{n})$ and hence, almost-everywhere agreement can be violated with probability $O(\frac{1}{n})$ in any individual execution. By taking a union bound over the $\lceil \frac{n}{k} \rceil + 1$ executions in the chain, we get

$$1 = \Pr[F] \leq \left(\left\lceil \frac{n}{k} \right\rceil + 1\right) O\left(\frac{1}{n}\right) = O\left(\frac{d^t}{(1-\epsilon')n}\right) + O\left(\frac{1}{n}\right) = o(1),$$

where we have used the bound (6) and where the final equality follows from the premise $t = o(\log_d n)$. This is a contradiction and completes the proof of Theorem 5.

## 5 EXPERIMENTAL EVALUATION

We have performed simulations of the $(k, \ell)$-majority algorithm for various network sizes and adversarial thresholds. As elaborated in more detail below, these results suggest that the algorithm reaches almost-everywhere agreement within $\leq 2\log(n)$ rounds (on average) while being resilient against up to $n/15$ adversarial attacks per round. Moreover, by just increasing the communication degree of each node from 6 to 12, i.e., executing the $(12, 3)$-majority algorithm, it turns out that agreement is achievable as long as the adversary blocks no more than $n/5$ nodes per round.

A detailed description of our setup can be found in the full version [37]. To briefly mention its most important aspects, the late adversary is, like each simulated node, modeled as a separately executing process who is informed by all participating nodes regarding their value at the start of the round, and then, at the end of the round, decides which nodes to block in the next round based on this information, trying to balance the distribution of 0s and 1s. The execution starts in a balanced state w.r.t. the input values and is terminated if either (1) the difference between the number of nodes supporting 0 and the number of nodes supporting 1 is $\geq (\frac{2}{3} - \epsilon)n$, or (2) at least $n/2$ nodes currently hold the reset value $\perp$. Case (1) represents reaching almost-everywhere agreement, while we assume that the adversary has succeeded if Case (2) holds and consider the trial as failed.

For each parameter setting, we performed 1000 independent runs of the $(k, \ell)$-majority algorithm. The first set of results concern the $(6, 3)$-majority algorithm and show that the algorithm succeeded to achieve almost-everywhere agreement in 100% of the trials as long as $\epsilon \leq 1/15$, i.e., when the adversary can block at most $n/15$ nodes in each round. The average number of rounds until termination is within $2\log(n)$ rounds, whereas the 95th percentile is bounded by $3\log(n)$. For $\epsilon \geq 1/14$, on the other hand, the success rate of the algorithm drops to approximately 80% and the 95th percentiles increase significantly. Since the algorithm fails when too many nodes hold the reset value $\perp$, which either occurs due to being blocked by the adversary or when a node does not receive sufficiently many messages from other nodes, we also investigated the impact of increasing the number of recipients that each node contacts to disseminate its value from 6 to 12. We observed that the $(12, 3)$-majority algorithm has a significantly higher resilience and achieved a.e. agreement in all trials for $\epsilon \leq 1/5$. It may be tempting to further increase the communication by instructing nodes to contact 24 peers in each round, however, in our simulations this did not provide any improvements regarding the resilience threshold compared to the (12, 3)-majority algorithm. The detailed simulation results can be found in the full version [37].

## 6 CONCLUSION AND FUTURE WORK

We have initiated the study of reaching agreement in the late adversarial model, where the adversary has a view that is outdated by 1 round. Our results raise the question if increasing the "lateness" of the adversary to a larger number of rounds results in improvement of the time complexity of our algorithms. Our lower bound gives a negative answer to this question. It would be interesting to investigate the impact of lateness on the complexity of distributed algorithms also for other problems, since it is realistic to assume that typically an adversary will not have the most up-to-date information about a distributed system.

## REFERENCES


[1] Marcos Kawazoe Aguilera, Wei Chen, and Sam Toueg. 2000. Failure detection and consensus in the crash-recovery model. *Distributed computing* 13, 2 (2000), 99–125.

[2] Mohamad Ahmadi, Abdolhamid Ghodselahi, Fabian Kuhn, and Anisur Rahaman Molla. 2015. The Cost of Global Broadcast in Dynamic Radio Networks. In *19th International Conference on Principles of Distributed Systems, OPODIS 2015, December 14-17, 2015, Rennes, France.* 7:1–7:17. DOI: http://dx.doi.org/10.4230/LIPIcs.OPODIS.2015.7

[3] Mohamad Ahmadi and Fabian Kuhn. 2016. Multi-message Broadcast in Dynamic Radio Networks. In *Algorithms for Sensor Systems - 12th International Symposium on Algorithms and Experiments for Wireless Sensor Networks, ALGOSENSORS 2016, Aarhus, Denmark, August 25-26, 2016, Revised Selected Papers.* 1–15. DOI: http://dx.doi.org/10.1007/978-3-319-53058-1_1

[4] Dana Angluin, James Aspnes, and David Eisenstat. 2007. A Simple Population Protocol for Fast Robust Approximate Majority. In *Proceedings of the 21st International Conference on Distributed Computing (DISC'07).* Springer-Verlag, Berlin, Heidelberg, 20–32. http://dl.acm.org/citation.cfm?id=2393794.2393801

[5] James Aspnes. 2003. Randomized protocols for asynchronous consensus. *Distributed Computing* 16, 2-3 (2003), 165–175.

[6] Hagit Attiya and Keren Censor-Hillel. 2010. Lower Bounds for Randomized Consensus under a Weak Adversary. *SIAM J. Comput.* 39, 8 (2010), 3885–3904. DOI: http://dx.doi.org/10.1137/090751906

[7] Hagit Attiya and Jennifer Welch. 2004. *Distributed Computing: Fundamentals, Simulations and Advanced Topics (2nd ed.).* John Wiley & Sons, Inc.

[8] John Augustine, Gopal Pandurangan, and Peter Robinson. 2013. Fast Byzantine agreement in dynamic networks. In *ACM Symposium on Principles of Distributed Computing, PODC '13, Montreal, QC, Canada, July 22-24, 2013.* 74–83. DOI: http://dx.doi.org/10.1145/2484239.2484275

[9] John Augustine, Gopal Pandurangan, Peter Robinson, and Eli Upfal. 2015. Distributed agreement in dynamic peer-to-peer networks. *J. Comput. Syst. Sci.* 81, 7 (2015), 1088–1109. DOI: http://dx.doi.org/10.1016/j.jcss.2014.10.005

[10] Baruch Awerbuch and Christian Scheideler. 2007. A Denial-of-Service Resistant DHT. In *Proc. of the 21st Intl. Symp. on Distributed Computing (DISC).* 33–47.

[11] Ziv Bar-Joseph and Michael Ben-Or. 1998. A tight lower bound for randomized synchronous consensus. In *Proceedings of the seventeenth annual ACM symposium on Principles of distributed computing.* ACM, 193–199.

[12] L. Becchetti, A. Clementi, E. Natale, F. Pasquale, and R. Silvestri. 2015. Plurality Consensus in the Gossip Model. In *Proceedings of the Twenty-sixth Annual ACM-SIAM Symposium on Discrete Algorithms (SODA '15).* Society for Industrial and Applied Mathematics, Philadelphia, PA, USA, 371–390. http://dl.acm.org/citation.cfm?id=2722129.2722156

[13] Luca Becchetti, Andrea Clementi, Emanuele Natale, Francesco Pasquale, Riccardo Silvestri, and Luca Trevisan. 2014. Simple Dynamics for Plurality Consensus. In *Proceedings of the 26th ACM Symposium on Parallelism in Algorithms and Architectures (SPAA '14).* ACM, New York, NY, USA, 247–256. DOI: http://dx.doi.org/10.1145/2612669.2612677

[14] L. Becchetti, A. Clementi, E. Natale, F. Pasquale, and L. Trevisan. 2016. Stabilizing Consensus with Many Opinions. In *Proceedings of the Twenty-seventh Annual ACM-SIAM Symposium on Discrete Algorithms (SODA '16).* Society for Industrial and Applied Mathematics, Philadelphia, PA, USA, 620–635. http://dl.acm.org/citation.cfm?id=2884435.2884481

[15] Michael Ben-Or. 1983. Another advantage of free choice (extended abstract): Completely asynchronous agreement protocols. In *Proceedings of the second annual ACM symposium on Principles of distributed computing.* ACM, 27–30.

[16] Petra Berenbrink, Tom Friedetzky, George Giakkoupis, and Peter Kling. 2016. Efficient Plurality Consensus, Or: the Benefits of Cleaning up from Time to Time. In *43rd International Colloquium on Automata, Languages, and Programming (ICALP 2016) (Leibniz International Proceedings in Informatics (LIPIcs)),* Vol. 55. Schloss Dagstuhl–Leibniz-Zentrum fuer Informatik, Dagstuhl, Germany, 136:1–136:14. DOI: http://dx.doi.org/10.4230/LIPIcs.ICALP.2016.136

[17] Benny Chor, Michael Merritt, and David B. Shmoys. 1989. Simple constant-time consensus protocols in realistic failure models. *J. ACM* 36, 3 (1989), 591–614. DOI: http://dx.doi.org/10.1145/65950.65956

[18] Benjamin Doerr, Leslie Ann Goldberg, Lorenz Minder, Thomas Sauerwald, and Christian Scheideler. 2011. Stabilizing consensus with the power of two choices. In *SPAA 2011: Proceedings of the 23rd Annual ACM Symposium on Parallelism in Algorithms and Architectures, San Jose, CA, USA, June 4-6, 2011.* 149–158. DOI: http://dx.doi.org/10.1145/1989493.1989516

[19] Danny Dolev and H. Raymond Strong. 1983. Authenticated Algorithms for Byzantine Agreement. *SIAM J. Comput.* 12, 4 (1983), 656–666. DOI: http://dx.doi.org/10.1137/0212045

[20] Maximilian Drees, Robert Gmyr, and Christian Scheideler. 2016. Churn- and DoS-resistant Overlay Networks Based on Network Reconfiguration. In *Proceedings of the 28th ACM Symposium on Parallelism in Algorithms and Architectures, SPAA 2016, Asilomar State Beach/Pacific Grove, CA, USA, July 11-13, 2016.* 417–427. DOI: http://dx.doi.org/10.1145/2935764.2935783

[21] Cynthia Dwork, David Peleg, Nicholas Pippenger, and Eli Upfal. 1988. Fault tolerance in networks of bounded degree. *SIAM J. Comput.* 17, 5 (1988), 975–988.

[22] Michael J Fischer, Nancy A Lynch, and Michael Merritt. 1986. Easy impossibility proofs for distributed consensus problems. *Distributed Computing* 1, 1 (1986), 26–39.

[23] Michael J. Fischer, Nancy A. Lynch, and M. S. Paterson. 1985. Impossibility of Distributed Consensus with one Faulty Process. *J. ACM* 32, 2 (April 1985), 374–382.

[24] Mohsen Ghaffari and Merav Parter. 2016. A Polylogarithmic Gossip Algorithm for Plurality Consensus. In *Proceedings of the 2016 ACM Symposium on Principles of Distributed Computing (PODC '16).* ACM, New York, NY, USA, 117–126. DOI: http://dx.doi.org/10.1145/2933057.2933097

[25] Seth Gilbert and Dariusz R. Kowalski. 2010. Distributed Agreement with Optimal Communication Complexity. In *Proceedings of the Twenty-First Annual ACM-SIAM Symposium on Discrete Algorithms, SODA 2010, Austin, Texas, USA, January 17-19, 2010.* 965–977. DOI: http://dx.doi.org/10.1137/1.9781611973075.78

[26] N. L. Johnson and S. Kotz. 1977. *Urn Models and Their Application.* John Wiley & Sons, New York.

[27] Valerie King and Jared Saia. 2011. Breaking the $O(n^2)$ bit barrier: Scalable byzantine agreement with an adaptive adversary. *J. ACM* 58, 4 (2011), 18:1–18:24. DOI: http://dx.doi.org/10.1145/1989727.1989732

[28] Valerie King, Jared Saia, Vishal Sanwalani, and Erik Vee. 2006. Towards secure and scalable computation in peer-to-peer networks. In *Foundations of Computer Science, 2006. FOCS'06. 47th Annual IEEE Symposium on.* IEEE, 87–98.

[29] Marek Klonowski, Dariusz R. Kowalski, and Jaroslaw Mirek. 2017. Ordered and Delayed Adversaries and How to Work against Them on Shared Channel. *CoRR* abs/1706.08366 (2017). http://arxiv.org/abs/1706.08366

[30] L Lamport and Clocks Time. 1978. the Ordering of Events in a Distributed System, Comms. (1978).

[31] Nancy Lynch. 1996. *Distributed Algorithms.* Morgan Kaufman Publishers, Inc., San Francisco, USA.

[32] M. Mitzenmacher and E. Upfal. 2004. *Probability and Computing: Randomized Algorithms and Probabilistic Analysis.* Cambridge University Press.

[33] Achour Mostéfaoui, Hamouma Moumen, and Michel Raynal. 2015. Signature-Free Asynchronous Binary Byzantine Consensus with t < n/3, $O(n^2)$ Messages, and O(1) Expected Time. *J. ACM* 62, 4 (2015), 31:1–31:21. DOI: http://dx.doi.org/10.1145/2785953

[34] Satoshi Nakamoto. 2008. Bitcoin: A peer-to-peer electronic cash system. (2008).

[35] Calvin C. Newport. 2014. Consensus with an abstract MAC layer. In *ACM Symposium on Principles of Distributed Computing, PODC '14, Paris, France, July 15-18, 2014.* 66–75. DOI: http://dx.doi.org/10.1145/2611462.2611479

[36] Michael O Rabin. 1983. Randomized byzantine generals. In *Foundations of Computer Science, 1983., 24th Annual Symposium on.* IEEE, 403–409.

[37] Peter Robinson, Christian Scheideler, and Alexander Setzer. 2018. Breaking the $\tilde{\Omega}(\sqrt{n})$ Barrier: Fast Consensus under a Late Adversary (full version). *ArXiv e-prints* (2018). arXiv:cs.DC/1805.00774 https://arxiv.org/abs/1805.00774

[38] C. Scheideler. 2000. *Probabilistic Methods for Coordination Problems.* HNI-Verlagsschriftenreihe 78, University of Paderborn.

[39] J. Schmidt, A. Siegel, and A. Srinivasan. 1995. Chernoff-Hoeffding bounds for applications with limited independence. *SIAM Journal on Discrete Mathematics* 8, 2 (1995), 223–250.

[40] Eli Upfal. 1992. Tolerating linear number of faults in networks of bounded degree. In *Proceedings of the eleventh annual ACM symposium on Principles of distributed computing.* ACM, 83–89.

# Intense Competition can Drive Selfish Explorers to Optimize Coverage*

Simon Collet
IRIF, CNRS and University Paris Diderot
Paris, France
simon.collet@irif.fr

Amos Korman
IRIF, CNRS and University Paris Diderot
Paris, France
amos.korman@irif.fr

## ABSTRACT

We consider a game-theoretic setting in which selfish individuals compete over resources of varying quality. The motivating example is a group of animals that disperse over patches of food of different abundances. In such scenarios, individuals are biased towards selecting the higher quality patches, while, at the same time, aiming to avoid costly collisions or overlaps. Our goal is to investigate the impact of collision costs on the parallel coverage of resources by the whole group.

Consider $M$ *sites*, where a site $x$ has *value* $f(x)$. We think of $f(x)$ as the reward associated with site $x$, and assume that if a single individual visits $x$ exclusively, it receives this exact reward. Typically, we assume that if $\ell > 1$ individuals visit $x$ then each receives at most $f(x)/\ell$. In particular, when competition costs are high, each individual might receive an amount strictly less than $f(x)/\ell$, which could even be negative. Conversely, modeling cooperation at a site, we also consider cases where each one gets more than $f(x)/\ell$. There are $k$ identical *players* that compete over the rewards. They independently act in parallel, in a one-shot scenario, each specifying a single site to visit, without knowing which sites are explored by others. The group performance is evaluated by the expected *coverage*, defined as the sum of $f(x)$ over all sites that are explored by at least one player. Since we assume that players cannot coordinate before choosing their site we focus on symmetric strategies.

The main takeaway message of this paper is that the optimal symmetric coverage is expected to emerge when collision costs are relatively high, so that the following "Judgment of Solomon" type of rule holds: If a single player explores a site $x$ then it gains its full reward $f(x)$, but if several players explore it, then neither one receives any reward. Under this policy, it turns out that there exists a unique symmetric Nash Equilibrium strategy, which is, in fact, evolutionary stable. Moreover, this strategy yields the best possible coverage among all symmetric strategies. Viewing the coverage measure as the social welfare, this policy thus enjoys a *(Symmetric) Price of Anarchy* of precisely 1, whereas, in fact, any other congestion policy has a price strictly greater than 1.

Our model falls within the scope of mechanism design, and more precisely in the area of incentivizing exploration. It finds relevance in evolutionary ecology, and further connects to studies on Bayesian parallel search algorithms.

## CCS CONCEPTS

• **Applied computing → Economics**; *Systems biology*;

## KEYWORDS

Algorithmic Game Theory, Mechanism Design, Ideal Free Distribution, Evolutionary Game Theory, Incentivizing Exploration, Congestion Games, Symmetric Strategies, Distributed Computing

**ACM Reference Format:**
Simon Collet and Amos Korman. 2018. Intense Competition can Drive Selfish Explorers to Optimize Coverage. In *SPAA '18: 30th ACM Symposium on Parallelism in Algorithms and Architectures, July 16–18, 2018, Vienna, Austria.* ACM, New York, NY, USA, 10 pages. https://doi.org/10.1145/3210377.3210405

## 1 INTRODUCTION

Studying the way humans and other animals distribute themselves in their environment is a cornerstone of ecology and the social sciences [4, 17, 19, 21]. In many of these contexts, dispersal is governed by two contradicting forces. On the one hand, individuals are biased towards selecting the higher quality patches, and, on the other hand, they aim to avoid costly collisions or overlaps, which can significantly deteriorate the value of a patch [16, 22, 44]. In nature, collision costs can be caused by various factors, including aggressive behavior, or merely due to sharing the patch equally between colliding individuals (a.k.a., scramble competition [32]). The purpose of this paper is to investigate the impact of collision costs on the overall coverage of resources by the whole group.

Understanding the impact of collisions on the overall parallel coverage can also have implications to the way centralized entities incentive individuals in human organizations. For example, research foundations are often interested in promoting specific research topics, and offer grants to attract researchers to such topics. The question of how to properly define a grant policy that is expected to yield a desirable distribution of researchers can have significant implication on the scientific community [23].

This paper proposes a framework to study the impact of collision on the group performances through an *algorithmic mechanism design* approach. We focus on a relatively simple scenario, which already provides interesting, and perhaps surprising, insights. See Section 5.1 for suggested generalizations left for future work.

*This work has received funding from the European Research Council (ERC) under the European Union's Horizon 2020 research and innovation programme (grant agreement No 648032).


*SPAA '18, July 16–18, 2018, Vienna, Austria*

ACM ISBN 978-1-4503-5799-9/18/07...$15.00
https://doi.org/10.1145/3210377.3210405

## 1.1 The Dispersal Game

Think about the following imaginary scenario. A group of individuals are searching for resources in some space. Eventually, they gather all resources found for the benefit of the public, and hence the group performances is defined as the sum of the resources values. In order to avoid the free-rider problem, the group incentivizes individuals by granting those who find more resource with higher social status. When an individual exclusively finds a resource of value $f$, a simple mechanism is to let its social status be proportional to $f$. However, how should the group define the social status of each of $\ell$ individuals in case they all found a resource simultaneously?

Formally, we have $M$ *sites* indexed by $x \in [1, M]$. Each site $x$ has some *importance value* $f(x)$, and we assume without loss of generality that sites are ordered such that lower index sites have higher values, i.e., $f(x) \geq f(x+1)$ for each $x < M$.

We have $k$ players that act a one-shot scenario, each specifying a cite $x$ to visit. Crucially, they cannot coordinate, and each player must commit to a site $x$, without knowing which sites are selected by other players [14]. Moreover, we assume that players cannot change their mind after committing. Formally, each player specifies an index $x$ according to some law, called *strategy*. This is simply a probability distribution, indicating, for each $x$, the probability $p(x)$ to explore $x$. A *strategy profile* is a vector of $k$ strategies, one for each player. It is called *symmetric* when all players play the same strategy. For short, we shall use the term *symmetric strategy* to refer to the strategy being played in the case of a symmetric strategy profile.

The group performance is evaluated by the *weighted coverage*, defined as the sum of the values $f(x)$ over visited sites $x$. With the lack of coordination between users, the most the group can hope for is the best achievable coverage among all symmetric strategies, that is, when assuming that all players play the same strategy. Formally, the *coverage* of a strategy $p$ is defined as:

$$\mathsf{Cover}(p) = \sum_{x=1}^{M} f(x)(1 - (1 - p(x))^k) \tag{1}$$

Let $p^\star$ be a strategy that maximizes $\mathsf{Cover}(p)$. Using a compactness argument, it is not difficult to show that such a strategy exists. The following observation implies that the optimal symmetric strategy $p^\star$ has coverage which is, up to a small constant factor, as good as the best achievable coverage in the full coordination case, when the $k$ users can be assigned to precisely cover the $k$ highest value sites.

Observation 1. $\mathsf{Cover}(p^\star) > (1 - \frac{1}{e}) \sum_{x=1}^{k} f(x)$.

Proof. Let $\hat{p}$ be the uniform distribution in $[k]$, that is, we have $\hat{p}(x) = 1/k$ for each $x \leq k$. Then, $\mathsf{Cover}(p^\star) \geq \mathsf{Cover}(\hat{p}) = \sum_{x=1}^{k} f(x) \left(1 - \left(1 - \frac{1}{k}\right)^k\right) > (1 - \frac{1}{e}) \sum_{x=1}^{k} f(x)$. □

A *reward policy* is a function $I(x, \ell)$ specifying the *payoff* (or reward) that a player exploring $x$ receives, given that $\ell - 1$ other players are also exploring $x$. We shall be particularly interested in *congestion* reward policies, which can be written as:

$$I(x, \ell) = f(x) \cdot C(\ell)$$

where $C(\cdot)$ is some *congestion* function, for which $C(1) = 1$, and $C$ is non-increasing. Note that the specification of the policy does not depend on the total number of players $k$, and is influenced only by the number of players that visit $x$.

The assumption that $C(1) = 1$ implies that a player visiting $x$ exclusively will gain exactly[1] $f(x)$. A natural example of a congestion policy is the *sharing policy* in which $C_{share}(\ell) = 1/\ell$, and hence if $\ell$ players select site $x$ in parallel then each receives a payoff of $f(x)/\ell$. This policy has received a lot of attention in both the ecology literature and algorithmic game theory community due to its simplicity [22, 23, 44]. Cases where $C(\ell) > 1/\ell$ can model cooperation, in the sense that the presence of several players at a site would result in each having more than their relative share. On the other extreme, note that we do not restrict $C$ to be a positive function. Taking $C(\ell)$ to be negative implies that the presence of $\ell$ players at $x$ damages each of them quite significantly. In the context of animals, this could represent aggressive behavior that increases with the amount of potential benefit $f(x)$ and could result in severe injuries.

Let $X_i$ be the site specified by player $i$. Given a policy $I$, the goal of each player $i$ is to maximize the *expected payoff* it receives, defined as

$$\mathbb{E}\left[I(X_i, \sum_j \mathbb{1}_{X_j = X_i})\right]$$

## 1.2 Evaluating Policies

The game we define is symmetric and possesses both mixed symmetric equilibria and pure non-symmetric equilibria. Most previous works dealing with such situations prefer to focus on pure equilibria (rather than on the mixed equilibria), because of their conceptual simplicity. The classical example of this situation is the well-know game "battle of the sexes" [34]. However we argue otherwise: the number of pure equilibria grows exponentially with the number of players, and choosing an equilibrium among those requires coordination between the players. In some contexts, because coordination is not possible or communication is too costly, it does not seem reasonable to expect that a pure equilibrium arises in practice, and instead, it is more natural to expect the emergence of a symmetric equilibrium. Since we focus on large distributed systems, where players do not always possess individual identities and often have identical behaviors, we will restrict our attention to symmetric equilibria, and disregard pure equilibria[2].

Viewing $p^\star$ as the symmetric strategy that maximizes the social welfare, we adopt an interpretation of the concept of Price of Anarchy to evaluate a policy $I(x, \ell)$, by measuring the coverage of

[1] Alternatively, we could have defined $C(1)$ to be any constant that doesn't depend on $x$. This would mean that the reward a single player gets when visiting $x$ exclusively is proportional to the value $f(x)$. (This assumption contrasts with the setting of [23], see more details in Section 1.6). Note that in this sense, $f(x)$ plays a double role - it has a meaning from the perspective of the group and a meaning from the perspective of an individual.

[2] At first glance, our focus on symmetric strategies may seem non-compatible with the fact that conspecific animals often appear not to have identical strategies. However, it is important to note that a symmetric strategy profile in the context of ESS (see Section 1.4) does not imply that every player follows the same strategy! Indeed, a symmetric strategy profile can arise also if the population contains pure strategies in proportions as specified by the mixed strategy. In this case, since the framework of ESS assumes that at each time $k$ players are selected at random from the population, each of the selected random players ends up having the same mixed strategy. For this reason, restricting attention to symmetric equilibria is in fact very common in the ecology literature [16, 22, 44].

the worst symmetric Nash Equilibrium under $I(x, \ell)$ in comparison with the coverage of $p^\star$. Specifically, let $C(\ell)$ be a congestion function, and $f(x)$ be an importance value function. Define

$$\mathsf{SPoA}(C, f) := \sup_{p \in \mathcal{P}(C,f)} \left\{ \frac{\mathsf{Cover}(p^\star)}{\mathsf{Cover}(p)} \right\},$$

where $\mathcal{P}(C, f)$ is the set of symmetric Nash Equilibrium under $I(x, \ell) = f(x) \cdot C(\ell)$. The *Symmetric Price of Anarchy* (SPoA) of the congestion function $C(\ell)$ is defined as the sup of $\mathsf{SPoA}(C, f)$ over all functions $f : [M] \to \mathbb{R}^+$, where we take the freedom to choose their domain $M$ as well, i.e.,

$$\mathsf{SPoA}(C) := \sup_{\substack{M \in \mathbb{N} \\ f:[M] \to \mathbb{R}^+}} \{\mathsf{SPoA}(C, f)\}$$

By definition, $\mathsf{SPoA}(C) \geq 1$ for any congestion function $C$. On the other hand, there exist congestion functions with much higher SPoA. For example, taking $C(\ell) \equiv 1$ yields SPoA of roughly $k$. Indeed, under this function, and assuming a strictly decreasing $f$, a strategy at equilibrium would explore the first site with probability 1, and for distributions $f$ that decrease very slowly (and thus are close to uniform), this would yield a gap $\Omega(k)$, with respect to, e.g., the uniform strategy. Note, however, that this policy is unlikely to occur in nature, as it implies that a value at a site is fully obtained by all visitors.

The PoA of the sharing policy $C_{share}$ was studied by Kleinberg and Oren in a somewhat similar model [23] (see also Section 1.6). Thanks to a more general result from Vetta [45], they showed that the SPoA of the sharing policy, defined as the ratio between the best achievable coverage and the worst coverage among Nash equilibria, is at most 2. Since the worst symmetric equilibrium coverage is at least as good as the worst equilibrium coverage, and the best achievable coverage is at least as good as the best achievable coverage with a symmetric strategy profile, this directly implies that our notion of SPoA also satisfies $\mathsf{SPoA}(C_{share}) \leq 2$.

## 1.3 Ideal Free Distribution (IFD)

The setting of animals competing over patches of resources, often referred to as *playing the field*, has been extensively studied in the ecology discipline through the theory of *Ideal Free Distribution (IFD)*, see reviews in [22, 44]. Introduced by Fretwell and Lucas [16], the standard model assumes that each individual follows the same distribution $p(\cdot)$ (i.e., a symmetric strategy) and hence the fraction of the population that is expected to occupy a site $x$ is $p(x)$.

An IFD is a probability distribution $p(\cdot)$ in which every site which is explored with positive probability yields the same payoff, and every other site yields a lower payoff if explored. More precisely, as before, let $I(x, \ell)$ denote the payoff received by an individual selecting a site $x$ together with $\ell - 1$ other individuals. Fix a player and let $P(x, \ell) = \binom{k-1}{\ell} p(x)^\ell (1 - p(x))^{k-\ell-1}$ be the probability that among $k-1$ players, $\ell$ of them selected site $x$. The $value_p$ of a site $x$ corresponds to the expected gain for exploring site $x$ and is defined as:

$$v_p(x) := \sum_{\ell=1}^{k} I(x, \ell) \cdot P(x, \ell - 1) \qquad (2)$$

By definition, the expected payoff that a player receives is $\sum_x p(x) \cdot v_p(x)$. The IFD is a distribution $p$, that for some integer $W$, satisfies the following *IFD conditions.*

- $p(x) > 0 \iff x \leq W$
- $v_p(1) = v_p(2) = \ldots = v_p(W) = v_p$, and for all $W + 1 \leq x$, we have $v_p > v_p(x)$

The following observation is well-known, see e.g., [8, 16]. For completeness, a sketch of the proof is provided in Appendix A.

Observation 2. *Assume that $I(x, \cdot)$ is non-increasing for any $x$ (note that this is indeed the case for congestion policies). There exists a unique strategy satisfying the IFD conditions. Moreover, this IFD is the only symmetric Nash Equilibrium of the game.*

## 1.4 Evolutionary Stable Strategy (ESS)

In addition to the notion of Nash Equilibrium, we shall adopt the stronger concept of an *Evolutionary Stable Strategy (ESS)* [3–5, 18, 28, 43]. This concept has become a cornerstone of evolutionary game theory, and has been extensively used to study the evolution of animal and human behavior [4, 28]. Informally, an ESS is a strategy $\sigma$ such that, in a population composed of a majority of $\sigma$-strategists and a minority of "mutants" playing strategy $\pi$, the $\sigma$-strategists have a higher payoff, provided that the proportion of mutants is not too high.

The standard view of ESS is to consider an infinite population whose individuals play repeatedly against each other in pairs, chosen uniformly at random. In our setting, individuals play in groups of $k$, and hence a generalization is required. One possible generalization is to consider a fixed population of $k$ individuals that play the game between themselves. Unfortunately, generalizing ESS to finite populations is quite challenging, and the known generalizations are often too restrictive to be applicable. Instead, we chose the generalization in which the population remains infinite and players are randomly matched in $k$-tuples, for any fixed $k \geq 2$, see e.g., the book [4]. Modeling biological settings, this generalization may correspond, for example, to scenarios in which a large colony of bats breaks on a daily basis into smaller groups, each of which forages in a different field of patched resources, see [10, 29].

Formally, let $\mathcal{E}(\rho; \sigma^\ell, \pi^{k-\ell-1})$ denote the payoff received by an individual playing strategy $\rho$ against $\ell$ players playing strategy $\sigma$ and $(k - \ell - 1)$ players playing strategy $\pi$. When $\sigma = \pi$, we use the abridged notation $\mathcal{E}(\rho; \sigma^{k-1})$. Consider a population in which a proportion $(1 - \epsilon)$ of it are playing strategy $\sigma$ and a proportion of $\epsilon$ are playing $\pi$. The average payoff of a player playing $\rho$ matched against $k - 1$ opponents drawn uniformly at random from this population is denoted by $\mathcal{U}[\rho; (1 - \epsilon)\sigma + \epsilon\pi]$, and is equal to

$$\mathcal{U}[\rho; (1 - \epsilon)\sigma + \epsilon\pi] = \sum_{\ell=0}^{k-1} \binom{k-1}{\ell} (1 - \epsilon)^\ell \epsilon^{k-\ell-1} \mathcal{E}(\rho; \sigma^\ell, \pi^{k-\ell-1})$$

A strategy $\sigma$ is an ESS if for every other strategy $\pi$, there exist $\epsilon_\pi > 0$ such that $\forall \epsilon \leq \epsilon_\pi$, $\mathcal{U}[\sigma, (1-\epsilon)\sigma+\epsilon\pi] > \mathcal{U}[\pi, (1-\epsilon)\sigma+\epsilon\pi]$, i.e., $\sigma$ cannot be "invaded" by $\pi$, as long as the proportion of $\pi$-strategists remains below $\epsilon_\pi$.

We also recall the following *characterization of ESS* [4]: a strategy $\sigma$ is an ESS if for every other strategy $\pi$, there is an integer $0 \leq m_\pi \leq k - 1$, such that both conditions below hold:

- $\mathcal{E}(\sigma;\sigma^{k-m_\pi-1},\pi^{m_\pi}) > \mathcal{E}(\pi;\sigma^{k-m_\pi-1},\pi^{m_\pi})$
- $\forall \ell,\ 0 \le \ell < m_\pi$, we have $\mathcal{E}(\sigma;\sigma^{k-\ell-1},\pi^{\ell}) = \mathcal{E}(\pi;\sigma^{k-\ell-1},\pi^{\ell})$

It should be clear from this definition that every ESS is a symmetric Nash equilibrium of the $k$-player game. Indeed, these conditions ensure that $\mathcal{E}(\sigma;\sigma^{k-1}) \ge \mathcal{E}(\pi;\sigma^{k-1})$ for every $\pi \ne \sigma$. Further details about the ESS notion appear in Section 5.1.

## 1.5 Our Results

We study the interplay between the congestions and the expected coverage of strategies at equilibrium. Our main takeaway message is that optimal coverage is expected to emerge by a congestion policy which is defined by a "Judgment of Solomon" type of rule: If a single player attempts to exploit a site then it gains the full reward $f(x)$, but when several players attempt to exploit it, they all receive nothing. Formally, define the *exclusive congestion function* as follows:

$$C_{exc}(\ell) = \begin{cases} 1 & \text{if } \ell = 1 \\ 0 & \text{otherwise} \end{cases}$$

and define the *exclusive reward policy* as

$$I_{exc}(\ell, x) = f(x) \cdot C_{exc}(\ell)$$

We identify $I_{exc}$ as a critical reward policy, in the sense that its IFD yields optimal coverage, while any other congestion policy yields strictly worse coverage.

More formally, let $\sigma^\star$ be the IFD for the exclusive reward policy. We first claim that under this policy, $\sigma^\star$ is not only a Nash Equilibrium but also an ESS.

Theorem 3. *$\sigma^\star$ is an ESS under $I_{exc}$.*

Next, we claim that $\sigma^\star$ yields the best possible coverage, among all symmetric strategies.

Theorem 4. *For any strategy $\sigma$, $\mathsf{Cover}(\sigma^\star) \ge \mathsf{Cover}(\sigma)$, with equality if and only if $\sigma = \sigma^\star$.*

Since the IFD is the only symmetric Nash Equilibrium under $I_{exc}$, the price of anarchy equals 1.

Corollary 5. $\mathsf{SPoA}(C_{exc}) = 1$.

We find the fact that $\mathsf{SPoA}(C_{exc}) = 1$ rather surprising. Indeed, although it appears intuitive that increasing the competition will result in better coverage, the exclusive policy $C_{exc}$ is, in fact, not the one with highest levels of competition. Indeed, one could define a congestion policy where in case of conflict, each of the colliding players receives a negative payoff (i.e., $C(\ell)$ being negative, see Section 1.1). This means that the competition level could significantly exceed the level of $C_{exc}$. The fact that the best coverage occurs exactly at that level is thus quite surprising. A second important factor to note is that even if one identifies the best policy (i.e., the one for which the SPoA is smallest), it is a priori unclear that the resulted coverage would actually be optimal among all symmetric strategies (including the non-competing ones), i.e., that SPoA = 1.

The criticality of $I_{exc}$ follows by the fact that among all congestion policies, it is the only one whose IFD yields optimal coverage for all value functions $f$.

Theorem 6. *For any congestion function $C \ne C_{exc}$, we have* $\mathsf{SPoA}(C) > 1$.

An informal discussion regarding the implications of our results in the context of animal behavior is presented in Section 5.2.

See Figure 1 for an illustration of the coverage as a function of the competition extent, in specific instances of 2 players and 2 sites.

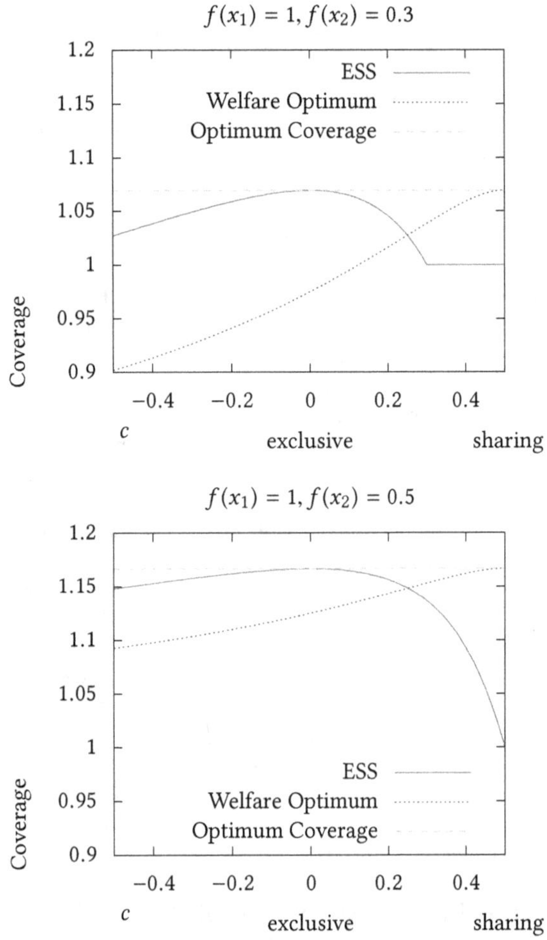


**Figure 1: Coverage as a function of the extent of competition (parametrized by $c$) for the case where two players complete over two sites $x_1$ and $x_2$. In the top figure (respectively, bottom) we consider the case where $f(x_1) = 1$ and $f(x_2) = 0.3$ (respectively, $f(x_2) = 0.5$). The $X$-axis represents a range of congestion functions $C_c$, defined as $C_c(1) = 1$ and $C_c(2) = c$, where $c \in [-0.5, 0.5]$. The case $c = 0$ corresponds to the exclusive function and the case $c = 0.5$ corresponds to the sharing function. The $Y$-axis represents the coverage. The red line corresponds to the coverage of the ESS, the green corresponds to the optimum coverage, taken over all symmetric strategies, and the blue corresponds to the coverage of the symmetric strategy that maximizes the individual payoffs.**

## 1.6 Related Work

A research theme that is currently quite popular in the Operations Research, and Economic Theory research communities goes by the name "incentivizing exploration". Similarly to us, such papers tend to focus on the problem of designing mechanisms to coordinate the activities of independent selfish agents exploring a space of alternatives [15, 25, 26, 35]. These papers however typically focus on sequential rather than simultaneous exploration, leading them to model the problem as a multi-armed bandit problem rather than a congestion game. For this reason, there is no real technical connection between the two lines of work, but there is nevertheless a thematic connection.

Closest to our work is the paper by Kleinberg and Oren [23] which considers a general model that is motivated by research foundations offering grants to incentivize researchers to work on particular topics. That paper proposes two mechanisms for selecting grant policies that are expected to incentivize researchers to adopt an optimal distribution, while assuming that researchers are restricted to the sharing policy. The first mechanism relies on the ability to freely choose the rewards (grants) associated with sites (topics), despite the fact that the significance of a site from the perspective of the group is fixed. In contexts of animals, however, the overall rewards (termed here as $f(x)$) correspond to the amount of food in patch $x$ and therefore cannot be modified. Moreover, implementing their mechanism of choosing rewards requires the knowledge of the number of players $k$, whereas the specification of the congestion policies studied here does not require this knowledge (see Section 1.1). The second mechanism proposed in [23] requires that the players receive different rewards, set in a particular way by the central entity, despite doing the same actions. This might be seen as unfair and unsatisfying. Moreover, implementing this would require high levels of coordination which again seem unlikely in the context of animals.

The settings of selfish routing, job scheduling, and congested games [30, 42] all bear similarities to the dispersal game, however, the measurement of the global performances considered here, namely, the coverage, is very different from the measures studied in the former frameworks, such as makespan or latency [1, 2, 9, 33].

Finally, many articles have informally mentioned the IFD as an example of an ESS [22, 31, 36, 37, 39, 40]. However, on a formal level, it is only recently that a rigorous proof was given [7], and even this proof was with respect a limited definition of ESS (essentially, in our notation, they proved the first item of the characterization with $m_\pi = k - 1$, without considering the second item). Since that paper, several other works have also addressed this question rigorously, but, to the best of our knowledge, they all considered either weaker versions than our ESS definition, or other contexts, such as continuous populations dynamics [6, 41].

## 2 THE EXCLUSIVE REWARD POLICY

This section considers the exclusive reward policy $I_{exc}$. In Section 2.1 we explicitly calculate the IFD for this policy, called $\sigma^\star$. Then, in Section 2.2, we prove that $\sigma^\star$ yields optimal coverage.

### 2.1 Algorithm $\sigma^\star$

Consider a strategy $p$ that satisfies the IFD conditions for the exclusive reward policy. We know that it exists by Observation 2 and we calculate it explicitly. In the context of $C_{exc}$, the $value_p$ of a site $x$, as given by Eq. (2), is:

$$v_p(x) = f(x)(1-p(x))^{k-1}$$

The second IFD condition implies that for any two $x, y \in [1, W]$, we have $f(x)(1-p(x))^{k-1} = f(y)(1-p(y))^{k-1}$, or in other words,

$$\frac{1-p(x)}{1-p(y)} = \left(\frac{f(y)}{f(x)}\right)^{1/(k-1)} \tag{3}$$

A natural guess for a distribution that satisfies this is the following Pareto distribution:

$$p(x) = \begin{cases} 1 - \alpha\, f(x)^{-\frac{1}{k-1}} & \text{if } x \leq W \\ 0 & \text{otherwise} \end{cases}$$

Since $p$ is a distribution, we must have $\sum_{x=1}^{W} p(x) = 1$, from which we can extract

$$\alpha = \frac{W-1}{\sum_{x \leq W} f(x)^{-\frac{1}{k-1}}}.$$

To complete the description of our candidate IFD strategy, it remains to calculate $W$. By the second IFD condition, we get that if $W < M$, then for every $x \leq W$:

$$f(x)(1-p(x))^{k-1} = v_p(x) > v_p(W+1) = f(W+1) \tag{4}$$

Rearranging, we get

$$p(x) < 1 - (f(W+1)/f(x))^{\frac{1}{k-1}}.$$

Since $p(x)$ is a distribution whose support is $[W] := \{1, \ldots, W\}$ we get

$$1 = \sum_{x \leq W} p(x) < \sum_{x \leq W} \left(1 - (f(W+1)/f(x))^{\frac{1}{k-1}}\right).$$

This means that we can define $W$ as the first index that satisfies the equation above, if one exists, or $M$ otherwise. Equivalently, we can define $W$ as the largest index that satisfies

$$\sum_{x \leq W} \left(1 - \left(\frac{f(W)}{f(x)}\right)^{\frac{1}{k-1}}\right) \leq 1$$

Altogether, this leads to strategy $\sigma^\star$, defined as follows.

$$\sigma^\star(x) = \begin{cases} 1 - \dfrac{\alpha}{f(x)^{\frac{1}{k-1}}} & \text{if } x \leq W \\ 0 & \text{otherwise} \end{cases}$$

where $W$ and the normalization factor $\alpha$ are calculated as follows.

$$W = \arg\max_{y \leq M} \left\{ \sum_{x \leq y} \left(1 - \left(\frac{f(y)}{f(x)}\right)^{\frac{1}{k-1}}\right) \leq 1 \right\}$$

$$\alpha = \frac{W-1}{\sum_{x \leq W} f(x)^{-\frac{1}{k-1}}}$$

**Pseudocode of Algorithm $\sigma^\star(x)$**

Interestingly, it turns out that algorithm $\sigma^\star$ is actually identical to the first round in the algorithm $A^\star$ used in [24] in the context of Bayesian search.

The following claim verifies that the constructed strategy is indeed the IFD.

CLAIM 7. *$\sigma^\star$ satisfies the IFD conditions under the exclusive reward policy $I_{exc}$.*

PROOF. The first IFD condition is satisfied by $\sigma^\star$ by construction. It remains to show that $v_p(1) = v_p(2) = \ldots = v_p(W)$, and for all $x > W$, we have $v_p(W) > v_p(x)$. Under the exclusive reward policy $I_{exc}$, the *value*$_p$ of a site $x \leq W$, as given by Eq. (2), is:

$$v_p(x) = f(x)(1 - \sigma^\star(x))^{k-1} = \alpha^{k-1}$$

which proves the first part. For the second part, we first derive $f(W+1) < \alpha^{k-1}$ as follows:

$$\sum_{x \leq W+1} \left(1 - \left(\frac{f(W+1)}{f(x)}\right)^{\frac{1}{k-1}}\right) > 1$$

$$\sum_{x \leq W} \left(1 - \left(\frac{f(W+1)}{f(x)}\right)^{\frac{1}{k-1}}\right) > 1$$

$$\sum_{x \leq W} \left(\frac{f(W+1)}{f(x)}\right)^{\frac{1}{k-1}} < W - 1$$

$$f(W+1)^{\frac{1}{k-1}} < \frac{W-1}{\sum_{x \leq W} f(x)^{-\frac{1}{k-1}}}$$

$$f(W+1) < \alpha^{k-1}$$

Now it suffices to observe that the *value*$_p$ of a site $x > W$ is $v_p(x) = f(x) \leq f(W+1) < \alpha^{k-1} = v_p(W)$. □

As claimed in Theorem 3 (and proved in Section 3), it turns out that under the exclusive policy $I_{exc}$, strategy $\sigma^\star$ is not only a Nash Equilibrium, but in fact an ESS.

## 2.2 $\sigma^\star$ has Optimal Coverage

In this subsection we prove Theorem 4, that is, we prove that for any strategy $\sigma$, $\texttt{Cover}(\sigma^\star) \geq \texttt{Cover}(\sigma)$, with equality if and only if $\sigma = \sigma^\star$. Before dwelling into the proof we note that algorithm $A^\star$ was shown in [24] to be optimal for the setting in which $k$ independent searchers are searching for a treasure placed in one of $M$ boxes, according to a Bayesian distribution. The proof therein is long and relies on deep techniques that were developed in [14]. Since $\sigma^*$ agrees with $A^\star$ on the first round of $A^\star$ and since there are some similarities between the search and the coverage objectives, it might be possible to translate the proof in [14, 24] to show the optimality of $\sigma^\star$ in terms of coverage. However, we managed to find a simple and concise proof of this fact, that can also be used to show the uniqueness of $\sigma^\star$. We provide it below.

Note that maximizing $\texttt{Cover}(p)$ is equivalent to minimizing $\mathcal{T}(p) = \sum_x f(x)(1 - p(x))^k$. We next show that $\sigma^\star$ minimizes the latter expression.

First observe that since the number of resources is finite, it follows by a compactness argument that the infimum of $\{\mathcal{T}(\sigma) \mid \sigma \text{ is a distribution}\}$ is attained by some distribution $\sigma_{\min}$. Assume by contradiction that $\sigma_{\min} \neq \sigma^\star$. Since both $\sigma_{\min}$ and $\sigma^\star$ are distributions, we must have some $x_0 \leq W$ such that $\sigma^\star(x_0) > \sigma_{\min}(x_0)$ and some $x_1$ such that $\sigma^\star(x_1) < \sigma_{\min}(x_1)$. For sufficiently small $\epsilon > 0$, let us define $\sigma'(x)$ which equals $\sigma_{\min}$ everywhere except that $\sigma'(x_1) = \sigma_{\min}(x_1) - \epsilon$ and $\sigma'(x_0) = \sigma_{\min}(x_0) + \epsilon$. In other words, we create $\sigma'$ from $\sigma_{\min}$ by shifting a small mass of probability from $x_1$ to $x_0$.

Aiming to contradict the minimality of $\sigma_{\min}$, our goal is to show that $\mathcal{T}(\sigma') < \mathcal{T}(\sigma_{\min})$. In other words, we aim to show that the following expression, which equals to $\mathcal{T}(\sigma_{\min}) - \mathcal{T}(\sigma')$, is positive.

$$f(x_0)\left((1 - \sigma_{\min}(x_0))^k - (1 - \sigma_{\min}(x_0) - \epsilon)^k\right) + f(x_1)\left((1 - \sigma_{\min}(x_1))^k - (1 - \sigma_{\min}(x_1) + \epsilon)^k\right)$$

By a Taylor expansion, for a small $\epsilon > 0$, we obtain:

$$\mathcal{T}(\sigma_{\min}) - \mathcal{T}(\sigma') \approx \epsilon k \left(f(x_0)(1 - \sigma_{\min}(x_0))^{k-1} - f(x_1)(1 - \sigma_{\min}(x_1))^{k-1}\right)$$

By Eq. (4) and the definitions of $x_0$ and $x_1$, we know that

$$f(x_0)(1 - \sigma_{\min}(x_0))^{k-1} > f(x_0)(1 - \sigma^\star(x_0))^{k-1} \geq f(x_1)(1 - \sigma^\star(x_1))^{k-1} > f(x_1)(1 - \sigma_{\min}(x_1))^{k-1}$$

Hence, for sufficiently small $\epsilon > 0$, we get that $\mathcal{T}(\sigma_{\min}) > \mathcal{T}(\sigma')$, contradicting the minimality of $\sigma_{\min}$. This establishes the fact that $\sigma^\star = \sigma_{\min}$, implying that $\sigma^\star$ maximizes the coverage $\texttt{Cover}(p)$.

Finally, the fact that $\sigma^\star = \sigma_{\min}$ also implies that the distribution that minimizes $\mathcal{T}(p)$ (and hence maximizes $\texttt{Cover}(p)$) is unique. Hence, $\texttt{Cover}(\sigma^\star) = \texttt{Cover}(\sigma)$ can occur only if $\sigma = \sigma^\star$. This concludes the proof of Theorem 4. □

# 3 THE IDEAL FREE DISTRIBUTION IS AN ESS

The goal of this section is to prove Theorem 3, i.e, we aim to show that under $I_{exc}$, strategy $\sigma^\star$ is an ESS.

Let $\sigma$ be a strategy, distinct from $\sigma^\star$. First note that, when playing against strategy $\sigma^\star$, because it is the IFD, the expression of $\mathcal{E}_k(\sigma; \sigma^{\star(k-1)})$ becomes :

$$\mathcal{E}_k(\sigma; \sigma^{\star(k-1)}) = \sum_{x=1}^{M} \sigma(x) v_{\sigma^\star}(x) = \sum_{x=1}^{W} \sigma(x) v_{\sigma^\star}(W) + \sum_{x=W+1}^{M} \sigma(x) f(x)$$

Since for every site $x > W$, we have $f(x) < v_{\sigma^\star}(W)$, it is clear that every strategy $\sigma$ whose support is not a subset of $[1, W]$ has

$$\mathcal{E}_k(\sigma; \sigma^{\star(k-1)}) < \mathcal{E}_k(\sigma^\star; \sigma^{\star(k-1)})$$

and therefore satisfies the ESS characterization conditions with $m_\sigma = 0$.

Next, let us assume that the support of $\sigma$ is included in $[1, W]$, and show that the ESS characterization conditions are satisfied for $m_\sigma = 1$, i.e., we aim to show that

$$\forall \ell, 1 \leq \ell \leq k-2, \text{ we have}$$

$$\mathcal{E}_k(\sigma^\star; \sigma^\ell, \sigma^{\star(k-\ell-1)}) > \mathcal{E}_k(\sigma; \sigma^\ell, \sigma^{\star(k-\ell-1)}), \quad (5)$$

$$\text{and } \mathcal{E}_k(\sigma^\star; \sigma^{\star(k-1)}) = \mathcal{E}_k(\sigma; \sigma^{\star(k-1)}). \quad (6)$$

In fact, to show that the ESS characterization conditions are satisfied for $m_\sigma = 1$, we need only the case $\ell = 1$ in Inequality (5), but we prove here a stronger stability criteria, showing that this inequality holds for every $1 \leq \ell \leq k-2$.

Eq. (6) follows quite simply from the observation above, coupled with the assumption that the support of $\sigma$ is in $[1, W]$, which gives both $\mathcal{E}_k(\sigma^\star; \sigma^{\star(k-1)}) = v_{\sigma^\star}$ and $\mathcal{E}_k(\sigma; \sigma^{\star(k-1)}) = v_{\sigma^\star}$.

Eq. (5) requires more elaboration. We first show that for every $1 \le \ell \le k-2$:

$$\mathcal{E}_k(\sigma^\star; \sigma^\ell, \sigma^{\star(k-\ell-1)}) \ge \mathcal{E}_k(\sigma; \sigma^\ell, \sigma^{\star(k-\ell-1)})$$

and then show that equality holds iff $\sigma = \sigma^\star$. We start with the following claim.

Claim 8. *Expanding each side in Eq. (5), we obtain:*

$$\mathcal{E}_k(\sigma^\star; \sigma^\ell, \sigma^{\star(k-\ell-1)}) =$$
$$\alpha^{k-\ell-1}\left(\sum_{x\le W} f(x)^{\frac{\ell}{k-1}}(1-\sigma(x))^\ell - \alpha \sum_{x\le W} f(x)^{\frac{\ell-1}{k-1}}(1-\sigma(x))^\ell\right),$$
$$\mathcal{E}_k(\sigma; \sigma^\ell, \sigma^{\star(k-\ell-1)}) =$$
$$\alpha^{k-\ell-1}\left(\sum_{x\le W} f(x)^{\frac{\ell}{k-1}}(1-\sigma(x))^\ell - \sum_{x\le W} f(x)^{\frac{\ell}{k-1}}(1-\sigma(x))^{\ell+1}\right)$$

*Proof of Claim 8.* We start by expanding the left hand side of Eq. (5).

$$\mathcal{E}_k(\sigma^\star; \sigma^\ell, \sigma^{\star(k-\ell-1)}) =$$
$$\sum_x f(x)\sigma^\star(x)(1-\sigma^\star(x))^{k-\ell-1}(1-\sigma(x))^\ell =$$
$$\sum_{x\le W} (f(x) - \alpha f(x)^{\frac{k-2}{k-1}})\alpha^{k-\ell-1} f(x)^{\frac{\ell+1-k}{k-1}}(1-\sigma(x))^\ell =$$
$$\alpha^{k-\ell-1}\sum_{x\le W} (f(x)^{\frac{\ell}{k-1}} - \alpha f(x)^{\frac{\ell-1}{k-1}})(1-\sigma(x))^\ell =$$
$$\alpha^{k-\ell-1}\left(\sum_{x\le W} f(x)^{\frac{\ell}{k-1}}(1-\sigma(x))^\ell - \alpha \sum_{x\le W} f(x)^{\frac{\ell-1}{k-1}}(1-\sigma(x))^\ell\right)$$

This establishes the first part of the claim.

Next, we expand the right hand side of Eq. (5).

$$\mathcal{E}_k(\sigma; \sigma^\ell, \sigma^{\star(k-\ell-1)}) =$$
$$\sum_x f(x)\sigma(x)(1-\sigma^\star(x))^{k-\ell-1}(1-\sigma(x))^\ell =$$
$$\sum_{x\le W} f(x)\sigma(x)(1-\sigma^\star(x))^{k-\ell-1}(1-\sigma(x))^\ell =$$
$$\sum_{x\le W} f(x)\sigma(x)\alpha^{k-\ell-1} f(x)^{\frac{\ell+1-k}{k-1}}(1-\sigma(x))^\ell =$$
$$\alpha^{k-\ell-1}\sum_{x\le W} \sigma(x) f(x)^{\frac{\ell}{k-1}}(1-\sigma(x))^\ell =$$
$$\alpha^{k-\ell-1}\left(\sum_{x\le W} f(x)^{\frac{\ell}{k-1}}(1-\sigma(x))^\ell - \sum_{x\le W} f(x)^{\frac{\ell}{k-1}}(1-\sigma(x))^{\ell+1}\right)$$

Concluding the proof of Claim 8.

By Claim 8, it follows that the desired inequality is equivalent to:

$$\alpha \sum_{x\le W} f(x)^{\frac{\ell-1}{k-1}}(1-\sigma(x))^\ell \le \sum_{x\le W} f(x)^{\frac{\ell}{k-1}}(1-\sigma(x))^{\ell+1}$$

By definition of $\alpha$, we rearrange this inequality into

$$(W-1)\sum_{x\le W} f(x)^{\frac{\ell-1}{k-1}}(1-\sigma(x))^\ell \le$$
$$\sum_{x\le W}\frac{1}{f(x)^{\frac{1}{k-1}}}\sum_{x\le W} f(x)^{\frac{\ell}{k-1}}(1-\sigma(x))^{\ell+1}$$

Decomposing $f(x)^{\frac{\ell-1}{k-1}} = \frac{f(x)^{\frac{\ell}{\ell+1}\cdot\frac{\ell}{k-1}}}{f(x)^{\frac{1}{(\ell+1)(k-1)}}}$, and applying Hölder's Inequality, we obtain:

$$\sum_{x\le W} f(x)^{\frac{\ell-1}{k-1}}(1-\sigma(x))^\ell \le$$
$$\left(\sum_{x\le W}\frac{1}{f(x)^{\frac{1}{k-1}}}\right)^{\frac{1}{\ell+1}}\left(\sum_{x\le W} f(x)^{\frac{\ell}{k-1}}(1-\sigma(x))^{\ell+1}\right)^{\frac{\ell}{\ell+1}}$$

This implies that to prove that Eq. (5) holds, it is sufficient to establish the following inequality:

$$(W-1)\left(\sum_{x\le W}\frac{1}{f(x)^{\frac{1}{k-1}}}\right)^{\frac{1}{\ell+1}} \le$$
$$\sum_{x\le W}\frac{1}{f(x)^{\frac{1}{k-1}}}\left(\sum_{x\le W} f(x)^{\frac{\ell}{k-1}}(1-\sigma(x))^{\ell+1}\right)^{\frac{1}{\ell+1}}$$

Using the fact that $\sigma$ is a distribution, and hence $\sum_{x\le W}(1-\sigma(x)) = W-1$, it suffices to prove that

$$\sum_{x\le W}(1-\sigma(x))\left(\sum_{x\le W}\frac{1}{f(x)^{\frac{1}{k-1}}}\right)^{\frac{1}{\ell+1}} \le$$
$$\sum_{x\le W}\frac{1}{f(x)^{\frac{1}{k-1}}}\left(\sum_{x\le W} f(x)^{\frac{\ell}{k-1}}(1-\sigma(x))^{\ell+1}\right)^{\frac{1}{\ell+1}}$$

Rearranging, this is equivalent to proving that

$$\sum_{x\le W}(1-\sigma(x)) \le$$
$$\left(\sum_{x\le W}\frac{1}{f(x)^{\frac{1}{k-1}}}\right)^{\frac{\ell}{\ell+1}}\left(\sum_{x\le W} f(x)^{\frac{\ell}{k-1}}(1-\sigma(x))^{\ell+1}\right)^{\frac{1}{\ell+1}} \tag{7}$$

Which finally follows by applying Hölder's Inequality.

The fact that the inequality is strict for $\ell \ge 1$ follows from the following.

Claim 9. *For $\ell \ge 1$,*
$\mathcal{E}_k(\sigma^\star; \sigma^\ell, \sigma^{\star(k-\ell-1)}) = \mathcal{E}_k(\sigma; \sigma^\ell, \sigma^{\star(k-\ell-1)}) \implies \sigma = \sigma^\star$.

*Proof of Claim 9.* The proof of the claim is based on the observation that the former equality implies, in particular, an equality in Hölder's inequality in Eq. (7). For $\ell \ge 1$, this can be the case only if the two sides are linearly dependent, i.e., for each $x \le W$, we have

$$f(x)^{\frac{\ell}{k-1}}(1-\sigma(x))^{\ell+1} = \frac{\beta^{\ell+1}}{f(x)^{\frac{1}{k-1}}}$$

where $\beta$ is some fixed constant. Together with the fact that the support of $\sigma$ is included in $[W]$, the strategy $\sigma$ must therefore be of the form

$$\sigma(x) = \begin{cases} 1 - \beta f(x)^{-\frac{1}{k-1}} & \text{if } x \le W \\ 0 & \text{otherwise} \end{cases}$$

Finally, we know that

$$\sum_{x \le W} \sigma(x) = \sum_{x \le W} \left(1 - \beta f(x)^{-\frac{1}{k-1}}\right) = 1$$

Solving this for $\beta$ gives

$$\beta = \frac{W-1}{\sum_{x \le W} f(x)^{-\frac{1}{k-1}}} = \alpha$$

and therefore $\sigma = \sigma^\star$. This completes the proof of Claim 9, and thus established the proof for Theorem 3. □

# 4 THE CRITICALITY OF THE EXCLUSIVE COLLISION COST FUNCTION

The goal in this section is to prove Theorem 6. That is, fixing a congestion function $C(\cdot) \neq C_{exc}(\cdot)$, we aim to show that $\mathsf{SPoA}(C) > 1$.

First recall that by definition of congestion functions, $C(\cdot)$ is non-increasing. Hence Observation 2 applies, and the existence of the IFD is guaranteed for every value function $f$. Our plan is to show that there exists a value function $f$, for which this IFD is different than $\sigma^\star$. Once this is established, the fact that $\mathsf{SPoA}(C) > 1$ follows from Theorem 4.

Assume, towards contradiction, that for every $f$, the IFD under $C(\cdot)$ is precisely $\sigma^\star$. Let $M \gg k$, and let $f$ be a strictly decreasing function, that, nevertheless, decreases very slowly, such that, e.g., for every $x \le y$ in $[1, M]$, we have $\frac{f(y)}{f(x)} \ge \frac{f(M)}{f(1)} > \left(1 - \frac{1}{2k}\right)^{k-1}$. Together with the definition of $W$ (see the pseudocode of Algorithm $\sigma^\star(x)$), we obtain that $W \ge 2k$.

Because $\sigma^\star$ is the IFD, we have that $\forall x \le W$, $\nu_p(x) = \nu_p(W)$. Let us develop this expression:

$$\nu_p(W) = f(x) \sum_{\ell=1}^{k} C(\ell) P(x, \ell - 1) =$$

$$f(x) \sum_{\ell=1}^{k} C(\ell) \binom{k-1}{\ell-1} \sigma^\star(x)^{\ell-1} (1 - \sigma^\star(x))^{k-\ell} =$$

$$f(x) \sum_{\ell=1}^{k} C(\ell) \binom{k-1}{\ell-1} \left(1 - \alpha f(x)^{-\frac{1}{k-1}}\right)^{\ell-1} \alpha^{k-\ell} f(x)^{-\frac{k-\ell}{k-1}} =$$

$$\sum_{\ell=1}^{k} C(\ell) \binom{k-1}{\ell-1} \left(1 - \alpha f(x)^{-\frac{1}{k-1}}\right)^{\ell-1} \alpha^{k-\ell} f(x)^{\frac{\ell-1}{k-1}}$$

The last line above is a polynomial equation in $f(x)^{\frac{1}{k-1}}$ of degree at most $k-1$. Note that this polynomial is not a constant. Indeed, since $C \neq C_{exc}$ and $C(1) = C_{exc}(1) = 1$, there must exist $\ell \ge 2$, such that $C(\ell) \neq 0$. Hence, the $\ell - 1$'st coefficient of the polynomial is non-zero, implying that this polynomial is not a constant. It follows that there are at most $k - 1$ of values for $f(x)$ that would satisfy this equation (recall that $f$ is strictly decreasing). This yields a contradiction since the equation is supposed to be true for every site $x \le W$, and $W \ge 2k$. This concludes the proof of Theorem 6. □

# 5 DISCUSSION

## 5.1 Conclusions and Future Directions

This paper studies the mechanism design challenges in the basic dispersal game inspired by animal behavior. Our focus is on congestion policies, where there is no control over the utility associated with a site, and only the price associated with congestion can vary. Indeed, for natural scenarios in particular, it makes sense that evolution would impact the competition levels but the values of sites would be determined by the environment. The definition of congestion policies neglects, however, a factor that might play a significant role in several scenarios, namely, the cost incurred when in visiting a site $x$ (e.g., the energetic cost consumed while traveling to $x$). Studying the more general model that takes into account this extra cost is left for future work.

This paper focuses on one-shot scenarios. Tackling the multi-round game appears to be challenging and is left for future work. The main difficulty lies in the fact that after one round, different players might have different views of the remaining game, as they have previously visited different sites.

The coverage measure can find relevance in contexts of animal foraging. This is because effective group coverage can indirectly contribute to the fitness of individuals, especially when the group is in competition with other groups over the same set of resources [17]. Indeed, in this case, the consumption of many resources by conspecifics reduces the fitness of individuals in the competing group and vice versa. It is therefore of interest to develop a more comprehensive game-theoretic perspective that would integrate into the individual fitness both the competition inside the group, and the competition between groups [11]. A plausible insight that can be learned from our results is that aggressive behavior between conspecifics, which appears to be wasteful or even harmful from the group's perspective, can in fact be effective on the group level, as it allows for better coverage. For further discussion on the interpretation of our results in the context of animals see Section 5.2.

Our definition of coverage assumes that a single player in a site $x$ suffices to consume the full utility $f(x)$. In natural settings, e.g., in animal foraging scenarios, this assumption might be too strong, and it is of interest to study relaxations of it. One possibility is to assume that there is a maximum capacity of consumption per individual. In some other cases, a more complex definition of coverage might be appropriate. We leave the study of such generalizations for future work.

Finally, game theory in computer science typically studies the notion of Nash Equilibrium as the main concept to capture stability. This notion was originally designed for games with small number of players. When considering games with thousands or even millions of players, it becomes less plausible to assume that all players are rational, and one may seek for stronger notions of stability. ESS, which was developed in the evolutionary game theoretical community, appears to be a good candidate to capture stability in large populations. We believe that this notion should be applied more in game theory works that correspond to large distributed settings.

## 5.2 Informal Discussion on Animal Dispersal

From the perspective of the group, consuming a large amount of food by all members together can indirectly increase the fitness of the group members and hence become significant for their survival. For example, when multiple species compete over the same patched resource, a thorough consumption of patches by one species implies less food remaining for the other. In this respect, it would be interesting to experiment on the interplay between two similar species that compete over the same set of resources, but differ in their level of aggressiveness toward conspecifics [38]. In cases where there is no direct contact between the species (e.g., when they feed at different times of the day), it may appear that the more aggressive species would be inferior as it induces unnecessary waste of energy and risks of injury. However, our results suggest that perhaps it is the aggressive species that would turn out to be the superior one. Indeed, its aggressive behavior incurs higher collisions costs, which may drive individuals to better cover the resources, on the expense of the more peaceful species.

During foraging, both selfish individuals and collaborating groups (e.g., ants or bees) share the basic challenge of balancing the need to exploit the more promising resources, while trying to avoid overlaps (or collisions) with conspecifics [12, 17]. This tradeoff, however, is manifested in the two cases in a manner that appears to be very different: While collaborative groups aim to optimize the tradeoff by setting the parameters in a somewhat "centralized" manner, the competing dynamics is governed by a selection process yielding an evolutionary stable strategy which need not be optimal for individuals. As suggested here, despite these differences, when colliding individuals are punished severely, the two perspectives yield similar strategies.

Finally, the alignment in behavior between collaborating and competing individuals, as reported here, may suggest a modest contribution to the theory of evolution of eusocial species. The currently dominated theory proposes that eusocial species have evolved from self motivated individuals due to kin selection [20]. An issue that is discussed less is that a shift in the "motivation focus" can potentially be accompanied by a shift in function and hence, perhaps, also in structure [27]. Indeed, in principle, while evolving from self-interested to altruistic, an individual which had evolved in a way that was tailored to its own needs, may now need to adapt to the collective needs. As these needs are on different scales, they may not necessarily be akin [13], and hence a long evolutionary process may be required in order to bridge this gap. In this respect, that seemingly cooperative behavior can arise in competing systems, as demonstrated here, suggests that the behavioral transition, at least in the context of dispersal or forage, may have been smoother than what one might expect.

*Acknowledgements.* The authors are thankful for Yoav Rodeh, Yossi Yovel, Yuval Emek, Lucas Boczkowski, Emanuele Natale, and Ofer Feinerman for useful discussions concerning both the model and its applications to biological contexts.

## REFERENCES


[1] Susanne Albers and Matthias Hellwig. 2013. Online Makespan Minimization with Parallel Schedules. *CoRR* abs/1304.5625 (2013). http://arxiv.org/abs/1304.5625

[2] Sayan Bhattacharya, Sungjin Im, Janardhan Kulkarni, and Kamesh Munagala. 2014. Coordination mechanisms from (almost) all scheduling policies. In *Innovations in Theoretical Computer Science, ITCS'14, Princeton, NJ, USA, January 12-14, 2014.* 121–134. https://doi.org/10.1145/2554797.2554811

[3] C. Cannings Broom, M. and G. Vickers. 1997. Multi-player matrix games. *Bulletin of Mathematical Biology* 59, 3 (1997), 931–952.

[4] Mark Broom and Jan Rychtár. 2013. *Game-theoretical models in biology.* CRC Press.

[5] Maciej Bukowski and Jacek Miekisz. 2004. Evolutionary and asymptotic stability in symmetric multi-player games. *International Journal of Game Theory* 33, 1 (2004), 41–54.

[6] Chris Cosner, Juan Dávila, and Salomé Martínez. 2012. Evolutionary stability of ideal free nonlocal dispersal. *Journal of Biological Dynamics* 6, 2 (2012), 395–405.

[7] Ross Cressman and Vlastimil Křivan. 2006. Migration dynamics for the ideal free distribution. *The American Naturalist* 168, 3 (2006), 384–397.

[8] Ross Cressman and Vlastimil Křivan. 2010. The ideal free distribution as an evolutionarily stable state in density-dependent population games. *Oikos* 119, 8 (2010), 1231–1242.

[9] Artur Czumaj and Berthold Vöcking. 2007. Tight Bounds for Worst-case Equilibria. *ACM Trans. Algorithms* 3, 1, Article 4 (Feb. 2007), 17 pages. https://doi.org/10.1145/1186810.1186814

[10] Dina K.N. Dechmann, Silke L. Heucke, Luca Giuggioli, Kamran Safi, Christian C. Voigt, and Martin Wikelski. 2009. Experimental evidence for group hunting via eavesdropping in echolocating bats. *Proceedings of the Royal Society of London B: Biological Sciences* 276, 1668 (2009), 2721–2728. https://doi.org/10.1098/rspb.2009.0473 arXiv:http://rspb.royalsocietypublishing.org/content/276/1668/2721.full.pdf

[11] Avigdor Eldar. 2011. Social conflict drives the evolutionary divergence of quorum sensing. *Proceedings of the National Academy of Sciences* 108, 33 (2011), 13635–13640. https://doi.org/10.1073/pnas.1102923108 arXiv:http://www.pnas.org/content/108/33/13635.full.pdf

[12] Ofer Feinerman and Amos Korman. 2017. The ANTS problem. *Distributed Computing* 30, 3 (2017), 149–168. https://doi.org/10.1007/s00446-016-0285-8

[13] Ofer Feinerman and Amos Korman. 2017. Individual versus collective cognition in social insects. *Journal of Experimental Biology* 220, 1 (2017), 73–82. https://doi.org/10.1242/jeb.143891 arXiv:http://jeb.biologists.org/content/220/1/73.full.pdf

[14] Pierre Fraigniaud, Amos Korman, and Yoav Rodeh. 2016. Parallel exhaustive search without coordination. In *Proceedings of the 48th Annual ACM SIGACT Symposium on Theory of Computing, STOC 2016, Cambridge, MA, USA, June 18-21, 2016.* 312–323. https://doi.org/10.1145/2897518.2897541

[15] Peter Frazier, David Kempe, Jon Kleinberg, and Robert Kleinberg. 2014. Incentivizing exploration. In *Proceedings of the fifteenth ACM conference on Economics and computation.* ACM, 5–22.

[16] Stephen Dewitt Fretwell and Henry L. Lucas Jr. 1969. On territorial behavior and other factors influencing habitat distribution in birds. *Acta biotheoretica* 19, 1 (1969), 16–32.

[17] Luc-Alain Giraldeau and Thomas Caraco. [n. d.]. Social Foraging Theory. *Princeton University Press* ([n. d.]).

[18] Chaitanya S Gokhale and Arne Traulsen. 2010. Evolutionary games in the multiverse. *Proceedings of the National Academy of Sciences* 107, 12 (2010), 5500–5504.

[19] Thomas Gregor, Koichi Fujimoto, Noritaka Masaki, and Satoshi Sawai. 2010. The Onset of Collective Behavior in Social Amoebae. *Science* 328, 5981 (2010), 1021–1025. https://doi.org/10.1126/science.1183415 arXiv:http://science.sciencemag.org/content/328/5981/1021.full.pdf

[20] William D. Hamilton. 1996. Narrow roads of geneland. Freeman. *Freeman* (1996).

[21] Thomas T Hills, Peter M Todd, David Lazer, A David Redish, Iain D Couzin, Cognitive Search Research Group, et al. 2015. Exploration versus exploitation in space, mind, and society. *Trends in cognitive sciences* 19, 1 (2015), 46–54.

[22] Martyn Kennedy and Russell D. Gray. 1993. Can Ecological Theory Predict the Distribution of Foraging Animals? A Critical Analysis of Experiments on the Ideal Free Distribution. *Oikos* 68, 1 (1993), 158–166. http://www.jstor.org/stable/3545322

[23] Jon Kleinberg and Sigal Oren. 2011. Mechanisms for (mis) allocating scientific credit. In *Proceedings of the forty-third annual ACM symposium on Theory of computing.* ACM, 529–538.

[24] Amos Korman and Yoav Rodeh. 2017. Parallel search without coordination. In *Proceedings of the 24th International Colloquium on Structural Information and Communication Complexity, SIROCCO 2017, Porquerolles, France, June 19-22, 2017.*

[25] Ilan Kremer, Yishay Mansour, and Motty Perry. 2014. Implementing the AgWisdom of the CrowdAh. *Journal of Political Economy* 122, 5 (2014), 988–1012.

[26] Yishay Mansour, Aleksandrs Slivkins, and Vasilis Syrgkanis. 2015. Bayesian incentive-compatible bandit exploration. In *Proceedings of the Sixteenth ACM Conference on Economics and Computation.* ACM, 565–582.

[27] John M. McNamara and Alasdair I. Houston. 2009. Integrating function and mechanism. *Trends in Ecology & Evolution* 24, 12 (2009), 670 – 675. https://doi.org/10.1016/j.tree.2009.05.011

[28] Linda Mealey. 1995. The sociobiology of sociopathy: An integrated evolutionary model. *Behavioral and Brain Sciences* 18(3) (1995), 523–541.

[29] Rodrigo A Medellin, Marina Rivero, Ana Ibarra, J Antonio de la Torre, Tania P Gonzalez-Terrazas, Leonora Torres-Knoop, and Marco Tschapka. 2018. Follow me: foraging distances of Leptonycteris yerbabuenae (Chiroptera: Phyllostomidae) in Sonora determined by fluorescent powder. *Journal of Mammalogy* 99, 2 (2018), 306–311. https://doi.org/10.1093/jmammal/gyy016 arXiv:/oup/backfile/content_public/journal/jmammal/99/2/-10.1093_jmammal_gyy016/1/gyy016.pdf
[30] Dov Monderer and Lloyd S Shapley. 1996. Potential games. *Games and economic behavior* 14, 1 (1996), 124–143.
[31] Douglas W Morris. 2003. Shadows of predation: habitat-selecting consumers eclipse competition between coexisting prey. *Evolutionary Ecology* 17, 4 (2003), 393–422.
[32] AJ Nicholson. 1954. An outline of the dynamics of animal populations. *Australian Journal of Zoology* (1954), 9–65.
[33] Noam Nisan, Tim Roughgarden, Eva Tardos, and Vijay V. Vazirani. 2007. *Algorithmic Game Theory.* Cambridge University Press.
[34] Martin J Osborne and Ariel Rubinstein. 1994. *A course in game theory.* MIT press.
[35] Yiangos Papanastasiou, Kostas Bimpikis, and Nicos Savva. 2017. Crowdsourcing exploration. *Management Science* (2017).
[36] Geoffrey A Parker. 1978. Searching for mates. *Behavioural ecology: an evolutionary approach* 1 (1978), 214–244.
[37] Geoffrey A Parker. 1984. Evolutionary stable strategies. *Behavioural ecology: an evolutionary approach* (1984), 30–61.
[38] Noa Pinter-Wollman, Tamar Dayan, David Eilam, and Noga Kronfeld-Schor. 2006. Can aggression be the force driving temporal separation between competing common and golden spiny mice? *Journal of Mammalogy* 87, 1 (2006), 48–53.
[39] H Ronald Pulliam and Thomas Caraco. 1984. Living in groups: is there an optimal group size. *Behavioural ecology: an evolutionary approach* 2 (1984), 122–147.
[40] H Ronald Pulliam and Brent J Danielson. 1991. Sources, sinks, and habitat selection: a landscape perspective on population dynamics. *The American Naturalist* 137 (1991), S50–S66.
[41] Nicanor Quijano and Kevin M Passino. 2007. The ideal free distribution: Theory and engineering application. *IEEE Transactions on Systems, Man, and Cybernetics, Part B (Cybernetics)* 37, 1 (2007), 154–165.
[42] Robert W Rosenthal. 1973. A class of games possessing pure-strategy Nash equilibria. *International Journal of Game Theory* 2, 1 (1973), 65–67.
[43] J. Maynard Smith and G. R. Price. 1973. The Logic of Animal Conflict. *Nature* 246(5427) (1973), 15–18.
[44] Tom Tregenza. 1995. Building on the ideal free distribution. *Adv. Ecol. Res* (1995), 253–307.
[45] Adrian Vetta. 2002. Nash equilibria in competitive societies, with applications to facility location, traffic routing and auctions. In *Foundations of Computer Science, 2002. Proceedings. The 43rd Annual IEEE Symposium on.* IEEE, 416–425.

# APPENDIX

## A PROOF SKETCH FOR OBSERVATION 2

The existence of the IFD follows by the fact that $v_p(x)$ is non-increasing with $p(x)$. By definition, the IFD is a symmetric Nash Equilibrium of the game. We now prove its uniqueness. Imagine there are two different symmetric Nash Equilibria, $\pi$ and $\pi'$, respectively associated with their values $v_\pi$ and $v_{\pi'}$. Note that for any fixed $x$, the $value_p$ $v_p(x)$ is a strictly decreasing function of $p(x)$. Therefore

$$\pi = \pi' \iff v_\pi = v_{\pi'}$$

Assume by contradiction that $v_\pi > v_{\pi'}$. This implies that for any $x \in [\pi]$, $\pi(x) < \pi'(x)$, where $[\pi]$ denotes the support of $\pi$, i.e the set of sites explored with positive probability. Summing over all sites in $[\pi]$, we get

$$\sum_{x \in [\pi]} \pi(x) < \sum_{x \in [\pi]} \pi'(x)$$

Since the left-hand size is equal to 1, we get a contradiction. This proves the uniqueness of the symmetric Nash Equilibrium, and of the IFD. □

# Massive-scale Streaming Analytics: Models, Parallelism, & Real-world Applications

Keynote Talk

David A. Bader
School of Computational Science and Engineering
College of Computing
Georgia Institute of Technology
Atlanta, GA 30332 USA

## ABSTRACT

Emerging real-world graph problems include: detecting and preventing disease in human populations; revealing community structure in large social networks; and improving the resilience of the electric power grid. Unlike traditional applications in computational science and engineering, solving these social problems at scale often raises new challenges because of the sparsity and lack of locality in the data, the need for research on scalable algorithms and development of frameworks for solving these real-world problems on high performance computers, and for improved models that capture the noise and bias inherent in the torrential data streams. Highlighting this keynote talk, Bader will discuss the opportunities and challenges in massive data-intensive computing for applications in social sciences, physical sciences, and engineering.

Focusing on parallel algorithm design and implementation, Bader formalizes a practical model for graph analysis on streaming data. In this model, a massive graph undergoes changes from an input stream of edge insertions and removals. The model supports concurrent updating of the graph while algorithms execute concurrently on the dynamic data structure. The talk introduces a concept of validity: an algorithm is valid if the output is correct for a graph consisting of the initial graph with some subset of concurrent changes. Practical examples of this model are given for valid implementations of breadth first search, connected components, PageRank, and triangle counting, all useful graph kernels in real-world applications. This is joint work with E. Jason Riedy and Chunxing Yin.

## KEYWORDS

Graph Algorithms; Parallel Computing.

**ACM Reference format:**

D.A. Bader. 2018. In *Proceedings of 30th ACM Symposium on Parallelism in Algorithms and Architectures, Vienna, Austria, July 2018 (SPAA '18),* 1 page. https://doi.org/10.1145/3210377.3210379

## ACKNOWLEDGMENTS

This work is supported in part by the Defense Advanced Research Projects Agency (DARPA) under Contract Number FA8750-17-C-0086. The content of the information in this document does not necessarily reflect the position or the policy of the Government, and no official endorsement should be inferred. The U.S. Government is authorized to reproduce and distribute reprints for Government purposes notwithstanding any copyright notation here on.


*SPAA '18, July 16-18, 2018, Vienna, Austria.*

ACM ISBN 978-1-4503-5799-9/18/07.
DOI: https://doi.org/10.1145/3210377.3210379

# Red-Blue Pebble Game: Complexity of Computing the Trade-Off between Cache Size and Memory Transfers

Erik D. Demaine
Computer Science and Artificial Intelligence Laboratory
Massachusetts Institute of Technology
edemaine@mit.edu

Quanquan C. Liu
Computer Science and Artificial Intelligence Laboratory
Massachusetts Institute of Technology
quanquan@mit.edu

## ABSTRACT

The red-blue pebble game was formulated in the 1980s [14] to model the I/O complexity of algorithms on a two-level memory hierarchy. Given a directed acyclic graph representing computations (vertices) and their dependencies (edges), the red-blue pebble game allows sequentially adding, removing, and recoloring red or blue pebbles according to a few rules, where red pebbles represent data in cache (fast memory) and blue pebbles represent data on disk (slow, external memory). Specifically, a vertex can be newly pebbled red if and only if all of its predecessors currently have a red pebble; pebbles can always be removed; and pebbles can be recolored between red and blue (corresponding to reading or writing data between disk and cache, also called I/Os or memory transfers). Given an upper bound on the number of red pebbles at any time (the cache size), the goal is to compute a game execution with the fewest pebble recolorings (memory transfers) that finish with pebbles on a specified subset of nodes (outputs get computed).

In this paper, we investigate the complexity of computing this trade-off between red-pebble limit (cache size) and number of recolorings (memory transfers) in general DAGs. First we prove this problem PSPACE-complete through an extension of the proof PSPACE-hardness of black pebbling complexity [13]. Second, we consider a natural restriction on the red-blue pebble game to forbid pebble deletions, or equivalently, forbid discarding data from cache without first writing it to disk. This assumption both simplifies the model and immediately places the trade-off computation problem within NP. Unfortunately, we show that even this restricted version is NP-complete. Finally, we show that the trade-off problem parameterized by the number of transitions is W[1]-hard, meaning that there is likely no algorithm running in a fixed polynomial for constant number of transitions.

## KEYWORDS

red-blue pebble game; external memory model; computational complexity


ACM ISBN 978-1-4503-5799-9/18/07...$15.00
https://doi.org/10.1145/3210377.3210387

**ACM Reference Format:**
Erik D. Demaine and Quanquan C. Liu. 2018. Red-Blue Pebble Game: Complexity of Computing the Trade-Off between Cache Size and Memory Transfers. In *SPAA '18: 30th ACM Symposium on Parallelism in Algorithms and Architectures, July 16–18, 2018, Vienna, Austria.* ACM, New York, NY, USA, 10 pages. https://doi.org/10.1145/3210377.3210387

## 1 INTRODUCTION

Pebble games were originally introduced to study compiler operations and programming languages. One example of such an application is when a directed acyclic graph (DAG) represents the computational dependencies between operations and the pebbles represent register or memory allocation. Minimizing the resources allocated to perform a computation is accomplished by minimizing the number of pebbles placed on the graph [17], and the time of computation is modeled by the number of pebbles moves the player makes in a strategy that ultimately pebbles the desired output vertices. In addition to the standard pebble game (also known as the black pebble game in the literature) that models register or memory allocation, there are several other pebble games that are useful for studying computation. The *red-blue pebble game* is used to study I/O complexity [14], the *reversible pebble game* is used to model reversible computation [2], and the *black-white pebble game* is used to model non-deterministic straight-line programs [5].

In this paper, we study the *red-blue pebble game* used to model the cost of programs in a two-level memory hierarchy. The two-level memory hierarchy model of [14] and the blocked version, the I/O model or external memory model [1], were introduced in the 1980s [1, 14] to capture the computational bottleneck of transferring data between a large but slow disk and a small but fast cache. (See [7] for more about the history.) The *red-blue pebble game* models the number of such data transitions that are necessary between cache and disk, as well as the limit of the cache size. The rules of the game are as follows:

**Red-Blue Pebble Game** [14]. Given a DAG $G = (V, E)$, the game works as follows:

(1) At the start, every source node has a blue pebble, and no other nodes have pebbles.
(2) The player can place a red pebble on a node if and only if all of its predecessors are currently pebbled with red pebbles.
(3) The player can recolor a blue pebble to red, or a red pebble to blue.
(4) The player can delete a pebble from a node at any time.

**Goal:** Pebble all sink nodes with blue pebbles.

Red pebbles represent data in cache and blue pebbles represent data in disk. We suppose (as in real systems) that there is a limited amount of cache and an unlimited amount of disk. In terms of the red-blue pebble game, this means that the number of red pebbles is limited by some upper bound $r$. Subject to this constraint, the goal is to pebble all target nodes while minimizing the number $k$ of pebble recolorings between red and blue, i.e., minimizing the number $k$ of memory transfers between cache and disk. Recoloring a pebble from red to blue corresponds to writing data out from cache to disk, while recoloring from blue to red corresponds to reading data in from disk to cache.

Much previous research has focused on proving lower and upper bounds on the pebbling cost (i.e., the number of pebbles and/or transitions used) of pebbling a given family of DAGs under the rules of the red-blue pebble game. Such upper and lower bounds are computed with respect to the number of transitions given a number of red pebbles, $r$, that are provided to pebble the graph. Such previous results include upper and lower bounds of $O(n \log n / \log r)$ and $\Omega(n \log n / \log r)$, respectively, on the minimum number of transitions needed to pebble an FFT graph. Upper and lower bounds on number of transitions for other graph classes such as $r$-pyramids, diamond graphs, butterfly graphs, and matrix multiplication graphs can be found in [11, 14, 16]. More recently, the model of one-shot red-blue pebble games was introduced in [3]. This pebble game is used to model I/O-complexity *without recomputating any calculations in cache.* They also show how to extend this model to the multi-level memory hierarchy case.

Despite somewhat extensive research on the upper and lower bounds of optimally pebbling a DAG in pebble games, the complexity of finding a minimum solution has fewer results. In fact, it is not yet known whether it is hard to find the minimum number of pebbles within a constant or logarithmic multiplicative approximation factor [4, 8]. It turns out that finding a strategy to optimally pebble a graph in the standard pebble game is computationally difficult even when each vertex is allowed to be pebbled only once. Specifically, finding the minimum number of black pebbles needed to pebble a DAG in the standard pebble game to within an additive $n^{1/3-\varepsilon}$ term is PSPACE-complete [8] and finding the minimum number of black pebbles needed in the one-shot case is NP-complete [17]. While much has been done in showing upper and lower bounds in pebbling price in terms of number of red pebbles and number of transitions of pebbling certain types of DAGs using the red-blue pebble game, the computational complexity of finding the exact number of minimum red pebbles used and the minimum number of transitions has not been studied in the past to the best of the authors' knowledge.

The purpose of this paper is twofold. We seek to answer the question of computational complexity of finding the optimal number of red pebbles and minimum number of transitions used. Secondly, we seek to motivate the study of finding lower bounds and optimal pebbling strategies for certain graph classes by showing that such hardness results even hold for the very restricted class of layered graphs. In this paper, we discuss the following new results:

(1) In Section 2, we show that the red-blue pebble game is PSPACE-complete, via a simple extension of the result of [13].
(2) In Section 3, we introduce a new red-blue pebble game and prove it NP-complete. Specifically, we consider the natural restriction to when all data must be kept somewhere, either in cache or on disk, or equivalently, the player cannot delete pebbles, only recolor them.
(3) In Section 4, we analyze the complexity of the red-blue pebble game when parameterized by the allowed number $t$ of transitions. We prove that this problem is W[1]-hard, so it does not have a fixed-parameter algorithm (with running time $f(t)n^{O(1)}$) unless FPT $= W[1]$. (Note that some PSPACE-complete problems are fixed-parameter tractable, so this result is not implied by our other results.)

Due to space constraints, all proofs which are not given in the main body of the paper can be found in the full version of our paper.

## 2 RED-BLUE PEBBLE GAME

We begin this section with a short proof that the red-blue pebble game *with deletion* is PSPACE-complete. We do not expand too much into the proof since it relies heavily on the proof given in [13] (and is almost identical to the proof provided there). Therefore we include this result first before our main result on red-blue pebbling *without deletions* whose proof we expand upon in more detail in the next section.

First, we define the *red-blue start-in-disk* game to be the version of the red-blue pebble game as defined in Section 1 (i.e. all source nodes contain blue pebbles at the beginning of the computation, i.e. at $t = 0$, and all inputs if deleted from cache must be obtained from disk and all outputs are written back to disk) and the *red-blue start-in-cache* game to be the version of the red-blue pebble game where we remove the condition that all source nodes contain blue pebbles at the beginning of the computation (i.e. essentially, all inputs start in cache) and red pebbles can be placed at any time on the source nodes–without the need of blue pebbles being on the source nodes first (i.e. inputs always stay in cache). Furthermore, for the *red-blue start-in-cache* game, we assume that all targets must be computed at least once in cache without the need to write the results back into disk (i.e. this is also known as a visiting pebbling in cache [15] in that the red pebbles do not need to be turned into blue pebbles even if they are deleted in cache).

Before we dive into the proofs, we first show that any red-blue pebbling of a DAG $G$ using the rules of the red-blue start-in-cache game that has minimum red pebble space usage $r$ and minimum number of transitions $k$ can be converted to a DAG $G'$ with minimum pebbling space usage $r+1$ and number of transitions $k+1+|T|$ (where $T$ is the target set or output nodes) using the rules of the red-blue start-in-disk game.

Theorem 1 (Red-Blue Disk to Cache). *Given a DAG, $G = (V, E)$ with target set $T$ and bounded in-degree 2 that uses a minimum of $r$ red pebbles and $k$ transitions to pebble using the rules of the red-blue start-in-cache game, we can convert it into a DAG, $G' = (V', E')$, that uses a minimum of $r + 1$ red pebbles and $k + 1 + |T|$ transitions to pebble using the rules of the red-blue start-in-disk game.*

Proof. First, create a node $u$ and let $V' = V \cup \{u\}$. Then, create a set of directed edges $U$ where we add an edge $(u, v)$ to $U$ for all

$v \in V$. Let $E' = E \cup U$. Graph $G'$ now potentially has vertices with in-degree up to 3. In the final step of creating $G'$, we replace all vertices with in-degree 3 with pyramids of height 3. Note that a pyramid of height 3 functions in the same manner as a node with in-degree 3 by normality of pebbling strategies proven in [13, 15].

Let $\mathcal{P}$ be the optimal strategy used to pebble $G$ using the rules of the red-blue start-in-cache game that results in a minimum of $r$ red pebbles and $k$ transitions.

Now, we prove that a minimum of $r + 1$ pebbles and $k + 1 + |T|$ transitions are necessary to pebble $G'$ using the rules of the red-blue start-in-disk game. By construction, $G'$ has one source (leaf) node where one blue pebble is placed on it at the beginning of the pebbling (at $t = 0$). Before any other pebbles can be placed on $G'$, we must use exactly 1 transition to turn the blue pebble on the source to a red pebble. The red pebble remains on the source, and we use strategy $\mathcal{P}$ to pebble the remaining nodes of $G'$.

We now consider the minimum number of transitions that can be used with at most $r + 1$ red pebbles and before all outputs are written back to disk. We show that in order to use a minimum of $k + 1$ transitions, the red pebble must remain on the source during the entire computation of $G'$. Suppose for contradiction, the red pebble is turned into a blue pebble (recall that all leaves must contain a pebble at all times–otherwise they can never be pebbled again using the rules of the red-blue start-in-disk game), then, in any future pebbling of any other nodes in $G'$, the blue pebble on the source must be turned into a red pebble, resulting in 2 additional transitions (a total of $k+3$ transitions) which exceeds the minimum allowed $k + 1$ transitions (since $\mathcal{P}$ uses a minimum of $k$ transitions and turning the pebble on $u$ to red requires 1 transition). Thus, given that the red pebble remains on the source during the entire pebbling of $G'$ (i.e. the red pebble on the source $u$ is present at time $t = \text{argmax}_{P_t \in \mathcal{P}} \{|P_t|\}$) where the maximum number of red pebbles are on the graph using strategy $\mathcal{P}$) the number of red pebbles necessary to pebble $G$ is then increased by 1, so a minimum of $r+1$ red pebbles are necessary to pebble $G'$ given that a minimum of $k + 1$ transitions are used before all outputs are written back into disk.

Finally, given the set $T$ of targets, one transition must be spent to turn a red pebble into a blue pebble on each $v_T \in T$. Thus, at least $|T|$ transitions must be spent in this case, resulting in a total of at least $k + 1 + |T|$ transitions. □

In the remaining sections of the paper, we prove all results with respect to the rules of the red-blue start-in-cache game, even if we do not explicitly state that we do so. Note that using Theorem 1, we can transform any graph $G$ we use in our hardness reductions into a graph $G'$ that can be used to show the corresponding hardness results for the red-blue start-in-disk game.

The red-blue start-in-cache pebble game as defined above is PSPACE-hard as a simple extension of the proof given in [13]. The formal definition of the problem is given below.

DEFINITION 1 (RED-BLUE PEBBLE GAME). *Given a DAG, $G(V, E)$ with $n = |V|$ vertices and $m = |E|$ edges, find a pebbling of $G$ following the red-blue start-in-cache pebbling rules as defined above such that at most $r$ red pebbles are present on $G$ at any time and the number of red-blue transitions, $k$, is minimized.*

The proof structure and the gadgets to show that the red-blue pebble game is PSPACE-hard can be constructed in the same way as the gadgets in the proof of the PSPACE-hardness of the standard pebble game as defined in [13]. The reduction would specify the number of red pebbles necessary to be one greater than the number of pebbles necessary in the proof presented by Gilbert et al. [13] and the number of transitions to be 0. We, thus, only need to show that the number of red pebbles necessary to pebble the gadgets in the construction is indeed one greater than the number necessary to pebble the construction provided in [13]. We show that the construction can be pebbled with one greater pebble in the red-blue pebble game using 0 transitions if and only if the construction in [13] can be pebbled using the rules of the standard pebble game; hence the red-blue pebble game is PSPACE-complete.

LEMMA 1. *The proof construction provided in [13] can be pebbled using $s$ pebbles in the standard pebble game if and only if it can be pebbled using $s + 1$ red pebbles and 0 transitions in the red-blue start-in-cache pebble game.*

THEOREM 2. *Determining the minimum pebbling cost and number of transitions is PSPACE-complete (even given constant number of transitions) to compute in the red-blue pebble game.*

By noticing that we can transform the above hardness construction to a layered graph by topologically sorting the vertices used in the construction and replacing each edge that go between non-consecutive layers by a path of length equal to the number of layers that the edge go between, we result in a multiplicative factor increase of at most $O(n^2)$ in the number of nodes in the graph since the number of layers is at most $O(n)$. It is trivial to see that all pebbling constraints are still preserved by replacing edges with paths.

COROLLARY 1. *Determining the minimum pebbling cost and number of transitions is PSPACE-complete to compute in the red-blue pebble game even for layered graphs.*

## 3 RED-BLUE PEBBLE GAME WITH NO DELETION

In this section, we introduce our model of the red-blue pebble game with *no deletion* and prove that it is NP-complete to determine the minimum number of red pebbles and transitions needed to pebble a given DAG under the rules of this game. The red-blue pebble game with no deletion is defined as follows:

(1) A red pebble can be placed on any vertex that has a blue pebble. (Transition move.)
(2) A blue pebble can be placed on any vertex that has a red pebble. (Transition move.)
(3) A red pebble can be placed on a vertex where all predecessors of the vertex contain red pebbles. (The red pebble can override preexisting pebble placements without using any additional transitions, i.e. the vertex already contains a blue pebble.)
(4) No pebbles can be deleted from a vertex.

As usual, red pebbles represent fast memory and blue pebbles represent slow memory; we assume that we have infinitely large slow memory, but only a bounded fast memory. The goal of this game is to pebble all vertices in $G$ while minimizing the number of *transition* moves. The motivation of this game is to determine the added computational complexity of allowing deletions to occur in the RAM. Suppose that one would like to limit the number of deletions or to minimize the number of transitions as well as deletions. Another motivation is to always maintain computed data in memory. For example, for certain persistent data structures, one always want to keep some form of computed values in memory at all times. This paper analyzes the computational complexity of such a model.

The formal statement of the game is almost identical to the definition of the red-blue pebble game and is the following:

Definition 2 (Red-Blue Pebble Game with No Deletions). *Given a DAG, $G(V, E)$ with $n = |V|$ vertices and $m = |E|$ edges, find a pebbling of $G$ following the red-blue with no deletion pebbling rules (given above) such that at most $r$ red pebbles are present on $G$ at any time and at most $k$ red-blue transitions are used.*

In the next few sections, we show that the Red-Blue Pebble Game is NP-complete.

## 3.1 Proof Overview

We provide a reduction broadly similar in concept to [13] except we reduce from Positive 1-in-3 SAT to show that our problem is NP-complete. The definition of Positive 1-in-3 SAT is given below:

Definition 3 (Positive 1-in-3 SAT [12]). *Given a set $U$ of variables and a collection $C$ of clauses over $U$ such that each clause $c \in C$ has size $|c| = 3$ and all literals in $c$ are positive, does there exist a truth assignment for $U$ such that each clause has exactly one true literal?*

The proof of NP-completeness of the red-blue pebble game with no deletions proceeds as follows. We create a set of variable gadgets that are pebbled with a set of red pebbles that determine whether the variable is set to true or false. The variable gadgets are then connected to clause and anti-clause gadgets that enforce the 1-in-3 condition on the literal truth settings. The variable gadgets are also connected to a *pebble sink path* that ensures that all variables are pebbled and set to a truth configuration before the clause gadgets are pebbled. Finally, the clause gadgets and variable gadgets are connected to a *pebble hold path* that ensures that all red pebbles are removed from these gadgets and are used to fill up the pebble hold path. Specifics about the gadgets and details of the proof construction will be given in the next few sections.

The pebbling of the gadgets occur in two phases: Phase 1 and Phase 2. During Phase 1 of the pebbling, all variables gadgets are set to a truth value. During Phase 2 of the pebbling, the portions of the variable gadgets that were not pebbled in Phase 1, leading to the pebbling of the target node. The gadgets are connected in the following way: all variable gadgets are connected to a pebble sink path (see $g_i$, $g_i'$, and $g_i''$ in Fig. 2) where the end of the path is connected to the first clause gadget; all clause gadgets are connected via a path and the last clause is connected to another pebble sink path (see $s_i$, $s_i'$, and $s_i''$ in Fig. 2) which is connected to the target node. Each variable gadget is also connected to the clause it appears in as well as the corresponding anti-clause. We define the pebbling of the clauses and anti-clauses to be the *clause verification phase.*

## 3.2 Gadgets

In this section, we introduce some gadget components that will be used in the proof that the red-blue pebble game with no deletions is NP-complete.

We define a *variable* gadget for every $x_i \in U$. The purpose of the variable gadget is to force a selection of variable assignments. In order to construct the variable gadget, we use a *pyramid* gadget introduced by previous work [13] that is used to "trap" a certain minimum number of pebbles that must be used to pebble the gadget. Henceforth, for every gadget, $g$, we introduce, we will specify the minimum number of red pebbles, $r_g$, that can remain on the gadget after it has been pebbled once and $t_g$, the minimum number of red-blue transitions that must be performed on the gadget after it is pebbled each time.

The pyramid graph has been proven to use $h$ pebbles where $h$ is the height (where a single node has height 1) of the pyramid graph using standard pebbling (with sliding pebbles) [6]. Let $\Pi_h$ be a pyramid graph with height $h$. It was proven in [15] that the standard pebbling price with no sliding is $h+1$ for a pyramid with height $h$. Here we prove that using the red-blue pebbling strategy with no deletions, the minimum pebbling price of a pyramid with height $h$ is $r_{\Pi_h} = h + 1$ and $t_{\Pi_h} = \frac{h(h+1)}{2}$. Let $PebRBD(\Pi_h)$ be the minimum pebbling price of a pyramid graph using the red-blue strategy with no deletions. The ending state of the pyramid has no red pebbles. We use this property of the pyramid graph in our proof in Section 3.3.

Lemma 2. *Given a pyramid graph of height $h$, the $PebRBD(\Pi_h)$ is $r_{\Pi_h} = h + 1$ and $t_{\Pi_h} = \frac{h(h+1)}{2}$ such that no red pebbles remain on the pyramid at the end of the pebbling.*

Fig. 1 shows the construction of the pyramid gadget and its associated symbol that will be used to denote it in all subsequent proofs in Section 3.3. One can see that the number of pebbles required to fill the pyramid gadget is also the number of leaves on the bottom layer plus one and the number of transitions is $\sum_{i=1}^{l} i$ where $l$ is the number of leaves in the gadget.

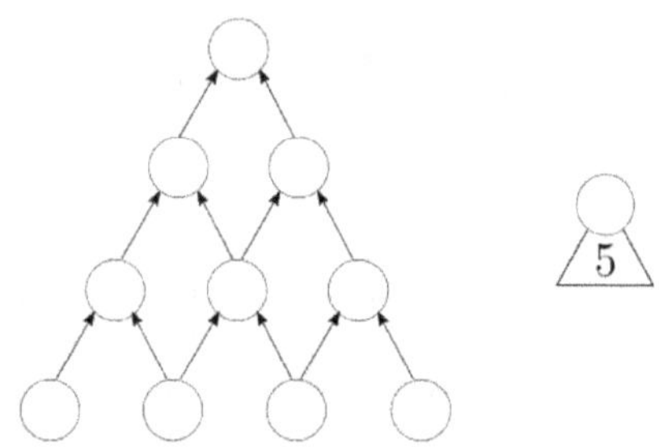


**Figure 1: Example of a pyramid gadget with $r_{\Pi_4} = 5$ and $t_{\Pi_4} = 10$.**

Using the pyramid gadget we can construct the variable gadget as in Fig. 2.

We define $a_i$ for all $x_i$ shortly. Each $x_i$ variable gadget requires $a_i$ pebbles since in order to choose an assignment for $x_i$, $a_i$ pebbles must be used to pebble the pyramid gadget attached to the variable. Since each $q_i$ is part of two variable gadgets, we define $q_{i-1}$ to be

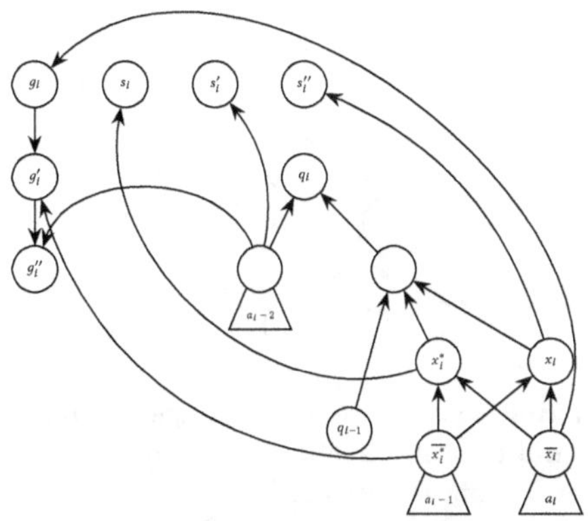

**Figure 2: Example of a variable gadget, $x_i$, with pyramid costs $a_i$, pebble sink path connections $g_i, g_i'$, and $g_i''$. The corresponding pebble sinks that correspond with this gadget are $s_i$, $s_i'$, and $s_i''$.**

part of variable gadget $x_i$ and $q_i$ to be part of the next variable gadget. We show that the gadget must be pebbled in the following way.

During Phase 1 of pebbling the variable gadget $x_i$, each pyramid gadget is pebbled. Then, the corresponding nodes in the pebble sink path can be pebbled in the order $g_i$, $g_i'$, and, then, $g_i''$. All nodes along the pebble sink path must be pebbled in order to pebble the clauses and proceed to the clause verification phase. First, $a_i$ pebbles must be used to pebble both $\overline{x_i}$ and $\overline{x_i^*}$ with red pebbles, converting all other pebbled vertices in each pyramid to contain blue pebbles. This then leaves $a_i - 2$ pebbles to pebble the other pyramid gadget, leaving one pebble at the apex of the gadget and converting all other pebbled vertices in the pyramid to contain blue pebbles. The apex of these pyramids are connected to *pyramid sink paths* which are paths of length $n$ occuring after each set of clause and two anti-clauses triples. Then, either the pair of nodes $x_i$ and $x_i^*$ is pebbled with red pebbles and $\overline{x_i}$ and $\overline{x_i^*}$ are converted to blue pebbles or $\overline{x_i}$ and $\overline{x_i^*}$ contain red pebbles and $x_i$ and $x_i^*$ are not pebbled. We show that at most 3 red pebbles can remain on each variable gadget.

In Phase 2, $q_{i-1}$ will be pebbled once all clauses are pebbled. Therefore, all other nodes of the variable gadget must be pebbled using the pebbles that remain on each pyramid gadget. If the red pebbles from Phase 1 are placed on $\overline{x_i^*}$ and $\overline{x_i}$, then $x_i$ and $x_i^*$ need to be pebbled in Phase 2. Furthermore, $s_i$, $s_i'$ and $s_i''$ need to be pebbled with red pebbles in Phase 2 by moving the red pebbles from each corresponding pyramid. The red pebbles will remain on $s_i$, $s_i'$, and $s_i''$ since no transitions are allowed to be spent on these nodes.

A *clause gadget* is created for each $c_j \in C$. The clause gadget is connected to every positive $x_i$ literal that is present in its respective clause $c_j$. An example clause gadget with $r_{c_i} = 6$ and $t_{c_i} = 29$ (here $r_{c_i}$ *does not* include the red pebble on the one true literal and the red pebble on $p_{i-1}$ and $t_{c_i}$ does not include the transition used to turn the pebble on $p_i$ to blue) is shown below in Fig. 3. The order of the clauses is determined arbitrarily and all clauses are duplicated and occur in the same topological order in the two sets (the original clauses and the duplicate clauses).

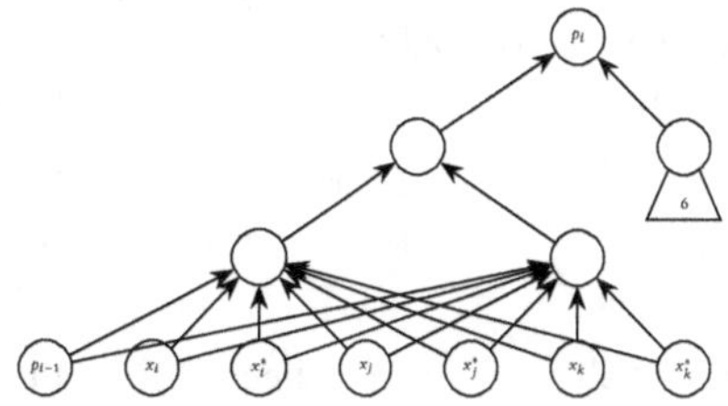

**Figure 3: Example of a clause gadget with $r_{c_i} = 2$ and $t_{c_i} = 29$ for clause $c_i = (x_i \vee x_j \vee x_k)$. The number of red pebbles that is needed to fill this gadget is 6 (excluding the two red pebbles that are present on the true literal and the red pebble on $p_{i-1}$).**

The clause gadget is accompanied by two *anti-clause* gadgets, $\overline{c_i}$ and $\overline{c_i}'$, that are used to enforce the exact 1-in-3SAT condition. The anti-clause gadgets should also be pebbled with $r_{\overline{c_i}} = 6$ and $t_{\overline{c_i}} = 64$. $\overline{c_i}$ contains all $\overline{x_i}$ literals and $\overline{c_i}'$ contains all $\overline{x_i^*}$ literals. First, the pyramids must be pebbled along the path leading up to $p_i$. Then, the one negative literal that is not pebbled must be pebbled with a red pebble by using 2 transitions. Finally, the remaining nodes of the gadget are pebbled once using 62 transitions resulting in $p_i$ being pebbled with a red pebble. An anti-clause gadget is shown in Fig. 5.

Each variable gadget is connected to a *pebble sink path* as shown in Fig. 4. The purpose of the pebble sink path is to ensure that all pyramids are pebbled by the end of Phase 1 of variable pebbling and that each variable only contains at most 3 red pebbles. The pebble sink path can be pebbled using $a_n - 3n$ red pebbles and the number of transitions needed to pebble this path is $3n + \frac{(a_n-3n+1)(a_n-3n)}{2}$. The number of transitions indicate that each node of the pebble sink path can only be pebbled once. Once the end of the pebble sink path is pebbled, the clause gadgets can be pebbled in the *clause verification phase.*

We now prove our claims above more formally. We begin by proving that the end of Phase 1, at most 3 red pebbles can remain on each of the variable gadgets.

LEMMA 3. *At most* $3n$ *red pebbles can remain on the variable gadgets at the end of Phase* 1 *and the beginning of the clause verification phase where* $n$ *is the number of variable gadgets.*

We prove a matching lower bound for the number of red pebbles that should remain on the variable gadgets after Phase 1.

LEMMA 4. *At least* 3 *red pebbles must remain on each variable gadget at the end of Phase* 1 *in order to be able to pebble the constructed graph using a minimum number of red pebbles and transitions.*

Using Lemma 3, we can now prove the number of red pebbles and transitions necessary to pebble the variable gadgets.

LEMMA 5. *The pebbling price of the variable gadget (not including* $s_i$, $s_i'$, $s_i''$, $g_i$, $g_i'$, $g_i''$ *or* $q_i$*) for variable* $x_i$ *is* $r_{x_i} = a_i$ *and* $t_{x_i} =$

$\sum_{j=1}^{3} \frac{(a_i-j+1)(a_i-j)}{2} + 4$ *assuming all red pebbles are removed from the gadget at the end of the pebbling. The transitions cost includes the cost of pebbling and removing red pebbles from all nodes as shown in Fig. 2 except* $s_i, s_i', s_i'', g_i, g_i', g_i''$ *and* $q_i$. *Assuming all variable gadgets are set to a truth value during Phase 1 and Phase 2 begins with the pebbling of* $q_0$ *and ends with red pebbles on* $s_i, s_i', s_i'', q_i$, *during Phase 1, the pebbling cost is* $r_{x_i} = a_i$ *and* $\sum_{j=1}^{3} \frac{(a_i-j+1)(a_i-j)}{2} - 3 \leq t \leq \sum_{j=1}^{3} \frac{(a_i-j+1)(a_i-j)}{2} - 1$. *Furthermore, during Phase 2 of the pebbling, the pebbling cost is* $r_{x_i} = 4$ *and* $5 \leq t_{x_i} \leq 7$ *and red pebbles remain only on* $s_i, s_i', s_i''$, *and* $q_i$.

We prove the following lemma to help us prove that all variable gadgets must be set in Phase 1.

Lemma 6. *If* $n'$ *variables do not have at least one of the two pairs,* $x_i^*$ *and* $x_i$ *or* $\overline{x_i}$ *and* $\overline{x_i^*}$, *pebbled at the end of the clause verification phase, then a total of at least* $\left(\sum_{i=1}^{n} \sum_{j=1}^{3} \frac{(a_i-j+1)(a_i-j)}{2} + 4\right) + n'$ *transitions are needed to pebble all variable gadgets in Phase 1 and Phase 2.*

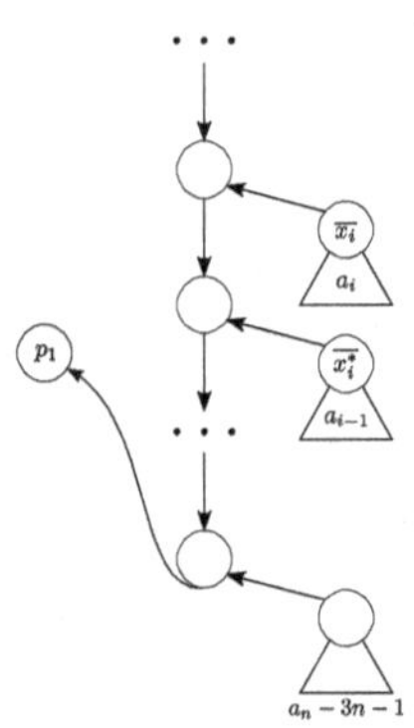


**Figure 4: Example pebble sink path. Each node is connected to the root of each pyramid in each variable gadget.**

Lemma 7. *Given* $r_{c_i} = 6$ *and* $t_{c_i} = 29$, *the clause gadget* $c_i$ *(shown in Fig. 3) cannot be pebbled if all three variable gadgets incident on* $c_i$ *are in the false configuration and no red pebbles remain on* $c_i$ *after it is pebbled (i.e. when* $p_i$ *is pebbled).*

Lemma 8. *Given* $r_{\overline{c_i}} = 6$ *and* $t_{\overline{c_i}} = 61$, *the anti-clause gadget cannot be pebbled if less than 2 negative literals are true.*

Lemma 9. *Each clause gadget must contain exactly one true literal pebbled with red pebbles and each anti-clause gadget must contain exactly two true literals pebbled with red pebbles at the end of Phase 1 before the clause verification phase.*

Given these gadgets, we are ready to proceed with the reduction from Positive 1-in-3 SAT.

## 3.3 Reduction from Positive 1-in-3 SAT

Given a Positive 1-in-3 SAT expression, $\phi$, we create a variable gadget for each of the $n$ variables and a clause and two anti-clause gadgets (one for $\overline{x_i}$ and one for $\overline{x_i^*}$) for each of the $m$ clauses. To see

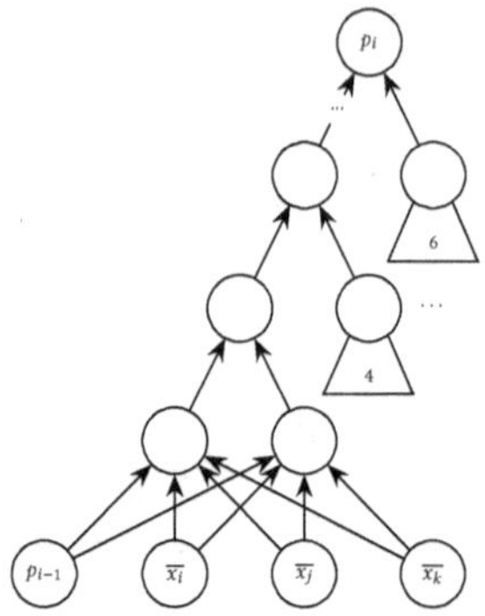


**Figure 5: Example of an anti-clause gadget with $r = 6$ and $t = 64$. The number of red pebbles that is needed to fill this gadget is 6 (excluding the two red pebbles that are present on the true negative literals).**

an example full construction, please refer to the full version of our paper. .

Each variable gadget is connected to the next by the set of vertices $Q$ consisting of nodes $q_i \in Q$. Each variable gadget is also connected to the pebble sink path consisting of vertices $g_i \in G$ and to the pebble hold nodes $s_i$, $s_i'$, and $s_i''$. For each clause gadget, we connect it with its corresponding anti-clause gadgets via the nodes in the set $p_i \in P$. The final anti-clause gadget in the chain of clause and anti-clause gadgets is connected to the bottom of the chain of variable gadgets. Finally, all variable gadgets are connected to pebble hold nodes, $s_i, s_i', s_i'' \in S$ that are also along a path and ensure that all red pebbles end on these set of nodes. There are no transitions allocated for these nodes; therefore, any red pebbles that are used to pebble these nodes must remain.

We let $a_n = 3n + 6$ and $a_i = a_{i-1} + 3$. Therefore, we set $r = 3n + 6$ and $t = 93m + 3n + 22 + \sum_{i=1}^{n} \sum_{j=1}^{3} \frac{(a_i-j+1)(a_i-j)}{2}$ for the entirety of the construction.

We now provide an argument that red-blue pebbling with no deletions is in NP.

Lemma 10. *Given a DAG* $G(V, E)$ *where* $n = |V|$, *and parameters* $r$ *and* $t$ *and a pebbling strategy, we can check whether the strategy works in time* $O(n^2)$.

Theorem 3. *Generalized red-blue no-deletion pebble game on a DAG with maximum in degree 7 is NP-complete by reduction from Positive 1-in-3 SAT.*

Corollary 2. *Generalized red-blue no-deletion pebble game on a DAG with maximum in degree 2 is NP-Complete by reduction from Positive 1-in-3 SAT.*

One can produce a reduction with indegree 2 graphs by replacing all nodes with indegree greater than 2 with pyramids with height equal to the indegree minus 1. Similar proofs can prove hardness in this case.

## 4 RED-BLUE PEBBLE GAME PARAMETERIZED BY TRANSITIONS

In this section, we prove that the red-blue pebble game with deletion where the number of red-to-blue or blue-to-red transitions is parameterized by $k$ is W[1]-hard by reduction from the W[1]-complete problem, Weighted $q$-CNF Satisfiability. It was previously shown by [9] that Weighted $q$-CNF Satisfiability is W[1]-complete for any fixed $q \geq 2$. In order to maximize the similarity to our previous reductions, we will be reducing from Weighted 3-CNF SAT via a parameterized reduction.

It has been noted that this result seems superfluous given the NP-hardness result for 0 transitions given in Section 2. However, we note that an NP-hardness result does not necessarily supersede a parameterized complexity result since they are different complexity domains. In fact, there exist NP-complete problems with natural parameterizations that have fixed-parameter tractable algorithms. Furthermore, the techniques presented in this section are techniques that could be important for future proofs of hardness or hard-to-pebble graph family constructions.

DEFINITION 4 (WEIGHTED $q$-CNF SATISFIABILITY [9, 10]). *Given a CNF formula, $\phi$, a set $U$ of variables ($n = |U|$), and a set $C$ of clauses ($m = |C|$) where the number of literals per clause is at most $q$, determine whether there is a satisfying assignment for $\phi$ of truth values to the variables in $U$ such that the number of variables that are true is $k$.*

Given a 3-CNF formula, we first create two clauses for each of the variables: for all $x_i \in U$ we add the clauses $(x_i \vee x_i \vee \overline{x_i}) \wedge (x_i \vee \overline{x_i} \vee \overline{x_i})$. Note that if a truth value is assigned to $x_i$, then both clauses must be true. The presence of these clauses is to ensure that each of the variable gadgets in the reduction are assigned a valid truth value.

The reduction transforms an instance of Weighted 3-CNF SAT with parameter $k$ to an instance of red-blue pebble game *with deletion* (note that this is a different model from the one presented in Section 3) such that the reduced instance is allowed $r = 7n - 4k + 1$ pebbles and $2k$ red-blue transitions.

We first provide an overview of our proof techniques. Then, we describe the gadgets used in our proof. Finally, we provide the proof that the red-blue pebble game defined in Section 2 is W[1]-hard.

## 4.1 Proof Overview

Given a Weighted 3-CNF SAT expression, $\phi$, we first duplicate all the variables and clauses until $n'$ the number of new variables including duplicates follows the rule $\frac{3n'}{4} > k$. From here onwards, we refer to $\phi$ to be the new 3-CNF expression (with the duplications) and $n$ to be the number of new variables.

As in the proof given in Section 3, we create a set of variable gadgets that are connected to a set of clause gadgets that check whether each clause is satisfied according to the truth settings of the variables. The $k$ true variables conditions is enforced by the *All-False* and *$k$-True-Variables* gadgets which first force all variable gadgets to be set to false, then picks exactly $k$ variables to set to true and uses exactly $2k$ transitions. The problem is parameterized by the number of transitions, $2k$, and the number of red pebbles is limited by some number that is polynomial in the number of variables in $\phi$. All of the transitions will be used before the clause gadgets are pebbled. Therefore, all pebblings of all gadgets after the variable gadgets, the All-False gadget, and the $k$-True-Variables gadget are pebbled using only red pebbles and no transitions.

We will now describe the gadgets that are used in the reduction.

## 4.2 Gadgets

*4.2.1 Variable Gadget.* The variable gadgets are used to represent the variables that are in $U$ and are present in $\phi$ (i.e. we do not create a variable gadget for variables that are not present in $\phi$). We again categorize the complete pebbling of the variable gadgets into three phases: Phase 1, Phase 2, and Phase 3. During Phase 1, each variable must be pebbled in the following way. The pyramid gadgets within each variable gadget are first pebbled with red pebbles and one red pebble remains on the apex of each pyramid gadget. See Fig. 6.

After all variable gadgets have been pebbled once (i.e. both $\overline{x_i'}$ and $\overline{x_i}$ are pebbled), the $x_i'$ nodes must be pebbled with red pebbles. In order to pebble the $x_i'$ nodes, the remaining red pebbles will be used as well as the red pebbles on $\overline{x_i'}$. The corresponding red pebble on $\overline{x_i'}$ is either turned to blue or removed. At most $k$ of these red pebbles may be turned to blue since we are given only $2k$ transitions and each of the blue pebbles must be reverted back to red at some point in the future (proof will be provided later). The three vertices representing $x_i$ remain un-pebbled and a red pebble remains on each $\overline{x_i}$. Each vertex of $x_i'$ as well as $\overline{x_i}$ are connected to the All False gadget (described below). The All False gadget must be pebbled after the variable gadgets since all other subsequent pebbling depends on the set of $2k + 1$ nodes that were pebbled during the pebbling of the All False gadget.

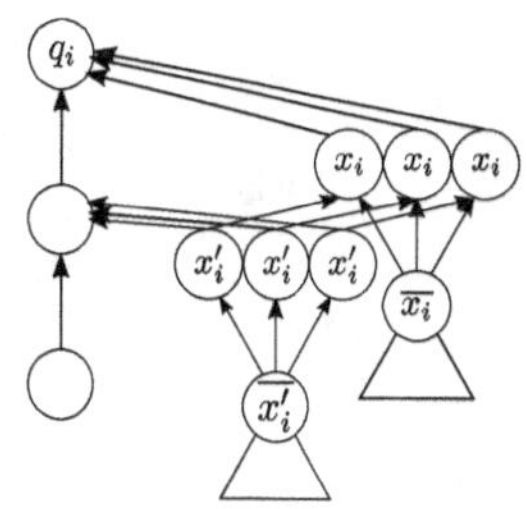


**Figure 6: Variable gadget.**

LEMMA 11. *All variable gadgets must be in the false configuration after Phase 1.*

During Phase 3 of pebbling the variable gadgets, the other nodes within the gadget are pebbled using the red pebbles that are left on the gadget from Phase 2. This phase requires no transitions since the extra red pebbles from the clause and pebble sink path gadgets can be used to pebble the variable gadgets during this phase.

*4.2.2 All False Gadget.* The All False gadget is used to check that all variables are initially set to false. See Fig. 7. It consists of $2k + 1$ vertices with unbounded indegree with predecessors $x_i'$ and $\overline{x_i}$ for all $i$. Furthermore, its predecessors also contain $a_n - 4n - i$ nodes for $i = \{0, \ldots, 2k\}$ to use up the other $a_n - 4n - i$ extra pebbles. The $2k + 1$ nodes from the All False gadget are then connected to the $k$-True-Variables gadget and all the clause gadgets.

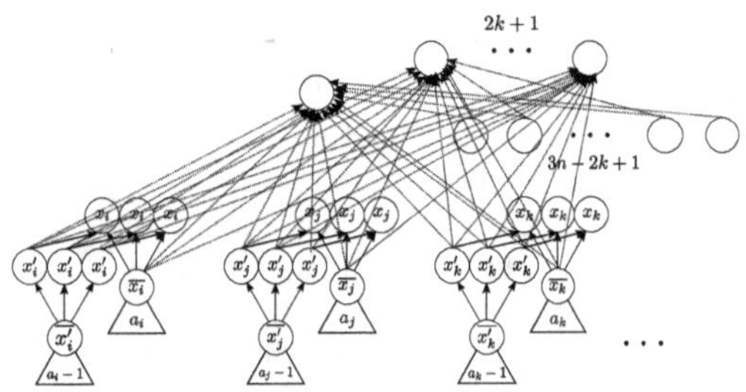


**Figure 7: The All False gadget consists of $2k + 1$ nodes that all have $x_i'$ and $\overline{x_i}$ as predecessors. Each of these $2k + 1$ nodes are connected to the $k$-True-Variables gadget and the clause gadgets.**

4.2.3 *$k$-True-Variables Gadget.* Phase 2 of the variable pebbling phases consists of resetting a set of $k$ variables to true. The $k$-True-Variables gadget is present to constrain the number of true variables to exactly $k$. The $k$-True-Variables gadget consists of a single unbounded indegree vertex with $x_i$ as predecessors for all $i$. After passing through the All False gadget, $k$ variable gadgets must be switched from the False position to the True position by moving $3k$ pebbles from $x_i'$ to $x_i$ and using $k$ transitions to move $k$ red pebbles to $\overline{x_i'}$. As we will show in the next few gadgets, $k$ transitions must be used to pebble $\overline{x_i'}$ nodes with red pebbles. See Fig. 8 for an example.

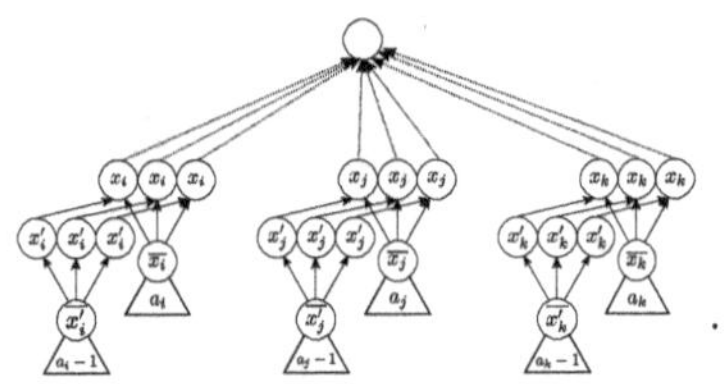

**Figure 8: $k$-True gadget connects to all $x_i$ for all $i$.**

LEMMA 12. *At the end of Phase 2, exactly k variable gadgets are set in the true configuration.*

4.2.4 *3-or-None Gadget.* The 3-or-None gadgets are used to ensure that every variable either has 3 pebbles on each $x_i$ or $x_i'$ or none on them. This is to ensure that the player cannot cheat by using less than 3 pebbles to set either $x_i'$ or $x_i$ true. A 3-or-None gadget is created for each variable. The 3-or-None gadget consists of sets of 2 vertices one picked from $x_i$ and the other picked from $x_i'$. All such pairings are connected to a path with vertices of indegree 5 (the other vertices are roots) so that only one pebble is allowed to go through the path. See Fig. 9 for an example of a 3-or-None gadget. This gadget can be pebbled using 5 pebbles. However, more pebbles will not ensure that the gadget can be pebbled if it does not satisfy the invariant as stated in Lemma 15. In other words, more pebbles does not guarantee that the gadget can be pebbled without using any transitions. Attached to each node of the 3-or-None gadget are $3n - 4k - 3$ roots that have outgoing edges to the nodes in the path in the gadget. The All-False termination node is also connected to every node in the path of the 3-or-None gadget.

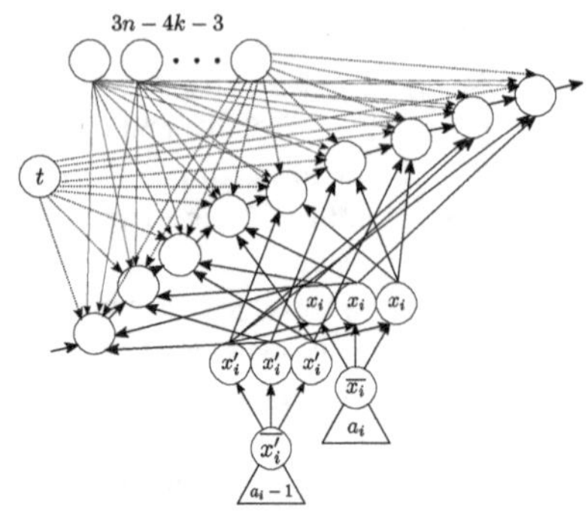


**Figure 9: 3-or-None gadget. One is created for every variable.**

LEMMA 13. *For every variable gadget that does not follow the condition specified in Lemma 15 and contains less than 6 red pebbles, at least two transitions are required to satisfy the gadget.*

LEMMA 14. *Suppose some variable gadgets are set in the configuration where $\overline{x_i}$ and $\overline{x_i'}$ are pebbled with red pebbles, then the number of transitions needed to pebble both the All-False gadget and the 3-or-None gadget is greater than $2k$.*

LEMMA 15. *In order to satisfy all 3-or-None gadgets using at most $2k$ transitions, the only possible configurations for all pebbles must be placed in one of the two pairs of components: $\overline{x_i'}$ and $\overline{x_i}$ or $x_i$ or $x_i'$.*

The remaining gadgets may be pebbled with red pebbles without using any transitions.

4.2.5 *Pebble Sink Path Gadget.* The Pebble Sink Path Gadget is used to take up $3n - 4k - 6$ pebbles that were used in the $k$-True-Variables gadget (and were left over after passing through the gadget) leaving only 5 pebbles for the remaining parts of the winning path. The Pebble Sink Path occurs directly after the clause gadgets path and must be pebbled before the clause gadgets are pebbled. This sink path consists of $3n - 4k - 6$ pyramid gadgets of successively smaller value starting from $3n - 4k - 1$. See Fig. 10 for an example.

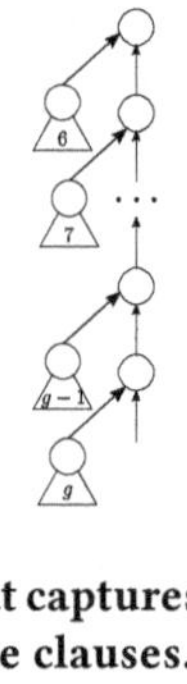


**Figure 10: Pebble sink that captures $3n-4k-6$ pebbles leaving 5 pebbles to be used in the clauses. Here $g = 3n - 4k - 1$.**

4.2.6 *Clause Gadget.* After the set of 3-or-None gadgets comes the Clause gadgets which are used to ensure that the 3SAT clauses are satisfied by the assignments. The clause gadget can only be pebbled with the 5 extra pebbles that remain after the pebble sink has been pebbled. Given that all $2k$ transitions are used in Phase 2 and/or the pebbling 3-or-None gadgets phase, no transitions can be spent in Phase 3 or pebbling the clause gadgets. The output of the clause path must be connected to each vertex of the Pebble Sink Path gadget. See Fig. 11.

Finally, the target vertex can be pebbled with a red pebble if and only if all previous gadgets are pebbled according to the necessary rules and conditions. The $2k + 1$ nodes from the All-False gadget are also predecessors of this target vertex.

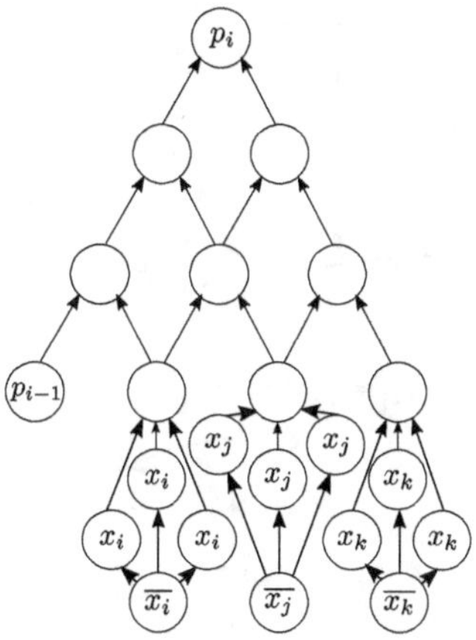


**Figure 11: Clause gadget.**

For an example reduction, see Fig. 12. The target vertex that must be pebbled is the one colored blue.

LEMMA 16. *The clause gadget can be pebbled with* 5 *pebbles (not including the red pebble on* $p_{i-1}$*) if and only if at least one of the variable gadgets that connects to it is set in the true configuration.*

## 4.3 Red-Blue Pebbling is W[1]-hard

In this section, we prove that red-blue pebbling parameterized by the number of transitions is W[1]-hard using the gadgets as specified in Section 4.2. An example construction is shown in Fig. 12. The order of the pebbling is given as the following. First, the variable gadgets are pebbled during Phase 1 of the pebbling which pebbles each pyramid gadget in each variable with a red pebble. Then, the All-False gadget is pebbled which results in all $x_i'$ and $\overline{x_i}$ nodes being pebbled with red pebbles. During Phase 2 of pebbling the variable gadgets, $k$ variables are switched from the false configuration to the true configuration. This in total uses the entirety of the allowed $2k$ transitions. To ensure the $2k$ transitions are used in this phase, the 3-or-None gadgets are pebbled using only 5 red pebbles and no transitions. After the 3-or-None gadgets are pebbled, we pebble the Pebble Sink Path gadget which consumes $3n - 4k - 6$ pebbles. The clause gadgets are pebbled with the remaining 5 pebbles not used in the pebble sink path. Finally, the variable gadgets are pebbled completely using all the pebbles during Phase 3 and the target node as indicated in Fig. 12 pebbled with a red pebble. The total number of red pebbles necessary is $r = 7n - 2k + 1$ and the total number of transitions is $t = 2k$.

THEOREM 4. *The red-blue pebble game parameterized by the number of transitions k is W[1]-hard.*

## 5 OPEN PROBLEMS

We conclude this paper with several open questions:

(1) Are red pebbling number and minimum number of transitions hard to approximate?
(2) Does there exist FPT algorithms for restricted class of graphs (such as bounded width graphs)?
(3) Is finding the red pebbling number W[1]-hard? Recall in this paper that we proved W[1]-hardness only for transitions, not for number of red pebbles.

*Acknowledgements.* This research was supported in part by NSF Graduate Research Fellowship grant 1122374.

## REFERENCES

[1] Alok Aggarwal and S. Vitter, Jeffrey. 1988. The Input/Output Complexity of Sorting and Related Problems. *Commun. ACM* 31, 9 (Sept. 1988), 1116–1127. https://doi.org/10.1145/48529.48535
[2] Charles H. Bennett. 1989. Time/Space Trade-offs for Reversible Computation. *SIAM J. Comput.* 18, 4 (Aug. 1989), 766–776. https://doi.org/10.1137/0218053
[3] Timothy Carpenter, Fabrice Rastello, P. Sadayappan, and Anastasios Sidiropoulos. 2016. Brief Announcement: Approximating the I/O Complexity of One-Shot Red-Blue Pebbling. In *Proceedings of the 28th ACM Symposium on Parallelism in Algorithms and Architectures (SPAA '16)*. ACM, New York, NY, USA, 161–163. https://doi.org/10.1145/2935764.2935807
[4] Siu Man Chan, Massimo Lauria, Jakob Nordström, and Marc Vinyals. 2015. Hardness of Approximation in PSPACE and Separation Results for Pebble Games. In *Proceedings of the IEEE 56th Annual Symposium on Foundations of Computer Science (FOCS '15)*. 466–485. https://doi.org/10.1109/FOCS.2015.36
[5] Stephen Cook and Ravi Sethi. 1974. Storage Requirements for Deterministic / Polynomial Time Recognizable Languages. In *Proceedings of the 6th Annual ACM Symposium on Theory of Computing (STOC '74)*. 33–39. https://doi.org/10.1145/800119.803882
[6] Stephen A. Cook. 1973. An Observation on Time-storage Trade off. In *Proceedings of the 5th Annual ACM Symposium on Theory of Computing (STOC '73)*. 29–33. https://doi.org/10.1145/800125.804032
[7] Erik D. Demaine. 2017. Lecture 22: History of memory models. In *6.851: Advanced Data Structures*. Massachusetts Institute of Technology. http://courses.csail.mit.edu/6.851/fall17/lectures/L22.html
[8] Erik D. Demaine and Quanquan C. Liu. 2017. Inapproximability of the Standard Pebble Game and Hard to Pebble Graphs. In *Proceedings of the 16th International Symposium on Algorithms and Data Structures, WADS '17 (Lecture Notes in Computer Science)*, Vol. 10389. Springer, 313–324.
[9] Rod G. Downey and Michael R. Fellows. 1995. Fixed-Parameter Tractability and Completeness I: Basic Results. *SIAM J. Comput.* 24, 4 (1995), 873–921. https://doi.org/10.1137/S0097539792228228 arXiv:https://doi.org/10.1137/S0097539792228228
[10] Rod G. Downey and Michael R. Fellows. 1995. Fixed-parameter Tractability and Completeness II: On Completeness for $W[1]$. *Theor. Comput. Sci.* 141, 1-2 (April 1995), 109–131. https://doi.org/10.1016/0304-3975(94)00097-3
[11] Venmugil Elango, Fabrice Rastello, Louis-Noël Pouchet, J. Ramanujam, and P. Sadayappan. 2015. On Characterizing the Data Access Complexity of Programs. In *Proceedings of the 42nd Annual ACM SIGPLAN-SIGACT Symposium on Principles of Programming Languages (POPL '15)*. 567–580. https://dl.acm.org/citation.cfm?id=2677010
[12] Michael R. Garey and David S. Johnson. 1990. *Computers and Intractability; A Guide to the Theory of NP-Completeness.* W. H. Freeman & Co., New York, NY, USA.
[13] John R. Gilbert, Thomas Lengauer, and Robert Endre Tarjan. 1980. The Pebbling Problem is Complete in Polynomial Space. *SIAM J. Comput.* 9, 3 (1980), 513–524. https://doi.org/10.1137/0209038 arXiv:https://doi.org/10.1137/0209038
[14] Hong Jia-Wei and H. T. Kung. 1981. I/O Complexity: The Red-blue Pebble Game. In *Proceedings of the 13th Annual ACM Symposium on Theory of Computing (STOC '81)*. 326–333. https://doi.org/10.1145/800076.802486
[15] Jakob Nordstrom. 2015. New Wine into Old Wineskins: A Survey of Some Pebbling Classics with Supplemental Results. https://www.csc.kth.se/~jakobn/research/PebblingSurveyTMP.pdf.
[16] Desh Ranjan, John E. Savage, and Mohammad Zubair. 2012. Upper and lower I/O bounds for pebbling $r$-pyramids. *J. Discrete Algorithms* 14 (2012), 2–12.
[17] Ravi Sethi. 1975. Complete Register Allocation Problems. *SIAM J. Comput.* 4, 3 (1975), 226–248. https://doi.org/10.1137/0204020

$$\phi = (x_1 \vee \overline{x_2} \vee \overline{x_3}) \wedge (x_2 \vee x_1 \vee \overline{x_4}) \wedge (\overline{x_2} \vee \overline{x_3} \vee \overline{x_4})$$

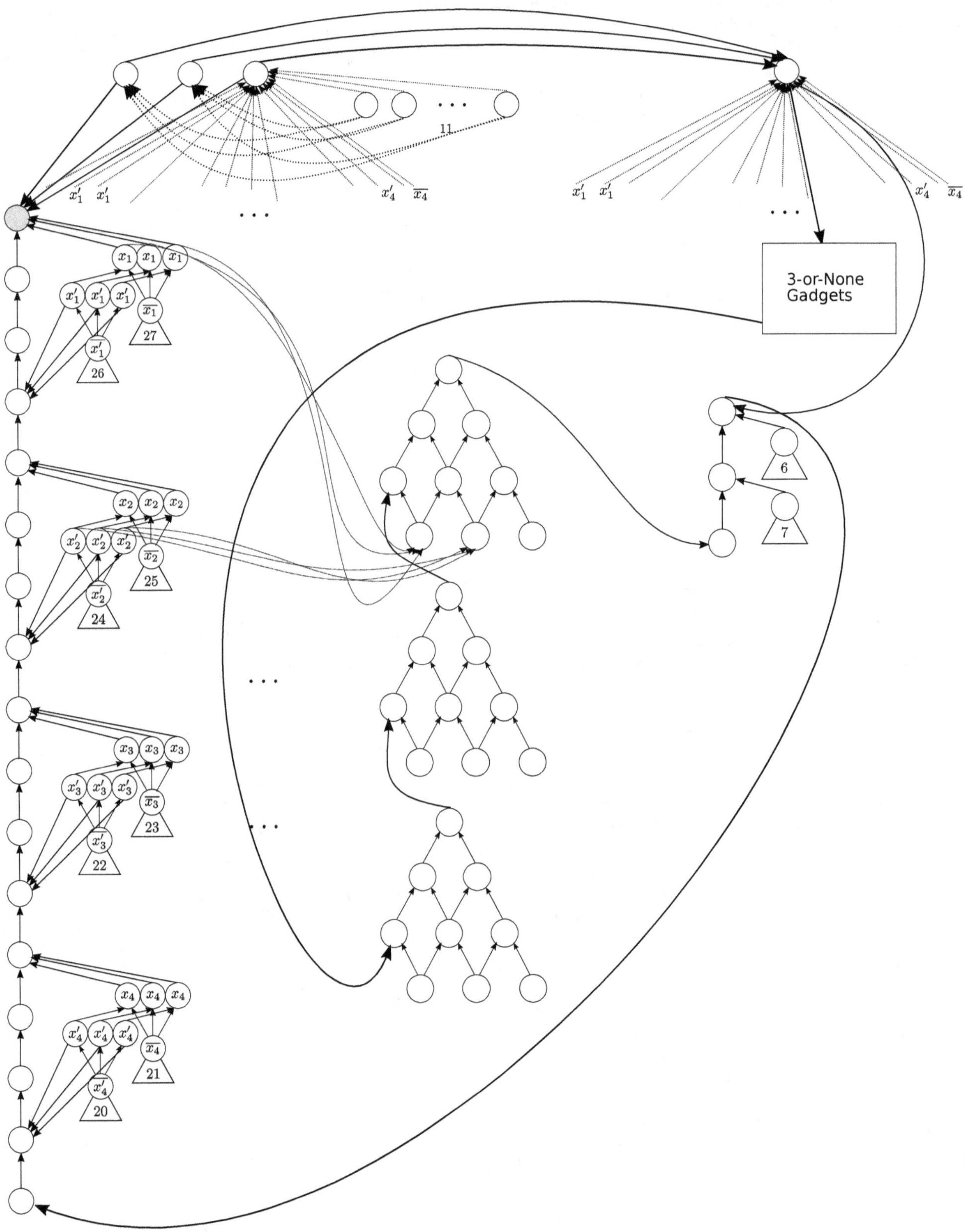


**Figure 12: Example W[1]-hardness reduction for the red-blue pebble game. The vertex colored blue is the vertex that must be pebbled at the end and can only be pebbled if and only if the 3SAT instance has a solution that sets exactly $k$ variables to True and uses at most $2k$ transitions.**

# Online Generalized Caching with Varying Weights and Costs

Regular Paper

Guy Even*
Tel Aviv University
guy@eng.tau.ac.il

Moti Medina
Ben Gurion University of the Negev
medinamo@bgu.ac.il

Dror Rawitz†
Bar Ilan University
dror.rawitz@biu.ac.il

## ABSTRACT

We present a new extension of the generalized caching/paging problem that allows the adversary to arbitrarily change the cost or weight of the currently requested page.

We present modifications of previous algorithms for generalized caching to handle varying page weights and page costs. In particular, a deterministic algorithm based on [5, 9] for an $(h, k)$-competitive algorithm with competitive ratio $k/(k - h + 1)$ is presented. In addition, a randomized algorithm based on [1, 2] with competitive ratio $O(\log k)$ is presented.

We present three applications that can be supported via reductions to generalized caching with varying page weights and page costs. These applications are: (1) support of subsets of pages that must be simultaneously present in the cache before entry to a critical section (i.e., working sets), (2) change of page size due to compression and decompression, (3) variable cache size (i.e., elastic caches).

## CCS CONCEPTS

• **Theory of computation → Online algorithms; Caching and paging algorithms;**

## KEYWORDS

online algorithms; competitive analysis; paging; caching

**ACM Reference Format:**
Guy Even, Moti Medina, and Dror Rawitz. 2018. **Online Generalized Caching with Varying Weights and Costs: Regular Paper. In *SPAA '18: 30th ACM Symposium on Parallelism in Algorithms and Architectures, July 16–18, 2018, Vienna, Austria.* ACM, New York, NY, USA, 8 pages. https://doi.org/10.1145/3210377.3210404**

## 1 INTRODUCTION

Consider a cache of size $k$ and requests for pages in each round $t$. In the generalized caching problem, each page $p$ has a weight $w(p)$ and a cost $c(p)$. The weight of a page specifies the size of the page so that the sum of the page weights in the cache cannot exceed $k$. The cost of a page specifies the cost of fetching the page. We denote the page that is requested in round $t$ by $p_t$. The goal of the caching algorithm is to decide which pages reside in the cache in each round. On one hand, the requested page $p_t$ must reside in the cache in round $t$. On the other hand, the sum of the weights of the pages in the cache is bounded by the cache size $k$. A request for a page $p_t$ that is not in the cache incurs a cost of $c(p_t)$ to pay for fetching $p_t$. If page $p_t$ is in the cache, then no cost is incurred. We consider the online version of the caching problem in which the caching algorithm does not have any information about the requests at time $t'$ greater than $t$.

In this paper, we consider a generalization in which the weight or cost of the currently requested page $p_t$ may be changed. Thus a request in round $t$ is a triple $r_t \triangleq \langle p_t, w_t(p_t), c_t(p_t)\rangle$, where $w_t(p_t)$ is the new weight of $p_t$ and $c_t(p_t)$ is the new cost of $p_t$. We refer to this problem as the generalized caching problem with varying page weights and page costs and denote it by GVWC.

**Our Results.** We present modifications of online algorithms for generalized caching so that they apply also to GVWC.

Our deterministic online algorithm is based on [5, 9]. This algorithm competes with an optimal (offline) solution that has a cache of size $h$. We refer to such an algorithm as an $(h, k)$-competitive caching algorithm. Our competitive ratio meets the previous competitive ratio of $(h, k)$-competitive algorithms for generalized caching. Namely, we obtain a competitive ratio of $k/(k - h + 1)$.

Our randomized online algorithm is based on [1, 2] and obtains the same competitive ratio of $O(\log k)$.

We present three applications of GVWC. These applications are (see Sec. 3 for more details): (1) Support of working sets for critical segments. In this application, before entering a critical segment, the operating system announces which pages will be accessed during the critical segment. This set of pages is called a working set. Cache misses are forbidden during the critical segment. Hence, the pages in the working set must be locked in the cache. Only after the critical segment ends, the pages of the working set are released and may be evicted. (2) Support of storage of pages in compressed form. To save I/O and storage, pages are stored in the (non-cache) memory in compressed format. Pages are decompressed after they are fetched to the cache. Since a compressed page is smaller than a decompressed page, the weight and cost of a compressed page is smaller than the weight and cost of a decompressed page. (3) Support of variable cache size. In this application the size of the cache is not fixed. In between requests for pages, directives for increasing or decreasing the cache size may be given.

*This research was supported by a grant from the United States-Israel Binational Science Foundation (BSF), Jerusalem, Israel, and the United States Science Foundation (NSF).
†Supported in part by the Israel Science Foundation (grant no. 497/14).


ACM ISBN 978-1-4503-5799-9/18/07...$15.00
https://doi.org/10.1145/3210377.3210404

We show how to reduce these applications to the GVWC problem. These reductions together with the algorithms imply online algorithms for these applications with the same competitive ratios.

## 2 PROBLEM FORMULATION

***Generalized caching with fixed weights and costs.*** The generalized caching problem with fixed page weights and costs is defined as follows. Consider a cache of size $k$ and a set $P$ of pages. Each page $p \in P$ has a weight $w(p)$ and a cost $c(p)$, both of which are real numbers which are assumed to be at least one.[1] For a subset $A \subseteq P$, let $w(A) \triangleq \sum_{p \in A} w(p)$ and $c(A) \triangleq \sum_{p \in A} c(p)$. The *state* of the cache in round $t$ is a subset of pages and is denoted by $A_t \subseteq P$. The input is a sequence of pages $\sigma \triangleq \{p_t\}_{t=1}^{T-1}$.

Definition 1. *A sequence $\{A_t\}_{t=0}^{T}$ of cache states is* valid *with respect to the input sequence $\sigma$ it satisfies the following properties:*

*(1) $A_0 = A_T = \emptyset$,*
*(2) for every $t \in [1:T]$, $w(A_t) \leq k$, and*
*(3) for every $t \in [1:T]$, $p_t \in A_t$.*

Note that we add a final empty cache state $A_T$ after the last page request $A_{T-1}$.

A page $p$ is *fetched* in round $t$ if $p \in A_t \setminus A_{t-1}$. The *fetch cost* of a sequence $\{A_t\}_{t=1}^{T}$ of cache states is defined by

$$\text{fetch}_{\text{cost}}(\{A_t\}_{t=1}^{T}) \triangleq \sum_{t=1}^{T} c(A_t \setminus A_{t-1}).$$

Let $\mathcal{V}(\sigma)$ denote the set of all valid sequences of cache states with respect to the input sequence $\sigma$. Let $\text{OPT}(\sigma) \in \mathcal{V}(\sigma)$ denote a valid sequence of cache states such that

$$\text{OPT}(\sigma) \triangleq \arg\min_{\mathcal{B} \in \mathcal{V}(\sigma)} \text{fetch}_{\text{cost}}(\mathcal{B}).$$

A sequence of cache states $\mathcal{A} \in \mathcal{V}(\sigma)$ is $\alpha$-competitive with respect to $\sigma$ if

$$\text{fetch}_{\text{cost}}(\mathcal{A}) \leq \alpha \cdot \text{fetch}_{\text{cost}}(\text{OPT}(\sigma)).$$

An online algorithm ALG is fed the requests of the input one-by-one. Before round $t$, the algorithm has already seen the prefix of requests $\{p_{t'}\}_{t'<t}$, and has computed the prefix of states $\{A_{t'}\}_{t'<t}$. In round $t$, ALG is input $p_t$, and it must compute $A_t$. In particular, if $w(A_{t-1} \cup \{p_t\}) > k$, then ALG must decide which of the pages in $A_{t-1}$ must be evicted. Formally, a page $p$ is evicted at round $t$ if $p \in A_{t-1} \setminus A_t$.

An online algorithm ALG has a *competitive ratio* of $\alpha$ if, for every input sequence $\sigma$, it computes a valid sequence of cache states $\mathcal{A}(\sigma) \in \mathcal{V}(\sigma)$ such that $\mathcal{A}$ is $\alpha$-competitive with respect to $\sigma$.

A randomized online algorithm need not output a fixed sequence of cache states. Instead, its output is drawn from a distribution $\mu(\sigma)$ over the set $\mathcal{V}(\sigma)$ of valid cache sequences. We say that ALG has a *competitive ratio* of $\alpha$ if, for every input sequence $\sigma$,

$$\mathbb{E}_{\mathcal{A} \sim \mu(\sigma)}[\text{fetch}_{\text{cost}}(\mathcal{A})] \leq \alpha \cdot \text{fetch}_{\text{cost}}(\text{OPT}(\sigma)).$$

***Generalized caching with varying weights and costs (GVWC).*** In this version of the caching problem, page weights and costs depend also on the round. Let $w_t(p)$ and $c_t(p)$ denote the weight and cost of page $p$ in round $t$. Now we allow costs and weights to be real numbers greater equal to one and "infinity". We do not allow the page weight and cost to change arbitrarily. The restriction is that the weight or cost of page $p$ may change in round $t$ only if $p = p_t$. Formally, initial page weights and costs are assigned to all the pages. We denote these weights and costs by $w_0(p)$ and $c_0(p)$, respectively. For every round $t \geq 1$ we require that the following holds.

$$w_t(p) \neq w_{t-1}(p) \Longrightarrow p = p_t$$
$$c_t(p) \neq c_{t-1}(p) \Longrightarrow p = p_t$$

The input in each round $t$ consists of three parts. The first part is $p_t$ as before. The second part is the (new) weight $w_t(p_t)$ and the third part is the (new) cost $c_t(p_t)$.

The update in the weight of $p_t$ means the following. The size of the fetched page $p_t$ is still its old size. Once it is in the cache, its size changes to the new weight (e.g, due to processing). Hence, for $1 \leq t < T$, a state $A_t$ of the cache is valid if

$$p_t \in A_t \text{ and } \max\{w_t(A_t), w_{t-1}(A_t)\} \leq k.$$

This means that the sum of the weights of the pages in $A_t$ is bounded by $k$ before and after the weight of $p_t$ has been updated.

The update in the cost of $p_t$ means that the future cost of fetching the page will change. Hence, the cost of fetching a page $p_t$ in round $t$ still equals $c_{t-1}(p_t)$. However, let $t'$ denote the next round that $p_t$ is requested (i.e., $p_{t'} = p_t$), if $p_t$ is not in the cache in the beginning of round $t'$, then the cost of fetching it will be $c_t(p_t)$.

Definition 2. *The* fetch cost *of a sequence $\{A_t\}_{t=1}^{T}$ of cache states with respect to varying page costs is defined by*

$$\text{fetch}_{\text{cost}}(\{A_t\}_{t=1}^{T}) \triangleq \sum_{t=1}^{T} c_{t-1}(A_t \setminus A_{t-1}).$$

### 2.1 Fetch Cost vs. Eviction Cost

The online paging algorithms of Bansal et al. [1–3] are competitive with respect to eviction cost rather than fetch cost. In this section we justify the task of competing with eviction cost even in the case of varying page weights and page costs.

Consider an input sequence $\sigma = \{(p_t, w_t(p_t), c_t(p_t))\}_{t=1}^{T-1}$. Denote the set of accessed pages by $B(T) \triangleq \{p \mid \exists t \in [1, T-1] : p = p_t\}$. Let $\mathcal{A} \triangleq \{A_t\}_{t=1}^{T}$ denote a sequence of valid cache states with respect to $\sigma$, i.e., $\mathcal{A} \in \mathcal{V}(\sigma)$.

Definition 3. *The* eviction cost *of a sequence $\{A_t\}_{t=1}^{T}$ of cache states with respect to varying page costs is defined by*

$$\text{evict}_{\text{cost}}(\{A_t\}_{t=1}^{T}) \triangleq \sum_{t=1}^{T} c_{t-1}(A_{t-1} \setminus A_t).$$

Definition 4. *A sequence $\mathcal{A}$ of cache states is* lazy with respect to fetches *(or simply* lazy*) if, for every $t \in [1, T-1]$ the following holds:*

$$p_t \in A_{t-1} \Longrightarrow A_t \subseteq A_{t-1}$$
$$p_t \notin A_{t-1} \Longrightarrow A_t \setminus A_{t-1} = \{p_t\}.$$

The following observation justifies focusing only on lazy sequences of cache states.

[1] In fact, zero weight pages do not create any problem because they do not consume cache space. Hence, we may allow weights to be zero, but not in the range (0, 1).

Observation 5. *For every $\mathcal{A} \in \mathcal{V}(\sigma)$, there exists a lazy sequence $\mathcal{A}' \in \mathcal{V}(\sigma)$ such that* $\text{fetch}_{\text{cost}}(\mathcal{A}') \leq \text{fetch}_{\text{cost}}(\mathcal{A})$ *and* $\text{evict}_{\text{cost}}(\mathcal{A}') \leq \text{evict}_{\text{cost}}(\mathcal{A})$.

Proof. Define $A'_0 = \emptyset$, and

$$A'_t \triangleq \begin{cases} A'_{t-1} \cap A_t & \text{if } p_t \in A'_{t-1} \\ \{p_t\} \cup (A'_{t-1} \cap A_t) & \text{if } p_t \notin A'_{t-1}. \end{cases}$$

Since $A'_t \subseteq A_t$ for all $t$ and since $\mathcal{A}$ is valid, it follows that $\max\{w_t(A'_t), w_{t-1}(A'_t)\} \leq k$. Since $p_t \in A'_t$ by definition it follows that $\mathcal{A}'$ is valid with respect to $\sigma$. In addition, $\mathcal{A}'$ is lazy with respect to fetches by definition. Now, $\text{fetch}_{\text{cost}}(\mathcal{A}') \leq \text{fetch}_{\text{cost}}(\mathcal{A})$ holds since the lazy algorithm fetches a page only if it is requested, and $\text{evict}_{\text{cost}}(\mathcal{A}') \leq \text{evict}_{\text{cost}}(\mathcal{A})$ holds due to Definition 3 and the fact that $A'_t \subseteq A_t$ for all $t$. □

Note that in the following claim the fetch cost equals the eviction cost if $c_0(p) = c_T(p)$, for every requested page $p$.

Claim 6.

$$\text{fetch}_{\text{cost}}(\{A_t\}_{t=1}^T) = \text{evict}_{\text{cost}}(\{A_t\}_{t=1}^T) + c_0(B(T)) - c_T(B(T)) \tag{1}$$

Proof. We may assume that $\{A_t\}_{t=1}^T$ is lazy. Hence, $B(T) = \bigcup_t A_t$. Fix a page $p$. Let $\text{fetch}_{\text{cost}p}$ denote the sum of all the fetch costs associated with fetching $p$. Similarly, let $\text{evict}_{\text{cost}p}$ denote the sum of all the eviction costs associated with evicting $p$. It suffices to prove that $\text{fetch}_{\text{cost}p} - \text{evict}_{\text{cost}p} = c_0(p) - c_T(p)$.

Let $f_i$ denote the index of the round in which $p$ is fetched for the $i$'th time. Let $e_i$ denote the index of the round in which $p$ is evicted for the $i$'th time. Let $\widetilde{t_i} = \max\{t < e_i \mid p = p_t\}$, namely the index of the last round $p$ was requested before it was evicted in round $e_i$. Let $\ell$ denote the number of times $p$ is fetched. Note that since $A_T = \emptyset$, the number of time $p$ is fetched equals the number of times $p$ is evicted.

Note that $f_i \leq \widetilde{t_i} < e_i$ and $p_t \neq p$ for every $t \in (\widetilde{t_i}, f_{i+1})$. Hence, the cost of fetching $p$ in round $f_{i+1}$ equals $c_{\widetilde{t_i}}(p)$. The cost of the first fetch (in round $f_1$) equals $c_0(p)$. We conclude that

$$\text{fetch}_{\text{cost}p} = c_0(p) + \sum_{i=1}^{\ell-1} c_{\widetilde{t_i}}(p). \tag{2}$$

On the other hand, the cost of evicting $p$ in round $e_i$ equals $c_{\widetilde{t_i}}$. Hence,

$$\text{evict}_{\text{cost}p} = \sum_{i=1}^{\ell} c_{\widetilde{t_i}}(p), \tag{3}$$

Since $c_{\widetilde{t_\ell}}(p) = c_T(p)$, we conclude that $\text{fetch}_{\text{cost}p} - \text{evict}_{\text{cost}p} = c_0(p) - c_T(p)$, as required. □

The following lemma states that an $\alpha$-competitive algorithm w.r.t. eviction cost is an $(\alpha + 1)$-competitive algorithm w.r.t. fetch cost. Note that if $c_0(p) = c_T(p)$, for every page $p$, then the algorithm is an $\alpha$-competitive w.r.t. fetch cost.

Lemma 7. *An online algorithm for generalized caching with varying page weights and costs that achieves a competitive ratio of $\alpha$ for the eviction cost also achieves a competitive ratio of $(1 + \alpha)$ for the fetch cost.*

Proof. By Obs. 5, we may assume that the algorithm computes a lazy sequence of cache states. By Claim 6, the fetch cost is at most the sum of the eviction cost and the initial costs of the pages that are requested. Since the cost of fetching $p$ for the first time is $c_0(p)$, we conclude that $c_0(\{p \mid \exists t : p = p_t\}) \leq \text{OPT}(\sigma)$, and the lemma follows. □

## 2.2 Advocacy of the Model

The model only allows changes in weight or cost of the currently requested page. Although this model may look limited at first, we show in the next section that this model is strong enough for the applications of GVWC. On the other hand, in this section we argue that relaxing the model to allow changes of weights and costs of pages which are not in OPT's cache can result with unbounded competitive ratio, as follows.

For randomized algorithms, consider the following scenario. The adversary introduces two page requests of weight $\frac{k}{2}$ and cost 0, followed by a page request of weight 1. Hence, the algorithm should evict either the first or the second page. Now, the adversary evicts the page that the algorithm is less likely to evict (in deterministic algorithms the adversary knows which page the algorithm is going to evict) and then increases its eviction cost to "infinity". This example uses the fact that the adversary can change pages which are not in its cache.

# 3 APPLICATIONS

We present three applications that are reducible to GVWC. In these applications, we consider an operating system (OS) or user application (APP) that may request pages, change the requested page weight or cost, or give other directives. The cache controller (our online algorithm or the optimal offline solution) decides which pages are fetched or evicted. However, the input sequence does not depend on the state of the cache (i.e., the input sequence is oblivious to whether a page has been evicted or not).

## 3.1 Working Sets

*Motivating Story.* Consider an APP or OS entering a "critical section" during which page faults are forbidden. Before entering the critical section, the set $S$ of pages to be accessed during the critical section is announced to the cache controller. The cache controller guarantees that the cache contains all the pages in $S$ during the critical section. Thus the pages in $S$ are announced as "unswappable". After leaving the critical section, the set $S$ is "released", allowing the cache controller to evict pages in $S$.

*Problem Definition.* The *Generalized Caching with Working Sets* problem is defined as follows. In addition to regular page requests, the input may contain working set requests. There are two types of working set requests: lock($S$) and unlock($S$), where $S$ is a subset of pages among the pages that have been already requested. The semantics of lock and unlock requests is that in the interval between lock($S$) and unlock($S$) every page $p \in S$ must be in the cache. To ensure feasibility, we assume that the weight of the locked pages is less than the size of the cache. We also assume that after every lock($S$) request an unlock($S$) request appears. (This is required so that the cache can be emptied in the last round.)

*Reduction to GVWC.* To support a lock($S$) request we simply insert a new request $\langle p, w_t(p) = w_{t-1}(p), c_t(p) = \infty\rangle$, for every $p \in S$. To support an unlock($S$) request we simply insert a new request $\langle p, w_t(p) = w_{t-1}(p), c_t(p) = c_{t'}(p)\rangle$, for every $p \in S$, where $t' < t$ is the last time $p$ was requested in original input.

*Formal Statement of Competitive Ratio.* Applying the reduction to GVWC and the GVWC algorithms yields an online randomized $O(\log k)$-competitive algorithm, as well as an online deterministic $(h, k)$-competitive algorithm with competitive ratio $k/(k - h + 1)$. We are not aware of previous analyses of online algorithms for working sets.

## 3.2 Compressed Pages

*Motivating Story.* A common means to reduce storage space is to store pages in compressed format. Of course, such compression incurs additional computation (see Douglis [6] for a study of the I/O delay vs. computation trade-off when compression is utilized). We consider the following setting: in the normal state of affairs pages are stored in (non-cache) memory in a compressed form. A fetched page is decompressed after it is fetched. If a page is evicted before it is compressed, then it is stored in a decompressed format. The last request for every page is a compress request, hence pages are finally evicted in their compressed format.

*Simplified abstraction.* In this setting we assume that the input sequence consists of regular page requests, decompression requests (i.e., make sure the page is in the cache and decompress it), and compression requests (i.e., make sure the page is in the cache and compress it). The cost of evicting a compressed page is smaller than the cost of evicting a decompressed page since the compressed page is shorter. Formally, a page $p$ is associated with two sets of parameters. In its compressed form, page $p$ has weight $w'(p)$ and a cost $c'(p)$. Similarly, in its decompressed form it has a weight $w''(p)$ and a cost $c''(p)$. Initially, all pages are assumed to be compressed, and the last request for every page is a compress request.

*Reduction to GVWC.* We model this setting as follows.

- Initial weights and costs are $w_0(p) = w'(p)$ and $c_0(p) = c'(p)$, for every page $p$.
- Page requests remain unchanged (in this application, a page retains its weight and cost in a regular request).
- A decompression request of a page $p$ is mapped to a request $\langle p, w_t(p) = w''(p), c_t(p) = 2 \cdot c''(p)\rangle$.
- A compression request of a page $p$ is mapped to a request $\langle p, w_t(p) = w'(p), c_t(p) = 2 \cdot c'(p)\rangle$.

We assume that each page is initially compressed and that the request sequence leaves all pages compressed. Since the cache state in the end is empty, all pages in the end are stored in compressed form in the memory.

Note that a page can be in the cache in compressed form. Compression and decompression are modeled by the change in the page parameters. For example, it may be the case that the OS decides to compress a page without evicting it. The updated page cost in compression and decompression requests are multiplied by 2 to account for both writing and reading the page in its corresponding state.

*Formal Statement of Competitive Ratio.* Consider a valid sequence of cache states $\mathcal{A} = \{A_t\}_{t=0}^{T}$ w.r.t. to an input sequence obtained by the reduction to GVWC. Let $\Gamma_t$ denote the subset of pages that are compressed at time $t$. The *real* cost of $\mathcal{A}$ is defined by

$$\text{real}_{\text{cost}}(\mathcal{A}) \triangleq \sum_{t=1}^{T}\left(\sum_{p\in(A_t \triangle A_{t-1})\cap\Gamma_t} c'(p) + \sum_{p\in(A_{t-1} \triangle A_t)\setminus\Gamma_t} c''(p)\right)$$

The following claim can be proved along the same lines as Claim 6. (Note that, for every page, the first request is a regular request and the last request is a compress request. In particular, $c_0(p) = c_T(p)$.)

Claim 8. *For every valid sequence of cache states $\mathcal{A}$*

$$\text{fetch}_{\text{cost}}(\mathcal{A}) = \text{evict}_{\text{cost}}(\mathcal{A}) = \text{real}_{\text{cost}}(\mathcal{A}).$$

The reduction of caching of compressed pages to GVWC together with the online GVWC-algorithms yields a randomized $O(\log k)$-competitive algorithm and a deterministic $(h, k)$-competitive algorithm with a competitive ratio of $k/(k - h + 1)$. We are not aware of a previous analysis of the competitive ratio of an online algorithm for caching of compressed pages.

### 3.2.1 *Extending to Asymmetric Fetch and Evict Costs.*

In this section we outline the adaptations required to support asymmetric fetch and evict costs in the context of the compressed pages application. Now, the set of parameters that is associated with each page captures the fact that the cost of fetching a page and writing a page are different. Formally, in its compressed form, page $p$ has weight $w'(p)$, a fetch cost $c'(p, r)$, and a evict cost $c'(p, w)$. Similarly, in its decompressed form it has a weight $w''(p)$, a fetch cost $c''(p, r)$, and a evict cost $c''(p, w)$. As before, initially, all pages are assumed to be compressed.

The reduction to GVWC is similar to the symmetric case, as follows.

- Initial weights and costs are $w_0(p) = w'(p)$ and $c_0(p) = c'(p, r) + c'(p, w)$, for every page $p$.
- Page requests remain unchanged (in this application, a page retains its weight and cost in a regular request).
- A decompression request of a page $p$ is mapped to a request $\langle p, w_t(p) = w''(p), c_t(p) = c''(p, r) + c''(p, w)\rangle$.
- A compression request of a page $p$ is mapped to a request $\langle p, w_t(p) = w'(p), c_t(p) = c'(p, r) + c'(p, w)\rangle$.

Now, the *real* cost of $\mathcal{A}$ is defined by

$$\text{real}_{\text{cost}}(\mathcal{A}) \triangleq \sum_{t=1}^{T}\left(\sum_{p\in\Gamma_t\cap(A_t\setminus A_{t-1})} c'(p, r) + \sum_{p\in\Gamma_t\cap(A_{t-1}\setminus A_t)} c'(p, w) + \sum_{p\in A_t\setminus(A_{t-1}\cup\Gamma_t)} c''(p, r) + \sum_{p\in A_{t-1}\setminus(A_t\cup\Gamma_t)} c''(p, w)\right)$$

Given the (re)definition of the real cost one can show that Claim 8 holds also with respect to the asymmetric case. Moreover, the competitiveness guarantees of the asymmetric case also apply to the symmetric case.

## 3.3 Elastic Paging

*Motivating story.* Elastic paging is an abstraction in which the size of a cache varies over time. Varying cache size occurs, for example, when multiple virtual machines (VMs) share the same cache. A disjoint part of the cache is allocated to each VM. The partitioning changes over time, and hence the individual cache size of a VM is not constant (see [8] for more applications).

*Simplified abstraction.* Peserico [8] considered an extension of the classical online caching model (with unit costs and weights) where the size $k$ of the cache is in the interval $[0 : K]$. Moreover, the size of the cache is part of the online input. Formally, the online sequence of page requests is augmented with two new symbols '+' and '−', the semantics of which are "increase or decrease cache size by 1". The initial and final size of the cache is assumed to be 0.

We assume that the input sequence is feasible, namely, $w_t(p_t)$ is never bigger than the current cache size.

*Reduction to GVWC.* We reduce elastic paging to GVWC as follows:

- Add a special page (called the *balloon*) that is never evicted. We denote the balloon by $s$. Insert two new requests in the beginning $r_1 = \langle s, w_0(s) = K, c_0(s) = 0\rangle$. Note that the balloon occupies the whole cache, and hence the cache's effective size is zero. The next request updates the balloon's cost so that it will not be evicted: $r_2 = \langle s, w_1(s) = K, c_1(s) = \infty\rangle$.
- Original page requests remain unchanged.
- A '+' symbol at time $t$ is mapped to a request $\langle s, w_t(s) = w_{t-1}(s) - 1, c_t(s) = \infty\rangle$.
- A '−' symbol at time $t$ is mapped to a request $\langle s, w_t(s) = w_{t-1}(s) + 1, c_t(s) = \infty\rangle$.
- Add a last request: $r_T = \langle s, w_T(s) = K, c_T(s) = 0\rangle$ to force the eviction of all pages and guarantee that $c_0(s) = c_T(s)$.

Observe that the cache size in round $t$ equals $K - w_t(s)$. (We also allow $w_t(s) = 0$ which is easily handled by the caching algorithm as $s$ is never evicted.)

*Formal Statement of Competitive Ratio.* Applying the reduction and GVWC algorithms yields an online randomized $O(\log K)$-competitive algorithm, as well as an online deterministic $(h, K)$-competitive algorithm that achieves a competitive ratio of $\frac{K}{K-h+1}$. Note that in an $(h, K)$-competitive algorithm for elastic caching, the cache size in round $t$ is $K - w_t(s)$ and the cache size of the competing optimal solution is $h - w_t(s)$.

*Comparison to previous results.* Peserico [8] obtained essentially the same result for deterministic elastic paging (with unit costs and weights. In particular, natural extensions of marking and conservative algorithms (see, e.g., [4]) are $K$-competitive for Elastic Paging (with unit costs and weights). Peserico also considered an algorithm with a resource augmentation version where the adversary's cache size is a $\frac{h}{K}$ fraction of the online algorithm's cache size in each round. In this case the competitive ratio is $\frac{K}{K-h+1}$.

# 4 A RANDOMIZED $O(\log k)$-COMPETITIVE ALGORITHM

Our randomized algorithm is based on the algorithms in [1, 2]. To obtain an $O(\log k)$ competitive ratio, we follow the version in [1].

## 4.1 LP Relaxation

*Notation.* Let $r(p, t)$ denote the number of times the page $p$ was requested in the interval $[1, t]$. Let $t(p, i)$ denote the index of the round in which $p$ was requested for the $i$th time. Formally,

$$r(p,t) \triangleq |\{t' \le t \mid p_{t'} = p\}|$$
$$t(p,i) \triangleq \text{argmin}\{t \mid r(p,t) = i\}$$
$$I(p,i) \triangleq (t(p,i), t(p,i+1))$$
$$B(t) \triangleq \{p \mid \exists t' \le t : p_t = p\}$$
$$H(t) \triangleq \{S \subseteq B(t) \mid w_t(S) > k\}.$$

For every prefix of rounds $[1, T]$, we have a primal LP $\mathcal{PLP}(T)$ and a dual LP $\mathcal{DLP}(T)$ (see Table 1). The primal variables are $x(p, i)$ and denote the extent to which page $p$ has been evicted from the cache during $I(p, i)$. The dual variables are $y(S, t)$, where $S \in H(t)$. Let $\widetilde{w}_t^S(p) \triangleq \min\{w_t(p), w_t(S) - k\}$ denote the truncated weight of $p$ with respect to $S$ in round $t$.

The following claim is a straightforward adaption of [2].

CLAIM 9. *The primal LP $\mathcal{PLP}$ is a fractional relaxation of GVWC with respect to evict costs.*

## 4.2 Algorithm Description

The algorithm works in two phases. The first phase is an online primal-dual algorithm that solves the fractional version. The fractional solution satisfies the following properties:

1. The dual variables $\{y(S, t)\}_{S,t}$ constitute a feasible solution of the dual LP.
2. The primal variables $\{x(p, i)\}_{p,i}$ do not necessarily constitute a feasible solution of the primal LP. However, the primal variables do satisfy the following conditions.
   (a) $x(p_t, r(p_t, t)) = 0$, in every round $t$.
   (b) $x(p, i) > 0$ implies that $x(p, i) \ge 1/k$.
   (c) Let $S_t \triangleq \{p \in B(t) \mid x(p, r(p, t)) < 1/16\}$. Then the covering constraint for $t$ and $S_t$ is satisfied.
   (d) Let $P(t') \triangleq \sum_{p \in B(t')} \sum_{i=1}^{r(p,t')} c_{t(p,i)}(p) \cdot x(p, i)$ denote the value of the primal solution in round $t'$. Let $D(t) \triangleq \sum_{t=1}^{t'} \sum_{S \in H(t)} (w_t(S) - k) \cdot y(S, t)$ denote the value of the dual solution in round $t'$. The primal and dual solutions satisfy $P(t') \le O(\log k) \cdot D(t')$, for every round $t'$. By weak duality, $D(T)$ is a lower bound on the optimal evict cost. We conclude that $P(t)$ is at most $O(\log k)$ times the cost of the optimal evict cost.

The primal-dual algorithm for computing the fractional version in [1] requires a few changes to deal with the varying page weights and costs. As this is a primal-dual algorithm, these modifications are dictated by the primal and dual LPs. We point out that each request $\langle p_t, w_t(p_t), c_t(p_t)\rangle$ is processed in three steps. First we process the request with the old weight and cost $\langle p_t, w_{t-1}(p_t), c_{t-1}(p_t)\rangle$. Second, if $w_t(p_t) > w_{t-1}(p_{t-1})$, we process the request with the new weight and old cost $\langle p_t, w_t(p_t), c_{t-1}(p_t)\rangle$. In this stage, more pages might be evicted. Finally, we process the request $\langle p_t, w_t(p_t), c_t(p_t)\rangle$. We point out that the third stage does not induce any change in the values of the variables (namely, in the third stage we only introduce the new cost of $p_t$). The reason for this is that: (1) The LHS of the

$$\mathcal{PLP}(T) : \min \sum_{p \in B(T)} \sum_{i=1}^{r(p,T)} c_{t(p,i)}(p) \cdot x(p,i)$$

s.t.

$$\forall t \in [1,T]\ \forall S \in H(t) : \quad \sum_{p \in S \setminus \{p_t\}} \widetilde{w}_t^S(p) \cdot x(p, r(p,t)) \geq w_t(S) - k$$

$$\forall p \in B(T)\ \forall i \leq r(p,T) : \quad x(p,i) \geq 0$$

$$\mathcal{DLP}(T) : \max \sum_{t=1}^{T} \sum_{S \in H(t)} (w_t(S) - k) \cdot y(S,t)$$

s.t.

$$\forall p \in B(T)\ \forall i \leq r(p,T) : \quad \sum_{t \in I(p,i)} \sum_{S \in H(t) | p \in S} \widetilde{w}_t^S(p) \cdot y(S,t) \leq c_{t(p,i)}(p)$$

$$\forall t \in [1,T]\ \forall S \in H(t) : \quad y(S,t) \geq 0$$

**Table 1: The primal and dual relaxations of GVWC**

dual constraint for $p_t$ and $i = r(p,t)$ equals zero because $I(p,t)$ is empty. (2) The change in the cost of $p_t$ does not influence the value of the primal solution because $x(p_t, r(p_t, t)) = 0$.

The second phase of the algorithm deals with rounding the fractional primal solution to an integral solution. This phase is executed by attaching a distribution $\mu_t$ over $k^2$ complements of valid cache states (i.e., "anti-configurations") in each round $t$. The challenge in the construction of the distributions is to maintain the invariant that the distance between $\mu_t$ and $\mu_{t-1}$ is bounded by $O(P(t) - P(t-1))$. The distance between $\mu_t$ and $\mu_{t-1}$ is the average "scaled" $\ell_1$-distance between the $i$th set in $\mu_t$ and the $i$th set in $\mu_{t-1}$, where scaling is by the page costs. Thus, the random algorithm initially picks an $i$ uniformly at random in $[1, k^2]$, and "sticks" to the $i$th set in every distribution. This implies that the expected cost of the rounding phase is $O(P(T))$.

We point out that the rounding step handles changes of weights and costs to the currently requested page $p_t$. The reason is that page $p_t$ must be in the cache. Hence, for every set $D$ in $\mu_t$, $p_t \notin D$. We conclude that the change in the weight or cost of $p_t$ does not affect the construction of $\mu_t$ based on $\mu_{t-1}$.

We conclude with the following theorem.

THEOREM 10. *There exists a randomized online algorithm for GVWC whose competitive ratio is $O(\log k)$.*

# 5 A DETERMINISTIC $k$-COMPETITIVE ALGORITHM

In this section we present a deterministic $(h,k)$-competitive algorithm for GVWC. The competitive ratio is $\frac{k}{k-h+1}$ if the initial cost and final cost are equal for every page. Our algorithm extends the algorithms by Young [9] and by Cao and Irani [5]. The analysis in this case is done with respect to fetch cost.

Algorithm **DynamicLandlord** receives an input sequence $\{\langle p_t, w_t(p_t), c_t(p_t)\rangle\}_{t=1}^{T-1}$. Every page $p$ has an initial weight $w_0(p)$ and cost $c_0(p)$. The initial cache state $A_0$ is empty. The algorithm proceeds as follows. Upon arrival of a request for a page $p_t$, the algorithm makes room for $p_t$ by evicting pages, if necessary. The eviction process is determined by page credits. When a page is requested, its credit is set to its cost. When there is not enough room in the cache, credits drop in proportion to weights, and when a page has zero credit it is evicted from the cache. The second step is to update the weight of the page $p_t$. If the weight increases, then we may need to evict more pages. Hence, the algorithm makes room for $\max\{w_{t-1}(p_t), w_t(p_t)\}$. The last step is to set the credit of $p_t$ to its current cost. Note that if there is no cache miss (i.e., $p_t \in A_{t-1}$), then the cache state is not changed. However, the credit of $p_t$ is reset to its cost. In round $T$, the contents of the cache are evicted so that $A_T = \emptyset$.

**Algorithm 1: Dynamic Landlord**

**Input:** A valid cache state $A_{t-1}$, page credits $\{\text{credit}_{t-1}(p)\}_{p \in A_{t-1}}$, and a request $(p_t, w_t(p_t), c_t(p_t))$
**Output:** A valid cache $A_t$ (i.e., $p_t \in A_t$ and $w_t(A_t) \leq k$)
**Invariants:** For every page $p \neq p_t$, we have $w_t(p) = w_{t-1}(p)$ and $c_t(p) = c_{t-1}(p)$. Credits satisfy $p \in A_t$ iff $\text{credit}_t(p) > 0$.

**begin**
  $S \leftarrow A_{t-1} \setminus \{p_t\}$;
  $\text{credit}_t(p) \leftarrow \text{credit}_{t-1}(p)$ for every page $p \in S$;
  **while** $w_t(S) > k - \max\{w_{t-1}(p_t), w_t(p_t)\}$ **do**
    $\Delta \leftarrow \min_{q \in S} \text{credit}_t(q)/w_t(q)$;
    $\text{credit}_t(p) \leftarrow \text{credit}_t(p) - \Delta \cdot w_t(p)$, for every $p \in S$;
    $S \leftarrow \{p \in S : \text{credit}_t(p) > 0\}$
  $A_t \leftarrow S \cup \{p_t\}$;
  $\text{credit}(p_t) \leftarrow c_t(p_t)$;

LEMMA 11. *Let $\{A_t\}_{t=0}^{T}$ denote the sequence of cache states of Algorithm Dynamic Landlord, and let $\{A_t^*\}$ denote any (optimal)* *sequence of valid cache states for a cache of size $h \le k$. Then,*

$$\text{fetch}_{\text{cost}}(\{A_t\}_{t=0}^T) \le \frac{k}{k-h+1} \cdot \text{fetch}_{\text{cost}}(\{A_t^*\}_{t=0}^T) + \frac{h-1}{k-h+1} \cdot \sum_{p \in B(T)} (c_T(p) - c_0(p)).$$

Proof. Let $A_t$ denote the state of the cache of Algorithm Dynamic Landlord at the end of round $t$. Let $A_t^*$ denote the state of the cache at the end of round $t$ of an optimal solution that is limited to a cache of size $h$. Define the potential function $\Phi_t$ by:

$$\Phi_t \triangleq \frac{k}{k-h+1} \cdot \sum_{p \in A_t^*} [c_t(p) - \text{credit}_t(p)] - \frac{h-1}{k-h+1} \cdot \sum_{p \in B(T)} [c_t(p) - \text{credit}_t(p)] .$$

Note that $c_t(p) \ge \text{credit}_t(p)$ and that $\text{credit}_t(p) > 0$ iff $p \in A_t$. The potential in the beginning and in the end satisfy:

$$\Phi_0 = -\frac{h-1}{k-h+1} \cdot \sum_{p \in B(T)} c_0(p)$$

$$\Phi_T \ge -\frac{h-1}{k-h+1} \cdot \sum_{p \in B(T)} c_T(p).$$

Let $d_t \triangleq c_{t-1}(A_t \setminus A_{t-1})$ denote the fetch cost incurred by the algorithm in round $t$. Similarly, define $d_t^* \triangleq c_{t-1}(A_t^* \setminus A_{t-1}^*)$. Let $a_t$ denote the *amortized* fetch cost incurred by the algorithm in round $t$.

$$a_t \triangleq d_t + \Phi_t - \Phi_{t-1}. \tag{4}$$

Claim 12. *For every round $t$, $a_t \le \frac{k}{k-h+1} \cdot d_t^*$.*

The proof of Claim 12 is based on a case analysis described below. The competitive ratio now follows because

$$\sum_{t=1}^T d_t = \sum_{t=1}^T (a_t + \Phi_{t-1} - \Phi_t) \le \frac{k}{k-h+1} \cdot \sum_{t=1}^T d_t^* + \Phi_0 - \Phi_T.$$

□

Proof of Claim 12. For the purpose of analyzing a single round, we partition the processing in round $t$ into 4 stages. Do avoid confusion we denote by $w_t^i(p), c_t^i(p), \text{credit}_t^i(p)$ the weight, cost, and credit of page $p$ at stage $i$ of round $t$, (1) The optimum solution serves the request by the transition from cache state $A_{t-1}^*$ to $A_t^*$. We emphasize, that at this stage $\textit{credit}_t^1(p) = \text{credit}_{t-1}(p)$, $c_t^1(p) = c_{t-1}(p)$, and $w_t^1(p) = w_{t-1}(p)$, for every page $p$, because nothing has been updated yet. (2) The algorithm serves the request $\langle p_t, w_{t-1}(p_t), c_{t-1}(p_t)\rangle$. We emphasize that at this stage $w_t^2(p_t) = w_{t-1}(p_t)$ and $c_t^2(p_t) = c_{t-1}(p_t)$. Credits of pages in $A_{t-1} \setminus \{p_t\}$ may be decreased, and $\text{credit}_t^2(p_t) \leftarrow c_{t-1}(p_t)$. (3) Both the algorithm and the optimal solution deal with the update of the page weight to $w_t(p_t)$. In fact, processing is required only if $w_t(p_t) > w_{t-1}(p_t)$. We emphasize that at this stage $w_t^3(p_t) = w_t(p_t)$, $c_t^3(p_t) = c_{t-1}(p_t)$ and $\text{credit}_t^3(p_t) = c_{t-1}(p_t)$. (4) The algorithm deals with the update of the page cost to $c_t(p_t)$. This means that $\text{credit}_t^4(p_t) \leftarrow c_t(p(t))$. Note that this partitioning assumes that the algorithm "makes room" for the $p_t$ with size $w_{t-1}(p_t)$ in the second stage. If $w_t(p_t) > w_{t-1}(p_t)$, then more room is obtained in the 3rd stage. We also assume that $\text{credit}(p_t)$ is first set to $c_{t-1}(p_t)$ in the 2nd stage, and then it is set to $c_t(p_t)$ in the 4th stage. Table 2 summarizes the values of the parameters in each stage.

| stage | $w_t^i(p)$ | $c_t^i(p)$ | $\text{credit}_t^i(p)$ |
|---|---|---|---|
| (1) | $w_{t-1}(p)$ | $c_{t-1}(p)$ | $\text{credit}_{t-1}(p)$ |
| (2) | $w_{t-1}(p)$ | $c_{t-1}(p)$ | $c_{t-1}(p_t)$ and $\text{credit}_t(p)$ for $p \ne p_t$ |
| (3) | $w_t(p)$ | $c_{t-1}(p)$ | $c_{t-1}(p_t)$ and $\text{credit}_t(p)$ for $p \ne p_t$ |
| (4) | $w_t(p)$ | $c_t(p)$ | $c_t(p_t)$ and $\text{credit}_t(p)$ for $p \ne p_t$ |

**Table 2: Weight, cost, and credit in each stage.**

We now analyze the effect of each stage on $a_t = d_t + \Phi_t - \Phi_{t-1}$ and $d_t^*$. In fact, let $d_t^i$ and $\Phi_t^i$ denote the algorithm fetch cost and potential at stage $i$ of round $t$. Thus, $a_t = (d_t^1 + \Phi_t^1 - \Phi_{t-1}) + (d_t^2 + \Phi_t^2 - \Phi_t^1) + \cdots + (d_t^4 + \Phi_t^4 - \Phi_t^3)$. We claim that $d_t^1 + \Phi_t^1 - \Phi_{t-1} \le \frac{k}{k-h+1} \cdot d_t^*$, and $d_t^i + \Phi_t^i - \Phi_t^{i-1} \le 0$ for $i = 2, 3, 4$.

(1) The adversary serves the request for $p_t$.
The algorithm does nothing in this stage, hence $d_t^1 = 0$. We may assume that $A_t^*$ is lazy (i.e., $A_t^* \setminus A_{t-1}^* \subseteq \{p_t\}$). If the optimal solution does not suffer a page miss (i.e. $p_t \in A_{t-1}^*$), then $A_t^* = A_{t-1}^*$ and $d_t^* = 0$. Moreover, page costs and credits are not updated at this stage, hence $\Phi_t^1 = \Phi_{t-1}$. Hence $d_t^1 + \Phi_t^1 - \Phi_{t-1} = d_t^* = 0$.
If a page miss occurs (i.e. $\{p_t\} = A_t^* \setminus A_{t-1}^*$), then $d_t^* = c_{t-1}(p_t)$. We analyze the effect of evictions as well as the fetching of $p_t$ on $\Phi_t^1 - \Phi_{t-1}$. Since $c_t(p) \ge \text{credit}_t(p)$, an eviction of a page $p$ (i.e., $p \in A_{t-1}^* \setminus A_t^*$) has a nonpositive contribution to $\Phi_t^1 - \Phi_{t-1}$. The fetching of $p_t$ contributes at most $c_t^1(p_t) \cdot k/(k-h+1)$ to $\Phi_t^1 - \Phi_{t-1}$. (Note that $\text{credit}_t^1(p_t) = \text{credit}_{t-1}(p_t)$ might equal zero.) Since $c_t^1(p_t) = c_{t-1}(p_t)$, we conclude that $d_t^1 + \Phi_t^1 - \Phi_{t-1} \le \frac{k}{k-h+1} \cdot d_t^*$, as required.

(2) The algorithm services a request for a page $p_t$.
We consider the case of no cache miss and a cache miss. If $p_t \in A_{t-1}$, then $A_t = A_{t-1}$ and $d_t^2 = 0$. At this point the weight of $p_t$ is still $w_{t-1}(p_t)$, hence no credit is modified, except for $\text{credit}_t^2(p_t) = c_{t-1}(p_t) \ge \text{credit}_{t-1}(p)$. This has a nonpositive contribution to $\Phi_t^2 - \Phi_t^1$ because $p_t \in A_t^*$ and $k \ge h$. Hence $d_t^2 + \Phi_t^2 - \Phi_t^1 \le 0$.
If $p_t \notin A_{t-1}$, then algorithm Dynamic Landlord lowers the credits of pages in $S$. Consider an iteration of the while loop, and observe that such an iteration occurs if $w_t^2(S) \ge k - w_{t-1}(p_t) + 1$. Moreover, notice that $w^2(A_t^* \cap S) \le h - w_{t-1}(p_t)$. Assume, for simplicity, that the while loop iterates only once (one can prove the same also for multiple iterations), then

(not taking into account the contribution of $p_t$)

$$\Phi_t^2 - \Phi_t^1 = \Delta \cdot \left[\frac{k}{k-h+1} \cdot w_t^2(S \cap A_t^*) - \frac{h-1}{k-h+1} \cdot w_t^2(S)\right]$$

$$\leq \frac{\Delta}{k-h+1} \cdot [k \cdot (h - w_{t-1}(p_t)) - (h-1) \cdot (k - w_{t-1}(p_t) + 1)]$$

$$\leq \frac{\Delta}{k-h+1} \cdot [k - h + 1 - w_{t-1}(p_t) \cdot (k - (h-1))] \leq 0,$$

because $w_{t-1}(p_t) \geq 1$.

Now, $d_t^2 = c_{t-1}(p_t)$ and the effect of fetching $p_t$ to $A_t$ is as follows. Since $p_t \notin A_{t-1}$, we conclude that $\text{credit}_t^1(p_t) = 0$. However, $\text{credit}^2(p_t) = c_{t-1}(p_t)$. Hence, taking into account the contribution of $p_t$ we get

$$d_t^2 + \Phi_t^2 - \Phi_t^1 \leq c_{t-1}(p_t) - \text{credit}_t^2(p_t) \cdot \frac{k-(h-1)}{k-h+1} = 0$$

(3) Weight change.
In this stage, $d_t^3$=0. If $w_t(p_t) \leq w_{t-1}(p_t)$, then both the algorithm and the optimal solution remain unchanged. If $w_t(p_t) > w_{t-1}(p_t)$, then both the optimal solution and the algorithm may need to evict some pages. Eviction of pages by the optimal solution does not increase the potential.
As for the algorithm, then the while-loop deals with decreasing credits to determine which pages are evicted. As we already saw in the analysis of stage (2), each iteration of the while-loop does not increase the potential.
We conclude that $d_t^3 + \Phi_t^3 - \Phi_t^2 \leq 0$, as required.

(4) Cost change.
In this stage $d_t^4 = 0$ and only the cost and the credit of $p_t$ are updated. However, $c^3(p_t) = \text{credit}^3(p_t) = c_{t-1}(p)$ and $c^4(p_t) = \text{credit}^4(p_t) = c_t(p_t)$. Hence, $d_t^4 + \Phi_t^4 - \Phi_t^3 = 0$, as required.

□

The following theorem is a direct consequence of Lemma 11.

Theorem 13. *If $c_T(p) = c_0(p)$ for every page $p \in B(T)$, then Algorithm **Dynamic Landlord** is $\frac{k}{k-h+1}$-competitive with respect to any (offline) solution that uses a cache of size h.*

## 6 FURTHER WORK

An open problem is to allow the page costs to depend on whether the page is in the cache or has been evicted. An example of such a setting is described in [7]. The cost model in [7] assumes that the cost of a page is a non-linear function of the total number of misses of the page over a given period of time. Another example of such a situation is the distinction between "dirty" pages (i.e., pages that have been modified) and "untouched" pages (i.e., unmodified pages). The eviction of a dirty page requires storing the page in the memory, while the eviction of an untouched page is for free.

## ACKNOWLEDGMENTS

The authors would like to thank Marcin Bienkowski and Gil Einziger for useful discussions. Part of this work was done while the authors were visiting the Max Planck Institute for Informatics.

## REFERENCES

[1] Anna Adamaszek, Artur Czumaj, Matthias Englert, and Harald Räcke. 2012. An O(log k)-competitive algorithm for generalized caching. In *23rd Annual ACM-SIAM Symposium on Discrete Algorithms*. 1681–1689.
[2] Nikhil Bansal, Niv Buchbinder, and Joseph Naor. 2012. Randomized Competitive Algorithms for Generalized Caching. *SIAM J. Comput.* 41, 2 (2012), 391–414.
[3] Nikhil Bansal, Niv Buchbinder, and Joseph Seffi Naor. 2008. Randomized competitive algorithms for generalized caching. In *40th annual ACM symposium on Theory of computing*. ACM, 235–244.
[4] Allan Borodin and Ran El-Yaniv. 2005. *Online computation and competitive analysis.* cambridge university press.
[5] Pei Cao and Sandy Irani. 1997. Cost-Aware WWW Proxy Caching Algorithms. In *1st USENIX Symposium on Internet Technologies and Systems*. 193–206.
[6] Fred Douglis. 1993. The Compression Cache: Using On-line Compression to Extend Physical Memory.. In *USENIX Winter*. Citeseer, 519–529.
[7] Ishai Menache and Mohit Singh. 2015. Online caching with convex costs. In *27th ACM symposium on Parallelism in Algorithms and Architectures*. ACM, 46–54.
[8] Enoch Peserico. 2013. Elastic paging. *ACM SIGMETRICS Performance Evaluation Review* 41, 1 (2013), 349–350.
[9] Neal E. Young. 2002. On-Line File Caching. *Algorithmica* 33, 3 (2002), 371–383.

# Cache-Adaptive Exploration: Experimental Results and Scan-Hiding for Adaptivity

Andrea Lincoln
Computer Science and Artificial Intelligence Laboratory
Massachusetts Institute of Technology
andreali@mit.edu

Quanquan C. Liu
Computer Science and Artificial Intelligence Laboratory
Massachusetts Institute of Technology
quanquan@mit.edu

Jayson Lynch
Computer Science and Artificial Intelligence Laboratory
Massachusetts Institute of Technology
jaysonl@mit.edu

Helen Xu
Computer Science and Artificial Intelligence Laboratory
Massachusetts Institute of Technology
hjxu@mit.edu

## ABSTRACT

Systems that require programs to share the cache such as shared-memory systems, multicore architectures, and time-sharing systems are ubiquitous in modern computing. Moreover, practitioners have observed that the cache behavior of an algorithm is often critical to its overall performance.

Despite the increasing popularity of systems where programs share a cache, the theoretical behavior of most algorithms is not yet well understood. There is a gap between our knowledge about how algorithms perform in a static cache versus a dynamic cache where the amount of memory available to a given program fluctuates.

Cache-adaptive analysis is a method of analyzing how well algorithms use the cache in the face of changing memory size. Bender *et al.* showed that optimal cache-adaptivity does not follow from cache-optimality in a static cache. Specifically, they proved that some cache-optimal algorithms in a static cache are suboptimal when subject to certain memory profiles (patterns of memory fluctuations). For example, the canonical cache-oblivious divide-and-conquer formulation of Strassen's algorithm for matrix multiplication is suboptimal in the cache-adaptive model because it does a linear scan to add submatrices together.

In this paper, we introduce scan hiding, the first technique for converting a class of non-cache-adaptive algorithms with linear scans to optimally cache-adaptive variants. We work through a concrete example of scan-hiding on Strassen's algorithm, a sub-cubic algorithm for matrix multiplication that involves linear scans at each level of its recursive structure. All of the currently known sub-cubic algorithms for matrix multiplication include linear scans, however, so our technique applies to a large class of algorithms.

We experimentally compared two cubic algorithms for matrix multiplication which are both cache-optimal when the memory size stays the same, but diverge under cache-adaptive analysis. Our findings suggest that memory fluctuations affect algorithms with the same theoretical cache performance in a static cache differently. For example, the optimally cache-adaptive naive matrix multiplication algorithm achieved fewer relative faults than the non-adaptive variant in the face of changing memory size. Our experiments also suggest that the performance advantage of cache-adaptive algorithms extends to more practical situations beyond the carefully-crafted memory specifications in theoretical proofs of worst-case behavior.

## CCS CONCEPTS

• **Theory of computation → Parallel computing models; Caching and paging algorithms;** • **General and reference →** *Experimentation;*

## KEYWORDS

cache adaptivity; scan hiding; adaptive constructions; external memory

**ACM Reference Format:**
Andrea Lincoln, Quanquan C. Liu, Jayson Lynch, and Helen Xu. 2018. Cache-Adaptive Exploration: Experimental Results and Scan-Hiding for Adaptivity. In *SPAA '18: 30th ACM Symposium on Parallelism in Algorithms and Architectures, July 16–18, 2018, Vienna, Austria.* ACM, New York, NY, USA, 10 pages. https://doi.org/10.1145/3210377.3210382


*SPAA '18, July 16–18, 2018, Vienna, Austria*

ACM ISBN 978-1-4503-5799-9/18/07...$15.00
https://doi.org/10.1145/3210377.3210382

## 1 INTRODUCTION

Since multiple processors may compete for space in a shared cache on modern machines, the amount of memory available to a single process may vary dynamically. Programs running on multicore architectures, shared-memory machines, and time-shared machines often experience memory fluctuations. For example, Dice, Marathe and Shavit [12] demonstrated that in practice, multiple threads running the same program will each get a different amount of access to a shared cache.

Experimentalists have recognized the problem of changing memory size in large-scale scientific computing and have developed heuristics [17–19] for allocation with empirical guarantees. Furthermore, researchers have developed adaptive sorting and join algorithms [10, 16, 20, 21, 27–29] that perform well empirically in environments with memory fluctuations. While most of these algorithms work well on average, they may still suffer from poor worst-case performance [4, 5].

In this paper, we continue the study of algorithmic design of external-memory algorithms which perform well in spite of memory fluctuations. Barve and Vitter [4, 5] initiated the theoretical analysis of such algorithms. Bender *et al.* [8] later formulated the "cache-adaptive model" to formally study the effect of such memory changes and analyzed specific "cache-adaptive" algorithms using this model. ***Cache-adaptive*** algorithms are algorithms that use the cache optimally in the face of memory fluctuations. They then introduced techniques for analyzing some classes of divide-and-conquer algorithms in the cache-adaptive model.

### *Cache Analysis Without Changing Memory*

Despite the reality of dynamic memory fluctuations, the majority of theoretical work on external-memory computation [25, 26] assumes a fixed cache size $\mathcal{M}$. The measure of interest in the external-memory model is the number of I/Os, or fetches from external memory, that an algorithm takes to finish its computation. Many I/O-efficient algorithms in the fixed-memory model suffer from poor performance when $\mathcal{M}$ changes due to thrashing if the available memory drops.

Cache-oblivious algorithms [11, 13, 14] provide insight about how to design optimal algorithms in the face of changing memory. Notably, cache-oblivious algorithms are not parameterized by the cache or cache line size. Instead, they leverage their recursive algorithm structure to achieve cache-optimality under static memory sizes. They are often more portable because they are not tuned for a specific architecture. Although Bender *et al.* [7] showed that *not all* cache-oblivious algorithms are cache-adaptive, many cache-oblivious algorithms are in fact also cache-adaptive. Because so many cache-oblivious algorithms are also cache-adaptive, this suggests that modifying the recursive structure of the non-adaptive cache-oblivious algorithms may be the key to designing optimally cache-adaptive algorithms.

Algorithms designed for external-memory efficiency may be especially affected by memory level changes as they depend on memory locality. Such programs include I/O-model algorithms, shared-memory parallel programs, database joins and sorts, scientific computing applications, and large computations running on shared hardware in cloud computing.

Practical approaches to alleviating I/O latency constraints include techniques such as *latency hiding*. Latency hiding [15, 24] is a technique that leverages computation time to hide I/O latency to improve overall program performance. Since our model counts computation as free (i.e. it takes no time), we cannot use latency hiding because it requires nonzero computation time.

### *Analysis of Cache-Adaptive Algorithms*

Prior work took important steps toward closing the separation between the reality of machines with shared caches and the large body of theoretical work on external-memory algorithms in a fixed cache. Existing tools for design and analysis of external-memory algorithms that assume a fixed memory size often cannot cope with the reality of changing memory.

Barve and Vitter [4, 5] initiated the theoretical study of algorithms with memory fluctuations by extending the DAM (disk-access machine) model to accommodate changes in cache size. Their work proves the existence of optimal algorithms in spite of memory changes but lacks a framework for finding such algorithms.

Bender *et al.* [8] continued the theoretical study of external-memory algorithms in the face of fluctuating cache sizes. They formalized the ***cache-adaptive model***, which allows memory to change more frequently and dramatically than Barve and Vitter's model, and introduced ***memory profiles***, which define sequences of memory fluctuations.

They showed that some (but not all) optimal cache-oblivious algorithms are optimal in the cache-adaptive model. At a high level, an algorithm is "optimal" in the cache-adaptive model if it performs well under all memory profiles. Specifically, if the I/O complexity for a recursive cache-oblivious algorithm fits in the form $T(n) = aT(n/b) + O(1)$, it is optimally cache-adaptive. They also showed that lazy funnel sort [9] is optimally cache-adaptive and does not fit into the given form. Despite the close connection between cache-obliviousness and cache-adaptivity, they show that neither external-memory optimality nor cache-obliviousness is necessary or sufficient for cache-adaptivity. The connections and differences between cache-oblivious and cache-adaptive algorithms suggest that cache-adaptive algorithms may one day be as widely used and well-studied as cache-oblivious algorithms.

In follow-up work, Bender *et al.* [7] gave a more complete framework for designing and analyzing cache-adaptive algorithms. Specifically, they completely characterize when a linear-space-complexity Master-method-style or mutually recursive linear-space-complexity Akra-Bazzi-style algorithm is optimal in the cache-adaptive model. For example, the in-place recursive naive[1] cache-oblivious matrix multiplication algorithm is optimally cache-adaptive, while the naive cache-oblivious matrix multiplication that does the additions upfront (and not in-place) is not optimally cache-adaptive. They provide a toolkit for the analysis and design of cache-oblivious algorithms in certain recursive forms and show how to determine if an algorithm in a certain recursive form is optimally cache-adaptive and if not, to determine how far it is from optimal.

Although these results take important steps in cache-adaptive analysis, open questions remain. The main contribution of Bender *et al.* [7] was an algorithmic toolkit for recursive algorithms in specific forms. At a high level, cache-oblivious algorithms that have long ($\omega(1)$ block transfers) scans[2] (such as the not-in-place $n^3$ matrix multiplication algorithm) in addition to their recursive calls are not immediately cache-adaptive. However, there exists an in-place, optimally cache-adaptive version of naive matrix multiplication. Is there a way to transform other algorithms that do $\omega(n/\mathcal{B})$ block transfers at each recursive call (where $\mathcal{B}$ is the cache line size in words), such as Strassen's algorithm [23], into optimally cache-adaptive algorithms? Our ***scan-hiding*** technique answers this question for Strassen and other similar algorithms. Furthermore, Bender *et al.* [8] gave a worst-case analysis in which the non-adaptive naive matrix multiplication is a $\Theta(\lg N)$ factor off from optimal. Does the predicted slow down manifest in reality? We begin to answer this question via experimental results in this paper.

[1] We use "naive" matrix multiplication to refer to the $O(n^3)$ work algorithm for matrix multiplication.

[2] That is, the recurrence for their cache complexity has the form $T(n) = aT(n/b) + \Omega(n/\mathcal{B})$ where $\mathcal{B}$ is the cache line size in words.

### Contributions

The contributions of this paper are twofold:

First, we develop a new technique called ***scan-hiding*** for making a certain class of non-cache-adaptive algorithms adaptive and use it to construct a cache-adaptive version of Strassen's algorithm for matrix multiplication in Section 4. Strassen's algorithm involves linear scans in its recurrence, which makes the algorithm as described non-adaptive via a theorem from Bender *et al.* [7]. We generalize this technique to many algorithms which have recurrences of the form $T(n) = aT(n/b) + O(n)$ in Section 3. This is the first framework in the cache-adaptive setting to transform non-adaptive algorithms into adaptive algorithms.

Next, we empirically evaluate the performance of various algorithms when subject to memory fluctuations in Section 5. Specifically, we compared cache-adaptive and non-adaptive naive matrix multiplication. We include additional experiments on external-memory sorting libraries in the full version of this paper. Our results suggest that algorithms that are "more adaptive" (i.e. closer to optimal cache-adaptivity) are more robust under memory changes. Moreover, we observe performance differences even when memory sizes do not change adversarially.

## 2 PRELIMINARIES

In this section we introduce the disk-access model (DAM) [3] for analyzing algorithms in a static cache. We review how to extend the disk-access model to the cache-adaptive model [8] with changing memory. Finally, this section formalizes mathematical preliminaries from [7] required to analyze scan-hiding techniques.

### Disk-Access Model

Aggarwal and Vitter [3] first introduced the disk-access model for analyzing algorithms in a fixed-size cache. This model describes I/O limited algorithms on single processor machines. Memory can reside in an arbitrarily large, but slow disk, or in a fast cache of size $M$. The disk and cache are divided into cache lines of size $\mathcal{B}$ (in bytes). Access to memory in the cache and operations on the CPU are free. If the desired memory is not in cache, however, a cache miss occurs at a cost of one unit of time. A line is evicted from the cache and the desired line is moved into cache in its place. We measure algorithm performance in this model by counting up the number of cache-line transfers. That is, algorithms are judged based on their performance with respect to $\mathcal{B}$ and $M$. Furthermore, we differentiate between algorithms which are parameterized by $\mathcal{B}$ or $M$, called ***cache-aware***, and those which do not make use of the values of the cache or line size, called ***cache-oblivious*** [13].

The ***cache-adaptive model*** [7, 8] extends the disk-access model to accommodate for changes in cache size over time. Since we use the cache-adaptive model and the same definitions for cache-adaptivity, we repeat the relevant definitions in this section.

### Cache-Adaptive Analysis

First, we will give a casual overview of how to do cache-adaptive analysis. This is meant to help guide the reader through the array of technical definitions that follow in this section, or perhaps to give enough sense of the definitions that one may follow the ideas, if not the details, in the rest of the paper. For a more thorough treatment of this topic, please see the paper *Cache-Adaptive Analysis* [7].

In general, we want to examine how well an algorithm is able to cope with a memory size which changes with time. We consider an algorithm $\mathcal{A}$ good, or "optimally cache-adaptive" if it manages to be constant-competitive with the same algorithm $\mathcal{A}^*$ whose scheduler was given knowledge of the memory profile ahead of time .

To give our non-omniscient algorithm a fighting chance we also allow ***speed-augmentation*** where $\mathcal{A}$ gets to perform a constant number of I/Os in a given time step, whereas $\mathcal{A}^*$ still runs at one I/O per time step.

To prove an algorithm is cache-adaptive, we instead show it has a stronger condition called optimally progressing. An optimally progressing algorithm has some measure of "progress" it has made, and it is constantly accomplishing a sufficient amount of progress. The "progress bound" does not have to resemble any sort of real work being done by the algorithm, but has more general constraints and can be thought of more as an abstraction that amortizes what $\mathcal{A}$ is accomplishing. We pick our progress bound to be an upper bound on our optimally scheduled algorithm and then show that our (speed-augmented) algorithm always accomplishes at least as much progress as $\mathcal{A}^*$.

Small slices of time or strangely-shaped cache sizes often make analyzing algorithms difficult in the cache-adaptive model. For simplicity, we instead consider ***square profiles***, which are memory profiles that stay at the same size for a number of time steps equal to their size. Thus, when we look at a plot of these profiles, they look like a sequence of squares. There are two important square profiles for each given memory profile $M$: one that upper bounds and another that lower bounds the progress $\mathcal{A}$ can accomplish in $M$. Bender *et al.* [7] showed that these square profiles closely approximate the exact memory profile.

In short, proving an algorithm is cache-adaptive involves:

(1) Picking a ***progress function*** to represent work done by our algorithms.
(2) Upper bound the progress $\mathcal{A}^*$ can make in a square of memory by a ***progress bound***.
(3) Show that a speed-augmented version of $\mathcal{A}$ can make at least as much progress as $\mathcal{A}^*$ given the same square of memory.

### Achieving Cache-Optimality on any Memory Profile

Since the running time of an algorithm is dependent on the pattern of memory size changes during its execution, we turn to competitive analysis to find "good" algorithms that are close to an optimal algorithm that knows the future set of memory changes. We will now formalize what makes an algorithm "good" and how to analyze algorithms in spite of cache fluctuations.

DEFINITION 2.1 (MEMORY PROFILE). *A* ***memory profile*** *$M$ is a sequence (or concatenation) of memory size changes. We represent $M$ as an ordered list of of natural numbers ($M \in \mathbb{N}^*$) where $M(t)$ is the value of the cache size (in words) after the $t$-th cache miss during the algorithm's execution. We use $m(t)$ to denote the number of cache lines at time $t$ of memory profile $M$ (i.e. $m(t) = M(t)/\mathcal{B}$).*

*The size of the cache is required to stay in integral multiples of the cache line size.*

In general, an optimal algorithm $\mathcal{A}^*$ takes at most a constant factor of time longer than any other algorithm $\mathcal{A}$ for a given problem on any given memory profile. Since a memory profile might be carefully constructed to drop almost all of its memory after some specific algorithm finishes, we allow the further relaxation that an optimal algorithm may be speed augmented. This relaxation allows an algorithm to complete multiple I/Os during one time step, and can be thought of in a similar manner to the memory augmentation allowed during the analysis of Least Recently Used. Speed augmentation relates to running lower latency memory access. Since memory augmentation (giving an online algorithm more space as described in Definition 2.3) is a key technique in the analysis of cache-oblivious algorithms, speed augmentation is an important tool for proving algorithms optimal in the cache-adaptive model.

We now formally define these notions of augmentation.

Definition 2.2 (Speed Augmentation [8]). *Let $\mathcal{A}$ be an algorithm. The c-**speed augmented** version of $\mathcal{A}$, $\mathcal{A}'$, performs c I/Os in each step of the memory profile.*

Bender *et al.* [7] extended the notions of memory augmentation and the tall-cache assumption, common tools in the analysis of cache-oblivious algorithms, to the cache-adaptive model. The tall-cache assumption specifies that $M$ must be a certain size in terms of $\mathcal{B}$, ensuring there are enough distinct cache lines in the cache for certain algorithms.

We assume page replacement is done according to a least-recently-used policy, which incurs at most a constant factor more page faults (and therefore I/Os) more than an optimal algorithm [6] under constant space-augmentation [22].

Definition 2.3 (Memory Augmentation [8]). *For any memory profile m, we define a c-**memory augmented** version of m as the profile $m'(t) = cm(t)$. Running an algorithm $\mathcal{A}$ with c-**memory augmentation** on the profile m means running $\mathcal{A}$ on the c-memory augmented profile of m.*

Definition 2.4 (H-tall [7]). *In the cache-adaptive model, we say that a memory profile M is H-**tall** if for all $t \geq 0$, $M(t) \geq H \cdot \mathcal{B}$ (where H is measured in lines).*

Definition 2.5 (Memory Monotone [7]). *A **memory monotone** algorithm runs at most a constant factor slower when given more memory.*

Intuitively, an optimally cache-adaptive algorithm for a problem $\mathcal{P}$ does as well as any other algorithm for $\mathcal{P}$ given constant speed augmentation.

Definition 2.6 (Optimally Cache-adaptive [8]). *An algorithm $\mathcal{A}$ that solves problem $\mathcal{P}$ is **optimal** in the cache-adaptive model if there exists a constant c such that on all memory profiles and all sufficiently large input sizes N, the worst-case running time of a c-speed-augmented $\mathcal{A}$ is no worse than the worst-case running time of any other (non-augmented) memory-monotone algorithm.*

Notably, this definition of optimal allows algorithms to query the memory profile at any point in time but not to query future memory sizes. Optimally cache-adaptive algorithms are robust under any memory profile in that they perform asymptotically (within constant factors) as well as algorithms that know the entire memory profile.

### *Approximating Arbitrary Memory Profiles with Square Profiles*

Since memory size may change at any time in an arbitrary memory profile $M$, Bender *et al.* [8] introduced ***square profiles*** to approximate the memory during any memory profile and simplify algorithm analysis in the cache-adaptive model. Square profiles are profiles where the memory size stays constant for a time range proportional to the size of the memory.

Definition 2.7 (Square Profile [8]). *A memory profile M or m is a **square profile** if there exist boundaries $0 = t_0 < t_1 < \ldots$ such that for all $t \in [t_i, t_{i+1})$, $m(t) = t_{i+1} - t_i$. In other words, a square memory profile is a step function where each step is exactly as long as it is tall. Let $\square_{M(t)}$ and $\square_{m(t)}$ denote a square of M and m, respectively, of size $M(t)$ by $M(t)$ words and $m(t)$ and $m(t)$ lines, respectively.*

Definition 2.8 (Inner Square Profile [8]). *For a memory profile m, the **inner square boundaries** $t_0 < t_1 < t_2 < \ldots$ of m are defined as follows: Let $t_0 = 0$. Recursively define $t_{i+1}$ as the largest integer such that $t_{i+1} - t_i \leq m(t)$ for all $t \in [t_i, t_{i+1})$.*

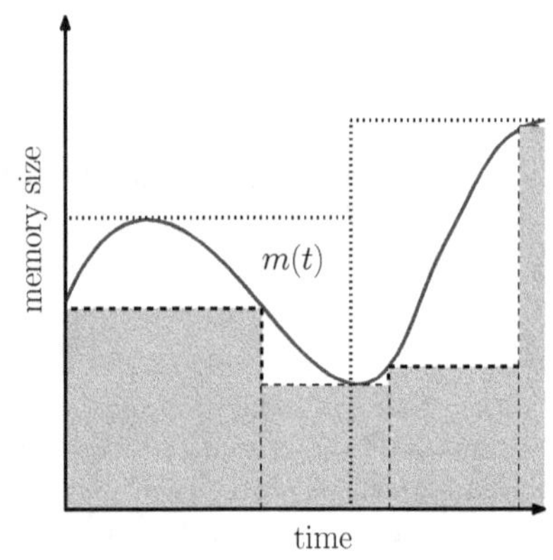


**Figure 1: A memory profile $m$ and its inner and outer square profiles. The red curving line represents the memory profile $m$, the grey dashed boxes represent the associated inner square profile, the dotted lines represent the outer square profile (as defined in [8]).**

Bender *et al.* [8] showed that for all timesteps $t$, the size of inner square profile $m'$ is at most a constant factor smaller than the size of the original memory profile $m$. If an algorithm is optimal on all square profiles, it is therefore optimal on all arbitrary profiles. Cache-adaptive analysis uses inner square profiles because they are easier to analyze than arbitrary profiles and closely approximate any memory profile. Figure 1 shows an example of a memory profile and its inner and outer square profiles.

Lemma 2.9 (Square Profile Usability [8]). *Let m be a memory profile where $m(t+1) \leq m(t) + 1$ for all t. Let $t_0 < t_1 < \ldots$ be the inner square boundaries of m, and $m'$ be the inner square profile of m.*

*(1) For all t, $m'(t) \leq m(t)$.*
*(2) For all i, $m'(t_{i+1}) \leq 2m'(t_i)$.*
*(3) For all i and $t \in [t_{i+1}, t_{i+2})$, $m(t) \leq 4(t_{i+1} - t_i)$.*

### *Optimally Progressing Algorithms are Optimally Cache-Adaptive*

We show an algorithm is optimally cache-adaptive by showing a stronger property: that it is "optimally progressing". The ***progress*** of an algorithm is the number of cache accesses that occurred during a time interval. (In other words, we assume the algorithm makes one unit of progress per cache access.)

Intuitively, an optimally progressing algorithm has some notion of work it needs to accomplish to solve the given problem, and for any given interval of the memory profile that algorithm does within a constant factor as much work as the optimal algorithm would. An optimally progressing algorithm is optimally cache-adaptive [7].

To show an algorithm is optimal in the DAM model, we require an upper and lower bound on the progress any algorithm can make for its given problem. Let $\mathcal{P}$ be a problem. A ***progress bound*** $\rho_{\mathcal{P}}(M(t))$ or $\rho_{\mathcal{P}}(m(t))$ is an upper bound on the amount of progress any algorithm can make on problem $\mathcal{P}$ given memory profiles $M$ or $m$ with $M(t)$ or $m(t)$ cache size at time $t$, respectively. $\rho_{\mathcal{P}}(M(t))$ and $\rho_{\mathcal{P}}(m(t))$ are defined in terms of number of words and number of cache lines, respectively. We use a "progress-requirement function" to bound from below the progress any algorithm must be able to make. A ***progress requirement function*** $R_{\mathcal{P}}(N)$ is a lower bound on the amount of progress an algorithm must make to be able to solve all instances of $\mathcal{P}$ of size at most $N$.

We combine square profiles with progress bounds to show algorithms are optimally progressing in the cache-adaptive model. Cache-adaptive analysis with square profiles is easier than reasoning about arbitrary profiles because square profiles ensure that memory size stays constant for some time. Since the performance of an algorithm on an inner square profile is close enough to its performance on the original memory profile, we use inner square profiles in our progress-based analysis.

Finally, we formalize notions of progress over changing memory sizes. At a high level, we define progress of an algorithm $\mathcal{A}$ on an inner square profile $\square_M$ such that the sum of the progress of $\mathcal{A}$ over all of the squares of $\square_M$ is within a constant factor of the total progress of $\mathcal{A}$ on $M$. We call our ***progress function*** over a single square of square profile $M$ and $m$, $\phi_{\mathcal{A}}(\square_M)$ or $\phi_{\mathcal{A}}(\square_m)$ since by definition a single square profile gives a cache size and our progress function $\phi_{\mathcal{A}}$ takes as input a cache size.

Definition 2.10 (Progress Function [7]). *Given an algorithm $\mathcal{A}$, a **progress function** $\phi_{\mathcal{A}}(M(t))$ and $\phi_{\mathcal{A}}(m(t))$ defined for $\mathcal{A}$ is the amount of progress that $\mathcal{A}$ can make given $M(t)$ words or $m(t)$ lines. We define the **progress function** given as input a memory profile $M$ and $m$ as $\Phi_{\mathcal{A}}(M)$ and $\Phi_{\mathcal{A}}(m)$ and it provides the amount of progress $\mathcal{A}$ can make on a given profile $M$ and $m$, respectively.*

Let $M_1 \| M_2$ indicate concatenation of profiles $M_1$ and $M_2$.

Definition 2.11 ([7]). *Let $M$ and $\mathcal{U}$ be any two profiles of finite duration. The duration of a profile $M$ is the length of the ordered list representing $M$. Furthermore, let $M_1 \| M_2$ indicate concatenation of profiles $M_1$ and $M_2$. We say that $M$ **is smaller than** $\mathcal{U}$, $M \prec \mathcal{U}$, if there exist profiles $\mathcal{L}_1, \mathcal{L}_2 \ldots \mathcal{L}_k$ and $\mathcal{U}_0, \mathcal{U}_1, \mathcal{U}_2 \ldots \mathcal{U}_k$, such that $M = \mathcal{L}_1 \| \mathcal{L}_2 \ldots \| \mathcal{L}_k$ and $\mathcal{U} = \mathcal{U}_0 \| \mathcal{U}_1 \| \mathcal{U}_2 \ldots \| \mathcal{U}_k$, and for each $1 \le i \le k$,*

**(i)** *If $d_i$ is the duration of $\mathcal{L}_i$, $\mathcal{U}_i$ has duration $\ge d_i$, and*

**(ii)** *as standalone profiles, $\mathcal{L}_i$ is always below $\mathcal{U}_i$ ($\mathcal{L}_i(t) \le \mathcal{U}_i(t)$ for all $t \le d_i$).*

Definition 2.12 (Monotonically Increasing Profiles [7]). *A function $f : \mathbb{N}^* \to \mathbb{N}$ which takes as its input a memory profile $M$ is **monotonically increasing** if for any profiles $M$ and $\mathcal{U}$, $M \prec \mathcal{U}$ implies $f(M) \le f(\mathcal{U})$.*

Definition 2.13 (Square Additive[7]). *A monotonically increasing function $f : \mathbb{N}^* \to \mathbb{N}$ which takes as its input a single square $\square_M$ of a square profile $M$ is **square-additive** if*

**(i)** *$f(\square_M)$ is bounded by a polynomial in $M$,*

**(ii)** *$f(\square_{M_1} \| \cdots \| \square_{M_k}) = \Theta(\sum_{i=1}^{k} f(\square_{M_i}))$.*

We now formally define progress bounds in the cache-adaptive model and show how to use progress bounds to prove algorithms are optimally cache-adaptive. Given a memory profile $M$, a ***progress bound*** $\rho_{\mathcal{P}}(M(t))$ or $\rho_{\mathcal{P}}(m(t))$ is a function that takes a cache size $M(t)$ or $m(t)$ and outputs the amount of progress any algorithm could possibly achieve on that cache size.

Definition 2.14 (Progress Bound [7]). *A problem $\mathcal{P}$ of size $N$ has a **progress bound** if there exists a monotonically increasing polynomial-bounded **progress-requirement function** $R : \mathbb{N} \to \mathbb{N}$ and a square-additive **progress limit function** $\mathrm{P}_{\mathcal{P}} : \mathbb{N}^* \to \mathbb{N}$ such that: For any profile $M$ or $m$, if $\mathrm{P}_{\mathcal{P}}(M) < R_{\mathcal{P}}(N)$, then no memory-monotone algorithm running under profile $M$ can solve all problem instances of size $N$. Let $\rho_{\mathcal{P}}(M(t))$ and $\rho_{\mathcal{P}}(m(t))$ for a problem $\mathcal{P}$ be a function $\rho_{\mathcal{P}} : \mathbb{N} \to \mathbb{N}$ that provides an upper bound on the amount of progress any algorithm can make on problem $\mathcal{P}$ given cache sizes $M(t)$ and $m(t)$. We also refer to both $\rho_{\mathcal{P}}$ and $\mathrm{P}_{\mathcal{P}}$ as the **progress bound** (although they are defined for different types of inputs).*

Throughout this paper, for purposes of clarity (when talking about a square profile), when we write $\rho_{\mathcal{P}}(\square_{M(t)})$ or $\rho_{\mathcal{P}}(\square_{m(t)})$, we mean $\rho_{\mathcal{P}}(M(t))$ and $\rho_{\mathcal{P}}(m(t)))$.

Furthermore, we limit our analysis to "usable" memory profiles. If the cache size increases faster than an algorithm can pull lines into memory, then some of that cache is inaccessible and cannot be utilized. Thus we consider ***usable*** memory profiles.

Definition 2.15 (Usable Profiles [8]). *An $h$-tall memory profile $m$ is **usable** if $m(0) = h(\mathcal{B})$ and if $m$ increases by at most 1 block per time step, i.e. $m(t+1) \le m(t) + 1$ for all $t$.*

Next, we formalize "feasible" and "fitting" profiles to characterize how long it takes algorithms complete on various memory profiles.

Definition 2.16 (Fitting and Feasibility [7]). *For an algorithm $\mathcal{A}$ and problem instance $I$ we say a profile $M$ of length $\ell$ is $I$-**fitting** for $\mathcal{A}$ if $\mathcal{A}$ requires exactly $\ell$ time steps to process input $I$ on profile $M$. A profile $M$ is $N$-**feasible for** $\mathcal{A}$ if $\mathcal{A}$, given profile $M$, can complete its execution on all instances of size $N$. We further say that $M$ is $N$-**fitting for** $\mathcal{A}$ if it is $N$-feasible and there exists at least one instance $I$ of size $N$ for which $M$ is $I$-fitting. (When $\mathcal{A}$ is understood, we will simply say that $M$ is $N$-feasible, $N$-fitting, etc.)*

We now have the necessary language to formally define ***optimally progressing*** algorithms. Intuitively, optimally progressing do about as well as any other algorithm for the same problem regardless of the memory profile.

Definition 2.17 (Optimally Progressing [7]). *For an algorithm $\mathcal{A}$ that solves problem $\mathcal{P}$, integer $N$, and $N$-feasible profile $M(t)$, let $M_N(t)$ denote the $N$-fitting prefix of $M$. We say that algorithm $\mathcal{A}$ with tall-cache requirement $H$ is* ***optimally progressing with respect to a progress bound*** $\mathrm{P}_{\mathcal{P}}$ *(or simply optimally progressing if $\mathrm{P}_{\mathcal{P}}$ is understood) if, for every integer $N$ and $N$-feasible $H$-tall usable profile $M$, $\mathrm{P}_{\mathcal{P}}(M_N) = O(R_{\mathcal{P}}(N))$. We say that $\mathcal{A}$ is* ***optimally progressing in the DAM model*** *if, for every integer $N$ and every constant $H$-tall profile $M$, $\mathrm{P}_{\mathcal{P}}(M_N) = O(R_{\mathcal{P}}(N))$.*

Bender *et al.* [7] showed that optimally progressing algorithms are optimally cache-adaptive.

Lemma 2.18 (Optimally Progressing Implies Adaptivity [7]). *If an algorithm A is optimally progressing, then it is optimally cache adaptive.*

### *Cache-adaptivity of Recursive Algorithms*

We focus on recursive algorithms which decompose into sections which are somewhat cache intensive and linear scans in Section 3.

Definition 2.19. *Let $f(n)$ be a function of an input size $n$. A* ***linear scan*** *of size $O(f(n))$ is a sequence of operations which sequentially accesses groups of memory which are $O(\mathcal{B})$ in size and performs $O(\mathcal{B})$ (and at least one) operations on each group before accessing the next group.*

Finally, [7] analyzes recursive algorithms analogous to those in the Master Theorem. We use the following theorem about $(a, b, c)$-regular algorithms.

Definition 2.20 ($(a, b, c)$-regular [7]). *Let $a \geq 1/b$, $0 < b < 1$, and $0 \leq c \leq 1$ be constants. A linear-space algorithm is $(a, b, c)$-* ***regular*** *if, for inputs of sufficiently large size $N$, it makes*

**(i)** *exactly $(a)$ recursive calls on subproblems of size $(N/b)$, and*

**(ii)** *$\Theta(1)$ linear scans before, between, or after recursive calls, where the size of the biggest scan is $\Theta(N^c)$.*

Finally, we specify which algorithms we can apply our "scan-hiding" technique to. Scan-hiding generates optimally-adaptive algorithms from non-optimally-adaptive recursive algorithms with linear (or sublinear) scans. We can apply scan-hiding to $(a, b, c)$-***scan regular algorithms***.

Definition 2.21 ($(a, b, c)$-scan regular [7]). *Let $a \geq 1/b$, $0 < b < 1$, and $C \geq 1$ be constants. A linear-space algorithm is $(a, b, c)$-* ***scan regular*** *if, for inputs of sufficiently large size $N$, it makes*

**(i)** *exactly $(a)$ recursive calls on subproblems of size $(N/b)$, and*

**(ii)** *$\Theta(1)$ linear scans before, between, or after recursive calls, where the size of the biggest scan is $\Theta(N^C)$ where $\log_b(a) > C$.*

Finally, we restate a theorem due to Bender *et al.* that determines which algorithms are immediately optimal and how far non-optimal algorithms are from optimal algorithms.

Theorem 2.22 ($(a, b, c)$-regular optimality [7]). *Suppose $\mathcal{A}$ is an $(a, b, c)$-regular algorithm with tall-cache requirement $H(\mathcal{B})$ and linear space complexity. Suppose also that, in the DAM model, $\mathcal{A}$ is optimally progressing for a problem with progress function $\phi_{\mathcal{A}}(\square_N) = \Theta(N^p)$, for constant $p$. Assume $\mathcal{B} \geq 4$. Let $\lambda = \max\{H(\mathcal{B}), ((1+\varepsilon)\mathcal{B}\log_{1/b}\mathcal{B})^{1+\varepsilon)}\}$, where $\varepsilon > 0$.*

*(1) If $c < 1$, then $\mathcal{A}$ is optimally progressing and optimally cache-adaptive among all $\lambda$-tall profiles.*

*(2) If $c = 1$, then $\mathcal{A}$ is $\Theta\left(\lg_{1/b}\frac{N}{\lambda}\right)$ away from being optimally progressing and $O\left(\lg_{1/b}\frac{N}{\lambda}\right)$ away from being optimally cache-adaptive.*

## 3 GENERALIZED SCAN HIDING

In this section, we present a generalized framework for *scan hiding* derived from the concept of our scan hiding Strassen algorithm above. Our generalized scan hiding procedure can be applied to Master Theorem style recursive algorithms $A$ that contain "independent" linear scans in each level of the recursion.

At a high level, scan hiding breaks up long (up to linear) scans at each level of a recursive algorithm and distributes the pieces evenly throughout the entire algorithm execution. We define a ***recursion tree*** as the tree created from a recursive algorithm $\mathcal{A}$ such that each node of the tree contains all necessary subprocesses for the subproblem defined by that node. Figure 2 shows an example of scan hiding on the recursion tree for Strassen's algorithm. Each node of the Strassen recursion tree contains a set of scans and matrix multiplication operations as its subprocesses.

We now formalize our generalized scan-hiding technique. The following proofs extend the example of Strassen's algorithm and theorems from Section 4 for a more general result. We apply scan hiding to Strassen's algorithm in Section 4 as a case study of our technique.

Strassen's algorithm for matrix multiplication is amenable to scan hiding due to its recursive structure. It is an $(a, b, c)$-regular algorithm with linear sized scans. Moreover, these scans must happen before or after a recursive function call, and might need to read in information from a parent call, but otherwise the scans are very independent.

More specifically, through our scan hiding approach, we can show algorithms that have the following characteristics to be cache-adaptive. We call this class of algorithms ***scan-hideable algorithms***.

Definition 3.1 (Scan Hideable Algorithms). *Algorithms that have the following characteristics are cache-adaptive:*

- *Let the input size be $n^C$. For most functions $C = 1$, however, for dense graphs and matrices $C = 2$.*
- *$\mathcal{A}$ is a $(a, b, c)$-scan regular algorithm and has a runtime that can be computed as a function that follows the Master Theorem style equations of the form $T(n) = aT(n/b) + O(n^C)$ in the DAM model where $\log_b(a) > C$ for some constants $a > 0$, $b \geq 1$, and $C \geq 1$.*
- *In terms of I/Os, the base case of $A$ is $T(M) = \frac{M}{\mathcal{B}}$ where $M$ is the cache size.*
- *We define* work *to be the amount of computation* in words *performed in a square profile of size $m$ by $m$ by some subprocess of $A$. A subprocess is more* work consuming *if it uses more work in a square profile of size $m$ by $m$. For example, a naive matrix multiplication subprocess is more work consuming than a scan since it uses $(m\mathcal{B})^{\log_2 3}$ work as opposed to a scan which uses $m\mathcal{B}$ work. At each level a linear scan is*

*performed in conjunction with a more work consuming subprocess (in the case of Strassen, for example, the linear scan is performed in conjunction with the more work consuming matrix multiplication).*

- *Each of the more work consuming subprocesses in each node of the recursion tree only depends on the the results of the scans performed in the subtrees to the left of the path from the current node to the root.*
- *If each node's scans depend on the result of the subprocesses of the ancestors (including the parent) of the current node in the computational DAG of the algorithm.*

Our scan hiding technique involves hiding all scans "inside" the recursive structure in subcalls. If an algorithm (e.g. Strassen) requires an initial linear scan for even the first subcall, we cannot hide the first scan in recursive subcalls. Therefore, we show that an algorithm $\mathcal{A}$ is optimally progressing even if $\mathcal{A}$ having an initial scan of $O(n^C)$ length. We will be using $\mathcal{A}_{\text{scan\_hiding}}$ as the name for the algorithm using this scan hiding technique.

Lemma 3.2. *If the following are true:*

- *The optimal A algorithm in the DAM model (i.e. ignoring wasted time due to scans) takes total work $n^{\lg_b(a)}$ and respects the progress bound $\rho(m(t)) = d_0(m(t)B)^{\log_b(a)/C}$ where $d_0$ is a constant greater than 0. Let m be a profile that starts at time step 0 and ends at time step T where the optimal A algorithm completes.*
- *Let us assign potential in integer units to accesses, much as we do for work.*
- *$\mathcal{A}_{\text{scan\_hiding}}$ is an algorithm which computes the solution to the problem and has total work $d_1 n^{\lg_b(a)}$ and has total potential $d_2 n^{\lg_b(a)}$ and completes $c_3(m\mathcal{B})^{\log_b(a)/C}$ work and potential in any m by m square profile where $d_1$, $d_2$ and $d_3$ are all constants greater than 0 and where $m\mathcal{B} < n^C$.*
- *Finally, $\mathcal{A}_{\text{scan\_hiding}}$ must also have the property that if the total work plus potential completed is $(d_1+d_2)n^{\lg_b(a)}$, $\mathcal{A}_{\text{scan\_hiding}}$ is guaranteed to have finished its last access.*

*Then $\mathcal{A}_{\text{scan\_hiding}}$ is cache-adaptive.*

Finally, we prove that algorithm $\mathcal{A}$ is optimally progressing. Specifically, we show that any algorithm $\mathcal{A}$ with running time of the form $T(n) = aT(n/b) + O(n^C)$ and with the characteristics specified in Definition 3.1 is optimally progressing,

Theorem 3.3. *Given an algorithm $\mathcal{A}$ with running time of the form $T(n) = aT(n/b)+O(n^C)$ and with the characteristics as specified in Definition 3.1, then A is optimally progressing with progress bound $\rho(m(t)) = (m(t)\mathcal{B})^{\frac{\log_b(a)}{C}}$. To manage all the pointers we also require $m(t) \geq \log_b n$ for all t.*

Since scan hiding amortizes the work of part of scan against each leaf node of the recursion tree, each leaf node must be sufficiently large to hide part of a scan. Therefore, we insist that $m(t) \geq \log_b n$. Note that given a specific problem one can usually find a way to split the scans such that this requirement is unnecessary. However, for the general proof we use this to make passing pointers to scans easy and inexpensive.

As an immediate consequence of Theorem 3.3 above, we get the following corollary.

Corollary 3.4. *Given an algorithm $\mathcal{A}$ with running time of the form $T(N) = aT(N/b) + O(N)$ and with the characteristics as specified in Definition 3.1, $\mathcal{A}$ is cache-adaptive. If a node's subprocesses depend on the scans of the nodes in the left subtree, then we also require $m(t) \geq \log n$.*

Note that this procedure directly broadens Theorem 7.3 in [7] to show cache-adaptivity for a specific subclass of Master Theorem style problems when $\log_b(a) > C$.

# 4 STRASSEN

In this section we apply scan hiding to Strassen's algorithm for matrix multiplication to produce an optimally cache-adaptive variant of Strassen from the classic non-optimal version. We detail how to spread the scans out throughout the algorithm's recursive structure and show that our technique results in an optimally adaptive algorithm.

Some of the most efficient matrix multiplication algorithms in practice for large matrices use Strassen's algorithm for matrix multiplicationfootnoteWe provide pseudocode for Strassen's matrix multiplication algorithm in the RAM model in the full version of the paper. [1, 2].

Doing all of the scans of Strassen's algorithm in-place as in the optimal naive matrix multiplication algorithm does not result in an optimally cache-adaptive versino of STrassen. In naive Strassen, each recursive call begins with an addition of matrices and ends with an addition of matrices (see the full version for a discussion of naive Strassen). Doing this work in place still leaves a recurrence of $T(n) = 7T(n/2) + O(n^2)$ which is not optimally progressing. Each of these sums relies on the sums that its parent computed. In naive matrix multiplication, the input to the small sub-problems generated by its recurrence can be read off of the original matrix. In Strassen, the sub-problems are formed by the multiplication of one submatrix and the sum of two submatrices. To produce the input for a sub-problem generated by Strassen of size 1 by 1, one would need to read off n values from the original matrix making the running time $O(n^{\lg(7)+1})$. Thus the inplace approach does not work for this problem.

### *Adaptive Strassen is Optimally Progressing*

We will now describe the high level idea of our adaptive Strassen algorithm. We depict the input and running of Strassen in Figure 4.

The primary issue with naive Strassen is the constraint that many of the summations in the algorithm must be computed before the next recursive call, leading to long blocks of cache-inefficient computation. The main insight behind our adaptive Strassen is that all of these summations do not need to be executed immediately prior to the recursive call that takes their result as input. We are thus able to spread out these calculations among other steps of the algorithm making its execution more "homogeneous" in its cache efficiency.

Pseudocode for the scan hiding procedure and a full proof of its cache adaptivity can be found in the full version of the paper.

Our algorithm requires an awareness of the size of the cache line $\mathcal{B}$, though it can be oblivious to the size of the cache ($m(t)$ or $M(t)$). We further require that the number of cache lines in $m(t)$ be at least $\lg(n)$ at any time ($m(t) = \Omega(\lg(n))$).

To begin, the algorithm takes as input a pointer to input matrices $X$ and $Y$. We are also given the side length of the matrix $n$ and a pointer $pZ$ to the location to write $X \times Y$.

At a high level, scan hiding "homogenizes" the long linear scans at the beginning of each recursive call across the entire algorithm. We will precompute each node's matrix sum by having an earlier sibling do this summation spread throughout its execution. Figure 2 shows an example of how to spread out the summations. We need to do some extra work to keep track of this precomputation, however. Specifically, we need to read in $O(\lg(n))$ bits and possibly incur $O(\lg(n))$ cache misses. As long as $M(t) = \Omega(\lg(n)\mathcal{B})$ our algorithm is optimally progressing.

We hide all "internal" scans throughout the algorithm and do the first scan required for the first recursive call of Strassen upfront. The first recursive call of Strassen does the precomputation and set up of $O(n^2)$ sized scans as well as the post-computation for the output which also consists of $O(n^2)$ scans. This algorithm is described in the full version of the paper. In the middle of this algorithm, it makes a call to the recursive `AdaptiveStrassenRecurse` algorithm. `AdaptiveStrassenRecurse` has pseudocode in the full version of the paper.

THEOREM 4.1. *Let $X, Y$ be two matrices of size $n^2$ (side length $n$). Adaptive Strassen is optimally cache adaptive over all memory profiles $m$ when $m(t) > \lg(n)\ \forall t$ and the algorithm is aware of the size of the cache line size $\mathcal{B}$ with respect to the progress function $\rho(m(t)) = (m(t)\mathcal{B})^{\lg(7)/2}$.*

PROOF. We can apply Theorem 3.3 where $a = 7$ and $b = 4$ and the recurrence is $T(N) = 7T(N/4) + O(N)$ to begin with when $N = n^2$.

For concreteness, the full version includes pseudocode and proofs referencing the details of the algorithm. □

## 5 EXPERIMENTAL RESULTS

We compare the faults and runtime of MM-SCAN and MM-INPLACE as described in [7] in the face of memory fluctuations. MM-INPLACE is the in-place divide-and-conquer naive multiplication algorithm, while MM-SCAN is not in place and does a scan at the end of each recursive call. MM-INPLACE is cache adaptive while MM-SCAN is not.

Each point on the graph in Figure 3 represents the ratio of the average number of faults (or runtime) during the changing memory profile to the average number of faults (or runtime) without the modified adversarial profile.

We found that the optimally cache-adaptive MM-INPLACE incurred fewer relative faults and a shorter runtime than the non-adaptive MM-SCAN, lending empirical support to the cache-adaptive model.

### *Naive Matrix Multiplication*

We implemented MM-INPLACE and MM-SCAN and tested their behavior on a variety of memory profiles. The worst-case profile as described by Bender*et al.* [8] took too long to complete on any reasonably large input size for MM-SCAN.

We measured the faults and runtime of both algorithms under a fixed cache size and under a modified version of the adversarial memory profile for naive matrix multiplication. Figure 3 shows the runtime and faults of both algorithms under a changing cache normalized against the runtime and faults of both algorithms under a fixed cache, respectively. We also provide details of the profile

Figure 3 shows that the relative number of faults that MM-SCAN incurs during the random profile is higher than the corresponding relative number of faults due to MM-INPLACE on a random profile drawn from the same distribution. As Bender *et al.* [7] show, MM-SCAN is a $\Theta(\lg N)$ factor from optimally progressing on a worst-case profile while MM-INPLACE is optimally progressing on all profiles.

The relative faults incurred by MM-SCAN grows at a non-constant rate. In contrast, the performance of MM-INPLACE decays gracefully in spite of memory fluctuations. The large measured difference between MM-SCAN and MM-INPLACE may be due to the overhead of repopulating the cache after a flush incurred by MM-SCAN.

### *System*

We ran experiments on a node with and tested their behavior on a node with a two core Intel® Xeon™ CPU E5-2666 v3 at 2.90GHz. Each core has 32KB of L1 cache and 256 KB of L2 cache. Each socket has 25 Megabytes (MB) of shared L3 cache.

*Acknowledgements.* This research was supported in part by NSF grants 1314547, 1740519, 1651838 and 1533644, a National Physical Sciences Consortium Fellowship, and National Science Foundation Graduate Research Fellowship grant 1122374.

We would like to thank Michael Bender and Rob Johnson for their writing input and technical comments. Thanks to Rishab Nithyanand for contributions to the experimental section. We would like to thank Rezaul Chowdhury, Rathish Das, and Erik D. Demaine for helpful discussions. Finally, thanks to the anonymous reviewers for their comments.

## REFERENCES

[1] [n. d.]. GMP FFT Multiplication. https://gmplib.org/manual/FFT-Multiplication.html. Accessed: 2018-02-01.
[2] [n. d.]. JAVA BigInteger Class. https://raw.githubusercontent.com/tbuktu/bigint/master/src/main/java/java/math/BigInteger.java. Accessed: 2018-02-01.
[3] Alok Aggarwal and Jeffrey S. Vitter. 1988. The Input/Output Complexity of Sorting and Related Problems. *Commun. ACM* 31, 9 (Sept. 1988), 1116–1127.
[4] Rakesh D. Barve and Jeffrey S. Vitter. 1998. *External Memory Algorithms with Dynamically Changing Memory Allocations.* Technical Report. Duke University.
[5] Rakesh D. Barve and Jeffrey S. Vitter. 1999. A Theoretical Framework for Memory-Adaptive Algorithms. In *Proc. 40th Annual Symposium on the Foundations of Computer Science (FOCS).* 273–284.
[6] Laszlo A. Belady. 1966. A Study of Replacement Algorithms for a Virtual-storage Computer. *IBM Journal of Research and Development* 5, 2 (June 1966), 78–101.
[7] Michael A. Bender, Erik D. Demaine, Roozbeh Ebrahimi, Jeremy T. Fineman, Rob Johnson, Andrea Lincoln, Jayson Lynch, and Samuel McCauley. 2016. Cache-adaptive Analysis. In *Proceedings of the 28th ACM Symposium on Parallelism in Algorithms and Architectures, SPAA 2016, Asilomar State Beach/Pacific Grove, CA, USA, July 11-13, 2016.* 135–144. https://doi.org/10.1145/2935764.2935798
[8] Michael A. Bender, Roozbeh Ebrahimi, Jeremy T. Fineman, Golnaz Ghasemiesfeh, Rob Johnson, and Samuel McCauley. 2014. Cache-adaptive Algorithms. In *Proc. 25th Annual ACM-SIAM Symposium on Discrete Algorithms (SODA).* 958–971.
[9] Gerth S. Brodal and Rolf Fagerberg. 2002. Cache Oblivious Distribution Sweeping. In *Proc. 29th International Colloquium on Automata, Languages and Programming (ICALP).* Springer-Verlag, 426–438.
[10] Kurt P. Brown, Michael J. Carey, and Miron Livny. 1993. Managing Memory to Meet Multiclass Workload Response Time Goals. In *Proc. 19th International Conference on Very Large Data Bases (VLDB).* Institute of Electrical & Electronics Engineers (IEEE), 328–328.

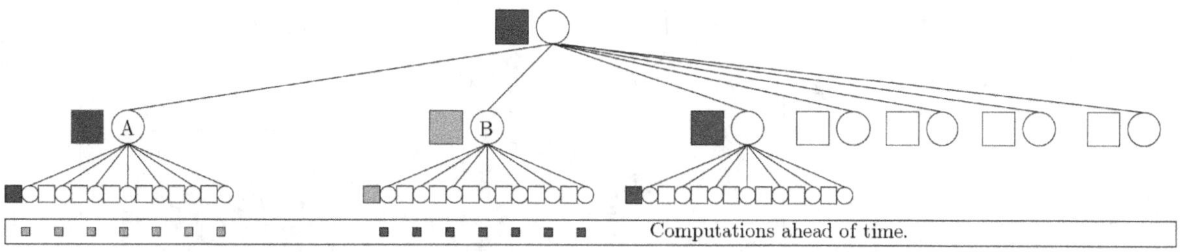


**Figure 2: The purple squares represent the scans on the rightmost path of the root. The orange squares represent the rightmost path of the second child of root. The scans represented in orange will be completed before the recursive call for $B$ is made. The scans will be completed by the leaf nodes under $A$. We represent the look-ahead computations as the small squares in the rectangle labeled *Computations ahead of time.***

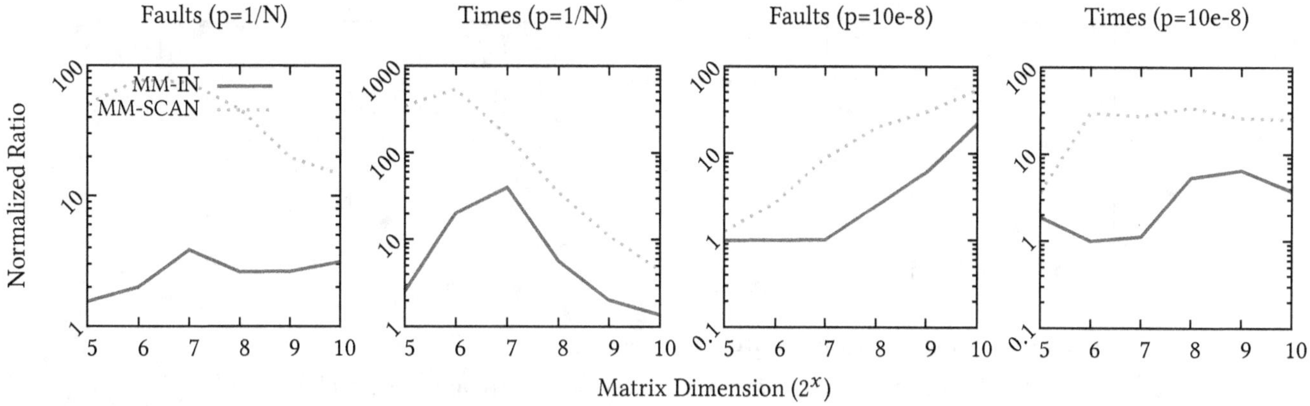


**Figure 3: An empirical comparison of faults and runtime of MM-SCAN and MM-INPLACE under memory fluctuations. Each plot shows the normalized faults or runtime under a randomized version of the worst-case profile.**
**The first two plots show the faults and runtime during a random profile where the memory drops with probability $p = 1/N$ at the beginning of each recursive call.**
**Similarly, in the last two plots, we drop the memory with probability $p = 5 \times 10^{-8}$ at the beginning of each recursive call. Recall that the theoretical worst-case profile drops the memory at the beginning of each recursive call.**


[11] Erik D. Demaine. 2002. Cache-Oblivious Algorithms and Data Structures. *Lecture Notes from the EEF Summer School on Massive Data Sets* 8, 4 (2002), 1–249.

[12] Dave Dice, Virendra J. Marathe, and Nir Shavit. 2014. Brief Announcement: Persistent Unfairness Arising from Cache Residency Imbalance. In *26th ACM Symposium on Parallelism in Algorithms and Architectures, SPAA '14, Prague, Czech Republic - June 23 - 25, 2014*. 82–83. https://doi.org/10.1145/2612669.2612703

[13] Matteo Frigo, Charles E. Leiserson, Harald Prokop, and Sridhar Ramachandran. 1999. Cache-Oblivious Algorithms. In *Proc. 40th Annual Symposium on the Foundations of Computer Science (FOCS)*. 285–298.

[14] Matteo Frigo, Charles E. Leiserson, Harald Prokop, and Sridhar Ramachandran. 2012. Cache-Oblivious Algorithms. *ACM Transactions on Algorithms* 8, 1 (2012), 4.

[15] Pieter Ghysels and Wim Vanroose. 2014. Hiding Global Synchronization Latency in the Preconditioned Conjugate Gradient Algorithm. *Parallel Comput.* 40, 7 (2014), 224 – 238. https://doi.org/10.1016/j.parco.2013.06.001 7th Workshop on Parallel Matrix Algorithms and Applications.

[16] Goetz Graefe. 2013. A New Memory-Adaptive External Merge Sort. Private communication.

[17] Richard T. Mills. 2004. *Dynamic Adaptation to CPU and Memory Load in Scientific Applications*. Ph.D. Dissertation. The College of William and Mary.

[18] Richard T. Mills, Andreas Stathopoulos, and Dimitrios S. Nikolopoulos. 2004. Adapting to Memory Pressure from within Scientific Applications on Multiprogrammed COWs. In *Proc. 8th International Parallel and Distributed Processing Symposium (IPDPS)*. 71.

[19] Richard T. Mills, Chuan Yue, Andreas Stathopoulos, and Dimitrios S. Nikolopoulos. 2007. Runtime and Programming Support for Memory Adaptation in Scientific Applications via Local Disk and Remote Memory. *Journal of Grid Computing* 5, 2 (01 Jun 2007), 213–234. https://doi.org/10.1007/s10723-007-9075-7

[20] HweeHwa Pang, Michael J. Carey, and Miron Livny. 1993. Memory-Adaptive External Sorting. In *Proc. 19th International Conference on Very Large Data Bases (VLDB)*. Morgan Kaufmann, 618–629.

[21] HweeHwa Pang, Michael J Carey, and Miron Livny. 1993. Partially Preemptible Hash Joins. In *Proc. 5th ACM SIGMOD International Conference on Management of Data (COMAD)*. 59.

[22] Daniel D. Sleator and Robert E. Tarjan. 1985. Amortized Efficiency of List Update and Paging Rules. *Commun. ACM* 28, 2 (February 1985), 202–208.

[23] Volker Strassen. 1969. Gaussian Elimination is Not Optimal. *Numer. Math.* 13, 4 (Aug. 1969), 354–356. https://doi.org/10.1007/BF02165411

[24] Volker Strumpen and Thomas L. Casavant. 1994. Exploiting Communication Latency Hiding for Parallel Network Computing: Model and Analysis. In *Proceedings of 1994 International Conference on Parallel and Distributed Systems*. 622–627. https://doi.org/10.1109/ICPADS.1994.590409

[25] Jeffrey Scott Vitter. 2001. External memory algorithms and data structures: dealing with massive data. *Comput. Surveys* 33, 2 (2001).

[26] Jeffrey Scott Vitter. 2006. Algorithms and Data Structures for External Memory. *Foundations and Trends in Theoretical Computer Science* 2, 4 (2006), 305–474.

[27] Hansjörg Zeller and Jim Gray. 1990. An Adaptive Hash Join Algorithm for Multiuser Environments. In *Proc. 16th International Conference on Very Large Data Bases (VLDB)*. 186–197.

[28] Weiye Zhang and Per-Åke Larson. 1996. A Memory-Adaptive Sort (MASORT) for Database Systems. In *Proc. 6th International Conference of the Centre for Advanced Studies on Collaborative research (CASCON)*. IBM Press, 41–.

[29] Weiye Zhang and Per-Äke Larson. 1997. Dynamic Memory Adjustment for External Mergesort. In *Proc. 23rd International Conference on Very Large Data Bases (VLDB)*. Morgan Kaufmann Publishers Inc., 376–385.

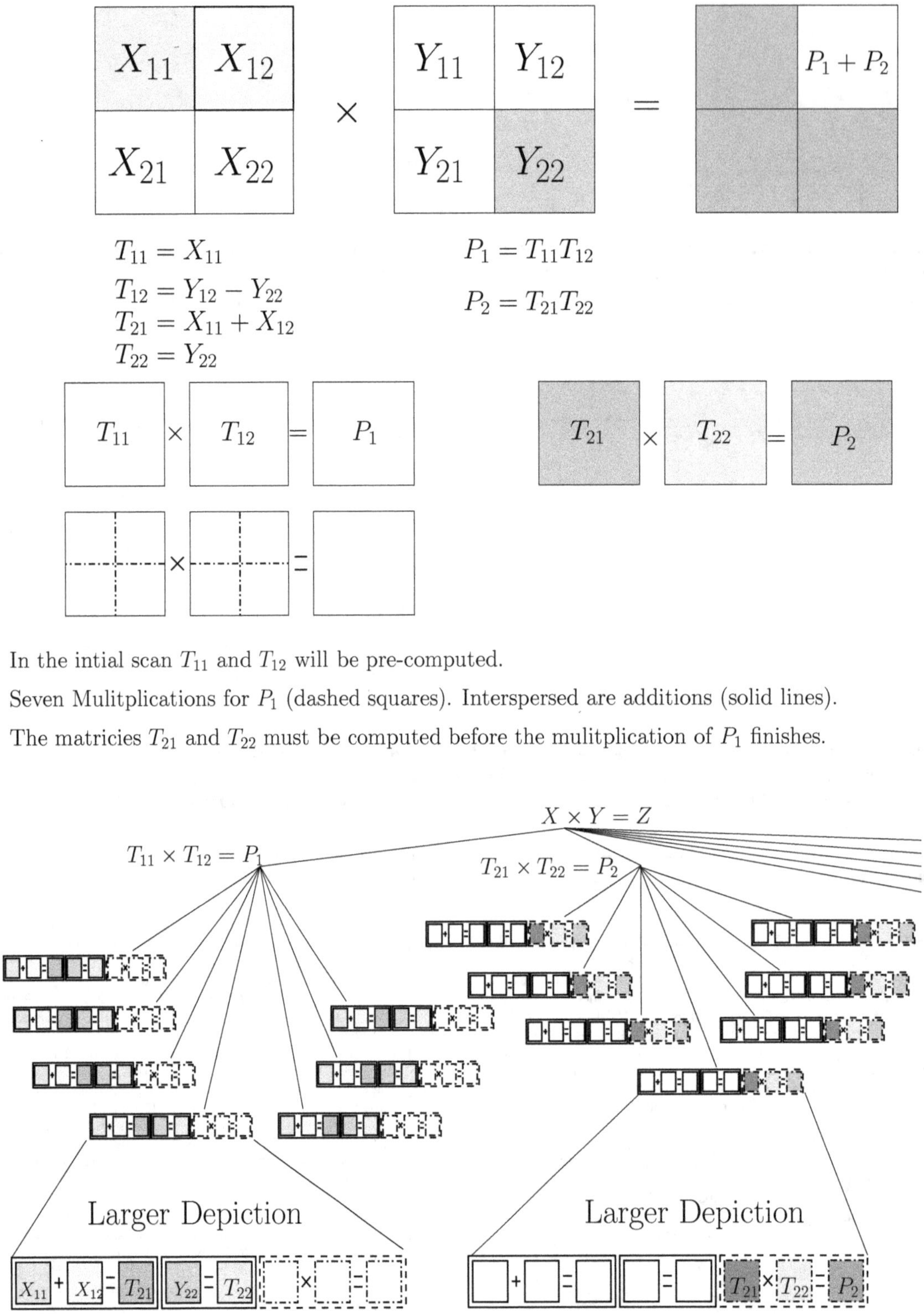


**Figure 4: The pre-computation scan of size $O(n^2)$ would in this case pre-compute $T_{11}$ and $T_{21}$. Then, all multiplications can be done. Assume that the smallest size of subproblem (3 small boxes) fit in memory. Then we show how the (dotted line boxes not filled in) multiplications needed for $P_1$ can be inter-spersed with the (complete line and colored in) additions or scans needed to pre-compute $T_{21}$ and $T_{22}$. Note that $T_{21}$ and $T_{22}$ will be done computing before we try to compute the multiplication of $P_2$. Thus, we can repeat the process of multiplies interspersed with pre-computation during the multiplication for $P_2$. The additions or scans during $P_2$ will be for the inputs to the next multiplication, $P_3$ (not listed here). The multiplications in $P_2$ are computed based on the pre-computed matrices $T_{21}$ and $T_{22}$ (dotted line boxes filled in).**

# Brief Announcement: Distributed Symmetry-Breaking with Improved Vertex-Averaged Complexity*

Leonid Barenboim
Open University of Israel
Department Of Computer Science
Ra'anana, Israel
leonidb@openu.ac.il

Yaniv Tzur
Open University of Israel
Department Of Computer Science
Ra'anana, Israel
yaniv.tzur@outlook.com

**ACM Reference Format:**
Leonid Barenboim and Yaniv Tzur. 2018. Brief Announcement: Distributed Symmetry-Breaking with Improved Vertex-Averaged Complexity. In *Proceedings of 30th ACM Symposium on Parallelism in Algorithms and Architectures (SPAA'18).* ACM, New York, NY, USA, 4 pages. https://doi.org/10.1145/3210377.3210660

## ABSTRACT

We study the distributed message-passing model in which a communication network is represented by a graph $G = (V, E)$. Usually, the measure of complexity that is considered in this model is the worst-case complexity, which is the largest number of rounds performed by a vertex $v \in V$. Often this is a reasonable measure, but in some occasions it does not express sufficiently well the actual performance of the algorithm. For example, an execution in which one processor performs $r$ rounds, and all the rest perform significantly less rounds than $r$, has the same running time as an execution in which all processors perform the same number of rounds $r$. On the other hand, the latter execution is less efficient in several respects, such as energy efficiency, task execution efficiency, local-neighborhood efficiency and simulation efficiency. Consequently, a more appropriate measure is required in these cases. Recently, the vertex-averaged complexity was proposed by [9]. In this measure, the running time is the worst-case average of rounds over the number of vertices. Feuilloley [9] showed that leader-election admits an algorithm with significantly better vertex-averaged complexity than worst-case complexity. On the other hand, for $O(1)$-coloring of rings, the worst-case and vertex-averaged complexities are the same. This complexity is $O(\log^* n)$ [9]. It remained open whether the vertex-averaged complexity of symmetry-breaking in general graphs can be better than the worst-case complexity.

In this paper we devise symmetry-breaking algorithms with significantly improved vertex-averaged complexity for general graphs, as well as specific graph families. Some algorithms of ours have significantly better vertex-averaged complexity than the best-possible worst case complexity. For example, for general graphs, we devise an $O(a^2)$-vertex-coloring algorithm with vertex-averaged complexity of $O(\log \log n)$, where the arboricity $a$ is the minimum number of forests that the graph's edges can be partitioned into. In the worst-case, this requires $\Omega(\log n)$ rounds [6].

*This research has been supported by ISF grant 724/15, and by the Open University of Israel research fund. The full version of this paper is available online on arXiv.org.


*SPAA'18, July 16–18, 2018, Vienna, Austria*

ACM ISBN 978-1-4503-5799-9/18/07.
https://doi.org/10.1145/3210377.3210660

## 1 INTRODUCTION

### 1.1 Background

We operate in the static, synchronous message passing model of distributed computation. In this model, an $n$ -vertex graph $G = (V, E)$ is given, where the vertex set $V$ represents the set of processors and the edge set $E$ represents the set of communication lines between processors in the underlying network. All processors operate in parallel, where they can pass messages of unbounded size to their neighbors in constant time, over the communication lines.

Also, we assume, in the static model, that no addition or deletion of vertices or edges is performed. Every algorithm in this model operates in synchronous rounds, where all vertices start simultaneously in round 0, and each vertex $v \in V$ starts the $i + 1$-th round only after all vertices have finished the $i$-th round.

Among the most important problems that have been studied in this model, are the problems of vertex coloring, edge coloring, finding a maximal independent set (also known as MIS) and finding a maximal matching (also known as MM). (See Section 2 for the definitions of these problems.) Many studies have been conducted since the mid 80's to try and find an efficient distributed solution to these problems. Notable early studies on these matters include [1, 8, 11–13, 15–17].

### 1.2 Related Work

Research in the field of distributed computing conducted since the 1980's, and until a few years ago, has focused mainly on the analysis of the time complexity of the developed algorithms in the *worst-case scenario.* On the other hand, during the past few years, several studies have been published, presenting new distributed algorithms with no improvement in the worst-case scenario, but a significant improvement in the average-case scenario ([9, 19]). In our review of related work, we will focus on [9].

In [9], the model is static, like the model used for analysis in this paper. Also, the running time of a vertex for a certain algorithm $\mathcal{A}$ is defined in one of two ways, which the author shows to be equivalent. We use a measure based on one of these definitions. The definition is as follows. The average running time of an algorithm is computed by summing up the running time of all vertices in the input graph and dividing the sum by the number of vertices in the graph. This measure of average running time is called by the author the *complexity of an ordinary node*, or *node-averaged complexity.* More formally, let there be a graph $G$, an algorithm $\mathcal{A}$ and let $\mathcal{ID}$ denote the set of legal ID assignments. Then, the above-mentioned measure of average running time is defined as $\bar{T}(G) = \max_{I \in \mathcal{ID}} \frac{1}{n} \sum_{v \in V(G)} r_{G,I,\mathcal{A}}(v)$, where $\bar{T}(G)$ denotes the average running time of the inspected distributed algorithm for a graph with $n$ vertices, $V(G)$ denotes the set of vertices of the graph $G$, and $r_{G,I,\mathcal{A}}(v)$ denotes the number of rounds until a vertex $v$ terminates in the execution of algorithm $\mathcal{A}$ on $G$ with ID assignment $I$.

In [9], the author mainly studies the average time complexity of algorithms on cycles and other specific sparse graphs. For the problem of leader election on cycles, the author showed the following positive result. There is an exponential gap between the vertex-averaged complexity, which is $O(\log n)$, and the worst-case time complexity, which is $O(n)$. However, for other problems, such as 3-coloring a cycle, the author shows the vertex-averaged complexity cannot be improved. The author also generalized this lower bound to a class of sparse graphs he called *q-sparse graphs.*

Our paper employs the first definition of [9] with a slight difference. Once a vertex has finished executing an algorithm and has decided upon a final output, it sends the output once to all its neighbors and terminates. In subsequent rounds, the vertex performs no further local computation or communication. For an algorithm $\mathcal{A}$, we name this time complexity measure, the *vertex-averaged complexity* of algorithm $\mathcal{A}$.

| Number of colors | Our vertex-averaged time | Previous running time |
|---|---|---|
| $O(a)$ | $O(a + \log^* n)$ (Det.) | $O(a \log n)$ (Det.) [6] |
| $O(a \log\log n)$ | $O(1)$ (Rand.) | $\Omega\left(\frac{\log n}{\log\log n}\right)$ (Det.) [6]<br>$O(a \log n)$ (Det.) [6]<br>$O\left(\log^2 n\right)$ (Rand.) [6][2] |
| $O(a^{1+\eta})$ | $O(\log a \log\log n)$ (Det.) | $O(\log a \log n)$ (Det.) [3] |
| $O(a^2 \log n)$ | $O(1)$ (Rand.) | $O\left(\frac{\log n}{\log\log n}\right)$ (Det.) [6] |
| $O(a^2)$ | $O(\log\log n)$ (Det.) | $O(\log n)$ (Det.) [6] |
| $O(ka^2)$ | $O(k \log^* n + \log^{(k+1)} n)$ (Det.) | $O(\log n)$ (Det.) [6] |
| $\Delta + 1$ | $O\left(\sqrt{a} \log^{2.5} a + \log^* n\right)$ (Det.) | $O(\sqrt{\Delta} \log^{2.5} \Delta + \log^* n)$ (Det.) [10] |
| $\Delta + 1$ | $O(1)$ (Rand.) | $2^{O\left(\sqrt{\log\log n}\right)}$ (Rand.) [7] |

**Table 1: Comparison of vertex-coloring algorithms.**

## 1.3 Open Questions Left by Existing Research

Despite some positive results obtained by the author of [9], it remained open for general graphs, and for sparse graphs not contained in the class studied in [9], for the above-mentioned important graph-theoretic problems, whether an improvement can be achieved in terms of vertex-averaged complexity. This is the subject of our paper.

## 1.4 Our Results and Comparison with Previous Work

Tables 1-2 present a comparison of previous work with results obtained in this paper. We note the following. In the case of all randomized algorithms presented in the tables, the time bound for each algorithm holds with high probability. Also, the time complexity of all results presented of previous work is a worst-case time complexity measure. However, no algorithms with better vertex-averaged complexities have been previously devised, to the best of our knowledge. On the other hand, the time complexity of results of this paper presented in the tables is a vertex-averaged complexity measure. In addition, where present, the parameters $\delta$,$\epsilon$ and $\eta$ denote an arbitrarily small positive constant. Also, "(Det.)" denotes "Deterministic" and "(Rand.)" denotes "Randomized".

## 1.5 Motivation

According to the worst-case complexity measure, the running time of an algorithm is the number of rounds of the processor that is the last one to terminate. Even if $n-1$ vertices terminate after just a single round, and the remaining $n$-th vertex performs $n$ rounds, the running time is $n$. According to this measure, exactly the same running time is achieved in the scenario where each of the $n$ processors perform $n$ rounds. The former scenario, however, is significantly better in several respects. These respects include a lower overall energy consumption when the network's vertices are fed by a common energy source, a faster running time of the majority of the network's processors when they need to execute two tasks, one after another, and a faster simulation of a large-scale network by a smaller number of processors, possibly even a single processor.

## 2 PRELIMINARIES

The *k-vertex coloring problem*, also referred to as "*graph coloring*", is the problem of assigning each vertex of an undirected graph a color, such that no two adjacent vertices share a color, using at most $k$ colors. The problem of *k-edge coloring* is the problem of assigning each edge a color from a set of $k$ different colors, such that each pair of edges which share an endpoint are assigned different colors. The problem of finding a *maximal independent set* in a graph is a problem, where given an undirected graph $G = (V, E)$, one needs to find a subset $I \subsetneq V$ such that no edge exists that connects any two different vertices $v_1, v_2 \in I$ and for each vertex $u \in V \setminus I$, if $u$ is added to $I$, then $I \cup \{u\}$ is no longer an independent set. The problem of finding a *maximal matching* in a given graph $G = (V, E)$ is the problem of finding a subset of edges $E' \subsetneq E$, such that for each pair of different edges $e_1, e_2 \in E'$, the two edges have no shared endpoint (vertex), and the addition of any edge $e$ from $E \setminus E'$ to $E'$ will result in the set $E' \cup \{e\}$ no longer being a matching. We call a vertex that has not yet finished executing a given distributed algorithm an *active vertex.* Accordingly, we call a vertex that has finished executing a given distributed algorithm and no longer takes part in it, an *inactive vertex.* For a graph $G = (V, E)$, we denote $\Delta(G) = \max_{v \in V} \deg(v)$, where $\deg(v)$ is the number of edges in

| Problem | Our vertex-averaged time | Previous running time |
|---|---|---|
| Maximal Independent Set<br>$(2\Delta - 1)$-edge-coloring<br>Maximal Matching | $O(a + \log^* n)$ (Det.) | $2^{O(\sqrt{\log n})}$ (Det.) [18]<br>$O\left(\frac{\log n}{\log \log n}\right)$ (for $a \le \log^{\frac{1}{2}-\delta} n$) (Det.) [4]<br>$O(a + \log n)$ for MM and $(2\Delta - 1)$-edge-coloring (Det.) [4, 5]<br>$O(a + a^{\epsilon} \log n)$ for MIS (Det.) [3, 4] |

**Table 2: Comparison of algorithms for the problems of MIS, $(2\Delta - 1)$-edge-coloring and maximal matching.**

$E$ incident on $v$. When the graph $G$ is clear from context, we simply write $\Delta$. Also, given a graph $G = (V, E)$ and a subset of vertices $V' \subseteq V$, we denote by $G(V')$ the subgraph of $G$ induced by $V'$.

# 3 BASIC TECHNIQUES

## 3.1 Procedure Partition

In this section we present a basic building block that is used by many of our algorithms. This is an algorithm devised in [6] (See also chapter 5 in [2]). The worst-case running time of the algorithm is $O(\log n)$. In this section, however, we demonstrate that its vertex-averaged complexity is significantly better, specifically, it is $O(1)$. The algorithm is Procedure Partition, which receives as input an undirected graph $G = (V, E)$, the arboricity $a$ of the graph and a constant $0 < \epsilon \le 2$ and produces as output a partitioning of the graph's vertices into $\ell = \lfloor \frac{2}{\epsilon} \log n \rfloor$ disjoint subsets $H_1, H_2, ..., H_\ell$ such that every vertex $v \in H_i$ has at most $A = (2 + \epsilon) \cdot a$ neighbors in the set $\bigcup_{j=i}^{\ell} H_j$. We call each such subset $H_i$ an *H-set*. Procedure Partition serves as a subroutine in Procedure Forest-Decomposition (also presented in [2]) which partitions the edges of an input graph into $O(a)$ directed forests. Procedure Forest-Decomposition is in turn used as a subroutine in additional algorithms presented in [2] for the problems mentioned in Section 1.1.

In Procedure Partition, all vertices begin in an active state at the start of the algorithm's execution. Every vertex with at most $(2+\epsilon)\cdot a$ active neighbors in the $i$-th round of the algorithm's execution joins a subset of vertices $H_i$ and then terminates, becoming inactive. It is shown in [2] that each vertex in the input graph eventually joins some subset $H_i$, and therefore, every vertex becomes inactive during some round. It is also shown in [2] that the algorithm executes for at most $\log_{\frac{2+\epsilon}{2}} n$ rounds. Therefore, the running time of Procedure Partition in the worst-case scenario is $O(\log_{\frac{2+\epsilon}{2}} n)$.

Let $n_i$ denote the number of active vertices in the input graph $G$ in round $i$ ($1 \le i \le \log_{\frac{2+\epsilon}{2}} n$) of the algorithm's execution. The following upper bound on $n_i$ that is provided in [2] is useful for our analysis.

Lemma 3.1. *[2] For $1 \le i \le \log_{\frac{2+\epsilon}{2}} n$, it holds that:*

$$n_i \le \left(\frac{2}{2+\epsilon}\right)^{i-1} n$$

Proof. According to [2], in each round $i$ of the algorithm's execution, for $1 \le i \le \log_{\frac{2+\epsilon}{2}} n$, at least $\frac{\epsilon}{2+\epsilon} n_i$ vertices with a degree of at most $(2 + \epsilon) \cdot a$ join $H_i$ simultaneously, subsequently becoming inactive. The result follows easily. □

Also, let *RoundSum*($V$) denote the sum of rounds of all vertices in $V$ in the execution of Procedure Partition. (For each vertex we count the number of rounds from the start until it terminates, and *RoundSum*($V$) is the sum of all these values over all vertices in $V$.) We observe that if a certain vertex $v \in V$ was active in rounds $1, 2, ..., i$ for some $1 \le i \le \log_{\frac{2+\epsilon}{2}} n$ then it adds 1 to the value of each of the terms $n_1, n_2, ..., n_i$. It follows that:

$$RoundSum(V) = \sum_{i=1}^{\log_{\frac{2+\epsilon}{2}} n} n_i \qquad (3.1)$$

One can easily infer the upper bound on *RoundSum*($V$) presented in the following lemma.

Lemma 3.2. *The term RoundSum($V$) satisfies RoundSum($V$) = $O(n)$.*

Lemmas 3.1, 3.2 imply the following theorem.

Theorem 3.3. *Suppose we are given an input graph $G = (V, E)$, where $|V| = n$. Then, the vertex-averaged complexity of Procedure Partition on $G$, denoted $\bar{T}(G)$, is $\bar{T}(G) = O(1)$.*

Proof. We observe , that by Lemma 3.2 , $\bar{T}(G)$ satisfies:

$$\bar{T}(G) = \frac{RoundSum(V)}{n} = \frac{O(n)}{n} = O(1)$$

□

The result of Theorem 3.3, contrasted with the worst-case running time of Procedure Partition of $O(\log n)$ rounds , implies that by creating, in each iteration of a new algorithm, a single $H$-set using Procedure Partition, and then invoking another subroutine on $G(H_i)$, one can parallelize many existing distributed algorithms, achieving a better vertex-averaged complexity.

## 3.2 Analysis of an Algorithm Composed of Procedure Partition and Another Distributed Algorithm

Let us define an algorithm $C$ consisting of $\ell = O(\log n)$ iterations as follows. In each iteration $1 \le i \le \ell$, we perform two steps. The first step is to execute a single round of Procedure Partition, producing a new $H$-set $H_i$. The second step is to have each vertex $v \in H_i$ and these vertices only execute an auxiliary algorithm $\mathcal{A}$ on the subgraph $G(H_i)$ induced by $H_i$. Also, let $T_{\mathcal{A}}$ denote the worst-case running time of algorithm $\mathcal{A}$. From these definitions and Theorem 3.3 the following corollary follows.

Corollary 3.4. *For an input graph $G = (V, E)$, let $C$ be an algorithm as described above. Then, algorithm $C$ has a vertex-averaged complexity of $O(T_{\mathcal{A}})$ rounds.*

Proof. We prove the corollary by deriving an upper bound of $O(n \cdot T_{\mathcal{A}})$ on the sum of rounds of communication carried out by all vertices of $V$, similarly to the proof of Lemma 3.2. We then divide the obtained expression by $n$, thus obtaining the required result. For a detailed proof, see the full version of this paper. □

It is important to note that though the $\ell$ executions of $\mathcal{A}$ are carried out sequentially on each $H$-set $H_i$, and not on all $H$-sets in parallel, the vertex-averaged complexity of $C$ is still $O(T_{\mathcal{A}})$.

In the following section, we present an example for an application of Corollary 3.4 by devising algorithms with improved vertex-averaged complexity.

# 4 DETERMINISTIC ALGORITHMS

## 4.1 An $O(a^2)$-Coloring in $O(\log\log n)$ Vertex-Averaged Complexity

In this section we devise an algorithm for $O(a^2)$-coloring that consists of two phases. The first phase lasts for $O(\log\log n)$ rounds, while the second phase lasts for $O(\log n)$ rounds. However, most vertices of the input graph terminate within the first phase, and so the average running time per vertex of the algorithm is only $O(\log\log n)$, in contrast to the best currently-known worst-case time complexity, which is $O(\log n)$. The algorithm proceeds as follows.

To begin with, we describe two helper procedures. First, we define a procedure called Procedure Parallelized-Forest-Decomposition. In this procedure, in each iteration $i$, we first execute a round of Procedure Partition. Subsequently, we orient each unoriented edge with an endpoint in the produced $H$-set $H_i$, towards the endpoint not yet in any $H$-set, if such an endpoint exists, and otherwise, towards the vertex with the higher ID value within the same $H$-set. We observe that invoking Procedure Parallelized-Forest-Decomposition on an input graph produces an $O(a)$-forests-decomposition of the graph (a decomposition of the graph's edges into $O(a)$ oriented forests). The second procedure is Procedure Arb-Linial from [6] (and based on [14]), that colors a graph using $O(a^2)$ colors. Computing the $O(a^2)$-vertex-coloring of a graph using the procedure from scratch requires $O(\log n)$ rounds in the worst case, but given an $O(a)$-forests-decomposition of the graph, the procedure requires only $O(\log^* n)$ rounds.

In the first phase, we execute $t = \lfloor c' \log\log n \rfloor$ iterations of Procedure Parallelized-Forest-Decomposition, for $c' = \log_{\frac{2+\epsilon}{2}} 2$. This invocation constructs $H$-sets $H_1, H_2, ..., H_t$, and orients and labels the edges with at least one endpoint in subset $H_i$, once $H_i$ has been formed, for iterations $i = 1, 2, ..., t$. Once $t = \lfloor c' \log\log n \rfloor$ sets have been formed, we run Procedure Arb-Linial on these $H$-sets. Then, we assign each vertex in the $t$ first $H$-sets formed so far a color $\langle c, 1 \rangle$ where $c$ is the color assigned by Procedure Arb-Linial. This completes the first phase of our algorithm.

In the second phase, we continue running Procedure Parallelized-Forest-Decomposition until every vertex has joined some $H$-set. Then, we run Procedure Arb-Linial for $O(\log^* n)$ rounds again on the sets $H_{t+1}, H_{t+2}, ..., H_\ell$. Finally, we assign $\langle c, 2 \rangle$ as the final coloring for each vertex in subsets $H_{t+1}, H_{t+2}, ..., H_\ell$.

We summarize the properties of the devised algorithm in the following theorem. Due to space constraints, we omit the proof, which can be found in the full version of this paper.

Theorem 4.1. *The devised algorithm properly colors an input graph using $O(a^2)$ colors with a vertex-averaged complexity of $O(\log\log n)$ rounds.*

We note that the above method can be generalized to produce an $O(ia^2)$-coloring within $O(i \log^* n + \log^{(i+1)} n)$ vertex-averaged complexity. Due to space constraints, a full explanation on this is given in the full version of the paper.

Theorem 4.2. *For $i = 1, 2, ...,$ we compute an $O(ia^2)$-coloring within $O(i \log^* n + \log^{(i+1)} n)$ vertex-averaged complexity.*

A plethora of additional results with improved vertex-averaged complexity is found in the full version of this paper.

# REFERENCES

[1] B. Awerbuch, M. Luby, A.V. Goldberg and S.A. Plotkin. Network Decomposition and Locality in Distributed Computation. In *Proc. of the 30th Annual Symposium on Foundations of Computer Science*, pages 364-369, 1989.
[2] L. Barenboim and M. Elkin. *Distributed Graph Coloring: Fundamentals and Recent Developments*. Morgan & Claypool Publishers, San Francisco, CA, 2013.
[3] L. Barenboim and M. Elkin. Deterministic Distributed Vertex Coloring in Polylogarithmic Time. *Journal of the ACM*, 58(5):23:1–23:25, 2011.
[4] L. Barenboim and M. Elkin. Sublogarithmic distributed MIS algorithm for sparse graphs using Nash-Williams decomposition. *Distributed Computing*, 22(5):363–379, 2010.
[5] L. Barenboim and M. Elkin. Distributed ($\Delta$+1)-coloring in Linear (in $\Delta$) Time. In *Proc. of the 41st Annual ACM Symposium on Theory of Computing*, pages 111-120, 2009.
[6] L. Barenboim and M. Elkin. Sublogarithmic Distributed MIS Algorithm for Sparse Graphs Using Nash-williams Decomposition. In *Proc. of the 27th ACM Symposium on Principles of Distributed Computing*, pages 25-34, 2008.
[7] Y. J. Chang, W. Li and S. Pettie. An Optimal Distributed ($\Delta$ + 1)-Coloring Algorithm? *arXiv.org*. Retrieved from https://arxiv.org/abs/1711.01361, 3 November 2017. Accessed 5 February 2018.
[8] R. Cole and U. Vishkin. Deterministic Coin Tossing and Accelerating Cascades: Micro and Macro Techniques for Designing Parallel Algorithms. In *Proc. of the 18th Annual ACM Symposium on Theory of Computing*, pages 206-219, 1986.
[9] L. Feuilloley. How Long It Takes for an Ordinary Node with an Ordinary ID to Output? In *Proceedings of the 24th International Colloquium on Structural Information and Communication Complexity (SIROCCO 2017)*, pages 263-282, 2017.
[10] P. Fraigniaud, M. Heinrich and A. Kosowski. Local Conflict Coloring. In *Proceedings of the 2016 IEEE 57th Annual Symposium on Foundations of Computer Science (FOCS)*, pages 625-634, 2016.
[11] A.V. Goldberg, S.A. Plotkin and G.E. Shannon. Parallel Symmetry-Breaking in Sparse Graphs. *SIAM Journal on Discrete Mathematics*, 1(4):434-446, 1988.
[12] A. Israel and A. Itai. A Fast and Simple Randomized Parallel Algorithm for Maximal Matching. *Information Processing Letters*, 22(2):77–80, 1986.
[13] A. Israeli and Y. Shiloach. An Improved Parallel Algorithm for Maximal Matching. *Information Processing Letters*, 22(2):57–60, 1986.
[14] N. Linial. Locality in Distributed Graph Algorithms. *SIAM Journal on Computing*, 21(1):193-201, 1992.
[15] N. Linial. Distributive Graph Algorithms Global Solutions from Local Data. In *Proc. of the 28th Annual Symposium on Foundations of Computer Science*, pages 331-335, 1987.
[16] M. Luby. Removing randomness in parallel computation without a processor penalty. *Journal of Computer and System Sciences*, 47(2):250-286, 1993.
[17] M. Luby. A Simple Parallel Algorithm for the Maximal Independent Set Problem. *SIAM Journal on Computing*, 15(4):1036-1053, 1986.
[18] A. Panconesi and A. Srinivasan. On the Complexity of Distributed Network Decomposition. *Journal of Algorithms*, 20(2):356–374, 1996.
[19] M. Parter, D. Peleg and S. Solomon. Local-on-average Distributed Tasks. In *Proc. of the 27th Annual ACM-SIAM Symposium on Discrete Algorithms*, pages 220-239, 2016.

# Brief Announcement: Hardware Transactional Persistent Memory

Ellis Giles
Rice University
Houston, TX, USA
erg@rice.edu

Kshitij Doshi
Intel Corporation
Chandler, AZ, USA
kshitij.a.doshi@intel.com

Peter Varman
Rice University
Houston, TX, USA
pjv@rice.edu

## ABSTRACT

This paper addresses the problem of creating durable transactions in byte-addressable Non-Volatile Memory or Persistent Memory (PM) when using Hardware Transactional Memory (HTM)-based concurrency control. It shows how HTM transactions can be ordered correctly and atomically into PM by the use of a novel software protocol combined with a Persistent Memory Controller, without requiring changes to processor cache hardware or HTM protocols. In contrast, previous approaches require significant changes to existing processor microarchitectures. Our approach compares well with standard (volatile) HTM transactions and yields significant gains in latency and throughput over other persistence methods.

**ACM Reference Format:**
Ellis Giles, Kshitij Doshi, and Peter Varman. 2018. Brief Announcement: Hardware Transactional Persistent Memory. In *SPAA '18: 30th ACM Symposium on Parallelism in Algorithms and Architectures, July 16–18, 2018, Vienna, Austria.* ACM, New York, NY, USA, 4 pages. https://doi.org/10.1145/3210377.3210656

## 1 INTRODUCTION

This paper provides a solution to the problems of adding *durability* to concurrent in-memory transactions that use Hardware Transactional Memory (HTM) for concurrency control while operating on data in byte-addressable Non-Volatile Memory or Persistent Memory (PM). In existing PM programming frameworks, transaction isolation is achieved in software within the rubric of an STM [1] or by using two-phase locking [2]; a log of updates is saved in persistent memory before the transaction completes, to permit failure recovery. However, logging based software approaches are problematic for HTM transactions (e.g., Intel TSX) which cannot bypass the caches in order to flush the log records synchronously into PM ahead of transaction closings. For these, PTM [3] proposes changes to processor caches while adding an on-chip scoreboard and global transaction id register to couple HTM with PM. Recent work [4–6] has attempted to provide inter-transactional isolation by employing processor based (HTM) [7, 8] mechanisms. However, these solutions require changes to the existing HTM semantics and implementations – [4] and [5] propose a new instruction to perform a non-aborting cacheline flush from within an HTM, while [6] proposes allowing non-aborting concurrent access to designated memory variables within an HTM. A software-based solution for this problem without any hardware changes or an external controller was presented in [9].

In this paper we provide a new solution to obtain durable consistency in Persistent Memory while using HTM for concurrency control. The solution does not alter the processor microarchitecture, but leverages a simple, external Persistent Memory Controller along with a persistence protocol, to supplement the existing HTM semantics and allowing HTM transactions to operate at the speed of in-memory volatile transactions. The solution, while it achieves the concurrency benefits of HTM for PM-based data, also applies to non-HTM transactions in a straightforward way.


*SPAA '18, July 16–18, 2018, Vienna, Austria*

ACM ISBN 978-1-4503-5799-9/18/07.
https://doi.org/10.1145/3210377.3210656

## 2 PERSISTENT HTM TRANSACTIONS

The code section between instructions **XBegin** and **XEnd** constitute an *HTM transaction* or simply a transaction. HTM ensures the *atomicity* and *isolation* of transaction execution. Within an HTM transaction, all updates are made to private locations in the cache, and the hardware guarantees that the updates are *not allowed* to propagate to their home locations in PM until **XEnd** completes.

**Atomic Persistence**: *Following crash recovery, ensure that all or none of the updates of an HTM transaction are stored in their PM home locations.* Following **XEnd**, transaction variables are subject to normal cache operations like evictions and write-back instructions. If the machine crashes before all the transaction updates are written back to PM, then on reboot, the values of these variables in PM will be inconsistent with the pre-crash transaction values. A common solution is to first log transaction updates in persistent storage before permitting updates to the PM home locations. However, with HTM the log can only be written to PM after **XEnd**, at which time the updates are also susceptible to uncontrolled cache evictions into PM. Hence there is no guarantee that the log has been persisted before transaction updates have percolated into PM.

**Persistence Ordering**: *Following crash recovery, ensure that the persistent state of any sequence of dependent transactions is consistent with their execution order.* For instance, if three dependent transactions A, B, C complete their **XEnd** in that order, we require that following crash recovery the PM variables reflect execution of either no transactions, {A}, {A, B}, or { A, B, C}. With HTM the logs can only be persisted after the transaction **XEnd** and the order in which log writes complete can differ from the transaction completion order. Approaches like ordering using a shared atomic counter within transactions are not practical due to the resulting HTM-induced aborts and serialization of transactions. Other papers have advocated changes to processor HTM semantics and implementation to allow selective writes to PM from within an HTM [4–6].

**Strict and Relaxed Durability**: *Following crash recovery, strict durability requires that the updates of a committed transaction are persistent in PM.* Strict durability is achieved in ACID databases by persisting transaction logs in order before commit. This is difficult to do for HTM transactions since transaction order and log completion order proceed independently. It is possible that an earlier transaction $X$ (on which $Y$ depends) to have completed but not yet persisted its log. During crash recovery the log of $Y$ should not be replayed since $X$ cannot be replayed.

We define a new property known as *relaxed durability* that allows an individual transaction to opt for an early commit immediately after it persists its log. The choice between relaxed or strict durability is made individually by a transaction based on its application requirements. Relaxed-durability transactions face a window of vulnerability after they commit, during which a crash may result in their transaction updates not being reflected in PM after recovery. The gain is reduced transaction latency. However, irrespective of individual durability choices, PM will always recover to a consistent state *i.e.* a prefix of every sequence of dependent transactions.

## 3 HTM+PM SOLUTION

We obtain durability of HTM transactions in PM using a coordinated protocol involving a back-end Persistent Memory Controller, transaction timestamps and logging, and the failure recovery procedure. The PM controller intercepts dirty cache lines evicted from the last-level processor cache (LLC) and holds them temporarily in a (volatile) FIFO queue within the controller. It delays the evicted cache lines from writing to PM until it can guarantee safety (atomicity and ordering) of the update. The controller is pre-programmed with the address range of a region of PM that is reserved for holding transaction logs. Addresses in the log region simply pass through the controller without intervention.

HTM+PM transactions execute independently. Within an outer-envelope that enforces consistency between updates to the volatile cache hierarchy and the durable state in PM, transactions use an unmodified HTM to serialize the computational portions of conflicting transactions. A transaction (1) notifies the controller when it opens and closes, (2) saves start and end timestamps in PM to enable consistent recovery after a failure, (3) performs its HTM operation, and (4) persists a log of its updates in PM before closing. A transaction requiring strict durability informs the controller during its closing step, and then waits for the go-ahead from the controller before committing. A relaxed-durability transaction can commit immediately after it closes.

The recovery routine is invoked after a system crash to restore the PM variables to a valid state *i.e.* a state that is consistent with the actual execution order of dependent transactions. It uses the saved logs to recover the values of the updated variables, and the saved start and end timestamps to determine which logs are eligible for replay and their replay order.

### 3.1 Transaction Lifecycle

A transaction can be viewed as progressing through five states: **OPEN**, **COMPUTE**, **LOG**, **CLOSE** and **COMMIT** as shown in Listing 1. When a transaction begins, it notifies the Persistent Memory Controller with a small unique integer (*wrapId*) that identifies the transaction. The controller adds *wrapId* to a set of Currently Open Transactions (referred to as COT) that it maintains. The transaction then allocates and initializes space in PM for its log and updates the *startTime* record of the log. The *startTime* is obtained by reading a system wide platform timer using the *RDTSCP* instruction implemented in the *ReadPlatformCounter* function. In addition to *startTime*, a log includes a second timestamp *persistTime* that will be set just prior to completing the HTM transaction. The *writeSet* is a sequence of $(address, value)$ pairs in the log that will be filled with the locations and values of the updates made by the HTM transaction. The log with its recorded *startTime* is then persisted using cache line write-back instructions (*clwb*) and *sfence*.

The transaction then enters the COMPUTE state by executing **XBegin** and entering the HTM code section. Within the HTM section, the transaction updates *writeSet* with the persistent variables that it writes. Note that the records in *writeSet* will be held in cache during the COMPUTE state since it occurs within an HTM and cannot be propagated to PM until **XEnd** completes. Immediately before **XEnd** the transaction obtains a second timestamp *persistTime* that will be used to order the transactions correctly. This timestamp is also obtained using the same *RDTSCP* instruction.

After executing **XEnd**, a transaction next enters the LOG state. It flushes its log records from cache hierarchy into PM using cache line write-back instructions (CLWB or CLFLUSHOPT), following the last of them with an SFENCE. This ensures that all the log records have been persisted. After the SFENCE following the log record flushes, the transaction enters the CLOSE state.

In the CLOSE state the transaction signals the Persistent Memory Controller that its log has been persisted in PM. The controller removes the transaction from its set, COT, of currently open transactions. It also reflects the closing in the state of evicted cache lines in its FIFO buffer as described below in Section 3.2. A transaction requiring strict durability informs the controller at this time; the controller will signal the transaction in due course when it is safe to commit *i.e.* its updates are guaranteed to be durable.

The transaction is then complete and enters the COMMIT state. If it requires strict durability it waits till it is signaled by the controller. Otherwise, it immediately commits and leaves the system.

### 3.2 Persistent Memory Controller

The Persistent Memory Controller is shown in Figure 1. While superficially similar to an earlier design [2, 10, 11], this controller handles races arising from the use of HTM rather than locking for concurrency control, and makes significant simplifications by delegating some PM state maintenance functions to the recovery protocol.

A primary function of the controller is to prevent a transaction's updates from reaching PM until it is safe for it to do so, without knowing which transactions generated a specific update. It does this by enforcing two requirements before allowing an evicted dirty cache line (representing a transaction's update) from proceeding to PM: (i) ensuring that the log of the transaction has been made persistent, and (ii) guaranteeing that the saved log will be replayed during recovery. The first condition is needed (but not sufficient) for atomic persistence by guarding against a failure that occurs after a partial subset of a transaction's updates have been persisted

**Listing 1: Transaction Structure**

```
Transaction Begin
----------  State: OPEN  ----------------
 1 NotifyPMController(open);
 2 Allocate a Log structure in PM;
 3 nowTime = ReadPlatformCounter();
 4 Log.startTime = nowTime;
 5 Log.writeSet = {};
 6 Persist Log in PM;
----------  State: COMPUTE  -------------
 XBegin
 // Transaction Body of HTM
 //   All reads and writes to transaction
 //  variables are performed and writes
 //  appended to  Log.writeSet.
 7   endTime = ReadPlatformCounter();
 XEnd

----------  State: LOG  ----------------
 8 Log.persistTime = endTime;
 9 Persist  Log in PM;

----------  State: CLOSE  ---------------
 10 NotifyPMController(close);

----------  State: COMMIT  --------------
11 If (strict durability requested)
        Wait for notification by controller;
12 Transaction End
```

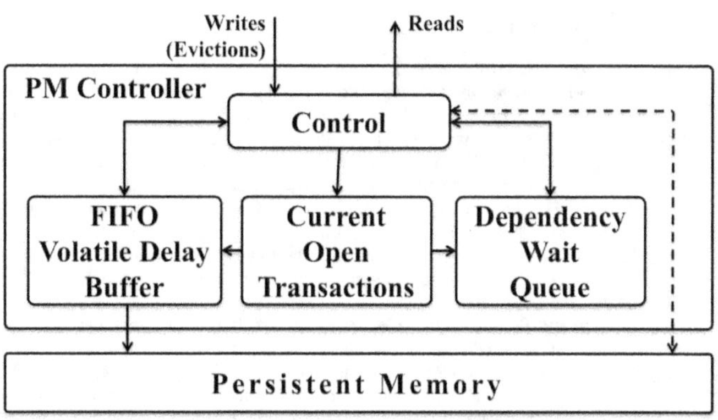


**Figure 1: PM Controller with Volatile Delay Buffer, Current Open Transactions Set, and Dependency Wait Queue**

in PM. The second requirement arises because transaction logs are persisted outside the HTM, and there is no relation between transaction dependency order and the order in which their logs are persisted. To maintain correct persistence ordering, the recovery routine may not be able to replay a saved log. We illustrate the issue in the example below.

**Example**: Consider two dependent transactions A and B, **A**: {w = 3; x=1;} and **B**: {y = w+1; z = 1;}. Assume that HTM transaction A executes before B, but that B persists its logs and closes before A. Suppose there is a crash just after B closes. The recovery routine will correctly refuse to replay either A and B, since the log of the earlier transaction A is not available.

Now consider the situation where $y$ (value 4) is evicted from the cache and then written to PM after B persists its log, just prior to a crash. Once again neither log will be replayed. However, atomic persistence is now violated since B's updates are partially reflected in PM. Note that this violation occurred even though the write back of $y$ to PM happened after B's log was persisted. The Persistent Memory Controller protocol prevents a write back to PM unless it can also guarantee that the log of the transaction creating the update will be played back on recovery (see Lemma C2 in Section 3.4).

The second function of the controller is to track when it is safe for a transaction requiring strict durability to commit. It is not sufficient to commit when a transaction's logs are persistent on PM since, as seen in the example above, the recovery routine may not replay the log if that would violate persistency ordering. The controller protocol effectively delays a strict-durability transaction $\tau$ from committing until the earliest open transaction has a *startTime* greater than the *persistTime* of $\tau$. This is because the recovery protocol will replay a log (see Section 3.3) if and only if all transactions with *startTime* less than its *persistTime* have closed.

**Implementation Overview**:

The controller tracks transactions by maintaining a set $S$ of currently open transactions (**COT**). When a transaction opens, its identifier is added to COT and when the transaction closes it is removed. The write to PM of a cache line $C$ evicted into the Persistent Memory Controller is deferred by placing it at the tail of a FIFO queue maintained by the controller. When $C$ enters the Persistent Memory Controller it is assigned a tag called its *dependency set* initialized to the current value of COT.

The controller holds the evicted instance of $C$ in the FIFO until all transactions that are in its dependency set (i.e. $S$) have closed. When a transaction closes it is removed from both the COT and from the dependency sets of all the FIFO entries. When the dependency set of a cache line in the FIFO becomes empty, it is eligible to be flushed to PM. One can see that the dependency sets will become empty in the order in which the cache lines were evicted, since a transaction that is still in the dependency set of $C$ when a new eviction enters the FIFO will also be in the dependency set of the new entry. This simple protocol guarantees that all transactions that opened before cache line $C$ was evicted into the controller (which must also include the transaction that last wrote $C$) must have closed and persisted their logs when $C$ becomes eligible to be written to PM. This also implies that all transactions with *startTime* less than the *persistTime* of the transaction that last wrote C would have closed, satisfying the condition for log replay. Hence the cache line can be safely written to PM without violating atomic persistence.

Note that the evicted cache lines intercepted by the controller do not hold any identifying transaction information and can occur at arbitrary times after the transaction leaves the COMPUTE state. The cache line could hold the update of a currently open transaction or could be from a transaction that has completed or even committed and left the system. To guarantee safety, the controller must perforce assume that the first situation holds.

### 3.3 Recovery

Each completed transaction saves its log in PM. The log holds records *startTime* and *persistTime* obtained by reading the platform timer using the RDTSCP instruction. We refer to these as the start and end timestamps of the transaction. The start timestamp is persisted *before* a transaction enters its HTM. This allows the recovery routine to identify a transaction that started but had not completed at the time of a failure. Note even though such a transaction has not completed, it could still have finished its HTM and fed values to a later dependent transaction which has completed and persisted its log. The end timestamp and the write set of the transaction are persisted *after* the transaction completes its HTM section, followed by an end of log marker. There can be an arbitrary delay between the end of the HTM and the time that its log is flushed from caches into PM and persisted.

The recovery procedure is invoked on reboot following a machine failure. The routine will restore PM values to a consistent state that satisfies persistence ordering by copying values from the *writeSets* of the logs of qualifying transactions to the specified addresses. A transaction qualifies for log replay if and only if all earlier transactions on which it depends (both directly and transitively) are also replayed.

**Implementation Overview**:

The recovery procedure first identifies the set of incomplete transactions $I$, which have started (as indicated by the presence of a *startTime* record in their log) but have not completed (indicated by the lack of a valid end-of-record marker). The remaining complete transactions (set $C$) are potential candidates for replay. Denote the smallest start timestamp of transactions in $I$ by $T_m$. A transaction in $C$ is valid (qualifies for replay) if its end timestamp (*persistTime*) is no more than $T_m$. All valid transactions are replayed in *increasing order of* their end timestamps *persistTime*.

### 3.4 Protocol Properties

We now summarize the invariants maintained by our protocol.

**Definition**: The precedence set of a transaction $T$, denoted by **prec**($T$), is the set of all dependent transactions that were ordered by the HTM before $T$.

**Lemma C1**: Consider a transaction $X$ with a precedence set **prec**($X$). For all transactions $Y$ in **prec**($X$), $startTime(Y) < persistTime(X)$.

**Lemma C2**: Consider transactions $X$ and $Y$ with $startTime(Y) < persistTime(X)$. If a cache line $C$ that is updated by $X$ is written to PM by the controller at time $t$, then $Y$ must have closed and persisted its log before $t$.

**Proof Sketch**: Suppose $C$ was evicted to the controller at time $t' \le t$. Now $t'$ must be later than the time $X$ completed HTM execution and set $persistTime(X)$; by assumption this is after $Y$ set its *startTime* at which time $Y$ must have been registered as an open transaction by the controller. Now, either $Y$ has closed before $t'$ or is still open at that time. In the latter case, $Y$ is included in the dependence set of $C$ at $t'$. Since $C$ can only be written to PM after its dependence set is empty, it follows that $Y$ must have closed and removed itself from the dependence set of $C$.

**Lemma C3** Any transaction $X$ whose update is written to PM at time $t$ will be replayed by the recovery routine if there is a crash any time after $t$.

**Proof** The recovery routine will replay a transaction $X$ if the only incomplete transactions (started but not closed) at the time of the crash started after $X$ completed; that is, there is no incomplete transaction $Y$ that has a $startTime(Y) \le persistTime(X)$. By Lemma C2 such an incomplete transaction cannot exist.

## 4 IMPLEMENTATION AND EVALUATION

In our full paper, we detail the implementation of the controller and user software library. We evaluate our approach using both micro-benchmarks and the STAMP suite. Our approach compares well with standard (volatile) HTM transactions. In comparison with persistent transactional locking, our approach performs 3x faster on standard benchmarks and almost 9x faster on a persistent Red-Black Tree data structure.

## 5 SUMMARY

In this paper we presented an approach that unifies HTM and PM to create durable, concurrent transactions. Our approach works with existing HTM and cache coherency mechanisms, does not require changes to existing processor caches or store instructions, and only utilizes logs for recovery. The solution correctly orders HTM transactions and atomically commits them to Persistent Memory by the use of a novel software protocol combined with a back-end Persistent Memory Controller.

## ACKNOWLEDGMENTS

Supported by NSF Grant CCF 1439075 and Intel SSG.

## REFERENCES

[1] H. Volos, A. J. Tack, and M. Swift, "Mnemosyne: Lightweight persistent memory," in *Proceedings of 16th International Conference on Architectural Support for Programming Languages and Operating Systems*. ACM Press, 2011, pp. 91–104.
[2] K. Doshi, E. Giles, and P. Varman, "Atomic Persistence for SCM with a Non-intrusive Backend Controller," in *The 22nd International Symposium on High-Performance Computer Architecture (HPCA)*. IEEE, March 2016.
[3] Z. Wang, H. Yi, R. Liu, M. Dong, and H. Chen, "Persistent transactional memory," *IEEE Computer Architecture Letters*, vol. 14, no. 1, pp. 58–61, Jan 2015.
[4] H. Avni, E. Levy, and A. Mendelson, "Hardware transactions in nonvolatile memory," in *International Symposium on Distributed Computing*. Springer, 2015, pp. 617–630.
[5] H. Avni and T. Brown, "PHyTM: Persistent hybrid transactional memory," *Proceedings of the VLDB Endowment*, vol. 10, no. 4, pp. 409–420, 2016.
[6] M. Liu, M. Zhang, K. Chen, X. Qian, Y. Wu, W. Zheng, and J. Ren, "DudeTM: building durable transactions with decoupling for persistent memory," in *Proceedings of the Twenty-Second International Conference on Architectural Support for Programming Languages and Operating Systems*. ACM, 2017, pp. 329–343.
[7] M. Herlihy and J. E. B. Moss, *Transactional Memory: Architectural support for lock-free data structures*. ACM, 1993, vol. 21,2.
[8] R. Rajwar and J. R. Goodman, "Speculative lock elision: Enabling highly concurrent multithreaded execution," in *Proceedings of the 34th annual ACM/IEEE international symposium on Microarchitecture*. IEEE Computer Society, 2001, pp. 294–305.
[9] E. Giles, K. Doshi, and P. Varman, "Continuous Checkpointing of HTM Transactions in NVM," in *Proceedings of the 2017 ACM SIGPLAN International Symposium on Memory Management*, ser. ISMM 2017. New York, NY, USA: ACM, 2017, pp. 70–81. [Online]. Available: http://doi.acm.org/10.1145/3092255.3092270
[10] ——, "Brief announcement: Hardware transactional storage class memory," in *Proceedings of the 29th ACM Symposium on Parallelism in Algorithms and Architectures*. ACM, 2017, pp. 375–378.
[11] L. Pu, K. Doshi, E. Giles, and P. Varman, "Non-Intrusive Persistence with a Backend NVM Controller," *IEEE Computer Architecture Letters*, vol. 15, no. 1, pp. 29–32, Jan 2016.

# Brief Announcement: Competitive Routing in Hybrid Communication Networks*

Daniel Jung
Heinz Nixdorf Institute & Computer Science Department
Paderborn University
Paderborn, Germany
jungd@hni.upb.de

Christina Kolb
Department of Computer Science
Paderborn University
Paderborn, Germany
ckolb@mail.upb.de

Christian Scheideler
Department of Computer Science
Paderborn University
Paderborn, Germany
scheideler@uni-paderborn.de

Jannik Sundermeier
Heinz Nixdorf Institute & Computer Science Department
Paderborn University
Paderborn, Germany
janniksu@mail.upb.de

## ABSTRACT

Routing is a challenging problem for wireless ad hoc networks, especially when the nodes are mobile and spread so widely that in most cases multiple hops are needed to route a message from one node to another. In fact, it is known that any online routing protocol has a poor performance in the worst case, in a sense that there is a distribution of nodes resulting in bad routing paths for that protocol, even if the nodes know their geographic positions and the geographic position of the destination of a message is known. The reason for that is that radio holes in the ad hoc network may require messages to take long detours in order to get to a destination, which are hard to find in an online fashion.

In this short paper, we assume that the wireless ad hoc network can make limited use of long-range links provided by a global communication infrastructure like a cellular infrastructure or a satellite in order to compute an abstraction of the wireless ad hoc network that allows the messages to be sent along near-shortest paths in the ad hoc network. We present distributed algorithms that compute an abstraction of the ad hoc network in $O\left(\log^2 n\right)$ time using long-range links, which results in $c$-competitive routing paths between any two nodes of the ad hoc network for some constant $c$ if the convex hulls of the radio holes do not intersect.

## CCS CONCEPTS

• **Networks** → **Mobile ad hoc networks**; *Overlay and other logical network structures*; • **Theory of computation** → **Distributed algorithms**; **Computational geometry**;

## KEYWORDS

greedy routing, ad hoc networks, convex hulls, $c$-competitiveness

**ACM Reference Format:**
Daniel Jung, Christina Kolb, Christian Scheideler, and Jannik Sundermeier. 2018. Brief Announcement: Competitive Routing in Hybrid Communication Networks. In *SPAA '18: 30th ACM Symposium on Parallelism in Algorithms and Architectures, July 16–18, 2018, Vienna, Austria.* ACM, New York, NY, USA, Article 4, 3 pages. https://doi.org/10.1145/3210377.3210663

## 1 INTRODUCTION

In a city center the density of cell phones would, in principle, be sufficiently high to set up a well-connected wireless ad hoc network spanning the entire city center, which could then be used for many interesting applications in the area of social networks, for example sending videos via Whatsapp. Wireless ad hoc networks have the advantage that there is no limit on the amount of data that can be exchanged while the amount of data that can be transferred at a reasonable rate via long-range links using the cellular infrastructure or satellite is limited or costly. However, routing in a mobile ad hoc network is challenging, even if the geographic position of the destination is known, since buildings or other obstacles like rivers may create radio holes that make it non-trivial to find a near-shortest routing path. So the question we address in this paper is: Can long-range links be used effectively to find near-shortest routing paths in the ad hoc network?

A simple solution to that problem would be that all nodes regularly post their geographic position and the nodes within their communication range to a server in the Internet. This would allow the server to compute optimal routing paths so that whenever a node wants to forward a message to a certain destination, the server can tell it which of the neighbors to send it to. An alternative approach that we are pursuing in this paper is a purely peer-to-peer based approach in which no other equipment other than the cell phones and an infrastructure for the long-range links needs to be used. To the best of our knowledge, our approach is the first one that is making use of a global communication infrastructure in a peer-to-peer manner in order to efficiently determine short routing paths for an ad hoc network. Wireless ad hoc networks have been considered before that utilize base stations in order to exchange messages more effectively, but there, messages will be

*This work was partially supported by the German Research Foundation (DFG) within the Collaborative Research Center 'On-The-Fly Computing' (SFB 901).


*SPAA '18, July 16–18, 2018, Vienna, Austria*

ACM ISBN 978-1-4503-5799-9/18/07.
https://doi.org/10.1145/3210377.3210663

sent via long-range links to bridge long distances while we will only allow messages to be sent via ad hoc links.

## 1.1 Model

We consider $V \subset \mathbb{R}^2$ to be a set of nodes in the Euclidean plane with unique IDs (e.g., phone numbers), where $|V| = n$. For any given pair of nodes $u = (u_x, u_y)$, $v = (v_x, v_y)$, we denote the Euclidean distance between $u$ and $v$ by $||uv|| = \sqrt{(u_x - v_x)^2 + (u_y - v_y)^2}$. We model our cell phone network as a hybrid directed graph $H = (V, E, E_{AH})$ where the node set $V$ represents the set of cell phones, an edge $(v, w)$ is in $E$ whenever $v$ knows the phone number (or simply *ID*) of $w$, and an edge $(v, w) \in E$ is also in the *ad hoc edge set* $E_{AH}$ whenever $v$ can send a message to $w$ using its Wifi interface. For all edges $(v, w) \in E \setminus E_{AH}$, $v$ can only use a long-range link to directly send a message to $w$. We adopt the *unit disk graph model* for the edges in $E_{AH}$, where for any point set $V \subseteq \mathbb{R}^2$ the *Unit Disk Graph* of $V$, UDG $(V)$, is a bi-directed graph that contains all edges $(u, v)$ with $||uv|| \leq 1$.

We assume UDG $(V)$ to be strongly connected so that a message can be sent from every node to every other node in $V$ by just using ad hoc edges. While the ad hoc edges $E_{AH}$ are fixed in Sections 1 – 4, the nodes can nevertheless change $E$ over time: If a node $v$ knows the IDs of nodes $w$ and $w'$, then it can send the ID of $w$ to $w'$, which adds $(w, w')$ to $E$. This procedure is called *ID-introduction*. Alternatively, if $v$ deletes the address of some node $w$ with $(v, w) \in E$, then $(v, w)$ is removed from $E$. There are no other means of changing $E$, i.e., a node $v$ cannot learn about an ID of a node $w$ unless $w$ is in $v$'s UDG-neighborhood or the ID of $w$ is sent to $v$ by some other node.

Moreover, we consider synchronous message passing in which time is divided into rounds. More precisely, we assume that every message initiated in round $i$ is delivered at the beginning of round $i + 1$, and a node can process all messages in a round that have been delivered at the beginning of that round.

## 1.2 Our Contributions

We consider any hybrid graph $G = (V, E, E_{AH})$ where the Unit Disk Graph of $V$ is connected and of bounded degree. Our main contribution is:

THEOREM 1.1. *For any distribution of the nodes in V that ensures that UDG(V) is connected and of bounded degree and that the convex hulls of the radio holes do not overlap, our algorithm computes an abstraction of UDG(V) in $O(\log^2 n)$ communication rounds using only polylogarithmic communication work at each node so that c-competitive paths between all source-destination pairs, that are positioned outside of convex hulls, can be found in an online fashion.*

The full version of this paper extends the protocols presented here in a way such that $c$-competitive paths between all source-destination pairs can be found, especially $c$-competitive paths between nodes which are located inside of convex hulls. In addition, we analyze the space requirements and prove that the majority of all nodes only has to store a constant number of references to other nodes. Nodes lying on the boundary of radio holes need to store references dependent on the size of the maximal radio hole. This is in general independent of the number of nodes in the network.

## 1.3 Related Work

Most research on routing in wireless networks has been done in the context of mobile ad-hoc networks, i.e., wireless networks that do not rely on some external infrastructure for their operation. There are basically two types of routing protocols for mobile ad hoc networks: table driven / proactive protocols, and on demand / reactive protocols. See, for example, [5] for a survey.

Proactive protocols only work well for small and relatively static ad hoc networks since otherwise the routing tables can get very large, and therefore the overhead of continuously updating them becomes prohibitively expensive. To reduce these problems, hierarchical and cluster-based strategies have been proposed like FSR and CGSR, but if the diameter of the ad hoc network is large, it may still take a long time for the tables to be up-to-date. Reactive protocols can produce a significantly lower overhead if messages are sent to only a small set of nodes. However, if many messages with different destinations are injected, the overhead of discovering routes can become prohibitively expensive. To reduce this problem, location-based variants have been proposed like LAR, but these only work well if the radio holes are not too large.

Unfortunately, greedy strategies like Compass routing [2] fail for graphs with radio holes, i.e., they might get stuck at a dead end. This can be avoided with the help of suitable virtual coordinates for the nodes (e.g., [7]), but computing these is quite expensive. Instead, Kuhn et al. [6] proposed GOAFR, a routing strategy that uses a combination of greedy and face routing, which can find paths with quadratic competitiveness [6]. They also proved that this is worst-case optimal. That is, it is not possible to design routing strategies which use only local knowledge and achieve a better competitiveness than quadratic. Their lower bound is based on the fact that a radio hole might have a complex structure, like a maze, making it hard to find a short path to a destination in an online fashion. To answer this question, we consider a hybrid communication model. A Hybrid Communication Network has been introduced in different contexts [3, 10]. To the best of our knowledge, we are the first ones that consider these types of networks for the purpose of finding paths in ad hoc networks.

# 2 PRELIMINARIES

In this work, we transform the ad hoc network into the *k-localized Delaunay Graph* $LDel^k(V)$, where a triangle $\triangle(u, v, w)$ for nodes $u, v, w$ of $V$ satisfies that all edges of $\triangle(u, v, w)$ have length at most 1 and the interior of the disk $\bigcirc(u, v, w)$ does not contain any node which can be reached within $k$ hops from $u, v$ or $w$ in UDG$(V)$. The *k-localized Delaunay Graph* $LDel^k(V)$ is defined to consist of all edges of $k$-localized triangles and all edges $(u, v)$ for which the circle with diameter $\overline{uv}$ does not contain any further node $w \in V$. Since we consider radio holes and 'near' shortest paths of the ad hoc network, we make use of the following definitions

*Definition 2.1 (Hole).* Let $V \in \mathbb{R}^2$. A *hole* is a face of $LDel^2(V)$ with at least 4 nodes.

*Definition 2.2.* A *path* $(v, \ldots, w)$ between two nodes $v$ and $w$ in a geometric graph $G$ is a *geometric c-spanning path* between $v$ and $w$, if its length is at most $c$ times the Euclidean distance between $w$ and $v$.

Classes of graphs that contain such paths for every pair of nodes are called geometric $c$-spanners.

## 3 HIGH LEVEL CONSTRUCTION

To prove Theorem 1.1, we use the following approach:

(1) Given the Unit Disk Graph, we compute the 2-localized Delaunay Graph. This only needs $O(1)$ communication rounds [8]. The 2-localized Delaunay Graph allows the nodes to detect whether they are at the boundary of a radio hole. Nodes at the boundary can then form a ring.

(2) Then, given a hole ring, we present a distributed convex hull algorithm which is based on Miller [9]. The protocol makes use of a pointer-jumping technique to transform a ring of nodes into a hypercube.

THEOREM 3.1. *Given a hole ring with $k$ nodes, the convex hull of this hole ring can be calculated in $O(\log k)$ communication rounds on expectation.*

(3) Afterwards, we make use of a recently developed distributed protocol by Gmyr et al. which is designed for Hybrid Communication Networks [4]. The protocol ensures that all nodes of the network are connected in a rooted tree via long-range links after $O(\log^2 n)$ communication rounds. The tree has a height of $O(\log n)$ and a constant degree. We introduce the nodes of the convex hulls to each other so that they form a clique. Based on the clique, they can compute a local Visibility graph such that they can determine the visibility of each pair of nodes in the ad hoc network only given the coordinates of the nodes. This will allow them to compute $c$-competitive paths for all source-destination pairs that are outside of a convex hull. The introduction requires $O(\log^2 n)$ communication rounds.

## 4 ROUTING PROTOCOL

Due to the existence of radio holes, we assume that the source and the target are not visible to each other. For visible nodes, the application of Chew's Algorithm [1] would directly find $c$-competitive paths. The following lemma gives the reason for considering convex hulls as an abstraction of radio holes.

LEMMA 4.1. *The shortest path between any pair of non-visible nodes of the 2-localized Delaunay Graph contains convex hull nodes.*

The routing protocol works as follows: A node $s$ sends its message via Chew's Algorithm into the direction of $t$. In case the message arrives at a hole node, it is directed to a convex hull node. The convex hull node inserts $t$ into its Visibility Graph and applies a shortest path algorithm. The resulting path is added to the message and used for forwarding the message in the ad hoc network. Between any pair of nodes on the received path, Chew's Algorithm is applied. This path has the following properties:

THEOREM 4.2. *Let $s$ and $t$ be two nodes of a 2-localized Delaunay Graph that do not lie inside of any convex hull. Further, let $(s = c_0, c_1, \ldots, c_{\ell-1}, c_\ell = t)$ be the shortest path in the Overlay Delaunay Graph via long-range links. Then we have*

(1) *There is a $\left(1.998 \cdot \sum_{m=0}^{\ell-1} d_m\right)$-path in the 2-localized Delaunay Graph from $s$ to $t$, where $d_m := \|c_m c_{m+1}\|$.*

(2) *By applying Chew's Algorithm, we obtain a $\left(5.9 \cdot \sum_{m=0}^{\ell-1} d_m\right)$-path in the 2-localized Delaunay Graph from $s$ to $t$, where $d_m := \|c_m c_{m+1}\|$.*

## 5 NODE MOVEMENT

As long as nodes do not leave and join the network, the Overlay tree remains valid as its structure does not depend on the position of the nodes. Once the Overlay tree for fast exchange of convex hull information is built, we can obtain new convex hull information (due to movement of nodes) in only $O(\log n)$ communication rounds since the dominating runtime of $O(\log^2 n)$ is only required for the Overlay tree.

## 6 CONCLUSION AND FUTURE WORK

We introduced the Hybrid Communication Network and presented a protocol to achieve knowledge about the ad hoc network in $O(\log n^2)$ time, as well as a routing protocol that chooses $c$-competitive paths. Since still fulfilling the results above, where convex hulls do not intersect and $s$ and $t$ are positioned within convex hulls is not trivial, investigating Hybrid Communication Networks under these assumptions is of high interest for future work. In addition, the join and leave of nodes could be investigated.

## REFERENCES


[1] Nicolas Bonichon, Prosenjit Bose, Jean-Lou De Carufel, Ljubomir Perkovic, and André van Renssen. 2017. Upper and Lower Bounds for Online Routing on Delaunay Triangulations. *Discrete & Computational Geometry* 58, 2 (2017), 482–504.

[2] Prosenjit Bose, Andrej Brodnik, Svante Carlsson, Erik D. Demaine, Rudolf Fleischer, Alejandro López-Ortiz, Pat Morin, and J. Ian Munro. 2000. Online Routing in Convex Subdivisions. In *Algorithms and Computation*, Gerhard Goos, Juris Hartmanis, Jan van Leeuwen, D. T. Lee, and Shang-Hua Teng (Eds.). Springer Berlin Heidelberg, Berlin, Heidelberg, 47–59.

[3] G. Cena, A. Valenzano, and S. Vitturi. 2008. Hybrid wired/wireless Networks for real-time Communications. *IEEE Industrial Electronics Magazine* 2, 1 (March 2008), 8–20.

[4] Robert Gmyr, Kristian Hinnenthal, Christian Scheideler, and Christian Sohler. 2017. Distributed Monitoring of Network Properties: The Power of Hybrid Networks. In *44th International Colloquium on Automata, Languages, and Programming (ICALP 2017) (Leibniz International Proceedings in Informatics (LIPIcs))*, Ioannis Chatzigiannakis, Piotr Indyk, Fabian Kuhn, and Anca Muscholl (Eds.), Vol. 80. Schloss Dagstuhl–Leibniz-Zentrum fuer Informatik, Dagstuhl, Germany, 137:1–137:15.

[5] Anuj K Gupta, Harsh Sadawarti, and Anil K Verma. 2011. Review of various routing protocols for MANETs. *International Journal of Information and Electronics Engineering* 1, 3 (2011), 251.

[6] Fabian Kuhn, Rogert Wattenhofer, and Aaron Zollinger. 2003. Worst-Case Optimal and Average-case Efficient Geometric Ad-hoc Routing. In *Proceedings of the 4th ACM International Symposium on Mobile Ad Hoc Networking &Amp; Computing (MobiHoc '03)*. ACM, New York, NY, USA, 267–278.

[7] S. Li, W. Zeng, D. Zhou, X. Gu, and J. Gao. 2016. Compact Conformal Map for Greedy Routing in Wireless Mobile Sensor Networks. *IEEE Transactions on Mobile Computing* 15, 7 (July 2016), 1632–1646.

[8] Xiang-Yang Li, G. Calinescu, and Peng-Jun Wan. 2002. Distributed Construction of a Planar Spanner and Routing for Ad Hoc Wireless Networks. In *Proceedings of the 21st Annual Joint Conference of the IEEE Computer and Communications Societies*, Vol. 3. IEEE Press., New York, NY, USA, 1268–1277 vol.3.

[9] R. Miller and Q. F. Stout. 1988. Efficient Parallel Convex Hull Algorithms. *IEEE Trans. Comput.* 37, 12 (Dec 1988), 1605–1618.

[10] Y. S. N. Murty. 1998. Hybrid Communication Networks for Power Utilities. In *Power Quality '98*. IEEE press, New York, NY, USA, 239–242.

# Parallel Write-Efficient Algorithms and Data Structures for Computational Geometry

Guy E. Blelloch
Carnegie Mellon University
guyb@cs.cmu.edu

Yan Gu
Carnegie Mellon University
yan.gu@cs.cmu.edu

Julian Shun
MIT CSAIL
jshun@mit.edu

Yihan Sun
Carnegie Mellon University
yihans@cs.cmu.edu

## ABSTRACT

In this paper, we design parallel write-efficient geometric algorithms that perform asymptotically fewer writes than standard algorithms for the same problem. This is motivated by emerging non-volatile memory technologies with read performance being close to that of random access memory but writes being significantly more expensive in terms of energy and latency. We design algorithms for planar Delaunay triangulation, $k$-d trees, and static and dynamic augmented trees. Our algorithms are designed in the recently introduced Asymmetric Nested-Parallel Model, which captures the parallel setting in which there is a small symmetric memory where reads and writes are unit cost as well as a large asymmetric memory where writes are $\omega$ times more expensive than reads. In designing these algorithms, we introduce several techniques for obtaining write-efficiency, including DAG tracing, prefix doubling, and $\alpha$-labeling, which we believe will be useful for designing other parallel write-efficient algorithms.

**ACM Reference Format:**
Guy E. Blelloch, Yan Gu, Julian Shun, and Yihan Sun. 2018. Parallel Write-Efficient Algorithms and Data Structures for Computational Geometry. In *SPAA '18: 30th ACM Symposium on Parallelism in Algorithms and Architectures, July 16–18, 2018, Vienna, Austria.* ACM, New York, NY, USA, 12 pages. https://doi.org/10.1145/3210377.3210380

## 1 INTRODUCTION

In this paper, we design a set of techniques and parallel algorithms to reduce the number of writes to memory as compared to traditional algorithms. This is motivated by the recent trends in computer memory technologies that promise byte-addressability, good read latencies, significantly lower energy and higher density (bits per area) compared to DRAM. However, one characteristic of these memories is that reading from memory is significantly cheaper than writing to it. Based on projections in the literature, the asymmetry is between 5–40 in terms of latency, bandwidth, or energy. Roughly speaking, the reason for this asymmetry is that writing to memory requires a change to the state of the material, while reading only requires detecting the current state. This trend poses the interesting question of how to design algorithms that are more efficient than traditional algorithms in the presence of read-write asymmetry.

There has been recent research studying models and algorithms that account for asymmetry in read and write costs [7, 8, 13, 14, 19, 20, 26, 27, 34, 42, 52, 53]. Blelloch et al. [8, 13, 14] propose models in which writes to the asymmetric memory cost $\omega \geq 1$ and all other operations are unit cost. The Asymmetric RAM model [8] has a small symmetric memory (a cache) that can be used to hold temporary values and reduce the number of writes to the large asymmetric memory. The Asymmetric NP (Nested Parallel) model [14] is the corresponding parallel extension that allows an algorithm to be scheduled efficiently in parallel, and is the model that we use in this paper to analyze our algorithms.

Write-efficient parallel algorithms have been studied for many classes of problems including graphs, linear algebra, and dynamic programming. However, parallel write-efficient geometric algorithms have only been developed for the 2D convex hull problem [8]. Achieving parallelism (polylogarithmic depth) and optimal write-efficiency simultaneously seems generally hard for many algorithms and data structures in computational geometry. Here, optimal write-efficiency means that the number of writes that the algorithm or data structure construction performs is asymptotically equal to the output size. In this paper, we propose two general frameworks and show how they can be used to design algorithms and data structures from geometry with high parallelism as well as optimal write-efficiency.

The first framework is designed for randomized incremental algorithms [21, 39, 45]. Randomized incremental algorithms are relatively easy to implement in practice, and the challenge is in simultaneously achieving high parallelism and write-efficiency. Our framework consists of two components: a DAG-tracing algorithm and a prefix doubling technique. We can obtain parallel write-efficient randomized incremental algorithms by applying both techniques together. The write-efficiency is from the DAG-tracing algorithm, that given a current configuration of a set of objects and a new object, finds the part of the configuration that "conflicts" with the new object. Finding $n$ objects in a configuration of size $n$ requires $O(n \log n)$ reads but only $O(n)$ writes. Once the conflicts have been found, previous parallel incremental algorithms (e.g. [15]) can be used to resolve the conflicts among objects taking linear reads and writes. This allows for a prefix doubling approach in which the number of objects inserted in each round is doubled until all objects are inserted.

Using this framework, we obtain parallel write-efficient algorithms for comparison sort, planar Delaunay triangulation, and $k$-d trees, all requiring optimal work, linear writes, and polylogarithmic depth. The most interesting result is for Delaunay triangulation (DT). Although DT can be solved in optimal time and linear writes sequentially using the plane sweep method [14], previous parallel DT algorithms seem hard to make write-efficient. Most are based


*SPAA '18, July 16–18, 2018, Vienna, Austria*

ACM ISBN 978-1-4503-5799-9/18/07...$15.00
https://doi.org/10.1145/3210377.3210380

on divide-and-conquer, and seem to inherently require $\Theta(n \log n)$ writes. Here we use recent results on parallel randomized incremental DT [15] and apply the above mentioned approach. For comparison sort, our new algorithm is stand-alone (i.e., not based on other complicated algorithms like Cole's mergesort [13, 22]). Due to space constraints, this algorithm is presented in the full version of this paper [16]. For $k$-d trees, we introduce the $p$-batched incremental construction technique that maintains the balance of the tree while asymptotically reducing the number of writes.

The second framework is designed for augmented trees, including interval trees, range trees, and priority search trees. Our goal is to achieve write-efficiency for both the initial construction as well as future dynamic updates. The framework consists of two techniques. The first technique is to decouple the tree construction from sorting, and introduce parallel algorithms to construct the trees in linear reads and writes after the objects are sorted (the sorting can be done with linear writes [13]). Such algorithms provide write-efficient constructions of these data structures, but can also be applied in the rebalancing scheme for dynamic updates—once a subtree is unbalanced, we reconstruct it. The second technique is $\alpha$-labeling. We subselect some tree nodes as critical nodes, and maintain part of the augmentation only on these nodes. By doing so, we can limit the number of tree nodes that need to be written on each update, at the cost of having to read more nodes.[1]

Using this framework, we obtain efficient augmented trees in the asymmetric setting. In particular, we can construct the trees in optimal work and writes, and polylogarithmic depth. For dynamic updates, we provide a trade-off between performing extra reads in queries and updates, while doing fewer writes on updates. Standard algorithms use $O(\log n)$ reads and writes per update ($O(\log^2 n)$ reads on a 2D range tree). We can reduce the number of writes by a factor of $\Theta(\log \alpha)$ for $\alpha \geq 2$, at a cost of increasing reads by at most a factor of $O(\alpha)$ in the worst case. For example, when the number of queries and updates are about equal, we can improve the work by a factor of $\Theta(\log \omega)$, which is significant given that the update and query costs are only logarithmic.

The contributions of this paper are new parallel write-efficient algorithms for comparison sorting, planar Delaunay triangulation, $k$-d trees, and static and dynamic augmented trees (including interval trees, range trees and priority search trees). We introduce two general frameworks to design such algorithms, which we believe will be useful for designing other parallel write-efficient algorithms.

## 2 PRELIMINARIES

### 2.1 Computation Models

**Nested-parallel model.** The algorithms in this paper is based on the nested-parallel model where a computation starts and ends with a single ***root*** task. Each task has a constant number of registers, and runs a standard instruction set from a random access machine, except it has one additional instruction called FORK. The FORK instruction takes an integer $n'$ and creates $n'$ ***child*** tasks, which can run in parallel. Child tasks get a copy of the parent's register values, with one special register getting an integer from 1 to $n'$ indicating which child it is. The parent task suspends until all its children finish at which point it continues with the registers in the same state as when it suspended, except the program counter advanced by one. We say that a computation has ***binary branching*** if $n' = 2$. In the model, a computation can be viewed as a (series-parallel) DAG in the standard way. We assume every instruction has a weight (cost). The ***work*** ($W$) is the sum of the weights of the instructions, and the ***depth*** ($D$) is the weight of the heaviest path.

**Asymmetric NP (Nested Parallel) model.** We use the Asymmetric NP (Nested Parallel) model [8], which is the asymmetric version of the nested-parallel model, to measure the cost of an algorithm in this paper. The memory in the Asymmetric NP model consists of (i) an infinitely large *asymmetric* memory (referred to as large-memory) accessible to all processors and (ii) a small private *symmetric* memory (small-memory) accessible only to one processor. The cost of writing to large memory is $\omega$, and all other operations have unit cost. The size of the small-memory is measured in words. In this paper, we assume the small memory can store a logarithmic number of words, unless specified otherwise. A more precise and detailed definition of the Asymmetric NP model is given in [8].

The ***work*** $W$ of a computation is the sum of the costs of the operations in the DAG, which is similar to the symmetric version but just has extra charges for writes. The ***depth*** $D$ is the sum of the weights on the heaviest path in the DAG. Since the depth can vary by a logarithmic factor based on specifics of the model (e.g. allowing binary or multiway branching), in this paper we show $O(\omega \cdot \text{polylog}(n))$ bounds for the depth of the algorithms, disregarding the particular power in the logarithm. Under mild assumptions, a work-stealing scheduler can execute an algorithm with work $W$ and depth $\omega \cdot \text{polylog}(n)$ in $W/P + O(\omega \cdot \text{polylog}(n))$ expected time on $P$ processors [8]. We assume concurrent-read, and concurrent-writes use priority-writes to resolve conflicts. In our algorithm descriptions, the number of ***writes*** refers only to the writes to the large-memory, and does not include writes to the small-memory. All reads and writes are to words of size $\Theta(\log n)$-bits for an input size of $n$.

### 2.2 Write-Efficient Geometric Algorithms

Sorting and searching are widely used in geometry applications. Sorting requires $O(\omega n + n \log n)$ work and $O(\omega \cdot \text{polylog}(n))$ depth [13]. Red-black trees with appropriate rebalancing rules require $O(\omega + \log n)$ amortized work per update (insertion or deletion) [51].

These building blocks facilitate many classic geometric algorithms. The planar convex-hull problem can be solved by first sorting the points by $x$ coordinates and then using Graham's scan that requires $O(\omega n)$ work [24]. This scan step can be parallelized with $O(\omega \cdot \text{polylog}(n))$ depth [28]. The output-sensitive version uses $O(n \log h + \omega n \log \log h)$ work and $O(\omega\, \text{polylog}(n))$ depth where $h$ is the number of points on the hull [8].

## 3 GENERAL TECHNIQUES FOR INCREMENTAL ALGORITHMS

In this section, we first introduce our framework for randomized incremental algorithms. Our goal is to have a systematic approach for designing geometric algorithms that are highly parallel and write-efficient.

[1] At a very high level, the $\alpha$-labeling is similar to the weight-balanced B-tree (WBB tree) proposed by Arge et al. [4, 5], but there are many differences and we discuss them in Section 6.

Our observation is that it should be possible to make randomized incremental algorithms write-efficient since each newly added object on expectation only conflicts with a small region of the current configuration. For instance, in planar Delaunay triangulation, when a randomly chosen point is inserted, the expected number of encroached triangles is 6. Therefore, resolving such conflicts only makes minor modifications to the configuration during the randomized incremental constructions, leading to algorithms using fewer writes. The challenges are in finding the conflicted region of each newly added object write-efficiently and work-efficiently, and in adding multiple objects into the configuration in parallel without affecting write-efficiency. We will discuss the general techniques to tackle these challenges based on the *history* graph [18, 31], and then discuss how to apply them to develop parallel write-efficient algorithms for planar Delaunay triangulation in Section 4 and $k$-d tree construction in Section 5. The application of these techniques to designing a write-efficient parallel comparison sorting algorithm is presented in the full version of this paper [16].

## 3.1 DAG Tracing

We now discuss how to find the conflict set of each newly added object (i.e., only output the conflict primitives) based on a history (directed acyclic) graph [18, 31] in a parallel and write-efficient fashion. Since the history graphs for different randomized incremental algorithms can vary, we abstract the process as a DAG tracing problem that finds the conflict primitives in each step by following the history graph.

*Definition 3.1 (DAG tracing problem).* The DAG tracing problem takes an element $x$, a DAG $G = (V, E)$, a root vertex $r \in V$ with zero in-degree, and a boolean predicate function $f(x, v)$. It computes the vertex set $S(G, x) = \{v \in V \mid f(x, v) \text{ and out-degree}(v) = 0\}$.

We call a vertex $v$ ***visible*** if $f(x, v)$ is true.

*Definition 3.2 (tracable property).* We say that the DAG tracing problem has the tracable property when $v \in V$ is visible only if there exists at least one direct predecessor vertex $u$ of $v$ that is visible.

| Variable | Description |
|---|---|
| $D(G)$ | the length of the longest path in $G$ |
| $R(G, x)$ | the set of all visible vertices in $G$ |
| $S(G, x)$ | the output set of vertices |

Theorem 3.3. *The DAG tracing problem can be solved in $O(|R(G, x)|)$ work, $O(D(G))$ depth and $O(|S(G, x)|)$ writes when the problem has the tracable property, each vertex $v \in V$ has a constant degree, $f(x, v)$ can be evaluated in constant time, and the small-memory has size $O(D(G))$. Here $R(G, x)$, $D(G)$, and $S(G, x)$ are defined in the previous table.*

Proof. We first discuss a sequential algorithm using $O(|R(G, x)|)$ work and $O(|S(G, x)|)$ writes. Because of the tracable property, we can use an arbitrary search algorithm to visit the visible nodes, which requires $O(R(G, x))$ writes since we need to mark whether a vertex is visited or not. However, this approach is not write-efficient when $|S| = o(|R(G, x)|)$, and we now propose a better solution.

Assume that we give a global ordering $<_v$ of the vertices in $G$ (e.g., using the vertex labels) and use the following rule to traverse the visible nodes based on this ordering: a visible node $v \in V$ is visited during the search of its direct visible predecessor $u$ that has the highest priority among all visible direct predecessors of $v$. Based on this rule, we do not need to store all visited vertices. Instead, when we visit a vertex $v$ via a directed edge $(u, v)$ from $u$, we can check if $u$ has the highest priority among all visible predecessors of $v$. This checking has constant cost since $v$ has a constant degree and we assume the visibility of a vertex can be verified in constant time. As long as we have a small-memory of size $O(D(G))$ that keeps the recursion stack and each vertex in $V$ has a constant in-degree, we can find the output set $S(G, x)$ using $O(|R(G, x)|)$ work and $O(|S(G, x)|)$ writes.

We note that the search tree generated under this rule is unique and deterministic. Therefore, this observation allows us to traverse the tree in parallel and in a fork-join manner: we can simultaneously fork off an independent task for each outgoing edges of the current vertex, and all these tasks can be run independently and in parallel. The parallel depth, in this case, is upper bounded by $O(D(G))$, the depth of the longest path in the graph. □

Here we assume the graph is explicitly stored and accessible, so we slightly modify the algorithms to generate the history graph, which is straightforward in all cases in this paper.

## 3.2 The Prefix-Doubling Approach

The sequential version of randomized incremental algorithms process one object (e.g., a point or vertex) in one iteration. The prefix-doubling approach splits an algorithm into multiple rounds, with the first round processing one iteration and each subsequent round doubling the number of iterations processed. This high-level idea is widely used in parallel algorithm design. We show that the prefix-doubling approach combined with the DAG tracing algorithm can reduce the number of writes by a factor of $\Theta(\log n)$ in a number of algorithms. In particular, our variant of prefix doubling first processes $n/\log n$ iterations using a standard write-inefficient approach (called as the ***initial round***). Then the algorithm runs $O(\log \log n)$ ***incremental rounds***, where the $i$'th round processes the next $2^{i-1}n/\log n$ iterations.

# 4 PLANAR DELAUNAY TRIANGULATION

A Delaunay triangulation (DT) in the plane is a triangulation of a set of points $P$ such that no point in $P$ is inside the circumcircle of any triangle (the circle defined by the triangle's three corner points). We say a point ***encroaches*** on a triangle if it is in the triangle's circumcircle, so the triangle will be replaced once this point is added to the triangulation. We assume for simplicity that the points are in general position (no three points on a line or four points on a circle).

Delaunay triangulation is widely studied due to its importance in many geometry applications. Without considering the asymmetry between reads and writes, it can be solved sequentially in optimal $\Theta(n \log n)$ work. It is relatively easy to generate a sequential write-efficient version that does $\Theta(n \log n)$ reads and only requires $\Theta(n)$ writes based on the plane sweep method [14]. There are several work-efficient parallel algorithms that run in polylogarithmic depth [6, 15, 17, 44]. More practical ones (e.g., [18, 31]) have linear depth. Unfortunately, none of them perform any less than $\Theta(n \log n)$

**Algorithm 1:** ParIncrementalDT

```
   Input: A sequence V = {v_1, ..., v_n} of points in the plane.
   Output: The Delaunay triangulation of V.
   Maintains: E(t), the points that encroach on each triangle t.
1  t_b ← a sufficiently large bounding triangle
2  E(t_b) ← V
3  M ← {t_b}
4  while E(t) ≠ ∅ for any t ∈ M do
5  |  parallel foreach triangle t ∈ M do
6  |  |  Let t_1, t_2, t_3 be the three neighboring triangles
7  |  |  if min(E(t)) ≤ min(E(t_1) ∪ E(t_2) ∪ E(t_3)) then
8  |  |  |  ReplaceTriangle(M, t, min(E(t)))
9  return M
10 function ReplaceTriangle(M,t,v)
11 |  foreach edge (u, w) ∈ t (three of them) do
12 |  |  if (u, w) is a boundary of v's encroached region then
13 |  |  |  t_o ← the other triangle sharing (u, w)
14 |  |  |  t' ← (u, w, v)
15 |  |  |  E(t') ← {v' ∈ E(t) ∪ E(t_o) | InCircle(v', t')}
16 |  |  |  M ← M ∪ {t'}
17 |  M ← M \ {t}
```

writes. In particular the divide-and-conquer algorithms [6, 17] seem to inherently require $\Theta(n \log n)$ writes since the divide or merge step requires generating an output of size $\Theta(n)$, and is applied for $\Theta(\log n)$ levels. The randomized incremental approach of Blelloch et al. (BGSS) [15], which improves the Boissonnat and Teillaud algorithm [18] to polylogarithmic depth, also requires $O(n \log n)$ writes for reasons described below.

In this section, we show how to modify the BGSS algorithm to use only a linear number of writes, while maintaining the expected $\Theta(n \log n)$ bound on work, and polylogarithmic depth. Algorithm 1 shows the pseudocode for the BGSS algorithm. In the algorithm, the vertices are labeled from 1 to $n$ and when taking a min over vertices (Lines 7–8) it is with respect to these labels. The algorithm proceeds in rounds the algorithm adds some triangles (Line 16) and removes others (Line 17) in each round.

In the algorithm, there are dependences between triangles so that some of them need to be processed before the other triangles can proceed. For a sequence of points $V$, BGSS define the dependence graph $G_T(V) = (T, E)$ for the algorithm in the following way. The vertices $T$ correspond to triangles created by the algorithm, and for each call to ReplaceTriangle$(M, t, v_i)$, we place an arc from triangle $t$ and its three neighbors ($t_1$, $t_2$, and $t_3$) to each of the one, two, or three triangles created by ReplaceTriangle. Every triangle $T$ with depth $d(T)$ in $G_T(V)$ is created by the algorithm in round $d(T)$. BGSS show that for a randomly ordered set of input points of size $n$, the depth of the dependence graph is $O(\log n)$ *whp*[2], and hence the algorithm runs in $O(\log n)$ rounds *whp*. Each round can be done in $O(\log n)$ depth giving an overall depth of $O(\log^2 n)$ *whp* on the nested-parallel model.

The algorithm, however, is not write-efficient. In particular, every point moves down the DAG through the rounds (on line 15), and therefore can be moved $O(\log n)$ times, each requiring a write.

[2] We say $O(f(n))$ with high probability (*whp*) to indicate $O(c \cdot f(n))$ with probability to be at least $1 - 1/n^c$ for any constant $c > 0$.

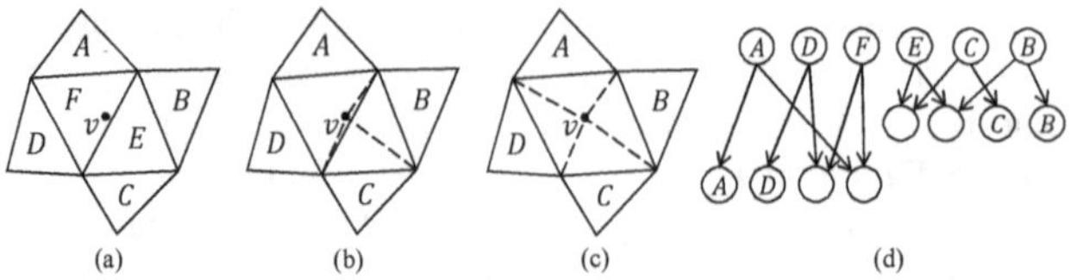

**Figure 1: An example of the tracing structure. Here a point $v$ is added and the encroaching region contains triangles $E$ and $F$ (subfigure (a)). Four new triangles will be generated and replace the two previous triangles. They may or may not be created in the same round, and in this example this is done in two substeps (subfigures (b) and (c)). Part of the tracing structure is shown in subfigure (d). Four neighbor triangles $A$, $B$, $C$, and $D$ are copied, and four new triangles are created. An arrow indicates that a point is encroached by the head triangle only if it is encroached by the tail triangle.**

**A Linear-Write Version.** We now discuss a write-efficient version of the BGSS algorithm. We use the DAG tracing and prefix-doubling techniques introduced in Section 3. The algorithm first computes the DT of the $n/\log_2 n$ earliest points in the randomized order, using the non-write-efficient version. This step requires linear writes. It then runs $O(\log \log n)$ incremental rounds and in each round adds a number of points equal to the number of points already inserted.

To insert points, we need to construct a search structure in the DAG tracing problem. We can modify the BGSS algorithm to build such a structure. In fact, the structure is effectively a subset of the edges of the dependence graph $G_T(V)$. In particular, in the algorithm the only InCircle test is on Line 15. In this test, to determine if a point encroaches $t'$, we need only check its two ancestors $t$ and $t_o$ (we need not also check the two other triangles neighboring $t$, as needed in $G_T(V)$). This leads to a DAG with depth at most as large as $G_T(V)$, and for which every vertex has in-degree 2. The out-degree is not necessarily constant. However, by noting that there can be at most a constant number of outgoing edges to each level of the DAG, we can easily transform it to a DAG with constant out-degree by creating a copy of a triangle at each level after it has out-neighbors. This does not increase the depth, and the number of copies is at most proportional to the number of initial triangles ($O(n)$ in expectation) since the in-degrees are constant. We refer to this as the *tracing structure*. An example of this structure is shown in Figure 1.

The tracing structure can be used in the DAG tracing problem (Definition 3.1) using the predicate $f(v, t) =$ InCircle$(v, t)$. This predicate has the traceable property since a point can only be added to a triangle $t'$ (i.e., encroaches on the triangle) if it encroached one of the two input edges from $t$ and $t_o$. We can therefore use the DAG tracing algorithm to find all of the triangles encroached on by a given point $v$ starting at the initial root triangle $t_b$.

We first construct the DT of the first $n/\log_2 n$ points in the initial round using Algorithm 1 while building the tracing structure. Then at the beginning of each incremental round, each point traces down the structure to find its encroached triangles, and leaves itself in the encroached set of that triangle. Note that the encroached set for a given point might be large, but the average size across points is constant in expectation.

We now analyze the cost of finding all the encroached triangles when adding a set of new points. As discussed, the depth of $G$ is upper bounded by $O(\log n)$ *whp*. The number of encroached triangles of a point $x$ can be analyzed by considering the degree of the point (number of incident triangles) if added to the DT. By Euler's formula, the average degree of a node in a planar graph is at most 6. Since we add the points in a random order, the expected value of $|S(G,x)|$ in Theorem 3.3 is constant. Finally, the number of all encroached (including non-leaf) triangles of this point is upper bounded by the number of INCIRCLE tests. Then $|R(G,x)|$, the expected number of visible vertices of $x$, is $O(\log n)$ (Theorem 4.2 in [15]).

After finding the encroached triangles for each point being added, we need to collect them together to add them to the triangle. This step can be done in parallel with a semisort, which takes linear expected work (writes) and $O(\omega \cdot \text{polylog}(m))$ depth *whp* [30], where $m$ is the number of inserted points in this round. Combining these results leads to the following lemma.

LEMMA 4.1. *Given $2m$ points in the plane and a tracing structure $T$ generated by Algorithm 1 on a randomly selected subset of $m$ points, computing for each triangle in $T$ the points that encroach it among the remaining $m$ points takes $O(m \log m + \omega m)$ work ($O(m)$ writes) and $O(\omega \cdot \text{polylog}(m))$ depth whp in the Asymmetric NP model.*

The idea of the algorithm is to keep doubling the size of the set that we add (i.e., prefix doubling). Each round applies Algorithm 1 to insert the points and build a tracing structure, and then the DAG tracing algorithm to locate the points for the next round. The depth of each round is upper bounded by the overall depth of the DAG on all points, which is $O(\log n)$ *whp*, where $n$ is the original size. We obtain the following theorem.

THEOREM 4.2. *Planar Delaunay triangulation can be computed using $O(n \log n + \omega n)$ work (i.e., $O(n)$ writes) in expectation and $O(\omega \cdot \text{polylog}(n))$ depth whp on the Asymmetric NP model with priority-writes.*

PROOF. The original Algorithm 1 in [15] has $O(\omega \cdot \text{polylog}(n))$ depth *whp*. In the prefix-doubling approach, the depth of each round is no more than $O(\omega \cdot \text{polylog}(n))$, and the algorithm has $O(\log \log n)$ rounds. The overall depth is hence $O(\omega \cdot \text{polylog}(n))$ depth *whp*.

The work bound consists of the costs from the initial round, and the incremental rounds. The initial round computes the triangulation of the first $n/\log_2 n$ points, using at most $O(n)$ INCIRCLE tests, $O(n)$ writes and $O(\omega n)$ work. For the incremental rounds, we have two components, one for locating encroached triangles in the tracing structure, and one for applying Algorithm 1 on those points to build the next tracing structure. The first part is handled by Lemma 4.1. For the second part we we can apply a similar analysis to Theorem 4.2 of [15]. In particular, the probability that there is a dependence from a triangle in the $i$'th point (in the random order) to a triangle added by a later point at location $j$ in the ordering is upper bounded by $24/i$. Summing across all points in the second half (we have already resolved the first half) gives:

$$\mathbb{E}[C] \leq \sum_{i=m+1}^{2m} \sum_{j=i+1}^{2m} 24/i = O(m)\,.$$

This is a bound on both the number of reads and the number of writes. Since the points added in each round doubles, the cost is dominated by the last round, which is $O(n \log n)$ reads and $O(n)$ writes, both in expectation. Combined with the cost of the initial round gives the stated bounds. □

## 5 SPACE-PARTITIONING DATA STRUCTURES

Space partitioning divides a space into non-overlapping regions.[3] This process is usually applied repeatedly until the number of objects in a region is small enough, so that we can afford to answer a query in linear work within the region. We refer to the tree structure used to represent the partitioning as the space-partitioning tree. Commonly-used space-partitioning trees include binary space partitioning trees, quad/oct-trees, $k$-d trees, and their variants, and are widely used in computational geometry [24, 33], computer graphics [3], integrated circuit design, learning theory, etc.

In this section, we propose write-efficient construction and update algorithms for $k$-d trees [9]. We discuss how to support dynamic updates write-efficiently in Section 5.2, and we discuss how to apply our technique to other space-partitioning trees in the full version of this paper [16].

### 5.1 $k$-d Tree Construction and Queries

$k$-d trees have many variants that facilitate different queries. We start with the most standard applications on range queries and nearest neighbor queries, and discussions for other queries are in the full version of this paper. A range query can be answered in $O(n^{(k-1)/k})$ worst-case work, and an approximate $(1+\epsilon)$-nearest neighbor (ANN) query requires $\log n \cdot O(1/\epsilon)^k$ work assuming bounded aspect ratio,[4] both in $k$-dimensional space. The tree to achieve these bounds can be constructed by always partitioning by the median of all of the objects in the current region either on the longest dimension of the region or cycling among the $k$ dimensions. The tree has linear size and $\log_2 n$ depth [24], and can be constructed using $O(n \log n)$ reads and writes. We now discuss how to reduce the number of writes to $O(n)$.

One solution is to apply the incremental construction by inserting the objects into a $k$-d tree one by one. This approach requires linear writes, $O(n \log n)$ reads and polylogarithmic depth. However, the splitting hyperplane is no longer based on the median, but the object with the highest priority pre-determined by a random permutation. The expected tree depth can be $c \log_2 n$ for $c > 1$, but to preserve the range query cost we need the tree depth to be $\log_2 n + O(1)$ (see details in Lemma 5.1). Motivated by the incremental construction, we propose the following variant, called $p$-batched incremental construction, which guarantees both write-efficiency and low tree depth.

**The $p$-batched incremental construction.** The $p$-batched incremental construction is a variant of the classic incremental construction where the dependence graph is a tree. Unlike the classic version, where the splitting hyperplane (splitter) of a tree node is

[3] The other type of partitioning is object partitioning that subdivides the set of objects directly (e.g., R-tree [32, 36], bounding volume hierarchies [29, 54]).

[4] The largest aspect ratio of a tree node on any two dimensions is bounded by a constant, which is satisfied by the input instances in most real-world applications.

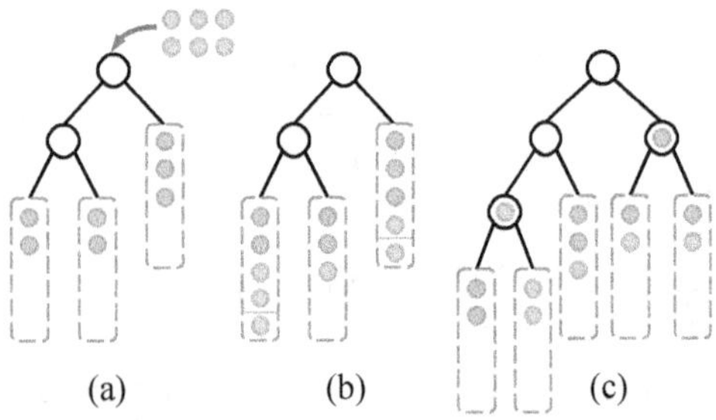


**Figure 2: An illustration of one round in the $p$-batched incremental construction for $p = 4$. Subfigure (a) shows the initial state of this round. Then the new objects (shown in orange) are added to the buffers in the leaves, as shown in subfigure (b). Two of the buffers overflow, and so we settle these two leaves as shown in subfigure (c).**

immediately set when inserting the object with the highest priority, in the $p$-batched version, each leaf node will buffer at most $p$ objects before it determines the splitter. We say that a leaf node *overflows* if it holds more than $p$ objects in its buffer. We say that a node is *generated* when created by its parent, and *settled* after finding the splitters, creating leaves and pushing the objects to the leaves' buffers.

The algorithm proceeds in rounds, where in each round it first finds the corresponding leaf nodes that the inserted objects belong to, and adds them into the buffers of the leaves. Then it settles all of the overflowed leaves, and starts a new round. An illustration of this algorithm is shown in Figure 2. After all objects are inserted, the algorithm finishes building the subtree of the tree nodes with non-empty buffers recursively. For write-efficiency, we require the small-memory size to be $\Omega(p)$, and the reason will be shown in the cost analysis.

We make a partition once we have gathered $p$ objects in the corresponding subregion based on the median of these $p$ objects. When $p = 1$, the algorithm is the incremental algorithm mentioned above, but the range query cost cannot be preserved. When $p = n$, the algorithm constructs the same tree as the classic $k$-d tree construction algorithm, but requires more than linear writes unless the small-memory size is $O(n)$, which is impractical when $n$ is large. We now try to find the smallest value of $p$ that preserves the query cost, and we analyze the cost bounds accordingly.

**Range query.** We use the following lemma to analyze the cost of a standard $k$-d range query (on an axis-aligned hypercube for $k \geq 2$).

Lemma 5.1. *A $k$-d range query costs $O(2^{((k-1)/k)h})$ using our $k$-d tree of height $h$.*

Proof Sketch. A $k$-d range query has at most $2k$ faces that generate $2k$ half-spaces, and we analyze the query cost of each half-space. Since each axis is partitioned once in every $k$ consecutive levels, one side of the partition hyperplane perpendicular to the query face will be either entirely in or out of the associated half-space. We do not need to traverse that subtree (we can either directly report the answer or ignore it). Therefore every $k$ levels will expand the search tree by a factor of at most $2^{k-1}$. Thus the query cost is $O(2^{((k-1)/k)h})$. □

Lemma 5.2. *For our $p$-batched $k$-d tree, $p = \Omega(\log^3 n)$ guarantees the tree height to be no more than $\log_2 n + O(1)$ whp.*

Proof. We now consider the $p$-batched incremental construction. Since we are partitioning based on the median of $p$ random objects, the hyperplane can be different from the actual median. To get the same cost bound, we want the actual number of objects on the two sides to differ by no more than a factor of $\epsilon$ *whp*. Since we pick $p$ random samples, by a Chernoff bound the probability that more than $1/2p$ samples are within the first $(1/2 - \epsilon/4)n$ objects is upper bounded by $e^{-p\epsilon^2/24}$. Hence, the probability that the two subtree weights of a tree node differ by more than a factor of $\epsilon$ is no more than $2e^{-p\epsilon^2/24}$. This $\epsilon$ controls the tree depth, and based on the previous analysis we want to have $n(\frac{1}{2} + \frac{\epsilon}{4})^{\log_2 n/p+O(1)} < p$. Namely, we want the tree to have no more than $\log_2 n/p+O(1)$ levels *whp* to reach the subtrees with less than $p$ elements, so the overall tree depth is bounded by $\log_2 n/p + O(1) + \log_2 p = \log_2 n + O(1)$. Combining these constraints leads to $\epsilon = O(1)/\log_2 n$ and $p = \Omega(\log^3 n)$. □

Lemma 5.2 indicates that setting $p = \Omega(\log^3 n)$ gives a tree height of $\log_2 n + O(1)$ *whp*, and Lemma 5.1 shows that the corresponding range query cost is $O(2^{((k-1)/k)(O(1)+\log_2 n)}) = O(n^{(k-1)/k})$, matching the standard range query cost.

**ANN query.** If we assume that the input objects are well-distributed and the $k$-d tree satisfies the bounded aspect ratio, then the cost of a $(1 + \epsilon)$-ANN query is proportional to the tree height. As a result, $p = \Omega(\log n)$ leads to a query cost of $\log n \cdot O(1/\epsilon)^k$ *whp*.[5]

**Parallel construction and cost analysis.** To get parallelism, we use the prefix-doubling approach, starting with $n/\log n$ objects in the first round. The number of reads of the algorithm is still $\Theta(n \log n)$, since it is lower bounded by the cost of sorting when $k = 1$, and upper bounded by $O(n \log n)$ since the modified algorithm makes asymptotically no more comparisons than the classic implementation. We first present the following lemma.

Lemma 5.3. *When a leaf overflows at the end of a round, the number of objects in its buffer is $O(p)$ whp when $p = \Omega(\log n)$.*

Proof Sketch. In the previous round, assume $n'$ objects were in the tree. At that time no more than $p - 1$ objects are buffered in this leaf node. Then in the current round another $n'$ objects are inserted, and by a Chernoff bound, the probability that the number of objects falling into this leaf node is more than $(c + 1)p$ is at most $e^{-c^2 p/2}$. Plugging in $p = \Omega(\log n)$ proves the lemma. □

We now bound the parallel depth of this construction. The initial round runs the standard construction algorithm on the first $n/\log_2 n$ objects, which requires $O(\omega \cdot \text{polylog}(n))$ depth. Then in each of the next $O(\log \log n)$ incremental rounds, we need to locate leaf nodes and a parallel semisort to put the objects into their buffers. Both steps can be done in $O(\omega \cdot \text{polylog}(n))$ depth *whp* [30]. Then we also need to account for the depth of settling the leaves after the incremental rounds. When a leaf overflows, by Lemma 5.3 we need to split a set of $O(p)$ objects for each leaf, which has a depth

[5] Actually the tree depth is $O(\log n)$ even when $p = 1$. However, for write-efficiency, we need $p = \Omega(\log n)$ to support efficient updates as discussed in Section 5.2 that requires the two subtree sizes to be balanced at every node.

of $O(\omega \cdot \text{polylog}(n))$ using the classic approach, and is applied for no more than a constant number of times *whp* by Lemma 5.3.

We now analyze the number of writes this algorithm requires. The initial round requires $O(n)$ writes as it uses a standard construction algorithm on $n/\log_2 n$ objects. In the incremental rounds, $O(1)$ writes *whp* are required for each object to find the leaf node it belongs to and add itself to the buffer using semisorting [30]. From Lemma 5.3, when finding the splitting hyperplane and splitting the object for a tree node, the number of writes required is $O(p)$ *whp*. Note that after a new leaf node is generated from a split, it contains at least $p/2$ objects. Therefore, after all incremental rounds, the tree contains at most $O(n/p)$ tree nodes, and the overall writes to generate them is $O((n/p) \cdot p) = O(n)$. After the incremental rounds finish, we need $O(n)$ writes to settle the leaves with non-empty buffers, assuming $O(p)$ cache size. In total, the algorithm uses $O(n)$ writes *whp*.

THEOREM 5.4. *A $k$-d tree that supports range and ANN queries efficiently can be computed using $O(n \log n + \omega n)$ expected work (i.e., $O(n)$ writes) and $O(\omega \cdot \text{polylog}(n))$ depth whp in the Asymmetric NP model. For range query the small-memory size required is $\Omega(\log^3 n)$.*

### 5.2 $k$-d Tree Dynamic Updates

Unlike many other tree structures, we cannot rotate the tree nodes in $k$-d trees since each tree node represents a subspace instead of just a set of objects. Deletion is simple for $k$-d trees, since we can afford to reconstruct the whole structure from scratch when a constant fraction of the objects in the $k$-d tree have been removed, and before the reconstruction we just mark the deleted node (constant reads and writes per deletion via an unordered map). In total, the amortized cost of each deletion is $O(\omega + \log n)$. For insertions, we discuss two techniques that optimize either the update cost or the query cost.

**Logarithmic reconstruction [41].** We maintain at most $\log_2 n$ $k$-d trees of sizes that are increasing powers of 2. When an object is inserted, we create a $k$-d tree of size 1 containing the object. While there are trees of equal size, we flatten them and replace the two trees with a tree of twice the size. This process keeps repeating until there are no trees with the same size. When querying, we search in all (at most $\log_2 n$) trees. Using this approach, the number of reads and writes on an insertion is $O(\log^2 n)$, and on a deletion is $O(\log n)$. The costs for range queries and ANN queries are $O(n^{(k-1)/k})$ and $\log^2 n \cdot O(1/\epsilon)^k$ respectively, plus the cost for writing the output.

If we apply our write-efficient $p$-batched version when reconstructing the $k$-d trees, we can reduce the writes (but not reads) by a factor of $O(\log n)$ (i.e., $O(\log n)$ and $O(1)$ writes per update).

When using logarithmic reconstruction, querying up to $O(\log n)$ trees can be inefficient in some cases, so here we show an alternative solution that only maintains a single tree.

**Single-tree version.** As discussed in Section 5.1, only the tree height affects the costs for range queries and ANN queries. For range queries, Lemma 5.2 indicates that the tree height should be $\log_2 n + O(1)$ to guarantee the optimal query cost. To maintain this, we can tolerate an imbalance between the weights of two subtrees by a factor of $O(1/\log n)$, and reconstruct the subtree when the imbalance is beyond the constraint. In the worst case, a subtree of size $n'$ is rebuilt once after $O(n'/\log n)$ insertions into the subtree. Since the reconstructing a subtree of size $n'$ requires $O(n' \log n' + \omega n')$ work, each inserted object contributes $O(\log n \log n' + \omega \log n)$ work to every node on its tree path, and there are $O(\log n)$ such nodes. Hence, the amortized work for an insertion is $O(\log^3 n + \omega \log^2 n)$. For efficient ANN queries, we only need the tree height to be $O(\log n)$, which can be guaranteed if the imbalance between two subtree sizes is at most a constant multiplicative factor. Using a similar analysis, in this case the amortized work for an insertion is $O(\log^2 n + \omega \log n)$.

## 6 AUGMENTED TREES

An ***augmented tree*** is a tree that keeps extra data on each tree node other than what is used to maintain the balance of this tree. We refer to the extra data on each tree node as the ***augmentation***. In this section, we introduce a framework that gives new algorithms for constructing both static and dynamic augmented trees including interval trees, 2D range trees, and priority search trees that are parallel and write-efficient. Using these data structures we can answer 1D stabbing queries, 2D range queries, and 3-sided queries (defined in Section 6.1). For all three problems, we assume that the query results need to be written to the large-memory. Our results are summarized in Table 1. We improve upon the traditional algorithms in two ways. First, we show how to construct interval trees and priority search trees using $O(n)$ instead of $O(n \log n)$ writes (since the 2D range tree requires $O(n \log n)$ storage we cannot asymptotically reduce the number of writes). Second, we provide a tradeoff between update costs and query costs in the dynamic versions of the data structures. The cost bounds are parameterized by $\alpha$. By setting $\alpha = O(1)$ we achieve the same cost bounds as the traditional algorithms for queries and updates. $\alpha$ can be chosen optimally if we know the update-to-query ratio $r$. For interval and priority trees, the optimal value of $\alpha$ is $\min(2 + \omega/r, \omega)$. The overall work without considering writing the output can be improved by a factor of $\Theta(\log \alpha)$. For 2D range trees, the optimal value of $\alpha$ is $2 + \min(\omega/r, \omega)/\log_2 n$.

We discuss two techniques in this section that we use to achieve write-efficiency. The first technique is to decouple the tree construction from sorting, and we introduce efficient algorithms to construct interval and priority search trees in linear reads and writes after the input is sorted. Sorting can be done in parallel and write-efficiently (linear writes).Using this approach, the tree structure that we obtain is perfectly balanced.

The second technique that we introduce is the $\alpha$-labeling technique. We mark a subset of tree nodes as *critical* nodes by a predicate function parameterized by $\alpha$, and only maintain augmentations on these critical nodes. We can then guarantee that every update only modifies $O(\log_\alpha n)$ nodes, instead of $O(\log n)$ nodes as in the classic algorithms. At a high level, the $\alpha$-labeling is similar to the weight-balanced B-tree (WBB tree) proposed by Arge et al. [4, 5] for the external-memory (EM) model [1]. However, as we discuss in Section 6.3, directly applying the EM algorithms [2, 4, 5, 47, 48] does not give us the desired bounds in our model. Secondly, our underlying tree is still binary. Hence, we mostly need no changes to the algorithmic part that dynamically maintains the augmentation in this trees, but just relax the balancing criteria so the underlying search trees can be less balanced. An extra benefit of our framework

| | Construction | Query | Update |
|---|---|---|---|
| **Classic interval tree** | $O(\omega n \log n)$ | $O(\omega k + \log n)$ | $O(\omega \log n)$ |
| **Our interval tree** | $O(\omega n + n \log n)$ | $O(\omega k + \alpha \log_\alpha n)$ | $O((\omega + \alpha) \log_\alpha n)$ |
| **Classic priority search tree** | $O(\omega n \log n)$ | $O(\omega k + \log n)$ | $O(\omega \log n)$ |
| **Our priority search tree** | $O(\omega n + n \log n)$ | $O(\omega k + \alpha \log_\alpha n)$ | $O((\omega + \alpha) \log_\alpha n)$ |
| **Classic range Tree** | $O(\omega n \log n)$ | $O(\omega k + \log^2 n)$ | $O((\log n + \omega) \log n)$ |
| **Our range tree** | $O((\alpha + \omega) n \log_\alpha n)$ | $O(\omega k + \alpha \log_\alpha n \log n)$ | $O((\alpha \log n + \omega) \log_\alpha n)$ |

**Table 1: A summary of the work cost of the data structures discussed in Section 6. In all cases, we assume that the tree contains $n$ objects (intervals or points). For interval trees and priority search trees, we can reduce the number of writes in the construction from $O(\log n)$ per element to $O(1)$. For dynamic updates, we can reduce the number of writes per update by a factor of $\Theta(\log \alpha)$ at the cost of increasing the number of reads in update and queries by a factor of $\alpha$ for any $\alpha \geq 2$.**

is that bulk updates can be supported in a straightforward manner. Such bulk updates seem complicated and less obvious in previous approaches. We propose algorithms on our trees that can support bulk updates write-efficiently and in polylogarithmic depth.

The rest of this section is organized as follows. We first provide the problem definitions and review previous results in Section 6.1. Then in Section 6.2, we introduce our post-sorted construction technique for constructing interval and priority search trees using a linear number of writes. Finally, we introduce the $\alpha$-labeling technique to support a tradeoff in query and update cost for interval trees, priority search trees, and range trees in Section 6.3.

## 6.1 Preliminaries and Previous Work

We define the *weight* or *size* of tree node or a subtree as the number of nodes in this subtree plus one. The "plus one" guarantees that the size of a tree node is always the sum of the sizes of its two children, which simplifies our discussion. This is also the standard balancing criteria used for weight-balanced trees [40].

**Interval trees and the 1D stabbing queries.** An *interval tree*[6] [24, 25, 37] organizes a set of $n$ intervals $S = \{s_i = (l_i, r_i)\}$ defined by their left and right endpoints. The key on the root of the interval tree is the median of the $2n$ endpoints. This median divides all intervals into two categories: those completely on its left/right, which then form the left/right subtrees recursively, and those covering the median, which are stored in the root. The intervals in the root are stored in two lists sorted by the left and right endpoints respectively. In this paper, we use red-black trees to maintain such ordered lists to support dynamic updates and refer to them as the *inner trees*. In the worst case, the previous construction algorithms scan and copy $O(n)$ intervals in $O(\log n)$ levels, leading to $O(n \log n)$ reads and writes.

The interval tree can be used to answer a 1D stabbing query: given a set of intervals, report a list of intervals covering the specific query point $p_q$. This can be done by searching $p_q$ in the tree. Whenever $p_q$ is smaller (larger) than the key of the current node, all intervals in the current tree node with left (right) endpoints smaller than $p_q$ should be reported. This can be done efficiently by scanning the list sorted by left (right) endpoints. The overall query cost is $O(\omega k + \log n)$ (where $k$ is the output size).

[6]There exist multiple versions of interval trees. In this paper, we use the version described in [24].

**2D Range trees and the 2D range queries.** The *2D range tree* [10] organizes a set of $n$ points $p = \{p_i = (x_i, y_i)\}$ on the 2D plane. It is a tree structure augmented with an inner tree, or equivalently, a two-level tree structure. The outer tree stores every point sorted by their $x$-coordinate. Each node in the outer tree is augmented with an inner tree structure, which contains all the points in its subtree, sorted by their y-coordinate.

The 2D range tree can be used to answer the 2D range query: given $n$ points in the 2D plane, report the list of points with $x$-coordinate between $x_L$ and $x_R$, and $y$-coordinate between $y_B$ and $y_T$. Such range queries using range trees can be done by two nested searches on $(x_L, x_R)$ in the outer tree and $(y_B, y_T)$ in at most $O(\log n)$ associated inner trees. Using balanced BSTs for both the inner and outer trees, a range tree can be constructed with $O(n \log n)$ reads and writes, and each query takes $O(\log^2 n + k)$ reads and $O(k)$ writes (where $k$ is the output size). A range tree requires $O(n \log n)$ storage so the number of writes for construction is already optimal.

**Priority search trees and 3-sided range queries.** The *priority search tree* [24, 38] (priority tree for short) contains a set of $n$ points $p = \{p_i = (x_i, y_i)\}$ each with a *coordinate* $(x_i)$ and a *priority* $(y_i)$. There are two variants of priority trees, one is a search tree on coordinates that keeps a heap order of the priorities as the augmented values [4, 38]. The other one is a heap of the priorities, where each node is augmented with a splitter between the left and right subtrees on the coordinate dimension [24, 38]. The construction of both variants uses $O(n \log n)$ reads and writes as shown in the original papers [24, 38]. For example, consider the second variant. The root of a priority tree stores the point with the highest priority in $p$. All the other points are then evenly split into two sets by the median of their coordinates which recursively form the left and right subtrees. The construction scans and copies $O(n)$ points in $O(\log n)$ levels, leading to $O(n \log n)$ reads and writes for the construction.

Many previous results on dynamic priority search trees use the first variant because it allows for rotation-based updates. In this paper, we discuss how to construct the second variant allowing reconstruction-based updates, since it is a natural fit for our framework. We also show that bulk updates can be done write-efficiently in this variant. For the rest of this section, we discuss the second variant of the priority tree.

The priority tree can be used to answer the 3-sided queries: given a set of $n$ points, report all points with coordinates in the range $[x_L, x_R]$, and priority higher than $y_B$. This can be done by traversing the tree, skipping the subtrees whose coordinate range do not overlap $[x_L, x_R]$, or where the priority in the root is lower than $y_B$. The cost of each query is $O(\omega k + \log n)$ for an output of size $k$ [24].

## 6.2 The Post-Sorted Construction

For interval trees and priority search trees, the standard construction algorithms [23–25, 37, 38] require $O(n \log n)$ reads and writes, even though the output is only of linear size. This section describes algorithms for constructing them in an optimal linear number of writes. Both algorithms first sort the input elements by their $x$-coordinate in $O(\omega n + n \log n)$ work and $O(\omega \cdot \text{polylog}(n))$ depth using the write-efficient comparison sort described in the full version of this paper [16]. We now describe how to build the trees in $O(n)$ reads and writes given the sorted input. For a range tree, since the standard tree has $O(n \log n)$ size, the classic construction algorithm is already optimal.

**Interval Tree.** After we sort all $2n$ coordinates of the endpoints, we can first build a perfectly-balanced binary search tree on the endpoints using $O(n)$ reads and writes and $O(\omega \cdot \text{polylog}(n))$ depth. We now consider how to construct the inner tree of each tree node.

We create a lowest common ancestor (LCA) data structure on the keys of the tree nodes that allows for constant time queries. This can be constructed in $O(n)$ reads/writes and $O(\omega \cdot \text{polylog}(n))$ depth [11, 35]. Each interval can then find the tree node that it belongs to using an LCA query on its two endpoints. We then use a radix sort on the $n$ intervals. The key of an interval is a pair with the first value being the index of the tree node that the interval belongs to, and the second value being the index of the left endpoint in the pre-sorted order. The sorted result gives the interval list for each tree node sorted by left endpoints. We do the same for the right endpoints. This step takes $O(n)$ reads/writes overall. Finally, we can construct the inner trees from the sorted intervals in $O(n)$ reads/writes across all tree nodes.

Parallelism is straightforward for all steps except for the radix sort. The number of possible keys can be $O(n^2)$, and it is not known how to radix sort keys from such a range work-efficiently and in polylogarithmic depth. However, we can sort a range of $O(n \log n)$ in $O(\omega n)$ expected work and $O(\omega \cdot \text{polylog}(n))$ depth *whp* [43]. Hence our goal is to limit the first value into a $O(\log n)$ range. We note that given the left endpoint of an interval, there are only $\log_2(2n)$ possible locations for the tree node (on the tree path) of this interval. Therefore instead of using the tree node as the first value of the key, we use the level of the tree node, which is in the range $[1, \ldots, O(\log n)]$. By radix sorting these pairs, so we have the sorted intervals (based on left or right endpoint) for each level. We observe that the intervals of each tree node are consecutive in the sorted interval list per level. This is because for tree nodes $u_1$ and $u_2$ on the same level where $u_1$ is to the left of $u_2$, the endpoints of $u_1$'s intervals must all be to the left of $u_2$'s intervals. Therefore, in parallel we can find the first and the last intervals of each node in the sorted list, and construct the inner tree of each node. Since the intervals are already sorted based on the endpoints, we can build inner trees in $O(n)$ reads and writes and $O(\omega \cdot \text{polylog}(n))$ depth [12].

**Priority Tree.** In the original priority tree construction algorithm, points are recursively split into sub-problems based on the median at each node of the tree. This requires $O(n)$ writes at each level of the tree if we explicitly copy the nodes and pack out the root node that is removed. To avoid explicit copying, since the points are already pre-sorted, our write-efficient construction algorithm passes indices determining the range of points belonging to a sub-problem instead of actually passing the points themselves. To avoid packing, we simply mark the position of the removed point in the list as invalid, leaving a hole, and keep track of the number of valid points in each sub-problem.

Our recursive construction algorithm works as follows. For a tree node, we know the range of the points it represents, as well as the number of valid points $n_v$. We then pick the valid point with the highest priority as the root, mark the point as invalid, find the median among the valid points, and pass the ranges based on the median and number of valid points (either $\lfloor (n_v - 1)/2 \rfloor$ or $\lceil (n_v - 1)/2 \rceil$) to the left and right sub-trees, which are recursively constructed. The base case is when there is only one valid point remaining, or when the number of holes is more than the valid points. Since each node in the tree can only cause one hole, for every range corresponding to a node, there are at most $O(\log n)$ holes. Since the size of the small-memory is $\Omega(\log n)$, when the number of valid points is fewer than the number of holes, we can simply load all of the valid points into the small-memory and construct the sub-tree.

To efficiently implement this algorithm, we need to support three queries on the input list: finding the root, finding the $k$-th element in a range (e.g., the median), and deleting an element. All queries and updates can be supported using a standard tournament tree where each interior node maintains the minimum element and the number of valid nodes within the subtree. With a careful analysis, all queries and updates throughout the construction require linear reads/writes overall. The details are provided in the full version of this paper [16].

The parallel depth is $O(\omega \cdot \text{polylog}(n))$—the bottleneck lies in removing the points. There are $O(\log n)$ levels in the priority tree and it costs $O(\omega \log n)$ for removing elements from the tournament tree on each level. For the base cases, it takes linear writes overall to load the points into the small-memory and linear writes to generate all tree nodes. The depth is $O(\omega \log n)$.

We summarize our result in this section in Theorem 6.1.

THEOREM 6.1. *An interval tree or a priority search tree can be constructed with pre-sorted input in $O(\omega n)$ expected work and $O(\omega \cdot \text{polylog}(n))$ depth whp on the Asymmetric NP model.*

## 6.3 Dynamic Updates using Reconstruction-Based Rebalancing

Dynamic updates (insertions and deletions) are often supported on augmented trees [23–25, 37, 38] and the goal of this section is to support updates write-efficiently, at the cost of performing extra reads to reduce the overall work. Traditionally, an insertion or deletion costs $O(\log n)$ for interval trees and priority search trees, and $O(\log^2 n)$ for range trees. In the asymmetric setting, the work is multiplied by $\omega$. To reduce the overall work, we introduce an approach to select a subset of tree nodes as *critical* nodes, and only update the balance information of those nodes (the augmentations are mostly unaffected). The selection of these critical nodes are done by the $\alpha$-labeling introduced in Section 6.3.1. Roughly speaking, for each tree path from the root to a leaf node, we have $O(\log_\alpha n)$ critical nodes marked such that the subtree weights of two consecutive marked nodes differ by about a factor of $\alpha \geq 2$. By doing so, we only need to update the balancing information in the critical nodes, leading to fewer tree nodes modified in an update.

Arge et al. [4, 5] use a similar strategy to support dynamic updates on augmented trees in the external-memory (EM) model, in which a block of data can be transferred in unit cost [1]. They use a $B$-tree instead of a binary tree, which leads to a shallower tree structure and fewer memory accesses in the EM model. However, in the Asymmetric NP model, modifying a block of data requires work proportional to the block size, and directly using their approach cannot reduce the overall work. Inspired by their approach, we propose a simple approach to reduce the work of updates for the Asymmetric NP model.

The main component of our approach is *reconstruction-based rebalancing* using the *$\alpha$-labeling* technique. We can always obtain the sorted order via the tree structure, so when imbalance occurs, we can afford to reconstruct the whole subtree in reads and writes proportional to the subtree size and polylogarithmic depth. This gives a unified approach for different augmented trees: interval trees, priority search trees, and range trees.

We introduce the $\alpha$-labeling idea in Section 6.3.1, the rebalancing algorithm in Section 6.3.2, and its work analysis in Section 6.3.3. We then discuss the maintenance of augmented values for different applications in Section 6.3.4. We mention how to parallelize bulk updates in Section 6.3.5 and in the full version of the paper [16].

*6.3.1 $\alpha$-Labeling.* The goal of the $\alpha$-labeling is to maintain the balancing information at only a subset of tree nodes, the critical nodes, such that the number of writes per update is reduced. Once the augmented tree is constructed, we label the node as a critical node if for some integer $i \geq 0$, (1) its subtree weight is between $2\alpha^i$ and $4\alpha^i - 2$ (inclusive); or (2) its subtree weight is $2\alpha^i - 1$ and its sibling's subtree weight is $2\alpha^i$. All other nodes are *secondary* nodes. As a special case, we always treat the root as a virtual critical node, but it does not necessary satisfy the invariants of critical nodes. Note that all leaf nodes are critical nodes in $\alpha$-labeling since they always have subtrees of weight 2. When we label a critical node, we refer to its current subtree weight (which may change after insertions/deletions) as its *initial weight.* Note that after the augmented tree is constructed, we can find and mark the critical nodes in $O(n)$ reads/writes and $O(\omega \log n)$ depth. After that, we only maintain the subtree weights for these critical nodes, and use their weights to balance the tree.

Fact 6.2. *For a critical node $A$, $2\alpha^i - 1 \leq |A| \leq 4\alpha^i - 2$ holds for some integer $i$.*

This fact directly follows the definition of the critical node.

For two critical nodes $A$ and $B$, if $A$ is $B$'s ancestor and there is no other critical node on the tree path between them, we refer to $B$ as $A$'s *critical child*, and $A$ as $B$'s *critical parent.* We define a *critical sibling* accordingly.

We show the following lemma on the initial weights.

Lemma 6.3. *For any two critical nodes $A$ and $B$ where $A$ is $B$'s critical parent, their initial weights satisfy* $\max\{(\alpha/2)|B|, 2|B| - 1\} \leq |A| \leq (2\alpha + 1)|B|$.

Proof. Based on Fact 6.2, we assume $2\alpha^i - 1 \leq |A| \leq 4\alpha^i - 2$ and $2\alpha^j - 1 \leq |B| \leq 4\alpha^j - 2$ for some integers $i$ and $j$. We first show that $i = j + 1$. It is easy to check that $j$ cannot be larger than or equal to $i$. Assume by contradiction that $j < i - 1$. With this assumption, we will show that there exists an ancestor of $B$, which we refer to it as $y$, which is a critical node. The existence of $y$ contradicts the fact that $A$ is $B$'s critical parent. We will use the property that for any tree node $x$ the weight of its parent $p(x)$ is $2|x| - 1 \leq |p(x)| \leq 2|x| + 1$.

Assume that $B$ does not have such an ancestor $y$. Let $z$ be the ancestor of $B$ with weight closest to but no more than $2\alpha^{i-1}$. We consider two cases: (a) $|z| \leq 2\alpha^{i-1} - 2$ and (b) $|z| = 2\alpha^{i-1} - 1$. In case (a) $z$'s parent $p(z)$ has weight at most $2|z|+1 = 4\alpha^{i-1} - 3$. $|p(z)|$ cannot be less than $2\alpha^{i-1}$ by definition of $z$, and so $y = p(z)$, leading to a contradiction. In case (b), $z$'s sibling does not have weight $2\alpha^{i-1}$, otherwise $y = z$. However, then $|p(z)| \leq 2|z| = 4\alpha^{i-1} - 2$, and either $z$ is not the ancestor with weight closest to $2\alpha^{i-1}$ or $y = p(z)$.

Given $i = j + 1$, we have $(\alpha/2)|B| \leq |A| \leq (2\alpha + 1)|B|$ (by plugging in $2\alpha^i - 1 \leq |A| \leq 4\alpha^i - 2$ and $2\alpha^{i-1} - 1 \leq |B| \leq 4\alpha^{i-1} - 2$). Furthermore, since $A$ is $B$'s ancestor, we have $2|B| - 1 \leq |A|$. Combining the results proves the lemma. □

*6.3.2 Rebalancing Algorithm based on $\alpha$-Labeling.* We now consider insertions and deletions on an augmented tree. Maintaining the augmented values on the tree are independent of our $\alpha$-labeling technique, and differs slightly for each of the three tree structures. We will further discuss how to maintain augmented values in Section 6.3.4.

We note that deletions can be handled by marking the deleted objects without actually applying the deletion, and reconstructing the whole subtree once a constant fraction of the objects is deleted. Therefore in this section, we first focus on the insertions only. We analyze single insertions here, and discuss bulk insertions in the full version of the paper [16]. Once the subtree weight of a critical node $A$ reaches twice the initial weight $s$, we reconstruct the whole subtree, label the critical nodes within the subtree, and recalculate the initial weights of the new critical nodes. An exception here is that, if $s \leq 4\alpha^i - 2$ and $2\alpha^{i+1} - 1 \leq 2s$ for a certain $i$, we do not mark the new root since otherwise it violates the bound stated in Lemma 6.4 (see more details in Section 6.3.3) with $A$'s critical parent. After this reconstruction, $A$'s original critical parent gets one extra critical child, and the two affected children now have initial weights the same as $A$'s initial weight. If imbalance occurs at multiple levels, we reconstruct the topmost tree node. An illustration of this process is shown in Figure 3.

We can directly apply the algorithms in Section 6.2 to reconstruct a subtree as long as we have the sorted order of the (end)points in this subtree. For interval and range trees, we can acquire the sorted order by traversing the subtree. using linear work and $O(\omega \cdot \text{polylog}(n))$ depth [8, 46]. For priority trees, since the tree nodes are not stored in-order, we need to insert all interior nodes into the tree in a bottom-up order based on their coordinates (without applying rebalancing) to get the total order on coordinates of all points (the details and cost analysis can be found in the full version of this

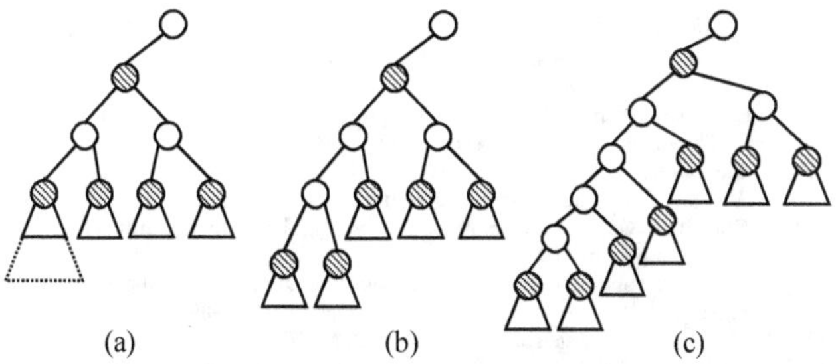

**Figure 3: An illustration of rebalancing based on $\alpha$-labeling. The critical nodes are shaded. The case after construction is shown in (a) with solid borders. After some insertions, the size of one of the subtrees grows to twice its initial weight (dashed lines in (a)), so the algorithm reconstructs the subtree, as shown in (b). As we keep inserting new nodes along the left spine, the tree will look like what is shown in (c), but Lemma 6.4 guarantees that the subtree of the topmost critical node will be reconstructed before it gets more than $4\alpha + 2$ critical children. The lemma also guarantees that on the path from a critical node to any of its critical children, there can be at most $4\alpha - 1$ secondary nodes.**

paper [16]). After we have the sorted order, a subtree of weight $n$ can be constructed in $O(\omega n)$ work and $O(\omega \cdot \text{polylog}(n))$ depth.

As mentioned, we always treat the root as a virtual critical node, but it does not necessary satisfy the invariants of critical nodes. By doing so, once the weight of the whole tree doubles, we reconstruct the entire tree. We need $\Omega(n)$ insertions for one reconstruction on the root (there can be deletions). The cost for reconstruction is $O(\omega n)$ for interval trees and priority trees, and $O(\omega n \log_\alpha n)$ for range trees (shown in Section 6.3.4). The amortized cost is of a lower order compared to the update cost shown in Theorem 6.8.

*6.3.3 Cost Analysis of the Rebalancing.* To show the rebalancing cost, we first prove some properties about our dynamic augmented trees.

Lemma 6.4. *In a dynamic augmented tree with $\alpha$-labeling, we have $\max\{(\alpha/4)|B|, (3/2)|B| - 1\} \leq |A| \leq (4\alpha + 2)|B|$ for any two critical nodes $A$ and $B$ where $A$ is $B$'s critical parent.*

Proof. For any critical node $A$ in the tree, the subtree weight of its critical child $B$ can grow up to a factor of 2 of $B$'s initial weight, after which the subtree is reconstructed to two new critical nodes with the same initial weight of $B$. $A$'s weight can grow up to a factor of 2 of $A$'s initial weight, without affecting $B$'s weight (i.e., all insertions occur in $A$'s other critical children besides $B$). Combining these observations with the result in Lemma 6.3 shows this lemma except for the $(3/2)|B| - 1 \leq |A|$ part. Originally we have $2|B| - 1 \leq |A|$ after the previous reconstruction. $|A|$ grows together when $|B|$ grows, and right before the reconstruction of $B$ we have $(3/2)|B| - 1 \leq |A|$. □

Lemma 6.4 shows that each critical node has at most $4\alpha + 2$ critical children, and so that there are at most $4n + 1$ secondary nodes to connect them. This leads to the following corollary.

Corollary 6.5. *The length of the path from a critical node to its critical parent is at most $4\alpha + 1$.*

Combining Lemma 6.4 and Corollary 6.5 gives the following result.

Corollary 6.6. *For a leaf node in a tree with $\alpha$-labeling, the tree path to the root contains $O(\log_\alpha n)$ critical nodes and $O(\alpha \log_\alpha n)$ nodes.*

Corollary 6.6 shows the number of reads during locating a node in an augmented tree, and the number of critical nodes on that path.

With these results, we now analyze the cost of rebalancing for each insertion. For a critical node with initial weight $W$, we need to insert at least another $W$ new nodes into this subtree before the next reconstruction of this critical node. Theorem 6.1 shows that the amortized cost for each insertion in this subtree is therefore $O(\omega)$ on this node. Based on Corollary 6.6, the amortized cost for each insertion contains $O(\log_\alpha n)$ writes and $O(\alpha \log_\alpha n)$ reads. In total, the work per insertion is $O((\alpha + \omega) \log_\alpha n)$, since we need to traverse $O(\alpha \log_\alpha n)$ tree nodes, update $O(\log_\alpha n)$ subtree weights, and amortize $O(\omega \log_\alpha n)$ work for reconstructions.

We note that any interleaving insertions can only reduce the amortized cost for deletions. Therefore, both the algorithm and the bound can be extended to any interleaving sequence of insertions and deletions. Altogether, we have the following result, which may be of independent interest.

Theorem 6.7. *Using reconstruction-based rebalancing based on the $\alpha$-labeling technique, the amortized cost of each update (insertion or deletion) to maintain the balancing information on a tree of size $n$ is $O((\omega + \alpha) \log_\alpha n)$.*

*6.3.4 Handling Augmented Values.* Since the underlying tree structure is still binary, minor changes to the trees are required for different augmentations.

*Interval trees.* We do not need any changes for the interval tree. Since we never apply rotations, we directly insert/delete the interval in the associated inner tree with a cost of $O(\log n + \omega)$.

*Range trees.* For the range tree, we only keep the inner trees for the critical nodes. As such, the overall augmentation weight (i.e., overall weights of all inner trees) is $O(n \log_\alpha n)$. For each update, we insert/delete this element in $O(\log_\alpha n)$ inner trees (Corollary 6.6), and the overall cost is $O((\log n + \omega) \log_\alpha n)$. Then each query may look into no more than $O(\alpha \log_\alpha n)$ inner trees each requiring $O(\log n)$ work for a 1D range query. The overall cost for a query is therefore $O(\omega k + \alpha \log_\alpha n \log n)$.

*Priority trees.* For insertions on priority trees, we search its coordinate in the tree and put it where the current tree node is of lower priority than the new point. The old subtree root is then recursively inserted to one of its subtrees. The cost can be as expensive as $O(\omega\alpha \log_\alpha n)$ when a point with higher priority than all tree nodes is inserted. To address this, points are only stored in the critical nodes, and the secondary nodes only partition the range, without holding points as augmented values. This can be done by slightly modifying the construction algorithm in Section 6.2. During the construction, once the current node is a secondary node, we only partition the range, but do not find the node with the highest priority. Since all leaf nodes are critical, the tree size is affected by at most a factor of 2. With this approach, each insertion modifies at most $O(\log_\alpha n)$ nodes, and so the extra work per insertion for maintaining augmented data is $O((\alpha + \omega)\log_\alpha n)$. A deletion on priority trees can be implemented symmetrically, and can lead to cascading promotions of the points. Once the promotions occur, we leave a dummy node in the original place of the last promoted point, so that all of the subtree sizes remain unchanged (and the tree is reconstructed once half one the nodes are dummy). The cost of a deletion is also $O((\alpha + \omega)\log_\alpha n)$.

Combining the results above gives the following theorem.

Theorem 6.8. *Given any integer $\alpha \geq 2$, an update on an interval or priority search tree requires $O((\omega + \alpha)\log_\alpha n)$ amortized work and a query costs $O(\omega k + \alpha \log_\alpha n)$; for a 2D range tree, the query and amortized update cost is $O((\alpha \log n + \omega)\log_\alpha n)$ and $O(\omega k + \alpha \log_\alpha n \log n)$.*

*6.3.5 Bulk Updates.* One of the benefits of the reconstruction-based approach is that bulk updates on our augmented trees can be directly supported. In this case we need to change the inner trees to be treaps to support efficient bulk insertions/deletions [12, 49, 50]. We discuss the details bulk updates in the full version of this paper [16]. The overall conclusion is that, given a bulk update of size $m$, we can process it in parallel using the same amount of work as applying the updates sequentially, and in $O(\omega \cdot \text{polylog}(n))$ depth.

## ACKNOWLEDGMENTS

This work was supported in part by NSF grants CCF-1408940, CCF-1533858, and CCF-1629444.

## REFERENCES


[1] A. Aggarwal and J. S. Vitter. The Input/Output complexity of sorting and related problems. *Communications of the ACM*, 31(9), 1988.
[2] D. Ajwani, N. Sitchinava, and N. Zeh. Geometric algorithms for private-cache chip multiprocessors. In *ESA*, 2010.
[3] T. Akenine-Möller, E. Haines, and N. Hoffman. *Real-time rendering*. CRC Press, 2008.
[4] L. Arge, V. Samoladas, and J. S. Vitter. On two-dimensional indexability and optimal range search indexing. In *PODS*, 1999.
[5] L. Arge and J. S. Vitter. Optimal external memory interval management. *SIAM Journal on Computing*, 32(6), 2003.
[6] M. Atallah and M. Goodrich. Deterministic parallel computational geometry. In *Synthesis of Parallel Algorithms*, pages 497–536. Morgan Kaufmann, 1993.
[7] A. Ben-Aroya and S. Toledo. Competitive analysis of flash-memory algorithms. In *ESA*, 2006.
[8] N. Ben-David, G. E. Blelloch, J. T. Fineman, P. B. Gibbons, Y. Gu, C. McGuffey, and J. Shun. Parallel algorithms for asymmetric read-write costs. In *SPAA*, 2016.
[9] J. L. Bentley. Multidimensional binary search trees used for associative searching. *Communications of the ACM*, 18(9), 1975.
[10] J. L. Bentley. Decomposable searching problems. *Information Processing Letters*, 8(5), 1979.
[11] O. Berkman and U. Vishkin. Recursive *-tree parallel data-structure. In *FOCS*, 1989.
[12] G. E. Blelloch, D. Ferizovic, and Y. Sun. Just join for parallel ordered sets. In *SPAA*, 2016.
[13] G. E. Blelloch, J. T. Fineman, P. B. Gibbons, Y. Gu, and J. Shun. Sorting with asymmetric read and write costs. In *SPAA*, 2015.
[14] G. E. Blelloch, J. T. Fineman, P. B. Gibbons, Y. Gu, and J. Shun. Efficient algorithms with asymmetric read and write costs. In *ESA*, 2016.
[15] G. E. Blelloch, Y. Gu, J. Shun, and Y. Sun. Parallelism in randomized incremental algorithms. In *SPAA*, 2016.
[16] G. E. Blelloch, Y. Gu, J. Shun, and Y. Sun. Parallel write-efficient algorithms and data structures for computational geometry. *arXiv preprint:1805.05592*, 2018.
[17] G. E. Blelloch, J. C. Hardwick, G. L. Miller, and D. Talmor. Design and implementation of a practical parallel Delaunay algorithm. *Algorithmica*, 24(3-4), 1999.
[18] J.-D. Boissonnat and M. Teillaud. On the randomized construction of the delaunay tree. *Theoretical Computer Science*, 112(2), 1993.
[19] E. Carson, J. Demmel, L. Grigori, N. Knight, P. Koanantakool, O. Schwartz, and H. V. Simhadri. Write-avoiding algorithms. In *IPDPS*, 2016.
[20] S. Chen, P. B. Gibbons, and S. Nath. Rethinking database algorithms for phase change memory. In *CIDR*, 2011.
[21] K. L. Clarkson and P. W. Shor. Applications of random sampling in computational geometry, II. *Discrete & Computational Geometry*, 4(5), 1989.
[22] R. Cole. Parallel merge sort. *SIAM J. Comput.*, 17(4), 1988.
[23] T. H. Cormen, C. E. Leiserson, R. L. Rivest, and C. Stein. *Introduction to Algorithms (3rd edition)*. MIT Press, 2009.
[24] M. de Berg, O. Cheong, M. van Kreveld, and M. Overmars. *Computational Geometry: Algorithms and Applications*. Springer-Verlag, 2008.
[25] H. Edelsbrunner. *Dynamic data structures for orthogonal intersection queries*. Technische Universität Graz/Forschungszentrum Graz. Institut für Informationsverarbeitung, 1980.
[26] D. Eppstein, M. T. Goodrich, M. Mitzenmacher, and P. Pszona. Wear minimization for cuckoo hashing: How not to throw a lot of eggs into one basket. In *SEA*, 2014.
[27] E. Gal and S. Toledo. Algorithms and data structures for flash memories. *ACM Computing Surveys*, 37(2), 2005.
[28] M. T. Goodrich. Finding the convex hull of a sorted point set in parallel. *Information Processing Letters*, 26(4), 1987.
[29] Y. Gu, Y. He, K. Fatahalian, and G. Blelloch. Efficient BVH construction via approximate agglomerative clustering. In *High-Performance Graphics Conference*, 2013.
[30] Y. Gu, J. Shun, Y. Sun, and G. E. Blelloch. A top-down parallel semisort. In *SPAA*, 2015.
[31] L. J. Guibas, D. E. Knuth, and M. Sharir. Randomized incremental construction of Delaunay and Voronoi diagrams. *Algorithmica*, 7(4):381–413, 1992.
[32] A. Guttman. R-trees: A dynamic index structure for spatial searching. In *SIGMOD*, 1984.
[33] S. Har-Peled. *Geometric approximation algorithms*, volume 173. American Mathematical Society, 2011.
[34] R. Jacob and N. Sitchinava. Lower bounds in the asymmetric external memory model. In *SPAA*, 2017.
[35] J. JaJa. *Introduction to Parallel Algorithms*. Addison-Wesley Professional, 1992.
[36] Y. Manolopoulos, A. Nanopoulos, A. N. Papadopoulos, and Y. Theodoridis. *R-trees: Theory and Applications*. Springer Science & Business Media, 2010.
[37] E. M. McCreight. Efficient algorithms for enumerating intersecting intervals and rectangles. Technical report, 1980.
[38] E. M. McCreight. Priority search trees. *SIAM Journal on Computing*, 14(2), 1985.
[39] K. Mulmuley. *Computational geometry–an introduction through randomized algorithms*. Prentice Hall, 1994.
[40] J. Nievergelt and E. M. Reingold. Binary search trees of bounded balance. *SIAM journal on Computing*, 2(1), 1973.
[41] M. H. Overmars. *The design of dynamic data structures*, volume 156. Springer Science & Business Media, 1983.
[42] H. Park and K. Shim. FAST: Flash-aware external sorting for mobile database systems. *Journal of Systems and Software*, 82(8), 2009.
[43] S. Rajasekaran and J. H. Reif. Optimal and sublogarithmic time randomized parallel sorting algorithms. *SIAM J. Comput.*, 18(3), 1989.
[44] J. H. Reif and S. Sen. Optimal randomized parallel algorithms for computational geometry. *Algorithmica*, 7(1-6):91–117, 1992.
[45] R. Seidel. Backwards analysis of randomized geometric algorithms. In *New Trends in Discrete and Computational Geometry*. 1993.
[46] J. Shun, Y. Gu, G. Blelloch, J. Fineman, and P. Gibbons. Sequential random permutation, list contraction and tree contraction are highly parallel. In *SODA*, 2015.
[47] N. Sitchinava. Computational geometry in the parallel external memory model. *SIGSPATIAL Special*, 4(2), 2012.
[48] N. Sitchinava and N. Zeh. A parallel buffer tree. In *SPAA*, 2012.
[49] Y. Sun and G. E. Blelloch. Parallel range and segment queries with augmented maps. *arXiv preprint:1803.08621*, 2018.
[50] Y. Sun, D. Ferizovic, and G. E. Blelloch. PAM: Parallel augmented maps. In *PPoPP*, 2018.
[51] R. E. Tarjan. Updating a balanced search tree in $O(1)$ rotations. *Information Processing Letters*, 16(5), 1983.
[52] S. D. Viglas. Adapting the $B^+$-tree for asymmetric I/O. In *ADBIS*, 2012.
[53] S. D. Viglas. Write-limited sorts and joins for persistent memory. *PVLDB*, 7(5), 2014.
[54] I. Wald, S. Boulos, and P. Shirley. Ray tracing deformable scenes using dynamic bounding volume hierarchies. *ACM Transactions on Graphics (TOG)*, 26(1), 2007.

# The Parallel Persistent Memory Model

Guy E. Blelloch* Phillip B. Gibbons* Yan Gu* Charles McGuffey* Julian Shun†

*Carnegie Mellon University †MIT CSAIL

## ABSTRACT

We consider a parallel computational model, the *Parallel Persistent Memory model*, comprised of $P$ processors, each with a fast local ephemeral memory of limited size, and sharing a large persistent memory. The model allows for each processor to fault at any time (with bounded probability), and possibly restart. When a processor faults, all of its state and local ephemeral memory is lost, but the persistent memory remains. This model is motivated by upcoming non-volatile memories that are nearly as fast as existing random access memory, are accessible at the granularity of cache lines, and have the capability of surviving power outages. It is further motivated by the observation that in large parallel systems, failure of processors and their caches is not unusual.

We present several results for the model, using an approach that breaks a computation into *capsules*, each of which can be safely run multiple times. For the single-processor version we describe how to simulate any program in the RAM, the external memory model, or the ideal cache model with an expected constant factor overhead. For the multiprocessor version we describe how to efficiently implement a work-stealing scheduler within the model such that it handles both soft faults, with a processor restarting, and hard faults, with a processor permanently failing. For any multithreaded fork-join computation that is race free, write-after-read conflict free and has $W$ work, $D$ depth, and $C$ maximum capsule work in the absence of faults, the scheduler guarantees a time bound on the model of $O\left(\frac{W}{P_A} + \frac{DP}{P_A}\left\lceil\log_{1/(Cf)} W\right\rceil\right)$ in expectation, where $P$ is the maximum number of processors, $P_A$ is the average number, and $f \leq 1/(2C)$ is the probability a processor faults between successive persistent memory accesses. Within the model, and using the proposed methods, we develop efficient algorithms for parallel prefix sums, merging, sorting, and matrix multiply.

**ACM Reference Format:**
Guy E. Blelloch* Phillip B. Gibbons* Yan Gu* Charles McGuffey* Julian Shun† . 2018. The Parallel Persistent Memory Model. In *SPAA '18: 30th ACM Symposium on Parallelism in Algorithms and Architectures, July 16–18, 2018, Vienna, Austria.* ACM, New York, NY, USA, 12 pages. https://doi.org/10.1145/3210377.3210381


*SPAA '18, July 16–18, 2018, Vienna, Austria*

ACM ISBN 978-1-4503-5799-9/18/07...$15.00
https://doi.org/10.1145/3210377.3210381

## 1 INTRODUCTION

In this paper, we consider a parallel computational model, the *Parallel Persistent Memory (Parallel-PM) model*, that consists of $P$ processors, each with a fast local ephemeral memory of limited size $M$, and sharing a large slower persistent memory. As in the external memory model [4, 5], each processor runs a standard instruction set from its ephemeral memory and has instructions for transferring blocks of size $B$ to and from the persistent memory. The cost of an algorithm is calculated based on the number of such transfers. A key difference, however, is that the model allows for individual processors to fault at any time. If a processor faults, all of its processor state and local ephemeral memory is lost, but the persistent memory remains. We consider both the case where the processor restarts (soft faults) and the case where it never restarts (hard faults).

The model is motivated by two complimentary trends. Firstly, it is motivated by upcoming non-volatile memories that are nearly as fast as existing random access memory (DRAM), are accessed via loads and stores at the granularity of cache lines, have large capacity (more bits per unit area than existing random access memory), and have the capability of surviving power outages and other failures without losing data (the memory is *non-volatile* or *persistent*). For example, Intel's 3D-Xpoint memory technology, currently available as an SSD, is scheduled to be available as such a random access memory in 2019. While such memories are expected to be the pervasive type of memory [50, 52, 56], each processor will still have a small amount of cache and other fast memory implemented with traditional *volatile* memory technologies (SRAM or DRAM). Secondly, it is motivated by the fact that in current and upcoming large parallel systems the probability that an individual processor faults is not negligible, requiring some form of fault tolerance [17].

In this paper, we first consider a single processor version of the model, the *PM model*, and give conditions under which programs are robust against faults. In particular, we identify that breaking a computation into "capsules" that have no write-after-read conflicts (writing a location that was read earlier within the same capsule) is sufficient, when combined with our approach to restarting faulting capsules from their beginning, due to its idempotent behavior. We then show that RAM algorithms, external memory algorithms, and cache-oblivious algorithms [31] can all be implemented asymptotically efficiently on the model. This involves a simulation that breaks the computations into capsules and buffers writes, which are handled in the next capsule. However, the simulation is likely not practical. We therefore consider a programming methodology in which the algorithm designer can identify capsule boundaries, and ensure that the capsules are free of write-after-read conflicts.

We then consider our multiprocessor counterpart, the Parallel-PM described above, and consider conditions under which programs are correct when the processors are interacting through the shared memory. We identify that if capsules are free of write-after-read conflicts and atomic, in a way that we define, then each capsule acts as if it ran once despite many possible restarts. Furthermore we identify that a compare-and-swap (CAS) instruction is not safe in the PM model, but that a compare-and-modify (CAM), which does not see its result, is safe.

The most significant result in the paper is a work-stealing scheduler that can be used on the Parallel-PM. Our scheduler is based on the scheduler of Arora, Blumofe, and Plaxton (ABP) [5]. The key challenges in adopting it to handle faults are (i) modifying it so that it only uses CAMs instead of CASs, (ii) ensuring that each stolen task gets executed despite faults, (iii) properly handling hard faults, and (iv) ensuring its efficiency in the presence of soft or hard faults. Without a CAS, and to avoid blocking, handling faults requires that processors help the processor that is part way through a steal. Handling hard faults further requires being able to steal a thread from a processor that was part way through executing the thread.

Based on the scheduler we show that any race-free, write-after-read conflict free multithreaded fork-join program with work $W$, depth $D$, and maximum capsule work $C$ will run in expected time:

$$O\left(\frac{W}{P_A} + D\left(\frac{P}{P_A}\right)\left\lceil \log_{1/(Cf)} W \right\rceil\right).$$

Here $P$ is the maximum number of processors, $P_A$ the average number, and $f \leq 1/(2C)$ an upper bound on the probability a processor faults between successive persistent memory accesses. This bound differs from the ABP result only in the $\log_{1/(Cf)} W$ factor on the depth term, due to faults along the critical path.

Finally, we present Parallel-PM algorithms for prefix-sums, merging, sorting, and matrix multiply that satisfy the required conditions. The results for prefix-sums, merging, and sorting are work-optimal, matching lower bounds for the external memory model. Importantly, these algorithms are only slight modifications from known parallel I/O efficient algorithms [15]. The main change is ensuring that they write their partial results to a separate location from where they read them so that they avoid write-after-read conflicts.

**Related Work.** Because of its importance to future computing, the computer systems community (including companies such as Intel and HP) have been hard at work trying to solve the issues arising when fast nonvolatile memories (such as caches) sit between the processor and a large persistent memory [10, 11, 19–21, 23, 28, 30, 32, 33, 36–39, 44–47, 51, 53, 55]. Standard caches are write-back, meaning that a write to a memory location will make it only as far as the cache, until at some later point the updated cache line gets flushed out to the persistent memory. Thus, when a processor crashes, some writes (those still in the cache) are lost while other writes are not. The above prior work includes schemes for encapsulating updates to persistent memory in either *transactions* or *lock-protected failure atomic sections* and using various forms of (undo, redo, resume) logging to ensure correct recovery. The intermittent computing community works on the related problem of small systems that will crash due to power loss [7, 16, 25, 26, 35, 48, 49, 54]. Lucia and Ransford [48] describe how faults and restarting lead to errors that will not occur in a faultless setting. Several of these works [25, 26, 48, 49, 54] break code into small chunks, referred to as *tasks*, and work to ensure progress at that granularity. Avoiding write-after-read conflicts is often the key step towards ensuring that tasks are idempotent. Because these works target intermittent computing systems, which are designed to be small and energy efficient, they do not consider multithreaded programs, concurrency, or synchronization. In contrast to this flurry of recent systems research, there is relatively little work from the theory/algorithms community aimed at this setting [27, 40, 41, 52]. David et al. [27] presents concurrent data structures (e.g., for skip-lists) that avoid the overheads of logging. Izraelevitz et al. [40, 41] presents efficient techniques for ensuring that the data in persistent memory captures a consistent cut in the happens-before graph of the program's execution, via the explicit use of instructions that flush cache lines to persistent memory (such as Intel's `CLFLUSH` instruction [38]). Nawab et al. [52] defines *periodically persistent* data structures, which combine mechanisms for tracking proper write ordering with a periodic flush of all cache lines to persistent memory. None of this work defines an algorithmic cost model, presents a work-stealing scheduler, or provides the provable bounds in this paper.

There is a very large body of research on models and algorithms where processors and/or memory can fault, but to our knowledge, none of it (other than the works mentioned above) fits the setting we study with its two classes of memory (local volatile and shared nonvolatile). Papers focusing on memory faults (e.g., [1, 22, 29] among a long list of such papers) consider models in which individual memory locations can fault. Papers focusing on processor faults (e.g., [6] among an even longer list of such papers) either do not consider memory faults or assume that all memory is volatile.

**Write-back Caches.** Note that while the PM models are defined using explicit external read and external write instructions, they are also appropriate for modeling the (write-back) cache setting described above, as follows. Explicit instructions, such as `CLFLUSH`, are used to ensure that an external write indeed writes to the persistent memory. Writes that are intended to be solely in local memory, on the other hand, could end up being evicted from the cache and written back to persistent memory. However, for programs that are race-free and well-formed, as defined in Section 3, our approach preserves its correctness properties.

## 2 THE PERSISTENT MEMORY MODEL

**Single Processor.** We assume a two-layer memory model with a small fast *ephemeral memory* of size $M$ (in words) and a large slower *persistent memory* of size $M_p \gg M$. The two memories are partitioned into blocks of $B$ words. Instructions include standard RAM instructions that work on single words within the processor registers (a processor has $O(1)$ registers) and ephemeral memory, as well as two *(external) memory transfer* instructions: an *external read* that transfers a block from persistent memory into ephemeral memory, and an *external write* that transfers a block from ephemeral memory to persistent memory. We assume that the words contain $\Theta(\log M_p)$ bits. These assumptions are effectively the same as in the $(M, B)$ external memory model [2].

We further assume that the processor can *fault* between any two instructions,[1] and that after faulting, the processor *restarts*. On restart, the ephemeral memory and processor registers can be in an arbitrary state, but the persistent memory is in the same state as immediately before the fault. To enable forward progress, we assume

[1]For simplicity, we assume that individual instructions are atomic.

there is a fixed memory location in the persistent memory referred to as the *restart pointer location*, containing a *restart pointer*. On restart, the processor loads the restart pointer from the persistent memory into a register, which we refer to as the *base* register, and then loads the location pointed to by the restart pointer (the *restart instruction*) and jumps to that location, i.e., sets it as the program counter. The processor then proceeds as normal. As it executes, the processor can update the restart pointer to be the current program counter, at the cost of an external write, in order to limit how far the processor will fall back on a fault. We refer to this model as the (single processor) $(M, B)$ persistent memory (PM) model.

The basic model can be parameterized based on the cost of the various instructions. Throughout this paper, and in the spirit of the external memory model [2] and the ideal cache model [31], we assume that external reads and writes take unit cost and all other instructions have no cost.[2] We further assume that the program is constant size and that either the program is loaded from persistent memory into ephemeral memory at restart, or that there is a small cache for the program itself, which is also lost in the case of a fault. Thus, faulting and restarting (loading the base register and jumping to the restart instruction, and fetching the code) takes a constant number of external memory transfers.

The processor's computation can be viewed as partitioned into *capsules*: each capsule corresponds to a maximally contiguous sequence of instructions running on the processor while the restart pointer location contains the same restart pointer. The last instruction of every capsule is therefore a write of a new restart pointer. We refer to writing a new restart pointer as *installing* a capsule. We assume that the next instructions after this write, which are at the start of the next capsule, do exactly the same as a restart does–i.e., load the restart pointer into the base pointer, load the start instruction pointed to by base pointer, and jump to it. The capsule is *active* while its restart pointer is installed. Whenever the processor faults, it will restart using the restart pointer of the active capsule, i.e., the capsule will be restarted as it was the first time. We define the *capsule work* to be the number of external reads and writes in the capsule, assuming no faults. Note that, akin to checkpointing, there is a tension between the desire for high work capsules that amortize the capsule start/restart overheads and the desire for low work capsules that lessen the repeated work on restart.

In our analysis, we consider two ways to count the total cost. We say that the *faultless work* (or *work*), $W$, is the number of external memory transfers assuming no faults. We say that the *total work* (or *fault-tolerant work*), $W_f$, is the number of external transfers for an actual run including all transfers due to having to restart. $W_f$ can only be defined with respect to an assumed fault model. In this paper, for analyzing costs, we assume that the probability of faulting by a processor between any two consecutive non-zero cost instructions (i.e., external reads or writes) is bounded by $f \leq 1/2$, and that faults are independent events. We will specify $f$ to ensure that a maximum work capsule fails with at most constant probability.

We assume throughout the paper that instructions are deterministic, i.e., each instruction is a function from the values of registers and memory locations that it reads to the registers and memory locations that it writes.

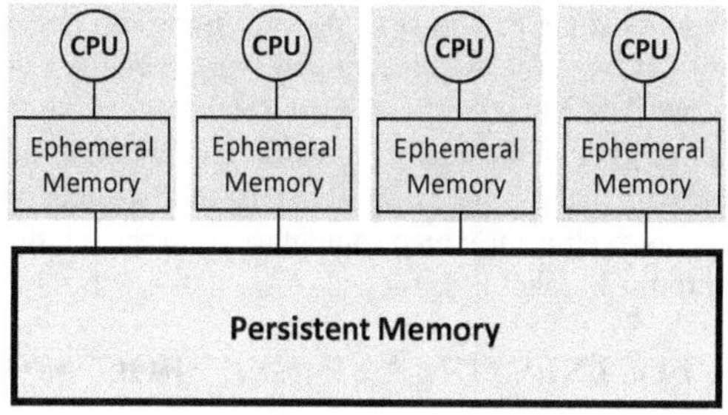


**Figure 1: The Parallel Persistent Memory Model**

**Multiple Processors.** The Parallel-PM consists of $P$ processors each with its own fast local ephemeral memory of size $M$, but sharing a single slower persistent memory of size $M_p$ (see Figure 1). Each processor works as in the single processor PM, and the processors run asynchronously. Any processor can fault between two of its instructions, and each has its own restart pointer location in the persistent memory. When a processor faults, the processor restarts like it would in the single processor case. We refer to this as a *soft fault*. We also allow for a *hard fault*, in which the processor faults and then never restarts—we say that such a processor is *dead*. We assume that other processors can detect when a processor has hard faulted using a liveness oracle `isLive(procId)`. We allow for concurrent reads and writes to the shared persistent memory, and assume that all instructions involving the persistent memory are sequentially consistent.

The Parallel-PM includes a compare-and-swap (CAS) instruction. The CAS takes a pointer to a location of a word in persistent memory and two values in registers. If the first value equals the value at the location, it atomically swaps the value at the location and the value in the second register, and the CAS is *successful*. Otherwise, no swap occurs and the CAS is *unsuccessful*. Even though the persistent memory is organized in blocks, we assume that the CAS is on a single word within a block.

The (faultless) work $W$ and the total work $W_f$ are as defined in the sequential model but summed across all processors. The (faultless) *time* $T$ (and the *fault-tolerant* or *total time* $T_f$) is the maximum faultless work (total work, respectively) done by any one processor. Without faults, this is effectively the same as the parallel external memory model [4]. In analyzing correctness, we allow for arbitrary delays between any two successive instructions by a processor. However, for our time bounds and our results on work stealing we make similar assumptions as made in [5]. These are described in Section 6.

**Multithreaded Computations.** Our aim is to support multithreaded dynamic parallelism layered on top of the Parallel-PM. We consider the same form of multithreaded computations as considered by Arora, Blumofe, and Plaxton (ABP) [5]. In the model, a computation starts as a single thread. On each step, a thread can run an instruction, fork a new thread, or join with another thread. Such a computation can be viewed as a DAG, with an edge between instructions, a pair of out-edges at a fork, and a pair of in-edges at a join. As with ABP, we assume that each node in the DAG has out-degree at most two. In the *multithreaded model*, the (faultless) work

[2]The results in this paper can be readily extended to a setting (an *Asymmetric PM model*) where external writes are more costly than external reads, as in prior work on algorithms for NVM [8, 9, 12, 13, 18, 42]; for simplicity, we study here the simpler PM model because such asymmetry is not the focus of this paper.

$W$ is the work summed across all threads in the absence of faults, and the total work $W_f$ is the summed work including faults. In addition, we define the (faultless) *depth* $D$ (and the *fault-tolerant* or *total depth* $D_f$) to be the maximum work (total work, respectively) along any path in the DAG. The goal of our work-stealing scheduler (Section 6) is to efficiently map computations in the multithreaded model into the Parallel-PM.

## 3 ROBUSTNESS ON A SINGLE PROCESSOR

In this section, we discuss how to run programs on the single processor PM model so that they complete the computation properly.

Our goal is to structure the computation and its partitioning into capsules in a way that is sufficient to ensure correctness regardless of faults. Specifically, our goal is that each capsule is a sequence of instructions that will look from an external view like it has been run exactly once after its completion, regardless of the number of times it was partially run due to faults and restarts. We say that a capsule is *idempotent* if, when it completes, regardless of how many times it faults and restarts, all modifications to the persistent memory are consistent with running once from the initial state (i.e., the state of the persistent memory, the ephemeral memory, and the registers at the start of the capsule).

There are various means to guarantee that a capsule is idempotent, and here we consider a natural one. We say that a capsule has a *write-after-read conflict* if the first transfer from a block in persistent memory is a read (called an "exposed" read), and later there is a write to the same block. Avoiding such a conflict is important because if a location in the persistent memory is read and later written, then on restart the capsule would see the new value instead of the old one. We say a capsule is *well-formed* if the first access to each word in the registers or ephemeral memory is a write. Being well-formed means that a capsule will not read the undefined values from registers and ephemeral memory after a fault. We say that a capsule is *write-after-read conflict free* if it is well-formed and had no write-after-read conflicts.

Theorem 3.1. *With a single processor, all write-after-read conflict free capsules are idempotent.*

Proof. On restarting, the capsule cannot read any persistent memory written by previous faults on the capsule, because we restart from the beginning of the capsule and the exposed read locations are disjoint from the write locations. Moreover, the capsule cannot read the state of the ephemeral memory because a write is required before a read (well-formedness). Therefore, the first time a capsule runs and every time a capsule restarts it has the same visible state, and because the processor instructions are deterministic, will repeat exactly the same instructions with the same results. □

An immediate question is whether a standard processing model such as the RAM can be simulated efficiently on the PM model. The following theorem, whose proof is in the full version of the paper [14], shows that the PM can simulate the RAM model with only constant overheads.

Theorem 3.2. *Any RAM computation taking $t$ time can be simulated on the $(O(1), B)$ PM model with $f \leq 1/c$ for some constant $c \geq 2$, using $O(t)$ expected total work, for any $B$ ($B = 1$ is sufficient).*

Although the RAM simulation is linear in the number of instructions, our goal is to create algorithms that require asymptotically fewer reads and writes to persistent memory. We therefore consider efficiently simulating external memory algorithms in the model.

Theorem 3.3. *Any $(M, B)$ external memory computation with $t$ external accesses can be simulated on the $(O(M), B)$ PM model with $f \leq B/(cM)$ for some constant $c \geq 2$, using $O(t)$ expected total work.*

Proof. The simulation consists of rounds each of which has a *simulation* capsule and a *commit* capsule. It maps the ephemeral memory of the source program to part of the ephemeral memory, and the external memory to the persistent memory. It keep the registers in the ephemeral memory, and keeps space for two copies of the simulated ephemeral memory and the registers in the persistent memory, which it swaps back and forth between.

The simulation capsule simulates some number of steps of the source program. It starts by reading in one of the two copies of the ephemeral memory and registers. Then during the simulation all instructions are applied within their corresponding memories, except for writes from the ephemeral memory to the persistent memory. These writes, instead of being written immediately, are buffered in the ephemeral memory. This means that all reads from the external memory have to first check the buffer. The simulation also maintains a count of the number of reads and writes to the external memory within a capsule. When this count reaches $M/B$, the simulation "closes" the capsule. The closing is done by writing out the simulated ephemeral memory, the registers, and the write buffer to persistent memory. For ephemeral memory and registers, this is the other copy from the one that is read. The capsule finishes by installing a commit capsule.

The commit capsule reads in the write buffer from the closed capsule to ephemeral memory, and applies all the writes to their appropriate locations of the simulated external memory in the persistent memory. When the commit capsule is done, it installs the next simulation capsule.

This simulation is write-after-read conflict free because the only writes during a simulation capsule are to the copy of ephemeral memory, registers, and write buffer. The write buffer has no conflicts since it is not read, and the ephemeral memory and registers have no conflicts since they swap back and forth. There are no conflicts in the commit capsules because they read from write buffer and write to the simulated external memory. The simulation is therefore write-after-read conflict free.

To see the claimed time and space bounds, we note that the ephemeral memory need only be a constant factor bigger than the simulated ephemeral memory because the write buffer can only contain $M$ entries. Each round requires only $O(M/B)$ reads and writes to the persistent memory because the simulating capsules only need the stored copy of the ephemeral memory, do at most $M/B$ reads, and then do at most $O(M/B)$ writes to the other stored copy. The commit capsule does at most $M/B$ simulated writes, each requiring a read from and write to the persistent memory. Because each round simulates $M/B$ reads and writes to external memory at the cost of $O(M/B)$ reads and writes to persistent memory, the faultless work across all capsules is bounded by $O(t)$. Because the probability that a capsule faults is bounded by the maximum capsule work, $O(M/B)$, times $f \leq B/(cM)$, there is a constant $c$ such that the probability of a capsule faulting is less than 1. Since the faults are independent, the expected total work is a constant factor greater than the faultless work, giving the stated bounds. □

It is also possible to simulate the ideal cache model [31] in the PM model. The ideal cache model is similar to the external memory model, but assumes that the fast memory is managed as a fully associative cache. It assumes a cache of size $M$ is organized in blocks of size $B$ and has an optimal replacement policy. The ideal cache model makes it possible to design cache-oblivious algorithms [31]. Due to the following result, whose proof is in the full version of the paper [14], these algorithms are also efficient in the PM model.

THEOREM 3.4. *Any $(M, B)$ ideal cache computation with $t$ cache misses can be simulated on the $(O(M), B)$ PM model with $f \leq B/(cM)$ for a constant $c \geq 2$, using $O(t)$ expected total work.*

## 4 PROGRAMMING FOR ROBUSTNESS

This simulation of the external memory is not completely satisfactory because its overhead, although constant, could be significant. It can be more convenient and certainly more efficient to program directly for the model. Here we describe one protocol for this purpose. It can greatly reduce the overhead of using the PM model. It is also useful in the context of the parallel model.

Our protocol is designed so capsules begin and end at the boundaries of certain function calls, which we refer to as *persistent function calls*. Non-persistent calls are ephemeral. We assume function calls can be marked as persistent or ephemeral, by the user or possibly compiler. Once a persistent call is made, the callee will never revert back further than the call itself, and after a return the caller will never revert back further than the return. All persistent calls require a constant number of external reads and writes on the call and on the return. In an ephemeral function call a fault in a callee can roll back to before the call, and similarly a fault after a return can roll back to before the return. All ephemeral calls are handled completely in the ephemeral memory and therefore by themselves do not require any external reads or writes. In addition to the persistent function call we assume a `commit` command that forces a capsule boundary at that point. As with a persistent call, the commit requires a constant number of external reads and writes.

We assume that all user code between persistent boundaries is write-after-read conflict free, or otherwise idempotent. This requires a style of programming in which results are copied instead of overwritten. For sequential programs, this increases the space requirements of an algorithm by at most a factor of two. Persistent counters can be implemented by placing a commit between reading the old value and writing the new. In the algorithms that we describe in Section 7, this style is very natural.

Implementing persistent function calls requires some care with a standard stack protocol. Here we outline one way to modify a standard stack discipline to work. We describe how to do this is some detail using closures [3] in the full paper [14].

The stack is organized in stack frames stored in the persistent memory. The first location in each stack frame is a pointer to the first instruction to run, and it is followed by slots for its arguments, for values returned to it, a pointer to the parent frame, and a pointer to code to execute for the parent when the function returns. When making a call, the parent can fill in the frame of the child. In particular the instruction to start at (in the first location), the arguments, a pointer to itself, and the instruction to run on return. As in standard protocols it must also save local variables to its own frame it needs on return. When making a call, the parent can install a the child frame as the new capsule.

On return, the child can fill in the result in the parent frame, and also fill in the instruction to run on return in the first slot of the parent frame. It can then install the parent frame as the new capsule. Arguments should not be modified in place since this would not be write-after-read conflict free. Local variable and return results that are available when returning from a function call must also not be modified for the same reason. A `commit` command can be implemented by creating a function for the code after the commit, and calling it. Standard tail-recursion optimizations can then return directly to the parent of the caller. The main difference of this calling convention from a standard one is keeping an instruction pointer with each frame, and ensuring local variables do not have any write-after-read conflicts. It also means the built in call/ret instruction on certain architectures likely cannot be used.

Memory allocation can be implemented in various ways in a write-after-read conflict free manner. One way is for the memory for a capsule to be allocated starting at a base pointer that is stored in the closure. Memory is allocated one after the other, using a pointer kept in local memory (avoiding the need for a write-after-read conflict to persistent memory in order to update it). In this way, the allocations are the same addresses in memory each time the capsule restarts. At the end of the capsule, the final value of the pointer is stored in the closure for the next capsule. For the Parallel-PM, each processor allocates from its own pool of persistent memory, using this approach. In the case where a processor takes over for a hard-faulting processor, any allocations while the taking-over processor is executing on behalf of the faulted processor will be from the pool of the faulted processor.

## 5 ROBUSTNESS ON MULTIPLE PROCESSORS

With multiple processors our previous definition of idempotent is inadequate since the other processors can read or write persistent memory locations while a capsule is running. For example, even though the final values written by a capsule $c$ might be idempotent, other processors can observe intermediate values while $c$ is running and therefore act differently than if $c$ was run just once. We therefore consider a stronger variant of idempotency that in addition to requiring that its final effects on memory are if it ran once, requires that it acts as if it ran atomically. The requirement of atomicity is not necessary for correctness, but sufficient for what we need and allows a simple definition. We give an example of how it can be relaxed at the end of the section.

More formally we consider the history of a computation, which is an interleaving of the persistent memory instructions from each of the processors, and which abides by the sequential semantics of the memory. The history includes the additional instructions due to faults (i.e., it is a complete trace of instructions that actually happened). A capsule within a history is *invoked* at the instruction it is installed and *responds* at the instruction that installs the next capsule on the processor. All instructions of a capsule, and possibly other instructions from other processors, fall between the invocation and response.

We say that a capsule in a history is *atomically idempotent* if

(1) (atomic) all its instructions can be moved in the history to be adjacent somewhere between its invocation and response without violating the memory semantics, and
(2) (idempotent) the instructions are idempotent at the spot they are moved to—i.e., their effect on memory is as if the capsule ran just once without fault.

As with a single processor, we now consider conditions under which capsules are ensured to be idempotent, in this case atomically. Akin to standard definitions of conflict, race, and race free, we say that two persistent memory instructions on separate processors *conflict* if they are on the same block and one is a write. For a capsule within a history we say that one of its instructions has a *race* if it conflicts with another instruction that is between the invocation and response of that capsule. A capsule in a history is *race free* if none of its instructions have a race.

Theorem 5.1. *Any capsule that is write-after-read conflict free and race free in a history is atomically idempotent.*

Proof. Because the capsule is race free we can move its instructions to be adjacent at any point between the invocation and response without affecting the memory semantics. Once moved to that point, the idempotence follows from Theorem 3.1 because the capsule is write-after-read conflict free. □

This property is useful for user code if one can ensure that the capsules are race free via synchronization. We use this extensively in our algorithms. However the requirement of being race free is insufficient in general because synchronizations themselves require races. In fact the only way to ensure race freedom throughout a computation would be to have no processor ever write a location that another processor ever reads or writes. We therefore consider some other conditions that are sufficient for atomic idempotence.

**Racy Read Capsule.** We first consider a *racy read capsule*, which reads one location from persistent memory and writes its value to another location in persistent memory. The capsule can have other instructions, but none of them can depend on the value that is read. A racy read capsule is atomically idempotent if all its instructions except for the read are race free. This is true because we can move all instructions of the capsule, with possible repeats due to faults, to the position of the last read. The capsule will then properly act like the read and write happened just once. Because races are allowed on the read location, there can be multiple writes by other processors of different values to the read location, and different such values can be read anytime the racy read capsule is restarted. However, because the write location is race free, no other processor can "witness" these possible writes of different values to the write location. Thus, the copy capsule is atomically idempotent. A copy capsule is a useful primitive for copying from a volatile location that could be written at any point into a processor private location that will be stable once copied. Then when the processor private location is used in a future capsule, it will stay the same however many times the capsule faults and restarts. We make significant use of this in the work-stealing scheduler.

**Racy Write Capsule.** We also consider a *racy write capsule*, for which the only instruction with a race is a write instruction to persistent memory, and the instruction races only with either read instructions or other write instructions, but not both kinds. Such a capsule can be shown to be atomically idempotent. In the former case (races only with reads), then in any history, the value in the write location during the capsule transitions from an old value to a new value exactly once no matter how many times the capsule is restarted. Thus, for the purposes of showing atomicity, we can move all the instructions of the capsule to immediately before the first read that sees the new value, or to the end of the capsule if there is no such read. Although the first time the new value is written (and read by other processors) may be part of a capsule execution that subsequently faulted, the effect on memory is as if the capsule ran just once without fault (idempotency). In the latter case (races only with other writes), then if in the history the racy write capsule is the last writer before the end of the capsule, we can move all the instructions of the capsule to the end of the capsule, otherwise we can move all the instructions to the beginning of the capsule, satisfying atomicity and idempotency.

**Compare-and-Modify (CAM) Instruction.** We now consider idempotency of the CAS instruction. Recall that we assume that a CAS is part of the machine model. We cannot assume the CAS is race free because the whole purpose of the operation is to act atomically in the presence of a race. Unfortunately it seems hard to efficiently simulate a CAS at the user level when there are faults. The problem is that a CAS writes two locations, the two that it swaps. In the standard non-faulty model one is local (a register) and therefore the CAS involves a single shared memory modification and a local register update. Unfortunately in the Parallel-PM model, the processor could fault immediately before or after the CAS instruction. On restart the local register is lost and therefore the information about whether it succeeded is lost. Looking at the shared location does not help since identical CAS instructions from other processors might have been applied to the location, and the capsule cannot distinguish its success from their success.

Instead of using a CAS, here we show how to use a weaker instruction, a *compare-and modify (CAM)*. A CAM is simply a CAS for which no subsequent instruction in the capsule reads the local result (i.e., the swapped value).[3] Furthermore, we restrict the usage of a CAM. For a capsule within a history we say a write $w$ (including a CAS or CAM) to persistent memory is *non-reverting* if no other conflicting write between $w$ and the capsule's response changes the value back to its value before $w$. We define a *CAM capsule* as a capsule that contains one non-reverting CAM and may contain other write-after-read conflict free and race free instructions.

Theorem 5.2. *A CAM capsule is atomically idempotent.*

Proof. Assume that the CAM is non-reverting and all other instructions in the capsule are write-after-read conflict free and race free. Due to faults the CAM can repeat multiple times, but it can only succeed in changing the target value at most once. This is because the CAM is non-reverting so once the target value is changed, it could not be changed back. Therefore if the CAM ever succeeds, for the purpose of showing atomicity, in the history we move all the

[3]Some CAS instructions in practice return a boolean to indicate success; in such cases, the boolean cannot be read either.

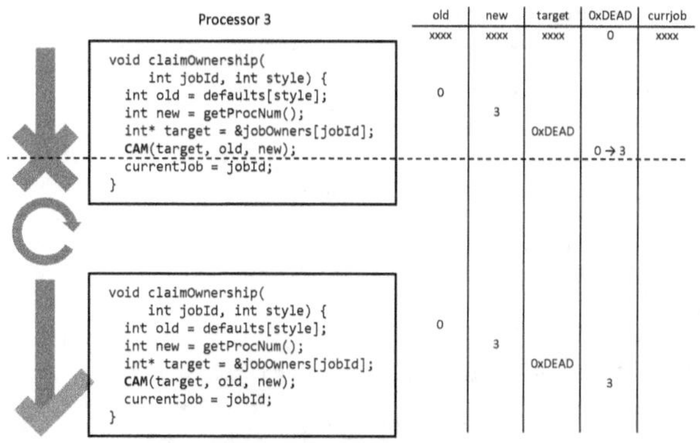


**Figure 2: CAM Capsule Example. In CAM capsules, earlier faulting runs of the capsule may perform work that is visible to the rest of the system.**

instructions of the capsule (including the instructions from faulty runs) to the point of the successful CAM. This does not affect the memory semantics because none of the other instructions have races, and any of the other CAMs were unsuccessful and therefore also have no affect on memory. At the point of the successful CAM the capsule acts like it ran once because it is write-after-read conflict free—other than the CAM, which succeeded just once. If the CAM never succeeds, the capsule is conflict free and race free because the CAM did not do any writes, so Theorem 5.1 applies. □

The example CAM capsule in Figure 2 shows one of the interesting properties of idempotence: unlike transactions or checkpointing, earlier runs that faulted can make changes to the memory that are seen or used by other processes. Similarly, these earlier runs can affect the results of the successful run, as long as the result is equivalent to a non-faulty run.

A CAM can be used to implement a form of test-and-set in a constant number of instructions. In particular, we will assume a location can either be *unset*, or the value of a process identifier or other unique identifier. A process can then use a CAM to conditionally swap such a location from *unset* to its unique identifier. The process can then check if it "won" by seeing if its identifier is in the location. We make heavy use of this in the work-stealing scheduler to atomically "steal" a job from another queue. It can also be used at the join point of two threads in fork-join parallelism to determine who got there last (the one whose CAM from *unset* was unsuccessful) and hence needs to run the code after the join.

**Racy Multiread Capsule.** It is also possible to design capsules that are idempotent without the requirement of atomicity. By way of example, we discuss the *racy multiread capsule.* This capsule consists of multiple racy read capsules that have been combined together into a single capsule. Concurrent processes may write to locations that the capsule is reading between reads, which violates atomicity. Despite this, a racy multiread capsule is idempotent since the results of the final successful run of the capsule will overwrite any results of partial runs. We make use of the snapshot capsule in the work-stealing scheduler to reduce the number of capsules required. It is not needed for correctness.

# 6 WORK STEALING

We show how to implement an efficient version of work stealing (WS) in the Parallel-PM model. Our results are based on the work-stealing scheduler of Arora, Blumofe, and Plaxton (ABP) [5] and therefore work in a multiprogrammed environment where the number of active processors can change. As in their work, we require some assumptions about the machine, which we summarize here.

The schedule is a two-level scheduler in which the work-stealing scheduler, under our control, maps threads to processes, and an adversarial operating system scheduler maps processes to processors. The OS scheduler can change the number of allocated processors and which processes are scheduled on those processors during the computation, perhaps giving processors to other users. The number of processes and the maximum number of processors used is given by $P$. The average number that are allocated to the user is $P_A$.

The quanta for scheduling is at least the time for two scheduling steps where each step takes a small constant number of instructions. In our case we cannot guarantee that the quanta is big enough to capture two steps since the processor could fault. However it is sufficient to show that with constant probability two scheduling steps complete within the quanta, which we can show.

The available instruction set contains a yield-to-all instruction. This instruction tells the OS that it must schedule all other processes that have not hard faulted before (or at the same time) as the process that executes the instruction. It is used to ensure that processors that are doing useful work have preference over ones who run out of work and need to steal.

Our schedule differs from the ABP scheduler in some crucial ways since our model allowing processors to fault. First, our scheduler cannot use a CAS, for reasons described in Section 5, and instead must use a CAM. ABP uses a CAS and we see no direct translation to using a CAM. Second, our scheduler has to handle soft faults anywhere in either the scheduler or the user program. This requires some care to maintain idempotence. Third, our scheduler has to handle hard faults. In particular it has to be able to steal from a processor that hard faults while it is running a thread. It cannot restart the thread from scratch, but needs to start from the previous capsule boundary (a thread can consist of multiple capsules).

Our scheduler is also similar to the ABP scheduler in some crucial ways. In particular it uses a work-stealing double ended work queue and takes a constant number of instructions for the popTop, popBottom, and pushBottom functions. This is important in proving the performance bounds and allows us to leverage much of their analysis. An important difference in the performance analysis is that faults can increase both the work and the span (critical path/depth). Because faults can happen anywhere this holds for the user work and for the scheduler. The expected work is only increased by a constant factor, which is not a serious issue. However, for span, expectations cannot be carried through the maximum implied by parallel execution. We therefore need to consider high probability bounds.

## 6.1 The Scheduler Interface

For handling faults, and in particular hard faults, the interaction of the scheduler and threads is slightly different from that of ABP.

We assume that when a thread finishes it jumps to the `scheduler`.[4] When a thread forks another thread, it calls a `fork` function, which pushes the new thread on the bottom of the work queue and returns to the calling thread. When the scheduler starts a thread it jumps to it (actually a capsule representing the code to run for the thread). Recall that when the thread is done it jumps back to the scheduler. These are the only interactions of threads and the scheduler—i.e. jumping to a thread from the scheduler, forking a new thread within a thread, and jumping back to the scheduler from a thread on completion. All of these occur at capsule boundaries, but a thread itself can consist of many capsules. We assume that at a join (synchronization) point of threads whichever one arrives last continues the code after the join and therefore that thread need not interact with the scheduler. The other threads that arrive at the join earlier finish and jump to the scheduler. In our setup, therefore, a thread is never blocked, assuming the `fork` function is non-blocking.

## 6.2 WS-Deque

A work-stealing deque (WS-deque) is a concurrent deque supporting a limited interface. Here we used a similar interface to ABP. In particular the interface supports popTop, pushBottom, and popBottom. Any number of concurrent processors can execute popTop, but only one process can execute either pushBottom or popBottom. The idea is only the process owning the deque will work on the bottom. The deque is linearizable except that popTop can return empty even if the deque is not-empty. However this can only happen if another concurrent popTop succeeds with a linearization point when the popTop is live, i.e., from invocation to response.

We provide an implementation of a idempotent WS-deque in Figure 3. Our implementation maintains an array of tagged entries that refer to threads that the processor has either enabled or stolen while working on the computation. The tag is simply a counter that is used to avoid the ABA problem [34]. An *entry* consists of one of the following states:

- *empty*: An empty entry is one that has not been associated with a thread yet. Newly created elements in the array are initialized to empty.
- *local*: A local entry refers to a thread that is currently being run by the processor that owns this WS-Deque. We need to track local entries to deal with processors that have a hard fault (i.e., never restart).
- *job*: A job entry is equivalent to the values found in the original implementation of the WS-Deque. It contains a thread (i.e., a capsule to jump to start the thread).
- *taken*: A taken entry refers to a thread that has already been or is in the process of being stolen. It contains a pointer to the entry that the thief is using to hold the stolen thread, and the tag of that entry at the time of the steal.

The transition table for the entry states is shown in Figure 4.

In addition to this array of entries, we maintain pointers to the top and the bottom of the deque, which is a contiguous region of the array. As new threads are forked by the owner process, new entries will be added to the bottom of the deque using the pushBottom function. The bottom pointer will be updated to these new entries. The top pointer will move down on the deque as threads are stolen. This implementation does not delete elements at the top of the

[4]Note that jumping to a thread is the same as installing a capsule.

```
P = number of procs
S  = stack size

struct procState {
  union entry = empty
              | local
              | job of continuation
              | taken of ⟨entry*,int⟩

  ⟨int,entry⟩ stack[S];
  int top;
  int bot;
  int ownerID;

  inline int getStep(i) { return stack[i].first; }

  inline void clearBottom() {
    stack[bot] = ⟨getStep(bot)+1, empty⟩; }

  void helpPopTop() {
    int t = top;
    switch(stack[t]) {
      case ⟨_, taken(ps,i)⟩:
        // Set thief state.
        CAM(ps, ⟨i,empty⟩, ⟨i+1,local⟩);
        CAM(&top, t, t+1);    // Increment top.
  } }

  // Steal from current process, if possible.
  // If a steal happens, location e is set to "local"
  // & a job is returned. Otherwise NULL is returned.
  continuation popTop(entry* e, int c) {
    helpPopTop();
    int i = top;
    ⟨int, entry⟩ old = stack[i];
    commit;
    switch(old) {
      // No jobs to steal and no ongoing local work.
      case ⟨j, empty⟩: return NULL;
      // Someone else stole in meantime.  Help it.
      case ⟨j, taken(_)⟩:
        helpPopTop(); return NULL;
      // Job available, try to steal it with a CAM.
      case ⟨j, job(f)⟩:
        ⟨int, entry⟩ new = ⟨j+1, taken(e,c)⟩;
        CAM(&stack[i], old, new);
        helpPopTop();
        if (stack[i] != new) return NULL;
        return f;
      // No jobs to steal, but there is local work.
      case ⟨j, local⟩:
        // Try to steal local work if process is dead.
        if (!isLive(ownerID) && stack[i] == old) {
          commit;
          ⟨int, entry⟩ new = ⟨j+1,taken(e,c)⟩;
          stack[i+1] = ⟨getStep(i+1)+1, empty⟩;
          CAM(&stack[i], old, new);
          helpPopTop();
          if (stack[i] != new) return NULL;
          return getActiveCapsule(ownerID);
        }
        // Otherwise, return NULL.
        return NULL;
  } }

  void pushBottom(continuation f) {
    int b = bot;
    int t1 = getStep(b+1);
    int t2 = getStep(b);
    commit;
    if (stack[b] == ⟨t2, local⟩) {
      stack[b+1] = ⟨t1+1, local⟩;
      bot = b + 1;
      CAM(&stack[b], ⟨t2, local⟩, ⟨t2+1, job(f)⟩
    } else if (stack[b+1].second == empty) {
      states[getProcNum()].pushBottom(f);
    }
    return;
  }
```

```
  continuation popBottom() {
    int b = bot;
    ⟨int, entry⟩ old = stack[b-1];
    commit;
    if (old == ⟨j, job(f)⟩) {
      CAM(&stack[b-1], old, ⟨j+1,local⟩);
      if (stack[b-1] == ⟨j+1, local⟩) {
        bot = b-1;
        return f;
      } }
    // If we fail to grab a job, return NULL.
    return NULL;
  }

  ^ findWork() {
    // Try to take from local stack first.
    continuation f = popBottom();
    if (f) GOTO(f);
    // If nothing locally, randomly steal.
    while (true) {
      yield();
      int victim = rand(P);
      int i = getStep(bot);
      continuation g
        = states[victim].popTop(&stack[bot],i);
      if (g) GOTO(g);
    }
  }
}

procState states[P]; // Stack for each process.

// User call to fork.
void fork(continuation f) {
  // Pushes job onto the correct stack.
  states[getProcNum()].pushBottom(f);
}

// Return to scheduler when any job finishes.
^ scheduler() {
  // Mark the completion of local thread.
  states[getProcNum()].clearBottom();
  // Find work on the correct stack.
  GOTO(states[getProcNum()].findWork());
}
```

**Figure 3: Fault-tolerant WS-Deque Implementation. Jumps are marked as GOTO and functions that are jumped to and do not return (technically continuations) are marked with a ^. All CAM instructions occur in separate capsules, similar to function calls.**

| | | New State | | | |
|---|---|---|---|---|---|
| | | Empty | Local | Job | Taken |
| Old State | Empty | - | ✓ | | |
| | Local | ✓ | - | ✓ | ✓ |
| | Job | | ✓ | - | ✓ |
| | Taken | | | | - |

**Figure 4: Entry state transition diagram**

deque, even after steals. This means that we do not need to worry about entries being deleted in the process of a steal attempt, but does mean that maintaining $P$ WS-Deques for a computation with span $T_\infty$ requires $O(PT_\infty)$ storage space.

Our implementation of the WS-Deque maintains a consistent structure that is useful for proving its correctness and efficiency. The elements of our WS-Deque are always ordered from the beginning to the end of the array as follows:

(1) A non-negative number of taken entries. These entries refer to threads that have been stolen, or possibly in the case of the last taken entry, to a thread that is in the process of being stolen.
(2) A non-negative number of job entries. These entries refer to threads that the process has enabled that have not been stolen or started since their enabling.
(3) Zero, one, or two local entries. If a process has one local entry, it is the entry that the process is currently working on. Processes can momentarily have two local entries during the pushBottom function, before the earlier one is changed to a job. If a process has zero local entries, that means the process has completed the execution of its local work and is in the process of acquiring more work through popBottom or stealing, or it is dead.
(4) A non-negative number of empty entries. These entries are available to store new threads as they are forked during the computation.

We can also relate the top and bottom pointers of the WS-Deque (i.e. the range of the deque) to this array structure. The top pointer will point to the last taken entry in the array if a steal is in process. Otherwise, it will point to the first entry after the taken entries. At the end of a capsule, the bottom pointer will point to the local entry if it exists, or the first empty entry after the jobs otherwise. The bottom pointer can also point to the last job in the array or the earlier local entry during a call to pushBottom.

## 6.3 Algorithm Overview and Rationale

We now give an overview and rationale of correctness of our work-stealing scheduler under the Parallel-PM.

Each process is initialized with an empty WS-Deque containing enough `empty` entries to complete the computation. The top and bottom pointers of each WS-Deque are set to the first entry. One process is assigned the root thread. This process installs the first capsule of this thread, and sets its first entry to `local`. All other processes install the `findWork` capsule.

Once computation begins, the adversary chooses processes to schedule according to the rules of the yield instruction described in ABP, with the additional restriction that dead processes cannot be scheduled. When a process is scheduled, it continues running its code. This code may be scheduler code or user code.

If the process is running user code, this continues until the code calls `fork` or terminates. Calls to `fork` result in the newly enabled thread being pushed onto the bottom of the process' WS-Deque. When the user code terminates, the process returns to the `scheduler` function.

The scheduler code works to find new threads for the process to work on. It begins by calling the `popBottom` function to try and find a thread on the owner's WS-Deque. If `popBottom` finds a thread, the process works on that thread as described above. Otherwise, the process begins to make steal attempts using the `popTop` function on random victim stacks. In a faultless setting, our work-stealing scheduler fuctions like that of ABP. We use the additional information stored in the WS-Deques and the configuration of capsule boundaries to provide fault tolerance.

We provide correctness in a setting with soft faults using idempotent capsules. Each capsule in the scheduler is an instance of one of the capsules discussed in Section 5. This means that processes can fault and restart without affecting the correctness of the scheduler.

Providing correctness in a setting with hard faults is more challenging. This requires the scheduler to ensure that work being done by processes that hard fault is picked up in the same capsule that the fault ocurred during by exactly one other process. We handle this by allowing thieves to steal `local` entries from dead processes. A process can check whether another process is dead using a liveness oracle `isLive(procId)`.

The liveness oracle might be constructed by implementing a counter and a flag for each process. Each process updates its counter after a constant number of steps (this does not have to be synchronized). If the time since a counter has last updated passes some threshold, the process is considered dead and its flag is set. If the process restarts, it can notice that it was marked as dead, clear its flag, and enter the system with a new empty WS-Deque. Constructing such an oracle does not require a global clock or tight synchronization.

By handling these high level challenges, along with some of the more subtle challenges that occur when trying to provide exactly-once semantics in the face of both soft and hard faults, we reach the following result.

THEOREM 6.1. *The implementation of work stealing provided in Figure 3 correctly schedules work according to the specification in Section 6.*

The proof, appearing in the full version of the paper [14], deals with the many possible code interleavings that arise when considering combinations of faulting and concurrency. We discuss our methods for ensuring that work is neither duplicated during capsule retries after soft faults or dropped due to hard faults. In particular, we spend considerable time ensuring that recovery from hard faults during interaction with the bottom of the WS-Deque happens correctly.

## 6.4 Time Bounds

We now analyze bounds on runtime based on the work-stealing scheduler under the assumptions mentioned at the start of the section (scheduled in fixed quanta, and supporting a yield-to-all instruction).

As with ABP, we consider the total amount of work done by a computation, and the depth of the computation, also called the critical path length. In our case we have $W$, the work assuming no faults, and $W_f$, the work including faults. In algorithm analysis the user analyzes the first, but in determining the runtime we care about the second. Similarly we have both $D$, a depth assuming no faults, and $D_f$, a depth with faults.

For the time bounds we can leverage the proof of ABP. In particular as in their algorithm our popTop, popBottom, and pushBottom functions all take $O(1)$ work without faults. With our deque, operations take expected $O(1)$ work. Also as with their version, our popTop is unsuccessful (returns Null when there is work) only if another popTop is successful during the attempt. The one place where their proof breaks down in our setup is the assumption that a constant sized quanta can always capture two steal attempts. Because our processors can fault multiple times, we cannot guarantee this. However in their proof this is needed to show that for every $P$ steal attempts, with probability at least 1/4, at least 1/4 of the non-empty deques are successfully stolen from ([5], Lemma 8). In our case a constant fraction $(1 - O(1) \cdot f)^2$ of adjacent pairs of steal attempts will not fault at all and therefore count as a steal attempt. For analysis we can assume that if either steals in a pair faults, then the steal is unsuccessful. This gives a similar result, only with a different constant, i.e., with probability at least 1/4, at least $(1 - O(1) \cdot f)^2/4$ of the non-empty deques are successfully stolen from. We note that hard faults affect the average number of active processors $P_A$. However they otherwise have no asymptotic affect in our bounds because a hard fault in our scheduler is effectively the same as forking a thread onto the bottom of a work-queue and then finishing.

ABP show that their work-stealing scheduler runs in expected time $O(W/P_A + DP/P_A)$. To apply their results we need to plug in $W_f$ for $W$ because that is the actual work done, and $D_f$ for $D$ because that is actual depth. While bounding $W_f$ to be within a constant factor of $W$ is straightforward, bounding $D_f$ is trickier because we cannot sum expectations to get the depth bound (the depth is a maximum over paths lengths). Instead we show that with some high probability no capsule faults more than some number of times $l$. We then simply multiply the depth by $l$. By making the probability sufficiently high, we can pessimistically assume that in the unlikely even that any capsule faults more than $l$ times then, the depth is as large as the work. This idea leads to the following theorem.

THEOREM 6.2. *Consider any multithreaded computation with $W$ work, $D$ depth, and $C$ maximum capsule work (all assuming no faults) for which all capsules are atomically idempotent. On the Parallel-PM with $P$ processors, $P_A$ average number of active processors, and fault probability bounded by $f \leq 1/(2C)$, the expected total time $T_f$ for the computation is*

$$O\left(\frac{W}{P_A} + D\left(\frac{P}{P_A}\right)\left\lceil \log_{1/(Cf)} W \right\rceil\right).$$

PROOF. We must account for faults in both the computation and the work-stealing scheduler. The work-stealing scheduler has $O(1)$ maximum capsule work, which we assume is at most $C$. Because we assume all faults are independent, the probability that a capsule will run $l$ or more times is upper bounded by $(Cf)^l$. Therefore if there are $\kappa$ capsules in the computation including the capsules executed as part of the scheduler, the probability that any one runs more than $l$ times is upper bounded by $\kappa(Cf)^l$ (by the union bound). If we want to bound this probability by some $\epsilon$, we have $\kappa(Cf)^l \leq \epsilon$. Solving for $l$ and using $\kappa \leq 2W$ gives $l \leq \lceil \log_{1/(Cf)}(2W/\epsilon)\rceil$. This means that with probability at most $\epsilon$, $D_f \leq D \log_{1/(Cf)}(2W/\epsilon)$. If we set $\epsilon = 2/W$ then $D_f \leq 2D \log_{1/(Cf)} W$. Now we assume that if any capsule faults $l$ times or more that the depth of the computation equals the work. This gives $(P/P_A)(2/W)W + (1 - 2/W)2D\lceil \log_{1/(Cf)} W\rceil)$ as the expected value of the second term of the ABP bound, which is bounded by $O((P/P_A)D\lceil \log_{1/(Cf)} W\rceil)$. Because the expected total work for the first term is $W_f \leq (1/(1 - Cf))W$, and given $Cf \leq 1/2$, the theorem follows. □

This time bound differs from the ABP bound only in the extra $\log_{1/(Cf)} W$ factor. If we assume $P_A$ is a constant fraction of $P$ then the expected time simplifies to $O(W/P + D\lceil \log_{1/(Cf)} W\rceil)$.

## 7 FAULT-TOLERANT ALGORITHMS

In this section, we outline how to implement several algorithms for the Parallel-PM model. The algorithms are all based on binary fork-join parallelism (i.e., nested parallelism), and hence fit within the multithreaded model. We state all results in terms of faultless work and depth. The results can be used with Theorem 6.2 to derive bounds on time for the Parallel-PM. Recall that in the Parallel-PM model, external reads and writes are unit cost, and all other instructions have no cost (accounting for other instructions would not be hard). The algorithms that we use are already race-free. Making them write-after-read conflict free simply involves ensuring that reads and writes are to different locations. All capsules of the algorithms are therefore atomically idempodent. The base case for each of our variants of the algorithms is done sequentially within the ephemeral memory.

**Prefix Sum.** Given $n$ elements $\{a_1, \cdots, a_n\}$ and an associative operator "+", the prefix sum algorithm computes a list of prefix sums $\{p_1, \cdots, p_n\}$ such that $p_i = \sum_{j=1}^{i} a_j$. Prefix sum is one of the most commonly-used building blocks in parallel algorithm design [43].

We note that the standard prefix sum algorithm [43] works well in our setting. The algorithm consists of two phases—the up-sweep phase and the down-sweep phase, both based on divide-and-conquer. The up-sweep phase bisects the list, computes the sum of each sublist recursively, adds the two partial sums as the sum of the overall list, and stores the sum in the persistent memory. After the up-sweep phase finishes, we run the down-sweep phase with the same bisection of the list and recursion. Each recursive call in this phase has a temporary parameter $t$, which is initiated as 0 for the initial call. Then within each function, we pass $t$ to the left recursive call and $t$ + *LeftSum* for the right recursive call, where *LeftSum* is the sum of the left sublist computed from the up-sweep phase. In both sweeps the recursion stops when the sublist has no more than $B$ elements, and we sequentially process it using $O(1)$ memory transfers. For the base case in the down-sweep phase, we set the first element $p_i$ to be $t + a_i$, and then sequentially compute the rest of the prefix sums for this block. The correctness of $p_i$ follows from how $t$ is computed along the path to $a_i$.

This algorithm fits the Parallel-PM model in a straightforward manner. We can place the body of each function call (without the recursive calls) in an individual capsule. In the up-sweep phase, a capsule reads from two memory locations and stores the sum back to another location. In the down-sweep phase, it reads from at most one memory location, updates $t$, and passes $t$ to the recursive calls. Defining capsules in this way provides write-after-read conflict-freedom and limits the maximum capsule workto a constant.

Theorem 7.1. *The prefix sum of an array of size $n$ can be computed in $O(n/B)$ work, $O(\log n)$ depth, and $O(1)$ maximum capsule work, using only atomically-idempotent capsules.*

**Merging.** A merging algorithm takes the input of two sorted arrays $A$ and $B$ of size $l_A$ and $l_B$ ($l_A + l_B = n$), and returns a sorted array containing the elements in both input lists. We use an algorithm on the Parallel-PM model based on the classic divide-and-conquer algorithm [15].

The first step of the algorithm is to allocate the output array of size $n$. Then the algorithm conducts dual binary searches of the arrays in parallel to find the elements ranked $\{n^{2/3}, 2n^{2/3}, 3n^{2/3}, \ldots, (n^{1/3} - 1)n^{2/3}\}$ among the set of keys from both arrays, and recurses on each pair of subarrays until the base case when there are no more than $B$ elements left (and we switch to a sequential version). We put each of the binary searches into a capsule, as well as each base case. These capsules are write-after-read conflict free because the output of each capsule is written to a different subarray. Based on the analysis in [15] we have the following theorem.

Theorem 7.2. *Merging two sorted arrays of overall size $n$ can be done in $O(n/B)$ work, $O(\log n)$ depth, and $O(\log n)$ maximum capsule work, using only atomically-idempotent capsules.*

**Sorting.** Using the merging algorithm in Section 7, we can implement a fault-tolerant mergesort with $O((n/B)\log(n/M))$ work and maximum capsule work $O(\log n)$. However, this is not optimal. We now outline a samplesort algorithm with improved work $O(n/B \cdot \log_M n)$, based on the algorithm in [15].

The sorting algorithm first splits the set of elements into $\sqrt{n}$ subarrays of size $\sqrt{n}$ and recursively sorts each of the subarrays. The recursion terminates when the subarray size is less than $M$, and the algorithm then sequentially sorts within a single capsule. Then the algorithm samples every $\log n$'th element from each subarray. These samples are sorted using mergesort, and $\sqrt{n}$ pivots are picked from the result using a fixed stride. The next step is to merge each $\sqrt{n}$-size subarray with the sorted pivots to determine bucket boundaries within each subarray. Once the subarrays have been split, prefix sums and matrix transposes are used to determine the location in the buckets where each segment of the subarray is to be sent. After that, the keys need to be moved to the buckets, using a bucket transpose algorithm. We can use our prefix sum algorithm and the divide-and-conquer bucket transpose algorithm from [15], where the base case is a matrix of size less than $M$, and in the base case the transpose is done sequentially within a single capsule (note that this assumes $M > B^2$ to be efficient). The last step is to recursively sort the elements within each bucket. All steps can be made write-after-read conflict free by writing to locations separate than those being read. By applying the analysis in [15] with the change that the base cases (for the recursive sort and the transpose) are when the size fits in the ephemeral memory, and that the base case is done sequentially, we obtain the following theorem.

Theorem 7.3. *Sorting $n$ elements can be done in $O(n/B \cdot \log_M n)$ work, $O((M/B+\log n)\log_M n)$ depth, and $O(M/B)$ maximum capsule work, using only atomically-idempotent capsules.*

It is possible that the $\log n$ term in the depth could be reduced using a sort by Cole and Ramachandran [24].

**Matrix Multiplication.** Due to space constraints, our Parallel-PM algorithm for matrix multiply is given in the full version of this paper [14], and here we only introduce our result.

Theorem 7.4. *Multiplying two square matrices of size $n$ can be done in $O(n^3/(B\sqrt{M}))$ work, $O(M/B + \log^2 n)$ depth, and $O(M/B)$ maximum capsule work, using only atomically-idempotent capsules.*

The algorithm is a slight modification of the classic 8-way divide-and conquer approach [31]. The computation is made race-free by setting correct capsule boundaries.

## 8 CONCLUSION

In this paper, we describe the Parallel Persistent Memory model, which characterizes faults as loss of data in individual processors and their associated volatile memory. For this paper, we consider an external memory model view of algorithm cost, but the model could easily be adapted to support other traditional cost models. We also provide a general strategy for designing programs based on capsules that perform properly when faults occur. We specify a condition of being atomically idempotent that is sufficient for correctness, and provide examples of atomic idempotent capsules that can be used to generate more complex programs. We use these capsules to build a work-stealing scheduler that can run programs in a parallel system while tolerating both hard and soft faults with only a modest increase in the total cost of the computation. We also provide several algorithms designed to support fault tolerance using our capsule methodology. We believe that the techniques in this paper can provide a practical way to provide the desirable quality of fault tolerance without requiring significant changes to hardware or software.

## ACKNOWLEDGEMENTS

This work was supported in part by NSF grants CCF-1408940, CCF-1533858, and CCF-1629444.

## REFERENCES


[1] Y. Afek, D. S. Greenberg, M. Merritt, and G. Taubenfeld. Computing with faulty shared memory. In *PODC*, 1992.

[2] A. Aggarwal and J. S. Vitter. The Input/Output complexity of sorting and related problems. *Communications of the ACM*, 31(9), 1988.

[3] A. W. Appel and T. Jim. Continuation-passing, closure-passing style. In *POPL*, 1989.

[4] L. Arge, M. T. Goodrich, M. Nelson, and N. Sitchinava. Fundamental parallel algorithms for private-cache chip multiprocessors. In *SPAA*, 2008.

[5] N. S. Arora, R. D. Blumofe, and C. G. Plaxton. Thread scheduling for multiprogrammed multiprocessors. *Theory of Computing Systems*, 34(2), Apr 2001.

[6] Y. Aumann and M. Ben-Or. Asymptotically optimal PRAM emulation on faulty hypercubes. In *FOCS*, 1991.

[7] D. Balsamo, A. S. Weddell, G. V. Merrett, B. M. Al-Hashimi, D. Brunelli, and L. Benini. Hibernus: Sustaining computation during intermittent supply for energy-harvesting systems. *IEEE Embedded Systems Letters*, 7(1), 2015.

[8] N. Ben-David, G. E. Blelloch, J. T. Fineman, P. B. Gibbons, Y. Gu, C. McGuffey, and J. Shun. Parallel algorithms for asymmetric read-write costs. In *SPAA*, 2016.

[9] N. Ben-David, G. E. Blelloch, J. T. Fineman, P. B. Gibbons, Y. Gu, C. McGuffey, and J. Shun. Implicit decomposition for write-efficient connectivity algorithms. In *IPDPS*, 2018.

[10] R. Berryhill, W. Golab, and M. Tripunitara. Robust shared objects for non-volatile main memory. In *Conf. on Principles of Distributed Systems (OPODIS)*, volume 46, 2016.

[11] K. Bhandari, D. R. Chakrabarti, and H.-J. Boehm. Makalu: Fast recoverable allocation of non-volatile memory. In *OOPSLA*, 2016.

[12] G. E. Blelloch, J. T. Fineman, P. B. Gibbons, Y. Gu, and J. Shun. Sorting with asymmetric read and write costs. In *SPAA*, 2015.

[13] G. E. Blelloch, J. T. Fineman, P. B. Gibbons, Y. Gu, and J. Shun. Efficient algorithms with asymmetric read and write costs. In *ESA*, 2016.

[14] G. E. Blelloch, P. B. Gibbons, Y. Gu, C. McGuffey, and J. Shun. The parallel persistent memory model. *arXiv preprint:1805.05580*, 2018.

[15] G. E. Blelloch, P. B. Gibbons, and H. V. Simhadri. Low depth cache-oblivious algorithms. In *SPAA*, 2010.

[16] M. Buettner, B. Greenstein, and D. Wetherall. Dewdrop: an energy-aware runtime for computational RFID. In *NSDI*, 2011.

[17] F. Cappello, G. Al, W. Gropp, S. Kale, B. Kramer, and M. Snir. Toward exascale resilience: 2014 update. *Supercomput. Front. Innov.: Int. J.*, 1(1), Apr. 2014.

[18] E. Carson, J. Demmel, L. Grigori, N. Knight, P. Koanantakool, O. Schwartz, and H. V. Simhadri. Write-avoiding algorithms. In *IPDPS*, 2016.

[19] D. R. Chakrabarti, H.-J. Boehm, and K. Bhandari. Atlas: Leveraging locks for non-volatile memory consistency. In *OOPSLA*, 2014.

[20] H. Chauhan, I. Calciu, V. Chidambaram, E. Schkufza, O. Mutlu, and P. Subrahmanyam. NVMove: Helping programmers move to byte-based persistence. In *INFLOW*, 2016.

[21] S. Chen and Q. Jin. Persistent b+-trees in non-volatile main memory. *Proceedings of the VLDB Endowment*, 8(7), 2015.

[22] B. S. Chlebus, A. Gambin, and P. Indyk. PRAM computations resilient to memory faults. In *ESA*, 1994.

[23] J. Coburn, A. M. Caulfield, A. Akel, L. M. Grupp, R. K. Gupta, R. Jhala, and S. Swanson. NV-Heaps: Making persistent objects fast and safe with next-generation, non-volatile memories. In *ASPLOS*, 2011.

[24] R. Cole and V. Ramachandran. Resource oblivious sorting on multicores. *ACM Transactions on Parallel Computing (TOPC)*, 3(4), 2017.

[25] A. Colin and B. Lucia. Chain: tasks and channels for reliable intermittent programs. *OOPSLA*, 2016.

[26] A. Colin and B. Lucia. Termination checking and task decomposition for task-based intermittent programs. In *International Conference on Compiler Construction*, 2018.

[27] T. David, A. Dragojevic, R. Guerraoui, and I. Zablotchi. Log-free concurrent data structures. EPFL Technical Report, 2017.

[28] M. A. de Kruijf, K. Sankaralingam, and S. Jha. Static analysis and compiler design for idempotent processing. In *PLDI*, 2012.

[29] I. Finocchi and G. F. Italiano. Sorting and searching in the presence of memory faults (without redundancy). In *STOC*, 2004.

[30] M. Friedman, M. Herlihy, V. J. Marathe, and E. Petrank. A persistent lock-free queue for non-volatile memory. In *ACM Symposium on Principles and Practice of Parallel Programming (PPOPP)*, 2018.

[31] M. Frigo, C. E. Leiserson, H. Prokop, and S. Ramachandran. Cache-oblivious algorithms. In *FOCS*, 1999.

[32] D. Grove, S. S. Hamouda, B. Herta, A. Iyengar, K. Kawachiya, J. Milthorpe, V. Saraswat, A. Shinnar, M. Takeuchi, and O. Tardieu. Failure recovery in resilient X10. Technical Report RC25660 (WAT1707-028), IBM Research, Computer Science, 2017.

[33] R. Guerraoui and R. R. Levy. Robust emulations of shared memory in a crash-recovery model. In *Inter. Conference on Distributed Computing Systems (ICDCS)*. IEEE, 2004.

[34] M. Herlihy and N. Shavit. *The Art of Multiprocessor Programming*. Morgan Kaufmann, 2012.

[35] J. Hester, K. Storer, and J. Sorber. Timely execution on intermittently powered batteryless sensors. In *Proc. ACM Conference on Embedded Network Sensor Systems*, 2017.

[36] T. C.-H. Hsu, H. Bruegner, I. Roy, K. Keeton, and P. Eugster. NVthreads: Practical persistence for multi-threaded applications. In *EuroSys*, 2017.

[37] Intel. Intel NVM library. https://github.com/pmem/nvml/.

[38] Intel. Intel architecture instruction set extensions programming reference. Technical Report 3319433-029, Intel Corporation, April 2017.

[39] J. Izraelevitz, T. Kelly, and A. Kolli. Failure-atomic persistent memory updates via JUSTDO logging. In *ASPLOS*, 2016.

[40] J. Izraelevitz, H. Mendes, and M. L. Scott. Brief announcement: Preserving happens-before in persistent memory. In *SPAA*, 2016.

[41] J. Izraelevitz, H. Mendes, and M. L. Scott. Linearizability of persistent memory objects under a full-system-crash failure model. In *DISC*, 2016.

[42] R. Jacob and N. Sitchinava. Lower bounds in the asymmetric external memory model. In *SPAA*, 2017.

[43] J. JaJa. *Introduction to Parallel Algorithms*. Addison-Wesley Professional, 1992.

[44] W.-H. Kim, J. Kim, W. Baek, B. Nam, and Y. Won. NVWAL: exploiting NVRAM in write-ahead logging. In *ASPLOS*, 2016.

[45] A. Kolli, S. Pelley, A. Saidi, P. M. Chen, and T. F. Wenisch. High-performance transactions for persistent memories. In *ASPLOS*, 2016.

[46] S. K. Lee, K. H. Lim, H. Song, B. Nam, and S. H. Noh. Wort: Write optimal radix tree for persistent memory storage systems. In *USENIX Conference on File and Storage Technologies (FAST)*, 2017.

[47] M. Liu, M. Zhang, K. Chen, X. Qian, Y. Wu, W. Zheng, and J. Ren. DudeTM: Building durable transactions with decoupling for persistent memory. In *ASPLOS*, 2017.

[48] B. Lucia and B. Ransford. A simpler, safer programming and execution model for intermittent systems. *PLDI*, 2015.

[49] K. Maeng, A. Colin, and B. Lucia. Alpaca: intermittent execution without checkpoints. *OOPSLA*, 2017.

[50] J. S. Meena, S. M. Sze, U. Chand, and T.-Y. Tseng. Overview of emerging non-volatile memory technologies. *Nanoscale Research Letters*, 9, 2014.

[51] A. Memaripour, A. Badam, A. Phanishayee, Y. Zhou, R. Alagappan, K. Strauss, and S. Swanson. Atomic in-place updates for non-volatile main memories with Kamino-Tx. In *EuroSys*, 2017.

[52] F. Nawab, J. Izraelevitz, T. Kelly, C. B. Morrey III, and D. R. C. amd Michael L. Scott. Dali: A periodically persistent hash map. In *DISC*, 2017.

[53] S. Pelley, P. M. Chen, and T. F. Wenisch. Memory persistency. In *ISCA*, 2014.

[54] J. Van Der Woude and M. Hicks. Intermittent computation without hardware support or programmer intervention. In *OSDI*, 2016.

[55] H. Volos, A. J. Tack, and M. M. Swift. Mnemosyne: Lightweight persistent memory. In *ASPLOS*, 2011.

[56] Yole Developpement. Emerging non-volatile memory technologies, 2013.

# The Inherent Cost of Remembering Consistently

Nachshon Cohen
EPFL

Rachid Guerraoui
EPFL

Igor Zablotchi
EPFL

## ABSTRACT

Non-volatile memory (NVM) promises fast, byte-addressable and durable storage, with raw access latencies in the same order of magnitude as DRAM. But in order to take advantage of the durability of NVM, programmers need to design *persistent* objects which maintain consistent state across system crashes and restarts. Concurrent implementations of persistent objects typically make heavy use of expensive persistent fence instructions to order NVM accesses, thus negating some of the performance benefits of NVM.

This raises the question of the minimal number of persistent fence instructions required to implement a persistent object. We answer this question in the deterministic lock-free case by providing lower and upper bounds on the required number of fence instructions. We obtain our upper bound by presenting a new universal construction that implements durably any object using at most one persistent fence per update operation invoked. Our lower bound states that in the worst case, each process needs to issue at least one persistent fence per update operation invoked.

**ACM Reference Format:**
Nachshon Cohen, Rachid Guerraoui, and Igor Zablotchi. 2018. The Inherent Cost of Remembering Consistently. In *SPAA '18: 30th ACM Symposium on Parallelism in Algorithms and Architectures, July 16–18, 2018, Vienna, Austria.* ACM, New York, NY, USA, 11 pages. https://doi.org/10.1145/3210377.3210400

## 1 INTRODUCTION

Non-volatile memory (NVM) is fast, byte-addressable memory that preserves its contents even in the absence of power. Recent years have seen significant research into NVM [33, 39, 41, 43], but the technology is only now starting to become commercially available.

NVM shares similarities with both traditional stable storage and DRAM. Like stable storage, NVM allows programs to persist their state across power failures or machine restarts. Unlike stable storage, NVM is byte-addressable and fast (with access times in the same order of magnitude as DRAM [47]). In this sense, NVM promises applications that are durable and fast, for they would not need to access slow storage to persist their state or during recovery.

Yet, the task of designing fast persistent objects (as building blocks of persistent applications) is complicated by two factors:

(1) Processor registers and caches are expected to remain volatile (transient) for the foreseeable future. Therefore, simply writing to a memory location is not sufficient to ensure the persistence of its contents (even if the memory location is in NVM), because the write instruction might, for instance, be satisfied in the cache and thus lost in the case of a crash.
(2) There is a priori no guarantee on the order in which cache lines are written back to NVM. However, program correctness might rely on such a guarantee, especially in a concurrent setting, which is the focus of this paper.

Due to these two factors, programming for NVM requires the use of flush instructions to force cache line write-backs, as well as of expensive fence instructions to ensure ordering among such flushes.

As we explain in Section 2, it is these latter fences that dominate the cost of NVM write-backs, which raises an interesting question: What is the minimum number of persistent fences required to implement a persistent object? In this paper, we answer this question for concurrent lock-free objects, by providing both upper and lower bounds on the number of fences required to implement them persistently.

We focus on the lock-free case because it provides an interesting trade-off. On the one hand, intuitively, lock-free objects can be implemented with a small number of fences, because they are already required to always be in a consistent state, such that progress can be made despite the failure of any number of processes. A priori, durability has the related requirement of an object state being consistent, no matter when a crash may occur. On the other hand, it is this very need for consistency that makes lock-free objects require at least a minimal number of fences for each operation invoked, as we show in the paper (we discuss lock-based objects in Section 8).

The correctness (safety) property we consider in this paper is durable linearizability [29]. Durably linearizable objects satisfy the standard linearizability property: every operation seems to happen instantaneously at a *linearization point* between its invocation and response, in separation from any other process in the system. In addition, after a full-system crash, the state of the object must reflect a consistent operation subhistory that includes all operations completed by the time of the crash.

For the upper bound, we propose a new universal construction called *Order Now, Linearize Later* (ONLL) that takes a deterministic sequential specification of an object $O$ and produces a lock-free durably linearizable implementation of $O$ that uses at most one fence per operation invoked, in the worst case. Our construction in fact guarantees detectable execution [15], an even stronger property than durable linearizability, which ensures in addition that, upon recovery, processes can determine which operations were linearized before the crash and which operations were not.

In our universal construction, we distinguish between read-only and update operations. An update operation *op* proceeds in 3 steps, called *order*, *persist* and *linearize*, respectively. First, *op* synchronizes with other update operations to establish the linearization order of *op*. This step uses a shared lock-free execution trace data structure, based on a lock-free queue, for determining this order in a lock-free manner. Second, *op* is stored in NVM by using a per-process persistent log. Crucial to this construction is the fact that the persistent


*SPAA '18, July 16–18, 2018, Vienna, Austria*

ACM ISBN 978-1-4503-5799-9/18/07...$15.00
https://doi.org/10.1145/3210377.3210400

log can be implemented with only one persistent fence per append operation [12]. A helping mechanism is used to ensure that delayed processes do not create inconsistencies in the state of the object. Third, *op* announces that it has completed the persistence step. This is also the linearization point [23] of *op* if it runs solo. When setting the linearization point, care is taken to respect the linearization order computed in Step 1. A read-only operation determines its return value based on the update that most recently announced completion of the persistence step.

Since persistent fences are only performed when appending one or more updates to a process' persistent log, it is clear that our construction uses at most one persistent fence per operation. Moreover, no process can prevent the system from making progress, thus the construction is lock-free.

Our lower bound states that any lock-free implementation of a persistent object has at least one execution in which all concurrent processes need to issue one fence instruction per update operation invoked. The intuition behind this result is that processes cannot always rely on each other to persist updates and must therefore sometimes persist these updates themselves. To see this, imagine that some process $p$ is designated to persist updates for one or more other processes but $p$ is delayed. In order for lock-freedom to be satisfied, those other processes cannot wait indefinitely for $p$, and so must persist their updates themselves, thus each incurring the cost of persistent fences.

To summarize, the contributions of this paper are:

(1) The ONLL universal construction, providing a lock-free durably linearizable implementation of any deterministic object. ONLL uses a single persistent fence per update operation and no persistent fences for read-only operations. ONLL also serves as upper bound on the number of persistent fences required to implement such objects.
(2) A lower bound on the number of persistent fences in a lock-free durably linearizable implementation of an object.

We also discuss extensions to our universal construction for wait-freedom, improved read performance and memory reclamation.

The rest of this paper is organized as follows. Section 2 recalls useful background. In Section 3, we give a high-level overview of our universal construction. In Section 4, we describe in detail the universal construction algorithm and we prove its correctness in Section 5. In Section 6, we present our lower bound result. We discuss relevant related work in Section 7 and conclude with an overview of possible extensions and future directions in Section 8.

# 2 BACKGROUND

## 2.1 NVM

So far, storage has been either slow but durable (e.g., SSD, hard disk, magnetic tape) or fast but volatile (e.g., DRAM). NVM promises to combine the best of both worlds through fast and durable storage. Several implementations of NVM are foreseen: Memristors [43], Phase Change Memory[33, 41] and 3D XPoint [39].

NVM is expected to be byte-addressable and attached directly to the memory bus of the CPU, accessible by standard load and store instructions. Thus, programming for NVM will probably be closer to programming for DRAM than for block-based storage. As argued in the introduction, the main difficulty in programming for NVM will likely stem from the fact that a priori there is no guarantee on when and in what order (volatile) cache lines will be written back to NVM. Therefore, programmers will need to use special instructions to ensure cache lines are written to the NVM.

One such instruction on Intel machines is `clflush` [27], which forces a cache-line to be written back to the NVM. This instruction is strongly ordered: a call to `clflush` returns only once the cache line is written-back to the NVM and is durable. Consequently, this instruction stalls the CPU for the entire duration of accessing the NVM, which is expected to be expensive in terms of CPU cycles.

Durability can also be ensured by using asynchronous write-back instructions, such as `clflushopt` or `clwb` [25]. We adopt this approach in this paper since it can be up to an order of magnitude faster than `clflush` [26]. Multiple invocations of these instructions are not ordered, so multiple cache lines can be flushed in parallel. Since these instructions do not stall the CPU and can be processed in the background, we consider the cost of invoking such instructions to be zero. Of course, this also means that invoking write-back asynchronous instructions is not sufficient to ensure durability.

In order to ensure that an asynchronous write-back completes and data is made durable, a *fence instruction* is required, which stalls the CPU until all active asynchronous write-back instructions complete. The fence instruction stalls the CPU for the entire duration for accessing the NVM, which can be expensive. Thus, our focus in this work is reducing the number of such fences. We emphasize the fact that that it is possible to execute a fence while no asynchronous cache line flush instructions are active, in which case the CPU does not (necessarily) access the NVM. We denote an execution of a fence while asynchronous cache line flushes are pending by *persistent fence*.

Additional details of the memory ordering model to the NVM are available in [12]. Briefly, two writes separated by a persistent fences are guaranteed to reach NVM in order. However, standard fences (e.g., `mfence`s) do not generally guarantee ordering to the NVM, unless all writes address the same cache line.

## 2.2 Processes and Operations

We consider a set of $n$ processes that communicate through shared memory access primitives. We make no assumptions on the relative speeds of the processes; in particular, at any point in time, processes may be delayed for arbitrary or even infinite amounts of time. As in previous work [29], we also assume that the whole system can crash at any point in time and potentially recover later. On such a full-system crash, we assume that the contents of NVM are preserved but that the contents of the processor's registers and caches are lost. Processes running at the time of the full-system crash also crash and are replaced by new processes after recovery. After a system recovers and before resuming normal operation, we assume that a (potentially empty) *recovery* routine is invoked in order to bring the persistent objects on the NVM back to a consistent state.

We classify operations on an object as *read-only* or *update*. Updates are operations that influence the result of subsequent operations; read-only operations do not influence later operations. Updates also read the state of the object and have return values. The *state* of the object is the sequence of update operations applied to the object; the first operation must be INITIALIZE. This definition implies that update operations are deterministic: applying the same sequence of updates on the object always results in the same state.

Our universal construction assumes the existence of a *compute* method. Given a read operation $r$ and the state of the object $s$ (i.e., the sequence of update operations on the object), this method computes the returned value of $r$ applied to $s$. For an update operation $u$, the returned value is computed on the state of the object $s$ immediately after appending $u$.

# 3 ONLL: A PRIMER

We give in this section a high-level view of ONLL, our universal construction that takes any deterministic object $O$ and produces a lock-free durably linearizable implementation of $O$ that requires at most one persistent fence per update operation and no persistent fence for read-only operations. Broadly, the execution of an operation under ONLL follows three stages: (1) *order* (in which the linearization order of the operations is established), (2) *persist* (in which the operation is made persistent) and (3) *linearize* (in which the operation is linearized)[1]. We first present the rationale behind these three stages and then give an overview of how ONLL works. We end the section with a concrete example, illustrating a shared counter implementation produced by ONLL.

## 3.1 Rationale

Not performing any persistent fences when reading is a highly desirable property. However, this imposes some constraints on the design of ONLL:

(1) The linearization point of an update operation cannot coincide with the time when the operation reaches NVM. This is because NVM can only be written using simple writes (as opposed to the cache that supports CAS), so it cannot in general serve as a synchronization point. A reader cannot distinguish whether data already reached NVM or not.
(2) The linearization order of update operations must be known before the operation is written to NVM. This is because NVM must contain enough information to replay this information in the correct (linearization) order.
(3) The linearization point of an update operation must happen after the write to NVM.

The last constraint was derived by the following contradiction. Suppose that the linearization point of an update does not happen after the write to the NVM. Then, a reader may observe the update operation before it reaches NVM. There are three cases, each leading to a different contradiction:

- The reader finishes its operation before the dependent update is persisted. This breaks linearizability if the reader performs an external operation (e.g., print) before the dependent update reaches NVM and the system crashes afterward. It is not possible to recover the update, but the dependent read was already observed.
- The reader waits for the dependent update to be persisted. This breaks lock-freedom since the process executing the update operation may stall arbitrarily long.
- The reader helps the dependent update to persist. This breaks the property of never executing a persistent fence for read-only operations.

[1]Formally, the linearization point of an operation can be reasoned about only after the entire event history is known. We say that the linearization point of an operation is at time $t$ if for any valid sequence of events after time $t$ the linearization point of the operation can be set to time $t$.

## 3.2 ONLL Design

The design of ONLL derives naturally from the above-mentioned constraints. Since the linearization order of an update operation must be known before the operation is made durable, and the operation must be made durable before it is linearized, an update operation $u$ under ONLL has three stages: order, persist, linearize.

First, in the order stage, a descriptor $d$ is created for $u$ and is appended to the tail of a shared *execution trace*. Second, in the persist stage, $u$ and operations preceding it that are not yet persistent are appended to a per-process persistent log (residing in NVM), along with the ordering information. Third, in the linearize stage, $u$ becomes visible to other operations when the available flag of $u$, or a later operation, is set. Finally, the returned value of $u$ is computed based on the state of the object according to the execution trace up to $d$. So $u$ is linearized at the linearize stage, after the write to NVM, but according to the order computed at the order stage.

For a read-only operation $r$, the execution trace is traversed, starting from the tail, until the first descriptor $d_{\text{first}}$ with a set available flag is reached. The return value of $r$ is then computed based on the object state up to $d_{\text{first}}$, as recorded in the execution trace.

This design ensures that the linearization point of an operation happens after the write to the NVM, so that readers are never required to wait or help with persisting the update operation. Moreover, after a crash, the NVM contains enough information to recover the state of the object in same order as the linearization points.

## 3.3 Illustration: Shared Counter

We illustrate how our ONLL universal construction works for a concrete shared object: a counter. A counter holds an integer value and has two operations: *increment* and *read*. The first is an update operation that increments the counter's value and returns the new value. Read is a read-only operation that returns the value of the counter. In what follows, we walk through several increasingly complex executions of the counter (shown in Figure 1), to illustrate various situations that can arise with our construction.

*Sequential update and read.* In the first execution, a single process $p_1$ executes an update operation (increment), followed by a read-only operation. Initially, both the execution trace and $p_1$'s persistent log is empty. Process $p_1$ creates a new node $n$ with execution index equal to 1 and available flag unset. Then, $p_1$ appends to the persistent log an entry containing all operations that have not been persisted yet (just $n$ in this case). To finalize the update, $p_1$ sets $n$'s available flag and returns the new value of the counter, 1. Next, $p_1$ performs a read operation by traversing the execution index from tail to head, stopping at the first node with a set available flag. In our case, there is only one node $n$, and its available flag is set. The read thus computes its return value based on the state of the counter at $n$. $n$ corresponds to a state in which one increment has been performed, so the read returns 1.

*Update concurrent with reads.* In the second execution, process $p_1$ is executing an update concurrently with two readers $r_1$ and $r_2$. The counter initially has value 1: there is already a node $n_1$ in the execution trace. The update appends a new node $n_2$ to the execution trace, appends the relevant entry to $p_1$'s persistent log, and then pauses. $r_1$ traverses the execution trace from tail to head, stopping at $n_1$, the first node with a set available flag. $p_1$ resumes

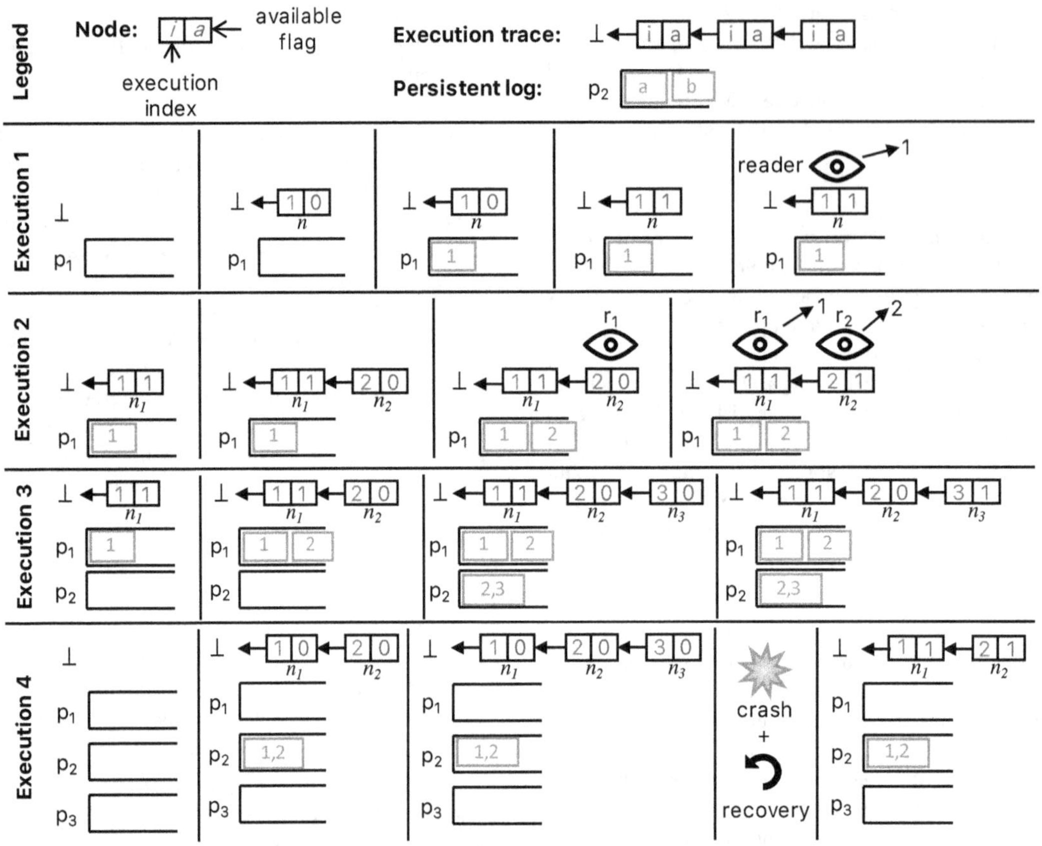

**Figure 1: Executions of a counter implemented using ONLL.**

execution and sets the available flag of $n_2$. $r_2$ begins traversing the execution trace and stops at $n_2$. Finally, the three operations return: $r_1$ returns 1, based on the state of the counter at $n_1$; $r_2$ returns 2, based on the state at $n_2$; $p_1$'s update returns 2, also based on the state at $n_2$.

*Update helping another update.* In the third execution, processes $p_1$ and $p_2$ are each executing an increment concurrently. Initially, the counter has value 1: the execution trace only contains node $n_1$. Process $p_1$ appends a node $n_2$ to the execution trace, adds the corresponding entry to the persistent log, and then pauses. $p_2$ also appends a node $n_3$ to the execution trace and then adds a persistent log entry containing all operations that have not been persisted yet: both $p_1$'s update and $p_2$'s update. Finally, $p_2$ sets the available flag of $n_3$ and returns 3. Any reader starting its traversal after $n_3$'s available flag has been set will return 3, even though the available flag of $n_2$ has not yet been set.

*Crash concurrent with updates and reads.* In the fourth execution, processes $p_1$, $p_2$ and $p_3$ are each executing an update operation. Initially, the counter has value 0 and the execution trace is empty. Process $p_1$ appends a node $n_1$ to the execution trace and then pauses for the rest of the execution. $p_2$ appends an execution trace node $n_2$, adds an entry to the persistent log corresponding to its own update and to the update of $p_1$, and then pauses without setting the available flag of $n_2$. $p_3$ also appends an execution trace node $n_3$, and starts adding a node to the persistent log corresponding to the updates of $p_1$, $p_2$ and $p_3$. The system crashes before any of the operations have returned.

After the crash, the state of the counter reflects the updates of $p_1$ and $p_2$. These can be reconstructed from $p_2$'s persistent log, even though no available flag was set during the execution. The post-crash state of the counter does not however reflect $p_3$'s update, because $p_3$ did not finish adding its persistent log entry.

Since no available flag was set during the execution, any reader concurrent with the updates will return 0, the initial value of the counter. Post-crash readers will return 2.

# 4 ONLL: A UNIVERSAL CONSTRUCTION

In this section, we first detail the data structures required by ONLL and then we describe the ONLL algorithm itself.

## 4.1 Data Structures

The ONLL algorithm depends on two basic building blocks: a single-fence persistent log and a lock-free queue.

We assume that an update operation can be stored in (persistent) memory by using an `operation` structure; input parameters are considered part of the operation and are thus also reflected in the operation structure.

*4.1.1 PERSISTENT LOG USAGE.* ONLL uses per-process persistent logs. We leverage the log implementation of Cohen et al. [12], which uses only one persistent fence per append. Each append invocation records up to *MAX-PROCESSES* operations, the number of recorded operations, and an execution index; pseudo code is

**Listing 1: recordEntry**

```
struct recordEntry{
    operation ops[MAX_PROCESSES];
    int num_ops; //between 1 and MAX_PROCESSES
    long executionIndex;
}
```

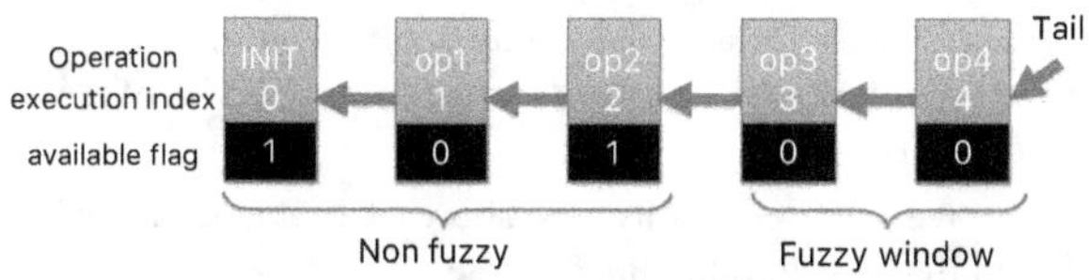


**Figure 2: The execution trace and the fuzzy window. Since op2 has a set available flag, all operations preceding it, including op1, are considered part of the non-fuzzy window. op3 and op4 have no later operation with a set available flag and so are the fuzzy window of the execution trace.**

provided in Listing 1. The first operation in the operation array is the current update operation executed by the process. The rest of the operations in the operation array are used to help other processes to persist their data. The `executionIndex` is a unique index that represents the ordering of the linearization point of the first operation. Operations in the array are sequential, so that the execution index of the $k$-th help operation is `executionIndex` $- k$.

*4.1.2 Transient Execution Trace.* The second data structure used by ONLL is a *transient* (i.e., not necessarily stored in NVM) execution trace of the object. This represents the sequence of all update operations applied to the object. Recall that the execution trace is equivalent to the state of the object. We emphasize that read-only operations do not appear in the execution trace of an object since they do not influence the state of the object; in our design, a read-only operation never writes to shared memory or to NVM.

The sequence of the update operations in the execution trace is partitioned into a *non-fuzzy* prefix and a *fuzzy window* postfix. The fuzzy window represents a set of currently executing operations that are not yet guaranteed to reside on NVM and their linearization point has not yet occurred. The non-fuzzy prefix consists of all other operations, which are guaranteed to reside on NVM and their linearization point has already occured. The fuzzy window is implemented by assigning an *available* flag for each operation in the execution trace. The fuzzy window spans from from the latest operation in the execution trace up to (but not including) the latest operation with available flag set. Available flags can be set in any order, depending on the speed of the relevant process. A set available flag is never cleared.

It is important to note that the fuzzy window is continuous: if an operation *op* has its available flag unset, but a later operation has its available flag set, then *op* is not part of the fuzzy window. An illustration appears in Figure 2.

The execution trace is implemented in a lock-free manner, based on a lock-free queue algorithm [38]. A slight difference from a traditional lock-free algorithm is the need to compute the *execution index* of each operation, which counts the number of update operations in the execution trace before the current operation. Pseudo code for the queue operation appears in Listing 2. Computing the execution index of a new operation is done at Line 34.

**Listing 2: Execution trace**

```
1  struct queueNode{
2      operation op;
3      long idx;
4      atomic<bool> available;
5      queueNode *next;
6      set<operation> getFuzzyOps(){
7          queueNode *curr=this;
8          set<operation> ops;
9          while(curr->available==false){
10             ops.add(curr->op);
11             curr=curr->next;
12         }
13         return ops;
14     }
15     queueNode *latestAvailable(){
16         queueNode *curr=this;
17         while(curr->available==false){
18             curr=curr->next;
19         }
20         return curr;
21 }}
22
23 class executionTrace{
24     atomic<queueNode *> tail;
25     executionTrace(){
26         tail=new operation(INITIALIZE, 0, true, null);
27         //also serves as a sentinel
28     }
29     void insert(queueNode *node){
30         queueNode *ltail;
31         node->available.store(false, memory_order_relaxed);
32         do{
33             ltail = tail;
34             node->idx = ltail->idx+1;
35             node->next = tail;
36         }while(tail.compare_exchange_weak(ltail, node))==false);
37     }
38     queueNode *latestAvailable(){
39         queueNode *curr=tail;
40         return curr->latestAvailable();
41 }}
```

The execution trace data structure supports the `latestAvailable` method for reading the latest operation with its available flag set (the latest operation in the non-fuzzy part of the execution trace). Pseudo code appears at Listing 2 Line 38. It is important to note that the `latestAvailable` method returns the latest *observed* available operation, which might not be the actual latest operation in the non-fuzzy part of the execution trace. This is because it is possible that while the `latestAvailable` method is traversing the operations with available flag unset, the availability of a later operation is set. In fact, it is possible that the returned node was never the latest operation in the non-fuzzy part. ONLL is correct despite this anomaly, as is described later (Proposition 5.9).

## 4.2 ONLL Algorithm

Our algorithms for updating the object and reading the object are presented in Listing 3 and Listing 4, respectively.

An update operation starts by adding a new node to the execution trace at Line 3. This corresponds to setting the linearization

**Listing 3: ONLL-update**

```
1  Update(operation op){
2      queueNode *node = new queueNode(op);
3      executionTrace.insert(node);
4      operation fuzzyOps[MAX_PROCESSES] =
5                                  node->getFuzzyOps();
6      persistentLog.append(fuzzyOps, node->idx);
7      node->available.store(true, memory_order_seq_cst);
8      return compute(node, op);
9  }
```

**Listing 4: ONLL-read**

```
Read(operation op){
    queueNode *node = executionTrace.latestAvailable();
    return compute(node, op);
}
```

**Listing 5: ONLL-recovery**

```
    executionTrace.insert(queueNode(INITIALIZE)).setAvailable();
    for(i=1; true; i++){
        Find log entry E with lowest execution index j : j ≥ i.
        if(E does not exist)
            break;
        operation op=E.ops[j-i];
        executionTrace.insert(queueNode(op)).setAvailable();
    }
```

order of the update operation without making it visible to read-only operations and without linearizing it[2]. At Line 5, the fuzzy window of the operation is computed. This corresponds to the set of operations preceding the current operation but are not yet guaranteed to be persistent. (We later show — Proposition 5.2 — that this computation is finite since there are at most *MAX-PROCESSES* nodes in the fuzzy window). Helping these operations to persist on the NVM prevents waiting for an unresponsive process. Then, the current operation and the helped operations are persisted by appending them to the private, persistent log (Line 6). The update part finishes by writing the available flag. This corresponds to the linearization point of the operation (unless another process helped it[3]) and makes the operation visible to read-only operations. Finally, if the update operation also returns a value, this value is computed and returned to the caller.

A read-only operation gets the latest node with available flag set. This node corresponds to the latest node in the non-fuzzy prefix of the object state. Then, the return value is computed based on this state and returned to the caller.

After a system crash, the transient execution trace is reconstructed from the persistent logs of all processes. The recovery process starts by adding the initialization operation to the execution trace, which serves as a sentinel node in the execution trace. Then, it iteratively searches for the next operation in the execution trace by looking into the persistent logs of all processes. If the operation *op* was not stored into any persistent log, the recovery process looks for an operation with a higher execution index and finds *op* by looking into the helped operations by the later operation. Finally, the found operation is pushed to the execution trace and the available flag is set. Recovery code is illustrated on Listing 5.

[2]We note that adding a new node uses a CAS instruction, which serves as a (concurrency) fence. However, no writes to the NVM are pending, so this fence does not count as a persistent fence.

[3]Helping is done by setting the available flag of a later operation, which logically linearizes the current operation. There is no help for setting the available flag: it is set only by the process executing the operation.

# 5 ONLL: CORRECTNESS

In this section, we prove the following theorem.

THEOREM 5.1. *For any deterministic object O, there exists a lock-free durably linearizable implementation of O that requires at most one persistent fence per update operation and no persistent fence per read-only operation.*

We prove the theorem by first showing that ONLL is lock-free and then that it is durably linearizable.

## 5.1 Lock-freedom

An implementation is *lock-free* if it guarantees that infinitely often, some operation returns in a finite number of steps. More specifically, if any process is permanently taking steps, some operation will eventually return.

The lock-freedom proof uses the following proposition, showing that traversing the size of a fuzzy window is bounded regardless of the initial node.

PROPOSITION 5.2. *At any time during any execution of* ONLL *and any MAX-PROCESSES+1 consecutive nodes in the execution trace, at least one has an available flag that is set.*

PROOF. Let $t$ be any time during the execution and let $S = \{n_i, \ldots, n_{i+MAX-PROCESSES}\}$ be *MAX-PROCESSES*+1 consecutive nodes in the execution trace. Clearly, there are at least two nodes $n_j, n_k \in S$ that correspond to two operations by the same process.

In our model, two operations cannot be executed by the same process at the same time: the first operation must return before the second operation can be invoked. Thus, let $n_j$ be the earlier operation and the $t'$ be the time it finished. Clearly, $t' < t$ since at time $t$ the operation corresponding to $n_k$ already appended itself to the execution trace, implying that it was already invoked.

According to Listing 3, an operation does not finish before setting the available flag and executing a memory fence. Thus, at least $n_j$ has a set available flag, as required. □

Recall that a set available flag is never unset; this property together with Proposition 5.2 imply that `getFuzzyOps` and `latestAvailable` are wait-free: they cannot be interfered with by other processes and they always finish in *O*(*MAX-PROCESSES*) steps.

LEMMA 5.3. *Suppose that compute — the function for computing the return value of an operation — always finishes in a finite time. Then* ONLL *is lock-free.*

PROOF. Reads first find the `latestAvailable` node and then execute *compute* on the resulting node. `latestAvailable` finishes in a bounded number of steps and is thus wait-free. *Compute* operates on a prefix of the execution trace starting with the `latestAvailable` node. This prefix is never modified by any process (except for the available flag, which is ignored by *compute*). Since we assume *compute* finishes in a bounded number of steps, it is also wait-free. Thus, reads are wait-free.

Next we consider updates. Appending to the execution trace is a lock-free operation. Getting the fuzzy window of an operation is wait-free since it always finishes in a bounded time. Appending to the process' private persistent log is also wait-free since an append is never interrupted by other processes and it finishes in a bounded number of steps. Finally, setting the available flag of a node is a wait-free operation. Thus, we conclude that updates are lock-free. □

## 5.2 Durable linearizability

We first recall the concept of durable linearizability and then proceed with the proof of durable linearizability in ONLL.

*5.2.1 Technical Preliminaries.* The execution of a concurrent system is modeled by a *history*, a sequence of events. Events can be operation *invocations* and *responses*. Each event is labeled with the process and with the object to which it pertains. A *subhistory* of a history $H$ is a subsequence of the events in $H$.

A response *matches* an invocation if they are performed by the same process on the same object. An operation in a history $H$ consists of an invocation and the next matching response. An invocation is *pending* in $H$ if no matching response follows it in $H$. An *extension* of $H$ is a history obtained by appending responses to zero or more pending invocations in $H$. $complete(H)$ denotes the subhistory of $H$ containing all matching invocations and responses.

For a process $p$, the *process subhistory* $H|p$ is the subhistory of $H$ containing all events labeled with $p$. The object subhistory $H|O$ is similarly defined for an object $O$. Two histories $H$ and $H'$ are equivalent if for every process $p$, $H|p = H'|p$.

A history $H$ is *sequential* if the first event of $H$ is an invocation, and each invocation, except possibly the last, is immediately followed by a matching response. A history is *well-formed* if each process subhistory is sequential.

A *sequential specification* of an object $O$ is a set of sequential histories called *legal* histories of $O$. A sequential history $H$ is *legal* if for each object $O$ appearing in $H$, $H|O$ is legal.

An operation $op_1$ *precedes* $op_2$ in $H$ (denoted $op_1 \rightarrow_H op_2$) if $op_1$'s response event appears in $H$ before $op_2$'s invocation event. Precedence defines a partial order on the operations of $H$.

*Definition 5.4 (Linearizability).* A history $H$ is *linearizable* if $H$ has an extension $H'$ and there is a legal sequential subhistory $S$ such that

**L1** $complete(H')$ is equivalent to $S$

**L2** if an operation $op_1$ precedes an operation $op_2$ in $H$, then the same holds in $S$.

Informally, this definition is equivalent to saying that an object is linearizable if every operation appears to take effect instantaneously at some point (the *linearization point*) between invocation and response. Incomplete operations (invocations without matching responses) may or may not have a linearization point.

Durable linearizability [29] captures the fact that an object's state should remain consistent even across crashes and recoveries, without "erasing" any completed operations.

*Definition 5.5 (Consistent cut).* Given a history $H$, a consistent cut of $H$ is a subhistory $P$ of $H$ such that if $op_2 \in P$ and $op_1 \rightarrow_H op_2$, then $op_1 \in P$ and $op_1 \rightarrow_P op_2$.

*Definition 5.6 (Durable linearizability).* An object $O$ is *durably linearizable* if its states immediately before and immediately after a crash and recovery reflect histories $H$ and $H'$ respectively such that (1) $H$ and $H'$ are linearizable and (2) $H'$ is a consistent cut of $H$ for which every complete operation $op$ in $H$ is also in $H'$.

In other words, all operations that completed before the crash must be included in $H'$, but some operations that had not yet completed may be excluded and thus not be reflected in the post-recovery state of the object. However, the operations in $H'$ must constitute a consistent cut of $H$, meaning that if some operation $op$ is included in $H'$, then so must all operations on which $op$ depends.

Informally, an object $O$ is durably linearizable if, in any history $H$ produced by $O$, every operation appears to take effect instantaneously at some point (the *linearization point*) between invocation and response. Incomplete operations (invocations without matching responses, either due to delayed processes or to system crashes) may or may not have linearization points. Operations concurrent with a crash may be reflected in the post-crash state of the object (in which case these operations have linearization points before the crash) or may not be reflected (in which case these operations have no linearization points).

*5.2.2 Durable Linearizability in ONLL.*

LEMMA 5.7. ONLL *is durably linearizable.*

The proof of durably linearizable for ONLL proceeds in 4 steps. First, we define linearization points for all update operations and define a time point for a crash (if a crash occurs). Second, we prove that the linearization point of an update falls between its invocation and response. Third, we show that a read is linearizable. Fourth, we show that the state of the object after crash and recovery matches the state of the object before recovery, according to the update operations linearized before the crash.

We start by defining a point in time where each update operation linearizes. When defining linearization points, we use the following convention. An integral time, denoted by $t_\square$, corresponds to a specific instruction executed on the durable shared object; a non-integral (i.e., fractional) time, denoted by $t_\square - a \cdot \epsilon$ denotes a linearization point that happens before time $t_\square$ but does not relate to a specific event during execution. We assume $\epsilon$ is sufficiently small and $a$ is a positive finite number so that $t_\square - 1 < t_\square - a \cdot \epsilon < t_\square$.

The linearization point of an update operation $op$ with execution index $i$ is the earlier between (1) the time $t_i$ the $i$-th available flag was set at the end of $op$ or (2) immediately before the time $t_j$ when the $j$-th available flag was set for $j > i$. To avoid distinguishing between these two cases, we consider the first $j$-th available flag that was set such that $j \geq i$. The linearization point of $op_i$ is $t_i = t_j - (j - i) \cdot \epsilon$ for a sufficiently small $\epsilon > 0$.

If a crash happens, let $t_{crash}$ be the time of the crash; we assume this time is higher by at least one than the last instruction executed before the crash. Clearly, operations that returned before the crash are included in the post-crash state of the object. We now examine operations that were ongoing at $t_{crash}$. Let $op_i$ be such an ongoing operation, with execution index $i$. We examine several cases:

(1) Some operation $op_j : j \geq i$ persisted $op_i$ and $op_j$ set its available flag at time $t_j$. Then $op_i$ is linearized at time $t_i = t_j - (j - i) \cdot \epsilon$ as discussed above.

(2) $op_i$ either (a) persisted itself, but did not set its flag, or (b) was persisted by one or more other operations (Listing 3 Line 6), but none of these operations set their flag. To establish the linearization point of $op_i$, let $op_l$ be the operation with highest execution index (= $l$) that finished persisting before $t_{crash}$. $op_i$ is linearized at $t_i = t_{crash} - (l - i) \cdot \epsilon$.

(3) $op_i$ was not persisted at all. That is, no operation $op_j : j \geq i$ finished appending to the persistent log at Listing 3 Line 6. Then, $op_i$ is not linearized and is lost in the crash.

Proposition 5.8. *The linearization point of an update operation falls between the invocation and the response of this operation.*

Proof. Consider an update operation $op_i$ and let $j \geq i$ be the first index such that the $j$-th available flag that was set. The linearization point of $op_i$ is $t_j - (j - i) \cdot \epsilon$.

When $op_i$ is inserted in the execution trace, the latest operation in the trace is $i - 1$; clearly, $op_j$ is inserted in the execution trace no earlier than $op_i$ was inserted in the execution trace (note that $i$ can be equal to $j$, in which case the times are equal). Setting the $j$-th available flag is done at time $t_j$. Inserting the $j$-th node in the execution trace happens earlier and is related to the execution of an actual instruction; thus, its time is at most $t_j - 1$. Recall that $\epsilon$ is small enough so that $t_j - 1 < t_j - (j - i) \cdot \epsilon$. Thus, $op_i$ is inserted in the execution trace before time $t_j - (j - i) \cdot \epsilon$. $op_i$ is invoked before is it inserted in the execution trace, establishing that the linearization point of $op_i$ happens after its invocation.

Operation $i$ does not finish before setting the $i$-th available flag. Clearly, the $i$-th available flag is set no earlier than the first $j$-th available flag is set, $j \geq i$. By definition of the linearization points, setting the $j$-th available flag happens at time $t_j$. Thus, the response to $op_i$ happens after time $t_j \geq t_j - (j - i) \cdot \epsilon$. □

Next we consider the linearization point of reads. If a reader were to traverse an atomic snapshot of the execution trace and found the last node in the non-fuzzy window, its linearization point would follow immediately from the definition of the linearization points of writes. But ONLL readers traverse the execution trace directly (and not an atomic snapshot thereof) and thus they may find a node corresponding to a concurrent update[4]. In this case, we show that the linearization point of the read can be set to immediately after the linearization point of the concurrent update operation.

Proposition 5.9. *A read-only operation has a linearization point between the invocation and the response of the operation, such that the return value of the operation corresponds to the state of the object at the linearization point.*

Proof. A read-only operation traverses the execution trace from the tail until it reaches a node with a set available flag. The resulting node is the state on which the returned value is computed. Suppose that the tail pointed to $op_j$ and the highest index operation with available flag set is $op_i : i \leq j$. Consider the time $t$ the read-only operation reads the tail (Line 7); either the $i$-th available flag was set at time $t$ or not. If the $i$-th available flag was set at time $t$, then the linearization point of the read is set to time $t$. This clearly falls between the invocation and the response. The state of the object at time $t$ contains $op_i$ since its available flag is set, but not any operation in the range $[i + 1, j]$ since their available flag is unset at time $t$. The latter is true since otherwise the traversal would find a later node $k \geq i + 1$ with a set available flag.

Next, consider the case that the $i$-th available flag was not set at time $t$. Denote by $t_e$ the time the read-only operation finds that the $i$-th available flag is set. At time $t$ all operations in the range $[i, j]$ have unset available flag and at time $t_e$ the $i$-th available flag is set. Thus, the linearization point of $op_i$ falls between time $t$ and $t_e$. We set the linearization time of the read-only operation to immediately after the linearization time of $op_i$ and before the linearization point of any other update operation[4]. Since the linearization point is between time $t$ and $t_e$, it is after the invocation of the read-only operation and before the response, as required. □

[4]For more details see our full paper [13, Appendix].

Proposition 5.10. *The state of the* ONLL *object after a crash includes all the operations that were linearized before the crash, executed in linearization order, and none of the operations that were not linearized before the crash.*

Proof. By definition of the linearization points before a crash, the state of the object just before $t_{crash}$ corresponds to the last operation that was written to the persistent log. After a crash, the recovery reconstructs the execution trace by traversing all persistent logs. Thus, the last node in the execution trace after recovery is the last operation that was written to the persistent log. The order of operations follows the `executionIndex`, which is stored on the persistent logs. Thus, the order of operations is equal before the crash and after recovery. It remains to show that all operations appearing in the execution trace before the crash also appear after recovery.

Suppose, by a way of contradiction, that an operation $i$ that appeared before the crash does not appear after the crash. Since the latest operation is the same, there exists an operation $op_j : j > i$ that appears both before the crash and after recovery. We pick the operation with smallest $j$ (that is larger than $i$). Operations that have a set available flag clearly appear in the log. Thus, all operations in the range $[i, j - 1]$ must have their available flag unset until $t_{crash}$. But since $op_j$ persisted in the persistent log before $t_{crash}$, it must have been added to the execution trace before $t_{crash}$. According to Proposition 5.2, there are at most *MAX-PROCESSES* - 1 operations between $op_i$ and $op_{j-1}$ since the available flag of $op_j$ is unset when it is appended to the execution trace.

But $op_j$ appended to the persistent log all operations in the range $[i, j]$, including $op_i$, so it appears in a persistent log. This contradicts our assumption that $op_i$ is not on the persistent log. □

The proof of Lemma 5.7 follows from Propositions 5.8, Proposition 5.9 and Proposition 5.10. The proof of Theorem 5.1 follows from Lemma 5.3 and Lemma 5.7.

Interestingly, ONLL also provides detectable execution [15]. After recovery, it is possible to check if a given update operation appears in the execution trace. The operation was linearized before the crash if and only if it appears in the execution trace after recovery.

## 6 LOWER BOUND

We show that in any lock-free implementation of a durably linearizable object, there exists some execution in which every update operation must issue at least one persistent fence. This is trivially true if operations are executed sequentially (otherwise a crash immediately after an operation $op$ would mean that $op$ is not reflected in the state of the object after recovery). Intuitively, the need for processes to persist their operations also manifests in some concurrent executions: if some process $p$ were to always rely on other processes to persist its operations, then $p$ might need to wait indefinitely if those other processes are delayed, thus violating lock-freedom.

We prove this intuition below, through several intermediate results, after defining relevant terminology.

*Terminology.* We say that a process $p$ *runs solo* between events $A$ and $B$ in an execution if $p$ is the only process taking steps between $A$ and $B$ in that execution. Two sequences of operations $H_1$ and $H_2$ are *equivalent* (denoted $H_1 \equiv H_2$) if any possible execution, when started from $H_1$ produces the same results (operation return values) as when started from $H_2$. We denote by $H_1 \cdot H_2$ the sequence obtained by executing sequence $H_2$ after sequence $H_1$. An operation $op$ is an *update* if there exists a sequence $H$ such that $H \cdot op \not\equiv H$. For ease of description, we define a *state* as a sequence of update operations, starting with INITIALIZE.

LEMMA 6.1. *Let $A$, $A'$ and $B$ be sequences of operations such that $A \cdot B \not\equiv A' \cdot B$. Then $A \not\equiv A'$.*

PROOF. Assume that $A \equiv A'$. Then, by definition of equivalence, $A \cdot B \equiv A' \cdot B$, a contradiction. □

LEMMA 6.2. *Let $op$ be any update and $H$ be any state such that $H \cdot op \not\equiv H$. Then, if for some $n \geq 2$, $H \cdot op^{n-1} \equiv H \cdot op^n$, the following property holds: $\forall j \geq 1, H \not\equiv H \cdot op^j$.*

PROOF. Assume by contradiction that $\exists j \geq 1 : H \equiv H \cdot op^j$. Then for all $k \in \mathbb{N}$, $H \cdot op^{kj} \equiv H$. Then (1) $H \cdot op^{n-1} \cdot op^{\lceil \frac{n}{j} \rceil j-(n-1)} \equiv H$ and (2) $H \cdot op^n \cdot op^{\lceil \frac{n}{j} \rceil j-(n-1)} \equiv H \cdot op$. The left sides of (1) and (2) are equivalent (because $H \cdot op^{n-1} \equiv H \cdot op^n$), but the right sides are not equivalent. We have reached a contradiction. □

THEOREM 6.3. *In a n-process system, for any lock-free durably linearizable implementation of an update operation op, there is an execution in which (1) all processes call op concurrently and (2) each process performs at least one persistent fence during its call to op.*

PROOF. By definition of an update operation, there exists a state $H$ such that $op$ applied from $H$ produces a different state $H \cdot op \not\equiv H$.

We now consider two cases: (1) $H \cdot op^{n-1} \not\equiv H \cdot op^n$ and (2) $H \cdot op^{n-1} \equiv H \cdot op^n$. For each case, we construct an execution in which the $n$ processes $p_1, ..., p_n$ call $op$ concurrently and all necessarily perform persistent fences.

*Case 1: $H \cdot op^{n-1} \not\equiv H \cdot op^n$.* We construct the following execution:

- Starting from $H$, let $p_1$ call $op$ and run solo until just before the response of $op$. $p_1$ will eventually reach this point, due to the lock-freedom of the implementation. $p_1$ will perform at least one persistent fence before being preempted. Otherwise, let $p_1$ resume and perform the very next step of returning from $op$; if a crash occurs after this response, after recovery the contents of persistent memory will be identical to that at $H$, which is inconsistent with the only possible linearization $H \cdot op \not\equiv H$.
- Let $p_2$ call $op$ and run solo until just before $op$ returns ($p_2$ eventually returns due to lock-freedom). $p_2$ performs at least one persistent fence during its call to $op$. Otherwise, let $p_2$ return from $op$ and let $p_1$ resume and perform the step of returning from $op$. If a crash occurs immediately after, at recovery the contents of memory will be identical to $H \cdot op \not\equiv H$, but the only possible linearization is $H \cdot op \cdot op$. By Lemma 6.1, $H \cdot op \cdot op \not\equiv H \cdot op$ (taking $A = H \cdot op$, $A' = H \cdot op \cdot op$ and $B = op^{n-2}$). We have reached a situation in which the only possible linearization is not compatible with the contents of memory, a contradiction; thus $p_2$ does indeed perform at least one persistent fence during its call to $op$.
- Continue with $p_3, ..., p_n$, each time calling $op$ and preempting the process just before returning. As with $p_2$, each process will perform at least one persistent fence before being preempted.

*Case 2: $H \cdot op^{n-1} \equiv H \cdot op^n$.* We construct the following execution:

- Starting from $H$, let $p_1$ call $op$ and run solo. If left to run solo long enough, $p_1$ will eventually perform a persistent fence. Otherwise, $p_1$ either never returns from $op$, violating lock-freedom, or returns from $op$ without performing a persistent fence. In the latter case, a crash may occur immediately after the response of $op$; upon recovery, the contents of persistent memory will be identical to those at $H$, which is inconsistent with the fact that $H \cdot op \not\equiv H$.
- Preempt $p_1$ just before the first persistent fence.
- Let $p_2$ call $op$ and run solo. If left to run solo long enough, $p_2$ will eventually perform a fence. Otherwise, if $p_2$ returns without a fence and the system crashes afterwards, the contents of persistent memory are identical to $H$ which is inconsistent with all the possible linearizations $H$, $H \cdot op$, $H \cdot op \cdot op$ due to Lemma 6.2.
- Continue in this way with processes $p_3, ..p_n$.
- For each process $p_n, ...p_1$, resume the process for one step—the persistent fence it was about to perform—then preempt it and move to the next process. □

Our lower bound result holds for detectable execution [15] as well, since it is a stronger criterion than durable linearizability (an implementation satisfying the former requires at least as many persistent fences as an implementation satisfying the latter).

## 7 RELATED WORK

*Safety criteria.* Several safety criteria have been proposed in the crash-recovery model. Persistent atomicity [18] requires any operation interrupted by a crash to be linearized or aborted before any later invocation by the pending process. In the same situation, recoverable linearizability [4] requires the operation to be linearized or aborted before any later invocation by the pending process on the same object. These two criteria assume that processes may crash and recover independently. However, it can be argued that this model is unnecessarily general, since processes typically crash together in a full-system crash (e.g., restart). In a more restricted model that only allows such full-system crashes, the two criteria become indistinguishable, and equivalent to durable linearizability [29], the safety condition adopted in this paper.

Work has been done on verifying linearizability for traditional transient objects [16, 35, 42]. It would be interesting to see if such verification techniques could be extended to verify durable linearizability for persistent objects.

Our upper bound algorithm relates in an interesting way to Section 4.1 of Izraelevitz et al. [29]. In that section, the authors state that the linearization point of an operation must happen before it is persisted. However, our ONLL construction linearizes an operation *op after* the time when *op* persisted and generates the linearization order before persisting, so that it knows what to persist. In fact, as discussed in Section 3, we argue that having the persist point earlier than the linearization point is necessary for any lock-free algorithm where readers never execute a persistent fence.

The same section of [29] contains a theorem (Theorem 2), which provides a set of sufficient conditions for an object to be durably linearizable. While at first glance it may seem that our ONLL algorithm contradicts this theorem, this is not the case: ONLL is durably linearizable, without satisfying the condition that operations are linearized before they are persisted.

*General transformations.* Related to the generality of our upper bound construction, there has been work [7, 9, 24] on generating correct persistent applications from existing code (designed for DRAM). However, in contrast to our work, these approaches assume the application is already multi-threaded and generally also assume lock-based code. Moreover, the focus in this work [7, 9, 24] is on lessening the programming effort necessary to transform applications, not on achieving optimality in terms of the number of persistent fences used.

In the same vein of generality, our work shares similarities with the universal construction of Herlihy [20, 21]. In both cases, the construction yields a correct concurrent implementation of an object from its sequential specification.

*Transactions.* Significant work has been done on transactions as a means of interacting with NVM [5, 8, 11, 14, 17, 28, 30, 32, 36, 37, 45]. These efforts share similarities to our work in the following sense: they strive for generality, they aim to reduce the cost of interacting with NVM, and they often use logging. Yet, these works do not consider lock-freedom as a progress guarantee. Also, whereas in transactions logging is used to help maintain the consistency of application state, in our construction, the log *is* the state.

*Persistent data structures.* A specific class of shared objects are concurrent data structures [22]. There has been some work on designing efficient data structures for NVM, focused mostly on indexing trees [10, 34, 40, 46]. This is natural, given that indexing trees are used extensively in data structures and file systems. Recently, Friedman et al. [15] have proposed three lock-free durable queue algorithms. These are specific approaches, not easily generalizable to other data structures or to other shared objects.

*Lower bounds.* Related to our lower bound result, Attiya et al. [1] have shown that linearizable implementations of strongly non-commutative operations cannot completely eliminate the use of expensive synchronization primitives such as memory barriers and atomic instructions (whose effects also include the effects of memory fences). This seems to imply that any implementation of a durably linearizable update operation requires (at least in some executions) two fences: one to account for the cited lower bound and one to account for our lower bound. However, since the effects of a memory fence also include stalling until pending cache line flushes have completed, a memory fence can also count as a persistent fence if flushes to NVM are pending. Thus, it might be possible in some cases to implement a persistent object using only one (memory) fence per update operation, accounting for both our lower bound result and that of Attiya et al. We leave open the questions of when and if such one-fence updates are indeed achievable.

## 8 CONCLUDING REMARKS

In the NVM era, programmers will need persistent and concurrent data structures. The performance of these is strongly influenced by the number of persistent fences executed for each operation. This paper shows that lock-free implementations require exactly one persistent fence for any update operation to ensure correctness. Our upper bound uses a novel ordering scheme to persist operations before their linearization points. Our lower bound captures the very fact that processes cannot rely on each other to persist updates and thus shows that one cannot hope to reduce the number of persistent fences while still guaranteeing durable linearizability and lock-freedom.

Below, we discuss possible extensions of our results and future directions left open by our work.

*Wait-freedom.* According to the proof of Lemma 5.3, the only operation in our ONLL construction that is not wait-free is the execution trace transient data structure. Since this data structure is transient, standard techniques such as the wait-free construction of Timnat and Petrank [44] can be used to derive a wait-free execution trace data structure. Alternatively, a wait-free execution trace can be based on the wait-free queue of Kogan et al. [31]. ONLL can thus easily be made wait-free.

*Compressing the execution trace.* An ONLL object stores its state as a sequence of all operations applied to this object. This representation could be improved for specific cases, as most practical objects have an object-specific representation of their state. For example, for the shared persistent counter discussed in Section 3, an object-specific representation would be an integer field corresponding to the current value of the counter.

If such a representation exists, one could consider a hybrid approach that combines a small ONLL execution trace for correctness with an object-specific representation for efficiency. As explained below, this approach would have the double benefit of (1) allowing better read performance and (2) enabling memory reclamation, thus reducing memory consumption.

Readers in ONLL traverse the entire execution trace; thus, reading an object's state implies traversing all update operations in the history of the object. ONLL read performance can be significantly improved by storing a local view per process, similarly to log-based systems [2, 3, 6]. The local view of process $p$ includes (1) a representation $r_p$ of the object up to some operation $op_p$ and (2) the execution index of $op$.

A read by process $p$ begins as before by finding the first execution trace node $n$ with a set available flag. Then, $p$ applies to its local representation $r_p$ all updates between $op_p$ and $n$. Then, $p$ updates its local execution index to that of $n$. Finally, the read is served directly from $r_p$.

In this way, the overhead of a read is the difference between the execution index of the local view and the execution index of the shared object, which is expected to be significantly smaller than the number of nodes in the execution trace.

Another effect of storing the entire execution trace in ONLL is the inability to reclaim memory. Both execution trace nodes and persistent log entries have to be kept forever. If the state can be stored as a small object-specific representation, however, then there is no need to remember all update operations and log entries, thus significantly reducing memory consumption.

Execution trace nodes can be reclaimed if we use the following scheme. As before, each process $p$ has a local transient representation of the object $r_p$, which $p$ brings up to date periodically. Note that once a process $p$ has applied an operation $op$ from the execution trace to $r_p$, $p$ will never need to read $op$ again. Thus, once all processes have updated their local representations past $op$, the execution trace prefix up to $op$ can be safely reclaimed.

We can go one step further and also reclaim persistent log entries. Each process $p$ periodically records its local representation $r_p$ in its persistent log, along with the execution index $n$ of $op_p$. Afterwards, $p$ can reclaim the memory of all persistent log entries with execution indexes smaller than $n$.

*Lock-based implementations.* At first glance, it might seem that by allowing implementations of persistent objects to be blocking, one could reduce the number of persistent fence instructions. For instance, the work of Cohen et al. [12] enables an implementation in which each process announces its operation and one of the processes applies all announced operations (similarly to flat combining [19]) using a single persistent fence. This implementation might seem to use only one persistent fence for every batch of concurrent operations. However, upon closer inspection, it is easy to realize that all pending operations pay the price of a persistent fence (by waiting while the combiner performs the fence), even without actually performing the fence.

## ACKNOWLEDGMENTS

We wish to thank the anonymous reviewers for their helpful comments on improving the paper. This work has been supported in part by the European Research Council (ERC) Grant 339539 (AOC).

## REFERENCES

[1] Hagit Attiya, Rachid Guerraoui, Danny Hendler, Petr Kuznetsov, Maged M. Michael, and Martin Vechev. Laws of Order: Expensive Synchronization in Concurrent Algorithms Cannot Be Eliminated. POPL 2011.

[2] Mahesh Balakrishnan, Dahlia Malkhi, John D. Davis, Vijayan Prabhakaran, Michael Wei, and Ted Wobber. CORFU: A Distributed Shared Log. TOCS 2013.

[3] Mahesh Balakrishnan, Aviad Zuck, Dahlia Malkhi, Ted Wobber, Ming Wu, Vijayan Prabhakaran, Michael Wei, John D. Davis, Sriram Rao, and Tao Zou. Tango: Distributed Data Structures Over a Shared Log. SOSP 2013.

[4] Ryan Berryhill, Wojciech Golab, and Mahesh Tripunitara. Robust Shared Objects for Non-Volatile Main Memory. OPODIS 2015.

[5] Hans-J. Boehm and Dhruva R. Chakrabarti. Persistence Programming Models for Non-volatile Memory. ISMM 2016.

[6] Irina Calciu, Siddhartha Sen, Mahesh Balakrishnan, and Marcos K. Aguilera. Black-box Concurrent Data Structures for NUMA Architectures. ASPLOS 2017.

[7] Dhruva R Chakrabarti, Hans-J Boehm, and Kumud Bhandari. Atlas: Leveraging Locks for Non-volatile Memory Consistency. OOPSLA 2014.

[8] Andreas Chatzistergiou, Marcelo Cintra, and Stratis D Viglas. Rewind: Recovery Write-ahead System for In-memory Non-volatile Data-structures. VLDB 2015.

[9] Himanshu Chauhan, Irina Calciu, Vijay Chidambaram, Eric Schkufza, Onur Mutlu, and Pratap Subrahmanyam. NVMove: Helping Programmers Move to Byte-Based Persistence. INFLOW 2016.

[10] Shimin Chen and Qin Jin. Persistent B+-trees in Non-volatile Main Memory. VLDB 2015.

[11] Joel Coburn, Adrian M Caulfield, Ameen Akel, Laura M Grupp, Rajesh K Gupta, Ranjit Jhala, and Steven Swanson. NV-Heaps: Making Persistent Objects Fast and Safe with Next-generation, Non-volatile Memories. ASPLOS 2011.

[12] Nachshon Cohen, Michal Friedman, and James R. Larus. Efficient Logging in Non-volatile Memory by Exploiting Coherency Protocols. OOPSLA 2017.

[13] Nachshon Cohen, Rachid Guerraoui, and Igor Zablotchi. The Inherent Cost of Remembering Consistently. *EPFL Technical Report*, 2018.

[14] Joel Edward Denny, Seyong Lee, and Jeffrey S. Vetter. Language-Based Optimizations for Persistence on Nonvolatile Main Memory Systems. IPDPS 2017.

[15] Michal Friedman, Maurice Herlihy, Virendra Marathe, and Erez Petrank. A Persistent Lock-free Queue for Non-volatile Memory. PPoPP 2018.

[16] Guy Golan-Gueta, G. Ramalingam, Mooly Sagiv, and Eran Yahav. Automatic Scalable Atomicity via Semantic Locking. *ACM Transactions on Parallel Computing*, 3(4), 2017.

[17] Yonatan Gottesman, Joel Nider, Ronen Kat, Yaron Weinsberg, and Michael Factor. Using Storage Class Memory Efficiently for an In-memory Database. SYSTOR 2016.

[18] Rachid Guerraoui and Ron R Levy. Robust Emulations of Shared Memory in a Crash-Recovery Model. ICDCS 2004.

[19] Danny Hendler, Itai Incze, Nir Shavit, and Moran Tzafrir. Flat combining and the synchronization-parallelism tradeoff. SPAA 2010.

[20] Maurice Herlihy. Wait-free Synchronization. *ACM Transactions on Programming Languages and Systems*, 13(1):124–149, 1991.

[21] Maurice Herlihy. A Methodology for Implementing Highly Concurrent Data Objects. *ACM Transactions on Programming Languages and Systems*, 1993.

[22] Maurice Herlihy and Nir Shavit. *The Art of Multiprocessor Programming, Revised Reprint*. Morgan Kaufmann Publishers Inc., San Francisco, CA, USA, 1st edition, 2012.

[23] Maurice Herlihy and Jeannette M Wing. Linearizability: A Correctness Condition for Concurrent Objects. *ACM Transactions on Programming Languages and Systems*, 12(3):463–492, 1990.

[24] Terry Ching-Hsiang Hsu, Helge Brügner, Indrajit Roy, Kimberly Keeton, and Patrick Eugster. NVthreads: Practical Persistence for Multi-threaded Applications. EuroSys 2017.

[25] Intel. Intel Architecture Instruction Set Extensions Programming Reference. https://software.intel.com/sites/default/files/managed/b4/3a/319433-024.pdf.

[26] Intel. Intel64 and IA-32 Architectures Optimization Reference Manual. https://www-ssl.intel.com/content/dam/www/public/us/en/documents/manuals/64-ia-32-architectures-optimization-manual.pdf.

[27] Intel. Intel64 and IA-32 Architectures Software Developers Manuals Combined. http://www.intel.com/content/www/us/en/processors/architectures-software-developer-manuals.html.

[28] Joseph Izraelevitz, Terence Kelly, and Aasheesh Kolli. Failure-atomic Persistent Memory Updates via JUSTDO Logging. ASPLOS 2016.

[29] Joseph Izraelevitz, Hammurabi Mendes, and Michael L Scott. Linearizability of Persistent Memory Objects Under a Full-System-Crash Failure Model. DISC 2016.

[30] Wook-Hee Kim, Jinwoong Kim, Woongki Baek, Beomseok Nam, and Youjip Won. NVWAL: Exploiting NVRAM in Write-ahead Logging. ASPLOS 2016.

[31] Alex Kogan and Erez Petrank. Wait-free Queues with Multiple Enqueuers and Dequeuers. PPoPP 2011.

[32] Aasheesh Kolli, Steven Pelley, Ali Saidi, Peter M Chen, and Thomas F Wenisch. High-performance Transactions for Persistent Memories. ASPLOS 2016.

[33] Benjamin C Lee, Engin Ipek, Onur Mutlu, and Doug Burger. Architecting Phase Change Memory as a Scalable DRAM Alternative. In *ACM SIGARCH Computer Architecture News*, volume 37, pages 2–13. ACM, 2009.

[34] Se Kwon Lee, K Hyun Lim, Hyunsub Song, Beomseok Nam, and Sam H Noh. WORT: Write Optimal Radix Tree for Persistent Memory Storage Systems. FAST 2017.

[35] Mohsen Lesani, Todd Millstein, and Jens Palsberg. Automatic Atomicity Verification for Clients of Concurrent Data Structures. CAV 2014.

[36] Mengxing Liu, Mingxing Zhang, Kang Chen, Xuehai Qian, Yongwei Wu, Weimin Zheng, and Jinglei Ren. DUDETM: Building Durable Transactions with Decoupling for Persistent Memory. ASPLOS 2017.

[37] Amirsaman Memaripour, Anirudh Badam, Amar Phanishayee, Yanqi Zhou, Ramnatthan Alagappan, Karin Strauss, and Steven Swanson. Atomic In-place Updates for Non-volatile Main Memories with Kamino-Tx. EuroSys 2017.

[38] Maged M. Michael and Michael L. Scott. Simple, Fast, and Practical Non-blocking and Blocking Concurrent Queue Algorithms. PODC 1996.

[39] Micron. 3D XPoint Technbology. https://www.micron.com/about/our-innovation/3d-xpoint-technology.

[40] Ismail Oukid, Johan Lasperas, Anisoara Nica, Thomas Willhalm, and Wolfgang Lehner. FPTree: A Hybrid SCM-DRAM Persistent and Concurrent B-tree for Storage Class Memory. SIGMOD 2016.

[41] Moinuddin K Qureshi, Vijayalakshmi Srinivasan, and Jude A Rivers. Scalable High Performance Main Memory System Using Phase-change Memory Technology. *ACM SIGARCH Computer Architecture News*, 37(3):24–33, 2009.

[42] Ohad Shacham, Eran Yahav, Guy Golan Gueta, Alex Aiken, Nathan Bronson, Mooly Sagiv, and Martin Vechev. Verifying Atomicity via Data Independence. ISSTA 2014.

[43] Dmitri B Strukov, Gregory S Snider, Duncan R Stewart, and R Stanley Williams. The Missing Memristor Found. *Nature*, 453(7191):80, 2008.

[44] Shahar Timnat and Erez Petrank. A Practical Wait-free Simulation for Lock-free Data Structures. PPoPP 2014.

[45] Haris Volos, Andres Jaan Tack, and Michael M Swift. Mnemosyne: Lightweight Persistent Memory. ASPLOS 2011.

[46] Jun Yang, Qingsong Wei, Cheng Chen, Chundong Wang, Khai Leong Yong, and Bingsheng He. NV-Tree: Reducing Consistency Cost for NVM-based Single Level Systems. FAST 2015.

[47] Yiying Zhang and Steven Swanson. A study of application performance with non-volatile main memory. MSSR 2015.

# Romulus: Efficient Algorithms for Persistent Transactional Memory

Andreia Correia
University of Neuchatel
andreia.veiga@unine.ch

Pascal Felber
University of Neuchatel
pascal.felber@unine.ch

Pedro Ramalhete
Cisco Systems
pramalhe@gmail.com

## ABSTRACT

Byte addressable persistent memory eliminates the need for serialization and deserialization of data, to and from persistent storage, allowing applications to interact with it through common store and load instructions. In the event of a process or system failure, applications rely on persistent techniques to provide consistent storage of data in non-volatile memory (NVM). For most of these techniques, consistency is ensured through logging of updates, with consequent intensive cache line flushing and persistent fences necessary to guarantee correctness. Undo log based approaches require store interposition and persistence fences before each in-place modification. Redo log based techniques can execute transactions using just two persistence fences, although they require store and load interposition which may incur a performance penalty for large transactions. So far, these techniques have been difficult to integrate with known memory allocators, requiring allocators or garbage collectors specifically designed for NVM.

We present Romulus, a user-level library persistent transactional memory (PTM) which provides durable transactions through the usage of twin copies of the data. A transaction in Romulus requires at most four persistence fences, regardless of the transaction size. Romulus uses only store interposition. Any sequential implementation of a memory allocator can be adapted to work with Romulus. Thanks to its lightweight design and low synchronization overhead, Romulus achieves twice the throughput of current state of the art PTMs in update-only workloads, and more than one order of magnitude in read-mostly scenarios.

## CCS CONCEPTS

• **Theory of computation** → *Concurrent algorithms*; • **Computer systems organization** → *Reliability*;

## KEYWORDS

Persistent memory; crash resilience; failure atomicity; transactions; concurrency

**ACM Reference Format:**

Andreia Correia, Pascal Felber, and Pedro Ramalhete. 2018. Romulus: Efficient Algorithms for Persistent Transactional Memory. In *SPAA '18: 30th ACM Symposium on Parallelism in Algorithms and Architectures, July 16–18, 2018, Vienna, Austria.* ACM, New York, NY, USA, 12 pages. https://doi.org/10.1145/3210377.3210392


ACM ISBN 978-1-4503-5799-9/18/07...$15.00
https://doi.org/10.1145/3210377.3210392

## 1 INTRODUCTION

Persistent mechanisms can provide resilience against power outages and non-corrupting software failures. The advent of storage-class memory or non-volatile memory (NVM) as a commercial product has brought this research to the front stage, allowing data and data structures to be directly persisted to NVM, avoiding serialization and deserialization of data, as is typically done for block devices. Non-volatile memory constitutes an opportunity to build applications that require resilience to failures with improved performance. Persistent application data is not guaranteed to be stored in a consistent state. A consistent state must satisfy application-level invariants or other correctness criteria.

To guarantee consistent persistence, in case of a failure during a modification of application data, one must ensure that only the following two scenarios can occur: either the modification is persisted in its entirety, or application data is reverted to the previous consistent state. This behavior of *all or nothing* fits naturally into the concept of a transaction.

Prior research on this topic has identified the same behavior and expose a persistent transactional memory (PTM) interface to the end user. Most of these PTMs use an underlying software transactional memory (STM), thus providing safe concurrent access in addition to durable transactions. These transactions are sometimes referred in the literature as failure-atomic-sections (FASEs).

To enable transactions, previous works on transactional persistence employ one of two logging techniques: write-ahead logging (WAL) with **undo** [7, 16, 20] or **redo** [16, 31] log. Both techniques require a log, containing the new value (redo log) or the current value (undo log) to be persisted. This adds complexity, given that the log used to revert to a consistent state must itself be allocated in persistent memory and be reverted in case of failure. Another approach is to use copy-on-write, which consists in copying the data in its existing state, applying the modifications to the new copy, and finally replacing the existing state with the new one with a single atomic operation. This technique is commonly used for disk storage and has also been considered for NVM [9, 26, 30]. Due to the lengthy copy procedure, the copy-on-write technique has not been deemed to be a viable alternative to in-place modifications via logging [1].

In this paper we present Romulus, a novel user-space library for consistent application recovery from a non-corrupting failure, which allows application developers to take advantage of byte-addressable non-volatile memory, with safe memory reclamation. Romulus was developed to be fast, lightweight and simple to use. Its code is written in processor-agnostic C++ and integrates a custom persistent memory allocator.

In short, with Romulus we make the following contributions.

- We introduce a novel PTM algorithm that relies on two copies of the data to be persisted, with three different algorithms that provide different trade-offs in terms of performance and sophistication. Unlike previous approaches, Romulus maintains a redo log in volatile memory instead of persisting it, hence significantly reducing overheads on log accesses. Romulus also allows concurrent access through a highly scalable reader-writer lock and a flat-combining array.
- We specifically address concurrency with a second implementation of Romulus that guarantees wait-free progress for read operations and blocking starvation-free update operations. Concurrent read-only transactions use lightweight synchronization mechanisms and are very efficient.
- Romulus performance is unprecedented with 4 persistence fences per transaction, independent of the transaction size and the number of threads. Another source of potential delay are the number of cache line flushes (pwb), which were also studied and significantly reduced.
- We formally present the different variants of the Romulus algorithm, study and discuss their properties, and give proofs of their correctness.
- Finally, we evaluate experimentally its performance in real-world use cases. In particular, we develop a fully-functional persistent key-value store, RomulusDB, and test it with state-of-the-art benchmarks.

The rest of the paper is organized as follows. We first discuss related work in §2. We then present background concepts in §3 before introducing the basic version of the Romulus algorithm in §4. We extend the original algorithm in §5 to efficiently handle concurrent transactions. We provide an in-depth evaluation of Romulus in §6 and finally conclude in §7.

## 2 RELATED WORK

Vista [20] was the first system to provide consistent persistent memory, using the Rio file cache. Vista does in-place modifications and guarantees consistent recovery through an undo log stored in persistent memory. To use transactions in Vista, the user must manually interpose every store to persistent memory. For every range of stores, the current value of those memory locations are saved in the log, requiring one persistence fence per range of stores. Each log entry in Vista uses at least three words: one word for the address, one word for the length of the range, and one word for the original value. Although not originally designed for NVM, Vista can be adapted to use it.

Atlas [4] also uses a WAL with an undo log. An entry in the undo log is created for every store to persistent memory. Each log entry has four words: the destination address of the store, the original value at the address, a pointer to the next node, and the size of the store combined with the log type. This implies that a persistent store in user code will cause a total of 5 stores to NVM. To minimize cache line flushes, Atlas uses a helper thread to aggregate memory locations and to guarantee that a consistent state is persisted to memory. As with any undo log approach, the algorithm has to guarantee that the log entry is made persistent before any in-place modification, which implies one persistence fence per log entry.

JustDo [16] uses WAL with a per-thread redo log that saves the last store and program counter. A failure recovery will re-execute the last store in the log, resuming the program at the exact point where it has stopped execution. The persistent store has to be idempotent, so that if the store is re-executed, it will result in the same modification on the destination address. This approach assumes that both the main memory and cache local memory are persistent. It requires that all memory loads and stores within FASEs access only persistent data, where a FASE, as in Atlas, encompasses the outermost critical sections of all acquired locks (nested or hand-over-hand). The log has two fixed entries, only one of which is active at a time, each contains the destination address of the store, the size of the write, and the value to be placed at the destination. An extra 64-bit variable holds the program counter with one bit indicating which of the two fixed entries is active. During a FASE, a persistence fence is needed after saving the new value and destination address, and another after saving the program counter.

NV-Heaps [7] uses an undo log system that provides extra functionality, like garbage collection and pointer safety, managing references from volatile to non-volatile memory and vice versa. It aims at facilitating the programmer's task of using persistent memory.

Mnemosyne [31] combines a redo log and the TinySTM [25] underlying STM. For every modified word it uses 8 words on the persisted log. The persistent data is modified only at commit time, which means that during a transaction, the data of variables stored in memory still contains unmodified data. When called to read data from persistence by the user code, the PTM interposes the load and checks if the data was modified. If so, it returns the new value from the log and not the value from memory. This approach can incur a high cost for large transactions because every load on the persistent memory region needs to first check for an updated value on the log. The longer the transaction, the bigger the log, and the longer it will take to search for the existence (and updated value) of a given variable. The authors of Mnemosyne mention that the choice of using a redo log was deliberately made, because it reduces the ordering constraints on writes to persistence, thus allowing this technique to perform only two persistence fences per transaction using a torn bit log. However, Mnemosyne's default implementation does not use the torn bit log technique, and therefore requires 4 persistence fences. Furthermore, in our benchmark experiments we noticed an increase in the number of persistence fences in concurrent settings; for example, with two concurrent threads, we identified transactions with more than 50 fences.

Table 1 summarizes the main features for failure-resilient transactional techniques, where $N_{ranges}$ represents the number of contiguous ranges of data modified during a transaction and $N_{stores}$ represents the number of word-sized stores to persistent memory done by the user code in the transaction. Some techniques are capable of logging a contiguous range of data instead of single word-sized stores, thus implying that $N_{ranges} \leq N_{stores}$.

The columns respectively indicate: which log type each of the techniques utilizes; the amount of persistent memory (in words) that may be used during a transaction associated with the persistence of the log; the number of persistence fences (pfence and

| | Log type | Persistent memory used per transaction | Nb. pfence+psync per transaction | Interposition type | Write amplification |
|---|---|---|---|---|---|
| Vista [20] | undo | $3 \times N_{ranges}$ | n/a | stores | 300% |
| Atlas [4] | undo | $4 \times N_{ranges}$ | $2 + 3 \times N_{ranges}$ | stores | 400% |
| JustDo [16] | done-to-here | 3 words | $2 + 3 \times N_{stores}$ | stores | 400% |
| Mnemosyne [31] | redo | $8 \times N_{stores}$ | 4 or more | loads + stores | 300 – 600% |
| Romulus | volatile redo | n/a | 4 | stores | 100% |

**Table 1: Comparison of the main transactional persistence techniques.**

psync) needed per transaction; how many stores are done to persistence, taking into account the stores done by the user code; whether the technique needs to interpose only stores, or both loads and stores to persistent memory; and the write amplification factor for each of the techniques (see §3). Notice that JustDo is the only algorithm in the table that requires specialized hardware.

## 3 BACKGROUND AND CONCEPTS

We briefly overview in this section the main concepts and features of persistent memory, as well as programming models and tools to exploit it in software.

### 3.1 Persistent memory

Persistent storage has been so far mainly based on disk persistence, with data being persisted through the whole I/O stack of the operating system, involving costly user/kernel mode switches from read/write system calls and data copying between kernel space and user space [6]. Recent studies propose to exploit high-performance next-generation NVM storage [6] for memory mapped file I/O. Mapping a file onto user memory space with an mmap system call enables users to access the file directly in the same way as data on memory. This approach minimizes overhead and simplifies application development, even though it suffers from some limitations, such as dynamically resizing the file and the pre-defined memory region to which it is mapped. Access to these new types of persistent memory using the direct access (DAX) feature available in both Linux and Windows allows for a much finer granularity of persistence at the cache line level.

For a correct understanding of the concepts used in the paper, we refer to the definitions proposed by Izraelitz et al. and extensively described in [16]. Failures are events that may corrupt application data, for example application process crash or an abrupt failure of the machine. We distinguish from corrupting and non-corrupting failures: corrupting failures cause damage to data required for recovery, which prevents restoring a consistent state, whereas non-corrupting failures allow for the recovery procedure to complete. Data are persistent if after a non-corrupting failure are accessible by the recovery procedure. The same is true for persistent memory locations and persistent cache lines where data resides. A persistent memory region is a contiguous range of persistent memory locations, and it is not guaranteed to be in a consistent state after a failure. Data are in a consistent state if the relevant application-level correctness criteria hold. Hereafter, we use the term *failure* to simply refer to a non-corrupting failure.

Another concept, more performance related, is *write amplification* described in [23]. *Write amplification* is the number of additional bytes written to persistent memory for every byte of user data stored in persistent memory during a transaction. Additional bytes are incurred by the log, whether undo or redo, and the memory allocator's metadata.

### 3.2 Interposition of memory accesses

PTMs require at least the interposition of stores to persistent memory. This interposition is necessary to flush modified cache lines to persistence and, in the case of an undo log, to save the original data. Techniques with a redo log need the interposition of loads from persistent memory as well. This load interposition is required so as to have the latest modified data during a transaction. There are three different ways of achieving interposition: *manual* interposition by the user, *compiler* interposition, and *language* interposition.

With *manual* interposition, it is up to the user to explicitly call a method before a store is done to persistent memory. Techniques like Vista [20] and Atlas [4] use manual interposition of stores. As the user must identify where the stores to persistent memory are done in the code within the transaction, this approach is prone to errors and may yield non-recoverable transactions if the user misses some of the stores.

With *compiler* interposition, the compiler will insert a call to the PTM method responsible for handling stores and loads. This can be achieved by modifying the compiler or by extending an existing framework like gnu-tm in gcc. Mnemosyne [31] uses compiler interposition for stores and loads.

With *language* interposition, instrumentation of the stores or loads is done at the level of the programming language itself, typically through operator overloading. When using a language like C++ that supports operator overloading, one can trigger a method responsible for persistence management upon every access to a variable that has been annotated as persistent. This method can, for instance, save the original value in a log. We use this approach in our implementation of the algorithms shown in this paper. Except for rare cases, programs written in C can also be compiled with a C++ compiler and, therefore, provide the same functionality.

## 4 THE BASIC ALGORITHM

We first describe in this section the basic Romulus algorithm. We will then introduce additional variants that improve on the basic design and work around some of its performance limitations (§5). Proofs of correctness can be found in a companion technical report.

### 4.1 Model and assumptions

In the following description of Romulus, we rely on the C++ memory model [11]. As in [17], we assume that threads control the ordering and timing of persistence using three special instructions:

*(i)* a persist write-back (pwb) initiates write-back of a specified location to persistent memory, but does not block; *(ii)* a subsequent persist fence (pfence) enforces an ordering between previous and subsequent writes-back in the current thread; finally, *(iii)* a persist sync (psync) blocks until all preceding pfences in the current thread have become persistent. In the absence of fences, pwb instructions are allowed to reorder with respect to both ordinary and synchronization instructions. The implementation of each of these instructions on Intel and ARM processors is summarized in the following table:

| | NVM on x86 | | NVM on ARM |
|---|---|---|---|
| pwb | CLFLUSH | CLWB or CLFLUSHOPT | DC CVAC |
| pfence | nop | SFENCE | DSB |
| psync | nop | SFENCE | DSB |

We also use the persistent cache store order (*PCSO*) protocol [8] that guarantees that: *(i)* each pwb is ordered with respect to each preceding or subsequent pfence in its thread; and *(ii)* for any given thread and location, each pwb is ordered with respect to each preceding pwb of the same location in the same thread.

## 4.2 Principle and architecture

The design of Romulus has the objective of minimizing the number of persistent fences, knowing that this is a slow operation and represents a bottleneck of existing approaches. To achieve 4 persistent fences per transaction independent of the number of modified memory locations, Romulus uses twin copies of the data stored in persistent memory, so that at every point in time at least one of these copies is consistent. We name these two copies main and back (see Figure 1).

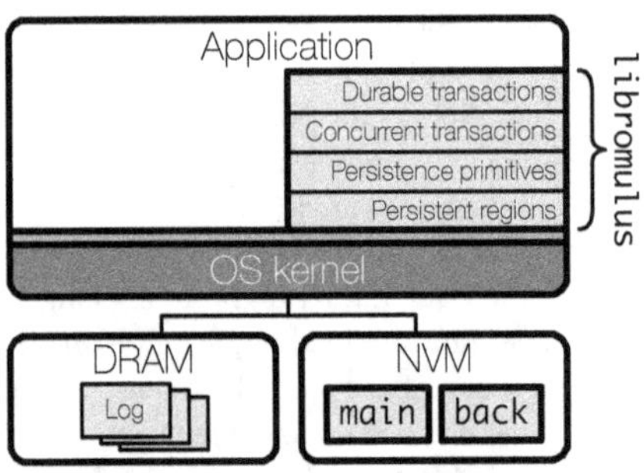


**Figure 1: Architecture of Romulus.**

The main region is where the user-code executes in-place modifications. At the end of a successful transaction, the modifications in main are copied over to back to bring it up-to-date. The back region is never accessed directly by the user-code and serves solely as a *backup* of the previous state of main. If the user code were to be allowed to access the back data, any pointer dereference would redirect to a memory location inside main.

In the event of a failure of the process that is mutating main, the recovery procedure will copy the contents of back over to main so as to revert any of the incomplete modifications done to main, thus restoring it to its previous consistent state. If a failure occurs during the copy from main to back, then the recovery procedure will copy the full contents of main to back.

Romulus follows a copy-on-write approach and will hence suffer from the associated performance issues when applied to large data sets. We will propose a variant of the algorithm to overcome these limitations in §5.

The architecture of Romulus is shown in Figure 1. The implementation of the algorithm and supporting libraries are entirely in user space, without any modification of the kernel. They are exposed to the application via a unified C/C++ library, libromulus, which provides support for durable and concurrent transactions, mediating all interactions with the NVM in a safe and consistent manner.

## 4.3 Data structures

The memory layout of Romulus is shown in Figure 2. The persistent memory area is separated into three regions: a persistent header (head) that is placed at the start of Romulus's persistent memory area, immediately followed by the main and back regions themselves.

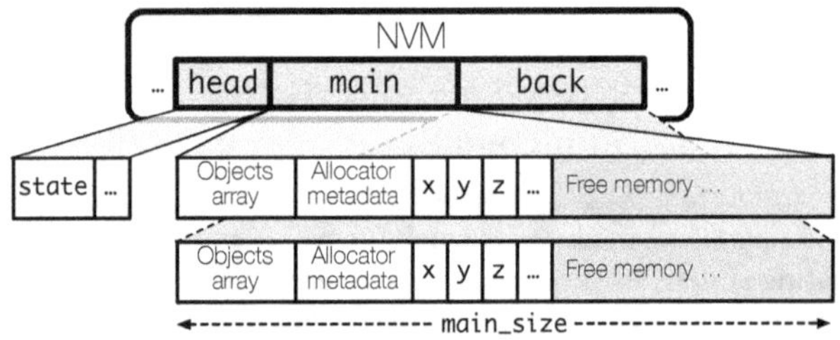


**Figure 2: Memory layout of Romulus.**

The persistent header holds medadata used to ensure consistency of persistent memory. It is initialized the first time a Romulus instance is created. The most important fields of the header are: *(i)* an atomic variable state that can take any of the three values indicating whether the current thread is executing outside a transaction (IDL), inside an active transaction (MUT), or immediately after the transaction has committed while modifications are being copied from main to back (CPY); *(ii)* a reference to the objects array—also designated as *root pointers*—maintained in the persistent memory region that allows user code to access persisted objects; *(iii)* a pointer to the metadata of the memory allocator, also maintained in the persistent memory region; *(iv)* the amount of bytes effectively used in the main region; *(v)* as well as internal variables to guarantee correct initialization of the header, maintain consistency of the data structure upon recovery, and perform bookkeeping operations.

As can be seen in Figure 2, the persistent header is not replicated to the back region, it is used to guarantee at initialization that the main region is in a valid consistent state before being accessed by user code. Furthermore, all the data present in the main region will be replicated at the end of the transaction, when calling end_transaction. The replication process is simply a raw copy of the bytes from the main to the back region. The back region is a snapshot of the previous consistent state of the main region and is never accessed directly by the user code. It does not contain a second copy of the objects present in the main region, but holds instead pointer values that refer to addresses in the main region.

## 4.4 Memory allocation and reclamation

One of the main challenges in designing and implementing transactional persistence is providing correct memory allocation and reclamation. Persistent transactions must recover from failures, even if those occur during memory management operations. For most PTMs described in the literature, a failure occurring while updating the allocator's metadata can lead to inconsistencies. These inconsistencies are categorized as *internal* or *external* with respect to the allocator [2]. Internal inconsistencies can often have disastrous consequences, such as failure to restart properly upon recovery, erroneous re-allocation of memory objects currently in use, or leakage of large chunks of memory. External inconsistencies can occur when a failure happens after a call to the allocator has returned a pointer to a newly allocated block, but before this pointer has been made persistent, thus causing memory leaks.

Previous PTMs in the literature [4, 20, 31] tend to ignore these issues, and for correctness they rely on specialized garbage collector like Makalu [2]. Mnemosyne deliberately accepts the possibility of leaking in the event of a failure for performance reasons [31]. None of the Romulus algorithms suffer from any of these issues and, therefore, can be used with any memory allocator.

The memory allocator used in our implementation is based in the sequential allocator designed by Doug Lea [19]. Both the memory allocator and `objects` refer to data structures that are placed in the persistent region and have to follow the same procedure as any other user code, where every store to a persistent data requires a subsequent `pwb`. This is achieved by wrapping all attributes of every data structure used by the memory allocator with the `persist` class. The `persist<T>` class is a wrapper that allows to interpose every access to the underlying data of type `T` that is meant to be persistent. Every mutative access to the underlying data has its update operation redefined inside of `persist`, where a call to `pwb` is done after executing the store on the persistent data. This technique, which is also used by PMDK [27], significantly reduces the amount of modifications when porting user code written for volatile memory, while not requiring a special compiler. We only had to modify 61 lines in the memory allocator's original code, and we expect that other standard sequential memory allocators can be just as easily adapted.

In our approach, allocating and reclaiming memory is itself part of the transaction, meaning that, in the event of a failure during a transaction, any modifications on the allocator's metadata will be rollbacked along with all modifications of user variables pertaining to that transaction.

**Algorithm 1** Basic Romulus algorithm.

```
void begin_transaction() {
    state.store(MUT, memory_order_relaxed);
    pwb(&state);
    pfence();
}

void end_transaction() {
    pfence();
    state.store(CPY, memory_order_relaxed);
    pwb(&state);
    psync();                 // Provide ACID durable modifications on 'main'
    copyMainToBack();                              // pwb() for each cache line
    pfence();                             // No need for durability on 'back'
    state.store(IDL, memory_order_relaxed);
}

void recover() {
    int lstate = state.load(memory_order_relaxed);
    if (lstate == IDL) return;
    if (lstate == CPY) {
        copyMainToBack();                          // pwb() for each cache line
    } else if (lstate == MUT) {
        copyBackToMain();                          // pwb() for each cache line
    }
    pfence();
    state.store(IDL, memory_order_relaxed);
}
```

## 4.5 The Romulus algorithm

Romulus provides a persistent transactional memory interface, shown in Algorithm 1, with two main methods `begin_transaction` and `end_transaction` surrounding critical sections of user code accessing persistent data. The transaction provides consistency for the persisted data modified within the critical section. The consistency of the data relies on the `state` variable that indicates in what stage the transaction is. Upon start, a transaction changes the state from `IDL` to `MUT` indicating it is in progress. Thereafter, every access to persistent data from the transaction's user code is instrumented using language interposition, in particular every modification triggers a call to `pwb` for the modified cache line. Once the user code has completed its execution, `end_transaction` updates the state from `MUT` to `CPY` indicating the transaction has already committed to persistent memory, but modifications are still being propagated to the `back` region. The `back` region serves as a consistent state for the next transaction in case a failure occurs during execution of the user code. Finally, state reverts to `IDL` after the transaction has ended.

In the event of a failure, the `recover` method is called upon restart to restore the persistent memory to a consistent state. The `state` variable indicates which of the `main` or `back` region is in a consistent state: when `IDL`, both regions are consistent; when `MUT`, the `back` region is consistent; and finally when `CPY`, the `main` region is consistent. Once the restore method has completed, both the `main` and `back` regions are in a consistent state, with `back` containing an exact byte per byte copy of `main`.

## 4.6 Romulus API

To illustrate the programming interface of Romulus, we provide in Algorithm 2 sample code for a persistent set implemented as a sorted single linked list. Every data structure that must be persisted by Romulus has to be wrapped within the `persist<T>` class; this ensures transparent interposition of accesses to its attributes.

Algorithm 3 illustrates how one can instantiate and invoke persistent objects with Romulus. The linked list must first be created and stored in the persistent memory region (lines 2–8). Thereafter it can be accessed using regular method invocations, with transparent interposition ensuring data persistence and consistency (lines 10–13). Finally, the list is deallocated and removed from persistent memory (lines 15–21). All three steps are wrapped within independent Romulus transactions.

**Algorithm 2** Romulus-based linked list.

```
struct Node {
  persist<K> key;                          // All node attributes are persisted
  persist<Node *> next;
  Node(const K& key) : key { key }, next{ nullptr } {}
};
persist<Node *> head { nullptr };          // Head and tail are also persisted
persist<Node *> tail { nullptr };

void find(const K& key, Node*& prev, Node*& node) {
  for (prev = head; (node = prev->next) != tail; prev = node) {
    if (node->key >= key) break;
  }
}

bool contains(const K& key) {
  bool found = false;
  Romulus::read_transaction([&] () {       // Read-only transaction
    Node *prev, *node;
    find(key, prev, node);
    found = (node != tail && node->key == key);
  });
  return found;
}

bool add(const K& key) {
  bool added = false;
  Romulus::update_transaction([&] () {     // Update transaction
    Node *prev, *node;
    find(key, prev, node);
    added = !(node != tail && key == node->key);
    if (!added) return;
    Node *n = Romulus::alloc<Node>(key);
    prev->next = n;
    n->next = node;
  });
  return added;
}
```

**Algorithm 3** Using Romulus-based linked list.

```
LinkedListSet<int> *set;
Romulus::begin_transaction();              // Allocate list in NVM
set = Romulus::get_object<LinkedListSet<int>>(0);
if (set == nullptr) {
  set = Romulus::alloc<LinkedListSet<int>>();
  Romulus::put_object(0, set);
}
Romulus::end_transaction();

Romulus::begin_transaction();              // Invoke operations on list
set->add(33);
assert(set->contains(33));
Romulus::end_transaction();

Romulus::begin_transaction();              // Deallocate list from NVM
set = Romulus::get_object<LinkedListSet<int>>(0);
if (set != nullptr) {
  Romulus::free(set);
  Romulus::put_object(0, nullptr);
}
Romulus::end_transaction();
```

### 4.7 Log optimization

One of the main drawbacks of Romulus, which is shared with other copy-on-write designs, is that it must copy the whole data from `main` to `back` on each transaction. While simplifying the algorithm, this approach inevitably reduces throughput and wastes resources by repeatedly copying many unchanged bytes. Furthermore, the performance penalty increases as the size of `main` grows and the length of transactions decrease.

To address this issue, we incorporate a logging technique into Romulus, where all persistent stores inside a transaction are logged for later replication to `back`. The redo log keeps the memory locations that are being modified by the current transaction. At the end of the transaction, only these memory locations are copied from `main` to `back` rather than the whole persistent region. The log is not required for consistency since, in the event of a failure, the recovery procedure can simply use the same strategy as Romulus (see algorithm 1). Therefore, the log is not stored in persistent memory, residing in faster volatile memory for optimized performance.

With the log optimization, every store done by the user code is interposed and an entry is added to the log, followed by the in-place modification on `main` and the final `pwb` instruction. The order of these three steps is not important as long as the `pwb` is done *after* the in-place modification on `main`.

Unlike other log-based approaches in the literature, Romulus log stores only the addresses and ranges of modified data, but not the actual data. Furthermore, whereas other techniques that rely on persistent logs suffer from high *write amplification* because each byte written to persistent memory causes several additional bytes to be persisted to the log, Romulus's persistent writes are limited to the replication of the `back` region. Another advantage is that, since the log resides in volatile memory, its size does not need to be fixed beforehand. In our implementation, we simply use a dynamic array of address/range pairs (pseudo-code omitted for space considerations).

## 5 ALGORITHM EXTENSIONS

We describe in this section extensions of the basic Romulus algorithm, focusing in particular on the efficient support of concurrent transactions. These extensions leverage scalable synchronization mechanisms for achieving good performance even when many threads contend on shared persistent data structures.

### 5.1 Concurrent transactions

Similarly to most other persistent memory frameworks (e.g., Vista [20], Atlas [4], JustDo [16] and PMDK [27]), Romulus provides durable transactions for single-threaded applications. Support for concurrency in such settings can be as simple as using mutual exclusion locks—typically a single global lock—to embed transactions within critical sections and serialize them. Mnemosyne [31] allows concurrent transactions by leveraging a software transactional memory (STM) library based on TinySTM [25]. NV-Heaps [7] embeds its own lock-based STM.

The global lock approach has the advantage to be simple to implement and reason about, but it does not scale well. On the other hand, the STM approach has the drawback of being tightly coupled with the underlying transactional memory mechanisms and capabilities, and that the price of concurrent synchronization must be paid for every transaction even in single-threaded applications.

Our approach is to provide two different APIs, one for concurrent usage in multi-threaded applications, and another one for single-threaded applications. We have developed two different concurrency mechanisms for Romulus, as described next. Each of these mechanisms provides two types of concurrent transactions, *update* and *read-only* transactions, which are both "irrevocable", i.e., they never need to abort and restart. Read-only transactions are by their very nature *disjoint-access parallel*, which theoretically allows them to scale.

## 5.2 C-RW-WP synchronization

Our first concurrency approach uses flat combining [12, 14], essentially replacing the mutual exclusion lock with a C-RW-WP reader-writer lock [3]. With flat combining, multiple update transactions can be aggregated and processed with a single lock acquisition and release. An update transaction first announces itself in the flat combining array by registering a pointer to its actual code. Thereafter, the C-RW-WP algorithm acquires the lock, traverses the array, executes all registered transactions, and finally releases the lock.

In our C-RW-WP implementation we replace the cohort lock by a simpler spin-lock, but thanks to the flat combining technique starvation-free progress [15] is still guaranteed for update transactions. We implement the C-RW-WP lock's "read indicator" as an array where each entry is statically assigned to a thread and extends over two cache lines, so as to avoid false sharing; this ensures low contention, and consequently low overhead and high scalability for read-only transactions. The coupling of flat combining with C-RW-WP is a novel approach which takes the best of both techniques, providing scalable read-only transactions and starvation-free update transactions.

All the variables used in the implementation of the C-RW-WP lock are stored in volatile memory, even though the lock protects data that may be persistent. A reader-writer lock grants exclusive access to a single writer. To guarantee *durable linearizability* [18], all modifications to persistent memory must be completely persisted before the lock is released by the writer, with their effects visible to other threads. In addition, reader-writer locks provide linearizability, only allowing visibility of operation effects to other threads after the release of the exclusive lock. As for other writer threads that have published their operations on the flat combine array, visibility and durability is guaranteed as soon as an operation is marked as executed by flushing the associated cache line and resetting its entry in the array (refer to actual code in [10] for implementation details). This approach provides complete separation between durability and linearizability: it allows the actual synchronization to *not* be persisted and avoids extra persistence fences that could adversely impact the performance of readers. No persistence fence is required for shared-lock acquisition.

## 5.3 Left-right synchronization

Romulus requires two persistent copies of the data to guarantee consistent recovery. The existence of these two copies makes it a natural fit for integration with the left-right (LR) [24] synchronization primitive. LR is a universal construct that provides wait-free population-oblivious progress for read-only operations, and blocking starvation-free progress for update operations. The integration of LR with Romulus creates the first persistent universal construct with partial non-blocking progress. Any user application will not only have durable linearizable transactions, but read-only transactions will also automatically profit from the scalability and low latency provided by wait-free population-oblivious progress.

The LR concurrency control technique is based on two replicas of the same data and allows an unlimited number of readers to access one instance, while a single writer modifies the other instance. This synchronization mechanism can be summarily described as follows, where the two instances of the data are referred as *left* and *right*. The synchronization is achieved using a control variable indicating to readers which of the two copies to access. The writer starts by modifying the *right* instance, whereas the *left* instance is attributed to the readers. Once the writer completes the modification, the control variable is changed and new readers will read from the *right* instance. The writer then waits for the completion of all the readers still running on the *left* instance and finally repeats its modification on the *left* instance, bringing both instances up-to-date. It is hence up to the writer to ensure that readers are always running on the instance that is not being modified.

This approach has some similarities with the basic Romulus algorithm, yet with one significant difference: for LR to work correctly both regions must be traversable by the read-only operations, whereas in Romulus only the `main` region can be traversed. Any attempt to traverse data in `back` will re-direct to memory locations in `main`, given that all pointers refer to objects within the `main`'s memory range. In other words, the two instances are *shallow* copies in LR while they are *byte-per-byte* copies in Romulus. Fortunately, we can overcome this limitation through the use of *synthetic pointers*.

Read-only traversals of the `back` instance are done with interposition of loads, such that an offset is added on every variable access. This offset is equal to the size of the `main` memory region, so as to create a synthetic pointer that refers to the equivalent memory location within `back` (see Figure 3). During a transaction, we use a thread-local variable to indicate to the load-interposing method which of the instances to use and adjust the offset appropriately. This synthetic pointer approach allows us to use an efficient raw memory copy operation at the end of transactions or during recovery, without the need to perform shallow copying.

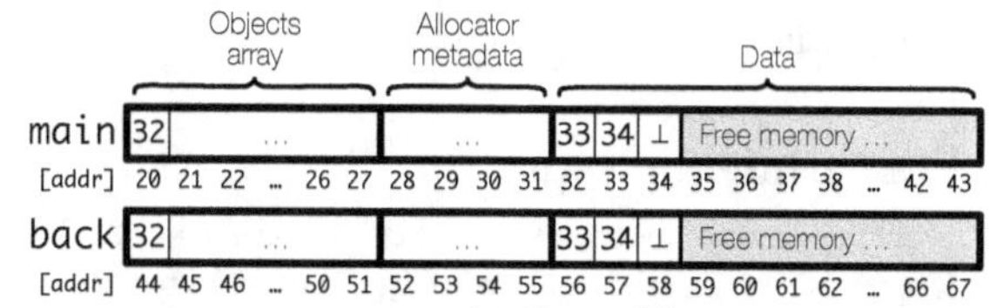


**Figure 3: Memory layout of RomulusLR for a minimal example of linked list with three nodes and values 32, 33, 34.**

Figure 3 shows an example of the memory layout with RomulusLR. In this specific example, each load instruction executed in the back region will be adjusted with an offset of 24 bytes added to references from the main region; for instance, address 32 + 24 = 56 refers to the head of the linked list. This transformation allows readers to always access data on the back region when they operate on that region.

Some adaptations to LR were also necessary for update transactions. While in the original LR algorithm writers can start execution on any of the two instances, in RomulusLR the control variable is toggled twice during an update transaction. This guarantees that update transactions always start execution on the `main` region and greatly simplifies the implementation because the memory allocator can operate on just the `main` region.

The integration of LR with Romulus requires that readers can only access the `main` region after it is guaranteed that all updates to that region are persisted by calling psync (see algorithm 1). Thereafter, accesses to the main region are durable linearizable and, in the event of a failure, the recovery method will complete the transaction by copying the entire `main` region to the back region. From this moment on, the effects of the current update transaction can be made visible and the control variable is changed so that new readers can start executing on the `main` region.

For both concurrent solutions proposed, there is always a single writer executing an update transaction that aggregates all mutations previously published by other writer threads in the flat combining array. All mutations are hence serialized and performed by a single writer. This approach minimizes lock acquisition and conflicts while providing starvation freedom for update operations. It is also less prone to cache line bouncing and generates less cache coherence traffic while maintaining cache locality for larger update transactions. Furthermore, the average number of persistent fences per mutation can be smaller than 4 because several updates are aggregated within a single update transaction. Regarding memory allocation, providing exclusive access to a single writer thread allows Romulus implementations to directly leverage state-of-the-art sequential memory allocators.

In the rest of the paper, Romulus refers to the basic algorithm with concurrent accesses synchronized using C-RW-WP; RomulusLog denotes the basic algorithm with volatile log optimization and C-RW-WP; and finally RomulusLR corresponds to the basic algorithm with volatile log optimization and LR synchronization.

# 6 EVALUATION

We present in this section a detailed evaluation of Romulus and compare it against other state-of-the-art techniques using both synthetic benchmarks and real-world applications.

## 6.1 Experimental setup

Our microbenchmarks were executed on a dual-socket 2.10 GHz Intel Xeon E5-2683 ("Broadwell") with a total of 32 hyper-threaded cores (64 HW threads), running Ubuntu LTS and using gcc 7.2 with the `-O3` optimization flag. The CPU does not support the CLFLUSHOPT and CLWB instructions and, therefore, we implement pwb with the CLFLUSH instruction and map the `pfence` and psync operations to NOP.

We compare Romulus against Mnemosyne [31] and PMDK [27] as they are considered to be the most generic and efficient approaches, they are representative of different designs (respectively redo and undo log), and their code is freely available. Mnemosyne was compiled using the latest available version on github (commit 855f452), which requires compilation with the `-O0` flag. As for PMDK, we use the latest `libpmemobj` from github (commit f697c52) executed with the environment variable `PMEM_IS_PMEM_FORCE=1`. Since PMDK does not provide built-in support for concurrent transactions, in our evaluation we protect concurrent accesses with a standard reader-writer lock (`std::shared_timed_mutex`) with reader preference. We rely on a memory-mapped file located in the `/dev/shm/` folder for all implementations.

Unless otherwise noted, our evaluations use DRAM to mimic systems that implement persistent memory using supercapacitor-backed DRAM (e.g., Viking NVDIMMs [28] or HPE NVDIMMs [29]), and no artificial delays are added. The data points labeled STT emulate STT-RAM persistent memory, with delays of 140, 200 and 200 ns respectively injected for each pwb, `pfence` and psync [5]. Data points labeled PCM emulate PCM-RAM, with delays of 340, 500 and 500 ns respectively injected for each pwb, `pfence` and psync. Similarly to Mnemosyne, delays are measured using `rdtsc` and no delays are added for loads from persistent memory. Each data point is the median of 5 runs with each run executing for 20 seconds, unless otherwise noted in the figure.

## 6.2 Data structures

Application data is typically stored in complex structures, such as a hash map or a tree, and therefore our benchmarks cover multiple data structures. We conduct evaluations on a linked list, a resizable hash map and a red-black tree, as representative examples of structures used by real-world applications to store data. Figure 4 shows throughput for update-only and read-only workloads (note the logarithmic scales) with data structures holding 1,000 entries.[1] An update operation is composed of two consecutive transactions, a removal followed by an insertion whereas a read operation is composed of two consecutive read-only transactions, each executes a search for an existing random key.

Looking at the performance of these data structures, we observe that the linked list has higher throughput than the red-back tree. This can be explained by the small size of the data structures and the fact that the linked list performs on average fewer stores, and hence fewer costly accesses to persistent memory. Further investigation shows that the linked list executes an average of 10 pwb instructions, while the red-black tree has a more disperse histogram, with two peaks at 50 and 130 pwbs per transaction. Another interesting finding is that most of the stores inside transactions are triggered by the memory allocator. RomulusLog performs generally at least 4× better than Mnemosyne thanks to its lower write amplification and lighter synchronization mechanism.

PMDK performs better than would be expected from an undo-log based technique, but one should keep in mind that the tests were conducted on a machine only supporting the CLFLUSH instruction. In this case, all the extra persistence fences that would be necessary to implement an undo log are omitted, because the CLFLUSH instructions already guarantee strict ordering between themselves. On a machine that provides solely CLFLUSH, performance is therefore mainly dominated by the number of pwb instructions per transaction. After investigation, it turns out that Romulus and PMDK

[1] This is the limit beyond which Mnemosyne starts becoming unstable and exhibits random crashes. In addition, Mnemosyne only support up to 31 threads and hence samples are missing beyond this point in scalability tests. We have been in touch with the authors to work around these limitations but did not manage to completely solve them for our experiments.

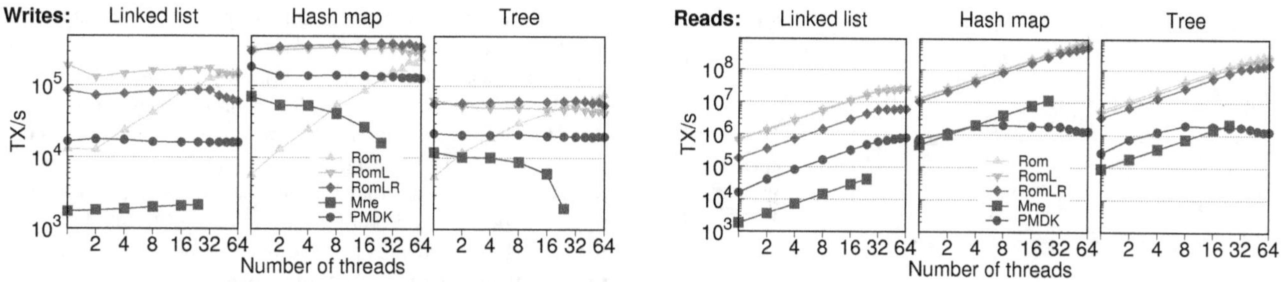


**Figure 4: Update (left) and read (right) operations on various data structures (Mnemosyne data points are one run of 20 s).**

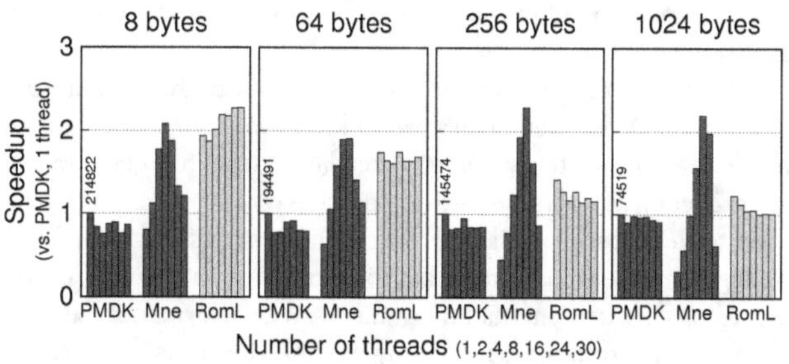


**Figure 5: Speedup of a hash map with 100 entries relative to single-treaded throughput of PMDK. Mnemosyne data points correspond to 1 run of 20s.**

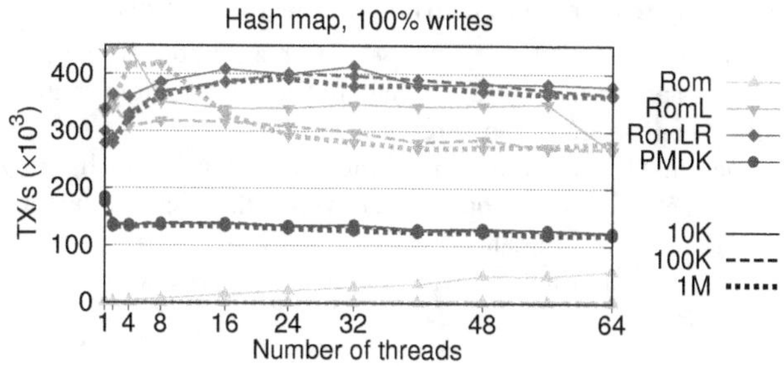


**Figure 6: Hash map with varying numbers of keys and threads executing update-only operations.**

execute a similar number of pwb instructions. The memory allocator of PMDK for the hash map issues only one CLFLUSH to allocate memory and one when memory is freed, for a total of 11 CLFLUSH instructions per transaction. This demonstrates that PMDK's memory allocator is highly optimized for small allocations and offers room for improvement for Romulus, which uses a much less efficient allocator. Even so, in update scenarios with small sized transactions, RomulusLog still provides the best results with at least twice the performance of PMDK.

As expected, read-only transactions represent a good example of workload for which Romulus excels. The throughput of Romulus is 10× to 400× higher than PMDK, while compared with Mnemosyne it is 25× to 50× higher. Indeed, read-only operations can be done in-place, either directly in main memory or more likely within the cache. Furthermore, the reader-writer lock and LR concurrency mechanism provide excellent performance and scalability with read-mostly workloads.

We were intrigued to find out that Mnemosyne's performance degraded on the hash map when increasing the number of threads, since the performance evaluation of the original paper exhibits good scalability. Therefore, in order to better reproduce these results, we have developed a second hash map implementation with a fixed number of 2,048 buckets. As one can observe in Figure 5, the throughput becomes much better for such a statically-dimensioned hash map. This difference can be explained as follows. On the one hand, Mnemosyne supports concurrent access using TinySTM, a software transactional memory that relies on fine grain locking to allow multiple threads executing disjoint transactions to progress. On the other hand, the implementation of our resizable hash map relies on a shared counter to keep track of the number of elements and determine when to resize. Modifications to the counter upon every update operation (insertion or removal) will generate contention and trigger conflicts, which in turn will cause transactions to abort and eventually hamper scalability. The Romulus implementations do not suffer from this issue as they rely on simpler synchronization primitives and transactions never abort.

We also evaluated scalability to larger data structures up to one million entries with update-only workloads.[2] The results, shown in Figure 6, do not differ much from those presented earlier for 1,000 entries and highlight that almost all implementations can support large data structures without performance penalty. As expected, the only exception is the basic Romulus algorithm, which suffers from the data size due to the longer copy procedure necessary to keep the back region up to date.

As previously mentioned, we also emulated STT-RAM persistent memory by injecting a delay for every instruction to persistent memory. Performance results, which are omitted because of space constraints, are highly similar to those shown in Figure 4. We believe this is due to the limited number of persistent stores per transaction and the fact that CLFLUSH is a costly instruction as compared to CLFLUSHOPT and CLWB, which are available on more recent processors. Note that our emulation only affects the throughput of update operations because load instructions have no added delay.

## 6.3 Read-dominated workloads

Figure 7 shows the number of transactions per second for the hash map data structure as the number of concurrent reader threads increases. A logarithmic scale is used for both axes. The left graph shows the number of read- and update-only transactions with 2 concurrent writer threads and an increasing number of reader threads, while the right graph has no writer thread and only runs read-only

[2] Mnemosyne is omitted as the publicly available implementation does not support allocation of sufficiently large amounts of data.

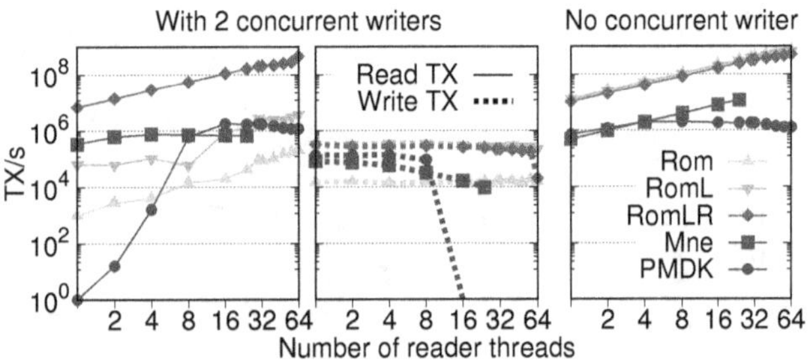


**Figure 7: Read operations with 2 concurrent writers (left) and no writer (right) on a hash map with 1,000 entries. Mnemosyne data points correspond to 1 run of 20s.**

transactions. Note that PMDK uses an unfair reader-writer lock that gives preference to readers and prevents writers from running with 16 concurrent reader threads or more.

RomulusLR is the only one of the tested techniques that provides scalability for read operations, even with concurrent update operations. This is possible thanks to the use of the left-right concurrency mechanism that provides wait-free progress for read-only transactions.

## 6.4 RomulusDB

Our three PTMs provide durable concurrent transactions with ACID properties (atomicity, consistency, isolation, durability) and durable linearizability when executed in concurrent settings. These PTMs can be straightforwardly applied to any sequential implementation of a *map* data structure and use it to construct a key-value store with persistence. We used RomulusLog to wrap a hash map and implement the same interface as the popular LevelDB [13] database. We named our persistent key-value store RomulusDB.

Unlike LevelDB, RomulusDB is capable of executing real transactions, with durability ensured for every transaction. By default, update operations in LevelDB are not immediately durable—unless the option `WriteOptions.sync` is enabled—which implies that in the event of a non-corrupting failure, a possibly large amount of recently completed operations may be lost. Furthermore, LevelDB does not provide transactional semantics, but provides instead the simpler model of *write batches.*

LevelDB benchmarks utilize 16-byte keys and 100-byte values. The `fillseq` benchmark measures the time for a thread to insert one million distinct key-value pairs in the database, using sequential keys. The `fillrandom` benchmark performs one million insertions of random keys per thread (note that existing key-value pairs may be overwritten because of the randomness). The `overwrite` benchmark is similar to `fillrandom` but starts from a pre-populated database. The `fillsync` benchmark measures the time to insert 1,000 key-value pairs in a database, with durability enforced by enabling the `WriteOptions.sync` option. `readseq` and `readreverse` do a single read-only iteration over the entire database.

Results are shown in Figure 8. For read-only operations RomulusDB performs extremely well independently of the read pattern (sequential or reverse). Indeed, the traversal order has no effect because the random accesses to a hash map have no particular extra cost. RomulusDB scales linearly with the number of threads for read operations, with an operation execution time remaining constant when increasing the number of threads. It outperforms LevelDB in all of the read benchmarks.

As for update operations, the only truly comparable benchmark is `fillsync` as it provides durable transactions on both systems. With LevelDB, enforcing durable transactions triggers execution of `fdatasync` on every transaction, which brings a huge penalty to key-value databases that rely on disk persistence. For the other update benchmarks, RomulusDB can be up to 50% slower than LevelDB, but it provides durable transactions whereas LevelDB flushes updates to disk approximately every 1,000 kB, hence providing a weaker consistency guarantee referred to in the literature as *buffered durability*. The measured number of `fdatasync` system calls per thread execution was less than 100 for one million insertions of 116-byte objects.

Finally, the `fill-100k` benchmark measures the time it takes to write 1,000 key-value pairs of 100 kB. LevelDB executes around 100 `fdatasync` system calls per thread execution for 1,000 transactions. In contrast, Romulus already persists on every transaction but executes less costly persistence fences instructions and can take advantage of large transaction sizes to aggregate writes and flush full cache lines, hence demonstrating impressive performance. LevelDB transaction throughput is 3× slower than RomulusDB in single-thread execution, as the number of threads increases, performance degrades even more to reach a factor of 25× for 64 threads.

## 6.5 Recovery cost

Recovery is a lengthy procedure that requires copying data from `main` to `back` or vice versa. Yet, because Romulus can copy only the region up to the last allocated object, the costs actually depend on the size of the data structures stored in persistent memory. Measurements on our machine for a hash map show that the recovery method takes about 114 $\mu s$ for 1,000 key-values and 127 ms for 1,000,000 key-value pairs. Recovering an entire 1 GB region takes around 1 second. This value grows linearly with the size of the persistent memory region, with the largest source of overhead being the `pwb` calls (measurements were done using `CLFLUSH`).

## 6.6 Overhead of different fences

To better study the cost of fences, we execute the simple SPS microbenchmark regularly used in the literature [7, 21, 22] that stores a large array of integers in PM and randomly swap some of its values. This benchmark allows us to understand the performance profile of each PTM under different transaction sizes. Each swap exchanges the values of two randomly selected entries of an array of 10,000 64-bit integers, hence modifying two memory words in PM.

Figure 9 shows the number of *swaps* executed per second as a function of the transaction size (logarithmic scale), with a single-threaded application running on a C5 compute-intensive instance of AWS supporting the `CLWB` instruction. The five plots represent different choices of fence implementations and/or delay injection: *(i)* `pwb` is mapped to a `CLWB` and `pfence/psync` to `SFENCE`; *(ii)* `pwb` is mapped to a `CLFLUSHOPT` and `pfence/psync` to a `SFENCE`; *(iii)* `pwb` is mapped to a `CLFLUSH` and `pfence/psync` to a nop; *(iv)* `pwb` is mapped to a delay of 140 ns and `pfence/psync` to a delay of 200 ns, so as to simulate STT-RAM; and *(v)* `pwb` is mapped to a delay of 340 ns and `pfence/psync` to a delay of 500 ns, so as to simulate

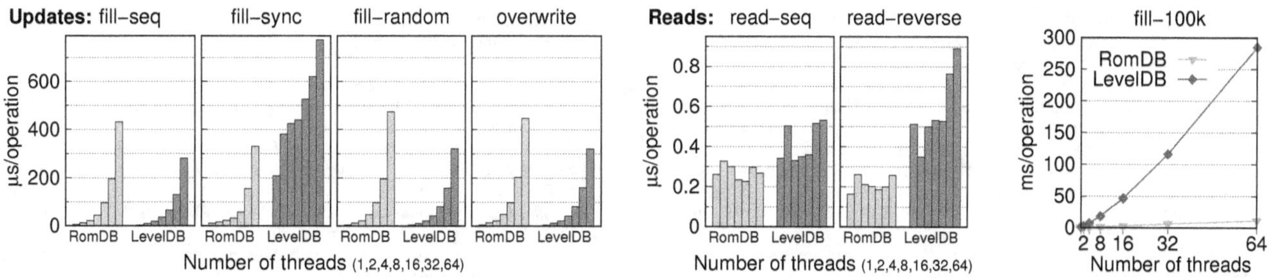


**Figure 8: One run of LevelDB benchmark with update (left) and read (center) operations, as well as with sequences of update operations (right).**

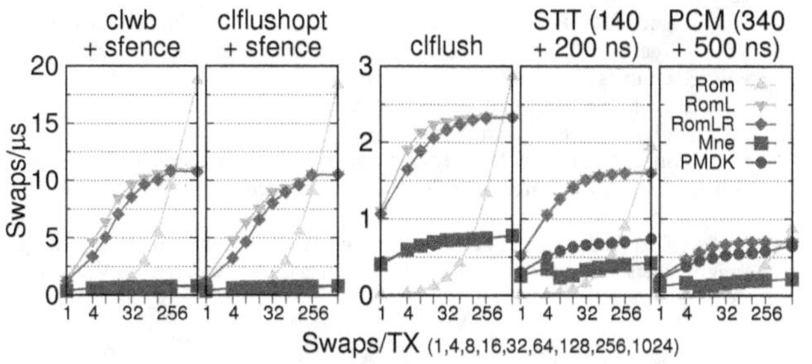


**Figure 9: SPS benchmark with varying transaction size for different types of fences. All data points correspond to 1 run of 20s.**

PCM-RAM. The timings for the injected delays were taken from previous work [5].

There is no memory allocation or de-allocation during execution of the SPS benchmark because it consists of swapping integers on an array. This allows us to examine the throughput of each algorithm, without being affected by the implementation of the NVM memory allocator specific to each PTM.

As observed previously, thanks to their small number of persistence fences and low synchronization overhead, the RomulusLog and RomulusLR perform best on all workloads except for high transaction sizes (1,024 swaps per transaction), where making a copy of the entire array becomes advantageous enough for Romulus to overtake them. When running short transactions, the pwbs constitute the main bottleneck of RomulusLog and RomulusLR and, as their cost increases, the difference between these two approaches and Mnemosyne or PMDK diminishes. This benchmark highlights that, when using the `CLWB` instruction instead of a more expensive `CLFLUSH`, the gains of Romulus over other approaches becomes even more important.

## 7 CONCLUSION

Romulus provides consistent recovery of persistent application data from non-corrupting failures. Persistent transactions in Romulus do not distinguish memory allocator metadata from user-defined application data. Any modification during a transaction will only be durable if the `main` region is left in a consistent state, otherwise the recovery procedure will revert to the consistent state at the start of the transaction. This approach, eliminates all issues inherent to NVM memory allocators, such as memory leaks and allocator metadata corruption.

Concurrent transactions in Romulus are durable linearizable. The two synchronization mechanisms integrated into Romulus, C-RW-WP and left-right, have low overhead. Read transactions require a single store-load fence and their announcement mechanism allows uncontended execution. Consequently, reader throughput scales linearly with the number of threads. Moreover, RomulusLR is the first PTM to provide wait-free progress for read-only transactions.

The low synchronization overhead, combined with a reduced number of persistence fences and low write amplification, contributes to the overall performance gains when compared with other solutions. Ultimately, our evaluation reveals that Romulus achieves twice the throughput of current state of the art PTMs in update-only workloads, and more than one order of magnitude in read-mostly scenarios.

## ACKNOWLEDGMENTS

This work is supported in part by the Swiss National Science Foundation (SNSF) under project number 200021-178822/1.

## REFERENCES


[1] Joy Arulraj, Andrew Pavlo, and Subramanya R Dulloor. 2015. Let's talk about storage & recovery methods for non-volatile memory database systems. In *Proceedings of the 2015 ACM SIGMOD International Conference on Management of Data*. ACM, 707–722.

[2] Kumud Bhandari, Dhruva R Chakrabarti, and Hans-J Boehm. 2016. Makalu: Fast recoverable allocation of non-volatile memory. In *Proceedings of the 2016 ACM SIGPLAN International Conference on Object-Oriented Programming, Systems, Languages, and Applications*. ACM, 677–694.

[3] Irina Calciu, Dave Dice, Yossi Lev, Victor Luchangco, Virendra J Marathe, and Nir Shavit. 2013. NUMA-aware reader-writer locks. In *ACM SIGPLAN Notices*, Vol. 48. ACM, 157–166.

[4] Dhruva R Chakrabarti, Hans-J Boehm, and Kumud Bhandari. 2014. Atlas: Leveraging locks for non-volatile memory consistency. *ACM SIGPLAN Notices* 49, 10 (2014), 433–452.

[5] Himanshu Chauhan, Irina Calciu, Vijay Chidambaram, Eric Schkufza, Onur Mutlu, and Pratap Subrahmanyam. 2016. NVMOVE: Helping Programmers Move to Byte-Based Persistence.. In *INFLOW@ OSDI*.

[6] Jungsik Choi, Jiwon Kim, and Hwansoo Han. 2017. Efficient Memory Mapped File I/O for In-Memory File Systems. In *9th USENIX Workshop on Hot Topics in Storage and File Systems (HotStorage 17)*. USENIX Association.

[7] Joel Coburn, Adrian M Caulfield, Ameen Akel, Laura M Grupp, Rajesh K Gupta, Ranjit Jhala, and Steven Swanson. 2011. NV-Heaps: making persistent objects fast and safe with next-generation, non-volatile memories. *ACM Sigplan Notices* 46, 3 (2011), 105–118.

[8] Nachshon Cohen, Michal Friedman, and James R Larus. 2017. Efficient logging in non-volatile memory by exploiting coherency protocols. *Proceedings of the ACM on Programming Languages* 1, OOPSLA (2017), 67.

[9] Jeremy Condit, Edmund B Nightingale, Christopher Frost, Engin Ipek, Benjamin Lee, Doug Burger, and Derrick Coetzee. 2009. Better I/O through byte-addressable, persistent memory. In *Proceedings of the ACM SIGOPS 22nd symposium on Operating systems principles*. ACM, 133–146.

[10] Andreia Correia, Pascal Felber, and Pedro Ramalhete. 2018. Romulus github. https://github.com/pramalhe/Romulus. (2018).
[11] CPP-ISO-committee. 2013. C++ Memory Order. http://en.cppreference.com/w/c/atomic/memory_order. (2013).
[12] Dave Dice, Virendra J Marathe, and Nir Shavit. 2011. Flat-combining NUMA locks. In *Proceedings of the twenty-third annual ACM symposium on Parallelism in algorithms and architectures.* ACM, 65–74.
[13] Sanjay Ghemawat and Jeff Dean. 2011. LevelDB. *URL: https://github. com/-google/leveldb,% 20http://leveldb. org* (2011).
[14] Danny Hendler, Itai Incze, Nir Shavit, and Moran Tzafrir. 2010. Flat combining and the synchronization-parallelism tradeoff. In *Proceedings of the twenty-second annual ACM symposium on Parallelism in algorithms and architectures.* ACM, 355–364.
[15] Maurice Herlihy and Nir Shavit. 2011. *The art of multiprocessor programming.* Morgan Kaufmann.
[16] Joseph Izraelevitz, Terence Kelly, and Aasheesh Kolli. 2016. Failure-atomic persistent memory updates via JUSTDO logging. In *ACM SIGPLAN Notices*, Vol. 51. ACM, 427–442.
[17] Joseph Izraelevitz, Hammurabi Mendes, and Michael L Scott. 2016. Brief Announcement: Preserving Happens-before in Persistent Memory. In *Proceedings of the 28th ACM Symposium on Parallelism in Algorithms and Architectures.* ACM, 157–159.
[18] Joseph Izraelevitz, Hammurabi Mendes, and Michael L Scott. 2016. Linearizability of persistent memory objects under a full-system-crash failure model. In *International Symposium on Distributed Computing.* Springer, 313–327.
[19] Doug Lea and Wolfram Gloger. 1996. A memory allocator. (1996).
[20] David E Lowell and Peter M Chen. 1997. Free transactions with rio vista. In *ACM SIGOPS Operating Systems Review*, Vol. 31. ACM, 92–101.
[21] Youyou Lu, Jiwu Shu, and Long Sun. 2015. Blurred persistence in transactional persistent memory. In *Mass Storage Systems and Technologies (MSST), 2015 31st Symposium on.* IEEE, 1–13.
[22] Youyou Lu, Jiwu Shu, Long Sun, and Onur Mutlu. 2014. Loose-ordering consistency for persistent memory. In *Computer Design (ICCD), 2014 32nd IEEE International Conference on.* IEEE, 216–223.
[23] Sanketh Nalli, Swapnil Haria, Mark D Hill, Michael M Swift, Haris Volos, and Kimberly Keeton. 2017. An Analysis of Persistent Memory Use with WHISPER. In *Proceedings of the Twenty-Second International Conference on Architectural Support for Programming Languages and Operating Systems.* ACM, 135–148.
[24] Pedro Ramalhete and Andreia Correia. 2015. Brief Announcement: Left-Right-A Concurrency Control Technique with Wait-Free Population Oblivious Reads. *Distributed* (2015), 663.
[25] T Riegel, P Felber, and C Fetzer. 2010. TinySTM. (2010).
[26] David Schwalb, Markus Dreseler, Matthias Uflacker, and Hasso Plattner. 2015. NVC-hashmap: A persistent and concurrent hashmap for non-volatile memories. In *Proceedings of the 3rd VLDB Workshop on In-Memory Data Mangement and Analytics.* ACM, 4.
[27] Pmem team. 2017. Persistent Memory Programming. http://pmem.io. (2017).
[28] Viking Technology. 2017. Persistent Memory Technologies. http://www.vikingtechnology.com/products/nvdimm/. (2017).
[29] Viking Technology. 2017. Persistent Memory Technologies. http://www.vikingtechnology.com/products/nvdimm/. (2017).
[30] Shivaram Venkataraman, Niraj Tolia, Parthasarathy Ranganathan, Roy H Campbell, et al. 2011. Consistent and Durable Data Structures for Non-Volatile Byte-Addressable Memory.. In *FAST*, Vol. 11. 61–75.
[31] Haris Volos, Andres Jaan Tack, and Michael M Swift. 2011. Mnemosyne: Lightweight persistent memory. In *ACM SIGARCH Computer Architecture News*, Vol. 39. ACM, 91–104.

# A Unified Rounding Algorithm For Unrelated Machines Scheduling Problems

Extended Abstract

Nikhil R. Devanur
Microsoft Research
Redmond, Washington
nikdev@microsoft.com

Janardhan Kulkarni
Microsoft Research
Redmond, Washington
jakul@microsoft.com

## ABSTRACT

The rise of cloud computing platforms has led to the study of many scheduling problems. Towards this, general algorithmic techniques that are applicable to a wide range of problems are highly valuable. We develop one such technique by a temporal generalization of the rounding algorithm of Shmoys and Tardos [23] for the generalized assignment problem. Our algorithm gives a bi-criteria approximation algorithm for a problem we introduce, called the generalized interval scheduling problem, on unrelated machines. The problem allows for each job, a specification of a collection of intervals on each machine, with the constraint that the job must be completely processed in one of the given intervals on a single machine. The assignment costs and the processing lengths are interval dependent.

Next we show how to get improved approximation factors for several classical scheduling problems, involving energy, $\ell_p$-norms of completion time, tardiness, and general delay costs by giving a reduction from these problems to the generalized interval scheduling problem with an appropriately defined assignment cost.

## KEYWORDS

ACM proceedings, LaTeX, text tagging

**ACM Reference Format:**

Nikhil R. Devanur and Janardhan Kulkarni. 2018. A Unified Rounding Algorithm For Unrelated Machines Scheduling Problems: Extended Abstract. In *SPAA '18: 30th ACM Symposium on Parallelism in Algorithms and Architectures, July 16–18, 2018, Vienna, Austria,* Jennifer B. Sartor, Theo D'Hondt, and Wolfgang De Meuter (Eds.). ACM, New York, NY, USA, Article 4, 8 pages. https://doi.org/10.1145/3210377.3210384

## 1 INTRODUCTION

With the rapid adoption of cloud computing, scheduling problems of many flavors have gained a renewed importance recently. General algorithmic techniques that can handle many of these variations are therefore very valuable. In this paper, we develop one such technique, generalizing the rounding algorithm of Shmoys and Tardos [23] for the generalized assignment problem (GAP). This problem and its special case of makespan minimization [16] are among the most fundamental problems in scheduling theory, and the rounding algorithm of Shmoys and Tardos [23] is a cornerstone of the theory of approximation algorithms.

We consider a substantial generalization of GAP, which we call the Generalized Interval Scheduling Problem (GISP). The problem allows us to specify that a job must be completed within one of many given intervals of time on a collection of heterogeneous machines. There may be multiple feasible intervals for a job on each machine. The processing length, and the assignment costs may depend on the interval in which the job is scheduled. These features allow us to model several practical scheduling constraints that arise in cloud settings: heterogeneity of machine models, varying cost of processing based on electricity cost, load of the cluster, or cost of renting VMs, etc. Within an interval, the job maybe preempted, but all of the job must be completed inside a single interval. The goal is to find a feasible schedule of minimum cost. We design a rounding algorithm for this problem that gives a bi-criteria approximation à la Shmoys and Tardos [23] rounding: it gives a schedule whose cost is at most that of the optimum, while violating the capacity constraints by a constant factor.[1]

While GISP is interesting on its own, our main motivation to study the problem comes from its applications to various classical problems in the unrelated machines setting – arguably the most general model of machine scheduling.

*We show that* GISP *captures the main technical challenge that underlies several classical scheduling problems in the unrelated machines setting. A novel aspect of our work is reducing many scheduling problems on unrelated machines to an instance of* GISP *with appropriately defined assignment costs and interval deadlines. Thus, the bi-criteria approximation algorithm for* GISP *leads to improved, and in many cases the first, approximation algorithms for many classical problems such as minimizing the $\ell_p$-norms of completion time, deadline scheduling to minimize energy, and minimizing the total weighted tardiness of jobs in the unrelated machines setting.*

We discuss more about the applications of GISP in 1.1.

Formally, in GISP we are given a set of $m$ machines. We assume that time is discrete, and machine $i \in [m]$ has a capacity $c_i(t) > 0$ at time $t$. A set of $n$ jobs needs to scheduled on these machines. For each job $j \in [n]$ we are given a set $L_{ij}$ of *disjoint* time intervals on machine $i$. Each interval $l \in L_{ij}$ is a continuous set of time slots between $[r_{ijl}, d_{ijl}]$. A job $j$ needs to be scheduled in exactly *one*

[1] Shmoys and Tardos [23]'s rounding algorithm guarantee is similar: it violated the capacity by at most a factor of 2.


*SPAA '18, July 16–18, 2018, Vienna, Austria*

ACM ISBN 978-1-4503-5799-9/18/07...$15.00
https://doi.org/10.1145/3210377.3210384

*interval on a single machine.* While a job cannot be scheduled on multiple machines or on multiple intervals, we allow preemption of a job within an interval. If a job $j$ is scheduled on machine $i$ in an interval $l \in L_{ij}$, it needs a total processing of $p_{ijl} \geq 0$ units and incurs an assignment cost of $h_{ijl} \geq 0$; We assume without loss of generality that all the values are distinct. We assume that $p_{ijl} \leq \sum_{t \in l} c_i(t)$; if this is not true, $j$ cannot be scheduled in the interval $l$ and we remove $l$ from $L_{ij}$. The goal is to assign each job to a *single interval on a single machine* so as to minimize the total assignment cost.

The problem is captured by an integer program, with the following notation. Let $x_{ijl}$ be a binary variable that denotes if a job $j$ is scheduled on machine $i$ in the interval $l \in L_{ij}$. Let $x_{ijlt}$ for $t \in [r_{ijl}, d_{ijl}]$ denote the amount of job $j$ that is scheduled at time slot $t$ in the interval $l$. The following integer program captures GISP.

$$\text{Minimize} \quad \textstyle\sum_j \sum_i \sum_{l \in L_{ij}} h_{ijl} x_{ijl} \tag{1}$$

$$\forall j, \quad \textstyle\sum_i \sum_l x_{ijl} = 1 \tag{2}$$

$$\forall j, \forall l \in L_{ij}, \quad \textstyle\sum_i \sum_{t \in l} \frac{x_{ijlt}}{p_{ijl}} = x_{ijl} \tag{3}$$

$$\forall i, t, \quad \textstyle\sum_{j, l: t \in l} x_{ijlt} \leq c_i(t) \tag{4}$$

$$\forall i, j, l, t, \quad x_{ijlt} \geq 0 \tag{5}$$

$$\forall i, j, l, \quad x_{ijl} \in \{0, 1\} \tag{6}$$

Our first main result of the paper is a bi-criteria approximation algorithm for GISP. It is based on the the linear programming (LP) relaxation of the integer program (1 - 6), where we replace the constraints (6) by $x_{ijl} \in [0, 1]$.

Theorem 1.1. *There is a* $(16, 1)$ *bi-criteria approximation algorithm for GISP. That is, if there exists a feasible solution to the LP relaxation above, our algorithm finds an assignment of jobs to intervals such that the total assignment cost is at most that of the optimal LP solution, and we violate the capacity of any time slot by at most a factor of 16.*

Note that minimizing makespan on unrelated machines [16] is a special case of GISP. Another important special case of the problem is the *deadline scheduling problem.* In the deadline scheduling problem, each job $j$ is associated with exactly one interval $[r_{ij}, d_{ij}]$ on each machine $i$. The cost of assigning a job $j$ to machine $i$ is equal to $h_{ij}$. Each machine has a uniform capacity of 1 at all time instants; that is, $c_i(t) = 1$ for all $i, t$. The goal is to assign each job $j$ to a single machine $i$ and specify a scheduling order on each machine such that the job is completely processed (preemptively) in the interval $[r_{ij}, d_{ij}]$, so as to minimize the assignment cost of jobs.

Corollary 1.2. *There is a polynomial time* $(16, 1)$ *bi-criteria approximation algorithm for the deadline scheduling problem on unrelated machines.*

GISP is related to the problem of machine minimization with interval constraints, studied by Chuzhoy et al [9]. In this problem, we are given a set of jobs, and associated with each job is a set of time intervals. The goal is to find the minimum number of machines needed such that every job is scheduled in exactly one of the time intervals on a single machine. An $O(\log n / \log \log n)$ approximation follows from a simple randomized rounding of a natural linear program. Better algorithms are known for some variants; see [9, 12] for more details. The machine minimization problem, however, is well defined only for the case when all the machines are identical, and is not a natural problem to study in scenarios where machines are heterogeneous.

## 1.1 Applications to Scheduling on Unrelated Machines

Now we show how Theorem 1.1 gives a unified framework to solve several problems in the unrelated machines setting such as minimizing the $\ell_p$-norms of completions times, deadline scheduling to minimize energy, and minimizing the total weighted tardiness. These problems have been extensively studied for more than 25 years, yet no results were known in the unrelated machines setting.

Recall that in the unrelated machines setting, a job $j$ has a processing length of $p_{ij}$ on machine $i$. Let $w_j$ denote the weight of job $j$. The goal of unrelated machines scheduling problems is to *assign each job to a single machine* and specify a scheduling policy on each machine, so as to minimize a certain objective function. Unless stated otherwise, all our algorithms produce preemptive schedules. We emphasize that the technical challenge of unrelated machine setting comes from the assignment question; If a job is allowed to be processed on multiple machines, i.e., if migration is allowed, then many of these problems can be solved easily including GAP [23].

*1.1.1 Minimizing $\ell_p$-norms of Completion times.* Let $C_j$ denote the completion time of job $j$. For a given $p \geq 1$, the $\ell_p$-norm of weighted completion times of a set of jobs is defined as

$$\left(\textstyle\sum_j w_j \cdot C_j^p\right)^{\frac{1}{p}}.$$

This classical optimization problem has been extensively studied for more than 25 years [11, 22, 24]. The values of $p > 1$, especially $p = 2, 3$, have been used to model fairness in job scheduling [14]. For $p = 1$, recent breakthrough results of Bansal, Srinivasan, and Svensson [8], and Li [17], achieve the best approximation factor that is strictly better than 1.5. For all values of $p$, the results of Im and Moseley [13], Anand, Garg, and Kumar [3] give $O(p)$-competitive online algorithms to the problem. In another recent result, Makarychev and Sviridenko [19] gave an improved $2 \cdot A_p^{1/p}$-approximation algorithm for all values $p > 1$ in the unrelated machines setting. Here $A_p$ is the $p$-th moment of the Poisson random variable with parameter 1 defined as $A_p = \sum_{t=1}^{\infty} t^p e^{-1}/t!$, which grows at least as $\Omega(\sqrt{p})$.

Despite the extensive research on the problem for more than two decades, no constant factor approximation algorithm is known. We close this gap.

Theorem 1.3. *For all $p \geq 1$, there is a polynomial time deterministic $O(1)$ approximation algorithm for the problem of minimizing $\ell_p$-norms of weighted completion times on unrelated machines. Our result holds even when jobs have release dates.*

The exact constant obtained by our algorithm is $p \cdot (\frac{16}{p-1})^{1-1/p} \cdot 64^{1/p}$. When $p = 1$ we get a 70-approximation algorithm, and as $p$ increases our approximation factor approaches 16. This gives a smooth interpolation between the completion time and the makespan objectives.

Our approach also gives a constant factor approximation algorithm to the problem of minimizing $\ell_p$-norms of machine loads, another well-studied problem. However, several constant factor approaximation algorithms are already known for the problem [4, 15, 19].

*1.1.2 Deadline Scheduling to Minimize Energy.* In this problem, we are given a set of $n$ jobs, and each job $j$ has a machine dependent deadline $d_{ij}$ and a release time $r_{ij}$. A job $j$ needs to be completely processed in the interval $[r_{ij}, d_{ij}]$ on some machine $i$. Each machine has a speed scalable processor that can be run at various speed levels. If a machine $i$ is run at a speed $s$ then it incurs an energy cost of $s^\alpha$, for some $\alpha > 1$. The goal of a scheduling algorithm is to process each $j$ in the interval $[r_{ij}, d_{ij}]$ on a single machine $i$ such that the energy cost is minimized. That is, minimize $\sum_i \sum_t (s_i(t))^\alpha$, where $s_i(t)$ is the speed at which machine $i$ is run at time $t$.

Since the seminal work of Yao, Demers, and Shenker [25], scheduling jobs to minimize energy has been an active area of research both in theory and practice; we refer the readers to [1, 20] for excellent surverys on the topic. The YDS algorithm [25] is optimal for the problem when there is only one machine; see [5] for an elegant analysis. For the unrelated machines setting, however, to the best of our knowledge we do not know of any algorithm for the problem.

Theorem 1.4. *There is a polynomial time $2 \cdot 32^\alpha$-approximation algorithm for the problem of deadline scheduling to minimize energy on unrelated machines.*

In practice $\alpha \in [2, 3]$ [2, 25], hence our result implies a constant factor approximation algorithm to the problem. The proof of above theorem relies crucially on the rounding used in GISP. However, the single machine scheduling algorithm and the analysis for the problem are quite different from GISP. One of the main differences between GISP and the deadline scheduling to minimize energy is that the length of the interval $[r_{ij}, d_{ij}]$ where the job $j$ needs to be scheduled can be shorter than the processing length of $j$. This poses several technical challenges that leads to a more involved single machine scheduling algorithm, and a careful analysis of the energy cost.

*1.1.3 General Cost Functions on Unrelated Machines.* As a final application of our Theorem 1.1, we consider the problem of minimizing general costs on unrelated machines. Much of the literature on unrelated machine scheduling has focused on a few natural measures of efficiency, e.g., makespan, flow-time, completion time, throughput, etc. However, none of them completely capture the scheduling problems that arise in large data centers. Typically in an industrial setup there are two kinds of jobs: 1) high priority jobs that need to be scheduled within a certain deadline and 2) low priority jobs for which one is interested in minimizing flow-times. In an influential work, Bansal and Pruhs [7] introduce the *general delay costs* as a way to model this problem. Here, for each job $j$ we are given a non-decreasing cost function $f_j$, and the cost of completing the job at time $t$ is equal to $f_j(t)$. The goal is to schedule jobs such that $\sum_j f_j(C_j)$ is minimized, where $C_j$ is the completion time of job $j$. Clearly, the *general delay costs* problem generalizes most scheduling objectives considered in the literature including makespan, (weighted) completion time, (weighted) flow-time, (weighted) tardiness, and deadline scheduling. In the same paper [7], the authors show an $O(\log \log P)$ approximation to the problem for single machine setting, where $n$ is the number of jobs and $P$ is the ratio of largest to smallest processing lengths of jobs.

In this paper we give the first non-trivial approximation for the problem of general delay costs on unrelated machines. We study the problem in the standard speed augmentation model, as speed augmentation is necessary to design algorithms with bounded approximation factors.

Theorem 1.5. *For any $0 < \epsilon \leq 16$, there exists a polynomial time $(16 + \epsilon)$-speed, $64/\epsilon$-approximation algorithm for the general delay costs problem on unrelated machines.*

As general delay costs captures $p$th power of $\ell_p$-norms of flow-time, we obtain a constant factor approximation algorithm for minimizing the weighted $\ell_p$-norms of flow-time in the speed augmentation model.

## 1.2 Our Techniques

The rounding algorithm of Theorem 1.1 has to deal with two main challenges:

(1) Keep the total volume of jobs assigned to a machine in *any time interval* as close to the LP solution as possible.
(2) Ensure that the jobs that are assigned to a machine do not have conflicting deadlines.

Maintaining both the invariants simultaneously turns out to be tricky and makes the rounding significantly more complex than the rounding for makespan problem or flow-time problems. Consider for example the iterated rounding of [6], which allows us to get property (1). However, it gives us little control over which set of jobs get assigned to a single interval; hence it is not clear how to enforce property (2) using this technique. It is also the reason why approaches such as randomized rounding [21], iterated rounding [6], and unsplittable flow-rounding [10] do not work for our problem. A rounding based on these methods may assign too many jobs with conflicting deadlines onto a single machine, hence forcing us to violate capacity constraints at certain time slots by a large amount. In fact, we can show that a straight forward application of these techniques can lead to violating the capacity constraints by a factor of $O(\log n)$.

We address these challenges by a temporal generalization of the rounding of Shmoys and Tardos [23]. Similar to their rounding, we rely on converting a fractional matching into an integral one, but our construction is more complex as jobs have release times and deadlines. Furthermore, we show how to maintain the load balancing property for any time interval $[t_1, t_2]$, while simultaneously ensuring that the jobs that are assigned to a machine do not have conflicting deadlines. This requires us to group jobs based on processing lengths, similar to the proof for flow-time in [6], and interleave Shmoys and Tardos rounding across various job groups and time intervals. At the end of our rounding we get a *tentative schedule* where each job is assigned to a single machine with the property that for any interval of time, the total size of jobs is roughly the same as what LP assigned.

This property alone, however, is not enough to guarantee that each job completes by its deadline. For the deadline scheduling we also need to ensure that the deadlines of the jobs assigned in each interval are feasible. In fact, the tentative schedule produced by our rounding can be infeasible in the sense that if we start processing the job from that point onwards we may not be able to complete the job even if we violate capacity constraints by a constant factor. In the final part of the proof we show how to convert the tentative schedule into a feasible schedule by appropriately *shifting* jobs without violating capacity constraints by more than a small constant factor.

## 1.3 Future directions

Although our rounding scheme is very general and gives a unified way to solve several important scheduling problems, it comes with one disadvantage: The constants obtained using our technique are not always tight. It is possible that one can improve approximation factor/speed augmentation required by tailoring the rounding algorithm to a specific problem. It is an interesting research direction to get better approximation algorithms for many problems considered in this paper. Note also that improving the approximation factor better than $(2, 1)$ in Theorem 1.1 would imply a better than 2 approximation for the makespan problem, which is a major open in approximation algorithms.

## 1.4 Organization of the Paper

We present the proof of Theorem 1.1 in main body of the paper. Omitted proofs of all the applications can be found in the full version of the paper on authors' websites.

# 2 THE GENERALIZED INTERVAL SCHEDULING PROBLEM

In this section we prove Theorem 1.1. To keep the notation simple and to convey the main technical ideas, we will assume that in the GISP instance each job only has *one feasible interval on each machine.* This case corresponds to the deadline scheduling problem. The proof of more general case follows immediately from our analysis, and can be found in the full version of the paper.

As each job has only one feasible interval on each machine, we drop the subscript $l$ from our notation. Recall that the input to the problem consists of a set of $n$ jobs and a set of $m$ machines. Each job $j \in [n]$ needs $p_{ij}$ units of processing time on machine $i$. For the rest of this section, we scale down the processing lengths of jobs to their nearest power of two. That is, for each job $j$, let $p'_{ij} = 2^k$ if $p_{ij} \in [2^k, 2^{k+1})$. Each job $j$ needs to be scheduled in the interval $[r_{ij}, d_{ij}]$ on machine $i$. Further, we are also given assignment costs for jobs; the cost of assigning a job $j$ to a machine $i$ is $h_{ij}$. The goal is to assign each job $j$ to a single machine $i$ and specify a schedule on each machine such that every job is processed in the interval $[r_{ij}, d_{ij}]$, and the total assignment cost of jobs is minimized. For this special case, LP(1 - 6) simplifies to:

$$\text{Minimize} \sum_j \sum_i h_{ij} \cdot \left(\sum_{t:t\geq r_{ij}}^{d_{ij}} x_{ijt}/p'_{ij}\right) \tag{7}$$

$$\forall j, \sum_i \sum_{t \geq r_{ij}}^{d_{ij}} \frac{x_{ijt}}{p'_{ij}} \geq 1 \tag{8}$$

$$\forall i,t, \sum_j x_{ijt} \leq 1 \tag{9}$$

$$\forall i,j,t \;:\; r_{ij} \leq t \leq d_{ij}, x_{ijt} = 0 \quad \text{if} \quad d_{ij} - r_{ij} < p'_{ij} \tag{10}$$

$$\forall i,j,t \;:\; r_{ij} \leq t \leq d_{ij}, x_{ijt} \geq 0 \tag{11}$$

For the remainder of this paper, we assume that all the input parameters are polynomially bounded and take integral values. This assumption can be removed easily. Clearly, if the instance is feasible then there is a solution to the linear program. The converse, however, is not true: the LP can schedule a job on multiple machines, hence need not produce a feasible schedule. In this section we prove the following lemma.

Lemma 2.1. *If there is a feasible solution to the linear program (7 - 11), then there is a polynomial time algorithm that when given a speed augmentation of 16 (i) assigns each job $j = 1, \ldots n$ exactly to one machine (ii) schedules a job $j$ that is assigned to machine $i$ in the interval $[r_{ij}, d_{ij}]$ (iii) incurs an assignment cost at most the LP cost.*

## 2.1 Rounding

Let $\mathbf{x} = \{x^*_{ijt}\}_{i,j,t}$ be an optimal solution to LP (7 - 11). For the rest of this section, we use $x_{ijt}$ to refer to the LP variables and $x^*_{ijt}$ for their values in $\mathbf{x}$. We give an algorithm to round $\mathbf{x}$ such that each job is assigned to a single machine. In this step, we also *tentatively* assign each job to an interval of time on a machine, which is intended to be the interval where the job gets processed. The main goal of this subsection is to prove Lemma 2.3, which states that in the tentative schedule for any time period $[t_1, t_2]$, any machine $i$ and class $k$, the total size of jobs belonging to class at most $k$ is less than $\text{SIZE-LP}(t_1, t_2) + 4 \cdot 2^k$. Given the lemma, we show in Section 2.2, how to convert this tentative schedule into a valid schedule by speed augmentation.

The tentative assignment of jobs to intervals is given by generalizing the rounding of Shmoys and Tardos [23]. We say that a job $j$ belongs to class $k$ on machine $i$ if $p'_{ij} = 2^k$. For each class $k$ and each machine $i$, we define intervals $I(i, k, *)$ that correspond to a contiguous set of time slots on machine $i$ with the property that the total size of class $k$ jobs processed in the interval in the LP solution $\mathbf{x}$ is equal to $2^k$. Since this may not always be possible, in our formal definition, $I(i, k, *)$ intervals correspond to a consecutive set of $x_{ijt}$ variables such that their total value is equal to $2^k$, which we achieve by appropriately modifying the $x_{ijt}$ variables. In spite of this, it is instructive to think of $I(i, k, *)$ simply as intervals of time that corresponds to 1 slot for a class $k$ job in the LP solution.

*Definition of $I(i, k, *)$ intervals.* Fix a machine $i$ and a class $k$. Formally, we define $I(i, k, *)$ intervals inductively as follows. Sort the $x^*_{ijt}$ variables in the increasing order of $t$ breaking ties in the lexicographic order of job indices. Let $t_0$ be the first time instant when $\sum_{t=0}^{t_0} \sum_{j:p'_{ij}=2^k} x^*_{ijt} \geq 2^k$. If the sum $\sum_{t=0}^{t_0} \sum_{j:p'_{ij}=2^k} x^*_{ijt} = 2^k$, then we define

$$I(i, k, 0) := \left\{ x_{ijt} \mid p'_{ij} = 2^k \text{ and } t \in [0, t_0] \right\}.$$

Let us look at the case when the sum is greater than $2^k$. Consider the set of $\{x_{ijt_0}\}_j$ variables, and let $j' \le n$ be the index of the first class $k$ job such that $\sum_{t=0}^{t_0-1}\sum_{j:p'_{ij}=2^k} x^*_{ijt} + \sum_{j:j\le j',p'_{ij}=2^k} x^*_{ijt_0} \ge 2^k$. We *split* the variable $x_{ij't_0}$ into two variables $x_{ij't_0}(1)$ and $x_{ij't_0}(2)$ and set

$$x^*_{ij't_0}(2) := \sum_{t=0}^{t_0-1}\sum_{j:p'_{ij}=2^k} x^*_{ijt} + \sum_{j:j\le j',p'_{ij}=2^k} x^*_{ijt_0} - 2^k$$

and $x^*_{ij't_0}(1) := x^*_{ij't_0} - x^*_{ij't_0}(2)$. This would imply that

$$\sum_{t=0}^{t_0-1}\sum_{j:p'_{ij}=2^k} x^*_{ijt} + \sum_{j:j\le j'-1,p'_{ij}=2^k} x^*_{ijt_0} + x^*_{ij't_0}(1) = 2^k.$$

We define $I(i,k,0)$ as the set of all $x_{ijt}$ variables in the interval $[0, t_0]$ up to $x_{ij't_0}(1)$. That is,

$$I(i,k,0) := \left\{x_{ijt} \mid p'_{ij} = 2^k \text{ and } t \in [0, t_0-1]\right\} \bigcup \left\{x_{ijt_0} \mid p'_{ij} = 2^k \text{ and } j < j'\right\} \bigcup \{x_{ij't_0}(1)\}$$

We call the job $j'$ as a *boundary job*, and we define the operation of breaking a variable $x_{ijt}$ into $x_{ijt}(1)$ and $x_{ijt}(2)$ as *splitting*. Note that each interval can have at most 2 split variables, one at each end of the interval. Further, we also associate the interval $[0, t_0]$ to $I(i,k,0)$, and call $t_0$ as the *right end point* and 0 as its *left end point*.

By splitting a boundary job if necessary, we inductively define $I(i,k,\ell)$ for $\ell > 0$ as the contiguous set of $x_{ijt}$ variables not belonging to the previous intervals such that the sum of their LP values is exactly equal to $2^k$. For an interval $I(i,k,\ell)$, we define the left end point $t_L(\ell)$ of the interval as smallest value of $t$ for which some $x_{ijt} \in I(i,k,\ell)$. Similarly, we define the right end point $t_R(\ell)$ of the interval as largest value of $t$ for which some $x_{ijt} \in I(i,k,\ell)$ (including the split variables).

To simplify notation, let $t_{\ell-1}$ (instead of $t_R(\ell-1)$) denote the right end point of the interval $(\ell-1)$ and $j'$ be the index of the boundary job at the right end point of the interval $(\ell-1)$. Let $t_\ell > t_{\ell-1}$ be the first time instant and $j'' \le n$ be the index of first class $k$ job such that

$$(x^*_{ij't_{\ell-1}}(2) + \sum_{j:j>j',p'_{ij}=2^k} x^*_{ijt_{\ell-1}} + \sum_{j:p'_{ij}=2^k}\sum_{t>t_{\ell-1}}^{t_\ell-1} x^*_{ijt} + \sum_{j:j\le j'',p'_{ij}=2^k} x^*_{ijt_\ell}) \ge 2^k.$$

We split the variable $x_{ij''t_\ell}$ into $x_{ij''t_\ell}(1)$ and $x_{ij''t_\ell}(2)$ (if necessary), and define $I(i,k,\ell)$ as the contiguous set of variables from $x^*_{ij't_{\ell-1}}(2)$ to $x^*_{ij''t_\ell}(1)$.

The last $I(i,k,\ell)$ interval on each machine $i$ and class $k$ contains the remaining $x_{ijt}$ variables even if their value do not sum up to $2^k$. We define the right end point of the last interval as $\max\{r_{ij}\} + \sum_j p_{ij}$.

*Summarizing $I(i,k,*)$ intervals.* Although in our formal definition we treat $I(i,k,\ell)$ as a collection of $x_{ijt}$ variables, it is instructive to think $I(i,k,\ell)$ as an interval of time from $[t_L, t_R]$ where the LP processed $2^k$ units of jobs belonging to class $k$. Keeping this picture in mind, we say the interval $I(i,k,\ell)$ intersects $[t_1,t_2]$ to mean $[t_1,t_2] \cap [t_L,t_R] \ne \emptyset$. Moreover, for every interval $I(i,k,\ell)$, we observe that $t_R - t_L \ge 2^k$. This follows from the capacity constraints of the LP (9) as at most 1 unit of jobs can be processed at each time slot. We also observe that two consecutive class $k$ intervals may overlap at only one time instant.

*Constructing bipartite graph.* Given the definition of intervals $I(i,k,\ell)$ for each class $k$ on each machine $i$, we define a bipartite graph $B = (J, M, E)$ as follows. The left side vertex set $J$ corresponds to the set of jobs; we create one vertex for each job $j = 1, \ldots n$. The right side vertex set $M$ corresponds to $I(i,k,\ell)$ intervals; We create a vertex $v_{ik\ell}$ for every interval $\{I(i,k,\ell)\}_{i,k,\ell}$, and define $M := \{v_{ik\ell} : \forall i,k,\ell\}$. Observe that for each $(i,k)$ pair, there are exactly $\left\lceil \sum_t \sum_{j:p'_{ij}=2^k} x^*_{ijt}/2^k \right\rceil$ vertices of type $v_{ik\ell} \in M$. This corresponds to the number of jobs of class $k$ processed on machine $i$.

There is an edge $e := (j, v_{ik\ell})$ in $E$ if job $j$ is of class $k$ on machine $i$ and $x_{ijt} \in I(i,k,\ell)$; there is also an edge $e := (j, v_{ik\ell})$ in $E$ if job $j$ is a boundary job and either $x_{ijt}(1) \in I(i,k,\ell)$ or $x_{ijt}(2) \in I(i,k,\ell)$. An edge $e := (j, v_{ik\ell})$ means that in the LP solution, the job $j$ belonging to class $k$ was scheduled on machine $i$ in the interval $I(i,k,\ell)$. Let $w_e$ denote the weight of edge $e$. We set $w_e$ as the total fraction of job $j$ that was scheduled in the interval $I(i,k,\ell)$. Formally, we define $w_e$ as follows:

If job $j$ is not a boundary job in the interval $I(i,k,\ell)$, then $w_e = (\sum_{t\in I(i,k,\ell)} x^*_{ijt})/p'_{ij}$. If job $j$ is a boundary job, we set $w_e$ as follows. If $x^*_{ijt_L}(2), x^*_{ijt_R}(1) \in I(i,k,\ell)$ then,

$$w_e := \left(x^*_{ijt_L}(2) + \sum_{t\in[t_L-1,t_R-1]} x^*_{ijt} + x^*_{ijt_R}(1)\right)/p'_{ij}.$$

If $x^*_{ijt_L}(2) \notin I(i,k,\ell), x^*_{ijt_R}(1) \in I(i,k,\ell)$ then we set

$$w_e := \left(\sum_{t\in[t_L,t_R-1]} x^*_{ijt} + x^*_{ijt_R}(1)\right)/p'_{ij}.$$

Finally, $x^*_{ijt_L}(2) \in I(i,k,\ell), x^*_{ijt_R}(1) \notin I(i,k,\ell)$ we define

$$w_e := \left(x^*_{ijt_L}(2) + \sum_{t\in[t_L-1,t_R]} x^*_{ijt}\right)/p'_{ij}.$$

where $t_L$ and $t_R$ denote the left and right end points of the interval $I(i,k,\ell)$.

Let $c_e$ denote the cost of edge $e$. For an edge $e := (j, v_{ik\ell})$, we set $c_e = h_{ij}$, where $h_{ij}$ is the cost of assigning job $j$ to machine $i$. From our construction

$$\sum_{e\in B} w_e \cdot c_e = \sum_j \sum_i h_{ij} \cdot (\sum_{t:t\ge r_{ij}}^{d_{ij}} x^*_{ijt}/p'_{ij}),$$

which is the assignment cost incurred by the LP solution $\mathbf{x}$.

Given an edge weighted bipartite graph, we say that a vertex is *fractionally matched* if the total weight of the edges incident on the vertex is equal to 1. From our construction of the bipartite graph $B$ and from the service constraints (8) of the LP , we observe that job nodes in $B$ are fractionally matched; That is, for all $u \in B$, $\sum_{e:e\to u} w_e = \sum_i \sum_{t:t>r_{ij}}^{d_{ij}} \frac{x^*_{ijt}}{p'_{ij}} = 1$. Now consider a vertex $v \in M$. Each such vertex corresponds to an $I(i,k,\ell)$ interval, and the set of edges incident on it are precisely from the class $k$ jobs whose $x_{ijt} \in I(i,k,\ell)$. Therefore, the total weight of edges incident on a vertex $v_{ik\ell}$ is also equal to 1. Only exception to this are the vertices corresponding to the last $I(i,k,\ell)$ intervals for each machine $i$ and class $k$, for which the total weight may be less than 1.

A beautiful result from matching theory states that if there is a fractional matching of vertices of $B$ then there is also an integral matching with the same cost [18].

THEOREM 2.2. *Let $G := (U,V,E)$ be a bipartite graph with edge weights $w_e : E \to [0,1]$ and edge costs $c_e : E \to \mathbb{R}^+$. Suppose $\forall u \in U$, $\sum_{e:e\to u} w_e = 1$ and $\forall v \in V$, $\sum_{e:\to v} w_e \le 1$. Then there exists an integral matching $\mathcal{M} : U \to V$, $\mathcal{M} \subseteq E$ such that 1) every vertex $u \in U$ is matched 2) $\sum_{e\in\mathcal{M}} c_e \le \sum_{e\in E} w_e c_e$.*

*Tentative Schedule.* Our assignment of jobs to machines is given by finding an integral matching $\mathcal{M}(B)$ on graph $B$ with the minimum cost. From Theorem 2.2 we have

$$\textstyle\sum_{e\in\mathcal{M}(B)} c_e \le \sum_j \sum_i h_{ij} \cdot (\sum_{t:t\ge r_{ij}}^{d_{ij}} x^*_{ijt}/p_{ij}). \tag{12}$$

Since our algorithm never changes the assignment of jobs to machines, it follows that the assignment cost of our solution is at most the LP cost. Therefore, it only remains to argue that every job completes by its deadline.

Observe that in our assignment of jobs to machines using $\mathcal{M}(B)$, each job is in fact matched to an interval $I(i,k,\ell)$. Our intention is to schedule the job in the interval $I(i,k,\ell)$ such that it does not miss the deadline. For now, we treat this as a *tentative schedule of jobs*. One of the problems with this tentative assignment is that the total size of jobs that are assigned within a time period may be more than the actual capacity. Although this is true, we argue that the total extra size of jobs assigned in any time period does not deviate too much from the actual LP solution.

*Bounding the load.* For the rest of the proof, we fix a machine $i$, and argue that all the jobs tentatively assigned to machine $i$ can be scheduled on that machine, given a constant speed up. For the rest of this subsection, for a given machine $i$, we show that no interval of time is too overloaded in a certain sense formalized in Lemma 2.3. For a fixed time period $[t_1,t_2]$ (on machine $i$) define

$$\text{SIZE-LP}(t_1,t_2) := \sum_j \sum_{t=t_1}^{t_2} x^*_{ijt} \tag{13}$$

$$\text{SIZE-LP}_k(t_1,t_2) := \sum_{j:p'_{ij}=2^k} \sum_{t=t_1}^{t_2} x^*_{ijt} \tag{14}$$

SIZE-LP denotes the total size of jobs scheduled in the interval $[t_1,t_2]$, and $\text{SIZE-LP}_k(t_1,t_2)$ denote the total size of jobs belonging to class $k$ scheduled in the interval $[t_1,t_2]$ in the LP solution on machine $i$. (For the sake of simplicity we drop the subscript $i$ from all notation.)

We define $\text{SIZE-TENT}_k$ as the total size of jobs belonging to class *at most* $k$ that are tentatively assigned to an interval intersecting $[t_1,t_2]$. For any $i,k$ and $\ell$, let $I^{-1}(i,k,\ell)$ denote the job $j$ that is assigned to the interval $I(i,k,\ell)$; more precisely, the job $j$ that got matched to the vertex $v_{ikl}$ in the matching $\mathcal{M}(B)$. Let $J_k(t_1,t_2)$ denote the set of jobs belonging to class at most $k$ that are tentatively assigned to an interval intersecting $[t_1,t_2]$. Formally,

$$J_k(t_1,t_2) := \{I^{-1}(i,k',\ell) : k' \le k, [t_1,t_2] \cap I(i,k',\ell) \ne \phi\}.$$

$$\text{SIZE-TENT}_k(t_1,t_2) := \textstyle\sum_{j\in J_k(t_1,t_2)} p'_{ij}.$$

LEMMA 2.3. *For any time period $[t_1,t_2]$, any machine $i$ and class $k$,*

$$\text{SIZE-TENT}_k(t_1,t_2) \le \text{SIZE-LP}(t_1,t_2) + 4\cdot 2^k$$

PROOF. We distinguish the intervals that intersect with $[t_1,t_2]$ into two types: Those that are completely contained in $[t_1,t_2]$ and those intervals that overlap the left and right end points. For each class $k' \le k$, let $I(i,k',\ell_L)$ and $I(i,k',\ell_R)$ denote the intervals that overlap at the left end point ($t_1$) and right end point ($t_2$). Let $J_L(t_1,t_2) \subseteq J_k(t_1,t_2)$ and $J_R(t_1,t_2) \subseteq J_k(t_1,t_2)$ denote the set of jobs that are assigned to the intervals that overlap at the boundaries of $[t_1,t_2]$. Let $J_1(t_1,t_2) = J_L(t_1,t_2) \cup J_R(t_1,t_2)$ and let $J_2(t_1,t_2) = J_k(t_1,t_2) \setminus J_1(t_1,t_2)$.

First, consider the jobs in $J_2(t_1,t_2)$, and using the definition of $J_2$ we have,

$$\begin{aligned}\sum_{j\in J_2(t_1,t_2)} p'_{ij} &= \sum_{k'\le k} \sum_{\ell:I(i,k',l)\subseteq[t_1,t_2]} p'_{iI^{-1}(i,k',l)} \\ &= \sum_{k'\le k} \sum_{\ell:I(i,k',\ell)\subseteq[t_1,t_2]} \sum_{x_{ijt}\in I(i,k',\ell)} x^*_{ijt} \qquad (15)\\ &\le \text{SIZE-LP}(t_1,t_2). \qquad (16)\end{aligned}$$

The proof of equality 15 follows from the definition of $I(i,k',\ell)$. The last inequality above follows from the observation that the $x_{ijt}$ variables contained in the intervals $I(i,k',\ell)$ for different $\ell$s are disjoint.

Now consider jobs in $J_1(t_1,t_2)$. For each class $k' \le k$ we can have at most 1 interval overlapping $[t_1,t_2]$ at the left end point and 1 interval at the right end point. Therefore we conclude,

$$\sum_{j\in J_1(t_1,t_2)} p'_{ij} \le 2\sum_{k'\le k} 2^{k'} \le 4\cdot 2^k. \tag{17}$$

Putting it all together, from inequalities 16 and 17, we get

$$\begin{aligned}\text{SIZE-TENT}_k(t_1,t_2) &= \sum_{j\in J_k(t_1,t_2)} p'_{ij} \\ &= \sum_{j\in J_1(t_1,t_2)} p'_{ij} + \sum_{j\in J_2(t_1,t_2)} p'_{ij} \\ &\le 4\cdot 2^k + \text{SIZE-LP}(t_1,t_2).\end{aligned}$$

□

## 2.2 Scheduling on Each Machine

Now we describe the algorithm we use to convert the tentative assignment into an actual schedule on each machine. Our algorithm consists of two parts: 1) we assign each job to an instant of time $t^*_j \ge r_j$ which is the first time at which we start to consider the job $j$ for scheduling. We say that a job $j$ is *ready* to be scheduled at time

$t$ if $t \geq t_j^*$ and it is not complete yet. 2) We assign priorities to jobs. The actual schedule is to simply process the highest priority job that is ready at that time.

- **Assigning intervals to each job:** Consider the tentative schedule produced by our LP rounding. Suppose job $j$ is assigned to the interval $I(i, k, \ell)$. Let $t_L$ and $t_R$ be the beginning and end points of this interval. Note that it cannot be that $[r_{ij}, d_{ij}] \subsetneq [t_L, t_R]$, since it would imply that the LP solution is infeasible. Further, from our construction of the bipartite graph, $[r_{ij}, d_{ij}] \cap [t_L, t_R] \neq \emptyset$. As a result the following set of cases in the definition of $t_j^*$ is mutually exhaustive.

$$t_j^* := \begin{cases} t_L & \text{if } [t_L, t_R] \subseteq [r_{ij}, d_{ij}] \\ r_{ij} & \text{if } r_{ij} > t_L \\ d_{ij} - p'_{ij} & \text{if } d_{ij} < t_R. \end{cases}$$

For every job $j$, we show that we can process the job in the interval $[t_j^*, t_j^* + p'_{ij}]$. We call $[t_j^*, t_j^* + p'_{ij}]$ the interval of job $j$, and denote it by $I_j^*$.

- **Assigning priorities to each job:** A job $j'$ can preempt a job $j$, denoted by $j' \succeq j$, if and only if the intervals of the jobs intersect: $I_{j'}^* \cap I_j^* \neq \emptyset$, and either $j'$ belongs to a smaller class than $j$, or they both belong to the same class and the interval $j'$ was assigned to in the tentative assignment precedes that assigned to $j$.

From the definition of our priority rules, it is easy to verify that it gives a total ordering on jobs that are ready at any time instant. Our algorithm at each time instant $t$ schedules the job with the highest priority. This completes the description of our scheduling policy. The following lemma follows directly from the definition of $I(i, k, \ell)$ intervals.

Lemma 2.4. *Let job $j$ be assigned to the interval $I(i, k, \ell)$ in the tentative schedule. If $I_j^* \cap I(i, k, \ell') \neq \emptyset$, then $\ell'$ is either $\ell - 1, \ell$ or $\ell + 1$.*

Proof. Proof of the lemma follows from the observation that for each $I(i, k, \ell)$ interval with $t_L$ and $t_R$ as the left and right end points, $t_R - t_L \geq 2^k$ and $p'_{ij} = 2^k$. □

*R.* emark: Once we define the deadline for each job as described above, we can schedule jobs in the earliest deadline first (EDF) order using a speed augmentation of 16. However, proving that EDF meets all deadlines is equivalent to the proof for our scheduling policy based on the job classes, which is, in our opinion, more intuitive and easy to visualize.

*Speed augmentation analysis.* It remains to show that every job is completely processed in the interval $I_j^* = [t_j^*, t_j^* + p'_{ij}]$, if we give each machine $O(1)$ extra speed. The main idea behind the proof is that if we consider the interval $[t_j^*, t_j^* + p'_{ij}]$, then Lemma 2.3 shows that the total size of jobs assigned in the tentative schedule is at most $p'_{ij} + 4 \cdot 2^k$, if job $j$ belongs to class $k$. However, our actual assignment of jobs to intervals may increase the volume due to shifting of jobs. Next we argue that this increase is not too much.

For a job $j$ belonging to class $k$ that is assigned to machine $i$, let $J_{>j}$ denote the set of jobs that can preempt $j$:

$$J_{>j} := \{j' : j' \succeq j\}.$$

Lemma 2.5. *For every job $j$*

$$\textstyle\sum_{j' \in J_{>j}} p'_{ij'} \leq 7 \cdot p'_{ij}$$

Proof. Once again, we partition $J_{>j}$ into two parts. The first set consists of those jobs whose tentative assignment intersects with $I_j^*$, and the rest of the jobs are in the second set. Recall that $J_k(t_1, t_2)$ denote the set of jobs belonging to class at most $k$ that are tentatively assigned to an interval intersecting $[t_1, t_2]$.

$$J_{>j}^1 := J_{>j} \cap J_k(t_j^*, t_j^* + p_{ij}) \text{ and } J_{>j}^2 := J_{>j} \setminus J_{>j}^1.$$

We can bound the total processing lengths of jobs in $J_{>j}^1$ and the job $j$ as follows.

$$\begin{aligned} p_{ij} + \textstyle\sum_{j' \in J_{>j}^1} p_{ij'} &\leq \text{SIZE-TENT}_k(t_j^*, t_j^* + p_{ij}) \\ &\leq \text{SIZE-LP}(t_j^*, t_j^* + p'_{ij}) + 4 \cdot 2^k \\ &\leq p'_{ij} + 4 \cdot 2^k \leq 5p'_{ij} \end{aligned} \tag{18}$$

The first inequality is by definition. The second one is an application of Lemma 2.3. The third one follows from the capacity constraints (9) of the LP. Since job $j$ belongs to class $k$, we have that $p'_{ij} = 2^k$, giving us the last inequality.

The processing lengths of jobs in $J_{>j}^2$ are bounded as follows. From Lemma 2.4, for each class $k' < k$, there are at most 2 jobs belonging to that class in $J_{>j}^2$, each of them contributing at most $2^{k'}$ to the sum. For the class $k$, there is at most 1 other job in that class that is also in $J_{>j}^2$. Hence the total length of such jobs is

$$\textstyle\sum_{j' \in J_{>j}^2} p'_{ij'} \leq \sum_{k' < k} 2 \cdot 2^{k'} + 2^k \leq 2 \cdot 2^k + 2^k \leq 3 \cdot p'_{ij}. \tag{19}$$

The lemma now follows from 19 and 18. □

Putting everything together, we get the proof of Lemma 2.1 which implies Corollary 1.2.

**Proof of Lemma 2.1.** From Equation 12, the assignment of cost our solution is at most the LP cost (7 - 11). From the definition of our algorithm, in the interval $[t_j^*, t_j^* + p'_{ij}]$, only jobs that can preempt job $j$ are the jobs in $J_{>j}$. From the above lemma, the total size of those jobs is at most $7 \cdot p'_{ij}$. Therefore, at most $8 \cdot p'_{ij}$ units of jobs is scheduled in the interval $[t_j^*, t_j^* + p'_{ij}]$. However, the actual processing length of a job $j$ can be at most $2p'_{ij}$. Thus, actual processing scheduled in the interval $[t_j^*, t_j^* + p'_{ij}]$ can be $16 \cdot p'_{ij}$. Since we are given a speed of 16 and the job $j$ is ready to be scheduled at time $t_j^*$, we will complete the job $j$ before $t_j^* + p'_{ij} \leq d_{ij}$. □

**Proof Of Theorem (1.1).** Note that Lemma 2.1 implies Theorem 1.1 for the case when each job has exactly one interval on each machine; thus it proves Corollary 1.2.

## REFERENCES


[1] Susanne Albers. 2009. Algorithms for Energy Saving. In *Efficient Algorithms, Essays Dedicated to Kurt Mehlhorn on the Occasion of His 60th Birthday*. 173–186. https://doi.org/10.1007/978-3-642-03456-5_12

[2] Susanne Albers and Hiroshi Fujiwara. 2007. Energy-efficient algorithms for flow time minimization. *ACM Transactions on Algorithms* 3, 4 (2007).

[3] S. Anand, Naveen Garg, and Amit Kumar. 2012. Resource augmentation for weighted flow-time explained by dual fitting. In *SODA*. 1228–1241.

[4] Yossi Azar and Amir Epstein. 2005. Convex programming for scheduling unrelated parallel machines. In *Proceedings of the thirty-seventh annual ACM symposium on Theory of computing*. ACM, 331–337.

[5] Nikhil Bansal, Tracy Kimbrel, and Kirk Pruhs. 2007. Speed scaling to manage energy and temperature. *J. ACM* 54, 1 (2007), 3:1–3:39.

[6] Nikhil Bansal and Janardhan Kulkarni. 2015. Minimizing Flow-Time on Unrelated Machines. In *Proceedings of the Forty-Seventh Annual ACM on Symposium on Theory of Computing, STOC 2015, Portland, OR, USA, June 14-17, 2015.* 851–860. https://doi.org/10.1145/2746539.2746601

[7] Nikhil Bansal and Kirk Pruhs. 2010. The Geometry of Scheduling. In *IEEE Symposium on the Foundations of Computer Science.* 407–414.

[8] Nikhil Bansal, Aravind Srinivasan, and Ola Svensson. 2016. Lift-and-round to improve weighted completion time on unrelated machines. In *Proceedings of the 48th Annual ACM SIGACT Symposium on Theory of Computing, STOC 2016, Cambridge, MA, USA, June 18-21, 2016.* 156–167. https://doi.org/10.1145/2897518.2897572

[9] Julia Chuzhoy, Sudipto Guha, Sanjeev Khanna, and Joseph Naor. 2004. Machine Minimization for Scheduling Jobs with Interval Constraints. In *45th Symposium on Foundations of Computer Science (FOCS 2004), 17-19 October 2004, Rome, Italy, Proceedings.* 81–90. https://doi.org/10.1109/FOCS.2004.38

[10] Yefim Dinitz, Naveen Garg, and Michel X. Goemans. 1999. On the Single-Source Unsplittable Flow Problem. *Combinatorica* 19, 1 (1999), 17–41. https://doi.org/10.1007/s004930050043

[11] Leslie A. Hall, David B. Shmoys, and Joel Wein. 1996. Scheduling to Minimize Average Completion Time: Off-line and On-line Algorithms. In *Proceedings of the Seventh Annual ACM-SIAM Symposium on Discrete Algorithms, 28-30 January 1996, Atlanta, Georgia.* 142–151.

[12] Sungjin Im, Shi Li, Benjamin Moseley, and Eric Torng. 2015. A Dynamic Programming Framework for Non-Preemptive Scheduling Problems on Multiple Machines [Extended Abstract]. In *Proceedings of the Twenty-Sixth Annual ACM-SIAM Symposium on Discrete Algorithms, SODA 2015, San Diego, CA, USA, January 4-6, 2015.* 1070–1086. https://doi.org/10.1137/1.9781611973730.72

[13] Sungjin Im and Benjamin Moseley. 2011. An Online Scalable Algorithm for Minimizing $\ell_k$-norms of Weighted Flow Time on Unrelated Machines. In *ACM-SIAM Symposium on Discrete Algorithms.*

[14] Sungjin Im and Benjamin Moseley. 2017. Fair Scheduling via Iterative Quasi-Uniform Sampling. In *Proceedings of the Twenty-Eighth Annual ACM-SIAM Symposium on Discrete Algorithms, SODA 2017, Barcelona, Spain, Hotel Porta Fira, January 16-19.* 2601–2615. https://doi.org/10.1137/1.9781611974782.171

[15] VS Kumar, Madhav V Marathe, Srinivasan Parthasarathy, and Aravind Srinivasan. 2009. A unified approach to scheduling on unrelated parallel machines. *Journal of the ACM (JACM)* 56, 5 (2009), 28.

[16] Jan K. Lenstra, David B. Shmoys, and Éva Tardos. 1990. Approximation Algorithms for Scheduling Unrelated Parallel Machines. *Math. Program.* 46 (1990), 259–271. https://doi.org/10.1007/BF01585745

[17] Shi Li. 2017. Scheduling to Minimize Total Weighted Completion Time via Time-Indexed Linear Programming Relaxations. *Accepted for publication in FOCS 2017* (2017).

[18] László Lovász and Michael D Plummer. 2009. *Matching theory.* Vol. 367. American Mathematical Soc.

[19] Konstantin Makarychev and Maxim Sviridenko. 2014. Solving Optimization Problems with Diseconomies of Scale via Decoupling. In *55th IEEE Annual Symposium on Foundations of Computer Science, FOCS 2014, Philadelphia, PA, USA, October 18-21, 2014.* 571–580.

[20] Kirk Pruhs. 2011. Green Computing Algorithmics. In *IEEE 52nd Annual Symposium on Foundations of Computer Science, FOCS 2011, Palm Springs, CA, USA, October 22-25, 2011.* 3–4. https://doi.org/10.1109/FOCS.2011.44

[21] Prabhakar Raghavan and Clark D. Thompson. 1987. Randomized rounding: a technique for provably good algorithms and algorithmic proofs. *Combinatorica* 7, 4 (1987), 365–374. https://doi.org/10.1007/BF02579324

[22] Andreas S. Schulz and Martin Skutella. 1997. Random-Based Scheduling: New Approximations and LP Lower Bounds. In *RANDOM.* 119–133.

[23] David Shmoys and Eva Tardos. 1993. An approximation algorithm for the generalized assignment problem. *Math. Program.* 62 (1993), 461–474.

[24] Martin Skutella. 2001. Convex quadratic and semidefinite programming relaxations in scheduling. *J. ACM* 48, 2 (2001), 206–242. https://doi.org/10.1145/375827.375840

[25] F. Yao, A. Demers, and S. Shenker. 1995. A Scheduling Model for Reduced CPU Energy. In *Proceedings of the 36th Annual Symposium on Foundations of Computer Science (FOCS '95).* IEEE Computer Society, Washington, DC, USA, 374–. http://dl.acm.org/citation.cfm?id=795662.796264

# Online Non-preemptive Scheduling on Unrelated Machines with Rejections

Giorgio Lucarelli
Univ. Grenoble Alpes, CNRS, Inria, Grenoble INP, LIG
Grenoble, France
giorgio.lucarelli@imag.fr

Benjamin Moseley
Carnegie Mellon University
moseleyb@andrew.cmu.edu

Nguyen Kim Thang
IBISC, Univ Évry, Université Paris-Saclay
Evry, France
thang@ibisc.fr

Abhinav Srivastav
Dépt. d'Informatique, ENS-Paris
LAMSADE, Univ. Paris-Dauphine
Paris, France
abhinavsriva@gmail.com

Denis Trystram
Univ. Grenoble Alpes, CNRS, Inria, Grenoble INP, LIG
Grenoble, France
denis.trystram@imag.fr

## ABSTRACT

When a computer system schedules jobs there is typically a significant cost associated with preempting a job during execution. This cost can be from the expensive task of saving the memory's state and loading data into and out of memory. There is a need for non-preemptive system schedulers to avoid the costs of preemption on desktops, servers and data centers. Despite this need, there is a gap between theory and practice. Indeed, few non-preemptive *online* schedulers are known to have strong foundational guarantees. This gap is likely due to strong lower bounds on any online algorithm for popular objectives. Indeed, typical worst case analysis approaches, and even resource augmented approaches such as speed augmentation, result in all algorithms having poor performance guarantees.

This paper considers online non-preemptive scheduling problems in the worst-case model where the algorithm is allowed to reject a small fraction of jobs. By rejecting only few jobs, this paper shows that the strong lower bounds can be circumvented. This model can be used to discover scheduling policies with desirable worst-case guarantees. Specifically, the paper presents algorithms for minimizing the total flow-time and minimizing the total weighted flow-time plus energy under the speed-scaling mechanism. The algorithms have a small constant competitive ratio while rejecting only a constant fraction of jobs. Beyond specific results, the paper asserts that alternative models beyond speed augmentation should be explored to aid in the discovery of good schedulers in the face of the requirement of being online and non-preemptive.

## CCS CONCEPTS

• **Theory of computation → Scheduling algorithms**; **Online algorithms**;

## KEYWORDS

Online algorithms; Non-preemptive scheduling; Rejections; Primal-dual; Energy

**ACM Reference Format:**
Giorgio Lucarelli, Benjamin Moseley, Nguyen Kim Thang, Abhinav Srivastav, and Denis Trystram. 2018. Online Non-preemptive Scheduling on Unrelated Machines with Rejections. In *SPAA '18: 30th ACM Symposium on Parallelism in Algorithms and Architectures, July 16–18, 2018, Vienna, Austria.* ACM, New York, NY, USA, 10 pages. https://doi.org/10.1145/3210377.3210402


ACM ISBN 978-1-4503-5799-9/18/07...$15.00
https://doi.org/10.1145/3210377.3210402

## 1 INTRODUCTION

Designing efficient system schedulers is critical for optimizing system performance. Many environments require the scheduler to be *non-preemptive*, ensuring each job is scheduled on a machine without interruption. The need for non-preemption arises because preemption requires saving the state of a program and writing the state to memory or disk. For large complex tasks, the overhead cost of saving state is so large that it has to be avoided entirely.

Designing theoretically efficient *online* non-preemptive schedulers is challenging. Strong lower bounds have been shown, even for simple instances [7, 13]. The difficulty lies in the pessimism of assuming the algorithm is online and must be robust to all problem instances combined with irrevocable nature of scheduling non-preemptive jobs.

In order to overcome strong theoretical barriers when designing scheduling algorithms, Kalyanasundaram and Pruhs [12] and Phillips et al. [15] proposed using resource augmentation in terms of *speed augmentation* and the *machine augmentation*, respectively. The idea is to either give the algorithm faster processors or extra machines versus the adversary. These models provide a tool to establish a theoretical explanation for the good performance of algorithms in practice. Indeed, many practical heuristics have been shown to be competitive in the online preemptive model where the algorithm is given resource augmentation. Non-preemptive environments have resisted the discovery of strong theoretical schedulers. Designing meaningful algorithms for non-preemptive problems is an important direction in scheduling [3]. Specifically, it is known that a non-preemptive algorithm cannot have a small reasonable competitive ratio using only speed or machine augmentation [14] for the popular average flow time objective.

Recently, Choudhury et al. [8] extended the resource augmentation model to allow *rejection* (some jobs need not be completed and are rejected). By combining rejection and speed augmentation, Lucarelli et al. [14] gave competitive algorithms for non-preemptive flow-time problems. An intriguing question is the power of rejection versus resource augmentation. Is there a competitive algorithm that only uses rejection? This would establish that theoretically rejection is more powerful since there are lower bounds using resource augmentation. This paper answers this question positively.

## 1.1 Models, Problems and Contribution

*Non-Preemptive Total Flow-time Minimization.* In this problem, we are given a set of unrelated machines $\mathcal{M}$ and jobs arrive online. Each job $j \in \mathcal{J}$ is characterized by a *release time* $r_j$ and it takes a different *processing time* $p_{ij}$ if it is executed on each machine $i \in \mathcal{M}$. The characteristics of each job become known to the algorithm only after its arrival. The jobs should be scheduled *non-preemptively*, that is a job is considered to be successfully executed only if it is executed on a machine $i \in \mathcal{M}$ for $p_{ij}$ continuous time units. Given a schedule $\mathcal{S}$, the *completion time* of a job $j \in \mathcal{J}$ is denoted by $C_j$. Then, its *flow-time* is defined as $F_j = C_j - r_j$, that is the total amount of time during which $j$ remains in the system. Our goal is to create a non-preemptive schedule that minimizes the total flow-times of all jobs, i.e., $\sum_j F_j$.

The problem has been studied in [14] in the model of speed augmentation and rejection. Specifically, Lucarelli et al. [14] gave a $O(1/(\epsilon_r \cdot \epsilon_s))$-competitive algorithm that uses machines with speed $(1+\epsilon_s)$ and reject at most $\epsilon_r$-fraction of jobs for arbitrarily small $\epsilon_r, \epsilon_s > 0$. A natural question is whether speed augmentation is necessary. Our main result answers positively this question.

Theorem 1.1. *For the non-preemptive total flow-time minimization problem, there exists a $2\left(\frac{1+\epsilon}{\epsilon}\right)^2$-competitive algorithm that removes at most $2\epsilon$ fraction of the total number of jobs, for any $\epsilon > 0$.*

The design and analysis of the algorithm follow the duality approach. At the release time of any job $j$, the algorithm defines the dual variables associated to the job and assigns $j$ to some machine based on this definition. The value of the dual variables associated to $j$ are selected in order to satisfy two key properties: (i) express the marginal increase of the total weighted flow-time due to the arrival of the job — the property that has been observed [2] and has become more and more popular in dual-fitting for online scheduling; and (ii) capture the information for a future decision of the algorithm whether job $j$ will be completed or rejected. Moreover, the dual variables are defined so as to stabilize the schedule and allows us to maintain a non-preemptive schedule (even with job arrivals and rejections in the future).

The decision about rejecting a job depends on the load of the recently released jobs that are waiting in the queue of each machine. The scheduler rejects a job when this load exceeds a given threshold. The rejected job is not necessarily the one that just arrived and caused the excess in the threshold. The following lemma shows that immediate rejection policies cannot improve the competitive ratio.

Lemma 1.2. *Any $\epsilon$-rejection policy which has to decide the rejection or not of each job immediately upon its arrival, has a competitive ratio of $\Omega(\sqrt{\Delta})$ for the non-preemptive total flow-time minimization problem even on a single machine environment, where $\Delta$ is the ratio of the maximum over the minimum processing time in the instance and $\epsilon > 0$.*

*Non-Preemptive Total Flow-time Plus Energy Minimization.* We next consider non-preemptive scheduling in the speed scaling model. In this model, each machine $i \in \mathcal{M}$ has a power function of the form $P(s_i(t)) = s_i(t)^\alpha$, where $s_i(t)$ is the speed of the machine $i$ at time $t$ and $\alpha > 1$ is a constant parameter (usually $\alpha \in (1,3]$). Each job $j \in \mathcal{J}$ is now characterized by its *weight* $w_j$, its *release date* $r_j$ and, for each machine $i \in \mathcal{M}$, a machine-dependent *volume* of execution $p_{ij}$. A *non-preemptive* schedule in the speed-scaling model is a schedule in which each job is processed continuously (without being interrupted) in a machine and a job has a constant speed during its execution. Note that in the model, it is allowed to process multiple jobs in parallel on the same machine. The objective is to schedule jobs non-preemptively so that minimizing the total weighted flow-time plus the energy consumed for all jobs, i.e. $\sum_j w_j F_j + \sum_i \int_0^\infty \left(s_i(t)\right)^\alpha dt$.

Building upon the resilient ideas and techniques from flow-time minimization, we derive a competitive algorithm for the problem. Note that this algorithm does not need to process multiple jobs in parallel on the same machine, although this is permissible by the described model.

Theorem 1.3. *For the non-preemptive total weighted flow-time plus energy minimization problem, there exists an $O\left(\left(1+\frac{1}{\epsilon}\right)^{\frac{\alpha}{\alpha-1}}\right)$-competitive algorithm that rejects jobs of total weight at most an $\epsilon$-fraction of the total weight of all jobs, for any $\epsilon > 0$.*

*Non-Preemptive Energy Minimization.* Subsequently, we consider the non-preemptive energy minimization scheduling problem in the speed scaling model. The setting is similar to the previous problem but a job $j \in \mathcal{J}$ now has a release date $r_j$, a deadline $d_j$ and a processing volume $p_{ij}$ if it is assigned to machine $i \in \mathcal{M}$. Every job has to be processed non-preemptively and to be completed before its deadline. The goal is to minimize the total energy consumption $\sum_i \sum_t P_i\left(s_i(t)\right)$ where $P_i$ is the power function of machine $i$. (In this case we consider the discrete time setting.)

No competitive algorithm is known in the non-preemptive multiple-machine environment. Despite of some similarities to the problem of minimizing energy plus flow-time, the main difference is that in the latter, one can make a trade-off between energy and flow-time and derive a competitive algorithm whereas for the energy minimization problem, one has to deal directly with a non-linear objective. The critical issue is that no linear program (LP) with relatively small integrality gap was known. In order to derive a competitive algorithm for this problem, we make use of the primal-dual approach based on configuration LP recently developed in [17]. The approach consists of introducing exponential number of variables to the natural formulation in order to reduce the integrality gap. Then, in contrast to current rounding techniques based on configuration LPs, the approach maintains greedily a competitive solution in the sense of primal-dual (without solving exponential size LPs). Interestingly, using this approach, the power functions are not required to be convex (a crucial property for prior analyses) and the competitive ratio is characterized by a notion of smoothness defined as follows.

*Definition 1.4.* A set function $f : 2^{\mathcal{N}} \to \mathbb{R}^+$ is $(\lambda, \mu)$-*smooth* if for any set $A = \{a_1, \ldots, a_n\} \subseteq \mathcal{N}$ and any collection $B_1 \subseteq B_2 \subseteq \ldots \subseteq B_n \subseteq B \subseteq \mathcal{N}$, the following inequality holds.

$$\sum_{i=1}^{n} \left[ f\big(B_i \cup a_i\big) - f\big(B_i\big) \right] \leq \lambda f\big(A\big) + \mu f\big(B\big)$$

THEOREM 1.5. *Assume that all power functions are $(\lambda, \mu)$-smooth. Then, there is a $\lambda/(1-\mu)$-competitive algorithm for the non-preemptive energy minimization scheduling problem. In particular, if $P_i(s) = s^{\alpha_i}$ for $\alpha_i \geq 1$ then the algorithm is $O(\alpha^\alpha)$-competitive where $\alpha = \max_i \alpha_i$.*

In the following lemma we consider the case of typical power functions of the form $P(s) = s^\alpha$, and we show that the above result is asymptotically optimal as a function of $\alpha$.

LEMMA 1.6. *Any deterministic algorithm is at least $(\alpha/9)^\alpha$-competitive for the non-preemptive energy minimization problem even in a single machine environment.*

## 1.2 Related Work

For the online non-preemptive scheduling problem of minimizing total weighted flow-time, any algorithm has at least $\Omega(n)$ competitive ratio, even for single machine where $n$ is the number of jobs (as mentioned in [7]). In identical machine environments, Phillips et al. [15] gave a constant competitive algorithm that uses $m \log P$ machines (recall that the adversary uses $m$ machines), where $P$ is the ratio of the largest to the smallest processing time. Moreover, an $O(\log n)$-machine $O(1)$-speed algorithm that returns the optimal schedule has been presented in [15] for the unweighted flow-time objective. Epstein and van Stee [11] proposed an $\ell$-machines $O(\min\{\sqrt[\ell]{P}, \sqrt[\ell]{n}\})$-competitive algorithm for the unweighted case on a single machine. This algorithm is optimal up to a constant factor for constant $\ell$. Recently, Lucarelli et al. [14] consider the problem in the model of speed augmentation and rejection. They showed that without rejection, no algorithm is competitive even on single machine with speed arbitrarily faster than that of adversary. Moreover, they gave a scalable $O(1/(\epsilon_r \cdot \epsilon_s))$-competitive algorithm that uses machines with speed $(1+\epsilon_s)$ and reject at most $\epsilon_r$ fraction of jobs for arbitrarily small $\epsilon_r, \epsilon_s > 0$.

For the online non-preemptive scheduling problem of minimizing total weighted flow-time plus energy, to the best of our knowledge, no competitive algorithm is known. However, the problem in the preemptive setting has been widely studied. Bansal et al. [5] gave an $O(\alpha/\log\alpha)$-competitive algorithm for weighted flow-time plus energy in a single machine where the energy function is $s^\alpha$. Based on linear programming and dual-fitting, Anand et al. [2] proved an $O(\alpha^2)$-competitive algorithm for unrelated machines. Subsequently, Nguyen [16] and Devanur and Huang [10] presented an $O(\alpha/\log\alpha)$-competitive algorithms for unrelated machines by dual fitting and primal dual approaches, respectively.

For the online non-preemptive scheduling problem of minimizing total energy consumption, no competitive algorithm is known. Even in the preemptive scheduling in which migration of jobs between machines are not allowed, no algorithm with provable performance is given. The difficulty, as mentioned earlier, is due to the integrality gap barrier of all currently known formulations. In single machine where the issue of non-migration does not exist, Bansal et al. [6] gave a $2\left(\frac{\alpha}{\alpha-1}\right)^\alpha e^\alpha$-competitive algorithm. Moreover, Bansal et al. [4] showed that no deterministic algorithm has competitive ratio less than $e^{\alpha-1}/\alpha$. Albers et al. [1] considered the case where jobs are allowed to be executed preemptively and migration between machines is permitted. For this problem, they proposed an algorithm based on the AVERAGE RATE algorithm [18] and they showed a competitive ratio of $(1+\epsilon)(\alpha^\alpha 2^{\alpha-1}+1)$.

## 2 MINIMIZE TOTAL FLOW-TIME

*Linear Programming Formulation.* In order to formulate our problem as a linear program, for each job $j \in \mathcal{J}$, machine $i \in \mathcal{M}$ and time $t \geq r_j$, we introduce a binary variable $x_{ij}(t)$ which is equal to one if $j$ is processed on $i$ at time $t$, and zero otherwise. We use two lower bounds on the flow-time of each job $j \in \mathcal{J}$, assuming that it is dispatched to machine $i$: its *fractional flow-time* which is defined as $\int_{r_j}^{\infty} \frac{t-r_j}{p_{ij}} x_{ij}(t)dt$ (see for example [2]), and its processing time $p_{ij} = \int_{r_j}^{\infty} x_{ij}(t)dt$. Then, the linear programming formulation for the problem of minimizing the total flow-time follows.

$$\begin{aligned}
\min \sum_{i\in\mathcal{M}} \sum_{j\in\mathcal{J}} \int_{r_j}^{\infty} \left(\frac{t-r_j}{p_{ij}} + 1\right) x_{ij}(t)dt & \\
\sum_{i\in\mathcal{M}} \int_0^{\infty} \frac{x_{ij}(t)}{p_{ij}} dt \geq 1 & \quad \forall j \\
\sum_{j\in\mathcal{J}} x_{ij}(t) \leq 1 & \quad \forall i, t \\
x_{ij}(t) \in \{0,1\} & \quad \forall i, j, t
\end{aligned}$$

Note that the objective value of the above linear program is at most twice that of the optimal non-preemptive schedule. We relax the above integer linear program by replacing the integrality constraints for each $x_{ij}(t)$ with $0 \leq x_{ij}(t) \leq 1$. The dual of the relaxed linear program is the following.

$$\begin{aligned}
\max \sum_{j\in\mathcal{J}} \lambda_j - \sum_{i\in\mathcal{M}} \int_0^{\infty} \beta_i(t) \quad & dt \\
\frac{\lambda_j}{p_{ij}} - \beta_i(t) \leq \frac{t-r_j}{p_{ij}} + 1 & \quad \forall i, j, t \\
\lambda_j \geq 0 & \quad \forall j \\
\beta_i(t) \geq 0 & \quad \forall i, t
\end{aligned}$$

In the *rejection model* considered in this article, we assume that the algorithm is allowed to reject some jobs. This can be interpreted in the primal linear program by considering only the variables corresponding to the non-rejected jobs, that is the algorithm does not have to satisfy the first constraint for the rejected jobs.

*The Algorithm and Definition of Dual Variables.* We next define the scheduling, the rejection and the dispatching policies of our algorithm which is denoted by $\mathcal{A}$. Let $\epsilon$, $0 < \epsilon < 1$, be an arbitrarily small constant which indicates the fraction of the total number of jobs that will be rejected. Each job is immediately dispatched to a machine upon its arrival. Let $U_i(t)$ be the set of *pending* jobs at time $t$ dispatched to machine $i \in \mathcal{M}$, that is the jobs dispatched to $i$ that have been released but not yet completed or rejected at time $t$. Moreover, let $q_{ij}(t)$ be the remaining processing time at time $t$ of a job $j \in \mathcal{J}$ which has been dispatched to the machine $i$.

Let $k$ be the job that is executed on machine $i$ at time $t$. We always consider the jobs in $U_i(t) \setminus \{k\}$ sorted in non-decreasing order with respect to their processing times; in case of ties, we consider the jobs in earliest release time order. We say that a job $j \in U_i(t) \setminus \{k\}$ precedes (resp. succeeds) a job $\ell \in U_i(t) \setminus \{k\}$ if $j$ appears before (resp. after) $\ell$ in the above order, and we write $j \prec \ell$ (resp. $j \succ \ell$). We use the symbols $\preceq$ and $\succeq$ to express the fact that $j$ may coincide with $\ell$. The *scheduling policy* of the algorithm $\mathcal{A}$ is the following: whenever a machine $i \in \mathcal{M}$ becomes idle at a time $t$, schedule on $i$ the job $j \in U_i(t)$ that precedes any other job in $U_i(t)$.

We use two different rules for defining our *rejection policy*. The first rule handles the arrival of a big group of jobs during the execution of a long job as in [14]. The second rule simulates and replaces the utility of speed-augmentation.

**Rejection Rule 1.** At the beginning of the execution of a job $j \in \mathcal{J}$ on machine $i$, we introduce a counter $v_j$ which is initialized to zero. Whenever a job $\ell$ is dispatched to machine $i$ during the execution of $j$, we increase $v_j$ by 1. Then, we interrupt and reject the job $j$ the first time when $v_j \geq \frac{1}{\epsilon}$.

**Rejection Rule 2.** For each machine $i \in \mathcal{M}$, we maintain a counter $c_i$ which is initialized to zero at $t = 0$. Whenever a job $j$ is dispatched to a machine $i$, we increase $c_i$ by 1. Then, we reject the job with the largest processing time in $U_i(t) \setminus \{k\}$ the first time when $c_i = 1 + \frac{1}{\epsilon}$, and we reset $c_i$ to zero.

Let $\mathcal{R}$ be the set of all rejected jobs. By slightly abusing the notation, we denote the rejection time of a job $j \in \mathcal{R}$ by $C_j$. Moreover, we define the flow-time of a rejected job $j \in \mathcal{R}$ to be the difference between its rejection time and its arrival time, and we denote it by $F_j$.

At the arrival of a new job $j \in \mathcal{J}$, let $\Delta_{ij}$ be the increase in the total flow-time if we decide to dispatch the job $j$ to the machine $i$. Fix a machine $i$ and let $k$ be the job that is executed on $i$ at $r_j$. Then, assuming that $j$ is dispatched to $i$ (i.e., assuming that $j \in U_i(r_j)$), we have that

$$\begin{aligned}\Delta_{ij} &= q_{ik}(r_j) \cdot \mathbb{1}_{\{\text{if } k \text{ is not rejected (due to Rule 1)}\}} + \sum_{\ell \preceq j} p_{i\ell} \\ &+ \sum_{\ell \succ j} p_{ij} \\ &- \Big(q_{ik}(r_j) + \sum_{\ell \neq j} q_{ik}(r_j)\Big) \cdot \mathbb{1}_{\{\text{if } k \text{ is rejected due to Rule 1}\}} \\ &- \Big(q_{ik}(r_j) + \sum_{\ell \neq j} p_{i\ell} + p_{ij_{\max}}\Big) \cdot \mathbb{1}_{\{\text{if } j_{\max} \text{ is rejected due to Rule 2}\}}\end{aligned}$$

where the first term corresponds to the flow-time of the new job $j$, the second term corresponds to the increase of the flow-time for the jobs in $U_i(r_j)$ due to the dispatching of $j$ to machine $i$, the third term corresponds to the decrease of the flow-time for the jobs in $U_i(r_j) \cup \{k\}$ due to the rejection of $k$ (according to Rule 1), and the forth term corresponds to the decrease of the flow-time of the largest job $j_{\max}$ due to its rejection (according to Rule 2). Based on the above, we define

$$\lambda_{ij} = \frac{1}{\epsilon} p_{ij} + \sum_{\ell \preceq j} p_{i\ell} + \sum_{\ell \succ j} p_{ij}$$

Then, our *dispatching policy* is the following: at the arrival of a new job $j$ at time $r_j$, dispatch $j$ to the machine $i^* = \text{argmin}_{i \in \mathcal{M}} \lambda_{ij}$.

The quantity $\lambda_{ij}$ is strongly related with the marginal increase $\Delta_{ij}$. However, all negative terms that appear in $\Delta_{ij}$ have been eliminated in $\lambda_{ij}$. Moreover, the positive quantity $q_{ik}(r_j)$ does not appear in $\lambda_{ij}$, but we have added the term $\frac{1}{\epsilon} p_{ij}$. The intuition for the definition of $\lambda_{ij}$ is to charge an upper bound to the marginal increase $\Delta_{ij}$ to the $\lambda_{i\ell}$ quantities of some jobs dispatched to $i$. Specifically, the quantity $\sum_{\ell \preceq j} p_{i\ell} + \sum_{\ell \succ j} p_{ij}$ is charged to $\lambda_{ij}$. If the positive quantity $q_{ik}(r_j)$ exists, then it is charged to the term $\frac{1}{\epsilon} p_{ik}$ of $\lambda_{ik}$ (i.e., to the job $k$ that is executed on $i$ at the arrival of $j$). The rejection Rule 1 guarantees that this term is sufficient for all jobs arrived and dispatched to $i$ during the execution of $k$.

In order to deal with the ignored negative terms, we expand the notion of completion time of each job $j \in \mathcal{J}$. Let $D_j$ be the set of jobs that are rejected due to Rule 1 after the release time of $j$ and before its completion or rejection (including $j$ in case it is rejected), that is the jobs that cause a decrease to the flow time of $j$ due to Rule 1. Moreover, we denote by $j_k$ the job released at the moment we reject a job $k \in \mathcal{R}$. Then, we say that a job $j \in \mathcal{J}$ which is dispatched to machine $i$ is *definitively finished* at the time

$$\begin{aligned}\tilde{C}_j &= C_j + \sum_{k \in D_j} q_{ik}(r_{j_k}) \\ &+ \Big(q_{ik}(r_{j_j}) + \sum_{\ell \neq j_j} p_{i\ell} + p_{ij}\Big) \cdot \mathbb{1}_{\{\text{if } j \text{ is rejected due to Rule 2}\}}\end{aligned}$$

Let $V_i(t)$ be the set of jobs that are completed or rejected at time $t$ but not yet definitively finished. Intuitively, at the completion or rejection of job $j$ at time $C_j$ is moved from the set of pending jobs $U_i(t)$ to the set of not yet definitively finished jobs $V_i(t)$, and it remains to this set until the time $\tilde{C}_j$. Let $R_i(t) \subseteq V_i(t)$ be the set of jobs that are already rejected due to Rule 2 at time $t$ but they are not yet definitively finished.

It remains to formally define the dual variables. At the arrival of a job $j \in \mathcal{J}$, we set $\lambda_j = \frac{\epsilon}{1+\epsilon} \min_{i \in \mathcal{M}} \lambda_{ij}$ and we never change this value again. Moreover, for each $i \in \mathcal{M}$ and $t \geq 0$, we set $\beta_i(t) = \frac{\epsilon}{(1+\epsilon)^2}(|U_i(t)| + |V_i(t)|)$. Note that, given any fixed time $t$, $\beta_i(t)$ may increase if a new job arrives at any time $t' < t$. However, $\beta_i(t)$ never decreases in the case of rejection since the rejected jobs are transferred to the set $V_i(t)$ where they remain until they are definitively finished.

*Analysis.* We first show the following lemma which relates all but $c_i$ jobs in $U_i(t)$ to some jobs in $R_i(t)$.

LEMMA 2.1. *Fix a machine $i$ and a time $t$. Consider the jobs in $R_i(t)$ sorted in non-decreasing order of the time they are definitively finished; let $k_1, k_2, \ldots, k_r$ be this order, where $r = |R_i(t)|$. There is a partition of the jobs in $U_i(t)$ into at most $r+1$ subsets, $U_i^1(t), U_i^2(t), \ldots, U_i^{r+1}(t)$ such that*

*(i) $|U_i^\ell(t)| \leq \frac{1}{\epsilon}$, for $1 \leq \ell \leq r$,*
*(ii) $|U_i^{r+1}(t)| \leq c_i$,*

*(iii) for each job $j \in U_i^\ell(t)$, $1 \le \ell \le r$, the estimated completion time of $j$ assuming that no other job is released after time $t$ is at most $\tilde{C}_{k_\ell}$.*

Proof. The proof is based on induction on time. We consider only times which correspond to discrete events that modify the sets $U_i(t)$ and $R_i(t)$, i.e., arrival of a new job, completion of a job, rejection of a job according to Rule 2 and definitive finish of a job in $R_i(t)$.

At the arrival of the first job dispatched to machine $i$, we have that $c_i = 1$ and the statement directly holds. Let us assume that the partition exists at an event which occurs at time $t$. We will show that this holds also for the next event at time $t' \ge t$. We consider the following three cases.

- If a job $j$ completes at time $t'$, then $j$ is removed from $U_i(t')$ without affecting the mapping implied by the statement of the lemma.
- If a job $j$ arrives at time $t'$, then $c_i$ is increased by one. Let $j_\ell$, $1 \le \ell \le r+1$, be the job with the largest processing time in $U_i^\ell(t)$. If $p_j \ge p_{j_r}$, then we set $U_i^\ell(t') = U_i^\ell(t)$ for $1 \le \ell \le r$ and $U_i^{r+1}(t') = U_i^{r+1}(t) \cup \{j\}$ and the partition is valid since $c_i$ is increased. Otherwise, find the biggest $z$, $1 \le z \le \ell$, such that $p_j < p_{j_z}$. We set $U_i^\ell(t') = U_i^\ell(t)$ for $1 \le \ell \le z-1$, $U_i^z(t') = U_i^z(t) \cup \{j\} \setminus \{j_z\}$, and $U_i^\ell(t') = U_i^\ell(t) \cup \{j_{\ell-1}\} \setminus \{j_\ell\}$ for $z+1 \le \ell \le r+1$. By these definitions, the first two items of the lemma are satisfied by the induction hypothesis since each set, except for $U_i^{r+1}$, has the same size at times $t$ and $t'$. For item (iii), we observe that the job that is added in each set $U_i^\ell$, $z \le \ell \le r$, has a shorter processing time than the job which is removed. Hence, the item (iii) holds by the definition of the scheduling policy. Moreover, if a job $k$ is rejected according to Rule 2 at time $t'$, then $R_i(t') = R_i(t) \cup \{k\}$ and $U_i^{|R_i(t')|}(t') = U_i^{r+1}(t)$. Therefore, the lemma holds since $c_i \le 1 + \frac{1}{\epsilon}$ and $k$ is the job with the largest processing time (and hence the largest estimated completion time) in $U_i^{r+1}(t)$.
- If the job $k_1$ is definitively finished at time $t'$, then assume that $U_i^1(t)$ is not empty. Then, by the induction hypothesis each job $j \in U_i^1(t)$ should complete before $t'$, which is a contradiction to the fact that $t'$ is the next event after $t$.

Therefore, the lemma follows. □

The following corollary is an immediate consequence of Lemma 2.1.

Corollary 2.2. *For each $t$, it holds that $|U_i(t)| \le \frac{1}{\epsilon}(|R_i(t)|+1)$.*

The following lemma guarantees that the definition of the dual variables lead always to a feasible solution for the dual program.

Lemma 2.3. *For all $i \in \mathcal{M}$, $j \in \mathcal{J}$ and $t \ge r_j$, the dual constraint is feasible.*

Proof. For a machine $i$ and a job $j$, observe that for any fixed $t \ge r_j$, the value of $\beta_i(t)$ may only increase during the execution of the algorithm. Hence, it is sufficient to prove the constraint assuming that no job arrives after $r_j$. Assume that the job $k$ is executed on the machine $i$ at the arrival of the job $j$. We have the following cases.

**Case 1:** The job $k$ is executed at $t$. By the definition of $\lambda_j$ and $\lambda_{ij}$, we have:

$$\begin{aligned}\frac{\lambda_j}{p_{ij}} &\le \frac{\epsilon}{1+\epsilon}\left(\frac{1}{\epsilon} + \frac{1}{p_{ij}}\sum_{\ell \le j} p_{i\ell} + \sum_{\ell > j} 1\right) \le \frac{\epsilon}{1+\epsilon}\left(\frac{1}{\epsilon} + \sum_{\ell \le j} 1 + \sum_{\ell > j} 1\right)\\ &\text{(since } p_{i\ell} \le p_{ij} \text{ for all } \ell \le j)\\ &\le \frac{\epsilon}{1+\epsilon}\left(\frac{1}{\epsilon} + |U_i(t)| + \frac{t-r_j}{p_{ij}}\right)\\ &\text{(since } t - r_j \ge 0)\end{aligned}$$

**Case 2:** A job $z \le j$ is executed at $t$. Then, we have $t - r_j \ge \sum_{\ell < z} p_{i\ell}$. Using the definition of $\lambda_j$ and $\lambda_{ij}$, we have:

$$\begin{aligned}\frac{\lambda_j}{p_{ij}} &\le \frac{\epsilon}{1+\epsilon}\left(\frac{1}{\epsilon} + \frac{1}{p_{ij}}\sum_{\ell \le j} p_{i\ell} + \sum_{\ell > j} 1\right)\\ &= \frac{\epsilon}{1+\epsilon}\left(\frac{1}{\epsilon} + \frac{1}{p_{ij}}\sum_{\ell < z} p_{i\ell} + \frac{1}{p_{ij}}\sum_{z \le \ell \le j} p_{i\ell} + \sum_{\ell > j} 1\right)\\ &\le \frac{\epsilon}{1+\epsilon}\left(\frac{1}{\epsilon} + \frac{t-r_j}{p_{ij}} + \sum_{z \le \ell \le j} 1 + \sum_{\ell > j} 1\right)\\ &\text{(since } p_{i\ell} \le p_{ij} \text{ for all } \ell \le j)\\ &\le \frac{\epsilon}{1+\epsilon}\left(\frac{1}{\epsilon} + \frac{t-r_j}{p_{ij}} + |U_i(t)|\right)\end{aligned}$$

**Case 3:** A job $z > j$ is executed at $t$. Then, we have $t - r_j \ge \sum_{\ell < z} p_{i\ell}$. Using the definition of $\lambda_j$ and $\lambda_{ij}$, we have:

$$\begin{aligned}\frac{\lambda_j}{p_{ij}} &\le \frac{\epsilon}{1+\epsilon}\left(\frac{1}{\epsilon} + \frac{1}{p_{ij}}\sum_{\ell \le j} p_{i\ell} + \sum_{\ell > j} 1\right)\\ &= \frac{\epsilon}{1+\epsilon}\left(\frac{1}{\epsilon} + \frac{1}{p_{ij}}\sum_{\ell < j} p_{i\ell} + \sum_{j < \ell < z} \frac{p_{i\ell}}{p_{i\ell}} + \sum_{\ell \ge z} 1\right)\\ &\le \frac{\epsilon}{1+\epsilon}\left(\frac{1}{\epsilon} + \frac{1}{p_{ij}}\sum_{\ell < j} p_{i\ell} + \sum_{j < \ell < z} \frac{p_{i\ell}}{p_{ij}} + \sum_{\ell \ge z} 1\right)\\ &\text{(since } p_{i\ell} > p_{ij} \text{ for all } \ell > j)\\ &\le \frac{\epsilon}{1+\epsilon}\left(\frac{1}{\epsilon} + \frac{t-r_j}{p_{ij}} + |U_i(t)|\right)\end{aligned}$$

Hence, in all the three cases we have:

$$\begin{aligned}\frac{\lambda_j}{p_{ij}} &\le \frac{\epsilon}{1+\epsilon}\left(\frac{1}{\epsilon} + \frac{t-r_j}{p_{ij}} + |U_i(t)|\right)\\ &= \frac{\epsilon}{1+\epsilon}\left(\frac{1}{\epsilon} + \frac{t-r_j}{p_{ij}} + \frac{|U_i(t)| + \epsilon|U_i(t)|}{1+\epsilon}\right)\\ &\le \frac{\epsilon}{1+\epsilon}\left(\frac{1}{\epsilon} + \frac{t-r_j}{p_{ij}} + \frac{|U_i(t)| + |R_i(t)| + 1}{1+\epsilon}\right)\\ &\text{(by Corollary 2.2)}\\ &\le \frac{1}{1+\epsilon} + \frac{\epsilon}{(1+\epsilon)^2} + \frac{\epsilon}{1+\epsilon}\frac{t-r_j}{p_{ij}} + \beta_i(t) < 1 + \frac{t-r_j}{p_{ij}} + \beta_i(t)\end{aligned}$$

and the lemma follows. □

Using the above results, we next prove Theorem 1.1.

Proof of Theorem 1.1. An immediate consequence of the definition of the two rejection rules is that the jobs rejected by algorithm $\mathcal{A}$ is at most a $2\epsilon$-fraction of the total number of jobs in $\mathcal{J}$. By Lemma 2.3, we know that the proposed definition of the dual variables leads to a feasible dual solution. For the objective value of the dual program, by the definition of $\lambda_j$ and $\tilde{C}_j$, we have that

$$\sum_{j\in\mathcal{J}} \lambda_j \geq \frac{\epsilon}{1+\epsilon}\sum_{j\in\mathcal{J}}(\tilde{C}_j - r_j)$$

Moreover, by the definition of $U_i(t)$, $V_i(t)$ and $\tilde{C}_j$, we have that

$$\sum_{i\in\mathcal{M}}\int_0^\infty \beta_i(t) = \frac{\epsilon}{(1+\epsilon)^2}\sum_{j\in\mathcal{J}}(\tilde{C}_j - r_j)$$

Then, the dual objective is at least

$$\left(\frac{\epsilon}{1+\epsilon}\right)^2\sum_{j\in\mathcal{J}}(\tilde{C}_j - r_j)$$

Let $F_j^{\mathcal{A}}$ be the flow time of a job $j \in \mathcal{J}$ in the schedule constructed by algorithm $\mathcal{A}$; recall that, for a rejected job $j \in \mathcal{R}$, $F_j^{\mathcal{A}}$ corresponds to the time between its release and its rejection. By definition, we have that $\tilde{C}_j - r_j \geq F_j^{\mathcal{A}}$, for each $j \in \mathcal{J}$. Therefore, taking into account that the objective value of our primal linear program is at most twice the value of an optimal non-preemptive schedule, the theorem follows. □

## 3 MINIMIZE TOTAL WEIGHTED FLOW TIME PLUS ENERGY

*Linear Programming Formulation.* Let $\delta_{ij} = \frac{w_j}{p_{ij}}$ be the *density* of a job $j \in \mathcal{J}$ on machine $i \in \mathcal{M}$. Let $s_{ij}(t)$ be a variable that represents the speed at which the job $j \in \mathcal{J}$ is executed on machine $i \in \mathcal{M}$ at time $t$. Given a constant $\gamma$ that will be defined later, we consider the following convex programming formulation for the problem of minimizing the total weighted flow time plus energy.

$$\min \sum_{i\in\mathcal{M}}\sum_{j\in\mathcal{J}}\int_{r_j}^\infty s_{ij}(t)\delta_{ij}(t - r_j + p_{ij})dt + \frac{\alpha}{\gamma(\alpha-1)}\sum_{i\in\mathcal{M}}\sum_{j\in\mathcal{J}} w_j^{\frac{\alpha-1}{\alpha}}\int_{r_j}^\infty s_{ij}(t)dt + \sum_{i\in\mathcal{M}}\int_{r_j}^\infty\Big(\sum_{j\in\mathcal{J}} s_{ij}(t)\Big)^\alpha dt$$

$$\sum_{i\in\mathcal{M}}\int_{r_j}^\infty \frac{s_{ij}(t)}{p_{ij}}dt \geq 1 \qquad \forall j\in\mathcal{J}$$

$$s_{ij}(t) \geq 0 \qquad \forall i\in\mathcal{M}, j\in\mathcal{J}, t\geq r_j$$

The first and the second [2] terms of the objective correspond to the weighted fractional flow time whereas the third term corresponds to the total energy consumed. In order to linearize the convex energy term, we use the following property which holds for any convex function $f(x)$: $f(x) \geq f(y) + f'(y)(x-y)$. Thus, we can relax the objective function by replacing its last term by

$$\sum_{i\in\mathcal{M}}\int_0^\infty(1-\alpha)\big(u_i(t)\big)^\alpha dt + \sum_{i\in\mathcal{M}}\int_0^\infty \alpha\big(u_i(t)\big)^{\alpha-1}\Big(\sum_{j\in\mathcal{J}} s_{ij}(t)\Big)dt$$

Note that the only variables in the above formulation are $s_{ij}(t)$. The quantities $u_i(t)$ are constants that will be defined later. In fact, $u_i(t)$'s will be treated as dual variables and they will be defined during the primal-dual procedure. The dual of the above LP is the following:

$$\max \textstyle\sum_{j\in\mathcal{J}}\lambda_j + \sum_{i\in\mathcal{M}}\int_0^\infty(1-\alpha)\big(u_i(t)\big)^\alpha dt$$

$$\frac{\lambda_j}{p_{ij}} \leq \delta_{ij}(t - r_j + p_{ij}) + \alpha\big(u_i(t)\big)^{\alpha-1} + \frac{\alpha}{\gamma(\alpha-1)}w_j^{\frac{\alpha-1}{\alpha}}$$

$$\forall i\in\mathcal{M}, j\in\mathcal{J}, t\geq r_j$$

*The Algorithm and Definition of Dual Variables.* In this section, we define the scheduling, the rejection and the dispatching policies of our algorithm which is denoted by $\mathcal{A}$. Let $0 < \epsilon < 1$ be some arbitrarily small constant which corresponds to the fraction of the rejected weights. Each job is immediately dispatched to some machine $i \in \mathcal{M}$ upon its arrival. Let $U_i(t)$ be the set of *pending* jobs at time $t$ dispatched to machine $i \in \mathcal{M}$, that is the jobs dispatched to $i$ that have been released but not yet completed or rejected at time $t$. Moreover, let $q_{ij}(t)$ be the remaining volume at time $t$ of job $j$ which is dispatched to machine $i$.

Let $k$ be the job that is being executed on machine $i$ at time $t$. We consider the jobs in $U_i(t) \setminus \{k\}$ sorted in non-increasing order with respect to their densities; in case of ties, we consider the jobs in earliest release time order. We say that a job $j \in U_i(t)\setminus\{k\}$ precedes (resp. succeeds) a job $\ell \in U_i(t)\setminus\{k\}$ if $j$ appears before (resp. after) $\ell$ in the above order, and we write $j \prec \ell$ (resp. $j \succ \ell$). We use the symbols $\preceq$ and $\succeq$ to express the fact that $j$ may coincide with $\ell$.

The *scheduling policy* of the algorithm $\mathcal{A}$ is the following: whenever a machine $i \in \mathcal{M}$ becomes idle at a time $t$, schedule on $i$ the job $j \in U_i(t)$ that precedes any other job in $U_i(t)$. The *speed* of the machine $i$ at the start time $j$ is defined as $s_{ij} = \gamma\Big(\sum_{\ell\in U_i(t)} w_\ell\Big)^{1/\alpha}$. Note that, the speed of $i$ is defined at the beginning of the execution of $j$ and does not change until $j$ is completed or rejected. Assuming that no other jobs arrive in the future, we can compute the expected speed of each remaining pending job $\ell \in U_i(t)$ which is equal to $\gamma\Big(\sum_{\ell'\succeq\ell} w_{\ell'}\Big)^{1/\alpha}$.

As soon as the machine $i$ starts executing a job $j$, we introduce a counter $v_j$ which is initialized to zero. Each time a job $\ell$ is released during the execution of $j$ and it is dispatched to machine $i$, we increase $v_j$ by $w_\ell$. Then, the *rejection policy* of the algorithm $\mathcal{A}$ is the following: interrupt the execution of $j$ and reject it the first time when $v_j > w_j/\epsilon$.

Assume that at the arrival of a new job $j$ at time $r_j$, the machine $i$ is executing the job $k$. For each $\ell \in U_i(t)\setminus\{k\}$, let $W_\ell = \sum_{\ell'\in U_i(t)\setminus\{k\}:\ell'\succeq\ell} w_{\ell'}$. We denote by $\Delta_{ij}$ the marginal increase in the total weighted flow time that will occur following the scheduling and rejection policies of $\mathcal{A}$, if we decide to dispatch the job $j$ to machine $i$. Then, $\Delta_{ij}$ can be bounded as follows (we ignore the increase of the speed and hence the decrease of the processing time for each job $\ell < j$)

$$\Delta_{ij} \le \begin{cases} w_j\left(\frac{q_{ik}(r_j)}{s_k} + \sum_{\ell \le j} \frac{p_{i\ell}}{\gamma W_\ell^{1/\alpha}}\right) + \left(\sum_{\ell > j} w_\ell\right)\frac{p_{ij}}{\gamma W_j^{1/\alpha}} & \text{if } v_k + w_j \le \frac{w_k}{\epsilon} \\ w_j\left(\sum_{\ell \le j} \frac{p_{i\ell}}{\gamma W_\ell^{1/\alpha}}\right) + \left(\sum_{\ell > j} w_\ell\right)\frac{p_{ij}}{\gamma W_j^{1/\alpha}} - \left(\sum_{\ell \ne j} w_\ell\right)\frac{q_{ik}(r_j)}{s_k} & \text{otherwise} \end{cases}$$

where in both cases, the first positive term correspond to the weighted flow time of the job $j$, while the second positive term correspond to the marginal increase of the weighted flow time of other jobs, that is the completion time of the jobs with density smaller than the density of $j$ is delayed by $p_{ij}/\gamma W_j^{1/\alpha}$. The negative term in the second case corresponds to the decrease in the weighted flow time of all jobs in $U_i(t)$ if the job $k$ is rejected. Then, we define a set of variables $\lambda_{ij}$, for all $i \in \mathcal{M}$, as: $\lambda_{ij} = w_j\left(\frac{p_{ij}}{\epsilon} + \sum_{\ell \le j} \frac{p_{i\ell}}{\gamma W_\ell^{1/\alpha}}\right) + \left(\sum_{\ell > j} w_\ell\right)\frac{p_{ij}}{\gamma W_j^{1/\alpha}}$. The *dispatching policy* is the following: dispatch the job $j$ to the machine $i^*$ such that $i^* = \text{argmin}_{i \in \mathcal{M}}\{\lambda_{ij}\}$.

We next define the dual variables $\lambda_j$ as well as the quantities $u_i(t)$. Based on the dispatching policy, we set $\lambda_j = \frac{\epsilon}{1+\epsilon}\min_{i\in\mathcal{M}}\{\lambda_{ij}\}$. For each job $j$, let $D_j$ be the set of the jobs rejected due to the rejection policy between $r_j$ and the time when $j$ is completed or rejected. Let $j_k$ denote the job released at the time when our policy rejects the job $k$. Then, we say that a job $j$ is *definitively finished* at the time $\sum_{k\in D_j} \frac{q_{ik}(r_{j_k})}{s_k}$ after its completion or rejection. For every job $\ell$, define the fractional weight $w_\ell(t)$ of $\ell$ at time $t$ as $w_\ell q_{i\ell}(t)/p_{i\ell}$. Let $Q_i(t)$ be the set of jobs that are dispatched to machine $i$ and are already completed or rejected but no yet definitively finished at time $t$. Let $V_i(t) = \sum_{\ell \in U_i(t) \cup Q_i(t)} w_\ell(t)$ be the total *fractional* weight of jobs that are not definitively finished on machine $i$ at time $t$. We define $u_i(t)$ as follows: $u_i(t) = \left(\frac{\epsilon}{\gamma(1+\epsilon)(\alpha-1)}\right)^{\frac{1}{\alpha-1}} V_i(t)^{1/\alpha}$. Note that when a job is rejected, it is transferred from $U_i(t)$ to $Q_i(t)$ where it remains until the time it is definitively finished.

Consider now two sets of jobs $I_1$ and $I_2$ assigned to machine $i$ such that they are identical except that there is only a job $j \in I_1 \setminus I_2$. Moreover, assume that no job is released after time $r_j$ in either of the instances. Then the algorithm $\mathcal{A}$ is said to be *monotonic* iff $\sum_{\ell\in I_2} w_\ell(t) \le \sum_{\ell \in I_1} w_\ell(t), \forall t$ where the jobs in $I_1$ and $I_2$ are scheduled according to $\mathcal{A}$. The following lemma shows the monotonicity of $V_i(t)$.

Lemma 3.1. *$V_i(t)$ is monotone for every machine i.*

Proof. Let $k$ be the job executing on machine $i$ at time $t$. Observe that $V_i(t)$ changes due to the arrival of a new job. Assume that a new job $j$ arrives at $t = r_j$. Then, it is sufficient to show that $V_i(t)$ is non-decreasing during anytime $t' \ge t$. Consider the jobs in $U_i(t) \setminus \{k\}$. Since all such jobs are scheduled in non-increasing order of their densities, the total fractional weight of jobs in $U_i(t) \setminus \{k\}$ is monotonic with respect to the arrival of a new job (refer to Lemma 6.1 in [2]).

In the case where $k$ is not rejected then for $t' < t + \frac{q_{ik}(r_j)}{s_j}$, the speed of the machine $i$ is a constant. Hence, $U_i(t')$ is a constant. Using Lemma 6.1 in [2], the lemma holds for this case. In the case where $k$ is rejected then $U_i(t)$ decreases due to the removal of $k$. Since all jobs in $U_i(t) \setminus \{j\}$ remain for at least $\frac{q_{ik}(r_j)}{s_j}$ time in $Q_i(t)$ after their completion or rejection from $U_i(t)$, the total fractional weight of jobs in $U_i(t) \cup Q_i(t)$ is monotonic with respect to the rejection of job $k$. Using this property with Lemma 6.1 in [2], the lemma holds. □

*Analysis.* The following lemma guarantees that the definition of the dual variables lead always to a feasible solution for the dual program.

Lemma 3.2. *For every $i \in \mathcal{M}, j \in \mathcal{J}$ and $t \ge r_j$, the dual constraint is feasible.*

Proof. Fix a machine $i$. By Lemma 3.1, $u_i(t)$'s do never decrease during the execution of the algorithm. Hence, it is sufficient to prove the inequality for the job $j$ at time $r_j$. Let $k$ be the job executed in machine $i$ at $r_j$ . Moreover, let $\bar{C}_j$ be the completion time of the job $j$ estimated at time $r_j$ if it is assigned to machine $i$. Specifically, if $k$ is rejected then $\bar{C}_j = r_j + \sum_{\ell \le j} \frac{p_{i\ell}}{\gamma W_\ell^{1/\alpha}}$; otherwise we have $\bar{C}_j = r_j + \frac{q_{ik}(r_j)}{s_k} + \sum_{\ell \le j} \frac{p_{i\ell}}{\gamma W_\ell^{1/\alpha}}$.

By the definitions of $\lambda_j$ and $\lambda_{ij}$, we have:

$$\frac{\lambda_j}{p_{ij}} \le \frac{\epsilon}{1+\epsilon}\frac{\lambda_{ij}}{p_{ij}} = \frac{\epsilon}{1+\epsilon}\left(\frac{w_j}{p_{ij}}\left(\frac{p_{ij}}{\epsilon} + \sum_{\ell \le j}\frac{p_{i\ell}}{\gamma W_\ell^{1/\alpha}}\right) + \left(\sum_{\ell > j} w_\ell\right)\frac{1}{\gamma W_j^{1/\alpha}}\right)$$

Let $w_n$ denote the weight of the latest job according to the precedence order defined above.

**Case 1:** $t \le \bar{C}_j$. Assume, first, that the job $k$ is running at time $t$. Hence, we have that

$$t - r_j = \frac{q_{ik}(r_j) - q_{ik}(t)}{s_k}$$

and thus

$$\begin{aligned} &\frac{\lambda_j}{p_{ij}} - \delta_{ij}(t - r_j + p_{ij}) \\ &\le \frac{\epsilon}{1+\epsilon}\left(\frac{w_j}{p_{ij}}\left(\frac{p_{ij}}{\epsilon} + \sum_{\ell \le j}\frac{p_{i\ell}}{\gamma W_\ell^{1/\alpha}}\right) + \left(\sum_{\ell > j} w_\ell\right)\frac{1}{\gamma W_j^{1/\alpha}}\right) \\ &\quad - \frac{w_j}{p_{ij}}\left(\frac{q_{ik}(r_j) - q_{ik}(t)}{s_k} + p_{ij}\right) \\ &\le \frac{\epsilon}{1+\epsilon}\left(\frac{w_j}{p_{ij}}\sum_{\ell \le j}\frac{p_{i\ell}}{\gamma W_\ell^{1/\alpha}} + \left(\sum_{\ell > j} w_\ell\right)\frac{1}{\gamma W_j^{1/\alpha}}\right) \\ &\quad - \frac{w_j}{p_{ij}} \cdot \frac{q_{ik}(r_j) - q_{ik}(t)}{s_k} \\ &\le \frac{\epsilon}{1+\epsilon}\left(\frac{w_j}{p_{ij}}\sum_{\ell \le j}\frac{p_{i\ell}}{\gamma W_\ell^{1/\alpha}} + \left(\sum_{\ell > j} w_\ell\right)\frac{1}{\gamma W_j^{1/\alpha}}\right) \end{aligned}$$

(since $t \ge r_j$ and hence $q_{ik}(r_j) - q_{ik}(t) \ge 0$)

$$\leq \frac{\epsilon}{1+\epsilon}\left(\sum_{\ell \leq j} \frac{w_\ell}{\gamma W_\ell^{1/\alpha}} + \left(\sum_{\ell > j} w_\ell\right)\frac{1}{\gamma W_j^{1/\alpha}}\right)$$

(since $\frac{w_\ell}{p_{i\ell}} \geq \frac{w_j}{p_{ij}}$ for any $\ell \leq j$)

$$\leq \frac{\epsilon}{1+\epsilon}\left(\sum_{\ell \leq j} \frac{w_\ell}{\gamma W_\ell^{1/\alpha}} + \sum_{\ell > j} \frac{w_\ell}{\gamma W_\ell^{1/\alpha}}\right)$$

$$= \frac{\epsilon}{1+\epsilon}\sum_{\ell \neq k} \frac{w_\ell}{\gamma W_\ell^{1/\alpha}}$$

$$\leq \frac{\epsilon}{1+\epsilon}\int_{w_n}^{V_i(t)+w_j} \frac{dz}{\gamma z^{1/\alpha}}$$

$$= \frac{\epsilon}{1+\epsilon}\cdot\frac{\alpha}{\gamma(\alpha-1)}\left(V_i(t)+w_j\right)^{\frac{\alpha-1}{\alpha}}$$

$$\leq \frac{\epsilon}{1+\epsilon}\cdot\frac{\alpha}{\gamma(\alpha-1)}\left(V_i(t)^{\frac{\alpha-1}{\alpha}} + w_j^{\frac{\alpha-1}{\alpha}}\right)$$

$$= \frac{\epsilon}{1+\epsilon}\cdot\frac{\alpha}{\gamma(\alpha-1)}\left(\frac{\gamma(1+\epsilon)(\alpha-1)}{\epsilon}\left(u_i(t)\right)^{\alpha-1} + w_j^{\frac{\alpha-1}{\alpha}}\right)$$

$$= \alpha\left(u_i(t)\right)^{\alpha-1} + \frac{\epsilon}{1+\epsilon}\cdot\frac{\alpha}{\gamma(\alpha-1)}w_j^{\frac{\alpha-1}{\alpha}}$$

$$\leq \alpha\left(u_i(t)\right)^{\alpha-1} + \frac{\alpha}{\gamma(\alpha-1)}w_j^{\frac{\alpha-1}{\alpha}}$$

Assume now that a job $h \neq k$ is executing at time $t$. Therefore, the machine $i$ has processed all the jobs which have density higher than $\delta_{ih}$. Moreover, the job $k$ is either completed or rejected. Hence, we have that

$$t - r_j \geq \sum_{\ell < h} \frac{p_{i\ell}}{\gamma {W_\ell}^{1/\alpha}} + \frac{p_{ih} - q_{ih}(t)}{\gamma {W_h}^{1/\alpha}}$$

and thus

$$\frac{\lambda_j}{p_{ij}} - \delta_{ij}(t - r_j + p_{ij})$$

$$\leq \frac{\epsilon}{1+\epsilon}\left(\frac{w_j}{p_{ij}}\left(\frac{p_{ij}}{\epsilon} + \sum_{\ell \leq j}\frac{p_{i\ell}}{\gamma W_\ell^{1/\alpha}}\right) + \left(\sum_{\ell > j} w_\ell\right)\frac{1}{\gamma W_j^{1/\alpha}}\right)$$

$$- \frac{w_j}{p_{ij}}\left(\sum_{\ell < h}\frac{p_{i\ell}}{\gamma {W_\ell}^{1/\alpha}} + \frac{p_{ih} - q_{ih}(t)}{\gamma {W_h}^{1/\alpha}} + p_{ij}\right)$$

$$= \frac{\epsilon}{1+\epsilon}\left(\frac{w_j}{p_{ij}}\sum_{h \leq \ell \leq j}\frac{p_{i\ell}}{\gamma W_\ell^{1/\alpha}} + \left(\sum_{\ell > j} w_\ell\right)\frac{1}{\gamma W_j^{1/\alpha}}\right)$$

$$- \frac{w_j}{p_{ij}}\left(\frac{1}{1+\epsilon}\cdot\sum_{\ell < h}\frac{p_{i\ell}}{\gamma W_\ell^{1/\alpha}} - \frac{\epsilon}{1+\epsilon}p_{ij} - \frac{p_{ih} - q_{ih}(t)}{\gamma {W_h}^{1/\alpha}}\right)$$

$$\leq \frac{\epsilon}{1+\epsilon}\left(\sum_{h \leq \ell \leq j}\frac{w_\ell}{\gamma W_\ell^{1/\alpha}} + \sum_{\ell > j}\frac{w_\ell}{\gamma W_\ell^{1/\alpha}}\right)$$

$$= \frac{\epsilon}{1+\epsilon}\sum_{\ell \geq h}\frac{w_\ell}{\gamma W_\ell^{1/\alpha}} \leq \frac{\epsilon}{1+\epsilon}\int_{w_n}^{V_i(t)+w_j}\frac{d_z}{\gamma z^{1/\alpha}}$$

$$\leq \alpha\left(u_i(t)\right)^{\alpha-1} + \frac{\alpha}{\gamma(\alpha-1)}w_j^{\frac{\alpha-1}{\alpha}}$$

**Case 2:** $t > \bar{C}_j$. Let $h$ be the job executing at time $t$. Thus, the machine $i$ has processed all the jobs which have density higher than $\delta_{ih}$. Hence, we have

$$t - r_j \geq \sum_{\ell < h}\frac{p_{i\ell}}{\gamma W_\ell^{1/\alpha}} + \frac{p_{ih} - q_{ih}(t)}{\gamma W_h^{1/\alpha}}$$

Thus

$$\frac{\lambda_j}{p_{ij}} - \delta_{ij}(t - r_j + p_{ij})$$

$$\leq \frac{\epsilon}{1+\epsilon}\left(\frac{w_j}{p_{ij}}\left(\frac{p_{ij}}{\epsilon} + \sum_{\ell \leq j}\frac{p_{i\ell}}{\gamma W_\ell^{1/\alpha}}\right) + \left(\sum_{\ell > j} w_\ell\right)\frac{1}{\gamma W_j^{1/\alpha}}\right)$$

$$- \frac{w_j}{p_{ij}}\left(\sum_{\ell < h}\frac{p_{i\ell}}{\gamma {W_\ell}^{1/\alpha}} + \frac{p_{ih} - q_{ih}(t)}{\gamma {W_h}^{1/\alpha}} + p_{ij}\right)$$

$$= \frac{\epsilon}{1+\epsilon}\left(\frac{w_j}{p_{ij}}\sum_{\ell \leq j}\frac{p_{i\ell}}{\gamma W_\ell^{1/\alpha}} + \left(\sum_{\ell > j} w_\ell\right)\frac{1}{\gamma W_j^{1/\alpha}}\right)$$

$$- \frac{w_j}{p_{ij}}\left(\frac{1}{1+\epsilon}\cdot\sum_{\ell < h}\frac{p_{i\ell}}{\gamma W_\ell^{1/\alpha}} - \frac{\epsilon}{1+\epsilon}p_{ij} - \frac{p_{ih} - q_{ih}(t)}{\gamma {W_h}^{1/\alpha}}\right)$$

$$\leq \frac{\epsilon}{1+\epsilon}\left(\sum_{\ell > h}\frac{w_\ell}{\gamma W_\ell^{1/\alpha}}\right)$$

$$= \frac{\epsilon}{1+\epsilon}\sum_{\ell \geq h}\frac{w_\ell}{\gamma W_\ell^{1/\alpha}} \leq \frac{\epsilon}{1+\epsilon}\int_{w_n}^{V_i(t)+w_j}\frac{d_z}{\gamma z^{1/\alpha}}$$

$$\leq \alpha\left(u_i(t)\right)^{\alpha-1} + \frac{\alpha}{\gamma(\alpha-1)}w_j^{\frac{\alpha-1}{\alpha}}$$

□

Based on this lemma we can prove Theorem 1.3.

Proof of Theorem 1.3. By Lemma 3.2, the proposed dual variables constitute a feasible solution for the dual program. Since each job $j \in \mathcal{J}$ is charged to at most one other job while a job $k$ is rejected the first time where $v_k > \frac{w_k}{\epsilon}$, the algorithm $\mathcal{A}$ rejects jobs of total weight at most $\epsilon\sum_{j\in\mathcal{J}} w_j$. Hence, it remains to give a lower bound for the dual objective based on the proposed dual variables.

Let $\mathcal{R}$ be the set of rejected jobs. We denote by $F_j^{\mathcal{A}}$ the flow-time of a job $j \in \mathcal{J} \setminus \mathcal{R}$ in the schedule of $\mathcal{A}$. By slightly abusing the notation, for a job $k \in \mathcal{R}$, we will also use $F_k^{\mathcal{A}}$ to denote the total time passed after $r_k$ until deciding to reject a job $k$, that is, if $k$ is rejected at the release of the job $j \in \mathcal{J}$ then $F_k^{\mathcal{A}} = r_j - r_k$. Denote by $j_k$ the job released at the moment we decided to reject $k$, i.e., for the counter $v_k$ before the arrival of job $j_k$ we have that $w_k/\epsilon - w_{j_k} < v_k < w_k/\epsilon$.

Let $\Delta_j$ be the total increase in the flow-time caused by the arrival of the job $j \in \mathcal{J}$, i.e., $\Delta_j = \Delta_{ij}$, where $i \in \mathcal{M}$ is the machine to which $j$ is dispatched by $\mathcal{A}$. For the objective function of the dual program we have

$$\sum_{j\in\mathcal{J}}\lambda_j + \sum_{i\in\mathcal{M}}\int_0^\infty (1-\alpha)\big(u_i(t)\big)^\alpha dt$$
$$\geq \frac{\epsilon}{1+\epsilon}\left(\sum_{j\in\mathcal{J}}\Delta_j + \sum_{k\in\mathcal{R}}\left(\frac{q_{ik}(r_{jk})}{s_k}\sum_{\ell\neq j_k} w_\ell\right)\right)$$
$$-(\alpha-1)\left(\frac{\epsilon}{\gamma(1+\epsilon)(\alpha-1)}\right)^{\frac{\alpha}{\alpha-1}} V_i(t)$$
$$\geq \left(\frac{\epsilon}{1+\epsilon} - (\alpha-1)\left(\frac{\epsilon}{\gamma(1+\epsilon)(\alpha-1)}\right)^{\frac{\alpha}{\alpha-1}}\right)F^*$$

The total weighted flow time plus energy is

$$2F^* + \left(\frac{\alpha}{\gamma(\alpha-1)}\right)F^* + \sum_i\int_0^\infty (s_i(t))^\alpha dt \leq \left(2 + \left(\frac{\alpha}{\gamma(\alpha-1)}\right) + \gamma^\alpha\right)F^*$$

.

Hence the competitive ratio is:

$$\frac{\left(2 + \left(\frac{\alpha}{\gamma(\alpha-1)}\right) + \gamma^\alpha\right)}{\left(\frac{\epsilon}{1+\epsilon}\right) - \left(\frac{\epsilon}{\gamma(1+\epsilon)}\right)^{\frac{\alpha}{\alpha-1}}(\alpha-1)^{\frac{-1}{\alpha-1}}}$$

We choose $\gamma = \left(\frac{\epsilon}{1+\epsilon}\right)^{\frac{1}{\alpha-1}} \frac{1}{\alpha-1}(\alpha - 1 + \ln(\alpha-1))^{\frac{\alpha-1}{\alpha}}$. Observe that denominator becomes $\frac{\epsilon}{1+\epsilon}(\frac{\ln(\alpha-1)}{\alpha-1+\ln(\alpha-1)})$ and the numerator becomes $2 + 2\left(\frac{1+\epsilon}{\epsilon}\right)^{\frac{1}{\alpha-1}} + \left(\frac{\epsilon}{1+\epsilon}\right)^2$. Hence the competitive ratio is at most $O\Big(\left(1+\frac{1}{\epsilon}\right)^{\frac{\alpha}{\alpha-1}}\Big)$. □

## 4 MINIMIZE TOTAL ENERGY CONSUMPTION

*Formulation.* In the problem, we consider the sets of discretized speeds $\mathcal{V}$ and times. We can do that and loose only a factor $(1+\epsilon)$ for $\epsilon$ arbitrarily small. In the non-preemptive model, the execution of a job is specified by three parameters: (1) a machine in which it is executed; (2) a starting time; and (3) a speed which is constant during its execution. Note that the parameters imply the completion time of job. A *valid* execution of a job $j$ must have the starting time and completion time in $[r_j, d_j]$. We say that a *strategy* of a job is a specification of a valid execution of the job. Formally, a strategy $s_{i,j,k}$ of a job $j$ in machine $i$ indicates the starting time of the job and its speed during the execution. Let $\mathcal{S}_j$ be a set of strategies of job $j$. As the sets of speeds and times are finite, so is the set of strategies $\mathcal{S}_j$ for every job $j$. Let $x_{i,j,k}$ be a variable indicating whether job $j$ is executed by strategy $s_{i,j,k} \in \mathcal{S}_j$. We say that $A$ is a *configuration* in machine $i$ if $A$ is a feasible schedule of a subset of jobs. Specifically, $A$ consists of tuples $(i,j,k)$ meaning that job $j$ is executed in machine $i$ following the strategy $s_{i,j,k}$. For configuration $A$ and machine $i$, let $z_{i,A}$ be a variable such that $z_{i,A} = 1$ if and only if for every triple $(i,j,k) \in A$, $x_{i,j,k} = 1$. In other words, $z_{i,A} = 1$ iff the schedule in machine $i$ is exactly $A$. The energy cost of a configuration $A$ of machine $i$ is $f_i(A) = \sum_t P_i(A(t))$ where $A(t)$ is the speed of the corresponding schedule at time $t$. We consider the following formulation and the dual of its relaxation.

$$\min \sum_{i,A} f_i(A) z_{i,A}$$
$$\sum_{i,k:s_{i,j,k}\in\mathcal{S}_j} x_{i,j,k} = 1 \qquad \forall j$$
$$\sum_{A:(i,j,k)\in A} z_{i,A} = x_{i,j,k} \qquad \forall i,j,k$$
$$\sum_A z_{i,A} = 1 \qquad \forall i$$
$$x_{i,j,k}, z_{i,A} \in \{0,1\} \qquad \forall i,j,k,A$$

$$\max \sum_j \delta_j + \sum_i \gamma_i$$
$$\delta_j \leq \beta_{i,j,k} \qquad \forall i,j,k$$
$$\gamma_i + \sum_{(i,j,k)\in A} \beta_{i,j,k} \leq f_i(A) \qquad \forall i,A$$

In the primal, the first constraint guarantees that a job $j$ has to be processed by some valid execution (in some machine). The second constraint ensures that if job $j$ follows strategy $s_{i,j,k}$ then in the solution, the schedule (configuration) on machine $i$ must contain the execution corresponding to strategy $s_{i,j,k}$. The third constraint says that in the solution, there is always a configuration (schedule) associated to machine $i$.

*Algorithm.* We first interpret intuitively the dual variables, dual constraints and derive useful observations for a competitive algorithm. Variable $\delta_j$ represents the increase of energy to the arrival of job $j$. Variable $\beta_{i,j,k}$ stands for the marginal energy if job $j$ follows strategy $s_{i,j,k}$. By this interpretation, the first dual constraint clearly indicates the greedy behavior of an algorithm. That is, if a new job $j$ is released, select a strategy $s_{i,j,k} \in \mathcal{S}_j$ that minimizes the marginal increase of the total energy.

Let $A_i^*$ be the set of current schedule of machine $i$. Initially, $A_i^* \leftarrow \emptyset$ for every $i$. At the arrival of job $j$, select a strategy $s_{i,j,k} \in \mathcal{S}_j$ that minimizes $\left[f_i(A_i^* \cup s_{i,j,k}) - f_i(A_i^*)\right]$ where $(A_i^* \cup s_{i,j,k})$ is the current schedule plus the execution of job $j$ which follows strategy $s_{i,j,k}$. Let $s_{i^*,j,k^*}$ be an optimal strategy. Then assign job $j$ to machine $i^*$ and process it according to the corresponding execution of $s_{i^*,j,k^*}$. In the algorithm, we never interrupt or modify the speed of a job.

We implement this algorithm as follows. Let $u_{it}$ be the speed of machine $i$ at time $t$. Initially, set $u_{it} \leftarrow 0$ for every machine $i$ and time $t$. At the arrival of a job $j$, compute the minimum energy increase if $j$ is assigned to machine $i$ and is executed with constant speed. This corresponds to the optimization problem

$$\min_i \min_{\tau,v} \sum_{t=\tau}^{\tau+p_{ij}/v}\left[f_i\big(u_{it}+v\big) - f_i\big(u_{it}\big)\right]$$
$$\text{s.t} \quad r_j \leq \tau \leq \tau + \frac{p_{ij}}{v} \leq d_j, \quad v \in \mathcal{V}$$

*Dual variables.* Assume that all energy power functions $f_i$ are $(\lambda,\mu)$-smooth for some fixed parameters $\lambda > 0$ and $\mu < 1$. We construct a dual feasible solution. Define $\delta_j$ as $1/\lambda$ times the the increase of the total cost due to the arrival of job $j$. For each machine $i$ and job $j$, define $\beta_{i,j,k} := \frac{1}{\lambda}\left[f_i(A^*_{i,<j} \cup s_{i,j,k}) - f_i(A^*_{i,<j})\right]$ where $A^*_{i,<j}$ is the schedule of $i$ (due to the algorithm) prior to the arrival of $j$. Finally, for every machine $i$ define dual variable $\gamma_i := -\frac{\mu}{\lambda} f_i(A^*_i)$ where $A^*_i$ is the schedule of machine $i$ (at the end of the instance).

Lemma 4.1. *The defined variables form a dual feasible solution.*

Proof. The first dual constraint follows immediately the definitions of $\delta_j, \beta_{i,j,k}$ and the decision of the algorithm. Specifically, the right-hand side of the constraint represents $1/\lambda$ times the increase of energy if a job $j$ follows a strategy $s_{i,j,k}$. This is larger than $1/\lambda$ times the minimum increase of energy optimized over all strategies in $\mathcal{S}_j$, which is $\delta_j$.

For the second constraint, fix a machine $i$ and an arbitrary configuration $A$ on machine $i$. Then,

$$-\frac{\mu}{\lambda} f_i(A^*_i) + \frac{1}{\lambda} \sum_{(i,j,k)\in A} \left[f_i(A^*_{i,<j} \cup s_{i,j,k}) - f_i(A^*_{i,<j})\right] \leq f_i(A) \Leftrightarrow$$

$$\sum_{(i,j,k)\in A} \left[f_i(A^*_{i,<j} \cup s_{i,j,k}) - f_i(A^*_{i,<j})\right] \leq \lambda f_i(A) + \mu f_i(A^*_i) \quad (1)$$

We argue that this inequality follows the $(\lambda, \mu)$-smoothness of energy power functions. We slightly abuse notation by defining $A^*_{i,<j}(t)$ as the speed of machine $i$ (due to the algorithm) at time $t$ before the arrival of job $j$ and $s_{i,j,k}(t)$ be the speed at time $t$ of job $j$ if it follows the strategy $s_{i,j,k}$. Observe that $A^*_{i,<j}(t)$ is the sum of speeds (according to the algorithm) at time $t$ of jobs assigned to machine $i$ prior to job $j$. For any time $t$, as the power $P_i$ is $(\lambda, \mu)$-smooth, we have

$$\sum_{(i,j,k)\in A} \left[P_i\left(A^*_{i,<j}(t) + s_{i,j,k}(t)\right) - P_i\left(A^*_{i,<j}(t)\right)\right]$$
$$\leq \lambda P_i\left(\sum_{(i,j,k)\in A} s_{i,j,k}(t)\right) + \mu P_i\left(A^*_i(t)\right)$$

Summing over all $t$, Inequality (1) holds and the lemma follows. □

We are now ready to prove the Theorem 1.5.

Proof of Theorem 1.5. By the definition of the dual variables, the dual objective is

$$\sum_j \delta_j + \sum_i \gamma_i = \sum_i \frac{1}{\lambda} f_i(A^*_i) - \sum_i \frac{\mu}{\lambda} f_i(A^*_i) = \frac{1-\mu}{\lambda} \sum_i f_i(A^*_i)$$

Besides, the cost of the solution due to the algorithm is $\sum_i f_i(A^*_i)$. Hence, the competitive ratio is at most $\lambda/(1-\mu)$.

In particular, the power functions of the form $P_i(s) = s^{\alpha_i}, \alpha_i > 1$, are $O\left(\alpha^{\alpha-1}, \frac{\alpha-1}{\alpha}\right)$-smooth where $\alpha = \max_i \alpha_i$. By the smooth inequalities in [9], for any sequences of non-negative real numbers $\{a_1, a_2, \ldots, a_n\}$ and $\{b_1, b_2, \ldots, b_n\}$ and for any $\alpha \geq 1$, it holds that

$$\sum_{i=1}^{n} \left[\left(b_i + \sum_{j=1}^{i} a_j\right)^\alpha - \left(\sum_{j=1}^{i} a_j\right)^\alpha\right] \leq \lambda(\alpha) \cdot \left(\sum_{i=1}^{n} b_i\right)^\alpha + \mu(\alpha) \cdot \left(\sum_{i=1}^{n} a_i\right)^\alpha$$

where $\mu(\alpha) = \frac{\alpha-1}{\alpha}$ and $\lambda(\alpha) = \Theta\left(\alpha^{\alpha-1}\right)$. That implies the competitive ratio $O\left(\alpha^\alpha\right)$. □

## 5 CONCLUSIONS

This paper considered designing online non-preemptive schedulers – a domain which has long resisted algorithms with strong worst case guarantees . The paper gave provably competitive algorithms in the rejection model. This shows how relaxed models can give rise to good algorithms for the non-preemptive setting. It is of significant interest to develop other realistic relaxations of worst case models (like rejection or resource augmentation) that give rise to strong algorithms for non-preemptive settings.

## ACKNOWLEDGMENTS

Nguyen Kim Thang is supported by the ANR project OATA n° ANR-15-CE40-0015-01, Hadamard PGMO and DIM RFSI. Abhinav Srivastav was supported by the PSL project Multi-Fac and is supported by the ANR project OATA n° ANR-15-CE40-0015-01. Benjamin Moseley was supported in part by a Google Research Award, and NSF Grants CCF-1617724, CCF-1733873 and CCF-1725661.

## REFERENCES

[1] Susanne Albers, Evripidis Bampis, Dimitrios Letsios, Giorgio Lucarelli, and Richard Stotz. 2016. Scheduling on power-heterogeneous processors. In *Latin American Symposium on Theoretical Informatics*. 41–54.
[2] S. Anand, Naveen Garg, and Amit Kumar. 2012. Resource augmentation for weighted flow-time explained by dual fitting. In *Symposium on Discrete Algorithms*. 1228–1241.
[3] Nikhil Bansal. 2017. Some Open Problems in Scheduling. In *Proc. 13th Workshop on Models and Algorithms for Planning and Scheduling Problems*.
[4] Nikhil Bansal, Ho-Leung Chan, Dmitriy Katz, and Kirk Pruhs. 2012. Improved Bounds for Speed Scaling in Devices Obeying the Cube-Root Rule. *Theory of Computing* 8, 1 (2012), 209–229.
[5] Nikhil Bansal, Ho-Leung Chan, and Kirk Pruhs. 2009. Speed scaling with an arbitrary power function. In *Proc. 20th ACM-SIAM Symposium on Discrete Algorithms*. 693–701.
[6] Nikhil Bansal, Tracy Kimbrel, and Kirk Pruhs. 2007. Speed scaling to manage energy and temperature. *J. ACM* 54, 1 (2007).
[7] Chandra Chekuri, Sanjeev Khanna, and An Zhu. 2001. Algorithms for minimizing weighted flow time. In *Proceedings of the thirty-third annual ACM symposium on Theory of computing*. 84–93.
[8] Anamitra Roy Choudhury, Syamantak Das, Naveen Garg, and Amit Kumar. 2015. Rejecting jobs to Minimize Load and Maximum Flow-time. In *Proc. Symposium on Discrete Algorithms*. 1114–1133.
[9] Johanne Cohen, Christoph Dürr, and Nguyen Kim Thang. 2012. Smooth inequalities and equilibrium inefficiency in scheduling games. In *International Workshop on Internet and Network Economics*. 350–363.
[10] Nikhil R. Devanur and Zhiyi Huang. 2014. Primal Dual Gives Almost Optimal Energy Efficient Online Algorithms. In *Proc. 25th ACM-SIAM Symposium on Discrete Algorithms*.
[11] Leah Epstein and Rob van Stee. 2006. Optimal on-line flow time with resource augmentation. *Discrete Applied Mathematics* 154, 4 (2006), 611–621.
[12] Bala Kalyanasundaram and Kirk Pruhs. 2000. Speed is as powerful as clairvoyance. *J. ACM* 47, 4 (2000), 617–643.
[13] Hans Kellerer, Thomas Tautenhahn, and Gerhard J. Woeginger. 1999. Approximability and Nonapproximability Results for Minimizing Total Flow Time on a Single Machine. *SIAM J. Comput.* 28, 4 (1999), 1155–1166.
[14] Giorgio Lucarelli, Nguyen Kim Thang, Abhinav Srivastav, and Denis Trystram. 2016. Online Non-preemptive Scheduling in a Resource Augmentation Model based on Duality. In *European Symposium on Algorithms (ESA)*, Vol. 57. 1–17.
[15] Cynthia A Phillips, Clifford Stein, Eric Torng, and Joel Wein. 2002. Optimal time-critical scheduling via resource augmentation. *Algorithmica* 32, 2 (2002), 163–200.
[16] Nguyen Kim Thang. 2013. Lagrangian Duality in Online Scheduling with Resource Augmentation and Speed Scaling. In *Proc. 21st European Symposium on Algorithms*. 755–766.
[17] Nguyen Kim Thang. 2017. Online Primal-Dual Algorithms with Configuration Linear Programs. *arXiv:1708.04903* (2017).
[18] Frances Yao, Alan Demers, and Scott Shenker. 1995. A scheduling model for reduced CPU energy. In *Proceedings. 36th Annual Symposium on Foundations of Computer Science*. 374–382.

# The Price of Bounded Preemption

Noga Alon*
Tel-Aviv University
Tel-Aviv, Israel
Princeton University
Princeton, New Jersey, USA
nogaa@post.tau.ac.il

Yossi Azar†
Tel-Aviv University
Tel-Aviv, Israel
azar@tau.ac.il

Mark Berlin
Tel-Aviv University
Tel-Aviv, Israel
markberlin@mail.tau.ac.il

## ABSTRACT

In this paper we provide a tight bound for the *price of preemption* for scheduling jobs on a single machine (or multiple machines). The input consists of a set of jobs to be scheduled and of an integer parameter $k \geq 1$. Each job has a release time, deadline, length (also called processing time) and value associated with it. The goal is to feasibly schedule a subset of the jobs so that their total value is maximal; while preemption of a job is permitted, a job may be preempted no more than $k$ times. The price of preemption is the worst possible (i.e., largest) ratio of the optimal non-bounded-preemptive scheduling to the optimal $k$-bounded-preemptive scheduling.

Our results show that allowing at most $k$ preemptions suffices to guarantee a $\Theta(\min\{\log_{k+1} n, \log_{k+1} P\})$ fraction of the total value achieved when the number of preemptions is unrestricted (where $n$ is the number of the jobs and $P$ the ratio of the maximal length to the minimal length), giving us an upper bound for the price; a specific scenario serves to prove the tightness of this bound. We further show that when no preemptions are permitted at all (i.e., $k = 0$), the price is $\Theta(\min\{n, \log P\})$.

As part of the proof, we introduce the notion of the *Bounded-Degree Ancestor-Free Sub-Forest (BAS)*. We investigate the problem of computing the maximal-value BAS of a given forest and give a tight bound for the loss factor, which is $\Theta(\log_{k+1} n)$ as well, where $n$ is the size of the original forest and $k$ is the bound on the degree of the sub-forest.

## CCS CONCEPTS

• **Mathematics of computing** → **Trees**; • **Theory of computation** → **Scheduling algorithms**;

## KEYWORDS

scheduling jobs; multiple machines; bounded preemptions; bounded-degree sub-forest

*Partially supported by the Israel Science Foundation (ISF) and the GIF.
†Partially supported by the ISF grant no. 1506/16 and by the ICRC Blavatnik Fund.


ACM ISBN 978-1-4503-5799-9/18/07...$15.00
https://doi.org/10.1145/3210377.3210407

**ACM Reference Format:**
Noga Alon, Yossi Azar, and Mark Berlin. 2018. The Price of Bounded Preemption. In *Proceedings of 30th ACM Symposium on Parallelism in Algorithms and Architectures (SPAA'18).* ACM, New York, NY, USA, 10 pages. https://doi.org/10.1145/3210377.3210407

## 1 INTRODUCTION

### 1.1 Background

We study the bounded preemption real-time scheduling problem in an off-line setting, modelled as follows. There is a set $J$ of $n$ jobs available for scheduling, each of the jobs is associated with a triplet $\langle r_j, d_j, p_j \rangle$, denoting its release time, deadline and length (also called processing time), respectively, and with a value val$(j)$. In addition, there is an integer $k > 0$. The jobs can be scheduled on a single machine as well as on multiple machines (for which we consider the migrative and non-migrative cases alike).

A *feasible k-bounded-preemptive schedule* is a scheduling of the jobs for execution in a way that at most one job is executed in every moment, the time constraints are not violated and that no job is preempted (i.e., its execution is stopped) more than $k$ times. The objective is to provide a feasible (in the sense defined in the last sentence) schedule for a subset of the jobs of maximum total value.

We want to investigate the *price* of bounding preemption to $k$, which is defined as PoBP $\triangleq \sup_J \frac{\text{OPT}_\infty(J)}{\text{OPT}_k(J)}$, i.e. the amount of value we lose by limiting the preemptions to $k$ with respect to the optimal $\infty$-preemptive scheduling. Also note that Lawler [21] has already found an optimal algorithm for the unbounded case on a single machine, which in turn can be extended to yield a constant factor approximation for the multiple identical machines setting; therefore, the price of bounded preemption and the approximation factor for the problem can be related to each other.

### 1.2 Motivation

The (NP-hard) problem of unbounded preemptive scheduling on multiple identical machines (denoted $P \,|\, pmtn, r_j \,|\, \sum_j (1 - U_j) W_j$, using the notation of [17]) was first analyzed by Lawler in [21], who found for the single-machine case an optimal solution in pseudo-polynomial time, which becomes polynomial for unit-value jobs. This (single-machine) solution can be transformed into an FPTAS using a technique developed by Pruhs and Woeginger [25].

This result can in turn be extended for multiple (identical) machines in the following way. First, one can use the same FPTAS iteratively on the residual jobs set [2], thus obtaining a $(2 + \epsilon)$-approximation for the non-migrative case. Then, this result can be further extended to the migrative case using the result of [18], thus obtaining a $(6+\epsilon)$-approximation.

However, in a real-world setting, preemption comes with a certain price tag (e.g., the sequence of operations required for a context switch), and so one would want to somehow limit its usage: hence the motivation to study the bounded preemption setting.

The *bounded* version of the problem was addressed using several different approaches (e.g., [11, 12, 27]; surveyed in [13]). The approach consisting of bounding the number of preemptions per job, which is also the approach studied in this paper, was first addressed by Albagli-Kim et al. [1], who showed an $O(1)$-approximation for the special cases of unit-value and unit-density.

Other approaches to the notion of the power of preemption (albeit without regard to specific $k$) were suggested in [26] (defining it in terms of makespan) and [16] (defining it in terms of cost).

### 1.3 Our Results

Our paper provides both lower and upper bounds for the price of $k$-bounded preemption in terms of $n \triangleq |J|$ (i.e., the number of jobs) and of $P \triangleq \frac{\max_j p_j}{\min_j p_j}$.

- First, we explore the problem of the $k$-Bounded Degree Ancestor-Free Sub-Forest ($k$-BAS) and find:
  - an optimal solution using Dynamic Programming;
  - a $\Theta(\log_{k+1} n)$ bound for the loss factor yielded by the optimal solution.
- We then proceed to bound the price of bounded preemption and achieve the following:
  - an upper bound of $PoBP_k = O(\log_{k+1} n)$, for single and multiple machines alike;
  - an upper bound of $PoBP_k = O(\log_{k+1} P)$, for single and multiple machines alike;
  - these above bounds are proven to be tight.
- We also show that for the special case of $k = 0$, i.e. when no preemptions are allowed for the machine, but an unbounded number of preemptions is allowed for a hypothetical competitor. We establish $PoBP_k = \Theta(\min\{n, \log P\})$ for this case.

### 1.4 Other Related Work

Recall that Lawler's solution for the non-bounded preemption problem on a single machine [21] can be transformed into an FPTAS, which in turn can be extended to a $(2+\epsilon)$-approximation for multiple non-migrative machines and to a $(6+\epsilon)$-approximation for multiple migrative machines (as described in subsection 1.2). Also, Baptiste et al. [5, 6] gave a polynomial algorithm for the special case of non-bounded preemption on a single machine with uniform processing time.

Recall also that Albagli-Kim et al. [1] established an $O(1)$-approximation (and price) for both the unit-value and the unit-density sub-problems. Their results can be easily extended, by Classify-and-Select, to yield $O(\log \rho)$ and $O(\log \sigma)$ approximations (and price) for the general bounded problem, respectively, where $\rho \triangleq \frac{\max_j \text{val}(j)}{\min_j \text{val}(j)}$, $\sigma \triangleq \frac{\max_j(\text{val}(j)/p_j)}{\min_j(\text{val}(j)/p_j)}$. However, their work gave no result with respect to either $n$ or $P$, a gap which our work attends to.

The on-line version of the problem with no bound on the preemption was analyzed by [14], whose upper bound for the competitiveness ratio was later proven to be tight by [3].

The non-preemptive real-time scheduling problem has been posited and studied already several decades ago, and has various flavours, several of which have also been solved since. Moore devised an $O(n \log n)$-time algorithm [24] solving the simplest version of the problem, maximizing the number of jobs meeting their deadline (equivalent to minimizing the number of late jobs), where all the jobs are unit-value and have the same release time. Later, Lawler [20] extended this technique for special sub-cases of the problem of weighted jobs with the same release time (known to be NP-hard in general by [19]), and again [22] – for special sub-cases of the problem of unit-value jobs with different release times (known to be NP-hard in general by [21]). Also, Lawler and Moore devised [23] an $O(n \sum p_j)$-time (pseudopolynomial) algorithm for maximizing the value of jobs meeting the deadline with the same release time.

Bar-Noy et al. [7, 8] showed a constant factor approximation for maximizing the value of jobs meeting their deadline with different release times; other approximations in this setting have been suggested prior to that, particularly [15].

A different approach was used by Bar-Yehuda et al. in [10], who consider the scheduling of jobs already divided into $k$ intervals which can be scheduled only at specific points in time. Using the *local ratio* technique first presented in [9], they achieve an $O(k)$ approximation for the problem itself and the APX-hard *Max-Weight Independent Set* (MWIS) problem to which it can be reduced.

## 2 PRELIMINARIES

### 2.1 Statement of Main Problem

Let $J$ be a set of $n$ *jobs* that should be scheduled for processing on a single machine (multiple non-migrating machines), and $k > 0$ an integer. Each of the jobs $j \in J$ has a *value* $\text{val}(j) > 0$, a *release time* $r_j$, a *deadline* $d_j$ and a *length* $p_j$.

*Definition 2.1.*

(a) A *feasible schedule of a job on a single machine* $j \in J$ is a set $G_j$ of pairwise-disjoint segments such that $\forall g \in G_j$ : $g \subseteq [r_j, d_j]$ and $\sum_{g \in G_j} |g| = p_j$.

(b) A *feasible schedule of a job set* $J$ *on a single machine* is a set of feasible schedules of jobs $\mathcal{G}_J = \{G_j | j \in J\}$, s.t. $\forall\, j_1, j_2 \in J$, $j_1 \neq j_2 : \forall\, g_1 \in G_{j_1}, g_2 \in G_{j_2} : g_1 \cap g_2 = \emptyset$.

(c) A *$k$-preemptive feasible schedule of a job set* $J$ *on a single machine* is a feasible schedule $\mathcal{G}_J$ s.t. $\forall j \in J, |G_j| \leq k+1$, i.e. no job is preempted more than $k$ times.

The above definitions can trivially be extended to multiple **non-migrating** machines by making the feasible schedule for multiple machines a union of feasible schedules on single machine, s.t. no job is scheduled twice on different machines.

Our objective is, given $J$, to find $J' \subseteq J$ and a k-preemptive feasible schedule $\mathcal{G}_{J'}$ s.t. $\text{val}(J') \triangleq \sum_{j \in J'} \text{val}(j)$ is maximal.

### 2.2 Useful Shorthands

We will denote the $i$-th segment of a job $j$ as $g_j^i = [s_j^i, t_j^i]$. Also, we will define the relation of *precedence* between any two segments $g_{j_1}^{i_1} = [s_{j_1}^{i_1}, t_{j_1}^{i_1}], g_{j_2}^{i_2} = [s_{j_2}^{i_2}, t_{j_2}^{i_2}]$ as follows: $g_{j_1}^{i_1} \prec g_{j_2}^{i_2} \iff t_{j_1}^{i_1} \leq s_{j_2}^{i_2}$.

Note, that since all the segments are disjoint, this relation induces a total order on the segments.

# 3 BOUNDED-DEGREE ANCESTOR-FREE SUB-FOREST

## 3.1 Statement of Problem

In order to solve the k-bounded preemption problem we first reduce it to the following problem of the k-Bounded Degree Ancestor-Free Sub-Forest ($k$-BAS). In this section, we denote by $T(u)$ the sub-tree of a tree $T$ which is rooted in the node $u \in T$ and by $C_T(u)$ the set of the children nodes of a tree node $u$. Also, the *degree* of a node $u$ in $T$ is defined to be the number of $u$'s children in $T$, i.e. $\deg_T(u) \triangleq |C_T(u)|$.

*Definition 3.1.* An *Ancestor-Free Sub-Forest* (AFSF) of a given forest (tree) $T(V, E)$ is a sub-forest $T'$ of $T$ s.t. for any two different connected components $C_1 \neq C_2$ of $T'$, for any $v_1 \in C_1, v_2 \in C_2$, $v_1$ is not a descendant of $v_2$ with respect to $E$.

*Definition 3.2.* A *k-Bounded-Degree Ancestor-Free Sub-Forest* ($k$-BAS) of a given forest (tree) $T(V, E)$ is an Ancestor-Free Sub-Forest $T'$ of $T$, s.t. $\forall v \in V', \deg_{T'}(v) \leq k$.

*Definition 3.3.* An *optimal k-BAS* of a given forest (tree) $T(V, E)$ with values val $: V \to \mathbb{R}^+$ is a $k$-BAS $T'$ of $T$ s.t. $\text{val}(V') \triangleq \sum_{v \in V'} \text{val}(v)$ is maximum.

Naturally, a $k$-BAS of a tree does not equal the whole tree in the general case, but has less nodes and hence less total value. We will formalize this through the notion of the *loss factor.*

*Definition 3.4.* The *loss factor* $\alpha_{\text{ALG}}$ of an algorithm ALG for the computation of a $k$-BAS of a tree (forest) is the ratio $\alpha_{\text{ALG}} \triangleq \sup_T \frac{\text{val}(T)}{\text{val}(\text{ALG}(T))}$.

Observation 3.5. *A max-value k-BAS of a forest T is the union of the max-value k-BASs of the trees constituting T.*

Corollary 3.6. *A loss factor α for an algorithm computing a k-BAS of a tree implies the same loss factor for the same algorithm applied to a forest.*

In the following sub-sections we will present an optimal algorithm for the computation of a $k$-BAS of a tree and bound its loss factor. By the above reasoning, this loss factor will hold for forests as well.

## 3.2 Dynamic Programming Solution

Trivially, in order to turn a given tree (of arbitrary degree) into a $k$-BAS, several of the nodes need to be deleted.

Lemma 3.7. *Let $T'(V', E')$ be an Ancestor-Free Sub-Forest of a forest (tree) $T(V, E)$. Then $v \in V \setminus V'$ iff all of its ancestors or all of its descendants are in $V \setminus V'$.*

Proof. Assume on the contrary that there is a node $v \in V \setminus V'$ s.t. both an ancestor of it $u$ and a descendant of it $w$ are $V'$. Since $T$ is a forest, and $v$ is deleted, it follows that $u, w$ belong to two different connected components of $T'$. But $w$ is a descendant of $u$, contrary to the definition of an AFSF. □

We therefore can divide the nodes of the tree into three groups as follows: (1) *retained* nodes, i.e. nodes that are retained in the k-BAS (however, some of their descendants might be deleted); (2) *pruned-up* nodes, i.e. nodes that are deleted with all their ancestors up to the root (in order to fulfill Ancestor-Freedom); (3) *pruned–down* nodes, i.e. nodes that are deleted with all their descendants.

Observation 3.8. *For any k-BAS:*

*(a) A* retained *node cannot have* pruned-up *descendants.*
*(b) A* pruned-up *node can have descendants of all types.*
*(c) A* pruned-down *node has only* pruned-down *descendants.*

For a node $v$, let us denote its *aggregate value* (i.e., the maximal possible value that can be salvaged from $T(v)$ after the pruning) as $t(v)$ in case $v$ is *retained*, and as $m(v)$ in case it is *pruned-up* (there is no need to introduce a notation for the aggregate value of $v$ in case it is *pruned-down*, since in that case it is discarded). Also, let us denote as $C_k(v)$ the nodes in $C(v)$ with $k$ highest $t(v)$. Observation 3.8 leads us to the following formula:

$$\begin{cases} t(u) = \text{val}(u) + \sum_{v_i \in C_k(u)} t(v_i) \\ m(u) = \sum_{v_i \in C(u)} \max(t(v_i), m(v_i)) \end{cases} \tag{3.1}$$

In order to compute the $k$-BAS of a tree rooted in $u$, we need to decide for each node in this tree whether it is better for it to be *retained* or *pruned-up* (it may, of course, so happen that a node is better *pruned-down* with all its value in order to allow for its parent node to be *retained*). This is done by computing $\langle t(u), m(u) \rangle$ using bottom-up traversal and then deciding which of them is better and applying the decision in reverse order for all its descendants. This scheme is, essentially, Dynamic Programming. For simplicity, the algorithm will be presented for a tree as an input, but it can be trivially extended to a forest by applying it separately to each of the trees of which the forest consists.

**Procedure** TM

**Input:** A tree $T(V, E)$ rooted in $u$.
**Output:** Two numbers, $t(u), m(u)$, being the maximal values attained for $u$ being designated *retained* or *removed*, respectively.

**if** $u$ *is leaf* **then**
  $t(u) \leftarrow \text{val}(u)$ ;
  $m(u) \leftarrow 0$ ;
**else**
  **foreach** $v_i \in C(u)$ **do**
    $(t(v_i), m(v_i)) \leftarrow \text{TM}(v_i)$ ;
  **end foreach**
  $t(u) \leftarrow \text{val}(u) + \sum_{v_i \in C_k(u)} t(v_i)$ ;
  $m(u) \leftarrow \sum_{v_i \in C(u)} \max(t(v_i), m(v_i))$ ;
**end if**
**return** $t(u), m(u)$;

ANALYSIS. The runtime of the algorithm is trivially $O(|V|)$. Since the algorithm implements exactly the formulae presented in equation 3.1, it is optimal, i.e. gives the maximal value k-BAS possible for a given tree (forest). □

### 3.3 Determining the Loss Factor

The analysis of the quality of the loss factor directly from the TM algorithm is difficult. We will therefore look at a different algorithm, which is easier to analyze and which we will call the algorithm of *levelled contraction*. Using it, we will prove the following theorem:

THEOREM 3.9. *The loss factor of the algorithm* TM *is at most* $\log_{k+1} n$.

We will make use of the simple observation, that a sub-tree with a degree $k$ can be viewed as a single large node, since from the point of view of the choice which node to retain there is no need to look at each of them individually, but all of them can be accommodated *en bloc*. Formally:

*Definition 3.10.* A node $u$ of a tree $T$ is $k$-*contractible* iff: **either** (i) it is a leaf; **or** (ii) it has no more than $k$ children, all which are *contractible* as well.

*Definition 3.11.* The $k$-*contraction* of a $k$-contractible node $u$ in a tree $T$ with values val : $T \to \mathbb{R}^+$ is deleting $T(u)$ from the tree and setting $\text{val}(u) \leftarrow \text{val}(T(u))$.

OBSERVATION 3.12. *Let $u$ be a $k$-contractible node in a forest $T(V, E)$ with values assigned to the nodes. Then the sub-tree $T(u)$ can be contracted to a single (leaf) job without loss of value.*

The contraction itself is done by a bottom-up marking of the nodes as *contractible*. The algorithm is described in the procedure MaxContract, which has the following properties:

OBSERVATION 3.13. *After the application of* MaxContract *to a tree, all non-leaf nodes have more than k descendants; i.e., the contraction is* maximal *(there are no more $k$-contractible nodes left).*

OBSERVATION 3.14. *A contraction (in particular, the application of* MaxContract*) cannot increase the number of leafs.*

If a node $u$ is not contractible, the number of leafs of $T(u)$ remains the same. If $u$ is contractible, then all the leafs of $T(u)$ are replaced by $u$ as a new leaf; but $T(u)$ trivially has at least one leaf. Thus, in either case the number of leafs does not increase.

The algorithm LevelledContraction uses MaxContract as a primitive in an iterative fashion: in each iteration it performs a maximal contraction, takes the set of leafs aside and continues to the next one. In the end, the algorithm returns the set of leafs with the maximal value. Each of such sets represents a $k$-BAS of the original tree, as shown in the following lemma.

OBSERVATION 3.15. *Let $S_i$ be the set of leafs $S$ after the contraction at the $i$-th iteration. Then at the beginning of the $i$-th iteration all the nodes $w_i^j \in S_i$ are $k$-contractible.*

LEMMA 3.16. *Let* $S_i = \left\{w_i^1, w_i^2, \dots w_i^{|S_i|}\right\}$ *be the set of leafs $S$ after the contraction at the $i$-th iteration, and let $T_i^j$ be the sub-forest of $T$ rooted in $s_i^j$ in the beginning of that iteration (which is contracted during it). Then the union* $T_i = \bigcup_{j=1}^{|S_i|} T_i^j$ *is a $k$-BAS.*

**Algorithm 1:** Levelled Contraction

```
Procedure MaxContract()
    Input: A tree T.
    Output: The tree T after maximal k-contraction.
    foreach node u of T in bottom-up order do
        if u is a leaf then mark u as true ;
        else if deg(u) ≤ k and all children of u are marked
          true then
            contract children of u ;
            set val(u) ← Σ_{v_i ∈ CN(u)} val(v_i) ;
            mark u as true ;
        else mark u as false ;
    end foreach
end
Procedure LevelledContraction()
    Input: A tree T.
    Output: A k-BAS S of T.
    𝒮 ← ∅ ;
    while T ≠ ∅ do
        MaxContract(T) ;
        S ← all leafs of T ;
        𝒮 ← 𝒮 ∪ {S} ;
        T ← T \ S ;
    end while
    return argmax_{S∈𝒮} val(S) ;
end
```

PROOF. $T_i$ is trivially a sub-forest of $T$. Thus, in order to prove it is a $k$-BAS of $T$, we need to prove that its degree is bounded by $k$ and that it is ancestor-free.
*Bounded Degree.* From observation 3.15 immediately follows that the degree of each $T_i^j$ is at most $k$, and therefore the same holds for their union $T_i$.
*Ancestor-Freedom.* Assume on the contrary that there exist $u_1 \in T_i^{j_1}, u_2 \in T_i^{j_2}$ s.t. $u_1$ is ancestor of $u_2$ in the original $T$. It therefore means that $w_i^{j_1}$ is ancestor of $u_2$ as well. However, $u_2$ was not contracted into $w_i^{j_1}$; therefore, on the (single) path from $u_2$ to $w_i^{j_1}$ there is a node with a degree higher than $k + 1$. This contradicts the fact that $w_i^{j_1}$ is $k$-contractible, by observation 3.15. □

LEMMA 3.17. *The value returned by* LevelledContraction *is not less than* $\frac{\text{val}(T)}{L}$*, where $L$ is the number of iterations.*

PROOF. Let $S_i$ be the set of leafs $S$ at the $i$-th iteration, and $S_i'$ the set of their parents. Also, let $T_i$ be the $k$-BAS of $T$ corresponding to $S_i$, as explained in lemma 3.16. Since the algorithm only performs contractions, by observation 3.12, no value is lost, i.e., $\text{val}(T) = \sum_{i=1}^{L} \text{val}(T_i) = \sum_{i=1}^{L} \text{val}(S_i)$. Therefore, the value returned by the algorithm is

$$\text{ALG} \geq \frac{\text{val}(T)}{L} . \tag{3.2}$$

□

**Figure 1: Rearranging a Lawler Schedule**

Lemma 3.18. *The number of iterations of* `LevelledContraction` *is less than* $\log_{k+1} n$.

Proof. Due to observation 3.13, $|S_i| \geq (k+1) \cdot |S'_i|$. After the removal of $S_i$ from the tree in the iteration's end, $S'_i$ becomes the set of the tree's leafs. By observation 3.14, a contraction cannot increase the number of leafs in a tree, and therefore $|S_{i+1}| \leq |S'_i|$. Combining these, we get that for every iteration $i$,

$$|S_{i+1}| \leq |S'_i| \leq \frac{1}{k+1} \cdot |S_i| \Rightarrow 1 = |S_L| \leq \frac{1}{(k+1)^{L-i}} \cdot |S_i|$$

where $L$ is the (maximum) number of iterations. Hence follows:

$$n \geq \sum_{i=1}^{L} |S_i| \geq \sum_{i=1}^{L} (k+1)^{L-i} = \frac{(k+1)^L - 1}{k} \geq (k+1)^{L-1} - 1 \ ,$$

which in turn implies

$$L \leq \log_{k+1} n \ .$$

Combining this result with equation 3.2 yields us:

$$\text{ALG} \geq \frac{\text{val}(T)}{L} \geq \frac{\text{val}(T)}{\log_{k+1} n} \ . \qquad \square$$

Corollary 3.19. *The loss factor of* `LevelledContraction` *is not larger than* $\log_{k+1} n$.

Proof of Theorem 3.9. Since algorithm TM is optimal, its loss factor cannot be worse than the loss factor of `LevelledContraction`. Therefore, it is at most $\log_{k+1} n$, i.e. the algorithm TM $(T)$ yields a k-BAS $T'$ such that $\text{val}(T') \geq \frac{1}{\log_{k+1} n} \cdot \text{val}(T)$. □

*Remark.* The runtime of `LevelledContraction` is trivially $O(|V|)$.

## 3.4 Tightness of Bound

Theorem 3.20. *The loss factor of the* TM *algorithm for the k-BAS problem in the general case is at least* $\log_{k+1} n$, *i.e. the loss factor established previously is tight.*

The proof of this lemma is presented in appendix A. □

# 4 THE MAIN PROBLEM

## 4.1 Reduction to $k$-BAS

Assume we are given an optimal solution for the case $k = \infty$. Observe, that if in a feasible schedule for a single machine segments of two jobs $A$ and $B$ interleave, i.e. $\exists g_A^{a_1}, g_A^{a_2} \in G_A, g_B^{b_1}, g_B^{b_2} \in G_B$ s.t. $g_A^{a_1} < g_B^{b_1} < g_A^{a_2} < g_B^{b_2}$, they can be re-arranged into $g_A^{a_1} < g_A^{a_2} < g_B^{b_1} < g_B^{b_2}$ without affecting the feasibility. This of course can be done independently for each machine in the multiple machine setting (if the machines are non-migrative). It therefore follows that any schedule (in particular, an optimal one) can be re-arranged (with no loss of value) into a form where a segment of $B$ is between two segments of $A$ iff there are no segments of $A$ between any two of the segments of $B$.

Note, that the described re-arrangement makes the *preempts* relation *laminar*. If we now present such a re-arranged schedule $\mathcal{G}_J$ as a graph $T(V, E)$, where the set of nodes $V = J$ is the set of jobs in the schedule, and the set of edges $E = \{(u, v) \in V \times V \mid v \text{ preempts } u\}$, the resulting (directed) graph is therefore a forest, which be will call a *Schedule Forest*. Let $T'(V', E')$ be a max-value $k$-BAS of $T$, computed using the algorithm TM described in subsection 3.2.

We will now describe the way of obtaining a new schedule $\mathcal{G}'_{J'}$ from $G'$; also, for the sake of simplicity, we will call the child nodes of a node (job) $j$ in $T$ the *sub-jobs* of $j$. The set of jobs $J'$ in the new schedule corresponds directly to $V'$. For each retained job $j \in V'$, its segments between two consecutive sub-jobs remain as is. If, however, a sub-job of $j$ is removed (pruned-down – see observation 3.8), the segments of $j$ surrounding it are merged to the left. This left-merge may affect several segments at once if several consecutive sub-jobs are removed.

Lemma 4.1. *The schedule* $\mathcal{G}'_{J'}$ *obtained as described from an original unbounded-preemption schedule* $\mathcal{G}_J$ *is a feasible* $k$*-bounded schedule as defined in definition 2.1.*

Proof.
*Feasibility of Individual Job Schedules.* The feasibility of the individual job schedules $G'_j \in \mathcal{G}_{J'}$ follows from the feasibility of the original $G_j \in \mathcal{G}_J$, as the segments of the jobs are either retained as is or merged to the left, i.e., earlier than the deadline, but nevertheless not earlier than the release time. Also, since segments are removed only as part of the removal of a job as a whole, the length constraint is kept as well.
*Feasibility of the Schedule Overall.* The unchanged segments do not intersect each other by feasibility of the original $\mathcal{G}_J$. The merged segments replace sub-jobs which are pruned-down, i.e. removed with all their descendants and therefore occupy a place which would otherwise be empty.
*Preemption Bound.* The segments of any job $j$ are scheduled so that between any two of them there is a sub-job of $j$ (because of the left-merge). Since by the definition of a $k$-BAS each $j \in J'$ has no more than $k$ sub-jobs, the number of segments of each job $j$ is not more than $k + 1$. □

*Remark.* In the multiple non-migrative machines setting the reduction can be applied to each machine separately. The forests obtained per machine are simply merged to a single forest. Since migration can be eliminated by using 6 times more machines [18], if we keep the number of machines constant, we retain at least the $\frac{1}{6}$-th part of the optimal solution after this elimination and prior to applying the reduction. Thus all the prices achieved below using this reduction stay the same in terms of $O$ notation.

*Remark.* The described reduction is **not** bidirectional, i.e. the optimal solution for the k-BAS problem is not necessarily optimal for the corresponding k-Bounded Preemptive Schedule problem. This due to the problem of adequately translating a case where a single job $A$ is preempted by a string of successive jobs. In this case $A$ is preempted only once, however if each of these other jobs is in turn preempted, say, $k+1$ times, we are forced to represent it in the tree as if $A$ were preempted more than once (modelling it as an infinitely small segment of $A$ between each of the jobs preempting it in succession), which may force us to forgo some of these jobs, which of course is not necessary in the schedule problem and thus the reverse reduction might yield a non-optimal solution. However, the reduction does provide an upper bound for the loss factor.

## 4.2 The Price of Bounded Preemption as Function of the Number of the Jobs

THEOREM 4.2. *$PoBP_k \leq \log_{k+1} n$.*

PROOF. Lemma 4.1 describes the transformation of an original optimal unbounded preemptive schedule $\mathcal{G}_J$ into a $k$-bounded preemption schedule $\mathcal{G}'_{J'}$. Trivially, the total value of the new set of jobs $J'$ is equal to the total value of the $V'$ of the max-value $k$-BAS $T'$, which in turn is optimal (see subsection 3.2) and obeys theorem 3.9. Thus,

$$PoBP_k \triangleq \sup_J \frac{\mathrm{OPT}_\infty(J)}{\mathrm{OPT}_k(J)} \leq \frac{\mathrm{val}(J)}{\mathrm{val}(J')} = \frac{\mathrm{val}(V)}{\mathrm{val}(V')} \leq \log_{k+1} n \quad \square$$

This bound is tight; the proof is presented in appendix B.

THEOREM 4.3. *$PoBP_k = \Theta(\log_{k+1} n)$.*

## 4.3 The Price of Bounded Preemption as Function of the Length-Ratio

In order to analyze the Price of Bounded Preemption as a function of the length ratio $P$, we will first introduce the notion of *relative laxity* of jobs.

*Definition 4.4.* The *relative laxity* of a job $j \in J$ is $\lambda_j \triangleq \frac{d_j - r_j}{p_j}$. We shall also denote $\lambda_{\max} \triangleq \max_{j \in J} \lambda_j$.

We will partition the set of jobs $J$ into two by their relative laxity (i.e., $J_1 = \{j \in J | \lambda_j \leq k+1\}$, $J_2 = \{j \in J | \lambda_j > k+1\}$) and solve each case separately. We show that in both cases the price bound is $\log_{k+1} P$, and hence it is $O(\log_{k+1} P)$ for the overall problem. Formally, we prove the following:

THEOREM 4.5. *$PoBP_k = O(\log_{k+1} P)$.*

*4.3.1 Strict Jobs.* Let us define the *window* of a scheduled job $j \in J_{in}$, denoted $w(j)$, as the time difference between its release time and its deadline. Trivially, $\forall j \in J, w(j) = p_j \cdot \lambda_j$.

Note that the window of a job necessarily includes the window of all its descendants in the original tree. Thus, if we look back at the proof of lemma 3.18 and define $W_i \triangleq \min_{j \in S_i} w(j)$, we have, by observation 3.13, that for every iteration $i$,

$$W_{i+1} \geq (k+1) \cdot W_i \Rightarrow p_{\max} \cdot \lambda_{\max} \geq W_L \geq (k+1)^{L-i} \cdot W_i$$

where $L$ is the (maximum) number of iterations. Hence follows:

$$p_{\max} \cdot \lambda_{\max} \geq (k+1)^L \cdot W_0 \geq (k+1)^L \cdot p_{\min}$$
$$L \leq \log_{k+1}(P \cdot \lambda_{\max})$$

By lemma 3.17, this in turn implies:

LEMMA 4.6. *For a tree $T$ created from a schedule satisfying $\lambda_{\max} \leq k+1$, the k-BAS $T'$ returned by algorithm* `Levelled-Contraction` *satisfies* $\mathrm{val}(T') \geq \frac{1}{\log_{k+1} P} \cdot \mathrm{val}(T)$. □

*4.3.2 Lax Jobs.* The treatment of the lax jobs is slightly different and requires a different algorithm. It also requires the establishment of several auxiliary lemmas presented below.

LEMMA 4.7. *Let $S$ be a set of intervals. There exists a subset $S' \subseteq S$ such that each point in $\bigcup_{I \in S} I$ is covered by at least one and at most two different intervals in $S$.*

PROOF. Assume WLOG $\bigcup_{I \in S} I$ is a single segment (otherwise apply the proof separately for each segment and all intervals contained in that segment). Let $I_0$ be the interval whose left endpoint is the leftmost among all intervals in $S$. We start with $S' \leftarrow I_0$ and iteratively add intervals to $S'$. Let $I_i$ be the interval whose right endpoint is the rightmost among all intervals in $S$ that intersect an interval in $S'$. Add $I_i$ to $S'$, that is $S' \leftarrow S' \cup \{I_i\}$. Repeat this procedure until $\bigcup_{I \in S'} I = \bigcup_{I \in S} I$. □

COROLLARY 4.8. *If we number the intervals in $S'$ by the order of their leftmost coordinate and divide them into two disjoint subsets $S'_E, S'_O$ by the parity of this numbering, then each of these subsets is a set of pairwise-disjoint intervals.*

PROOF. Assume on the contrary WLOG that $S'_E$ does not satisfy the above. Then $\exists k$ s.t. $I_{2k} \cap I_{2k+2} \neq \emptyset$. By construction, $I_{2k} \cap I_{2k+1} \neq \emptyset$ and $I_{2k+2} \cap I_{2k+1} \neq \emptyset$. However, since $I_{2k+1}$ is contiguous, this necessary implies the existence of a point belonging to all three at once, in contradiction of the previous lemma. □

The following lemma was proven in [4]:

LEMMA 4.9. *Given a sequence $\{a_1, ..., a_n\}$, a non-increasing non-negative sequence $\{b_1, ..., b_n\}$ and two sets $X, Y \subseteq \{1, ..., n\}$, let $X^i = X \cap \{1, ..., i\}$ and $Y^i = Y \cap \{1, ..., i\}$. Then*

$$\forall 1 \leq i \leq n: \sum_{j \in X^i} a_j > \alpha \sum_{j \in Y^i} a_j \Longrightarrow \sum_{j \in X} a_j b_j > \alpha \sum_{j \in Y} a_j b_j$$

Let us now return to the main problem. Recall that we assume all the jobs are lax, specifically $\forall j \in J, \lambda_j > k+1$. We will prove the following:

LEMMA 4.10. *For a given set of jobs $J$ exclusively of jobs for which $\lambda_j \geq k+1$, the algorithm* `LSA_CS` *yields a feasible $k$-preemptive schedule $\mathcal{G}_{J_{in}}$ s.t.* $\mathrm{val}(J_{in}) \geq \frac{1}{6 \cdot \log_{k+1} P} \cdot \mathrm{val}(J)$.

In order to prove this theorem, we will present the Leftmost-Schedule Algorithm (LSA) suggested by [1], with the difference that the jobs will be sorted by their *density* $\sigma_j \triangleq \frac{\mathrm{val}(j)}{p_j}$ rather than by value. In the following analysis we will use the same terminology of *busy-segment* (a maximal subset $g^*$ of the timeline s.t. $\exists j \in J: \exists g \in G_j : g^* \cap g \neq \emptyset$) and *idle-segment* (a maximal subset $g^*$ of the timeline s.t. $\forall j \in J : \forall g \in G_j : g^* \cap g = \emptyset$). Also, for the sake of brevity, we introduce the notation $J_{out} \triangleq J \setminus J_{in}$.

**Algorithm 2:** The Leftmost Schedule Algorithm

**Procedure** LSA_CS()
  **Input:** A set of lax jobs $J$ (i.e., satisfying $\forall j \in J, \lambda_j \geq k+1$).
  **Output:** A feasible schedule for jobs $J_{in} \subseteq J$, s.t. $\text{val}(J_{in}) \geq \frac{\text{val}(J_{\text{OPT}})}{6 \cdot \log_{k+1} P}$.
  Separate all jobs in $J$ into classes $J_c, 1 \leq c \leq log_{k+1}P$ by length, s.t. $\forall\ 1 \leq c \leq log_{k+1}P$, $\forall\ j \in J_c,\ (k+1)^{c-1} \leq p_j \leq (k+1)^c$ ;
  **foreach** $1 \leq c \leq \log_{k+1} P$ **do**
    $\langle J_{c,in}, \mathcal{G}_{J_{c,in}} \rangle \leftarrow$ LSA($J_c$) ;
  **end foreach**
  **return** $\langle J_{c^*,in}, \mathcal{G}_{J_{c^*,in}} \rangle$, s.t. $\text{val}(J_{c^*,in})$ is maximal among the $J_{c,in}$ ;
**end**

**Procedure** LSA()
  **Input:** A set of lax jobs $J$ (satisfying $P \leq k+1$).
  **Output:** A feasible schedule for jobs $J_{in} \subseteq J$ (s.t. $\text{val}(J_{in}) \geq \frac{1}{6} \cdot \text{val}(J_{\text{OPT}})$).
  Sort $J$ in descending order of the jobs *density* ;
  **foreach** $j \in J$ **do**
    $S \leftarrow k+1$ leftmost *idle segments* in $[r_j, d_j]$ ;
    **repeat**
      **if** *$j$ fits into the segments in $S$* **then**
        Schedule $j$ in members of $S$ in the leftmost possible way ;
        **break**;
      **else**
        Remove shortest segment from $S$ and replace it with the next *idle segment* in $[r_j, d_j]$ ;
      **end if**
    **until** *all* idle segments *are exhausted*;
  **end foreach**
**end**

Lemma 4.11. *The length of each busy-segment in the schedule created by* LSA *is at least the length of the shortest job.*

Proof is omitted and will be presented in the full paper. □

Now let $j$ be a discarded job. If it was discarded, it means that already at the moment of its discarding in the span of time $[r_j, d_j]$ which is at least $p_j \cdot (k+1)$ long there could be found no $k+1$ idle segments of total cumulative length $p_j$.

Let us denote the the number of the idle segments in $[r_j, d_j]$ as $f$. We will look at two distinct cases. Either (i) $f \leq k+1$; or (ii) $f > k+1$.

In case (i), since the total length of the busy segments and idle segments in $[r_j, d_j]$ is equal to $d_j - r_j \geq p_j \cdot (k+1)$, and the total length of (all) the idle segments is less than $p_j$, it necessarily means that the total length of the busy segments is more than $p_j \cdot k$, and so in the worst case we have that $\text{val}(J') \geq \frac{k}{k+1} \cdot \text{val}(J)$.

In case (ii), $f > k+1$, yet $j$ could not be scheduled; this implies that the sum of the $k+1$ longest idle segments in $[r_j, d_j]$ is less than $p_j$. Therefore, if we denote the total cumulative length of all idle segments in $[r_j, d_j]$ as $L_{idle}$, it holds that $L_{idle} \leq \frac{f}{k+1} \cdot p_j$. On the other hand, the number of busy segments in $[r_j, d_j]$ is trivially at least $f-1$, making their total length $L_{busy} \geq f-1$ (by lemma 4.11). It holds that:

$$\left.\begin{aligned} L_{idle} &\leq \frac{f}{k+1} \cdot p_j \\ L_{busy} &\geq f-1 \end{aligned}\right\} \Rightarrow \frac{L_{idle}}{L_{busy}} \leq \frac{f}{f-1} \cdot \frac{p_j}{k+1} \leq \frac{2P}{k+1}$$

$$\frac{L_{busy}}{L_{busy} + L_{idle}} = \frac{1}{1 + \frac{L_{idle}}{L_{busy}}} \geq \frac{1}{1 + \frac{2P}{k+1}} = \frac{k+1}{2P+k+1},$$

meaning that the busy segments constitute at least the $\frac{k+1}{2P+k+1}$-th part of the span $[r_j, d_j]$. We have thus proved the following lemma:

Lemma 4.12. *Given set of jobs $J$ s.t. $\forall j \in J, \lambda_j \geq k+1$, algorithm* LSA *yields a feasible $k$-preemptive schedule $\mathcal{G}_{J_{in}}$ s.t. $\forall j \in J_{out}$, the timespan $[r_j, d_j]$ is at least $b_0$-loaded, where $b_0 = \frac{k+1}{2P+k+1}$.* □

*Remark.* Since in LSA we operate under classify and select, in each class $P(J_c) \leq k+1$, and therefore $b_0 \geq \frac{1}{3}$.

Now let us assume WLOG that all the union of the rejected jobs' timespans $U = \bigcup_{j \in J_{out}} [r_j, d_j]$ is a single contiguous time segment. Applying to $U$ the construction described in lemmas 4.7, 4.8, we get two disjoint sets of pairwise disjoint timespans $U'_E, U'_O$, in which in turn correspond to two disjoint sets of jobs $J'_E, J'_O$. Let us denote the timespans set with the larger total length $U^*$, and the corresponding job set $J^*$. By lemma 4.12, the timespan of every job in $J_{out}$, and in particular of every job $j$ in $J^* \subseteq J_{out}$, is at least $b_0$-loaded by jobs from $J_{in}$. Since the timespans of jobs in $J^*$ are disjoint, we can safely claim that

$$\sum_{j \in J_{\text{OPT}}} p_j \leq |U| \leq 2 \cdot |U^*| = 2 \cdot \sum_{j \in J^*} \lambda_j p_j \leq \frac{2}{b_0} \cdot \sum_{j \in J_{in}} p_j .$$

Note that since we made no special assumptions, this inequality applies to every contiguous subset of $U$ involving at least two timespans (and by linearity, to every union of disjoint pairs of timespans) and to the corresponding subsets of $J_{\text{OPT}}, J_{in}$. (For subsets of $U$ consisting of a single timespan the stricter lemma 4.12 holds.) Let us assume an order on $J$ by the jobs' densities from the largest to the smallest; since algorithm LSA considers the jobs in the same order, and so the corresponding members of $J_{in}$ are always considered prior to the corresponding members of $J_{\text{OPT}}$, we can claim that this inequality applies to all the prefixes of $J_{\text{OPT}}, J_{in}$ by this order. Now we will utilize lemma 4.9 to achieve:

$$\text{OPT}_\infty(J) = \sum_{j \in J_{\text{OPT}}} \sigma_j p_j \leq \frac{2}{b_0} \cdot \sum_{j \in J_{in}} \sigma_j p_j = \frac{2}{b_0} \cdot \text{val}(J_{in})$$

Note that since LSA operates on classes of jobs separately, this inequality holds for every class $J_c$.

Proof of Lemma 4.10. Recall that LSA_CS divides the lax jobs into $\log_{k+1} P$ classes $J_c$, for each of which the above inequality holds with $b_0 \geq \frac{1}{3}$. Therefore, for each class $J_c$ the application of the internal function LSA will yield $J_{c,in}$ s.t. $\forall c, \text{val}(J_{c,in}) \geq \frac{1}{6} \cdot \text{val}(J_{c,\text{OPT}})$. Since necessarily $\exists c^* \in [\log_{k+1} P]$ s.t. $\text{val}(J_{c^*,\text{OPT}}) \geq$

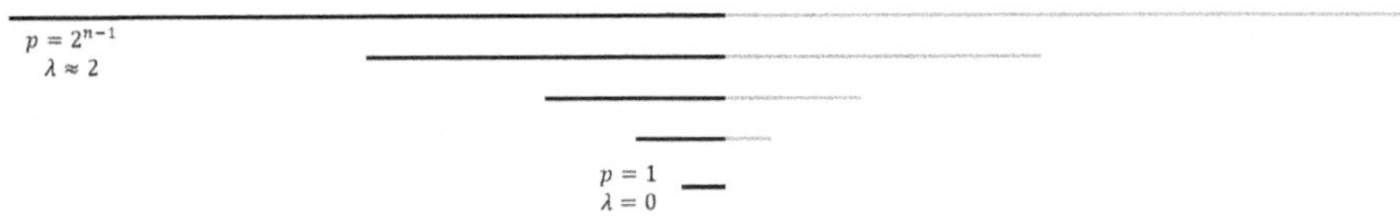


**Figure 2: Lower bound for k=0**

$\frac{1}{\log_{k+1} P} \cdot \text{val}(J_{\text{OPT}})$, it follows that $\text{val}(J_{c^*,in}) \geq \frac{1}{6} \cdot \text{val}(J_{c^*,\text{OPT}}) \geq \frac{1}{6} \cdot \frac{1}{\log_{k+1} P} \cdot \text{val}(J_{\text{OPT}})$.

Thus, classifying all the lax jobs as described, running LSA separately for each of the classes and taking the best result will yield us $J_{in}$ s.t. $\text{val}(J_{in}) \geq \frac{1}{6 \cdot \log_{k+1} P} \cdot \text{val}(J_{\text{OPT}})$. □

*4.3.3 Overall Price of Preemption.* To conclude the proof, we combine the results of lemmas 4.6 and 4.10 into a single algorithm.

**Algorithm 3:** k-PreemptionCombined

**Input:** A pair $\langle J, \mathcal{G}_J \rangle$, where $J$ is a set of jobs, and $\mathcal{G}_J$ is a feasible $\infty$-preemptive schedule for them.

**Output:** A feasible $k$-preemptive schedule $\mathcal{G}'_{J'}$ for $J' \subseteq J$, s.t. $\text{val}(J') \geq O(\frac{1}{\log_{k+1} P}) \cdot \text{val}(J_{\text{OPT}})$.

$J_1, \mathcal{G}_{J_1} \leftarrow$ all jobs $j$ and schedules $G_j$ for which $\lambda_j \leq k+1$ ;
$J_2, \mathcal{G}_{J_2} \leftarrow$ all jobs $j$ and schedules $G_j$ for which $\lambda_j > k+1$ ;
$J'_1 \leftarrow$ LevelledContraction($J_1$) ;
$J'_2 \leftarrow$ LSA_CS($J_2$) ;
**return** $\max(J'_1, J'_2)$ ;

Analysis. Since $J_1, J_2$ are a *partition* of $J$, one of them has at least half the total value of $J$; similarly, the optimal unbounded preemptive scheduling for one of them is at least half of the optimal one for the whole. Since both algorithms yield the $O(\log_{k+1} P)$-th fraction of the input's optimal unbounded preemption's value, the total value of at least one of $J'_1, J'_2$ is a $O(\log_{k+1} P)$-th fraction of $\text{val}(J_{\text{OPT}})$ itself. Choosing the better result ensures this factor further. □

*Remark.* Like in subsection 4.1, we can eliminate migration and retain a least a $\frac{1}{6}$ of the optimal job set prior to applying the algorithm LSA_CS. Thus, the price of the migrative setting is still $O(\log_{k+1} P)$.

From the above we can conclude the proof of theorem 4.5.

Proof of Theorem 4.5.

$$PoBP_k \triangleq \sup_J \frac{\text{OPT}_\infty(J)}{\text{OPT}_k(J)}$$
$$\leq \frac{2 \cdot \max\left(\text{OPT}_\infty(J_1), \text{OPT}_\infty(J_2)\right)}{\max\left(\text{val}(J'_1), \text{val}(J'_2)\right)} = O(\log_{k+1} P) .$$ □

This bound is tight, as we will prove in appendix B:

Theorem 4.13. *The Price of Bounded Preemption for k preemptions is $\Theta(\log_{k+1} P)$.*

*4.3.4 Extending to Multiple Machines.* The result for strict jobs can be trivially extended to multiple non-migrative machines by applying the reduction from subsection 4.1 and algorithm TM for each machine separately, which yields the same bound on the price.

As for the lax jobs, the LSA_CS algorithm can be extended to multiple non-migrative machines in the following way. In each iteration $i$, the $i$-th machine is assigned the schedule given by LSA_CS for the jobs remaining (formally, $J_i = J \setminus \bigcup_{k=1}^{i-1} J'_k$). By a known result from [2], this adds at most 1 to the price, thus preserving the $O(\log_{k+1} P)$ ratio (price).

This overall result for non-migrative machines, being constructive, promptly implies an approximation with the same $O(\log_{k+1} P)$ factor. This approximation can be further extended to the migrative machines setting using the results of [18], which adds a multiplicative factor to the quality of the approximation. This approximation (relative to $\leq J_{\infty,\text{OPT}}$) immediately implies a $O(\log_{k+1} P)$ price for the migrative setting as well (since necessarily $J_{k,\text{OPT}} \leq J_{\infty,\text{OPT}}$ and therefore the price is smaller than the approximation factor).

## 5 SPECIAL CASE: $k = 0$

Note that the expressions $\log_{k+1} n, \log_{k+1} P$ are defined only for $k \geq 1$. To complete our work, let us now look at the special case where $k = 0$, i.e. we are not allowed to preempt at all whereas the optimal algorithm can preempt as much as is required.

Let us look at a specific example of a series of unit-value jobs as presented in figure 2. Since the jobs' lengths form a geometrical progression with $q = 2$, it is clear that even with one preemption per job allowed, all of the jobs can be accommodated. On the other hand, if no preemptions are allowed, one can only accommodate a single job. Therefore the price of bounding preemption in this case is $n$ and also, due to the nature of the example, $\log P$; these are the lower bounds for the price in case $k = 0$.

These lower bounds can be trivially extended to multiple machines by simply multiplying the setting by the number of machines (along a third axis, so to speak); the bound of $\log P$ remains the same, whereas the bound of $n$ becomes $O(n)$ for any fixed number of machines.

The $n$ lower bound for the price is trivially tight, since we can always choose from a set of jobs the one with the maximal value and thus achieve a feasible schedule; however, the tightness of the $\log P$ approximation ratio should be examined further.

Let us utilize the algorithm LSA_CS, from subsection 4.3, adjusting it for the case $k = 0$, i.e. mandating scheduling to be made solely *en bloc* and classifying the jobs s.t. $\forall J_c, P(J_c) \leq 2$. Lemma 4.11 still holds in this setting.

Let us now look at the set $J_{out} \triangleq J \setminus J'$; specifically, let us look at $j \in J_{out}$ at the moment of its rejection. Again, since the algorithm schedules the jobs in descending order of density, it suffices to

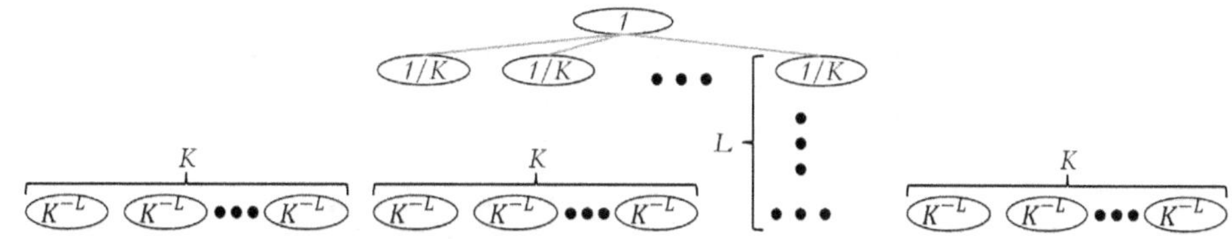


**Figure 3: $k$-BAS lower bound**

compare the total lengths of the busy and idle segments. If $j$ is rejected, this means that the total length of the idle segments in $[r_j, d_j]$ is less than $p_j$, i.e.$L_I \le P$. On the other hand, trivially $L_B \ge 1$, since if there were no busy segments in the span, it would be possible to schedule $j$. Thus

$$\left.\begin{array}{l} L_I \le P \\ L_B \ge 1 \end{array}\right\} \Rightarrow \frac{L_I}{L_B} \le P$$

$$b_0 = \frac{L_B}{L_B + L_I} = \frac{1}{1 + \frac{L_I}{L_B}} \ge \frac{1}{1+P} \;.$$

By the same technique as in subsection 4.3 this yields us val$(J_{in}) \ge \frac{1}{1+P} \cdot$val$(J_{\text{OPT}})$ for each class. Since (in this case) we classify the jobs so that $P \le 2$, by the same reasoning as before, taking the maximal-value $J_{c,in}$ yields us in the overall val$(J_{in}) \ge \frac{1}{3 \cdot \log P} \cdot$ val$(J_{\text{OPT}})$. By the same logic as in 4.3.4, this result remains the same for the multiple machines setting.

Thus the upper bound for the price in case $k = 0$ is established to be $O(\log P)$, and in conjunction with the previous, it means that this bound is tight. □

## REFERENCES


[1] S. Albagli-Kim, B. Schieber, H. Shachnai, and T. Tamir. Real-time k-bounded preemptive scheduling. In *Proc. of the 18th Workshop on Algorithm Engineering and Experiments (ALENEX)*, pages 127–137, 2016.

[2] B. Awerbuch, Y. Azar, A. Fiat, S. Leonardi, and A. Rosén. On-line competitive algorithms for call admission in optical networks. *Algorithmica*, 31(1):29–43, 2001.

[3] Y. Azar and O. Gilon. Scheduling with deadlines and buffer management with processing requirements. *Algorithmica*, 78(4):1246–1262, 2017.

[4] Y. Azar and O. Regev. Combinatorial algorithms for the unsplittable flow problem. *Algorithmica*, 44(1):49–66, 2006.

[5] P. Baptiste. Polynomial time algorithms for minimizing the weighted number of late jobs on a single machine with equal processing times. *Journal of Scheduling*, 2:245–252, 1999.

[6] P. Baptiste, M. Chrobak, C. Dürr, W. Jawor, and N. Vakhania. Preemptive scheduling of equal-length jobs to maximize weighted throughput. *Operations Research Letters*, 32(3):258–264, 2004.

[7] A. Bar-Noy, R. Bar-Yehuda, A. Freund, J. Naor, and B. Schieber. A unified approach to approximating resource allocation and scheduling. *J. ACM*, 48(5):1069–1090, 2001.

[8] A. Bar-Noy, S. Guha, J. Naor, and B. Schieber. Approximating the throughput of multiple machines in real-time scheduling. *SIAM J. Comput.*, 31(2):331–352, 2001.

[9] R. Bar-Yehuda and S. Even. A local ratio theorem for approximating the weighted vertex cover problem. *Ann. Discrete Math.*, 25:27–46, 1985.

[10] R. Bar-Yehuda, M. M. Halldórsson, J. S. Naor, H. Shachnai, and I. Shapira. Scheduling split intervals. *SIAM J. Comput.*, 36(1):1–15, 2006.

[11] S. Baruah. The limited-preemption uniprocessor scheduling of sporadic task systems. In *Proc. 17th Euromicro Conf. Real-Time Syst. (ECRTS)*, pages 137–144, 2005.

[12] R. J. Bril, J. J. Lukkien, and W. F. J. Verhaegh. Worst-case response time analysis of real-time tasks under fixed-priority scheduling with deferred preemption revisited. In *Proc. 19th Euromicro Conf. RealTime Syst. (ECRTS)*, pages 269–279, 2007.

[13] G. C. Buttazzo, M. Bertogna, and G. Yao. Limited preemptive scheduling for real-time systems. a survey. *IEEE Transactions on Industrial Informatics*, 9(1):3–15, 2013.

[14] R. Canetti and S. Irani. Bounding the power of preemption in randomized scheduling. *SIAM J. Comput.*, 27(4):993–1015, 1998.

[15] S. Dauzère-Pérès. Minimizing late jobs in the general one machine scheduling problem. *European Journal of Operational Research*, 81(1):134–142, 1995.

[16] L. Epstein, A. Levin, A. J. Soper, and V. A. Strusevich. Power of preemption for minimizing total completion time on uniform parallel machines. *SIAM J. Discrete Math.*, 31(1):101–123, 2017.

[17] R. Graham, E. L. Lawler, J. Lenstra, and A. R. Kan. Optimization and approximation in deterministic sequencing and scheduling: A survey. *Arm. Discr. Math.*, 5:75–90, 1979.

[18] B. Kalyanasundaram and K. Pruhs. Eliminating migration in multi-processor scheduling. *J. Algorithms*, 38(1):2–24, 2001.

[19] R. M. Karp. Reducibility among combinatorial problems. In R. E. Miller and J. W. Thatcher, editors, *Complexity of Computer Computations*, pages 85–103. Plenum Press, New York, 1972.

[20] E. L. Lawler. Sequencing to minimize the weighted number of tardy jobs. *Rev. Française d'Automatique, Informatique, Recherche Opérationnel*, 10:27–33, 05 1976.

[21] E. L. Lawler. A dynamic programming algorithm for preemptive scheduling of a single machine to minimize the number of late jobs. *Annals of Operations Research*, 26:125–133, 1990.

[22] E. L. Lawler. Knapsack-like scheduling problems, the moore-hodgson algorithm and the 'tower of sets' property. *Mathl. Comput. Modelling*, 20(2):91–106, 1994.

[23] E. L. Lawler and J. M. Moore. A functional equation and its application to resource allocation and sequencing problems. *Management Science*, 16:77–84, 1969.

[24] J. M. Moore. Sequencing n jobs on one machine to minimize the number of tardy jobs. *Management Science*, 15:102–109, 1968.

[25] K. Pruhs and G. J. Woeginger. Approximation schemes for a class of subset selection problems. *Theoretical Computer Science*, 382:151–156, 2007.

[26] A. J. Soper and V. A. Strusevich. Power of Preemption on Uniform Parallel Machines. In K. Jansen, J. D. P. Rolim, N. R. Devanur, and C. Moore, editors, *Approximation, Randomization, and Combinatorial Optimization. Algorithms and Techniques (APPROX/RANDOM 2014)*, volume 28 of *Leibniz International Proceedings in Informatics (LIPIcs)*, pages 392–402, Dagstuhl, Germany, 2014. Schloss Dagstuhl–Leibniz-Zentrum fuer Informatik.

[27] Y. Wang and M. Saksena. Scheduling fixed-priority tasks with preemption threshold. In *Proc. 6th IEEE Int. Conf. Real-Time Comput. Syst. Appl. (RTCSA)*, pages 328–335, 1999.


## A LOWER BOUND FOR LOSS FACTOR IN $k$-BAS

In this appendix we establish the lower bound for the loss factor of the k-BAS by providing a specific example, as shown in figure 3. All the claims in this subsection pertain solely to said example.

The nodes of the tree are arranged in $\lfloor \log_K n \rfloor + 1$ *levels*, numbered from 0 (the topmost) to $L \triangleq \lfloor \log_K n \rfloor$ (the lowermost). In each level $i$, the number of nodes is $K^i$ and the value of each of them $K^{-i}$. Every node has exactly $K$ children. $K$ is taken to be an arbitrary integer number strictly larger than $k$ (later, we will assign it a specific value); in particular, since $k \ge 1$, this implies $K > 1$.

Observation A.1. *The total value of all the nodes in a level of the tree is 1; thus the total value of all the nodes in the tree is $L + 1$.*

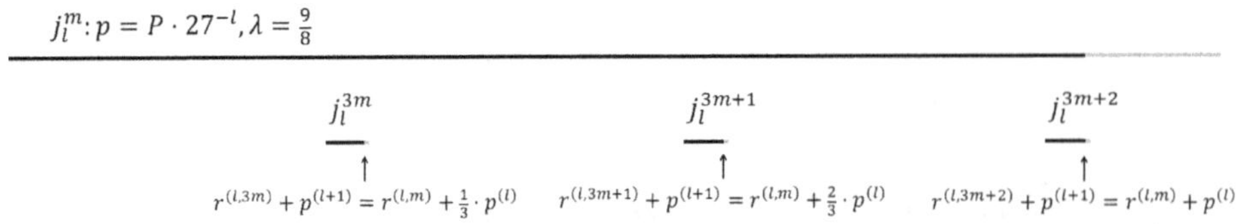


**Figure 4: General lower bound: example for $K = 3$**

LEMMA A.2. *For each node $v$ on level $i$, algorithm* TM *yields*

$$t(v) = K^{-i} \cdot \sum_{j=0}^{L-i} \left(\frac{k}{K}\right)^j, \quad m(v) = K^{-i} \cdot \sum_{j=0}^{L-(i+1)} \left(\frac{k}{K}\right)^j.$$

*Note that this implies that for every node $v$ at level $i$, $t(v) > m(v)$.*

PROOF. By induction on the application of the algorithm TM (from level $L$ up to 0).
*Base:* For each leaf $v$ ($i = L$), $t(v) = K^{-L}$, $m(v) = 0$.
*Hypothesis:* For a node (job) $v$ at level $i$,

$$t(v) = K^{-i} \cdot \sum_{j=0}^{L-i} \left(\frac{k}{K}\right)^j, \quad m(v) = K^{-i} \cdot \sum_{j=0}^{L-(i+1)} \left(\frac{k}{K}\right)^j.$$

*Step:* Let $u$ be a job at level $i - 1$. Then:

$$t(u) = \text{val}(u) + \sum_{v_i \in CN_k(u)} t(v_i) = K^{1-i} + k \cdot K^{-i} \cdot \sum_{j=0}^{L-i} \left(\frac{k}{K}\right)^j = K^{1-i} \cdot \sum_{j=0}^{L-i+1} \left(\frac{k}{K}\right)^j$$

$$m(u) = \sum_{v_i \in CN(u)} \max(t(v_i), m(v_i)) = K \cdot K^{-i} \cdot \sum_{j=0}^{L-i} \left(\frac{k}{K}\right)^j = K^{1-i} \cdot \sum_{j=0}^{L-i} \left(\frac{k}{K}\right)^j$$

□

COROLLARY A.3. *The total value of the $k$-BAS returned by* TM *on the example is less than $\frac{K}{K-k}$.*

PROOF. Denote the root node $v_0$. The total value of the $k$-BAS is

$$\text{ALG} = \max\{t(v_0), m(v_0)\} = t(v_0) = \sum_{j=0}^{L} \left(\frac{k}{K}\right)^j < \frac{1}{1 - \frac{k}{K}} = \frac{K}{K-k}.$$

□

PROOF OF THEOREM 3.20. We have established in subsection 3.2 that the TM algorithm yields the optimal result. If we take the example and set $K = 2k$, we get:

$$\left.\begin{array}{l} \text{OPT}_\infty = \lfloor \log_{k+1} n \rfloor + 1 \\ \text{OPT}_k < \frac{2k}{2k-k} = 2 \end{array}\right\} \Rightarrow \frac{\text{OPT}_\infty}{\text{OPT}_k} = \Omega(\log_{k+1} n)$$

□

# B LOWER BOUND FOR PRICE IN $k$-BOUNDED PREEMPTION PROBLEM

In this appendix we establish the lower bound for the price of $k$-bounded preemption by providing a specific example, as shown in figure 4. All the claims in this section pertain solely to said example.

The example is constructed as follows:

- All the jobs are arranged in $L + 1$ *levels* numbered from 0 to $L$, where $L \triangleq \lfloor \log_{3K^2} P \rfloor$. Level $l$ contains $K^l$ jobs, numbered from 0 to $K^l - 1$. The $m$-th job at the $l$-th level is denoted $j_l^m$.
- The value of a job $j_l^m$ is $K^{-l}$.
- The length of a job $j_l^m$ is $p^{(l)} = P \cdot (3K^2)^{-l}$.
- The relative laxity of all the jobs is $\lambda = 1 + \frac{1}{3K-1}$.
- For a job $j_l^m$, the jobs $\{j_{l+1}^{m'} \mid mK \le m' \le (m+1)K - 1\}$ are called the *child jobs* of $j_l^m$. This term can be trivially extended to introduce the notion of a *descendant job*.
- The release times are given by the recursive formula $r^{(l+1,m')} = r^{(l,m)} + (m' - mK + 1) \cdot \frac{p^{(l)}}{K} - p^{(l+1)}$, where $mK \le m' \le (m+1)K - 1$ and $r^{(0,0)} = 0$.
- The deadline times are given by $d^{(l,m)} = r^{(l,m)} + p^{(l)} \cdot \lambda$.

From the above construction one can deduce the following (proofs are omitted and will be presented in the full version of the paper):

LEMMA B.1. *For every job $j_l^m$, a single preemption allows the scheduling of at most one of $j_l^m$'s child jobs. Therefore, in a feasible solution, a job is scheduled with at most $k$ child jobs.*

LEMMA B.2.

$$\begin{cases} \text{OPT}_\infty = L + 1 > \log_{3K^2} P = \frac{\log_K P}{\log_K (3K^2)} > \frac{1}{3} \cdot \log_K P \\ \text{OPT}_k = \sum_{i=0}^{L} \left(\frac{k}{K}\right)^i = \frac{1 - \left(\frac{k}{K}\right)^{L+1}}{1 - \frac{k}{K}} < \frac{1}{1 - \frac{k}{K}} = \frac{K}{K-k} \end{cases}$$

PROOF OF THEOREM 4.13. Let us choose $K = 2k$; then:

$$\left.\begin{array}{l} \text{OPT}_\infty > \frac{1}{3} \cdot \log_{2k} P \\ \text{OPT}_k < \frac{2k}{2k-k} = 2 \end{array}\right\} \Rightarrow PoBP_k > \Omega(\log_{k+1} P)$$

□

PROOF OF THEOREM 4.3. We use the same example. Then

$$n = \sum_{l=0}^{L} K^l = \frac{K^{L+1} - 1}{K - 1} < \frac{K \cdot K^L}{K - 1} \le \frac{3}{2} \cdot K^L \Rightarrow \log_K n < L,$$

and if we, as in the previous paragraph, choose $K = 2k$, we get

$$\left.\begin{array}{l} \text{OPT}_\infty > \log_{2k} n \\ \text{OPT}_k < \frac{2k}{2k-k} = 2 \end{array}\right\} \Rightarrow PoBP_k > \Omega(\log_{k+1} n)$$

□

*Remark.* For the multiple machine setting, this example can be multiplied "along a third axis", effectively forcing to solve the same basic example for each machine separately. The $\Omega(\log_{k+1} P)$ bound will hold as is; the $\Omega(\log_{k+1} n)$ will hold for any fixed number of machines.

# Accurate Traffic Splitting on Commodity Switches

Ori Rottenstreich
Technion

Yossi Kanizo
Tel-Hai College

Haim Kaplan
Tel Aviv University

Jennifer Rexford
Princeton University

## ABSTRACT

Traffic splitting is essential for load balancing over multiple servers, middleboxes, and paths. Often the target traffic distribution is not uniform (e.g., due to heterogeneous servers or path capacities). A natural approach is to implement traffic split in existing rule matching tables in commodity switches. In this paper we suggest an analytical study of such an approach. To do that, we relate the description of distributions in switches to signed representations of positive integers. We suggest an optimal algorithm that minimizes the number of rules needed to represent a weighted traffic distribution. Since switches often have limited rule-table space, the target distribution cannot always be exactly achieved. Accordingly, we also develop a solution that, given a restricted number of rules, finds a distribution that can be implemented within the limited space. To select among different solutions, we describe metrics for quantifying the accuracy of an approximation. We demonstrate the efficiency of the solutions through extensive experiments.

**ACM Reference Format:**
Ori Rottenstreich, Yossi Kanizo, Haim Kaplan, and Jennifer Rexford. 2018. Accurate Traffic Splitting on Commodity Switches. In *SPAA '18: 30th ACM Symposium on Parallelism in Algorithms and Architectures, July 16–18, 2018, Vienna, Austria.*

## 1 INTRODUCTION

Traffic splitting is a commonly required capability in modern networks for balancing traffic over multiple network paths or servers. Traditionally, load balancers rely on dedicated middleboxes, servers or hardware switches for traffic splitting [6, 14]. Equal-cost multipath routing (ECMP) [8, 9] is a common approach to achieve a uniform distribution by hashing the packet header. While ECMP achieves a uniform distribution, sometimes the desired distribution is not uniform. When servers are heterogeneous, more traffic should be sent to servers with more resources (e.g., CPU, memory, and storage). In irregular topologies, the network may need to split traffic unevenly among output ports when different paths have different costs. Furthermore, even regular topologies (e.g., fat-trees) can become irregular upon a link or switch failure.

WCMP (weighted cost multipathing) [20] generalizes ECMP for non uniform distributions. While also relying on hashing, a variable number of entries is required for implementing the different distributions. Achieving high accuracy for skewed distributions, sometimes requires an unrealistic number of memory entries (e.g., at least proportional to the ratio between the largest and smallest weights).

Recently, several schemes capitalize on the rule matching tables (implemented typically by Ternary Content Addressable Memory (TCAMs)), commonly available in commodity switches, to implement traffic splitting (e.g., [19] and Niagara [10]). A part of the packet header (e.g., the destination or the source IP field) is compared in parallel against a list of rules and traffic is forwarded according to the highest-priority matching rule. (Priority is usually implemented by ordering the rules, early rules in the order are of higher priority.) We address the problem of how to construct such tables that implement exactly or approximately a given distribution. We restrict the tables to consist of prefix rule (wildcards are consecutive at the end of the rule). For prefix rules, more specific rules are of higher priority.

Assume traffic has to be split into $k = 3$ servers in ratio of 2:3:5 based on matching $W = 8$ bits of the header. This implies a target (unnormalized) distribution of $C = (0.2 \cdot 2^W, 0.3 \cdot 2^W, 0.5 \cdot 2^W)$. Assume that the $W = 8$ traffic bits are uniformly distributed with values in $\{00000000, \ldots, 11111111\}$. As illustrated in Table 1, with three allowed rules, our target distribution $C$ is best approximated as $D_1 = (64, 64, 128) = (0.25 \cdot 2^W, 0.25 \cdot 2^W, 0.5 \cdot 2^W)$ meaning that 64 bit combinations are mapped to server 1, another 64 bit combinations are mapped to server 2, and the remaining 128 are sent to server 3. With four rules a distribution of $D_2 = (48, 80, 128) = (0.1875 \cdot 2^W, 0.3125 \cdot 2^W, 0.5 \cdot 2^W)$ can be implemented, with a higher *similarity* to $C$ (as formally defined later). With six rules an even closer distribution $D_3 = (51, 77, 128) \approx (0.1992 \cdot 2^W, 0.3008 \cdot 2^W, 0.5 \cdot 2^W)$ to $C$ can be implemented.

While an application might require a representation of high accuracy, little is known about the number of rules required to perform traffic split to within some prespecified accuracy, and how to optimally utilize a given number of rules to maximize accuracy. There are two previous papers, which we are aware of that address the problem of how to split traffic by rule matching. The work of [19], uses disjoint rules, that is each packet is matched only by a single rule. This unnecessary restriction increases the table size. The work of Kang et al. [10] suggests an algorithm named Niagara. Theoretical guarantees have not been provided for Niagara but it was demonstrated empirically that Niagara efficiently generates compact tables. Intuitively, Niagara iteratively adds a matching rule directing traffic from the server with the maximal amount of excess traffic to the server that lacks the largest amount. We conjecture that Niagara (or a slight variation of it) does compute the smallest


*SPAA '18, July 16–18, 2018, Vienna, Austria*

ACM ISBN 978-1-4503-5799-9/18/07...$15.00
https://doi.org/10.1145/3210377.3210412

| Target distribution $C = (0.2 \cdot 2^W, 0.3 \cdot 2^W, 0.5 \cdot 2^W) \approx (51, 77, 128)$ | | |
|---|---|---|
| $n_1 = 3$ rules | $n_2 = 4$ rules | $n_3 = 6$ rules |
| 00****** $\to$ 1 | 0000**** $\to$ 2 | 00000000 $\to$ 1 |
| 01****** $\to$ 2 | 00****** $\to$ 1 | 0000001* $\to$ 1 |
| 1******* $\to$ 3 | 01****** $\to$ 2 | 0000**** $\to$ 2 |
| | 1******* $\to$ 3 | 00****** $\to$ 1 |
| | | 01****** $\to$ 2 |
| | | 1******* $\to$ 3 |
| Output distribution $D$ | | |
| $D_1 = (64, 64, 128)$ | $D_2 = (48, 80, 128)$ | $D_3 = (51, 77, 128)$ |

**Table 1: Approximating the target distribution $C$ with a limited number of $n$ rules. Rules are defined on $W = 8$ bits and are ordered according to their priorities. The first matching rule applies.**

set of rules required to exactly implement a given distribution (in which the probabilities are multiples of $1/2^W$).

The restriction to use only prefix rules is common in works about TCAM, and is made by [19] and [10] as well as in other related works such as [12, 15]. TCAMs that support general wildcard matching are often considered expensive and power-hungry. Accordingly, for efficiency, recently suggested programmable switch architectures such as RMT and Intel's FlexPipe combine multiple match-action tables of different kinds and include tables dedicated to prefix matching [3, 13]. We believe that relaxing this constraint makes the problem much harder and we leave it for future work. We note that if we consider a related problem in which one needs to find the most concise representation of a given function (rather than a distribution), then in the case where only prefix rules are allowed, there exists an efficient optimal algorithm [4], in contrast to the general case where this problem becomes NP-hard [11]. Furthermore, considering only prefix rules is more natural and is likely to show up in other contexts beyond ours.

**Our contributions.** In Section 2 we formalize and consider the following two basic optimization problems, 1) Find the smallest set of prefix rules that implement a given target distribution (assuming it is implementable). We refer to this problem as the *Exact* problem. 2) Given $n$ and a target distribution $C$, find a set of $n$ rules that defines a distribution which is "closest" to $C$ among all distributions defined by $n$ rules. We consider two metrics to measure the distance between distributions. One is the classical $L_1$ distance (or the variation distance), and the other is a variation of $L_\infty$ in which we consider only servers to which we direct more traffic than the target. We refer to this problem as the *Approximate* problem (the metric we use would be clear from the context).

We first consider the case of splitting traffic to two servers ($k = 2$) in Section 3. In this case we give efficient algorithms computing optimal solutions for the *Exact* and *Approximate* problems (for both metrics). We show a connection between the optimal solution for the *Exact* problem to particular signed bit representations of integers [1, 16]. Specifically, we characterize the number of rules in the optimal solution of the *Exact* problem in terms of the smallest weights of a signed bit representations of the integers specifying the (unnormalized) distribution. This characterization also suggests how to obtain an optimal set of rules in $O(W)$ time. In addition we prove that one can always obtain a set of rules that maps a prefix of the bit combinations to server 1 and the corresponding suffix to server 2. One can verify that the solution computed by Niagara for $k = 2$ obeys our characterization and is therefore optimal. For the *Approximate* problem we observe that for $k = 2$ our two metrics are the same, and we use the relation with the signed representations to give an algorithm for this problem that runs in $O(W)$ time.

We generalize our approach to the case of an arbitrary number of servers in Section 4. We introduce a representation of a distribution over multiple servers by a *vector set*. Then we show that we can restrict our vector-sets to be of a restricted kind. In Section 5 we use this to describe an optimal algorithm for the *Exact* problem. Our algorithm runs in $O(W2^{2k})$ time and therefore is not efficient when the number of servers is large. In all our experiments we observed that the number of rules that our algorithm computes is identical to the number of rules computed by Niagara, which supports the conjecture we made above. Finding an optimal polynomial time algorithm for the case of an arbitrary number of servers (or proving that it is NP-hard) is an intriguing open question. Due to space constraints part of the proofs are omitted.

## 2 TRAFFIC SPLITTING PROBLEM

The input is a target traffic distribution $C = (c^1, \ldots, c^k)$ describing the relative amount of traffic required by each of the $k$ servers $[1, k]$. Traffic is split between servers based on matching rules examining a field in the packet header. Let $W$ describe the length in bits of this field in the header. We assume that $c^i > 0$ ($\forall i \in [1, k]$) and $\sum_i c^i = 2^W$, so the target distribution $C = (c^1, \ldots, c^k)$ is already "rounded" and specified by integers $c^i$'s that sum up to $2^W$, which is the total number of bit combinations in the designed header field. For instance, if traffic is split based on the destination IP, $W = 32$ in IPv4 and $W = 128$ in IPv6.

The field value is assumed to be uniformly distributed. That is every bit combination among the $2^W$ possible ones has the same probability to appear in traffic. While this assumption is not generally true, we observe that: (i) There are some bits for which this is true, e.g., the least significant bits in many cases. That's enough for us and we can simply refer only to those bits; (ii) in some applications such bits can be achievable through the use of hash function (supported in recent versions of the P4 switch programming language [2]); Or (iii) there are ways to generalize some of our schemes to work around known non-uniformities which we will address in future work.

A matching rule is of the form $(s_1 \ldots s_W) \to a$ where $s_i \in \{0, 1, *\}$ and the wildcard $*$ stands for a don't care. It is composed of a matching pattern $(s_1 \ldots s_W)$ and an index $a \in [1, k]$ of a server. Rules are assumed to be of the form of *prefix rules* where we refer to the matching pattern simply as a prefix. A prefix rule has a prefix of length $\ell \in [0, W]$ describing the number of first bits it examines and $s_i = *$ for $i \in [\ell + 1, W]$. We say that a packet with a bit combination $b_1 \ldots b_W$ (as its field value) matches a rule $s_1 \ldots s_W$ iff $s_i = b_i \ \forall i \in [1, \ell]$. Intuitively, a prefix rule of length $\ell \in [0, W]$ corresponds to a subtree of size $2^{W-\ell}$ in the $W$-bits trie. The subtree includes the bit combinations the rule matches. The rule matching process relies on a semantics named *Longest Prefix Match (LPM)*.

In case of a match in multiple rules, the longer more specific one is prioritized. Rules are ordered in a non-increasing order of their prefix lengths so that the first among multiple matches is with the longest prefix.

We refer to the number of bit patterns which are first matched by a rule as the *effective weight* of this rule. The effective weight determines the amount of traffic sent to the corresponding server based on the rule. We assume that all traffic is matched by at least one rule. We can see the set of rules as defining a function that maps each of the $2^W$ bit combinations $[0, 2^W - 1]$ in the header space to one of the $k$ possible server indices. We refer to the distribution implied by the selected rules as $D = (d^1, \ldots, d^k)$ where $d^i \geq 0$ is the total amount of traffic to server $i$, i.e., the sum of the effective weights of rules pointing to server $i \in [1, k]$. We say that $D$ is the *output distribution.* Since all traffic is assumed to be matched by at least one rule, $D$ satisfies that $\sum_i d^i = 2^W$. Ideally, we would like to have $D = C$, meaning that $d^i = c^i, \forall i \in [1, k]$. Therefore our first optimization problem is defined as follows.

Problem 1. *Given a target distribution C for k servers. Find an* exact *representation of the function within a minimal number of rules.*

In many scenarios, the number of available rules is limited and it may be impossible to realize a specific target distribution $C$ with the number of available rules. We define two metrics to measure the dissimilarity of $C$ and $D$ when $D \neq C$. The first is the maximum deviation of a server $i$ *above* its target load $c^i$. The second is the average deviation or the $\ell_1$ norm of $D - C$.

*Definition 2.1.* (Dissimilarity Metrics) Consider a target distribution $C$ for $k$ servers. For a given output distribution $D$, a metric $G$ examines the maximal amount of excess traffic in a server,

$$G(D) = \max_{i \in [1,k]} \left( \max \left( d^i - c^i, 0 \right) \right) = \max_{i \in [1,k]} \left( d^i - c^i \right).$$

Likewise, a metric $H$ examines the average amount of error in the required traffic amount,

$$H(D) = \frac{1}{k} \cdot \sum_{i=1}^{k} |d^i - c^i|.$$

In the second optimization problem we are interested in a distribution with a constrained number of rules.

Problem 2. *Given a target distribution C for k servers and an upper bound n on the number of rules. Find a distribution D represented by at most n rules that minimizes G(D) or H(D).*

In particular, when we can implement $C$ with at most $n$ rules then $D = C$ and we have $G(D) = H(D) = 0$. Larger rule number $n$ can enable finding a distribution closer to the target distribution, achieving smaller dissimilarities, for both metrics. For a given target distribution $C$ and a number of allowed rules $n$ we denote by $G_{OPT}, H_{OPT}$ the optimal values of the metrics $G(D)$ and $H(D)$, respectively.

The same output distribution can be achieved by implementing different functions. For instance, the distribution $(\frac{1}{4} \cdot 2^W, \frac{3}{4} \cdot 2^W)$ can be obtained by the rules (00*...*** → server 1, ***...*** → server 2) as well as by the rules (11*...*** → server 1, ***...*** → server 2), describing two different mappings. Accordingly, *the requirement for a specific traffic distribution does not imply a unique mapping.*

This flexibility leads to an inherent difficulty. While it is easy to find a representation with a minimal number of (prefix) rules for a *particular mapping* (e.g., by the ORTC algorithm or similar alternatives [4, 18]), finding the most concise (exact) representation of a *target distribution* can be challenging since many possible mappings have to be considered. Furthermore, finding a closest representation given a specific number of rules can be even harder.

Since our model requires that all traffic is matched by the set of rules, we assume without loss of generality that the last among the $n$ rules is a match-all (default) rule with a matching pattern **...**. In any set of rules we can replace the last rule to be a match-all (without modifying its target) and get an equivalent set of rules of the same size.

Finally, throughout this paper, when looking for optimal rule sets, we can consider only sets given in a *compressed form* as defined below.

*Definition 2.2.* A compressed-form prefix rule set is an ordered set of rules, where for each rule $r_i$ in the set, the first colliding lower-priority rule $r_j$ (i) has a shorter prefix, i.e. a larger number of wildcards, and, (ii) is mapped to a different server.

By the above property of two intersecting prefixes, if condition *(i)* in Definition 2.2 is not met then $r_j$ can be removed from the set, while if condition *(ii)* is not met then $r_i$ can be removed; both remove operations do not affect the mapping that the original rule set implements. Note that a compressed form is not necessarily the most concise way to represent a function.

## 3 THE CASE OF TWO SERVERS

In this section we consider the case of two servers. We present a simple mapping that realizes a given target distribution with a minimal number of prefix rules. This enables us to calculate the number of required rules for realizing a target distribution. Such information can help a network designer to estimate the number of rules available in a switch for other common tasks such as forwarding and traffic measurements. Furthermore, given a specific number of rules, we describe how to select them so that the distribution $D$ which they realize minimizes $G(D)$ and $H(D)$. Let $OPT_C$ be the minimal number of prefix rules required to obtain an output distribution that equals a target distribution $C = (c^1, c^2)$.

### 3.1 Representation as a range function

Different functions can be implemented to realize $C$. The next theorem shows that an optimal number of rules can always be achieved by a function that partitions the address space $[0, 2^W - 1]$ to two consecutive ranges, such that bit combinations from the first range are mapped to server 1 and bit combinations from the second range are mapped to server 2.

Theorem 3.1. *For a given target distribution $C = (c^1, c^2)$ with $k = 2$ servers, there exists a set of $OPT_C$ rules implementing a function $F_C$ satisfying $F_C(x) = 1$ for $x \in \left[0, c^1 - 1\right]$ and $F_C(x) = 2$ for $x \in \left[c^1, 2^W - 1\right]$.*

Proof. Consider an ordered set $S$ of prefix rules that realizes the distribution $C = (c^1, c^2)$. We show how to construct an ordered set of prefix rules $R$ implementing the function $F_C$ such that *(i)* $F_C$ satisfies $F_C(x) = 1$ for $x \in \left[0, c^1 - 1\right]$ and $F_C(x) = 2$ for $x \in \left[c^1, 2^W - 1\right]$, and *(ii)*, $|R| \leq |S|$.

Recall our Definition 2.2 regarding the compressed-form requirement. Furthermore, without loss of generality we assume that the last match-all rule in $S$ is mapped to server 2. Thus, we can express the number of distinct bit combinations $c^1$ that are mapped to server 1 by using a linear combination of powers of two. Let $b_i$ be the number of wildcards in the $i$-th rule, and define $a_i$ as follows:

$$a_i = \begin{cases} 1 & i\text{-th rule is mapped to server 1,} \\ -1 & i\text{-th rule is mapped to server 2.} \end{cases}$$

Then, we get that

$$c^1 = \sum_{j=0}^{W-1} q_j \cdot 2^j, \tag{1}$$

where $q_j = \sum_{i, b_i = j} a_i$, that is, $q_j$ equals the total number of prefix rules with $j$ wildcards that are mapped to server 1, minus those with $j$ wildcards that are mapped to server 2.

We denote by $Q = (q_{W-1}, \ldots, q_1, q_0)$ the vector of the coefficients of the powers of two in Equation (1). Note that the shortest prefix, that is, the one with the largest number of wildcards, excluding the last match-all rule, may have at most $W - 1$ wildcards.

The elements in $Q$ will be used to construct the alternative ordered set of prefix rules $R$ that satisfies the required properties of this theorem. In this construction, in addition to a match-all rule, the number of rules in $R$ will be exactly as the sum of the absolute values of the elements in $Q$. By the definition of $Q$, the number of rules in $R$ will be at most the number of the rules in $S$.

We further simplify $Q$ by operations on its elements:

- For $j \in [0, W - 2]$ such that $q_j \geq 2$ set $q_j := q_j - 2$ and $q_{j+1} := q_{j+1} + 1$.
- For $j \in [0, W - 2]$ such that $q_j \leq -2$ set $q_j := q_j + 2$ and $q_{j+1} := q_{j+1} - 1$.

Each of these two operations preserves Equation (1), and it lowers the sum of absolute values of the elements in $Q$ by at least 1. We perform either of these operations repetitively until they do not apply anymore. The resulting vector $Q$ satisfies that

- For the largest $j$ for which $q_j \neq 0$, $q_j = 1$.
- The vector $Q$ has at most $W$ elements.
- For each $j \in 0, \ldots, W - 1$, $\left|q_j\right| \leq 1$.

Finally, we construct the prefix rule set $R$. We first select the last match-all rule as in $S$ (mapped to server 2), and then we add rules with an increasing order of their priority by going over the elements of $Q$.

Specifically, set $u = 0$, and for each of the elements of $Q$ (from $j = W - 1$ to $j = 0$):

- If $q_j = 1$, add the rule $\left[u, u + 2^j - 1\right] \to 1$, and set $u := u + 2^j$.
- If $q_j = -1$, add the rule $\left[u - 2^j, u - 1\right] \to 2$, and set $u := u - 2^j$.
- Skip if $q_j = 0$.

In the last construction, the number of rules in $R$ is not larger than that of $S$, and the function $F_C$ defined by the rule set $R$ satisfies

| # | rule | mapping |
|---|---|---|
| 1 | 11010 | server 2 |
| 2 | 0011* | server 1 |
| 3 | 1101* | server 1 |
| 4 | 001** | server 2 |
| 5 | 101** | server 1 |

| # | rule | mapping |
|---|---|---|
| 6 | 110** | server 2 |
| 7 | 10*** | server 2 |
| 8 | 00*** | server 1 |
| 9 | 1**** | server 1 |
| 10 | ***** | server 2 |

(a) Input rule set (with 10 rules, defined over $W = 5$ bits), that yields a distribution of (15, 17) of the $2^W = 32$ bit combinations.

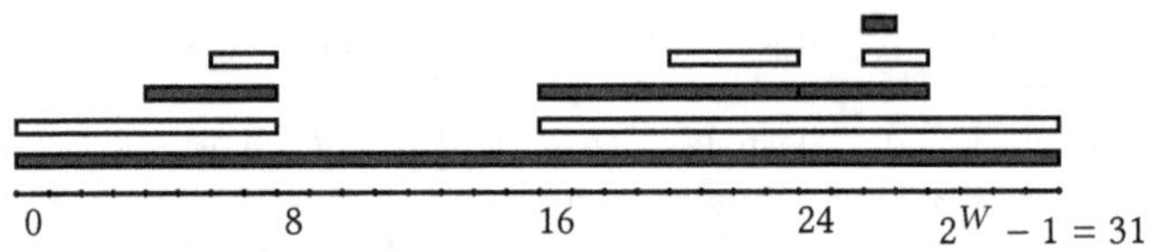


(b) graphical illustration of the input rule set

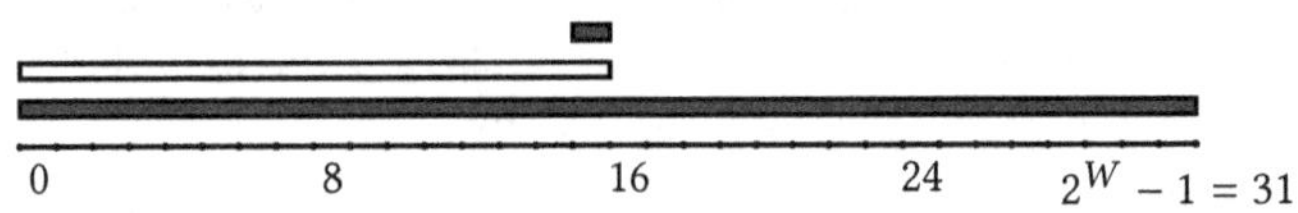


(c) graphical illustration of the resulting rule set (with 3 rules) that describes a simpler function and yields the same distribution (15,17)

**Figure 1: An example of the technique described in the proof of Theorem 3.1: (a) an example rule set given in a compressed form defined over $W = 5$ bits, (b) a graphical illustration of the rule set, and (c) a graphical illustration of the resulting rule set (01111 → server 2, 0**** → server 1, ***** → server 2). Clear white and solid blue rectangles correspond to rules mapped to server 1 and server 2, respectively.**

$F_C(x) = 1$ for $x \in \left[0, c^1 - 1\right]$ and $F_C(x) = 2$ for $x \in \left[c^1, 2^W - 1\right]$. Therefore, the theorem follows. □

The construction of the new rule set $R$ given the rule set $S$ as described in the proof of Theorem 3.1 is illustrated in the following example.

*Example 3.2.* Given the rule set $S$ in Fig. 1(a) which is illustrated graphically in Fig. 1(b), the vector $Q = (q_4, q_3, q_2, q_1, q_0)$ is initially equal to $(1, 0, -1, 2, -1)$. The reason $q_2 = -1$ is due to the rules with 2 wildcards which are rules 4, 5, and 6. These rules are mapped to servers 2,1, and 2, respectively. Therefore, $a_4 = -1$, $a_5 = 1$, and $a_6 = -1$, which sum up to $q_2 = -1$. The number of bit combinations that are mapped to server 1 is given by $c^1 = 1 \cdot 2^4 + 0 \cdot 2^3 - 1 \cdot 2^2 + 2 \cdot 2^1 - 1 \cdot 2^0 = 15$.

The only element with an absolute value greater or equal to 2 is $q_1$. Therefore, we apply the simplification process on $q_1$ and get that $q_1 := q_1 - 2 = 0$ and $q_2 := q_2 + 1 = 0$. The resulting vector $Q = (1, 0, 0, 0, -1)$ has no element with an absolute value greater than 1. Hence, this process is over.

To construct the rule set $R$, we first take the match-all rule as in $S$ (mapping to server 2). We set $u = 0$, and go from left to right over the elements of $Q$. For $q_4$ we add the rule $\left[0, 2^4 - 1\right] \to 1$, and set $u = 16$. We skip $q_3$, $q_2$, and $q_1$ since they equal 0, and last, for $q_0$, we add the rule $\left[2^4 - 2^0, 2^4 - 1\right] \to 2$. Fig. 1(c) shows a graphical illustration of the resulting rule set $S$ = (01111 → server 2, 0**** → server 1, ***** → server 2).

### 3.2 Calculating the cost of a given distribution with signed representations of positive integers

Following Theorem 3.1, we express the minimal number of prefix rules $OPT_C$ required to (exactly) follow a target distribution $C = (c^1, c^2)$ by relating it to signed representations of positive integers. As mentioned, this can be useful for a network designer to determine the number of rules available for other tasks such as forwarding and traffic measurements.

Unlike the regular binary representation, in the signed-bit representation an integer is described as a sum of positive and negative powers of two. We now define it formally, following the terminology of [1].

*Definition 3.3.* A signed-bit representation of $y \in \mathbb{Z}$ is given by a sequence $Q = (q_t, q_{t-1}, \ldots, q_0)$, such that $y = \sum_{i=0}^{t} q_i \cdot 2^i$ and $\forall i \in [0, t-1], q_i \in \{-1, 0, 1\}$ and $q_t \in \{-1, 1\}$. We refer to $t+1$ as the length of the representation and to the number of non-zero $q_i$'s as the *weight* of the representation. The integer 0 is represented by the empty sequence denoted by ().

Unlike the regular binary representation, which is unique, there are multiple signed-bit representations for a given integer $y \in \mathbb{Z}$. Consider for instance the integer $y = 7$. While the unique binary representation $(1,1,1)$ is also a signed-bit representation (satisfying $7 = 4 + 2 + 1 = 2^2 + 2^1 + 2^0$), another signed-bit representation is $(1,0,0,-1)$ (satisfying $7 = 8 - 1 = 2^3 - 2^0$). The last representation has a property captured in the following definition.

*Definition 3.4.* A signed-bit representation of an integer $y \in \mathbb{Z}$ is said to be in a *non-adjacent form* if there are no two non-zero adjacent signed bits, that is, $\forall i \in [1, t]$, if $q_i \neq 0$ then $q_{i-1} = 0$.

By [1] positive integers have a unique non-adjacent form. This can be easily generalized for any integer.[1]

PROPERTY 1. *All integers have a unique non-adjacent form representation.*

It is easy to derive the non-adjacent signed-bit form representation of an integer. Start with its binary representation and while beginning from the right bit, replace any sequence of $0, 1, 1, \ldots, 1, 1$ by the sequence $1, 0, 0, \ldots, 0, -1$ of the same length (where the most significant 1 bit of the assigned sequence can be considered as the least significant 1 bit of the next sequence to be replaced).

As we show later, we are interested in the weight of the representation since it relates to the number of prefix rules required to follow a distribution. The following property is due to [1].

PROPERTY 2. *For all integers, the non-adjacent form has a minimal weight among all signed-bit representations.*

Notice that for some integers, in addition to the unique non-adjacent form, there can be additional signed-bit representations that also achieve the minimal weight.

[1]Clearly, this property of positive integers applies for any integer since we can negate a represented number by negating the signed bits in its signed-bit representation. Similarly, there is only one representation for 0.

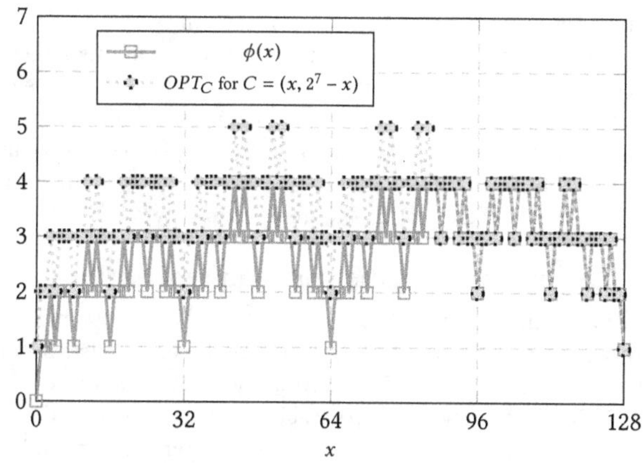


**Figure 2: The value of $\phi(x)$ and the number of rules $OPT_C$ required to describe a distribution $C = (x, 2^7 - x)$ for an integer $x \in [0, 2^7]$.**

For an integer $x$, we denote by $\phi(x)$ the weight of its non-adjacent form representation. It is easy to calculate $\phi(x)$ by the above computation of the non-adjacent form. Clearly, $\phi(x) = \phi(-x)$. Notice that for a distribution $C = \left(c^1, c^2\right)$ of $k = 2$ servers, we have $c^1 + c^2 = 2^W$ and accordingly $|\phi(c^1) - \phi(c^2)| \leq 1$. To represent $c^j$ in a signed bit representation we can always negate a representation of the other value $c^{3-j}$ and add a coefficient of $2^W$ (achieving a representation with a weight that is at most larger by one and thus by Property 2 the weight of a non-adjacent form cannot be larger). We characterize the minimal required number of rules to exactly represent a distribution.

THEOREM 3.5. *Consider a target distribution $C = \left(c^1, c^2\right)$. The minimal number of rules $OPT_C$ required to realize $C$, is given by* $\min(\phi(c^1), \phi(c^2)) + 1$.

PROOF. We first show that we can realize $C$ with $\min(\phi(c^1), \phi(c^2)) + 1$ rules. Without loss of generality assume that the minimum is attained by $\phi(c^1)$. We use $\phi(c^1)$ rules (mapping prefixes either to server 1 or to server 2) to map $c^1$ bit combinations to server 1. If the last rule is not a match-all rule, we add a last match-all rule to map the other $c^2 = 2^W - c^1$ bit combinations to server 2. Thus $OPT_C \leq \min(\phi(c^1), \phi(c^2)) + 1$. For the opposite inequality, assume $C$ is realized with $OPT_C$ rules. Let's assume, without loss of generality, that the last is an all-match rule that maps to server 2. The value $c^1$ must correspond to the number of bit combinations matched by the rules that map to server 1 among the first $OPT_C - 1$ rules. We can derive from these rules a signed bit representation with a weight $OPT_C - 1$ for $c^1$. Thus $\phi(c^1) \leq OPT_C - 1$. □

Interestingly, the values of $\phi(x)$ (for non-negative values) have been widely investigated, and the values $\{\phi(x) \mid x \geq 0\}$ have been described as a sequence in the Encyclopedia of Integer Sequences [16]. Applications of the sequence have been suggested for instance for minimizing communication between processors as well as for routing in peer-to-peer networks [7, 17]. Bounds and recursive formulas for the value of $\phi(x)$ were suggested. An illustration of the values of $\phi(x)$ and $OPT_C$ of a distribution $C = (x, 2^7 - x)$ for $x \in [0, 128]$ is given in Fig. 2. This graph can give an intuition on the representation cost of a distribution. It is easy to observe the symmetry of $OPT_C$, i.e., the same rule count is required for $(x, 2^7 - x)$ and $(2^7 - x, x)$. We can also see that $OPT_C \in [\phi(x), \phi(x) + 1]$ and that the only distributions that can be described by at most two rules are those where $x$ or $2^7 - x$ are powers of two.

## 3.3 Approximated distribution realization

Consider a target distribution $C = (c^1, c^2)$ and a given number of allowed rules $n$. We study the case where the target distribution cannot necessarily be realized accurately by at most $n$ rules (i.e., $n < OPT_C$). Instead, we find a realizable distribution with a minimal dissimilarity value with the target. By Theorem 3.5, the output distribution $D = (d^1, d^2)$ must satisfy $\min(\phi(d^1), \phi(d^2)) + 1 \le n$. For the metric $G$, considering the maximal amount of excess traffic in a server, among the realizable distributions $(d^1, d^2)$ we would like to find the one minimizing $|d^1 - c^1| = |d^2 - c^2|$. For the metric $H$, considering the average amount of error, we would like to minimize the sum $0.5 \cdot (|d^1 - c^1| + |d^2 - c^2|) = |d^1 - c^1|$. It follows that for $k = 2$ servers the two metrics are minimized by the same distributions. In the rest of this section we describe an efficient algorithm that achieves a target distribution minimizing the two metrics.

We start with a statement on the number of bits required to represent an integer in its non-adjacent form. Intuitively, it shows that given $t + 1$ bits, the largest integer that can be represented (in its non-adjacent form) is $y_u = 2^t + 2^{t-2} + \ldots$, that is starting with 1 in the most significant bit and alternating between 1 and 0 when going from left to right. Likewise, the smallest integer that can be represented is $y_d = -y_u = -2^t - 2^{t-2} - \ldots$. Furthermore, the next lemma shows that the non-adjacent form of any integer in the range $[y_d, y_u]$ has no more than $t + 1$ bits.

Lemma 3.6. *An integer $y$ has a non-adjacent form representation of at most $t + 1$ bits iff*

*(i) $|y| \le 2^t + 2^{t-2} + \ldots + 1$ for an even $t$,*
*(ii) $|y| \le 2^t + 2^{t-2} + \ldots + 2$ for an odd $t$.*

Recall that we aim at finding a set of at most $n$ rules that best approximates the target distribution $\left(c^1, c^2\right)$. The following lemma significantly reduces the search space for the output distribution $D = \left(d^1, d^2\right)$.

Lemma 3.7. *Given an integer $y = x \cdot 2^a$, with $a, x \in \mathbb{N}$, and let $U_a = \sum_{i=1}^{\lfloor a/2 \rfloor} 2^{a-2\cdot i}$. Then,*

$$\min\left\{\phi(y - U_a), \ldots, \phi(y), \ldots, \phi(y + U_a)\right\} = \phi(y) = \phi(x).$$

*Moreover, the value of $\phi(y)$ is uniquely retrieved for $y$.*

To find a distribution $D = (d^1, d^2)$ satisfying $\min(\phi(d^1), \phi(d^2)) + 1 \le n$, we consider four scenarios such that at least one of them occurs (the scenarios are not necessarily disjoint). We explain how to find $D$ of a minimal dissimilarity under each scenario. They are *(i)* $d^1 \ge c^1$ and $\phi(d^1) = \min(\phi(d^1), \phi(d^2))$, *(ii)* $d^1 \le c^1$ and $\phi(d^1) = \min(\phi(d^1), \phi(d^2))$, *(iii)* $d^1 \ge c^1$ and $\phi(d^2) = \min(\phi(d^1), \phi(d^2))$, *(iv)* $d^1 \le c^1$ and $\phi(d^2) = \min(\phi(d^1), \phi(d^2))$.

Since for $k = 2$ servers the two metrics $G$ and $H$ are minimized by the same distributions, we arbitrarily focus on the metric $G$ and the optimality follows also for the metric $H$. We discuss scenario *(i)*. We consider $W + 1$ disjoint ranges for the value $d^1 \in [c^1, 2^W]$. The ranges are denoted by $R_0, R_1, \ldots, R_W$ such that $R_a = [\lceil c^1/2^a \rceil \cdot 2^a - U_a, \lceil c^1/2^a \rceil \cdot 2^a + U_a]$ for $a \in [0, W]$. Let $\phi_a$ be the minimal value of $\phi$ for values in $R_a$. By Lemma 3.7 it satisfies $\phi_a = \phi(\lceil c^1/2^a \rceil \cdot 2^a)$. We take the minimal value of $a$ that satisfies $\phi_a \le n - 1$. Notice that for $a \in [0, W - 1]$ it satisfies $\phi_a - \phi_{a+1} \le 1$. This is since the two values $\lceil c^1/2^a \rceil \cdot 2^a, \lceil c^1/2^{a+1} \rceil \cdot 2^{a+1}$ are either equal or differ by the power of two $2^a$. For the selected value of $a$, we set $d^1$ as $\lceil c^1/2^a \rceil \cdot 2^a$ and we have that this value minimizes the error while satisfying the constraint of $n$. The scenario of *(ii)* is similar. We consider $W + 1$ disjoint ranges for the value $d^1 \in [0, c^1]$. They are $R_0, R_1, \ldots, R_W$ such that $R_a = [\lfloor c^1/2^a \rfloor \cdot 2^a - U_a, \lfloor c^1/2^a \rfloor \cdot 2^a + U_a]$. We find the first range for which $\phi_a = \phi(\lfloor c^1/2^a \rfloor \cdot 2^a) \le n - 1$. Then we set $d^1 = \lfloor c^1/2^a \rfloor \cdot 2^a$. For *(iii), (iv)* we repeat $(i), (ii)$ by replacing $c^1, c^2$. Finally, among the four options, we select the one minimizing $|d^i - c^i|$.

# 4 THE VECTOR-SET REPRESENTATION FOR MULTIPLE SERVERS

We study the case of an arbitrary number of servers. Our ultimate goal is to develop also for this scenario solutions for an exact representation with minimal rules or the best representation for a given number of rules. Towards this goal, while relying on an analytic model, we suggest a novel representation of a given rule set which can be manipulated to construct an alternative low-cost rule set that yields the same distribution. Then, in Section 5 we use this tool to develop algorithms for both problems.

In Section 3, for the case of two servers, we used the vector $Q = (q_{W-1}, \ldots, q_1, q_0)$ with coefficients of powers of two for summarizing a set of rules involving two servers. In this section, we generalize this representation for multiple servers. We refer to this generalization as a *vector set*, denote it by $\hat{Q}$ and explain that a vector set implies a single distribution. In Section 4.1, we formally define the vector set, explain how to construct it for a given set of rules and study its properties. Then, in section 4.2, we explain how to process a vector set while keeping the distribution it implies, so that it can be realized into a set of rules of a small size.

## 4.1 Construction and basic properties

A vector set $\hat{Q}$ consists of $k^2$ vectors denoted as $\left\{Q^{ij}\right\}$ with $i, j \in [1, k]$. Each vector $Q^{ij} = \left(q^{ij}_{W-1}, \ldots, q^{ij}_0\right)$ has $W$ elements. A given set of rules, can be associated with a vector set $\hat{Q}$, described in the following. Informally, a vector $Q^{ij}$ represents the amount of traffic (number of bit combinations) that server $i$ "takes" from server $j$. Thus, a vector set $\hat{Q}$ represents the entire relation (in that manner) between the servers.

We explain a way to construct a vector set from a general compressed-form rule set $S$ for representing its structure. Formally, consider a general ordered set $S$ of prefix rules. We assume that the rule set $S$ adheres to the compressed-form requirement described in Definition 2.2 and that the last match-all rule is mapped to server $k$. Following Definition 2.2, for each rule $r$ in the set, the first colliding

| # | rule | mapping |
|---|---|---|
| 1 | 11011 | server 2 |
| 2 | 0011* | server 1 |
| 3 | 1101* | server 3 |
| 4 | 001** | server 2 |
| 5 | 110** | server 1 |
| 6 | 10*** | server 2 |
| 7 | 01*** | server 1 |
| 8 | ***** | server 3 |

$$\begin{aligned} Q^{12} &= (0,0,0,1,0) \\ Q^{13} &= (0,1,1,-1,0) \\ Q^{23} &= (0,1,1,0,1) \end{aligned}$$

**Figure 3: Rule set example (left) and its corresponding vector set representation (right). The output distribution is $D = (12, 11, 9)$.**

lower-priority rule, that is, the rule that $r$ "takes" traffic from, *(i)* has more wildcards, and *(ii)* maps to a different server.

The construction of the vectors in $\hat{Q}$, given a set of rules is defined by the following process: Initiate all vectors in $\hat{Q}$ to zero, and repeat the following for each rule starting from the highest priority rule (excluding the match-all rule). For each rule, denote by $i$ the server it maps to and by $z$ its number of wildcards. Find its first lower-priority colliding rule and denote its server by $j$. Then, increment $q_z^{i,j}$ and decrement $q_z^{j,i}$, both by one. These operations reflect the fact that server $i$ eliminates $2^z$ bit combinations from server $j$.

By the definition of the above construction, for all $i, j \in [1,k]$ and $z \in [0, W-1]$, $q_z^{i,j} = -q_z^{j,i}$. Moreover, since for each rule (excluding the match-all rule), its first lower-priority colliding rule is mapped to a different server then for all $i \in [1,k]$ and $z \in [0, W-1]$, $q_z^{i,i} = 0$.

Fig. 3 shows an example of a rule set $S$ and its corresponding vector set representation $\hat{Q}$. Since $Q^{21}$, $Q^{31}$ and $Q^{32}$ are the element-wise negation of $Q^{12}$, $Q^{13}$ and $Q^{23}$, only the latter vectors are shown; the vectors $Q^{11}$, $Q^{22}$, and $Q^{33}$ are all zeroed.

The construction of the vectors (initialized with zeros) starts with the first rule 11011 that has 0 wildcards and maps to server 2. Its first lower-priority colliding rule is rule number 3 (1101∗, mapped to server 3). Therefore, we increment by one $q_0^{2,3}$ (and decrement $q_0^{3,2}$). Next, the first colliding rule of rule number 2 (mapping to server 1, with a single wildcard) is rule number 4 (mapping to server 2), then we increment $q_1^{1,2}$ (and decrement $q_1^{2,1}$). This process continues for all rules (excluding the match-all rule).

Intuitively, if one keeps track on the exact function implemented by considering only the last $t$ rules for $t = 1, 2, ..., k$, the vector set $\hat{Q}$ represents succinctly, using cancellation, the number of times there is a change in the function implemented by the rule set. In particular, a vector $Q^{ij}$ represents the times the change in function involves server $i$ and $j$.

Accordingly, one can count the number of bit combinations mapped to each server. Let $T^{ij} = \sum_{t=0}^{W-1} q_t^{ij} \cdot 2^t$. The value $T^{ij}$ counts the total number of bit combinations server $i$ takes from server $j$. Given these values one can count for each server $i$ the total number of bit combinations $d^i$ that the function maps to:

$$d^i = \begin{cases} \sum_{j=1}^{k} T^{ij} & 1 \le i \le k-1 \\ 2^W + \sum_{j=1}^{k} T^{ij} & i = k \end{cases}$$

$$\begin{aligned} Q^{ix} &= (\_,\_,\ge 1,\_,\_) & & \Delta Q^{ix} = (\_,\_,-1,\_,\_) \\ Q^{iy} &= (\_,\_,\_,\_,\_) & \Rightarrow & \Delta Q^{iy} = (\_,\_,+1,\_,\_) \\ Q^{xy} &= (\_,\_,\ge 1,\_,\_) & & \Delta Q^{xy} = (\_,\_,-1,\_,\_) \end{aligned}$$

(a) step I

$$Q^{ix} = (\_,\_,\ge 2,\_,\_) \Rightarrow \Delta Q^{ix} = (\_,+1,-2,\_,\_)$$

(b) step II

$$\begin{aligned} Q^{ix} &= (\_,\_,\ge 1,\_,\_) & & \Delta Q^{ix} = (\_,+1,-1,\_,\_) \\ Q^{iy} &= (\_,\_,\ge 1,\_,\_) & \Rightarrow & \Delta Q^{iy} = (\_,\_,-1,\_,\_) \\ Q^{xy} &= (\_,\_,\_,\_,\_) & & \Delta Q^{xy} = (\_,\_,+1,\_,\_) \end{aligned}$$

(c) step III

**Figure 4: Illustration of the simplification process of the vector set $\hat{Q}$, describing the delta (addition) to each of the vectors. The output distribution is preserved in each of these changes.**

For each vector $Q^{ij}$, we further define a partial (weighted) sum series of its elements. For $v \in [0, W-1]$, representing prefix length, let $T_v^{ij} = \sum_{t=v}^{W-1} q_t^{ij} \cdot 2^t$ and $T_W^{ij} = 0$. An equivalent more intuitive definition is through using the following recursion: Let $T_{W-1}^{ij} = q_{W-1}^{ij} \cdot 2^{W-1}$, and for $v \in [0, W-2]$, $T_v^{ij} = T_{v+1}^{ij} + q_v^{ij} \cdot 2^v$. Last, we define the number of bit combinations mapped to each server by rules with prefix length of at most $W - 1 - v$ (namely more than $v$ wildcards), as represented by the vectors in $\hat{Q}$:

$$d_v^i = \begin{cases} \sum_{j=1}^{k} T_v^{ij} & 1 \le i \le k-1 \\ 2^W + \sum_{j=1}^{k} T_v^{ij} & i = k \end{cases}$$

We capture a simple property of a vector set.

Theorem 4.1. *Given a compressed-form prefix rule set $S$, the values $d_v^i$ for the vector set $\hat{Q}$ associated with the rule set, satisfy $d_v^i \ge 0$ for all $i \in [1,k], v \in [0,W]$.*

## 4.2 Processing and realization

We describe a technique to reduce the number of rules required to achieve the output distribution of a vector set. In the next theorem we show that the vector set can be manipulated, preserving its original implemented distribution, such that for each prefix length and for each server there is at most one rule that changes the number of bit combinations mapped to the server.

Theorem 4.2. *Any vector set $\hat{Q}$, with $d_v^i \ge 0$ for all $i \in [1,k]$ and $v \in [0, W-1]$, can be processed, preserving the original distribution and the non-negativity of its partial sums such that $q_t^{ix} \in \{-1, 0, 1\}$ for all $i, x, t$. Further, for all $t$ and $i$, if for some $x$, $q_t^{ix} \ne 0$, then for all $j \ne x$, $q_t^{ij} = 0$ (and $q_t^{ji} = 0$).*

Proof Outline. The processing has two main phases, each composed of several steps among steps I-III, as illustrated in Fig. 4. Each of the steps maintains the output distribution $D$. We verify that along the processing, for all $i \in [1,k], v \in [0,W]$ the partial sums satisfy $d_v^i \ge 0$. Phase 1 relies on steps I and II. In step I, for instance, illustrated in Fig. 4(a), we consider $t \in [0, W-1]$. Assume there exist $i, x, y$ such that $q_t^{ix}, q_t^{xy} > 0$. We reduce $q_t^{ix}, q_t^{xy}$ by one and

| # | rule | mapping |
|---|---|---|
| 1 | 11000 | server 2 |
| 2 | 1100* | server 3 |
| 3 | 100** | server 1 |
| 4 | 00*** | server 1 |
| 5 | 1**** | server 2 |
| 6 | ***** | server 3 |

$$Q^{12} = (0,0,1,0,0)$$
$$Q^{13} = (0,1,0,0,0)$$
$$Q^{23} = (1,0,0,-1,1)$$

**Figure 5: The rule set $S$ and the corresponding vector set representation $\hat{Q}$ derived after the processing of the rule set from Fig. 3. The output distribution is again $D = (12, 11, 9)$.**

| $B_u^i$ | $q_u^i$ | server-state for bit $u$ |
|---|---|---|
| 0 | -1 | positive |
| 0 | 0 | invalid |
| 0 | 1 | invalid |
| 1 | -1 | negative / zero |
| 1 | 0 | positive |
| 1 | 1 | invalid |

**Table 2: Server state transition: Dependency of the state of server $i$ for bit $u$ on $B_u^i$ and $q_u^i$, given a positive-state for bit index $u + 1$.**

increase $q_t^{iy}$ by one (and update $q_t^{xi}, q_t^{yx}, q_t^{yi}$ correspondingly). In phase 1, we repeat steps I and II, column by column for $t \in [0, W-2]$ and then apply step I for $t = W - 1$. In phase 2, steps I and III are repeated, column by column for $t \in [0, W - 2]$ and then step I is applied for $t = W - 1$. We explain that following phases 1 and 2, the vector set has the required form in all columns besides maybe the most-left one. To satisfy the property also for that column, we might have to replace the default server by another server. □

The next theorem shows that when a simple condition on a vector set holds, there exists a set of rules (in a compressed form) for which the vector set corresponds.

THEOREM 4.3. *Consider a vector set $\hat{Q}$ satisfying: (i) $d_v^i \geq 0$ for all $i \in [1, k], v \in [0, W]$. (ii) $q_t^{ix} \in \{-1, 0, 1\}$ for all $i, x, t$. (iii) for all $t$ and $i$, if for some $x$, $q_t^{ix} \neq 0$, then for all $j \neq x$, $q_t^{ij} = q_t^{ji} = 0$. Then, vector set can be realized to a compressed-form prefix rule set.*

Note that the number of required (non-default) rules in the construction of the proof of Theorem 4.3 equals half the sum of the absolute values of all elements (i.e. $0.5 \cdot \sum_{i,j \in [1,k]} |q^{i,j}|$). Fig. 5 describes the set of rules obtained after the processing of the vector set from Fig. 3. While maintaining the output distribution, the number of rules is reduced from 8 to 6.

## 5 SOLUTIONS FOR MULTIPLE SERVERS

Inspired by the representation of a distribution for multiple servers through a vector set from Section 4, we turn to design algorithms that find an exact representation with minimal rules (in Section 5.1) and the most accurate representation for a given number of rules (in Section 5.2).

### 5.1 Exact distribution realization

We describe an algorithm to find an exact representation with the minimal possible number of rules for any given target distribution. We start with properties that relate the vector set to the output distribution it yields. For space constraints we provide the high-level details of the algorithm.

THEOREM 5.1. *Let $\hat{Q}$ be a vector set with an output distribution $D = (d^1, \ldots, d^k)$ for which the processing from Theorem 4.2 was applied. For all $i \in [1, k], u \in [0, W - 1]$, let $h_u^i = \lfloor d^i / 2^u \rfloor \cdot 2^u$ be the number encoded in the binary representation of $d^i$ when clearing bits with bit indices lower than $u$. Then, the value $d_u^i$, expressed by the indices higher or equal to $u$ in the vector set $\hat{Q}$, satisfies $d_u^i = h_u^i$ or $d_u^i = h_u^i + 2^u$.*

We define the notion of a *server state*. Given a vector set $\hat{Q}$, a server $i \in [1, k]$ is associated with a state for every bit index $u \in [0, W - 1]$. Intuitively, the state examines the difference between the allocation of a server following the complete vector set $\hat{Q}$ and its allocation as expressed by some high-indexed bits of $\hat{Q}$. For $u \in [0, W - 1]$,

- A server $i$ is in a *zero-state* for $u$ if $d_u^i = h_u^i$, and $d_u^i = d^i$.
- In a *negative-state* for $u$ if $d_u^i = h_u^i$, but $d_u^i < d^i$.
- In a *positive-state* for $u$ if $d_u^i = h_u^i + 2^u$. This implies that $d^i < d_u^i$.

In other words, the server $i$ is in a positive-state for a bit index $u$ if all rules involving it with number of don't-care bits higher or equal to $u$ encode a specific number that is larger than the total number of bit combinations when considering all rules. It is in a negative-state if these rules encode a specific number that is lower than the total number of bit combinations when considering all rules, and it is in a zero-state if both numbers are equal. By Theorem 5.1, there are no other possibilities.

The above statement is true for every vector set $Q$. In particular, it is true for all sets that match the target distribution. Let us focus on all such vector sets that match the target distribution.

Assuming that none of the servers has a target number of zero bit combinations, then by convention we define that for bit index $u = W$ all servers are in a negative-state, except for the server that is assigned with the default rule which is in a positive-state.

For each of the servers, its states (either negative, positive, or zero) over the bit indices are related to each other.

Given the state of server $i$ for some bit index $u + 1$ where $u \in [0, W - 1]$, its state for $u$ can be determined based on $B_u^i \in \{0, 1\}$, and $q_u^i \in \{-1, 0, 1\}$, where $B_u^i$ is the bit located at index $u$ in the binary representation of $d^i$, and $q_u^i = \sum_{j=1}^{k} q_u^{ij} \in \{-1, 0, 1\}$ as indicated by Theorem 4.2.

Table 2 captures this dependency given a server that is in a positive-state for a bit index $u+1$. For example, given that the server is in a positive-state for bit $u + 1$, meaning that $d_{u+1}^i = h_{u+1}^i + 2^{u+1}$, then if $B_u^i = 0$ (meaning $h_{u+1}^i = h_u^i$) and $q_u^i = -1$ (meaning $d_u^i = d_{u+1}^i - 2^u$), we get that $d_u^i = h_u^i + 2^u$ using simple substitution operations. Therefore, the server stays in a positive-state for bit index $u$. On the other hand, if $B_u^i = 0$ and $q_u^i = 0$, we get neither of the defined states. Similar transition tables given a negative-state and a zero-state for bit $u$ can be obtained.

**Algorithm 1:** Algorithm for computing the optimal number of rules given server $p$ gets the default rule

**Input**: A target traffic distribution $C = (c^1, \ldots, c^k)$. Server $p$ gets the default rule.
**Output**: An optimal number of rules realizing $C$

```
iSS.count = 0; iSS.state = all servers in a negative-state, except
for server p which is in a positive-state;
A_W = {iSS};
For all i,u, B^i_u = u^th binary bit of c^i;
for u ∈ {0,...,W − 1} in reverse order do
    A_u = ∅
    for cSS ∈ A_{u+1} do
        • Find for each server optional rule additions
        • Consider balanced options to calculate the
          possible next super-state added to A_u
Find SS ∈ A_0 with k servers in zero-state that minimizes
SS.count.
return SS.count
```

Consequentially, for each server, based on its state for bit index $u+1$ and the value of $B^i_u$, we can describe whether a rule that refers to it should be added, and if so whether this can be a positive rule (increasing $q^i_u$ by one) or a negative rule (decreasing $q^i_u$ by one). The result state of the server for bit index $u$ depends on this choice.

We refer to the set of all server states for some bit index $u$ as a *super-state* for bit $u$. Our suggested search algorithm operates on these super-states. Initially, for bit $W$, there is only one super-state where all servers are in negative-states except for the server who gets the default rule and is in a positive-state. Then, it iterates over the bit indices $u \in \{0, 1, \ldots, W-1\}$ in reversed order, where at the step corresponding to bit index $u$ it considers all super-states it arrived at the step corresponding to bit index $u+1$, and constructs all reachable super-states by assigning possible values to $q^i_u$ under the constraint that the number of servers that are assigned with $q^i_u = 1$ is equal to the number of servers that are assigned with $q^i_u = -1$. Last, it also collects for each such reachable super-state the minimal number of rules needed to reach that super-state.

Since for every $u \in \{0, 1, \ldots, W-1\}$, each server can have one of three possible states, the number of super-states is clearly bounded by $3^k$. In our experiments we observe that the number of reachable states is in practice often much smaller although still exponential in the number of servers.

The pseudo-code of this algorithm is described in Algorithm 1. We use *iSS*, *cSS* and *SS* that stand for the initial, the current and a general super-state, respectively. For the sake of brevity, the algorithm described only computes the optimal rule count. The distribution is determined by the super-states for $u = 0$. In particular, to correctly represent the target distribution we need all $k$ servers to be of a zero-state. The required rules number is the count associated with this super-state. By Theorem 4.2 the solution can be realized, where the actual realization can be performed by Theorem 4.3. The minimality of the representations in each iteration implies the optimality of the algorithm. Last, one may iterate over all $p \in \{1, \ldots, k\}$ and select the server leading to the optimal number of rules upon pointing of the default rule to the server.

For computing the actual vector set $\hat{Q}$, one need to keep track for each super-state, the super-state it was reached from. By the chain of the super-states the vector set $\hat{Q}$ can be recovered. In each bit index $u$, the added rules transfer traffic from servers with values $q^i_u = -1$ to those of values $q^i_u = 11$ where pairing can be arbitrary.

## 5.2 Approximated distribution realization

Given a restriction on the rule number, a simple approach is to take the $n$ first added (lowest priority) rules in an optimal solution for an exact representation. However, we conclude by the following example that this approach is not optimal.

*Example 5.2.* Consider the target distribution $C = (2, 3, 3, 8)$. In its first two rules, the solution for exact representation applies a default rule to the last server, and the next rule as a rule of size $2^3$ mapping to server 3 and eliminating traffic from server 4, resulting in a maximum excess traffic $G(D)$ of 5 (to server 3). However, using two rules one can achieve a value $G(D) = 4$, by replacing the second rule in the above solution to be of size $2^2$.

Our approach is based on intuition taken from study of properties of the algorithm for optimal exact realization. We provide the high level ideas. We basically follow the exact same steps as the algorithm for exact realization where we keep record of the maximum excess traffic $G(D)$ of any distribution that is encoded by each super-state the algorithm arrives at. We find for each number of rules, the super-state that minimizes the maximum excess traffic $G(D)$.

For a more accurate consideration of the super-states we arrive at, we also consider transitions between super-states that involves more than one rule, for which we carefully, in a separate sub-routine, add the involved rules one by the other, where the next rule to be added is the one that results in the minimal $G(D)$. For each such sub-step we also record the value of $G(D)$.

The algorithm then outputs for each number of rules the minimal $G(D)$ encountered and its corresponding distribution (along with the corresponding super-state or the corresponding sub-step of a transition between super-states).

# 6 EXPERIMENTAL RESULTS

## 6.1 Effect of number of servers on exact realization size

In this section we examine the optimal rules number needed for an exact realization of a distribution given by the algorithm from Section 1.

Fig. 6 shows the average and maximum optimal number of rules over 500 random traffic allocations for each $k \in \{5, 6, \ldots, 12\}$ servers and a number of bits $W \in \{10, 15, 20, 25\}$. For given values of $k$ and $W$, randomization was performed such that the traffic distribution is uniformly distributed over the vectors with fixed sum of $2^W$. These vectors were created using results related to Dirichlet distribution [5], where first we generated $a^1, \ldots, a^k$ uniformly distributed numbers in $[0, 1]$. Then the allocation $c^i$ for a server is given by the closest integer of $2^W \cdot \log a^i / (\sum_{j=1}^k \log a^j)$ with last small corrections due to rounding so that their sum is $2^W$. The

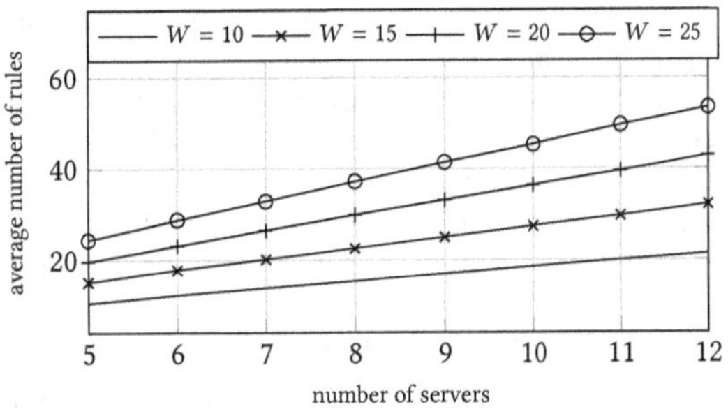


(a) average number of rules

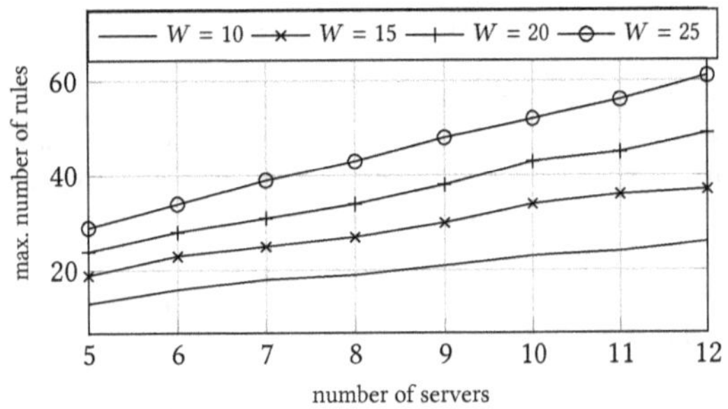


(b) maximum number of rules

**Figure 6: Average and maximum optimal number of rules over 500 uniformly distributed traffic allocations as a function of the number of servers $k$ and the number of bits $W$.**

results show a linear increase in the rule number as a function of the number of servers.

Last, we note that in all instances that we tested we obtained the exact same optimal number of rules as Niagara [10], although the later one is not proven to be optimal.

## 6.2 Approximate realization of single flow

We now investigate the number of rules needed to achieve a given normalized maximum amount of expense $G(D)$.

We used the same method presented in Section 6.1 for creating uniformly distributed fixed sum target traffic distribution. Fig. 7 shows the average of the (normalized) maximum allocation expense $G(D)$ found by our algorithm for approximating traffic allocation over 1000 such random instances with $k = 10$ servers and for $W \in \{10, 15, 20, 25\}$ bits. Interestingly, the normalized maximum allocation expense $G(D)$ drops exponentially with the same exponent regardless of the number of bits. This is because our algorithm deals first with the most significant bit and then considers lower bits, making it indifference to the actual number of bits.

## 7 CONCLUSIONS AND FUTURE WORK

In this paper, we studied the representation of traffic distributions in commodity switches. We explained the tight connection of the problem to signed representations of positive integers. This observation allows us to construct representations with optimality guarantees. As a future work, we would like to find also optimal limited size representations with a minimal error. We would also like to examine whether this link can help to understand more the expressiveness of switch memory for other typical tasks such as traffic measurement and policy enforcement.

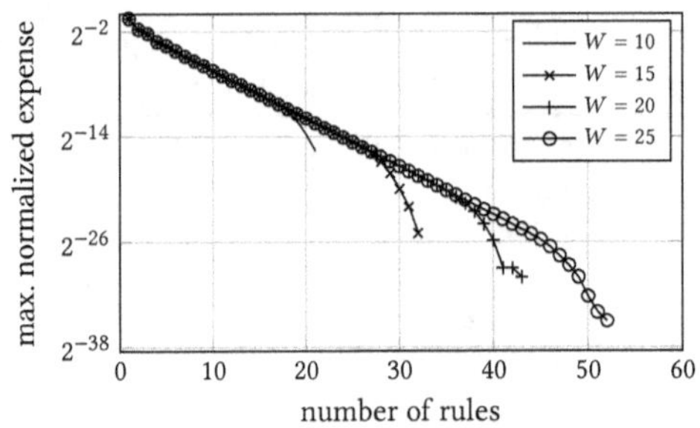


**Figure 7: Expectation of the normalized maximum expense $G(D)$ over 1000 random instances with $k = 10$ servers and $W \in \{10, 15, 20, 25\}$ bits.**

## REFERENCES


[1] Wieb Bosma. 2001. Signed bits and fast exponentiation. *Journal de théorie des nombres de Bordeaux* 13, 1 (2001), 27–41.

[2] Pat Bosshart, Dan Daly, Glen Gibb, Martin Izzard, Nick McKeown, Jennifer Rexford, Cole Schlesinger, Dan Talayco, Amin Vahdat, George Varghese, and David Walker. 2014. P4: Programming protocol-independent packet processors. *Computer Communication Review* 44, 3 (2014), 87–95.

[3] Pat Bosshart, Glen Gibb, Hun-Seok Kim, George Varghese, Nick McKeown, Martin Izzard, Fernando A. Mujica, and Mark Horowitz. 2013. Forwarding metamorphosis: Fast programmable match-action processing in hardware for SDN. In *ACM SIGCOMM*.

[4] Richard Draves, Christopher King, Srinivasan Venkatachary, and Brian Zill. 1999. Constructing optimal IP routing tables. In *IEEE Infocom*.

[5] Paul Emberson, Roger Stafford, and Robert I Davis. 2010. Techniques for the synthesis of multiprocessor tasksets. In *WATERS*. 6–11.

[6] Rohan Gandhi, Hongqiang Harry Liu, Y. Charlie Hu, Guohan Lu, Jitendra Padhye, Lihua Yuan, and Ming Zhang. 2014. Duet: Cloud scale load balancing with hardware and software. In *ACM SIGCOMM*.

[7] Prasanna Ganesan and Gurmeet Singh Manku. 2004. Optimal routing in Chord. In *ACM-SIAM SODA*.

[8] C. Hopps. 2000. Analysis of an equal-cost multi-path algorithm. RFC 2992.

[9] C. Hopps and D. Thaler. 2000. Multipath issues in unicast and multicast next-hop selection. RFC 2991.

[10] Nanxi Kang, Monia Ghobadi, John Reumann, Alexander Shraer, and Jennifer Rexford. 2015. Efficient traffic splitting on commodity switches. In *ACM CoNEXT*.

[11] Rick McGeer and Praveen Yalagandula. 2009. Minimizing Rulesets for TCAM Implementation. In *IEEE Infocom*.

[12] Tal Mizrahi, Ori Rottenstreich, and Yoram Moses. 2017. TimeFlip: Using Timestamp-Based TCAM Ranges to Accurately Schedule Network Updates. *IEEE/ACM Trans. Netw.* 25, 2 (2017), 849–863.

[13] Recep Ozdag. 2012. Intel®Ethernet Switch FM6000 Series-Software Defined Networking. *Intel Coroporation* (2012).

[14] Parveen Patel, Deepak Bansal, Lihua Yuan, Ashwin Murthy, Albert G. Greenberg, David A. Maltz, Randy Kern, Hemant Kumar, Marios Zikos, Hongyu Wu, Changhoon Kim, and Naveen Karri. 2013. Ananta: Cloud scale load balancing. In *ACM SIGCOMM*.

[15] Ori Rottenstreich and János Tapolcai. 2017. Optimal Rule Caching and Lossy Compression for Longest Prefix Matching. *IEEE/ACM Trans. Netw.* 25, 2 (2017), 864–878.

[16] N. J. A. Sloane and Simon Plouffe. 1995. The Encyclopedia of Integer Sequences.

[17] Ion Stoica, Robert Morris, David Liben-Nowell, David R. Karger, M. Frans Kaashoek, Frank Dabek, and Hari Balakrishnan. 2003. Chord: A scalable peer-to-peer lookup protocol for Internet applications. *IEEE/ACM Trans. Netw.* 11, 1 (2003), 17–32.

[18] Subhash Suri, Tuomas Sandholm, and Priyank Ramesh Warkhede. 2003. Compressing two-dimensional routing tables. *Algorithmica* 35, 4 (2003), 287–300.

[19] Richard Wang, Dana Butnariu, and Jennifer Rexford. 2011. OpenFlow-based server load balancing gone wild. In *USENIX Hot-ICE*.

[20] Junlan Zhou, Malveeka Tewari, Min Zhu, Abdul Kabbani, Leon Poutievski, Arjun Singh, and Amin Vahdat. 2014. WCMP: Weighted cost multipathing for improved fairness in data centers. In *ACM EuroSys*.

# Parallel Working-Set Search Structures

Kunal Agrawal
Washington University in St. Louis

Seth Gilbert
National University of Singapore

Wei Quan Lim
National University of Singapore

## Abstract

In this paper we present two versions of a parallel working-set map on $p$ processors that supports searches, insertions and deletions. In both versions, the total work of all operations when the map has size at least $p$ is bounded by the *working-set bound*, i.e., the cost of an item depends on how recently it was accessed (for some linearization): accessing an item in the map with recency $r$ takes $O(1+\log r)$ work. In the simpler version each map operation has $O\big((\log p)^2+\log n\big)$ span (where $n$ is the maximum size of the map). In the pipelined version each map operation on an item with recency $r$ has $O\big((\log p)^2+\log r\big)$ span. (Operations in parallel may have overlapping span; span is additive only for operations in sequence.)

Both data structures are designed to be used by a dynamic multithreading parallel program that at each step executes a unit-time instruction or makes a data structure call. To achieve the stated bounds, the pipelined version requires a weak-priority scheduler, which supports a limited form of 2-level prioritization. At the end we explain how the results translate to practical implementations using work-stealing schedulers.

To the best of our knowledge, this is the first parallel implementation of a *self-adjusting* search structure where the cost of an operation adapts to the access sequence. A corollary of the working-set bound is that it achieves *work static optimality*: the total work is bounded by the access costs in an optimal static search tree.

The full version of this paper is at http://arxiv.org/abs/1805.05787.

**ACM Reference Format:**

Kunal Agrawal, Seth Gilbert, and Wei Quan Lim. 2018. Parallel Working-Set Search Structures. In *SPAA '18: 30th ACM Symposium on Parallelism in Algorithms and Architectures, July 16–18, 2018, Vienna, Austria.* ACM, New York, NY, USA, 12 pages. https://doi.org/10.1145/3210377.3210390

## 1 Introduction

**Map** (or **dictionary**) data structures, such as binary search trees and hash tables, support inserts, deletes and searches/updates (collectively referred to as accesses) and are one of the most used and studied data structures. In the comparison model, balanced binary search trees such as AVL trees and red-black trees provide a performance guarantee of $O(\log n)$ worst-case cost per access for a tree with $n$ items. Other kinds of balanced binary trees provide probabilistic or amortized performance guarantees, such as treaps and weight-balanced trees.


*SPAA '18, July 16–18, 2018, Vienna, Austria*

ACM ISBN 978-1-4503-5799-9/18/07...$15.00
https://doi.org/10.1145/3210377.3210390

**Self-adjusting maps**, such as splay trees [37], adapt their internal structure to the sequence of operations to achieve better performance bounds that depend on various properties of the access pattern (see [20] for a hierarchical classification). Many of these data structures make it cheaper to search for recently accessed items (temporal locality) or items near to previously accessed items (spatial locality). For instance, the working-set structure described by Iacono in [29] has the working-set property (which captures temporal locality); it takes $O(\log r+1)$ time per operation with access rank $r$ (Definition 1), so its total cost satisfies the working-set bound (Definition 2).

**Definition 1 (Access Rank).** Define the **access rank** of an operation in a sequence of operations on a map $M$ as follows. The access rank for a successful search for item $x$ is the number of distinct items in $M$ that have been searched for or inserted since the last prior operation on $x$ (including $x$ itself). The access rank for an insertion, deletion or unsuccessful search is always $n+1$, where $n$ is the current size of $M$.

**Definition 2 (Working-Set Bound).** Given any sequence $L$ of $N$ map operations, we shall use $W_L$ to denote the **working-set bound** for $L$, defined by $W_L = \sum_{i=1}^{N}(\log r_i+1)$ where $r_i$ is the access rank of the $i$-th operation in $L$ when $L$ is performed on an empty map.

### Parallel search structures

Our goal in this paper is to design efficient self-adjusting search structures that can be used by parallel programs. Even designing a non-adjusting parallel or concurrent search structure is quite challenging, and there has been a lot of research on the topic.

There are basically two approaches. In the concurrent computing world, processes independently access the data structure using some variety of concurrency control (e.g., locks) to prevent conflicts. In the parallel computing world, data structures are designed to support executing operations in parallel, either individually or in batches.

For example, in the concurrent computing world, Ellen et al. [19] show how to design a non-blocking binary search tree, with later work generalizing this technique [13] and analyzing the amortized complexity [18]. However, these data structures do not maintain balance in the tree (i.e., the height can get large) and their cost depends on the number of concurrent operations.

An alternate approach (that bears some similarity to the implicit batching that we use) is software combining [22, 28, 32], where each processor inserts a request in a shared queue and a single processor sequentially executes all outstanding requests later. These works provide empirical efficiency but not worst-case bounds.

Another notable example is the CBTree [1, 2], a concurrent splay tree that in real experiments achieves surprisingly good performance — leading to an interesting hypothesis that self-adjustment may be even more valuable (in practice) in concurrent settings than sequential settings. However, the CBTree does not guarantee that it maintains the proper 'frequency balance', and hence does not provide the guarantees of a splay tree (despite much experimental success).

In the parallel computing world, there are several classic results in the PRAM model. Paul et al. [34] devised a parallel 2-3 tree such that $p$ synchronous processors can perform a batch of $p$ operations on a parallel 2-3 tree of size $n$ in $O(\log n + \log p)$ time. Blelloch et. al [8] show how pipelining can be used to increase parallelism of tree operations. Also, (batched) parallel priority queues [12, 15, 16, 36] have been utilized to give efficient parallel algorithms such as for shortest-path and minimum spanning tree [12, 16, 33].

More recently, in the dynamic multithreading model, there have been several elegant papers on parallel treaps [9] and how to parallelize a variety of different binary search trees [7] supporting unions and intersections, and also work on how to achieve batch parallel search trees with optimal work and span [4]. Other batch parallel search trees include red-black trees [23] and weight-balanced B-trees [21]. (We are unaware of any batched self-adjusting data structures.)

And yet, such concurrent/parallel map data structures can be difficult to use; the programmer cannot simply treat it as a black box and use atomic map operations on it from within an ordinary parallel program. Instead, she must carefully coordinate access to the map.

### Implicit batching

Recently, Agrawal et al. [3] introduced the idea of **implicit batching**. Here, the programmer writes a parallel program that uses a black box data structure, treating calls to the data structure as basic operations. In addition, she provides a data structure that supports batched operations (e.g., search trees in [7, 9]). The runtime system automatically stitches these two components together, ensuring efficient running time by creating batches on the fly and scheduling them appropriately. This idea of implicit batching provides an elegant solution to the problem of parallel search trees.

### Our goals

Our goal is to extend the idea of implicit batching to self-adjusting data structures — and more generally, to explore the feasibility of the implicit batching approach for a wider class of problems. In [3], they show how to apply the idea to uniform-cost data structures (where every operation has the same cost). [1] In a self-adjusting structure, some operations are much cheaper than others, and additionally every operation may modify the data structure (unlike say AVL/red-black trees where searches have no effect on the structure), which makes parallelizing it much harder.

We present in this paper, to the best of our knowledge, the first parallel self-adjusting search structure that is distribution-sensitive with worst-case guarantees. In particular, we design two versions of a parallel map whose total work is essentially bounded by the Working-Set Bound for some linearization $L$ of the operations (that respects the dependencies between them).

### Parallel Programming Model

The parallel data structures in this paper can be used in the scenario where a parallel program accesses data structures expressed through **dynamic multithreading** (see [14, Ch. 27]), which is the case in many parallel languages and libraries, such as Cilk dialects [24, 30], Intel TBB [35], Microsoft Task Parallel Library [38] and subsets of OpenMP [31]. The programmer expresses algorithmic parallelism through parallel programming primitives such as fork/join (also spawn/sync), parallel loops and synchronized methods, and does not provide any mapping from subcomputations to processors.

[1] They also provide some bounds for amortized data structures, where queries do not modify the data structure.

These types of programs are typically scheduled using a **greedy scheduler** [11, 27] or a nearly greedy scheduler such as **work-stealing scheduler** (e.g., [10]) provided by the runtime system. A greedy scheduler guarantees that at each time step if there are $k$ available tasks then $\min(k, p)$ of them are completed.

We analyze our two data structures in the context of a greedy scheduler and a weak-priority scheduler (respectively). A **weak-priority scheduler** has two priority levels, and at each step at least half the processors greedily choose high-priority tasks and then low-priority tasks — if there are at most $\frac{1}{2}p$ high-priority tasks, then all are executed. We discuss in Section 8 how to adapt these results for work-stealing schedulers.

## 2 Main Results

We present two parallel working-set maps that can be used with any parallel program $P$, whose actual execution is captured by a **program DAG** $D$ where each node is a unit-time instruction or a call to some data structure $M$, called an **$M$-call**, that blocks until the answer is returned, and each edge represents a dependency due to the parallel programming primitives. Let $T_1$ be the total number of nodes in $D$, and $T_\infty$ be the number of nodes on the longest path in $D$.

Both designs take work nearly proportional to the Working-Set Bound $W_L$ for some legal linearization $L$ of $D$, while having good parallelism. (We assume that each key comparison takes $O(1)$ steps.)

The first design, called $M_1$, is a simpler batched data structure.

**Theorem 3** (**$M_1$ Performance**). If $P$ uses only $M_1$ (i.e., no other data structures), then its running time on $p$ processes using any greedy scheduler is

$$O\left(\frac{T_1 + W_L + e_L \cdot \log p}{p} + T_\infty + d \cdot \left((\log p)^2 + \log n\right)\right)$$

(as $n, p \to \infty$) for some linearization $L$ of $D$, where $d$ is the maximum number of $M_1$-calls on any path in $D$, and $n$ is the maximum size of the map, and $e_L$ is the number of **small-ops**, defined as operations in $L$ that are performed on the map when its size is less than $p$.

Notice that if $M_1$ is replaced by an ideal concurrent working-set map (one that does the same work as the sequential working-set map if we ran the program according to linearization $L$), then running $P$ on $p$ processors according to the linearization $L$ takes $\Omega(T_{opt})$ worst-case time where $T_{opt} = \frac{T_1 + W_L}{p} + T_\infty$. Also, we very likely have $e_L \ll \frac{W_L}{\log p}$ in practice, and so can usually ignore the $e_L \cdot \log p$ term. Thus $M_1$ gives an essentially optimal time bound except for the "span term" $d \cdot \left((\log p)^2 + \log n\right)$, which adds $O\left((\log p)^2 + \log n\right)$ time per $M_1$-call along some path in $D$. In short, the parallelism of $M_1$ is within a factor of $O\left((\log p)^2 + \log n\right)$ of the optimal.

The second design, called $M_2$, uses a more complex pipelined data structure design as well as a weak-priority scheduler (see Section 7.2) to provide a better bound on the "span term".

**Theorem 4** (**$M_2$ Performance**). If $P$ uses only $M_2$, then its running time on $p$ processes using any weak-priority scheduler is

$$O\left(\frac{T_1 + W_L + e_L \cdot \log p}{p} + T_\infty + d \cdot (\log p)^2 + s_L\right)$$

for some linearization $L$ of $D$, where $d, e_L$ are defined as in Theorem 3, and $s_L$ is the weighted span of $D$ where each map operation is weighted by its cost according to $W_L$. Specifically, each map operation in $L$ with access rank $r$ is given the weight $\log r + 1$, and $s_L$ is the maximum weight of any path in $D$.

Compared to $M_1$, the "work term" $\frac{T_1+W_L+e_L\cdot\log p}{p}$ is unchanged, but the "span term" for $M_2$ has no $\log n$ term. Since running $P$ on $p$ processors according to the linearization $L$ takes $\Omega(T_{opt}+s_L)$ worst-case time, $M_2$ gives an essentially optimal time bound up to an extra $O((\log p)^2)$ time per map operation along some path in $D$, and hence $M_2$ has parallelism within an $O((\log p)^2)$ factor of optimal.

# 3 Central Ideas

We shall now sketch the intuitive motivations behind $M_1$ and $M_2$.

It starts with ***Iacono's sequential working-set structure***, which contains a sequence of balanced binary search trees $t_1, t_2, ..., t_l$ where tree $t_i$ for $i < l$ contains $2^{2^i}$ items and hence has height $\Theta(2^i)$. The invariant maintained is that the $r$ most recently accessed items are in the first $\log\log r$ trees. A search on a key proceeds by searching in each tree in the sequence in order until the key is found in tree $t_k$. After a search, the item is moved to $t_1$ and then for each $i < k$, the least recently accessed item from tree $t_i$ is moved to tree $t_{i+1}$. By the invariant, any item in the map with recency $r$ will take $O(\log r + 1)$ time to access. Each insertion or deletion can be easily carried out in $O(\log(n+1)+1)$ time while preserving the invariant.

***The challenge is to 'parallelize' this working-set structure while preserving the total work.*** The first step is to ***process operations in batches***, using a batched search structure in place of each 'tree'.

The problem is that, if there are $b$ searches for the same item in the last tree, then according to the working-set bound these $b$ operations should take $O(\log n + b)$ work. But if these operations all happen in parallel and end up in the same batch, and we execute this batch naively, then each operation will go through the entire structure leading to $\Omega(b\cdot\log n)$ work.

Therefore, in order to get the desired bound, we must ***combine duplicate accesses*** in each batch. But naively sorting a batch of $b$ operations takes $\Theta(b\cdot\log b)$ work. To eliminate this as well, $M_1$ (Section 6) uses a novel ***entropy-sorting algorithm***, and a careful analysis yields the desired work bound.

Next, we cannot simply apply the generic "implicit batching" transformation in [3] to $M_1$, because the Batcher Bound (Theorem 1 in [3]) would give an expected running time of $O\big(\frac{T_1+W+N\cdot s}{p}+T_\infty+d\cdot s\big)$ for $N$ map operations, where $W$ is the work done by $M_1$, and $s$ is the worst-case span of a size-$p$ batch. The problem is that $s$ is $\Omega(\log n)$, because a batch with a search for an item in the last tree has span $\Omega(\log n)$.

Firstly, this means that the $N\cdot s$ term would be $\Omega(N\cdot\log n)$, and so the Batcher Bound would be no better than for a batched binary search tree. Secondly, the $d\cdot s$ term would be $\Omega(d\cdot\log n)$. $M_1$ has the same span term, because if a cheap operation is 'blocked' by the previous batch that has an expensive operation, then the span of the cheap operation could be $\Omega(\log n)$. To reduce this, we improve $M_1$ to $M_2$ using an intricate ***pipelining scheme*** (explained in Section 7) so that a cheap operation is 'blocked' less by the previous batch.

# 4 Parallel Computation Model

In this section, we describe how the parallel program $P$ generates an execution DAG, how we measure the cost of a given execution DAG, and issues related to the chosen memory model.

## Execution DAG

The actual complete execution of $P$ can be captured by the **execution DAG** $E$ (which may be schedule-dependent), in which each node is a unit-time instruction and the directed edges represent the underlying computation flow (such as constrained by forking/joining of threads and acquiring/releasing of locks). At any point during the execution of $P$, a node in the program/execution DAG is said to be **ready** if its parent nodes have been executed. An **active thread** is simply a ready node in $E$, while a **suspended thread** is a terminal node in $E$.

The **program DAG** $D$ captures the high-level execution of $P$, but interaction between data structure calls is only captured by the execution DAG. We further assume that all the data structures are (implicitly) batched data structures, and that the number of data structures in use is bounded by some constant. To support implicit batching, each data structure call is automatically handled by a **parallel buffer** for the data structure. (See Appendix Section A.1.)

The execution DAG $E$ consists of **core nodes** and **ds nodes**, which are dynamically generated as follows. At the start $E$ has a single core node, corresponding to the start of the program $P$. Each node could be a **local instruction** or a **synchronization instruction** (including fork/join and acquire/release of a lock). Each core node could also be a data structure call. When a node is executed, it may generate child nodes or terminate. A join instruction also generates edges that linearize all the join operations according to the actual execution. Likewise, simultaneous operations on a non-blocking lock generate child nodes that are linearized by edges. For a blocking lock, a release instruction generates a child node that is simply the **resumed thread** that next acquires the lock (if any), with an edge to it from the node corresponding to the originally suspended thread.

The core nodes are further classified into **program nodes** and **buffer nodes**. The program nodes (here ***P*-nodes**) correspond to nodes in the program DAG $D$, and they generate only program nodes except for data structure calls. An $M$-call generates a **buffer node** corresponding to passing the call to the parallel buffer. This buffer node generates more buffer nodes, until at some point it generates an $M$-node (every ***M*-node** is a ds node), corresponding to the actual operation on $M$, which passes the **input batch** to $M$. That $M$-node generates only $M$-nodes except for when it returns the result of some operation in the batch (generating a program node with an edge to it from the original $M$-call), or when it becomes ready for input (generating a buffer node that initiates flushing of the parallel buffer).

## Effective Cost

We shall now precisely define the notion of effective work/span/cost for a parallel data structure used by a (terminating) parallel program.

**Definition 5 (Effective Work/Span/Cost).** Take any program $P$ using a batched data structure $M$ on $p$ processors. Let $E$ be the actual execution DAG of $P$ using $M$. Then the **effective work** taken by $M$ (as used by $P$) is the total number $w$ of $M$-nodes in $E$. And the **effective span** taken by $M$ is the maximum number $v$ of $M$-nodes on a path in $E$. And the **effective cost** of $M$ is $\frac{w}{p}+v$.

The effective cost has the desired property that it is **subadditive** across multiple parallel data structures. This implies that our results are **composable** with other data structures in this model, since we actually show the following for some linearization $L$:

- ✧ (Theorem 12 and Theorem 13) $M_1$ takes $O(W_L+e_L\cdot\log p)$ effective work and $O\big(\frac{W_L}{p}+d\cdot((\log p)^2+\log n)\big)$ effective span (using any scheduler).

- (Theorem 22 and Theorem 25) $M_2$ takes $O(W_L + e_L \cdot \log p)$ effective work and $O(\frac{W_L}{p} + d \cdot (\log p)^2 + s_L)$ effective span (using a weak-priority scheduler (Section 7.2)).

Interestingly, the bound for the effective cost of $M_1$ is independent of the scheduler, while the effective cost bound for $M_2$ requires a weak-priority scheduler. In addition, using any greedy scheduler, the parallel buffer for either map $M$ has effective cost (analogously defined) at most $O(\frac{T_1 + w_M}{p} + d \cdot \log p)$ where $w_M$ is the effective work taken by $M$ (Appendix Theorem 26). Therefore our main results (Theorem 3 and Theorem 4) follow from the above claims.

### Memory Model

Unless otherwise stated, we work within the **pointer machine model** for parallel programs given by Goodrich and Kosaraju [26] [2]. But instead of having synchronous processors, we introduce a new more realistic [3] **QRMW** model with queued read-modify-write operations (including read, write, test-and-set, fetch-and-add, compare-and-swap) as described in [17], where multiple memory requests to the same memory cell are FIFO-queued and serviced one at a time, and the processor making each memory request is blocked until the request has been serviced. Our data structures can hence be implemented and used in the dynamic multithreading paradigm.

This QRMW pointer machine model supports **binary fork/join** primitives. It cannot support constant-time random-access locks, but it supports **non-blocking locks** (try-locks), where attempts to acquire the lock are serialized but do not block. Acquiring a non-blocking lock succeeds if the lock is not currently held but fails otherwise, and releasing always succeeds. If $k$ threads concurrently access a non-blocking lock, then each access completes within $O(k)$ time steps. Non-blocking locks can be used to support **activation calls** to a process, where **activating** a process will start its execution iff it is not already executing and it is ready (some condition is satisfied), and the process can optionally reactivate itself on finishing.

We can also implement a **dedicated lock**, which is a blocking lock initialized with keys $[1..k]$ for some constant $k$, such that simultaneous acquisitions must be made using distinct keys. When a thread attempts to acquire a dedicated lock, it is guaranteed to obtain the lock after at most $O(1)$ other threads that attempt to acquire the lock at the same time or later.

## 5 Amortized Sequential Working-set Map

In this section we explain the amortized sequential working-set map $M_0$, which is similar to Iacono's working-set structure [29], but does not move an accessed item all the way to the front. This ***localization of self-adjustment*** is the basis for parallelizing it as in $M_2$.

$M_0$ keeps the items in a list with segments $S[0..l]$. Each segment $S[k]$ has capacity $2^{2^k}$ and every segment is full except perhaps the last. Items in each segment are stored in both a key-map and a recency-map, each of which is a BBT (balanced binary tree), sorted by key and by recency respectively. Consider any item $x$ currently in segment $S[k]$. On a search of $x$, if $k = 0$ then $x$ is moved to the front (most recent; i.e. first in the recency-map) of $S[0]$, otherwise $x$ is moved to the front of $S[k-1]$ and the last (least recent) item of $S[k-1]$ is shifted to the front of $S[k]$. On a deletion of $x$, it is removed and for each $i \in [k..l-1]$ the first (most recent) item of $S[i+1]$ is moved to the back of $S[i]$. On an insertion, the item is added at the back of $S[l]$ (if $S[l]$ is full, then it is added to a new segment $S[l+1]$).

We now prove an abstract lemma about a list with operations and costs that mimic $M_0$. We will later use this same lemma to analyze $M_1$ and $M_2$ as well.

**Lemma 6 (Working-Set Cost Lemma).** Take any sequence $L$ of operations on an abstract list $R$, each of which is a search, insert, delete or demote (described below), and a constant $d \geq 0$, such that the following hold (where $n$ is the current size of $R$):

- Searching for an item with rank $q$ in $R$ costs $O(\log q + 1)$ and it is pulled forward to within the first $2^d \cdot q^{1/2}$ items in $R$.
- Searching for an item not in $R$ costs $O(\log(n+1)+1)$.
- Inserting or deleting an item costs $O(\log(n+1)+1)$.
- Demoting an item in $R$ costs 0 and pushes it backward in $R$, but that item subsequently can only be demoted or deleted.

Then the total cost of performing $L$ on $R$ is $O(W_L)$, where demotions are ignored in computing $W_L$ (they are not counted as accesses).

*Proof.* We shall perform the analysis via the accounting method; each operation on $L$ has a budget according to $W_L$, and we must use those credits to pay for that operation, possibly saving surplus credits for later. Define the $R$-recency of an item $x$ in $R$ to be the number of items in $R$ that have been inserted before or pulled forward past $x$ in $R$ since the last operation on $x$. Clearly, for each search/insertion/deletion of an item $x$ in $L$, its access rank (actual recency) is at least the $R$-recency of $x$. Each item in $R$ has some stored credit, and we shall maintain the invariant that every item in $R$ with $R$-recency $r$ and stored credit $c$ is within the first $2^{c+2d+1} + r$ items in $R$ or has been demoted. The invariant trivially holds at the start.

First we show that, on every operation on an item $x$, the invariant can be preserved for $x$ itself. For insertion/deletion or unsuccessful search for $x$, the budget of $\Theta(\log(n+1)+1)$ can pay for the operation and (for insertion) also pay for the stored credit for $x$. For successful search for $x$, it is as follows. Let $c$ be the stored credit and $r$ be the $R$-recency of $x$ before the operation, and let $q$ be the rank of $x$ in $R$ after that. By the invariant, $x$ was within the first $2^{c+2d+1} + r$ items in $R$ before the operation. Also the budget is $\Omega(\log r + 1)$. If $r \geq 2^{c+2d+1}$, then $q \leq 2^d \cdot \sqrt{2r}$ and so the budget can pay for both the operation cost and a new stored credit of $\log\sqrt{2r}$. If $r \leq 2^{c+2d+1}$, then $q \leq 2^d \cdot \sqrt{2^{c+2d+1} \cdot 2} = 2^{c/2+2d+1}$ and so the stored credit can pay for the operation cost and a new stored credit of $c/2$.

Finally we check that the invariant is preserved for every other item $y$ in $M$. For search/insertion of $x$, the rank of $y$ in $R$ changes by the same amount as its $R$-recency. For deletion of $x$, if $x$ is after $y$ in $R$ then $y$ is more recent than $x$ and so the $R$-recency of $y$ does not change, and if $x$ is before $y$ in $R$ then the rank of $y$ in $R$ decreases by 1 and its $R$-recency decreases by at most 1. For a demotion, every other item's rank in $R$ does not increase. ◇

This lemma implies that $M_0$ has the desired working-set property.

**Theorem 7 ($M_0$ Performance).** The cost of $M_0$ satisfies the working-set bound.

*Proof.* Let $n$ be the number of items in $M_0$. By construction, $2^{l-1} \leq \log(n+1)$, and each operation on $M_0$ takes $O(2^k)$ time on segment $S[k]$. Thus each insertion/deletion takes $O(\log(n+1)+1)$ time, and each access/update of an item with rank $q$ in $M_0$ (in order of segment

[2] In short, the main memory can be accessed only via pointers, which can only be stored, dereferenced or tested for equality (no pointer arithmetic).

[3] Exclusive reads/writes (EREW) is too strict, while concurrent reads/writes (CRCW) does not realistically model the cost of contention, as stated in [25].

followed by order in the recency-map) takes $O(\log q + 1)$ time. Also, on each access of an item $x$ with rank $q$ in $M_0$, its new rank $q'$ is at most $2q^{1/2}$, because if $x$ is in $S[0..1]$ then $q' = 1$, and if $x$ is in $S[k]$ for some $k > 1$ then $q \geq 2^{2^{k-1}}$ and $q' \leq 2^{2^{k-2}} \cdot 2$. Thus by the Working-Set Cost Lemma (Lemma 6) we are done. ◇

# 6 Simple Parallel Working-Set Map

We now present our simple batched working-set map $M_1$. The idea is to use the amortized sequential working-set map $M_0$ (Section 5) and execute operations in batches [4]. In order to get the bound we desire, however, we must combine operations in a batch that access the same item. In particular, for consecutive accesses to the same item, all but the first one should cost $O(1)$. Therefore, we must sort the batch (efficiently) using the Parallel Entropy Sort (Appendix Definition 29), to 'combine duplicates'. We also control the size of batches — if batches are too small, then we lose parallelism; if the batches are too large, then the sorting cost is too large.

## 6.1 Description of $M_1$

As described in the Section 4, $M_1$-calls in the program are put into the parallel buffer for $M_1$. When $M_1$ is ready (i.e. the previous batch is done), we flush the parallel buffer to obtain the next input batch $I$, which we cut and store in a **feed buffer**, which is a queue of bunches (a **bunch** is a set supporting $O(1)$ addition of a batch and $O(\log b)$-span conversion to a batch if it has size $b$) [5] each of size $p^2$ except possibly the last. Specifically, we divide $I$ into small batches of size $p^2$ except possibly the first and last, the first having size $\min(b, p^2 - q)$, where $b$ is the size of $I$ and $q$ is the size of the last bunch $F$ in the feed buffer. Next we add that first small batch to $F$, and append the rest as bunches to the feed buffer. Let $n$ be the current size of $M_1$. Then we remove the first $\lceil \frac{\log n}{p} \rceil$ bunches from the feed buffer, convert them into batches, merge them in parallel into a **cut batch** $B$, and process it as follows.

First we sort $B$ using the Parallel Entropy Sort (Appendix Definition 29). Then we combine all operations on each item into one **group-operation** [6] that is treated as a single operation with the same effect as the whole group of operations in the given order.

We pass the resulting batch (of group-operations) through each segment from $S[0]$ to $S[l]$. At segment $S[k]$, first we search for the relevant items. For insertions, if the item is found then we treat it as an update. For successful searches/updates, we return the results immediately, and shift the items (keeping their relative order) to the front of the previous segment $S[k-1]$ ($S[0]$ if $k = 0$). For deletions, if the item is found then we delete the item. Next, we restore the capacity invariant for $S[0..k-1]$ — for each segment $S[i]$ from $S[k]$ to $S[1]$, we transfer the appropriate number of items between the front of $S[i]$ and the back of $S[i-1]$ so that either $S[0..i-1]$ have total size $\sum_{j=0}^{i-1} 2^{2^j}$ or $S[i]$ is empty. Then we pass the unfinished (unreturned) operations (including all deletions) on to the next segment.

At the end, we handle the remaining insertions. First we insert at the back of $S[l]$ up to its capacity. If there are leftover items, we create segments $S[l+1..l']$ with just enough capacity, and carve out the correct amount for each segment from $S[l']$ to $S[l+1]$ in that order.

Finally, we return the results for the insertions/deletions and the unsuccessful searches/updates, and we are done processing the batch.

To parallelize the above, we need to be able to efficiently delete, from each segment, any sorted batch of items or any number of the most/least recent items. For this we replace each BBT by a Batched Parallel 2-3 Tree (Appendix Section A.2), where each leaf in the key-map also has a direct pointer to the corresponding leaf in the recency-map, and vice versa. Given a sorted batch of items, we can find them by one batch operation on the key-map, and then we have a batch of direct pointers to the leaves for these items in the recency-map, and hence can perform one reverse-indexing operation on the recency-map to obtain a sorted batch of indices for those leaves, with which we can perform one batch operation to delete them. Similarly, to remove the $b$ most recent items from a segment, we find them via the recency-map, and then do a reverse-indexing operation on the key-map to obtain them in sorted order, whence we can delete them.

## 6.2 Analysis of $M_1$

We first bound the cost of parallel entropy-sorting each batch (Lemma 10). To do so, we will find a batch-preserving linearization (Definition 8) $L$ such that for each batch of size $b$, the entropy bound is at most the insert working-set bound (Definition 9), which we in turn bound by the cost according to the working-set bound $W_L$, plus $O(\log b)$ per operation when the map is small (i.e. has size $b^{O(1)}$). This extra cost arises when a batch has many operations on distinct items while the map is small, which according to $W_L$ are cheap.

**Definition 8 (Batch-Preserving Linearization).** Take any sequence $I$ of batches of operations on a map $M$. We say that $L$ is a **batch-preserving linearization** of $I$ if $L$ is a permutation of the operations in $I$ that preserves the ordering of batches and (within each batch) the ordering of operations on the same item.

**Definition 9 (Insert Working-Set Bound).** The **insert working-set bound** $IW_L$ for any sequence $L$ of map operations is the working-set bound for 'inserting' the items in $L$ in the given order (ignoring the actual operations) into an empty map, namely for each item first searching for it and then inserting it iff it is absent.

**Lemma 10 (Batch-Sorting Cost Lemma).** Take any sequence $I$ of batches of operations on a map $M$, and any constant $\varepsilon > 0$. Then there is a batch-preserving linearization $L$ of $I$ such that parallel entropy-sorting (Appendix Definition 29) each batch in $I$ takes $O(W_L + \sum_{B \in L} e_B \cdot \log b_B)$ total work over all batches, where each batch $B$ in $L$ has size $b_B$ and has $e_B$ operations that are performed when $M$ has size less than $b_B{}^{\varepsilon}$ (when $L$ is performed on $M$).

*Proof.* Let $L$ be a batch-preserving linearization of $I$ such that each batch $B$ in $L$ has the maximum insert working-set bound $IW_B$ (Definition 9). By the Worse-case Working-set Bound (Appendix Theorem 28) $IW_B$ is at least the entropy bound for $B$. Thus parallel entropy-sorting $B$ takes $O(IW_B)$ work (Appendix Theorem 30).

Let $b$ be the size of $B$, and $u$ be the number of distinct items (accessed by operations) in $B$. Partition $B$ into subsequences $B_0$ and $B_1$ such that $B_0$ has only the first operation of every distinct item in $B$. For each $i \in \{0,1\}$, let $C_i$ be the cost of the operations in $B_i$ according to $W_L$, and let $IC_i$ be the cost of the operations in $B_i$ according to $IW_B$, so $IW_B = IC_0 + IC_1$. Let $e_B$ be the number of operations in $B$ performed when $M$ has size less than $b^{\varepsilon}$ (according to $L$).

Note that $IC_1 \leq C_1$ because every operation in $B_1$ is a successful search according to $IW_B$ with access rank no more than according to $W_L$. Thus it suffices to show that $IC_0 \in O(C_0 + e_B \cdot \log b)$.

---

[4] Each batch is stored in a leaf-based balanced binary tree for efficient processing.

[5] A bunch is implemented using a complete binary tree with batches at the leaves, with a linked list threaded through each level to support adding a leaf in $O(1)$ steps.

[6] Each group-operation stores the original operations as a batch.

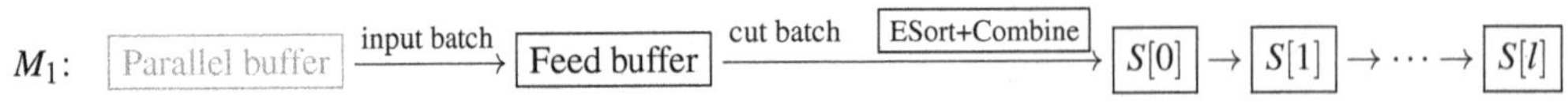


**Figure 1: $M_1$ Outline**

If $e_B > \frac{1}{2}u$, then obviously $IC_0 \in O(e_B \cdot \log b)$.

If $e_B \le \frac{1}{2}u$, then at least $\frac{1}{2}u$ operations in $B_0$ are performed when $M$ has size at least $b^\varepsilon$. So according to $W_L$, each of those operations has access rank at least $b^\varepsilon$ and hence costs $\log(b^\varepsilon) \in \Omega(\log u)$. Thus $C_0 \in \Omega(u \cdot \log u)$. Also, $IC_0 \in O(u \cdot \log u)$, since any insertion on a map with at most $u$ items has access rank $O(u)$. ◇

Next we prove a simple lemma that allows us to divide the work done on the segments among the operations.

**Lemma 11** (**$M_1$ Segment Work**)**.** Each segment $S[k]$ takes $O(2^k)$ work per operation that reaches it.

*Proof.* Searching/deleting/shifting the relevant items in the parallel 2-3 trees takes $O(2^k)$ work per operation. Also, for each $i \le k$, the number of transfers (to restore the capacity invariant) between $S[i-1]$ and $S[i]$ is at most the number of operations, and each transfer takes $O(2^i)$ work because there are always at most $\sum_{j=0}^{i} 2^{2^j} \le 2 \cdot 2^{2^i}$ items in $S[0..i]$. Thus the transfers take $O(2^k)$ total work. ◇

Then we can prove the desired effective work bound for $M_1$.

**Theorem 12** (**$M_1$ Effective Work**)**.** $M_1$ takes $O(W_L + e_L \cdot \log p)$ effective work for some linearization $L$ of $D$.

*Proof.* Cutting the input batch of size $b$ from the parallel buffer into small batches takes $O(b)$ work. Adding the first small batch to the last bunch in the feed buffer takes $O(1)$ work. Inserting the bunches into the feed buffer takes $O(b)$ work. Forming a cut batch of size $b'$ (converting the bunches and merging the results) takes $O(b')$ work. So all this buffering work adds up to $O(1)$ per map operation.

Sorting the (cut) batches takes $O(W_L + e_L \cdot \log p)$ total work (over all batches) for some linearization $L$, by the Batch-Sorting Cost Lemma (Lemma 10). Specifically, we choose $\varepsilon = \frac{1}{3}$. For each batch $B$, let $n$ be the size of $M_1$ just before that batch, and then $B$ has size $b^* \le \lceil \frac{\log n}{p} \rceil \cdot p^2 \le p \cdot \log n + p^2$ and:

- ✧ If $n \le 3p^2$, then $b^* \le p \cdot \log n + p^2 \le p \cdot \log(3p^2) + p^2 \le 4p^2$ and so $b^{*\varepsilon} \le p$ (as $p \ge 4$).
- ✧ If $n > 3p^2$, then $n > p \cdot \log n + p^2 + p \ge b^* + p$ so none of the operations in that batch can be small-ops.

It now suffices to show that the work on segments is $O(W_{L'})$ for some linearization $L'$ (since either $L$ or $L'$ suffices for the final bound). For this, we pretend that a deleted item is marked rather than removed, and when a segment is filled to capacity all marked items are simultaneously transferred to the next segment, and at the last segment the marked items are removed. This takes more work than what $M_1$ actually does, but is easier to bound.

We shall now use the Working-Set Cost Lemma (Lemma 6) on the list $R$ of the items in $M_1$ (including the marked items) in order of segment followed by recency within the segment, where $R$ is updated after the batch has passed through each segment in the actual execution $A$ of $M_1$, and after we finish processing the batch.

We simulate the updates to $R$ by list operations as follows:

- ✧ Shift successfully searched/updated items in $A$: Search for them in reverse order (from back to front in $R$).
- ✧ Shift marked (to-be-deleted) items in $A$: Demote them.
- ✧ Insert items in $A$: Insert in the desired positions.
- ✧ Remove marked items in $A$: Delete them.

This simulation yields a sequence $G$ of list operations on $R$, to which we can then apply the Working-Set Cost Lemma.

For each search for an item $x$ with rank $q$ in $R$, $x$ is found in $S[0]$ or some segment $S[k+1]$ such that $2^{2^k} < q$, and so by $M_1$ Segment Work (Lemma 11) the search takes $O(\log q + 1)$ work in $A$, after which $x$ has new rank in $R$ at most $2q^{1/2}$, like in $M_0$ (Theorem 7). After each batch $B$, let $n'$ be the final size of $M_1$ and $S[l']$ be the new last segment, and then each insertion in $B$ takes $O\left(\sum_{i=0}^{l'} 2^i\right) \subseteq O(\log n' + 1)$ work in $A$. Each deletion takes $O(\log n + 1)$ work in $A$.

Thus by Lemma 6, $M_1$ takes $O(W_G)$ work on segments. Now let $L'$ be the same as $G$ but with each group-operation expanded to its original sequence of operations. Clearly $W_G \le W_{L'}$, since each group-operation is on the same item, so we are done. ◇

And now we turn to bounding the effective span.

**Theorem 13** (**$M_1$ Effective Span**)**.** $M_1$ takes $O\left(\frac{N}{p} + d \cdot \left((\log p)^2 + \log n\right)\right)$ effective span, where $N$ is the number of operations on $M_1$, and $n$ is the maximum size of $M_1$.

*Proof.* First we bound the the span of processing each cut batch (i.e. the span of the corresponding execution subDAG). Let $s(b)$ denote the maximum span of processing a cut batch of size $b$. Take any cut batch $B$ of size $b$ and let $n_B$ be the size of $M_1$ just before $B$. $B$ takes $O\left(\frac{b}{p^2} + \log b\right)$ span to be removed and formed from the feed buffer, and $O\left((\log b)^2\right)$ span to be sorted. $B$ then takes $O\left(\log b + 2^k\right)$ span in each segment $S[k]$ (because shifting between parallel 2-3 trees of size $O(2^h)$ or cutting a batch of size $O(2^h)$ takes $O(h)$ span), which adds up to $O(\log b \cdot \log\log b + \log n_B)$ span over all segments, since $\log b < 2^k$ when $k > \log\log b$. Returning the results for each group-operation takes $O(\log b)$ span. Thus $s(b) \in O\left(\frac{b}{p} + (\log b)^2 + \log n_B\right)$. If $b \le p^2$ then $s(b) \in O\left(\frac{b}{p} + (\log p)^2 + \log n_B\right)$. If $b \ge p^2$ then $(\log b)^2 \in O\left(\frac{b}{p}\right)$ and hence $s(b) \in O\left(\frac{b}{p} + \log n_B\right)$.

Now let $E$ be the actual execution DAG for $P$ using $M_1$ (on $p$ processors). Then the effective span of $M_2$ is simply the time taken to execute $E$ on an unlimited number of processors when each $M_1$-node in $E$ takes unit time while every other node takes zero time, since $E$ captures all relevant behaviour of $P$ using $M_1$ including all the dependencies created by the locks. In this execution, we put a counter at each $M_1$-call in the program DAG $D$, initialized to zero, and at each step we increment the counter at every pending $M_1$-call (i.e., the result is not yet returned). Then the total number of steps is at most the final counter-weighted span of $D$, which we now bound.

Take any path $C$ in $D$. Consider each $M_1$-call $X$ on $C$. We trace the 'journey' of $X$ from the parallel buffer as an operation in an uncut batch $U$ of size $u$ to a cut batch $B$ of size $b$ to the end of $M_1$.

Observe that any batch of size $u$ takes $O(\log p + \log u)$ span to be flushed from the parallel buffer, and $O\left(\log u + \frac{u}{p^2}\right)$ span to be cut and added/appended to the bunches in the feed buffer, which in total is at most $O(\log p + \frac{u}{p})$ span.

So, first of all, $X$ waits for the preceding uncut batch of size $u'$ to be processed, taking $O\left(\log p + \frac{u'}{p}\right)$ span. Next, $X$ waits for the current cut batch $B'$ of size $b'$ to be processed, taking $s(b')$ span. After that, $U$ is processed, taking $O(\log p + \frac{u}{p})$ span. Then $X$ waits for intervening cut batches (between $B'$ and $B$) with $i$ operations in total. Each intervening batch $B^*$ has some size $b^* \geq \max(p^2, p \cdot \log n_{B^*})$ and hence $s(b^*) \in O(\frac{b^*}{p})$. Finally, $B$ is processed, taking $s(b)$ span. Thus $X$ takes $O\left(\log p + \frac{u}{p} + \frac{u'}{p} + s(b) + s(b') + \frac{i}{p}\right)$ span in total.

Note that no two $M_1$-calls on the path $C$ can wait for the same intervening batch, because the second can be executed only after the first has returned. Thus over all counters at $M_1$-calls on $C$, each of $u, u', b, b', i$ will sum up to at most $N$. Therefore the final counter-weighted span of $D$ is at most $O\left(\frac{N}{p} + d \cdot ((\log p)^2 + \log n)\right)$. ◇

# 7 Faster Parallel Working-Set Map

To reduce the effective span of $M_1$, we intuitively have to:

- ✧ Shift each accessed item near enough to the front, so that accessing it again soon would be cheap.
- ✧ Pipeline the batches somehow, so that an expensive access in a batch does not hold up the next batch.

Naive pipelining will not work, because operations on the same item may take too much work. Hence we shall use a **filter** before the pipelined segments to ensure that operations proceeding through them are on distinct items, namely we pass all operations through the filter and only allow an operation through if there is not already another operation on the same item in the pipeline.

For similar reasons as in $M_1$, we must control both the batch size and filter size to achieve enough parallelism, and so we choose the filter capacity to be $\Theta(p^2)$. However, we cannot put the filter before the first segment, because accessing the filter requires $\Omega(\log p)$ work per operation, whereas to meet the working-set bound we need operations with $O(1)$ access rank to cost only $O(1)$ work.

Therefore, we divide the segments into the **first slab** and the **final slab**, where the first slab comprises the first $\log \Theta(\log p)$ segments and the final slab contains the rest, and put the filter after the first slab. Only operations that do not finish in the first slab are passed through the filter, and so the filtering cost per operation is bounded by the $\Theta(\log p)$ work already incurred in going through the first slab. Furthermore, we shift accessed items to the front of the final slab, and 'cascade' the excess items only when a later batch passes.

We cannot pipeline the first slab, but since the first slab is essentially a copy of $M_1$ but with only $\log O(\log p)$ trees, its non-pipelined span turns out to be bounded by the $O((\log p)^2)$ span of sorting. To allow operation on items in the first slab to finish quickly, we need to allow the first slab to run while the final slab is running, but only when the filter has size at most $p^2$, so that the filter size is always $O(p^2)$.

We also use **special locking schemes** to guarantee that the first slab and the segments in the final slab can process the operations at a consistent pace without interfering with one another. Finally, we shall **weakly prioritize** the execution of the final slab, to prevent excessive work from being done in the first slab on an item $x$ if there is already an operation on $x$ in the final slab.

## 7.1 Description of $M_2$

We shall now give the details for implementing this (see Figure 2), making considerable use of the Batched Parallel 2-3 Tree (Appendix Section A.2). $M_2$ has the same segments as in $M_1$, where segment $S[k]$ has assigned capacity $2^{2^k}$ but may be under-full or over-full. We shall group the first $m = \lceil \log\log(2p^2) \rceil + 1$ segments into the **first slab**, and the other segments into the **final slab**. $M_2$ uses a **feed buffer** (like $M_1$; see Section 6.1), which is a queue of bunches [5] each of size $p^2$ except possibly the last.

The $M_2$ interface is ready iff both the following hold:

- ✧ The parallel buffer or feed buffer is non-empty.
- ✧ The filter has size at most $p^2$.

When the $M_2$ interface is activated (and ready), it does the following (in sequence) on its run (the locks are described later):

(1) Let $q$ be the size of the last bunch $F$ in the feed buffer. Flush the parallel buffer and cut the input batch of size $b$ into small batches of size $p^2$ except possibly the first and last, where the first has size $\min(b, p^2 - q)$. Add that first small batch to $F$, and append the others as bunches to the feed buffer. Remove the first bunch from the feed buffer and convert it into a batch $B$, which we shall call a **cut batch**.

(2) Sort $B$ using the Parallel Entropy Sort (Appendix Definition 29), combining operations on the same item [6], as in $M_1$.

(3) Pass $B$ through the first slab, which processes the operations as in $M_1$. Successful searches/updates immediately finish, while the rest finish only if there was no final slab. Successful deletions are tagged to indicate success. But just before running $S[m-1]$ (if it exists) to process the remaining batch at that segment, acquire the neighbour-lock shared with $S[m]$ (as shown in Figure 2) and then acquire the front-lock $FL[0]$.

(4) If there was a final slab, then pass the (sorted) batch of unfinished operations through the filter (including successful deletions), insert the filtered batch into the buffer before $S[m]$, and fork (a child thread) to activate $S[m]$.

(5) Release $FL[0]$ and the neighbour-lock shared with $S[m]$.

(6) Reactivate itself.

The **filter** is used to ensure that at any point all the operations in the final slab are on distinct items. It is implemented using a batched parallel 2-3 tree that stores items, each tagged with a list of operations on that item (in the order they arrive at the filter) and their cumulative **effect** (as a single equivalent map operation).

When a batch is passed through the filter, each operation on an item in the filter is appended to the list for it (the effect is also updated) and filtered out of the batch, whereas each operation on an item not in the filter is added to the filter and put into the buffer of $S[m]$.

The final slab is pipelined in the following way. Between every pair of consecutive segments is a **neighbour-lock**, which is a dedicated lock (see Section 4 Memory Model) with 1 key for each arrow to it in Figure 2. Since each segment needs to access the filter and

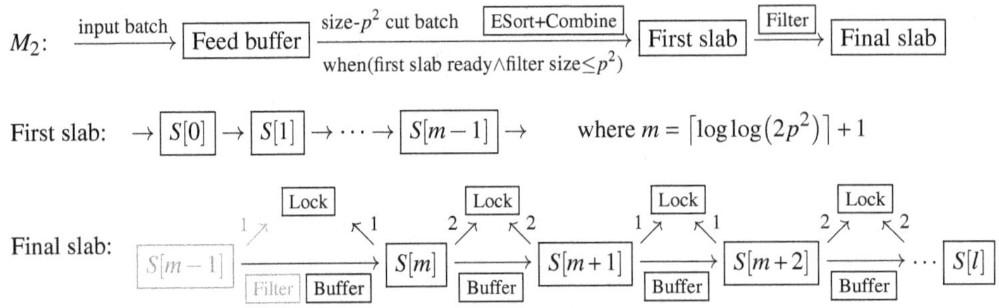


**Figure 2: $M_2$ Outline**

the contents of $S[m]$, those accesses will also be guarded by a front-locking scheme using a series of **front-locks** $FL[0..l-m]$, each of which is a dedicated lock with 1 key for each arrow to it in Figure 3. (This will be fully spelt out below.)

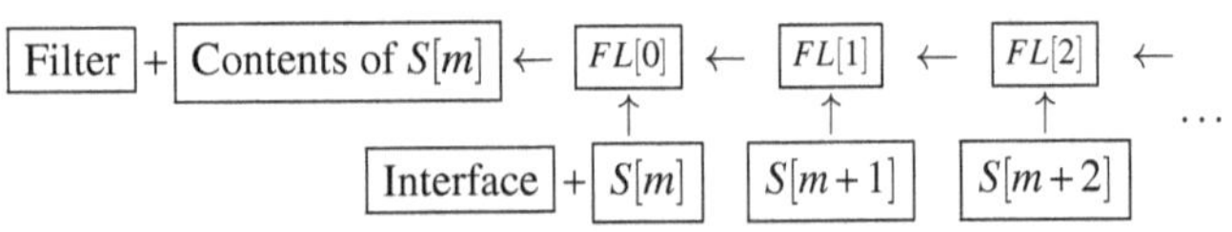


**Figure 3: Front-locking**

Each final slab segment $S[k]$ has a **sorted buffer** before it (for operations from $S[k-1]$), which is a batched parallel 2-3 tree. $S[k]$ is ready iff its buffer is non-empty, and when activated (and ready) it runs as follows (front-locking is highlighted):

(1) Acquire the neighbour-locks (between $S[k]$ and its neighbours) in the order given by the arrow number in Figure 2.
(2) If $k = m$, acquire $FL[0]$.
(3) If $S[k]$ is the terminal segment and $S[k-1,k]$ have total size exceeding their total capacity, create a new terminal segment $S[k+1]$.
(4) Flush and process the operations in its buffer as follows:
  (a) Search for the accessed items $A$ in $S[k]$ (by performing one batch operation on the key-map in $S[k]$). Let $R$ be the (sorted batch of) items in $A$ that are found in $S[k]$, and delete $R$ from $S[k]$.
  (b) If $k > m$, acquire $FL[k-m]$ to $FL[0]$ in that order.
  (c) Search for $R$ in the filter to determine what to do with it. Let $R'$ be the items in $R$ to be searched or updated, and delete $R'$ from the filter. (Insertions on items in $R$ are treated as updates.) Perform all the updates on items in $R$.
  (d) Let $m' = \min(k-1, m)$. Fork to return the results for operations on $R'$, and insert $R'$ at the front of $S[m']$. If $S[k]$ is (now) the terminal segment, perform all insertions at the front of $S[m']$, and delete $A \setminus R'$ from the filter, and fork to return the results for operations on $A \setminus R'$.
  (e) If the filter size is at most $p^2$, fork to activate the interface.
  (f) If $k > m$, release $FL[0]$ to $FL[k-m]$ in that order.
  (g) If $S[k-1]$ is over-full, transfer items from the back of $S[k-1]$ to the front of $S[k]$ so that $S[k-1]$ is full.
  (h) If $S[k-1]$ is under-full by $i$ items and $S[k]$ has $c$ items and $A$ has $d$ successful deletions, transfer $\min(i,c,d)$ items from the front of $S[k]$ to the back of $S[k-1]$.
  (i) If $S[k]$ is not the terminal segment, insert the operations on $A \setminus R'$ (with successful deletions tagged as such) into the buffer of $S[k+1]$, then fork to activate $S[k+1]$.
(5) If $S[k]$ is the terminal segment and is empty, remove $S[k]$ to make $S[k-1]$ the new terminal segment.
(6) If $k = m$, release $FL[0]$.
(7) Release both neighbour-locks and reactivate itself.

### 7.2 Weak-priority scheduler

It turns out that, ignoring the sorting cost, all we need to achieve the working-set bound is that, for each operation on an item $x$ in the final slab, the work 'done' by the first slab on $x$ can be counted against the work done in the final slab. This can be ensured using a **weak-priority scheduler**. A weak-priority scheduler has two queues $Q_1$ and $Q_2$, where $Q_1$ is the high-priority queue, and each ready node is assigned to either $Q_1$ or $Q_2$, and at every step the following hold:

- ✧ If there are $k$ ready nodes, then $\min(k, \frac{1}{2}p)$ of them are executed.
- ✧ If queue $Q_1$ has $k$ ready nodes, then $\min(k, \frac{1}{2}p)$ of them are executed (and so $Q_1$ nodes are weakly-prioritized).

The $M_2$-nodes generated for the final slab are assigned to $Q_1$, while all other $M_2$-nodes are assigned to $Q_2$. Specifically, each (forked) activation call to $S[m]$ and all nodes generated by that are assigned to $Q_1$, except for activation calls to the $M_2$ interface (which are assigned to $Q_2$). Any suspended thread is put back into its original queue when it is resumed (i.e. the resuming node is assigned to the same queue as the acquiring node).

### 7.3 Analysis of $M_2$

For each computation (subDAG of the actual execution DAG), we shall define its **delay**, which intuitively captures the minimum possible time it needs, including all waiting on locks. Each blocked acquire of a dedicated lock corresponds to an **acquire-stall node** $\alpha$ in the execution DAG whose child node $\rho$ is created by the release just before the successful acquisition of the lock. Let $\Delta(\alpha)$ be the ancestor nodes of $\rho$ that have not yet executed at the point when $\alpha$ is executed. Then we define delay as follows.

**Definition 14 (Computation Delay).** The **delay** of a computation $\Gamma$ is recursively defined as the weighted span of $\Gamma$, where each acquire-stall node $\alpha$ in $\Gamma$ is weighted by the delay of $\Delta(\alpha)$ (to capture the total waiting at $\alpha$), and every other node has unit weight.

Also, we classify each operation as **segment-bound** iff it finishes in some segment, and **filter-bound** otherwise (namely filtered out due to a prior operation on the same item that finishes in the final slab).

The ***key lemma*** (Lemma 19) is that any operation that finishes in segment $S[m+k]$ takes $O(2^{m+k})$ delay to be processed by the final slab, which is ensured (Lemma 18) by the front-locking scheme and the balance invariants (Lemma 16).

Then $M_2$ takes $O(W_L + e_L \cdot \log p)$ effective work for some linearization $L$ of $D$, and here is the intuitive proof sketch:

(1) The work divides into **segment work** (done by the slabs) and **non-segment work** (cutting and sorting batches, and filtering).
(2) The segment work can be divided per operation; segment $S[k]$ does $O(2^k)$ work per operation that reaches it (Lemma 20).
(3) The cutting work is $O(1)$ per operation, and the (overall) sorting work is $O(W_L + e_L \cdot \log p)$ for some linearization $L$ of $D$ (Lemma 10). The filtering work is $O(\log p)$ per filtered operation, which can be ignored since each filtered operation already took $\Omega(\log p)$ work in the first slab. Similarly we can ignore the work done in passing the batch through $S[m-1]$.
(4) The segment work on segment-bound operations is $O(W_{L'})$ for some linearization $L'$ of $D$ (Lemma 21; proven using Lemma 6 like we did for $M_1$).
(5) The segment work on filter-bound operations is $O(W_{L'})$ too:
   (a) We can ignore work during **high-busy steps** (where $Q_1$ has at least $\frac{1}{2}p$ ready nodes), because the final slab takes $O(W_{L'})$ work and so there are $O\left(\frac{W_{L'}}{p}\right)$ high-busy steps.
   (b) We can ignore **high-busy runs** of $S[0..m-2]$ (namely with at least half its steps high-busy), because its work is $O(1)$ times the work during high-busy steps.
   (c) High-idle runs of $S[0..m-2]$ take $O(W_{L'})$ total work.
      (i) Every filter-bound operation is filtered out due to some operation in the final slab. So take any operation $X$ on item $x$ that finishes in a final slab segment $S[k]$.
      (ii) During each high-idle run (which takes $\Omega(\log p)$ high-idle steps), the processing of $X$ is not blocked by any $Q_2$-thread (since $S[0..m-2]$ does not hold any neighbour-lock or filter-lock), so each high-idle step 'reduces' its remaining delay, which by the *key lemma* (Lemma 19) is $O(2^k)$.
      (iii) Therefore the work done on $x$ by high-idle runs while $X$ is in the final slab is $O(1)$ times the work done by the final slab on $X$.

Moreover, $M_2$ takes $O(\frac{W_L}{p} + d \cdot (\log p)^2 + s_L)$ effective span for some linearization $L$ of $D$:

(1) The effective span is the time taken to run the execution DAG on infinitely many processors, where each $M_2$-node takes unit time while every other node takes zero time.
(2) There are $O\left(\frac{W_{L'}}{p}\right)$ **filter-full steps** (steps in which the filter has size at least $p$). To see why, let every operation in the final slab consume a token on each step. Then each filter-full step consumes at least $p$ tokens. But by the *key lemma* (Lemma 19) the total token consumption is just $O(1)$ times the total work in the final slab, which amounts to $O(W_{L'})$ (Lemma 21).
(3) There are $O(\frac{N}{p} + d \cdot (\log p)^2 + s_{L^*})$ **filter-empty steps** (filter size at most $p$) for some linearization $L^*$ of $D$, where $N$ is the number of $M_2$-calls, because each operation essentially has the following path: It waits $O\left((\log p)^2\right)$ filter-empty steps for the current cut batch in the first slab. Then it waits $O\left(\frac{b^*}{p}\right)$ filter-empty steps per intervening cut batch of size $b^* = p^2$. Finally it takes $O\left((\log p)^2 + \log r\right)$ steps to pass through the slabs where $r$ is its access rank according to $L^*$, by the *key lemma* and the rank invariant (Lemma 24).

We shall now give the details. For the purpose of our analysis, we consider a segment to be **running** iff it has acquired all neighbour-locks and has not released them. We also consider an operation to be **in** segment $S[k]$ exactly when it is in the buffer of $S[k]$ or is being processed by $S[k]$ up to step 4h (inclusive). Likewise, we consider an item that is found in $S[k]$ and to be searched/updated to remain in $S[k]$ until it is **shifted** to $S[m']$ (in step 4d).

We begin by showing that $M_2$ remains 'balanced'; each non-terminal segment has size not too far from capacity.

**Definition 15 ($M_2$ Segment Holes).** We say that a segment $S[k]$ has $c$ **holes** if $S[k]$ is not the terminal segment but has $c$ fewer items than its capacity. (If $S[k]$ exceeds capacity then it has no holes.)

**Lemma 16 ($M_2$ Balance Invariants).** The following balance invariants hold:

(1) If $S[m]$ is not running or does not exist, then $S[m-1]$ does not exceed capacity (if it exists).
(2) If the interface is not running, $S[0..m-2]$ has no holes, and $S[m-1]$ has at most $d$ holes where $d$ is the number of successful deletions in $S[m]$.
(3) Each final slab segment $S[k]$ has at most $3 \cdot 2^{2^k}$ items.
(4) If a final slab segment $S[k]$ is not running, $S[0..k-1]$ is at most $2p^2$ below capacity.

*Proof.* Let $f$ be the filter size. Then $f \leq 2p^2$ always, since the interface only runs if $f \leq p^2$, on a batch of size at most $p^2$.

Invariant 1

$S[m-1]$ can only exceed capacity when $S[m]$ runs, and $S[m]$ restores the invariant (in step 4g) before it finishes running.

Invariant 2

Only the interface creates more holes in $S[0..m-1]$ (in step 3), each corresponding to a unique successful deletion that is inserted into the buffer of $S[m]$, and so just after the interface finishes running $S[0..m-1]$ has at most $d$ holes where $d$ is the number of successful deletions in $S[m]$, and all the holes must be in $S[m-1]$ since $d \leq 2p^2 \leq 2^{2^{m-1}}$. Once $S[m]$ runs, $S[m-1]$ will have no holes, because either $S[m]$ was the terminal segment or $S[m]$ had at least $2^{2^m} - 2p^2 \geq d$ items by Invariant 4.

Invariants 3,4

To establish Invariants 3,4, we can prove sharper invariants. Let $e(k)$ be the total size of $S[0..k-1]$ minus their total capacity. Let $u(k)$ be the number of unfinished operations in $S[k+1..l]$. Let $d(k)$ be the number of successful deletions in $S[m..k]$. Then the following invariants hold:

(A) If a final slab segment $S[k]$ is not running, $e(k) + u(k) \leq 2p^2$.
(B) For each final slab segment $S[k]$, we always have $e(k) \leq 4p^2$.
(C) $e(l+1) \leq 2p^2$.
(D) If a final slab segment $S[k]$ is not running, $e(k) + d(k) \geq 0$.

Their proofs can be found at http://arxiv.org/abs/1805.05787.

Using these we can establish Invariants 3,4. By both (B) and (C), for each final slab segment $S[k]$ we have $e(k+1) \leq 4p^2$, and hence $S[k]$ has size at most $\sum_{i=m}^{k} 2^{2^i} + 4p^2 \leq 2 \cdot 2^{2^k} + 4p^2 \leq 3 \cdot 2^{2^k}$. By (D), if a final slab segment $S[k]$ is not running, then $-e(k) \leq d(k) \leq f \leq 2p^2$ and hence $S[0..k-1]$ is at most $2p^2$ below capacity. ◇

**Corollary 17** (**$M_2$ Segment Access Bound**). Each batch operation on a parallel 2-3 tree in segment $S[k]$ where $k \geq m-1$ takes $\Theta(2^k)$ work per operation in the batch and $\Theta(\log p^2 + 2^k) \subseteq \Theta(2^k)$ span.

Now we can prove a delay bound on the 'front access' (through the front-locks) by each final slab segment.

**Lemma 18** (**$M_2$ Front Access Bound**). Any segment $S[m+k]$ takes $O(2^{m+k})$ total delay to acquire the front-locks $FL[0..k]$ and run the front-locked section (in-between) and then release $FL[0..k]$. And similarly the interface takes $O(2^m)$ delay to acquire $FL[0]$ and run the front-locked section and then release $FL[0]$.

*Proof.* The front-locked section takes $O(2^m)$ delay, since each operation on a parallel 2-3 tree in $S[m-1,m]$ takes $O(2^m)$ span by Corollary 17. We shall show by induction that any segment $S[i]$ that has acquired $FL[k]$ will release $FL[k]$ within $c \cdot 2^{m+k}$ delay, where $c$ is a constant chosen to make it true when $k=0$. If $k>0$, then $S[i]$ next attempts to acquire $FL[k-1]$, and if it fails then $S[m+k-1]$ must now be holding it and will release it within $c \cdot 2^{m+k-1}$ delay by induction, and then $S[i]$ will actually acquire $FL[k-1]$ and then will release $FL[k]$ within $c \cdot 2^{m+k-1}$ delay by induction, which in total amounts to $c \cdot 2^{m+k}$ delay. Therefore any segment $S[m+k]$ that attempts to acquire $FL[k]$ will wait at most $c \cdot 2^{m+k}$ delay for any current holder of $FL[k]$ to release it, and then take at most $c \cdot 2^{m+k}$ delay to run its front-locked section and release $FL[0..k]$, which is in total $O(2^{m+k})$ delay. Similarly for when the interface attempts to acquire $FL[0]$. ◇

Then we can prove the *key lemma*:

**Lemma 19** (**$M_2$ Final Slab Bound**). Take any segment $S[k]$ where $k \geq m$, and any operation $X$. Then $S[k]$ runs within $O(2^k)$ delay. So if $X$ finishes in segment $S[k]$ then the processing of $X$ in the final slab takes $O(2^k)$ delay.

*Proof.* Once any $S[k]$ acquires the second neighbour-lock, it will finish within $O(2^k)$ delay, since the operations on the parallel 2-3 trees takes $O(2^k)$ span by Corollary 17, the front access take $O(2^k)$ delay by Lemma 18, and inserting the unfinished operations into the buffer of $S[k+1]$ takes $O(\log p)$ span. Thus once any $S[k]$ acquires the first lock, it waits $O(2^k)$ delay for the holder of the second lock to finish, and then itself finishes within $O(2^k)$ delay. And once the interface acquires the lock shared with $S[m]$, it will finish within $O(2^m)$ delay by Lemma 18. Thus any $S[k]$ when run will acquire both locks within $O(2^k)$ delay, and then itself finish within $O(2^k)$ delay. Therefore, the final slab takes $O(\sum_{i=m}^{k} 2^i) \subseteq O(2^k)$ delay to process any operation that finishes in $S[k]$. ◇

To bound the total work, we begin by partitioning it per operation:

**Lemma 20** (**$M_2$ Segment Work**). We can divide the **segment work** (work done on segments) in $M_2$ among the operations in the following natural way — each segment $S[k]$ does $\Theta(2^k)$ work per operation it processes.

*Proof.* If $k<m$, then the proof is the same as for $M_1$ Segment Work (Lemma 11). So consider only $k \geq m$. The front-locking takes $O(k) \subseteq O(2^k)$ work, and both accessing the filter and inserting into the buffer of $S[k+1]$ take $O(\log p) \subseteq O(2^k)$ work per operation. Accessing the parallel 2-3 trees takes $\Theta(2^k)$ work per item by Corollary 17. Thus searching for the accessed items in $S[k]$ takes $O(2^k)$ work per operation, and frontward transfers (in step 4h) can be paid for by the successful deletions.

All that remains is to pay for the rearward transfers (in step 4g). Define the charge for a rearward transfer from $S[k-1]$ to $S[k]$ to be $2^{k-1}$. Let $C$ be the minimum total charge for rearward transfers needed to make every segment not exceed capacity. Then each search/update/insertion that finishes in $S[k]$ increases $C$ by at most the total charge for a cascade of rearward transfers that returns the shifted/inserted item to its original segment, which is less than $2^k$. And each rearward transfer done by $S[k]$ is necessary to make $S[k-1]$ not exceed capacity, so it decreases $C$ by at least $2^k$. Therefore the searches/updates/insertions can pay for the rearward transfers. ◇

We are now ready to bound the core work done by $M_2$:

**Lemma 21** (**$M_2$ Core Work**). $M_2$ takes $O(W_L)$ segment work on segment-bound operations, for some linearization $L$ of $D$.

*Proof.* The proof is basically the same as for $M_1$ (see Theorem 12), and can be found at http://arxiv.org/abs/1805.05787. ◇

We now have the needed lemmas to bound the effective work of $M_2$.

**Theorem 22** (**$M_2$ Effective Work**). $M_2$ takes $O(W_L + e_L \cdot \log p)$ effective work for some linearization $L$ of $D$.

*Proof.* We shall follow the same techniques as in the proof of $M_1$ Effective Work. We can ignore the work done to transform the input batches from the parallel buffer into cut batches of size $p^2$, since it takes $O(1)$ work per operation. Sorting the cut batches takes $O(W')$ work where $W' = W_L + e_L \cdot \log p$ for some linearization $L$ by Batch-Sorting Cost Lemma (Lemma 10) with the choice of $\varepsilon = \frac{1}{2}$.

We divide the segment work done among the operations as per Lemma 20. Then the segment-bound operations take $O(W_{L'})$ total segment work for some linearization $L'$ of $D$, by $M_2$ Core Work (Lemma 21). We can ignore the work done by $S[m-1]$ and the filter, since that is $O(\log p)$ work per operation, each of which had already taken $\Omega(\log p)$ segment work in $S[0..m-2]$. Thus we just have to show that the filter-bound operations take $O(W_{L'})$ total work in $S[0..m-2]$.

We classify each time step as a **high-busy step** iff $Q_1$ has at least $\frac{1}{2}p$ ready nodes, and as a **high-idle step** otherwise. On each high-busy step, $\frac{1}{2}p$ ready nodes generated for the final slab will be executed (by the weak-priority scheduler). Since the final slab takes $O(W_{L'})$ work in total by the preceding analysis, there can be only $O\left(\frac{W_{L'}}{p}\right)$ high-busy steps, which hence take $O(W_{L'})$ work.

Now consider each first slab run ($M_2$ interface step 3) as comprising an $S[0..m-2]$ run and then an $S[m-1]$ run (where only the latter is neighbour-locked and front-locked). We classify each $S[0..m-2]$ run as a **high-busy run** iff at least half the time steps during the run are high-busy steps, and as a **high-idle run** otherwise. During each high-busy run, the total work is $O(1)$ times the work during high-busy steps, since every high-busy step does $\Theta(p)$ work. Thus we can ignore the work done during high-busy runs, and it remains to show that high-idle runs do $O(W_{L'})$ work on filter-bound operations.

Note that every filter-bound operation is trapped in the filter due to some operation that finishes in the final slab. So take any operation $X$ on item $x$ that finishes in segment $S[k]$ in the final slab, and consider the time interval $Z$ when $X$ is in the final slab (after being put in the buffer for $S[m]$). Let $\Gamma$ be the remaining computation for the processing of $X$, which initially has delay $O(2^k)$ by $M_2$ Final Slab Bound (Lemma 19), and note the following:

- At any high-idle step, all ready $Q_1$-nodes are executed.
- During any $S[0..m-2]$ run, the interface is not holding any neighbour-lock or front-lock.

These imply that during $\Gamma$, at any high-idle step during an $S[0..m-2]$ run, the delay of $\Delta(\alpha)$ is reduced for each acquire-stall node $\alpha$ in $\Gamma$ (by structural induction), and hence the delay of $\Gamma$ is reduced. Thus there are $O(2^k)$ such steps during $Z$. Finally observe that each $S[0..m-2]$ run takes $\Omega(\log p)$ high-idle steps, and hence at most $O\left(1+\frac{2^k}{\log p}\right)$ $S[0..m-2]$ runs overlap $Z$, and they do at most $O(\log p+2^k) \subseteq O(2^k)$ work on $x$, which is $O(1)$ times the work done on $X$. Summing over all operations $X$ that finish in the final slab, at most $O(W_{L'})$ total work is done during $S[0..m-2]$ runs on filter-bound operations. ◇

At last, we tackle the effective span bound for $M_2$.

**Definition 23 ($M_2$ Time Linearization).** We say that a linearization $L$ of $D$ is a **time linearization** if the following hold:

(1) $L$ orders operations by when they finish (for those finished by the final slab this is defined to be when step 4d is run).
(2) For operations that finish at the same time in the same segment, $L$ puts searches/updates/insertions in reverse order of how the items are inserted into $S[m']$ (in step 4d).

**Lemma 24 ($M_2$ Rank Invariant).** Every item $x$ in the final slab is within the first $r$ items of the final slab, where $r$ is the number of distinct items searched/updated/inserted since the last (combined) operation that shifted/inserted $x$ (in step 4d), according to any time linearization.

*Proof.* The shifts/inserts can be simulated by individual shifts/inserts of items in the same order as the time linearization, such that every item $x$ that is shifted/inserted is placed at the front of $S[m']$, at which point the invariant is preserved for $x$. Between consecutive accesses to $x$, every item searched/updated/inserted can move $x$ rearward in $M_2$ by at most 1 position. ◇

**Theorem 25 ($M_2$ Effective Span).** $M_2$ takes $O\left(\frac{W_L}{p}+d\cdot(\log p)^2 + s_L\right)$ effective span for some linearization $L$ of $D$.

*Proof.* See the Section 7.3 outline for the proof sketch. To expand a little on point 3:

Take any path $C$ in the program DAG $D$. Let $L$ be the time linearization of $D$ that puts each $M_2$-call along $C$ before all the other operations that finish together with it (in step 4d). Then take any search/update $X$ along $C$ with access rank $r$ according to $L$.

If $X$ finishes in the first slab, it takes $O((\log p)^2)$ steps.

If $X$ finishes in some final slab segment $S[k]$, then just before that $S[k]$ run, the item is within the first $r$ items of the final slab by $M_2$ Rank Invariant (Lemma 24). Thus $2^{2^m}+r \geq 2^{2^{k-1}}-2p^2$ because $S[0..k-1]$ is at most $2p^2$ below capacity by $M_2$ Balance Invariants (Lemma 16), and hence by $M_2$ Final Slab Bound (Lemma 19) $X$ takes $O(2^k) \subseteq O(\log p+\log r)$ steps to pass through the final slab. Similarly if $X$ finishes in the filter (gets filtered out due to some prior operation $Y$ on the same item that finishes in the final slab).

The full details are at http://arxiv.org/abs/1805.05787. ◇

This concludes our analysis of $M_2$.

# 8 Practical Schedulers

The bounds on the effective work and span in Section 6 and Section 7 apply if we use a greedy scheduler for $M_1$ and a weak-priority scheduler (Section 7.2) for $M_2$. In practice, we do not have such schedulers. But a work-stealing scheduler for $M_1$ gives the desired time bound (Theorem 3) on average, as essentially shown in [5, 10]. As for $M_2$, dedicating $\frac{1}{2}p$ processors to a greedy scheduler for $Q_1$-nodes and the other $\frac{1}{2}p$ processors to another greedy scheduler for $Q_2$-nodes gives a weak-priority scheduler as required for $M_2$. Replacing each greedy scheduler by a work-stealing scheduler would yield the desired time bound (Theorem 4) on average.

# Appendix

Here we spell out the data structures, locking mechanisms and supporting theorems that we have used in our paper. More details and proofs can be found at http://arxiv.org/abs/1805.05787.

## A.1 Parallel Buffer

We can use any parallel buffer implementation that takes $O(p+b)$ work and $O(\log p+\log b)$ span per batch of size $b$, and is such that (regardless of the scheduler) any operation that arrives will be included in the batch that is being flushed or in the next batch, and it always has at most $\frac{1}{2}p+q$ ready nodes (active threads) where $q$ is the number of operations that are currently buffered or being flushed. Then the parallel buffer overhead is given by the following theorem.

**Theorem 26 (Parallel Buffer Cost).** Take any program $P$ using a batched data structure $M$ on $p$ processors using any greedy scheduler. Let $E$ be the actual execution DAG of $P$ using $M$. The buffer's effective cost (see Definition 5) is $O\left(\frac{T_1+w_M}{p}+d\cdot\log p\right)$, where $w_M$ is the effective work taken by $M$ and $d$ is the maximum number of $M$-calls on any path in the program DAG $D$ for $P$.

## A.2 Batched Parallel 2-3 Tree

A batched parallel 2-3 tree $M$ supports the following batched operations (where $n$ is the number of items in $M$ before the batch):

(1) **Normal operation** on an item-sorted batch $B$ of $b$ operations on distinct items: $M$ performs all the operations in $B$, and returns (as a batch) the results in the same order as in $B$, all within $O(b\cdot\log n)$ work and $O(\log b+\log n)$ span. The **result** for each operation is a direct pointer to the item in $M$ (or *null* if deleted).
(2) **Reverse-indexing operation** on an (unsorted) input batch $B$ of $b$ direct pointers to distinct items in $M$: $M$ returns the item-sorted batch of the items pointed to by the direct pointers in $B$, all within $O(b\cdot\log n)$ work and $O(\log b+\log n)$ span.

The batched parallel 2-3 tree that we use can be adapted from the parallel 2-3 dictionary described in [34].

## A.3 Sorting Theorems

Let $S$ be the set of items in the search problem, linearly ordered by a given comparison function. We assume that $\#(S)>1$.

**Definition 27 (Normalized Frequencies).** We say that $q_{1..u}$ are **normalized frequencies** if $q_{1..u}\in\mathbb{R}^+$ and $\sum_{i=1}^{u} q_i = 1$. Let $\mathrm{Seq}(n,q)$ be the class of sequences in $S^n$ with normalized item frequencies $q$.

**Theorem 28 (Worse-case Working-set Bound).** Take any normalized frequencies $q_{1..u}$, and let $C=\mathrm{Seq}(n,q)$. Then the working-set bound for inserting some sequence $I\in C$ is $\Omega(n\cdot H+n)$ where $H=\sum_{i=1}^{u}\left(q_i\cdot\ln\frac{1}{q_i}\right)$.

**Definition 29 (Parallel Entropy Sort).** Let *PESort* be the following parallel variant of Quicksort:

> Use the Parallel Pivot Algorithm to pick a pivot from the middle half of the input list. Parallel partition the list into a lower, a middle (equal to the pivot) and an upper part. Then sort the lower and upper parts recursively. Finally concatenate the three parts.

**Theorem 30** (*PESort* **Performance).** Take any normalized frequencies $q_{1..u}$, and let $C = \text{Seq}(n,q)$. Then *PESort* sorts every sequence from $C$, taking $O(n \cdot H + n)$ work and $O\big((\log n)^2\big)$ span, where $H = \sum_{i=1}^{u}\big(q_i \cdot \ln \frac{1}{q_i}\big)$.

**Theorem 31 (Parallel Pivot Algorithm).** Let *PPivot* be the following parallel algorithm:

> Partition the input list of size $k$ into blocks $B[1..c]$ of size $\log k$ except perhaps the last block. For each $i$ in $[1..c]$ in parallel, find the median $m[i]$ of $B[i]$ using the linear-time algorithm. Then use an optimal parallel sorting algorithm (such as adapted from [6, 26]) to sort $m[1..c]$ and output their median.

Then *PPivot* outputs an item that is in the two middle quartiles of any input list of size $k$, taking $O(k)$ work and $O(\log(k))$ span.

## Acknowledgments

This research was supported in part by Singapore MOE AcRF Tier 1 grant T1 251RES1719 and National Science Foundation grants CCF-1150036, CCF-1733873 and CCF-1725647.

## References


[1] Yehuda Afek, Haim Kaplan, Boris Korenfeld, Adam Morrison, and Robert Endre Tarjan. 2012. CBTree: A Practical Concurrent Self-Adjusting Search Tree. In *Distributed Computing - 26th International Symposium, DISC 2012, Salvador, Brazil, October 16-18, 2012. Proceedings*. 1–15. https://doi.org/10.1007/978-3-642-33651-5_1

[2] Yehuda Afek, Haim Kaplan, Boris Korenfeld, Adam Morrison, and Robert Endre Tarjan. 2014. The CB tree: a practical concurrent self-adjusting search tree. *Distributed Computing* 27, 6 (2014), 393–417. https://doi.org/10.1007/s00446-014-0229-0

[3] Kunal Agrawal, Jeremy T Fineman, Kefu Lu, Brendan Sheridan, Jim Sukha, and Robert Utterback. 2014. Provably good scheduling for parallel programs that use data structures through implicit batching. In *Proceedings of the 26th ACM symposium on Parallelism in algorithms and architectures*. ACM, 84–95.

[4] Yaroslav Akhremtsev and Peter Sanders. 2016. Fast Parallel Operations on Search Trees. In *23rd IEEE International Conference on High Performance Computing, HiPC 2016, Hyderabad, India, December 19-22, 2016*. 291–300. https://doi.org/10.1109/HiPC.2016.042

[5] Nimar S Arora, Robert D Blumofe, and C Greg Plaxton. 2001. Thread scheduling for multiprogrammed multiprocessors. *Theory of computing systems* 34, 2 (2001), 115–144.

[6] Mikhail J Atallah, Richard Cole, and Michael T Goodrich. 1989. Cascading divide-and-conquer: A technique for designing parallel algorithms. *SIAM J. Comput.* 18, 3 (1989), 499–532.

[7] Guy E. Blelloch, Daniel Ferizovic, and Yihan Sun. 2016. Just Join for Parallel Ordered Sets. In *Proceedings of the 28th ACM Symposium on Parallelism in Algorithms and Architectures, SPAA 2016, Asilomar State Beach/Pacific Grove, CA, USA, July 11-13, 2016*. 253–264. https://doi.org/10.1145/2935764.2935768

[8] Guy E. Blelloch and Margaret Reid-Miller. 1997. Pipelining with Futures. In *Proceedings of the ACM Symposium on Parallel Algorithms and Architectures (SPAA '97)*. ACM, New York, NY, USA, 249–259. https://doi.org/10.1145/258492.258517

[9] Guy E. Blelloch and Margaret Reid-Miller. 1998. Fast Set Operations Using Treaps. In *SPAA*. 16–26. https://doi.org/10.1145/277651.277660

[10] Robert D Blumofe and Charles E Leiserson. 1999. Scheduling multithreaded computations by work stealing. *Journal of the ACM (JACM)* 46, 5 (1999), 720–748.

[11] R. P. Brent. 1974. The Parallel Evaluation of General Arithmetic Expressions. *J. ACM* (1974), 201–206.

[12] Gerth Stølting Brodal, Jesper Larsson Träff, and Christos D. Zaroliagis. 1998. A Parallel Priority Queue with Constant Time Operations. *J. Parallel and Distrib. Comput.* (1998), 4–21.

[13] Trevor Brown, Faith Ellen, and Eric Ruppert. 2014. A general technique for non-blocking trees. In *ACM SIGPLAN Symposium on Principles and Practice of Parallel Programming, PPoPP '14, Orlando, FL, USA, February 15-19, 2014*. 329–342. https://doi.org/10.1145/2555243.2555267

[14] Thomas H. Cormen, Charles E. Leiserson, Ronald L. Rivest, and Clifford Stein. 2009. *Introduction to Algorithms* (third ed.). The MIT Press.

[15] A. Crauser, K. Mehlhorn, U. Meyer, and P. Sanders. 1998. A Parallelization of Dijkstra's Shortest Path Algorithm. In *Proceedings of the International Symposium on Mathematical Foundations of Computer Science (MFCS)*. Springer, 722–731.

[16] James R. Driscoll, Harold N. Gabow, Ruth Shrairman, and Robert E. Tarjan. 1988. Relaxed heaps: an alternative to Fibonacci heaps with applications to parallel computation. *Commun. ACM* 31 (1988), 1343–1354. Issue 11.

[17] Cynthia Dwork, Maurice Herlihy, and Orli Waarts. 1997. Contention in shared memory algorithms. *Journal of the ACM (JACM)* 44, 6 (1997), 779–805.

[18] Faith Ellen, Panagiota Fatourou, Joanna Helga, and Eric Ruppert. 2014. The amortized complexity of non-blocking binary search trees. In *ACM Symposium on Principles of Distributed Computing, PODC '14, Paris, France, July 15-18, 2014*. 332–340. https://doi.org/10.1145/2611462.2611486

[19] Faith Ellen, Panagiota Fatourou, Eric Ruppert, and Franck van Breugel. 2010. Non-blocking Binary Search Trees. In *Proceedings of the 29th ACM SIGACT-SIGOPS Symposium on Principles of Distributed Computing (PODC '10)*. ACM, New York, NY, USA, 131–140. https://doi.org/10.1145/1835698.1835736

[20] Amr Elmasry, Arash Farzan, and John Iacono. 2013. On the hierarchy of distribution-sensitive properties for data structures. *Acta informatica* 50, 4 (2013), 289–295.

[21] Stephan Erb, Moritz Kobitzsch, and Peter Sanders. 2014. Parallel Bi-Objective Shortest Paths using Weight-Balanced B-Trees with Bulk Updates. In *Proceedings of the Symposium on Experimental Algorithms (SEA)*. to appear.

[22] Panagiota Fatourou and Nikolaos D. Kallimanis. 2012. Revisiting the combining synchronization technique. In *PPoPP*. 257–266. https://doi.org/10.1145/2145816.2145849

[23] Leonor Frias and Johannes Singler. 2007. Parallelization of Bulk Operations for STL Dictionaries. In *Euro-Par Workshops (LNCS)*, Vol. 4854. Springer, 49–58.

[24] Matteo Frigo, Charles E. Leiserson, and Keith H. Randall. 1998. The Implementation of the Cilk-5 Multithreaded Language. In *Proceedings of the ACM SIGPLAN Conference on Programming Language Design and Implementation (PLDI)*. 212–223.

[25] Phillip B Gibbons, Yossi Matias, and Vijaya Ramachandran. 1998. The Queue-Read Queue-Write PRAM model: Accounting for contention in parallel algorithms. *SIAM J. Comput.* 28, 2 (1998), 733–769.

[26] Michael T Goodrich and S Rao Kosaraju. 1996. Sorting on a parallel pointer machine with applications to set expression evaluation. *Journal of the ACM (JACM)* 43, 2 (1996), 331–361.

[27] R. L. Graham. 1969. Bounds on Multiprocessing Anomalies. *SIAM J. Appl. Math.* (1969), 17(2):416–429.

[28] Danny Hendler, Itai Incze, Nir Shavit, and Moran Tzafrir. 2010. Flat combining and the synchronization-parallelism tradeoff. In *Proceedings of the ACM Symposium on Parallelism in Algorithms and Architectures (SPAA)*. 355–364. https://doi.org/10.1145/1810479.1810540

[29] John Iacono. 2001. Alternatives to splay trees with O(log n) worst-case access times. In *Proceedings of the twelfth annual ACM-SIAM symposium on Discrete algorithms*. Society for Industrial and Applied Mathematics, 516–522.

[30] Intel Corporation 2013. *Intel Cilk Plus Language Extension Specification, Version 1.1*. Intel Corporation. Document 324396-002US. Available from http://cilkplus.org/sites/default/files/open_specifications/Intel_Cilk_plus_lang_spec_2.htm.

[31] OpenMP Architecture Review Board. 2013. OpenMP Application Program Interface, Version 4.0. Available from http://www.openmp.org/mp-documents/OpenMP4.0.0.pdf.

[32] Y. Oyama, K. Taura, and A. Yonezawa. 1999. Executing Parallel Programs With Synchronization Bottlenecks Efficiently. In *Proceedings of the International Workshop on Parallel and Distributed Computing for Symbolic and Irregular Applications (PDSIA)*. 182–204.

[33] Richard C. Paige and Clyde P. Kruskal. 1985. Parallel Algorithms for Shortest Path Problems. In *Int. Conference on Parallel Processing*. 14–20.

[34] Wolfgang Paul, Uzi Vishkin, and Hubert Wagener. 1983. Parallel dictionaries on 2–3 trees. *Automata, Languages and Programming* (1983), 597–609.

[35] James Reinders. 2007. *Intel Threading Building Blocks: Outfitting C++ for Multi-Core Processor Parallelism*. O'Reilly.

[36] Peter Sanders. 1998. Randomized Priority Queues for Fast Parallel Access. *Journal of Parallel Distributed Computing* 49, 1 (1998), 86–97.

[37] Daniel Dominic Sleator and Robert Endre Tarjan. 1985. Self-adjusting binary search trees. *Journal of the ACM (JACM)* 32, 3 (1985), 652–686.

[38] tpl 2007. The Task Parallel Library. http://msdn.microsoft.com/en-us/magazine/cc163340.aspx. http://msdn.microsoft.com/en-us/magazine/cc163340.aspx

# Improved Worst-Case Deterministic Parallel Dynamic Minimum Spanning Forest

Tsvi Kopelowitz
Bar-Ilan University
Ramat-Gan, Israel
kopelot@gmail.com

Ely Porat
Bar-Ilan University
Ramat-Gan, Israel
porately@cs.biu.ac.il

Yair Rosenmutter
Bar-Ilan University
Ramat-Gan, Israel
yapoke@gmail.com

## ABSTRACT

This paper gives a new deterministic algorithm for the dynamic Minimum Spanning Forest (MSF) problem in the EREW PRAM model, where the goal is to maintain a MSF of a weighted graph with $n$ vertices and $m$ edges while supporting edge insertions and deletions. We show that one can solve the dynamic MSF problem using $O(\sqrt{n})$ processors and $O(\log n)$ worst-case update time, for a total of $O(\sqrt{n}\log n)$ work. This improves on the work of Ferragina [IPPS 1995] which costs $O(\log n)$ worst-case update time and $O(n^{2/3}\log\frac{m}{n})$ work.

**ACM Reference Format:**
Tsvi Kopelowitz, Ely Porat, and Yair Rosenmutter. 2018. Improved Worst-Case Deterministic Parallel Dynamic Minimum Spanning Forest. In *SPAA '18: 30th ACM Symposium on Parallelism in Algorithms and Architectures, July 16–18, 2018, Vienna, Austria.* ACM, New York, NY, USA, 9 pages. https://doi.org/10.1145/3210377.3210403

## 1 INTRODUCTION

In the *dynamic minimum spanning forest* (MSF) problem, the goal is maintain a MSF $F$ of an undirected dynamic graph $G = (V, E)$ with weight function $w : E \to \mathbb{R}$, while supporting edge insertions and deletions. The dynamic MSF problem is one of the most fundamental dynamic graph problems, and has been used as a subroutine for solving many other graph problems ([1],[3],[21],[22]). The first sequential algorithm solving the dynamic MSF problem has a worst-case update time of $O(\sqrt{m})$, where $m$ is the number of edges, and was introduced by Frederickson [6]. Using the sparsification technique of Eppstein et al. [3, 4] on Fredrickson's algorithm reduces the worst-case update time to $O(\sqrt{n})$, where $n$ is the number of vertices. Both of these results are deterministicWhile there have been several improvements on the time cost when using randomization or allowing amortization, the $O(\sqrt{n})$ time bound is the best known for deterministic worst-case dynamic MSF.

*Dynamic MSF in the PRAM model.* While the dynamic MSF problem in sequential models has received a lot of attention from researchers, there has been no progress since the 90s in the PRAM Model. Das and Ferragina [2] presented a dynamic MSF algorithm in the EREW PRAM model, which is based on Frederickson's [6] sequential algorithm, that uses $O(\frac{m^{2/3}}{\log n})$ processors, $O(\log n)$ worst-case time, and $O(m^{2/3})$ work. Ferragina [5] showed how to parallelize the sparsification technique of Eppstein et al. ([3], [4]), thereby obtaining a fully dynamic MSF algorithm in the EREW PRAM model, that uses $O\left(\frac{n^{2/3}\log\frac{m}{n}}{\log n}\right)$ processors, $O(\log n)$ worst-case time, and $O(n^{2/3}\log\frac{m}{n})$ work. Liang and McKay [16] proposed a different parallel algorithm for dynamic MSF that uses $O(n^{2/3})$ processors and has $O(\log n \cdot \log\frac{m}{n})$ parallel worst-case time.

*Our results.* In this paper we give the first improvement on dynamic MSF in the EREW PRAM model in over 20 years (in terms of deterministic worst-case update times). The main result is summarized by the following theorem.

THEOREM 1.1. *There exists a deterministic algorithm for the dynamic MSF problem in the EREW PRAM model that uses $O(\sqrt{n})$ processors and has a parallel worst-case update time of $O(\log n)$. The resulted work of the algorithm is $O(\sqrt{n}\log n)$.*

*Dynamic MSF and Dynamic Connectivity.* In the *dynamic connectivity* problem the goal is to maintain a dynamic graph $G$ with edge insertions and deletions, while supporting connectivity queries: "given two vertices in $G$, are the vertices in the same connected component?". The dynamic connectivity problem is a weaker version of the dynamic MSF problem, since one way of solving dynamic connectivity is to maintain a spanning forest of $G$ and using dynamic connectivity data structures for forests such as [20]. Thus, Frederickson's algorithm together with the sparsification techinque yield a $O(\sqrt{n})$ worst-case deterministic update time for dynamic connectivity. Recently, Kejlberg-Rasmussen et al. [14] reduced the runtime slightly to $O\left(\sqrt{\frac{n(\log\log n)^2}{\log n}}\right)$. The proof of Theorem 1.1 is based on the approach used by Kejlberg-Rasmussen et al. [14] for solving dynamic connectivity.

### 1.1 Algorithmic Overview

Throughout the paper we apply the standard assumption that the graph is *sparse*, i.e., the graph has $m = O(n)$ edges. In the sequential case this assumption is permissable due to the sparsification technique of [4]. We later show how to extend the sparsification technique for dynamic MSF to the EREW PRAM model. We also assume throughout the paper that the maximum degree in $G$ is 3 by applying the techniques of Frederickson [6]. This last assumption costs an $O(1)$ worst-case time additive overhead per operation.

We are now ready to provide an overview of our techniques. We emphasize that our overview sacrifices accuracy for the sake of


*SPAA '18, July 16–18, 2018, Vienna, Austria*

ACM ISBN 978-1-4503-5799-9/18/07...$15.00
https://doi.org/10.1145/3210377.3210403

intuition. An accurate description of the techniques that we use is given in the rest of the paper. We believe it is best to first discuss a sequential version of our dynamic MSF algorithm, which is an $O(\sqrt{\log n})$ factor slower than the algorithm of Frederickson [6] after applying the sparsification technique of [4]. Nevertheless, the proof of the following theorem is helpful for understanding our proof of Theorem 1.1.

THEOREM 1.2. *There exists a sequential deterministic algorithm for the dynamic MSF problem, which has a worst-case update time of* $O(\sqrt{n \log n})$.

*Euler tours and lists.* The proof of Theorem 1.2 is based on the dynamic connectivity algorithm presented in [14]. The basic technique is to maintain *Euler tours* of the trees in $F$, which is the MSF of $G$. An *Eulerian circuit* in a directed graph is a tour on the edges of the graph, starting and ending on the same vertex, in which each edge is visited exactly once. There is an Eulerian circuit if and only if for every vertex $u$ in the graph the out-degree of $u$ is the same as the in-degree of $u$. For a tree $T$ in a spanning forest of an undirected graph $G$, an Euler tour of $T$ is a list of the edges in $T$. The Euler tour of $T$ is created by treating each undirected edge as two directed edges in different directions, so that for every vertex $u$ in $T$ the out-degree of $u$ is the same as the in-degree of $u$. The authors of [14] showed how to reduce the problem of maintaining Euler tours to that of supporting splits and merges of linked lists, and finding a *minimum weight replacement* (MWR) edge in the case of deleting an edge in $G$ that is also in $F$. While supporting operations on lists is generally straightforward, being able to find a MWR edge is the challenging aspect. Nevertheless, lists turns out to be very convenient for parallelization since different processors can focus on different parts of the list.

*Chunks and LSDS..* In order to be able to manipulate the lists efficiently, we partition each list into *chunks* of size $K = O(\sqrt{n \log n})$, so that there are $J = O(\sqrt{n/\log n})$ chunks. The lists contain copies of vertices as they appear in the Euler tour, and so, by our assumptions, every chunk $c$ has as most $O(K)$ edges touching vertices with copies in $c$. Throughout the execution of the algorithm chunks are merged and split, either due to a list splitting at a chunk or in order to guarantee that every chunk is of size at most $O(K)$. Above the chunks, we use a tree-like data structure, called the *list sum data structure* (LSDS) that has at most $J$ leaves (one for each chunk) and height $O(\log J)$.

The basic idea is to separately aggregate useful information for finding MWR edges from all of the elements in each chunk, and then use the LSDS to aggregate all of the information from all of the chunks. The information stored for a chunk $c$ is an array $CAdj_c$ of size $J$ that stores the connectivity information between $c$ and every other chunk. The array stores one entry for each chunk such that the $i$'th entry in all of these arrays represents the chunk with id $i$. This information stored in $CAdj_c$ is derived from the at most $O(K)$ edges touching vertices that have a copy in $c$. The information stored at an LSDS tree vertex $u$ is an array $CAdj_u$ of size $J$ which stores the aggregate of all of the chunk information of chunks in the subtree of $u$.

When a chunk $c$ is the outcome of either a split or merge of chunks, $CAdj_c$ is updated by scanning the elements of $c$ in $O(K)$ worst-case time (since each chunk contains at most $O(K)$ elements). Then, for every other chunk $c'$ the connectivity information between $c'$ and $c$ that needs to be stored in $CAdj_{c'}$ is derived from $CAdj_c$. Since there are $O(J)$ chunks, this takes $O(J)$ worst-case time. The information in $CAdj_c$ is then propagated up the LSDS tree to the ancestors of $c$, spending $O(J)$ worst-case time per ancestor for a total of $O(J \log J) = O(K)$ worst-case time. Finally, the entries corresponding to $c$ in *all* of the vertices of the LSDS tree are updated by scanning the LSDS tree while only accessing the entries in the arrays that correspond to $c$. This last part spends $O(1)$ worst-case time per tree vertex for a total of $O(J)$ worst-case time. Thus, the cost of merging and splitting chunks ends up being $O(J + K) = O(\sqrt{n \log n})$.

In addition to the splitting and merging of chunks, the algorithm will sometimes need to split or merge LSDS structures. These splits and merges are standard tree operations, and each such tree operation touches $O(\log n)$ tree-vertices. The time cost is dominated by updating the $CAdj$ arrays (of size $O(J)$ each) of the vertices touched during the tree operations, for a total of $O(\sqrt{n \log n})$ worst-case time.

*Finding a MWR edge.* The method for finding a MWR edge is to find the lightest edge connecting the vertices with copies in one list $L_1$ and the vertices with copies in a second list $L_2$. We remark that there are some crucial details of this process which we skip in the overview description here.

The algorithm uses the $CAdj$ array stored at the root of the LSDS for $L_2$, which specifically contains the connectivity information between the chunks in $L_2$ and all other chunks. The MWR edge is found by scanning the $O(J)$ chunks of $L_1$, and for each such chunk $c$ we look at the entry corresponding to $c$ in the $CAdj$ array of the root of $L_2$. The chunk in $L_1$ that has the smallest entry in the $CAdj$ array contains the lightest edge connecting $L_1$ and $L_2$, and the algorithm scans all of the $O(K)$ edges touching vertices with copies in that chunk in order to find the MWR edge. The entire process costs $O(J + K) = O(\sqrt{n \log n})$ worst-case time.

*Parallel dynamic MSF..* One of the advantages of our new sequential MSF algorithm is that it leads to an improved parallel dynamic MSF algorithm. The reason for the time cost being $O(\sqrt{n \log n})$ in the sequential algorithm is due to scanning all of the elements in a chunk, scanning all of the chunks of a list, and scanning all of the vertices in an LSDS. By utilizing several tournament like trees, we show how all of these tasks can be executed in parallel, with a cost of $O(\log n)$ parallel worst-case time.

*Parallel sparsification.* The sparsification method of Eppstein et al. [4] allows one to reduce the dependency of the sequential time cost for dynamic MSF in terms of the number of edges. In particular, this method admits a conversion of any algorithm for solving dynamic MSF with polynomial sequential time cost $f(m)$ to be reduced to a time cost of $f(n)$ by focusing on the special case in which $m = O(n)$. Roughly speaking, the method uses a tree based data structure that has $O(\log n)$ levels where the number of edges associated with a tree vertex at level $i$ is $n/2^i$. Each update necessitates at most one update at each level and so the total time cost becomes $\sum_{i=1}^{O(\log n)} f(n/2^i)$.

Unfortunately, the sequential sparsification does not transfer immediately to the parallel setting. In the sequential algorithm of Section 2 the time cost on a graph with $O(n')$ edges is $f(n') = O(\sqrt{n' \log n'})$, and so using the sparsification method we have that $\sum_{i=1}^{O(\log n)} \sqrt{(n/2^i)\log(n/2^i)} = O(\sqrt{n \log n})$. However, in the parallel algorithm, since $f(n') = O(\log n')$ we have that the total cost is $\sum_{i=1}^{O(\log n)} \log(n/2^i) = O(\log^2 n)$. This adds an $O(\log n)$ factor to the cost.

Ferragina [5] introduced a parallel technique to apply the sparsification data structure of Eppstein et al. [3] to any parallel algorithm solving the fully dynamic MSF problem, with a $O(\log \frac{m}{n})$ factor to the total work. However, we are interested in a parallel sparsification method that does not increase any of the asymptotic costs of the dynamic MSF data structure. Thus, we introduce an augmentation of the Eppstein et al. [4] sparsification method which achieves this goal. This augmentation requires a more detailed description of how the spasification data structure works, which we detail in the full version [15].

## 1.2 Other Related Work

*Related work on sequential dynamic MSF..* In the sequential setting, the fastest deterministic worst-case algorithm for dynamic MSF has an $O(\sqrt{n})$ worst-case update time [4, 6]. Henzinger and King [8] showed a deterministic algorithm for dynamic MSF with amortized update time of $O(n^{1/3} \log n)$. Holm et al. [9] designed another deterministic algorithm which has an amortized update time of $O(\log^4 n)$, and later Holm et al [10] improved the amortized update time to $O(\frac{\log^4 n}{\log \log n})$. When allowing randomization, Wulff-Nilsen [25] gave a randomized Las-Vegas algorithm for dynamic MSF with an expected worst-case update time of $O(n^{\frac{1}{2}-\epsilon})$ for some constant $\epsilon > 0$, and Nanongkai et al. [18] gave a randomized Las-Vegas algorithm with an expected worst-case update time of $n^{O(\log \log \log n / \log \log n)}$. Pătraşcu et al. [19] proved a lower bound of $\Omega(\log n)$ update time for dynamic connectivity, which is also a lower bound for dynamic MSF.

*Related work on sequential dynamic connectivity.* Notice that an algorithm for dynamic MSF is also an algorithm for dynamic connectivity. However, often there are faster dynamic connectivity algorithms. For the related dynamic connectivity problem, as mentioned above, the fastest deterministic worst-case time algorithm has an $O\left(\sqrt{\frac{n(\log \log n)^2}{\log n}}\right)$ worst-case update time [14]. When allowing randomization, Kapron, King, and Mountjoy [13] gave a Monte Carlo randomized structure with update time $O(c \log^5 n)$ and one-sided error probability $n^{-c}$. The update time was later improved to $O(c \log^4 n)$ independently by Gibb et al. [7] and Wang [23]. When allowing amortization Wulff-Nilsen [24] discovered a *deterministic* data structure with $O(\log^2 n / \log \log n)$ amortized update time. Recently, Huang et al. [11] showed that if both randomization and amortization are allowed then dynamic connectivity can be solved in expected $O(\log n (\log \log n)^2)$ amortized time. Recently, Nanongkai and Saranurak [17] presented a randomized Las-Vegas algorithm for dynamic MSF with an expected worst-case update time of $O(n^{\frac{1}{2}-\epsilon})$ for some constant $\epsilon > 0$.

## 1.3 Organization

In Section 2 we give a formal detailed description of the sequential dynamic MSF algorithm proving Theorem 1.2. In Section 3 we give a formal detailed description of the EREW PRAM dynamic MSF algorithm for sparse graphs, thereby proving Theorem 1.1 for the special case of $m = O(n)$. Due to space considerations, the description of how to extend the sparsification technique of Eppstein et al. [4] to the EREW PRAM model, without affecting the costs, is given in the full version [15]. This technique completes the proof of Theorem 1.1 for general graphs.

# 2 SEQUENTIAL DYNAMIC MSF - PROOF OF THEOREM 1.2

The goal of this section is to present a deterministic sequential algorithm for dynamic MSF in *sparse graphs*, where $m = O(n)$. Theorem 1.2 is proved by applying the sparsification technique of Eppstein et al. [4] to the presented algorithm, allowing the algorithm to also work for general graphs, without changing the time cost.

## 2.1 Preliminaries

Each tree $T$ in the MSF is represented as an Euler tour *Euler*$(T)$, and each Euler tour (which is a list of edges) is stored as a list of vertices whose order is defined by the Euler tour such that every two adjacent vertices in the list represent an edge in the tour. We say that an edge in the MSF is a *tree edge*. When a new edge $e = (u, v)$ is added to the graph, if $e$ connects two different trees in the MSF then $e$ becomes a tree edge, and the two corresponding Euler tours are merged. Otherwise, let $e'$ be the heaviest edge on the path between $u$ and $v$ in the MSF prior to the update. If $w(e) < w(e')$ then the algorithm removes $e'$ from the MSF and adds $e$ instead, thereby rearranging Euler tours. When a non-tree edge is deleted, there are no changes to any of the Euler tours. However, when a tree edge is deleted, the algorithm looks for a *Minimum Weight Replacement* (MWR) edge to reconnect the MSF, thereby rearranging Euler tours. Thus, the task of rearranging Euler tours is reduced to *surgical operations* of splitting or merging lists, as expressed in the following lemma (proven in [14]).

Lemma 2.1 ([14], Lemma 2.1). *Let $G$ be an undirected graph with MSF $F$. Let $T \in F$ be a MST in $F$ that contains a tree edge $e$. If $e$ is deleted, and $T = T_0 \cup e \cup T_1$, then Euler$(T_0)$ and Euler$(T_1)$ are constructed from Euler$(T)$ with $O(1)$ surgical operations. In the opposite direction, from Euler$(T_0)$ and Euler$(T_1)$, Euler$(T_0 \cup e \cup T_1)$ is constructed with $O(1)$ surgical operations. It takes $O(1)$ worst-case time to determine which surgical operations to perform.*

Notice that during the sequence of surgical operations (of splitting or merging lists) that take place during splitting or merging Euler tours (as expressed in Lemma 2.1), the lists of vertices may temporarily not be valid Euler tours.

The discussion above together with Lemma 2.1 reduces the dynamic MSF problem to the following three subproblems: (1) finding the heaviest edge between two given vertices in a dynamic forest, (2) finding a MWR edge, and (3) implementing surgical operations on lists. The first subproblem is solved by applying the dynamic tree data structure of Sleator and Tarjan [20], which costs $O(\log n)$

worst-case time per forest update or path query. The rest of the description focuses on solving the last two subproblems. We emphasize that implementing the surgical operations on lists can be done in a straightforward manner costing $O(1)$ worst-case time per operation, but such an implementation does not seem to support an efficient implementation of finding a MWR edge.

## 2.2 The Data Structure

*Principal copies.* For a graph vertex $u$ there could be several copies of $u$ in the list of vertices containing $u$ (since the purpose of the list is to represent an Euler tour). The algorithm designates one copy to be the *principal copy* of $u$, denoted by $pc_u$, and vertex $u$ stores a bidirectional pointer to $pc_u$.

*Chunks.* Each list of vertices is partitioned into consecutive *chunks* of vertices, so that each chunk $c$ contains $O(K)$ vertices and there are $O(K)$ edges incident to vertices whose principal copy is in $c$, for a carefully chosen parameter $K$. We say that an edge is *adjacent to* or *touches* chunk $c$ if the edge touches a graph vertex whose principal copy is in $c$. The algorithm maintains Invariant 1 for all chunks (recall that the maximum degree in the graph is 3):

INVARIANT 1. *For chunk $c$ let $n_c$ be the sum of the number of vertices in $c$ and the number of edges adjacent to $c$. Then $n_c \leq 3K$, and if $c$ is not the only chunk in the list containing $c$ then $K \leq n_c$.*

Notice that when Invariant 1 is violated, a standard technique of merging and/or splitting $O(1)$ adjacent chunks is used in order to restore the invariant. We describe the process for merging and splitting chunks in the proof of Lemma 2.2.

We assume for now that every list contains at least two chunks. The special case of lists containing only one chunk is addressed in the full version [15].Thus, we denote the maximum number of possible chunks by $J = O(n/K)$. Each chunk $c$ is assigned a unique id $id_c \in [J]$, and each vertex in $c$ stores $id_c$. In order to support quick lookups of chunks, the algorithm stores a $J$ sized array called *chunks* such that $chunks[id_c] = c$. Each chunk $c$ maintains two $J$-length vectors called $CAdj_c$ and $Memb_c$. $CAdj_c[id_{c'}]$ contains the minimum weight of an edge $(u, v)$ such that $pc_u$ is in $c$ and $pc_v$ is in $c'$. If no such edge exists then we denote $CAdj_c[id_{c'}] = \infty$. In the $Memb_c$ vector, all of the entries are set to 0 except for the entry at $id_c$ which is set to 1.

*The LSDS..* For each list $L$, the data structure stores a *list sum data structure* (LSDS) which is implemented as a 2-3 tree whose leaves correspond, in order, to the chunks of $L$. The LSDS supports logarithmic worst-case time inserts, deletes, splits and joins. Each internal vertex $z$ maintains two $J$-length vectors, $Memb_z$ and $CAdj_z$. $Memb_z$ is the entry-wise OR of all the *Memb* vectors of chunks contained in leaves in the subtree of $z$. $CAdj_z$ is the entry-wise minimum of all the *CAdj* vectors of chunks contained in leaves in the subtree of $z$, as shown in Figure 1.

In order to efficiently perform surgical operations on lists, we describe an efficient implementation for splitting and merging chunks (Section 2.3) and an efficient implementation of LSDS operations (Section 2.4). We then use these implementations to show how to efficiently implement the surgical operations and how to find a MWR edge (Section 2.5).

## 2.3 Splitting and Merging Chunks

LEMMA 2.2. *There exists a data structure on chunks that supports splits and merges such that each operation costs $O(J + K)$ worst-case time.*

PROOF. *Splitting.* Splitting a chunk $c$ can happen for one of two reasons: (1) either the list containing $c$ needs to be split at a given vertex $u$ that is in $c$, or (2) $n_c > 3K$ thereby violating Invariant 1. In the second case, the split location is located by scanning $c$ in $O(K)$ worst-case time. Thus, we assume from now that the algorithm knows the split location $u$.

Splitting the list of vertices in $c$ at vertex $u$ takes $O(1)$ worst-case time. Let $c_1$ and $c_2$ be the resulting chunks where $c_1$ contains the first part of the list of vertices from $c$ and $c_2$ contains the second part. The algorithm sets $id_{c_1} = id_c$ and allocates a new (unique) id for $c_2$. Next, the algorithm scans all of the vertices in $c_2$ and updates their chunk id. The new *CAdj* arrays for $c_1$ and $c_2$ are created by iterating over all edges adjacent to $c_1$ and $c_2$, respectively, in $O(K)$ worst-case time. Finally, for each chunk $c'$, the algorithm updates $CAdj_{c'}[id_{c_1}]$ to be $CAdj_{c_1}[id_{c'}]$ and $CAdj_{c'}[id_{c_2}]$ to be $CAdj_{c_2}[id_{c'}]$, which takes $O(J)$worst-case time. Thus, the cost for splitting a chunk is $O(J+K)$ worst-case time.

*Merging.* Merging the lists of vertices of adjacent chunks $c_1$ and $c_2$ takes $O(1)$ worst-case time. Let $c$ denote the resulting chunk containing the concatenation of the two lists. The algorithm sets $id_c = id_{c_1}$, and in $O(K)$ worst-case time the algorithm scans all of the vertices in $c$ in order to update their chunk id. The new *CAdj* array for $c$ is created by iterating over all edges incident to $c$ in $O(K)$ worst-case time. Finally, for each chunk $c'$, the algorithm updates $CAdj_{c'}[id_c]$ to be $CAdj_c[id_{c'}]$ and sets $CAdj_{c'}[id_{c_2}] = \infty$, which takes $O(J)$ worst-case time. Thus, the cost for merging two adjacent chunks $O(J + K)$ worst-case time. □

## 2.4 Implementing The LSDS Operations

The LSDS supports the following operations:

- `LSInsert`$(c, c')$ - Add a new leaf for chunk $c$ after chunk $c'$.
- `LSDelete`$(c)$ - Destroy chunk $c$.
- `LSJoin`$(LS_1, LS_2)$ - Concatenate two lists of chunks represented by LSDS $LS_1$ and LSDS $LS_2$.
- `LSSplit`$(c)$ - Split the LSDS at chunk $c$.
- `UpdateAdj`$(c)$ - (Takes place immediately after an update to $CAdj_c$ and $CAdj_{c'}[id_c]$ for all chunks $c' \neq c$.) Update the *CAdj* vectors for ancestors of $c$ in the LSDS, and update the $id_c$'th entry of the *CAdj* vectors for all of the vertices in the LSDS.

LEMMA 2.3. *There exists an implementation of the LSDS where each of the operations* `LSInsert`, `LSDelete`, `LSJoin`, `LSSplit` *and* `UpdateAdj` *take $O(J \log J)$ worst-case time.*

PROOF. *All operations except for* `UpdateAdj`. Basic tree operations on the LSDS, including access, insertion, deletion, splitting and joining cost $O(\log J)$ worst-case time each (since each LSDS supports at most $J$ chunks). Thus, each basic tree operation touches at most $O(\log J)$ vertices in the tree. For every vertex $z$ in the LSDS, updating a *single* entry in $CAdj_z$ or $Memb_z$ costs $O(1)$ worst-case time (since the number of children is $O(1)$), and so updating the

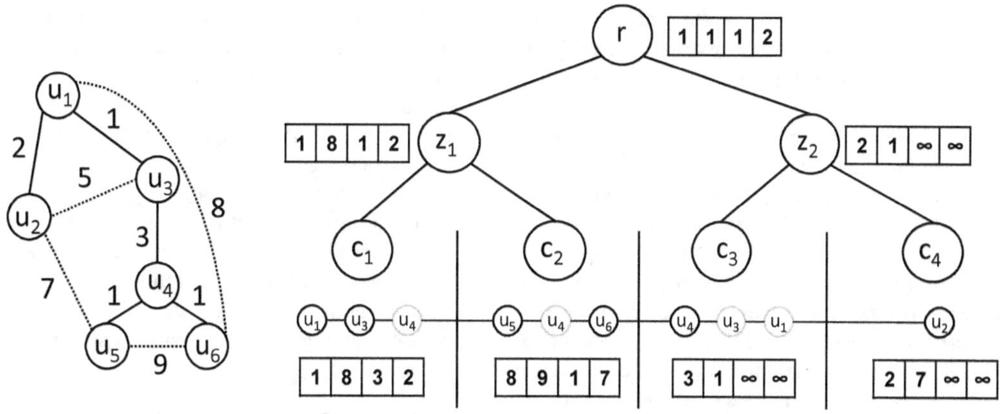

**Figure 1: The left part of the figure is a graph where the tree edges are solid edges and the non-tree edges are the dotted edges. The right part of the figure is a LSDS tree whose leaves are chunks of the list of vertices representing the Euler tour for the graph. Each chunk contains a sublist of the Euler tour. The principal copies are the black vertices. The arrays in each chunk and next to internal tree vertices are the *CAdj* vectors.**

*CAdj* and *Memb* arrays for the $O(\log J)$ vertices touched during a basic tree operation takes at most $O(J \log J)$ worst-case time.

*Operation* UpdateAdj. Updating the *CAdj* vectors in the path from the leaf representing $c$ to the root takes $O(J \log J)$ worst-case time. Updating the $id_c$'th entry of every *CAdj* array in the tree takes $O(J)$ worst-case time (since the 2-3 tree contains at most $O(J)$ vertices). Thus, the total cost of UpdateAdj is $O(J \log J)$ worst-case time. □

## 2.5 Surgical Operations

LEMMA 2.4. *There exists an algorithm in which each surgical operation on lists costs $O(J \log J + K)$ worst-case time and finding a MWR edge costs $O(J + K)$ worst-case time.*

PROOF. *Splitting a list.* Suppose we split list $L$ at vertex $u$ of chunk $c$ into two parts, $L_1$ and $L_2$. Let $LS$ be the LSDS representing $L$. The algorithm splits $c$ at vertex $u$ into $c_1$ and $c_2$, inserts $c_2$ into $LS$ after the leaf representing $c_1$ and calls UpdateAdj($c_1$) and UpdateAdj($c_2$) in order to update all *CAdj* vectors in $LS$. Next, the algorithm splits $LS$ into $LS_1$ and $LS_2$, where the last chunk of $LS_1$ is $c_1$ and the first chunk of $LS_2$ is $c_2$. If Invariant 1 is violated at either $c_1$ or $c_2$, then the algorithm executes $O(1)$ splits and merges (followed by $O(1)$ LSDS operations) on $c_1$ or $c_2$ together with their adjacent chunks in $L_1$ or $L_2$, respectively, thereby preserving Invariant 1. Thus, splitting a list costs $O(J \log J + K)$ worst-case time.

*Joining two lists.* Suppose we join two lists, $L_1$ and $L_2$, into a single list $L$. Let $LS_1$ ($LS_2$) be the corresponding LSDS of $L_1$ ($L_2$). The algorithm calls LSJoin($LS_1$, $LS_2$) to merge $LS_1$ and $LS_2$ into $LS$, which costs $O(J \log J)$ worst-case time.

*Finding a MWR edge.* Notice that the algorithm looks for a MWR edge between two Euler tours $ET_1$ and $ET_2$ *only immediately* after splitting Euler tour $ET$ into $ET_1$ and $ET_2$. Let $LS_1$ ($LS_2$) be the LSDS corresponding to the list of $ET_1$ ($ET_2$). Let $r_1$ and $r_2$ be the roots of $LS_1$ and $LS_2$, respectively.

The algorithm constructs an array $\gamma$ of length $J$ in $O(J)$ worst-case time such that if $Memb_{r_2}[i] = 0$ then $\gamma[i] = \infty$, and otherwise $\gamma[i] = CAdj_{r_1}[i]$. Thus, $\gamma[id_c] < \infty$ if and only if there exists some edges between vertices in $ET_1$ and vertices in chunk $c$ (which must be in $ET_2$). Moreover, if $\gamma[id_c] < \infty$ then the weight of the minimum weight edge between $ET_1$ and chunk $c$ is $\gamma[id_c]$. Let $\hat{c} = \arg\min_{\text{chunk } c}\{\gamma[id_c]\}$. Thus, the minimum weight edge between $ET_1$ and $ET_2$ touches a graph vertex $u$ such that $pc_u \in \hat{c}$. The algorithm computes $id_{\hat{c}}$ in $O(J)$ worst-case time by scanning $\gamma$ and looking for the smallest entry. Then, the algorithm scans all of the $O(K)$ edges touching $\hat{c} = chunks[id_{\hat{c}}]$, and for each such edge $e = (u, v)$ where $pc_u \in \hat{c}$, the algorithm verifies whether the chunk $c_v$ containing $pc_v$ is in $LS_1$ or not by looking at $Memb_{r_1}[id_{c_v}]$. Finally, the algorithm picks the lightest edge that passes the verification. Thus, the total cost of finding the MWR edge is $O(J + K)$ worst-case time. □

## 2.6 Graph Updates

PROOF OF THEOREM 1.2. *Edge insertion.* Suppose we insert a new edge $e = (u, v)$ with weight $w(e)$ to the graph. Let $c_1$ and $c_2$ be the chunks containing $pc_u$ and $pc_v$, respectively, and let $LS_1$ and $LS_2$ be the LSDSes containing $c_1$ and $c_2$, respectively. The algorithm begins by updating $CAdj_{c_1}[id_{c_2}]$ and $CAdj_{c_2}[id_{c_1}]$. Next, the algorithm calls UpdateAdj($c_1$) and UpdateAdj($c_2$) in order to update the *CAdj* vectors in $LS_1$ and $LS_2$. In case of a violation to Invariant 1, the algorithm executes $O(1)$ splits and merges on $c_1$ or $c_2$ together with their respective adjacent chunks, followed by $O(1)$ LSDS operations.

If $LS_1 \neq LS_2$ then $u$ and $v$ are in different Euler tours, and so by Lemma 2.1 a series of $O(1)$ surgical operations takes place in order to merge the two Euler tours containing $u$ and $v$ into a single Euler tour. The algorithm also adds $e$ to the dynamic tree structure of Sleator and Trajan [20] in $O(\log n)$ worst-case time.

If $LS_1 = LS_2$, then $u$ and $v$ are in the same Euler tour. In this case, the algorithm uses the dynamic tree structure to locate the heaviest edge $e'$ on the path from $u$ to $v$ in the current MSF. Finding $e'$ takes $O(\log n)$ worst-case time. If $w(e) < w(e')$ then the algorithm removes $e'$ from the MSF, inserts $e$ into the MSF, and updates the dynamic tree structure which costs $O(\log n)$ worst-case time. Thus, the total worst-case time for inserting an edge is $O(J \log J + K + \log n)$.

*Edge deletion.* Suppose we delete edge $e = (u, v)$ from the graph. Let $c_1$ be the chunk containing $pc_u$ and let $c_2$ be the chunk containing $pc_v$. Let $LS$ be the LSDS containing $c_1$ and $c_2$. The algorithm begins by updating $CAdj_{c_1}[id_{c_2}]$ and $CAdj_{c_2}[id_{c_1}]$ in $O(K)$ worst-case time by scanning all edges touching $c_1$. Next, the algorithm calls `UpdateAdj`($c_1$) on $LS$ to update all $CAdj$ vectors in $LS$. If $e$ is a tree edge, then the algorithm first removes $e$ from the dynamic tree structure in $O(\log n)$ worst-case time, and then executes a series of $O(1)$ surgical operations in order to split the Euler tour containing $u$ and $v$. Let $ET_u$ and $ET_v$ be the resulting two Euler tours containing $u$ and $v$, respectively. Finally, the algorithm looks for a MWR edge between $ET_u$ and $ET_v$ in $O(J + K)$ worst-case time, and if such an edge $e'$ is found, then the algorithm adds $e'$ to the dynamic tree structure and executes another series of $O(1)$ surgical operations reconnecting $ET_u$ and $ET_v$. Thus, the cost of deleting an edge is $O(J \log J + K + \log n)$ worst-case time.

*Time cost.* By setting $K = O(\sqrt{n \log n})$ and since $J = O(n/K)$, the insertion and deletion costs become $O(J \log J + K + \log n) = O(\sqrt{n \log n})$ worst-case time. □

# 3 PARALLEL DYNAMIC MSF ON SPARSE GRAPHS

In this section we prove the following theorem.

THEOREM 3.1. *There exists a deterministic algorithm for the dynamic MSF problem in the EREW PRAM model on sparse graphs with $m = O(n)$ edges that uses $O(\sqrt{n})$ processors and has a parallel worst-case update time of $O(\log n)$. The resulted work of the algorithm is $O(\sqrt{n} \log n)$.*

The new parallel sparsification technique (details in the full version [15]), extends Theorem 3.1 to work for general graphs, thereby proving Theorem 1.1.

*The data structure.* The algorithm uses the same data structure as described in Section 2.2 with three changes. The first change is that for each chunk $c$, the list of vertices in $c$ is augmented with a balanced 2-3 tree, denoted by $BT_c$, whose leaves are elements of the list that are in $c$. The height of $BT_c$ is $O(\log K)$. Each vertex $v$ in $BT_c$ stores an *edge counter* $ec_v$ which is the total number of edges incident to graph vertices whose principal copy is in the subtree of $v$; see Figure 2. The order of leaves in $BT_c$ together with an order of the at most 3 edges incident to each graph vertex whose principal copy is in $c$ defines an order on the edges touching $c$.

The second change is due to the requirements from the EREW PRAM model. In particular, for any chunk $c$, we cannot support constant worst-case time access to the entries of $CAdj_c$ (or $Memb_c$) in parallel through a single pointer from $c$ to the array $CAdj_c$, due to the exclusive reading requirement. Instead, we use a two dimensional matrix $C$ of size $J \times J = O(n)$ (at the end of this section we set $K = \sqrt{n}$) such that the entries of the $j$'th row of $C$ are exactly the entries of $CAdj_c$ where $id_c = j$. From now on, we let $CAdj_c[i]$ denote $C[id_c, i]$. We also use the same exact method for $Memb$ arrays.

The third change, which is also due to the exclusive reading requirement, is in the $CAdj$ and $Memb$ arrays in the LSDS. Instead of using one tree LSDS $LS$, we now use $J$ trees $S_1, S_2, \ldots, S_J$ for each LSDS, where the $j$'th tree corresponds to the chunk with id $j$. For chunk $c$, the $id_c$'th leaf of $S_j$ contains both $CAdj_c[j]$ and $Memb_c[j]$. We also store a pointer from $CAdj_c[j]$ and $Memb_c[j]$ to the $id_c$'th leaf of $S_j$, thereby providing direct access to that leaf. Finally, in order to provide direct access to the root of each $S_j$, we store a matrix of size $J \times J = O(n)$ where the $(j, i)$ entry contains a pointer to the root of $S_i$ used in the $j$'th LSDS.

As in the sequential algorithm, the special case of lists containing only one chunk in the new parallel algorithm is addressed in the full version [15].

*Assigning edges.* Our algorithm will often perform the task of assigning a different processor to each edge touching chunk $c$. This assignment is implemented by a parallel operation $getEdge_c(k)$ in which processor $p_k$ accesses the $k$'th edge incident to chunk $c$. The operation $getEdge_c(k)$ uses the edge counters in $BT_c$ together with an array $vertex$ of size $3K$ where each entry is a pointer to a vertex in $BT_c$. We describe the implementation from the perspective of processor $p_k$ for $1 \le k \le 3K$. We emphasize that in order to implement $getEdge_c(k)$, only $p_1$ will require access to $c$

Let $root_c$ be the root of $BT_c$. The implementation has $h$ phases where $h = O(\log K)$ is the height of $BT_c$. Processor $p_k$ participates in the $i$'th phase if and only if $vertex[k] \neq NULL$ at the beginning of the $i$'th phase. Moreover, the participating processors in each phase are assigned to different vertices in $BT_c$. In particular, processor $p_k$ is assigned to the vertex $v = vertex[k]$ with the guarantee that the rank of the rightmost edge in the subtree of $v$ is $k$.

To initialize the process, each $p_k$ sets $vertex[k] = NULL$ and if $k = 1$ then $p_k$ sets $vertex[ec_{root_c}] = root_c$. Now we begin the phases for $i = 1, 2, \ldots, h$. For the $i$'th phase, if $vertex[k] = v$, then $p_k$ accesses the at most 3 children of $v$ and looks at their edge counters. Based on these edge counters, $p_k$ computes in constant worst-case time the rank of the rightmost edge in each one of the subtrees of the children of $v$. If the rightmost edge in the subtree of a child $u$ of $v$ is $r$, then $p_k$ sets $vertex[r] = u$. Notice that $p_k$ necessarily sets $vertex[k]$ to be the rightmost child of $v$. After $h$ phases all of the vertices in $vertex$ are leaves of $BT_c$, but some of the entries of $vertex$ may still be set to $NULL$. An entry $vertex[k] = NULL$ can occur due to one of two reasons: either $k$ is larger than the number of edges touching $c$, or the principal copy of the edge that $p_k$ is accessing is also the principal copy of another edge which is being accessed by a different processor. However, due to the invariant that the rank of the rightmost edge in the subtree of $vertex[k]$ is $k$ and the fact that the maximum degree in the graph is 3, the principal copy that $p_k$ is looking for is either in $vertex[k+1]$ or $vertex[k+2]$. Thus, within 3 more steps, $p_k$ is able to access the principal copy and complete the task. Thus, the operation $getEdge_c(k)$ costs $O(\log K)$ worst-case time.

## 3.1 Splitting and Merging Chunks

LEMMA 3.2. *There exists an algorithm in the EREW PRAM model that supports splits and merges of chunks such that each operation costs $O(\log K)$ parallel worst-case time, using $O(J + K)$ processors.*

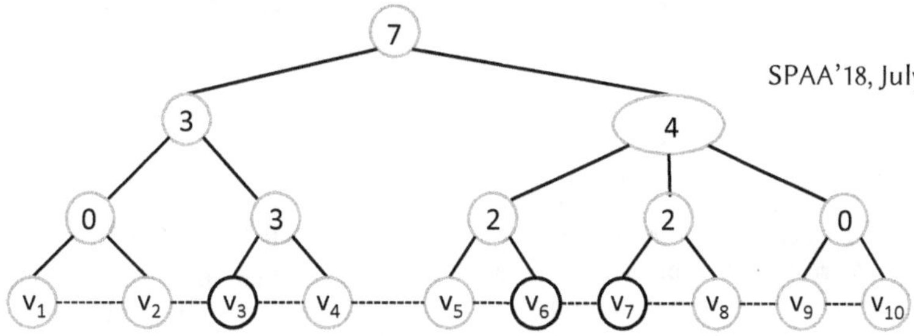


**Figure 2: The 2-3 tree $BT_c$ built on the list of vertices inside chunk $c$. $v_3$, $v_6$ and $v_7$ are the principal copies inside chunk $c$, and the number of edges touching $v_3$, $v_6$ and $v_7$ is 3, 2, and 3, respectively. The numbers inside the inner tree vertices are the edge counters.**

Proof. *Splitting.* Recall that splitting a chunk $c$ can happen for one of two reasons: (1) either the list containing $c$ needs to be split at a given vertex $u$ that is in $c$, or (2) $n_c > 3K$ thereby violating Invariant 1. In the second case, processor $p_1$ locates the split location in $O(\log K)$ worst-case time by traversing down $BT_c$ using the edge counters. Thus, we assume from now that the algorithm knows the split location $u$.

Processor $p_1$ splits $BT_c$ at vertex $u$ in $O(\log K)$ worst-case time. Let $c_1$ and $c_2$ be the resulting chunks where $c_1$ contains the first part of $BT_c$ and $c_2$ contains the second part. Processor $p_1$ sets $id_{c_1} = id_c$ and allocates a new (unique) id for $c_2$. We now focus on creating $CAdj_{c_1}$, since $CAdj_{c_2}$ is created in the same manner.

The sequential algorithm for constructing $CAdj_{c_1}$ (in the proof of Theorem 1.2) scans all of the $O(K)$ edges touching $c_1$. In the parallel setting, accessing all of the edges in parallel does not suffice since there could be several edges touching both $c_1$ and $\hat{c}$ for some other chunk $\hat{c}$, and the algorithm needs to store only the minimum weight of such an edge. To solve this issue we do the following.

The algorithm uses $J$ balanced binary tournament trees, denoted by $T_1, T_2, \ldots, T_J$, where each tree has $3K$ leaves. Each vertex $z$ in $T_j$ stores a value $A_z$ initialized to $\infty$[1]. The algorithm uses an iterative process for implementing a special tournament-like process. During the iterative process, each processor will initially be *active* until the processor decides to become *inactive* and no longer participates in the process. The iterative process implicitly uses an *exclusive-assignment property* which states that each participating processor is assigned to a vertex in some tree $T_j$ such that there are no two processors that are assigned to the same vertex. At the beginning of the $i$'th iteration the active processors are assigned to vertices whose height is $i-1$.

The initialization of the iterative process is as follows. For each $1 \leq k \leq 3K$, processor $p_k$ sets itself as active and executes the $getEdge_{c_1}(k)$ operation thereby gaining access to $e_k = (u_k, v_k)$, which is the $k$'th edge adjacent to chunk $c_1$. Assume without loss of generality that $pc_{u_k} \in c_1$. Let $c_{v_k}$ be the chunk such that $pc_{v_k} \in c_{v_k}$, and denote $id = id_{c_{v_k}}$. Processor $p_k$ assigns itself in $O(1)$ worst-case time (using a lookup table) to the $k$'th leaf of $T_{id}$, denoted by $\ell_k$, and sets $A_{\ell_k} = w(e_k)$. Thus, the exclusive-assignment property holds.

Each iteration has four *synchronous* phases. Recall that only active processors continue to participate in the process.

- *Phase 1.* If $p_k$ is assigned to a vertex $z$ that is the *left* child of its parent $parent(z)$ then $p_k$ sets $A_{parent(z)} = w(e_k)$.
- *Phase 2.* If $p_k$ is assigned to a vertex $z$ that is the *right* child of its parent $parent(z)$ then: if $A_{parent(z)} > w(e_k)$ then $p_k$ sets $A_{parent(z)} = w(e_k)$ and otherwise $p_k$ becomes inactive.
- *Phase 3.* If $p_k$ participated in the first phase and $A_{parent(z)} < w(e_k)$ then $p_k$ becomes inactive.
- *Phase 4.* If $parent(z)$ is the root of a tournament tree, then the iterative process ends. Otherwise, $p_k$ is assigned to $parent(z)$.

Notice that by the exclusive-assignment property we are guaranteed that during the first two phases no two processors are writing to the same location in memory at the same time. Also, we are guaranteed that if two processors are assigned to sibling vertices, then after the third phase the processor that is assigned to the lighter edge remains active, with ties favoring the left vertex, while the other processor becomes inactive. Thus, after the third phase, if $p_k$ is still active then there is no other active processor $p_{\hat{k}}$ that is currently assigned to $z$, and so after the fourth phase the exclusive-assignment property holds. At the end of the iterative process, the processor that is at the root of $T_j$ sets $CAdj_{c_1}[j] = A_{root(T_j)}$.

Finally, for each chunk $c'$, the algorithm sets $CAdj_{c'}[id_{c_1}] = CAdj_{c_1}[id_{c'}]$ and sets $CAdj_{c'}[id_{c_2}] = CAdj_{c_2}[id_{c'}]$, which takes $O(1)$ parallel worst-case time using $O(J)$ processors. Thus, the cost for splitting a chunk is $O(\log K)$ parallel worst-case time, using $O(J+K)$ processors.

*Merging.* Processor $p_1$ merges $BT_{c_1}$ and $BT_{c_2}$ in $O(\log K)$ worst-case time. Let $c$ denote the resulting chunk containing the concatenation of the lists of vertices represented by $BT_{c_1}$ and $BT_{c_2}$. Processor $p_1$ sets $id_c = id_{c_1}$. The new $CAdj$ array for $c$ is created by performing an entry-wise minimum of $CAdj_{c_1}$ and $CAdj_{c_2}$ in $O(1)$ parallel worst-case time using $O(J)$ processors. Finally, for each chunk $c'$, the algorithm sets $CAdj_{c'}[id_c] = CAdj_c[id_{c'}]$ and sets $CAdj_{c'}[id_{c_2}] = \infty$, which takes $O(1)$ parallel worst-case time using $O(J)$ processors. Thus, the cost for merging a chunk is $O(\log K)$ parallel worst-case time, using $O(J)$ processors. □

### 3.2 LSDS Operations

Lemma 3.3. *There exists an implementation of the LSDS in the EREW PRAM model using $O(J)$ processors where each of the operations* `LSInsert`, `LSDelete`, `LSJoin`, `LSSplit` *and* `UpdateAdj` *takes $O(\log J)$ parallel worst-case time.*

Proof. *All operations except for* `UpdateAdj`. Recall that in the proof of Lemma 2.3 each basic tree operation touches at most $O(\log J)$ vertices in the tree. We use a similar implementation as in Lemma 2.3, but now processor $p_j$ for $1 \leq j \leq J$ performs the basic tree operations on $S_j$. Thus, the total parallel worst-case time for each operation except for UpdateAdj is $O(\log J)$.

*Operation* `UpdateAdj(c)`. We again use a similar implementation as in Lemma 2.3, with the following changes. For each $S_j$, updating the path from the leaf representing $c$ to the root of $S_j$ costs $O(\log J)$

[1]Reusing and initializing a temporary data structure in the parallel setting is implemented by either using a timestamp for each word of memory or rolling back all of the memory changes after the operation completes, thereby allowing the cost analysis to ignore the initialization cost.

parallel worst-case time using $O(J)$ processors. In order to update $S_{id_c}$, processor $p_j$ for $1 \leq j \leq J$ is responsible for handling the leaf representing $chunks[j]$, which is accessible through the pointer stored in $CAdj_{chunks[j]}[id_c]$. We now need to sweep up $S_{id_c}$ in parallel, starting from all of the leaves of $S_{id_c}$. This process is described next.

The algorithm begins an iterative process where at the beginning of the $i$'th iteration there is a unique processer assigned to each vertex of height $i-1$ in $S_{id_c}$. At the $i$'th iteration, suppose $p_j$ is assigned to vertex $z$ of height $i-1$. Then $p_j$ is reassigned to $parent(z)$ only if $z$ is the *leftmost* child of $parent(z)$. If $z$ is *not* the leftmost child of $parent(z)$, then $p_j$ halts. Thus, each vertex at height $i$ is assigned to exactly one processor. If $p_j$ did not halt then $p_j$ updates the value stored in $parent(z)$ in $O(1)$ worst-case time. The iterative process ends at the root, which happens after $O(\log J)$ steps. The parallel worst-case time cost *per level* is $O(1)$ and $O(\log J)$ worst-case time for the entire procedure. The number of processors used is $O(J)$. □

## 3.3 Surgical Operations

Lemma 3.4. *There exists an algorithm in the EREW PRAM model in which each surgical operation on lists costs* $O(\log J + \log K)$ *parallel worst-case time using* $O(J + K)$ *processors and finding a MWR edge costs* $O(\log J + \log K)$ *parallel worst-case time using* $O(J + K)$ *processors.*

Proof. The implementation of both splitting and merging lists remains the same as in the proof of Lemma 2.4, but this time applying Lemma 3.2 instead of Lemma 2.2. So the operation of splitting a list costs $O(\log K)$ parallel worst-case time using $O(J + K)$ processors, and the operation of merging two lists costs $O(\log J + \log K)$ parallel worst-case time using $O(J + K)$ processors.

*Finding a MWR edge.* The algorithm constructs the array $\gamma$, as defined in the proof of Lemma 2.4, but now processor $p_j$ for $j \in [J]$ computes $\gamma[j]$ in $O(1)$ parallel worst-case time by accessing the root of $S_j$ in each LSDS in constant worst-case time (using the lookup matrix). Let $\hat{c} = \arg\min_{\text{chunk } c}\{\gamma[id_c]\}$. Recall that the minimum weight edge between $ET_1$ and $ET_2$ (as defined in the proof of Lemma 2.4) touches a vertex $u$ such that $pc_u \in \hat{c}$. The algorithm in the proof of Lemma 2.4 computes $id_{\hat{c}}$ in $O(J)$ worst-case time by scanning $\gamma$ and finding the smallest entry. In the EREW PRAM model, the algorithm uses a tournament tree to find the smallest entry, which costs $O(\log J)$ parallel worst-case time using $O(J)$ processors. Next, processor $p_k$ for $k \in [3K]$ accesses edge $e_k = getEdge_{\hat{c}}(k)$. Let $e_k = (u, v)$ where $pc_u \in \hat{c}$. In the CREW PRAM model, processor $p_k$ verifies in $O(1)$ whether the chunk $c_v$ containing $pc_v$ is in $LS_1$ (as defined in the proof of Lemma 2.4) by looking at the $Memb$ value in the root of $S_{id_{c_v}}$ of $LS_1$. Using the reduction of [12], this process costs $O(\log K)$ worst-case time in the EREW model. Finally, the algorithm picks the lightest edge via a tournament tree algorithm whose participants are the processors whose edge passed the verification. The algorithm for finding the MWR edge takes $O(\log J + \log K)$ parallel worst-case time, using $O(J)$ processors. □

## 3.4 Graph Updates

Proof of Theorem 1.1. *Edge insertion.* The algorithm for inserting an edge is the same as in the sequential algorithm in the proof of Theorem 1.2, but this time applying Lemmas 3.2, 3.3, and 3.4 instead of Lemmas 2.2, 2.3, and 2.4. The parallel worst-case update time is $O(\log J + \log K)$, by using $O(J + K)$ processors.

*Edge deletion.* The algorithm for deleting an edge is the same as in the sequential algorithm in the proof of Theorem 1.2, except for two changes: (1) the edge deletion algorithm applys Lemmas 3.2, 3.3, and 3.4 instead of Lemmas 2.2, 2.3, and 2.4, and (2) the new minimum weight edge connecting chunks $c_1$ and $c_2$ (as defined in the edge deletion operation in the proof of Theorem 1.2) is found in the EREW PRAM model by using a tournament tree which costs $O(\log K)$ parallel worst-case time using $O(K)$ processors. The parallel worst-case update time is $O(\log J + \log K)$, by using $O(J + K)$ processors.

*Time cost.* By setting $K = O(\sqrt{n})$, the insertion and deletion costs become $O(\log n)$ parallel worst-case time using $O(\sqrt{n})$ processors, for a total work of $O(\sqrt{n}\log n)$. □

# 4 CONCLUSION

We described an algorithm for solving dynamic MSF on sparse graphs in the EREW PRAM model that uses $O(\sqrt{n})$ processors and has $O(\log n)$ worst-case update time. The resulted work of the algorithm is $O(\sqrt{n}\log n)$. By extending the sparsification technique to work in the EREW PRAM model (see [15]), the algorithm can be used for solving dynamic MSF on general graphs with the same complexities. Thus, the total work is $O(\sqrt{n}\log n)$. We leave open the task of designing a solution that has a parallel $O(\log n)$ worst-case update time, but only $O(\sqrt{n})$ work, thereby matching the amount of work used in the sequential solutions.

# 5 ACKNOWLEDGMENTS

This work is supported in part by ISF grant 1278/16. This project has received funding from the European Research Council (ERC) under the European Union Horizon 2020 research and innovation programme (grant agreement No 683064).

# REFERENCES

[1] Ittai Abraham, David Durfee, Ioannis Koutis, Sebastian Krinninger, and Richard Peng. On fully dynamic graph sparsifiers. In *IEEE 57th Annual Symposium on Foundations of Computer Science, (FOCS)*, pages 335–344, 2016.

[2] Sajal K. Das and Paolo Ferragina. An o(n) work EREW parallel algorithm for updating MST. In *2'nd Annual European Symposium on Algorithms, (ESA)*, pages 331–342, 1994.

[3] David Eppstein, Zvi Galil, Giuseppe F. Italiano, and Amnon Nissenzweig. Sparsification-a technique for speeding up dynamic graph algorithms (extended abstract). In *33rd Annual Symposium on Foundations of Computer Science, (FOCS)*, pages 60–69, 1992.

[4] David Eppstein, Zvi Galil, Giuseppe F. Italiano, and Amnon Nissenzweig. Sparsification - a technique for speeding up dynamic graph algorithms. *J. ACM*, 44(5):669–696, 1997.

[5] Paolo Ferragina. An EREW PRAM fully-dynamic algorithm for MST. In *The 9th International Parallel Processing Symposium, (IPPS)*, pages 93–100, 1995.

[6] Greg N. Frederickson. Data structures for on-line updating of minimum spanning trees, with applications. *SIAM J. Comput.*, 14(4):781–798, 1985.

[7] D. Gibb, B. M. Kapron, V. King, and N. Thorn. Dynamic graph connectivity with improved worst case update time and sublinear space. *CoRR*, abs/1509.06464, 2015.

[8] Monika Rauch Henzinger and Valerie King. Maintaining minimum spanning trees in dynamic graphs. In *Automata, Languages and Programming, 24th International Colloquium, (ICALP)*, pages 594–604, 1997.

[9] Jacob Holm, Kristian de Lichtenberg, and Mikkel Thorup. Poly-logarithmic deterministic fully-dynamic algorithms for connectivity, minimum spanning tree, 2-edge, and biconnectivity. *J. ACM*, 48(4):723–760, 2001.
[10] Jacob Holm, Eva Rotenberg, and Christian Wulff-Nilsen. Faster fully-dynamic minimum spanning forest. In *Algorithms - 23rd Annual European Symposium, (ESA), Proceedings*, pages 742–753, 2015.
[11] Shang-En Huang, Dawei Huang, Tsvi Kopelowitz, and Seth Pettie. Fully dynamic connectivity in $O(\log n(\log\log n)^2)$ amortized expected time. In *Proceedings of the Twenty-Eighth Annual ACM-SIAM Symposium on Discrete Algorithms, (SODA)*, pages 510–520, 2017.
[12] Joseph JťaJťa. An introduction to parallel algorithms. In *Addison-Wesley*, 1992.
[13] Bruce M. Kapron, Valerie King, and Ben Mountjoy. Dynamic graph connectivity in polylogarithmic worst case time. In *Proceedings of the Twenty-Fourth Annual ACM-SIAM Symposium on Discrete Algorithms, (SODA)*, pages 1131–1142, 2013.
[14] Casper Kejlberg-Rasmussen, Tsvi Kopelowitz, Seth Pettie, and Mikkel Thorup. Faster worst case deterministic dynamic connectivity. In *24th Annual European Symposium on Algorithms, (ESA)*, pages 53:1–53:15, 2016.
[15] Tsvi Kopelowitz, Ely Porat, and Yair Rosenmutter. Improved worst-case deterministic parallel dynamic minimum spanning forest. *CoRR*, abs/1805.06151, 2018.
[16] W. Liang and B.D. McKay. Fully dynamic maintenance of minimum spanning trees by using a sublinear number of processors. In *Unpublished Manuscripts*, 1994.
[17] Danupon Nanongkai and Thatchaphol Saranurak. Dynamic spanning forest with worst-case update time: adaptive, las vegas, and $o(n^{1/2-\epsilon})$-time. In *Proceedings of the 49th Annual ACM SIGACT Symposium on Theory of Computing, (STOC)*, pages 1122–1129, 2017.
[18] Danupon Nanongkai, Thatchaphol Saranurak, and Christian Wulff-Nilsen. Dynamic minimum spanning forest with subpolynomial worst-case update time. In *58th IEEE Annual Symposium on Foundations of Computer Science, (FOCS)*, pages 950–961, 2017.
[19] Mihai Pătraşcu and Erik D. Demaine. Logarithmic lower bounds in the cell-probe model. *SIAM J. Comput.*, 35(4):932–963, 2006.
[20] Daniel Dominic Sleator and Robert Endre Tarjan. A data structure for dynamic trees. *J. Comput. Syst. Sci.*, 26(3):362–391, 1983.
[21] Mikkel Thorup. Dynamic graph algorithms with applications. In *7th Scandinavian Workshop on Algorithm Theory, (SWAT)*, pages 1–9, 2000.
[22] Mikkel Thorup. Fully-dynamic min-cut. *Combinatorica*, 27(1):91–127, 2007.
[23] Zhengyu Wang. An improved randomized data structure for dynamic graph connectivity. *CoRR*, abs/1510.04590, 2015.
[24] Christian Wulff-Nilsen. Faster deterministic fully-dynamic graph connectivity. In *Proceedings of the Twenty-Fourth Annual ACM-SIAM Symposium on Discrete Algorithms, (SODA)*, pages 1757–1769, 2013.
[25] Christian Wulff-Nilsen. Fully-dynamic minimum spanning forest with improved worst-case update time. In *Proceedings of the 49th Annual ACM SIGACT Symposium on Theory of Computing, (STOC)*, pages 1130–1143, 2017.

# Brief Announcement: Approximation Algorithms for Preemptive Resource Allocation

Kanthi Sarpatwar
IBM T. J. Watson Research Center
Yorktown Heights, New York
sarpatwa@us.ibm.com

Baruch Schieber
IBM T. J. Watson Research Center
Yorktown Heights, New York
sbar@us.ibm.com

Hadas Shachnai
Technion, Computer Science Dept.
Haifa, Israel
hadas@cs.technion.ac.il

## ABSTRACT

Cloud services require the allocation of scarce resources to multiple user requests (jobs) in a setting that facilitates preemption and migration, while respecting resource and timing constraints. This gives rise to the following variants of the classical *resource allocation problem* (RAP). The input is a set $J$ of jobs and a set $M$ of homogeneous hosts, each has available amount of some resource. A job is associated with a release time, a due date, a weight and a given length, as well as its resource requirement. A *feasible* schedule is an allocation of the resource to a subset of the jobs, satisfying the job release times/due dates as well as the resource constraints.

We consider two essential objectives: *throughput maximization* (MaxT), which seeks a maximum weight subset of the jobs that can be feasibly scheduled on the hosts in $M$, and *resource minimization* (MinR), that is finding the minimum number of (homogeneous) hosts needed to feasibly schedule all jobs. Both problems are known to be NP-hard. We address these fundamental problems, which have been studied previously in the *non-preemptive* model, and develop novel techniques for tackling them. In the full version of the paper, we present an $\Omega(1)$-approximation algorithm for MaxT, assuming there is sufficient slack for each job to be completed in its time window. For MinR we study a more general setting with $d$ resources and derive an $O(\log d)$-approximation for any fixed $d \geq 1$, under the assumption that time windows are not too small. This assumption can be removed leading to a slightly worse ratio of $O(\log d \log^* T)$, where $T$ is the maximum due date of any job.

## CCS CONCEPTS

• **Mathematics of computing → Approximation algorithms**;

## KEYWORDS

Preemptive resource allocation, throughput maximization, resource minimization, real-time scheduling, approximation algorithms

**ACM Reference Format:**

Kanthi Sarpatwar, Baruch Schieber, and Hadas Shachnai. 2018. Brief Announcement: Approximation Algorithms for Preemptive Resource Allocation. In *Proceedings of 30th ACM Symposium on Parallelism in Algorithms and Architectures (SPAA'18)*. ACM, New York, NY, USA, 3 pages. https://doi.org/10.1145/3210377.3210666


ACM ISBN 978-1-4503-5799-9/18/07.
https://doi.org/10.1145/3210377.3210666

## 1 BACKGROUND

A key challenge in cloud services is the allocation of available resources, such as processor cycles, storage space, and network bandwidth to user requests (jobs), so that each job is completed within its time window. The use of *virtual machines*, which can be assigned at different times to different hosts, enables non-consecutive allocation of resources to jobs, and also implies the possible migration of a job to another host throughout its execution.

This modern setting defines the following variants of the classic *resource allocation problem* (RAP) [4, 7, 25]. The input is a set of jobs $J$ that need to be scheduled on a set of hosts $M$, where each host has a limited (w.l.o.g., unit) amount of one or more resources. Each job $j \in J$ has a length, $p_j$, along with a required amount of the resource, $s_j$, and a time window in which it can be processed. The goal is to schedule jobs to the hosts within their time windows such that, at any given time, the total amount of resource required by the jobs assigned to any host does not exceed the available resource. A schedule may use preemption and job migration.

In the *maximum throughput* (MaxT) variant, we are given a set of homogeneous hosts $M$ and a set of jobs $J$, such that each job $j$ has a profit $w_j$ and attributes $(p_j, s_j, r_j, d_j)$; $r_j$ and $d_j$ are the release times and due dates of $j$, respectively. We seek a subset $S \subseteq J$ of jobs of maximum profit $\sum_{j \in S} w_j$ that can be feasibly scheduled on $M$.

In the *resource minimization* (MinR) variant, we assume that each job $j$ has a resource requirement vector $\bar{s}_j \in [0, 1]^d$ as one of the attributes, where $d \geq 1$ is the number of available resources. A schedule that assigns a set of jobs $S_{i,t}$ to a host $i \in M$ at time $t$ is feasible if $\sum_{j \in S_{i,t}} \bar{s}_j \leq \bar{1}^d$. Given a set of jobs $J$ with attributes $(p_j, \bar{s}_j, r_j, d_j)$, we seek a set of (homogeneous) hosts $M$ of minimum cardinality such that all of the jobs can be scheduled feasibly on $M$.

Indeed, a classic RAP instance can be viewed as MaxT with a *single* host. In this aspect, our setting is better suited for cloud services, where resources are distributed (also geographically) among multiple hosts. Further, MaxT allows non-consecutive allocation of the resource to each job. This renders significant structural differences between MaxT and RAP, as discussed below.

Another classical problem of interest in our setting is *vector packing* (VP), in which a set of $d$-dimensional items needs to be feasibly packed into a minimum number of $d$-dimensional bins of unit size in each dimension (i.e., the vector sum of all the items packed into each bin is less than $\bar{1}^d$). VP is the special case of MinR with unit processing times, where for all jobs $j \in J$, $r_j = 0$, $d_j = 1$ and $p_j = 1$.

We provide a first step in the study of *preemptive* RAP. In the full version of this paper, we present approximation algorithms for general inputs of MaxT and MinR, with better results for some special cases.

## 2 OUR CONTRIBUTIONS

### 2.1 Throughput Maximization

The non-preemptive version of MaxT, classical RAP, was studied earlier. To see the structural differences between the two problems, consider their natural linear programming relaxations. In the case of RAP, it is sufficient to have a single indicator variable $x_{jt}$ for each job $j$ and time slot $t$ to represent its start time. This allows the application of a natural randomized rounding algorithm, where job $j$ is scheduled to start at time $t$ with probability $x_{jt}$. On the other hand, in MaxT, a job can be preempted several times; therefore, each job requires multiple indicator variables. Further, these variables must be rounded in an *all-or-nothing* fashion, i.e., either we schedule all parts of a job or none of them. Our approach to handle this situation is to, somewhat counter-intuitively, "dumb down" the linear program by not committing the jobs to a particular schedule; instead, we choose a subset of jobs that satisfy certain knapsack constraints and construct the actual schedule in a subsequent phase.

We first consider a *laminar* variant of the problem, where the time windows for the jobs are chosen from a laminar family of intervals. This setting includes several important special cases, such as (*i*) all jobs are released at $t = 0$ but have different due dates, or (*ii*) jobs are released at different times, but all must be completed by a given due date.

Our algorithm for the laminar case relies on a combination of a *packing* phase and a *scheduling* phase. While the first phase ensures that the output solution has high profit, the second phase guarantees its feasibility. To facilitate a successful completion of the selected jobs, we formulate a set of conditions that must be satisfied in the packing phase. Both phases make use of the structural properties of a *laminar* family of intervals. In the packing phase, we apply our rounding procedure (for the LP solution) to the tree representation of the intervals. We further use this tree in the scheduling phase, to feasibly assign the resource to the selected jobs in a bottom-up fashion. We first handle instances satisfying some slackness condition; that is, for some constant $\lambda \in (0, 1)$, $p_j \leq \lambda(d_j - r_j + 1)$ for any job $j$. Thus, the time windows for processing the jobs are large enough. Such an assumption is quite reasonable in scenarios arising in our applications. We show that the two-phase algorithm yields a constant approximation for laminar instances.

Using a simple transformation of an arbitrary instance to laminar, we extend the result to general instances. Let $m = |M|$ be the number of hosts.

Theorem 1. *For any $\lambda < \frac{1}{4} - \frac{1}{2(m+2)}$, there exists a $\frac{1}{8} - \lambda\left(\frac{1}{2} + \frac{1}{m}\right)$-approximation algorithm for* MaxT *with slackness parameter $\lambda$.*

We further show that the dependence of the slackness parameter $\lambda$ on $m$ can be eliminated, i.e., MaxT admits a constant approximation for instances with *any* constant slackness parameter $\lambda \in (0, \frac{1}{4})$.

### 2.2 Maximizing Utilization

A central goal in allocating scarce resources is to maximize resource utilization. This is the special case of MaxT where the weight of each job is equal to its total resource requirement (or, *area*), i.e., $w_j = s_j p_j$ for all $j \in J$. For such instances, we obtain a constant approximation guarantee, building on an algorithm of Chen, Hassin and Tzur [10].

Theorem 2. *There is a polynomial time $\Omega(1)$-approximation for any instance of MaxT where $w_j = s_j p_j$ for all $j \in J$.*

### 2.3 General MaxT Instances

Our approach for tackling general instances (with no assumption on slackness) is to distinguish between jobs with 'large' and 'small' resource requirements. For jobs with requirements at least $\delta \in (0, 1)$, we show the existence of an $\Omega(\frac{1}{\log(1/\delta)})$-approximation. Thus, taking $\delta = \frac{1}{n}$, we obtain a solution $S_1$ that is an $\Omega(\frac{1}{\log n})$-approximation for the large jobs. The second solution, $S_2$, consists of all the small jobs, whose total sum of requirements is smaller than 1. Selecting the highest profit solution between $S_1$ and $S_2$, we obtain a logarithmic approximation ratio.

Theorem 3. *There is a polynomial time $\Omega(\frac{1}{\log n})$-approximation algorithm for MaxT.*

### 2.4 Resource Minimization

Our approach for solving MinR builds on a formulation of the problem as a configuration LP, inspired by the works of [2, 15]. However, we quickly deviate from these prior approaches, in order to handle the time windows and the extra constraints. Our algorithm involves two main phases: *a maximization phase* and *residual phase*. A *configuration* is a subset of jobs that can be feasibly assigned to a host at a given time slot $t$. Given the minimum number of hosts, $m$, obtained from an optimal solution for the LP, we choose for each $t$ $O(m \log d)$ configurations with probabilities proportional to their LP-values. In this phase, jobs may be allocated the resource only for part of their processing length. In the second phase, we construct a residual instance based on the amount of time each job has been processed. A key challenge is to show that, for any time window $[r_j, d_j]$, the total "area" of jobs left to be scheduled is at most $1/d$ of the original total area. We use this property to solve the residual instance. We obtain the next result.

Theorem 4. *Given an instance of* MinR *with slackness parameter $\lambda \in (0, \frac{1}{4})$, fix an $\epsilon \in (0, 1)$. Then there is a polynomial time algorithm that yields an $O(\log d \log^* T)$ approximation ratio with probability at least $1 - \epsilon$.*

## 3 RELATED WORK

The classical problem of preemptively scheduling a set of jobs with attributes ($p_j, s_j = 1, r_j, d_j$) on a single machine so as to maximize throughput can be cast as a special case of MaxT with a single host, where each job requires all of the available resource. Lawler [23] showed that in this special case MaxT admits a PTAS, and the problem is polynomially solvable for uniform job weights. For multiple hosts (i.e., $m = |M| > 1$), this special case of MaxT ($s_j = 1$ for all $j \in J$) admits a $\frac{1}{6+\varepsilon}$-approximation, for any fixed $\varepsilon > 0$. This follows from a result of Kalyanasundaram and Pruhs [20].

Another special case of MaxT was studied in the context of advertisement placement. The *ad placement* problem, introduced by Adler *et al.* [1], can be viewed as preemptive RAP with a single host, where all jobs have the same release time and due date. Ad placement was widely studied (see, e.g., [13, 14, 17, 21, 22] and the comprehensive survey in [24]). Freund and Naor [17] presented a $(\frac{1}{3} - \varepsilon)$-approximation for the maximum throughput (MaxT) version of the problem.

Fox and Korupula [16] recently studied our preemptive scheduling model, with job attributes $(p_j, s_j, r_j, d_j)$, under another popular objective, namely, minimizing weighted flow-time. Their work differs from ours in two ways: while they focus on the online versions, we consider our problems in an offline setting. Further, as they note, while the throughput and resource minimization objectives are also commonly considered metrics, their techniques only deal with flow-time. In fact, these objectives are fundamentally different and we need novel algorithms to tackle them.

The non-preemptive variant of MaxT, known as the *resource allocation problem* (RAP), was introduced by Phillips *et al.* [25], and later studied by many authors (see, e.g., [5–8, 10, 18] and the references therein).[1] Chakaravarthy *et al.* [8] consider a generalization of RAP and obtain a constant approximation based on a primal-dual algorithm.

As mentioned above, MinR generalizes the classic vector packing (VP) problem. The first non-trivial $O(\log d)$-approximation algorithm for VP was presented by Chekuri and Khanna [9], for any fixed $d \geq 1$. This ratio was improved by Bansal, Caprara and Sviridenko [2] to a randomized algorithm with asymptotic approximation ratio arbitrarily close to $\ln d + 1$. Bansal, Eliás and Khan [3] recently improved this ratio further to $0.807 + \ln(d + 1)$. A "fractional variant" of MinR was considered by Jansen and Porkolab [19], where time was assumed to be continuous. For this problem, in the case of a single host, they obtain a polynomial time approximation scheme (PTAS), by solving a configuration linear program (rounding the LP solution is not necessary because time is continuous in their case).

Resource minimization was considered also in the context of the ad placement problem. In this variant, a set of ads must be scheduled, and the objective is to minimize the total amount of resource (i.e., width of the display area) required to make this possible. Freund and Naor [17] gave a 2-approximation algorithm for the problem, which was later improved by Dawande *et al.* [14] to $\frac{3}{2}$. This implies a 3-approximation for MinR instances with $d = 1$, where all jobs have the same release time and due date. For this special case of MinR we show that the ratio can be improved, namely, the jobs can be feasibly scheduled on $2OPT + 1$ hosts, where $OPT$ is the optimal number of hosts.

Another line of work relates to the non-preemptive version of MinR, where $d = 1$ and the requirement of each job is equal to 1 (see, e.g. [11, 12]); thus, at most one job can be scheduled on each host at any time.

## ACKNOWLEDGMENTS

H. Shachnai's work was conducted during a visit to DIMACS partially supported by the National Science Foundation under grant number CCF-1445755.

## REFERENCES

[1] Micah Adler, Phillip B Gibbons, and Yossi Matias. 2002. Scheduling space-sharing for internet advertising. *Journal of Scheduling* 5, 2 (2002), 103–119.
[2] Nikhil Bansal, Alberto Caprara, and Maxim Sviridenko. 2009. A New Approximation Method for Set Covering Problems, with Applications to Multidimensional Bin Packing. *SIAM J. Comput.* 39, 4 (2009), 1256–1278.
[3] Nikhil Bansal, Marek Eliáš, and Arindam Khan. 2016. Improved approximation for vector bin packing. In *Proceedings of the 27th Annual ACM-SIAM Symposium on Discrete Algorithms.* 1561–1579.
[4] Nikhil Bansal, Zachary Friggstad, Rohit Khandekar, and Mohammad R Salavatipour. 2014. A logarithmic approximation for unsplittable flow on line graphs. *ACM Transactions on Algorithms* 10, 1 (2014), 1:1–1:15.
[5] Amotz Bar-Noy, Reuven Bar-Yehuda, Ari Freund, Joseph Naor, and Baruch Schieber. 2001. A unified approach to approximating resource allocation and scheduling. *J. ACM* 48, 5 (2001), 1069–1090.
[6] Amotz Bar-Noy, Sudipto Guha, Joseph Naor, and Baruch Schieber. 2001. Approximating the Throughput of Multiple Machines in Real-Time Scheduling. *SIAM J. Comput.* 31, 2 (2001), 331–352.
[7] Gruia Călinescu, Amit Chakrabarti, Howard J. Karloff, and Yuval Rabani. 2011. An improved approximation algorithm for resource allocation. *ACM Trans. Algorithms* 7, 4 (2011), 48:1–48:7.
[8] Venkatesan T Chakaravarthy, Anamitra R Choudhury, Shalmoli Gupta, Sambuddha Roy, and Yogish Sabharwal. 2014. Improved algorithms for resource allocation under varying capacity. In *Proceedings of the 22nd Annual European Symposium on Algorithms.* Springer, 222–234.
[9] Chandra Chekuri and Sanjeev Khanna. 2004. On multidimensional packing problems. *SIAM journal on computing* 33, 4 (2004), 837–851.
[10] Bo Chen, Refael Hassin, and Michal Tzur. 2002. Allocation of bandwidth and storage. *IIE Transactions* 34, 5 (2002), 501–507.
[11] Julia Chuzhoy and Paolo Codenotti. 2009. Resource minimization job scheduling. In *Approximation, Randomization, and Combinatorial Optimization. Algorithms and Techniques, Proceedings of the 12th Annual APPROX 2009, and 13th Annual RANDOM.* Springer, 70–83.
[12] Julia Chuzhoy, Sudipto Guha, Sanjeev Khanna, and Joseph Naor. 2004. Machine minimization for scheduling jobs with interval constraints. In *Proceedings of the 45th Annual IEEE Symposium on Foundations of Computer Science.* 81–90.
[13] Milind Dawande, Subodha Kumar, and Chelliah Sriskandarajah. 2003. Performance bounds of algorithms for scheduling advertisements on a web page. *Journal of Scheduling* 6, 4 (2003), 373–394.
[14] Milind Dawande, Subodha Kumar, and Chelliah Sriskandarajah. 2005. Scheduling web advertisements: a note on the minspace problem. *Journal of Scheduling* 8, 1 (2005), 97–106.
[15] Lisa Fleischer, Michel X. Goemans, Vahab S. Mirrokni, and Maxim Sviridenko. 2011. Tight Approximation Algorithms for Maximum Separable Assignment Problems. *Math. Oper. Res.* 36, 3 (2011), 416–431.
[16] Kyle Fox and Madhukar Korupolu. 2013. Weighted flowtime on capacitated machines. In *Proceedings of the 24th annual ACM-SIAM symposium on Discrete algorithms.* 129–143.
[17] Ari Freund and Joseph Naor. 2004. Approximating the advertisement placement problem. *Journal of Scheduling* 7, 5 (2004), 365–374.
[18] Navendu Jain, Ishai Menache, Joseph Naor, and Jonathan Yaniv. 2015. Near-optimal scheduling mechanisms for deadline-sensitive jobs in large computing clusters. *ACM Transactions on Parallel Computing* 2, 1 (2015), 3.
[19] Klaus Jansen and Lorant Porkolab. 2002. On preemptive resource constrained scheduling: polynomial-time approximation schemes. In *Proceedings of the 9th International Conference on Integer Programming and Combinatorial Optimization.* 329–349.
[20] Bala Kalyanasundaram and Kirk Pruhs. 2001. Eliminating Migration in Multi-processor Scheduling. *J. Algorithms* 38, 1 (2001), 2–24.
[21] Arshia Kaul, Sugandha Aggarwal, Anshu Gupta, Niraj Dayama, Mohan Krishnamoorthy, and PC Jha. 2017. Optimal advertising on a two-dimensional web banner. *International Journal of System Assurance Engineering and Management* (2017), 1–6.
[22] Subodha Kumar, Milind Dawande, and Vijay Mookerjee. 2007. Optimal scheduling and placement of internet banner advertisements. *IEEE Transactions on Knowledge and Data Engineering* 19, 11 (2007).
[23] Eugene L Lawler. 1990. A dynamic programming algorithm for preemptive scheduling of a single machine to minimize the number of late jobs. *Annals of Operations Research* 26, 1 (1990), 125–133.
[24] Shinjini Pandey, Goutam Dutta, and Harit Joshi. 2017. Survey on Revenue Management in Media and Broadcasting. *Interfaces* 47, 3 (2017), 195–213.
[25] Cynthia A. Phillips, R. N. Uma, and Joel Wein. 2000. Off-line admission control for general scheduling problems. In *Proceedings of the 11th Annual ACM-SIAM Symposium on Discrete Algorithms.* 879–888.

[1] RAP is also known as the *bandwidth allocation problem.*

# Brief Announcement: A Greedy 2 Approximation for the Active Time Problem

Saurabh Kumar*
Google
Mountain View, CA
saurabhkb@google.com

Samir Khuller†
University of Maryland
College Park, MD
samir@cs.umd.edu

## ABSTRACT

In this note, we give a simple 2 approximation for the active time problem - we are given a set of pre-emptible jobs, each with an integral release time, deadline and required processing length. The jobs need to be scheduled on a machine that can process at most $g$ distinct job units at any given integral time slot, in such a way that we minimize the time the machine is on i.e the active time. Our algorithm matches the state of the art bound obtained by a significantly more involved LP rounding scheme.

## KEYWORDS

Scheduling Algorithms

**ACM Reference Format:**

Saurabh Kumar and Samir Khuller. 2018. Brief Announcement: A Greedy 2 Approximation for the Active Time Problem. In *SPAA '18: 30th ACM Symposium on Parallelism in Algorithms and Architectures, July 16–18, 2018, Vienna, Austria.* ACM, New York, NY, USA, 3 pages. https://doi.org/10.1145/3210377.3210659

## 1 INTRODUCTION

In this paper, we consider the problem of scheduling jobs on a machine while minimizing the total time that the machine is on. This is captured by the active time model.

Active Time Model: We have a set of $n$ jobs say $J = \{1, 2, ..., n\}$ where each job $j$ has a processing time $p_j$ and must be scheduled in a window defined by a release time $r_j$ and deadline $d_j$ ($p_j, r_j, d_j$ are integers). Jobs are pre-emptible at integral points within their window. Time is divided into integral units. We are given a single machine that can process at most $g$ distinct job units in parallel. The machine is considered on i.e *active* in a particular time unit when it is processing at least one job in that time unit. Our goal is to feasibly schedule the jobs in $J$ while minimizing the *active time* (i.e the number of time units that the machine is on).

Chang et. al. [2] solve the problem exactly when jobs all have unit length. They show that the problem is NP hard when a job can have multiple disjoint windows but the complexity of the case where each job has a single contiguous window as is considered here is unknown. The unit length version of this problem has been considered in other contexts such as in scheduling jobs with precedence constraints [6], finding a minimum b-clique cover in an interval graph [1], and rectangle stabbing [4].

The general problem with arbitrary integral job lengths was considered by Chang et. al. [3] where the authors show that a minimal feasible solution is a 3 approximation. The authors also describe a more complicated 2 approximation based on LP rounding which is the current best known upper bound for the problem.

The main result in this paper is a simple combinatorial algorithm which achieves a 2 approximation for the active time problem, matching the upper bound obtained by the LP rounding scheme described by Chang et. al. [3].

*This work is based on the master's thesis of Kumar supervised by Khuller

†Supported by NSF Award CNS 1560193



*SPAA '18, July 16–18, 2018, Vienna, Austria*



ACM ISBN 978-1-4503-5799-9/18/07.
https://doi.org/10.1145/3210377.3210659

## 2 PRELIMINARIES

A job $j$ is said to be *live* at slot $t$ if $t \in [r_j, d_j]$. A slot is *open* if a job can be or has been scheduled in it. It is *closed* otherwise. An open slot is *full* if there are $g$ jobs assigned to it. It is *non-full* otherwise.

A feasible solution is given by a set of open time slots into which the jobs can be feasibly scheduled. Given a set of slots, we can find a feasible assignment of jobs or determine that no schedule is possible by performing a simple flow computation (described in the appendix).

## 3 GREEDY ALGORITHM

All time slots are assumed to be open initially. Consider time slots from left to right (i.e in increasing order). At a given time slot, close the slot and check if a feasible schedule exists in the open slots. If so, leave the slot closed, otherwise, open it again. Continue to the next slot.

THEOREM 3.1. *The greedy algorithm described above gives a 2 approximation to the active time problem.*

The remainder of this section is devoted to proving Theorem 3.1. We will bound the number of full and non-full slots separately. Let $S$ and $S^*$ denote the final greedy and optimal schedules respectively. Let $|S|$ and $|S^*|$ denote the number of open slots in $S$ and $S^*$ respectively. We first left shift the job units in $S$ as much as possible while maintaining feasibility. This is captured by the following lemma.

LEMMA 3.1. *For any job $j$ in time slot $t$, $j$ must be present in every non-full slot in the window of $j$ earlier than $t$ i.e in the interval $[r_j, t]$.*

PROOF. The proof follows from left shifting. For any non-full slot $t'$ earlier than $t$ in the window of job $j$, a unit of $j$ must be present in $t'$ since otherwise we would have left shifted the unit from $t$ into $t'$ (this would have been feasible since $t'$ is in $j$'s window and is non-full). □

For the proofs of the remaining lemmas and the definitions of $a$, $b$, $a^*$ and $b^*$, we assume that all job units have been left shifted as much as possible in $S$. Let $b_t[j]$ and $b^*_t[j]$ denote the number of units of any job $j \in J$ scheduled by $S$ and $S^*$ respectively at or before $t$ i.e in time interval $[r_j, t]$. Let $a_t[j]$ and $a^*_t[j]$ denote the amount of job $j$ scheduled by $S$ and $S^*$ respectively in the time interval $[t, d_j]$. So, $b_t[j] + a_{t+1}[j] = b^*_t[j] + a^*_{t+1}[j] = p_j$. Let $T$ be the latest deadline of all the jobs.

Lemma 3.2. *For any non-full slot $t$ opened by $S$, there must exist at least one job $j$ scheduled by $S$ in $t$ such that $b^*_t[j] \geq b_t[j]$.*

Proof. If possible, assume that $b^*_t[j] < b_t[j]$ for all $j$ scheduled by $S$ in $t$ (as depicted in Figure 1). While moving left to right in our greedy algorithm, we would encounter $t$. At this point, by definition, we have already scheduled $b_t[j]$ of each job in $[0, t]$. We still need to schedule $a_{t+1}[j]$ of each job $j$ in the interval $[t + 1, T]$.

Now, if we were to close $t$, then we would need to feasibly schedule the following in the interval $[t + 1, T]$:

(1) $a_{t+1}[j] + 1$ units[1] of each $j$ scheduled by $S$ in $t$. By our assumption, since $b_t[j] > b^*_t[j]$ we have $a_{t+1}[j] < a^*_{t+1}[j]$ and so $a_{t+1}[j] + 1 \leq a^*_{t+1}[j]$.
(2) $a_{t+1}[j]$ units of each $j$ that is live at $t$ but not scheduled by $S$ in $t$. Since $j$ is not scheduled in $t$, all units of $j$ must have been scheduled by $S$ earlier than $t$ since otherwise we could have left shifted $j$ into $t$ as it is non-full[2]. Therefore, $b_t[j] = p_j$ and $a_{t+1}[j] = 0$. So $a_{t+1}[j] \leq a^*_{t+1}[j]$.
(3) $a_{t+1}[j]$ units of each $j$ with $r_j > t$. Clearly $a_{t+1}[j] = p_j = a^*_{t+1}[j]$. So $a_{t+1}[j] \leq a^*_{t+1}[j]$.

It can be seen that if the greedy algorithm had closed $t$, the mass of each job $j$ that it would need to schedule in $[t + 1, T]$ (either $a_{t+1}[j]$ or $a_{t+1}[j] + 1$ units) is less than or equal to the mass of that job that OPT feasibly schedules in that interval ($a^*_{t+1}[j]$ units). When moving from left to right in our algorithm, when we reached $t$, all the slots in $[t + 1, T]$ were open to schedule jobs. This means that, had we closed $t$ in $S$, we would still have been able to find a feasible schedule of the remaining job units in $[t + 1, T]$, since OPT could find an optimal schedule for them in $[t + 1, T]$. Therefore, we would have closed $t$ greedily while constructing $S$. Since we did not, our original assumption must have been incorrect. □

Lemma 3.3. *The number of non-full slots in $S$ cannot exceed $|S^*|$.*

Proof. Start at the right most non-full slot in $S$, say $t$. From Lemma 3.2, we can find one job $j$ in $t$ such that $b^*_t[j] \geq b_t[j]$. By Lemma 3.1, $j$ must be present in every non-full slot in $[r_j, t]$. This means that the number of non-full slots in $[r_j, t]$ cannot exceed $b_t[j]$ ($\leq b^*_t[j]$). So we can charge every non-full slot of $S$ in $[r_j, t]$ to a distinct slot in $S^*$ in $[r_j, t]$. Now, move to the latest non-full slot opened by $S$ strictly earlier than $r_j$ and repeat this process. In this way, we can charge every non-full slot in $S$ to distinct slots in $S^*$. □

[1] The extra unit comes from the slot $t$ which we are attempting to close.
[2] Here, we use the fact that $t$ is non-full. If $t$ was full, this point may not have been true since the left shifting argument would not hold.

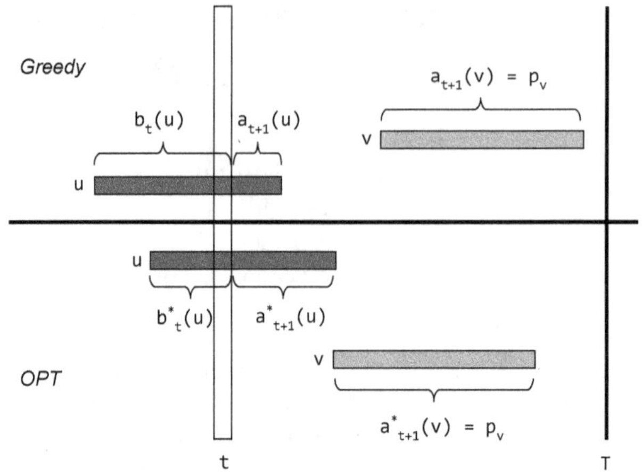


**Figure 1: The top half depicts $S$ and the bottom half $S^*$. Job $u$ is scheduled by $S$ in $t$ such that $b^*_t[u] < b_t[u]$. If this was true for all such jobs $u$ scheduled by $S$ in $t$, then in $[t + 1, T]$, $S^*$ would schedule as much as or more of every job that $S$ would have scheduled there even after closing $t$.**

Lemma 3.4. *The number of full slots in $S$ cannot exceed $|S^*|$.*

Proof. Let the number of full slots in $S$ be $|S_f|$. Since the maximum amount of job mass in any slot is $g$, the amount of job mass present in $S_f$ is $g|S_f|$. Similarly, the total job mass OPT scheduled is at most $g|S^*|$. By the conservation of job mass, $g|S_f| \leq g|S^*|$ and the lemma follows. □

The total cost of our schedule is the sum of the full and non-full slots, and therefore, from Lemmas 3.3 and 3.4, this sum cannot exceed $2|S^*|$. This proves Theorem 3.1.

# 4 CONCLUSION

In this paper, we prove that a simple greedy algorithm matches the best known approximation ratio for the active time problem. The complexity status of this problem is still open as is breaking the 2 upper bound barrier. A possible avenue to achieving this is via a local search technique which we briefly sketch in the appendix.

# REFERENCES

[1] Hans L Bodlaender and Klaus Jansen. 1995. Restrictions of graph partition problems. Part I. *Theoretical Computer Science* 148, 1 (1995), 93–109.
[2] Jessica Chang, Harold N Gabow, and Samir Khuller. 2012. A model for minimizing active processor time. In *European Symposium on Algorithms*. Springer, 289–300.
[3] Jessica Chang, Samir Khuller, and Koyel Mukherjee. 2014. LP rounding and combinatorial algorithms for minimizing active and busy time. In *Proceedings of the 26th ACM symposium on Parallelism in algorithms and architectures*. ACM, 118–127.
[4] Guy Even, Retsef Levi, Dror Rawitz, Baruch Schieber, Shimon Moni Shahar, and Maxim Sviridenko. 2008. Algorithms for capacitated rectangle stabbing and lot sizing with joint set-up costs. *ACM Transactions on Algorithms (TALG)* 4, 3 (2008), 34.
[5] Saurabh Kumar. 2016. *Combinatorial Algorithms for the Active Time and Busy Time Problems*. Master's thesis. University of Maryland, College Park.
[6] Christos H. Papadimitriou and Mihalis Yannakakis. 1979. Scheduling interval-ordered tasks. *SIAM J. Comput.* 8, 3 (1979), 405–409.

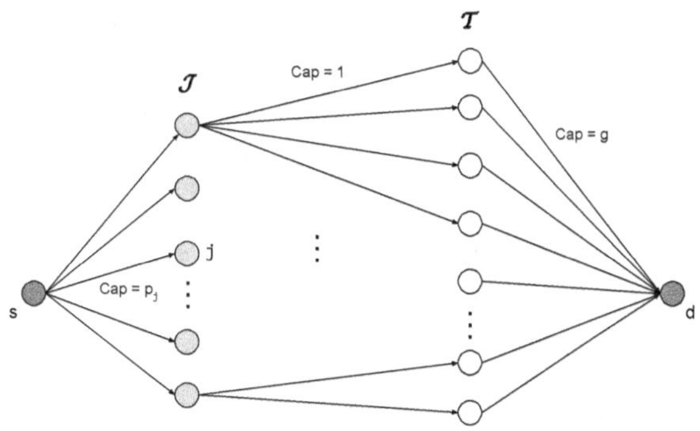


Figure 2: Flow network $G$. An integral flow of value $\sum_{j\in J} p_j$ corresponds to a feasible schedule.

# A APPENDIX

## A.1 Verifying a feasible schedule exists

Define a graph $G$ with vertex set consisting of one node for every job $j$, one node for every *open* time slot $t$ and a source and destination node ($s$ and $d$ respectively). Add edges from $s$ to each job node $j$ with capacity $p_j$. Add edges from each open time slot node $t$ to $d$ with capacity $g$. For each job $j$, for each time slot $t$ in its window, add an edge from job node $j$ to time slot node $t$ with unit capacity. The graph structure is shown in Figure 2. An active time instance has a feasible schedule on the set of open time slots iff the maximum flow (integral since capacities are integral) from $s$ to $d$ has value $\sum_{j\in J} p_j$. Furthermore, if a feasible schedule is possible, the unit capacity edges with non-zero flow give the mapping of job units to time slots.

## A.2 Tight Example

The tight example consists of the following set of jobs - one job of length $g$ with window $[1, 2g]$, $g$ unit length jobs with window $[1, g+1]$ and $g-1$ rigid jobs[3] of length $g$ with window $[2, g+1]$. OPT would have opened time slot $t = 1$, scheduled all unit jobs there and therefore been able to schedule the $g$ length job above the rigid jobs. This gives a total cost of $g+1$. However, our greedy algorithm closes time slot $t = 1$ since that is still feasible. So the unit jobs are forced to be scheduled above the rigid jobs, thereby pushing the long job out. This gives a total cost of $2g$. Thus, we get a lower bound of $\frac{2g}{g+1}$ which approaches 2 as $g$ becomes large. The two schedules are depicted in Figure 3 (reprinted from [5]).

## A.3 Local Search

Local search involves repeatedly performing local optimizations of the form - close $b$ slots and open at most $b-1$, for an integer constant $b\ (\geq 2)$. The only lower bound we currently have is $1+\frac{1}{b-1}$ as shown in Figure 4. Suppose in the left block we schedule $H = \frac{(b-1)g+1}{b}$ jobs each of length $\frac{gL}{2H}$ for some $L$, and we do the same in the right block with $H$ different jobs. From the figure, it can be seen that the jobs cannot be rearranged. If we take any $b$ columns, the total job mass amounts to $(b-1)g+1$ which cannot be scheduled in at most $b-1$ slots (so the schedule represents a local optimum). However, OPT can schedule all the jobs in the middle block of length $L$. This gives a lower bound of $\frac{bg}{(b-1)g+1}$ which approaches $1+\frac{1}{b-1}$ as $g$ becomes large.

[3]A rigid job is one whose processing length is equal to its window size. A rigid job cannot be moved in its window.

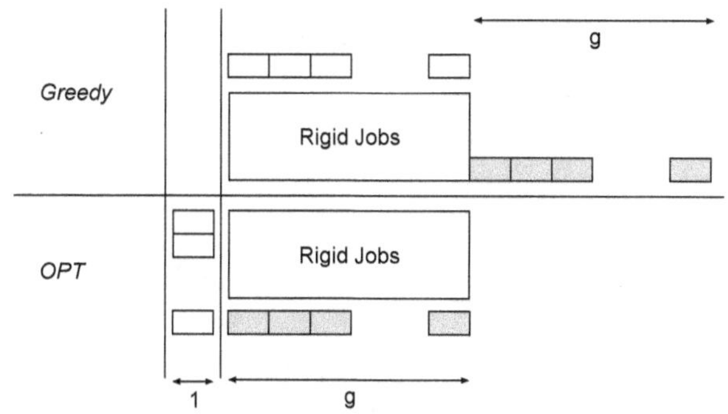


Figure 3: Tight Example for the Greedy Algorithm.

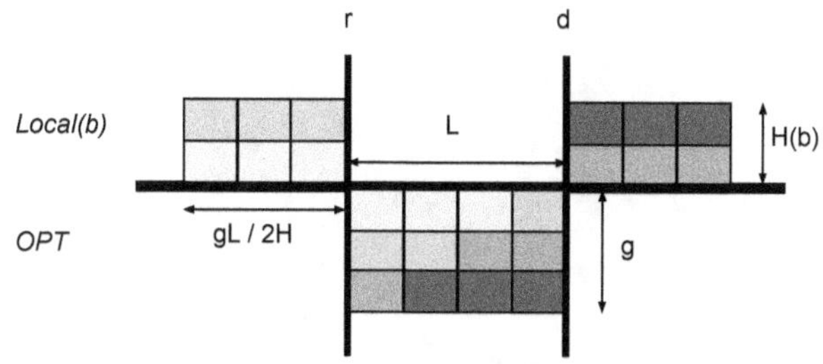


Figure 4: Lower bound for Local Search with parameter $b$. The jobs in the left block have deadline $d$ and those in the right have release time $r$.

# Brief Announcement: Open Cilk

Tao B. Schardl
MIT CSAIL
Cambridge, MA, USA
neboat@mit.edu

I-Ting Angelina Lee
Washington University in St. Louis
St. Louis, MO, USA
angelee@wustl.edu

Charles E. Leiserson
MIT CSAIL
Cambridge, MA, USA
cel@mit.edu

## ABSTRACT

Open Cilk is a new open-source platform to support Cilk multithreaded programming, especially for researchers and teachers. Open Cilk aims to provide a full-featured implementation of Cilk that is easy to modify and extend. Based on the award-winning Tapir/LLVM compiler, Open Cilk will provide a streamlined runtime system and feature comprehensive static instrumentation for dynamic-analysis tools. As a community-infrastructure project, Open Cilk encourages contributions from researchers in the areas of languages, compilers, runtime systems, tools, libraries, and benchmarks.

## CCS CONCEPTS

**• Theory of computation → Parallel algorithms; • Computing methodologies → Parallel programming languages; • Software and its engineering → Parallel programming languages; Compilers; Runtime environments; Software testing and debugging;**

## KEYWORDS

Cilk; multicore programming; parallel algorithms; parallel languages; productivity tools

**ACM Reference Format:**
Tao B. Schardl, I-Ting Angelina Lee, and Charles E. Leiserson. 2018. Brief Announcement: Open Cilk. In *SPAA '18: 30th ACM Symposium on Parallelism in Algorithms and Architectures, July 16–18, 2018, Vienna, Austria.* ACM, New York, NY, USA, 3 pages. https://doi.org/10.1145/3210377.3210658

## 1. Introduction

For years Cilk [6, 11, 19, 33, 42] has offered software developers a high-performance multithreaded programming environment while providing researchers with a platform for investigating a wide range of topics in multicore computing. When Cilk research began at MIT in 1994, it was conceived [5, 6, 10, 11, 26, 41] as a parallel-programming extension to the C programming language [28]. In 2006, at the advent of the multicore revolution, MIT spun off Cilk into the start-up Cilk Arts, Inc., which produced the open-source Cilk++ platform [33] as an extension to C++ [51]. Intel Corporation acquired Cilk Arts in 2009, added vectorization directives, and rechristened Cilk++ as Cilk Plus [19, 42], making it available commercially in the ICC compiler and in open-source implementations for the GCC [2, 13] and LLVM [21] compilers.

But Intel was unable to maintain a strong internal Cilk-development group. By 2013, attrition among Intel's Cilk team caused Intel to cease active development of the Cilk Plus product and focus solely on maintenance. In August 2017, Intel announced [23] that it would no longer even maintain Cilk Plus. Since Intel also maintained the open-source GCC implementation, GCC announced it was dropping its support for Cilk as well [14].

### *Cilk Hub and Open Cilk*

In January 2018, a group of us decided to address the flagging support for Cilk by creating a community-driven organization called ***Cilk Hub*** (http://cilkhub.org) to maintain and develop the Cilk technology. Cilk Hub provides a technically superior ***Open Cilk*** system to serve the needs of software developers, multicore and parallel-computing researchers, and teachers of parallel computing. Open Cilk features a new compiler based on Tapir/LLVM [45], comprehensive static instrumentation, and a suite of productivity tools. Cilk Hub provides external documentation of the Open Cilk system, offers workshops and tutorials, and coordinates annual meetings. Cilk Hub has formed an Advisory Board of leading researchers in multicore computing to set directions and priorities.

Cilk Hub will be active in developing Open Cilk as an open-source community project. Project enhancements include a lean-and-mean runtime system, new linguistics, new productivity tools, and libraries and benchmarks. Cilk Hub will manage integration of community-proposed enhancements to Open Cilk to ensure that it remains an efficient and malleable platform for multicore-programming research. Cilk Hub will produce a cloud VM that will allow researchers, teachers, and programmers to use Open Cilk technology — including the compiler, runtime system, libraries, and tools — without elaborate installation.

## 2. The Open Cilk system

Open Cilk is a full-featured, open-source implementation of Cilk designed to run on Linux and other Unix-like systems. Open Cilk provides a platform onto which researchers and teachers currently using Cilk Plus can migrate their ongoing research and educational materials with minimal effort. Open Cilk also serves as a vehicle for future research on Cilk programming and parallel-language technology.

### *Language*

Open Cilk is fully compatible with Cilk Plus, minus its vector notation. Open Cilk also enhances Cilk Plus by, for example, providing support for spawning statement blocks, instead of just functions. Going forward, we plan to improve the Cilk language based on input

This research was supported in part by NSF Grants 1314547, 1527692, 1533644, and 1733873.


*SPAA '18, July 16–18, 2018, Vienna, Austria*

ACM ISBN 978-1-4503-5799-9/18/07.
https://doi.org/10.1145/3210377.3210658

from the community. As we develop Cilk, we will strive to maintain its simplicity and ensure that all new language features work seamlessly with existing features. Some of the language features to be considered include simple linguistics for reducer hyperobjects [12] and a more efficient implementation of reducer hyperobjects in the Open Cilk runtime system [31], as well as linguistic and runtime support for on-the-fly pipeline parallelism [32], speculative parallelism [8], async-finish parallelism as in X10 [7], amorphous parallelism [39], and vectorization and data parallelism [17].

### *Compiler*

Open Cilk's compiler is based on the Tapir/LLVM compiler [45] and its Cilk/Clang front end. Tapir/LLVM embeds fork-join parallelism into LLVM's intermediate representation (IR). The resulting simple extension to LLVM's IR, called ***Tapir***, allows compiler optimizations for serial code to operate on parallel code with minimal changes. Integrating Tapir into LLVM required only adding or modifying about 6000 source lines of code, compared to LLVM's 4-million-line codebase. These few changes enable the Open Cilk compiler to produce more efficient parallel executables than other compilers for parallel languages.

### *Runtime system*

Although the Open Cilk system currently uses the Cilk Plus runtime system, we plan to develop a new open-source work-stealing runtime system for Open Cilk to suit the needs of researchers studying parallel runtime systems. The Open Cilk runtime system will implement the core runtime functionality of the existing Cilk Plus runtime system, but feature a smaller, simpler codebase and extensive documentation. We plan to enhance the runtime system with new capabilities. Among the considerations are support for long-latency operations such as file I/O [37] and interoperability with the system environment, including debuggers [1] and Pthreads [18].

### *Comprehensive static instrumentation*

To support productivity tools for parallelism, the Open Cilk compiler provides comprehensive compiler instrumentation based on the CSI framework [44]. CSI provides a simple application program interface (API) consisting of hooks (functions) that are automatically called at salient points throughout the program-under-test, such as function calls, basic blocks, and memory operations. A tool writer can implement a "CSI-tool" as a library, without modifying the compiler, by simply defining the semantics of the various API hooks. Undefined hooks are elided, minimizing the overhead of the CSI-tool. Whereas the original CSI framework operated on serial programs, the Open Cilk compiler extends CSI to instrument Tapir, giving tool writers additional hooks that correspond to `cilk_spawn`, `cilk_sync`, and other important points in parallel programs.

### *Productivity tools*

The Open Cilk system includes two open-source CSI-tools: the Cilksan nondeterminacy detector, and the Cilkscale scalability analyzer. Cilksan implements the core functionality of Intel's closed-source Cilkscreen tool [20], and Cilkscale implements the core functionality of Intel's closed-source Cilkview tool [16]. We plan to enhance Open Cilk's suite of productivity tools with performance and functionality enhancements [38, 40, 54, 56] to existing tools, as well as with implementations of additional productivity tools, such as the Cilkprof scalability profiler [43] and a tool to support record and replay [30, 55].

### *Libraries and benchmarks*

Open Cilk will incorporate an expansive collection of libraries and benchmark programs. We plan to build this collection by drawing from the extensive body of community-developed parallel libraries and benchmarks [3, 4, 9, 11, 15, 22, 24, 25, 27, 29, 34–36, 46–50, 52, 53, 57].

## 3. The architecture of Open Cilk

Open Cilk is architected to provide a robust platform for professional application development and for next-generation multicore-computing research and education. The design and implementation of Open Cilk exhibits five central software qualities: compatibility, open source, componentization, integration, and reliability.

### *Compatibility*

Open Cilk provides support for modern C++ features and existing Cilk Plus applications and libraries. To ensure that Cilk can parallelize large applications, Open Cilk supports crucial features, such as using C++ exceptions in Cilk programs. Open Cilk provides support for existing Cilk Plus libraries, including reducer hyperobjects [12] and deterministic parallel random-number generators [35].

### *Open source*

The entire Open Cilk implementation is open source. Open Cilk thus allows researchers to develop enhancements to all parts of the system: compiler, runtime system, libraries, and productivity tools. Cilk Hub manages the process of integrating community-proposed innovations into Open Cilk so that applications researchers and professional developers can exploit the enhancements.

### *Componentization*

The Open Cilk system is divided into distinct software components with well-defined interfaces. This design allows researchers to experiment with alternative implementations of different individual components.

### *Integration*

The components of Open Cilk are integrated to ensure that they all work together correctly. Cilk Hub aims for consistency and compatibility among all components with each system release. Cilk Hub will produce a cloud VM so that researchers, teachers, and programmers can use Open Cilk technology in the cloud without elaborate installation, confident that all components will interoperate.

### *Reliability*

To ensure that Open Cilk releases are stable, fast, and free of serious bugs, Open Cilk includes an extensive suite of unit tests, regression tests, and benchmarks, all of which it will continue to develop. We also plan to develop a cloud-based testing infrastructure for continuous testing and integration of changes to Open Cilk.

## 4. Conclusion

Cilk Hub welcomes contributions to Open Cilk. To stay abreast of further developments, please visit http://cilkhub.org.

## REFERENCES


[1] P. Alves, J. Brobecker, D. Evans, T. Tromey, and E. Zaretskii. GDB: The GNU project debugger. http://www.gnu.org/software/gdb/, Oct. 2014. Viewed Nov 3, 2014.

[2] B. Ayer. Intel Cilk Plus is now available in open-source and for GCC 4.7! http://www.cilkplus.org, 2011. The source code for the compiler and its associated runtime is available at http://gcc.gnu.org/svn/gcc/branches/cilkplus.

[3] C. Bienia, S. Kumar, J. P. Singh, and K. Li. The PARSEC benchmark suite: Characterization and architectural implications. In *PACT*, pages 72–81, 2008.

[4] G. E. Blelloch, J. T. Fineman, P. B. Gibbons, and J. Shun. Internally deterministic parallel algorithms can be fast. In *PPoPP*, pages 181–192, 2012.

[5] R. D. Blumofe. *Executing Multithreaded Programs Efficiently.* PhD thesis, Department of Electrical Engineering and Computer Science, Massachusetts Institute of Technology, Cambridge, Massachusetts, Sept. 1995. Available as MIT Laboratory for Computer Science Technical Report MIT/LCS/TR-677.

[6] R. D. Blumofe, C. F. Joerg, B. C. Kuszmaul, C. E. Leiserson, K. H. Randall, and Y. Zhou. Cilk: An efficient multithreaded runtime system. *Journal of Parallel and Distributed Computing*, 37(1):55–69, 1996.

[7] P. Charles, C. Grothoff, V. Saraswat, C. Donawa, A. Kielstra, K. Ebcioglu, C. von Praun, and V. Sarkar. X10: An object-oriented approach to non-uniform cluster computing. In *OOPSLA*, 2005.

[8] D. Dailey and C. E. Leiserson. Using Cilk to write multiprocessor chess programs. *The Journal of the International Computer Chess Association*, pages 25–52, 2002.

[9] L. Dhulipala, G. Blelloch, and J. Shun. Julienne: A framework for parallel graph algorithms using work-efficient bucketing. In *SPAA*, pages 293–304, 2017. ISBN 978-1-4503-4593-4.

[10] M. Frigo. A fast Fourier transform compiler. *ACM SIGPLAN Notices*, 34(5):169–180, May 1999.

[11] M. Frigo, C. E. Leiserson, and K. H. Randall. The implementation of the Cilk-5 multithreaded language. In *PLDI*, pages 212–223, 1998.

[12] M. Frigo, P. Halpern, C. E. Leiserson, and S. Lewin-Berlin. Reducers and other Cilk++ hyperobjects. In *SPAA*, pages 79–90, 2009.

[13] GCC Team. GCC 4.9 release series changes, new features, and fixes. Available at https://gcc.gnu.org/gcc-4.9/changes.html, 2014.

[14] GGC Team. GCC 7 release series: Changes, new features, and fixes. Available at https://gcc.gnu.org/gcc-7/changes.html, 2017.

[15] W. Hasenplaugh, T. Kaler, T. B. Schardl, and C. E. Leiserson. Ordering heuristics for parallel graph coloring. In *SPAA*, pages 166–177, 2014.

[16] Y. He, C. E. Leiserson, and W. M. Leiserson. The Cilkview scalability analyzer. In *SPAA*, pages 145–156, 2010.

[17] W. D. Hillis and G. L. Steele Jr. Data parallel algorithms. *Commun. ACM*, 29(12): 1170–1183, Dec. 1986.

[18] Institute of Electrical and Electronic Engineers. Information technology — Portable Operating System Interface (POSIX) — Part 1: System application program interface (API) [C language]. IEEE Standard 1003.1, 1996 Edition, 1996.

[19] Intel Corporation. *Intel Cilk Plus Language Specification*, 2010. Document Number: 324396-001US. Available from http://software.intel.com/sites/products/cilk-plus/cilk_plus_language_specification.pdf.

[20] Intel Corporation. Intel Cilk Plus software development kit. Available from http://software.intel.com/en-us/articles/intel-cilk-plus-software-development-kit/, Dec. 2011.

[21] Intel Corporation. Cilk Plus/LLVM: an implementation of the Intel Cilk Plus C/C++ language extensions in LLVM. Available from http://cilkplus.github.io/, 2016.

[22] Intel Corporation. Intel Cilk Plus samples. Available from https://software.intel.com/en-us/code-samples/intel-compiler/intel-compiler-features/intelcilkplus, 2016.

[23] Intel Corporation. Intel Cilk Plus. Available at https://www.cilkplus.org, sep 2017.

[24] Intel Corporation. *Reference Manual for Intel Math Kernel Library 2018 — C*, 2017. URL https://software.intel.com/en-us/mkl-reference-manual-for-c.

[25] S. Itzhaky, R. Singh, A. Solar-Lezama, K. Yessenov, Y. Lu, C. Leiserson, and R. Chowdhury. Deriving divide-and-conquer dynamic programming algorithms using solver-aided transformations. In *OOPSLA*, pages 145–164, 2016. ISBN 978-1-4503-4444-9.

[26] C. F. Joerg. *The Cilk System for Parallel Multithreaded Computing.* PhD thesis, Department of Electrical Engineering and Computer Science, Massachusetts Institute of Technology, Cambridge, Massachusetts, Jan. 1996. Available as MIT Laboratory for Computer Science Technical Report MIT/LCS/TR-701.

[27] T. Kaler, W. Hasenplaugh, T. B. Schardl, and C. E. Leiserson. Executing dynamic data-graph computations deterministically using chromatic scheduling. *Transactions on Parallel Computing*, 3(1):2:1–2:31, 2016. ISSN 2329-4949.

[28] B. W. Kernighan and D. M. Ritchie. *The C Programming Language.* Prentice Hall, Inc., second edition, 1988.

[29] M. Kulkarni, M. Burtscher, C. Cascaval, and K. Pingali. Lonestar: A suite of parallel irregular programs. In *ISPASS*, pages 65–76, 2009.

[30] T. J. LeBlanc and J. M. Mellor-Crummey. Debugging parallel programs with Instant Replay. *IEEE Transactions on Computers*, C-36(4):471–482, Apr. 1987.

[31] I.-T. A. Lee, A. Shafi, and C. E. Leiserson. Memory-mapping support for reducer hyperobjects. In *SPAA*, pages 287–297, 2012.

[32] I.-T. A. Lee, C. E. Leiserson, T. B. Schardl, Z. Zhang, and J. Sukha. On-the-fly pipeline parallelism. *ACM TOPC*, 2(3):17:1–17:42, 2015.

[33] C. E. Leiserson. The Cilk++ concurrency platform. *Journal of Supercomputing*, 51(3):244–257, 2010.

[34] C. E. Leiserson and T. B. Schardl. A work-efficient parallel breadth-first search algorithm (or how to cope with the nondeterminism of reducers). In *SPAA*, pages 303–314. ACM, June 2010.

[35] C. E. Leiserson, T. B. Schardl, and J. Sukha. Deterministic parallel random-number generation for dynamic-multithreading platforms. In *PPoPP*, 2012.

[36] M. M. Maza and Y. Xie. Balanced dense polynomial multiplication on multi-cores. *ACM Communications on Computer Algebra*, 43(3/4):85–87, June 2010. ISSN 1932-2240.

[37] S. K. Muller and U. A. Acar. Latency-hiding work stealing: Scheduling interacting parallel computations with work stealing. In *SPAA*, pages 71–82. ACM, 2016. ISBN 978-1-4503-4210-0.

[38] D. Oktay and S. Kamali, May 2017. Private communication.

[39] K. Pingali, D. Nguyen, M. Kulkarni, M. Burtscher, M. A. Hassaan, R. Kaleem, T.-H. Lee, A. Lenharth, R. Manevich, M. Méndez-Lojo, D. Prountzos, and X. Sui. The Tao of parallelism in algorithms. In *PLDI*, pages 12–25, 2011.

[40] R. Raman, J. Zhao, V. Sarkar, M. Vechev, and E. Yahav. Efficient data race detection for async-finish parallelism. *Formal Methods in Systems Design*, 41(3):321–347, Dec. 2012.

[41] K. H. Randall. *Cilk: Efficient Multithreaded Computing.* PhD thesis, Department of Electrical Engineering and Computer Science, Massachusetts Institute of Technology, May 1998.

[42] A. D. Robison and C. E. Leiserson. Cilk Plus. In P. Balaji, editor, *Programming Models for Parallel Computing*, chapter 13, pages 323–352. The MIT Press, Cambridge, MA, 2015.

[43] T. B. Schardl, B. C. Kuszmaul, I.-T. A. Lee, W. M. Leiserson, and C. E. Leiserson. The Cilkprof scalability profiler. In *SPAA*, pages 89–100, 2015.

[44] T. B. Schardl, T. Denniston, D. Doucet, B. C. Kuszmaul, I.-T. A. Lee, and C. E. Leiserson. The CSI framework for compiler-inserted program instrumentation. *Proc. ACM Meas. Anal. Comput. Syst.*, 1(2):43:1–43:25, Dec. 2017. ISSN 2476-1249.

[45] T. B. Schardl, W. S. Moses, and C. E. Leiserson. Tapir: Embedding fork-join parallelism into LLVM's intermediate representation. In *PPoPP*, pages 249–265, 2017. ISBN 978-1-4503-4493-7.

[46] J. Shun. *Shared-Memory Parallelism Can be Simple, Fast, and Scalable.* Morgan & Claypool, 2017.

[47] J. Shun and G. E. Blelloch. Ligra: A lightweight graph processing framework for shared memory. In *PPoPP*, pages 135–146, 2013.

[48] J. Shun, G. E. Blelloch, J. T. Fineman, P. B. Gibbons, A. Kyrola, H. V. Simhadri, and K. Tangwongsan. Brief announcement: the Problem Based Benchmark Suite. In *SPAA*, pages 68–70, 2012.

[49] J. Shun, L. Dhulipala, and G. E. Blelloch. Smaller and faster: Parallel processing of compressed graphs with Ligra+. In *DCC*, pages 403–412, 2015.

[50] G. L. Steele Jr., D. Lea, and C. H. Flood. Fast splittable pseudorandom number generators. In *OOPSLA*, pages 453–472, New York, NY, USA, 2014. ACM. ISBN 978-1-4503-2585-1.

[51] B. Stroustrup. *The C++ Programming Language.* Addison-Wesley, Boston, MA, third edition, 2000.

[52] Y. Tang, R. You, H. Kan, J. J. Tithi, P. Ganapathi, and R. A. Chowdhury. Cache-oblivious wavefront: Improving parallelism of recursive dynamic programming algorithms without losing cache-efficiency. In *PPoPP*, pages 205–214, 2015. ISBN 978-1-4503-3205-7.

[53] S. Toledo. TAUCS: A library of sparse linear solvers. Available on the Web from http://www.cs.tau.ac.il/~stoledo/taucs/, 2003.

[54] R. Utterback, K. Agrawal, J. T. Fineman, and I.-T. A. Lee. Provably good and practically efficient parallel race detection for fork-join programs. In *SPAA*, pages 83–94, 2016.

[55] R. Utterback, K. Agrawal, I.-T. A. Lee, and M. Kulkarni. Processor-oblivious record and replay. In *PPoPP*, pages 145–161, 2017.

[56] Y. Xu, I.-T. A. Lee, and K. Agrawal. Efficient parallel determinacy race detection for two-dimensional dags. In *PPoPP*, 2018. To appear.

[57] B. Zhang, J. Huang, N. P. Pitsianis, and X. Sun. RECFMM: recursive parallelization of the adaptive fast multipole method for Coulomb and screened Coulomb interactions. *Communications in Computational Physics*, 20(2):534–550, 2016.

# Brief Announcement: Stamp-it, a more Thread-efficient, Concurrent Memory Reclamation Scheme in the C++ Memory Model

Manuel Pöter
TU Wien, Faculty of Informatics
Vienna, Austria
manuel@manuel-poeter.at

Jesper Larsson Träff
TU Wien, Faculty of Informatics
Vienna, Austria
traff@par.tuwien.ac.at

## ABSTRACT

We present *Stamp-it*, a new, general, portable, lock-less concurrent memory reclamation scheme with amortized, constant-time (thread-count independent) reclamation overhead. Stamp-it has been implemented and proved correct in the C++ memory model using as weak memory-consistency assumptions as possible. We have (re)implemented six other comparable reclamation schemes. By a detailed performance comparison, we show that Stamp-it performs favorably, sometimes better, but at least as good as these other schemes while being able to reclaim free memory nodes earlier.

**ACM Reference Format:**

Manuel Pöter and Jesper Larsson Träff. 2018. Brief Announcement: Stamp-it, a more Thread-efficient, Concurrent Memory Reclamation Scheme in the C++ Memory Model. In *Proceedings of 30th ACM Symposium on Parallelism in Algorithms and Architectures, Vienna, Austria, July 16–18, 2018 (SPAA '18),* 4 pages.
https://doi.org/10.1145/3210377.3210661

## 1 INTRODUCTION

The *memory reclamation problem* is to determine, for any given allocated *memory node*, when it is safe to return it to the memory management system. In a concurrent setting, the memory reclamation problem is non-trivial, since there may be more than one thread referencing an allocated node unbeknownst to the other threads, in this case making it *unsafe* to give back the node.

Concurrent memory reclamation is an active research area with a number of proposals with different properties and issues. Our contribution is a new, lock-less, general, portable reclamation scheme, called *Stamp-it*, which, in contrast to almost all other schemes, allows reclamation to be done in *amortized constant time* per node, independently of the number of threads. Stamp-it is *general* in that it makes no assumptions on the structure of the allocated nodes or on the way nodes are used in concurrent data structures, and *portable* in that it neither relies on support from the operating system nor makes use of double-word atomic operations that may not be available on all architectures. Stamp-it is *lock-less* meaning that a stalled thread cannot block the progress of all other threads; but a stalled thread can prevent reclamation of otherwise reclaimable memory nodes. We call this (undesirable) property that most general schemes have *reclamation-blocking*; a notable exception is HPR [4]; other non-blocking schemes become non-blocking by sacrificing generality, e.g., DBERA+ [1]. In the following, we give a detailed, high-level explanation of Stamp-it, and argue for its main correctness properties. Details, including the extensive performance comparison to six other schemes, can be found in [5–8].


ACM ISBN 978-1-4503-5799-9/18/07.
https://doi.org/10.1145/3210377.3210661

## 2 A HIGH-LEVEL VIEW OF STAMP-IT

*Stamp-it* is an *epoch-based* reclamation scheme conceptually similar to NER [3] and therefore provides many of the same properties. As in ER/NER, the programmer has to define *critical regions* that are entered and left explicitly. A thread is only allowed to access shared memory nodes inside such regions. Our implementation is based on the C++ interface proposed by Robison [9], slightly extended for marking entry and exit from critical regions.

We now give a high-level overview of the algorithm behind Stamp-it. It maintains thread-local and one global *retire-list* of memory nodes that can potentially be reclaimed. It relies on an abstract lock-free, linearizable data structure that we call the *Stamp Pool* that efficiently supports the following operations:

(1) Add an element and assign it a new stamp (`push`). Stamps are strictly increasing, but not necessarily consecutive.
(2) Remove a specific element, return `true` if this element was the one with the lowest stamp at that point in time (`remove`).
(3) Get the highest stamp assigned to an element so far, i.e., the last stamp that has been assigned.
(4) Get the lowest stamp of all elements currently in the pool.

The Stamp-it algorithm uses the Stamp Pool as follows. Upon entering a critical region, the thread adds itself to the pool, and gets a new stamp value. Stamp values are strictly increasing, and therefore define a total order according to which threads have entered their respective critical region. When a thread retires a node, it requests the highest stamp from the Stamp Pool, stores it in the node and appends the node to the end of its local retire-list.

Upon leaving a critical region, the thread removes itself from the data structure and performs a *reclaim operation* on its local retire-list. The reclaim operation requests the now lowest stamp from the Stamp Pool, and can safely reclaim all nodes with a smaller stamp value. Since nodes are appended to the end of the retire-list, they are ordered by their stamp values, and reclamation can be performed by a linear scan of the retire list up to the first element with a higher time stamp than the currently lowest. No time is wasted on nodes that cannot yet be reclaimed. The working of Stamp-it is illustrated in Figure 1.

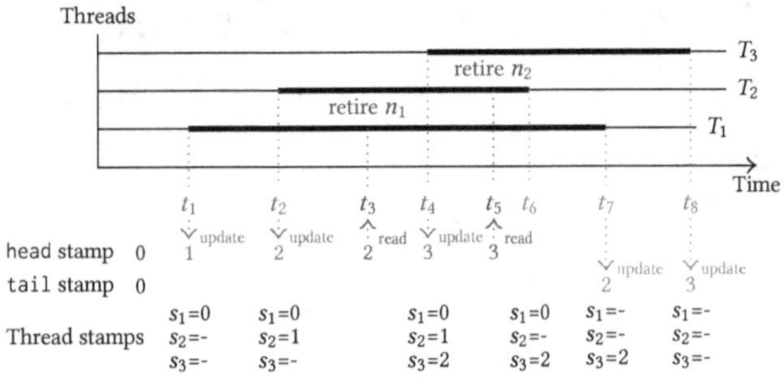


**Figure 1: An example sequence of Stamp-it pool operations. Thick lines indicate critical regions. Node $n_1$ can be reclaimed at time $t_7$, node $n_2$ at time $t_8$.**

If the remove operation returns false and the number of nodes in the local retire-list exceeds some threshold, the thread pushes all remaining, not reclaimed entries to the global retire-list as an ordered sublist. If remove returns true and the thread was the last one, (i.e., it entered its critical region the earliest) it performs a reclaim operation on the global retire-list. The global retire-list is a list of ordered sublists, so each sublist needs to be scanned only up to the node which has a stamp larger than or equal to the currently lowest stamp. Therefore, the resulting total runtime is $O(n + m)$ where $n$ is the total number of reclaimable nodes and $m$ is the number of ordered sublists; we will see later how this can be reduced to $O(n)$.

# 3 ALGORITHM AND IMPLEMENTATION DETAILS

The key ingredient of Stamp-it is the Stamp Pool data structure which should support the four operations in a lock-free manner, and in constant-time in the absence of conflicts. Our implementation is derived from the lock-free, doubly-linked list by Sundell and Tsigas [10]. It requires static dummy nodes, head and tail, which are also used to manage the highest and lowest stamp values. The highest stamp is stored in head and the lowest one in tail. In contrast to [10], we only need to add a node from one direction of the list (next to head), but nodes can be removed at any time and from any position. Each thread has a single, local thread_control_block that acts as a node in the list, i.e., the nodes are reused and we therefore have to consider the possibility that nodes might reappear at different positions without causing an ABA problem. From now on, we refer to these thread_control_blocks in the list as *blocks* (not to be confused with reclaimable memory nodes).

To insert or delete a block from the list one has to update the prev and next pointers. This must be done consistently, but not necessarily all at once. The solution in [10] is to treat the doubly-linked list as a singly-linked list with auxiliary information in the prev pointers. The next pointers always form a consistent, singly-linked list, but the prev pointers only give hints for where to find the previous block. We use the same approach, but with reversed directions: the prev list is kept consistent, and the next pointers are hints with auxiliary information. This is more suited to the use in Stamp-it. It is therefore possible that a block which is already in the prev list, does not occur (yet) in the next list (and the other way round in case of removal).

Both next and prev pointers have a DeleteMark (in the least significant bit) to prevent conflicting updates from concurrent insert and delete operations.

To avoid the ABA problem, we reserve additional 17 bits for a *version tag* in both pointers in addition to the delete mark. These bits store a tag that is incremented with every change to the pointer value. There is still a very small chance for an ABA problem to occur when the version tag wraps around, but in order for this to happen there have to be *exactly* $2^{17}$ updates to the pointer by other threads between the initial read and the subsequent update operation. We ensure that the allocated blocks are properly aligned to make these lower 18 bits available. This adds some memory overhead but ensures portability.

## 3.1 Stamp Pool data structure

The Stamp Pool keeps track of which threads have entered a critical region and in which order. Each thread_control_block, including head and tail, holds a *stamp counter*. When a new block is inserted, it loads head's prev pointer and stores it in its local prev, increases head's stamp by a *fetch-and-add* (FAA) operation, stores the returned value in its local stamp and then performs a *compare-and-swap* (CAS) on head->prev in order to insert itself into the prev list. This ensures that head always holds the highest stamp and that the stamps in the prev direction are strictly decreasing, i.e., that the stamp of the newly added block is greater than all other blocks (except head). The only exception to this is the tail block, which should always reflect the stamp value of its immediate predecessor in the prev direction. This way we can easily fetch the lowest stamp value from tail.

Even though the next pointers only act as hints, it is guaranteed that they only point to blocks with a higher stamp value, i.e., that the stamps in the next direction are strictly increasing (with the tail block again being an exception). More specifically, the next pointer of some block $b$ can point to:

- head, which is the case either when head is the predecessor of $b$ (in prev direction), or when some other block $c$ has inserted itself between head and $b$, but did not yet update $b$'s next pointer. Note that when $b$ has already marked its prev pointer, it can no longer be updated by $c$, so this inconsistency can only be resolved once $b$ is fully removed from both lists.
- a block $c$ which is still in the prev list. This is the "normal case", i.e., usually $c$ is the predecessor of $b$ in prev direction.
- a block $c$ which is removed from the prev list. This is an intermediate state when $c$ has been removed from the prev list, but not yet from the next list. So prev->next points to $c$, but $c$ is no longer the immediate predecessor of $b$ in the prev direction when starting from head. However, by following $c$'s next pointer (and potentially those of other removed blocks) one can find $b$'s new predecessor.

This is illustrated in Figure 2. The links of the blocks $T_1$, $T_3$ and $T_4$ are all marked so they cannot be updated. The block $T_3$ is already fully removed, i.e., is not referenced by any prev or next pointer in the list. The blocks $T_1$ and $T_4$ are marked for deletion, but are not yet fully removed; $T_1$ has been removed from the prev list, but is still

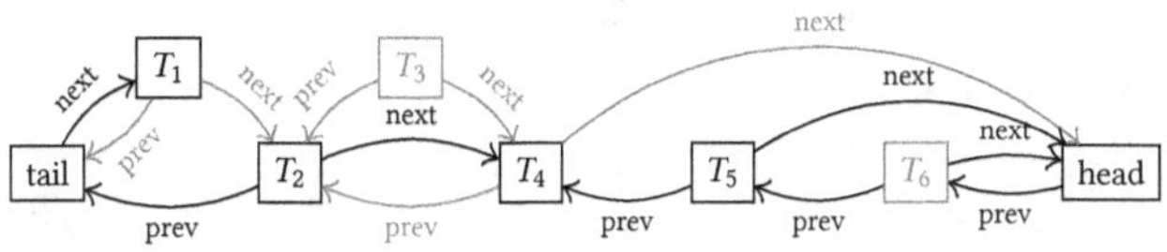


**Figure 2: Example of blocks with their links; green blocks are not yet fully inserted, red blocks are removed; red links are marked.**

in the next list; $T_4$ is still fully linked. Block $T_5$ already finished its push operation (not green), but the next pointer of its successor, $T_4$, still points to head. This indicates that $T_4$'s next pointer was already marked, so that it could not be updated by $T_5$. On the other hand, $T_6$ is currently in the push operation (green); it has successfully inserted itself in the prev list, but the update of $T_5$'s next pointer is still pending.

The two lowest bits of the stamp counter are used to embed flags to track a block's state. The PendingPush flag indicates that the block is currently being inserted into the prev list, while the NotInList flag is set when the block has been completely removed and is no longer part of neither prev nor next list. This also implies that the owning thread is no longer inside a critical region. The two flags are mutually exclusive, so they cannot both be set at the same time.

## 3.2 The Stamp Pool operations

We now explain how to support the Stamp Pool operations on the doubly-linked list data structure correctly in a lock-free manner.

*3.2.1 The push operation.* To insert a block we first set the block's next pointer to head implicitly clearing the DeleteMark of next. Then we perform an FAA on head->stamp, getting the new stamp for the block we are about to insert. This new stamp value is modified to have the PendingPush flag set before it is stored in our block. Then we set the block's prev pointer and attempt a CAS operation to update head->prev with our own block. When the CAS is successful, our block has been inserted in the prev list. We can therefore reset the PendingPush flag, and perform a final CAS-loop to update our successor's next pointer.

*3.2.2 The remove operation.* The remove operation first marks the prev and next pointers before removing the block from both lists. Afterwards it sets the NotInList flag and checks if this thread was the last one, i.e., if the block's prev pointer points to tail. If that is the case, it tries to update tail's stamp to that of the new "last" thread.

Marking the two pointers signals to other threads that this block is about to be removed, and also prevents the pointers from being updated by CAS operations from threads that did not yet see the mark. In order to remove a block $b$ from the prev list, the thread has to find its predecessor, i.e., the block $c$ with the prev pointer pointing to $b$, and update $c$'s prev pointer with the value of $b$'s prev pointer. But it can of course happen that $c$'s prev pointer is also marked and can therefore not be updated. In this case we have to find $c$'s predecessor and *help* remove $c$ before we can continue with the removal of $b$. By removing $c$, we get a new predecessor for $b$. We can then restart the loop and try to remove it again. The same idea is applied when removing a block from the next list.

Since a block $b$ can only be removed from the prev list when its immediate predecessor is not marked, any marked immediate predecessor has to be removed before $b$ can be removed. Therefore, whenever a thread that tries to remove a marked block $b$ encounters another block $c$ which is supposed to come *after* $b$ in the prev direction, we can conclude that $b$ has already been removed from both lists.

Since $c$ was encountered *after* $b$ in the prev direction, it is supposed to have a lower stamp than $b$; it can only have a larger stamp if it was removed and then reinserted. But since all blocks between $c$ and $b$ are marked, $c$ could not have been removed without first removing all those blocks, including $b$. The same holds for the case when the NotInList flag is set, as the flag is only set once the block has been fully removed.

The remove operation keeps track of three different pointers:

- ***prev*** is a reference to the next *unmarked* block in prev direction, i.e., the block that we want to set as the new value for our predecessor's prev pointer. We get to this block by following our own prev pointer and the prev pointers of other marked blocks (if any).
- ***next*** is a reference to some block that precedes our own block in prev direction. By following this block's prev pointer we should end up at our own block, unless some other thread has removed it already. This way we can efficiently find our immediate predecessor to update its prev pointer.
- ***last*** is a reference to a helper block that is used to remove potentially marked predecessors of our own block. When this pointer is not null, it should be the immediate predecessor of the *next* block in the prev direction.

The order of the blocks in the prev direction should be as follows: *last* (if it is set), *next*, our own block $b$, and *prev*. Each of these blocks (except $b$) can potentially be removed and reinserted at any time. For *next* and *last* we have to consider this possibility and take appropriate actions. However, when we recognize that *prev* has been removed or reinserted, we can stop since we know that $b$ must have been removed already as well.

The operation to remove $b$ from the prev list essentially consists of a loop that keeps track of the three mentioned blocks, while trying to find the direct predecessor of $b$. Once that predecessor is found, we try to update its prev pointer in order to remove $b$. There are several conditions that lead to the termination of this loop. In some of these cases we can conclude that $b$ is already removed from *both* lists, in other cases we know that $b$ has been removed from the prev list, but we still need to ensure that it is also removed from the next list.

In case we could not conclude that $b$ is already removed from both lists, we still have to remove it from the next list. The operation to remove $b$ from the next list is quite similar; It also keeps track of the same three pointers, where the initial values for *prev* and *next* are those that were returned by the previous operation that removed the block from the prev list. This allows us to continue from where we left, reducing the amount of work to find the blocks we need to update in many cases.

In this method we have to set *next* to the last unmarked block with a stamp greater than *b*'s `stamp`, and *prev* to the first unmarked block with a stamp less or equal to *b*'s `stamp` (both in the `prev` direction), i.e., the two blocks that would be the predecessor and successor of *b* if *b* would still be part of the `prev` list. This entails that *next*'s `prev` pointer must reference *prev*. Once we have found these blocks, we can attempt a CAS to update *prev*'s `next` pointer in order to finish removal of *b* from the `next` list. If the CAS succeeds, we have successfully removed *b*. However, we still have to make sure that the *prev* block has not been marked in the meantime. If this is the case, we have to continue and help remove *prev* from both lists in order to maintain the previously described condition, which lets us conclude that a block has been fully removed if we recognized that the successor block has been fully removed.

### 3.3 Correctness and Progress Conditions

We now state and briefly argue for the main properties of Stamp-it.

PROPOSITION 1. *Stamp-it is* reclamation safe*: A node is reclaimed only when it is referenced by no thread.*

Assume that some thread retires (want to reclaim) some node *n*. It fetches the currently highest stamp from the data structure, stores this stamp value in *n* and adds *n* to its local retire-list. Now, *n* can safely be reclaimed once all threads that were in a critical region at the time *n* was removed have left their respective critical regions. The lowest stamp in the data structure is smaller than or equal to the stamp of the last thread, so *n*'s stamp being less than this lowest stamp implies that all threads currently inside critical regions (if any) have entered their respective critical region *after n* was retired, and therefore *n* can safely be reclaimed (no references).

PROPOSITION 2. *Stamp-it reclaims any node in amortized constant time in the number of data structure operations.*

Assume that $q$ threads are inside critical regions, when thread $T_1$ is leaving its critical region and thus removing itself from the data structure. All nodes in $T_1$'s local retire-list can be reclaimed once these $q$ threads have left their critical regions. Thread $T_1$ can possibly add its local retire-list as sublist to the global retire-list, deferring reclamation of its nodes to the *last* thread to leave its critical region. The global retire-list is traversed only when this last thread removes itself from the data structure. In the worst case, the $q$ threads remove themselves in the same order as they have entered their critical regions, resulting in $q$ traversals of the global retire-list. We can therefore achieve amortized constant time by only adding local retire-lists that hold more than $q$ nodes (threshold); the sublist might be touched up to $q$ times to reclaim at least $q$ nodes.

PROPOSITION 3. *Stamp-it is* lock-less*, and all methods used for entering and leaving critical regions (*`push`, `remove`*), and all helper functions are lock-free. If threads do not conflict, the expected average runtime of the operations is constant.*

For the Stamp Pool operations lock-freeness was argued above; for full details we refer to [5]. Stamp-it is, however, reclamation-blocking in the sense that a stalled thread can prevent an unbounded number of nodes from being reclaimed. The term for this is to say that Stamp-it is a *lock-less* reclamation scheme.

PROPOSITION 4. *The implementation is correct under the C++ memory model.*

All atomic operations are relaxed as far as possible without sacrificing correctness with the appropriate C++ memory model annotations. For the detailed arguments, we refer to [5] which also contains full C++ implementations of the six other schemes chosen for comparison.

## 4 CONCLUDING REMARKS

This brief announcement explained *Stamp-it*, a new, lock-less, general, portable memory reclamation scheme with attractive features. To the best of our knowledge, it is the first non-reference counting based scheme that does not have to scan all other threads to determine reclaimability of a node. Stamp-it has been implemented in C++ using the C++ memory-model, and experimentally evaluated against six other, comparable, general and portable schemes (LFRC [11], HPR [4], ER [2], NER [3], QSR, DEBRA [1]), all (re)implemented portably in a similar fashion using the standardized C++ interface proposed by Robison [9]. Full source code is available at https://github.com/mpoeter/emr. Our empirical results show that Stamp-it matches or outperforms the other analyzed reclamation schemes in almost all cases. For the actual results, we have to refer to the technical reports [6, 8].

For future work it would be interesting to look for other data structures that could replace the doubly-linked list with less overhead, while providing all the required properties. We might also try to relax some of these properties (e.g., use a partial order instead of a strict order for the stamps) in order to reduce contention on the Stamp Pool.

## REFERENCES


[1] Trevor Alexander Brown. 2015. Reclaiming Memory for Lock-Free Data Structures: There Has to Be a Better Way. In *Proceedings of the 2015 ACM Symposium on Principles of Distributed Computing (PODC)*. ACM, 261–270.

[2] Keir Fraser. 2004. *Practical lock-freedom.* Ph.D. Dissertation. University of Cambridge Computer Laboratory.

[3] Thomas E. Hart, Paul E. McKenney, Angela Demke Brown, and Jonathan Walpole. 2007. Performance of Memory Reclamation for Lockless Synchronization. *J. Parallel and Distrib. Comput.* 67, 12 (2007), 1270–1285.

[4] Maged M. Michael. 2004. Hazard Pointers: Safe Memory Reclamation for Lock-Free Objects. *IEEE Transactions on Parallel and Distributed Systems* 15, 6 (2004), 491–504.

[5] Manuel Pöter. 2018. *Effective Memory Reclamation for Lock-Free Data Structures in C++.* Master's thesis. TU Wien, Vienna, Austria.

[6] Manuel Pöter and Jesper Larsson Träff. 2017. A new and five older Concurrent Memory Reclamation Schemes in Comparison (Stamp-it). (2017). arXiv:1712.06134.

[7] Manuel Pöter and Jesper Larsson Träff. 2018. POSTER: Stamp-it, Amortized Constant-time Memory Reclamation in Comparison to five other Schemes. In *23rd ACM SIGPLAN Symposium on Principles and Practice of Parallel Programming (PPoPP).* ACM, 413–414.

[8] Manuel Pöter and Jesper Larsson Träff. 2018. Stamp-it: A more Thread-efficient, Concurrent Memory Reclamation Scheme in the C++ Memory Model. (2018).

[9] Arch D. Robison. 2013. Policy-Based Design for Safe Destruction in Concurrent Containers. C++ standards committee paper, http://www.open-std.org/jtc1/sc22/wg21/docs/papers/2013/n3712.pdf. (2013).

[10] Håkan Sundell and Philippas Tsigas. 2008. Lock-free deques and doubly linked lists. *J. Parallel and Distrib. Comput.* 68, 7 (2008), 1008–1020.

[11] John D. Valois. 1995. *Lock-Free Data Structures.* Ph.D. Dissertation. Rensselaer Polytechnic Institute.

# Brief Announcement: Communication in Systems of Home Based Mobile Agents*

Friedhelm Meyer auf der Heide
Paderborn University
Heinz Nixdorf Institute
Paderborn, Germany
fmadh@uni-paderborn.de

Johannes Schaefer
Paderborn University
Heinz Nixdorf Institute
Paderborn, Germany
jschaef@mail.uni-paderborn.de

## ABSTRACT

We consider a scenario where agents have to exchange data in a wireless ad-hoc network, although it is not connected. We assume that each agent has a static home base. To improve connectivity, each agent is allowed to move away from his home base, but only for a limited distance which may be different for different agents. These distances might be dictated by limited batteries of the agents, which forces them to return to their home charging station after a while. An application currently widely considered in literature (and in projects and applications) is disaster management, where helpers are equipped with smartphones to submit important local information to a coordinating station. In case of the network being disconnected, mobile "postmen" are used for long distance connections.

In this paper, we focus on the aspect of "communication by postmen". We model such a scenario by a weighted directed graph. It consists of $n$ (static) nodes describing the home bases of the agents. A directed edge from base $v_i$ to base $v_j$ with weight $w(v_i, v_j)$ indicates that agent $a_i$ can walk from his home base to the home base of $a_j$, which needs time $w(v_i, v_j)$. If agent $a_j$ is at home when agent $a_i$ arrives, they can exchange messages. Alongside with the introduction of the model, we present a randomized distributed algorithm for all-to-all message dissemination and show that its performance is, in many cases, close to optimal.

**ACM Reference Format:**
Friedhelm Meyer auf der Heide and Johannes Schaefer. 2018. Brief Announcement: Communication in Systems of Home Based Mobile Agents. In *SPAA '18: 30th ACM Symposium on Parallelism in Algorithms and Architectures, July 16–18, 2018, Vienna, Austria.* ACM, New York, NY, USA, 3 pages. https://doi.org/10.1145/3210377.3210662

## 1 INTRODUCTION

Consider a scenario of a group of $n$ agents where the telecommunication infrastructure fails, and only ad-hoc communication among the smartphones of the agents is possible. Such scenarios might appear in situations like a blackout or other disaster scenarios. To manage such a disaster, communication among the agents has to be maintained, even if the ad-hoc network given by the agents and their smartphones is not connected. In this case, agents might decide to move small distances away from their homes to carry messages and connect to neighbors, i.e., act as postmen. Such scenarios are currently investigated in several projects and real applications dealing with disaster management.

Inspired by such scenarios, we introduce a model of home based mobile agents: every agent has a home base, neighbors, and short ranged communication capabilities. The agents can move away from their home bases, but these movements come with some cost, typically proportional to the moving distance. Moreover, the maximum distance they are allowed to move away from their home is bounded. Two agents can only exchange information if they are sufficiently close to each other. Their knowledge about the network is limited to a local view, which allows to see the home bases of neighboring agents, but forbids to observe the current positions of these agents. In this paper, we propose a suitable model and present an algorithm for a classic communication task, namely all-to-all message dissemination.

### Related Work

A vast amount of research is done on ad-hoc networks in general, as seen for instance in the recent survey by Conti et al. [1], as well as work specialized in routing messages in inhabited regions, especially as part of Delay Tolerant Networks [12]. Mobile ad-hoc networks are also of high interest for (post-)disaster communication in research [3–5, 7, 9, 11], as well as in practically oriented projects[1]. An important area of interest, for disaster communication as well as infrastructure-less communication in general, is the problem of connecting cut-off network regions by allowing some agents to be mobile, thus being able to connect to such cut-off regions. In a more general setting where all agents may be mobile, the notion of a dynamic diameter was introduced. This dynamic diameter turns out to be well-suited to characterize the time needed for all-to-all message dissemination in mobile ad-hoc networks (see [8]). More application oriented research deals with the efficient positioning of nodes that provide connectivity (e.g., unmanned aerial vehicles [5]), or moving the nodes to make the network strongly connected [2] . In the context of sensor networks there is also the concept of

*This work was partially supported by the Federal Ministry of Education and Research (BMBF) as part of the poject "Resilience by Spontaneous Volunteers Networks for Coping with Emergencies and Disaster" (RESIBES), (grant no 13N13955 to 13N13957), and by the German Research Foundation (DFG) within the Collaborative Research Centre "On-The-Fly Computing" (SFB 901).


*SPAA '18, July 16–18, 2018, Vienna, Austria*

ACM ISBN 978-1-4503-5799-9/18/07.
https://doi.org/10.1145/3210377.3210662

[1] Open source projects e.g. "The Serval Project" (www.servalproject.org), government funded "RESIBES" (http://www.resibes.de), "NICER" (https://www.nicer.tu-darmstadt.de/en/) and "smarter" (http://www.smarter-projekt.de)

data ferries. These are mobile nodes that collect data from static sensor nodes and deliver it to some sink node ([6, 10]).

## 2 MODEL AND RESULTS

In this section, we define our model of systems of home based mobile agents, and present and analyze our algorithm for all-to-all message dissemination in such systems.

### 2.1 Our Model of Systems of Home Based Mobile Agents

Consider a directed, weakly connected graph $G = (V, E)$ with $V = \{v_1, \ldots, v_n\}$. Every directed edge $(v_i, v_j) \in E$ is given a weight $w(v_i, v_j) \in \mathbb{N}$. Each node $v_i \in V$ is the home base of exactly one agent $a_i$. Time is divided into synchronous time steps. In every such time step an agent can either stay at his current position or move along an incident edge. The agent $a_i$ needs $w(v_i, v_j)$ time steps to move from its home $v_i$ to the home $v_j$ of a neighboring agent $a_j$, or back. Agents carry messages. If agent $a_j$ is at his home when $a_i$ arrives there, they exchange their messages. The problem we want to solve in this setting is all-to-all message dissemination: at the beginning of time step zero, every agent is in his home base and holds exactly one message. We aim at minimizing the time needed until every agent holds a copy of every message. In general, we might allow message exchanges whenever agents are close to each other. In the current work we consider the more restricted variant described above. One reason is that our restriction allows agents to switch off their devices during trips to save battery. Furthermore, our lower bounds for the two variants of message exchange only differ by a constant factor.

Algorithms for all-to-all message dissemination have to describe when an agent moves to which of his neighbors. Our algorithm is distributed; decisions are solely based on very limited local knowledge: an agent knows his home base and the weights of all outgoing edges of his home. He can observe whether a neighbor is at home only when he visits that neighbor's home base.

### 2.2 The WaitOrWalk Algorithm

Every agent $a_i$ divides the time into *round trip intervals for $a_i$*. Such an interval has length $R_i$, the *round trip time for $a_i$*. This is the time needed to visit all his neighbors, and to finally go back home. Formally,

$$R_i = 2 \cdot \sum_{j:(v_i, v_j) \in E} w(v_i, v_j).$$

If $v_i$ has no outgoing edges, then $R_i = 1$.

Algorithm WaitOrWalk works as follows:

*Every agent $a_i$ repeats the following: at the beginning of every round trip interval of $a_i$, agent $a_i$ tosses an unbiased coin to decide whether he stays at home during this round trip interval, or visits all his neighbors. If an agent decides to visit his neighbors, he visits them in an arbitrary, but fixed, order. Agents without outbound neighbors always stay at home. If $a_i$ meets a neighbor $a_j$ in his home base, they exchange all their messages.*

In the following we express dissemination times in terms of RTD($G$), the *round trip based diameter of $G$*. This value is closely related to the graph diameter, which is a lower bound for all-to-all message dissemination, as shown in the next section.

RTD($G$) is defined as follows. We define the *round trip based length of a path* $p = (v_{j_0}, v_{j_1}, \ldots, v_{j_k})$ as the sum $\mathrm{RTL}(p) = \sum_{i=0}^{k} R_{j_i}$ of the round trip times of all nodes on that path. For two nodes $v_i$ and $v_j$, we define their *round trip based distance* $\mathrm{RTL}(v_i, v_j)$ as the minimum round trip based length of any path from $v_i$ to $v_j$.

The round trip based diameter of a graph, RTD($G$), is defined as the maximum round trip based distance between any pair of nodes in that graph. Using this notion, we obtain an upper bound on the time for message dissemination with the WaitOrWalk algorithm:

Theorem 2.1. *Algorithm WaitOrWalk solves the all-to-all message dissemination problem on any weakly connected graph $G$ in time $O(\mathrm{RTD}(G) \cdot \log n)$ with high probability*[2].

Proof. We start with the following observation: given two agents $a_i$ and $a_j$ such that there exists an edge $(v_i, v_j)$ between their home bases, consider some round trip interval $I$ for $a_i$. Let $c(I)$ denote the target interval of $I$, i.e., the (unique) roundtrip interval for $a_j$ in which $a_i$ visits the home base of $a_j$ if he decides to perform a round trip in $I$.

Observation 1. *Agents $a_i$ and $a_j$ exchange messages in the home base of $a_j$ in the time interval $c(I)$ with probability at least 1/4.*

The observation is true because the message exchange takes place if and only if $a_i$ decides to perform a roundtrip in $I$, and $a_j$ decides to stay at home in $c(I)$.

Now fix some integer $k$.

If $R_i > R_j$, then consider $k$ consecutive round trip intervals $I_1, \ldots, I_k$ for $a_i$. As the target intervals $c(I_1), \ldots, c(I_k)$ are all different, the $k$ message-exchange events are independent.

If $R_i \leq R_j$, then consider $k$ consecutive round trip intervals $I'_1, \ldots, I'_k$ for $a_j$. Each of them is the target interval for at least one round trip interval for $a_i$. Now we choose one such interval for each $I'_l$, resulting in $k$ independent message-exchange events.

Therefore, by Observation 1, the probability that $a_i$ and $a_j$ do not exchange messages during $k$ consecutive intervals of length $\max(R_i, R_j)$ is at most $(3/4)^k$.

Thus we may conclude:

Lemma 2.2. *The probability that $a_i$ and $a_j$ do not exchange messages in a given time interval of length $c \cdot \max(R_i, R_j) \cdot \log_{4/3} n$ is at most $1/n^c$, where $c > 0$ can be chosen arbitrarily.*

Now we can easily conclude the theorem: Lemma 2.2 yields immediately that, for every path $p$ from $v_i$ to $v_j$ in $G$, $a_j$ knows the initial message of $a_i$ after $2c \cdot RTL(p) \cdot \log_{4/3} n$ steps with probability at least $1 - 1/n^{c-1}$. Applying the union bound to the round trip based distances between all pairs of home bases yields the stated result. □

### 2.3 Performance Evaluation in Terms of Lower Bounds

In classical communication networks, the diameter of the underlying graph is a lower bound for the all-to-all message dissemination

[2]With probability $1 - \frac{1}{n^c}$, for an arbitrary constant $c > 1$ that appears as a factor in the runtime bound.

time. Since the nature of communication in our model allows bidirectional communication by passively being visited, i.e., against the direction of an edge, the all-to-all message dissemination time can be lower than the network diameter. For example, consider a graph with two nodes $v_i$ and $v_j$, and edges $(v_i, v_j)$ and $(v_j, v_i)$ with weights of 1 and 100. The diameter of this graph is 100, while the time needed to exchange messages between the two nodes is only 1 (let $a_i$ visit $v_j$).

Therefore, we consider the undirected version $G^u$ of G. This graph has edges between all pairs $\{v_i, v_j\}$ of nodes that have at least one directed edge connecting them in G. The edge $\{v_i, v_j\}$ in $G^u$ gets as weight the minimum of the weights of the (at most two) edges connecting $v_i$ and $v_j$ in G. It is easy to see:

Observation 2. *The diameter of $G^u$ is a lower bound for the time needed for all-to-all message dissemination in G.*

We can compare path lengths for a path $p$ in $G^u$ (and thus the lower bound for communicating along that path) with RTL($p$) using the following properties of $G$: let

$$\rho = \frac{\max_{(u,v)\in E} w(u,v)}{\min_{(u,v)\in E} w(u,v)}$$

be called the *maximal edge weight ratio*, and let $d$ be the maximal out-degree of any node in $G$. Then we obtain the following relation.

Lemma 2.3. *If a graph G has a maximum degree d and maximum edge weight ratio of $\rho$, then* $\mathrm{RTD}(G) \leq 2 \cdot \mathrm{diam}(G^u) \cdot \rho \cdot d$.

Together with Theorem 2.1 and Observation 2, we obtain the following:

Corollary 2.4. *If G is weakly connected and has a maximum out-degree d and maximum edge weight ratio $\rho$, then Algorithm WaitOrWalk solves the all-to-all message dissemination problem in time $O(\mathrm{diam}(G^u) \cdot \rho \cdot d \cdot \log n)$ with high probability. Thus, its runtime is only by a factor $O(\rho \cdot d \cdot \log n)$ larger than the lower bound.*

Corollary 2.5. *If G is weakly connected, has constant out-degree and uniform weights, then the runtime needed by algorithm WaitOrWalk (with high probability) is only a factor* $\log n$ *worse than the lower bound.*

For lines we can show the asymptotic optimality of the expected time for the case that the edge weights are symmetric, i.e., $w(u, v) = w(v, u)$.

Theorem 2.6. *If G is a line with symmetric edge weights, then algorithm WaitOrWalk solves the all-to-all message dissemination problem in (asymptotically optimal) expected time $O(\mathrm{diam}(G^u))$.*

Proof. The expected time needed for a message to be exchanged between neighboring nodes $v_i$ and $v_{i+1}$ is at most $4 \cdot \max(R_i, R_{i+1})$. This is because a successful message exchange happens in the maximum of the two round trip lengths with a probability of at least 1/4 (compare proof of Theorem 2.1). Due to linearity of expectations the expected time to pass a message along the complete line is $\sum_{i=1}^{n-1} 4 \cdot \max(R_i, R_{i+1})$, which is at most $12 \cdot \sum_{i=1}^{n-1} w(v_i, v_{i+1})$. Since the diameter of the graph is the sum of all edge weights, the theorem follows. □

A result with high probability seems to need an additional factor of $\log n$.

## 3 OUTLOOK

In addition to the all-to-all message dissemination problem, we suggest to analyze other common network tasks such as leader election, or, motivated by the disaster scenario, local data aggregation, where nodes should hold up to date aggregated data about their surroundings. We propose to look into several relaxations of the restrictions of our current model. To name a few:

The setting could be a plane, where every movement is allowed, in opposition to just moving on fixed edges as we allow now. Giving agents the ability to observe their neighborhood enables them to more cooperative behavior. In an extended model the communication could be possible for all agents that have a certain distance to another.

Additionally, the model could be more restricted to be more realistic, for instance by requiring agents to recharge for some time at their home bases after moving for a (limited) distance.

## REFERENCES


[1] Marco Conti and Silvia Giordano. 2014. Mobile ad hoc networking: milestones, challenges, and new research directions. *IEEE Communications Magazine* 52, 1 (2014), 85–96.

[2] Erik D. Demaine, Mohammadtaghi Hajiaghayi, Hamid Mahini, Amin S. Sayedi-Roshkhar, Shayan Oveisgharan, and Morteza Zadimoghaddam. 2009. Minimizing movement. *ACM Transactions on Algorithms* 5, 3 (2009), 1–30.

[3] Marco Di Felice, Luca Bedogni, Angelo Trotta, Luciano Bononi, Fabio Panzieri, Giuseppe Ruggeri, Gianluca Aloi, Valeria Loscri, and Pasquale Pace. 2013. Smartphones like stem cells: Cooperation and evolution for emergency communication in post-disaster scenarios. *Proceedings of the 1st International Black Sea Conference on Communications and Networking* (2013), 28–33.

[4] Marco Di Felice, Angelo Trotta, Luca Bedogni, Luciano Bononi, Fabio Panzieri, Giuseppe Ruggeri, Valeria Loscri, and Pasquale Pace. 2013. STEM-mesh: Self-organizing mobile cognitive radio network for disaster recovery operations. *Proceedings of the 9th International Wireless Communications and Mobile Computing Conference* (2013), 602–608.

[5] Marco Di Felice, Angelo Trotta, Luca Bedogni, Kaushik Roy Chowdhury, and Luciano Bononi. 2014. Self-organizing aerial mesh networks for emergency communication. *Proceedings of the 25th Annual International Symposium on Personal, Indoor, and Mobile Radio Communication* (2014), 1631–1636.

[6] Ting He, Kang-Won Lee, and Ananthram Swami. 2010. Flying in the dark: Controlling autonomous data ferries with partial observations. *Proceedings of the 11th ACM International Symposium on Mobile Ad Hoc Networking and Computing* (2010), 141–150.

[7] Theus Hossmann, Franck Legendre, Paolo Carta, Per Gunningberg, and Christian Rohner. 2011. Twitter in Disaster Mode: Opportunistic Communication and Distribution of Sensor Data in Emergencies. (2011), 1:1–1:6.

[8] Fabian Kuhn and Rotem Oshman. 2011. Dynamic networks: models and algorithms. *ACM SIGACT News* 42, 1 (2011), 82–96.

[9] Quang Minh, Kien Nguyen, Cristian Borcea, and Shigeki Yamada. 2014. On-the-fly establishment of multihop wireless access networks for disaster recovery. *IEEE Communications Magazine* 52, 10 (2014), 60–66.

[10] Rahul C. Shah, Sumit Roy, Sushant Jain, and Waylon Brunette. 2003. Data MULEs: modeling and analysis of a three-tier architecture for sparse sensor networks. *Ad Hoc Networks* 1, 2 (2003), 215 – 233.

[11] Md Yusuf Sarwar Uddin, Hossein Ahmadi, Tarek Abdelzaher, and Robin Kravets. 2013. Intercontact routing for energy constrained disaster response networks. *IEEE Transactions on Mobile Computing* 12, 10 (2013), 1986–1998.

[12] Ying Zhu, Bin Xu, Xinghua Shi, and Yu Wang. 2013. A survey of social-based routing in delay tolerant networks: Positive and negative social effects. *IEEE Communications Surveys and Tutorials* 15, 1 (2013), 387–401.

# Optimal Algorithms for Right-Sizing Data Centers*

Susanne Albers
Technical University of Munich
albers@in.tum.de

Jens Quedenfeld
Technical University of Munich
jens.quedenfeld@in.tum.de

## ABSTRACT

Electricity cost is a dominant and rapidly growing expense in data centers. Unfortunately, much of the consumed energy is wasted because servers are idle for extended periods of time. We study a capacity management problem that dynamically right-sizes a data center, matching the number of active servers with the varying demand for computing capacity. We resort to a data-center optimization problem introduced by Lin, Wierman, Andrew and Thereska [17, 19] that, over a time horizon, minimizes a combined objective function consisting of operating cost, modeled by a sequence of convex functions, and server switching cost. All prior work addresses a continuous setting in which the number of active servers, at any time, may take a fractional value.

In this paper, we investigate for the first time the discrete data-center optimization problem where the number of active servers, at any time, must be integer valued. Thereby we seek truly feasible solutions. First, we show that the offline problem can be solved in polynomial time. Our algorithm relies on a new, yet intuitive graph theoretic model of the optimization problem and performs binary search in a layered graph. Second, we study the online problem and extend the algorithm *Lazy Capacity Provisioning* (LCP) by Lin et al. [17, 19] to the discrete setting. We prove that LCP is 3-competitive. Moreover, we show that no deterministic online algorithm can achieve a competitive ratio smaller than 3. Hence, while LCP does not attain an optimal competitiveness in the continuous setting, it does so in the discrete problem examined here. We prove that the lower bound of 3 also holds in a problem variant with more restricted operating cost functions, introduced by Lin et al. [17].

Finally, we address the continuous setting and give a lower bound of 2 on the best competitiveness of online algorithms. This matches an upper bound by Bansal et al. [5]. A lower bound of 2 was also recently shown by Antoniadis and Schewior [3]. We develop an independent proof that extends to the scenario with more restricted operating cost.

## KEYWORDS

Homogeneous servers; polynomial-time offline algorithm; online algorithm; lower bounds; discrete setting.

*Work supported by the European Research Council, Grant Agreement No. 691672.


ACM ISBN 978-1-4503-5799-9/18/07.
https://doi.org/10.1145/3210377.3210385

**ACM Reference Format:**
Susanne Albers and Jens Quedenfeld. 2018. Optimal Algorithms for Right-Sizing Data Centers. In *SPAA '18: SPAA '18: 30th ACM Symposium on Parallelism in Algorithms and Architectures, July 16–18, 2018, Vienna, Austria.* ACM, New York, NY, USA, 10 pages. https://doi.org/10.1145/3210377.3210385

## 1 INTRODUCTION

Energy conservation in data centers is a major concern for both operators and the environment. In the U.S., about 1.8% of the total electricity consumption is attributed to data centers [22]. In 2015, more than 416 TWh (terawatt hours) were used by the world's data centers, which exceeds the total power consumption in the UK [7]. Electricity cost is a significant expense in data centers [9]; about 18–28% of their budget is invested in power [8, 13]. Remarkably, the servers of a data center are only utilized 20–40% of the time on average [4, 6]. Even worse, when idle and in active mode, they consume about half of their peak power [21]. Hence, a promising approach for energy conservation and capacity management is to transition idle servers into low-power sleep states. However, state transitions, and in particular power-up operations, also incur energy/cost. Therefore, dynamically matching the number of active servers with the varying demand for computing capacity is a challenging optimization problem. In essence, the goal is to right-size a data center over time so as to minimize energy and operation costs.

**Problem Formulation.** We investigate a basic algorithmic problem with the objective of dynamically resizing a data center. Specifically, we resort to a framework that was introduced by Lin, Wierman, Andrew and Thereska [17, 19] and further explored, for instance, in [1–3, 5, 18, 20, 23].

Consider a data center with $m$ homogeneous servers, each of which has an active state and a sleep state. An optimization is performed over a discrete, finite time horizon consisting of time steps $t = 1, \ldots, T$. At any time $t$, $1 \leq t \leq T$, a non-negative convex cost function $f_t(\cdot)$ models the operating cost of the data center. More precisely, $f_t(x_t)$ is the incurred cost if $x_t$ servers are in the active state at time $t$, where $0 \leq x_t \leq m$. This operating cost captures, e.g., energy cost and service delay, for an incoming workload, depending on the number of active servers. Furthermore, at any time $t$ there is a switching cost, taking into account that the data center may be resized by changing the number of active servers. This switching cost is equal to $\beta(x_t - x_{t-1})^+$, where $\beta$ is a positive real constant and $(x)^+ = \max(0, x)$. Here we assume that transition cost is incurred when servers are powered up from the sleep state to the active state. A cost of powering down servers may be folded into this cost. The constant $\beta$ incorporates, e.g., the energy needed to transition a server from the sleep state to the active state, as well as delays resulting from a migration of data and connections. We assume that at the beginning and at the end of the time horizon all servers are in the sleep state, i.e. $x_0 = x_{T+1} = 0$. The goal is to determine a vector $X = (x_1, \ldots, x_T)$ called *schedule*, specifying at any time the number of active servers, that minimizes

$$\sum_{t=1}^{T} f_t(x_t) + \beta \sum_{t=1}^{T} (x_t - x_{t-1})^+. \quad (1)$$

In the offline version of this data-center optimization problem, the convex functions $f_t$, $1 \le t \le T$, are known in advance. In the online version, the $f_t$ arrive over time. At time $t$, function $f_t$ is presented. Recall that the operating cost at time $t$ depends for instance on the incoming workload, which becomes known only at time $t$.

All previous work on the data-center optimization problem assumes that the server numbers $x_t$, $1 \le t \le T$, may take fractional values. That is, $x_t$ may be an arbitrary real number in the range $[0, m]$. From a practical point of view this is acceptable because a data center has a large number of machines. Nonetheless, from an algorithmic and optimization perspective, the proposed algorithms do not compute feasible solutions. Important questions remain if the $x_t$ are indeed integer valued: (1) Can optimal solutions be computed in polynomial time? (2) What is the best competitive ratio achievable by online algorithms? In this paper, we present the first study of the data-center optimization problem assuming that the $x_t$ take integer values and, in particular, settle questions (1) and (2).

**Previous Work.** As indicated above, all prior work on the data-center optimization problem assumes that the $x_t$, $1 \le t \le T$, may take fractional values in $[0, m]$. First, Lin et al. [19] consider the offline problem. They develop an algorithm based on a convex program that computes optimal solutions. Second, Lin et al. [19] study the online problem. They devise a deterministic algorithm called *Lazy Capacity Provisioning (LCP)* and prove that it achieves a competitive ratio of exactly 3. Algorithm LCP, at any time $t$, computes a lower bound and an upper bound on the number of active servers by considering two scenarios in which the switching cost $\beta$ is charged, either when a server is powered up or when it is powered down. The LCP algorithm lazily stays within these two bounds. The tight bound of 3 on the competitiveness of LCP also holds if the algorithm has a finite prediction window $w$, i.e. a time $t$ it knows the current as well as the next $w$ arriving functions $f_t, \ldots, f_{t+w}$. Furthermore, Lin et al. [19] perform an experimental study with two real-world traces evaluating the savings resulting from right-sizing in data centers.

Bansal et al. [5] presented a 2-competitive online algorithm and showed that no deterministic or randomized online strategy can attain a competitiveness smaller than 1.86. Recently, Antoniadis and Schewior [3] improved the lower bound to 2. Bansal et al. [5] also gave a 3-competitive memoryless algorithm and showed that this is the best competitive factor achievable by a deterministic memoryless algorithm. The data-center optimization problem is an online convex optimization problem with switching costs. Andrew et al. [1] showed that there is an algorithm with sublinear regret but that $O(1)$-competitiveness and sublinear regret cannot be achieved simultaneously. Antoniadis et al. [2] examine generalized online convex optimization, where the values $x_t$ selected by an algorithm may be points in a metric space, and relate it to convex body chasing.

Further work on energy conservation in data center includes, for instance, [14, 15]. Khuller et al. [14] introduce a machine activation problem. There exists an activation cost budget and jobs have to be scheduled on the selected, activated machines so as to minimize the makespan. They present algorithms that simultaneously approximate the budget and the makespan. A second paper by Li and Khuller [15] considers a generalization where the activation cost of a machine is a non-decreasing function of the load. In the more applied computer science literature, power management strategies and the value of sleep states have been studied extensively. The papers focus mostly on experimental evaluations. Articles that also present analytic results include [10–12].

**Our Contribution.** We conduct the first investigation of the *discrete* data-center optimization problem, where the values $x_t$, specifying the number of active servers at any time $t \in \{1, \ldots, T\}$, must be integer valued. Thereby, we seek truly feasible solutions.

First, in Section 2 we study the offline algorithm. We show that optimal solutions can be computed in polynomial time. Our algorithm is different from the convex optimization approach by Lin et al. [19]. We propose a new, yet natural graph-based representation of the discrete data-center optimization problem. We construct a grid-structured graph containing a vertex $v_{t,j}$, for each $t \in \{1, \ldots, T\}$ and $j \in \{0, \ldots, m\}$. Edges represent right-sizing operations, i.e. changes in the number of active servers, and are labeled with operating and switching costs. An optimal solution could be determined by a shortest path computation. However, the resulting algorithm would have a pseudo-polynomial running time. Instead, we devise an algorithm that improves solutions iteratively using binary search. In each iteration the algorithm uses only a constant number of graph layers. The resulting running time is $O(T \log m)$.

The remaining paper focuses on the online problem and develops tight bounds on the competitiveness. In Section 3 we adapt the LCP algorithm by Lin et al. [19] to the discrete data-center optimization problem. We prove that LCP is 3-competitive, as in the continuous setting. We remark that our analysis is different from that by Lin et al. [19]. Specifically, our analysis resorts to the discrete structure of the problem and identifies respective properties. The analysis by Lin et al. [19] relates to their convex optimization approach that characterizes optimal solutions in the continuous setting.

In Section 4 we devise lower bounds. We prove that no deterministic online algorithm can obtain a competitive ratio smaller than 3. Hence, LCP achieves an optimal competitive factor. Interestingly, while LCP does not attain an optimal competitiveness in the continuous data-center optimization problem (where the $x_t$ may take fractional values), it does so in the discrete problem. We prove that the lower bound of 3 on the best possible competitive ratio also holds for a more restricted setting, originally introduced by Lin et al. [17] in the conference publication of their paper. Specifically, the problem is to find a vector $X = (x_1, \ldots, x_T)$ that minimizes

$$\sum_{t=1}^{T} x_t f(\lambda_t / x_t) + \beta \sum_{t=1}^{T} (x_t - x_{t-1})^+, \quad (2)$$

subject to $x_t \ge \lambda_t$, for $t \in \{1, \ldots, T\}$. Here $\lambda_t$ is the incoming workload at time $t$ and $f(z)$ is a non-negative convex function representing the operating cost of a single server running with load $z \in [0, 1]$. Since $f$ is convex, it is optimal to distribute the jobs equally to all active servers, so that the operating cost at time $t$ is $x_t f(\lambda_t / x_t)$. This problem setting is more restricted in that there is only a single function $f$ modeling operating cost over the

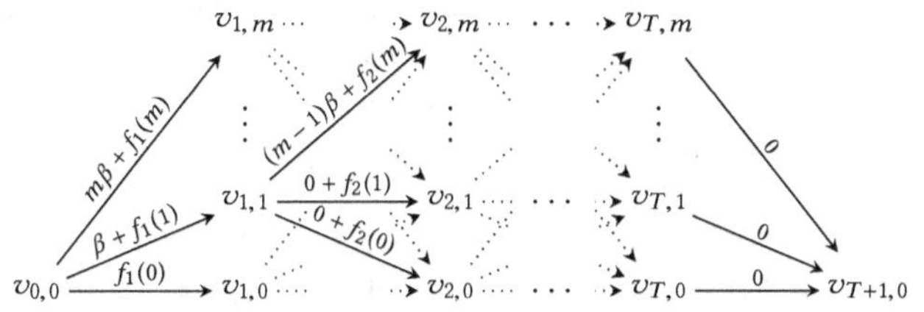


**Figure 1: Construction of the graph.**

time horizon. Nonetheless it is well motivated by real data center environments.

Furthermore, in Section 4 we address the continuous data-center optimization problem and prove that no deterministic online algorithm can achieve a competitive ratio smaller than 2. The same result was shown by Antoniadis and Schewior [3]. We develop an independent proof that can again be extended to the more restricted optimization problem stated in (2), i.e. the lower bound of 2 on the best competitiveness holds in this setting as well.

Finally, in Section 4 we analyze online algorithms with a finite prediction window, i.e. at time $t$ an online algorithm knows the current as well as the next $w$ arriving functions $f_t, \dots, f_{t+w}$. We show that all our lower bounds, for both settings (continuous and discrete) and both models (general and restricted), still hold.

## 2 AN OPTIMAL OFFLINE ALGORITHM

In this section we study the offline version of the discrete data-center optimization problem. We develop an algorithm that computes optimal solutions in $O(T \log m)$ time.

### 2.1 Graph-based approach

Our algorithm works with an underlying directed, weighted graph $G = (V, E)$ that we describe first. Let $[k] := \{1, 2, \dots, k\}$ and $[k]_0 := \{0, 1, \dots, k\}$ with $k \in \mathbb{N}$. For each $t \in [T]$ and each $j \in [m]_0$, there is a vertex $v_{t,j}$, representing the state that exactly $j$ servers are active at time $t$. Furthermore, there are two vertices $v_{0,0}$ and $v_{T+1,0}$ for the initial and final states $x_0 = 0$ and $x_{T+1} = 0$. For each $t \in \{2, \dots, T\}$ and each pair $j, j' \in [m]_0$, there is a directed edge from $v_{t-1,j}$ to $v_{t,j'}$ having weight $\beta(j'-j)^+ + f_t(j')$. This edge weight corresponds to the switching cost when changing the number of servers between time $t-1$ and $t$ and to the operating cost incurred at time $t$. Similarly, for $t = 1$ and each $j' \in [m]_0$, there is a directed edge from $v_{0,0}$ to $v_{1,j'}$ with weight $f_1(j') + \beta(j')^+$. Finally, for $t = T$ and each $j \in [m]_0$, there is a directed edge from $v_{T,j}$ to $v_{T+1,0}$ of weight 0. The structure of $G$ is depicted in Figure 1.

In the following, for each $j \in [m]_0$, vertex set $R_j = \{v_{t,j} \mid t \in [T]\}$ is called *row* $j$. For each $t \in [T]$, vertex set $C_t = \{v_{t,j} \mid j \in [m]_0\}$ is called *column* $t$.

A path between $v_0$ and $v_{T+1}$ represents a schedule. If the path visits $v_{t,j}$, then $x_t = j$ servers are active at time $t$. Note that a path visits exactly one vertex in each column $C_t$, $1 \le t \le T$, because the directed edges connect adjacent columns. The total length (weight) of a path is equal to the cost of the corresponding schedule. An optimal schedule can be determined using a shortest path computation, which takes $O(Tm)$ time in the particular graph $G$. However, this running time is not polynomial because the encoding length of an input instance is linear in $T$ and $\log m$, in addition to the encoding of the functions $f_t$.

In the following, we present a polynomial time algorithm that improves an initial schedule iteratively using binary search. In each iteration the algorithm constructs and uses only a constant number of rows of $G$.

### 2.2 Polynomial time algorithm

An instance of the data-center optimization problem is defined by the tuple $\mathcal{P} = (T, m, \beta, F)$ with $F = (f_1, \dots, f_T)$. We assume that $m$ is a power of two. If this is not the case we can transform the given problem instance $\mathcal{P} = (T, m, \beta, F)$ to $\mathcal{P}' = (T, m', \beta, F')$ with $m' = 2^{\lceil \log m \rceil}$ and

$$f'_t(x) = \begin{cases} f_t(x) & x \le m \\ x \cdot (f_t(m) + \epsilon) & \text{otherwise} \end{cases}$$

with $\epsilon > 0$. The term $x \cdot f_t(m)$ ensures that $f'_t(x)$ is a convex function, since the greatest slope of $f_t$ is $f_t(m) - f_t(m-1) \le f_t(m)$. The inequality holds because $f_t(x) \ge 0$ for all $x \in [m]_0$. The additional term $x \cdot \epsilon$ ensures that it is adverse to use a state $x > m$, because the cost of $f_t(m)$ is always smaller.

Our algorithm uses $\log m - 1$ iterations denoted reversely by $k = K := \log m - 2$ for the first iteration and $k = 0$ for the last iteration. The states used in iteration $k$ are always multiples of $2^k$. For the first iteration we use the rows $R_0, R_{m/4}, R_{m/2}, R_{3m/4}, R_m$, so that the graph of the first iteration contains the vertices

$$V^K := \{v_{0,0}, v_{T+1,0}\} \cup \left\{v_{t,\xi \cdot m/4} \mid t \in [T], \xi \in \{0, 1, 2, 3, 4\}\right\}.$$

The optimal schedule for this simplified problem instance can be calculated in $O(T)$ time, since each column contains only five states. Given an optimal schedule $\hat{X}^k = (\hat{x}^k_1, \dots, \hat{x}^k_T)$ of iteration $k$, let

$$V^{k-1}_t := \left\{\hat{x}^k_t + \xi \cdot 2^{k-1} \mid \xi \in \{-2, -1, 0, 1, 2\}\right\} \cap [m]_0$$

be the states used in the $t$-th column of the next iteration $k-1$. Thus the iteration $k-1$ uses the vertex set

$$V^{k-1} := \{v_{0,0}, v_{T+1,0}\} \cup \left\{v_{t,j} \mid t \in [T], j \in V^{k-1}_t\right\}.$$

Note that the states with $\xi \in \{-2, 0, 2\}$ were already used in iteration $k$ and we just insert the intermediate states $\xi = -1$ and $\xi = 1$. If $\hat{x}^k_t = 0$ (or $\hat{x}^k_t = m$), then $\xi \in \{-2, -1\}$ (or $\xi \in \{1, 2\}$) leads to negative states (or to states larger than $m$), thus the set $V^{k-1}_t$ is cut with $[m]_0$ to ensure that we only use valid states.

The last iteration ($k = 0$) provides an optimal schedule for the original problem instance as shown in the next section. The runtime of the algorithm is $O(T \cdot \log m)$ and thus polynomial.

### 2.3 Correctness

To prove the correctness of the algorithm described in the previous section we have to introduce some definitions:

Given the original problem instance $\mathcal{P} = (T, m, \beta, F)$, we define $\mathcal{P}_k$ (with $k \in [K]_0 := [\log m - 2]_0$) as the data-center optimization problem where we are only allowed to use the states that are multiples of $2^k$. Let $M_k := \{n \in [m]_0 \mid n \bmod 2^k = 0\}$, so $X$ is a feasible schedule for $\mathcal{P}_k$ if $x_t \in M_k$ holds for all $t \in [T]$. To express $\mathcal{P}_k$ as a tuple, we need another tuple element called $M$ which describes the allowed states, i.e. $x_t \in M$ for all $t \in [T]$. The original problem instance can be written as $\mathcal{P} = (T, m, \beta, F, [m]_0)$ and $\mathcal{P}_k = (T, m, \beta, F, M_k)$. Note that $\mathcal{P}_0 = \mathcal{P}$. Let $\hat{X}^k = (\hat{x}_1^k, \dots, \hat{x}_T^k)$ denote an optimal schedule for $\mathcal{P}_k$. In general, for any given problem instance $Q = (T, m, \beta, F, M)$, let $\Phi_k(Q) := (T, m, \beta, F, M \cap \{i \cdot 2^k \mid i \in \mathbb{N}\})$, so $\Phi_k(\mathcal{P}) = \mathcal{P}_k$.

Instead of using only states that are multiple of $2^k$ we can also scale a given problem instance $Q = (T, m, \beta, F, M)$ as follows. Let

$$\Psi_l(Q) := (T, m/2^l, \beta \cdot 2^l, F', M')$$

with $M' := \{x/2^l \mid x \in M\}$, $F' = (f_1', \dots, f_T')$ and $f'(x)_t := f_t(x \cdot 2^l)$. Given a schedule $X = (x_1, \dots, x_T)$ for $Q$ with cost $C^Q(X)$, the corresponding schedule $X' = (x_1/2^l, \dots, x_T/2^l)$ for $\Psi_l(Q)$ has exactly the same cost, i.e. $C^Q(X) = C^{\Psi_l(Q)}(X')$. Note that the problem instance $\Psi_k(\mathcal{P}_k)$ uses all integral states less than or equal to $m/2^l$, so there are no gaps.

Furthermore, we introduce a continuous version of any given problem instance $Q$ where fractional schedules are allowed. Let $\bar{Q} = (T, m, \beta, \bar{F}, [0, m])$ with $\bar{F} = (\bar{f}_1, \dots, \bar{f}_T)$ be the continuous extension of the problem instance $Q = (T, m, \beta, F, M)$, where $x_t \in [0, m]$, $\bar{f}_t : [0, m] \to \mathbb{R}_{\geq 0}$ and

$$\bar{f}_t(x) := \begin{cases} f_t(x) & \text{if } x \in M \\ (\lceil x \rceil - x) f_t(\lfloor x \rfloor) + (x - \lfloor x \rfloor) f_t(\lceil x \rceil) & \text{else.} \end{cases}$$

The operating cost of the fractional states is linearly interpolated, thus $\bar{f}_t$ is convex for all $t \in [T]$. Let $X^* = (x_1^*, \dots, x_T^*) \in [0, m]^T$ be an optimal schedule for $\bar{\mathcal{P}}$.

The set of all optimal schedules for a given problem instance $Q$ is denoted by $\Omega(Q)$. Let $C^Q_{[a,b]}(X) := \sum_{t=a}^b f_t(x_t) + \sum_{t=a+1}^b \beta(x_t - x_{t-1})^+$ be the cost during the time interval $\{a, a+1, \dots, b\}$. We define $f_0(x) := 0$, so $C^Q_{[0,T]}(X) = C^Q(X)$.

Now, we are able to prove the correctness of our algorithm. We begin with a simple lemma showing the relationship between the functions $\Phi$ and $\Psi$.

Lemma 2.1. *The problem instances $\Phi_{k-l}(\Psi_l(\mathcal{P}_l))$ and $\Psi_l(\mathcal{P}_k)$ are equivalent.*

The lemma can be proven by simple calculations using the definitions of $\Phi$ and $\Psi$ as shown in the full version of this paper. The next technical lemma will be needed later. Informally, it demonstrates that optimal solutions of the reduced discrete problem and the above continuous problem behave similarly.

Lemma 2.2. *Let $Y \in \Omega(\mathcal{P}_k)$ be an optimal schedule for $\mathcal{P}_k$ with $k \in [K]_0$. There exists an optimal solution $X^* \in \Omega(\bar{\mathcal{P}})$ such that*

$$(y_t - y_{t-1}) \cdot (x_t^* - x_{t-1}^*) \geq 0 \tag{3}$$

*holds for all $t \in [T]$ with $|y_t - x_t^*| \geq 2^k$ or $|y_{t-1} - x_{t-1}^*| \geq 2^k$.*

The proof (see full paper) consists of a careful case distinction according to the relations of $y_{t-1}, y_t, x_{t-1}$ and $x_t$. By using this lemma, we can show that an optimal solution for a discrete problem instance $\mathcal{P}_k$ cannot be very far from an optimal solution of the continuous problem instance $\bar{\mathcal{P}}$.

Lemma 2.3. *Let $\hat{X}^k \in \Omega(\mathcal{P}_k)$ be an arbitrary optimal schedule for $\mathcal{P}_k$ with $k \in [K]_0$. There exists an optimal schedule $X^* \in \Omega(\bar{\mathcal{P}})$ for $\bar{\mathcal{P}}$ such that $|\hat{x}_t^k - x_t^*| < 2^k$ holds for all $t \in [T]$. Formally,*

$$\forall k \in [K]_0 : \forall \hat{X}^k \in \Omega(\mathcal{P}_k) : \exists X^* \in \Omega(\bar{\mathcal{P}}) : \forall t \in [T] : |\hat{x}_t^k - x_t^*| < 2^k.$$

Proof. To get a contradiction, we assume that there exists a $\hat{X}^k \in \Omega(\mathcal{P}_k)$ with $k \in [K]_0$ such that for all optimal schedules $X^* \in \Omega(\bar{\mathcal{P}})$ there is at least one $t \in [T]$ with $|\hat{x}_t^k - x_t^*| \geq 2^k$. Let $X^* \in \Omega(\bar{\mathcal{P}})$ be arbitrary. Given the schedule $\hat{X}^k$, let $J_1, \dots, J_l \subseteq [T]$ be the inclusion maximal time intervals such that $|\hat{x}_t^k - x_t^*| \geq 2^k$ holds for all $t \in J_j$ and the sign of $\hat{x}_t^k - x_t^*$ remains the same during $J_j$. The set of all $J_j$ with $j \in [l]$ is denoted by $\mathcal{J}$. If $\mathcal{J}$ is empty, then the condition $|\hat{x}_t^k - x_t^*| < 2^k$ is fulfilled for all $t \in [T]$. We divide $\mathcal{J}$ into the disjunct sets $\mathcal{J}^+$ and $\mathcal{J}^-$ such that $\mathcal{J}^+$ contains the intervals where $\hat{x}_t^k - x_t^*$ is positive and $\mathcal{J}^-$ the others.

Given a schedule $X$, the corresponding interval set is denoted by $\mathcal{J}(X)$, the set of all time slots by $S(X) := \{t \in J \mid J \in \mathcal{J}(X)\}$, and the number of time slots in $\mathcal{J}$ by $L(X) := |S(\mathcal{J}(X))| = \sum_{J \in \mathcal{J}} |J|$.

We will use a recursive transformation $\phi$ that reduces $L(X)$ at least by one for each step, while the cost of $X$ is not increased. Formally, we have to show that $L(\phi(X)) \leq L(X) - 1$ and $C^{\bar{\mathcal{P}}}(\phi(X)) \leq C^{\bar{\mathcal{P}}}(X)$ holds. The first inequality ensures that the recursive procedure will terminate. The transformation described below will produce fractional schedules, however for each $t \in [T] \setminus S(X)$ it is ensured that $x_t \in M_k$. Therefore, if $L(X) = 0$, the corresponding schedule fulfills $|x_t - x_t^*| < 2^k$ and $x_t \in M_k$ for all $t \in [T]$.

To describe the transformation, we will use the following notation: A given schedule $Y = (y_1, \dots, y_T)$ with $L(Y) > 0$ is transformed to $Z = \phi(Y) = (z_1, \dots, z_T)$.

Let $J := (t_i + 1, \dots, t_{i+1} - 1) \in \mathcal{J}(Y)$. We differ between two cases, in case 1 we handle the intervals in $\mathcal{J}^+$, i.e. $y_t > x_t^* + 2^k$ holds for all $t \in J$ and in case 2 we handle the intervals in $\mathcal{J}^-$, i.e. $y_t < x_t^* - 2^k$. We will handle case 1 first.

Let $\lceil x \rceil_n := n \cdot \lceil x/n \rceil$ with $x \in \mathbb{R}$ and $n \in \mathbb{N}$ be the smallest value that is divisible by $n$ and greater than or equal to $x$. The schedule $Y$ is transformed to $Z$ with

$$z_t := \begin{cases} y_t & \text{if } t \notin J \\ \lambda \cdot y_t + (1 - \lambda) \cdot x_t^* & \text{if } t \in J \end{cases}$$

where $\lambda \in [0, 1]$ is as small as possible such that $z_t \geq \lceil x_t^* \rceil_{2^k}$ holds for all $t \in J$, so at least one time slot $t_= \in J$ satisfies this condition with equality. This transformation ensures that $L(Z) \leq L(Y) - 1$ holds, because the interval $J$ is split into at least two intervals and one time slot ($t_=$) between them that fulfills $|z_{t_=} - x_{t_=}^*| < 2^k$.

We still have to show that the total cost is not increased by this operation. The total cost can be written as

$$\begin{aligned} C^{\bar{\mathcal{P}}}(X) = {} & C^{\bar{\mathcal{P}}}_{[0,t_i]}(X) + \beta(x_{t_i+1} - x_{t_i})^+ + C^{\bar{\mathcal{P}}}_{[t_i+1, t_{i+1}-1]}(X) \\ & + \beta(x_{t_{i+1}} - x_{t_{i+1}-1})^+ + C^{\bar{\mathcal{P}}}_{[t_{i+1}, T]}(X). \end{aligned} \tag{4}$$

We have $C^{\bar{\mathcal{P}}}_{[0,t_i]}(Y) = C^{\bar{\mathcal{P}}}_{[0,t_i]}(Z)$ and $C^{\bar{\mathcal{P}}}_{[t_{i+1},T]}(Y) = C^{\bar{\mathcal{P}}}_{[t_{i+1},T]}(Z)$.

Consider the time slot $t_i$. By the definition of the interval $J$, the condition $|y_{t_i+1} - x_{t_i+1}^*| \geq 2^k$ is fulfilled. Thus we can apply Lemma 2.2 which says that the terms $(y_{t_i+1} - y_{t_i})$ and $(x_{t_i+1}^* - x_{t_i}^*)$ are both either non-negative or non-positive, so in Equation (4) the term $\beta(x_{t_i+1} - x_{t_i})^+$ can be replaced by $\beta(x_{t_i+1} - x_{t_i})$ or zero, respectively. Analogously, for the time slot $t_{i+1}$, the condition $|y_{t_{i+1}-1} - x^*_{t_{i+1}-1}| \geq 2^k$ is fulfilled, so by Lemma 2.2 the term $\beta(x_{t_{i+1}} - x_{t_{i+1}-1})^+$ in Equation (4) can be replaced by $\beta(x_{t_{i+1}} - x_{t_{i+1}-1})$ or zero. In the former cases, the cost function is

$$C^{\bar{\mathcal{P}}}(X) = C^{\bar{\mathcal{P}}}_{[0,t_i]}(X) + \beta x_{t_i+1} - \beta x_{t_i} + C^{\bar{\mathcal{P}}}_{[t_i+1,t_{i+1}-1]}(X) + \beta x_{t_{i+1}} - \beta x_{t_{i+1}-1} + C^{\bar{\mathcal{P}}}_{[t_{i+1},T]}(X).$$

Given a schedule $X = (x_1, \ldots, x_t)$, we define $X_{[a,b]} := (x_a, \ldots, x_b)$ and $X_J = X_{[t_i+1,t_{i+1}-1]}$. Since there is no summand that contains both $x_{t_i}$ and $x_{t_i+1}$, the function

$$D_{X^*}((x'_{t_i+1}, \ldots, x'_{t_{i+1}-1})) := C^{\bar{\mathcal{P}}}_{[0,t_i]}(X^*) - \beta x^*_{t_i} + \beta x'_{t_i+1} + C^{\bar{\mathcal{P}}}_{[t_i+1,t_{i+1}-1]}(X') + \beta x'_{t_{i+1}} - \beta x^*_{t_{i+1}-1} + C^{\bar{\mathcal{P}}}_{[t_{i+1},T]}(X^*)$$

with $x'_{t_i+1} \geq x^*_{t_i+1}$ and $x'_{t_{i+1}-1} \geq x^*_{t_{i+1}-1}$ is convex and has a minimum at $X^{\min}_J := (x^*_{t_i+1}, \ldots, x^*_{t_{i+1}-1})$.

Due to convexity, $D_{X^*}(Y_J) \geq D_{X^*}(Z_J) \geq D_{X^*}(X^{\min}_J)$, because $Z_J = \lambda Y_J + (1-\lambda)X^{\min}_J$. Therefore $C^{\bar{\mathcal{P}}}(Z) \leq C^{\bar{\mathcal{P}}}(Y)$ holds. If $\beta(x_{t_i+1} - x_{t_i})^+ = 0$ or $\beta(x_{t_{i+1}} - x_{t_{i+1}-1})^+ = 0$ we can use the same argument.

We still have to handle the second case, i.e. $y_t < x^*_t$. The proof works almost analogously, the difference is that we choose $\lambda$ as small as possible such that $z_t \leq \lfloor x^*_t \rfloor_{2^k}$ (where $\lfloor x \rfloor_n := n \cdot \lfloor x/n \rfloor$). Then we have a time slot $t_=$ with $z_{t_=} = \lfloor x^*_{t_=} \rfloor_{2^k}$, so $L(Z) \leq L(Y) - 1$. The proof that shows $C^{\bar{\mathcal{P}}}(Z) \leq C^{\bar{\mathcal{P}}}(Y)$ holds for both cases.

We use the transformation $\phi$ until $L(Z) = 0$. Then $\mathcal{J}(Z)$ is empty, so all states of $Z$ are multiples of $2^k$, i.e. $z_t \in M_k$ for all $t \in [T]$. Since $\hat{X}^k$ was defined to be optimal, $C^{\bar{\mathcal{P}}}(\hat{X}^k) = C^{\bar{\mathcal{P}}}(Z)$ holds. By our assumption, $Z \neq \hat{X}^k$ holds (because otherwise $|\hat{x}^k_t - x^*_t| < 2^k$ would be fulfilled for all $t \in [T]$), so there was a transformation with $\lambda < 1$. Thus we moved towards the optimal schedule, however by $C^{\bar{\mathcal{P}}}(\hat{X}^k) = C^{\bar{\mathcal{P}}}(Z)$, the cost does not change. As $D_{X^*}(X')$ is a convex function, $C^{\bar{\mathcal{P}}}(\hat{X}^k) = C^{\bar{\mathcal{P}}}(Z)$ implies that $C^{\bar{\mathcal{P}}}(Z) = C^{\bar{\mathcal{P}}}(X^*)$, because $X^*$ minimizes $C^{\bar{\mathcal{P}}}$. In this case $\hat{X}^k$ is also optimal for $\bar{\mathcal{P}}$, so the condition $|\hat{x}^k_t - x^*_t| < 2^k$ is already fulfilled.

In all cases we get a contradiction, so our assumption was wrong and the lemma is proven. □

The next lemma shows how an optimal fractional schedule can be rounded to an integral schedule such that it is still optimal.

Lemma 2.4. *Let $X^* \in \Omega(\bar{\mathcal{P}})$. The schedules $\lfloor X^* \rfloor := (\lfloor x^*_1 \rfloor, \ldots, \lfloor x^*_T \rfloor)$ and $\lceil X^* \rceil := (\lceil x^*_1 \rceil, \ldots, \lceil x^*_T \rceil)$ are optimal too, i.e. $\lfloor X^* \rfloor, \lceil X^* \rceil \in \Omega(\bar{\mathcal{P}})$.*

Proof. Let $X^* \in \Omega(\bar{\mathcal{P}})$ be arbitrary. Let $\mathcal{I}(X^*) = \{I_1, \ldots, I_l\}$ be the set of time intervals such that for each $I_i := \{a_i, a_i + 1, \ldots, b_i\}$ with $i \in [l]$ the following conditions are fulfilled

(1) All states of $X^*$ have the same value during $I_i$, i.e. $x^*_t = v_i$ for all $t \in I_i$.
(2) The value is fractional, i.e. $v_i \notin \mathbb{N}$.
(3) Each $I_i$ is inclusion maximal, i.e. $x^*_{a_i-1} \neq v_i$ and $x^*_{b_i+1} \neq v_i$.
(4) The intervals are sorted, i.e. $b_i < a_{i+1}$ for all $i \in [l-1]$.

If $\mathcal{I}(X^*) = \emptyset$, then $X^*$ is an integral schedule, so $\lfloor X^* \rfloor = X^* = \lceil X^* \rceil$. Otherwise let $I_i \in \mathcal{I}(X^*)$ be an arbitrary interval. We will transform $X^*$ to $X'$ by changing the states at $I_i$ such that $|\mathcal{I}(X')| < |\mathcal{I}(X^*)|$ and $\lfloor x^*_t \rfloor \leq x'_t \leq \lceil x^*_t \rceil$ for all $t \in I_i$. Let $g(x) := \sum_{t=a_i}^{b_i} \bar{f}_t(x)$. Since each $\bar{f}_t(x)$ is linear for $x \in [\lfloor v_i \rfloor, \lceil v_i \rceil]$, the slope of $g(x)$ is constant for $x \in [\lfloor v_i \rfloor, \lceil v_i \rceil]$ and denoted by $g'(v_i)$. According to $I_i$, we have to differ between different cases:

(1) $x^*_{a_i-1} < v_i < x^*_{b_i+1}$
Let $\tilde{x}^*_{a_i-1} := \max\{x^*_{a_i-1}, \lfloor v_i \rfloor\}$ and $\tilde{x}^*_{b_i+1} := \min\{x^*_{b_i+1}, \lceil v_i \rceil\}$. By using any schedule with $x'_{a_i} = x'_{a_i+1} = \cdots = x'_{b_i} \in [\tilde{x}^*_{a_i-1}, \tilde{x}^*_{b_i+1}]$ (and $x'_t = x^*_t$ otherwise), the switching cost is unchanged. Since $I_i$ is inclusion maximal and $X^*$ is optimal, we can conclude that $g'(v_i) = 0$, so $C(X') = C(X^*)$. To show that $\lfloor X^* \rfloor$ is optimal, we set $x'_t = \tilde{x}^*_{b_i+1}$ for all $t \in I_i$. To show that $\lceil X^* \rceil$ is optimal, we set $x'_t = \tilde{x}^*_{a_i-1}$ for all $t \in I_i$.
(2) $x^*_{a_i-1} > v_i > x^*_{b_i+1}$
This case works analogously to the first case
(3) $x^*_{a_i-1} > v_i < x^*_{b_i+1}$
Let $v^+ = \min\{x^*_{a_i-1}, x^*_{b_i+1}, \lceil v_i \rceil\}$. Let $v'_i \in [\lfloor v_i \rfloor, v^+]$. By using the schedule $x'_{a_i} = x'_{a_i+1} = \cdots = x'_{b_i} = v'_i$ for all $t \in I_i$, the switching cost is increased by $\beta(v_i - v'_i)$, but the operating cost is reduced by $g'(v_i) \cdot (v_i - v'_i)$. Since $v_i$ is fractional, $v_i \notin \{x^*_{a_i-1}, x^*_{b_i+1}\}$. As $X^*$ is optimal, we can conclude that $g'(v_i) = \beta$, so the total cost of $X'$ does not change for $v'_i \in [\lfloor v_i \rfloor, v^+]$. To show that $\lfloor X^* \rfloor$ is optimal, we set $x'_t = \lfloor v_i \rfloor$ for all $t \in I_i$. To show that $\lceil X^* \rceil$ is optimal, we set $x'_t = v^+$ for all $t \in I_i$.
(4) $x^*_{a_i-1} < v_i > x^*_{b_i+1}$
This case works analogously to the third case, but $\lfloor x \rfloor$ and $\lceil x \rceil$ are swapped as well as min and max. Furthermore, $g'(v_i) = -\beta$ and we replace $(v_i - v'_i)$ with $(v'_i - v_i)$.

By using the transformation described above, we can reduce the number $|\mathcal{I}|$ of fractional intervals is at least reduced by 1. By applying the transformation several times until $|\mathcal{I}| = 0$, we receive $\lfloor X^* \rfloor$ or $\lceil X^* \rceil$. The total cost is not increased by the operations. □

So far, we have shown in Lemma 2.3 that for each optimal solution of the discrete problem instance $\mathcal{P}_k$ there is an optimal solution of the continuous problem instance $\bar{\mathcal{P}}$ that is not far away. In the following lemma we expand this statement: Given an optimal solution for $\mathcal{P}_k$, there is not only a fractional solution for $\bar{\mathcal{P}}$ that is not far away, but also an optimal solution of the discrete problem instance $\mathcal{P}_l$ for the subsequent iterations $l < k$.

Lemma 2.5. *Let $k > l$ with $k, l \in [K]_0$. Let $\hat{X}^k \in \Omega(\mathcal{P}_k)$ be an arbitrary optimal schedule for $\mathcal{P}_k$ with $k \in [K]_0$. There exists an optimal schedule $\hat{X}^l \in \Omega(\mathcal{P}^l)$ for $\mathcal{P}^l$ such that $|\hat{x}^k_t - \hat{x}^l_t| \leq 2^k$ for all $t \in [T]$. Formally, $\forall k \in [K]_0 : \forall l \in [k-1] : \forall \hat{X}^k \in \Omega(\mathcal{P}_k) : \exists \hat{X}^l \in \Omega(\mathcal{P}_l) : \forall t \in [T] : |\hat{x}^k_t - \hat{x}^l_t| \leq 2^k$.*

Proof. Consider the reduced problem instance $Q := \Psi_l(\mathcal{P}_l)$ as well as the problem instance $Q_{k-l} := \Phi_{k-l}(\Psi_l(\mathcal{P}_l))$ which is equivalent to $\Psi_l(\mathcal{P}_k))$ due to Lemma 2.1. Let $\hat{X}^{k-l}_Q = (\hat{x}^k_1/2^l, \ldots, \hat{x}^k_T/2^l)$ be an optimal schedule for $Q_{k-l}$. We apply Lemma 2.3, but we use $\hat{X}^{k-l}_Q$ and $Q$ instead of $\hat{X}^k$ and $\mathcal{P}$. By Lemma 2.3, there exists an optimal fractional schedule $X^*_Q = (x^*_1, \ldots, x^*_T)$ for $\bar{Q}$ such that $|\hat{x}^k_t/2^l - x^*_t| \le 2^{k-l}$. By Lemma 2.4, $\lfloor X^*_Q \rfloor$ is also an optimal schedule for $\bar{Q}$ and therefore it is also optimal for $Q$. The inequality $|\hat{x}^k_t/2^l - \lfloor x^*_t \rfloor| \le 2^{k-l}$ still holds, because the terms $\hat{x}^k_t/2^l$ and $2^{k-l}$ are integral and therefore adding a value less than 1 to the left side cannot invalidate the inequality. Let $\hat{X}^l := (\lfloor x^*_1 \rfloor \cdot 2^l, \ldots, \lfloor x^*_T \rfloor \cdot 2^l)$. As $\lfloor X^*_Q \rfloor$ is optimal for $Q$, $\hat{X}^l$ must be optimal for $\mathcal{P}_l$. Furthermore $\lfloor x^*_t \rfloor = \hat{x}^l_t/2^l$ holds, so we can insert it into the above inequality and get $|\hat{x}^k_t/2^l - \hat{x}^l_t/2^l| \le 2^{k-l}$ which is equivalent to $|\hat{x}^k_t - \hat{x}^l_t| \le 2^k$. □

Now, we have proven all parts to show the correctness of our polynomial-time algorithm:

THEOREM 2.6. *The algorithm described in Section 2.2 is correct.*

PROOF. We will show the correctness by induction. In the first iteration, the algorithm finds an optimal schedule for $\mathcal{P}_K$, because all states of $M_K$ are considered.

Given an optimal schedule $\hat{X}^k$, in the next iteration the algorithm only considers the states $x_t$ with $|\hat{x}^k_t - x_t| \le 2^k$. By Lemma 2.5, there exists an optimal schedule $\hat{X}^l$ with $l = k-1$ such that $|\hat{x}^k_t - \hat{x}^l_t| \le 2^k$ holds. Therefore the schedule found in iteration $k-1$ must be optimal for $\mathcal{P}_{k-1}$ (although some states are ignored by the algorithm). Thus, by induction, the algorithm will find an optimal schedule for $\mathcal{P}_0 = \mathcal{P}$ in the last iteration. □

## 3 AN OPTIMAL ONLINE ALGORITHM

Lin et. al. [17, 19] developed an algorithm called *Lazy Capacity Provisioning* (LCP) that achieves a competitive ratio of 3 for the continuous setting (i.e. $x_t \in \mathbb{R}$). In this section we adapt LCP to the discrete data-center optimization problem and prove the algorithm is 3-competitive for this problem as well.

The general approach of our proof is similar to the proof of the continuous setting in [17]. Some lemmas (e.g., Lemma 3.1 and 3.6) were adopted, however, their proofs are completely different. Lin et. al. use the properties of the convex program, especially duality and the complementary slackness conditions. This approach cannot be adapted to the discrete setting.

### 3.1 Algorithm

First, we will define lower and upper bounds for the optimal offline solution that can be calculated online. For a given time slot $\tau$ let $X^L_\tau := (x^L_{\tau,1}, \ldots, x^L_{\tau,\tau})$ be the vector that minimizes

$$C^L_\tau(X) = \sum_{t=1}^{\tau} f_t(x_t) + \beta \sum_{t=1}^{\tau} (x_t - x_{t-1})^+ \quad (5)$$

with $X = (x_1, \ldots, x_\tau)$. This term describes the cost of a workload that ends at $\tau \le T$. For $\tau = T$ this equation is equivalent to (1) . Let $x^L_\tau := x^L_{\tau,\tau}$ be the last state for this truncated workload. If there is more than one vector that minimizes (5), then $x^L_\tau$ is defined as the smallest possible value.

Similarly, let $X^U_\tau := (x^U_{\tau,1}, \ldots, x^U_{\tau,\tau})$ be the vector that minimizes

$$C^U_\tau(X) = \sum_{t=1}^{\tau} f_t(x_t) + \beta \sum_{t=1}^{\tau} (x_{t-1} - x_t)^+. \quad (6)$$

The difference to the equation (5) is that we pay the switching cost for powering down. Powering up does not cost anything. The last state is denoted by $x^U_\tau := x^U_{\tau,\tau}$. If there is more than one vector that minimizes (6), then $x^U_\tau$ is the largest possible value.

Define $[x]^b_a := \max\{a, \min\{b, x\}\}$ as the projection of $x$ into the interval $[a, b]$. The LCP algorithm is defined as follows:

$$x^{\mathrm{LCP}}_\tau := \begin{cases} 0, & \tau = 0 \\ [x^{\mathrm{LCP}}_{\tau-1}]^{x^U_\tau}_{x^L_\tau}, & \tau \ge 1 \end{cases} \quad (7)$$

Before we can prove that this algorithm is 3-competitive, we have to introduce some notation.

### 3.2 Notation

Let $X^* = (x^*_1, \ldots, x^*_T)$ be an optimal offline solution that minimizes equation (1) (i.e. the whole workload). Note that $C^L_\tau(X^*)$ indicates the cost of the optimal solution until $\tau$.

Let $R_\tau(X) := \sum_{t=1}^{\tau} f_t(x_t)$ with $X = (x_1, \ldots, x_\tau)$ denote the operating cost until $\tau$, let $S^L_\tau(X) := \beta \sum_{t=1}^{\tau} (x_t - x_{t-1})^+$ denote the switching cost in $C^L_\tau(X)$ and let $S^U_\tau(X) := \beta \sum_{t=1}^{\tau} (x_{t-1} - x_t)^+$ denote the switching cost in $C^U_\tau(X)$. Note that $C^L_\tau(X) = R_\tau(X) + S^L_\tau(X)$ and $C^U_\tau(X) = R_\tau(X) + S^U_\tau(X)$. Furthermore,

$$S^L_\tau(X) = S^U_\tau(X) + \beta x_\tau \quad (8)$$

as well as $C^L_\tau(X) = C^U_\tau(X) + \beta x_\tau$ holds, because in $C^L_\tau$ we have to pay the missing switching cost to reach the final state $x_\tau$. Note that $\beta x_\tau$ equals the cost for powering up in $C^L_\tau$ minus the cost for powering down in $C^U_\tau$.

Given an arbitrary function $f : [m] \to \mathbb{R}$, we define

$$\Delta f(x) := f(x) - f(x-1)$$

as the slope of $f$ at $x$. Let

$$\hat{C}^Y_\tau(x) := \min_{x_1, \ldots, x_{\tau-1}} C^Y_\tau((x_1, \ldots, x_{\tau-1}, x))$$

with $Y \in \{L, U\}$ be the minimal cost achievable with $x_\tau = x$.

### 3.3 Competitive ratio

In this section we prove that the LCP algorithm described by equation (7) achieves a competitive ratio of 3. First, we show that the optimal solution is bounded by the upper and lower bounds defined in the previous section.

LEMMA 3.1. *For all $\tau$, $x^L_\tau \le x^*_\tau \le x^U_\tau$ holds.*

PROOF. We prove both parts of the inequality by contradiction:

**Part 1 ($x^L_\tau \le x^*_\tau$):** Assume that $x^L_\tau > x^*_\tau$. By the definition of the lower bound, $C^L_\tau(X^L_\tau) < C^L_\tau(X^*)$ holds and we can replace $(x^*_1, \ldots, x^*_\tau)$ by $(x^L_{\tau,1}, \ldots x^L_{\tau,\tau})$. This reduces the total cost of $x^*$, because the cost up to $\tau$ is reduced and for $\tau+1$ there are no additional switching costs because $x^L_\tau > x^*_\tau$ holds. Thus $x^*$ would not be an optimal solution which is a contradiction, so $x^L_\tau \le x^*_\tau$ must be fulfilled.

**Part 2 ($x^*_\tau \le x^U_\tau$):** Assume that $x^*_\tau > x^U_\tau$. By definition of the upper bound, $C^U_\tau(X^U_\tau) < C^U_\tau(X^*)$ and, thus,

$$R_\tau(X^U_\tau) + S^U_\tau(X^U) < R_\tau(X^*) + S^U_\tau(X^*) \quad (9)$$

holds. The cost of the optimal solution until $\tau$ is $R_\tau(X^*) + S^L_\tau(X^*)$. If the states $(x^*_1, \dots, x^*_\tau)$ are replaced by $X^U_\tau$ and afterwards $x^*_\tau - x^U_{\tau,\tau}$ servers are powered up (to ensure that we end in the same state), then the cost is $R_\tau(X^U_\tau) + S^L_\tau(X^U) + \beta(x^*_\tau - x^U_{\tau,\tau})$. This cost must be greater than or equal to the cost of the optimal solution, so

$$R_\tau(X^U_\tau) + S^L_\tau(X^U) + \beta(x^*_\tau - x^U_{\tau,\tau}) \geq R_\tau(X^*) + S^L_\tau(X^*)$$

holds. By using equation (8), we get

$$R_\tau(X^U_\tau)+S^U_\tau(X^U)+\beta x^U_{\tau,\tau}+\beta(x^*_\tau-x^U_{\tau,\tau}) \geq R_\tau(X^*)+S^U_\tau(X^*)+\beta x^*_\tau.$$

We eliminate identical terms and get

$$R_\tau(X^U_\tau) + S^U_\tau(X^U) \geq R_\tau(X^*) + S^U_\tau(X^*)$$

which is a contradiction to inequality (9). Therefore our assumption was wrong, so $x^*_\tau \leq x^U_\tau$ must be fulfilled. □

The following four lemmas show important properties of $\hat{C}^L_\tau(x)$. First, we prove that the relation between $C^L_\tau(X)$ and $C^U_\tau(X)$ described by equation (8) still holds for $\hat{C}^L_\tau(x)$ and $\hat{C}^U_\tau(x)$.

Lemma 3.2. *For all $\tau$, $\hat{C}^L_\tau(x) = \hat{C}^U_\tau(x) + \beta x$ holds.*

Proof. Let $X^L$ be a corresponding solution for $\hat{C}^L_\tau(x)$ such that $C^L_\tau(X^L) = \hat{C}^L_\tau(x)$ and let $X^U$ be a corresponding solution for $\hat{C}^U_\tau(x)$ such that $C^U_\tau(X^U) = \hat{C}^U_\tau(x)$. Note that the last state of $X^L$ and $X^U$ is $x$. Since $X^U$ is optimal for $C^U_\tau$, the inequality $C^U_\tau(X^U) \leq C^U_\tau(X)$ holds for all $X = (x_1, \dots, x_{\tau-1}, x)$. By equation (8), we get

$$C^L_\tau(X^U) - \beta x \leq C^L_\tau(X) - \beta x$$

which is equivalent to $C^L_\tau(X^U) \leq C^L_\tau(X)$. With $X := X^L$ we get $C^L_\tau(X^U) \leq C^L_\tau(X^L)$. Since $X^L$ is optimal for $C^L_\tau$, $X^U$ must be optimal too, so $C^L_\tau(X^U) = C^L_\tau(X^L)$ holds. All in all, we get

$$\hat{C}^L_\tau(x) = C^L_\tau(X^L) = C^L_\tau(X^U) = C^U_\tau(X^U) + \beta x = \hat{C}^U_\tau(x) + \beta x. \quad \square$$

Obviously, the cost functions $C^L_\tau(X)$ and $C^U_\tau(X)$ are convex, since convexity is closed under addition. The following lemma shows that also $\hat{C}^L_\tau(x)$ and $\hat{C}^U_\tau(x)$ are convex.

Lemma 3.3. *For all $\tau$ and $Y \in \{L, U\}$, $\hat{C}^Y_\tau(x)$ is a convex function.*

Lemma 3.4. *The slope of $\hat{C}^L_\tau(x)$ is at most $\beta$ for $x \leq x^U_\tau$ and at least $\beta$ for $x > x^U_\tau$, i.e. $\Delta\hat{C}^L_\tau(x^U_\tau) \leq \beta$ and $\Delta\hat{C}^L_\tau(x^U_\tau + 1) \geq \beta$*

The proof of Lemma 3.3 and 3.4 can be found in the full paper.

Lemma 3.5. *For $x \leq x^U_\tau$, the slope of $\hat{C}^L_\tau(x)$ is at most $\beta$, i.e. $\Delta\hat{C}^L_\tau(x) \leq \beta$ holds.*

Proof. By Lemma 3.4 $\Delta\hat{C}^L_\tau(x^U_\tau) \leq \beta$ holds and by Lemma 3.3 $\hat{C}^L_\tau$ is convex, so $\Delta\hat{C}^L_\tau(x) \leq \beta$ for $x \leq x^U_\tau$. □

The next lemma characterizes the behavior of the optimal solution backwards in time.

Lemma 3.6. *A solution vector $(\hat{x}_1, \dots, \hat{x}_T)$ that fulfills the following recursive equality for all $t \in \{1, \dots, T\}$ is optimal:*

$$\hat{x}_t := \begin{cases} 0, & t = T+1 \\ [\hat{x}_{t+1}]^{x^U_t}_{x^L_t}, & t \leq T \end{cases}$$

Proof. We will prove the lemma by induction in reverse time. Powering down does not cost anything, so setting $\hat{x}_{T+1} = 0$, does not produce any additional costs. Assume that $(\hat{x}_{\tau+1}, \dots, \hat{x}_T)$ can lead to an optimal solution, i.e. there exists an optimal solution $X^*$ with $x^*_t = \hat{x}_t$ for $t \geq \tau+1$. We will show that the vector $(\hat{x}_\tau, \dots, \hat{x}_T)$ can still lead to an optimal solution.

We have to examine three cases:

**Case 1:** If $\hat{x}_{\tau+1} < x^L_\tau$, then $\hat{x}_\tau = x^L_\tau$. By Lemma 3.1, $x^*_\tau \geq x^L_\tau$ holds. Since $X^L_\tau$ minimizes $C^L_\tau$, we know that $C^L_\tau(X^L_\tau) \leq C^L_\tau(X)$ for all $X = (x_1, \dots, x_\tau)$. Thus there is no benefit to use a state $x' \geq x^L_\tau$, because afterwards we have to power down some servers to reach $\hat{x}_{\tau+1}$. Therefore $\hat{x}_\tau = x^L_\tau$ can still lead to an optimal solution.

**Case 2:** If $\hat{x}_{\tau+1} > x^U_\tau$, then $\hat{x}_\tau = x^U_\tau$. By Lemma 3.1, $x^*_\tau \leq x^U_\tau$ holds. Since $X^U_\tau$ minimizes $C^U_\tau$, we know that $C^U_\tau(X^U_\tau) \leq C^U_\tau(X)$ for all $X$. By using the solution $X^U_\tau$ and then switching to state $\hat{x}_{\tau+1}$, the resulting cost is

$$\begin{aligned} & C^L_\tau(X^U_\tau) + \beta(\hat{x}_{\tau+1} - x^U_\tau) + f_{\tau+1}(\hat{x}_{\tau+1}) \\ = & C^U_\tau(X^U_\tau) + \beta\hat{x}_{\tau+1} + f_{\tau+1}(\hat{x}_{\tau+1}) \\ \leq & C^U_\tau(X) + \beta\hat{x}_{\tau+1} + f_{\tau+1}(\hat{x}_{\tau+1}) \\ = & C^L_\tau(X) + \beta(\hat{x}_{\tau+1} - x_\tau) + f_{\tau+1}(\hat{x}_{\tau+1}). \end{aligned}$$

The last line describes the cost until $\tau + 1$ by using the vector $X = (x_1, \dots, x_\tau)$ with $x_\tau \leq x^U_\tau$ instead of $X^U_\tau$. The cost is not reduced by using $X$, so $\hat{x}_\tau = x^U_\tau$ can still lead to an optimal solution.

**Case 3:** If $x^L_\tau \leq \hat{x}_{\tau+1} \leq x^U_\tau$, then $\hat{x}_\tau = \hat{x}_{\tau+1}$. Assume that there is a better state $\hat{x}^-_\tau < \hat{x}_\tau$ with $\hat{C}^L_\tau(\hat{x}^-_\tau) < \hat{C}^L_\tau(\hat{x}_\tau)$. Since $\hat{x}_{\tau+1}$ leads to an optimal solution, after the time slot $\tau$ we have to power up $\hat{x}_\tau - \hat{x}^-_\tau$ servers, so even $\hat{C}^L_\tau(\hat{x}^-_\tau) + \beta(\hat{x}_\tau - \hat{x}^-_\tau) < \hat{C}^L_\tau(\hat{x}_\tau)$ holds. By Lemma 3.5, we know that the slope of $\hat{C}^L_\tau(x)$ is at most $\beta$ for $x \leq x^U_\tau$. This leads to the contradiction $\hat{C}^L_\tau(\hat{x}_\tau) \leq \hat{C}^L_\tau(\hat{x}^-_\tau) + \beta(\hat{x}^-_\tau - \hat{x}_\tau)$. Therefore there is no $\hat{x}^-_\tau$ with the desired properties.

The other direction is more simple: Assume that there is a better state $\hat{x}^+_\tau > \hat{x}_\tau$ with $\hat{C}^L_\tau(\hat{x}^+_\tau) < \hat{C}^L_\tau(\hat{x}_\tau)$, then $x^L_\tau$ (which minimizes $\hat{C}^L_\tau$) must be greater than $\hat{x}_\tau$, because by Lemma 3.3, $\hat{C}^L_\tau$ is a convex function. However, this is a contradiction to $x^L_\tau \leq \hat{x}_{\tau+1} = \hat{x}_\tau$. □

In the following $X^* = (x^*_1, \dots, x^*_T)$ denotes an optimal solution that fulfills the recursive equality of Lemma 3.6. The next lemma describes time slots where $X^{\text{LCP}}$ and $X^*$ are in same state. Informally, the lemma says that if the LCP curve cuts the optimal solution, then there is one time slot $\tau$ where both solutions are in the same state.

Lemma 3.7. *If $x^{\text{LCP}}_{\tau-1} < x^*_{\tau-1}$ and $x^{\text{LCP}}_\tau \geq x^*_\tau$, then $x^{\text{LCP}}_\tau = x^*_\tau$.*
*If $x^{\text{LCP}}_{\tau-1} > x^*_{\tau-1}$ and $x^{\text{LCP}}_\tau \leq x^*_\tau$, then $x^{\text{LCP}}_\tau = x^*_\tau$.*

Proof. We will only show the first statement of the lemma, since the other one works exactly analogously. Assume that $x^{\text{LCP}}_{\tau-1} < x^*_{\tau-1}$ and $x^{\text{LCP}}_\tau \geq x^*_\tau$ holds. We differ between two cases.

**Case 1:** If $x^{\text{LCP}}_{\tau-1} < x^{\text{LCP}}_\tau$, then $x^{\text{LCP}}_\tau = x^L_\tau$ (by the definition of the LCP algorithm). By $x^{\text{LCP}}_\tau \geq x^*_\tau$ and Lemma 3.1 (which says that $x^L_\tau \leq x^*_\tau$), we get $x^{\text{LCP}}_\tau = x^*_\tau$.

**Case 2:** If $x^{\text{LCP}}_{\tau-1} \geq x^{\text{LCP}}_\tau$, then $x^*_{\tau-1} > x^*_\tau$. By Lemma 3.6, $x^*_{\tau-1} = x^L_{\tau-1}$ holds which is a contradiction to $x^*_{\tau-1} > x^{\text{LCP}}_{\tau-1} \geq x^L_{\tau-1}$. □

The time slots where $x^{\text{LCP}}_t = x^*_t$ are denoted by $0 = t_0 < t_1 < \dots < t_\kappa$. Between these time slots it is not possible that $X^{\text{LCP}}$

powers one or more servers down and $X^*$ powers servers up or vice versa. In the following $[a : b]$ with $a, b \in \mathbb{N}$ denotes the set $\{a, a+1, \dots, b\}$. Analogously, we define $[a : b[ := \{a, a+1 \dots, b-1\}$, $]a : b] := \{a+1, a+2, \dots, b\}$ and $]a : b[ := \{a+1, a+2, \dots b-1\}$.

LEMMA 3.8. *For all time intervals* $]t_i : t_{i+1}[$ *with* $i \geq 0$, *either*

(i) $x_\tau^{LCP} > x_\tau^*$ *and both* $x_\tau^{LCP}$ *and* $x_\tau^*$ *are non-increasing for all* $\tau \in ]t_i : t_{i+1}[$, *or*
(ii) $x_\tau^{LCP} < x_\tau^*$ *and both* $x_\tau^{LCP}$ *and* $x_\tau^*$ *are non-decreasing for all* $\tau \in ]t_i : t_{i+1}[$.

PROOF. First, we consider the case (i), i.e. $x_\tau^{\text{LCP}} > x_\tau^*$.

If $x_{\tau+1}^{\text{LCP}} > x_\tau^{\text{LCP}}$, then $x_{\tau+1}^L = x_{\tau+1}^{\text{LCP}}$ by the LCP algorithm and $x_{\tau+1}^* \geq x_{\tau+1}^L$ by Lemma 3.1. By Lemma 3.6, we get $x_\tau^U = x_\tau^*$ which leads to the contradiction $x_\tau^U = x_\tau^* < x_\tau^{\text{LCP}} \leq x_\tau^U$ (the last inequality uses the definition of the LCP algorithm). Thus $x_\tau^{\text{LCP}}$ is non-increasing for all $\tau \in ]t_i : t_{i+1}[$.

If $x_{\tau+1}^* > x_\tau^*$, then $x_\tau^* = x_\tau^U$ by Lemma 3.6 which is a contradiction to $x_\tau^U \geq x_\tau^{\text{LCP}} > x_\tau^*$, so $x_\tau^*$ is also non-increasing for all $\tau \in ]t_i : t_{i+1}[$. By Lemma 3.7 the inequality $x_\tau^{\text{LCP}} > x_\tau^*$ is fulfilled for all $\tau \in ]t_i : t_{i+1}[$.

Case (ii) works analogously. □

Now we can calculate the switching cost of the LCP algorithm.

LEMMA 3.9. $S_T^L(X^{LCP}) \leq S_T^L(X^*)$

PROOF. By Lemma 3.8, both $x_\tau^{\text{LCP}}$ and $x_\tau^*$ are either non-increasing or non-decreasing until there is a time slot $t$ with $x_t^{\text{LCP}} = x_t^*$. Therefore, the switching cost during the time interval $[t_i : t_{i+1}]$ is $\beta(x_{t_i}^* - x_{t_{i-1}}^*)^+$ for both $X^{\text{LCP}}$ and $X^*$. At the end of the workload, $X^{\text{LCP}}$ and $X^*$ are maybe in different states. If $x_T^{\text{LCP}} < x_T^*$, then $x_\tau^{\text{LCP}}$ and $x_\tau^*$ are non-decreasing in the corresponding time interval $[t_\kappa : T]$, so the switching cost of LCP is less than the switching cost of the optimal solution. If the $x_T^{\text{LCP}} > x_T^*$, both $x_\tau^{\text{LCP}}$ and $x_\tau^*$ are non-increasing, so there are no switching costs for this time interval. All in all, we get $S_T^L(X^{\text{LCP}}) \leq S_T^L(X^*)$. □

Lemma 3.8 divides the intervals $[t_i : t_{i+1}[$ into two sets: Intervals of case (i) are called *decreasing* intervals, the set of those intervals is denoted by $\mathcal{T}^-$. Intervals of case (ii) are called *increasing* intervals and the set is denoted by $\mathcal{T}^+$. The following lemma is needed to estimate the operating cost of the LCP algorithm.

LEMMA 3.10. *For all* $\tau \in [t_i : t_{i+1}[ \in \mathcal{T}^+$,

$$\hat{C}_\tau^L(x_\tau^{LCP}) + f_{\tau+1}(x_{\tau+1}^{LCP}) \leq \hat{C}_{\tau+1}^L(x_{\tau+1}^{LCP}). \tag{10}$$

*Analogously, for all* $\tau \in [t_i : t_{i+1}[ \in \mathcal{T}^-$,

$$\hat{C}_\tau^U(x_\tau^{LCP}) + f_{\tau+1}(x_{\tau+1}^{LCP}) \leq \hat{C}_{\tau+1}^U(x_{\tau+1}^{LCP}). \tag{11}$$

The lemma can be proven by using the properties of $\hat{C}_\tau^L$ and $\hat{C}_\tau^U$ shown in Lemma 3.3 and 3.5, the detailed proof can be found in the full version of this paper. We can use Lemma 3.10 to estimate the operating cost of the LCP algorithm.

LEMMA 3.11. $R_T(X^{LCP}) \leq R_T(X^*) + \beta \sum_{t=1}^T |x_t^* - x_{t-1}^*|$

PROOF. Consider the time interval $[t_i : t_{i+1}[ \in \mathcal{T}^+$. By adding the inequalities of Lemma 3.10 for $\tau \in [t_i : t_{i+1}[$, we get

$$\sum_{t=t_i}^{t_{i+1}-1} \hat{C}_t^L(x_t^{\text{LCP}}) + \sum_{t=t_i}^{t_{i+1}-1} f_{t+1}(x_{t+1}^{\text{LCP}}) \leq \sum_{t=t_i}^{t_{i+1}-1} \hat{C}_{t+1}^L(x_{t+1}^{\text{LCP}})$$

Subtracting the first sum gives

$$\sum_{t=t_i}^{t_{i+1}-1} f_{t+1}(x_{t+1}^{\text{LCP}}) \leq \hat{C}_{t_{i+1}}^L(x_{t_{i+1}}^{\text{LCP}}) - \hat{C}_{t_i}^L(x_{t_i}^{\text{LCP}})$$

$$= \hat{C}_{t_{i+1}}^L(x_{t_{i+1}}^*) - \hat{C}_{t_i}^L(x_{t_i}^*) = \sum_{t=t_i}^{t_{i+1}-1} f_{t+1}(x_{t+1}^*) + \beta(x_{t_{i+1}}^* - x_{t_i}^*) \tag{12}$$

The first equality holds because $x_{t_i}^{\text{LCP}} = x_{t_i}^*$ and $x_{t_{i+1}}^{\text{LCP}} = x_{t_{i+1}}^*$. Considering the time interval $[t_i : t_{i+1}[ \in \mathcal{T}^-$ yields to the following inequality:

$$\sum_{t=t_i}^{t_{i+1}-1} f_{t+1}(x_{t+1}^{\text{LCP}}) \leq \hat{C}_{t_{i+1}}^U(x_{t_{i+1}}^{\text{LCP}}) - \hat{C}_{t_i}^U(x_{t_i}^{\text{LCP}})$$

$$= \hat{C}_{t_{i+1}}^U(x_{t_{i+1}}^*) - \hat{C}_{t_i}^U(x_{t_i}^*) = \sum_{t=t_i}^{t_{i+1}-1} f_{t+1}(x_{t+1}^*) + \beta(x_{t_i}^* - x_{t_{i+1}}^*) \tag{13}$$

In both (12) and (13) the factor after $\beta$ is positive, so we can write

$$\sum_{t=t_i}^{t_{i+1}-1} f_{t+1}(x_{t+1}^{\text{LCP}}) \leq \sum_{t=t_i}^{t_{i+1}-1} f_{t+1}(x_{t+1}^*) + \beta|x_{t_{i+1}}^* - x_{t_i}^*|$$

$$= \sum_{t=t_i}^{t_{i+1}-1} f_{t+1}(x_{t+1}^*) + \beta \sum_{t=t_i}^{t_{i+1}-1} |x_{t+1}^* - x_t^*|$$

By adding all intervals in $\mathcal{T}^+ \cup \mathcal{T}^-$ we get

$$\sum_{t=1}^T f_t(x_t^{\text{LCP}}) \leq \sum_{t=1}^T f_t(x_t^*) + \beta \sum_{t=1}^T |x_t^* - x_{t-1}^*|$$ □

The term $\beta \sum_{t=1}^T |x_t^* - x_{t-1}^*|$ in Lemma 3.11 is upper bounded by twice the switching cost of the optimal schedule:

LEMMA 3.12. $\beta \sum_{t=1}^T |x_t^* - x_{t-1}^*| \leq 2 \cdot S_T^L(X^*)$

This lemma can be proven with simple calculations (see full paper). Now, we are able to show that LCP is 3-competitive.

THEOREM 3.13. *The LCP algorithm is 3-competitive.*

PROOF. By using Lemma 3.9, 3.11 and 3.12 we get

$$\begin{aligned} C_T^L(X^{\text{LCP}}) &= R_T(X^{\text{LCP}}) + S_T^L(X^{\text{LCP}}) \\ &\leq R_T(X^*) + \beta \sum_{t=1}^T |x_t^* - x_{t-1}^*| + S_T^L(X^*) \\ &\leq R_T(X^*) + 3 \cdot S_T^L(X^*) \leq C_T^L(X^*). \end{aligned}$$ □

## 4 LOWER BOUNDS

In this section we will show lower bounds for both the discrete and continuous data-center optimization problem. First, we prove that there is no deterministic online algorithm that achieves a competitive ratio better than 3 for the discrete problem. This lower bound demonstrates that the LCP algorithm analyzed in the previous section is optimal. Afterwards, we show that this lower bound also holds for Lin's model (introduced in [17]) that is a bit more restricted than the general model investigated in the previous sections. A formal definition of Lin's model is given in Section 4.2. Moreover, we give a lower bound for the continuous setting and show that this lower bound holds again for Lin's model. A lower bound of 2 for the general continuous setting was independently shown by Antoniadis et. al. [3]. Finally, we extend our lower bounds to the scenario that an online algorithm has a finite prediction window.

To simplify the analysis, the switching costs are paid for both powering up and powering down. At the end of the workload all servers have to be powered down. This ensures that the total cost remains the same. We will set $\beta = 2$, so changing a server's state will cost $\beta/2 = 1$. Thus the cost of a schedule is defined by

$$C(X) := \sum_{t=1}^{T} f_t(x_t) + \sum_{t=1}^{T+1} |x_t - x_{t-1}|$$

with $x_0 := x_{T+1} := 0$.

## 4.1 Discrete setting

First, we analyze the discrete setting.

Theorem 4.1. *There is no deterministic online algorithm that achieves a competitive ratio of $c < 3$ for the discrete data-center optimization problem.*

Proof. Assume that there is a deterministic algorithm $\mathcal{A}$ that is $(3-\delta)$-competitive with $\delta > 0$. The adversary will use the functions $\varphi_0(x) = \epsilon|x|$ and $\varphi_1(x) = \epsilon|x-1|$ with $\epsilon \to 0$, so we only need the states 0 and 1, there is no benefit to use other states. If $\mathcal{A}$ is in state 0 or 1, the adversary will send $\varphi_1$ or $\varphi_0$, respectively.

Let $S$ be the number of time slots where algorithm $\mathcal{A}$ changes the state of a server, i.e. $S$ is the switching cost of $\mathcal{A}$. Let $T$ be length of the whole workload (we will define $T$ later), so for $T - S$ time slots the operating costs of $\mathcal{A}$ are $\epsilon$. Thus, the total cost of $\mathcal{A}$ is

$$C(\mathcal{A}) = (T - S)\epsilon + S.$$

The cost of the optimal offline schedule can be bounded by the minimum of the following two strategies. The first strategy is to stay at one state for the whole workload. If $\varphi_0$ is sent more often than $\varphi_1$, then this is state 0, else it is state 1. The operating cost is at most $T\epsilon/2$, the switching cost is at most 2, because if we use state 1, we have to switch the state at the beginning and end of the workload. The second strategy is to always switch the state, such that there are no operating costs. In this case the switching cost is at most $S + 2$, because we switch the state after each time $\mathcal{A}$ switches its state as well as possibly at the beginning and the end of the workload. Thus, the cost of the optimal offline schedule is

$$C(X^*) \leq \min(T\epsilon/2 + 2, S + 2). \tag{14}$$

We want to find a lower bound for the competitive ratio $\frac{C(\mathcal{A})}{C(X^*)}$. We distinguish between $S \geq T\epsilon/2$ (case 1) and $S < T\epsilon/2$ (case 2).

In **case 1** the competitive ratio of $\mathcal{A}$ is

$$\begin{aligned}\frac{C(\mathcal{A})}{C(X^*)} &\overset{(14)}{\geq} \frac{(T-S)\epsilon + S}{T\epsilon/2 + 2} = 2 + \frac{S(1-\epsilon) - 4}{T\epsilon/2 + 2} \\ &\geq 2 + \frac{(T\epsilon/2)(1-\epsilon) - 4}{T\epsilon/2 + 2} = 2 + (1-\epsilon) - \frac{2(1-\epsilon) + 4}{T\epsilon/2 + 2}\end{aligned}$$

The last inequality uses $S \geq T\epsilon/2$ that holds for case 1. By setting $T \geq \frac{1}{\epsilon^2}$, we get $\lim_{\epsilon \to 0} T\epsilon = \infty$ and thus $\lim_{\epsilon \to 0} \frac{C(\mathcal{A})}{C(X^*)} = 3$.

In **case 2**, we get

$$\begin{aligned}\frac{C(\mathcal{A})}{C(X^*)} &\overset{(14)}{\geq} \frac{(T-S)\epsilon + S}{S+2} = (1-\epsilon) + \frac{T\epsilon - 2(1-\epsilon)}{S+2} \\ &\geq (1-\epsilon) + \frac{T\epsilon - 2(1-\epsilon)}{T\epsilon/2 + 2} = 3 - \epsilon - \frac{2(1-\epsilon) + 4}{T\epsilon/2 + 2}\end{aligned}$$

Again, we set $T \geq \frac{1}{\epsilon^2}$ and get $\lim_{\epsilon \to 0} \frac{C(\mathcal{A})}{C(X^*)} = 3$.

Therefore there is no algorithm with a competitive ratio that is less than 3. We can set $T$ to an arbitrarily large value, so the total cost of $\mathcal{A}$ converges to infinity. □

## 4.2 Discrete setting: Lin's model

Lin et. al. [17] introduced a more restricted setting as described by equation (2). In this section we show that the lower bound of 3 still holds for this model. The essential differences of Lin's model to the general model are: (1) There is only one convex function for the whole problem instance and (2) there is the additional condition that $x_t \geq \lambda_t$. The different definition of the switching cost does not influence the total cost as already mentioned in the beginning of Section 4.

Theorem 4.2. *There is no deterministic online algorithm for the discrete setting of Lin's model with a competitive ratio of $c < 3$.*

Proof. The general model (examined in the previous sections) is denoted by $\mathcal{G}$ and Lin's model is denoted by $\mathcal{L}$. The states of the model $\mathcal{X} \in \{\mathcal{G}, \mathcal{L}\}$ are indicated by $x_t^{\mathcal{X}}$. We will use the same idea as in the proof of Theorem 4.1, but we have to modify it such that it fits for Lin's model.

We use 2 servers, so the states are $x_t^{\mathcal{L}} \in \{0, 1, 2\}$. Instead of switching between the states 0 and 1 in $\mathcal{G}$, we will switch between 1 and 2 in $\mathcal{L}$, so for $t \in \{1, \ldots, T\}$ we have $x_t^{\mathcal{L}} = x_t^{\mathcal{G}} + 1$. In $\mathcal{L}$ the state 0 is only used at the beginning ($t = 0$) of the workload. This leads to additional switching costs of 1 for both the optimal offline solution and the online algorithm. However, for a sufficiently long workload the total cost converges to infinity, so the constant extra cost does not influence the competitive ratio.

We will apply the same adversary strategy used in the proof of Theorem 4.1. Let $f(z) := \epsilon|1 - 2z|$ with $\epsilon \to 0$, let $\beta = 2$. If the adversary in $\mathcal{G}$ sends $\varphi_0(x) = \epsilon|x|$ as function, then we will use $\lambda_t = l_0 := 0.5$ which leads to operating cost of

$$x_t^{\mathcal{L}} f\left(l_0/x_t^{\mathcal{L}}\right) = x_t^{\mathcal{L}} \cdot \epsilon \left|1 - \frac{1}{x_t^{\mathcal{L}}}\right| = \epsilon \left|x_t^{\mathcal{L}} - 1\right| = \epsilon \left|x_t^{\mathcal{G}}\right|$$

If the adversary sends $\varphi_1(x) = \epsilon|1 - x|$, then we will use $\lambda_t = l_1 = 1$ which leads to operating cost of

$$x_t^{\mathcal{L}} f\left(l_1/x_t^{\mathcal{L}}\right) = x_t^{\mathcal{L}} \cdot \epsilon \left|1 - \frac{2}{x_t^{\mathcal{L}}}\right| = \epsilon \left|x_t^{\mathcal{L}} - 2\right| = \epsilon \left|1 - x_t^{\mathcal{G}}\right|$$

Thus the difference (1) between both models is solved.

For $t \geq 1$ it is not allowed to use the state $x_t^{\mathcal{L}} = 0$, because both $l_0$ and $l_1$ are greater than 0. For $x_t^{\mathcal{L}} \in \{1, 2\}$ the inequality $x_t \geq \lambda_t$ is always fulfilled, so the difference (2) is solved too. □

### 4.3 Continuous setting

In this section we analyze the continuous setting of the data-center optimization problem.

THEOREM 4.3. *There is no deterministic online algorithm for the continuous data-center optimization problem that achieves a competitive ratio that is less than 2.*

The proof consists of two parts. First we will construct an algorithm $\mathcal{B}$ whose competitive ratio is greater than $2 - \delta$ for an arbitrary small $\delta$. Then we will show that the competitive ratio of any deterministic algorithm that differs from $\mathcal{B}$ is greater than 2.

For the first part we use an adversary that uses $\varphi_0(x) = \epsilon|x|$ and $\varphi_1(x) = \epsilon|1 - x|$ as functions where $\epsilon \to 0$. Let $b_t$ be the state of $\mathcal{B}$ at time $t$. If the function $\varphi_0$ arrives, then the next state $b_{t+1}$ is $\max\{b_t - \epsilon/2, 0\}$. If $\varphi_1$ arrives, the next state is $b_{t+1} := \min\{b_t + \epsilon/2, 1\}$. The algorithm starts at $b_0 = 0$, so $b_t \in [0, 1]$ is fulfilled for all $t$. Note that algorithm $\mathcal{B}$ is equivalent to Bansal's algorithm given in [5] for the special case of $\varphi_0$ and $\varphi_1$ functions. As shown in the full version of this paper, the competitive ratio of $\mathcal{B}$ is at least 2.

For the second part we use the following adversary strategy. Let $a_t$ be the state of $\mathcal{A}$ at time $t$. If $a_t < b_t$ or $a_t = 0$, the adversary sends $\varphi_1$ as next function. If $a_t > b_t$ or $a_t = 1$, the adversary sends $\varphi_0$. For the other cases the adversary can choose an arbitrary function. By doing this, it can be shown that the cost of $\mathcal{A}$ is always greater than or equal to the cost of $\mathcal{B}$, so the competitive ratio of $\mathcal{A}$ is at least 2. The detailed analysis can be found in the full paper.

### 4.4 Continuous setting: Lin's model

Analogously to the discrete setting, in this section we want to show that the lower bound of 2 for the continuous data-center optimization problem still holds for Lin's model described in Section 4.3.

THEOREM 4.4. *There is no deterministic online algorithm for the continuous setting of Lin's model with a competitive ratio of $c < 2$.*

To prove this theorem we will apply the same adversary strategy used in the previous section. We set $f(z) := \epsilon|1-kz|$ with $\epsilon \to 0$ and $k \to \infty$. If the adversary in the general model sends $\varphi_0(x) = \epsilon|x|$ as function, then we will use $\lambda_t = 0$, if it sends $\varphi_1(x) = \epsilon|1 - x|$, then we will use $\lambda_t = 1/k$. As shown in the full paper, this leads to the same operating cost functions as in the general model.

### 4.5 Online algorithms with prediction window

So far, we have considered online algorithms that at time $t$ only know the arriving function $f_t$ in determining the next state. In contrast, an offline algorithm knows the whole function sequence $F$. There are models between these edge cases. An online algorithm with a *prediction window* of length $w$, at any time $t$, can not only use the function $f_t$ but the function set $\{f_t, \ldots, f_{t+w}\}$ to choose the state $x_t$. This problem extension was also defined by Lin et al. [17, 19]. If $w$ has a constant size (i.e. $w$ is independent of $T$), then the lower bounds developed in the previous sections still holds as the following theorem shows. We develop the lower bounds for Lin's model so that they hold for the general model as well.

THEOREM 4.5. *Let $w \in \mathbb{N}$ and $\delta > 0$ be arbitrary constants. There is no deterministic online algorithm with a prediction window of length $w$ that achieves a competitive ratio of $3 - \delta$ in the discrete setting or $2 - \delta$ in the continuous setting for Lin's model.*

The basic idea for proving this theorem is to use a worst case workload for online algorithms without prediction window and send a scaled version of each function several times (dependent on $w$), such that there is no advantage in knowing the next $w$ functions. Details can be found in the full version of this paper.

## REFERENCES

[1] L.L.H. Andrew, S. Barman, K. Ligett, M. Lin, A. Meyerson, A. Roytman and A. Wierman. A tale of two metrics: Simultaneous bounds on competitiveness and regret. *Proc. 26th Annual Conference on Learning Theory (COLT'13)*, 741–763, 2013.

[2] A. Antoniadis, N. Barcelo, M. Nugent, K. Pruhs, K. Schewior and M. Scquizzato. Chasing convex bodies and functions. *Proc. 12th Latin American Symposium on Theoretical Informatics (LATIN'16)*, 68–81, 2016.

[3] A. Antoniadis and K. Schewior. A tight lower bound for online convex optimization with switching costs. Announced at the *15th Workshop on Approximation and Online Algorithms (WAOA'17)*, 2017.

[4] M. Armbrust, A. Fox, R. Griffith, A.D. Joseph, R.H. Katz, A. Konwinski, G. Lee, D.A. Patterson, A. Rabkin, I. Stoica and M. Zaharia. Above the clouds: A Berkeley view of cloud computing. Technical Report No. UCB/EECS-2009-28. EECS Department, University of California, Berkeley, 2009.

[5] N. Bansal, A. Gupta, R. Krishnaswamy, K. Pruhs, K. Schewior and C. Stein. A 2-competitive algorithm for online convex optimization with switching costs. *Proc. 18th. International Workshop on Approximation Algorithms for Combinatorial Optimization Problems (APPROX15)*, 96–109, 2015.

[6] L.A. Barroso and U. Hölzle. The case for energy-proportional computing. *IEEE Computer*, 40(12):33–37, 2007.

[7] T. Bawden. Global warming: Data centres to consume three times as much energy in next decade, experts warn. http://www.independent.co.uk/environment/global-warming-data-centres-to-consume-three-times-as-much-energy-in-next-decade-experts-warn-a6830086.html, 2016.

[8] K.G. Brill. The Invisible Crisis in the Data Center: The Economic Meltdown of Moore's Law. *white paper, Uptime Institute*, 2–5, 2007.

[9] M. Dayarathna, Y. Wen and R. Fan. Data center energy consumption modeling: A survey. *IEEE Communications Surveys and Tutorials*, 18(1):732–794, 2016.

[10] A. Gandhi and M. Harchol-Balter. How data center size impacts the effectiveness of dynamic power management. *49th Annual Allerton Conference*, 1164–1169, 2011.

[11] A. Gandhi, M. Harchol-Balter and I.J.B.F. Adan. Server farms with setup costs. *Perform. Eval.*, 67(11):1123–1138, 2010.

[12] Z.J. Haas and S. Gu. On power management policies for data centers. *Proc. IEEE Int. Conf. on Data Science and Data Intensive Systems (DSDIS)*, 404–411, 2015.

[13] J. Hamilton. Cost of Power in Large-Scale Data Centers. http://perspectives.mvdirona.com/2008/11/cost-of-power-in-large-scale-data-centers/

[14] S. Khuller, J. Li and B. Saha. Energy efficient scheduling via partial shutdown. *Proc. 21st Annual ACM-SIAM Symposium on Discrete Algorithms*, 1360–1372, 2010.

[15] J. Li and S. Khuller. Generalized machine activation problems. *Proc. 22nd Annual ACM-SIAM Symposium on Discrete Algorithms*, 80–94, 2011.

[16] M. Lin, Z. Liu, A. Wierman and L.L.H. Andrew. Online algorithms for geographical load balancing. *Proc. International Green Computing Conference (IGCC'12)*, 1–10, 2012.

[17] M. Lin, A. Wierman, L.L.H. Andrew and E. Thereska. Dynamic right-sizing for power-proportional data centers. *Proc. 30th IEEE International Conference on Computer Communications (INFOCOM'11)*, 1098–1106, 2011.

[18] M. Lin, A. Wierman, L.L.H. Andrew and E. Thereska. Online dynamic capacity provisioning in data centers. *Proc. 49th Annual Allerton Conference on Communication, Control, and Computing*, 1159–1163, 2011.

[19] M. Lin, A. Wierman, L.L.H. Andrew and E. Thereska. Dynamic right-sizing for power-proportional data centers. *IEEE/ACM Trans. Netw.*, 21(5):1378–1391, 2013.

[20] Z. Liu, M. Lin, A. Wierman, S.H. Low, L.L.H. Andrew. Greening geographical load balancing. *IEEE/ACM Trans. Netw.*, 23(2):657–671, 2015.

[21] P. Schmid and A. Roos. Overclocking Core i7: Power Versus Performance. Idle/Peak Power Consumption Analysis. http://www.tomshardware.com/reviews/overclock-core-i7,2268-10.html, 2009.

[22] A. Shehabi, S. Smith, D. Sartor, R. Brown, M. Herrlin, J. Koomey, E. Masanet, N. Horner, I. Azevedo and W. Lintner. United States data center energy usage report. Lawrence Berkeley National Laboratory, LBNL-1005775, 2016.

[23] K. Wang, M. Lin, F. Ciucu, A. Wierman and C. Lin. Characterizing the impact of the workload on the value of dynamic resizing in data centers. *Perform. Eval.*, 85-86:1–18, 2015.

# Online Facility Location with Mobile Facilities*

Björn Feldkord
Heinz Nixdorf Institute & Computer Science Dept.,
Paderborn University
Paderborn, Germany
bjoernf@mail.upb.de

Friedhelm Meyer auf der Heide
Heinz Nixdorf Institute & Computer Science Dept.,
Paderborn University
Paderborn, Germany
fmadh@upb.de

## ABSTRACT

We examine the Online Facility Location Problem in an augmented version, where the online algorithm is allowed to adapt the position of the facilities for costs proportional to the distance by which the position is changed. In this setting, it is possible to construct online algorithms which deal with the lower bound instances of Online Facility Location much more effectively. Fotakis showed a lower bound of $\Omega(\frac{\log n}{\log \log n})$ for the original Online Facility Location Problem, where $n$ denotes the number clients. This bounds holds even on the real line and for randomized algorithms against oblivious adversaries. In contrast, we are able to achieve competitive ratios independent of $n$ in our model.

We propose randomized online algorithms in two settings: We consider the Euclidean space (of arbitrary dimension) and allow the facilities to either move arbitrarily or to move at most a constant distance $m$ in each time step. The costs for moving a facility from $a$ to $b$ is $D \cdot d(a, b)$ where $D \geq 1$ is a constant. Our algorithms are memoryless w.r.t. past requests and only make local modifications to at most one facility in each time step. In the case of arbitrary movement, the competitive ratio only depends on $D$. In the case of limiting the movement to a constant distance $m$, the competitive ratio additionally depends on the opening cost $c_f$ of facilities and $m$. We show that our results are asymptotically tight on the real line. For the Euclidean space of higher dimensions, the competitive ratio of our algorithms is tight with respect to $D$, $c_f$ and $m$, but is additionally impacted by the number of optimal facilities.

## KEYWORDS

Facility Location, Resource Augmentation, Competitive Analysis, Online Algorithms

**ACM Reference Format:**

Björn Feldkord and Friedhelm Meyer auf der Heide. 2018. Online Facility Location with Mobile Facilities. In *SPAA '18: SPAA '18: 30th ACM Symposium on Parallelism in Algorithms and Architectures, July 16–18, 2018, Vienna, Austria.* ACM, New York, NY, USA, 9 pages. https://doi.org/10.1145/3210377.3210389

*This work was partially supported by the German Research Foundation (DFG) within the Collaborative Research Centre "On-The-Fly Computing" (SFB 901).



*SPAA '18, July 16–18, 2018, Vienna, Austria*

ACM ISBN 978-1-4503-5799-9/18/07...$15.00
https://doi.org/10.1145/3210377.3210389

## 1 INTRODUCTION

In the Metric Facility Location Problem, we are given a set of clients and a set of possible facility locations which both are part of the same metric space. For each of the possible facility locations, we are also given an opening cost. The goal is to select a subset of the facility locations such that the sum of the implied opening costs and the sum of the distances of each client to the closest facility is minimized. The Facility Location Problem is a basic and well studied optimization problem with many applications in areas such as clustering and network design.

The Facility Location Problem has been studied in many variants, including the Online Facility Location Problem [16] in which the clients are not given in advance but arrive over time. In each time step, new clients must be irrevocably assigned to a facility. This assumption is suitable for a lot of the applications mentioned above, i.e. a data set for clustering might grow over time and it may be to costly to split up already existing clusters.

While there exist many algorithms which approximate the offline version of Facility Location within a constant factor (see [18] for a survey), Meyerson showed that it is not possible to achieve a competitive ratio for the online version which is independent of the number of clients (and therefore time) [16]. This lower bound was later improved by Fotakis to $\Omega(\frac{\log n}{\log \log n})$, where $n$ is the number of clients [10]. In the same work, it was shown that this bound is tight for both deterministic and randomized algorithms and holds even for simple metrics like the 1-dimensional Euclidean space.

The lower bound constructions of Meyerson and Fotakis are both based on a sequence of clients which converges towards a point unknown to the online algorithm, but which is the location of the optimal facility for the offline case. This sequence naturally relies on the order in which the clients are revealed to the online algorithm in order to maximize its costs. In fact, Meyerson showed that if the clients arrive in a uniform random order there exists a randomized online algorithm with expected constant competitive ratio [16].

In this paper, we tackle the problem of the specific worst-case sequences from a different angle: Since the high costs of the online algorithm stems from the placement of facilities on points which are effectively rendered useless over time, it is only natural to ask whether the performance of an online algorithm improves asymptotically when it is allowed to make corrections to the position of its placed facilities. Divékih and Imreh [6] considered such a variant in which the online algorithm may move the facilities to an arbitrary new position in each time step and without incurring any additional cost for moving. Their algorithm computes an offline approximation of the optimal solution in each time step and moves the facilities accordingly. While they achieve a constant competitive ratio in this scenario, their model also has a major drawback: Since movement of facilities comes for free, a misplaced facility can be moved to an optimal point without any disadvantage for the algorithm from the initial error.

We propose a model where the online algorithm may make corrections to the positions of its facilities, but instead of this being free, it incurs cost proportional to the distance a facility is moved. In this way, bigger changes to the current configuration of the algorithm are more costly and may therefore be less advantageous than smaller corrections to the position, even if this does not result in an optimal configuration w.r.t. the offline solution. Furthermore, we consider a variant where the facilities may not be moved to arbitrary positions but can only be moved a constant maximum distance in each time step. This allows to measure the improvement of the solution of an online algorithm dependent on the amount of correction it makes in every step, thus getting a more refined view on the matter.

The extension of the Facility Location Problem by movement might also be of independent interest for scenarios in which we deal with resources which are mobile in the sense that they can be reconfigured to better fit incoming requests or are actually mobile in a physical sense. An example for the latter case may be the usage of mobile relay stations to provide network access in certain disaster scenarios, where the commonly used infrastructure in the area has collapsed. For theses cases, our algorithm presents a solution on how to best approximate an optimal, static configuration.

## 1.1 Related Work

The Online Facility Location Problem was introduced by Meyerson [16] who gave a simple randomized algorithm for the problem which achieves a competitive ratio of $O(\frac{\log n}{\log\log n})$. Fotakis later proved that this competitive ratio is asymptotically optimal and also gave a deterministic online algorithm achieving the same competitive ratio, fixing the ratio to $\Theta(\frac{\log n}{\log\log n})$ for both the deterministic and the randomized case [10]. In addition to the complex deterministic algorithm which achieves the optimal competitive ratio, there are deterministic algorithms which are much simpler to implement and achieve an almost optimal competitive ratio of $O(\log n)$ [1, 9].

In the same paper where the Online Facility Location Problem was introduced, Meyerson also showed that it is possible to achieve a constant competitive ratio if the demand points are given in a random order [16]. Other works in the area tackle the lower bound of Online Facility Location by allowing the algorithm to make some adjustment to the solution over time.

The model closest to our work is by Divéki and Imreh [6] who allow an online algorithm to arbitrarily change the position of already opened facilities without incurring any additional costs. They achieve a competitive ratio of at most 2 for arbitrary metrics when given black box access to optimal algorithms for facility location and $k$-median. Otherwise their competitive ratio depends on the approximation ratios of the algorithms for these problems.

A variant in which some of the facility placements can be revoked completely is the Incremental Facility Location Problem [8]: Motivated by applications to clustering, existing facilities may be merged into one while the clients which were previously assigned to the merged facilities are then assigned all to the same facility. In this setting, a constant competitive ratio can be achieved. A survey covering various algorithms for both the Online and Incremental Facility Location Problem can be found in [11].

Our cost model for the movement of facilities is derived from the Page Migration Problem [5] for which the currently best known algorithms achieve competitive ratios of 4 in the deterministic case [4] and 2.618 for randomized algorithms against oblivious adversaries [19]. In our work, we use, as a subroutine, an algorithm for a variant of this problem called the Mobile Server Problem, in which the page may only be moved a constant distance in each time step. As a result, the page (or server in the terminology of the problem) needs to be moved in every time step as opposed to the phase-based algorithms for page migration. This algorithm and its analysis can be found in [7].

Other concepts of movement related to Facility Location include models where the number of facilities is fixed and they have to be moved to service clients which appear over time [13], a variant where both the clients and facilities may be moved in a network such that each client arrives at the node of a facility [12] and a mobile version in which a set of clients moves over time and the movement for a fixed set of facilities has to be determined to fulfill a given property [3]. In all of these models, the focus lies on the movement of a fixed number of facilities, and thus the aspect of placement of new facilities is not contained in them. Hence the techniques used for these problems are of limited use for our problem, in which the initial placement (and the cost for the facilities) are still a major concern.

## 1.2 Our Contribution

We propose an augmentation of the Online Facility Location Problem in which facilities may be moved by the online algorithm for costs proportional to the moved distance. In particular, we define two variants of the problem: One, where the algorithm may move the facilities an arbitrary distance in each time step and one where the moving distance is restricted to a constant $m$ in each time step. For a formal description of these problems see Section 2.

We give randomized online algorithms for both variants of the problem. Our results for the real line as a metric are as follows: For the case of unlimited movement, we achieve an expected competitive ratio of $O(\frac{\log D}{\log\log D})$ where $D \geq 1$ is a constant determining the ratio by which moving a facility over some distance is more expensive then serving a request over the same distance. In the case of limiting the movement of a facility to some constant $m$ in each time step, we achieve an expected competitive ratio of $O(\max\{\frac{\log(c_f/m)}{\log\log(c_f/m)}, \frac{\log D}{\log\log D}\})$ where $c_f$ is the cost of opening a new facility. We extend our result to the Euclidean space of arbitrary dimension, where we achieve a competitive ratio with an additional additive $O(\sqrt{k})$ term, where $k$ is the number of facilities in the optimal solution.

Finally, we give lower bounds for both the unlimited and limited movement case which show that our algorithms are asymptotically optimal for the line. As in the original Online Facility Location Problem, these lower bounds hold even in the case if there is only a single facility in the optimal solution.

## 2 MODEL & NOTATION

We first define the Facility Location Problem in the Euclidean space (of arbitrary dimension). The input is a sequence of requests $(r_1, \ldots, r_n)$ which are represented as points in the Euclidean space. A feasible solution is a non-empty subset $F$ of facilities. For a facility $f \in F$, $p(f)$ denotes the position of $f$ in the Euclidean space. The cost of the solution $F$ is $c(F) = |F| \cdot c_f + \sum_{t=1}^{n} \min_{f \in F} d(p(f), r_t)$, where $d(x, y)$ denotes the Euclidean distance between two points $x$ and $y$, and $c_f$ is a constant called the opening cost of a facility. Our goal is to find a set $F$ minimizing $c(F)$.

In the Online Facility Location Problem, the requests $(r_1, \ldots, r_n)$ arrive over time and each request must be served by connecting it to an open facility in that time step, i.e. if $F_t$ represents the set of open facilities in step $t$ the costs for serving the request $r_t$ is $\min_{f \in F_t} d(p(f), r_t)$. As a measure of performance for an online algorithm we use the (expected) competitive ratio. Let $E[C_{Alg}]$ be the expected cost of an online algorithm *ALG* and $C_{Opt}$ the cost of an optimal offline solution. We say *ALG* is *c*-competitive if $E[C_{Alg}] \leq c \cdot C_{Opt}$. For our randomized algorithms, we consider the input sequences to be generated by a so-called *oblivious adversary*, which knows the description of our algorithm but not the outcome of the random choices in a specific instance.

In our augmented variant of the Online Facility Location Problem, an online algorithm may move currently open facilities to a different position in each time step. In the unlimited version, the new position of a facility may be arbitrary, while in the limited version, the new position may only have a distance from the old position of at most a constant $m$. A solution now formally consists of sets $F_1 \subseteq F_2 \subseteq \ldots \subseteq F_n$ and positions $p_t(f)$ for all $f \in F_t$, where $d(p_t(f), p_{t+1}(f)) \leq m$ for all $t$ with $f \in F_t$ in the limited movement variant. The cost of such a solution is $c(F_1, \ldots, F_n, p_1, \ldots, p_n) = |F_n| \cdot c_f + \sum_{t=1}^{n} \min_{f \in F_t} d(p(f), r_t) + \sum_{t=1}^{n-1} \sum_{f \in F_t} D \cdot d(p_t(f), p_{t+1}(f))$ for some constant $D \geq 1$. The competitive ratio of an online algorithm is defined as in other resource augmentation settings, where the optimal offline solution does not use the additional power given to the online algorithm, which in our case is the ability to move facilities between time steps.

## 3 ALGORITHMS

In this section, we present randomized algorithms for our augmented Online Facility Location Problem. We first give a technical overview explaining the main ideas of our algorithms and how they are reflected in the analysis. Afterwards, we present an algorithm for the case of unlimited movement on the real line and its analysis in detail. We extend this algorithm to the case of limited movement and to the Euclidean space of higher dimensions in the subsequent sections, reusing many ideas from the first case for the analysis.

Note that due to the cost function for moving facilities, the algorithm by Divékih and Imreh [6] does not achieve an asymptotically optimal competitive ratio if $D$ is large. Their algorithm, called Opt-Follow (OFW), computes the optimal solution in every time step and moves its facilities accordingly if it has as many or less facilities than the optimum. If the algorithm has already more facilities than the optimal solution, it moves them to the optimal solution of the respective $k$-median problem where $k$ is the number of currently owned facilities. We show that this strategy is $\Omega(D)$-competitive even on the line.

THEOREM 3.1. *The OFW algorithm can not achieve a better competitive ratio than $\frac{1}{2}(1 + \frac{D}{4})$ on the real line.*

PROOF. We construct the following input sequence by identifying points on the line with real numbers: We create a total of $n$ requests where the $i$'th request appears at position $\frac{c_f}{2^i}$. The optimal solution has cost less than $2c_f$ which can be achieved by placing a single facility at point 0.

The OFW algorithm places a facility at point $\frac{c_f}{2}$ in the first time step which induces cost $c_f$. For $n \geq 4$ the optimal solution w.r.t. the input so far, after the $n$'th request, will place a single facility at a point identified with a real number at most $\frac{c_f}{4}$, hence the OFW algorithm will move its facility by a distance at least $\frac{c_f}{4}$, inducing costs $D \cdot \frac{c_f}{4}$. The lower bound directly follows from comparing the costs of the two solutions. □

### 3.1 Technical Overview

When considering the lower bound constructions for the Online Facility Location Problem in [10, 16], we observe that they rely on an input sequence which converges towards a (previously unknown) point which is optimal for the offline algorithm (similar to the sequence used in the proof of Theorem 3.1). The online algorithm can not place facilities in points "ahead" in the sequence (since subsequent points are randomly determined) and therefore incurs significantly higher costs by requiring the placement of many facilities along the convergence path.

Our first main idea to circumvent the lower bound constructions is to move the facilities along the convergence path rather than placing new ones. In accordance with our cost function for moving facilities, we regard the requests associated with one facility as an instance of the Page Migration Problem. In order to create those instances, we divide the space as follows: Whenever we place a new facility, we remember its original location called *facility origin* and divide the given space in a way that each point is associated to the closest facility origin. A facility will serve all requests on points associated to its origin by moving a $1/D$ fraction towards them. This resembles the algorithm for the Mobile Server Problem presented in [7] (see Section 1.1).

Assume for now that we treat all requests in the described way. The problem of our division of the space is that it might not be the same as in the optimal solution and therefore requests which the online algorithm regards as part of the same Page Migration Problem instance are served by different facilities in the optimal solution. Hence when referring to the optimal solution in our virtual Page Migration Problem, we would have an offline solution which switches positions without incurring any costs. It is clear that no online algorithm can be competitive against such an adversary.

Although guessing the optimal division of the space seems hard at first, we show that we can approximate the proper division during the execution fast enough by randomly placing new facilities at current requests where the probability to place a new facility is proportional to the costs which would otherwise occur by serving this request. We analyze this placement strategy by defining so-called *prohibited areas* for pairs of facilities. For a pair of two facilities $f$

and $f'$ the prohibited area of $f'$ to $f$ represents all points which are much closer to $f'$ than $f$. These points should not be served by a facility of the online algorithm for which the origin is placed near $f$ since in this case the serving costs for the online algorithm would be much higher then for the optimal solution. We show that a facility of the online algorithm associated to $f$ will, after a small amount of requests, no longer serve requests within the prohibited area of $f'$ since a new facility is then placed within that area. The total costs for this separation of optimal facilities are bound by explicitly utilizing the structure of the solution in the 1-dimensional case. For the Euclidean space of higher dimensions, we need a more complex, combinatorial argument to achieve a better bound than the trivial bound which can be achieved by simply counting the maximum costs for the separation for each pair of optimal facilities. This simple counting would only result in a bound of $O(k)$ where $k$ denotes the number of optimal facilities.

Now assume we have properly separated the optimal facilities from one another. If we use the ideas described so far for serving the requests as part of a virtual Page Migration instance, we would obtain an $O(D)$-competitive algorithm where the worst case essentially occurs when a facility is placed far away from an optimal facility and has to be moved all the way towards the optimal point (cf. the lower bound for the OFW algorithm, Theorem 3.1). To further improve the algorithm, we want to utilize the movement only for requests which are close to the optimal facility. We achieve this by dividing the requests into two categories called *large* and *short* which is determined by their distance to the closest facility origin of the online algorithm. Short requests, i.e. requests which are close to a facility origin, are treated as part of a Page Migration instance and are therefore served by a mobile facility which moves towards the request as described above. Large requests are served by an additional static facility which never moves and is located at the corresponding facility origin. With this categorization of the requests we reduce the amount of movement done by facilities and obtain a competitive ratio of $O(\frac{\log D}{\log \log D})$ for the real line. In Section 4, we show that this is asymptotically the best possible ratio achievable by any algorithm.

## 3.2 A Randomized Algorithm for Unlimited Movement

We present a randomized online algorithm for the real line which uses unlimited movement of the facilities. Both clients and facilities will be denoted as real numbers corresponding to a point on the line. For two points $x$ and $y$, we denote by $d(x, y) := |x - y|$ the Euclidean distance between $x$ and $y$. For $x \neq y$, we say that $x$ is to the left of $y$ if $x < y$, otherwise $x$ is to the right of $y$.

During the execution, our algorithm maintains a set of *facility origins* $\mathcal{F} \subseteq \mathbb{R}$. Whenever a new facility is placed at a point $a$ by the algorithm, $a$ will be added to $\mathcal{F}$. We say a point $x \in \mathbb{R}$ *belongs to* $a \in \mathcal{F}$ if $d(a, x) \leq d(a', x)$ for all $a' \in \mathcal{F}$.

In the further description of the algorithm, we refer to placing a new facility origin at point $a$. In these cases, the following happens: The algorithm places one *static facility* at $a$, which will never be moved, and a *mobile facility* at $a$, which is assigned to the points which belong to $a$. Hence for every $a \in \mathcal{F}$ there exist 2 facilities in the solution of the online algorithm.

*Unlimited Algorithm.* Let $r$ be a request and $a \in \mathcal{F}$ such that $r$ belongs to $a$. We say $r$ is *short* if $d(a, r) \leq 2\frac{c_f}{D}$, otherwise we say that $r$ is *large*.

Upon arrival of a request $r$, the online algorithm determines $a \in \mathcal{F}$ such that $r$ belongs to $a$. If $r$ is a large request, we set the *servicing facility* to the static facility located at $a$. If $r$ is short, the servicing facility is the mobile facility assigned to the area of $a$. Let $v$ be the position of the servicing facility. Place a new facility origin with probability $\frac{d(v,r)}{c_f}$ on $r$. If no new facility was placed on $r$, then either service $r$ directly if $v$ is static ($r$ is large) or move $v$ a distance of $\frac{d(v,r)}{D}$ towards $r$ and then service $r$ if $v$ is mobile ($r$ is short).

In the following, we analyze the competitive ratio of the online algorithm based on the ideas from the previous section. The costs for short and large requests can by analyzed independently of one another.

Lemma 3.2. *The costs of the online algorithm for large requests are at most $O(\frac{\log D}{\log \log D})$ times the costs of the optimal solution.*

Proof. Consider a facility $f$ placed by the optimal offline algorithm. We refer to the interval of $f$ as all points for which $f$ is the closest facility of the optimal solution. Define the inner zone of $f$ as all points in its interval which have a distance less than $\frac{c_f}{D}$ to $f$. The set of outer zones of $f$ consists of zones $1, \ldots, h$ where each zone $j$ contains the points in the interval of $f$ which are at a distance in $[\frac{c_f}{x^j}, \frac{c_f}{x^{j-1}})$ from $f$. We set $x := \frac{\log D}{\log \log D}$ and $h := \Theta(\frac{\log D}{\log \log D})$ such that $x^h = D$. Note that each point in the interval of $f$ now either belongs to the inner zone or one of the outer zones of $f$.

For each of the zones of $f$, there exists a facility origin of the online algorithm in the respective zone after expected costs at most $c_f$ incurred by requests within that zone. After a facility origin is placed within the inner zone of $f$, large requests can only appear in outer zones since the origin has a distance of at most $\frac{c_f}{D}$ to $f$ and a large request must have a distance of at least $2\frac{c_f}{D}$ to every origin. For the outer zones of $f$ where a facility origin is already placed, the distance from a request $r$ to the origin $a \in \mathcal{F}$ is at most $2 \cdot d(f, r) + x \cdot d(f, r) = O(\frac{\log D}{\log \log D}) \cdot d(f, r)$. Combined with the fact that there are at most $h + 1$ zones for each optimal facility this implies a competitive ratio of $O(\frac{\log D}{\log \log D})$ for the large requests. □

We further divide the short requests by their distance to their respective optimal facility. The competitive ratio on short requests which are far from the optimal facilities is easy to obtain. Note that the movement in these cases would not be necessary, since the movement only improves the performance when the facility origin is already reasonably close to the optimal facility (i.e. the convergence point in the lower bound sequences), but also does not increase the costs of any request by more than a constant factor.

Lemma 3.3. *Consider the short requests served by a mobile facility of the online algorithm belonging to a facility origin with distance at least $4\frac{c_f}{D}$ to the nearest optimal facility. The costs for serving these requests are at most $O(1)$ times the cost of the optimal solution.*

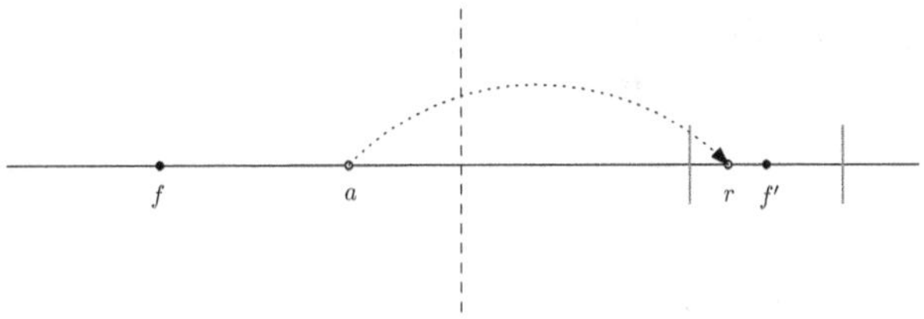


**Figure 1: The marked interval on the right contains the prohibited area of $f'$ to $f$. If the request $r$ is served by a facility with origin $a$, then $r$ is a prohibited request.**

Proof. Consider a facility origin $a$ with $d(f, a) \geq 4\frac{c_f}{D}$, where $f$ is the closest facility in the optimal solution to $a$. For all short requests served by a mobile facility assigned to this origin, the optimal costs will be at least $2\frac{c_f}{D}$. On the other hand, the costs of the online algorithm will be no more than $\Theta(\frac{c_f}{D})$ for each of those requests by definition. Note that this is also true for short requests which are served by a different optimal facility $f'$ than $f$ since the space is parted equally between $f$ and $f'$ and hence $d(f', a) \geq d(f, a)$. □

We finally turn our attention to short requests which occur in close proximity to a facility of the optimal solution. As explained in the previous section, those requests should not be served by a facility of the online algorithm which originates in the interval of a different optimal facility, since in that case the costs of the online algorithm are much higher than the costs of the optimal solution. We formally classify those type of requests as follows: For optimal facilities $f$ and $f'$, we define the prohibited area of $f'$ to $f$ to contain all points $r$ for which $d(f', r) \leq \frac{1}{8} \cdot d(f, f')$ holds. It is easy to see that if there is a facility origin within the red area of $f'$ to $f$, no facility with origin in the interval of $f$ will serve a request in the red area of $f'$ to $f$. If this is the case, we say that $f'$ is separated from $f$.

Consider a facility origin $a$ in the interval of $f$. We call a request $r$ in the prohibited area of $f'$ to $f$ for which $a$ is the closest facility origin a prohibited request. The concepts of prohibited areas and requests are illustrated in Figure 1.

Lemma 3.4. *Consider the short requests served by a mobile facility of the online algorithm belonging to a facility origin with distance less than $4\frac{c_f}{D}$ to the nearest optimal facility. The costs for serving these requests are at most $O(1)$ times the cost of the optimal solution excluding prohibited requests.*

Proof. For each of the mobile facilities for which the origin is placed by the online algorithm in the interval of an optimal facility $f$ we define an instance of the page migration problem consisting of all requests served by that facility. We may assume that all requests, which are not in the prohibited area of a different facility $f'$ to $f$, are served by $f$ with only a constant factor loss, since for a request $r$ served by $f'$ it holds $d(f, r) \leq d(f, f') + d(f', r) \leq 9d(f', r)$. Let $v$ be the current position of the mobile facility of the algorithm for this instance. We define the potential associated with the instance to be $\phi = 2D \cdot d(f, v)$.

When a mobile facility is placed along with a new facility origin on a point $a$, the potential $\phi$ is initialized with $2D \cdot d(f, r)$. Since $d(f, r) \leq 4\frac{c_f}{D}$, the cost for placing the new facility increases by at most a constant factor. Additionally, due to the probability of placing new facility origins, the expected costs for placing new facilities are not more than a constant times the cost for serving the current request and hence we omit these costs in the further analysis. In order to apply the potential argument properly, the change in potential must be accounted for every time the respective mobile facility is moved, including the times when it does so to serve prohibited requests. We show that including the potential in these costs does not increase them by more than a constant factor. When a mobile facility is moved from a point $v$ to $v'$ to serve any request $r$, we get $\Delta\phi = 2D \cdot (d(f, v') - d(f, v)) \leq 2D \cdot d(v, v') \leq 2d(v, r)$. Hence, including the potential argument does not increase the costs of any request by more than a constant factor.

We now consider the requests which are part of one virtual Page Migration instance but not prohibited. When the algorithm serves a request $r$ with a facility which is moved from $v$ to $v'$, the costs are $C_{Alg} = D \cdot d(v, v') + d(v', r)$, while $C_{OPT} = d(f, r)$. First consider the case that $d(v', r) > d(f, r)$. The potential difference is $\Delta\phi = 2D \cdot (d(f, v') - d(f, v)) \leq -2d(v, r)$. The costs of the algorithm can be estimated by $C_{Alg} = D \cdot \frac{1}{D} d(v, r) + d(v', r) \leq 2 \cdot d(v, r)$ and hence $C_{Alg} + \Delta\phi \leq 0$.

If $d(v', r) \leq d(f, r)$, we distinguish the following cases:
If $d(f, v') - d(f, v) \leq -\frac{1}{2} d(f, v)$, then $\Delta\phi \leq -D \cdot d(f, v)$ and $C_{Alg} \leq d(v, f) + 2d(f, r)$, hence $C_{Alg} + \Delta\phi \leq 2C_{Opt}$.
Else, $d(f, v) < 2d(f, v')$ holds which implies $\Delta\phi \leq 2D \cdot d(v, v') \leq 2(d(v, f) + d(f, r)) \leq 10d(f, r)$ and $C_{Alg} \leq 5d(f, r)$. □

So far, we have bounded all costs either incurred by large requests or by short requests not part of the prohibited area of an optimal facility $f'$ to the optimal facility $f$ in whose interval the servicing facility is originating. For short request which remain to be analyzed, i.e. the prohibited requests, the costs of the online algorithm may be much higher than the optimal costs for the same requests. However, we show that when considering all such requests, the total costs are bounded within a constant factor of the costs for facilities in the optimal solution.

Lemma 3.5. *The expected costs for prohibited requests is bounded by $O(k \cdot c_f)$ on the real line, where $k$ is the number of facilities in the optimal solution.*

Proof. Consider two optimal facilities $f$ and $f'$. W.l.o.g. assume that $f'$ is located to the right of $f$. After expected cost at most $O(c_f)$ for requests in the prohibited area of $f'$ to $f$ a facility origin is placed in that area, preventing any facility originating in the interval of $f$ or to the left of it from entering the prohibited area of $f'$ to $f$ again.

Now number the optimal facilities $f_1, \ldots, f_k$ from left to right, i.e. if $f_i$ refers to a position expressed as a real number we have $f_1 < f_2 < \ldots < f_k$. Consider facilities $f_i, f_j$ with $i < j$ for which the algorithm has a facility origin placed in the intervals of those facilities but no facility of the algorithm originates in the intervals of $f_{i+1}, \ldots, f_{j-1}$. We define the following type of events:

(a) The algorithm places a facility origin in the interval of a facility $f_\ell, \ell \in \{i+1, \ldots, j-1\}$.

(b) The algorithm places a facility origin in the prohibited area of $f_i$ to $f_j$ or vice versa.

Note that we can view these events as being charged by requests in the respective intervals or prohibited areas. After charging the event with expected costs $O(c_f)$, it then actually occurs.

For events of type (a), we observe that after expected costs of $O(c_f)$ in the interval of $f_\ell$ overall, a facility is placed in this interval. When that is the case, facilities originating from intervals of $f > f_\ell$ do no longer serve requests in intervals of facilities $f' < f_\ell$. For events of type (b), there are two of them in such a sequence and only occur once as argued above. Furthermore, any event of type (a) stops the events from happening. Hence, after an event of type (a) occurs, we can split the sequence of facilities in two parts $f_i, \ldots, f_\ell$ and $f_\ell, \ldots, f_j$ and apply the same arguments.

It follows that regarding the complete sequence $f_1, \ldots, f_k$, event (a) occurs at most $k$ times and between each of such events, at most 2 events of type (b) occur. Hence the costs for the events of type (a) and (b) on expectation sum up to at most $3k \cdot O(c_f)$. □

Summarizing all lemmas in this section, we have bound the costs of the online algorithm for all possible types of requests independently and can hence conclude the analysis.

THEOREM 3.6. *The online algorithm stated above is* $O(\frac{\log D}{\log\log D})$*-competitive on the real line.*

It is noteworthy that our algorithm is in fact $O(1)$-competitive on short requests, implying that we have an overall $O(1)$-competitive algorithm if all requests are at a distance of at most $O(\frac{c_f}{D})$ from the nearest optimal facility. In contrast, the lower bound for the classical Online Facility Location problem would still hold in that scenario for a sufficiently large number of clients $n$; in fact, the distances in the lower bound decrease with growing $n$.

## 3.3 Extension to Limited Movement

We extend the algorithm from the previous section to only utilize a maximum moving distance of $m$ in each time step. The algorithm considers two major cases: If $D$ is large, then the algorithms works as in the unlimited case. Else, we need to alter the definition of small and large requests to fit the restriction of the movement for handling the short requests.

*Limited Algorithm.* We classify a request $r$ by its distance to the closest facility origin $a \in \mathcal{F}$. The classification differs based on the parameters: If $D \geq \sqrt{c_f/m}$ we use the same classification as in the unlimited case, namely $r$ is short if $d(a,r) \leq 2\frac{c_f}{D}$ and large otherwise. If $D < \sqrt{c_f/m}$ we classify $r$ as short if $d(a,r) \leq 2m$ and large otherwise. The servicing facility of $r$ is either the static facility at $a$ if $r$ is large or the mobile facility assigned to the area in which $r$ lies if $r$ is short. When servicing a short request $r$ from a mobile facility at point $v$, we move the facility by a distance of $\frac{d(v,r)}{2D}$ towards $r$ and then service the request. Large requests simply get served by the static facility without any movement.

Note that the movement of the algorithm is possible in all cases under the restriction of a maximum movement distance $m$ since $r$ is short:

If $D \geq \sqrt{c_f/m}$ then $\frac{d(v,r)}{2D} \leq \frac{2c_f}{2D^2} \leq m$.
If $D < \sqrt{c_f/m}$ then $\frac{d(v,r)}{2D} \leq \frac{2m}{2D} \leq m$.

THEOREM 3.7. *The online algorithm with limited movement stated above is* $O(\max\{\frac{\log(c_f/m)}{\log\log(c_f/m)}, \frac{\log D}{\log\log D}\})$*-competitive on the real line.*

PROOF. The structure of the proof follows the analysis of the previous section. We only consider the case $D < \sqrt{c_f/m}$ for which we need to show that the algorithm is $O(\frac{\log(c_f/m)}{\log\log(c_f/m)})$-competitive. In case $D \geq \sqrt{c_f/m}$ the algorithm works the same as in the unlimited case and hence Theorem 3.6 directly gives the desired bound.

We begin by analyzing only large requests, i.e. requests with a distance greater than $2m$ to their closest facility origin. The analysis works essentially the same as in Lemma 3.2. Consider an optimal facility $f$. Requests with distance at most $m$ to $f$ incur expected costs at most $O(c_f)$ before a facility origin is placed within that area and hence no further large requests appear. The other points can be divided into $h = \Theta(\frac{\log(c_f/m)}{\log\log(c_f/m)})$ outer zones, where the $i$'th zone contains all points within a distance $[\frac{c_f}{x^i}, \frac{c_f}{x^{i-1}})$ from $f$ where $x = \frac{\log(c_f/m)}{\log\log(c_f/m)}$. After placing a facility origin in an outer zone of $f$, it is clear that all large requests in the same outer zone can be served for at most $3x$ times the optimal cost. From this, the bound for large requests follows.

We partition short requests into multiple instances of the Page Migration Problem as before, i.e. all requests served by one mobile facility form an instance. There are two kinds of instances we need to consider: If the mobile facility has its origin at a distance at least $4m$ from the optimal facility $f$, then the optimal solution has costs at least $2m$ for each request and the costs of the algorithm are at most $4m$ (cf. Lemma 3.3).

For instances where the origin is a distance less than $4m$ from $f$, we use a potential argument similar as in the proof of Lemma 3.4: Let $v$ be the current position of the mobile facility. The potential is defined as $\phi(f,v) = 2D \cdot d(f,v)$. For the initial potential it holds $\phi_0 \leq 2Dm \leq 2c_f$, hence the costs for placing a new facility does not increase more than a constant factor. The analysis for requests which are part of the instance served by the mobile facility outside of prohibited areas of other facilities to $f$ works as in Lemma 3.4. The bound on costs for prohibited requests can also be derived exactly as in the former case (Lemma 3.5). In total, we have shown that the online algorithm is $O(1)$-competitive on short requests and $O(\max\{\frac{\log(c_f/m)}{\log\log(c_f/m)}\})$-competitive on large requests, implying the desired bound. □

## 3.4 Extension to Higher-Dimensional Spaces

In this section, we turn our attention to the Euclidean space of higher dimensions. We use the same algorithms as before. Note, that most of the arguments presented in Sections 3.2 and 3.3 still hold in this case, however it should be obvious that the arguments presented in the proof of Lemma 3.5 no longer apply since they make explicit use of the linear structure of the space. Hence we present a new bound of the costs incurred by prohibited requests which relies more on the combinatorial aspects of the separation

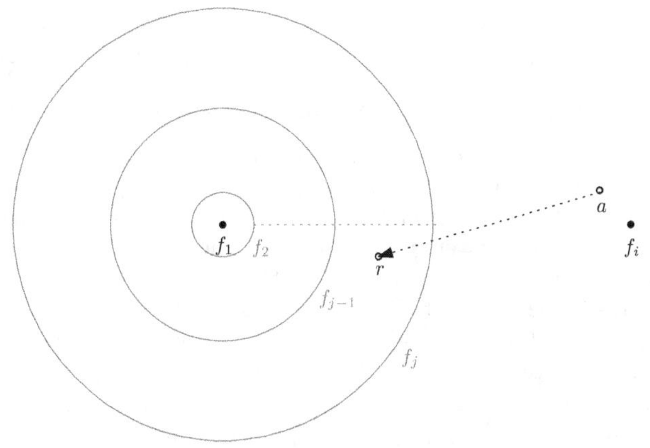


**Figure 2: A depiction of an event as described in (1) and (2). The circles mark the prohibited areas of $f_1$ to the other facilities indicated by their labels.**

taking place over time rather than the structure of the underlying space.

LEMMA 3.8. *The expected costs for prohibited requests is bounded by $O(k^{3/2} \cdot c_f)$, where $k$ is the number of facilities in the optimal solution.*

PROOF. For two optimal facilities $f$ and $f'$ we write $f \mid f'$ if an online facility origin is located in the prohibited area of $f'$ to $f$, i.e. $f$ is separated from $f'$. Recall that this implies that no prohibited requests in the interval of $f'$ will be served by facilities with their origin in the interval of $f$. We use the same notation with sets of facilities, in which the separation holds pairwise.

Consider the optimal facilities $f_1, \ldots, f_k$ sorted by their distance to $f_1$, i.e. $d(f_1, f_2) \leq d(f_1, f_3) \leq \ldots \leq d(f_1, f_k)$. Now consider a request $r$ which is served by an online facility associated to $f_i$ (meaning the closest optimal facility to its origin is $f_i$). Let $f_1$ be the closest optimal facility to $r$ and let $r$ be located in the prohibited area of $f_1$ to $f_i$. Furthermore, consider the minimal $j \leq i$ such that $r$ lies within the prohibited area of $f_1$ to $f_j$.

Now consider an optimal facility $f_\ell$ with $j - 1 \geq \ell \geq 2$. If $d(f_\ell, r) \geq \frac{1}{8} \cdot d(f_i, f_\ell)$, then $d(f_i, r) \leq 9d(f_\ell, r) \leq 9(d(f_\ell, f_1) + d(f_1, r)) \leq 9^2 \cdot d(f_1, r)$. Hence we may still assume that $r$ is served by $f_i$ in the optimal solution with the loss of only a constant factor. If on the other hand no such $\ell$ exists, than $d(f_\ell, r) < \frac{1}{8} \cdot d(f_i, f_\ell)$ and hence if a facility origin is placed on $r$, online facilities associated to $f_i$ will no longer serve requests located in the prohibited area of $f_\ell$ to $f_i$ for all $j - 1 \geq \ell \geq 2$. We assume this to be the case from here on.

We collect the impacts of a new facility origin being placed on $r$. Most obviously, all $f_\ell$ with $\ell \geq j$ are now separated from $f_1$, i.e.

$$\{f_j, f_{j+1}, \ldots, f_i, \ldots, f_k\} \mid f_1. \tag{1}$$

Additionally, as argued above, we get

$$f_i \mid \{f_1, \ldots, f_{j-1}\}. \tag{2}$$

The position of $r$ in relation to the facilities is depicted in Figure 2.

We refer to the placement of such a facility origin as an event, and each request which has the potential to trigger such an event due to its location is referred to as contributing to an event. After expected costs of $O(c_f)$ incurred by requests contributing to any of the events characterized above one the events occurs.

We now collect these type of events in a $k \times k$ matrix $A$, where each entry $a_{ij}$ represents an event in the area of $f_j$ served from a facility originating in the area of $f_i$. Note that the implied ordering of the facilities within the matrix does not correspond to the ordering used to describe the events as above, since that ordering may be different in each of the events. Each entry $a_{ij} \in \{1, \ldots, k-1\}$ represents the number of facilities $f_i$ separates itself from in the respective event, i.e. the number of elements on the right side of (2). If the entry is 0 there was no such an event. Since $f_i$ can separate itself from each facility only once, the sum of entries in a row is at most $k - 1$. We say that each $f_i$ has a budget of $k - 1$ and each element $a_{ij}$ draws from the budget of $f_i$.

Furthermore, each number in $\{1, \ldots, k-1\}$ can only appear once per column. This is since each entry $a_{ij}$ in column $j$ implies that $k - a_{ij}$ facilities are separated from $f_j$ after the respective event (the elements on the left side of (1)). Each event however must increase the number of facilities separated from $f_j$ by at least 1, since it at least separates itself from $f_j$.

If we consider the budget of all facilities to be $k \cdot (k-1)$ we can derive that one event draws a total budget of $a_{ij}$. Since each $a_{ij}$ can appear at most $k$ times, the number of non-zero entries is maximized by first choosing $k$ elements to be 1, then $k$ elements to be 2, etc. The total budget is spent after $O(\sqrt{k})$ rounds of this assignment, yielding a total of $O(k^{3/2})$ entries which are not 0. □

We finally collect the results to achieve the following result for our algorithm in the Euclidean space of arbitrary dimension.

THEOREM 3.9. *The algorithm is $O(\frac{\log D}{\log \log D} + \sqrt{k})$-competitive in the unlimited case and for a maximum moving distance of $m$, the limited algorithm is $O(\max\{\frac{\log(c_f/m)}{\log\log(c_f/m)}, \frac{\log D}{\log\log D}\} + \sqrt{k})$-competitive in the Euclidean space of arbitrary dimension, where $k$ denotes the number of optimal facilities.*

PROOF. We sort the requests into categories as before and collect the results for each of them. Large requests can be analyzed as in Lemma 3.2 for the unlimited case and as in Theorem 3.7 for the limited case. For short requests which are served by a facility with origin more than a distance $4\frac{c_f}{D}$ (or $4m$ in the limited case) from the nearest optimal facility we may apply the analysis of Lemma 3.3 and for short requests which are not prohibited we use Lemma 3.4. Finally, for prohibited requests we bound the costs via Lemma 3.8. □

## 4 LOWER BOUNDS

In this section, we provide lower bounds on the competitive ratio for algorithms in our model. The bounds illustrate that our algorithms from the previous section achieve an asymptotically tight competitive ratio in both the unlimited and limited movement versions on the real line.

Both lower bounds closely follow the structure of the original lower bound by Fotakis [10] and utilize Yao's Min-Max Principle [20], i.e. we construct a randomized sequence of demands independently of a deterministic online algorithm processing the input. We construct complete binary trees as an underlying metric where the distances are chosen in a way that utilizing the movement becomes essentially useless for the online algorithm. We show that such trees can be embedded onto the real line with all necessary properties staying intact.

THEOREM 4.1. *No randomized algorithm whose competitive ratio does not depend on n can be better than* $\Omega(\frac{\log D}{\log\log D})$*-competitive even on the real line and against an oblivious adversary.*

PROOF. We construct a complete binary tree with depth $x := \lfloor \frac{\log D}{\log\log D} \rfloor$. The distance between the root and its children is $\frac{c_f}{x}$ and the distance between nodes at level $i-1$ and nodes at level $i$ is $\frac{c_f}{x^i}$. We choose a simple path $v_0, \ldots, v_x$ from the root $v_0$ to a leaf $v_x$ by succinctly choosing a child $v_{i+1}$ of $v_i$ uniformly at random. The input sequence is divided into $x+1$ phases where in phase $i \in \{0, \ldots, x\}$ there are $x^i$ requests on $v_i$. The optimal solution can place a facility at $v_x$ and pays at most $c_f + \sum_{i=0}^{x-1} x^i \cdot \sum_{j=i+1}^{x} \frac{c_f}{x^j} \leq 3c_f$.

Let $T_v$ be the sub-tree rooted at node $v$. Consider an online algorithm at the end of phase $i \in \{0, \ldots, x-1\}$. If the algorithm has not placed a facility on $T_{v_i}$ or on the edge $(v_{i-1}, v_i)$, the costs are at least $x^i \cdot \frac{c_f}{x^i} = c_f$. Otherwise, if the algorithm placed a new facility within $T_{v_i}$, it will not be part of $T_{v_{i+1}}$ with probability at least $\frac{1}{2}$. Hence, the costs for facilities not in $T_{v_{i+1}}$ are at least $\frac{c_f}{2}$. Finally, if the algorithm has moved a facility by a distance $\delta$, it holds for the costs $D \cdot \delta > x^i \cdot \delta$. Hence moving a facility in order to reduce the costs for the requests of one phase does not pay off. Furthermore $D \cdot \frac{c_f}{x^i} > c_f$, hence moving a facility along any edge within the tree has costs more than $c_f$ and does not pay off. We conclude that for every $i$, the online algorithm pays $c_f$ for requests and facilities not in $T_{v_{i+1}}$. It follows that the costs of the online algorithm are $\Omega(x \cdot c_f)$ which implies the competitive ratio on the given tree metric.

It remains to describe how to embed the tree onto the real line such that all necessary properties for the lower bound are preserved. We choose the same embedding as in [10] which puts the tree root at point 0, and succinctly maps the children of a node $v$ at level $i$ which is located at position $p_v$ to positions $p_v + \frac{c_f}{x^{i+1}}$ and $p_v - \frac{c_f}{x^{i+1}}$. With this embedding it was shown in [10] that no pairwise distance increases and hence the value of the optimal solution does not increase. Furthermore the relevant distances from the algorithm's perspective are maintained in the classical setting, i.e. without the option to move a facility. It remains to argue that the embedding does not invalidate the arguments about facility movement. Consider a facility at node $v_i$. With probability $\frac{1}{2}$, all nodes in the sub-tree $T_{v_{i+1}}$ are located at a distance at least $\frac{c_f}{x^{i+1}}$ from $v_i$ and hence moving a facility inside this sub-tree is more expensive then constructing a new facility. It follows that the arguments from above still hold in the embedding. □

THEOREM 4.2. *No randomized algorithm whose competitive ratio does not depend on n and whose movement is restricted to m per time step can be better than* $\Omega(\frac{\log(c_f/m)}{\log\log(c_f/m)})$*-competitive.*

PROOF. We construct a similar binary tree as in the proof of Theorem 4.1 where the distance between nodes at level $i-1$ and $i$ is $\frac{c_f}{x^i}$ with $x := \lfloor \frac{\log\sqrt{c_f/m}}{\log\log\sqrt{c_f/m}} \rfloor$. The input sequence is again constructed by choosing a simple path $v_0, \ldots, v_x$ from the root $v_0$ to a leaf $v_x$ by succinctly choosing a child $v_{i+1}$ of $v_i$ uniformly at random. The input sequence is divided into $x+1$ phases where in phase $i \in \{0, \ldots, x\}$ there are $x^i$ requests on $v_i$. The optimal solution can place a facility at $v_x$ and pays at most $3c_f$.

Let $T_v$ be the sub-tree rooted at node $v$. Consider an online algorithm at the end of phase $i \in \{0, \ldots, x-1\}$. If the algorithm has not placed a facility on $T_{v_i}$ or on the edge $(v_{i-1}, v_i)$, the costs are at least $x^i \cdot \frac{c_f}{x_i} = c_f$. Otherwise, if the algorithm placed a new facility within $T_{v_i}$, it will not be part of $T_{v_{i+1}}$ with probability at least $\frac{1}{2}$. Hence, the costs for facilities not in $T_{v_{i+1}}$ are at least $\frac{c_f}{2}$.

Finally, we have to argue that movement does not help the algorithm. Suppose the algorithm has a facility on $v_{i-1}$ at the beginning of phase $i$. The cost for requests on $v_i$ are minimized if the algorithm moves the facility on $v_{i-1}$ by a distance $m$ towards $v_i$. In this case, the costs are at least $\sum_{j=1}^{x^i}(\frac{c_f}{x^i} - jm) \geq c_f - m\frac{x^{2i}}{2} \geq \frac{c_f}{2}$. The embedding onto the real line works the same as in Theorem 4.1 and the lower bound holds using the same arguments. □

Note, that the lower bound in Theorem 4.1 also holds for the limited movement case and the bound in Theorem 4.2 holds independent of the value of $D$. Hence, an online algorithm in the limited movement setting can not achieve a better competitive ratio than the maximum of $\Omega(\frac{\log D}{\log\log D})$ and $\Omega(\frac{\log(c_f/m)}{\log\log(c_f/m)})$.

## 5 FUTURE WORK

Our algorithm achieves a competitive ratio independent of the number of clients, surpassing the lower bound of the Online Facility Location problem without movement. For the real line, the competitive ratio is tight in both the unlimited and limited movement case. For higher dimensions, it is still open whether a competitive ratio independent of the number of facilities in the optimal solution can be achieved. We conjecture that the competitive ratios achieved by our randomized algorithms can also be achieved with deterministic algorithms, although those algorithms may have to use more complex policies with regards to placing new facilities. A good candidate algorithm would be to adapt the deterministic algorithm for the Online Facility Location problem by Fotakis [10], although the algorithm would then loose the property of working essentially without memory of past requests.

Regarding different models, it might be interesting to consider the leasing variant of Facility Location [17] in which facilities are rented for a fixed time period instead of bought permanently. In this model, the competitive ratio can be formulated in terms of the length of the longest lease instead of the number of clients [14]. It would be interesting to explore whether our techniques would also help to remove the dependence of the competitive ratio on this parameter.

Furthermore, it seems natural to consider a variant where the adversary may move the facilities for the same cost as the online algorithm. This model would then be closer related to the $k$-Page

Migration problem and variants of the $k$-Server Problem, specifically the $(h, k)$-Server Problem [2, 15] where the online algorithm has more servers available than the offline solution. Therefore the question arises whether it would be possible to achieve competitive ratios independent of the number of optimal facilities even on simple metrics as the real line.

## REFERENCES


[1] Aris Anagnostopoulos, Russell Bent, Eli Upfal, and Pascal Van Hentenryck. 2004. A simple and deterministic competitive algorithm for online facility location. *Inf. Comput.* 194, 2 (2004), 175–202. https://doi.org/10.1016/j.ic.2004.06.002

[2] Nikhil Bansal, Marek Eliáš, Lukasz Jez, and Grigorios Koumoutsos. 2017. The (h, k)-Server Problem on Bounded Depth Trees. In *Proceedings of the 28th Annual ACM-SIAM Symposium on Discrete Algorithms, SODA 2017, Barcelona, Spain, Hotel Porta Fira, January 16-19.* 1022–1037. https://doi.org/10.1137/1.9781611974782.65

[3] Sergei Bespamyatnikh, Binay K. Bhattacharya, David G. Kirkpatrick, and Michael Segal. 2000. Mobile facility location. In *Proceedings of the 4th International Workshop on Discrete Algorithms and Methods for Mobile Computing and Communications (DIAL-M 2000), Boston, Massachusetts, USA, August 11, 2000.* 46–53. https://doi.org/10.1145/345848.345858

[4] Marcin Bienkowski, Jaroslaw Byrka, and Marcin Mucha. 2017. Dynamic Beats Fixed: On Phase-Based Algorithms for File Migration. In *Proceedings of the 44th International Colloquium on Automata, Languages, and Programming, ICALP 2017, July 10-14, 2017, Warsaw, Poland.* 13:1–13:14. https://doi.org/10.4230/LIPIcs.ICALP.2017.13

[5] David L. Black and Daniel D. Sleator. 1989. *Competitive Algorithms for Replication and Migration Problems.* Technical Report CMU-CS-89-201. Department of Computer Science, Carnegie-Mellon University.

[6] Gabriella Divéki and Csanád Imreh. 2011. Online facility location with facility movements. *CEJOR* 19, 2 (2011), 191–200. https://doi.org/10.1007/s10100-010-0153-8

[7] Björn Feldkord and Friedhelm Meyer auf der Heide. 2017. The Mobile Server Problem. In *Proceedings of the 29th ACM Symposium on Parallelism in Algorithms and Architectures, SPAA 2017, Washington DC, USA, July 24-26, 2017.* 313–319. https://doi.org/10.1145/3087556.3087575

[8] Dimitris Fotakis. 2006. Incremental algorithms for Facility Location and k-Median. *Theor. Comput. Sci.* 361, 2-3 (2006), 275–313. https://doi.org/10.1016/j.tcs.2006.05.015

[9] Dimitris Fotakis. 2007. A primal-dual algorithm for online non-uniform facility location. *J. Discrete Algorithms* 5, 1 (2007), 141–148. https://doi.org/10.1016/j.jda.2006.03.001

[10] Dimitris Fotakis. 2008. On the Competitive Ratio for Online Facility Location. *Algorithmica* 50, 1 (2008), 1–57. https://doi.org/10.1007/s00453-007-9049-y

[11] Dimitris Fotakis. 2011. Online and incremental algorithms for facility location. *SIGACT News* 42, 1 (2011), 97–131. https://doi.org/10.1145/1959045.1959065

[12] Zachary Friggstad and Mohammad R. Salavatipour. 2011. Minimizing movement in mobile facility location problems. *ACM Trans. Algorithms* 7, 3 (2011), 28:1–28:22. https://doi.org/10.1145/1978782.1978783

[13] Abdolhamid Ghodselahi and Fabian Kuhn. 2015. Serving Online Requests with Mobile Servers. In *Proceedings of the 26th International Symposium on Algorithms and Computation, ISAAC 2015, Nagoya, Japan, December 9-11, 2015, Proceedings.* 740–751. https://doi.org/10.1007/978-3-662-48971-0_62

[14] Peter Kling, Friedhelm Meyer auf der Heide, and Peter Pietrzyk. 2012. An Algorithm for Online Facility Leasing. In *Proceedings of the19th International Colloquium on Structural Information and Communication Complexity, SIROCCO 2012, Reykjavik, Iceland, June 30-July 2, 2012, Revised Selected Papers.* 61–72. https://doi.org/10.1007/978-3-642-31104-8_6

[15] Elias Koutsoupias. 1999. Weak Adversaries for the k-Server Problem. In *Proceedings of the 40th Annual Symposium on Foundations of Computer Science, FOCS '99, 17-18 October, 1999, New York, NY, USA.* 444–449. https://doi.org/10.1109/SFFCS.1999.814616

[16] Adam Meyerson. 2001. Online Facility Location. In *Proceedings of the 42nd Annual Symposium on Foundations of Computer Science, FOCS 2001, 14-17 October 2001, Las Vegas, Nevada, USA.* 426–431. https://doi.org/10.1109/SFCS.2001.959917

[17] Chandrashekhar Nagarajan and David P. Williamson. 2013. Offline and online facility leasing. *Discrete Optimization* 10, 4 (2013), 361–370. https://doi.org/10.1016/j.disopt.2013.10.001

[18] David B. Shmoys. 2000. Approximation algorithms for facility location problems. In *Proceedings of the 3rd International Workshop on Approximation Algorithms for Combinatorial Optimization, APPROX 2000, Saarbrücken, Germany, September 5-8, 2000, Proceedings.* 27–33. https://doi.org/10.1007/3-540-44436-X_4

[19] Jeffery Westbrook. 1994. Randomized Algorithms for Multiprocessor Page Migration. *SIAM J. Comput.* 23, 5 (1994), 951–965. https://doi.org/10.1137/S0097539791199796

[20] Andrew Chi-Chih Yao. 1977. Probabilistic Computations: Toward a Unified Measure of Complexity (Extended Abstract). In *Proceedings of the 18th Annual Symposium on Foundations of Computer Science, Providence, Rhode Island, USA, 31 October - 1 November 1977.* 222–227. https://doi.org/10.1109/SFCS.1977.24

# The Transactional Conflict Problem

Dan Alistarh
IST Austria

Syed Kamran Haider
UConn

Raphael Kübler
ETH Zurich

Giorgi Nadiradze
ETH Zurich

## ABSTRACT

The *transactional conflict* problem arises in transactional systems whenever two or more concurrent transactions clash on a data item. While the standard solution to such conflicts is to immediately abort one of the transactions, some practical systems consider the alternative of *delaying* conflict resolution for a short interval, which may allow one of the transactions to commit. The challenge in the transactional conflict problem is to choose the optimal length of this delay interval so as to minimize the overall running time penalty for the conflicting transactions.

In this paper, we propose a family of optimal online algorithms for the transactional conflict problem. Specifically, we consider variants of this problem which arise in different implementations of transactional systems, namely "requestor wins" and "requestor aborts" implementations: in the former, the recipient of a coherence request is aborted, whereas in the latter, it is the requestor which has to abort. Both strategies are implemented by real systems. We show that the *requestor aborts* case can be reduced to a classic instance of the ski rental problem, while the *requestor wins* case leads to a *new* version of this classical problem, for which we derive optimal deterministic and randomized algorithms. Moreover, we prove that, under a simplified adversarial model, our algorithms are constant-competitive with the offline optimum in terms of throughput. We validate our algorithmic results empirically through a hardware simulation of hardware transactional memory (HTM), showing that our algorithms can lead to non-trivial performance improvements for classic concurrent data structures.

**ACM Reference Format:**
Dan Alistarh, Syed Kamran Haider, Raphael Kübler, and Giorgi Nadiradze. 2018. The Transactional Conflict Problem. In *SPAA '18: 30th ACM Symposium on Parallelism in Algorithms and Architectures, July 16–18, 2018, Vienna, Austria.* ACM, New York, NY, USA, 10 pages. https://doi.org/10.1145/3210377.3210406

## 1 INTRODUCTION

Several interesting tools and techniques have been developed to address the challenge of making correct decisions about the future while holding limited information, also known as *online decision-making* [3–5, 7, 14]. In this context, the *ski rental problem* [21] is the question of choosing between continuing to pay a recurring cost, and paying a larger one-time cost which eliminates or reduces the recurring cost. The standard setting of the problem is as follows. A person goes skiing for an unknown number of days $D$. On each day he or she can decide whether or not to buy skis for a fixed price $B$. If the person decides not to buy the skis, he or she has to rent them for a fixed cost per day $i < B$, where $i$ is usually equal to 1. The challenge is to find an algorithm that minimizes the expected cost of the ski tour over the number of days $D$.

In this paper, we phrase the problem of resolving conflicts efficiently in hardware transactional systems [19] as an online decision problem. We abstract this task as the following *transactional conflict* problem. Consider a database or hardware transactional system, which allows concurrent executions of transactions. The following scenario often arises in practice: a transaction $T_1$ accesses a set of data items, and is assigned ownership of a subset of these data items (usually the items in its write set). Assume that $T_1$ is executing concurrently with another transaction $T_2$, whose dataset intersects with that of $T_1$. In this case, this conflict of ownership is detected by the transactional system at runtime, and the transactional implementation usually makes one of two choices to resolve the conflict. The first strategy, usually called *requestor wins* [17, 24], will have the transaction $T_2$ abort the transaction $T_1$, while $T_2$ takes ownership of the contended data item. The second strategy, called *requestor aborts* [17], has transaction $T_2$ abort, resolving the conflict in favor of $T_1$.

To mitigate the high number of aborts caused by such conflicts, a number of hardware proposals, e.g. [16, 24] allow the following strategy: instead of aborting one of the transactions immediately, we allow the transaction a *grace period* $x$, *before* aborting it. From the algorithmic perspective, assume our objective is to maximize the likelyhood of a commit, while minimizing the expected value of the delay added to the running time of the two transactions. By introducing a grace period, we increase the running time of the delayed transaction $T_2$. Yet, since aborts are expensive, if $T_1$ commits during the grace period, we may gain in terms of the *sum of runtime costs*, since we could significantly *decrease* the total running time of $T_1$ if we do not abort it. Clearly, given this cost model, the question of optimally setting the grace period $x$ is an online decision problem.

**Contribution.** Our results are as follows.

- We formalize the *transactional conflict problem* for both the *requestor wins* and the *requestor aborts* conflict resolution strategies (Section 4).
- We give optimal deterministic and randomized solutions for both variants (Section 5). Further, we analyze the performance of both schemes in the setting where *additional information* is provided, in the form of the mean of the underlying distribution of transaction lengths, and when *chains* of


*SPAA '18, July 16–18, 2018, Vienna, Austria*

ACM ISBN 978-1-4503-5799-9/18/07...$15.00
https://doi.org/10.1145/3210377.3210406

transactions might conflict. We provide closed-form optimal solutions in this case (Section 5.2).

- We show that, under an adversarial transaction scheduling model, our algorithms are *globally* constant competitive in terms of the sum of running times of the transactions, i.e. inverse of throughput. (Section 6) Further, we discuss strategies to add probabilistic progress guarantees to our algorithms (Section 7).
- We validate our strategy on a hardware simulator implementation of HTM [19] and in synthetic tests, showing that it can yield throughput improvements of up to 4×, and that it is competitive with a finely-tuned manual approach (Section 8).

**The Transactional Conflict Problem.** In more detail, the transactional conflict problem presents the following trade-off. (Please see Figure 1 for an illustration.) Assume transaction $T_1$ is interrupted by a conflicting transaction $T_2$, in a *requestor wins* implementation. We have the choice of aborting $T_1$ immediately, or delaying the abort by a grace period $x$, in the hope that the transaction will commit before $x$ expires. If the transaction $T_1$ *commits* after some additional time $y < x$, then we have added $y$ time steps to the running time of $T_2$; yet, since $T_1$ commits, we do not incur any additional time penalty for this transaction. If the transaction $T_1$ has not committed within the $x$ grace period, then we will abort it. In this case, we wasted $2x$ time units in terms of the total running time of the transactions: one $x$ for which we have delayed $T_2$, and one $x$ for which we have increased the total running time of $T_1$, without committing it. (Since $T_1$ will have to redo all its computation in case of abort, none of the executed steps is useful.) In addition, we assume that we always incur a (large) cost $B$ for having aborted the transaction.

In sum, given the unknown remaining running time $y$ of the transaction $T_1$, the task is to compute the grace period $x$ which optimizes the trade-off between the cost $y$ we pay in the case where $y < x$, and the cost $2x + B$ which we pay in the case where $x \leq y$. This problem clearly appears to be related to the ski rental problem, and it is tempting to think that its solution follows by simple reduction.

However, this is not the case, due to the *different structure of the cost function.* Perhaps surprisingly, we show that this difference significantly alters the optimal strategy, as well as the competitive ratio. For example, for two transactions and a *requestor wins* implementation, we prove that the optimal strategy is a *uniform random* choice in the interval $[0, B)$, and its competitive ratio is 2. By contrast, the optimal strategy for *requestor aborts* implementations, which coincides with the classic ski rental problem, is the exponentially decaying probability distribution, with competitive ratio $e/(e-1)$. This trade-off becomes more complex for conflict chains involving more than two transactions. We also consider this case in this paper.

**Extensions and Techniques.** We consider and solve two natural extensions of the problem. The first is to consider larger conflict chains, when more than two distinct transactions may be involved in a conflict. The second is the case where the length of each transaction is assumed to come from an arbitrary probability distribution, whose mean $\mu$ is *known.* For instance, this corresponds to a profiler which records the empirical mean over all successful executions of a transaction, and uses this information when deciding the grace period length.

On the technical side, we give a unified technique for optimally solving parametrized instances of this online decision problem; in particular, we provide closed-form solutions for the general case with arbitrarily many conflicting transactions and mean constraints. Our main analytic tool is a non-trivial instance of the method of Lagrange multipliers tailored to this problem, building on an analysis by Khanafer et al. [8] for the ski rental problem.

**Order-Optimality.** Starting from the competitiveness of local decisions, we show that, under a simplified adversarial conflict model for a system of $n$ threads executing concurrent transactions, the algorithms we propose are globally competitive with an offline-optimal solution in terms of the sum of running times of transactions (intuitively, the inverse of throughput). Specifically, if the timing of conflicts between transactions is decided by an adversary, then we prove that the running time penalty incurred by all transactions using our scheme is *constant-competitive* with a perfect-information algorithm, which knows the remaining running time of each transaction at conflict time.

**Experimental Results.** We validate our results empirically, using both a synthetic testbed, and an implementation of a requestor-wins hardware transactional memory (HTM) system on top of the MIT Graphite processor simulator [23], executing data structure and transactional benchmarks. The synthetic experiments closely match our theoretical results. The HTM experiments suggest that adding delays can improve performance in HTM implementations under contention, and does not adversely impact performance in uncontended ones. Of note, we observe that our algorithms perform well even when compared with a finely-tuned approach, which uses knowledge about the application and implementation to manually fine-tune the delays.

**Implications.** The general problem of *contention management* in the context of transactional memory has been considered before [15], and several efficient strategies are known, e.g. [15, 18]. The main distinction from our setting is that contention managers (for instance in software TM) are usually assumed to have global knowledge about the set of running transactions, and possibly their abort history. By contrast, in our setting, decisions are entirely *local,* as well as immediate and unchangeable. In this context, our algorithms implement a *distributed, online* contention manager. We find it surprising that constant-competitive throughput bounds can be obtained in this restrictive setting.

A second implication of our work concerns *requestor wins* versus *requestor aborts* conflict resolution. Most systems only implement one such strategy, but our analytic results show a trade-off between contention and the performance of these two paradigms. In particular, *requestor aborts* is more efficient under low contention, whereas *requestor wins* is more efficient when conflicts involve more than two transactions. This suggests that a hybrid strategy, which can alternate between the two, would perform best.

## 2 RELATED WORK

The ski rental problem was introduced by Karlin, Manasse, Rudolph, and Sleator in [22], where the authors give optimal deterministic 2-competitive algorithms for the classic version of the ski rental problem. Follow-up work by Karlin et al. [21] showed that randomized algorithms can improve on this competitive ratio to $e/(e-1)$, which is optimal [25]. Several variants of this problem have been studied, e.g. [5, 8, 13, 20], with strong practical applications, e.g. [8, 13]. We refer the reader to the excellent survey by Albers [6] for an overview of the area, and to Section 3.3 for technical background on the problem.

The work that is technically closest to ours is by Khanafer et al. [8]: they define a *constrained* version of the ski rental problem, in which constraints such as the mean and variance of the underlying distribution from which the unknown parameter is chosen are added [1] The authors provide bounds on the improvement in terms of competitive ratio provided by these additional constraints. The basic technical ingredients we employ, notably the method of Lagrange multipliers, are similar to those of this work. However, we consider a significantly more complex instance of the problem, which requires a more involved analysis.

The problem of designing efficient contention management in the context of transactional memory [19] has received significant research attention, especially since such systems are already present in hardware by major vendors [1]. Several applied papers, e.g. [10, 12, 17, 24] discuss the trade-offs involved in implementing transactional protocols in hardware, and the performance pathologies of such systems. Reference [24] explicitly discusses the possibility of adding delays to hardware transactions, and implements and compares heuristics for tuning these delays. We believe we are the first to abstract the problem of setting the delays while minimizing running time impact, and to solve it optimally. As noted, the contention management problem has been abstracted by [15] in the context of software TM (STM), and there is a considerable amount of work on this topic, e.g. [11, 15, 18, 26]. However, to our understanding, all these systems assume a contention manager module with global knowledge about the set of running transactions, which is reasonable in the context of STM; by contrast, we analyze a setting where only local, immediate, and unchangeable decisions are possible, which is the case for HTM.

## 3 MODEL AND PRELIMINARIES

### 3.1 Shared-Memory Transactions

We consider an asynchronous shared-memory model in which $n$ processors communicate by performing atomic operations to shared memory. We assume that standard read-write atomic operations are available to the processors.

We are interested in a setting where processors execute sequences of basic read-write operations *atomically*, as *transactions*. Specifically, a transaction is a set of read and write operations, which are guaranteed to be executed atomically if the transaction *commits*. Otherwise, if the transaction *aborts*, then none of the operations is applied to shared memory. Many hardware implementations of transactional memory use some version of the pattern shown in Algorithm 1 below.

**Algorithm 1** Simplified Pseudocode for Hardware Transactional Memory implementation.

**function** TRANSACTION(code)
  *// Use a MESI cache coherence protocol, except each cache line has an additional bit. This additional bit is set if cache line is used by transaction. In this case, cache line is called transactional and it resides in the transactional cache.*
  *// Execution phase*
  **if** at any point transactional cache line is evicted, abort transaction.
  **if** transaction is aborted, invalidate all transactional cache lines.
  **for** each access in code **do**
    **if** read **then**
      Try to acquire the transactional cache line in a shared or exclusive state.
      **Conflict** arises if some transaction has the required cache line in its transactional cache in a modified state.
    **if** write **then**
      Try to invalidate all existing copies of the required cache line, then change a state of the cache line to modified.
      **Conflict** arises if some transaction has a copy of the line in its tranactional cache.
  *// Commit phase*
  **if** transaction is not aborted in the execution phase, then **commit**, by clearing additional bits in all transactional cache lines.

Notice that, if several transactions with overlapping read and write sets may execute or attempt to commit at the same time, then they may conflict in the commit phase. In particular, consider the following example, involving transactional objects $A$, $B$ and $C$:

A transaction $T_1$ performing $[A \leftarrow B+1; C = 3]$ and a transaction $T_2$ performing $[A \leftarrow B + 2]$ from an initial state of $A = B = 0$ can conflict in the commit phase as follows. Imagine $T_1$ holds variable $A$ in Exclusive state locally, and is in the process of acquiring variable $B$ in Exclusive state, so that it can commit. Then $T_2$ starts executing its Commit phase, and sends a coherence message to $T_1$, asking for $A$ in Exclusive state. At this point, $T_1$ has two choices: it can either relinquish exclusive access of $A$, and abort its transaction (see Figure 1a), or delay the request by $A$ for some time, hoping that it will commit soon (see Figure 1b). In the following, we will look at algorithms for making this choice. Note that we will use both terms algorithm and strategy meaning the same thing from now on.

### 3.2 Conflict and Cost Models

**Transaction Conflict Scheduling.** As described, we have $n$ threads, each of which has a virtually infinite sequence of transactions to execute. Threads proceed to execute these transactions in parallel. At arbitrary times during the execution, an adversary can interrupt a pair of transactions, and put them in conflict: one of them will be the *requestor*, and the other one is the *receiver*. The algorithm has

[1] In this paper we adopt the original terminology used in [8], even though stochastic ski rental problem might be a better name for this version of the problem.

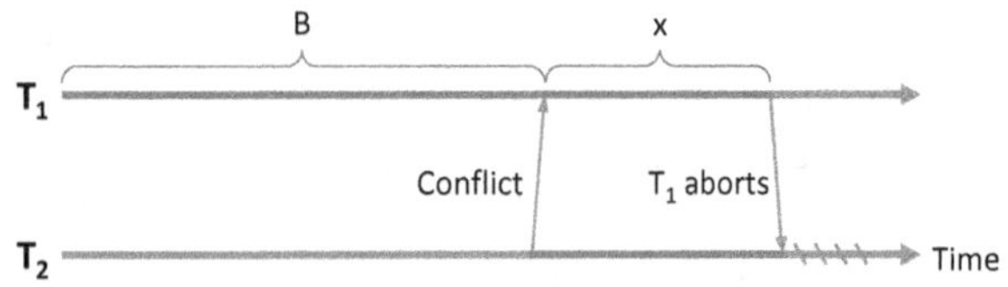


**(a) Requestor wins scenario. Here, $T_1$ has been running for $B$ time steps when a conflict with $T_2$ is detected. $T_1$ has the possibility of delaying $T_2$'s message response for $x$ steps before aborting itself. The "wasted" time added to the execution of both transactions in case $T_1$ aborts is shown in red.**

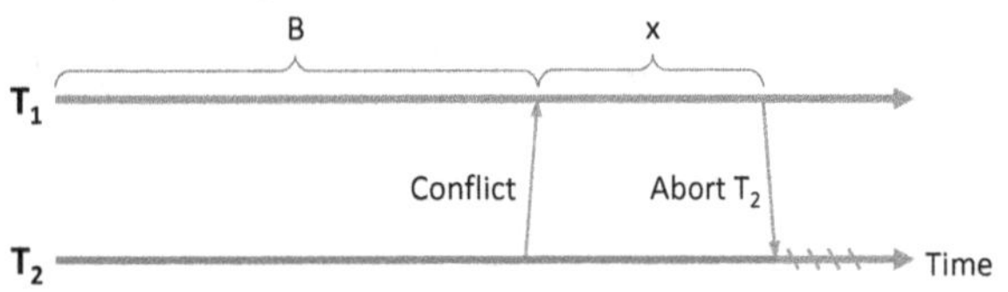


**(b) Requestor aborts scenario. Again, $T_1$ has been running for $B$ time steps when a conflict with $T_2$ is detected. $T_1$ has the possibility of delaying $T_2$'s message response for $x$ steps before aborting $T_2$. The "wasted" time added to the execution of both transactions in case $T_2$ aborts is shown in red.**

**Figure 1: The transactional conflict problem for the two conflict resolution strategies.**

the choice of resolving the conflict immediately, by aborting one of the transactions, or to postpone the abort for a grace period $\Delta$. The cost model is specified for each conflict resolution strategy in Section 4.

Upon aborting a transaction, the thread will restart its execution immediately. Initially, the conflicted transaction will no longer be in conflict with any other transaction, although it may become conflicted if chosen by the adversary. Upon committing a transaction, the thread moves to the next transaction in its input. During its grace period, a receiver transaction may become conflicted as a requestor with another transaction, since it may need to access some new data item.

**Additional Assumptions.** In the following, we assume a simplified version of the conflict model, and analyze the global competitiveness of our strategies. In particular, we assume that (a) a transaction that is part of a conflict as a requestor cannot become part of a new conflict as a receiver, (b) a transaction that is currently during its grace period cannot be conflicted again as a receiver by the adversary (but the transaction may be conflicted as a requestor), and (c) that conflicts cannot be cyclic. Assumptions (a) and (b) are in some sense necessary given our strong adversarial model: we wish to ensure that the adversary can only inflict the same set of conflicts on the offline optimal strategy as to the online decision algorithm. We note that assumption (c) is implemented by some real-world HTM implementations, which actively detect conflict cycles, and abort all transactions involved upon such events [2].

**Cost Model.** Given the above setup, our cost model is defined as follows. Fix an adversarial conflict strategy $S$, and a (possibly randomized) algorithm $\mathcal{A}$ for resolving conflicts. For each transaction $T$, define $\Gamma(T, \mathcal{A})$ be the expected length of the interval between $T$'s starting time (i.e., the first time it is invoked) and its eventual commit time, assuming conflicts induced by $S$. We analyze strategies for deciding the grace period, which minimize the *expected sum of running times of transactions.* Formally, we wish to find an algorithm $\mathcal{A}$ such that, for any adversarial strategy $S$, $\sum_T \Gamma(T, \mathcal{A})$ is minimized.

## 3.3 Background on the Ski Rental Problem

We recall the definition of the ski rental problem [21]: a person goes skiing for an unknown number of days $y$. On each day, he or she can decide whether or not to buy skis for a fixed price $B$. If the person decides to not buy the skis, he or she has to rent them for a fixed cost per day $c < B$, which we will choose w.l.o.g. to be equal to 1. The challenge is to find an algorithm that minimizes the expected cost of the ski tour over the number of days $y$. The optimal cost with foresight for this problem is clearly $\min(y, B)$, and the optimal online deterministic strategy has cost $2B - 1$ if $y \geq B$. So the deterministic competitive ratio is basically 2. It is known that one can do better by employing a randomized strategy [21]:

Theorem 1. *Consider a strategy where, for each day $i \geq 1$, with probability $p(i)$ we rent skis on day $i$. Then, if we take $p(i) = \left(\frac{B-1}{B}\right)^{B-i} \frac{1}{B[1-(1-1/B)^B]}$, for days $i \leq B$, and 0 otherwise, we pay expected total cost $\left(\frac{e}{e-1}\right) \min(y, B)$.*

Using additional knowledge about the adversarial distribution, e.g. the mean $\mu$, it is known that one can improve the strategy further [8]:

Theorem 2. *Knowledge of the mean $\mu$ of the adversarial function $\pi(y)$ yields a new randomized strategy $p(x)$ for the standard ski rental problem, namely if $\frac{\mu}{B} < 2\frac{e-2}{e-1}$, then*

$$p(x) = \begin{cases} \frac{1}{B(e-2)} e^{\frac{x}{B}} - 1, & 0 \leq x \leq B \\ 0, & else. \end{cases}$$

*The competitive ratio improves to $1 + \frac{\mu}{2B(e-2)}$. Otherwise, the previous strategy is optimal.*

# 4 THE TRANSACTIONAL CONFLICT PROBLEM

We now formalize our problem, assuming the transactional model in Section 3. As the cost metric is different depending on the contention resolution strategy, we define the problem differently for each case. For simplicity, we will start by defining the problem for the case with two conflicting transactions, and then extend to the case with longer conflict chains.

## 4.1 Problem Statement for Requestor Wins

**Two Conflicting Transactions.** Assume that an executing transaction $T_1$ (the receiver) is interrupted by a transaction $T_2$ (the requestor), and that we have the choice between aborting $T_1$ immediately, and postponing $T_1$'s abort by $x$ steps, in the hope that it commits. Assume that $T_1$ still has to execute for $y$ time steps (unknown) to commit, and that aborting $T_1$ immediately incurs a fixed cost $B$.[2] We define the *conflict cost* as follows: (1) **If** $y < x$,

[2] In practice, the cost $B$ will consist of the time for which the transaction $T_1$ has already been running when interrupted, plus a fixed non-trivial cleanup cost.

then transaction $T_1$ commits before $x$, and we only pay the time by which we delayed $T_2$, which is $y$. In terms of the sum of running times, our delay decision added $y$ to the total cost. (2) **If** $y \geq x$, then transaction $T_1$ has not committed before $x$, and we will abort $T_1$, allowing $T_2$ to continue. We will pay the abort cost $B$, the additional time $x$ by which we ran $T_1$, and the additional time $x$ by which $T_2$ was delayed. This sums up to $2x + B$.

**The General Case.** In general, the conflict chain may be longer, as several transactions may be delayed if we decide to extend $T_1$'s execution. For example, a third transaction $T_3$ may already be waiting on $T_2$ to commit at the point where $T_2$ conflicts with $T_1$. Assume that $k \geq 2$ transactions, including $T_1$, are conflicting, forming a conflict chain. This means that delaying $T_1$'s abort by *one* step will add $k - 1$ time steps to the total running time of all transactions. In this case, the cost metric becomes:

- If $y < x$, then $T_1$ commits, and we pay the time by which we delayed all transactions other than $T_1$, which is $(k - 1)y$.
- If $y \geq x$, then we abort $T_1$, and pay the abort cost $B$ and the additional time $x$ by which we ran $T_1$, as well as the additional time $(k - 1)x$ by which other transactions are delayed. This sums up to $kx + B$.

We will first focus on decision algorithms which optimize the expected cost *of each conflict*. Later, in Section 6, we will show how to use competitive bounds on individual conflict cost to obtain competitive bounds on the throughput. We are trying to identify the probability distribution $p$ which minimizes the expected decision cost under arbitrary adversarial choices $y$. Formally, for arbitrary $y$, and fixed $k$ and $B$ as above,

$$p = \text{argmin}_p \text{Cost}(p(x), y), \text{ where}$$

$$\text{Cost}(p(x), y) = \int_0^y (kx + B)p(x)dx + (k-1)\int_y^{\frac{B}{k-1}} yp(x)dx,$$

where we have noticed that for $y > B/(k - 1)$ the algorithm will always abort. Notice that the offline optimum is $\min(B, (k - 1)y)$.

## 4.2 Problem Statement for Requestor Aborts

**Two Conflicting Transactions.** The converse case is when the receiving transaction $T_1$ can abort or delay any requestor transaction $T_2$. Again, we might choose to delay the conflict resolution by a grace period of $x$ steps. Assume that $T_1$ still has to execute for $y$ steps to commit, where $y$ is unknown. The conflict cost is now as follows:

- If $y < x$, then transaction $T_1$ commits at or before $x$, and we only pay the time by which we delayed the incoming transaction $T_2$, i.e., $y$.
- If $y \geq x$, then transaction $T_1$ has not committed at $x$, and we will abort $T_2$ and continue. In this case, we pay as extra cost $B$, a fixed abort cost, plus the time by which $T_2$ was delayed, i.e. total cost $x + B$.

Notice that the optimal cost with foresight is $\text{OPT} = \min(B, y)$. By comparing variables we realize that there exists a direct mapping between the ski rental problem and the requestor aborts version of the transactional conflict problem:

The point where the requesting transaction $T_2$ interrupts transaction $T_1$ marks day 0 of the ski rental problem. Furthermore, we have that $y$, the unknown number of steps until $T_1$ would eventually commit, denotes the day on which the adversary chooses to stop us from skiing. The choice of $x$, i.e., the length of the grace period by which $T_1$ delays $T_2$, is the same as to choose that we buy skis on day $x$. Finally, the fixed extra cost $B$ in the transactional conflict problem is the equivalent to the cost $B$ of buying the skis. Figure 1b illustrates this case. The results in Theorems 1 and 2 apply to this case.

Generalizing to conflicts of size $k > 2$ is also possible. Due to space limitations, this variant of the problem and its analysis are deferred to a full version of the paper [9].

# 5 ANALYSIS FOR REQUESTOR WINS

In the following, we focus on analyzing optimal strategies for the *requestor wins* strategy. In particular, we will examine the optimal deterministic strategy for the *unconstrained case*, in which no additional information about the adversarial distribution is known, and optimal *randomized strategies* for the *constrained case*, in which the first moment of the adversarial length distribution is known. (This case also convers the randomized unconstrained case, so we solve them together.)

## 5.1 The Deterministic Unconstrained Case

Since the algorithm is deterministic, it has to choose a time step $x$ at which to abort. Denote by $y$ the time step at which the transaction would commit, if allowed to execute. Throughout the rest of this section, unless stated otherwise, the expression *we abort* means that the receiving transaction aborts.

Observe that the optimal cost is $\min((y(k - 1), B)$. For simplicity, let us assume that $\frac{B}{k-1}$ is an integer. There are two cases we need to examine. The first one is $x \leq y$, in which we pay cost $kx + B$. The second one is $x > y$, in which we pay cost $(k - 1)y$. Note that the adversary knows after which time step $x$ we decided to abort, and thus will never choose to set the end of transaction after $x$. The following result characterizes the optimal deterministic strategy.

THEOREM 3. *The optimal deterministic strategy always chooses to abort after $\frac{B}{k-1}$ time steps. This strategy has total cost $\left(2 + \frac{1}{k-1}\right) \min((y(k - 1), B)$.*

PROOF. Let $x$ denote the time step on which we chose to abort. We first notice that we can reduce the case where $x \leq y$ to $x = y$, since our cost will not increase after the abort. Thus, delaying the end of transaction can only decrease the competitive ratio. The competitive ratio for $x = y$ looks as follows

$$\frac{kx + B}{\min((k - 1)x, B)} \tag{1}$$

For $x > y$ we get

$$\frac{y(k - 1)}{\min(y(k - 1), B)}$$

as the competitive ratio. This clearly is a non-decreasing function, thus the adversary would choose $y = x - 1$ to maximize our cost. Therefore, we have competitive ratio $\frac{(x-1)(k-1)}{\min((x-1)(k-1),B)}$. Because this is at most $\frac{kx+B}{\min((k-1)x,B)}$, the adversary will always prefer $y = x$. We obtain that our strategy will always yield competitive ratio (1). Observe that $\frac{kx+B}{\min((k-1)x,B)}$ is strictly decreasing when $(k-1)x \leq B$ and it is strictly increasing when $(k-1)x \geq B$, thus it is minimized for $x = \frac{B}{k-1}$, yielding ratio:

$$2 + \frac{1}{k-1}. \tag{2}$$

□

## 5.2 Randomized Strategies for Transactional Conflict

In this section, we discuss the transactional conflict problem where we have some knowledge about the distribution $\pi(y)$ of the adversarial function. For simplicity, we will consider the case where $k = 2$, i.e. the conflict involves only two transactions, and address the general case in a later section. Our goal is to prove the following.

THEOREM 4. *For arbitrary adversarial distributions, the following randomized strategy* $p(x)$ *is optimal:* $p(x) = 1/B$ for $0 \leq x \leq B$, and 0,*otherwise. This yields competitive ratio* 2 *for the conflict cost.*

*Knowledge of the mean* $\mu$ *of the adversarial function* $\pi(y)$ *yields the following strategy* $p(x)$ *for the transactional conflict problem. If* $\frac{\mu}{B} < 2(\ln 4 - 1)$, *then the optimal strategy is*

$$p(x) = \begin{cases} \frac{\ln \frac{B+x}{x}}{B(\ln 4-1)}, & 0 \leq x \leq B \\ 0, & \textit{otherwise.} \end{cases}$$

*In this case, the competitive ratio improves to* $1 + \frac{\mu}{2B(\ln 4-1)}$. *If* $\frac{\mu}{B} \geq 2(\ln 4 - 1)$, *then the unconstrained strategy is optimal.*

PROOF. It is easy to show that for arbitrary adversarial distributions above randomized strategy yields competitive ratio 2. Optimality of this strategy can be proven using the same techniques as in [8]. Note that for $k > 2$, the following strategy is optimal and 2-competitive: $p(x) = (k-1)/B$ for $0 \leq x \leq B/(k-1)$, and 0, otherwise. Proof is analogous to $k = 2$ case.

Let $x$ be a time step at which we decide to abort and let $y$ be a time step at which we would finish the computation. $x$ is chosen with the distribution $p$ and $y$ is chosen with the distribution $\pi$. Notice that we will always abort at or before time step $B$, because otherwise our cost will be greater than if we had aborted at time step 0. If $y < x$, we pay $y$. Otherwise, we pay $2x + B$. Let $Cost(p(x), y)$ be the expected cost for the fixed $y$. We have that

$$\text{Cost}(p(x), y) = \int_0^y (2x + B)p(x)dx + y \cdot \int_y^B p(x)dx.$$

We know that the optimal cost is $\min(y, B)$. This gives us a necessity to introduce non-zero probability $\pi_K$ for $y$ to be chosen from outside the interval $[0, B]$, because otherwise the trivial optimal strategy is to never abort. Our goal is to minimize the ratio

$$\mathcal{G}(p(x), \pi(y)) = \int_0^B \frac{\text{Cost}(p(x), y)}{y}\pi(y)dy + \pi_K \cdot \int_0^B \frac{2x + B}{B}p(x)dx.$$

Considering that we want to find the best possible solution under the worst case distribution $\pi(y)$ of the adversary our problem looks as follows

$$\min_{p(x)} \max_{\pi(y)} \mathcal{G}(p(x), \pi(y)). \tag{3}$$

We will give a closed-form solution for this as follows. We first construct the Lagrangian function $\mathcal{L}$ for the maximization problem in (3). Afterwards we will construct its dual to get the necessary constraints. We will then differentiate one of the constraints twice, leaving us with a first order differential equation for $p(x)$. Solving this yields the desired PDF $p(x)$. Finally, we substitute $p(x)$ into the constraints to solve for the Lagrangian multipliers.

The Lagrangian function $\mathcal{L}$ takes as inputs the probability distribution $\pi(y)$ of the adversary and the two Lagrange multipliers $\lambda_1$ and $\lambda_2$. The two multipliers act as weights for the constraints given by the fact that $\pi(y)$ is a PDF with the mean $\mu$. Thus, we get the following Lagrangian for the maximization problem:

$$\begin{aligned} \mathcal{L}(\pi(y), \lambda_1, \lambda_2) = & \int_0^B \frac{\text{Cost}(p(x), y)}{y}\pi(y)dy \\ & + \pi_K \cdot \int_0^B \frac{2x + B}{B}p(x)dx \\ & - \lambda_1 \cdot \left[\int_0^B \pi(y)dy + \pi_K - 1\right] \\ & - \lambda_2 \cdot \left[\int_0^B y\pi(y)dy + K \cdot \pi_K - \mu\right] \\ = & \int_0^B \left(\frac{\text{Cost}(p(x), y)}{y} - \lambda_1 - \lambda_2 y\right) \cdot \pi(y)dy \\ & + \pi_K \cdot \left(\int_0^B \frac{2x + B}{B}p(x)dx - \lambda_1 - \lambda_2 K\right) \\ & + (\lambda_1 + \lambda_2 \mu). \end{aligned}$$

Therefore, its dual is $h(\lambda_1, \lambda_2) = \sup_{\pi(y)} \mathcal{L}(\pi(y), \lambda_1, \lambda_2)$. We note that, since the adversarial strategy is arbitrary and we want to minimize the dual function, we will need constraints $\frac{\text{Cost}(p(x),y)}{y} - \lambda_1 - \lambda_2 y = 0$ and $\int_0^B \frac{2x+B}{B}p(x)dx - \lambda_1 - \lambda_2 K = 0$, to ensure that the Lagrangian function does not depend on the choice of $\pi(y)$. Therefore we get the following minimization problem:

$$\min_{p(x), \lambda_1, \lambda_2} \lambda_1 + \lambda_2 \mu \text{ s.t.}$$

$$\frac{\int_0^y (2x + B)p(x)dx + y \cdot \int_y^B p(x)dx}{y} = \lambda_1 + \lambda_2 y \tag{4}$$

$$\int_0^B \frac{2x + B}{B}p(x)dx = \lambda_1 + \lambda_2 K \tag{5}$$

$$\forall \lambda_1, \lambda_2 \geq 0 \text{ and } y \in [0, B]$$

Because the constraint (4) holds for every $y \in [0, B]$, we can differentiate it twice with respect to $y$ and after we substitute $y$ with $x$ we get the first order differential equation $p'(x) = \frac{1}{B+x} 2\lambda_2$. Solving this yields our strategy $p(x) = \alpha + 2\lambda_2 \ln(B + x)$. Using the fact that $p(x)$ is a PDF we get that $\alpha = \frac{1}{B} - 2\lambda_2(\ln B + \ln 4 - 1)$.

Since $\forall x, p(x) \geq 0$ and $\lambda_2 \geq 0$ we further have $0 \leq \lambda_2 \leq \frac{1}{2B(\ln 4-1)}$. Thus our problem becomes:

$$\min_{\lambda_1,\lambda_2} \lambda_1 + \lambda_2\mu \text{ such that}$$

$$[(4\ln 2B - 4\ln 4B + 2)B]\,\lambda_2 + 2 = \lambda_1 \quad (6)$$

$$[(4\ln 2B - 4\ln 4B + 3)B - K]\,\lambda_2 + 2 = \lambda_1 \quad (7)$$

$$\forall \lambda_1 \geq 0, 0 \leq \lambda_2 \leq \frac{1}{2B(\ln 4 - 1)}$$

We immediately realize that for $\lambda_2 \neq 0$ we must have $K = B$ in order to satisfy (6) and (7) simultaneously. We remind ourselves that the solutions to this linear program have to form a convex polytope and that each basic feasible solution is a corner point of that polytope. Therefore we get two corner points $c_1 = (2, 0)$ and $c_2 = \left(1, \frac{1}{2B(\ln 4-1)}\right)$ with corresponding competitive ratios $C_1 = 2$ and $C_2 = 1 + \frac{\mu}{2B(\ln 4-1)}$. Notice that for $\lambda_2 = 0$ we do not take the mean into account and thus are left with the solution for the unconstrained ski rental problem. For $\lambda_2 \neq 0$ we realize that $C_2 < C_1$ is only valid for small values of $\mu$. More precisely, $C_2 < C_1$, for $\frac{\mu}{B} < 2(\ln 4 - 1)$. Thus, if $\frac{\mu}{B} < 2(\ln 4 - 1)$ the optimal PDF is:

$$p(x) = \begin{cases} \frac{\ln \frac{B+x}{B}}{B(\ln 4-1)}, & 0 \leq x \leq B \\ 0, & \text{otherwise.} \end{cases}$$

Otherwise, the unconstrained strategy is optimal. □

## 5.3 Discussion

**Competitive Ratio Comparison.** We compare this result with the requestor aborts case (classic ski rental) [8]. Depending on the case distinction, we get:

- inequality holds: In this case we have a competitive ratio of $1+\frac{\mu}{2B(\ln 4-1)}$ for requestor wins and $1+\frac{\mu}{2B(e-2)}$ for requestor aborts. Clearly, requestor aborts outperforms requestor wins. Additionally, we get that the inequality which has to hold in order for this strategy to be applicable, is less strict for the requestor aborts case.
- inequality does not hold: If the inequality does not hold we get competitive ratio 2 for the requestor wins strategy and $\frac{e}{e-1}$ for the requestor aborts strategy. Again, we notice that the competitive ratio of requestor aborts is smaller than the one for requestor wins.

Thus, we can conclude that with respect to the competitive ratio for a single waiting transaction ($k = 2$), the transactional conflict problem should be tackled by the requestor aborts strategy. We note that this may no longer be the case for $k \geq 3$.

**Abort probability.** We now examine the probability that a transaction aborts, in the case where $y \leq B$. (Otherwise, it is more advantageous to abort the current transaction than to delay the system for $> B$ steps.) Notice that in this case, the adversary's best strategy is to set $y = B$. We obtain the following by direct computation:

- requestor wins: $1 - p(B) = 1 - \frac{\ln 2}{B(\ln 4-1)} \simeq 1 - 1.8/B$
- requestor aborts: $1 - p(B) = 1 - \frac{e-1}{B(e-2)} \simeq 1 - 2.4/B$.

Hence, the requestor aborts optimal strategy is less likely to abort a transaction, under the same conditions.

## 5.4 Constrained Problem for Conflict Size $k > 2$

A more involved analysis solves the general case where conflicts are of size $k > 2$. See a full version of the paper [9] for the proof.

THEOREM 5. *Consider an instance of requestor-wins transactional conflict where $k \geq 3$ transactions are involved. Given the fixed cost $B > 0$, and the mean of the adversarial distribution $\mu > 0$, then the optimal PDF $p(x)$ is as follows.*
*If $\frac{\mu}{B} \leq \frac{k^{k-1}-2(k-1)^{k-1}}{(k-2)(k^{k-1}-(k-1)^{k-1})}$, then:*

$$p(x) = \begin{cases} \frac{(B+x)^{k-2}(k-1)^k\left(2(k-1)^{k-1}+k^{k-1}\right)}{B^{k-1}\left(k^{k-1}-(k-1)^{k-1}\right)\left(k^{k-1}-2(k-1)^{k-1}\right)} - \frac{4(k-1)^k}{B\left(k^{k-1}-2(k-1)^{k-1}\right)}, & 0 \leq x \leq \frac{B}{k-1}, \\ 0, & \textit{otherwise}. \end{cases}$$

*Otherwise, or if the mean is unknown, the optimal PDF is :*

$$p(x) = \begin{cases} \frac{(B+x)^{k-2}(k-1)^k}{B^{k-1}\left(k^{k-1}-(k-1)^{k-1}\right)}, & 0 \leq x \leq \frac{B}{k-1}, \\ 0, & \textit{otherwise}. \end{cases}$$

# 6 COMPETITIVE ANALYSIS FOR THE SUM OF RUNNING TIMES

Given an adversarial strategy $S$, and an algorithm $\mathcal{A}$, recall that $\Gamma(T, \mathcal{A})$ is the expected time between the start of the transaction's execution, and the time it committed. We define the *commit cost* $\rho_T$ of a transaction $T$ the number of consecutive time steps it has to execute for in isolation in order to commit.

Given the optimal decision algorithm, a transaction $T$, and an adversarial strategy $S$, let the *abort cost* $\alpha_T(S)$ under an adversarial strategy be the length of time that the algorithm spends executing $T$ *minus* the commit cost $\rho_T$. Notice that, in the optimal algorithm, every time a transaction is interrupted by the adversary's strategy, the choice of whether to continue or not is deterministic, based on the length of time for which the transaction has already executed, on the abort cost, and on the remaining length of time for which the transaction has to execute. Given an adversarial strategy $S$, define $w(S)$ as the *waste* of the optimal algorithm given $S$, defined as $\sum_T \alpha_T(S) / \sum_T \rho_T$.

COROLLARY 1. *Under the above conflict model, let $\mathcal{A}$ be the randomized requestor wins strategy, and let OPT be the offline optimal algorithm. Then we have that*

$$\frac{\sum_T \Gamma(T, \mathcal{A})}{\sum_T \Gamma(T, OPT)} \leq \frac{2w(S) + 1}{w(S) + 1}.$$

PROOF. Let $C$ be a conflict which arises for algorithm $\mathcal{A}$ following strategy $S$. From our conflict model, we know that the same conflict $C$ must arise for the optimal decision algorithm as well, although the decision may be different. We know that there is one *receiver* transaction $T$ involved in the conflict, to which we will *amortize the cost of this conflict*. For our algorithm $\mathcal{A}$, let $Cost(C, \mathcal{A})$ be the conflict cost, that is, the sum of delays caused by transaction

$T$, plus the abort cost and delay to $T$ incurred in case $T$ does not commit.

Analogously, let $Cost(C, OPT)$ be the cost of a conflict $C$ for the optimal decision algorithm. We get that the sum $\sum_C Cost(C, OPT) = \sum_T \alpha_T(S)$. Because of the way we defined $Cost(C, OPT)$ and $Cost(C, \mathcal{A})$ we know from the properties of the local decision algorithm that

$$\frac{Cost(C, \mathcal{A})}{Cost(C, OPT)} \leq 2.$$

Therefore, we also have that

$$\frac{\sum_C Cost(C, \mathcal{A})}{\sum_C Cost(C, OPT)} \leq 2.$$

Finally, notice that:

$$\frac{\sum_T \Gamma(T, \mathcal{A})}{\sum_T \Gamma(T, OPT)} = \frac{\sum_T \rho_T + \sum_C Cost(C, \mathcal{A})}{\sum_T \rho_T + \sum_C Cost(C, OPT)} \leq \frac{\sum_T \rho_T + 2\sum_T \alpha_T}{\sum_T \rho_T + \sum_T \alpha_T} = \frac{2w(S) + 1}{w(S) + 1},$$

which concludes the proof. □

# 7 THROUGHPUT VERSUS PROGRESS

As described, our framework optimizes solely for throughput, and does not provide any progress guarantees. In particular, a transaction $T$ which consistently incurs conflicts at a time when its abort cost $B$ is smaller than its remaining execution time will always abort, since it is more advantageous for the system overall to abort this transaction than to delay. However, we can easily adapt our scheme in a backoff-like manner to address this issue: upon abort, a transaction can increase its future abort cost $B$ by an additive or multiplicative amount, and therefore be less likely to abort on its next execution. We consider the multiplicative case here, and obtain the following probabilistic progress guarantee for every transaction:

Corollary 2. *A transaction $T$ which encounters $\gamma$ conflicts during its execution and has a running time $y$, commits after at most* $\log y + \log \gamma + \log k - \log B + 2$ *attemps, with probability at least* $\frac{1}{2}$.

Proof. We consider the unconstrained case, where we do not have any knowledge about $y$. Notice that it is enough to prove that the bounds hold for requestor wins scenario, since requestor aborts strategy is less likely to abort the transaction. As noted in Theorem 4, the optimal 2-competitive strategy in this case is: $p(x) = (k-1)/B$ for $0 \leq x \leq B/(k-1)$, and 0, otherwise. Consider the situation after the transaction aborts $\log y + \log \gamma + \log k - \log B + 1$ times. Let $B'$ be the current abort cost. Since we double this cost every time transaction aborts, we have that $B' \geq 2ky\gamma$. Upon each conflict, the probability that we do not abort transaction is :

$$\frac{\frac{B'}{k-1} - y}{\frac{B'}{k-1}} = 1 - \frac{y(k-1)}{B'} \geq 1 - \frac{1}{2\gamma}.$$

Thus, the probability that transaction $T$ commits after $\log y + \log \gamma + \log k - \log B + 2$ attempts is at least:

$$(1 - \frac{1}{2\gamma})^{\gamma} \geq 1/2,$$

where in the last step we used Bernoulli's inequality. □

# 8 EXPERIMENTS

## 8.1 Synthetic Tests

In this section, we examine how various strategies perform for different types of distributions, in the case where two transactions are conflicting. We will use the following abbreviations:

- *RRW*($\mu$) denotes the randomized strategy that we derived for requestor wins using the constraint on the mean.
- *RRA*($\mu$) denotes the randomized strategy for requestor aborts using the constraint on the mean.
- *RRW* denotes the randomized strategy for requestor wins we derived without using constraints.
- *RRA* denotes the randomized strategy for requestor aborts without using constraints.
- *DET* denotes the deterministic strategy which we also derived for requestor wins without using constraints.
- *OPT* denotes the optimal strategy.

We benchmarked the decision algorithms in Python, as follows: First, we draw the length of the transaction $r$ from a given length distribution. We then pick an index $i$ u.a.r. from that length, which will be the point of interrupt in the ski rental problem. Note that $r - i$ is the equivalent to the mean in the ski rental problem. Then, the algorithm picks an index $j$ according to the above strategies, which will be the time at which we abort. Finally, we calculate the cost of this choice. The following length distributions were used in the experiment: Geometric, Normal, Uniform, Exponential and Poisson. The results are shown in Figures 2a and 2b.

Note that $\mu$ stands for the mean of the length distribution and that $B$ denotes the fixed cost that we pay for an abort. Notice that, in Figure 2a, *DET* performs quite well. The intuitive reason is these distributions are not adversarial. Therefore, since we choose a large cost $B$ compared to $\mu$, we (almost) never abort with *DET*. The second observation is that *RRW*($\mu$) and *RRA*($\mu$) perform significantly better than *RRW* and *RRA*. The reason is that the inequality $\frac{\mu}{B} < 2(\ln 4 - 1)$ / $\frac{\mu}{B} \leq 2\frac{e-2}{e-1}$ holds. The last observation that the cost of *RRW* and *RRA* is (almost) exactly 2, respectively $\frac{e}{e-1}$ times the optimal cost, as predicted by the analysis.

Figure 2b represents the case where the fixed cost $B$ is smaller than $\mu$. This has the following effects on cost: first, *DET* performs notably worse than before. The reason is that *DET* decides to abort based on the cost, and falls short of this value with higher frequency. Also notice that *RRW*($\mu$) and *RRA*($\mu$) and *RRW* and *RRA* perform similarly, since the threshold inequality does not hold most of the time. Further, we notice that the strategies for requestor aborts, i.e. *RRA*($\mu$) and *RRA*, outperform their respective counterparts from strategy requestor wins. Figure 2c illustrates cost under the worst-case distribution for *DET*.

## 8.2 Hardware Simulation

**Methodology**. We use Graphite [23], a tiled multi-core system simulator, to experiment with real applications. We extend Graphite's directory-based MSI cache coherence protocol for private-L1 shared-L2 cache hierarchy to implement a simple functional equivalent of hardware transactional memory with a requestor-wins policy and lazy validation. In particular, the L1 cache controller logic (at the cores) is modified for this purpose, while the directory logic did not

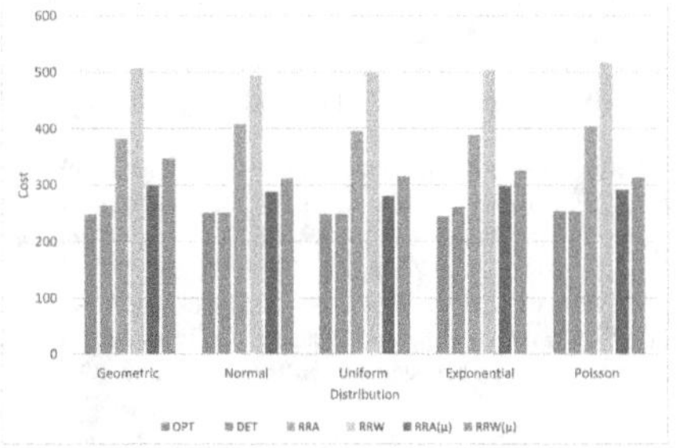

(a) Average cost of various strategies in the case with high fixed cost. Here, the fixed abort cost is $B = 2000$, and the mean is $\mu = 500$.

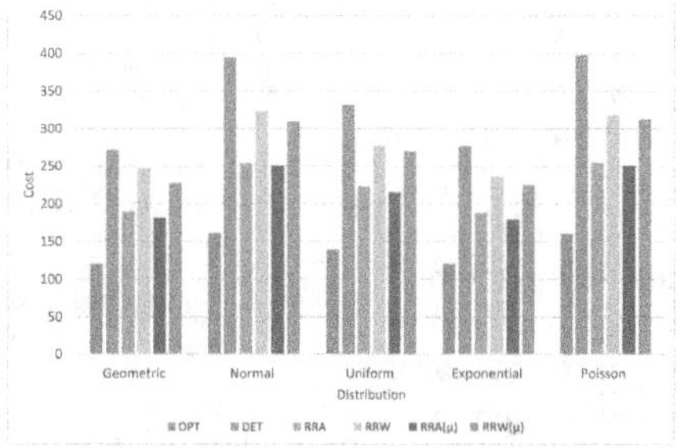

(b) Average cost of various strategies in the case with low fixed cost. Here, the fixed abort cost is $B = 200$ and the mean is $\mu = 500$.

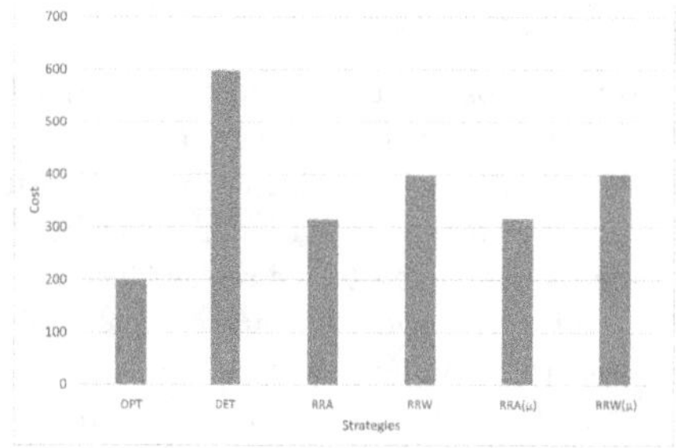

(c) Average cost of various strategies if the adversary uses the worst-case distribution for the deterministic strategy.

**Figure 2: Results of synthetic tests.**

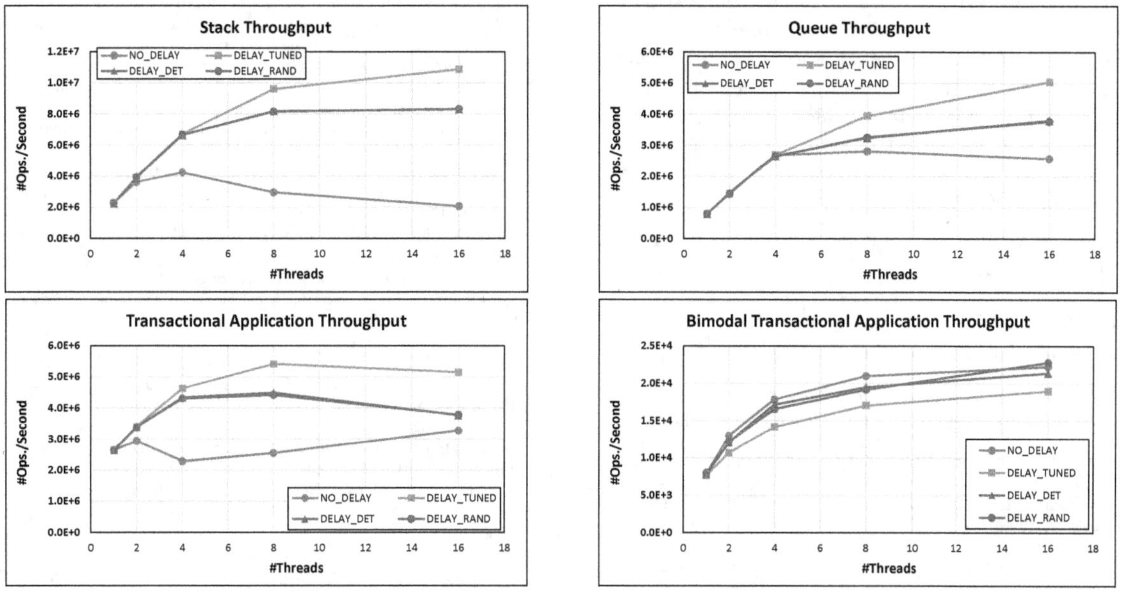


**Figure 3: Throughput results for lock-free stack, queue, and TL2 benchmark.**

have to be modified in any way. We test various conflict resolution techniques on top of this setup. In particular, we implement the randomized and deterministic delay-setting strategies, as well as a hand-tuned version, which decides on the amount of delay based on knowledge of the dataset and implementation. We experiment with two contended data structures implemented using HTM in this setting: a stack and a queue, as well as a simple transactional application. The stack and the queue use lock-free designs as "slow path" backups. The stack and the queue simply alternate inserts and deletes. The transactional application executes transactions which need to jointly acquire and modify two out of a set of 64 objects in order to commit.

**Results**. Please see Figure 3 for the results. The contended data structures are meant to illustrate a setting where the transaction lengths are short and stable. In this case, the hand-tuned algorithm does predictably well, since we are able to identify the exact average fast-path length of transactions. Its performance is closely followed by the two online algorithms, which improve significantly on the version which does not implement delays. We observe similar results for the transactional application with uniform transaction lengths. When the transactional application alternates between short and long transactions (the bimodal experiment, in which transactions alternate between short and very long transactions), we notice that the hand-tuned implementation loses performance, as the transaction length is less predictable. At the same time, the version with no delays performs well, since it tends to abort long transactions, which favors short ones. Of note, the randomized algorithm outperforms all other strategies at high contention and high variance, as expected.

## 9 CONCLUSION

This paper considered the problem of resolving conflicts between transactions using online decision techniques, and presented optimal algorithms for various scenarios arising in real implementations. Our results outline a difference between the performance of the requestor aborts and requestor wins strategies in different contention scenarios, and suggest that adding delays can lead to improvements in terms of practical performance of transactional systems. In particular, the online algorithms we develop appear to be competitive with offline hand-tuned algorithms. We note that the simplicity of the optimal requestor wins strategy–which just chooses a delay uniformly at random within some interval–may lend itself to simple implementation in real systems.

In terms of future work, we plan to further investigate the practicality of our designs through a more precise HTM implementation, and on a wider series of benchmarks. Due to the complexity of implementing a realistic version of RTM [1] accurately on a multiprocessor simulator, this task is beyond the scope of the current work. Second, we aim to further refine our conflict model, and to examine whether it is possible to provide guarantees on the competitive ratio under more general conflict models.

## 10 ACKNOWLEDGMENTS

Giorgi Nadiradze was supported by the Swiss National Fund Ambizione Project PZ00P2 161375.

## REFERENCES

[1] Intel architecture instruction set extensions programming reference, chapter 8, 2013.
[2] William cleaburn hasenplaugh, personal communication, 2017.
[3] Santosh Vempala Adam Kalai. Efficient algorithms for online decision problems. *Journal of Computer and System Sciences*, 71:291–307, 2005.
[4] Susanne Albers. Better bounds for online scheduling. *SIAM Journal on Computing*, 29:459–473, 1999.
[5] Susanne Albers. Generalized connection caching. *Theory of Computing Systems*, 35:251–267, 2002.
[6] Susanne Albers. *Online Algorithms: A Survey*. Springer-Verlag, 2003.
[7] Susanne Albers and Jeffery Westbrook. Self-organizing data structures. In *In*, pages 13–51. Springer, 1998.
[8] Murali Kodialamy Ali Khanafer and Krishna P. N. Puttaswamy. The constrained ski-rental problem and its application to online cloud cost optimization. In *INFOCOM, 2013 Proceedings IEEE*, 2013.
[9] Dan Alistarh, Syed Kamran Haider, Raphael Kübler, and Giorgi Nadiradze. The transactional conflict problem, 2018. arXiv:1804.00947.
[10] Adrià Armejach, Ruben Titos-Gil, Anurag Negi, Osman S. Unsal, and Adrián Cristal. Techniques to improve performance in requester-wins hardware transactional memory. *ACM Trans. Archit. Code Optim.*, 10(4):42:1–42:25, December 2013.
[11] Hagit Attiya and Alessia Milani. Transactional scheduling for read-dominated workloads. In *Proceedings of the 13th International Conference on Principles of Distributed Systems*, OPODIS '09, pages 3–17, Berlin, Heidelberg, 2009. Springer-Verlag.
[12] Jayaram Bobba, Kevin E. Moore, Haris Volos, Luke Yen, Mark D. Hill, Michael M. Swift, and David A. Wood. Performance pathologies in hardware transactional memory. In *Proceedings of the 34th Annual International Symposium on Computer Architecture*, ISCA '07, pages 81–91, New York, NY, USA, 2007. ACM.
[13] Daniel R Dooly, Sally A Goldman, and Stephen D Scott. Tcp dynamic acknowledgment delay (extended abstract): theory and practice. In *Proceedings of the thirtieth annual ACM symposium on Theory of computing*, pages 389–398. ACM, 1998.
[14] Ravid Y. Fiat A., Rabani Y. Competitive k-server algorithms. In *31st Annual IEEE Symposium on Foundations of Computer Science*, pages 454–463, 1990.
[15] Rachid Guerraoui, Maurice Herlihy, and Bastian Pochon. Toward a theory of transactional contention managers. In *Proceedings of the twenty-fourth annual ACM symposium on Principles of distributed computing*, pages 258–264. ACM, 2005.
[16] Syed Kamran Haider, William Hasenplaugh, and Dan Alistarh. Lease/release: Architectural support for scaling contended data structures. *SIGPLAN Not.*, 51(8):17:1–17:12, February 2016.
[17] Amin Firozshahian Omid Azizi J. Peter Stevenson Heiner Litz, David Cheriton. Si-tm: Improving transactional memory abort rates through snapshot isolation. In *19th International Conference on Architectural Support for Programming Languages and Operating Systems (ASPLOS'14)*, March 2014.
[18] Maurice Herlihy, Victor Luchangco, Mark Moir, and William N. Scherer, III. Software transactional memory for dynamic-sized data structures. In *Proceedings of the Twenty-second Annual Symposium on Principles of Distributed Computing*, PODC '03, pages 92–101, New York, NY, USA, 2003. ACM.
[19] Maurice Herlihy and J. Eliot B. Moss. Transactional memory: Architectural support for lock-free data structures. *SIGARCH Comput. Archit. News*, 21(2):289–300, May 1993.
[20] Anna R Karlin, Claire Kenyon, and Dana Randall. Dynamic tcp acknowledgement and other stories about e/(e-1). In *Proceedings of the thirty-third annual ACM symposium on Theory of computing*, pages 502–509. ACM, 2001.
[21] Anna R Karlin, Mark S Manasse, Lyle A McGeoch, and Susan Owicki. Competitive randomized algorithms for nonuniform problems. *Algorithmica*, 11(6):542–571, 1994.
[22] Anna R. Karlin, Mark S. Manasse, Larry Rudolph, and Daniel D. Sleator. Competitive snoopy caching. In *Proceedings of the 27th Annual Symposium on Foundations of Computer Science*, SFCS '86, pages 244–254, Washington, DC, USA, 1986. IEEE Computer Society.
[23] Jason E Miller, Harshad Kasture, George Kurian, Charles Gruenwald III, Nathan Beckmann, Christopher Celio, Jonathan Eastep, and Anant Agarwal. Graphite: A distributed parallel simulator for multicores. In *High Performance Computer Architecture (HPCA), 2010 IEEE 16th International Symposium on*, pages 1–12. IEEE, 2010.
[24] S. Park, M. Prvulovic, and C. J. Hughes. Pleasetm: Enabling transaction conflict management in requester-wins hardware transactional memory. In *2016 IEEE International Symposium on High Performance Computer Architecture (HPCA)*, pages 285–296, March 2016.
[25] Steven S. Seiden. A guessing game and randomized online algorithms. In *Proceedings of the Thirty-second Annual ACM Symposium on Theory of Computing*, STOC '00, pages 592–601, New York, NY, USA, 2000. ACM.
[26] Richard M. Yoo and Hsien-Hsin S. Lee. Adaptive transaction scheduling for transactional memory systems. In *Proceedings of the Twentieth Annual Symposium on Parallelism in Algorithms and Architectures*, SPAA '08, pages 169–178, New York, NY, USA, 2008. ACM.

# Theoretically Efficient Parallel Graph Algorithms Can Be Fast and Scalable

Laxman Dhulipala
Carnegie Mellon University
ldhulipa@cs.cmu.edu

Guy E. Blelloch
Carnegie Mellon University
guyb@cs.cmu.edu

Julian Shun
MIT CSAIL
jshun@mit.edu

## ABSTRACT

There has been significant recent interest in parallel graph processing due to the need to quickly analyze the large graphs available today. Many graph codes have been designed for distributed memory or external memory. However, today even the largest publicly-available real-world graph (the Hyperlink Web graph with over 3.5 billion vertices and 128 billion edges) can fit in the memory of a single commodity multicore server. Nevertheless, most experimental work in the literature report results on much smaller graphs, and the ones for the Hyperlink graph use distributed or external memory. Therefore, it is natural to ask whether we can efficiently solve a broad class of graph problems on this graph in memory.

This paper shows that theoretically-efficient parallel graph algorithms can scale to the largest publicly-available graphs using a single machine with a terabyte of RAM, processing them in minutes. We give implementations of theoretically-efficient parallel algorithms for 13 important graph problems. We also present the optimizations and techniques that we used in our implementations, which were crucial in enabling us to process these large graphs quickly. We show that the running times of our implementations outperform existing state-of-the-art implementations on the largest real-world graphs. For many of the problems that we consider, this is the first time they have been solved on graphs at this scale. We provide a publicly-available benchmark suite containing our implementations.

**ACM Reference Format:**
Laxman Dhulipala, Guy E. Blelloch, and Julian Shun. 2018. Theoretically Efficient Parallel Graph Algorithms Can Be Fast and Scalable. In *SPAA '18: 30th ACM Symposium on Parallelism in Algorithms and Architectures, July 16–18, 2018, Vienna, Austria.* ACM, New York, NY, USA, 12 pages. https://doi.org/10.1145/3210377.3210414

## 1 INTRODUCTION

Today, the largest publicly-available graph, the Hyperlink Web graph, consists of over 3.5 billion vertices and 128 billion edges [61]. This graph presents a significant computational challenge for both distributed and shared memory systems. Indeed, very few algorithms have been applied to this graph, and those that have often take hours to run [26, 45, 54], with the fastest times requiring between 1–6 minutes using a supercomputer [84, 85]. In this paper, we show that a wide range of fundamental graph problems can be solved quickly on this graph, often in minutes, on a single commodity shared-memory machine with a terabyte of RAM.[1] For example, our $k$-core implementation takes under 3.5 minutes on 72 cores, whereas Slota et al. [85] report a running time of about 6 minutes for *approximate* $k$-core on a supercomputer with over 8000 cores. They also report that they can identify the largest connected component on this graph in 63 seconds, whereas we can identify *all* connected components in 38.3 seconds. Another recent result by Stergiou et al. [86] solves connectivity on the Hyperlink 2012 graph in 341 seconds on a 1000 node cluster with 12000 cores and 128TB of RAM. Compared to this result, our implementation is 8.9x faster on a system with 128x less memory and 166x fewer cores. However, we note that they are able to process a significantly larger private graph that we would not be able to fit into our memory footprint. A more complete comparison between our work and existing work, including disk-based systems [26, 45, 54], is given in Section 6.

Importantly, all of our implementations have strong theoretical bounds on their work and depth. There are several reasons that algorithms with good theoretical guarantees are desirable. For one, they are robust as even adversarially-chosen inputs will not cause them to perform extremely poorly. Furthermore, they can be designed on pen-and-paper by exploiting properties of the problem instead of tailoring solutions to the particular dataset at hand. Theoretical guarantees also make it likely that the algorithm will continue to perform well even if the underlying data changes. Finally, careful implementations of algorithms that are nearly work-efficient can perform much less work in practice than work-inefficient algorithms. This reduction in work often translates to faster running times on the same number of cores [28]. We note that most running times that have been reported in the literature on the Hyperlink Web graph use parallel algorithms that are not theoretically-efficient.

In this paper, we present implementations of parallel algorithms with strong theoretical bounds on their work and depth for connectivity, biconnectivity, strongly connected components, low-diameter decomposition, maximal independent set, maximal matching, graph coloring, single-source shortest paths, betweenness centrality, minimum spanning forest, $k$-core decomposition, approximate set cover, and triangle counting. We describe the techniques used to achieve good performance on graphs with billions of vertices and hundreds of billions of edges and share experimental results for the Hyperlink 2012 and Hyperlink 2014 Web crawls, the largest and second largest publicly-available graphs, as well as several smaller real-world graphs at various scales. Some of the algorithms we


*SPAA '18, July 16–18, 2018, Vienna, Austria*

ACM ISBN 978-1-4503-5799-9/18/07...$15.00
https://doi.org/10.1145/3210377.3210414

[1] These machines are roughly the size of a workstation and can be easily rented in the cloud (e.g., on Amazon EC2).

| Problem | (1) | (72h) | (SU) | Algorithm | Model | Work | Depth |
|---|---|---|---|---|---|---|---|
| Breadth-First Search (BFS) | 649 | 10.7 | 60 | – | TS | $O(m)$ | $O(\text{diam}(G)\log n)$ |
| Integral-Weight SSSP (weighted BFS) | 3770 | 58.1 | 64 | [28] | PW | $O(m)$ expected | $O(\text{diam}(G)\log n)$ w.h.p.† |
| General-Weight SSSP (Bellman-Ford) | 4010 | 59.4 | 67 | [25] | PW | $O(\text{diam}(G)m)$ | $O(\text{diam}(G)\log n)$ |
| Single-Source Betweenness Centrality (BC) | 2260 | 37.1 | 60 | [19] | FA | $O(m)$ | $O(\text{diam}(G)\log n)$ |
| Low-Diameter Decomposition (LDD) | 1150 | 19.6 | 58 | [63] | TS | $O(m)$ expected | $O(\log^2 n)$ w.h.p. |
| Connectivity | 2080 | 38.3 | 54 | [79] | TS | $O(m)$ expected | $O(\log^3 n)$ w.h.p. |
| Biconnectivity | 9860 | 165 | 59 | [87] | FA | $O(m)$ expected | $O(\max(\text{diam}(G)\log n, \log^3 n))$ w.h.p. |
| Strongly Connected Components (SCC)* | 8130 | 185 | 43 | [12] | PW | $O(m\log n)$ expected | $O(\text{diam}(G)\log n)$ w.h.p. |
| Minimum Spanning Forest (MSF) | 9520 | 187 | 50 | [90] | PW | $O(m\log n)$ | $O(\log^2 n)$ |
| Maximal Independent Set (MIS) | 2190 | 32.2 | 68 | [11] | FA | $O(m)$ expected | $O(\log^2 n)$ w.h.p. |
| Maximal Matching (MM) | 7150 | 108 | 66 | [11] | PW | $O(m)$ expected | $O(\log^3 m/\log\log m)$ w.h.p. |
| Graph Coloring | 8920 | 158 | 56 | [40] | FA | $O(m)$ | $O(\log n + L\log\Delta)$ |
| $k$-core | 8515 | 184 | 46 | [28] | FA | $O(m)$ expected | $O(\rho\log n)$ w.h.p. |
| Approximate Set Cover | 5630 | 98.4 | 57 | [14] | PW | $O(m)$ expected | $O(\log^3 n)$ w.h.p. |
| Triangle Counting (TC) | – | 1470 | – | [81] | - | $O(m^{3/2})$ | $O(\log n)$ |

**Table 1: Running times (in seconds) of our algorithms on the symmetrized Hyperlink2012 graph where (1) is the single-thread time, (72h) is the 72-core time using hyper-threading, and (SU) is the parallel speedup. Theoretical bounds for the algorithms and the variant of the MT-RAM used are shown in the last three columns. We mark times that did not finish in 5 hours with –. *SCC was run on the directed version of the graph. †We say that an algorithm has $O(f(n))$ cost *with high probability (w.h.p.)* if it has $O(k \cdot f(n))$ cost with probability at least $1 - 1/n^k$.**

describe are based on previous results from Ligra, Ligra+, and Julienne [28, 76, 80], and other papers on efficient parallel graph algorithms [11, 40, 81]. However, most existing implementations were changed significantly in order to be more memory efficient. Several algorithm implementations for problems like strongly connected components, minimum spanning forest, and biconnectivity are new, and required implementation techniques to scale that we believe are of independent interest. We also had to extend the compressed representation from Ligra+ [80] to ensure that our graph primitives for mapping, filtering, reducing and packing the neighbors of a vertex were theoretically-efficient. We note that using compression techniques is crucial for representing the symmetrized Hyperlink 2012 graph in 1TB of RAM, as storing this graph in an uncompressed format would require over 900GB to store the edges alone, whereas the graph requires 330GB in our compressed format (less than 1.5 bytes per edge). We show the running times of our algorithms on the Hyperlink 2012 graph as well as their work and depth bounds in Table 1. To make it easy to build upon or compare to our work in the future, we describe a benchmark suite containing our problems with clear I/O specifications, which we have made publicly-available.[2]

We present an experimental evaluation of all of our implementations, and in almost all cases, the numbers we report are faster than any previous performance numbers for any machines, even much larger supercomputers. We are also able to apply our algorithms to the largest publicly-available graph, in many cases for the first time in the literature, using a reasonably modest machine. Most importantly, our implementations are based on reasonably simple algorithms with strong bounds on their work and depth. We believe that our implementations are likely to scale to larger graphs and lead to efficient algorithms for related problems.

## 2 RELATED WORK

**Parallel Graph Algorithms.** Parallel graph algorithms have received significant attention since the start of parallel computing, and many elegant algorithms with good theoretical bounds have been developed over the decades (e.g., [3, 8, 21, 32, 44, 49, 53, 62–64, 68, 69, 75, 87]). A major goal in parallel graph algorithm design is to find *work-efficient* algorithms with polylogarithmic depth. While many suspect that work-efficient algorithms may not exist for all parallelizable graph problems, as inefficiency may be inevitable for problems that depend on transitive closure, many problems that are of practical importance do admit work-efficient algorithms [48]. For these problems, which include connectivity, biconnectivity, minimum spanning forest, maximal independent set, maximal matching, and triangle counting, giving theoretically-efficient implementations that are simple and practical is important, as the amount of parallelism available on modern systems is still modest enough that reducing the amount of work done is critical for achieving good performance. Aside from intellectual curiosity, investigating whether theoretically-efficient graph algorithms also perform well in practice is important, as theoretically-efficient algorithms are less vulnerable to adversarial inputs than ad-hoc algorithms that happen to work well in practice.

Unfortunately, some problems that are not known to admit work-efficient parallel algorithms due to the transitive-closure bottleneck [48], such as strongly connected components (SCC) and single-source shortest paths (SSSP) are still important in practice. One method for circumventing the bottleneck is to give work-efficient algorithms for these problems that run in depth proportional to the diameter of the graph—as real-world graphs have low diameter, and theoretical models of real-world graphs predict a logarithmic diameter, these algorithms offer theoretical guarantees in practice [12, 72]. Other problems, like $k$-core are P-complete [4], which rules out polylogarithmic-depth algorithms for them unless P = NC [38]. However, even $k$-core admits an algorithm with strong theoretical guarantees that is efficient in practice [28].

**Parallel Graph Processing Frameworks.** Motivated by the need to process very large graphs, there have been many graph processing frameworks developed in the literature (e.g., [36, 52, 56, 65, 76] among many others). We refer the reader to [59, 89] for surveys of existing frameworks. Several recent graph processing systems evaluate the scalability of their implementations by solving problems on massive graphs [26, 28, 45, 54, 84, 86]. All of these systems report running times either on the Hyperlink 2012 graph or Hyperlink 2014 graphs, two web crawls released by the WebDataCommons that are the largest and second largest publicly-available graphs respectively. We describe these recent systems and give a detailed comparison of how our implementations perform compare to their codes in Section 6. We review existing parallel graph algorithm benchmarks in the full version of our paper [29].

[2]https://github.com/ldhulipala/gbbs

## 3 PRELIMINARIES

**Graph Notation.** We denote an unweighted graph by $G(V, E)$, where $V$ is the set of vertices and $E$ is the set of edges in the graph. A weighted graph is denoted by $G = (V, E, w)$, where $w$ is a function which maps an edge to a real value (its weight). The number of vertices in a graph is $n = |V|$, and the number of edges is $m = |E|$. Vertices are assumed to be indexed from 0 to $n-1$. For undirected graphs we use $N(v)$ to denote the neighbors of vertex $v$ and $deg(v)$ to denote its degree. For directed graphs, we use $in\text{-}deg(v)$ and $out\text{-}deg(v)$ to denote the in and out-neighbors of a vertex $v$. We use $\mathsf{diam}(G)$ to refer to the diameter of the graph, or the longest shortest path distance between any vertex $s$ and any vertex $v$ reachable from $s$. $\Delta$ is used to denote the maximum degree of the graph. We assume that there are no self-edges or duplicate edges in the graph. We refer to graphs stored as a list of edges as being stored in the ***edgelist*** format and the compressed-sparse column and compressed-sparse row formats as ***CSC*** and ***CSR*** respectively.

**Atomic Primitives.** We use three common atomic primitives in our algorithms: test-and-set (TS), fetch-and-add (FA), and priority-write (PW). A TEST-AND-SET(&$x$) checks if $x$ is 0, and if so atomically sets it to 1 and returns *true*; otherwise it returns *false*. A FETCH-AND-ADD(&$x$) atomically returns the current value of $x$ and then increments $x$. A PRIORITY-WRITE(&$x, v, p$) atomically compares $v$ with the current value of $x$ using the priority function $p$, and if $v$ has higher priority than the value of $x$ according to $p$ it sets $x$ to $v$ and returns *true*; otherwise it returns *false*.

**Model.** In the analysis of algorithms we use the following work-depth model, which is closely related to the PRAM but better models current machines and programming paradigms that are asynchronous and allow dynamic forking. We can simulate the model on the CRCW PRAM equipped with the same operations with an additional $O(\log^* n)$ factor in the depth due to load-balancing. Furthermore, a PRAM algorithm using $P$ processors and $T$ time can be simulated in our model with $PT$ work and $T$ depth.

The *Multi-Threaded Random-Access Machine (MT-RAM)* [10] consists of a set of threads that share an unbounded memory. Each thread is basically equivalent to a Random Access Machine—it works on a program stored in memory, has a constant number of registers, and has standard RAM instructions (including an end to finish the computation). The MT-RAM extends the RAM with a `fork` instruction that takes a positive integer $k$ and forks $k$ new child threads. Each child thread receives a unique integer in the range $[1, \dots, k]$ in its first register and otherwise has the identical state as the parent, which has a 0 in that register. They all start by running the next instruction. When a thread performs a `fork`, it is suspended until all the children terminate (execute an end instruction). A computation starts with a single root thread and finishes when that root thread ends. This model supports what is often referred to as nested parallelism. If the root thread never does a fork, it is a standard sequential program.

A computation can be viewed as a series-parallel DAG in which each instruction is a vertex, sequential instructions are composed in series, and the forked subthreads are composed in parallel. The ***work*** of a computation is the number of vertices and the ***depth*** is the length of the longest path in the DAG. We augment the model with three atomic instructions that are used by our algorithms: test-and-set (TS), fetch-and-add (FA), and priority-write (PW) and discuss our model with these operations as the TS, FA, and PW variants of the MT-RAM. As is standard with the RAM model, we assume that the memory locations and registers have at most $O(\log M)$ bits, where $M$ is the total size of the memory used. More details about the model can be found in [10].

**Parallel Primitives.** The following parallel procedures are used throughout the paper. ***Scan*** takes as input an array $A$ of length $n$, an associative binary operator $\oplus$, and an identity element $\bot$ such that $\bot \oplus x = x$ for any $x$, and returns the array $(\bot, \bot \oplus A[0], \bot \oplus A[0] \oplus A[1], \dots, \bot \oplus_{i=0}^{n-2} A[i])$ as well as the overall sum, $\bot \oplus_{i=0}^{n-1} A[i]$. Scan can be done in $O(n)$ work and $O(\log n)$ depth (assuming $\oplus$ takes $O(1)$ work) [44]. ***Reduce*** takes an array $A$ and a binary associative function $f$ and returns the sum of the elements in $A$ with respect to $f$. ***Filter*** takes an array $A$ and a predicate $f$ and returns a new array containing $a \in A$ for which $f(a)$ is true, in the same order as in $A$. Reduce and filter can both be done in $O(n)$ work and $O(\log n)$ depth (assuming $f$ takes $O(1)$ work).

**Ligra, Ligra+, and Julienne.** We make use of the Ligra, Ligra+, and Julienne frameworks for shared-memory graph processing in this paper and review components from these frameworks here [28, 76, 80]. Ligra provides data structures for representing a graph $G = (V, E)$, ***vertexSubset***s (subsets of the vertices). We make use of the EDGEMAP function provided by Ligra, which we use for mapping over edges. EDGEMAP takes as input a graph $G(V, E)$, a vertexSubset $U$, and two boolean functions $F$ and $C$. EDGEMAP applies $F$ to $(u, v) \in E$ such that $u \in U$ and $C(v) = true$ (call this subset of edges $E_a$), and returns a vertexSubset $U'$ where $u \in U'$ if and only if $(u, v) \in E_a$ and $F(u, v) = true$. $F$ can side-effect data structures associated with the vertices. EDGEMAP runs in $O(\sum_{u \in U} deg(u))$ work and $O(\log n)$ depth assuming $F$ and $C$ take $O(1)$ work. EDGEMAP either applies a ***sparse*** or ***dense*** method based on the number of edges incident to the current frontier. Both methods run in $O(\sum_{u \in U} deg(u))$ work and $O(\log n)$ depth. We note that in our experiments we use an optimized version of the dense method which examines in-edges sequentially and stops once $C$ returns *false*. This optimization lets us potentially examine significantly fewer edges than the $O(\log n)$ depth version, but at the cost of $O(in\text{-}deg(v))$ depth.

## 4 ALGORITHMS

In this section we describe I/O specifications of our benchmark, discuss related work and present the theoretically-efficient algorithm we implemented for each problem. We cite the original papers that our algorithms are based on in Table 1. We mark implementations based on prior work with a † and discuss the related work, algorithms, and implementations for these problems in the full version of our paper [29]. The full version also contains self-contained descriptions of all of our algorithms.

**Shortest Path Problems**†

---

Problem: Breadth-First Search (BFS)
Input: $G = (V, E)$, an unweighted graph, SRC $\in V$.
Output: $D$, a mapping where $D[v]$ is the shortest path distance from SRC to $v$ in $G$ and $\infty$ if $v$ is unreachable.

---

Problem: Integral-Weight SSSP (weighted BFS)

Input: $G = (V, E, w)$, a weighted graph with integral edge weights, $\text{SRC} \in V$.
Output: $D$, a mapping where $D[v]$ is the shortest path distance from SRC to $v$ in $G$ and $\infty$ if $v$ is unreachable.

---

Problem: General-Weight SSSP (Bellman-Ford)
Input: $G = (V, E, w)$, a weighted graph, $\text{SRC} \in V$.
Output: $D$, a mapping where $D[v]$ is the shortest path distance from SRC to $v$ in $G$ and $\infty$ if $v$ is unreachable. All distances must be $-\infty$ if $G$ contains a negative-weight cycle reachable from SRC.

---

Problem: Single-Source Betweenness Centrality (BC)
Input: $G = (V, E)$, an undirected graph, $\text{SRC} \in V$.
Output: $S$, a mapping from each vertex $v$ to the centrality contribution from all $(\text{SRC}, t)$ shortest paths that pass through $v$.

---

**Low-Diameter Decomposition**†

---

Input: $G = (V, E)$, a directed graph, $0 < \beta < 1$.
Output: $\mathcal{L}$, a mapping from each vertex to a cluster ID representing a $(O(\beta), O((\log n)/\beta))$ decomposition. A $(\beta, d)$-decomposition partitions $V$ into $V_1, \ldots, V_k$ such that the shortest path between two vertices in $V_i$ using only vertices in $V_i$ is at most $d$, and the number of edges $(u, v)$ where $u \in V_i, v \in V_j, j \neq i$ is at most $\beta m$.

---

**Connectivity**†

---

Input: $G = (V, E)$, an undirected graph.
Output: $\mathcal{L}$, a mapping from each vertex to a unique label for its connected component.

---

**Biconnectivity**

---

Input: $G = (V, E)$, an undirected graph.
Output: $\mathcal{L}$, a mapping from each edge to the label of its biconnected component.

---

Sequentially, biconnectivity can be solved using the Hopcroft-Tarjan algorithm [42]. The algorithm uses depth-first search (DFS) to identify articulation points and requires $O(m + n)$ work to label all edges with their biconnectivity label. It is possible to parallelize the sequential algorithm using a parallel DFS, however, the fastest parallel DFS algorithm is not work-efficient [2]. Tarjan and Vishkin present the first work-efficient algorithm for biconnectivity [87] (as stated in the paper the algorithm is not work-efficient, but it can be made so by using a work-efficient connectivity algorithm). Another approach relies on the fact that biconnected graphs admit open ear decompositions to solve biconnectivity efficiently [57, 70].

In this paper, we implement the Tarjan-Vishkin algorithm for biconnectivity in $O(m)$ work and $O(\max(\text{diam}(G) \log n, \log^3 n))$ depth on the FA-MT-RAM. Our implementation first computes connectivity labels using the algorithm from Section 4, which runs in $O(m)$ work and $O(\log^3 n)$ depth w.h.p. and picks an arbitrary source vertex from each component. Next, we compute a spanning forest rooted at these sources using breadth-first search, which runs in $O(m)$ work and $O(\text{diam}(G) \log n)$ depth. We note that the connectivity algorithm can be modified to compute a spanning forest in the same work and depth as connectivity, which would avoid the breadth-first-search. We compute *Low*, *High*, and *Size* for each vertex by running leaffix and rootfix sums on the spanning forests produced by BFS with fetch-and-add, which requires $O(n)$ work and $O(\text{diam}(G))$ depth. Finally, we compute an implicit representation of the biconnectivity labels for each edge, using an idea from [7]. This step computes per-vertex labels by removing all critical edges and computing connectivity on the remaining graph. The resulting vertex labels can be used to assign biconnectivity labels to edges by giving tree edges the connectivity label of the vertex further from the root in the tree, and assigning non-tree edges the label of either endpoint. Summing the cost of each step, the total work of this algorithm is $O(m)$ in expectation and the total depth is $O(\max(\text{diam}(G) \log n, \log^3 n))$ w.h.p.

**Minimum Spanning Forest**

---

Input: $G = (V, E, w)$, a weighted graph.
Output: $T$, a set of edges representing a minimum spanning forest of $G$.

---

Borůvka gave the first known sequential and parallel algorithm for computing a minimum spanning forest (MSF) [18]. Significant effort has gone into finding linear-work MSF algorithms both in the sequential and parallel settings [21, 47, 68]. Unfortunately, the linear-work parallel algorithms are highly involved and do not seem to be practical. Significant effort has also gone into designing practical parallel algorithms for MSF; we discuss relevant experimental work in Section 6. Due to the simplicity of Borůvka, many parallel implementations of MSF use variants of it.

In this paper, we present an implementation of Borůvka's algorithm that runs in $O(m \log n)$ work and $O(\log^2 n)$ depth on the PW-MT-RAM. Our implementation is based on a recent implementation of Borůvka by Zhou [90] that runs on the edgelist format. We made several changes to the algorithm which improve performance and allow us to solve MSF on graphs stored in the CSR/CSC format, as storing an integer-weighted graph in edgelist format would require well over 1TB of memory to represent the edges in the Hyperlink2012 graph alone. Our code uses an implementation of Borůvka that works over an edgelist; to make it efficient we ensure that the size of the lists passed to it are much smaller than $m$. Our approach is to perform a constant number of *filtering* steps. Each filtering step solves an approximate $k$'th smallest problem in order to extract the lightest $3n/2$ edges in the graph (or all remaining edges) and runs Borůvka on this subset of edges. We then filter the remaining graph, packing out any edges that are now in the same component. This idea is similar to the theoretically-efficient algorithm of Cole et al. [21], except that instead of randomly sampling edges, we select a linear number of the lowest weight edges. Each filtering step costs $O(m)$ work and $O(\log m)$ depth, but as we only perform a constant number of steps, they do not affect the work and depth asymptotically. In practice, most of the edges are removed after 3–4 filtering steps, and so the remaining edges can be copied into an edgelist and solved in a single Borůvka step. We also note that as the edges are initially represented in both directions, we can pack out the edges so that each undirected edge is only inspected once (we noticed that earlier edgelist-based implementations stored undirected edges in both directions).

**Strongly Connected Components**

Input: $G(V, E)$, a directed graph.
Output: $\mathcal{L}$, a mapping from each vertex to the label of its strongly-connected component.

Tarjan's algorithm is the textbook sequential algorithm for computing the strongly connected components (SCCs) of a directed graph [25]. As it uses depth-first search, we currently do not know how to efficiently parallelize it [2]. The current theoretical state-of-the-art for parallel SCC algorithms with polylogarithmic depth reduces the problem to computing the transitive closure of the graph. This requires $\tilde{O}(n^3)$ work using combinatorial algorithms [35], which is significantly higher than the $O(m+n)$ work done by sequential algorithms. As the transitive-closure based approach performs a significant amount of work even for moderately sized graphs, subsequent research on parallel SCC algorithms has focused on improving the work while potentially sacrificing depth [12, 24, 34, 72]. Conceptually, these algorithms first pick a random pivot and use a reachability-oracle to identify the SCC containing the pivot. They then remove this SCC, which partitions the remaining graph into several disjoint pieces, and recurse on the pieces.

In this paper, we present the first implementation of the SCC algorithm from Blelloch et al. [12]. Our implementation runs in $O(m \log n)$ expected work and $O(\text{diam}(G) \log n)$ depth w.h.p. on the PW-MT-RAM. One of the challenges in implementing this SCC algorithm is how to compute reachability information from multiple vertices simultaneously and how to combine the information to (1) identify SCCs and (2) refine the subproblems of visited vertices. In our implementation, we explicitly store $\mathcal{R}_F$ and $\mathcal{R}_B$, the forward and backward reachability sets for the set of centers that are active in the current phase, $C_A$. The sets are represented as hash tables that store tuples of vertices and center IDs, $(u, c_i)$, representing a vertex $u$ in the same subproblem as $c_i$ that is visited by a directed path from $c_i$. We explain how to make the hash table technique practical in Section 5. The reachability sets are computed by running simultaneous breadth-first searches from all active centers. In each round of the BFS, we apply EDGEMAP to traverse all out-edges (or in-edges) of the current frontier. When we visit an edge $(u, v)$ we try to add $u$'s center IDs to $v$. If $u$ succeeds in adding any IDs, it test-and-set's a visited flag for $v$, and returns it in the next frontier if the test-and-set succeeded. Each BFS requires at most $O(\text{diam}(G))$ rounds as each search adds the same labels on each round as it would have had it run in isolation.

After computing $\mathcal{R}_F$ and $\mathcal{R}_B$, we deterministically assign (with respect to the random permutation of vertices generated at the start of the algorithm) vertices that we visited in this phase a new label, which is either the label of a refined subproblem or a unique label for the SCC they are contained in. We first intersect the two tables and perform, for any tuple $(v, c_i)$ contained in the intersection, a priority-write with min on the memory location corresponding to $v$'s SCC label with $c_i$ as the label. Next, for all pairs $(v, c_i)$ in $\mathcal{R}_F \oplus \mathcal{R}_B$ we do a priority-write with min on $v$'s subproblem label, which ensures that the highest priority search that visited $v$ sets its new subproblem.

We implemented an optimized search for the first phase, which just runs two regular BFSs over the in-edges and out-edges from a single pivot and stores the reachability information in bit-vectors instead of hash-tables. It is well known that many directed real-world graphs have a single massive strongly connected component, and so with reasonable probability the first vertex in the permutation will find this giant component [20]. We also implemented a 'trimming' optimization that is reported in the literature [60, 83], which eliminates trivial SCCs by removing any vertices that have zero in- or out-degree. We implement a procedure that recursively trims until no zero in- or out-degree vertices remain, or until a maximum number of rounds are reached.

**Maximal Independent Set and Maximal Matching**

Problem: Maximal Independent Set
Input: $G = (V, E)$, an undirected graph.
Output: $U \subseteq V$, a set of vertices such that no two vertices in $U$ are neighbors and all vertices in $V \setminus U$ have a neighbor in $U$.

Problem: Maximal Matching
Input: $G = (V, E)$, an undirected graph.
Output: $E' \subseteq E$, a set of edges such that no two edges in $E'$ share an endpoint and all edges in $E \setminus E'$ share an endpoint with some edge in $E'$.

Maximal independent set (MIS) and maximal matching (MM) are easily solved in linear work sequentially using greedy algorithms. Many efficient parallel maximal independent set and matching algorithms have been developed over the years [3, 8, 11, 43, 49, 53]. Blelloch et al. show that when the vertices (or edges) are processed in a random order, the sequential greedy algorithms for MIS and MM can be parallelized efficiently and give practical algorithms [11]. Recently, Fischer and Noever showed an improved depth bound for this algorithm [33].

In this paper, we implement the rootset-based algorithm for MIS from Blelloch et al. [11] which runs in $O(m)$ expected work and $O(\log^2 n)$ depth w.h.p. on the FA-MT-RAM. To the best of our knowledge this is the first implementation of the rootset-based algorithm; the implementations from [11] are based on processing appropriately-sized prefixes of an order generated by a random permutation $P$. Our implementation of the rootset-based algorithm works on a priority-DAG defined by directing edges in the graph from the higher-priority endpoint to the lower-priority endpoint. On each round, we add all roots of the DAG into the MIS, compute $N(\mathit{roots})$, the neighbors of the rootset that are still active, and finally decrement the priorities of $N(N(\mathit{roots}))$. As the vertices in $N(\mathit{roots})$ are at arbitrary depths in the priority-DAG, we only decrement the priority along an edge $(u, v)$, $u \in N(\mathit{roots})$ if $P[u] < P[v]$. The algorithm runs in $O(m)$ work as we process each edge once; the depth bound is $O(\log^2 n)$ as the priority-DAG has $O(\log n)$ depth w.h.p. [33], and each round takes $O(\log n)$ depth. We were surprised that this implementation usually outperforms the prefix-based implementation from [11], while also being simple to implement.

Our maximal matching implementation is based on the prefix-based algorithm from [11] that takes $O(m)$ expected work and $O(\log^3 m / \log\log m)$ depth w.h.p. on the PW-MT-RAM (using the improved depth shown in [33]). We had to make several modifications to run the algorithm on the large graphs in our experiments. The original code from [11] uses an edgelist representation, but we cannot directly use this implementation as uncompressing all edges would require a prohibitive amount of memory for large graphs. Instead, as in our MSF implementation, we simulate the prefix-based approach by performing a constant number of *filtering* steps. Each filter step packs out $3n/2$ of the highest priority edges, randomly permutes them, and then runs the edgelist based algorithm on the prefix. After computing the new set of edges that are added to the matching, we filter the remaining graph and remove all edges that are incident to matched vertices. In practice, just 3–4 filtering steps are sufficient to remove essentially all edges in the graph. The last step uncompresses any remaining edges into an edgelist and runs the prefix-based algorithm. The filtering steps can be done within the work and depth bounds of the original algorithm.

**Graph Coloring**

Input: $G = (V, E)$, an undirected graph.
Output: $C$, a mapping from each vertex to a color such that for each edge $(u, v) \in E$, $C(u) \neq C(v)$, using at most $\Delta + 1$ colors.

As graph coloring is NP-hard to solve optimally, algorithms like greedy coloring, which guarantees a $(\Delta + 1)$-coloring, are used instead in practice, and often use much fewer than $(\Delta + 1)$ colors on real-world graphs [40, 88]. Jones and Plassmann (JP) parallelize the greedy algorithm using linear work, but unfortunately adversarial inputs exist for the heuristics they consider that may force the algorithm to run in $O(n)$ depth. Hasenplaugh et al. introduce several heuristics that produce high-quality colorings in practice and also achieve provably low-depth regardless of the input graph. These include LLF (largest-log-degree-first), which processes vertices ordered by the log of their degree and SLL (smallest-log-degree-last), which processes vertices by removing all lowest log-degree vertices from the graph, coloring the remaining graph, and finally coloring the removed vertices. For LLF, they show that it runs in $O(m + n)$ work and $O(L \log \Delta + \log n)$ depth, where $L = \min\{\sqrt{m}, \Delta\} + \log^2 \Delta \log n / \log \log n$ in expectation.

In this paper, we implement a synchronous version of Jones-Plassmann using the LLF heuristic in Ligra, which runs in $O(m + n)$ work and $O(L \log \Delta + \log n)$ depth on the FA-MT-RAM. The algorithm is implemented similarly to our rootset-based algorithm for MIS. In each round, after coloring the roots we use a fetch-and-add to decrement a count on our neighbors, and add the neighbor as a root on the next round if the count is decremented to 0.

**$k$-core**

Input: $G = (V, E)$, an undirected graph.
Output: $D$, a mapping from each vertex to its coreness value.

$k$-cores were defined independently by Seidman [73], and by Matula and Beck [58] who also gave a linear-time algorithm for computing the *coreness* value of all vertices, i.e. the maximum $k$-core a vertex participates in. Anderson and Mayr showed that $k$-core (and therefore coreness) is in NC for $k \leq 2$, but is P-complete for $k \geq 3$ [4]. The Matula and Beck algorithm is simple and practical—it first bucket-sorts vertices by their degree, and then repeatedly deletes the minimum-degree vertex. The affected neighbors are moved to a new bucket corresponding to their induced degree. As each edge in each direction and vertex is processed exactly once, the algorithm runs in $O(m+n)$ work. In [28], the authors give a parallel algorithm based on bucketing that runs in $O(m+n)$ expected work, and $\rho \log n$ depth w.h.p. $\rho$ is the peeling-complexity of the graph, defined as the number of rounds to peel the graph to an empty graph where each peeling step removes all minimum degree vertices.

Our implementation of $k$-core in this paper is based on the implementation from Julienne [28]. One of the challenges to implementing the peeling algorithm for $k$-core is efficiently computing the number of edges removed from each vertex that remains in the graph. A simple approach is to just fetch-and-add a counter per vertex, and update the bucket of the vertex based on this counter, however this incurs significant contention on real-world graphs with vertices with large degree. In order to make this step faster in practice, we implemented a work-efficient histogram which compute the number of edges removed from remaining vertices while incurring very little contention. We describe our histogram implementation in Section 5.

**Approximate Set Cover**[†]

Input: $G = (V, E)$, an undirected graph representing a set cover instance.
Output: $S \subseteq V$, a set of sets such that $\cup_{s \in S} N(s) = V$ with $|S|$ being an $O(\log n)$-approximation to the optimal cover.

**Triangle Counting**[†]

Input: $G = (V, E)$, an undirected graph.
Output: $T_G$, the total number of triangles in $G$.

## 5 IMPLEMENTATIONS AND TECHNIQUES

In this section, we introduce several general implementation techniques and optimizations that we use in our algorithms. Due to lack of space, we describe some techniques, such as a more cache-friendly sparse EDGEMAP that we call EDGEMAPBLOCKED, and compression techniques in the full version of our paper [29].

**A Work-efficient Histogram Implementation.** Our initial implementation of the peeling-based algorithm for $k$-core algorithm suffered from poor performance due to a large amount of contention incurred by fetch-and-adds on high-degree vertices. This occurs as many social-networks and web-graphs have large maximum degree, but relatively small degeneracy, or largest non-empty core (labeled $k_{max}$ in Table 2). For these graphs, we observed that many early rounds, which process vertices with low coreness perform a large number of fetch-and-adds on memory locations corresponding to high-degree vertices, resulting in high contention [77]. To reduce contention, we designed a work-efficient histogram implementation that can perform this step while only incurring $O(\log n)$ contention w.h.p. The ***Histogram*** primitive takes a sequence of $(K, T)$ pairs, and an associative and commutative operator $R : \mathrm{T} \times \mathrm{T} \to \mathrm{T}$ and computes a sequence of $(K, T)$ pairs, where each key $k$ only appears once, and its associated value $t$ is the sum of all values associated with keys $k$ in the input, combined with respect to $R$.

A useful example of histogram to consider is summing for each $v \in N(F)$ for a vertexSubset $F$, the number of edges $(u, v)$ where $u \in F$ (i.e., the number of incoming neighbors from the frontier). This operation can be implemented by running histogram on a sequence where each $v \in N(F)$ appears once per $(u, v)$ edge as a tuple $(v, 1)$

using the operator +. One theoretically efficient implementation of histogram is to simply semisort the pairs using the work-efficient semisort algorithm from [39]. The semisort places pairs from the sequence into a set of *heavy* and *light* buckets, where heavy buckets contain a single key that appears many times in the input sequence, and light buckets contain at most $O(\log^2 n)$ distinct keys $(k, v)$ keys, each of which appear at most $O(\log n)$ times w.h.p. (heavy and light keys are determined by sampling). We compute the reduced value for heavy buckets using a standard parallel reduction. For each light bucket, we allocate a hash table, and hash the keys in the bucket in parallel to the table, combining multiple values for the same key using $R$. As each key appears at most $O(\log n)$ times w.h.p, we incur at most $O(\log n)$ contention w.h.p. The output sequence can be computed by compacting the light tables and heavy arrays.

While the semisort implementation is theoretically efficient, it requires a likely cache miss for each key when inserting into the appropriate hash table. To improve cache performance in this step, we implemented a work-efficient algorithm with $O(n^\epsilon)$ depth based on radix sort. Our implementation is based on the parallel radix sort from PBBS [78]. As in the semisort, we first sample keys from the sequence and determine the set of heavy-keys. Instead of directly moving the elements into light and heavy buckets, we break up the input sequence into $O(n^{1-\epsilon})$ blocks, each of size $O(n^\epsilon)$, and sequentially sort the keys within a block into light and heavy buckets. Within the blocks, we reduce all heavy keys into a single value and compute an array of size $O(n^\epsilon)$ which holds the starting offset of each bucket within the block. Next, we perform a segmented-scan [9] over the arrays of the $O(n^{1-\epsilon})$ blocks to compute the sizes of the light buckets, and the reduced values for the heavy-buckets, which only contain a single key. Finally, we allocate tables for the light buckets, hash the light keys in parallel over the blocks and compact the light tables and heavy keys into the output array. Each step runs in $O(n)$ work and $O(n^\epsilon)$ depth. Compared to the original semisort implementation, this version incurs fewer cache misses because the light keys per block are already sorted and consecutive keys likely go to the same hash table, which fits in cache. We compared our times in the histogram-based version of $k$-core and the fetch-and-add-based version of $k$-core and saw between a 1.1–3.1x improvement from using the histogram.

**Techniques for overlapping searches.** In this section, we describe how we compute and update the reachability labels for vertices that are visited in a phase of our SCC algorithm. Recall that each phase performs a graph traversal from the set of active centers on this round, $C_A$, and computes for each center $c$, all vertices in the weakly-connected component for the subproblem of $c$ that can be reached by a directed path from it. We store this reachability information as a set of $(u, c_i)$ pairs in a hash-table, which represent the fact that $u$ can be reached by a directed path from $c_i$. A phase performs two graph traversals from the centers to compute $\mathcal{R}_F$ and $\mathcal{R}_B$, the out-reachability set and in-reachability sets respectively. Each traversal allocates an initial hash table and runs rounds of EDGEMAP until no new label information is added to the table.

The main challenge in implementing one round in the traversal is (1) ensuring that the table has sufficient space to store all pairs that will be added this round, and (2) efficiently iterating over all of the pairs associated with a vertex. We implement (1) by performing a parallel reduce to sum over vertices $u \in F$, the current frontier, the number of neighbors $v$ in the same subproblem, multiplied by the number of distinct labels currently assigned to $u$. This upper-bounds the number of distinct labels that could be added this round, and although we may overestimate the number of actual additions, we will never run out of space in the table. We update the number of elements currently in the table during concurrent insertions by storing a per-processor count which gets incremented whenever the processor performs a successful insertion. The counts are then summed together at the end of a round and used to update the count of the number of elements in the table.

One simple implementation of (2) is to simply allocate $O(\log n)$ space for every vertex, as the maximum number of centers that visit any vertex during a phase is at most $O(\log n)$ w.h.p. However, this will waste a significant amount of space, as most vertices are visited just a few times. Instead, our implementation stores $(u, c)$ pairs in the table for visited vertices $u$, and computes hashes based only on the ID of $u$. As each vertex is only expected to be visited a constant number of times during a phase, the expected probe length is still a constant. Storing the pairs for a vertex in the same probe-sequence is helpful for two reasons. First, we may incur fewer cache misses than if we had hashed the pairs based on both entries, as multiple pairs for a vertex can fit in the same cache line. Second, storing the pairs for a vertex along the same probe sequence makes it extremely easy to find all pairs associated with a vertex $u$, as we simply perform linear-probing, reporting all pairs that have $u$ as their key until we hit an empty cell. Our experiments show that this technique is practical, and we believe that it may have applications in similar algorithms, such as computing least-element lists or FRT trees in parallel [12, 13].

# 6 EXPERIMENTS

In this section, we describe our experimental results on a set of real-world graphs and also discuss related experimental work. Tables 1 and 3 show the running times for our implementations on our graph inputs. For compressed graphs, we use the compression schemes from Ligra+ [80], which we extended to ensure theoretical efficiency. We describe these modifications and also other statistics about our algorithms (e.g., number of colors used, number of SCCs, etc.) in the full version of the paper [29].

**Experimental Setup.** We run all of our experiments on a 72-core Dell PowerEdge R930 (with two-way hyper-threading) with 4 × 2.4GHz Intel 18-core E7-8867 v4 Xeon processors (with a 4800MHz bus and 45MB L3 cache) and 1TB of main memory. Our programs use Cilk Plus to express parallelism and are compiled with the g++ compiler (version 5.4.1) with the `-O3` flag. By using Cilk's work-stealing scheduler we are able obtain an expected running time of $W/P + O(D)$ for an algorithm with $W$ work and $D$ depth on $P$ processors [16]. For the parallel experiments, we use the command `numactl -i all` to balance the memory allocations across the sockets. All of the speedup numbers we report are the running times of our parallel implementation on 72-cores with hyper-threading over the running time of the implementation on a single thread.

**Graph Data.** To show how our algorithms perform on graphs at different scales, we selected a representative set of real-world graphs of varying sizes. Most of the graphs are Web graphs and

| Graph Dataset | Num. Vertices | Num. Edges | diam | $\rho$ | $k_{max}$ |
|---|---|---|---|---|---|
| *LiveJournal* | 4,847,571 | 68,993,773 | 16 | ~ | ~ |
| *LiveJournal-Sym* | 4,847,571 | 85,702,474 | 20 | 3480 | 372 |
| *com-Orkut* | 3,072,627 | 234,370,166 | 9 | 5,667 | 253 |
| *Twitter* | 41,652,231 | 1,468,365,182 | 65* | ~ | ~ |
| *Twitter-Sym* | 41,652,231 | 2,405,026,092 | 23* | 14,963 | 2488 |
| *3D-Torus* | 1,000,000,000 | 6,000,000,000 | 1500* | 1 | 6 |
| *ClueWeb* | 978,408,098 | 42,574,107,469 | 821* | ~ | ~ |
| *ClueWeb-Sym* | 978,408,098 | 74,744,358,622 | 132* | 106,819 | 4244 |
| *Hyperlink2014* | 1,724,573,718 | 64,422,807,961 | 793* | ~ | ~ |
| *Hyperlink2014-Sym* | 1,724,573,718 | 124,141,874,032 | 207* | 58,711 | 4160 |
| *Hyperlink2012* | 3,563,602,789 | 128,736,914,167 | 5275* | ~ | ~ |
| *Hyperlink2012-Sym* | 3,563,602,789 | 225,840,663,232 | 331* | 130,728 | 10565 |

**Table 2: Graph inputs, including vertices and edges.** diam **is the diameter of the graph. For undirected graphs, $\rho$ and $k_{max}$ are the number of peeling rounds, and the largest non-empty core (degeneracy). We mark** diam **values where we are unable to calculate the exact diameter with * and report the effective diameter observed during our experiments, which is a lower bound on the actual diameter.**

social networks—low diameter graphs that are frequently used in practice. To test our algorithms on large diameter graphs, we also ran our implementations 3-dimensional tori where each vertex is connected to its 2 neighbors in each dimension.

We list the graphs used in our experiments, along with their size, approximate diameter, peeling complexity [28], and degeneracy (for undirected graphs) in Table 2. ***LiveJournal*** is a directed graph of the social network obtained from a snapshot in 2008 [17]. ***com-Orkut*** is an undirected graph of the Orkut social network. ***Twitter*** is a directed graph of the Twitter network, where edges represent the follower relationship [51]. ***ClueWeb*** is a Web graph from the Lemur project at CMU [17]. ***Hyperlink2012*** and ***Hyperlink2014*** are directed hyperlink graphs obtained from the WebDataCommons dataset where nodes represent web pages [61]. ***3D-Torus*** is a 3-dimensional torus with 1B vertices and 6B edges. We mark symmetric (undirected) versions of the directed graphs with the suffix -Sym. We create weighted graphs for evaluating weighted BFS, Borůvka, and Bellman-Ford by selecting edge weights between $[1, \log n)$ uniformly at random. We process LiveJournal, com-Orkut, Twitter, and 3D-Torus in the uncompressed format, and ClueWeb, Hyperlink2014, and Hyperlink2012 in the compressed format.

**SSSP Problems.** Our BFS, weighted BFS, Bellman-Ford, and betweenness centrality implementations achieve between a 8–67x speedup across all inputs. We ran all of our shortest path experiments on the *symmetrized* versions of the graph. Our experiments show that our weighted BFS and Bellman-Ford implementations perform as well as or better than our prior implementations from Julienne [28]. Our running times for BFS and betweenness centrality are the same as the times of the implementations in Ligra [76]. We note that our running times for weighted BFS on the Hyperlink graphs are larger than the times reported in Julienne. This is because the shortest-path experiments in Julienne were run on directed version of the graph, where the average vertex can reach many fewer vertices than on the symmetrized version. We set a flag for our weighted BFS experiments on the ClueWeb and Hyperlink graphs that lets the algorithm switch to a dense EDGEMAP once the frontiers are sufficiently dense, which lets the algorithm run within half of the RAM on our machine. Before this change, our weighted BFS implementation would request a large amount of amount of memory when processing the largest frontiers which then caused the graph to become partly evicted from the page cache.

In an earlier paper [28], we compared the running time of our weighted BFS implementation to two existing parallel shortest path implementations from the GAP benchmark suite [6] and Galois [55], as well as a fast sequential shortest path algorithm from the DIMACS shortest path challenge, showing that our implementation is between 1.07–1.1x slower than the $\Delta$-stepping implementation from GAP, and 1.6–3.4x faster than the Galois implementation. Our old version of Bellman-Ford was between 1.2–3.9x slower than weighted BFS; we note that after changing it to use the EDGEMAPBLOCKED optimization, it is now competitive with weighted BFS and is between 1.2x faster and 1.7x slower on our graphs with the exception of 3D-Torus, where it performs 7.3x slower than weighted BFS, as it performs $O(n^{4/3})$ work on this graph.

**Connectivity Problems.** Our low-diameter decomposition (LDD) implementation achieves between 17–58x speedup across all inputs. We fixed $\beta$ to 0.2 in all of the codes that use LDD. The running time of LDD is comparable to the cost of a BFS that visits most of the vertices. We are not aware of any prior experimental work that reports the running times for an LDD implementation.

Our work-efficient implementation of connectivity achieves 25–57x speedup across all inputs. We note that our implementation does not assume that vertex IDs in the graph are randomly permuted and always generates a random permutation, even on the first round, as adding vertices based on their original IDs can result in poor performance. There are several existing implementations of fast parallel connectivity algorithms [67, 78, 79, 83], however, only the implementation from [79], which presents the algorithm that we implement in this paper, is theoretically-efficient. The implementation from Shun et al. was compared to both the Multistep [83] and Patwary et al. [67] implementations, and shown to be competitive on a broad set of graphs. We compared our connectivity implementation to the work-efficient connectivity implementation from Shun et al. on our uncompressed graphs and observed that our code is between 1.2–2.1x faster in parallel.

Despite our biconnectivity implementation having $O(\text{diam}(G))$ depth, our implementation achieves between a 20–59x speedup across all inputs, as the diameter of most of our graphs is extremely low. Our biconnectivity implementation is about 3–5 times slower than running connectivity on the graph, which seems reasonable as our current implementation performs two calls to connectivity, and one breadth-first search. There are a several existing implementations of biconnectivity. Cong and Bader [22] parallelize the Tarjan-Vishkin algorithm and demonstrated speedup over the Hopcroft-Tarjan (HT) algorithm. Edwards and Vishkin [31] also implement the Tarjan-Vishkin algorithm using the XMT platform, and show that their algorithm achieves good speedups. Slota and Madduri [82] present a BFS-based biconnectivity implementation which requires $O(mn)$ work in the worst-case, but behaves like a linear-work algorithm in practice. We ran the Slota and Madduri implementation on 36 hyper-threads allocated from the same socket, the configuration on which we observed the best performance for their code, and found that our implementation is between 1.4–2.1x faster than theirs. We used a DFS-ordered subgraph corresponding to the largest connected component to test their code, which

| Application | LiveJournal-Sym (1) | LiveJournal-Sym (72h) | LiveJournal-Sym (SU) | com-Orkut (1) | com-Orkut (72h) | com-Orkut (SU) | Twitter-Sym (1) | Twitter-Sym (72h) | Twitter-Sym (SU) | 3D-Torus (1) | 3D-Torus (72h) | 3D-Torus (SU) | ClueWeb-Sym (1) | ClueWeb-Sym (72h) | ClueWeb-Sym (SU) | Hyperlink2014-Sym (1) | Hyperlink2014-Sym (72h) | Hyperlink2014-Sym (SU) |
|---|---|---|---|---|---|---|---|---|---|---|---|---|---|---|---|---|---|---|
| Breadth-First Search (BFS) | 0.59 | 0.018 | 32.7 | 0.41 | 0.012 | 34.1 | 5.45 | 0.137 | 39.7 | 301 | 5.53 | 54.4 | 106 | 2.29 | 46.2 | 250 | 4.50 | 55.5 |
| Integral-Weight SSSP (weighted BFS) | 1.45 | 0.107 | 13.5 | 2.03 | 0.095 | 21.3 | 33.4 | 0.995 | 33.5 | 437 | 18.1 | 24.1 | 736 | 14.4 | 51.1 | 1390 | 22.3 | 62.3 |
| General-Weight SSSP (Bellman-Ford) | 1.96 | 0.086 | 22.7 | 3.98 | 0.168 | 23.6 | 48.7 | 1.56 | 31.2 | 6280 | 133 | 47.2 | 1050 | 16.2 | 64.8 | 1460 | 22.9 | 63.7 |
| Single-Source Betweenness Centrality (BC) | 1.66 | 0.049 | 33.8 | 2.52 | 0.057 | 44.2 | 26.3 | 3.26 | 8.06 | 496 | 12.5 | 39.6 | 569 | 27.7 | 20.5 | 866 | 16.3 | 53.1 |
| Low-Diameter Decomposition (LDD) | 0.54 | 0.027 | 20.0 | 0.33 | 0.019 | 17.3 | 8.48 | 0.186 | 45.5 | 275 | 7.55 | 36.4 | 176 | 3.62 | 48.6 | 322 | 6.84 | 47.0 |
| Connectivity | 1.20 | 0.050 | 24.0 | 1.64 | 0.056 | 29.2 | 26.1 | 0.807 | 32.3 | 351 | 14.3 | 24.5 | 552 | 11.2 | 49.2 | 990 | 17.1 | 57.8 |
| Biconnectivity | 5.36 | 0.261 | 20.5 | 7.31 | 0.292 | 25.0 | 146 | 4.86 | 30.0 | 1610 | 59.6 | 27.0 | 2250 | 48.7 | 46.2 | 3520 | 71.5 | 49.2 |
| Strongly Connected Components (SCC)* | 1.61 | 0.116 | 13.8 | ~ | ~ | ~ | 13.3 | 0.495 | 26.8 | ~ | ~ | ~ | 1240 | 38.1 | 32.5 | 2140 | 51.5 | 41.5 |
| Minimum Spanning Forest (MSF) | 3.64 | 0.204 | 17.8 | 4.58 | 0.227 | 20.1 | 61.8 | 3.02 | 20.4 | 617 | 23.6 | 26.1 | 2490 | 45.6 | 54.6 | 3580 | 71.9 | 49.7 |
| Maximal Independent Set (MIS) | 1.18 | 0.034 | 34.7 | 2.23 | 0.052 | 42.8 | 34.4 | 0.759 | 45.3 | 236 | 4.44 | 53.1 | 551 | 8.44 | 65.2 | 1020 | 14.5 | 70.3 |
| Maximal Matching (MM) | 2.42 | 0.095 | 25.4 | 4.65 | 0.183 | 25.4 | 46.7 | 1.42 | 32.8 | 403 | 11.4 | 35.3 | 1760 | 31.8 | 55.3 | 2980 | 48.1 | 61.9 |
| Graph Coloring | 4.69 | 0.392 | 11.9 | 9.05 | 0.789 | 11.4 | 148 | 6.91 | 21.4 | 350 | 11.3 | 30.9 | 2050 | 49.8 | 41.1 | 3310 | 63.1 | 52.4 |
| $k$-core | 3.75 | 0.641 | 5.85 | 8.32 | 1.33 | 6.25 | 110 | 6.72 | 16.3 | 753 | 6.58 | 114.4 | 2370 | 62.9 | 37.6 | 3480 | 83.2 | 41.8 |
| Approximate Set Cover | 4.65 | 0.613 | 7.58 | 4.51 | 0.786 | 5.73 | 66.4 | 3.31 | 20.0 | 1429 | 40.2 | 35.5 | 1490 | 28.1 | 53.0 | 2040 | 37.6 | 54.2 |
| Triangle Counting (TC) | 13.5 | 0.342 | 39.4 | 78.1 | 1.19 | 65.6 | 1920 | 23.5 | 81.7 | 168 | 6.63 | 25.3 | – | 272 | – | – | 568 | – |

**Table 3: Running times (in seconds) of our algorithms over symmetric graph inputs on a 72-core machine (with hyper-threading) where (1) is the single-thread time, (72h) is the 72 core time using hyper-threading, and (SU) is the parallel speedup (single-thread time divided by 72-core time). We mark experiments that are not applicable for a graph with ~, and experiments that did not finish within 5 hours with –. *SCC was run on the directed versions of the input graphs.**

produced the fastest times. Using the original order of the graph affects the running time of their implementation, causing it to run between 2–3x slower as the amount of work performed by their algorithm depends on the order in which vertices are visited.

Our strongly connected components implementation achieves between a 13–43x speedup across all inputs. Our implementation takes a parameter $\beta$, which is the base of the exponential rate at which we grow the number of centers added. We set $\beta$ between 1.1–2.0 for our experiments and note that using a larger value of $\beta$ can improve the running time on smaller graphs by up to a factor of 2x. Our SCC implementation is between 1.6x faster to 4.8x slower than running connectivity on the graph. There are several existing SCC implementations that have been evaluated on real-world directed graphs [41, 60, 83]. The Hong et al. algorithm [41] is a modified version of the FWBW-Trim algorithm from McLendon et al. [60], but neither algorithm has any theoretical bounds on work or depth. Unfortunately [41] do not report running times, so we are unable to compare our performance with them. The Multistep algorithm [83] has a worst-case running time of $O(n^2)$, but the authors point-out that the algorithm behaves like a linear-time algorithm on real-world graphs. We ran our implementation on 16 cores configured similarly to their experiments and found that we are about 1.7x slower on LiveJournal, which easily fits in cache, and 1.2x faster on Twitter (scaled to account for a small difference in graph sizes). While the multistep algorithm is slightly faster on some graphs, our SCC implementation has the advantage of being theoretically-efficient and performs a predictable amount of work.

Our minimum spanning forest implementation achieves between 17–50x speedup over the implementation running on a single thread across all of our inputs. Obtaining practical parallel algorithms for MSF has been a longstanding goal in the field, and several existing implementations exist [5, 23, 66, 78, 90]. We compared our implementation with the union-find based MSF implementation from PBBS [78] and the implementation of Borůvka from [90], which is one of the fastest implementations we are aware of. Our MSF implementation is between 2.6–5.9x faster than the MSF implementation from PBBS. Compared to the edgelist based implementation of Borůvka from [90] our implementation is between 1.2–2.9x faster.

**MIS, Maximal Matching, and Graph Coloring.** Our MIS and maximal matching implementations achieve between 31–70x and 25–70x speedup across all inputs. The implementations by Blelloch et al. [11] are the fastest existing implementations of MIS and maximal matching that we are aware of, and are the basis for our maximal matching implementation. They report that their implementations are 3–8x faster than Luby's algorithm on 32 threads, and outperform a sequential greedy MIS implementation on more than 2 processors. We compared our rootset-based MIS implementation to the prefix-based implementation, and found that the rootset-based approach is between 1.1–3.5x faster. Our maximal matching implementation is between 3–4.2x faster than the implementation from [11]. Our implementation of maximal matching can avoid a significant amount of work, as each of the filter steps can extract and permute just the $3n/2$ highest priority edges, whereas the edgelist-based version in PBBS must permute all edges. Our coloring implementation achieves between 11–56x speedup across all inputs. We note that our implementation appears to be between 1.2–1.6x slower than the asynchronous implementation of JP in [40], due to synchronizing on many rounds which contain few vertices.

**$k$-core, Approximate Set Cover, and Triangle Counting.** Our $k$-core implementation achieves between 5–46x speedup across all inputs, and 114x speedup on the 3D-Torus graph as there is only one round of peeling in which all vertices are removed. There are several recent papers that implement parallel algorithms for $k$-core [27, 28, 46, 71]. Both the ParK algorithm [27] and Kabir and Madduri algorithm [46] implement the peeling algorithm in $O(k_{\max}n + m)$ work, which is not work-efficient. Our implementation is between 3.8–4.6x faster than ParK on a similar machine configuration. Kabir and Madduri show that their implementation achieves an average speedup of 2.8x over ParK. Our implementation is between 1.3–1.6x faster than theirs on a similar machine configuration.

Our approximate set cover implementation achieves between 5–57x speedup across all inputs. Our implementation is based on the implementation presented in Julienne [28]; the one major modification was to regenerate random priorities for sets that are active on the current round. We compared the running time of our implementation with the parallel implementation from [15] which is available in the PBBS library. We ran both implementations with

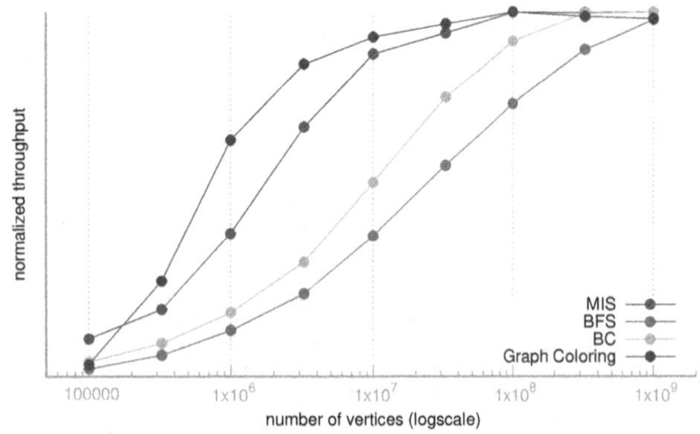


**Figure 1: Log-linear plot of normalized throughput vs. vertices for MIS, BFS, BC, and coloring on the 3D-Torus graph family.**

$\epsilon = 0.01$. Our implementation is between 1.2x slower to 1.5x faster than the PBBS implementation on our graphs, with the exception of 3D-Torus. On 3D-Torus, the implementation from [15] runs 56x slower than our implementation as it does not regenerate priorities for active sets on each round causing worst-case behavior. Our performance is also slow on this graph, as nearly all of the vertices stay active (in the highest bucket) during each round, and using $\epsilon = 0.01$ causes a large number of rounds to be performed.

Our triangle counting (TC) implementation achieves between 39–81x speedup across all inputs. Unfortunately, we are unable to report speedup numbers for TC on our larger graphs as the single-threaded times took too long due to the algorithm performing $O(m^{3/2})$ work. There are a number experimental papers that consider multicore triangle counting [1, 37, 50, 52, 74, 81]. We implement the algorithm from [81], and adapted it to work on compressed graphs. We note that in our experiments we intersect directed adjacency lists sequentially, as there was sufficient parallelism in the outer parallel-loop. There was no significant difference in running times between our implementation and the implementation from [81]. We ran our implementation on 48 threads on the Twitter graph to compare with the times reported by EmptyHeaded [1] and found that our times are about the same.

**Performance on 3D-Torus.** We ran experiments on a family of 3D-Torus graphs with different sizes to study how our diameter-bounded algorithms scale relative to algorithms with polylogarithmic depth. We were surprised to see that the running time of some of our polylogarithmic depth algorithms on this graph, like LDD and connectivity, are 17–40x more expensive than their running time on Twitter and Twitter-Sym, despite 3D-Torus only having 4x and 2.4x more edges than Twitter and Twitter-Sym. Our slightly worse scaling on this graph can be accounted for by the fact that we stored the graph ordered by dimension, instead of storing it using a local ordering. It would be interesting to see how much improvement we could gain by reordering the vertices.

In Figure 1 we show the normalized throughput of MIS, BFS, BC, and graph coloring for 3-dimensional tori of different sizes, where throughput is measured as the number of edges processed per second. The throughput for each application becomes saturated before our largest-scale graph for all applications except for BFS, which is saturated on a graph with 2 billion vertices. The throughput curves show that the theoretical bounds are useful in predicting how the half-lengths[3] are distributed. The half-lengths are ordered as follows: coloring, MIS, BFS, and BC. This is the same order as sorting these algorithms by their depth with respect to this graph.

| Algorithm | Cycles Stalled | LLC Hit Rate | LLC Misses | BW | Time |
|---|---|---|---|---|---|
| $k$-core (histogram) | 9 | 0.223 | 49 | 96 | 62.9 |
| $k$-core (fetch-and-add) | 67 | 0.155 | 42 | 24 | 221 |
| weighted BFS (blocked) | 3.7 | 0.070 | 19 | 130 | 14.4 |
| weighted BFS (unblocked) | 5.6 | 0.047 | 29 | 152 | 25.2 |

**Table 4: Cycles stalled while the memory subsystem has an outstanding load (trillions), LLC hit rate and misses (billions), bandwidth in GB/s (bytes read and written from memory, divided by running time), and running time in seconds. All experiments are run on the ClueWeb graph using 72 cores with hyper-threading.**

**Locality.** While our algorithms are efficient on the MT-RAM, we do not analyze their cache complexity, and in general they may not be efficient in a model that takes caches into account. Despite this, we observed that our algorithms have good cache performance on the graphs we tested on. In this section we give some explanation for this fact by showing that our primitives make good use of the caches. Our algorithms are also aided by the fact that these graph datasets often come in highly local orders (e.g., see the *Natural* order in [30]). Table 4 shows metrics for our experiments measured using Open Performance Counter Monitor (PCM).

Due to space limitations, we only report numbers for the ClueWeb graph. We observed that using a work-efficient histogram is 3.5x faster than using fetch-and-add in our $k$-core implementation, which suffers from high contention on this graph. Using a histogram reduces the number of cycles stalled due to memory by more than 7x. We also ran our wBFS implementation with and without the EDGEMAPBLOCKED optimization, which reduces the number of cache-lines read from and written to when performing a sparse EDGEMAP. The blocked implementation reads and writes 2.1x fewer bytes than the unoptimized version, which translates to a 1.7x faster runtime. We disabled the dense optimization for this experiment to directly compare the two implementations of a sparse EDGEMAP.

**Processing Massive Web Graphs.** In Tables 1 and 3, we show the running times of our implementations on the ClueWeb, Hyperlink2014, and Hyperlink2012 graphs. To put our performance in context, we compare our 72-core running times to running times reported by existing work. Table 5 summarizes the existing results in the literature. Most results process the *directed* versions of these graphs, which have about half as many edges as the symmetrized version. Unless otherwise mentioned, all results from the literature use the directed versions of these graphs. To make the comparison easier we show our running times for BFS, SSSP (weighted BFS), BC and SCC on the directed graphs, and running times for Connectivity, $k$-core and TC on the symmetrized graphs in Table 5.

FlashGraph [26] reports disk-based running times for the Hyperlink2012 graph on a 4-socket, 32-core machine with 512GB of memory and 15 SSDs. On 64 hyper-threads, they solve BFS in 208s, BC in 595s, connected components in 461s, and triangle counting in 7818s. Our BFS and BC implementations are 12x faster and 16x faster, and our triangle counting and connectivity implementations are 5.3x faster and 12x faster than their implementations, respectively. Mosaic [54] report in-memory running times on the

[3] The graph size when the system achieves half of its peak-performance.

| Paper | Problem | Graph | Memory | Hyper-threads | Nodes | Time |
|---|---|---|---|---|---|---|
| Mosaic [54] | BFS* | 2014 | 0.768 | 1000 | 1 | 6.55 |
| | Connectivity* | 2014 | 0.768 | 1000 | 1 | 708 |
| | SSSP* | 2014 | 0.768 | 1000 | 1 | 8.6 |
| FlashGraph [26] | BFS* | 2012 | .512 | 64 | 1 | 208 |
| | BC* | 2012 | .512 | 64 | 1 | 595 |
| | Connectivity* | 2012 | .512 | 64 | 1 | 461 |
| | TC* | 2012 | .512 | 64 | 1 | 7818 |
| BigSparse [45] | BFS* | 2012 | 0.064 | 32 | 1 | 2500 |
| | BC* | 2012 | 0.064 | 32 | 1 | 3100 |
| Slota et al. [85] | Largest-CC* | 2012 | 16.3 | 8192 | 256 | 63 |
| | Largest-SCC* | 2012 | 16.3 | 8192 | 256 | 108 |
| | Approx $k$-core* | 2012 | 16.3 | 8192 | 256 | 363 |
| Stergiou et al. [86] | Connectivity | 2012 | 128 | 24000 | 1000 | 341 |
| This paper | BFS* | 2014 | 1 | 144 | 1 | 5.71 |
| | SSSP* | 2014 | 1 | 144 | 1 | 9.08 |
| | BFS* | 2012 | 1 | 144 | 1 | 16.7 |
| | BC* | 2012 | 1 | 144 | 1 | 35.2 |
| | Connectivity | 2012 | 1 | 144 | 1 | 38.3 |
| | SCC* | 2012 | 1 | 144 | 1 | 185 |
| | $k$-core | 2012 | 1 | 144 | 1 | 184 |
| | TC | 2012 | 1 | 144 | 1 | 1470 |

**Table 5: System configurations (memory in terabytes, hyper-threads, and nodes) and running times (seconds) of existing results on the Hyperlink graphs. The last section shows our running times. *These problems are run on directed versions of the graph.**

Hyperlink2014 graph; we note that the system is optimized for external memory execution. They solve BFS in 6.5s, connected components in 700s, and SSSP (Bellman-Ford) in 8.6s on a machine with 24 hyper-threads and 4 Xeon-Phis (244 cores with 4 threads each) for a total of 1000 hyper-threads, 768GB of RAM, and 6 NVMes. Our BFS and connectivity implementations are 1.1x and 40x faster respectively, and our SSSP implementation is 1.05x slower. Both FlashGraph and Mosaic compute weakly connected components, which is equivalent to connectivity. BigSparse [45] report disk-based running times for BFS and BC on the Hyperlink2012 graph on a 32-core machine. They solve BFS in 2500s and BC in 3100s. Our BFS and BC implementations are 149x and 88x faster than their implementations, respectively.

Slota et al. [85] report running times for the Hyperlink2012 graph on 256 nodes on the Blue Waters supercomputer. Each node contains two 16-core processors with one thread each, for a total of 8192 hyper-threads. They report they can find the *largest* connected component and SCC from the graph in 63s and 108s respectively. Our implementations find *all* connected components 1.6x faster than their largest connected component implementation, and find *all* strongly connected components 1.6x slower than their largest-SCC implementation. Their largest-SCC implementation computes two BFSs from a randomly chosen vertex—one on the in-edges and the other on the out-edges—and intersects the reachable sets. We perform the same operation as one of the first steps of our SCC algorithm and note that it requires about 30 seconds on our machine. They solve approximate $k$-cores in 363s, where the approximate $k$-core of a vertex is the coreness of the vertex rounded up to the nearest powers of 2. Our implementation computes the *exact* coreness of each vertex in 184s, which is 1.9x faster than the approximate implementation while using 113x fewer cores.

Stergiou et al. [86] describe a connectivity algorithm that runs in $O(\log n)$ rounds in the BSP model and report running times for the symmetrized Hyperlink2012 graph. They implement their algorithm using a proprietary in-memory/secondary-storage graph processing system used at Yahoo!, and run experiments on a 1000 node cluster. Each node contains two 6-core processors that are 2-way hyper-threaded and 128GB of RAM, for a total of 24000 hyper-threads and 128TB of RAM. Their fastest running time on the Hyperlink2012 graph is 341s on their 1000 node system. Our implementation solves connectivity on this graph in 38.3s–8.8x faster on a system with 128x less memory and 166x fewer cores. They also report running times for solving connectivity on a private Yahoo! webgraph with 272 billion vertices and 5.9 trillion edges, over 26 times the size of our largest graph. While such a graph seems to currently be out of reach of our machine, we are hopeful that techniques from theoretically-efficient parallel algorithms can help solve problems on graphs at this scale and beyond.

## 7 CONCLUSION

In this paper, we showed that we can process the largest publicly-available real-world graph on a single shared-memory server with 1TB of memory using theoretically-efficient parallel algorithms. We outperform existing implementations on the largest real-world graphs, and use much fewer resources than the distributed-memory solutions. On a per-core basis, our numbers are significantly better. Our results provide evidence that theoretically-efficient shared-memory graph algorithms can be efficient and scalable in practice.

## ACKNOWLEDGEMENTS

Thanks to the reviewers and to Lin Ma for helpful comments. This work was supported in part by NSF grants CCF-1408940, CCF-1533858, and CCF-1629444.

## REFERENCES


[1] C. R. Aberger, A. Lamb, S. Tu, A. Nötzli, K. Olukotun, and C. Ré. Emptyheaded: A relational engine for graph processing. *ACM Trans. Database Syst.*, 2017.
[2] A. Aggarwal, R. J. Anderson, and M.-Y. Kao. Parallel depth-first search in general directed graphs. In *STOC*, 1989.
[3] N. Alon, L. Babai, and A. Itai. A fast and simple randomized parallel algorithm for the maximal independent set problem. *J. Algorithms*, 1986.
[4] R. Anderson and E. W. Mayr. A P-complete problem and approximations to it. Technical report, 1984.
[5] D. A. Bader and G. Cong. Fast shared-memory algorithms for computing the minimum spanning forest of sparse graphs. *JPDC*, 2006.
[6] S. Beamer, K. Asanovic, and D. A. Patterson. The GAP benchmark suite. *CoRR*, abs/1508.03619, 2015.
[7] N. Ben-David, G. E. Blelloch, J. T. Fineman, P. B. Gibbons, Y. Gu, C. McGuffey, and J. Shun. Implicit decomposition for write-efficient connectivity algorithms. In *IPDPS*, 2018.
[8] M. Birn, V. Osipov, P. Sanders, C. Schulz, and N. Sitchinava. Efficient parallel and external matching. In *Euro-Par*, 2013.
[9] G. E. Blelloch. Prefix sums and their applications. *Synthesis of Parallel Algorithms*, 1993.
[10] G. E. Blelloch and L. Dhulipala. Introduction to parallel algorithms 15-853: Algorithms in the real world. 2018.
[11] G. E. Blelloch, J. T. Fineman, and J. Shun. Greedy sequential maximal independent set and matching are parallel on average. In *SPAA*, 2012.
[12] G. E. Blelloch, Y. Gu, J. Shun, and Y. Sun. Parallelism in randomized incremental algorithms. In *SPAA*, 2016.
[13] G. E. Blelloch, Y. Gu, and Y. Sun. A new efficient construction on probabilistic tree embeddings. In *ICALP*, 2017.
[14] G. E. Blelloch, R. Peng, and K. Tangwongsan. Linear-work greedy parallel approximate set cover and variants. In *SPAA*, 2011.
[15] G. E. Blelloch, H. V. Simhadri, and K. Tangwongsan. Parallel and I/O efficient set covering algorithms. In *SPAA*, 2012.
[16] R. D. Blumofe and C. E. Leiserson. Scheduling multithreaded computations by work stealing. *J. ACM*, 46(5), Sept. 1999.
[17] P. Boldi and S. Vigna. The WebGraph framework I: Compression techniques. In *WWW*, 2004.

[18] O. Borůvka. O jistém problému minimálním. *Práce Mor. Přírodověd. Spol. v Brně III*, 3, 1926.
[19] U. Brandes. A faster algorithm for betweenness centrality. *Journal of mathematical sociology*, 25(2), 2001.
[20] A. Broder, R. Kumar, F. Maghoul, P. Raghavan, S. Rajagopalan, R. Stata, A. Tomkins, and J. Wiener. Graph structure in the web. *Computer networks*, 33(1-6), 2000.
[21] R. Cole, P. N. Klein, and R. E. Tarjan. Finding minimum spanning forests in logarithmic time and linear work using random sampling. In *SPAA*, 1996.
[22] G. Cong and D. A. Bader. An experimental study of parallel biconnected components algorithms on symmetric multiprocessors (SMPs). In *IPDPS*, 2005.
[23] G. Cong and I. G. Tanase. Composable locality optimizations for accelerating parallel forest computations. In *HPCC*, 2016.
[24] D. Coppersmith, L. Fleischer, B. Hendrickson, and A. Pinar. A divide-and-conquer algorithm for identifying strongly connected components. 2003.
[25] T. H. Cormen, C. E. Leiserson, R. L. Rivest, and C. Stein. *Introduction to Algorithms (3. ed.)*. MIT Press, 2009.
[26] D. M. Da Zheng, R. Burns, J. Vogelstein, C. E. Priebe, and A. S. Szalay. Flashgraph: Processing billion-node graphs on an array of commodity SSDs. In *FAST*, 2015.
[27] N. S. Dasari, R. Desh, and M. Zubair. ParK: An efficient algorithm for $k$-core decomposition on multicore processors. In *Big Data*, 2014.
[28] L. Dhulipala, G. E. Blelloch, and J. Shun. Julienne: A framework for parallel graph algorithms using work-efficient bucketing. In *SPAA*, 2017.
[29] L. Dhulipala, G. E. Blelloch, and J. Shun. Theoretically efficient parallel graph algorithms can be fast and scalable. *CoRR*, abs/1805.05208, 2018.
[30] L. Dhulipala, I. Kabiljo, B. Karrer, G. Ottaviano, S. Pupyrev, and A. Shalita. Compressing graphs and indexes with recursive graph bisection. In *KDD*, 2016.
[31] J. A. Edwards and U. Vishkin. Better speedups using simpler parallel programming for graph connectivity and biconnectivity. In *PMAM*, 2012.
[32] J. T. Fineman. Nearly work-efficient parallel algorithm for digraph reachability. In *STOC*, 2018.
[33] M. Fischer and A. Noever. Tight analysis of parallel randomized greedy MIS. In *SODA*, 2018.
[34] L. K. Fleischer, B. Hendrickson, and A. Pinar. On identifying strongly connected components in parallel. In *IPDPS*, 2000.
[35] H. Gazit and G. L. Miller. An improved parallel algorithm that computes the BFS numbering of a directed graph. *Information Processing Letters*, 28(2), 1988.
[36] J. E. Gonzalez, Y. Low, H. Gu, D. Bickson, and C. Guestrin. PowerGraph: Distributed graph-parallel computation on natural graphs. In *OSDI*, 2012.
[37] O. Green, L. M. Munguia, and D. A. Bader. Load balanced clustering coefficients. In *PPAA*, 2014.
[38] R. Greenlaw, H. J. Hoover, and W. L. Ruzzo. *Limits to Parallel Computation: P-completeness Theory*. Oxford University Press, Inc., 1995.
[39] Y. Gu, J. Shun, Y. Sun, and G. E. Blelloch. A top-down parallel semisort. In *SPAA*, 2015.
[40] W. Hasenplaugh, T. Kaler, T. B. Schardl, and C. E. Leiserson. Ordering heuristics for parallel graph coloring. In *SPAA*, 2014.
[41] S. Hong, N. C. Rodia, and K. Olukotun. On fast parallel detection of strongly connected components (SCC) in small-world graphs. In *SC*, 2013.
[42] J. Hopcroft and R. Tarjan. Algorithm 447: efficient algorithms for graph manipulation. *Communications of the ACM*, 1973.
[43] A. Israeli and Y. Shiloach. An improved parallel algorithm for maximal matching. *Inf. Process. Lett.*, 1986.
[44] J. Jaja. *Introduction to Parallel Algorithms*. Addison-Wesley Professional, 1992.
[45] S. W. Jun, A. Wright, S. Zhang, S. Xu, and Arvind. BigSparse: High-performance external graph analytics. *CoRR*, abs/1710.07736, 2017.
[46] H. Kabir and K. Madduri. Parallel k-core decomposition on multicore platforms. In *IPDPSW*, 2017.
[47] D. R. Karger, P. N. Klein, and R. E. Tarjan. A randomized linear-time algorithm to find minimum spanning trees. *J. ACM*, 42(2), Mar. 1995.
[48] R. M. Karp and V. Ramachandran. Handbook of theoretical computer science (vol. a). chapter Parallel Algorithms for Shared-memory Machines. MIT Press, Cambridge, MA, USA, 1990.
[49] R. M. Karp and A. Wigderson. A fast parallel algorithm for the maximal independent set problem. In *STOC*, 1984.
[50] J. Kim, W.-S. Han, S. Lee, K. Park, and H. Yu. OPT: A new framework for overlapped and parallel triangulation in large-scale graphs. In *SIGMOD*, 2014.
[51] H. Kwak, C. Lee, H. Park, and S. Moon. What is twitter, a social network or a news media? In *WWW*, 2010.
[52] Y. Low, J. Gonzalez, A. Kyrola, D. Bickson, C. Guestrin, and J. M. Hellerstein. GraphLab: A new parallel framework for machine learning. In *UAI*, 2010.
[53] M. Luby. A simple parallel algorithm for the maximal independent set problem. *SIAM J. Comput.*, 1986.
[54] S. Maass, C. Min, S. Kashyap, W. Kang, M. Kumar, and T. Kim. Mosaic: Processing a trillion-edge graph on a single machine. In *EuroSys*, 2017.
[55] S. Maleki, D. Nguyen, A. Lenharth, M. Garzarán, D. Padua, and K. Pingali. DSMR: A parallel algorithm for single-source shortest path problem. In *ICS*, 2016.
[56] G. Malewicz, M. H. Austern, A. J. Bik, J. C. Dehnert, I. Horn, N. Leiser, and G. Czajkowski. Pregel: A system for large-scale graph processing. In *SIGMOD*, 2010.
[57] Y. Maon, B. Schieber, and U. Vishkin. Parallel ear decomposition search (EDS) and st-numbering in graphs. *Theoretical Computer Science*, 47, 1986.
[58] D. W. Matula and L. L. Beck. Smallest-last ordering and clustering and graph coloring algorithms. *J. ACM*, 30(3), July 1983.
[59] R. R. McCune, T. Weninger, and G. Madey. Thinking like a vertex: A survey of vertex-centric frameworks for large-scale distributed graph processing. *ACM Comput. Surv.*, 48(2), Oct. 2015.
[60] W. Mclendon Iii, B. Hendrickson, S. J. Plimpton, and L. Rauchwerger. Finding strongly connected components in distributed graphs. *Journal of Parallel and Distributed Computing*, 65(8), 2005.
[61] R. Meusel, S. Vigna, O. Lehmberg, and C. Bizer. The graph structure in the web–analyzed on different aggregation levels. *The Journal of Web Science*, 1(1), 2015.
[62] U. Meyer and P. Sanders. Δ-stepping: a parallelizable shortest path algorithm. *J. Algorithms*, 49(1), 2003.
[63] G. L. Miller, R. Peng, and S. C. Xu. Parallel graph decompositions using random shifts. In *SPAA*, 2013.
[64] G. L. Miller and V. Ramachandran. A new graph triconnectivity algorithm and its parallelization. *Combinatorica*, 12(1), Mar 1992.
[65] D. Nguyen, A. Lenharth, and K. Pingali. A lightweight infrastructure for graph analytics. In *SOSP*, 2013.
[66] S. Nobari, T.-T. Cao, P. Karras, and S. Bressan. Scalable parallel minimum spanning forest computation. In *PPoPP*, 2012.
[67] M. Patwary, P. Refsnes, and F. Manne. Multi-core spanning forest algorithms using the disjoint-set data structure. In *IPDPS*, 2012.
[68] S. Pettie and V. Ramachandran. A randomized time-work optimal parallel algorithm for finding a minimum spanning forest. *SIAM J. Comput.*, 31(6), 2002.
[69] V. Ramachandran. A framework for parallel graph algorithm design. In *Optimal Algorithms*, 1989.
[70] V. Ramachandran. Parallel open ear decomposition with applications to graph biconnectivity and triconnectivity. In *Synthesis of Parallel Algorithms*, 1993.
[71] A. E. Sariyuce, C. Seshadhri, and A. Pinar. Parallel local algorithms for core, truss, and nucleus decompositions. *CoRR*, abs/1704.00386, 2017.
[72] W. Schudy. Finding strongly connected components in parallel using $O(\log^2 N)$ reachability queries. In *SPAA*, 2008.
[73] S. B. Seidman. Network structure and minimum degree. *Soc. Networks*, 5(3), 1983.
[74] M. Sevenich, S. Hong, A. Welc, and H. Chafi. Fast in-memory triangle listing for large real-world graphs. In *Workshop on Social Network Mining and Analysis*, 2014.
[75] Y. Shiloach and U. Vishkin. An $O(\log n)$ parallel connectivity algorithm. *J. Algorithms*, 1982.
[76] J. Shun and G. E. Blelloch. Ligra: A lightweight graph processing framework for shared memory. In *PPoPP*, 2013.
[77] J. Shun, G. E. Blelloch, J. T. Fineman, and P. B. Gibbons. Reducing contention through priority updates. In *SPAA*, 2013.
[78] J. Shun, G. E. Blelloch, J. T. Fineman, P. B. Gibbons, A. Kyrola, H. V. Simhadri, and K. Tangwongsan. Brief announcement: the Problem Based Benchmark Suite. In *SPAA*, 2012.
[79] J. Shun, L. Dhulipala, and G. E. Blelloch. A simple and practical linear-work parallel algorithm for connectivity. In *SPAA*, 2014.
[80] J. Shun, L. Dhulipala, and G. E. Blelloch. Smaller and faster: Parallel processing of compressed graphs with Ligra+. In *DCC*, 2015.
[81] J. Shun and K. Tangwongsan. Multicore triangle computations without tuning. In *ICDE*, 2015.
[82] G. M. Slota and K. Madduri. Simple parallel biconnectivity algorithms for multicore platforms. In *HiPC*, 2014.
[83] G. M. Slota, S. Rajamanickam, and K. Madduri. BFS and coloring-based parallel algorithms for strongly connected components and related problems. In *IPDPS*, 2014.
[84] G. M. Slota, S. Rajamanickam, and K. Madduri. *Supercomputing for Web Graph Analytics*. Apr 2015.
[85] G. M. Slota, S. Rajamanickam, and K. Madduri. A case study of complex graph analysis in distributed memory: Implementation and optimization. In *IPDPS*, 2016.
[86] S. Stergiou, D. Rughwani, and K. Tsioutsiouliklis. Shortcutting label propagation for distributed connected components. In *WSDM*, 2018.
[87] R. E. Tarjan and U. Vishkin. An efficient parallel biconnectivity algorithm. *SIAM Journal on Computing*, 1985.
[88] D. J. Welsh and M. B. Powell. An upper bound for the chromatic number of a graph and its application to timetabling problems. *The Computer Journal*, 1967.
[89] D. Yan, Y. Bu, Y. Tian, and A. Deshpande. Big graph analytics platforms. *Foundations and Trends in Databases*, 7, 2017.
[90] W. Zhou. A practical scalable shared-memory parallel algorithm for computing minimum spanning trees. Master's thesis, KIT, 2017.

# On the Distributed Complexity of Large-Scale Graph Computations

Gopal Pandurangan
University of Houston
Houston, TX, USA
gopalpandurangan@gmail.com

Peter Robinson
McMaster University
Hamilton, Canada
peter.robinson@mcmaster.ca

Michele Scquizzato
KTH Royal Institute of Technology
Stockholm, Sweden
mscq@kth.se

## ABSTRACT

Motivated by the increasing need to understand the distributed algorithmic foundations of large-scale graph computations, we study some fundamental graph problems in a message-passing model for distributed computing where $k \geqslant 2$ machines jointly perform computations on graphs with $n$ nodes (typically, $n \gg k$). The input graph is assumed to be initially randomly partitioned among the $k$ machines, a common implementation in many real-world systems. Communication is point-to-point, and the goal is to minimize the number of communication *rounds* of the computation.

Our main contribution is the *General Lower Bound Theorem*, a theorem that can be used to show non-trivial lower bounds on the round complexity of distributed large-scale data computations. The General Lower Bound Theorem is established via an information-theoretic approach that relates the round complexity to the minimal amount of information required by machines to solve the problem. Our approach is generic and this theorem can be used in a "cook-book" fashion to show distributed lower bounds in the context of several problems, including non-graph problems. We present two applications by showing (almost) tight lower bounds for the round complexity of two fundamental graph problems, namely *PageRank computation* and *triangle enumeration*. Our approach, as demonstrated in the case of PageRank, can yield tight lower bounds for problems (including, and especially, under a stochastic partition of the input) where communication complexity techniques are not obvious. Our approach, as demonstrated in the case of triangle enumeration, can yield stronger round lower bounds as well as message-round tradeoffs compared to approaches that use communication complexity techniques.

We then present distributed algorithms for PageRank and triangle enumeration with a round complexity that (almost) matches the respective lower bounds; these algorithms exhibit a round complexity which scales superlinearly in $k$, improving significantly over previous results for these problems [Klauck et al., SODA 2015]. Specifically, we show the following results:

- *PageRank:* We show a lower bound of $\tilde{\Omega}(n/k^2)$ rounds, and present a distributed algorithm that computes the PageRank of all the nodes of a graph in $\tilde{O}(n/k^2)$ rounds.
- *Triangle enumeration:* We show that there exist graphs with $m$ edges where any distributed algorithm requires $\tilde{\Omega}(m/k^{5/3})$ rounds. This result also implies the first non-trivial lower bound of $\tilde{\Omega}(n^{1/3})$ rounds for the *congested clique* model, which is tight up to logarithmic factors. We then present a distributed algorithm that enumerates all the triangles of a graph in $\tilde{O}(m/k^{5/3} + n/k^{4/3})$ rounds.

## CCS CONCEPTS

• **Theory of computation → Massively parallel algorithms; Distributed algorithms;**

**ACM Reference Format:**
Gopal Pandurangan, Peter Robinson, and Michele Scquizzato. 2018. On the Distributed Complexity of Large-Scale Graph Computations. In *Proceedings of SPAA '18: 30th ACM Symposium on Parallelism in Algorithms and Architectures (SPAA '18)*. ACM, New York, NY, USA, 10 pages. https://doi.org/10.1145/3210377.3210409

## 1 INTRODUCTION

The focus of this paper is on the distributed processing of large-scale data, in particular, *graph data*, which is becoming increasingly important with the rise of massive graphs such as the Web graph, social networks, biological networks, and other graph-structured data and the consequent need for fast distributed algorithms to process such graphs. Several large-scale graph processing systems such as Pregel [23] and Giraph [1] have been recently designed based on the *message-passing* distributed computing model [22, 30]. In these systems, the input graph, which is simply too large to fit into a single machine, is distributed across a group of machines that are connected via a communication network and the machines jointly perform computation in a distributed fashion by sending/receiving messages. A key goal in distributed large-scale computation is to minimize the amount of communication across machines, as this typically dominates the overall cost of the computation.

We study fundamental graph problems in a message-passing distributed computing model and present almost tight bounds on the number of communication rounds needed to solve these problems. In the model, called the $k$-machine model [19] (explained in detail in Section 1.1), the input graph (or more generally, any other type of data) is distributed across a group of $k$ machines that are pairwise interconnected via a communication network. The $k$ machines jointly perform computations on an arbitrary $n$-vertex input graph (where typically $n \gg k$) distributed among the machines. The communication is point-to-point via message passing. The goal is to minimize the *round complexity*, i.e., the number of *communication rounds*, given some (bandwidth) constraint on the amount of data that each link of the network can deliver in one round. We address


*SPAA '18, July 16–18, 2018, Vienna, Austria*

ACM ISBN 978-1-4503-5799-9/18/07...$15.00
https://doi.org/10.1145/3210377.3210409

a fundamental issue in distributed computing of large-scale data: What is the distributed (round) complexity of solving problems when each machine can see only *a portion of the input* and there is a *limited bandwidth* for communication? We would like to quantify the round complexity of solving problems as a function of the *size of the input* and the *number of machines* used in the computation.

A main contribution of this paper is a technique that can be used to show non-trivial lower bounds on the distributed complexity (number of communication rounds) of large-scale data computations, and its application to graph problems.

## 1.1 The Model

We now describe the adopted model of distributed computation, the *k-machine model* (a.k.a. the *Big Data model*), introduced in [19] and further investigated in [3, 7, 27, 29, 32]. The model consists of a set of $k \geqslant 2$ machines $\{M_1, M_2, \ldots, M_k\}$ pairwise interconnected by bidirectional point-to-point communication links. Each machine executes an instance of a distributed algorithm. The computation advances in synchronous rounds where, in each round, machines can exchange messages over their communication links and perform some local computation. Each link is assumed to have a bandwidth of $B$ bits per round; unless otherwise stated, we assume $B = \Theta(\text{polylog}\, n)$. Machines do not share any memory and have no other means of communication. We assume that each machine has access to a private source of true random bits. We say that algorithm $\mathcal{A}$ has *$\epsilon$-error* if, in any run of $\mathcal{A}$, the output of the machines corresponds to a correct solution with probability at least $1-\epsilon$. The *round complexity of $\mathcal{A}$* is defined to be the worst-case number of rounds required by any machine when executing $\mathcal{A}$.

Local computation within a machine is considered to happen instantaneously at zero cost, while the exchange of messages between machines is the costly operation. However, we note that in all the algorithms of this paper, every machine in every round performs lightweight computations; in particular, these computations are bounded by a polynomial (typically, even linear) in the size of the input assigned to that machine.

Although the $k$-machine model is a general model of distributed computation that can be applied to study any (large-scale data) problem, in this paper we focus on investigating graph problems in it. Specifically, we are given an input graph $G$ with $n$ vertices, each associated with a unique integer ID from $[n]$, and $m$ edges. To avoid trivialities, we will assume that $n \geqslant k$ (typically, $n \gg k$). Initially, the entire graph $G$ is not known by any single machine, but rather partitioned among the $k$ machines in a "balanced" fashion, i.e., the nodes and/or edges of $G$ must be partitioned approximately evenly among the machines. We assume a *vertex-partition* model, whereby vertices (and their incident edges) are partitioned across machines. Specifically, the type of partition that we will assume throughout is the *random vertex partition (RVP)*, i.e., vertices (and their incident edges) of the input graph are assigned randomly to machines. This is the typical way used by many real graph processing systems, such as Pregel [23] and Giraph [1, 6], to partition the input graph among the machines; it is easy to accomplish, e.g., via hashing.

More formally, in the *random vertex partition* model each vertex of $G$ is assigned independently and uniformly at random to one of the $k$ machines. If a vertex $v$ is assigned to machine $M_i$ we say that $M_i$ is the *home machine* of $v$ and, with a slight abuse of notation, write $v \in M_i$. When a vertex is assigned to a machine, all its incident edges are known to that machine as well, i.e., the home machine initially knows the IDs of the neighbors of that vertex as well as the identities of their home machines (and the weights of the corresponding edges in case $G$ is weighted). For directed graphs, we assume that out-edges of vertices are known to the assigned machine. (However, we note that our lower bounds hold even if both in- and out-edges are known to the home machine.) An immediate property of the RVP model is that the number of vertices at each machine is *balanced*, i.e., each machine is the home machine of $\tilde{\Theta}(n/k)$ vertices with high probability (see [19]); we shall assume this throughout the paper.

## 1.2 Our Results

We present a general information-theoretic approach for showing non-trivial round lower bounds for certain graph problems in the $k$-machine model. This approach can be useful in the context of showing round lower bounds for many other (including non-graph) problems in a distributed setting where the input is partitioned across several machines and the output size is large. Using our approach we show almost tight (up to logarithmic factors) lower bounds for two fundamental, seemingly unrelated, problems, namely PageRank computation and triangle enumeration. These lower bounds apply to distributed computations in essentially all point-to-point communication models, since they apply even to a synchronous complete network (where $k = n$), and *even* when the input is partitioned *randomly*, and thus they apply to worst-case balanced partitions as well (unlike some previous lower bounds, e.g., [39], which apply only under some worst-case partition).

To demonstrate the near-tightness of our lower bounds we present optimal (up to polylog($n$) factors) distributed algorithms for such problems. The round complexity of these algorithms scales *superlinearly* in $k$, improving significantly over previous results.

**1. PageRank Computation.** In Section 2.3 we show an almost tight lower bound of $\tilde{\Omega}(n/k^2)$ rounds.[1] In Section 3.1 we present an algorithm that computes the PageRank of all nodes of a graph in $\tilde{O}(n/k^2)$ rounds, thus improving over the previously known bound of $\tilde{O}(n/k)$ rounds [19].

**2. Triangle Enumeration.** In Section 2.4 we show that there exist graphs with $m$ edges where any distributed algorithm requires $\tilde{\Omega}(m/k^{5/3})$ rounds. In Section 3.2 we present an algorithm that enumerates all the triangles of a graph in $\tilde{O}(m/k^{5/3}+n/k^{4/3})$ rounds. This improves over the previously known bound of $\tilde{O}(n^{7/3}/k^2)$ rounds [19].

Our technique can be used to derive lower bounds in other models of distributed computing as well. Specifically, the approach used to show the lower bound for triangle enumeration can be adapted for the popular congested clique model (discussed in Section 1.4), yielding an $\Omega(n^{1/3}/\log n)$ lower bound for the same problem.[2] (Notice that this does not contradict the impossibility result of [12],

[1]Notation $\tilde{\Omega}$ hides a $1/\text{polylog}(n)$ factor, and $\tilde{O}$ hides a polylog($n$) factor and an additive polylog($n$) term.

[2]A preliminary version of this paper, appeared on arXiv [28], contained a slightly worse lower bound of the form $\Omega(n^{1/3}/\log^3 n)$; later, a subsequent work by Izumi and Le Gall [16] showed a lower bound of the form $\Omega(n^{1/3}/\log n)$ using our information-theoretic approach.

which states that any super-constant lower bound for the congested clique would give new lower bounds in circuit complexity: because of the size required by any solution for triangle enumeration, Remark 3 in [12] does not apply.) To the best of our knowledge, this is the first *super-constant* lower bound known for the congested clique model. (Previous bounds were known for weaker versions of the model, e.g., which allowed only broadcast communication, or which applied only to deterministic algorithms [12], or for implementations of specific algorithms [5].)

Our bounds for triangle enumeration also apply to the problem of enumerating all the *open triads*, that is, all the sets of three vertices with exactly two edges. Our techniques and results can be generalized to the enumeration of other small subgraphs such as cycles and cliques.

Due to lack of space, full proofs and additional details are deferred to the full version of the paper.

## 1.3 Overview of Techniques

**Lower Bounds.** In Theorem 2.1 we prove a general result, the *General Lower Bound Theorem*, which relates the round complexity in the $k$-machine model to the minimal amount of information required by machines for correctly solving a problem. While PageRank and triangle enumeration are fundamentally different problems, we derive lower bounds for both problems via the "information to running time" relationship of Theorem 2.1. The General Lower Bound Theorem gives two probabilistic bounds that must be satisfied in order to obtain a lower bound on the round complexity of any problem. The two bounds together capture the decrease in uncertainty (called *surprisal*, see Section 2) that happens to some machine as a result of outputting the solution. We can show that this "surprisal change" represents the maximum expected "Information Cost" over all machines which can be used to lower bound the run time. The proof of the General Lower Bound Theorem makes use of information-theoretic machinery, yet its application requires no use of information theory.

We conjecture that Theorem 2.1 can be used to obtain lower bounds for various problems (including non-graph problems) that have a relatively *large output size* (e.g., shortest paths, sorting, matrix multiplication, etc.) thus complementing the approach based on communication complexity (see, e.g., [9, 12, 13, 19, 24–27, 31] and references therein). In fact, our approach, as demonstrated in the case of triangle enumeration, can yield stronger round lower bounds as well as message-round tradeoffs compared to approaches that use communication complexity techniques (more on this in the next paragraph). Our approach, as demonstrated in the case of PageRank, can yield tight lower bounds for problems (including, and especially, under a stochastic/random partition of the input) where communication complexity techniques are not obvious. In fact, for many problems, applying the General Lower Bound Theorem gives non-trivial lower bounds in a fairly straightforward way that are not (at least easily) obtainable by communication complexity techniques. To give an example, the work of Klauck et al. [19] showed a lower bound of $\tilde{\Omega}(n/k^2)$ for connectivity by appealing to random partition communication complexity—this involved proving the classical set disjointness lower bound *under random input partition*, which involved non-trivial work. On the other hand, the same lower bound of $\tilde{\Omega}(n/k^2)$ for MST can be shown directly[3] via the General Lower Bound Theorem (this bound is tight due to the algorithm of [27]). To give another example, consider the problem of distributed sorting (see, e.g., [26]), whereby $n$ elements are randomly distributed across the $k$ machines and the requirement is that, at the end, the $i$-th machine must hold the $(i-1)k+1, (i-1)k+2, \ldots, i \cdot k$-th order statistics. One can use the General Lower Bound Theorem to show a $\tilde{\Omega}(n/k^2)$ lower bound for this problem (and this is tight, as there exists an $\tilde{O}(n/k^2)$-round sorting algorithm). Note that the same lower bound (under a random partition) is harder to show using communication complexity techniques.

We also note that tight *round* complexity lower bounds do not always directly follow from exploiting *message (bit)* complexity lower bounds obtained by leveraging communication complexity results. For example, for the problem of triangle enumeration, even assuming the highest possible message lower bound of $\Omega(m)$, this would directly imply a *round* lower bound of $\tilde{\Omega}(m/k^2)$ (since $\Theta(k^2)$ messages can be exchanged in one round) and not the tight $\tilde{\Omega}(m/k^{5/3})$ shown in this paper. Furthermore, our approach can show round-message *tradeoffs* giving stronger message lower bounds for algorithms constrained to run in a prescribed round bound compared to what one can obtain using communication complexity approaches. In particular, for triangle enumeration, we show that any round-optimal algorithm that enumerates all triangles with high probability in the $k$-machine model needs to exchange a total of $\tilde{\Omega}(mk^{1/3})$ messages in the worst case.

We emphasize that our General Lower Bound theorem gives non-trivial lower bounds only when the output size is large enough, but it still works seamlessly across all output sizes. To illustrate this, we note that the triangle enumeration lower bound of $\tilde{\Omega}(m/k^{5/3})$ is true only for dense graphs, i.e., $m = \Theta(n^2)$. In fact, the real lower bound derived through our theorem is $\tilde{\Omega}((t/k)^{2/3}/k)$, where $t$ is the number of triangles in the input graph; this bound can be shown to apply even for sparse (random) graphs by extending our analysis.

Entropy-based information-theoretic arguments have been used in prior work [19]. However, there is a crucial difference, as explained next. In [19], it was shown that $\tilde{\Omega}(n/k)$ is a lower bound for computing a spanning tree (ST) of a graph. However, this lower bound holds under the criterion that the machine which hosts the vertex (i.e., its home machine) must know at the end of the computation the status of all of its incident edges (whether they belong to a ST or not) and output their respective status. The lower bound proof exploits this criterion to show that any algorithm will require some machine receiving $\Omega(n)$ bits of information, and since any machine has $k-1$ links, this gives a $\tilde{\Omega}(n/k)$ lower bound. This argument fails if we require the final status of each edge to be known by *some* machine (different machines might know the status of different edges); indeed under this output criterion, it can be shown that MST can be solved in $\tilde{O}(n/k^2)$ rounds [27]. On the other hand, the lower bound proof technique of this paper applies to the less restrictive (and more natural) criterion that any machine can output any part of the solution. In [4], a direct sum theorem is shown that yields a communication complexity lower bound for set disjointness. The method of [4] can be applied to obtain lower bounds for functions

[3]The lower bound graph can be a complete graph with random edge weights.

$F$ that can be "decomposed" as $F(\mathbf{x}, \mathbf{y}) = f(g(x_1, y_1), \ldots, g(x_n, y_n))$, by reduction from the information complexity of the function $g$. These methods do not seem applicable to our setting as we are considering problems where the output size is large.

**Upper Bounds.** The Conversion Theorem of [19] directly translates algorithms designed for a message passing model for network algorithms to the $k$-machine model, and almost all the previous algorithms [7, 19, 32] were derived using this result. In contrast, the present paper does not use the Conversion Theorem; instead, it gives direct solutions for the problems at hand, leading to improved algorithms with significantly better round complexity.

While our algorithms use techniques specific to each problem, we point out a simple, but key, unifying technique that proves very useful in designing fast algorithms, called *randomized proxy computation.*[4] Randomized proxy computation is crucially used to distribute communication *and* computation across machines to avoid congestion at any particular machine, which instead is redistributed evenly across all the machines. This is achieved, roughly speaking, by re-assigning the *executions* of individual nodes uniformly at random among the machines. Proxy computation allows one to move away from the communication pattern imposed by the topology of the input graph, which can cause congestion at a particular machine, to a more balanced communication overall.

## 1.4 Related Work

For a comparison of the $k$-machine model with other parallel and distributed models proposed for large-scale data processing, including Bulk Synchronous Parallel (BSP) model [37], MapReduce [18], and the congested clique, we refer to [38]. In particular, according to [38], "Among all models with restricted communication the "big data" [$k$-machine] model is the one most similar to the MapReduce model".

Klauck et al. [19] present lower and upper bounds for several fundamental graph problems in the $k$-machine model. In particular, they presented weaker upper bounds for PageRank and triangle verification (which also works for triangle enumeration), which are substantially improved in this paper. They do not present any non-trivial lower bound for any of these problems. Also, as pointed out earlier, some lower bounds shown in [19], most notably the $\Omega(n/k^2)$ lower bound of MST (under random input partition and under the requirement that each MST edge has to be output by *some* machine), can be shown in a simpler way using the General Lower Bound Theorem of this paper. Pandurangan et al. [27] showed $\tilde{O}(n/k^2)$-round algorithms in the $k$-machine model for connectivity, MST, approximate min-cut, and other graph verification problems. The algorithmic techniques used in that paper (except for the randomized proxy computation) cannot be applied for PageRank and triangle enumeration.

The $k$-machine model is closely related to the BSP model [37]; it can be considered to be a simplified version of BSP, where local computation is ignored and synchronization happens at the end of every round (the synchronization cost is ignored). Unlike BSP which has a lot of different parameters (which typically makes it harder to prove rigorous theoretical bounds [38]), the $k$-machine model is characterized by one parameter (the number of machines) which allows one to develop and prove clean bounds and serves as a basis for comparing various distributed algorithms.

The $k$-machine model is also closely related to the classical CONGEST model [30], and in particular to the *congested clique* model, which recently has received considerable attention (see, e.g., [5, 12, 14, 15, 17, 20, 21]). The main difference is that the $k$-machine model is aimed at the study of large-scale computations, where the size $n$ of the input is significantly bigger than the number of available machines $k$, and thus many vertices of the input graph are mapped to the same machine, whereas the two aforementioned models are aimed at the study of distributed network algorithms, where $n = k$ and each vertex corresponds to a dedicated machine. More "local knowledge" is available per vertex (since it can access for free information about other vertices in the same machine) in the $k$-machine model compared to the other two models. On the other hand, all vertices assigned to a machine have to communicate through the links incident on this machine, which can limit the bandwidth (unlike the other two models where each vertex has a dedicated processor). These differences manifest in the design of fast algorithms for these models. In particular, the best distributed algorithm in the congested clique model may not directly yield the fastest algorithm in the $k$-machine model [27].

# 2 LOWER BOUNDS

## 2.1 A General Lower Bound Theorem

In this section we present a result, called *General Lower Bound Theorem*, which provides a general way to obtain round lower bounds in the $k$-machine model. In Section 2.2 we provide the full of this result. We will then apply it to derive lower bounds for two graph problems, namely, PageRank computation (Section 2.3) and triangle enumeration (Section 2.4).

Consider an $n$-vertex input graph $G$ partitioned across the machines via the random-vertex partition in the $k$-machine model. Note that the input graph $G$ is sampled from a probability distribution on a (suitably chosen) set of graphs $\mathcal{G}$. (For example, in the case of PageRank, $\mathcal{G}$ is the set of all possible instantiations of the lower bound graph $H$ shown in Figure 1.) Consider a partition $\mathbf{p} = (p_1, \ldots, p_k)$ of an input graph $G$. We use boldface $\mathbf{p}$ to denote a vector and $p_i$ to denote the $i$-th entry of $\mathbf{p}$, which corresponds to the subgraph assigned to machine $M_i$. In our analysis, we frequently condition on the event that a subgraph $p_i \subseteq G$ is assigned to a certain machine $M_i$. To simplify the notation, we also use $p_i$ to denote the event that this happens, e.g., $\Pr[E \mid p_i]$ is the probability of event $E$ conditioned on the assignment of $p_i$ to machine $M_i$.

Let $\Pi_i$ be the random variable representing the transcript of the messages received by machine $M_i$ across its $k-1$ links when executing a given algorithm $\mathcal{A}$ for (at most) $T$ rounds, and let $\mathcal{GP}$ be the set of all possible partitions of the graphs in $\mathcal{G}$ among the $k$ machines. The execution of algorithm $\mathcal{A}$ is fully determined by the given input partitioning $\mathbf{p} \in \mathcal{GP}$ and the public random bit string $R \in \mathcal{RS}$, where $\mathcal{RS}$ is the set of all possible strings that are used as random bit string by the algorithm. Note that $R$ is itself a random variable. Similarly to above, we write $\Pr[E \mid p_i, r]$ when conditioning event $E$ on the events that the public random string is $r$ and machine $M_i$ obtains subgraph $p_i$ as its input, where

[4]Similar ideas have been used in parallel and distributed computation in different contexts, see, e.g., [35, 36].

$\mathbf{p} = (p_1, \ldots, p_i, \ldots, p_k)$ and $(\mathbf{p}, r) \in \mathcal{GP} \times \mathcal{RS}$. We use $\mathcal{A}_i(\mathbf{p}, r)$ to denote the output of machine $M_i$, when executing the algorithm for a given $(\mathbf{p}, r)$. For technical reasons, we assume that the output $\mathcal{A}_i(\mathbf{p}, r)$ also includes $M_i$'s initial graph input $p_i$ and the random string $r$.

Theorem 2.1 (General Lower Bound Theorem). *Let* IC $=$ IC$(n, k)$ *be a positive integer-valued function called* information cost, *and let $Z$ be a random variable depending only on the input graph. Consider a $T$-round $\epsilon$-error algorithm $\mathcal{A}$, for some $\epsilon = o(\text{IC}/\mathbb{H}[Z])$, where $\mathbb{H}[Z]$ is the entropy of $Z$. Let Good $\subseteq \mathcal{GP} \times \mathcal{RS}$ be a set of pairs $(\mathbf{p}, r)$ where $\mathbf{p} = (p_1, \ldots, p_k) \in \mathcal{GP}$ is an input partition and $r \in \mathcal{RS}$ is a public random string, and $|Good| \geqslant (1 - \epsilon - n^{-\Omega(1)})|\mathcal{GP} \times \mathcal{RS}|$. Suppose that, for every $(\mathbf{p}, r) \in$ Good, there exists a machine $M_i$ receiving input graph $p_i$ and outputting $\mathcal{A}_i(\mathbf{p}, r)$, such that*

$$Pr[Z = z \mid p_i, r] \leqslant \left(\tfrac{1}{2}\right)^{\mathbb{H}[Z] - o(\text{IC})}, \tag{1}$$

$$Pr[Z = z \mid \mathcal{A}_i(\mathbf{p}, r), p_i, r] \geqslant \left(\tfrac{1}{2}\right)^{\mathbb{H}[Z] - \text{IC}}, \tag{2}$$

*for every $z$ that has nonzero probability conditioned on events $Out_i = \mathcal{A}_i(\mathbf{p}, r)$, $P_i = p_i$, and $R = r$. Then, if $B$ denotes the per-round communication link bandwidth, it holds that*

$$T = \Omega\left(\frac{\text{IC}}{Bk}\right). \tag{3}$$

**Intuition.** We can think of Premise (1) as bounding the initial knowledge of the machines about the random variable $Z$. On the other hand, Premise (2) says that at least one machine is able to increase its knowledge on the value of $Z$ eventually, which we formalize by conditioning on its output in addition to the initial knowledge. Then, if there is a large set (called *Good*) of inputs where these premises hold, then our theorem says that the worst-case time of the algorithm must be sufficiently large. These insights are formally captured by the *self-information* or *surprisal* of an event $E$, which is defined as $\log_2(1/\Pr[E])$ [33] and measures the "amount of surprise" or information contained in observing $E$. Premises (1) and (2) imply that, from some machine $M_i$'s point of view, the occurrence of $\{Z = z\}$ is "$\Omega$(IC) more surprising" given its initial knowledge, compared to observing this event after computing the output. We can show that this surprisal change IC bounds from below the maximum communication cost over all machines. In this light, (3) says that the run time of the algorithm is roughly a $(1/kB)$-fraction of the maximum expected information cost.

## 2.2 Proof of the General Lower Bound Theorem

In the proof of Theorem 2.1 we make use of some standard definitions in information theory, such as entropy, denoted with $\mathbb{H}$, and mutual information, denoted with $\mathbb{I}$ (see, e.g., [8]).

**Critical Index.** For a given input graph partition $\mathbf{p}$ and a random string $r$, we are interested in identifying the machine that has the maximum expected value of the amount of information that its output reveals about the random variable $Z$. This motivates us to define the *critical index* function as

$$\ell(\mathbf{p}, r) := \arg\max_{1 \leqslant i \leqslant k} \mathbb{I}[Out_i; Z \mid p_i, r], \tag{4}$$

and define random variables $\Pi_*(\mathbf{p}, r) = \Pi_{\ell(\mathbf{p}, r)}(\mathbf{p}, r)$ and $Out_*(\mathbf{p}, r) = Out_{\ell(\mathbf{p}, r)}(\mathbf{p}, r)$. Intuitively speaking, for each $(\mathbf{p}, r) \in \mathcal{GP} \times \mathcal{RS}$, the random variable $Out_*$ is the output of the machine $M_i$ (where $i$ depends on $\mathbf{p}, r$) that attains the maximum mutual information between its output and the random variable $Z$. For a given $(\mathbf{p}, r)$, we use $p_* = p_{\ell(\mathbf{p}, r)}$ to denote the input partition of machine $M_{\ell(\mathbf{p}, r)}$. Note that $Z$ depends *only* on the input graph, whereas $\Pi_*$, $P_*$, and $Out_*$ depend on the input graph and, in addition, also on the chosen partition $\mathbf{p}$ and random string $r$. From (4), we immediately obtain the following property of the critical index.

Observation 1. *For all $(\mathbf{p}, r) \in \mathcal{GP} \times \mathcal{RS}$, and for all $i \in [k]$, it holds that*

$$\mathbb{I}[Out_*; Z \mid p_*, r] \geqslant \mathbb{I}[Out_i; Z \mid p_i, r],$$

*where $p_* = p_{\ell(\mathbf{p}, r)}$ and $\mathbf{p} = (p_1, \ldots, p_{\ell(\mathbf{p}, r)}, \ldots, p_k)$.*

Lemma 2.2. *For every $(\mathbf{p}, r) \in \mathcal{GP} \times \mathcal{RS}$ where $\mathbf{p} = (p_1, \ldots, p_*, \ldots, p_k)$, it holds that*

$$\mathbb{I}[\Pi_*; Z \mid p_*, r] \geqslant \mathbb{I}[Out_*; Z \mid p_*, r].$$

Lemma 2.3. *For all $(\mathbf{p}, r) \in$ Good where $\mathbf{p} = (p_1, \ldots, p_k)$, there is an $i \in [k]$ (which satisfies (1) and (2) in the premise of the theorem) such that $\mathbb{I}[Out_i; Z \mid p_i, r] \geqslant \text{IC} - o(\text{IC})$.*

Proof. For a given $(\mathbf{p}, r) \in$ *Good*, let $M_i$ be a machine satisfying (2) (in addition to (1)). By definition,

$$\mathbb{I}[Out_i; Z \mid p_i, r] = \mathbb{H}[Z \mid p_i, r] - \mathbb{H}[Z \mid Out_i, p_i, r]. \tag{5}$$

We will now bound the terms on the right-hand side. By definition, we obtain

$$\begin{aligned} \mathbb{H}[Z \mid p_i, r] &= -\sum_z \Pr[Z = z \mid p_i, r] \log_2 \Pr[Z = z \mid p_i, r] \\ &\geqslant (\mathbb{H}[Z] - o(\text{IC})) \sum_z \Pr[Z = z \mid p_i, r] \qquad \text{(by (1))} \\ &= \mathbb{H}[Z] - o(\text{IC}), \end{aligned} \tag{6}$$

where the last inequality follows from $\sum_z \Pr[Z = z \mid p_i, r] = 1$.

In the remainder of the proof, we derive an upper bound on $\mathbb{H}[Z \mid Out_i, p_i, r]$. Since

$$\mathbb{H}[Z \mid Out_i, p_i, r] \leqslant \mathbb{H}[Z \mid Out_i], \tag{7}$$

we will proceed by proving an upper bound on the latter term. To simplify the notation, we use "$\mathcal{A}_i(\mathbf{p}, r)$" as a shorthand for the event "$Out_i = \mathcal{A}_i(\mathbf{p}, r)$". By definition, we have

$$\begin{aligned} \mathbb{H}[Z \mid Out_i] &= \sum_{(\mathbf{p}, r)} \Pr[\mathcal{A}_i(\mathbf{p}, r)]\, \mathbb{H}[Z \mid \mathcal{A}_i(\mathbf{p}, r)] \\ &= \sum_{(\mathbf{p}, r) \in Good} \Pr[\mathcal{A}_i(\mathbf{p}, r)]\, \mathbb{H}[Z \mid \mathcal{A}_i(\mathbf{p}, r)] \\ &\quad + \sum_{(\mathbf{p}, r) \notin Good} \Pr[\mathcal{A}_i(\mathbf{p}, r)]\, \mathbb{H}[Z \mid \mathcal{A}_i(\mathbf{p}, r)] \\ &\leqslant \sum_{(\mathbf{p}, r) \in Good} \Pr[\mathcal{A}_i(\mathbf{p}, r)]\, \mathbb{H}[Z \mid \mathcal{A}_i(\mathbf{p}, r)] \\ &\quad + \mathbb{H}[Z] \left( \sum_{(\mathbf{p}, r) \notin Good} \Pr[\mathcal{A}_i(\mathbf{p}, r)] \right), \end{aligned} \tag{8}$$

where the last inequality follows from $\mathbb{H}[Z] \geqslant \mathbb{H}[Z \mid \mathcal{A}_i(\mathbf{p}, r)]$. Intuitively speaking, the first sum in (8) represents the remaining uncertainty of $Z$ upon termination, assuming machines start with a hard input assignment (i.e., in *Good*), whereas the second term is weighted by the probability that either the input was easy or the algorithm failed (i.e. $\notin$ *Good*). The following claim bounds the entropy term in the first sum of (8), where $(\mathbf{p}, r)$ is restricted to the set *Good*.

CLAIM 1. $\mathbb{H}[Z \mid \mathcal{A}_i(\mathbf{p}, r)] \leqslant \mathbb{H}[Z] - \text{IC}$.

We will now derive an upper bound on the second sum in (8).

CLAIM 2. $\sum_{(\mathbf{p},r)\notin Good} \Pr[\mathcal{A}_i(\mathbf{p}, r)] \leqslant \epsilon + n^{-\Omega(1)}$.

Plugging the bounds in Claims 1 and 2 into (8), we get

$$\mathbb{H}[Z \mid Out_i] \leqslant (\mathbb{H}[Z] - \text{IC}) \sum_{(\mathbf{p},r)\in Good} \Pr[\mathcal{A}_i(\mathbf{p}, r)] + \mathbb{H}[Z]\left(\epsilon + n^{-\Omega(1)}\right)$$
$$\leqslant (\mathbb{H}[Z] - \text{IC}) + \mathbb{H}[Z]\left(\epsilon + n^{-\Omega(1)}\right).$$

Assuming a sufficiently large constant in the exponent of $n^{-\Omega(1)}$, we observe that $\mathbb{H}[Z] \cdot n^{-\Omega(1)} = o(1)$ since $Z$ depends only on the input graph. By the premise of Theorem 2.1, we have $\epsilon = o(\text{IC}/\mathbb{H}[Z])$ and $\text{IC} \leqslant \mathbb{H}[Z]$, hence $\epsilon \cdot \mathbb{H}[Z] = o(\text{IC})$. From this and (7) we conclude that

$$\mathbb{H}[Z \mid Out_i, p_i, r] \leqslant \mathbb{H}[Z] - \text{IC} + o(\text{IC}).$$

Plugging this upper bound and the lower bound of (6) into the right-hand side of (5), completes the proof of Lemma 2.3. □

Recall that Lemma 2.2 holds for any $(\mathbf{p}, r) \in \mathcal{GP} \times \mathcal{RS}$; in particular, even if we restrict our choice to the set *Good*. Thus, for $(\mathbf{p}, r) \in Good$, where $\mathbf{p} = (p_1, \ldots, p_k)$, let $i \in [k]$ be the index for which Lemma 2.3 holds (which is the index of the machine satisfying Premises (1) and (2)). This yields

$$\begin{aligned}\mathbb{H}[\Pi_* \mid p_*, r] &\geqslant \mathbb{I}[\Pi_*; Z \mid p_*, r] \\ &\geqslant \mathbb{I}[Out_*; Z \mid p_*, r] && \text{(by Lemma 2.2)} \\ &\geqslant \mathbb{I}[Out_i; Z \mid p_i, r] && \text{(by Obs. 1)} \\ &\geqslant \text{IC} - o(\text{IC}), && (9)\end{aligned}$$

where the last inequality follows from Lemma 2.3. To complete the proof of Theorem 2.1, we will argue that the worst-case run time needs to be large, as otherwise the entropy of machine $M_{\ell(\mathbf{p},r)}$'s transcript $\Pi_*$ would be less than IC$-o$(IC). The value of $\mathbb{H}[\Pi_* \mid p_*, r]$ is maximized if the distribution of $(\Pi_* \mid p_*, r)$ is uniform over all possible choices. In the next lemma we show that, during $T$ rounds of the algorithm, the transcript can take at most $2^{(B+1)(k-1)T}$ distinct values, and thus

$$\mathbb{H}[\Pi_* \mid p*, r] \leqslant \log_2\left(2^{(B+1)(k-1)T}\right) = O(B\,k\,T). \quad (10)$$

LEMMA 2.4. *Suppose that some machine $M_i$ can receive a message of at most $B$ bits on each of its $k-1$ links in a single round. Let $\Gamma$ be the bits received by $M_i$ over its $k-1$ links during $T$ rounds. Then, $\Gamma$ can take at most $2^{(k-1)(B+1)T}$ distinct values.*

Recall that the run time $T$ is the maximum time required by any machine $M_i$, over all random strings and input assignments, i.e., $T = \max_{(\mathbf{p},r)} T(\mathbf{p}, r)$. Combining (9) and (10), it follows that

$$T = \max_{(\mathbf{p},r)} T(\mathbf{p}, r) = \Omega\left(\frac{IC}{Bk}\right).$$

## 2.3 A Lower Bound for PageRank Computation

THEOREM 2.5. *Let $\mathcal{A}$ be an algorithm that computes a $\delta$-approximation of the* PageRank *vector of an $n$-node graph for a small constant $\delta > 0$ (depending on the reset probability), and suppose that $\mathcal{A}$ succeeds with probability $\geqslant 1 - o(1/k)$. Then, the run time of $\mathcal{A}$ is $\Omega\left(\frac{n}{B\cdot k^2}\right)$, assuming a communication link bandwidth of $B$ bits per round and $k = \Omega(\log^2 n)$ machines. This holds even when the input graph is assigned to the machines via random vertex partitioning.*

We first give a high-level overview of the proof. As input graph $G$, we construct a weakly connected directed graph where the direction of certain "important" edges is determined by a random bit vector, and assign random IDs to all the vertices. Flipping the direction of an important edge changes the PageRank of connected vertices by a constant factor and hence any (correct) algorithm needs to know about these edge directions. It is crucial that the vertex IDs are chosen randomly, to ensure that knowing just the direction of important edges is not sufficient for computing the PageRank of the adjacent nodes, as these random vertex IDs "obfuscate the position" of a vertex in the graph. This means that a machine needs to know both, the direction of an important edge and the IDs of the connected vertices to be able to output a correct result. By using a Chernoff bound, we can show that the random vertex partitioning of the input graph does not reveal too many edge-directions together with the matching vertex IDs to a single machine. This sets the stage for applying our generic lower bound theorem (Theorem 2.1) to obtain a lower bound on the run time.

**The Lower Bound Graph.** We consider the following directed graph $H$ (see Figure 1) of $n$ vertices and $m = n - 1$ edges; for simplicity, assume that $m/4$ is an integer. Let $X = \{x_1, x_2, \ldots, x_{m/4}\}$, $U = \{u_1, u_2, \ldots, u_{m/4}\}$, $T = \{t_1, t_2, \ldots, t_{m/4}\}$, $V = \{v_1, v_2, \ldots, v_{m/4}\}$, and let $V(G) = \{X \cup U \cup T \cup V \cup \{w\}\}$. The edges between these vertices are given as follows: For $1 \leqslant i \leqslant m/4$, there is a directed edge $u_i \to t_i$, a directed edge $t_i \to v_i$, and a directed edge $v_i \to w$. The edges between $u_i$ and $x_i$ (these are the "important" edges mentioned above) are determined by a bit vector $\mathbf{b}$ of length $m/4$ where each entry $b_i$ of $\mathbf{b}$ is determined by a fair coin flip: If $b_i = 0$ then there is an edge $u_i \to x_i$, otherwise there is an edge $x_i \to u_i$. Lemma 2.6 shows that, for any $1 \leqslant i \leqslant m/4$ and for any $\epsilon < 1$, there is a constant factor separation between the PageRank of any node $v_i$ if we switch the direction of the edge between $x_i$ and $u_i$.

LEMMA 2.6. *The following holds for the* PageRank *value of vertices $v_i$ of $G$, for $1 \leqslant i \leqslant n/4$: If $b_i = 0$, then* $\text{PageRank}(v_i) = \frac{(2.5-2\epsilon+\epsilon^2/2)\epsilon}{n}$. *Otherwise, if $b_i = 1$, then* $\text{PageRank}(v_i) \geqslant \frac{(3-3\epsilon+\epsilon^2)\epsilon}{n}$. *For any $\epsilon < 1$, there is a constant factor (where the constant depends on $\epsilon$) separation between the two cases.*

**The Input Graph Distribution.** We now build our input graph $G$ as follows. Let $m = n - 1$, and let $ID$ be the random variable representing a set of $n$ unique integers chosen uniformly at random from $\{S \subset [1, \text{poly}(n)] : |S| = n\}$. Assigning each vertex of $H$ a unique integer from $ID$ (in an arbitrary predetermined way) yields a graph $G$. Let $\mathcal{G}$ denote the set of graphs $G$ determined by all possible (different) ID assignments to all possible instances of $H$ considering all possible edge directions. Let $\mathcal{GP}$ be the set of all input graph partitions (i.e., the set of all graphs in $\mathcal{G}$ and all their possible input partitions) among the $k$ machines, and let $\mathcal{RS}$ be

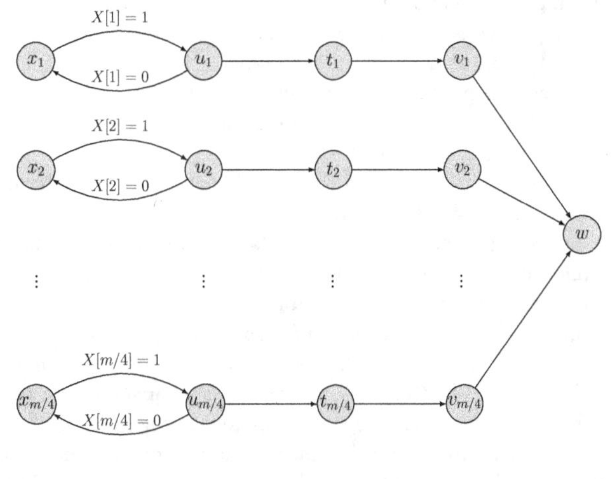


**Figure 1: The graph $H$ used to derive a lower bound on the round complexity of PageRank computations.**

the set of all random strings used by a given PageRank algorithm $\mathcal{A}$. Let $Bal \subseteq \mathcal{GP}$ be the set of all input partitions where each machine receives $\tilde{\Theta}(n/k)$ vertices of the input graph. Note that $(\mathbf{p}, r) \in \mathcal{GP} \times \mathcal{RS}$ fully determines the run of $\mathcal{A}$. We assume that each machine $M_i$ outputs a set $\{(\pi_1, id_1), \ldots, (\pi_\ell, id_\ell)\}$, where $\pi_j$ refers to the PageRank value of the vertex with ID $id_j$. Note that we do not make assumptions neither on which machine being the one that outputs the PageRank of a specific vertex $v$ (which could be a machine that holds no initial knowledge about $v$ and its ID), nor on the individual sizes of these output sets.

**Discovering Weakly Connected Paths of Vertices.** By the random vertex partitioning, each machine $M_i$ initially holds $\tilde{\Theta}(n/k)$ vertices in total. More specifically, $M_i$ receives random sets $X_i \subseteq X$, $U_i \subseteq U$, $T_i \subseteq T$, and $V_i \subseteq V$, each containing $O(n\log(n)/k)$ vertices. As machine $M_i$ also gets to know the incident edges of these vertices, $M_i$ can locally check if a path induced by some $(x_{j_1}, u_{j_2}, t_{j_3}, v_{j_4}) \in X_i \times U_i \times T_i \times V_i$ is weakly connected, i.e., $j_1 = \cdots = j_4$. Since $M_i$ learns the output pair $(\text{PageRank}(v), id_v)$ at zero cost, we upper bound the number of such paths that the machines learn initially by using a Chernoff bound. That is, we show that each machine learns at most $O\left(\frac{n \log n}{k^{3/2}}\right)$ paths.

Lemma 2.7. *With probability at least $1 - n^{-4}$, the initial graph partition reveals at most $O\left(\frac{n\log n}{k^2}\right)$ weakly connected paths between vertices in $X$ and $V$ to every machine.*

**Good Inputs.** We define $Good \subseteq Bal \times \mathcal{RS}$ to be the set of all (balanced) inputs and random strings where (1) $\mathcal{A}$ correctly outputs the PageRank of each vertex, (2) partition $\mathbf{p}$ is "balanced", i.e., each machine is assigned $O(n \log n/k)$ vertices (and hence $O(n\log n/k)$ edges since $m = O(n)$), and (3) the partitioning is such that each machine knows at most $O((n\log n)/k^2)$ weakly connected paths initially; we define $Bad = \mathcal{GP} \times \mathcal{RS} \setminus Good$.

Lemma 2.8. *(A) For any $(\mathbf{p}, r) \in Good$, algorithm $\mathcal{A}$ is correct and there must be at least one machine $M_i$ whose output list contains $\Omega(n/k)$ vertices of $V$. (B) $|Good| \geqslant \left(1 - o(1/k) - n^{-\Omega(1)}\right)|\mathcal{GP}\times\mathcal{RS}|$.*

To instantiate Theorem 2.1, we show in Lemma 2.9 and Lemma 2.10 that we can satisfy the Premises (1) and (2), by setting IC $= m/4k = \Theta(n/k)$. Plugging the above value of IC in (3) then gives the claimed lower bound.

Lemma 2.9. *Let $Z$ be the random variable representing the set of pairs $\{(b_1, v_1), \ldots, (b_{m/4}, v_{m/4})\}$, where $b_j$ refers to the direction of the edge $(x_j, u_j)$ in the weakly connected path $(x_j, u_j, t_j, v_j)$ of the input graph of Figure 1. Then, for each $(\mathbf{p}, r) \in Good$, where $\mathbf{p} = (p_1, \ldots, p_k)$, and for every possible choice of $z$, it holds that $Pr[Z = z \mid p_i, r] \leqslant 2^{-(m/4 - O(n\log(n)/k^2))}$.*

Lemma 2.10. *For each $(\mathbf{p}, r) \in Good$, where $\mathbf{p} = (p_1, \ldots, p_k)$, there exists a machine $M_i$ with output $\mathcal{A}_i(\mathbf{p}, r)$ such that, for every choice of $z$ for $Z$ (defined in Lemma 2.9) that has nonzero probability conditioned on $\mathcal{A}_i(\mathbf{p}, r), p_i, r$, it holds that $Pr[Z = z \mid \mathcal{A}_i(\mathbf{p}, r), p_i, r] \geqslant 1/2^{\frac{m}{4} - \frac{m}{4k}}$.*

## 2.4 A Lower Bound for Triangle Enumeration

We first give a high-level overview of the proof. The input graphs that we use for our lower bounds are sampled according to the $G_{n,1/2}$ Erdös-Renyi random graph model. We will argue that enumerating triangles implies a large reduction of the entropy of the characteristic vector of edges $Z$, i.e., $Z$ is a bit vector whose entries reflect the presence/absence of an edge in the input graph. We prove that initially the machines do not have significant knowledge of $Z$, which is equivalent to having a small probability for the event $\{Z = z\}$, for any $z$. Then, we show that any machine that outputs $t/k$ triangles, for a parameter $t$, must have reduced its uncertainty about $Z$ by approximately $(t/k)^{2/3}$ bits. In other words, the information obtained by such a machine throughout the course of the algorithm is high. We apply Theorem 2.1 to obtain a lower bound on the run time of any algorithm. This yields the following result.

Theorem 2.11. *There exists a class of graphs $\mathcal{G}$ of $n$ nodes for which every distributed algorithm that solves triangle enumeration in the $k$-machine model has a time complexity of $\Omega\left(\frac{n^2}{B \cdot k^{5/3}}\right)$, assuming a link bandwidth of $B$ bits per round, $k = \Omega(\log n)$ machines, and an error probability of $\epsilon = o(k^{-2/3})$. This holds even when the input graph is assigned to the machines via random vertex partitioning.*

**The Input Graph Distribution.** We choose our input graphs according to the Erdös-Renyi random graph model $G_{n,1/2}$, which samples an $n$-node graph where each possible edge is included independently with probability $1/2$. We use $\mathcal{GP}$ to denote the set of all possible partitions of all possible sampled $n$-node graphs and, similarly to before, denote the set of all random strings used by the algorithm by $\mathcal{RS}$.

Let $Z$ be the characteristic vector of the edges[5] of the input graph $G$. Note that the execution of $\mathcal{A}$ is fully determined by the given graph input partition $\mathbf{p} = (p_1, \ldots, p_k) \in \mathcal{GP}$ and the shared (among all machines) random bit string $r \in \mathcal{RS}$, where $\mathcal{RS}$ is the set of all possible strings that are used as random bit string by the algorithm. Hence we have $|\mathcal{GP} \times \mathcal{RS}|$ possible outcomes when running $\mathcal{A}$ on a graph sampled from $\mathcal{G}$.

[5] The characteristic vector specifies the graph $G$. Order the $\binom{n}{2}$ possible edges in some fixed ordering; if the $j$th edge in this ordering appears in $G$, then $Z_j = 1$, otherwise it is 0.

**Good Inputs.** We define $Good \subseteq \mathcal{GP} \times \mathcal{RS}$ to be the set of input pairs $(\mathbf{p}, r)$ such that (1) $\mathcal{A}$ performs correctly for the graph partition $\mathbf{p}$ of graph $G$ and the random string $r$, (2) partition $\mathbf{p}$ is "balanced", i.e., each machine is assigned $O(n \log(n)/k)$ vertices (and hence $O(n^2 \log(n)/k)$ edges), and (3) $G$ has $\geqslant t$ triangles, for some fixed $t = \Theta(\binom{n}{3})$.

Similarly as for Theorem 2.5, we prove that $\Pr[Z = z \mid p_i, r] \leqslant 1/2^{\binom{n}{2} - O(n^2 \log n/k)}$ and $\Pr[Z = z \mid o_i, p_i, r] \geqslant 1/2^{\binom{n}{2} - \frac{1}{3}\left(\frac{t}{k} - O\left(\frac{n^2 \log n}{k}\right)\right)^{2/3}}$. Then, setting $\text{IC} = \Theta(n^2/k^{2/3})$, and applying Theorem 2.1, completes the proof of Theorem 2.11.

**A tight lower bound in the congested clique.** Our analysis extends in a straightforward way to the congested clique model where, in a synchronous complete network of $n$ machines, every machine $u$ receives exactly one input vertex of the input graph and gets to know all its incident edges. Together with the deterministic upper bound of $O(n^{1/3})$ shown in [11], we have the following.

Corollary 2.12. *The round complexity of enumerating all triangles in the congested clique of $n$ nodes with high probability of success is $\Omega\left(\frac{n^{1/3}}{B}\right)$, assuming a link bandwidth of $B$ bits. This bound is tight up to logarithmic factors.*

**Message lower bounds.** We have the following.

Corollary 2.13. *Let $\mathcal{A}$ by any algorithm that enumerates all triangles with high probability and terminates in $\tilde{O}(\frac{n^2}{k^{5/3}})$ rounds. Then, the total message complexity in the $k$-machine model of $\mathcal{A}$ is $\tilde{\Omega}(n^2 k^{1/3})$. For $\tilde{O}(n^{1/3})$-rounds algorithms in the congested clique, the message complexity is $\tilde{\Omega}(n^{7/3})$.*

# 3 UPPER BOUNDS

## 3.1 An Almost Optimal Algorithm for PageRank Computation

In this section we present a simple distributed algorithm to compute the PageRank vector of an input graph in the $k$-machine model. This algorithm has a round complexity of $\tilde{O}(n/k^2)$, which significantly improves over the previous $\tilde{O}(n/k)$-round solution [19].

We first recall the distributed random walk-based Monte-Carlo algorithm for computing PageRank, for a given reset probability $\epsilon$, as described in [10]. This algorithm is designed and analyzed in the standard CONGEST model, where each vertex of the graph executes the algorithm. The algorithm is as follows. Initially, each vertex creates $c \log n$ random walk tokens, where $c = c(\epsilon)$ is a parameter defined in [10] ($c(\epsilon)$ is inversely proportional to $\epsilon$), which are then forwarded according to the following process: when a node $u$ receives some random walk token $\rho$, it terminates the token with probability $\epsilon$ and, with probability $1-\epsilon$, forwards it to a neighbor of $u$ chosen uniformly at random. Each node keeps a variable $\psi_v$, for each of its nodes $v$, which counts the number of random walk tokens that were addressed to $v$ (i.e., the total number of all random walks that visit $v$). Each node $v$ then estimates its PageRank by computing $\frac{\epsilon \psi_v}{cn \log n}$. It can be shown that this estimate gives a $\delta$-approximation, for any constant $\delta > 0$, to the PageRank value of each node $v$ with high probability, and that this algorithm terminates in $O(\log n/\epsilon)$ rounds with high probability [10]. The key idea to obtain such a fast runtime is to send only the *counts* of the random walks, instead of keeping track of the random walks from different sources. Clearly, only the number (i.e., count) of the random walks visiting a node at any step is required to estimate the PageRank. In the full paper, we describe why a naïve implementation of the above approach only yields a running time of $\tilde{O}(n/k)$.

To avoid the pitfalls of a naïve implementation, we describe an approach that directly exploits the $k$-machine model. On the one hand, our goal is to reduce the total amount of communication while, on the other hand, we need to ensures that the incurred message complexity is balanced for the available machines. This motivates us to treat vertices differently depending on how many tokens they hold. We say that a vertex $u$ has *low-load in iteration* $r$ if, conceptually, the machine that hosts $u$ considers $\geqslant k$ tokens to be held at $u$. Otherwise, we say that $u$ has *high-load in iteration* $r$. Note that, throughout the course of our algorithm, the value of tokens$[v]$ depends on the topology of the input graph and hence a vertex can change its status w.r.t. being a high-load or low-load vertex.

In our algorithm (Algorithm 1), each machine $M$ stores an array tokens$[u]$, which has an entry for each vertex $u$ hosted at $M$. Initially, we generate $\Theta(\log n)$ tokens for each vertex which we use as the initialization value of tokens. Then, we mimic the (parallel) random walk steps of [10] by performing $\Theta(\log(n)/\epsilon)$ iterations where, in each iteration, each machine $M$ first considers the tokens stored for its low-load vertices. For each such token held at one of its vertices $u$, $M$ uniformly at random selects a neighboring vertex $v$ and keeps track of how many tokens have chosen $v$ in a separate array $\alpha[v]$. In particular, $M$ also increments the same entry $\alpha[v]$ if $v$ is chosen as the destination for some token of a distinct low-load vertex $w$ at $M$. Then, $M$ sends a message $\langle \alpha[v], \text{dest:}v \rangle$ for each $v$ where $\alpha[v]$ is nonzero, which is subdelivered to the destination machine using random routing (cf. Lemma 3.2). This ensures that all the messages are delivered in $\tilde{O}(n/k^2)$ rounds.

We now describe how high-load vertices are processed, each of which can hold up to $O(n \log n)$ tokens. To avoid potentially sending a large number of messages for a single high-load vertex $u$, machine $M$ considers the index set $I$ of machines that host at least one neighbor of $u$. Then, for each token of $u$, machine $M$ samples an index from $I$ and keeps track of these counts in an array $\beta$, which has an entry for each machine in $I$. Finally, $M$ generates one message of type $\langle \beta[j], \text{src:}u \rangle$, for each entry $j$ where $\beta[j] > 0$ and sends this count message directly to the respective destination machine. We show that these messages can be delivered in $\tilde{O}(n/k^2)$ rounds by proving that, with high probability, each machine holds $\tilde{O}(n/k^2)$ high-load vertices in any given iteration of the algorithm.

Lemma 3.1. *Every machine $M_i$ sends at most $\tilde{O}(n/k)$ messages in any iteration $r$ with high probability.*

A key ingredient in the analysis of the algorithm is the following simple lemma, which quantifies how fast some specific routing can be done in the $k$-machine model.

Lemma 3.2. *Consider a complete network of $k$ machines, where each link can carry one message of $O(\text{polylog}\, n)$ bits at each round. If each machine is source of $O(x)$ messages whose destinations are distributed independently and uniformly at random, or each machine is*

**Algorithm 1** Computing the PageRank with reset probability $\epsilon > 0$. Code for machine $M_i$.

```
Let V_i denote the vertices hosted by machine M_i
Initalize array tokens[u] ← ⌈c log n⌉, for u ∈ V_i, where c > 0
    is a suitable constant        ▷ tokens[u] represents the current
    number of tokens at vertex u
for Θ(log(n)/ϵ) iterations do
    for u ∈ V_i do
        sample t from distribution Binomial(tokens[u], ϵ)
        tokens[u] ← tokens[u] − t        ▷ Terminate each token
    with probability ϵ

    Initialize array α[v] ← 0, for each v ∈ V        ▷ Process the
    low-load vertices
    for each vertex u ∈ V_i where tokens[u] < k do
        let N_u ⊆ V be the set of neighbors of vertex u
        while tokens[u] > 0 do
            sample v uniformly at random from N_u
            α[v] ← α[v] + 1
            tokens[u] ← tokens[u] − 1
    for each v ∈ V_i where α[v] > 0 do
        send message ⟨α[v], dest: v⟩ to the machine hosting
    vertex v using random routing

    for each vertex u ∈ V_i where tokens[u] ⩾ k do    ▷ Process
    the high-load vertices
        let I ⊆ [k] be the index set of the machines that host a
    neighbor of u
        initialize array β[j] ← 0, for each j ∈ I
        while tokens[u] > 0 do
            let n_{j,u} be number of neighbors of u hosted at ma-
    chine M_j and let d_u be u's degree
            sample index j from distribution (n_{1,u}/d_u, ..., n_{k,u}/d_u)
            β[j] ← β[j] + 1
            tokens[u] ← tokens[u] − 1
        for each j ∈ I where β[j] > 0 do
            send message ⟨β[j], src: u⟩ to machine M_j

    for each received message of type ⟨c_w, dest: w⟩ do
        tokens[w] ← tokens[w] + c_w
    for each received message of type ⟨c_v, src: v⟩ do
        while c_v > 0 do
            let N_v ⊆ V be the set of neighbors of v hosted at M_i
            sample w uniformly at random from N_v
            tokens[w] ← tokens[w] + 1
            c_v ← c_v − 1
```

*destination of $O(x)$ messages whose sources are distributed independently and uniformly at random, then all the messages can be routed in $O((x \log x)/k)$ rounds w.h.p.*

Lemma 3.3. *Consider any iteration $r$ of Algorithm 1. Then, with high probability, all messages generated at iteration $r$ can be delivered in $\tilde{O}(n/k^2)$ rounds.*

From Lemma 3.3 we conclude that all messages generated in a single iteration of Algorithm 1 can be delivered in $\tilde{O}(n/k^2)$ rounds with high probability. A union bound implies the following result.

Theorem 3.4. *Algorithm 1 computes a $\delta$-approximation of the PageRank vector of an $n$-node graph in the $k$-machine model with high probability in $\tilde{O}(n/k^2)$ rounds, for any constant $\delta > 0$.*

## 3.2 An Almost Optimal Algorithm for Triangle Enumeration

In this section we present a randomized algorithm that enumerates all the triangles of an input graph $G = (V, E)$, and that terminates in $\tilde{O}(m/k^{5/3} + n/k^{4/3})$ rounds w.h.p. This bound does not match the (existential) $\tilde{\Omega}(m/k^{5/3})$ lower bound provided in Section 2.4 only for very sparse graphs.

Our algorithm is a generalization of the algorithm TriPartition of Dolev et al. for the congested clique model [11], with some crucial differences explained next. The key idea, which in its generality can be traced back to [2], is to partition the set $V$ of nodes of $G$ in $k^{1/3}$ subsets of $n/k^{1/3}$ nodes each, and to have each of the $k$ machines to examine the edges between pairs of subsets in one of the $(k^{1/3})^3 = k$ possible triplets of subsets (repetitions are allowed).

The algorithm is as follows. Each node picks independently and uniformly at random one color from a set $C$ of $k^{1/3}$ distinct colors through a hash function $h : V \to C$ initially known by all the machines. This gives rise to a color-based partition of the vertex set $V$ into $k^{1/3}$ subsets of $\tilde{O}(n/k^{1/3})$ nodes each, w.h.p. A deterministic assignment of triplets of colors, hard-coded into the algorithm, logically assigns each of the $k$ possible triplets of such subsets to one distinct machine. Each machine then collects all the edges between pairs of subsets in its triplet. This is accomplished in two steps: (1) For each of the edges it holds, each machine designates one random machine (among the $k$ machines) as the *edge proxy* for that edge, and sends all its edges to the respective edge proxies. The designation of an edge itself is done by the following *proxy assignment rule* (this is necessary to avoid congestion at any one machine): A machine that has a node $v$ whose degree is at least $2k \log n$ requests all other machines to designate the respective edge proxies for each of the incident edges of node $v$. If two machines request each other to designate the same edge (since their endpoints are hosted by the respective machines), then such a tie is broken randomly. (2) In the second step, all the machines collect their required edges from the respective proxies: since each edge proxy machine knows the hash function $h$ as well as the deterministic assignment of triplets, it can send each edge to the machines where it is needed. Then, each machine simply enumerates all the triangles in its local subgraph.

We now argue that the above algorithm correctly enumerates all the triangles of a graph $G$, and analyze its round complexity. A key step in the analysis of the complexity is to bound from above the number of edges assigned to each machine. Observe that the number of edges between pairs of subsets of one triplet is no larger than the number of edges in the subgraph of $G$ induced by the nodes of one triplet; in turn, because of the random color-based partition of the vertices made by the algorithm, the latter quantity is asymptotically equivalent to the number of edges in the subgraph of $G$ induced by a set of (in this case, $\tilde{O}(n/k^{1/3})$) randomly-chosen nodes of a graph. Thus, we shall concentrate on the latter quantity (which is of interest in its own right). To this end, we will use the following concentration result due to Rödl and Ruciński [34].

PROPOSITION 3.5 ([34, PROPOSITION 1]). *Let, for a graph $G = (V, E)$, $m < \eta n^2$, and let $R$ be a random subset of $V$ of size $|R| = t$ such that $t \geqslant 1/3\eta$. Let $e(G[R])$ denote the number of edges in the subgraph induced by $R$. Then, for some $c > 0$,*

$$\Pr\left[e(G[R]) > 3\eta t^2\right] < t \cdot e^{-ct}$$

We are now ready to analyze the algorithm.

THEOREM 3.6. *There is a distributed algorithm for the $k$-machine model that enumerates all the triangles of an $n$-node, $m$-edge graph in $\tilde{O}(m/k^{5/3} + n/k^{4/3})$ rounds with high probability.*

## 4 CONCLUSIONS

We presented a general technique for proving lower bounds on the round complexity of distributed computations in a general message-passing model for large-scale computation, and showed its application for two prominent graph problems, PageRank and triangle enumeration. We also presented near-optimal algorithms for these problems, which can be efficiently implemented in practice.

Our lower bound technique works by relating the size of the output to the number of communication rounds needed, and could be useful in showing lower bounds for other problems where the output size is large (significantly more than the number of machines), such as sorting, matrix multiplication, shortest paths, matching, clustering, and densest subgraph.

## ACKNOWLEDGMENTS

This project has received funding from the European Research Council (ERC) under the European Union's Horizon 2020 research and innovation programme under grant agreement No 715672. G. Pandurangan and M. Scquizzato were also supported, in part, by NSF grants CCF-1527867, CCF-1540512, IIS-1633720, CCF-1717075, and by BSF grants 2008348 and 2016419. P. Robinson acknowledges the support of the Natural Sciences and Engineering Research Council of Canada (NSERC).

## REFERENCES

[1] Giraph, http://giraph.apache.org/.

[2] F. N. Afrati and J. D. Ullman. Optimizing multiway joins in a Map-Reduce environment. *IEEE Trans. Knowl. Data Eng.*, 23(9):1282–1298, 2011.

[3] S. Bandyapadhyay, T. Inamdar, S. Pai, and S. V. Pemmaraju. Near-optimal clustering in the $k$-machine model. In *Proceedings of the 19th International Conference on Distributed Computing and Networking (ICDCN)*, pages 15:1–15:10, 2018.

[4] Z. Bar-Yossef, T. S. Jayram, R. Kumar, and D. Sivakumar. An information statistics approach to data stream and communication complexity. *J. Comput. Syst. Sci.*, 68(4):702–732, 2004.

[5] K. Censor-Hillel, P. Kaski, J. H. Korhonen, C. Lenzen, A. Paz, and J. Suomela. Algebraic methods in the congested clique. In *Proceedings of the 34th ACM Symposium on Principles of Distributed Computing (PODC)*, pages 143–152, 2015.

[6] A. Ching, S. Edunov, M. Kabiljo, D. Logothetis, and S. Muthukrishnan. One trillion edges: Graph processing at facebook-scale. *PVLDB*, 8(12):1804–1815, 2015.

[7] F. Chung and O. Simpson. Distributed algorithms for finding local clusters using heat kernel pagerank. In *Proceedings of the 12th Workshop on Algorithms and Models for the Web-graph (WAW)*, pages 77–189, 2015.

[8] T. M. Cover and J. A. Thomas. *Elements of Information Theory*. Wiley, 2006.

[9] A. Das Sarma, S. Holzer, L. Kor, A. Korman, D. Nanongkai, G. Pandurangan, D. Peleg, and R. Wattenhofer. Distributed verification and hardness of distributed approximation. *SIAM J. Comput.*, 41(5):1235–1265, 2012.

[10] A. Das Sarma, A. R. Molla, G. Pandurangan, and E. Upfal. Fast distributed PageRank computation. *Theor. Comput. Sci.*, 561:113–121, 2015.

[11] D. Dolev, C. Lenzen, and S. Peled. "Tri, tri again": Finding triangles and small subgraphs in a distributed setting. In *Proceedings of the 26th International Symposium on Distributed Computing (DISC)*, pages 195–209, 2012.

[12] A. Drucker, F. Kuhn, and R. Oshman. On the power of the congested clique model. In *Proceedings of the 33rd ACM Symposium on Principles of Distributed Computing (PODC)*, pages 367–376, 2014.

[13] M. Elkin, H. Klauck, D. Nanongkai, and G. Pandurangan. Can quantum communication speed up distributed computation? In *Proceedings of the 33rd ACM Symposium on Principles of Distributed Computing (PODC)*, pages 166–175, 2014.

[14] M. Ghaffari and M. Parter. MST in log-star rounds of congested clique. In *Proceedings of the 2016 ACM Symposium on Principles of Distributed Computing (PODC)*, pages 19–28, 2016.

[15] J. W. Hegeman, G. Pandurangan, S. V. Pemmaraju, V. B. Sardeshmukh, and M. Scquizzato. Toward optimal bounds in the congested clique: Graph connectivity and MST. In *Proceedings of the 34th ACM Symposium on Principles of Distributed Computing (PODC)*, pages 91–100, 2015.

[16] T. Izumi and F. Le Gall. Triangle finding and listing in CONGEST networks. In *Proceedings of the ACM Symposium on Principles of Distributed Computing (PODC)*, pages 381–389, 2017.

[17] T. Jurdzinski and K. Nowicki. MST in $O(1)$ rounds of congested clique. In *Proceedings of the 29th Annual ACM-SIAM Symposium on Discrete Algorithms (SODA)*, pages 2620–2632, 2018.

[18] H. J. Karloff, S. Suri, and S. Vassilvitskii. A model of computation for MapReduce. In *Proceedings of the 21st annual ACM-SIAM Symposium on Discrete Algorithms (SODA)*, pages 938–948, 2010.

[19] H. Klauck, D. Nanongkai, G. Pandurangan, and P. Robinson. Distributed computation of large-scale graph problems. In *Proceedings of the 26th Annual ACM-SIAM Symposium on Discrete Algorithms (SODA)*, pages 391–410, 2015.

[20] C. Lenzen. Optimal deterministic routing and sorting on the congested clique. In *Proceedings of the 32nd ACM Symposium on Principles of Distributed Computing (PODC)*, pages 42–50, 2013.

[21] Z. Lotker, B. Patt-Shamir, E. Pavlov, and D. Peleg. Minimum-weight spanning tree construction in $O(\log \log n)$ communication rounds. *SIAM J. Comput.*, 35(1):120–131, 2005.

[22] N. A. Lynch. *Distributed Algorithms*. Morgan Kaufmann Publishers Inc., 1996.

[23] G. Malewicz, M. H. Austern, A. J. C. Bik, J. C. Dehnert, I. Horn, N. Leiser, and G. Czajkowski. Pregel: a system for large-scale graph processing. In *Proceedings of the 2010 ACM International Conference on Management of Data (SIGMOD)*, pages 135–146, 2010.

[24] D. Nanongkai, A. D. Sarma, and G. Pandurangan. A tight unconditional lower bound on distributed randomwalk computation. In *Proceedings of the 30th ACM Symposium on Principles of Distributed Computing (PODC)*, pages 257–266, 2011.

[25] R. Oshman. Communication complexity lower bounds in distributed message-passing. In *Proceedings of the 21st International Colloquium on Structural Information and Communication Complexity (SIROCCO)*, pages 14–17, 2014.

[26] G. Pandurangan, D. Peleg, and M. Scquizzato. Message lower bounds via efficient network synchronization. In *Proceedings of the 23rd International Colloquium on Structural Information and Communication Complexity (SIROCCO)*, pages 75–91, 2016.

[27] G. Pandurangan, P. Robinson, and M. Scquizzato. Fast distributed algorithms for connectivity and MST in large graphs. In *Proceedings of the 28th ACM Symposium on Parallelism in Algorithms and Architectures (SPAA)*, pages 429–438, 2016.

[28] G. Pandurangan, P. Robinson, and M. Scquizzato. Tight bounds for distributed graph computations. *CoRR*, abs/1602.08481, 2016.

[29] G. Pandurangan, P. Robinson, and M. Scquizzato. Fast distributed algorithms for connectivity and MST in large graphs. *ACM Trans. Parallel Comput.*, 2018.

[30] D. Peleg. *Distributed Computing: A Locality-Sensitive Approach*. Society for Industrial and Applied Mathematics, 2000.

[31] D. Peleg and V. Rubinovich. A near-tight lower bound on the time complexity of distributed minimum-weight spanning tree construction. *SIAM J. Comput.*, 30(5):1427–1442, 2000.

[32] J. Qiu, S. Jha, A. Luckow, and G. C. Fox. Towards HPC-ABDS: An initial high-performance big data stack, in building robust big data ecosystem. 2014.

[33] F. M. Reza. *An introduction to information theory*. Courier Corporation, 1961.

[34] V. Rödl and A. Ruciński. Random graphs with monochromatic triangles in every edge coloring. *Random Struct. Algorithms*, 5(2):253–270, 1994.

[35] C. Scheideler. *Universal Routing Strategies for Interconnection Networks*, volume 1390 of *Lecture Notes in Computer Science*. Springer, 1998.

[36] L. G. Valiant. A scheme for fast parallel communication. *SIAM J. Comput.*, 11(2):350–361, 1982.

[37] L. G. Valiant. A bridging model for parallel computation. *Commun. ACM*, 33(8):103–111, 1990.

[38] S. Vassilvitskii. Models for parallel computation (a hitchhikers' guide to massively parallel universes), http://grigory.us/blog/massively-parallel-universes/, 2015.

[39] D. P. Woodruff and Q. Zhang. When distributed computation is communication expensive. *Distrib. Comput.*, 30(5):309–323, 2017.

# Laika: Efficient In-Place Scheduling for 3D Mesh Graph Computations

Predrag Gruevski
Kensho Technologies, Inc.
predrag@kensho.com

William Hasenplaugh
CSAIL MIT
whasenpl@alum.mit.edu

David Lugato
CEA Cesta
david.lugato@cea.fr

James J. Thomas
CS Stanford
jjthomas@stanford.edu

## ABSTRACT

Scientific computing problems are frequently solved using ***data-graph computations*** – algorithms that perform local updates on application-specific data associated with vertices of a graph, over many time steps. The data-graph in such computations is commonly a ***mesh graph***, where vertices have positions in 3D space, and edges connect physically nearby vertices. A ***scheduler*** controls the parallel execution of the algorithm. Two classes of parallel schedulers exist: double-buffering and in-place. Double-buffering schedulers do not incur synchronization overheads due to an absence of read-write conflicts, but require two copies of the vertices, as well as a higher iteration count due to a slower convergence rate. Computations for which this difference in convergence rate is significant (e.g., multigrid method) are frequently performed using an in-place scheduler, which incurs synchronization overheads to avoid read-write conflicts on the single copy of vertex data.

We present LAIKA, a deterministic in-place scheduler we created using a principled three-step design strategy for high-performance schedulers. LAIKA reorders the input graph using a Hilbert space-filling curve to improve cache locality and minimizes parallel coordination overhead by explicitly curbing excess execution parallelism. Consequently, LAIKA has significantly lower scheduling overhead than alternative in-place schedulers and is even faster per iteration than the parallel double-buffered implementation on a reordered input graph.

We derive an improved bound on the expected number of cache misses incurred during a traversal of a graph reordered using a space-filling curve. We also prove that on a mesh graph $G = (V, E)$, LAIKA performs $O(|V| + |E|)$ total work and achieves linear expected speedup with $P = O(|V|/\log^2|V|)$ workers. On 48 cores, LAIKA yields 38.4x parallel speedup and empirically fares well against comparably well-engineered alternatives: it runs 6.97–12.60 times faster in geometric mean over a suite of input graphs than other parallel schedulers and 222.57 times faster than the baseline serial implementation.


ACM ISBN 978-1-4503-5799-9/18/07.
https://doi.org/10.1145/3210377.3210395

## KEYWORDS

Data-graph computations; multithreading; parallel programming; scheduling; work-stealing; cache locality

**ACM Reference Format:**
Predrag Gruevski, William Hasenplaugh, David Lugato, and James J. Thomas. 2018. Laika: Efficient In-Place Scheduling for 3D Mesh Graph Computations. In *SPAA '18: 30th ACM Symposium on Parallelism in Algorithms and Architectures, July 16–18, 2018, Vienna, Austria.* ACM, New York, NY, USA, 12 pages. https://doi.org/10.1145/3210377.3210395

## 1 INTRODUCTION

Practitioners frequently use numerical methods, such as the multigrid and finite-element methods, to solve problems in many domains, such as computer graphics or computational fluid dynamics. Such computations simulate physical processes by iteratively performing a computation on a ***mesh data graph***, denoted $G = (V, E)$. In this graph, vertices have positions in 3D space as well as other computation-specific physical quantities, and edges connect physically-nearby vertices. A common way (e.g., used in Simit [24], a domain-specific language for physical simulations) to express the data-graph computation is via an ***update function*** which modifies the data at a given vertex $v$ based on the data contained by its neighbors, denoted $N(v)$. This update function is applied to all vertices over many time steps, until reaching a physical or numerical convergence. A ***scheduler*** controls the (potentially parallel) invocation order of these update functions. For example, the ***serial baseline*** scheduler used in Simit simply iterates over the vertices, serially executing the update function at each vertex.

Two classes of parallel schedulers exist: ***in-place***, where the scheduler always applies the update function on the newest data for each vertex, and ***double-buffering***, where the scheduler keeps two copies of each vertex, reading from one and writing to the other in alternating iterations. Double-buffering (Jacobi) often has better per-iteration speed [30] at the cost of doubled memory usage. Meanwhile, in-place (Gauss-Seidel) approaches generally converge faster [3] – up to 8 times faster in some multigrid method computations [6]. Practitioners weigh the tradeoffs and opt for an in-place scheduler only when the improved convergence rates offset the per-iteration performance loss.

While in-place methods are already preferred in many applications [1–3, 6, 11, 13, 22, 34] we can widen their use by decreasing their per-iteration synchronization overhead relative to double-buffering. Recent research has explored improving in-place scheduler performance: GraphLab [26] uses a nondeterministic, mutual-exclusion-based scheduler; Prism [21] offers determinism via ***chromatic scheduling*** [1, 3, 4, 25]. A chromatic scheduler colors the input graph such that no edges exist between vertices of the same color. Then, all vertices of a given color may be updated in parallel without causing a determinacy race [12]. The scheduler serially processes all colors, executing all vertices of each color in parallel without the overhead of mutual-exclusion locks or atomic operations. While chromatic scheduling is frequently the preferred in-place method due to its high parallelism without synchronization operations, it suffers from highly inefficient cache usage [2, 3].

***DAG scheduling*** [20] is an alternative to chromatic scheduling that explicitly tracks dependencies between vertices and has better cache behavior in practice. A DAG scheduler uses a priority function $\rho : V \rightarrow \mathbb{R}$ to transform the graph $G = (V, E)$ into a directed acyclic graph (DAG) $G' = (V, E')$. Each edge $(v, w) \in E$ is oriented as $(v, w) \in E'$ if $\rho(v) < \rho(w)$, and as $(w, v)$ if $\rho(v) > \rho(w)$, breaking ties randomly. The vertices are then processed in DAG order — a vertex $v$ may be processed once all of its predecessors $v.pred = \{w \in N(v) : \rho(w) < \rho(v)\}$ have been processed. We consider the Jones-Plassmann [20] parallel DAG scheduler (henceforth, JP), which uses a dependency counter at each vertex $v$ initialized with the number of its predecessors $|v.pred|$ in the DAG $G'$. For each updated vertex $v$, the scheduler atomically decrements the counters for all successors $v.succ = N(v) \setminus v.pred$, and recursively updates any successors whose dependency counters drop to zero. While the DAG scheduler has a caching advantage due to the opportunity to update vertices shortly after their neighbors, in practice, the synchronization overhead of the atomic decrement operations results in a significant performance penalty.

We present the following contributions:

- **an improved upper bound on the cache miss rate** of traversals of locally-connected arbitrary-volume random graphs, reordered with a recursive (e.g., Hilbert) space-filling curve;
- **a principled design strategy** for high-performance schedulers for iterative data-graph computations;
- Laika, **a parallel, in-place scheduler** for data-graph computations on 3D mesh graphs, which offers deterministic, provably scalable execution with 6.97–12.60 times the performance of other parallel schedulers.

As using recursive space-filling curves to reorder input data for better locality is an established practice [16, 17, 27, 33], we first consider the cache miss rate of the traversal of a reordered random cube graph — $n$ vertices uniformly randomly distributed in the unit cube and connected to all other vertices within a distance $r$. The best prior upper bound for misses of an $M$-vertex cache during a traversal of such a graph is $O(M^{-1/4})$ [29]. We show a tighter bound of $O(M^{-1/3})$, and then extend the analysis from random cubes to ***arbitrary-volume random graphs***. Relying on this result as the basis of a principled design strategy for high-performance in-place schedulers, we point out synergies between three techniques:

- ***Proximity-preserving reordering*** — the graph's input data is reordered such that $N(v)$ are likely to be near $v$ in memory. Similar techniques are used in [16, 17, 27, 33].
- ***Execution locality*** — if a core is currently executing the update function on $v$, it is likely to choose one of $N(v)$ to update next. The JP scheduler [20] exhibits this behavior.
- ***Synchronization-overhead minimization*** — the scheduler's parallel execution order has minimal overhead caused by synchronization between processor cores. The double-buffering (Jacobi) and chromatic schedulers exhibit this behavior.

These three techniques address mostly orthogonal sources of performance problems at three levels of scope: a single update function, a single processor core, and all processor cores in the system. Proximity-preserving reordering creates spatial locality in update function executions, drastically reducing cache miss rates. Execution locality encourages temporal locality across update functions (i.e., most accesses of a vertex happen close in time), allowing efficient per-core execution through reuse of cached data. Synchronization-overhead minimization ensures near-linear parallel speedup by reducing the use of expensive coordination primitives, such as locks and atomics. Our design strategy posits that each of these techniques can make the subsequent ones more effective: execution locality is created easily on a well-ordered graph, and significantly less synchronization is required when the workload has both spatial and temporal locality.

Even though the three techniques above are complementary, no existing scheduler achieves all three properties *simultaneously*. Hence, we designed Laika— a new scheduler for data-graph computations on 3D mesh graphs executed on a shared-memory multicore computer. Laika is a variation of DAG scheduling that offers deterministic, cache-efficient, and provably scalable execution. For proximity-preserving reordering, Laika follows the established practice [16, 27, 33] of using a Hilbert space-filling curve [19]. To maximize execution locality and minimize expensive atomic updates of dependency counters, Laika explicitly limits the maximum parallelism of the execution via a compile-time constant.

We present both theoretical and empirical evidence of Laika's good performance. Using work-span analysis [10, Ch. 27], we show that Laika is work-efficient, with $O(|V| + |E|)$ work per time step on any input graph. Despite its explicit upper bound on parallelism, we prove that Laika achieves linear expected speedup on random cube graphs with $O(|V|/\log^2|V|)$ parallel workers. Our analysis considers computations with serial Update($v$) functions with $O(N(v))$ work for all $v$. We then compare Laika's empirical performance against four commonly-used alternative parallel schedulers: a double-buffering (Jacobi) scheduler, a chromatic scheduler, the JP DAG scheduler, a mutual-exclusion-based scheduler, as well as against a simple serial baseline scheduler. We use a set of four input graph topologies, each in five sizes ranging from 20MB to 5.4GB.

On 48 processors and in geometric mean across a set of four input topologies, Laika demonstrates a parallel speedup of 38.41, runs 6.97–12.60 times faster than the alternative parallel schedulers, and is 222.57 times faster than the serial baseline scheduler. Laika incurs 7.8 times fewer LLC misses than the chromatic scheduler, while also avoiding approximately 99% of the atomic operations required by the DAG scheduler. Laika also captures 54% of the theoretical upper-bound parallel performance[1] achievable on our workload

[1] We calculate the theoretical upper-bound parallel performance by dividing the runtime of the serial baseline scheduler by the number of processor cores in the system.

with 48 processor cores. Finally, LAIKA is 4% faster per iteration than the double-buffering scheduler running on the LAIKA-reordered input graph, as during execution of our workload on 48 cores, LAIKA's synchronization overhead appears to be less costly than the double-buffering scheduler's need to read and write two copies of vertex data. While our implementation [14] does not currently support it, our approach should naturally extend to distributed memory systems, as they merely deepen the memory hierarchy and would therefore derive even more benefit from LAIKA's proximity-preserving reordering and minimal synchronization overhead.

## 2 REORDERING VERTICES

In this section, we improve the theoretical upper bound on the miss rate of an $M$-vertex cache during a traversal of a Hilbert-reordered random cube graph, tightening it from $O(M^{-1/4})$ in [29] to $O(M^{-1/3})$. We include evidence that the new $O(M^{-1/3})$ bound is tight in practice, then build a generalized empirical model that accurately estimates the miss rate of a traversal of arbitrary-volume tetrahedralized mesh graphs [28].

### 2.1 Reordering with a Hilbert curve

To reorder a 3D mesh graph with a $k$-th order Hilbert curve, we first normalize the graph such that the 3D unit cube becomes its bounding box. We then divide up the unit cube into $2^k \times 2^k \times 2^k$ equal-sized blocks, numbered according to the $k$-th order Hilbert curve. Figure 1 depicts the 2D analog of this process, for $k = 2$. Finally, we assign each vertex to the block that encloses its position in 3D space, then sort the vertices in linear time using a counting sort. We aim for each of the $2^{3k}$ blocks to contain $O(1)$ vertices; frequently, simply setting $k$ such that $2^{3k} = O(|V|)$ will suffice. For input graphs with highly non-uniform vertex density, simply choosing a value of $k$ appropriate for the highest-density region would suffice. Setting $k$ to an unnecessarily high value is not a concern, since it has minimal negative impact:

- Computations on such a reordered input graph are no less efficient than ones with a more appropriate value of $k$.
- Increasing $k$ does not meaningfully increase the reordering process' runtime, since assigning vertices to locations on the Hilbert curve is an embarrassingly parallel problem, and therefore the sorting operation dominates the reordering runtime.
- Even on the largest (5.4GB, 27M vertex) input graphs, the reordering process takes no more than 10s — a trivial amount of time compared to the thousands of seconds required for the data-graph computation to reach convergence.

We approximate the cache behavior of the computation with a traversal of the graph that visits each vertex in order. With an $M$-vertex cache, at each vertex $v$ the cache contains all vertices in the range $[v - M/2, v + M/2)$. Any neighbor of $v$ outside that range would incur a cache miss. We can see in Figure 2 that reordering the vertices results in significantly lower cache miss rates across all cache sizes $M$. We also see that the miss rate as a function of the cache size is better captured by our tighter $O(M^{-1/3})$ bound than the prior $O(M^{-1/4})$ bound in [29].

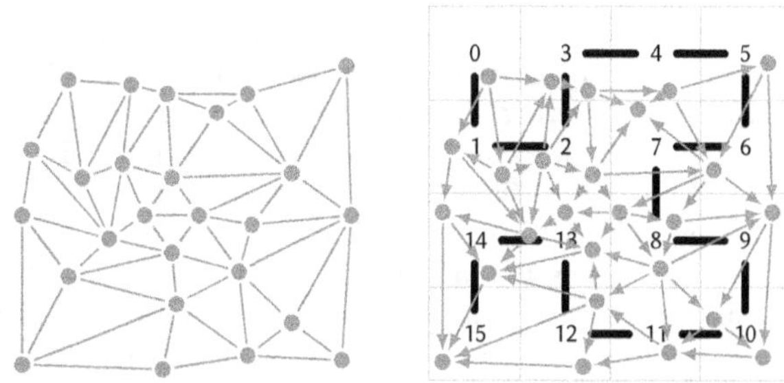


**Figure 1: Mapping a mesh graph to a DAG via a second-order Hilbert curve. Grid points in the discretized Hilbert curve are numbered in black. Each vertex $v$ is mapped to its closest grid point $H(v)$, then the input graph is reordered according to this mapping: if $H(v) < H(w)$ for $v, w \in V$, then $v$ appears before $w$ in the reordered output. Ties between vertices mapped to the same grid point are broken randomly.**

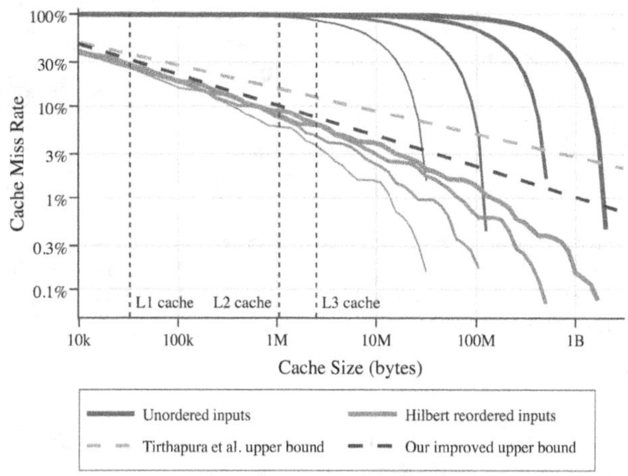


**Figure 2: Theoretical upper-bounds and empirical measurements of cache miss rates during a traversal of the input graph across four different sizes of random cube graph, from 20MB (thinnest line) to 1.3GB (thickest line), as detailed in Section 4. Vertical lines show our test system's memory hierarchy — the three lines correspond to one core's share of the total L1, L2 and L3 cache capacity of our 48-core system, respectively. We show a per-core share even of the shared L3 cache (LLC), since all cores in a parallel execution load data into cache and must therefore share the space in the LLC. Hilbert-reordering significantly reduces the number of cache misses across all input and cache sizes, and our improved upper bound on the cache miss rate is significantly tighter than the prior bound in [29].**

### 2.2 Improved expected miss rate bound

Recall that the $l^p$ norm of a vector $\vec{t} = (t_1, t_2, \dots, t_m)$ is:

$$\|\vec{t}\|_p = \begin{cases} \sum_{i=1}^{m} |t_i| & \text{for } p = 0 \\ \left(|t_1|^p + |t_2|^p + \dots |t_m|^p\right)^{1/p} & \text{for } 0 < p < \infty \\ \max_{i=1}^{m} |t_i| & \text{for } p = \infty \end{cases}$$

DEFINITION 1. *The position $\vec{x}_v$ of each vertex $v$ in an $n$-vertex* ***random cube graph*** *is chosen uniformly randomly in the unit cube and the edge set $E = \{(u, v) \in V \times V : \|\vec{x}_u - \vec{x}_v\|_p < r\}$ connects vertices within non-negative $l^p$ distance $r$.*

The expected degree of a vertex $v$ in a random cube graph is at most the expected number of vertices that fall within a ball of radius $r$. Since the vertices in $G$ are distributed uniformly randomly in the unit cube, the expected degree of a vertex is equal to the volume of the radius $r$ ball in the $l^p$ norm times the number of potential neighbors $|V|$.

Consider a vertex $v$ in a sub-cube $C$ of size $2^{-j} \times 2^{-j} \times 2^{-j}$ for some $j$, within the unit cube and aligned with the recursive decomposition of the space-filling curve, as depicted in Figure 3. We calculate the probability that another vertex $w$ in the random cube graph is connected to $v$, yet lies outside $C$.

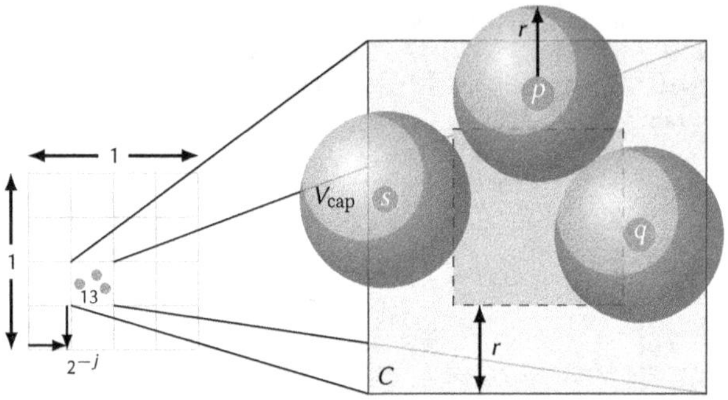


**Figure 3: The sub-cube $C$ at H(13) of Figure 1, with three vertices $s$, $p$, and $q$ with a different distance to the border. The probability that another vertex is placed outside of $C$, but within a radius $r$, is equal to the volume of the corresponding spherical cap $V_{cap}$.**

Lemma 1. *Let $G = (V, E)$, a random cube graph with $l^p$ distance parameter $r$, be decomposed into a grid of $2^j \times 2^j \times 2^j$ sub-cubes. The expected number of total edges connecting vertices in different sub-cubes is at most $6r^4|V|^2 2^j$.*

Proof. Consider two vertices $v$ and $w$; let $v$ be in sub-cube $C$. The probability that $w$ is placed within a distance $r$ of $v$, yet outside $C$, is equal to the fraction of the volume of the radius-$r$ ball under the $l^p$ norm centered on $v$ that lies outside of $C$. This volume is at most the sum of the volume of the spherical caps — the section of a ball on one side of a plane intersecting the ball — that lie outside of $C$. We first consider a single face of $C$: let the spherical cap be centered a distance of $h$ from the particular face of $C$. Recall that, since a ball in the $l^\infty$ norm is a cube, the corresponding spherical cap in $l^\infty$ is a rectangular prism and across all $l^p$ has maximal volume: $4r^2(r-h)$. Therefore, for any $l^p$, $V_{cap}(h) \le 4r^2(r-h)$ for $h \in [0, r]$, and $V_{cap}(h) = 0$ elsewhere. As $v$ is uniformly randomly located in $C$, we multiply by the area of the face $2^{-2j}$ and marginalize $h$ out, getting $E\left[V_{cap}\right] \le 2r^4 2^{-2j}$.

Each sub-cube has 6 faces and there are $2^{3j}$ total sub-cubes, so by the union bound, the probability that a particular pair of vertices is connected but lie in different sub-cubes is then at most $6 \times 2^{3j} \times 2r^4 2^{-2j} = 12r^4 2^j$. There are at most $|V|^2/2$ pairs of vertices, so the expected number of edges crossing between different sub-cubes is $6r^4|V|^2 2^j$. □

Definition 2. *Given a graph with $n$ vertices and cache size $M \in \mathbb{N}$, define $j_M \in \mathbb{N}$ as the minimum $j$ such that $M \ge 2^{-3j}n\left(1 + \sqrt{(9\ln n)/(2^{-3j}n)}\right)$.*

Lemma 2. *Given a graph with $n$ vertices and $M \ge 100 \ln n$, then $\sqrt{(9\ln n)/(2^{-3j_M}n)} \le 1$ and $2^{j_M} \le \sqrt[3]{16n/M}$.*

Proof. As $M < 2^{-3(j_M-1)}n\left(1 + \sqrt{(9\ln n)/(2^{-3(j_M-1)}n)}\right)$ (otherwise, $j_M$ would not be minimal) and $100 \ln n \le M$, we have $2^{-3j_M}n > 9 \ln n$ by a quadratic inequality manipulation and thus $\sqrt{(9\ln n)/(2^{-3j_M}n)} \le 1$. Factoring out 8, we have $M < 8 \cdot 2^{-3j_M}n\left(1 + \sqrt{1/8}\sqrt{(9\ln n)/(2^{-3j_M}n)}\right) < 16 \cdot 2^{-3j_M}n$, and thus $2^{j_M} \le \sqrt[3]{16n/M}$. □

Lemma 3. *Given an $M$-vertex cache and a random cube graph $G = (V, E)$ divided into $2^{-j_M} \times 2^{-j_M} \times 2^{-j_M}$ sub-cubes, the probability that any sub-cube holds more than $M$ vertices is at most $|V|^{-2}$ for all $M \ge 100 \ln|V|$.*

Proof. Let $X_v$ be an indicator variable which indicates that vertex $v$ is in a particular sub-cube $C$. Let $n = |V|$ and $X = {}_v X_v$. Set $\mu = E[X] = 2^{-3j_M}n$ and $\sigma = \sqrt{(9\ln n)/(2^{-3j_M}n)}$ ($\sigma \le 1$ by Lemma 2), then apply the Chernoff bound [8]:

$$\Pr\{X \ge (1+\sigma)\mu\} \le \exp\left(-\sigma^2\mu/3\right) \quad \forall \sigma \in [0, 1].$$

Combining with the definition of $j_M$, we get that $\Pr\{X \ge M\} \le n^{-3}$. There are at most $n$ sub-cubes, so by the union bound, the probability that any hold more than $M$ vertices is at most $n \cdot n^{-3} = |V|^{-2}$. □

Theorem 4. *For any cache of $M \ge 100 \ln|V|$ vertices and random cube graph $G = (V, E)$ with $l^p$ distance parameter $r$ such that $E[|E|/|V|] = d$ is constant, a traversal of $G$, reordered using a Hilbert curve, incurs $O(M^{-1/3})$ expected misses per vertex.*

Proof. Let $n = |V|$. Let $C_i$ be the number of vertices held by the $i$th sub-cube. If $C_i < M\ \forall i$, then all neighbors within a sub-cube would hit in the cache, so the number of misses is at most the expected number of edges connecting vertices in different sub-cubes, which is itself at most $6r^4n^2 2^{j_M}$ by Lemma 1. The probability that not all sub-cubes hold fewer than $M$ vertices $\Pr\left\{\overline{C_i < M\ \forall i}\right\}$ is at most $n^{-2}$ by Lemma 3, and as the number of edges is at most $n^2$, the expected number of total misses is at most

$$\Pr\{C_i < M\ \forall i\} \cdot 6r^4n^2 2^{j_M} + n^{-2} \cdot n^2 \le 6r^4n^2 2^{j_M} + 1.$$

Dividing by $n$ vertices and substituting using Lemma 2, the expected number of misses per vertex is $O\left(r^4 n \sqrt[3]{n/M}\right)$.

The expected number of edges per vertex $d$ in a random cube graph is equal to the volume of the radius-$r$ ball under the $l^p$ norm, times the number of vertices $n$. To upper bound the number of expected misses, we find the maximum $r$ across all norms such that the volume of the radius-$r$ ball equals $d$. This occurs when $l^p = l^1$ and the volume is $(4/3)r^3$, thus $r \le \sqrt[3]{3d/(4n)}$ for all $l^p$. Since $d = O(1)$, the expected number of misses per vertex is at most

$$O\left(\frac{3dn}{4n}\sqrt[3]{\frac{3dn}{4nM}}\right) = O\left(M^{-1/3}\right).$$

□

### 2.3 Generalizing to arbitrary volumes

To simulate graphs with complex volumes, we extend our analysis to random arbitrary-volume graphs.

DEFINITION 3. *The position $\vec{x}_v$ of each vertex $v$ in an $n$-vertex* ***random cube graph*** *is chosen uniformly randomly within a volume enclosed by a surface $\mathcal{S}$ and the edge set $E = \{(u, v) \in V \times V : \|\vec{x}_u - \vec{x}_v\|_p < r\}$ connects vertices within non-negative $l^p$ distance $r$.*

Each such graph has a fill-factor $\rho$, the fraction of the unit cube that is occupied by the surface after scaling it so that the unit cube is the surface's bounding cube.

THEOREM 5. *Let $G$ be a random arbitrary-volume graph filling a fraction $\rho \in (0, 1]$ of the unit cube. Given a cache of $M \geq 100 \ln|V|$ vertices, for all $l^p$ and all $r = O\left((\rho/|V|)^{1/3}\right)$, a traversal of $G$ reordered using a Hilbert curve incurs $O\left((1/\rho)M^{-1/3}\right)$ misses per vertex.*

PROOF. Let the vertices of $G$ lie within a volume enclosed by a surface $\mathcal{S}$. We start with a random cube graph ordered using a Hilbert curve, and remove all vertices that lie outside the volume enclosed by $\mathcal{S}$. Each removal of a vertex makes the distance between all remaining vertex pairs either stay the same or decrease by one. Thus the total expected number of misses of an $M$-vertex cache is no more than with a $(|V|/\rho)$-vertex random cube graph, $O\left((r^4|V|^2/\rho^2)\sqrt[3]{|V|/\rho M}\right)$. Since $G$ has $|V|$ vertices, the expected number of misses per vertex is $O\left((r^4|V|/\rho^2)\sqrt[3]{|V|/\rho M}\right)$.

To maximize the expected number of misses, we maximize $r = O\left((\rho/|V|)^{1/3}\right)$, the value of $r$ that would yield a $(|V|/\rho)$-vertex random cube graph with $O(1)$ expected degree by Theorem 4. Then, the expected number of misses per vertex is $O\left((1/\rho)M^{-1/3}\right)$. □

By plugging in the fill-factor $\rho$ of a real-world graph into the above bound, we can estimate that graph's expected cache miss rate. Figure 4 confirms that these predictions are quite accurate across a variety of real-world graph topologies.

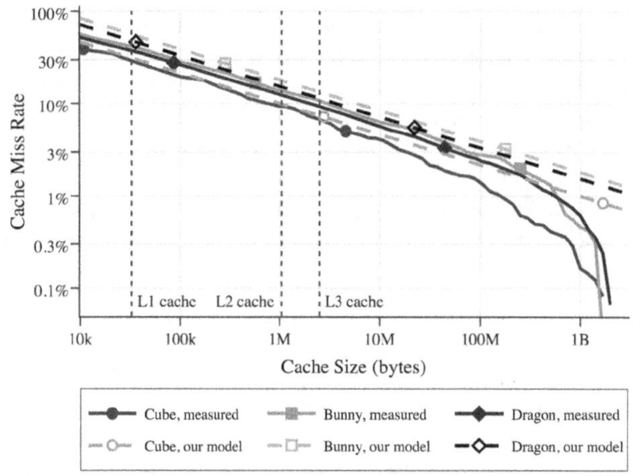


**Figure 4: Model estimates and empirical measurements of cache miss rates during a traversal of the bunny, dragon, and cube graphs described in Section 4. Estimates are calculated based on the input graph's fill-factor, as described in Section 2.3. The empirical measurements closely follow the model's estimates across all cache sizes.**

## 3 THE LAIKA SCHEDULER

We now describe LAIKA, a new in-place DAG scheduling algorithm. While it still uses a dependency counter at each vertex, LAIKA intentionally limits the exposed parallelism in the computation, thereby eliminating up to 99% of the coordination overhead caused by atomic counter decrements.

### 3.1 Laika algorithm

The algorithm breaks up the vertex array into contiguous chunks of size $2^b$. Following the rule of thumb defined in [10, p. 783] that a program with at least $10P$ parallelism should achieve nearly perfect linear speedup on $P$ processors, we set $b$ to the maximum integer such that $|V|/2^b > 10P$. Chunks are equally divided in two phases. Phases are processed serially, and in each phase chunks are processed in parallel. A barrier between the two phases obviates the need to protect against a data race between neighboring vertices from different phases. Due to the proximity-preserving Hilbert reordering of the vertices, most of the neighbors of any vertex $v$ are nearby in memory. Only edges between vertices that simultaneously are in different chunks and in the same phase require atomic decrements — empirically, 1–2% of all edges for the maximal-sized graphs in Section 4. The remaining 98–99% of all edges do not require *any scheduling computation whatsoever* — this is how LAIKA avoids the bulk of the coordination overhead incurred by JP. LAIKA uses a sawtooth-like priority function (see Figure 5) to ensure that edges between vertices in a single chunk are directed to create *forward dependencies*. Vertices near the beginning of a chunk (e.g., $v$ in chunk 3) may have successors at the end of the previous chunk (i.e., chunk 2) and so a *backward dependency*. Forward dependencies within the same chunk are implicitly satisfied by the serial processing of chunks. The proximity-preserving reordering causes many backward dependencies to fall in the opposite phase of an adjacent chunk, implicitly satisfying them.

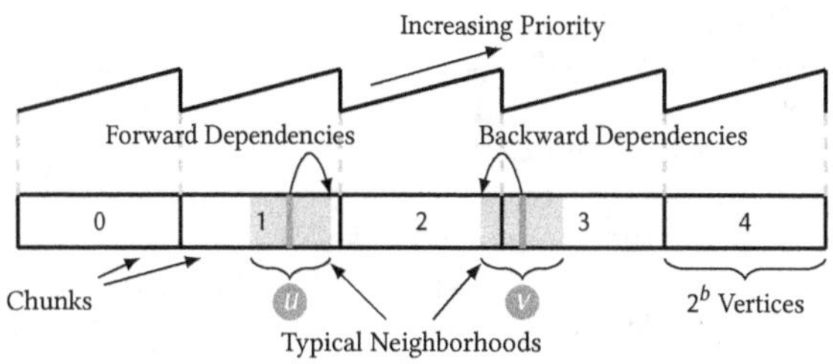


**Figure 5: Visualization of the LAIKA scheduling algorithm. Hilbert proximity-preserving reordering makes the neighbors of the vertices labeled $u$ and $v$ predominantly lie in the shaded regions surrounding them ("typical neighborhoods").**

LAIKA uses an explicit randomized work-stealing scheduler (Figure 6), to coordinate chunk processing among $P$ workers. Workers claim work from a set of $P$ heap-allocated concurrent queues, all of which are visible to all workers. Each worker executes the function LAIKA-WORKER in parallel, coordinating their work through the work queues, $Q[0{:}P\text{-}1]$, and a shared counter *activeChunks* initialized in the parent function LAIKA.

In Figure 7, each worker independently counts the rounds of the data-graph computation and the two phases of each round. Each phase begins with all workers pushing the chunks that nominally "belong" to them into their respective queues, as implemented in the function PUSH-CHUNKS in Figure 8. For example, we assume without loss of generality that $P$ evenly divides $|V|$, there are $N = |V|/P$ chunks per worker and worker $p$ pushes chunks $[N \cdot p, N \cdot (p+1) - 1]$ into $Q[p]$ on line 9. Workers then independently steal work from randomly selected queues on line 11; a successful steal retrieves the pair $\langle c, idx \rangle$, where $c$ is a chunk and $idx$ is the index of the next vertex in $c$ to be processed, on line 14. The worker will work on chunk $c$, as implemented by the function PROCESS-CHUNK in Figure 8, until it either finishes the last vertex in the phase or it cannot proceed due to an unmet dependency. Let $w$ be the next vertex to be processed in chunk $c$, and consider the case where it has a dependency counter greater than 0. The worker must prematurely stop processing $c$, and $c$ is ***shelved***. The worker indicates that $c$ has been shelved by decrementing the dependency counter of $w$. Thus, when the last predecessor of $w$ is processed, $w$'s dependency counter will be decremented to a value of $-1$, indicating that $w$'s chunk $c$ had been shelved when $w$ was the next vertex to be processed.

```
LAIKA(G, b, rounds)
1  let G = (V, E)
2  parallel for v ∈ V
3      N'(v) = {w ∈ N(v) :
4          SAME-PHASE(w, v) ∧ DIFFERENT-CHUNK(w, v)}
5      v.pred = {w ∈ N'(v) : ρ(w) < ρ(v)}
6      v.counter = |v.pred|
7      v.succ = {w ∈ N'(v) : ρ(w) > ρ(v)}
8  P = GET-NUM-WORKERS()
9  Q = ALLOCATE-QUEUES(P)
10 activeChunks = 0
11 for p = 1 to P
12     spawn LAIKA-WORKER(G, Q, b, activeChunks, rounds, P)
```

**Figure 6: The LAIKA data-graph computation scheduling algorithm. DIFFERENT-CHUNK$(w, v)$ returns TRUE iff $w$ and $v$ are in different chunks (i.e., $\lfloor w/2^b \rfloor \neq \lfloor v/2^b \rfloor$). SAME-PHASE$(w, v)$ returns TRUE iff $w$ and $v$ are in the same phase (i.e., $\lfloor (w \bmod 2^b)/2^{b-1} \rfloor == \lfloor (v \bmod 2^b)/2^{b-1} \rfloor$). The priority function and these two helper functions allow LAIKA to find, for each vertex $v$, the predecessor and successor vertex sets that require explicit dependency tracking.**

```
LAIKA-WORKER(G, Q, b, activeChunks, rounds, P)
1  let G = (V, E)
2  p = GET-WORKER-ID()
3  start[0] = 0; start[1] = 2^(b-1)
4  end[0] = 2^(b-1); end[1] = 2^b
5  N = |V|/P
6  for round = 1 to rounds
7      for phase = 0 to 1
8          ATOMIC-ADD(activeChunks, N)
9          PUSH-CHUNKS(Q[p], N · p, N, start[phase])
10         while activeChunks > 0
11             ⟨c, idx⟩ = POP(Q[RAND() (mod P)])
12             if c ≠ NIL
13                 v = V[idx + c · 2^b]
14                 if PROCESS-CHUNK(v, Q[p], b) == end[phase]
15                     ATOMIC-DEC(activeChunks)
16         BARRIER()
```

**Figure 7: The LAIKA-WORKER function executed by each worker. Each worker independently maintains the round and phase number (lines 6 and 7) via a shared variable, *activeChunks*. Each chunk is initially pushed onto its corresponding work queue on line 9, and the shared counter *activeChunks* is incremented for each chunk on line 8.**

Figure 8 shows that the function PROCESS-CHUNK$(v, Q, b)$ sequentially processes each vertex in the chunk, starting with $v$, until it cannot proceed due to an unmet dependency, as detected by the two logical clauses on line 1. If $v$ is ready for processing (i.e., all vertices in the set $v.pred$ have been updated), then the user-supplied UPDATE$(v)$ function is called and the counter $v.counter$ is reset to $|v.pred|$, on lines 2 and 3, respectively. If any post-decrement counter value $w.counter$ equals $-1$, then $w$'s chunk had been previously shelved and is now re-enabled, and so must be pushed onto its work queue on line 8. Finally, PROCESS-CHUNK moves on to the next vertex on line 9 and tests if the new vertex marks the start of a new phase on line 10, in which case the function returns.

```
PUSH-CHUNKS(Q, chunk, numChunks, start)
1  parallel for c = 0 to numChunks − 1
2      PUSH(Q, ⟨chunk + c, start⟩)

PROCESS-CHUNK(v, Q, b)
1  while v.counter == 0 or DEC-AND-FETCH(v.counter) == −1
2      UPDATE(v)
3      v.counter = |v.pred|
4      for w ∈ v.succ
5          if DEC-AND-FETCH(w.counter) == −1
6              c = ⌊w/2^b⌋
7              idx = w mod 2^b
8              PUSH(Q, ⟨c, idx⟩)
9      v = v + 1
10     if v ≡ 0 (mod 2^(b-1))
11         return v
12 return v
```

**Figure 8: Helper functions for LAIKA. PUSH-CHUNKS merely pushes onto the work queues $Q$ the range of chunks $[chunk, chunk + numChunks - 1]$ "belonging" to the worker calling the function, each with the index within the chunk of its starting vertex, *start*. PROCESS-CHUNK attempts to make as much progress as possible on the chunk, starting with vertex $v$, until it either finishes the chunk, on line 10, or reaches a vertex whose counter value indicates unmet dependencies, on line 1. If another worker happens to satisfy $v$'s last dependency and perform the final decrement to $v.counter$, then DEC-AND-FETCH will return $-1$, which indicates that all dependencies for $v$ have been met.**

## 3.2 Analysis of Laika

We make the reasonable assumption that the data-graph computation is ***ordinary*** — i.e. the UPDATE($v$) function executes serially in $O(N(v))$ time for all $v \in V$.

THEOREM 6. *LAIKA is work-efficient for any ordinary data-graph computation on any graph $G = (V, E)$.*

PROOF. LAIKA calls UPDATE once per vertex per iteration, just as in the baseline serial execution. Furthermore, there are at most $|E|$ calls to DEC-AND-FETCH made on counters on line 5. Finally, shelving and reactivating a chunk costs $O(1)$ work, and any vertex $v$ can only cause at most one shelving, so the total cost of shelving chunks is $O(|V|)$. Therefore, LAIKA performs $O(|V| + |E|)$ work and is work-efficient. □

LEMMA 7. *Let $G = (V, E)$ be a random cube graph with expected degree $d$. For any $c > 0$, the maximum degree $\max_{v \in V} |N(v)|$ is greater than $2d+3(4+c)\ln|V|$ with probability no more than $|V|^{-(3+c)}$.*

PROOF. Let $r$ be the distance parameter of $G$ — the radius of the sphere such that vertices within a distance $r$ are connected by an edge. Consider a vertex $v$ of $G$, and let $X_w$ be a indicator variable where $X_w == 1$ denotes the event that a vertex $w$ is connected to vertex $v$. For any $w \neq v$, the probability of an edge between $v$ and $w$ is $d/|V|$. We use now the Chernoff bound [8] for deviations of more than 1 times the mean:

$$\Pr\{D \geq (1+\beta) \cdot \mathrm{E}[D]\} \leq \exp(-(\beta/3)\mathrm{E}[D]) \quad \forall \beta > 1,$$

where $D = {}_w X_w$ [10, p. 1203]. By definition, $D = |N(v)|$, and $\mathrm{E}[|N(v)|] = d$. Let $\beta = (d + 3(4+c)\ln|V|)/d$. Then,

$$\Pr\{|N(v)| \geq 2d + 3(4+c)\ln|V|\} \leq |V|^{-(4+c)}.$$

We use the union bound across all $|V|$ vertices to see that $G$ has maximum degree greater than $2d + 3(4+c)\ln|V|$ with probability at most $|V| \cdot |V|^{-(4+c)} = |V|^{-(3+c)}$. □

LEMMA 8. *Let $G = (V, E)$ be a graph with maximum degree $\Delta$, let $n_G = |V|$, and let $G_\rho$ be a priority DAG induced on $G$ by a random priority function $\rho$. For any $c > 0$, there exists a directed path of length $e^2 \cdot \max\{\Delta, (4+c)\ln n\}$ in $G_\rho$ for any $n \geq n_G$ with probability at most $n^{-(3+c)}$.*

PROOF. For any $v_1, v_2, \ldots, v_k$, $p = \langle v_1, v_2, \ldots, v_k \rangle$ is a directed path in $G_\rho$ with probability at most $1/k! \leq (e/k)^k$, by Stirling's approximation [10, p. 57], There are at most $n_G \Delta^k$ paths in $G$ — $n_G$ potential starting points, and at most $\Delta$ potential neighbors of each vertex. By the union bound, $G_\rho$ can contain a directed path of length $k \geq e^2 \cdot \max\{\Delta, (4+c)\ln n\}$ with probability at most

$$\begin{aligned} n_G \left(\frac{e\Delta}{k}\right)^k &\leq n_G \cdot \exp\left(-k \ln\left(\frac{e^2 \max\{\Delta, (4+c)\ln n\}}{e\Delta}\right)\right) \\ &\leq n_G \cdot \exp(-k) \\ &\leq n_G \cdot \exp\left(-(e^2 \max\{\Delta, (4+c)\ln n\})\right) \\ &\leq n^{-(3+c)}. \end{aligned}$$

□

THEOREM 9. *Let $G = (V, E)$ be a random cube graph with expected degree $d$. Let $n = |V|$. For any $c > 0$ and $0 \leq b < \lg n - 1$, LAIKA with chunk size $2^b$ executes an ordinary data-graph computation on $G$ with span greater than $e^2(2d + 3(4+c)\ln n)^2 2^b$ with probability less than $n^{-(2+c)}$.*

PROOF. Consider LAIKB, an modification of LAIKA where the $k$th vertex from all chunks must be processed before the $k + 1$st vertex from any chunk. LAIKA is always at least as fast as LAIKB, so it suffices to prove that LAIKB satisfies the lemma. LAIKA randomly directs edges between vertices at equal positions within their chunks, so at each chunk position $k$, such dependent edges form the priority DAG $G_k$ of Lemma 8. Then, LAIKB's span will be less than the product of:

- the maximum degree (as UPDATE($v$) is serial with $|N(v)|$ work);
- the maximum depth among the $2^b$ random priority DAGs $\{G_1, G_2, \ldots, G_{2^b}\}$; and
- the total number of priority DAGs, $2^b$.

Let $A_\Delta$ be the event that the maximum degree in $G$ exceeds $\Delta = 2d + 3(4+c)\ln n$ and let $A_{G_k}$ be the event that the depth of the priority DAG $G_k$ exceeds $e^2\Delta$, for all $k \in [1, 2^b]$. The event $\overline{A_\Delta} \cap \{\forall_k \overline{A_{G_k}}\}$ would imply that the overall span of LAIKB applied to $G$ is at most $e^2(2d + 3(4+c)\ln n)^2 2^b$, since $\Delta > (4+c)\ln n$ when $\overline{A_\Delta}$ is true, as required by Lemma 8. We use De Morgan's law to find the negation of this event, and following from Lemmas 7 and 8, we see that the probability of the event $A_\Delta \cup \{\forall_k A_{G_k}\}$ is at most $n^{-(2+c)}$. □

COROLLARY 10. *Let $n = |V|$. With $P = O(n/\log^2 n)$ workers, LAIKA produces linear expected speedup.*

PROOF. The expected work of one iteration of the data-graph computation is $\mathrm{E}[{}_{v \in V}|N(v)|] = d|V| = 2|E|$. Let $A_S$ denote the event that the computation has span exceeding $e^2(2d + 3(4+c)\ln n)^2$. By Theorem 9, this occurs with probability at most $n^{-(2+c)}$, letting $2^b$ equal 1. Thus, the expected parallelism (the ratio of work to span) is at least

$$\begin{aligned} &\geq \Pr\{\overline{A_S}\} \frac{2|E|}{e^2(2d + 3(4+c)\ln n)^2} + \Pr\{A_S\} \cdot 1 \\ &\geq \left(1 - n^{-(2+c)}\right) \frac{2|E|}{e^2(2d + 3(4+c)\ln n)^2} + n^{-(2+c)} \cdot 1 \\ &\geq \left(1 - n^{-(2+c)}\right) \left(\frac{2|E|}{e^2(2d + 3(4+c)\ln n)^2} - 1\right) \\ &= \Omega(n/\log^2 n). \end{aligned}$$

LAIKA is a randomized work-stealing scheduler [5], so the expected runtime is at most the work $O(|V| + |E|)$ divided by the number $P$ of workers, plus the span $e^2(2d + 3(4+c)\ln n)^2$. Constraining $P$ to be less than the parallelism makes the first term dominate and thus LAIKA runs in $O((|V| + |E|)/P)$ time. A similar analysis holds for smaller values of $P$ and correspondingly larger values of $2^b$. □

## 4 EMPIRICAL EVALUATION

We compare LAIKA across four graph topologies against the serial baseline and four alternative parallel schedulers:

**BSP** — A deterministic Jacobi-type scheduler that uses double-buffering to avoid determinacy races [12]. BSP stands for bulk-synchronous parallel execution [31].

**LOCKS** — An in-place scheduler that simply updates all vertices in parallel with reader-writer locks for concurrency control, yielding a nondeterministic result [26].

**CHROMA** — A chromatic scheduler that colors the graph and serially loops through the colors, updating all vertices of the given color in parallel without the need for mutual-exclusion locks or atomic operations [21].

**JP** — A parallel DAG scheduler [20] built on a recursive function that updates a vertex once all of its predecessors have been updated using atomic operations.

These alternative schedulers satisfy at most one of the three properties outlined in our optimization strategy: CHROMA and BSP exhibit synchronization-overhead minimization due to their efficient parallelization, while JP exhibits execution locality as it recursively executes neighboring vertices' update functions.

To evaluate LAIKA, we conduct four studies:

**PER-ITERATION RUNTIME** — A per-iteration runtime analysis shows that LAIKA maintains nearly-linear parallel speedup across input sizes and topologies, and is 6.97–12.60x faster per iteration than the alternative parallel schedulers. None of the alternative schedulers match LAIKA's performance, even with Hilbert-reordered inputs.

**SCALABILITY** — We analyze the scalability of each scheduler by measuring its parallel speedup on 12, 24, 36, and 48 cores, as shown in Figure 13. On 48 cores, we measured a parallel speedup of 38.4x for LAIKA, whereas all other schedulers scale less well. BSP, in particular, only achieves 28.05x speedup on 48 cores, even with Hilbert-reordered inputs. We also corroborate our theoretical analysis in Section 2 by collecting hardware performance counters in each operating regime.

**CONVERGENCE RATE** — We present evidence supporting the conventional wisdom [3, 6, 30] that in-place executions generally require fewer iterations to converge than double-buffered executions. LAIKA consistently converges faster in wall-clock time than alternative schedulers, including the double-buffered BSP scheduler.

**IDEALIZED PERFORMANCE** — We show that LAIKA captures 54% of the theoretical upper bound of available performance, as defined by an ideal scheduler that achieves perfect linear speedup over the serial baseline scheduler.

### Experimental setup

We implemented LAIKA and the other schedulers with a similar level of performance engineering in Cilk and C++, compiled them with `GCC 7.3.0` with with these switches: `-fcilkplus -std=c++11 -O3 -Wall -m64 -march=native -mtune=native -pthread -ffast-math -fgcse-las`. All tests were executed on an Amazon EC2 m5.24xlarge cloud instance, a dual-socket system consisting of two 2.5GHz Intel Xeon Platinum 8175 (Skylake) CPU

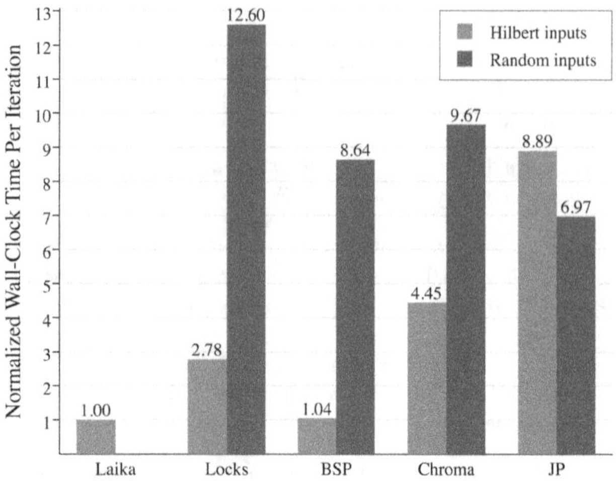


**Figure 9: Comparison of per-iteration wall-clock runtimes for each scheduler, in geometric mean across all topologies of the largest (5.4GB) input graphs, and normalized to LAIKA's runtime. For each alternative scheduler, the left bar (labeled "Hilbert inputs") represents the scheduler's performance when using Hilbert-reordered input data, while the right bar (labeled "Random inputs") represents the performance when using the original input order of each graph. LAIKA's per-iteration runtime is faster than any other scheduler, and remains 2.78–8.89 times faster than the other in-place schedulers even when they are provided Hilbert-reordered inputs.**

chips with a total of 48 physical processor cores. While we were not able to disable hyperthreading on the system, we used the `taskset` command to prevent execution of experiment code on hyperthreads. We disabled transparent huge pages system-wide, as the associated kernel activity can introduce measurement errors. Amazon EC2 instances enable dynamic frequency scaling, and unfortunately do not allow this setting to be changed. Our code is available online [14].

We intentionally chose an UPDATE function that is difficult to schedule efficiently, since it executes only 2.22 instructions per byte of data. Such an update function exposes scheduler overheads; in the absence of good cache locality the computation will quickly become memory-bound on even a few cores [32]. This update function also presents difficulty for in-place execution, as the double-buffered execution requires only 1.1–1.5 times as many iterations compared to an in-place execution. For comparison, this iterations ratio can be as high as 8x for some multigrid method [6] computations. Our UPDATE function performs a physical simulation named Mass-Spring-Dashpot [18], simulating a set of weights of unit mass (vertices) in 3D space, connected by springs (edges). Each vertex experiences air drag proportional to its velocity, as well as spring restoration forces under compression or tension.

We used four different graph topologies, each in five different sizes between 20MB (100k vertices) and 5.4GB (27M vertices). Each size increases the number of vertices roughly by a factor of 4, while retaining an average of 11–15 edges per vertex. The graph topology named *rand* is a random cube graph. The graphs named *dragon*, *bunny*, and *cube* were generated using `TetGen` [28], a tetrahedralizing mesh refinement engine that converts a 2D surface mesh (e.g.,

| *Scheduler* | *Size* | $T_{1,H}/\lvert E\rvert$ | $T_{48,H}/\lvert E\rvert$ | $T_{1,H}/T_{48,H}$ |
|---|---|---|---|---|
| LAIKA | 20MB | 11.39 | 0.83 | 13.80 |
| | 80MB | 11.31 | 0.48 | 23.72 |
| | 330MB | 15.87 | 0.40 | 39.25 |
| | 1.3GB | 12.61 | 0.31 | 40.47 |
| | 5.4GB | 11.93 | 0.31 | 38.41 |

**Table 10: Geometric mean of LAIKA runtimes across all graph topologies for each Hilbert-reordered input size. $T_1/|E|$ and $T_{48}/|E|$ denotes the runtime, in nanoseconds, of one iteration with 1 and 48 workers, normalized by the number of edges in the input. $T_1/T_{48}$ is the parallel speedup on 48 cores. The 20MB inputs fit within L2 cache, whereas the 80MB inputs fit within L3 cache. As soon as the input graph's size exceeds L3 cache, LAIKA is able to capture over 80% of the perfect parallel speedup possible on 48 cores.**

| *Scheduler* | *Graph* | $T_{1,H}/\lvert E\rvert$ | $T_{48,H}/\lvert E\rvert$ | $T_{1,H}/T_{48,H}$ |
|---|---|---|---|---|
| LAIKA | dragon | 12.26 | 0.29 | 42.00 |
| | bunny | 11.58 | 0.34 | 34.06 |
| | cube | 12.32 | 0.29 | 41.76 |
| | rand | 11.58 | 0.32 | 36.45 |

**Table 11: LAIKA runtimes across all graph topologies, using the largest, 5.4GB-sized input sets. The measurement column headings are equivalent to Table 10.**

a surface tessellated by triangles) into a corresponding 3D volume mesh tessellated by non-overlapping tetrahedra.

All measurements ignore the time taken to read the graph input files from disk, and any time taken for Hilbert curve reordering of the input. For the largest input graphs, Hilbert reordering took less than 9 seconds, whereas merely reading the graph from disk took 27 seconds; both times are a negligible fraction of the hours of wall-clock time of computation required to reach convergence.

## 4.1 Per-iteration runtime behavior

We measured the per-iteration execution runtimes of each scheduler across different graph topologies and sizes to determine the speedup of LAIKA versus other in-place, deterministic schedulers (CHROMA and JP), as well as the performance penalty of in-place updates and determinism relative to BSP and LOCKS, respectively. Using input graphs reordered with the Hilbert curve, Table 10 demonstrates how as soon as the graph is large enough to not fit in the system's cache, LAIKA shows good parallel speedup; Table 11 indicates that this speedup is insensitive to the specific bounding volume and topology (i.e., bunny versus dragon). Table 12 shows that LAIKA, using a Hilbert-reordered graph, is significantly faster (6.97–12.60x) than any alternative scheduler running on a randomly-ordered graph, and yields a 222.57x speedup over the serial baseline.

Even with LAIKA's Hilbert curve reordering, all other in-place schedulers remain slower than LAIKA, as we see in Figure 9 and Table 12. Per iteration, LAIKA is 4.45 times faster than CHROMA, 8.89 times faster than JP, and 2.78 times faster than LOCKS. As LAIKA outperforms the nondeterministic LOCKS scheduler, LAIKA's cost of determinism is *negative*. LAIKA is also 28.38 times faster than the

| *Scheduler* | $\frac{T_{1,R}}{T_{1,L}}$ | $\frac{T_{48,R}}{T_{48,L}}$ | $\frac{T_{1,R}}{T_{48,L}}$ | $\frac{T_{1,H}}{T_{1,L}}$ | $\frac{T_{48,H}}{T_{48,L}}$ | $\frac{T_{1,H}}{T_{48,L}}$ |
|---|---|---|---|---|---|---|
| LOCKS | 8.51 | 12.60 | 326.78 | 2.60 | 2.78 | 100.25 |
| BSP | 5.79 | 8.64 | 222.57 | 0.74 | 1.04 | 28.38 |
| CHROMA | 6.32 | 9.67 | 242.59 | 1.68 | 4.45 | 64.39 |
| JP | 4.29 | 6.97 | 164.64 | 1.36 | 8.89 | 52.36 |
| LAIKA | 6.38 | 9.60 | 245.28 | 1.00 | 1.00 | 38.41 |

**Table 12: Relative speedup of LAIKA compared to alternative schedulers on the largest input set in geometric mean across all graph topologies. $T_{k,R}$ and $T_{k,H}$ refer to an execution using $k$ workers of a Randomly or Hilbert-reordered input. $T_{k,L}$ refers to a $k$-worker execution of the Hilbert-reordered input graph using LAIKA.**

serial baseline scheduler applied to Hilbert-reordered graphs. Finally, the cost of LAIKA's in-place updates appear to be outweighed by BSP's cost of accessing two copies of vertex state: LAIKA is actually 4% faster per iteration than BSP with Hilbert-reordered inputs, while enabling further wall-clock speedups due to the superior convergence properties of in-place updates. For instance, as discussed in Section 4.3, LAIKA fully converges (to a remaining fraction of graph's initial energy of $1.18x10^{-8}$) on the largest *rand* input graph 28.6% faster than BSP.

## 4.2 Scalability

Figure 13 illustrates LAIKA's superior scalability compared to all other schedulers, even on Hilbert-reordered inputs. LAIKA continues to achieve linear speedup with as many as 48 cores, whereas BSP with Hilbert inputs is already straining to maintain linear speedup with only 24 cores. It is tempting to extrapolate that LAIKA would continue to scale well at least in a weak-scaling regime [15], while BSP has nearly saturated memory and cross-socket communication bandwidth and will have trouble scaling much further. Figure 13 hints that CHROMA is already in this situation: even though Hilbert reordering improves its per-iteration wall-clock speed, it comes at a significant scaling penalty starting at 24 cores.

We used the Linux `perf stat` utility to measure a variety of CPU performance countersand provide further insight into the differences in scalability across schedulers. We also measured the parallel speedup on 48 cores for unordered (random-order) and Hilbert-reordered inputs, and the relative speedup afforded by the reordering process; Table 14 shows our results.

Without reordering, all schedulers show evidence of poor cache utilization as predicted in Section 2 — their parallel speedup is only 23.49–26.05x on 48 cores, while incurring 0.53–1.27 LLC misses per edge and roughly 0.5 dTLB misses per edge. The dTLB is a small cache of translations between virtual and physical memory. If the virtual address being loaded is not present in the dTLB, a "page walk" occurs. The page walk traverses a tree structure that resides in memory and is cached in the LLC, just as any other memory state — competing for cache space with the data of the application itself. Therefore, each dTLB miss imposes a high latency penalty and frequently causes additional LLC misses. Given unordered input, all schedulers except for JP tend to suffer over 1 LLC miss for each edge they read; JP's recursive structure tends to reuse some cached vertex data regardless of input order, making it suffer only about half as many misses as the other schedulers.

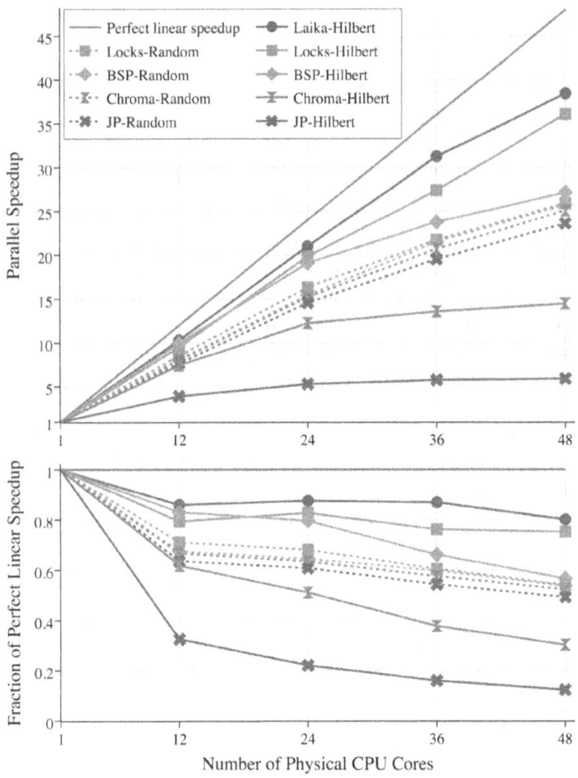


**Figure 13: Scalability (achieved parallel speedup) of different schedulers as a function of the number of physical CPU cores of the execution, in geometric mean across all topologies of the largest (5.4GB) input graphs. The top plot represents the measured parallel speedup, while the bottom plot shows the achieved fraction of perfect linear speedup. Dashed lines (labeled ending in "Random") correspond to schedulers using the original input order, whereas solid lines (labeled ending in "Hilbert") correspond to schedulers using our proximity-preserving reordered graph. LAIKA shows better scalability than any other scheduler, even when the alternative schedulers are provided Hilbert-reordered inputs. LAIKA always captures 80%+ of the ideal parallel speedup, achieving 38.4x speedup on 48 cores. Meanwhile, BSP's doubled memory usage, CHROMA's high cache miss rate, and JP's expensive atomic instructions cause these three schedulers to only capture less than 60% of the ideal parallel speedup with 48 cores, even on Hilbert-reordered inputs.**

Hilbert-reordered inputs significantly reduce all schedulers' LLC and dTLB miss rates, as a consequence of the cache advantages examined theoretically in Section 2 and empirically measured as shown in Table 14. For example, LAIKA with Hilbert ordering incurs 7.38 times fewer cache misses and 104.73 times fewer dTLB misses, making it 9.36 times faster overall. Reordering also appears to render prefetchers more effective, likely due to a more regular memory access pattern. However, the lower miss rates do not benefit all schedulers equally, and may in fact make performance worse! The reordering cannot alleviate JP's execution of expensive atomic decrements: the same recursive structure that improved its reuse of cached data now exacerbates memory contention between those atomic instructions, causing JP on 48 cores with Hilbert inputs to only achieve 77% of the performance of using unordered inputs.

| *Scheduler* | LLC Misses / Edge *R* / *H* | dTLB Misses / Edge *R* / *H* | $\frac{T_{1,R}}{T_{48,R}}$ | $\frac{T_{1,H}}{T_{48,H}}$ | $\frac{T_{48,R}}{T_{48,H}}$ |
|---|---|---|---|---|---|
| LOCKS | 1.27 / 0.154 | 0.514 / 5.50e-3 | 26.05 | 36.85 | 4.71 |
| BSP | 1.08 / 0.132 | 0.504 / 2.79e-3 | 25.62 | 28.05 | 8.85 |
| CHROMA | 1.17 / 0.655 | 0.517 / 2.25e-2 | 25.00 | 16.12 | 2.36 |
| JP | 0.53 / 0.165 | 0.226 / 2.68e-2 | 23.49 | 5.67 | 0.77 |
| LAIKA | 1.10 / 0.149 | 0.509 / 4.86e-3 | 25.71 | 36.45 | 9.36 |

**Table 14: Speedup and hardware performance counter measurements of data-graph computation schedulers executing the Mass-Spring-Dashpot model with 48 workers on the maximal-sized *rand* graph. The data under the subheadings *R* and *H* is taken with a Random and Hilbert ordering, respectively. The "LLC Misses / Edge" and "dTLB Misses / Edge" columns show the average number of load and store misses per edge use per iteration. LAIKA with Hilbert ordering incurs fewer LLC and dTLB misses than any other in-place scheduler. For example, LAIKA incurs 4.4 times fewer LLC misses and 4.6 times fewer dTLB misses than CHROMA.**

Similarly, the spatial locality produced by the reordering cannot alleviate CHROMA's poor temporal execution locality — it still incurs 0.655 LLC misses per edge as it reads each vertex in the graph approximately once for every color needed to color the graph, typically 3–5 colors for mesh graphs. While this is enough to improve performance by a factor of 2.36 relative to using unordered input, it is not sufficient to ensure good scalability, as the high LLC miss rate consumes large amounts of memory bandwidth.

In contrast, Hilbert-reordered inputs allows LOCKS, BSP, and LAIKA to achieve much better performance on 48 cores than with unordered input graphs. Because of their predominantly sequential vertex access pattern and Hilbert reordering, these schedulers now display good execution locality. In addition, BSP and LAIKA have minimal coordination (much less often than once per edge), while the once-per-edge coordination in LOCKS mostly consists of uncontended reader lock acquisitions. As LAIKA was explicitly designed with well-ordered input in mind, it exhibits the highest reordering-related performance gain (9.36 times). While Hilbert reordering somewhat relieves the memory bandwidth bottleneck suffered by BSP using unordered graphs, its scalability is ultimately limited by the fact that BSP's double buffering execution reads twice as much vertex data as the in-order schedulers.

## 4.3 Convergence rate

As our chosen physical simulation dissipates energy with each iteration via air drag on the moving point masses, it converges as the remaining kinetic energy in the system decreases to a small fraction of the total energy present at the beginning of the computation.

We recorded the number of iterations and the required wall-clock runtime (up to 14 hours) for all schedulers to reach a given fraction of the initial energy in the system. We show part of these results on the largest (5.4GB, 27M vertices) *rand* graph in Figure 15: LAIKA (solid blue line) reaches any energy fraction significantly faster than any alternative scheduler (dashed lines), and remains faster to most energy levels versus the alternative schedulers running on Hilbert-reordered inputs (remaining solid lines). The colored markers denoting increments of 10,000 iterations in Figure 15 show

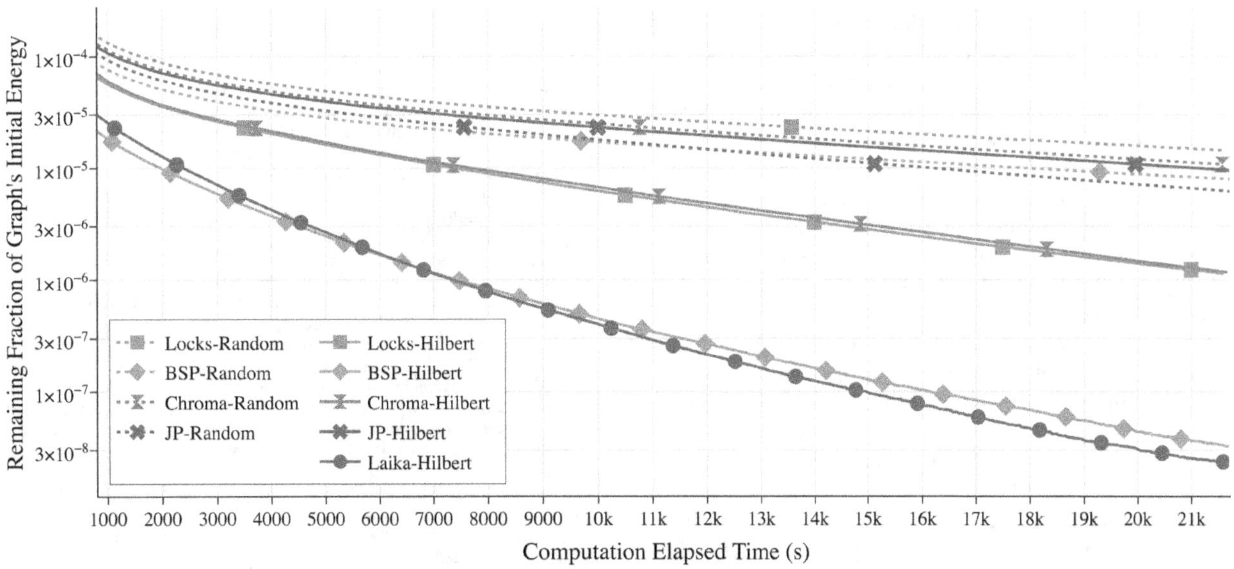


**Figure 15: Remaining fraction of initial kinetic energy, as a function of wall-clock time, for different schedulers on the 5.4GB (27M vertices) *rand* input graph. Dashed lines (labeled ending in "Random") correspond to schedulers using the original input order of the graph. Solid lines (labeled ending in "Hilbert") correspond to schedulers using our proximity-preserving reordered graph. For scale convenience, we stopped execution after six hours (21,600s) of wall-clock time. Colored markers denote multiples of 10,000 iterations for each scheduler, starting with the 10,000th iteration. Even on Hilbert-reordered inputs, all existing in-place schedulers take 2.6–8.8 times longer than Laika to reach any energy level.**

that in any fixed number of iterations, all in-place schedulers reach almost the same energy fraction, regardless of implementation or input reordering.

Furthermore, we see that for our physical simulation, all in-place schedulers exhibit superior per-iteration convergence rates compared to double-buffering: starting around energy fraction $3 \times 10^{-6}$ (approx. 4000s into the experiment), the colored markers of BSP with Hilbert-reordered data start appearing at higher energy fractions than the corresponding markers of in-place schedulers. Even though Laika's iterations are only 4% faster than BSP's iterations with Hilbert inputs, this difference in per-iteration convergence rates widens the performance gap between them with every iteration. After 14 hours of wall-clock execution time, the energy fraction that BSP with Hilbert data reaches is one that Laika achieved in only 10.86 hours — a performance gap of 28.6%. This effect is not unexpected, since many computations experience faster per-iteration convergence with in-place execution compared to double-buffering [3]. In fact, this difference in convergence rates in favor of in-place scheduling can be significantly higher than our physical simulation experiences — as high as 8x in some multigrid method computations [6].

## 4.4 Idealized performance

To estimate the remaining potential for improvement upon Laika's performance, we construct a theoretical model of an idealized scheduler that achieves perfect linear speedup, suffers no coordination overhead, and does no work other than executing update functions.

Our idealized scheduler is a physical manifestation of the *work law* from work-span analysis [10, p. 780]: the *serial baseline* scheduler already performs no coordination and has no other scheduling overhead; its perfectly-linear parallelization yields our idealized scheduler. Thus, if $T_{1,\text{SB}}$ denotes the serial baseline's runtime, the upper-bound on parallel performance with $P$ processors is $T_{1,\text{SB}}/P$, hence $T_{48,\text{IDEAL}} = T_{1,\text{SB}}/48$. In practice, this performance level is unattainable since a serial execution makes use of the entire LLC, whereas a parallel execution requires cores to share the LLC.

In geometric mean across all topologies of the largest, 5.4GB Hilbert-reordered input graphs, we calculate the ratio between the runtimes of Laika and the idealized scheduler: $T_{48,\text{LAIKA}}/T_{48,\text{IDEAL}} = 0.540$. Therefore, Laika captures 54% of the theoretical upper-bound performance, while providing both determinism and in-place execution. BSP with Hilbert-reordered inputs captures 51.7% of the upper-bound, while sacrificing in-place execution and its potential convergence rate advantages discussed in Section 4.3. The other in-place schedulers, even with Hilbert-reordered inputs, fall short: Locks achieves only 19.4% of the upper-bound while sacrificing determinism, while Chroma and JP provide deterministic execution but only manage 12.1% and 6.07%, respectively.

# 5 CONCLUSION

Practical high-performance data-graph computations are a challenging problem because they require both performance-engineering and domain-specific expertise. Attempting to improve usability, projects like Simit [24] and Prism [21] abstract away the scheduler and require the practitioner to only implement a serial update function for their computation. While we believe this is a good model, we have shown that the ability to adapt the scheduler to the particular input and computation can result in further performance gains for a variety of schedulers — up to 9.36x speedup in the case of simply Hilbert-reordering a mesh graph input.

Modular schedulers designed according to our three-step design strategy maximize performance by allowing practitioners to incorporate domain-specific expertise into the scheduler. For example, LAIKA relies on Hilbert curves for proximity-preserving reordering as we were able to prove their cache-efficiency on mesh graph inputs; however, with different inputs, one may wish to instead use a graph partitioning scheme like METIS [23], PT-Scotch [9], or Zoltan [7]. Similarly, if future research uncovers a more efficient technique for synchronization-overhead minimization, that part of the scheduler can be upgraded with minimal impact on the other scheduler components.

Such modularity also allows schedulers to adapt to different hardware architectures. While this paper focuses on shared-memory data-graph computations, the same ideas can in principle be applied to, e.g., high-performance distributed computing systems: Synchronization-overhead minimization and spatial and temporal locality become even more important when the worst-case latency costs increase by orders of magnitude, from RAM access to network access. We look forward to further exploring the potential performance gains stemming from this flexibility in our future work.

## ACKNOWLEDGMENTS

We would like to thank Charles E. Leiserson, Tao B. Schardl, and Tim Kaler from the Supertech group at MIT. They continue to be very generous with insights, humor, and technical assistance. We would like to thank Fredrik Kjølstad who inspired us to schedule data-graph computations on 3D mesh graphs and provided much needed context on real applications. Thanks to Leonid Taycher at Kensho Technologies for his patience, support, and understanding while this work was in progress. This work is sponsored in part by the Direction Générale de l'Armement, Kensho Technologies, and MIT's SuperUROP program; we thank them for their support.

## REFERENCES

[1] L. Adams and J. Ortega. 1982. A multi-color SOR method for parallel computation. In *International Conference on Parallel Processing*. 53–56.

[2] Mark Adams, Marian Brezina, Jonathan Hu, and Ray Tuminaro. 2003. Parallel Multigrid Smoothing: Polynomial versus Gauss-Seidel. *J. Comp. Phys* 188 (2003), 593–610.

[3] Mark F. Adams. 2001. A Distributed Memory Unstructured Gauss-Seidel Algorithm for Multigrid Smoothers. In *Proceedings of the 2001 ACM/IEEE Conference on Supercomputing (SC '01)*. ACM, New York, NY, USA, 4–4. https://doi.org/10.1145/582034.582038

[4] Dimitri P. Bertsekas and John N. Tsitsiklis. 1989. *Parallel and Distributed Computation: Numerical Methods*. Prentice-Hall, Upper Saddle River, NJ, USA.

[5] Robert D. Blumofe and Charles E. Leiserson. 1999. Scheduling Multithreaded Computations by Work Stealing. *J. ACM* 46, 5 (1999), 720–748. https://doi.org/10.1145/324133.324234

[6] William L. Briggs, Van Emden Henson, and Steve F. McCormick. 2000. *A Multigrid Tutorial*. SIAM: Society for Industrial and Applied Mathematics.

[7] Ümit V. Çatalyürek, Erik G. Boman, Karen D. Devine, Doruk Bozdag, Robert Heaphy, and Lee Ann Riesen. 2007. Hypergraph-based Dynamic Load Balancing for Adaptive Scientific Computations. In *Proc. of 21st International Parallel and Distributed Processing Symposium (IPDPS'07)*. IEEE.

[8] Herman Chernoff. 1952. A Measure of Asymptotic Efficiency for Tests of a Hypothesis Based on the sum of Observations. *The Annals of Mathematical Statistics* 23, 4 (1952), 493–507.

[9] Cédric Chevalier and François Pellegrini. 2008. PT-Scotch: A tool for efficient parallel graph ordering. *Parallel Comput.* 34, 6 (2008), 318 – 331. Parallel Matrix Algorithms and Applications.

[10] Thomas H. Cormen, Charles E. Leiserson, Ronald L. Rivest, and Clifford Stein. 2009. *Introduction to Algorithms, Third Edition* (3rd ed.). The MIT Press.

[11] D. J. Evans. 1984. Parallel S.O.R. Iterative Methods. *Parallel Comput.* 1, 1 (Aug. 1984), 3–18. https://doi.org/10.1016/S0167-8191(84)90380-6

[12] Mingdong Feng and Charles E. Leiserson. 1997. Efficient Detection of Determinacy Races in Cilk Programs. In *Proceedings of the Ninth Annual ACM Symposium on Parallel Algorithms and Architectures (SPAA '97)*. ACM, New York, NY, USA, 1–11. https://doi.org/10.1145/258492.258493

[13] Björn Gmeiner, Harald Köstler, Markus Stürmer, and Ulrich Rüde. 2014. Parallel multigrid on hierarchical hybrid grids: a performance study on current high performance computing clusters. *Concurrency and Computation: Practice and Experience* 26, 1 (2014), 217–240. https://doi.org/10.1002/cpe.2968

[14] Predrag Gruevski, William Hasenplaugh, and James J. Thomas. 2018. Laika: Efficient In-Place Scheduling for 3D Mesh Graph Computations. https://github.com/data-graph-computations/laika.

[15] John L. Gustafson. 1988. Reevaluating Amdahl's Law. *Commun. ACM* 31, 5 (May 1988), 532–533. https://doi.org/10.1145/42411.42415

[16] Gundolf Haase, Manfred Liebmann, and Gernot Plank. 2007. A Hilbert-order Multiplication Scheme for Unstructured Sparse Matrices. *Int. J. Parallel Emerg. Distrib. Syst.* 22, 4 (Jan. 2007), 213–220. https://doi.org/10.1080/17445760601122084

[17] Daniel F. Harlacher, Harald Klimach, Sabine Roller, Christian Siebert, and Felix Wolf. 2012. Dynamic Load Balancing for Unstructured Meshes on Space-Filling Curves. In *Proceedings of the 2012 IEEE 26th International Parallel and Distributed Processing Symposium Workshops & PhD Forum (IPDPSW '12)*. IEEE Computer Society, Washington, DC, USA, 1661–1669. https://doi.org/10.1109/IPDPSW.2012.207

[18] William Hasenplaugh. 2016. *Parallel Algorithms for Scheduling Data-Graph Computations*. Ph.D. Dissertation. MIT.

[19] David Hilbert. 1891. Über die stetige abbildung einer linie auf ein flächenstück. *Math. Ann.* (1891).

[20] Mark T. Jones and Paul E. Plassmann. 1993. A Parallel Graph Coloring Heuristic. *SIAM J. Sci. Comput.* 14, 3 (May 1993), 654–669. https://doi.org/10.1137/0914041

[21] Tim Kaler, William Hasenplaugh, Tao B. Schardl, and Charles E. Leiserson. 2014. Executing Dynamic Data-graph Computations Deterministically Using Chromatic Scheduling. In *Proceedings of the 26th ACM Symposium on Parallelism in Algorithms and Architectures (SPAA '14)*. ACM, New York, NY, USA, 154–165. https://doi.org/10.1145/2612669.2612673

[22] Kab Seok Kang. 2015. Scalable Implementation of the Parallel Multigrid Method on Massively Parallel Computers. *Comput. Math. Appl.* 70, 11 (Dec. 2015), 2701–2708. https://doi.org/10.1016/j.camwa.2015.07.023

[23] George Karypis and Vipin Kumar. 1998. A Fast and High Quality Multilevel Scheme for Partitioning Irregular Graphs. *SIAM Journal on Scientific Computing* 20, 1 (1998), 359–392. https://doi.org/10.1137/S1064827595287997 arXiv:http://dx.doi.org/10.1137/S1064827595287997

[24] Fredrik Kjølstad, Shoaib Kamil, Jonathan Ragan-Kelley, David I. W. Levin, Shinjiro Sueda, Desai Chen, Etienne Vouga, Danny M. Kaufman, Gurtej Kanwar, Wojciech Matusik, and Saman Amarasinghe. 2016. Simit: A Language for Physical Simulation. *ACM Trans. Graph.* 35, 2, Article 20 (March 2016), 21 pages. https://doi.org/10.1145/2866569

[25] Yucheng Low, Danny Bickson, Joseph Gonzalez, Carlos Guestrin, Aapo Kyrola, and Joseph M. Hellerstein. 2012. Distributed GraphLab: A Framework for Machine Learning and Data Mining in the Cloud. *Proc. VLDB Endow.* 5, 8 (April 2012), 716–727. https://doi.org/10.14778/2212351.2212354

[26] Yucheng Low, Joseph Gonzalez, Aapo Kyrola, Danny Bickson, Carlos Guestrin, and Joseph M. Hellerstein. 2010. GraphLab: A New Parallel Framework for Machine Learning. In *Conference on Uncertainty in Artificial Intelligence (UAI)*. Catalina Island, California.

[27] Bongki Moon, H. V. Jagadish, Christos Faloutsos, and Joel H. Saltz. 2001. Analysis of the clustering properties of the Hilbert space-filling curve. *IEEE Transactions on Knowledge and Data Engineering* 13 (2001), 2001.

[28] Hang Si. 2015. TetGen, a Delaunay-Based Quality Tetrahedral Mesh Generator. *ACM Trans. Math. Softw.* 41, 2 (January 2015).

[29] Srikanta Tirthapura, Sudip Seal, and Srinivas Aluru. 2006. A Formal Analysis of Space Filling Curves for Parallel Domain Decomposition. In *Proceedings of the 2006 International Conference on Parallel Processing (ICPP '06)*. IEEE Computer Society, Washington, DC, USA, 505–512. https://doi.org/10.1109/ICPP.2006.7

[30] John N. Tsitsiklis. 1989. A comparison of Jacobi and Gauss-Seidel parallel iterations. *IEEE Trans. Aut. Control* 2 (1989), 325–332.

[31] Leslie G. Valiant. 1990. A Bridging Model for Parallel Computation. *Commun. ACM* 33, 8 (Aug. 1990), 103–111. https://doi.org/10.1145/79173.79181

[32] Samuel Webb Williams, Andrew Waterman, and David A. Patterson. 2008. *Roofline: An Insightful Visual Performance Model for Floating-Point Programs and Multicore Architectures*. Technical Report UCB/EECS-2008-134. University of California at Berkeley.

[33] Albert Jan Nicholas Yzelman and Dirk Roose. 2014. High-Level Strategies for Parallel Shared-Memory Sparse Matrix-Vector Multiplication. *IEEE Transactions on Parallel and Distributed Systems* 25 (Jan 2014), 116–125. https://doi.org/10.1109/TPDS.2013.31

[34] Jinshan Zeng, Zhimin Peng, and Shaobo Lin. 2015. A Gauss-Seidel Iterative Thresholding Algorithm for lq Regularized Least Squares Regression. *CoRR* abs/1507.03173 (2015). http://arxiv.org/abs/1507.03173

# Author Index

# NOTES

www.ingramcontent.com/pod-product-compliance
Lightning Source LLC
LaVergne TN
LVHW080009210926
848481LV00011B/2975